THE
Shakespeare
KEY

THE

Shakespeare

KEY

A COMPREHENSIVE GUIDE
TO ALL FEATURES OF SHAKESPEARE'S STYLE,
DRAMATIC CONSTRUCTION,
AND EXPRESSION

Charles and Mary Cowden Clarke

FREDERICK UNGAR PUBLISHING CO.
NEW YORK

Printed in the United States of America

Library of Congress Catalog Card No. 61-13631

PREFACE.

SHAKESPEARE'S style, so masterly in power of effect, so vigorous in expression, so full of varied resource, so marked with bold originality, yet so accordant with pure English diction, offers supreme advantage in its careful study to the thinkers, the writers, and the orators in his native language. A man possessed of good intellect and education, who moulds his composition and speech on the model afforded by Shakespeare's works, can hardly fail of being an able writer and speaker; and even a moderately gifted and moderately educated man, who is in the habit of reading and thoughtfully appreciating Shakespeare, is likely to become capable of expressing himself with strength and clearness —the best eloquence—whether in writing or speaking.

Never was author who combined so many different words in his single writings—and not only so many different words, but so many varied forms and uses of words—as Shakespeare; never was author who comprised so many different phrases and sentences, with varied constructional forms of phrases and sentences, as Shakespeare; therefore it is that the possession of a ready means for inspecting these must needs be an advantage to students of the English language. More particularly must it be valuable to *dramatic* writers; whose object it is to produce prompt and imme-diate impression upon those who *hear* sentences uttered, without the opportunity to re-scan and weigh which reading affords. Of the same value is it to public speakers; since they also have to choose such expressions as will at once convey their meaning in the most full and forcible manner: and where can such expressions be found in larger number and more pregnant with significance than in Shakespeare's writings?

To afford ready access to every peculiar feature of this rich Shakespeare style, so that at a moment any particular mode of expression used by him may be referred to and found, is the object of the present work. It grew out of the necessity which its authors felt, while they were engaged in preparing their various editions of Shakespeare, for some accurate and facile means of recurring to his manifold beauties and peculiarities of diction : it assumed form first in the shape of innumerable jotted-down memoranda from daily examination for more than thirty years of Shakespeare's text ; it accumulated from minute observation of his varied niceties of phraseology, and gained bulk from the perpetual need of carefully noting these in all their different details. That which was so useful to our own joint task of editorship would naturally prove useful to general students of the great Poet, who might, so to say, become their own editors, if furnished with such a clue as we possessed to his component essentials of style. It will be of immense value to authors—especially dramatic authors—as showing the particular means whereby Shakespeare produces some of his best, most artistic, most characteristic, and most individual effects. It will be of essential aid as a philological work to those who carefully study the English language : showing Shakespeare's multiform use of the same word ; his nice shades of meaning, and gradations of distinctive impression, in selection of words ; his coined words ; his classical use of words, in their primitive and strict signification ; his invention in the formation of terms suited to his purpose and to the exact expression of his ideas ; his choice of epithets, appropriate, accurately descriptive, forcible, polished, comprehensively elliptical, consonant in pictorial or tonal effect— containing absolute colour and shape in some, melody and music in others : showing too his sentential construction—his robust and energetic conciseness, where brevity is needed; or his opulence of amplitude, where enlargement is requisite.

The work is so sorted and arranged as to give under different headings the divers specialities of Shakespeare's style, and to assemble thereunder the several passages presenting evidence of each speciality ; the whole placed alphabetically : therefore this book will afford the same clue to the infinite variety of features in Shakespeare's style that the "Concordance" affords to his every word and sentence; and thus the two books will, in fact, form companion volumes, the one to the other.

A peculiar advantage possessed by the present work is that it places *collectively* before the eye comparative evidence heretofore *scattered* in notes, glossaries, and other forms of animadversion on Shakespeare's style; so that it may be seen *at one view* how he uses the same word or form of expression, and thus frequently he becomes an interpreter to himself. Consequently, " The Shakespeare Key " will aid in determining various disputed readings and readings suspected of error, by showing *assembled together* several similar passages to the one in question; thus affording proof of its being in accordance with Shakespeare's peculiar style. Notes have been placed in several pages of this work, drawing attention to points of the kind here meant.

A special feature of the book will be found under the heading, DRAMATIC TIME, which discusses and denotes the system (invented by himself) upon which our greatest Dramatist moulded his style in this particular.

On this occasion it may perhaps be permitted us to congratulate our readers (who have proved to be more like *friends* in their constant and kind partiality towards us) as well as ourselves upon the prolonged and intimate knowledge we have maintained throughout the course of our lives with our greatest National Poet: as compiler of the "Concordance"—a task of sixteen years—as essayist and lecturer for a good half-century, as glossarist and editor of several editions for America and England; " The Shakespeare Key," forming the condensed result of these loving Shakespearian labours, wherewith, affectionately and gratefully, we take our leave.

CHARLES AND MARY COWDEN CLARKE.

Villa Novello, Genoa.

ADDED PREFACE.

These additional prefatory words are penned by the survivor of the Author-pair who put their names to the Preface originally written for this work, that she may explain why and how it has been modified since then.

The work was written happily *together*. After it was finished, Illness—Death—set their iron hands against its production in print. While it lay thus chained in manuscript, an extremely comprehensive Lexicon was brought out, which included many verbal points discussed in our work; and I resolved to sacrifice these points, amounting to no fewer than 639 pages of written labour. I also condensed much matter, which incurred fresh toil. But the result of this extra care bestowed upon our work has had the effect, I trust and believe, of rendering it more usefully valuable to its readers as a work of reference strictly to Shakespeare's *style;* and this belief amply repays the increased trouble it has cost her who signs herself

The faithfully devoted and loving servant of
Shakespeare and of all good Shakespearians,

MARY COWDEN CLARKE.

Villa Novello, Genoa,
1879.

TABLE OF CONTENTS.

THE SHAKESPEARE KEY.

ABRUPT COMMENCEMENTS.

SHAKESPEARE often begins a scene with an abrupt commencement ; with a conversation already begun, and in course of progress, at the time the speakers enter upon the scene. It serves to give an effect of great naturalness and ease to the dialogue :—

> If you misdoubt me that I am not she.—*All's W.*, iii. 7.
> We did observe.—*R. II.*, i. 4.
> Well said, my noble Scot.—1 *H. IV.*, iv. 1.
> His grace is bold, to trust these traitors.—*H. V.*, ii. 2.
> I warrant it is to knight you, captain.—*Ibid.*, iv. 8.
> Not for that neither : here 's the pang.—*H. VIII.*, ii. 3.
> But Montague is bound as well as I.—*R. & Jul.*, i. 2.
> Who, the Lord Timon ?—*Timon*, iii. 2.
> Will you think so ?—*Oth.*, iv. 1.
> It is the cause, it is the cause, my soul.—*Ibid.*, v. 2.
> So much for this, sir: now shall you see the other.—*Hamlet*, v. 2.

He occasionally makes a character enter with an abruptly commenced remark, as if in continuation of some speech addressed to the person accompanying the speaker, and not to those already on the scene :—

> 'Tis true, fair daughter ; and this blessed day.—*John*, iii. 1.
> Oh, sir, you are not right : have you not.—*Coriol.*, ii. 3.

He sometimes allows his speakers to make abrupt reference to some subject that has been talked of apart by two or more persons while others are occupied more prominently on the scene ; as where Polixenes says to the old Shepherd, in reply to something asked by the latter during the dance :—

> Oh, father, you 'll know more of that hereafter.—*W. T.*, iv. 3.

Or where Camillo refers to some difficulty that has been suggested by Florizel while Autolycus soliloquises :—

> Nay, but my letters, by this means being there
> So soon as you arrive, shall clear that doubt.—*Ibid.*, iv. 3.

Or where Brutus says, in reply to something Lucilius has said to him while Cassius and Messala have been engaged in spoken dialogue :—

> Even so, Lucilius.—*Jul. C.*, v. 1.

Or where Duncan responds to something which Banquo has said in praise of Macbeth's valour, while the two former have been conversing apart during the latter's soliloquy :—

> True, worthy Banquo—he is full so valiant.—*Macb.*, i. 4.

He sometimes commences a scene with abrupt reference to some unnamed but thoroughly understood person or persons, by allowing the speaker to use only the pronoun " he," " his," " him," " her," " them," or " their," as the case may be ; and the mode in which he employs this expedient of dramatic art occasionally serves as an admirable resource for producing emotional impression. As, for example, where Leontes bursts into the presence of his wife, furiously inquiring in reference to the escaped Polixenes :—

> Was *he* met there ? *his* train ? Camillo with *him* ?—*W. T.*, ii. 1.

Or where Queen Gertrude shudderingly refuses to admit the poor distracted Ophelia to an interview :—

> I will not speak with *her.*—*Hamlet*, iv. 5.

Or where the Duke of Cornwall, enraged against the supposed treachery of Gloster, says :—

> I will have my revenge, ere I depart *his* house.—*Lear*, iii. 5.

Or where Salisbury agitatedly alludes to his determination to join the Dauphin, in the words :—

> I will meet *him* at Saint Edmund's-Bury.—*John*, iv. 3.

Or where Antony angrily tells his wife Octavia of her brother's breach of faith towards him :—

> *He* hath wag'd new wars 'gainst Pompey.—*Ant. & C.*, iii. 4.

Or where Cleopatra comes in hurriedly asking for Antony :—

> Where is *he ?*—*Ibid.*, i. 3.

Or where Octavius and Antony are made to refer to each other in mutual wrath :—

> *He* calls me boy ; and chides, as *he* had power to.—*Ibid.*, iv. 1.
> *He* will not fight with me, Domitius.—*Ibid.*, iv. 2.
> We have beat *him* to *his* camp.—*Ibid.*, iv. 8.
> Go to *him*, Dolabella, bid *him* yield.—*Ibid.*, v. 1.

In certain instances, Shakespeare has employed the little word "he" with singularly impressive effect, to indicate purposely vague mention of an intended victim by murderous speakers :—

> That we may be admitted where *he* is.—*R. III.*, i. 3.
> *He* that 's coming must be provided for.—*Macb.*, i. 5.
> *He* 's here in double trust.—*Ibid.*, i. 7.
> *He* has almost supp'd.—*Ibid.*, i. 7.

The same indefinite monosyllable, used with pointed effect in reference to an understood though unnamed person, is employed where Macbeth seeks to rouse the two Murderers into belief of Banquo's having injured them, when the speaker incites them to undertake Banquo's assassination :—

Know that it was *he*, in the times past, which held you so under fortune.—*Macb.*, iii. 1.

Also, in the infamous Goneril's letter to Edmund, which is found in the slain Oswald's pocket by Edgar ; where the writer refers to her injured husband :—

You have many opportunities to cut *him* off: . . . if *he* return the conqueror: then am I the prisoner, and *his* bed my gaol.—*Lear*, iv. 6.

Also, where the tribunes, half fearful and repenting of their deed in causing Coriolanus to be banished, creep back from the city gates, alluding to the people and to the object of their excited enmity thus :—

Bid *them* all home; *he 's* gone.—*Coriol.*, iv. 2.

In some passages "them" is used abruptly with dramatic and passionate effect :—

Let *them* [the mob] pull all about mine ears.—*Ibid.*, iii. 2.
Let *them* [meaning his disaffected nobles] fly all.—*Macb.*, v. 3.

In the dark grop'd I to find out *them* [the base agents of the king's treachery against the speaker].—*Hamlet*, v. 2.

The pronouns "him" and "their" are employed abruptly, with characteristically reluctant effect, by Gloster in reference to the unnatural conduct of the Duke and Duchess of Cornwall towards the poor old king :—

When I desired *their* leave that I might pity *him*.—*Lear*, iii. 3.

One of Shakespeare's natural touches of abrupt reference and introduction of subject has exquisitely pathetic and characteristic effect. Although there has been no previous mention of conjugal infidelity in the scene, yet both Desdemona and Emilia use the word "such" in a manner to show that the subject has been in their thoughts, that it has lain at the root of their dread that Othello is jealous, and that it is perfectly present to their mind in this unushered allusion :—

Dost thou in conscience think,—tell me, Emilia,—
That there be women do abuse their husbands
In *such* gross kind ?
    Emil.   There be some *such*, no question.
    Des. Would'st thou do *such* a deed for all the world ?—*Oth.*, iv. 3.

He even occasionally opens a play with an abrupt commencement that gives excellent dramatic effect of spirit and vigour :—

As I remember, Adam, *it* was upon this fashion.—*As You L.*, i. 1.
Never tell me; I take it much unkindly
That thou, Iago, who hast had my purse
As if the strings were thine, should'st know of *this*.—*Oth.* i. 1.
Nay, but *this* dotage of our general's.—*Ant. & C.*, i. 1.
[*See* SOLILOQUIES.]

ABUNDANT IMAGERY.

Shakespeare is so exuberant in fancy, so overflowing with thought and idea, that he occasionally floods a passage with images ; sometimes even to the obscuring of its direct drift. See, among many others that might be cited in illustration :—

> Oh, will you eat no grapes, my royal fox ?
> Yes, but you will my noble grapes, an if
> My royal fox could reach them : I have seen
> A medicine that's able to breathe life into a stone,
> Quicken a rock, and make you dance canary
> With spritely fire and motion ; whose simple touch
> Is powerful to araise King Pepin, nay,
> To give great Charlemain a pen in 's hand,
> And write to her a love-line.—*All's W.*, ii. 1.

> This is his uncle's teaching : this is Worcester,
> Malevolent to you in all aspects ;
> Which makes him prune himself, and bristle up
> The crest of youth against your dignity.—1 *H. IV.*, i. 1.

> All furnish'd, all in arms ;
> All plum'd like estridges (that with the wind
> Bated, like eagles having lately bath'd) ;
> Glittering in golden coats, like images ;
> As full of spirit as the month of May,
> And gorgeous as the sun at midsummer ;
> Wanton as youthful goats, wild as young bulls.
> I saw young Harry—with his beaver on,
> His cuisses on his thighs, gallantly arm'd—
> Rise from the ground like feather'd Mercury,
> And vaulted with such ease into his seat,
> As if an angel dropp'd down from the clouds,
> To turn and wind a fiery Pegasus,
> And witch the world with noble horsemanship.—*Ibid.*, iv. 1.

In the above glowing passage, so richly full of illustration are the sentences—even giving a simile within a simile—that the author's scope has been missed by some emendators ; Rowe, and others, changing " with " to " wing." That clause of the passage, " that with the wind bated, like eagles having lately bath'd," is the speaker's comment upon the effect produced on his sight by the appearance he is imaging to his hearers. He describes the prince and his military companions as all " plum'd like estridges," and then, incidentally, gives the impression which these youthful warriors produced upon his sight by the fluttering of their plumed crests ; then resumes his more direct description of the men, by the words " glittering in golden coats." If the construction of the passage caused by Rowe's substituted word be adopted, we have the awkward effect of the warriors having " bated " ; if however we accept the construction afforded by the original word, we have the poetical effect of their plumes and those of the estridges to whom theirs are compared having " bated " with the wind. To "bate" is a term in falconry, meaning the fluttering or beating the wings of a hawk (French, *battre*, to beat); also the sedulous spreading and ruffling of the feathers of most birds after bathing, in order that the air may speedily dry them. "Estridges" is an old form of "ostriches," and the plumes of this bird are most appropriately introduced here, as they figure in the armorial cognisance of the Prince of Wales.

> As weeds before
> A vessel under sail, so men obey'd,
> And fell below his stem : his sword (death's stamp)
> Where it did mark, it took ; from face to foot
> He was a thing of blood, whose every motion
> Was tim'd with dying cries : alone he enter'd
> The mortal gate of the city, which he painted
> With shunless destiny ; aidless came off,
> And with a sudden re-inforcement struck
> Corioli like a planet.—*Coriol.*, ii. 2.

> Our poesy is as a gum, which oozes
> From whence 'tis nourish'd : the fire i' the flint
> Shows not till it be struck ; our gentle flame
> Provokes itself, and, like the current, flies
> Each bound it chafes.—*Timon*, i. 1.

> His two chamberlains
> Will I with wine and wassail so convince,
> That memory, the warder of the brain,
> Shall be a fume, and the receipt of reason
> A limbeck only.—*Macb.*, i. 7.

> We
> Must lave our honours in these flattering streams ;
> And make our faces vizards to our hearts,
> Disguising what they are.—*Ibid.*, iii. 2.

AFFECTED PHRASEOLOGY.

Our dramatist has given several different specimens of affected phraseology. Of the courtier's euphuism and high-flown diction, as in Le Beau ; where his nervous horror at holding acquaintance with one in court disgrace is shown, when he magnificently assures Orlando that he shall be happy to include him among his intimates in heaven :—

> Sir, fare you well :
> Hereafter, in a better world than this,
> I shall desire more love and knowledge of you.—*As You L.*, i. 3.

In Osric ; dreading to differ in opinion with the prince who has first observed that the weather is " very cold," and then that it is very " hot " :—

> Exceedingly, my lord ; it is very sultry,—as 'twere,—I cannot tell how.

And bringing the royal invitation to the fencing-match with that flourish of verbal trumpet :—

> Sir, here is newly come to court Laertes ; believe me, an absolute gentleman, full of most excellent differences, of very soft society, and great showing : indeed, to speak feelingly of him, he is the card and calendar of gentry ; for you shall find in him the continent of what part a gentleman would see.

The prince at once humours and quietly mocks Osric by replying in even an exaggerated strain of fantastic expression :—

> Sir, his definement suffers no perdition in you ; though, I know, to divide him inventorially would dizzy the arithmetic of memory ; and yet but raw, neither, in respect of his quick sail. But, in the verity of extolment, I take him to be a soul of great article ; and his infusion of such dearth and rareness, as, to make true diction of

him, his semblable is his mirror; and who else would trace him, his umbrage, nothing more.

The rejoinder to this shows that Osric perceives nothing of the subtle mockery, but accepts it as genuine elegance in expression; saying:—

> Your lordship speaks most infallibly of him.

For a moment the affected talker is posed by the prince's ultra extravagance in the question :—

> The concernancy, sir? why do we wrap the gentleman in our more rawer breath?

and is perplexed by Horatio's joining in Hamlet's banter. Nevertheless, he soon recovers his wonted glib frippery of language, and thus delivers the remainder of his message :—

> The king, sir, hath wagered with him six Barbary horses: against the which he has imponed, as I take it, six French rapiers and poniards, with their assigns, as girdle, hangers, and so: three of the carriages, in faith, are very dear to fancy, very responsive to the hilts, most delicate carriages, and of very liberal conceit.—*Hamlet*, v. 2.

A slight touch of courtierly finicalness in phraseology is given where the gentleman answers Edgar's inquiry, " How near's the other army?" by replying :—

> Near, and on speedy foot; the main descry
> Stands on the hourly thought.—*Lear*, iv. 6.

In the brief dialogue between Sir Toby and Viola (disguised as the page Cesario), an example is given of the periphrastic language affected by fine gentlemen and professed swordmen :—

> *Sir To.* Will you encounter the house? my niece is desirous you should enter, if your trade be to her.
> *Vio.* I am bound to your niece, sir; I mean, she is the list of my voyage.
> *Sir To.* Taste your legs, sir; put them to motion.
> *Vio.* My legs do better understand me, sir, than I understand what you mean by bidding me taste my legs.
> *Sir To.* I mean, to go, sir; to enter.
> *Vio.* I will answer you with gait and entrance.—*Tw. N.*, iii. 1.

Also of the affected and overbearing style of professed duellists; whom Mercutio scoffs at in the person of Tybalt, when he exclaims against—

> Such antic, lisping, affecting fantasticoes; these new tuners of accents! " By Jesu, a very good blade!—a very tall man!"—*R. & Jul.*, ii. 4.

Again, of the would-be soldierly bluffness and curtness, with use of a hackneyed word or phrase, that were adopted by military adventurers:—

> *Bard.* My captain, sir, commends him to you; my captain, Sir John Falstaff, a tall gentleman, by heaven, and a most gallant leader.

And when Shallow inquires " How my lady his wife doth?" answers:—

> Sir, pardon; a soldier is better accommodated than with a wife.

And finishes by thus vindicating his use of the expression which Shallow has patronised :—

> Pardon me, sir; I have heard the word. Phrase, call you it? by this good day, I know not the phrase; but I will maintain the word with my sword to be a soldier-like word, and a word of exceeding good command, by heaven. Accommodated; that is, when a man is, as they say, accommodated; or, when a man is, being, whereby,—he may be thought to be accommodated; which is an excellent thing.
> *2 H. IV.*, iii. 2.

Likewise in Nym's surly threats, and pretended recklessness :—

For my part, I care not; I say little; but when time shall serve, there shall be smiles ;—but that shall be as it may. I dare not fight; but I will wink, and hold out mine iron: it is a simple one; but what though? it will toast cheese, and it will endure cold as another man's sword will: and there an end. . . .
Faith, I will live so long as I may, that 's the certain of it ; and when I cannot live any longer, I will do as I may : that is my rest, that is the rendezvous of it. . . .
I cannot tell : things must be as they may : men may sleep, and they may have their throats about them at that time ; and, some say, knives have edges. It must be as it may : though patience be a tired mare, yet she will plod. There must be conclusions. Well, I cannot tell. . . .
I am not Barbason; you cannot conjure me. I have a humour to knock you indifferently well. If you grow foul with me, Pistol, I will scour you with my rapier, as I may, in fair terms: if you would walk off, I would prick your guts a little, in good terms, as I may: and that 's the humour of it. . . .
I will cut thy throat, one time or other, in fair terms: that is the humour of it.

H. V., ii. 1.

Then there is the conventional jargon of the painter and the poetaster. Each affecting to commend the other's production, while occupied in puffing his own, and making ostentatiously modest disclaimers, while urging praise :—

> *Pain.* You are rapt, sir, in some work, some dedication
> To the great lord.
> *Poet.* A thing slipp'd idly from me.
> Our poesy is as a gum, which oozes
> From whence 'tis nourish'd: the fire i' the flint
> Shows not, till it be struck; our gentle flame
> Provokes itself, and, like the current, flies
> Each bound it chafes. What have you there?
> *Pain.* A picture, sir. When comes your book forth?
> *Poet.* Upon the heels of my presentment, sir.
> Let 's see your piece.
> *Pain.* 'Tis a good piece.
> *Poet.* So 'tis: this comes off well, and excellent.
> *Pain.* Indifferent.
> *Poet.* Admirable! How this grace
> Speaks his own standing! what a mental power
> This eye shoots forth! how big imagination
> Moves in this lip! to the dumbness of the gesture
> One might interpret.
> *Pain.* It is a pretty mocking of the life.
> Here is a touch; is 't good?
> *Poet.* I 'll say of it,
> It tutors nature: artificial strife
> Lives in these touches, livelier than life.
>
>   *   *   *   *   *
>
> I have, in this rough work, shap'd out a man,
> Whom this beneath world doth embrace and hug
> With amplest entertainment: my free drift
> Halts not particularly, but moves itself
> In a wide sea of wax: no levell'd malice
> Infects one comma in the course I hold;
> But flies an eagle flight, bold, and forth on,
> Leaving no tract behind.
> *Pain.* How shall I understand you?
> *Poet.* I will unbolt to you
> You see how all, &c.—*Timon*, i. 1.

And thus the versifier goes on, expatiating upon his own performance; the painter endeavouring to interpose with hints of how
much better his own art would suffice to demonstrate the subject in
question.   But the other perseveres, will not be interrupted, im-
patiently exclaiming: "Nay, sir, but hear me on;" and continues
his analytical harangue.

Elsewhere Shakespeare gives the affectation of pedantry, the self-
glorification of empty-headed dealers in scraps of learning, displayed
with florid absurdity :—

Hol. The deer was, as you know, *sanguis*,—in blood; ripe as a pomewater, who
now hangeth like a jewel in the ear of *cælo*,—the sky, the welkin, the heaven; and
anon falleth like a crab on the face of *terra*,—the soil, the land, the earth.

Nath. Truly, Master Holofernes, the epithets are sweetly varied, like a scholar at
the least: but, sir, I assure ye, it was a buck of the first head.

Hol. Sir Nathaniel, *haud credo*.

Dull. 'Twas not a *haud credo;* 'twas a pricket.

Hol. Most barbarous intimation! yet a kind of insinuation, as it were, *in via*, in way,
of explication; *facere*, as it were, replication, or, rather, *ostentare*, to show, as it were,
his inclination, after his undressed, unpolished, uneducated, unpruned, untrained, or
rather, unlettered, or ratherest, unconfirmed fashion,—to insert again my *haud credo*
for a deer.

Dull. I said the deer was not a *haud credo;* 'twas a pricket.

Hol. Twice-sod simplicity, *bis coctus!* Oh, thou monster Ignorance, how deformed
dost thou look!

Nath. Sir, he hath never fed of the dainties that are bred in a book; he hath not
eat paper, as it were; he hath not drunk ink: his intellect is not replenished; he is
only an animal, only sensible in the duller parts: and such barren plants are set before
us, that we thankful should be—which we of taste and feeling are—for those parts that
do fructify in us more than he.—*Love's L. L.,* iv. 2.

And so on, through the whole of the scenes and dialogue wherein
Sir Nathaniel and Holofernes figure.

In the same play there is yet another sample of affected phraseology,
—that of the personage who is described as :—

> A man in all the world's new fashion planted,
>   That hath a mint of phrases in his brain;
> One whom the music of his own vain tongue
>   Doth ravish like enchanting harmony.—*Ibid.,* i. 1.

The following is the style in which this Armado describes the
struggles of his passion for the country girl, Jaquenetta, with his late-
made vow and his long devotion to deeds of arms:—

I do affect the very ground, which is base, where her shoe, which is baser, guided by
her foot, which is basest, doth tread.   I shall be forsworn, which is a great argument
of falsehood, if I love: and how can that be true love which is falsely attempted?
Love is a familiar; Love is a devil; there is no evil angel but Love.   Yet was Samson
so tempted, and he had excellent strength; yet was Solomon so seduced, and he
had a very good wit.   Cupid's butt-shaft is too hard for Hercules' club; and therefore
too much odds for a Spaniard's rapier.   The first and second cause will not serve my
turn; the passado he respects not, the duello he regards not: his disgrace is to be
called boy; but his glory is to subdue men.   Adieu, valour! rust, rapier! be still, drum!
for your manager is in love; yea, he loveth.   Assist me, some extemporal god of
rhyme, for I am sure I shall turn sonneteer.   Devise, wit; write, pen; for I am for
whole volumes in folio.—*Ibid.,* i. 2.

ALLEGED ANACHRONISMS, DISCREPANCIES, &c.

Various have been the charges brought against Shakespeare for anachronisms, inappropriatenesses, discrepancies, forgetfulnesses, inaccuracies, &c.; but we think that in each instance where he has been accused of oversight or error, the insufficient attention or knowledge will be found to be rather that of the critic than of the author. In giving the following passages, to which objections have been made by previous commentators, we shall append our own view of each passage, as our answer in vindication of Shakespeare's intention therein:—

A piece many years in doing, and now newly performed by that rare Italian master, Julio Romano.—*W. T.*, v. 2.

The introducing this compliment to the greatest artist of his time, by the greatest dramatist of all time, into a play where Apollo's oracle is consulted, has been denounced as a strange absurdity of anachronism. As well might objection be taken against the allusion to him (Judas Iscariot) "that did betray the best," which occurs in this same play. But the dramatist refers to Julio Romano as the type of artistic excellence, and to Judas Iscariot as the type of treacherous betrayal; knowing that typical truth in impression is superior to rigidity in accuracy of chronological detail, where dramatic effect is concerned.

The thunder of my cannon shall be heard.—*John*, i. 1.

As John's reign commenced in 1199, and cannon are said to have been first used at the battle of Cressy in 1346, our author is here liable to the charge of anachronism; but Shakespeare spoke of engines of war in the terms most readily understood by his audience.

A half-faced groat five hundred pound a year !—*Ibid.*, i. 1.

Here again is the poet taxed with anachronism, because groats and half-groats, with faces of the king in profile upon them, were not coined until the reign of Henry VII.; whereas the dramatist purposely mentions a piece of money familiar to his audience.

Report of fashions in proud Italy,
Whose manners still our tardy apish nation
Limps after, in base imitation.—*R. II.*, ii. 1.

Whereupon Johnson finds Shakespeare guilty of " charging the times of Richard with a folly not perhaps known then, but very frequent in Shakespeare's time." It is precisely for this reason that the great playwright satirises and denounces it.

That sprightly Scot of Scots, Douglas, that runs o' horseback up a hill perpendicular,
—He that rides at high speed and with his pistol kills a sparrow flying.—*1 H. IV.*, ii. 4.

Here Johnson is severe upon Shakespeare's speaking of a weapon that was not known in the time of Henry IV., although the critic simultaneously observes that pistols were in the poet's time "eminently used by the Scots." Of course this was why the dramatist introduced the point, because he knew it was a piece of national characterisation sure to be understood and appreciated by the audience for whom he wrote, and because accuracy in characterisation always weighed with him above strictness in chronology.

> Thy place in council thou hast rudely lost.—1 *H. IV.*, iii. 2.

Steevens and Malone point out an anachronism in this passage, because the event of the Prince of Wales's removal from his post of President of the Council in consequence of his having struck the Lord Chief Justice Gascoigne on the bench, occurred some years later than is here represented; but Shakespeare anticipated the period for dramatic purposes.

> Shall not thou and I, between Saint Denis and Saint George, compound a boy, half French, half English, that shall go to Constantinople and take the Turk by the beard ?—*H. V.*, v. 2.

Theobald informs us that " Shakespeare has here committed an anachronism. The Turks were not possessed of Constantinople before the year 1453, when Henry V. had been dead thirty-one years." But by allusion to this antedated circumstance, the poet gives animation to his character and dialogue.

> And whereas, before, our forefathers had no other books but the score and the tally, thou hast caused printing to be used.—2 *H. VI.*, iv. 7.

Johnson here arraigns the poet for being a " little too early with this accusation," since printing was not invented and introduced till some years later than the period here supposed; but who would wish a passage that has so much dramatic propriety to have been unwritten because of its chronological impropriety?

> And set the murderous Machiavel to school.—3 *H. VI.*, iii. 2.

Inasmuch as this allusion to the Italian politician involves an anachronism, Warburton prefers the adoption of " the aspiring Catiline," which are the three words that occur in parallel passages of the old play that formed the basis of his present drama. But since Machiavel was popularly known in our dramatist's time as the exemplar of astute political strategists, he in all probability designedly made the substituted allusion, a probability that is confirmed by his having made reference to Machiavel (with the same typical force) in two other of his plays, " The Merry Wives of Windsor " (iii. 1), and " The First Part of King Henry VI." (v. 4).

> Not much
> Unlike young men, whom Aristotle thought
> Unfit to hear moral philosophy.—*Tr. & Cr.*, ii. 2.

That Hector should cite Aristotle's opinion may subject Shakespeare to the charge of having committed an anachronism; but, such as it is, he found it in many of the classical poems and old romances that evidently were known to him. Moreover, if a point did but suit the general appropriateness of the theme, this sufficed for Shakespeare as well as for the writers who preceded him.

> Bull-bearing Milo his addition yield
> To sinewy Ajax.—*Ibid.*, ii. 3.

Malone observes: "Our author, here, as usual, pays no regard to chronology. Milo of Croton lived long after the Trojan war." On the contrary, Shakespeare, though usually having regard to chronology, knew when it was better to employ an incident for the sake of apt illustration than to pay strict attention to relative dates.

> Thou wast a soldier even to Cato's wish.—*Coriol.*, i. 4.

Shakespeare, basing the play upon Plutarch's Life of Coriolanus, and adopting this among many other passages therefrom, occasions Theobald to remark: "The poet, hereby following the historian, is fallen into a great chronological inpropriety;" but it is very possible that the poet, although he knew the historian used an illustration which anticipated a later period, yet chose to employ the illustration because it would be dramatically effective.

> The most sovereign prescription in Galen is but empiricutic.—*Ibid.*, ii. 1.

This is denounced by Grey as "an anachronism of near 650 years." That Galen was known to Shakespeare's audiences as one of the most celebrated authorities of antique times was quite sufficient for the dramatist's purpose; who puts the name into Menenius's mouth with appropriate effect, if not with chronological propriety.

> Matrons flung gloves,
> Ladies and maids their scarfs and handkerchiefs,
> Upon him as he pass'd.—*Ibid.*, ii. 1.

Because it was not a custom among the Romans, and because it was a custom in the age of Shakespeare, for successful tilters at tournaments to have these marks of female favour thrown upon them as they rode round or from the lists, Malone complains that "here our author has attributed some of the customs of his own age to a people who were wholly unacquainted with them." But it was exactly this reason, that his audience would at once comprehend the form of approbation showered upon Coriolanus as a victorious warrior, which induced the dramatist to write the passage as it stands.

> When he might act the woman in the scene.—*Ibid.*, ii. 2.

Steevens's note on this passage, stating that "the parts of women were, in Shakespeare's time, represented by the most smooth-faced young men to be found among the players," is followed up by a note from Malone, declaring that "here is a great anachronism. There were no theatres at Rome for the exhibition of plays for above 250 years after the death of Coriolanus." But it appears to us that the line may be taken to imply, 'When his youth might have warranted his behaving with no more martial prowess than a woman'; although the habit of seeing boys enact women's characters, of course, gave farther force of effect to the line with those for whom it was written.

> I would they would forget me, like the virtues
> Which our divines lose by them.—*Ibid.*, ii. 3.

By using the term "divines" here, Shakespeare has brought upon himself the disdain of one critic, Mr. Singer, who calls it "another amusing instance of anachronism." But though it happens to have been applied to ministers of the Gospel in Christian times, it is surely an expression of sufficiently wide signification to admit of being aptly employed in designating interpreters of Divine Nature and Divine Wisdom, in whatever creed or age of the world recognised.

> The noble house o' the Marcians, from whence came
> That Ancus Marcius, Numa's daughter's son,
> Who, after great Hostilius, here was king;
> Of the same house Publius and Quintus were,
> That our best water brought by conduits hither;
> And Censorinus, darling of the people,
> And nobly nam'd so, twice being censor,
> Was his great ancestor.—*Coriol.*, ii. 3.

This passage has caused Shakespeare to be taunted as " he who would disregard such anachronisms, or rather he to whom they were not known " by Malone ; and to be twitted with " haste" and " inadvertency " by Warburton.   But although Censorinus, Publius, and Quintus, were in fact descendants, not ancestors, of Coriolanus ; yet the passage in Plutarch (from whose book Shakespeare derived his historic material for this play) is worded with sufficient latitude in expression to warrant the poet in supposing, or choosing to represent, them as being predecessors of the hero—Plutarch saying : " Of the same house " and " also came of that family."

> He sits in his state, as a thing made for Alexander.—*Ibid.*, v. 4.

It has been pointed out that this is an anachronism, inasmuch as Alexander was not born until 355 B.C., and Coriolanus died 488 B.C. Nevertheless, the poet is dramatically correct in citing Alexander the Great as a type of human grandeur ; Shakespeare ever preferring dramatic fitness in typical expression to rigid fidelity in historic chronology.

> Peace! count the clock.
> The clock hath stricken three.—*Jul. C.*, ii. 1.

Clocks and watches being unknown to the Romans, Shakespeare has been accused of here committing an anachronism.   It is true they measured their time by sun-dials and clepsydræ ; but a sun-dial would not have suited the poet's purpose in a night-scene, and a clepsydra would have been an unknown instrument to the dramatist's audience. Judging from the free allusion to " clock" which is to be found in many of his plays—even such plays as " Comedy of Errors," " Winter's Tale," and " Cymbeline," where the supposed period of the action renders the allusion, strictly speaking, an anachronism—we believe that Shakespeare uses the word as an acknowledged and readily understood time-measurer, which was what his object required.

> In going back to school in Wittenberg.—*Hamlet*, i. 2.

Malone points out that " the University of Wittenberg was not founded till 1502, consequently did not exist in the time to which this play is referred;" but inasmuch as the University of Wittenberg was known by Shakespeare's hearers to exist when he wrote and they listened to his plays, he introduced the allusion.

> The music, ho!
> Let it alone ; let us to billiards.—*Ant. & C.*, ii. 5.

Malone says, " This is one of the numerous anachronisms that are found in these plays. This game was not known in ancient times." The latter is mere vague assertion ; for, there are many probabilities that *billiards* is only a modern form of an antique pastime. But were it still affirmed that the more recent term is improper in a drama of remote period, we contend that the term which most readily conveys to a modern audience the idea intended to be conveyed of the luxurious pursuits of that " Serpent of old Nile," Cleopatra, would be the best that could here be employed.

> If I can get him within my pistol's length,
> I'll make him sure.—*Per.*, i. 1.

As well might Shakespeare have been taxed with anachronism for introducing mention of a " pistol " in the present passage, as in the case objected to by Johnson from " 1 Henry IV.," ii. 4; and though the same defence cannot be set up for the poet here as we advanced for him there, yet it may be urged that he merely names a weapon familiarly known to his audience, and therefore one that they would recognise as fit for the mention and use of an assassin.

> By the bare scalp of Robin Hood's fat friar.—*Two G. of V.*, iv. 1.

That this allusion to Robin Hood and Friar Tuck, outlaws of Sherwood Forest, should be put into the mouth of the outlaws in a Mantuan forest need shock no one's sense of appropriateness who bears in mind the poet's privilege to introduce all that may serve to heighten impression ; and reference to a well-known English outlaw would infallibly impress Shakespeare's English hearers with extra vivid consciousness of outlaw presence.

> Look here what I found on a palm-tree.—*As You L.*, iii. 2.

Mr. Steevens appends the following remark to this passage :—" A *palm-tree* in the forest of *Arden* is as much out of its place as the *lioness* in a subsequent scene." The commentator first takes for granted that—because the scene of Lodge's novel (on which the present play is founded) is laid in France, because the novel makes the place of exile " the forest of Arden," and because there is a real forest of Ardenne or Ardennes in French Flanders—Shakespeare meant this same Flemish forest, and then asserts that he made a great mistake in introducing a palm-tree and a lioness there. Now we believe that Shakespeare, by his " forest of Arden," meant no special or actual forest, but a typical and ideal forest ; a forest that represents a poetical forest generally, where lovers, dukes, lords, shepherds, jesters, natural philosophers and artificial philosophers, lions and lambs, serpents and goats, oaks and olives, palm-trees and osiers, may all flourish contentedly and plausibly, without disturbing the peace of those whose imaginations accept the truths of poetry as universal truth, not mere geographical, animal, or botanical literalities. The old English word " Arden " originally signified woodiness ; it was applied to a large wooded district in Warwickshire, called the Forest of Arden ; and it was the maiden name of Shakespeare's own mother, Mary Arden, whose ancient family derived their name from this very forest of their county. Well might it in the poet's mind—as it should in the minds of his readers—serve well for the name of the archetype of poetic and romantic forests.

> Near twenty years ago, in Genoa,
> Where we were lodgers at the Pegasus.—*Tam of S.*, iv. 4.

Here Steevens flippantly scoffs at Shakespeare for having " taken a sign out of London, and hung it up in Padua." In the first place the commentator might be taunted with making a mistake in citing " Padua " instead of " Genoa "; in the next place, he might have bethought him, that the classical winged horse of poesy was likely to be as popular a sign in the classic land of Italy (where, to this day, classical allusions and classical tokens abound) as we learn that it was in the metropolis of England at the period when Shakespeare wrote.

> Or the bells of Saint Bennet, sir, may put you in mind; one, two, three.—*Tw. N.*, v. 1.

Johnson sneers at the "impropriety" of introducing the bells of Saint Bennet here, as if there could be only an English church of that name with a peal of bells. Not merely are there churches dedicated to San Benedetto to be found in Italy ; monasteries of Benedictine monks and convents of Benedictine nuns sufficiently abound there to make the Clown's allusion to some neighbouring church, monastery, or convent locally correct ; while, moreover, any one acquainted with the perpetual clang and jangle of bells pertaining to Italian religious houses of every kind, can bear witness to the appropriateness of the allusion in this respect also.

> Our ship hath touch'd
> Upon the deserts of Bohemia.—*W. T.* iii. 3.

Johnson is severe upon the " geographical error, by which Bohemia is supposed to be a maritime country." The poet was not troubled by such " errors," which he found in the story whence he derived the plot of this exquisite play ; for the story describes Bohemia as having a sea-coast, and Delphos as an island. He knew well that in a romantic tale or play such deviations from truth and geography detract nothing from the truth of romance and poetry. Nevertheless, for the comfort of persons more solicitous respecting these nice points, we may state that the author of " Consuelo " has attempted to save Shakespeare's credit in this particular, by recording that Ottokar II. possessed, in addition to Bohemia, Austria, Carniola, Istria, and Styria, part of Carynthia, and even a *sea-port* which he purchased on the Adriatic ; this sea-port being possibly the little port of Naon, bought by King Ottokar with the ostentatious view of asserting that his dominions extended to the shores of the Adriatic.

That our dramatist could adhere to strictest accuracy where accuracy is needful to art-verity, we know; therefore we may infer that, where he makes accuracy subservient to typical and poetic truth in productions purely romantic, he has excellent reason for so doing. In the present play he has purposely brought together a host of allusions which, however incongruous if judged according to actual existence, are nowise ill-assorted, if beheld through the medium of imagination ; and thus no violence is done to our sense of poetic propriety or to our poetic credence, by finding, assembled together in the "Winter's Tale," reference to Apollo's oracle, an emperor of Russia, a king of Sicilia, a puritan who "sings psalms to hornpipes," "one Mistress Taleporter," "Whitsun-pastorals" and a baptismal "bearing-cloth." Each of these things, in their several introduction, serve the art-purpose of vividly idealising the subject treated ; and are therefore poetically, if not prosaically, correct.

> Who should withhold me?
> Not fate, obedience, nor the hand of Mars
> Beckoning with fiery truncheon my retire.—*Tr. & Cr.*, v. 3.

Steevens observes, " We have here but a modern Mars. Antiquity acknowledges no such ensign of command as a *truncheon*." And though the commentator has the grace to add, " the spirit of the passage however is such as might atone for a greater impropriety," we can scarcely assent to the imputation of " impropriety "; since Shakespeare, throughout this play, has adopted the terms and attributes of chivalrous times which he found applied to the Greek and Trojan heroes in the Gothic and romantic versions of the story by Lydgate and Caxton, wherefrom he drew the groundwork for his drama, as well as from the more primitive and purely simple sources of Homer and Chaucer. Some of the expressions thus taken by the dramatist from the two first-named sources give a knightly effect to the characters : so that we find mention made of Troilus's " varlet " (the term used for an attendant upon a knight), of Hector's " armourer "; Æneas words his challenge to the Greeks in the true chivalric tone, ending with the phrase " not worth the splinter of a lance "; Nestor speaks of his " beaver " and his " vantbrace "; Achilles says " that Hector, by the fifth hour of the sun, will, with a trumpet, 'twixt our tents and Troy, to-morrow morning call some knight to arms "; Diomed bids his servant take the steed which he has won in battle to Cressid as a token that he is her " knight by proof "; and we hear that Hector " fights on Galathè his horse ": all of which, in combination, render the use of the term " truncheon " no impropriety, as belonging to those usages of knight-errantry with which the antique times of Troy and Greece in this drama are consociated by the author, for the sake of giving colour and refinement to his picture.

> I am attended at the cypress grove: I pray you
> ('Tis south the city mills) bring me word thither
> How the world goes.—*Coriol.*, i. 10.

Tyrwhitt inquires, " Where could Shakespeare have heard of these *mills* at Antium ? " And Steevens replies, " Shakespeare is seldom careful about such little improprieties." But is there any " impropriety " at all—is there not rather propriety and vividness of effect— in introducing a touch of local detail that gives force and naturalness to the dialogue and situation ?

> To beg of Hob and Dick, that do appear,
> Their needless vouches?—*Ibid.*, ii. 3.

Malone, with amusing severity, says, " By strange inattention our poet has here given the names (as in many other places he has attributed the customs) of England to ancient Rome. It appears that these were some of the most common names among the people in Shakespeare's time." Precisely so; and this is why the great play-writer, with his usual attention to dramatic fitness, introduced names that were so familiar to his audience as to be employed to express the rabble generally—" Jack, Tom, and Harry," or " Hob and Dick."

They are worn, lord consul, so.—Coriol., iii. 1.

Again Malone is severe upon Shakespeare, because he " has here, as in other places, attributed the usage of England to Rome. In his time the title of *lord* was given to many officers of state who were not peers; thus, *lords* of the council, *lord* ambassador, *lord* general, &c." This was exactly a reason for the dramatist to employ an expression which he knew would be at once understood by the public whom he addressed, and therefore would well impress upon their mind the point he wished to emphasise—Coriolanus's new title and dignity.

Let them pull all about mine ears; present me
Death on the wheel, or at wild horses' heels;
Or pile ten hills on the Tarpeian rock.—Ibid., iii. 2.

Malone takes great pains to show that neither breaking on the wheel nor tearing to pieces by wild horses were punishments known to the Romans; and therefore he objects to their being introduced here. As well might it be said that to " pile ten hills on the Tarpeian rock " was never known to be done in Rome as a means of punishing by death. For the purposes of poetic and dramatic effect, Shakespeare's putting these words into Coriolanus's mouth has a truth of appropriateness far beyond that demanded by the accuracies of chronological fact.

Clubs, bills, and partisans!—R. & Jul., i. 1.

To those who cavil at our poet's introducing this well-known rallying cry of old London streets into Verona streets, we may reply that the fact of its familiarity to the hearers of the play rendered it appropriate from the dramatist's pen, as the surest means of conveying to their minds the incident of a popular brawl in a public thoroughfare.

Stay not to question, for the watch is coming.—Ibid., v. 3.

It has been objected that no such establishment as that of night-watchmen existed in Italian cities; nevertheless, not only did Shakespeare find mention of " the watch " in the old poem whence he took the story of this play; but much the same remarks apply to the present passage as we appended to the previous one.

Believe me, I had rather have lost my purse full of cruzadoes.—Oth., iii. 4.

Douce observes, " The cruzado was not current, as it should seem, at Venice, though it certainly was in England in the time of Shakespeare, who has here indulged his usual practice of departing from national costume." On the contrary, Shakespeare has here followed his usual practice of making the accuracies of national costume a secondary consideration to that of facile popular comprehension of foreign allusions. That " cruzadoes " were foreign coins well known to English people, sufficed for the dramatist's purpose.

> This new governor
> Awakes me all the enrolled penalties
> Which have, like unscour'd armour, hung by the wall
> So long that nineteen zodiacs have gone round
> And none of them been worn.—*M. for M.*, i. 3.

Because the duke, in the next scene, is made to speak of these penalties as having been left " fourteen years " unenforced, Theobald complains of the discrepancy here, and says he makes no scruple of changing " fourteen " to " nineteen." But Shakespeare occasionally has similiar variations in statement, such as we find in Nature, whom he copied with the implicitness of a Chinese artificer and the fidelity of a true poet. That a young fellow like Claudio should carelessly mention *somewhere about* the period in question, while the staid duke cites it exactly, is most natural and characteristic.

> When last the young Orlando parted from you,
> He left a promise to return again
> Within an hour.—*As You L.*, iv. 3.

Johnson authoritatively says, " We must read, ' within two hours ; ' " because when Orlando parts from the forest youth in act iv., sc. i., he has said, " For these two hours, Rosalind, I will leave thee." But similar discrepancies of stated times are not unfrequently made on purpose by Shakespeare, where he wishes to produce the effect of vague period or indefinite lapse from epoch to epoch.

> Bid him shed tears, as being overjoy'd
> To see her noble lord restor'd to health,
> Who for this seven years hath esteemed him
> No better than a poor and loathsome beggar.
>   *Tam. of S., Induc.* i.

In order to make this passage agree with those in the following scene, where " fifteen years " are mentioned as the period of Sly's supposed delusion, Theobald altered " this seven years " to " twice seven years." But we have shown how Shakespeare intentionally gives these varied statements in time ; and in the present instance we think he did so to impart a natural and characteristically humorous effect in the servant's exaggeration of his lord's commands.

> My youngest boy, and yet my eldest care.—*Com. of E.*, i. i.

Mason says, " Shakespeare has here been guilty of a little forget fulness. Ægeon had said that the *youngest son* was that which his wife had taken care of :—

> My wife, more careful for the *latter-born*,
> Had fasten'd him unto a small spare mast.

It appears to us that the " forgetfulness " is the commentator's, not the dramatist's. Mr. Mason forgets that though the description states that the wife fastened the latter-born to the mast, it does not state that she fastened herself to the same end of the mast with her youngest son : on the contrary, the account of the arrangement of the two pair of twin children, with their parents as their protectors bound at

" either end the mast," and then the accident which divided the mast in twain, is so managed by the dramatist as to allow of some latitude in construing the mode in which the two sets of persons are saved ; thus, when we afterwards find that it was the elder son who escaped with the mother, and the younger son with the father, there is no violation of consistency. Moreover, " eldest " here bears the sense of ' most important,' ' first needing attention.' [*See* ELDER, ELDEST, &c.]

> Take what wife you will.—*Mer. of V.*, ii. 9 (*schedule*).

Upon this passage Johnson remarks, " Perhaps the poet had forgotten that he who missed Portia was never to marry any woman." But " Take what wife you will " does not so much mean " take in future " as " might at any time have taken ; " and even if the " will " be strictly accepted as referring to a coming period, it would be but an added gibe in the mocking " schedule "—a reminder of that wedlock which is henceforth forbidden.

> Methought you said
> You saw one here in court could witness it.—*All's W.*, v. 3.

Blackstone sharply says, " The poet has here forgot himself. Diana has said no such thing." No ; the poet here remembers his own dramatic practice of occasionally allowing certain points to be understood, for the sake of succinctness in explanation ; more particularly so towards the close of his plays and during a winding-up scene,—as in the present instance. [*See* CLOSING SCENES : BRIEF SCENES.]

> Thou wouldst have poison'd good Camillo's honour,
> To have him kill a king.—*W. T.*, iii. 2.

Malone scoffingly inquires, " How should Paulina know this ? No one had charged the king with this crime except himself, while Paulina was absent attending on Hermione. The poet seems to have forgotten this circumstance." Rather, the critic seems to have forgotten, or to have been ignorant, that Shakespeare sometimes permits such points as these, which are perfectly known to the audience, to be taken for granted as known to the persons speaking.

> Would I had been by, to have helped the old man !—*Ibid.*, iii. 3.

Steevens is contemptuously lenient with Shakespeare for having " inadvertently given this knowledge " [that Antigonus was old] " to the Shepherd who had never seen him." The inadvertency is the commentator's, who not only fails in being sure that the tone of the Clown's description allows age and incapacity for escape to be inferred, but also fails in the perception that the dramatist is here following a usual artistic practice of his. That this is an artistic practice, and not a " forgetfulness," or " oversight," or " carelessness," or " inadvertence"—each of which have been such favourite accusations against him—our present collected passages suffice evidently to show.

> I would to heaven,
> So my untruth had not provok'd him to it,
> The king had cut off my head with my brother's.—*R. II.*, ii. 2.

Ritson points out that " none of York's brothers had his head cut off, either by the king or any one else," adding, " the Duke of Gloster, to whose death he probably alludes, was secretly murdered at Calais, being smothered between two beds." And Singer suggests that "the poet may have confounded the death of Arundel, who was beheaded, with that of Gloster." In our opinion, York is here made by the dramatist to refer to the king's threat of having Gaunt beheaded at the time he was dying (in the previous scene); and that, in his present state of fluster, York confusedly recalls the circumstance with the incoherence and agitation that characteristically mark his utterance at this perplexing juncture.

> But which of you was by
> (You, cousin Nevil, as I may remember),
> When Richard, with his eye brimful of tears—
> Then check'd and rated by Northumberland—
> Did speak these words, now prov'd a prophecy?—2 *H. IV.*, iii. 1.

Johnson observes, "whether the king's or the author's memory fails him, so it was, that Warwick was not present at that conversation." That there was no failure of memory on the part of the author is shown by his care to insert the words "as I may remember," which imply that the king is speaking with avowed latitude.

> Since his majesty went into the field.—*Macb.*, v. 1.

Here Steevens remarks, "This is one of Shakespeare's oversights. He forgot that he had shut up Macbeth in Dunsinane and surrounded him with besiegers," afterwards adding, "our poet, in the haste of finishing his play, forgot his plan." The charge of oversight and forgetfulness lies surely with more propriety against the fault-finder, who overlooks the circumstance that it has been before mentioned how Macbeth "prepares for some attempt of war," and that Rosse says, "I saw the tyrant's power a-foot," and also forgot that the warlike usurper would be sure to superintend these military preparations ere he inclosed himself in his stronghold to await the expected assailants.

> How long hast thou been a grave-maker?—
> Of all the days i' the year, I came to 't that day that our last King Hamlet o'ercame Fortinbras.—
> How long is that since?—
> Cannot you tell that? every fool can tell that: it was the very day that young Hamlet was born; . . .
> I have been sexton here, man and boy, thirty years.—*Hamlet*, v. 1.

Blackstone says, "By this scene it appears that Hamlet was then thirty years old, and knew Yorick well, who had been dead twenty-two years. And yet in the beginning of the play he is spoken of as a *very young* man, one that designed to go back to school, *i.e.*, to the University of Wittenberg. The poet in the fifth act had forgot what he wrote in the first." Not at all; Shakespeare employed the term, "going to school," which was in his time used for attending college, or being an academic student. He has made Hamlet a man of thirty, to account for his mature reflections; but he has also made him possessed of the attractions of a still young man, and has taken care to associate the idea of youth all through the play with the various mentions of the prince. The dramatist's story, his development of character, demanded that the hero of this play should be, so to say, both youthful and mature; both personally young and mentally experienced; and

Shakespeare has, with his wonted felicity of conveying blended impressions, contrived to present this dual combination in the individuality of Hamlet.

> Althea dreamed she was delivered of a firebrand.—2 *H. IV.*, ii. 2.

Johnson observes, "Shakespeare is here mistaken in his mythology, and has confounded Althea's fire-brand with Hecuba's." Not so; Shakespeare has elsewhere proved (in two passages: one in "The Second Part of Henry VI.," i. 1., where York says, "As did the fatal brand Althea burn'd unto the prince's heart of Calydon"; and one in "Troilus and Cressida," ii. 2., where Cassandra says, "Our *fire-brand* brother, Paris, burns us all,") that he perfectly knew both these mythological stories; but he, like the true dramatist that he is, intentionally put the blunder into the mouth of Falstaff's page, who may be supposed to have picked up a smattering knowledge of mythological allusion from associating with his master and Prince Hal. Shakespeare has even taken care to draw attention to its being *a purposed mistake*, by making the prince give the boy a crown in reward for what he ironically terms his "*good interpretation.*"

> How chance the prophet could not at that time
> Have told me, I being by, that I should kill him.—*R. III.*, iv. 2.

Malone sneeringly says, "The Duke of Gloster was not by when Henry uttered the prophecy. Our author seldom took the trouble to turn to the plays to which he referred." That Shakespeare, of all dramatists, should be accused of *seldom taking trouble* is truly absurd; the very care and skill with which he made strictness of historic fact subordinate to the requirements of dramatic art, suffice to absolve him from the charge. In the present instance, he but gives effect to Richard's scoff by making him misstate the attendant circumstances of the prophecy he is citing.

> I, that was washed to death with fulsome wine.—*Ibid.*, v. 3.

Steevens pertly remarks, "Shakespeare seems to have forgot himself. The duke (as appears from act i., sc. 4) was killed before he was thrown into the malmsey-butt, and consequently could not be *wash'd to death.*" Had Mr. Steevens carefully scanned the scene he refers to, he might have perceived that the First Murderer stabs Clarence twice, saying, "If all this will not do, *I'll drown you in the malmsey-butt within;*" and immediately carries off his victim. Thus, the dramatist gives us ground to suppose that the dying man hears these words, and, half-murder'd, is flung into the wine to be finally "wash'd to death."

> More dances my rapt heart
> Than when I first my wedded mistress saw
> Bestride my threshold.—*Coriol.*, iv. 5.

Steevens observes, "Shakespeare was unaware that a Roman bride, on her entry into her husband's house, was prohibited from *bestriding* his threshold; and that, lest she should even touch it, she was always lifted over it." Instead of proving that Shakespeare was "unaware" of the custom in question, we think the present passage indicates that he knew there was a classical ceremonial in receiving a bride at the entrance of her bridegroom's house ; and that by making Aufidius advert thus particularly to the occasion, the poet evinces his perfect consciousness that there was a solemn rite therewith connected. May it not be Mr. Steevens betrays that he was " unaware " of the sense in which Shakespeare here uses the word " bestride " ? which, in the present passage, is not to be taken literally for " step across," but is to be accepted as meaning "pass over," "cross over." Shakespeare thus uses the word " stride," in " Cymbeline," iii. 3, where we find :—

> A prison for a debtor, that not dares
> To *stride* a limit.

Meaning to *overpass* a prescribed bound.

> How has the ass broke the wall, that thou art out of the city?—
> Yonder comes a poet and a painter: the plague of company light upon thee.—
> *Timon*, iv. 3.

Because the commentators assume " yonder " to indicate a spot within view, they blame our author's dramatic arrangement here ; and Reed speaks of " the negligence of Shakespeare," while Malone says, " Shakespeare was not very attentive to these minute particulars." But we find a much better solution of the difficulty than imputing negligence and inattention to the most finished dramatist ever known, by believing that "yonder" is here used for "over there," "from that place"; since Shakespeare often uses the word " yonder " in passages where the object spoken of is not seen by the speaker.

> When she first met Mark Antony, she pursed up his heart, upon the river of Cydnus.—*Ant. & C.*, ii. 2.

Mason says, " This is a strange instance of negligence and inattention. Enobarbus is made to say that Cleopatra gained Antony's heart on the river Cydnus ; but it appears from the conclusion of his own description that Antony had never seen her there ; that, whilst she was on the river, Antony was sitting alone, enthroned in the market-place." Surely, it might be retorted that the negligence and inattention are the commentator's ; since he did not perceive that " upon the river Cydnus " is here used to signify the district on the shores of the river Cydnus, including the " city " which " cast her people out upon her," and its " market-place " wherein " Antony " sat " enthron'd." The idiom " upon the Seine," or " upon the river Thames," is employed to express the adjacent shores of those streams, the country in their neighbourhood, the land on their banks.

> The herbs that have on them cold dew o' the night
> Are strewings fitt'st for graves. Upon their faces.
> You were as flowers, now withered: even so
> These herblets shall, which we upon you strow.—*Cym.*, iv. 2.

Malone observes, " Shakespeare did not recollect when he wrote these words, that there was but *one* face on which the flowers could be strewed "; and Singer remarks, " It is one of the poet's lapses of thought." For our parts, we can rather imagine a passage of Shakespeare's to be misapprehended by its peruser than that he himself " did not recollect " what he was about, or that he wrote with any

" lapse of thought." It seems to us that here " Upon their faces " does not refer so much to the faces of the two bodies now lying before the speaker as to the faces of corses generally, when prepared for burial, and having flowers strewn upon them, or when already in their " graves," and having " strewings " scattered upon that portion of the mound of earth beneath which the head and face lie.

> Or I 'll be buried in the king's highway,
> Some way of common trade where subjects' feet
> May hourly trample on their sovereign's head.—*R. II.*, iii. 3.

Johnson's note on this passage contains the singular sentence, " Shakespeare is very apt to deviate from the pathetic to the ridiculous ; " (! ! !) and expresses the wish that the speech of Richard had ended at the line last quoted. The dramatist knew, what the critic could not discern, that lengthy lamentation and diffuse self-pityings are the very characteristics of the weak king's diction.

> That fought with us upon Saint Crispin's day.—*H. V.*, iv. 3.

The spirited speech which concludes with the above line is pronounced by Johnson to be " too long" !

> Give me another horse : bind up my wounds.
> Have mercy, Jesu ! Soft ! I did but dream.—*R. III.*, v. 3.

Upon the wonderfully conceived speech of a terror-stricken conscience, commencing with these two lines, Johnson observes, " There is in this, as in many of our author's speeches of passion, something very trifling, and something very striking. Richard's debate whether he should quarrel with himself is too long continued."

> O proper stuff !
> This is the very painting of your fear.—*Macb.*, iii. 4.

At the conclusion of Lady Macbeth's energetic remonstrance, commencing thus, Johnson appends the remark, " This speech is rather too long for the circumstances in which it is spoken." Now, if reference be made to the above-cited four speeches against which Johnson brings the charge that each of them is too long, we think the referrer will agree with us that the fittest response to the commentator is the one made by Hamlet to Polonius :—" It shall to the barber's, with your beard."

One would not be rough or trenchant with a critic who has so good a claim to our respect in many points as Dr. Johnson ; but when we recall some of his own rough and trenchant animadversions upon our beloved Shakespeare, we cannot help feeling somewhat of bitterness. As a vindication of our resentment, and as an apt climax to our present heading, we will quote Johnson's concluding note upon " Cymbeline" : " This play has many just sentiments, some natural dialogues, and some pleasing scenes, but they are obtained at the expense of much incongruity. To remark the folly of the fiction, the absurdity of the conduct, the confusion of names and manners of different times, and the impossibility of the events in any system of life, were to waste criticism upon unresisting imbecility (! ! ! !), upon faults too evident for detection and too gross for aggravation." To our thinking, on the contrary, the incongruities of Druidical, Pagan, and Christian that may be traced in this enchanting romantic drama—among other minor so-called inconsistencies—were purposely here co-introduced by the dramatist as essential to his high art-purpose of depicting the existence of purest religion and purest morals amid primitive forms. How should it be objected that Imogen in one single exclamation combines an address to a Pagan god and to a Christian institution ("O Jove! I think, *Foundations** fly the wretched") when we perceive the manner in which the poet has made her a perfect exemplar of peerless woman-hood, combining the simplicity of Druid times, the nobleness of antique classical times, and the charity of Christian times? Why should we take exception against the ancient Briton, Posthumus, uttering so Christian a sentiment as this: "Kneel not to me: the power that I have on you is to spare you; the malice towards you to forgive you: live, and deal with others better," when we recall that the speaker's character has been drawn throughout with a view to show how the spirit of Christianity prevails to inspire a man during his gradual growth from Pagan vindictiveness and revenge into tolerance and for-bearance, with forgiveness of injury? Need we care that Belarius couples an allusion to Saracenic giants, who "keep their impious tur-bands on, without good-morrow to the sun," in the same sentence with his admonition to the two princely boys "to adore the heavens" with holiest morning worship, when we remember how divinely our Shakespeare has denoted natural piety, reverence of youth to age, instinctive affection, and all generous impulses of innate goodness in these young born princes peasant-bred? We cannot help thinking that "Cymbeline," instead of being one of Shakespeare's least con-gruously conducted plays, is rather one of those in which he best carries out his own supreme dramatic law of unity in moral design and impression.

ALLITERATION

Shakespeare satirises the over-use of alliteration in style, which was in his time a fashionable affectation. Holofernes—reading aloud to Sir Nathaniel the verses he has composed in honour of the princess's hunting, which he calls "an *extemporal epitaph* on the *death* of the *deer*"—says, "I will something *affect the letter*, for it argues facility" and then proceeds :—

> The *preyful princess pierc'd* and *prick'd* a *pretty pleasing pricket :*
>   *Some say* a *sore*, or else *sorel*, till now made *sore* with *shooting.*
> The dogs did yell: put l to *sore*, then *sorel* jumps from thicket ;
>   Or pricket, *sore*, or else *sorel ;* the people fall a-hooting,
> If *sore* be *sore*, then l to *sore* makes fifty *sores*: O *sore* l!
> Of one *sore* I a hundred make, by adding but one more l.—*Love's L. L.*, iv. 2.

---

* Establishments founded by charitable persons, with a settled revenue, where alms and relief were given.

Again in the specimen which Nick Bottom selects for the purpose of showing how well he can spout and rant :—

> The *raging rocks*
> And *shivering shocks*
> Shall break the locks
> Of prison-gates ;
> And Phibbus' car
> Shall shine from far
> And *make* and *mar*
> The *foolish fates.—Mid. N. D.*, i. 2.

Shakespeare himself occasionally uses alliteration for a special purpose of effect. As where Biron is railing at love :—

> This *wimpled, whining*, purblind, *wayward* boy ; . . .
> Th' anointed *sovereign* of *sighs* and groans,
> *Liege* of all *loiterers* and malcontents,
> Dread *prince* of *plackets.—Love's L. L.*, iii. 1.

And where Biondello is heaping up contumelious description on the steed which brings Petruchio to the wedding :—

> *Sped* with *spavins* . . . *stark spoiled* with the *staggers, begnawn* with the *bots, swayed* in the back, and *shoulder-shotten* ; . . . two letters for her name fairly *set* down in *studs*, and here and there *pieced* with *packthread.—Tam. of S.*, iii. 2.

Also, where Mercutio is jeeringly citing some of the noted beauties of antiquity, as compared with Romeo's charmer, Rosaline :—

> *Laura* to his *lady* was a kitchen-wench ; . . . *Dido*, a *dowdy* ; . . . *Helen* and *Hero, hildings* and *harlots.—R. & Jul.*, ii. 4.

Likewise, where the insolent Iago is coarsely goading Brabantio into alarm at his daughter's elopement with the Moor :—

> You 'll have your *nephews neigh* to you ; you 'll have *coursers* for *cousins*, and *gennets* for *germans.—Oth.*, i. 1.

And, again, where he is rollickingly describing the powers of the English in drinking, as an incitement to Cassio to get drunk :—

> I learned it in England, where, indeed, they are most *potent* in *potting.—Ibid.*, ii. 3.

ANTITHETICAL STYLE.

Shakespeare, among the many varied resources of expressive style, has availed himself of antithesis in several forms. He sometimes introduces words, antithetical to each other, in the same sentence :—

> I forget :
> But these sweet thoughts do even refresh my labours ;
> *Most* busy, *least* when I do it.*—Temp.*, iii. 1.

> Love, therefore, and tongue-tied simplicity
> In *least* speak *most*, to my capacity.—*Mid. N. D.*, v. 1.

---

* The Folio prints " lest " for " least " in this passage ; and many substitutions have been made for this word by various commentators. But we think that the other instances here cited by us of passages similarly constructed, serve to prove that the antithesis of " most " and " least " was intended by Shakespeare in the present instance.

Chewing the food of *sweet* and *bitter* fancy.—*As You L.,* iv. 3.
Hold *little* faith, though thou hast *too much* fear.—*Tw. N.,* v. 1.
Then poor Cordelia !

And yet not so ; since, I am sure, my love's
More *richer* than my tongue.—*Lear,* i. 1.
I could have given *less* matter a *better* ear.—*Ant. & C.,* ii. 1.
The *scriptures* of the loyal Leonatus,
All turn'd to *heresy* ?—*Cym.,* iii. 4.
But to *win* time, to *lose* so bad employment.—*Ibid.,* iii. 4.

Sometimes he uses an epithet that is antithetical with the noun to
which it is appended. [*See* LOVE-EXAGGERATIONS] :—

This *senior-junior, giant-dwarf,* Dan Cupid.—*Love's L. L.,* iii. 1.
According to the fool's bolt, sir, and such *dulcet diseases.*—*As You L.,* v. 4.
Dead life, blind sight, poor mortal *living ghost.*—*R. III.,* iv. 4.
Courteous destroyers, affable wolves, meek bears.—*Timon,* iii. 6.
O thou *sweet king-killer,* and *dear divorce*
'Twixt natural son and sire ! thou *bright defiler.*—*Ibid.,* iv. 3.
And come down with *fearful bravery.*—*Jul. C.,* v. 1.
Such a *holy witch,* that he enchants societies.—*Cym.,* i. 7.
O most delicate fiend !

Who is 't can read a woman ?—*Ibid.,* v. 5.
How now, *wholesome iniquity.*—*Per.,* iv. 6.

And he sometimes links antithetical terms together in a sentence :—

Thy speaking of my tongue, and I thine, most *truly falsely,* must needs be granted
to be much at one.—*H. V.,* v. 2.

Ignorance itself knows is so *abundant scarce.*—*Tr. & Cr.,* ii. 3.
Turn all her mother's *pains and benefits*
To laughter and contempt.—*Lear,* i. 4.

Sometimes he has entire passages of antithetical diction :—

The king's a beggar, now the play is done :
All is well ended, if this suit be won,
That you express content ; which we will pay,
With strife to please you, day exceeding day :
Ours be your patience then, and yours our parts ;
Your gentle hands lend us, and take our hearts.—*All's W.,* v. 3.
Woe's scene, world's shame, *grave's due by life usurp'd,*
Brief abstract and record of tedious days,
Rest thy unrest on England's lawful earth,
Unlawfully made drunk with innocent blood !—*R. III.,* iv. 4.
Bids the wind blow the earth into the sea,
*Or swell the curled waters 'bove the main.**—*Lear,* iii. 1.
But that your royalty

Holds idleness your subject, I should take you
For idleness itself.—
'Tis sweating labour

To bear such idleness so near the heart.—*Ant. & C.,* i. 3.
The borders maritime

Lack blood to think on 't, and *flush youth* revolt.—*Ibid.,* i. 4.
The breaking of so great a thing should make
A greater crack : the round world
Should have *shook lions into civil streets,*
And citizens to their dens.—*Ibid.,* v. 1.

---

* " Main " here used for the mainland.

There are several instances of Shakespeare using the words " general " and " particular " antithetically ; in the same way that he uses " beast " and " man " [*See* BEAST AND MAN] :—

> My brother *general*, the commonwealth,
> To brother born a household cruelty,
> I make my quarrel in *particular*.—*2 H. IV.*, iv. 1.
>
> Where 's our *general ?*
> Here I am, thou *particular* fellow.—*2 H. VI.*, iv. 2.
>
> Now let the *general* trumpet blow his blast,
> *Particularities* and petty sounds
> To cease !—*Ibid.*, v. 2.
>
> For the success,
> Although *particular*, shall give a scantling
> Of good or bad unto the *general*.—*Tr. & Cr.*, i. 3.
>
> Our *general* doth salute you with a kiss.
> Yet is the kindness but *particular ;*
> 'Twere better she were kiss'd in *general*.—*Ibid.*, iv. 5.
>
> You hear what he hath said,
> Which was sometime his *general ;* who lov'd him
> In a most dear *particular*.—*Coriol.*, v. 1.
>
> Of him that, his *particular* to foresee,
> Smells from the *general* weal.—*Timon*, iv. 3.
>
> Though in *general* part we were oppos'd,
> Yet our old love made a *particular* force,
> And made us speak like friends.—*Ibid.*, v. 3.
>
> Shall in the *general* censure take corruption
> From that *particular* fault.—*Hamlet*, i. 4.
>
> Nor doth the *general* care
> Take hold of me ; for my *particular* grief
> Is of so flood-gate and o'erbearing nature.—*Oth.*, i. 3.

Shakespeare has some passages where there is an effect given of an intended antithesis, but where there is no real antithesis existing :—

> *If you be not mad*, be gone; *if you have reason*, be brief.—*Tw. N.*, i. 5.
>
> *Are you not mad indeed ?* or *do you but counterfeit ?*—*Ibid.*, iv. 2.
>
> But let him say so then, and *let him go ;*
> But let him swear so, and *he shall not stay*.—*W. T.*, i. 2.
>
> *If I thought it were a piece of honesty* to acquaint the king withal, I would not do't: *I hold it the more knavery* to conceal it; and therein am I constant to my profession.— *Ibid.*, iv. 3.
>
> Then say at once *if I maintained the truth ;*
> Or else* *was wrangling Somerset in error ?*—*1 H. VI.*, ii. 4.
>
> Speak, Prince of Ithaca; *and be 't of less expect*
> *That matter needless, of importless burden,*
> *Divide thy lips* than *we are confident,*
> *When rank Thersites opes his mastiff jaws,*
> *We shall hear music, wit, and oracle*—*Tr. & Cr.*, i. 3.
>
> Tullus Aufidius, is he within your walls ?—
> No, *nor a man that fears you less than he,*
> *That's lesser than a little*.—*Coriol.*, i. 4.

Promise me friendship, but perform none : *if thou wilt not promise*, the gods plague thee, for thou art a man ! *if thou dost perform*, confound thee, for thou art a man !— *Timon*, iv. 3.

> *If thou hadst not been born the worst of men,*
> *Thou hadst been a knave and flatterer.*—*Ibid.*, iv. 3.

If I bring you no sufficient testimony that I have enjoyed the dearest bodily part of

---

* " Or else " is here used to express " or, in other words."

your mistress, my ten thousand ducats are yours ; so is your diamond too ; *if I come off, and leave her in such honour as you have trust in,* she your jewel, this your jewel, and my gold are yours.—*Cym., i.* 5.

If you can penetrate her with your fingering, so ; we'll try with tongue too : if none will do, *let her remain ;* but *I'll never give o'er.—Ibid.,* ii. 3.

> *If you will swear you have not done 't,* you lie ;
> And I will kill thee, *if thou dost deny.—Ibid.,* ii. 4.

In the following passage there is the real antithesis between " inn " (which originally meant an abode, or dwelling ; and here implies a stately dwelling) and " alehouse " (as meaning a lowly house of entertainment) : while, at the same time, there is the effect of antithesis between " inn " (in its more usual and exclusive acceptation) and " alehouse," as being both houses of wayside entertainment, though superior in grade the one to the other :—

> Thou map of honour, thou King Richard's tomb,
> And not King Richard ; thou most beauteous *inn,*
> Why should hard-favour'd grief be lodg'd in thee,
> When triumph is become an *alehouse* guest.—*R. II.,* v. 1.

APPRECIATION OF FRIENDSHIP: INTIMACY.

The intensity of strength wherewith Shakespeare appreciated the sentiment of friendship, the passionate fervour with which he depicts its attachment and glorifies its object, as evidenced in various passages in his plays, serve not only to denote his own warmth of nature and might of heart, but also serve to illustrate many of the ardent expressions that abound in his sonnets,—those veiled yet glowingly demonstrative outpourings of his own affection. The diction of his time permitted much more lavish utterance of feeling, the habits of his time allowed much more marked and open token of preference, between man and man, than the diction and habits of modern times permit ; and when we read the following eloquently effusive passages, we cannot but rejoice that William Shakespeare lived and wrote in an age that gave scope to unrestricted words and behaviour from one man-friend towards another. Thus passionately does he make Antonio, the noble-hearted and romantic-spirited sea-captain, express himself towards the youth for whom he has conceived a devoted personal attachment after saving him from perishing at sea :—

If you will not murder me for my love, let me be your servant. . . . The gentleness of all the gods go with thee ! . . . I do adore thee so.—*Tw. N.,* ii. 2.

> I could not stay behind you : my desire,
> More sharp than filed steel, did spur me forth ;
> And not all love to see you (though so much
> As might have drawn one to a longer voyage)
> But jealousy what might befall your travel,
> Being skilless in these parts ; which to a stranger,
> Unguided and unfriended, often prove
> Rough and unhospitable : my willing love,
> The rather by these arguments of fear,
> Set forth in your pursuit. . . . Hold, sir, here's my purse. . . .
> Haply your eye shall light upon some toy
> You have desire to purchase ; and your store,
> I think, is not for idle markets, sir.—*Ibid.,* iii. 3.

Is 't possible that my deserts to you
Can lack persuasion ?   Do not tempt my misery,
Lest that it make me so unsound a man
As to upbraid you with those kindnesses
That I have done for you. . . .
Let me speak a little.   This youth that you see here
I snatch'd one half out of the jaws of death ;
Reliev'd him with such sanctity of love,
And to his image, which methought did promise
Most venerable worth, did I devotion. . . .
But, O, how vile an idol proves this god !
Thou hast, Sebastian, done good feature shame.
In nature there 's no blemish but the mind ;
None can be call'd deform'd but the unkind :
Virtue is beauty ; but the beauteous evil
Are empty trunks, o'erflourish'd by the devil !—*Tw. N.*, iii. 4.

                A witchcraft drew me hither ;
That most ingrateful boy there, by your side,
From the rude sea's enrag'd and foamy mouth
Did I redeem ; a wreck past hope he was :
His life I gave him, and did thereto add
My love, without retention or restraint,
All his in dedication ; for his sake
Did I expose myself, pure for his love,
Into the danger of this adverse town ;
Drew to defend him when he was beset.—*Ibid.*, v. 1.

In reference to William Shakespeare himself might aptly be quoted his own words,—" You have a noble and a true conceit of godlike amity."   Thus earnestly, with the simple yet firm manliness of truth in an esteeming as well as loving attachment, does Hamlet speak to his bosom friend Horatio :—

Since my dear soul was mistress of her choice,
And could of men distinguish, her election
Hath seal'd thee for herself : for thou hast been
As one, in suffering all, that suffers nothing ;
A man that fortune's buffets and rewards
Hast ta'en with equal thanks : and bless'd are those
Whose blood and judgment are so well co-mingled,
That they are not a pipe for Fortune's finger
To sound what stop she please.   Give me that man
That is not passion's slave, and I will wear him
In my heart's core, ay, in my heart of heart,
As I do thee.—*Hamlet*, iii. 2.

The terms in which men-friends addressed each other were formerly scarcely less fond and caressing than those employed between lovers :—

Cease to persuade, *my loving Proteus.* . . .
         . . . *Sweet Valentine*, adieu !
Think on *thy Proteus*, when thou haply see'st
Some rare noteworthy object in thy travel. . . .
Sweet Proteus, no ; now let us take our leave.—*Two G. of V.*, i. 1.

One of his young court friends says to Bertram :—

O *my sweet lord*, that you will stay behind us !—*All's W.*, ii. 1.

And Parolles says to Bertram :—

What is the matter, *sweet-heart ?* . . . What, what, *sweet-heart ?*—*Ibid.*, ii. 3.

And Poins says to Prince Hal :—

Now, *my good sweet honey lord*, ride with us.—1 *H. IV.*, i. 2.

Coriolanus says of Menenius :—

> This man, Aufidius,
> Was *my belov'd* in Rome.—*Coriol.*, v. 2.

And Antony says of the friendship entertained by Cæsar for Brutus :—

> For Brutus, as you know, was Cæsar's *angel :*
> Judge, oh, you gods, how dearly Cæsar lov'd him !—*Jul. C.*, iii. 2.

And thus affectionate are the terms used by the friends and brothers-in-law, when they are reconciled after their temporary heat of quarrel:—

> *Cas.*   Hath Cassius liv'd
> To be but mirth and laughter to *his Brutus,*
> When grief, and blood ill-temper'd, vexeth him ?
> *Bru.* When I spoke that, I was ill-temper'd too.
> *Cas.* Do you confess so much ?   Give me your hand.
> *Bru.* And my heart too.
> *Cas.*   O Brutus !
> *Bru.*   What 's the matter ?
> *Cas.* Have not you love enongh to bear with me,
> When that rash humour which my mother gave me
> Makes me forgetful ?
> *Bru.*   Yes, Cassius ; and, from henceforth,
> When you are over-earnest with *your Brutus,*
> He 'll think your mother chides, and leave you so.—*Ibid.*, iv. 3.

Not unfrequently the word "lover" was formerly used for "friend ":—

> How true a gentleman you send relief,
> How dear a *lover* of my lord, your husband, . . .
> Which makes me think that this Antonio,
> Being the bosom *lover* of my lord.—*Mer. of V.*, iii. 4.
> Farewell, my lord : I as your *lover* speak.—*Tr. & Cr.*, iii. 3.
> Thy general is my *lover.*—*Coriol.*, v. 2.
> As I slew my best *lover* for the good of Rome.—*Jul. C.*, iii. 2.

And " friend " was sometimes formerly used for ' lover ":—

> He hath got his *friend* with child.—*M. for M.*, i. 5.
> Lady, will you walk about with your *friend.*—*M. Ado*, ii. 1.
> Art thou gone so ? my lord, my love, my *friend* !—*R. & Jul.*, iii. 5.
> Or to be naked with her *friend* abed an hour or more.—*Oth.*, iv. 1.
> So she from Egypt drive her all-disgracèd *friend* !—*Ant. & C.*, iii. 10.
> Though I profess myself her adorer, not [merely] her *friend.* . . .
> You are a *friend*, and therein the wiser.—*Cym.*, i. 5.

The demonstrations between men-friends were often formerly of extreme tenderness, without being felt to impair manly dignity ; and of this kind are the indications of attachment between Antonio and Bassanio:—

> I saw Bassanio and Antonio part :
> Bassanio told him he would make some speed
> Of his return : he answer'd, " Do not so ;
> Slubber not business for my sake, Bassanio,
> But stay the very riping of the time ;
> And for the Jew's bond which he hath of me,
> Let it not enter in your mind of love :
> Be merry ; and employ your chiefest thoughts
> To courtship, and such fair ostents of love
> As shall conveniently become you there:"
> And even there, *his eye being big with tears,*
> *Turning his face,* he put his hand behind him,
> *And with affection wondrous sensible,*
> *He wrung Bassanio's hand ;* and so they parted.—
> I think, he only loves the world for him.—*Mer. of V.*, ii. 8.

> Give me your hand, Bassanio : fare you well !
> Grieve not that I am fallen to this for you ; . . .
> Commend me to your honourable wife:
> Tell her the process of Antonio's end ;
> *Say how I lov'd you*, speak me fair in death ;
> And, when the tale is told, bid her be judge
> *Whether Bassanio had not once a love.*
> Repent not you that you shall lose your friend,
> And *he repents not that he pays your debt ;*
> For, if the Jew do cut but deep enough,
> I'll pay it instantly *with all my heart.—Mer. of V.*, iv. 1.

And also this description of York and Suffolk, dying together on the battle-field, while the describer, Exeter, and the hearer, King Harry V., are not afraid to own the manly tears they feel it forces from them:—

> Suffolk first died: and York, all haggled over,
> Comes to him, where in gore he lay insteep'd,
> And takes him by the beard; *kisses the gashes*
> That bloodily did yawn upon his face;
> And cries aloud, " *Tarry, dear cousin Suffolk !*
> *My soul shall thine keep company to heaven;*
> *Tarry, sweet soul, for mine, then fly abreast;*
> As in this glorious and well-foughten field
> We kept together in our chivalry ! "
> Upon these words I came and cheer'd him up:
> He smiled me in the face, raught me his hand,
> And, with a feeble gripe, says, " Dear my lord,
> Commend my service to my sovereign."
> So did he turn, and *over Suffolk's neck*
> *He threw his wounded arm and kiss'd his lips;*
> And so, *espous'd to death, with blood he seal'd*
> *A testament of noble-ending love.*
> *The pretty and sweet manner of it forc'd*
> *Those waters from me, which I would have stopp'd ;*
> But I had not so much of man in me,
> And all my mother came into mine eyes,
> And gave me up to tears.—
>   *I blame you not ;*
> *For, hearing this, I must perforce compound*
> *With mistful eyes, or they will issue too.—H. V.*, iv. 6.

That the usage existed in England in Shakespeare's time—as it still exists on the Continent—of men embracing each other when they meet or take leave, we have many indications in his contemporary writers as well as in his own writings.

The martial Coriolanus says to his fellow-general, Cominius :—

> O, *let me clip you*
> *In arms* as sound as when I woo'd.—*Coriol.*, i. 6.

And the warlike Aufidius, rejoicing to find his old opponent Coriolanus under his roof at Antium, exclaims :—

> *Let me twine*
> *Mine arms about that body*, where against
> My grained ash a hundred times hath broke,
> And scar'd the moon with splinters: *here I clip*
> *The anvil of my sword.—Ibid.*, iv. 5.

Biron, on discovering that he, the king, and the two companion noblemen, are all in love, cries joyfully :—

> Sweet lords, sweet lovers, O, *let us embrace !—Love's L. L.*, iv. 3.

Petruchio, meeting on the road the father of his brother-in-law, thus salutes the gentleman:—

> Let me embrace with old Vincentio.—*Tam. of S.,* iv. 5.

And Mark Antony, taking leave of Octavius Cæsar, says:—

> Come, sir, come;
> *I 'll wrestle with you in my strength of love:*
> *Look, here I have you; thus I let you go,*
> And give you to the gods.—*Ant. & C.,* iii. 2.

As a token of the extreme intimacy and familiarity of intercourse that subsisted formerly between men-friends, we find denotement that they often occupied the same bed-room, and even the same bed together.

Exeter, speaking indignantly of Lord Scroop's treason towards the king, says:—

> Nay, but the man that was *his bedfellow,**
> Whom he hath dull'd and cloy'd with gracious favours—
> That he should, for a foreign purse, so sell
> His sovereign's life to death and treachery!—*H. V.,* ii. 2.

Owing to this custom, the term became used to express close intimacy and affectionate companionship:—

> He loves your people;
> But tie him not to be their *bedfellow.—Coriol.,* ii. 2.

And the following passage again serves to show how common was the custom:—

> Oh, world, thy slippery turns! Friends now fast sworn,
> Whose double bosoms seem to wear one heart,
> Whose hours, *whose bed,* whose meal, and exercise,
> Are still together, who twin, as 'twere, in love
> Unseparable, shall within this hour,
> On a dissension of a doit, break out
> To bitterest enmity.—*Ibid.,* iv. 4.

Finally, Iago says:—

> *I lay with Cassio lately;*
> And, being troubled with a raging tooth,
> I could not sleep.
> There are a kind of men so loose of soul,
> That in their sleeps will mutter their affairs
> One of this kind is Cassio:
> *In sleep I heard him say, &c.,—Oth.,* iii. 3.

BEAST AND MAN.

Shakespeare frequently uses "beast" and "man" in contradistinction each to each—the one as the type of inhumanity, the other of humanity—or the one as representing unintelligence, the other intelligence; and his practice in this respect serves to show that the original is the right reading in the disputed instance of the passage

---

* Holinshed records this circumstance: "The said Lord Scroop was in such favour with the king that he admitted him sometime to be his bedfellow."

from " Macbeth," which we have cited among the rest to show how it
is but one of many parallel cases occurring in his works :—

O powerful love! that, in some respects, makes a *beast* a *man ;* in some other, a *man*
a *beast.*—*Merry W.*, v. 5.

When he is best, he is little worse than a *man ;* and when he is worst, he is little
better than a *beast.*—*Mer. of V.*, i. 2.

I think he be transformed into a *beast ;*
For I can no where find him like a *man.*—*As You L.*, ii. 7.

Whiles the eye of *man* did woo me,
That could do no vengeance to me.
Meaning me a *beast.*—*Ibid.*, iv. 3.

A king of *beasts*, indeed; if aught but *beasts*,
I had been still a happy king of *men.*— *R. II.*, v. 1.

What, ho ! you *men*, you *beasts.*—*R. & Jul.*, i. 1.

Art thou a *man ?* thy form cries out thou art.
Thy tears are womanish ; thy wild acts denote
The unreasonable fury of a *beast ;*
Unseemly woman in a seeming *man !*
Or ill-beseeming *beast* in seeming both.—*Ibid.*, iii. 3.

Timon will to the woods ; where he shall find
Th' unkindest *beast* more kinder than *mankind.*—*Timon*, iv. 1.

A *beast*, as thou art.   The canker gnaw thy heart,
For showing me again the eyes of *man !*— *Ibid.*, iv. 3.

What wouldst thou do with the world, Apemantus, if it lay in thy power ?—
Give it the *beasts*, to be rid of the *men.*—
Wouldst thou have thyself fall in the confusion of *men*, and remain a *beast* with
the *beasts ?*—*Ibid.*, iv. 3.

O, thou touch of hearts !
Think, thy slave *man* rebels ; and by thy virtue
Set them into confounding odds, that *beasts*
May have the world in empire !—*Ibid.*, iv. 3.

We cannot live on grass, on berries, water,
As beasts, and birds, and fishes.—
Nor on the *beasts* themselves, the birds, and fishes;
You must eat *men.*—*Ibid.*, iv. 3.

Timon is dead.   Who hath outstretch'd his span—
Some *beast*—read this ; there does not live a *man.*
Ibid., v. 4 (*Inscription*).

O, judgment, thou art fled to brutish *beasts*,
And *men* have lost their reason !—*Jul. C.*, iii. 2.

I dare do all that may become a *man ;*
Who dares do more is none.—
What *beast* was 't, then,
That made you break this enterprise to me?
When you durst do it, then you were a *man ;*
And, to be more than what you were, you would
Be so much more the *man.*—*Macb.*, i. 7.

What is a *man*,
If his chief good and market of his time
Be but to sleep and feed? a *beast*, no more.—*Hamlet*, iv. 4.

While I may 'scape,
I will preserve myself: and am bethought
To take the basest and most poorest shape,
That ever penury, in contempt of *man*,
Brought near to *beast.*—*Lear*, ii. 3.

> Allow not nature more than nature needs,
> *Man's* life is cheap as *beast's.—Ibid.*, ii. 4.
> Would you would bear your fortune like a *man* !—
> A horned *man's* a monster and a *beast.*—
> There's many a *beast*, then, in a populous city,
> And many a civil monster.—
> Did he confess it ?—
> > Good sir, be a *man.—Oth.*, iv. 1.
> Kingdoms are clay: our dungy earth alike
> Feeds *beast* as *man.—Ant. & C.*, i. 1.

Shakespeare puts the word "beast" into a woman's mouth as a term of strongest reprobation for *unmanliness* and *unnaturalness :—*

> > Sweet sister, let me live:
> What sin you do to save a brother's life,
> Nature dispenses with the deed so far
> That it becomes a virtue.—
> > > O, you *beast !*
> O, faithless coward!   O, dishonest wretch!
> Wilt thou be made a *man* out of my vice ?—*M. for M.*, iii. 1.

And into another woman's mouth to express 'a creature devoid of natural feeling,' ' an inhuman monster ' :—

> O, what a *beast* was I to chide at him !—*R. & Jul.*, iii. 2.

BITTER PUNS AND PLAYS ON WORDS : CONCEITS.

With his marvellous insight into the hidden springs of human passion as well as its effusive vents, the sources of emotion as well as its external signs, Shakespeare could hardly fail of denoting—among other fantastic shapes that human feeling takes—the proneness of some natures in moments of acute mental suffering to seek relief from the utterance of some bitter jest or whimsical quibble.   He has a passage that directly draws attention to this practice.   When the dying John of Gaunt, desperately grieving at his nephew King Richard's blindly pursued downward course, makes punning illustrations in reference to his own name, "Gaunt," the king exclaims, "Can sick men play so nicely with their names ?"   And Gaunt replies, "No, *misery makes sport to mock itself.*"   ("Richard II.," act ii., sc. 1.)   And on reference to this scene, a long string of instances will be found in addition to the following, which serve to show Shakespeare's sagacity in knowing as well as indicating this phase of passionate expression :—

> > For life, I prize it
> As I weigh grief, which I would *spare :* for honour,
> 'Tis a derivative from me to mine;
> And only that I stand for.—*W. T.*, iii. 2.

This is said by Hermione, a woman of strong self-control ; and she uses the word "spare" with concentratedly witty felicity of varied significance, partly in its sense of ' part with,' ' do without,' ' let go,' partly in that of ' forbear from destroying,' or ' shield from destruction,' and partly in that of ' avoid encountering ; ' so that her sentence tersely implies, ' I estimate life as. I estimate grief—things that I could willingly part with, while the one I would avoid destroying and the other I would avoid encountering.'

> You have beguil'd me with a *counterfeit*
> Resembling majesty, which, being touch'd and tried,
> Proves valueless.—*John*, iii. 1.

It is the impetuous-natured Constance who says this; using the word "counterfeit" in both the senses which it formerly bore of a 'portrait' and a 'false coin,' and thus flinging a double scoff at the king who has failed in his promise to her.

> Oh, lawful let it be
> That I have *room* with *Rome* to curse awhile!—*Ibid.*, iii. 1.

Again, it is the vehement Constance who avails herself of the mode in which "Rome" was sometimes pronounced, to give vent to a contemptuous utterance of her stung feeling.

> My sovereign lord, bestow yourself with speed:
> The French are *bravely* in their battles set,
> And will with all expedience charge on us.—*H. V.*, iv. 3.

Here it is Salisbury, one of the English warriors in the desperate condition of small numbers reduced by hard fighting and famine against a fresh and numerous force, who by using the word "bravely" indulges in a fleer at the 'bravingly boastful and defiant' enemy as well as at their 'showily arranged, smartly set forth' ranks.

> For *Suffolk's* duke, may he be *suffocate*,
> That dims the honour of this warlike isle!—*2 H. VI.*, i. 1.

Richard Plantagenet, Duke of York, in his wrath at Suffolk's betrayal of England's glory, utters this taunting pun.

> Foul wrinkled witch, what *mak'st* thou in my sight?—
> But repetition of what thou hast marr'd;
> That will I *make* before I let thee go.—*R. III.*, i. 3.

Gloster uses the word "mak'st" in the sense of 'dost'; but Margaret replies to it in its sense of 'achiev'st,' as used in juxta-position with "marr'd": her keen sense of wrong goading her into this sharpness of expression.

> My lord, my lord,
> I am a simple woman, much too weak
> To oppose your cunning. You're meek and humble-mouth'd;
> You sign your place and calling, in full seeming,
> With meekness and humility; but your heart
> Is cramm'd with arrogancy, spleen, and pride.
> You have by fortune and his highness' favours,
> Gone slightly o'er low steps, and now are mounted
> Where *powers* are your retainers; and your *words*,
> Domestics to you, serve your will as 't please
> Yourself pronounce their office.—*H. VIII.*, ii. 4.

It is the high-spirited and noble-hearted Queen Katharine, who pours forth this outspoken denouncement of the all-powerful Wolsey; and she uses two words therein with a double meaning,—"powers" in the duplicate sense of powerful 'persons' and 'powers of intellect'—and "words" in the duplicate sense of 'commands' and 'speech.' She tells him that by his own good fortune and the king's favours he has passed easily over the first steps from his original low position, and is now mounted to a height where potentates are at his disposal and direction, and where the powers of his own intellect are employed to promote his influence ; and his commands, as mere servitors, suffice to insure obedience to his will in whatever he desires to effect, while his speech serves his purpose by assuming whatever appearance of justice, truth, and candour he chooses to feign.   We the rather repeat our interpretation of the double meaning here borne by these two words, because they have been challenged as incorrect by other commentators.

> The more shame for ye ! holy men I thought ye,
> Upon my soul, two reverend *cardinal* virtues ;
> But *cardinal* sins and hollow hearts I fear ye.—*H. VIII.*, iii. 1. .

It is again Queen Katharine who, addressing the two Cardinals, Wolsey and Campeius, thus plays upon the word " cardinal " in its sense of ' chief ' and as used for their own ecclesiastical title.

> Oh, my lord,
> Press not a falling man too far ! 'tis virtue :
> His faults lie open to the laws ; let them,
> Not you, correct him.   My heart weeps to see him
> So *little* of his *great* self. . . .
> So *fare you well*, my *little good* lord cardinal.—
> So *farewell* to the *little good* you bear me.
> Farewell, a long farewell, to all my *greatness !*—*Ibid.*, iii. 2.

Norfolk's parting sneer comprises the double meaning of 'my good lord cardinal possessed of so little goodness,' and ' my good lord cardinal looking so little in this hour of exposure.'   It is used in reference to the Chamberlain's compassionate words, " my heart weeps to see him so *little* of his *great* self " ; and Wolsey uses the words " little good " in rejoinder to signify ' small amount of good-will.'   The immediate sequence of the word " greatness " in Wolsey's speech serves to show the link that is maintained between the Chamberlain's expression, Norfolk's sneer, and the Cardinal's reply.   This kind of play upon words, marking Shakespeare's style even in some of his gravest scenes, is perfectly consistent with nature ; especially in a case like the present, where men of intellect are dealing in sarcasm and sarcastic retort.

> These times of *woe* afford no time to *woo*.—*R. & Jul.*, iii. 4.

Paris, addressing Lord and Lady Capulet when mourning for their kinsman Tybalt, yet applying to them for the hand of their daughter, Juliet, permits himself thus much of sportiveness in phraseology.

> Some say the lark makes sweet *division ;*
> This doth not so, for she *divideth* us.—*Ibid.*, iii. 5.

Here the grief of Juliet, even in the hour of parting with her new-made husband, takes the wayward course of quibbling on the word " division " in its double sense of brilliant sequences of notes sung by a bird, and of ' separation.'   Such are the tricks played by the imagination, even at moments when the heart is most sorely tried ; and being such, Shakespeare so denotes them.

> Noting this penury, to myself I said,
> An if a man did *need* a poison now, ·
> Whose sale is present death in Mantua,
> Here lives a caitiff wretch would sell it him.
> Oh, this same thought did but forerun my *need* :
> And this same *needy* man must sell it me.—*Ibid.*, v. 1.

Romeo's inner thought being absorbed by the one image of his Juliet's death, his surface thought of obtaining the poison which will enable him to rejoin her takes the most capricious form of expression ; not only playing on the words " need " and " needy," but dallying with verbal repetitions, in " sell it him," " sell it me," " this same thought," and " this same man." Precisely the mode in which the process of surface-thought plays in fluctuating waves of vagary over the one deep unmoving torturing thought.

> All our *bills.*—
> *Knock me down with 'em ; cleave me to the girdle.*—Timon, iii. 4.

In the wrath of seeing the men all pressing upon him with their written demands, Timon grimly plays upon the word " bills," in its sense of weapons.

> No place will please me so, no mean of death,
> As here *by* Cæsar, and *by* you cut off.—*Jul. C.*, iii. 1.

Antony, in the mingled grief and indignation of seeing Cæsar lying there murdered, takes a kind of scornful pleasure in thus quibbling upon the word " by " ; first in its sense of ' by the side of' or ' beside' ; and secondly in its sense of ' by your means,' or ' through you.'

> Pardon me, Julius ! Here wast thou bay'd, brave *hart*;
> Here didst thou fall ; and here thy hunters stand,
> Sign'd in thy spoil, and crimson'd in thy lethe.
> O world, thou wast the forest to this *hart ;*
> And this, indeed, O world, the *heart* of thee.
> How like a *deer*, stricken by many princes,
> Dost thou here lie !—*Ibid.*, iii, 1.

Here Antony, still in the mood for taking refuge in conceits and plays upon words from the sting of his suppressed indignation against Cæsar's assassins, lets his fancy run riot in a figurative image that shall aggrandise his dead friend to the utmost. And yet Coleridge has denounced the two lines in this passage commencing " O world," &c., affirming them to be an interpolation ; while another critic has pronounced them to be a " a foul blemish "!

> *No eyes* in your head, nor *no money* in your purse ? Your *eyes are in a heavy case,* your *purse in a light :* yet you *see* how this world goes.—I *see* it *feelingly.*—Lear, iv. 6.

Gloster's attempt to reply, in a mood of quibbling correspondent with Lear's, is intensely pathetic ; and hardly a stronger instance than the present could be cited of the affecting power with which bitter puns and conceits may be introduced by a true poet into the most serious and even tragic scenes.

> No, *my heart is turned to stone ;* I strike it, and *it hurts my hand.*—Oth., iv. 1.

This wilfulness of an imagination writhing in anguish, and twisting itself into contortions of figurative speech, seems to us deeply moving ; and yet it provokes Mr. Steevens to remark that by it Shakespeare " counteracts his pathos " (!)

> Do not talk to me, Emilia ;
> I cannot *weep ;* nor answer have I none,
> But what should *go by water.*—*Ibid.*, iv. 2.

Desdemona stunned and bewildered, her eyes dry and tearless, from the effect of her husband's cruel usage and mysterious reproaches, can only try, with quivering lips and an attempted smile, to rouse herself from her stupor of grief; and the exact effect of this is conveyed by the dramatist's introduction of this slight play on the word here.

> Be witness to me, O thou blessed moon !
> When men revolted shall upon record
> Bear hateful memory, poor Enobarbus did
> Before thy face repent. . . .
> O sovereign mistress of true melancholy !
> The poisonous damp of night dispunge upon me,
> That life, a very rebel to my will,
> May hang no longer on me ; *throw my heart*
> *Against the flint and hardness of my fault ;*
> *Which, being dried with grief, will break to powder,*
> And finish all foul thoughts.—*Ant. & C.,* iv. 9.

Only on the principle that different natures are affected differently by the same causes, can be explained the reason why this passage—which occasions Dr. Johnson to resent what he calls "the intrusion of a conceit so far-fetched and unaffecting"—strikes us as being profoundly affecting and true to nature ; the anguish of the speaker's remorse goading him into the very necessity for his imagination to take refuge in forms of fantastic figurativeness.

> But, come, come, Antony,
> Help me, my women—*we must draw thee up ;*
> Assist good friends.—
> Oh, quick, or I am gone.—
> *Here 's sport,* indeed ! *How heavy weighs my lord !*
> Our *strength* is all gone into *heaviness,*
> That makes the *weight :* had I great Juno's *power,*
> The *strong-wing'd* Mercury should *fetch thee up,*
> And set thee by Jove's side.—*Ibid.,* iv. 13.

Though the whole passage bears token that Cleopatra is in that bitter mood of mind which prompts her to turn cruel earnest into mocking pastime, yet several emendators have proposed other words instead of " sport " here, which, we think, is manifestly correct.

> And so, great powers,
> If you will take this *audit,* take this life,
> And cancel these cold *bonds.*—*Cym.,* v. 4.

Dr. Johnson observes, that " this equivocal use of 'bonds' is another instance of our author's *infelicity in pathetic speeches* " (!); but, to our mind, it is in precise keeping with the whole tenor of Posthumus's passionately repentant speech—emotional, mournful, and highly imaginative in its lonely self-communing.

Into one of his most serious scenes our prince of dramatists has introduced a slight and very familiar touch, with extremely natural effect, turning it to excellent account as a means of stirring a father's heart, agitating it with wild thoughts, and prompting fierce plays on words and bitter puns. No one but a poet like Shakespeare would have ventured upon using such means as a passing black, a flying particle of smut resting upon a child's nose, for such a purpose, it would have been deemed beneath the dignity of tragedy by any but

the fearless delineator of nature in all her varied phases of tragic event
and feeling :—

> What, *hast smutch'd thy nose?*
> They say, it is a copy out of mine.   Come, captain,
> We must be *neat;* not *neat,* but *cleanly,* captain :
> And yet the steer, the heifer, and the calf,
> Are all call'd *neat.*—*W. T.,* i. 2.

And into one of his most deeply tragic scenes he has introduced a
homely touch, inexpressibly affecting and significant. It not only
serves to show the swelling and heaving of the heart that gives the dying
man a sense of intolerable oppression [*See* PHYSICAL INDICATIONS] ;
but it also serves to indicate the native courtesy of the old king, and
the gentleness of speech that has at length succeeded to his former
vehemence and violence when insane. It aids in reconciling us to his
death, as the peaceful end to so much unrest and distraction :—

> Thou 'lt come no more,
> Never, never, never, never, never!
> *Pray you, undo this button: thank you, sir.*—*Lear,* v. 3.

CANT TERMS.

In Shakespeare's works we find some of the cant terms and thieves'
jargon that were in use at the time he wrote ; and it will be perceived
that a few of them have still survived in modern slang :—

At last I spied *an ancient angel* ['a good old soul,' 'a worthy old chap'; a 'fellow
easily to be cajoled'] coming down the hill, will serve the turn.—*Tam. of S.,* iv. 2.

The wisest *aunt* ['good old dame,' 'worthy old woman'], telling the saddest tale,
sometime for three-foot stool mistaketh me.—*Mid. N. D.,* ii. 1.

Are summer songs for me and my *aunts* ['wanton women'].—*W. T.,* iv. 2 (*Song*).

We knew where the *bona-robas* ['good-looking bad women'] were, and had the best
of them at commandment. . . . She was then a *bona-roba.*—*2 H. IV.,* iii. 2.

You filthy *bung* [a cant term for a 'purse' and for a 'pocket'; but, by using it as a
nick-name for Pistol, Doll not only calls him a pickpocket, but insinuates that he is
saturated with the fumes of the beer-barrel], away !—*Ibid.,* ii. 4.

I knew by that piece of service, the men would *carry coals* ['put up with insults,'
'endure indignities,' 'submit tamely to affronts.'].—*H. V.,* iii. 2.

Gregory, o' my word, we 'll not *carry coals.*—*R. & Jul.,* i. 1.

Ye shall have a hempen *caudle* ['death by the rope,' or 'hanging'] then, and the
help of hatchet [this is Shakespeare's variation of an old slang phrase, 'pap with a
hatchet,' which signified 'the stroke of the headsman's axe']. [*See* PASSAGES WHERE AN
ORIGINAL WORD IS INTRODUCED INTO A USUAL FORM OF PHRASE.]—*2 H. VI.,* iv. 7.

Could I come near your beauty with my nails,
I 'd set my *ten commandments* ['fingers,' 'hands'] in your face.—*Ibid.,* i. 3.

There is no remedy, I must *coney-catch* ['cheat,' 'practise sharping'] ; I must shift.
—*Merry W.,* i. 3.

Take heed, Signior Baptista, lest you be *coney-catched* ['cheated'] in this business.—
Tam. of S., v. 1.

And against your *coney-catching* ['cheating'] rascals.—*Merry. W.,* i. 1.

Come, you are so full of *coney-catching* ['tricking waggery,' 'jocular deception'].—
Tam. of S., iv. 1.

"*Convey*" ['steal,' 'filch,' 'pilfer,' 'purloin,' 'rob'], the wise it call. "Steal!" foh! a fico for the phrase!—*Merry W.*, i. 3.

Since Henry's death, I fear, there is *conveyance* ['fraudulent dealing,' 'knavery,' 'sly and tricking practice'].—1 *H. VI.*, i. 3.

Would we could see you at *Corinth* ['our brothel,' 'our house of free-living.' See "Corinthian," subsequently cited and explained].—*Timon*, ii. 2.

O, nuncle, *court holy-water* ['flattering protestations,' 'favouring phrases'] in a dry house is better than this rain-water out o' door.—*Lear*, iii. 2.

I think thee now some common *customer* ['bad woman,' 'a woman who infamously trades on her beauty']—*All's W.*, v. 3.

I marry her! what? a *customer!*—*Oth.*, iv. 1.

I'll thrust my knife in your mouldy chaps, an you play the saucy *cuttle* ['the knife used by thieves and cutpurses'] with me.—2 *H. IV.*, ii. 4.

He, sir, that takes pity on decayed men, and gives them *suits of durance* ['captivity,' 'imprisonment'].—*Com. of E.*, iv. 3.

Is not a buff jerkin a most sweet *robe of durance?*—1 *H. IV.*, i. 2.

They call drinking deep, *dying scarlet.*—*Ibid.*, ii. 4.

I will retort the sum in *equipage* ['stolen goods'].—*Merry W.*, ii. 2.

And, being *fap* ['maudlin drunk'], sir, was, as they say, *cashier'd* ['turned out'— his pockets, and then himself].—*Ibid.*, i. 1.

I am joined with no *foot land-rakers* ['footpads,' 'those who rob on foot'].— 1 *H. IV.*, ii. 1.

Thou diest on point of *fox* ['sword:' originating in the circumstance that Andrea Ferrara, and other foreign sword-cutlers, adopted a fox as the blade-mark of their weapons].—*H. V.*, iv. 4.

He woos both high and low, both rich and poor,
Both young and old, one with another, Ford:
He loves the *gally-mawfry* ['heterogeneous collection,' 'hotch-potch,' 'medley'].— *Merry W.*, ii. 1.

And they have a dance which the wenches say is a *gally-mawfry* of gambols, because they are not in 't.—*W. T.*, iv. 3.

      She's impudent, my lord;
And was a common *gamester* ['wanton woman'] to the camp.—*All's W.*, v. 3.

  Were you a *gamester* at five, or at seven?—*Per.*, iv. 6.

  He is drunk now: where had he wine?
  And Trinculo is reeling ripe: where should they
  Find this grand liquor that hath *gilded*
['intoxicated:' besides implying by this cant term for being drunk that they are in liquor, "gilded" here includes allusion to being enriched by the alchemist's elixir (which was a preparation of gold), as a fleer at their having become yellowed over by the "filthy mantled pool" through which they have been led by Ariel]
         them?—*Temp.*, v. 1.

Nay, I can *gleek* ['gibe,' 'jeer:' in modern slang, 'chaff.' The expression originated in the name for a game of cards, called "gleek:" in which game "a gleek" was the term for a set of three particular cards; "to gleek," for gaining an advantage over; and "to be gleeked," for being tricked, cheated, duped, or befooled. Hence, the words "gleek," and "gleeking" became used, for being tauntingly or hectoringly jocose] upon occasion.—*Mid. N. D.*, iii. 1.

What will you give us?—No money, on my faith, but the *gleek*; I will give you the minstrel.—*R. & Jul.*, iv. 5.

I have seen you *gleeking* and galling at this gentleman twice or thrice.—*H. V.*, v. 1.

Now where's the Bastard's braves, and Charles his *gleeks?*—1 *H. VI.*, iii. 2.

Let vultures gripe thy guts! for *gourd* and *fullam.* holds,
And *high* and *low* ['false dice'] beguile the rich and poor.—*Merry W.*, i. 3.

Ere I would say, I would drown myself for the love of *a guinea-hen* ['a woman who may be bought for money'], I would change my humanity with a baboon.— *Oth.*, i. 3.

> What comfortable hour canst thou name,
> That ever grac'd me in thy company?
> Faith, none, but *Humphrey hour*

[' hungry hour:' we believe this to have been a cant term, arising out of the proverbial phrase, " to dine with Duke Humphrey "; which originated in the circumstance that one of the aisles in the ancient cathedral of St. Paul's was called Duke Humphrey's Walk, where those who had no means of procuring a dinner used to loiter, as if business, and not the passing away their hour for hunger, brought them there],

> that call'd
> Your grace to breakfast once forth of my company.—*R. III.*, iv. 4.

Some *jay* [' courtesan:' it is noteworthy that the Italian word for the bird of this name and for a hireling woman is the same—'*putta*'] of Italy, whose mother was.—*Cym.*, iii. 4.

We'll teach him to know turtles from *jays*.—*Merry W.*, iii. 3.

> He wears his honour in a box unseen,
> That hugs his *kicky-wicky* [' unruly jade:' employed by the coarse Parolles as a synonyme for ' wife'] here at home.—*All's W.*, ii. 3.

I, a *lost mutton* [' scapegrace fellow,' ' a stray sheep from the fold of righteousness'], gave your letter to her, a *laced mutton* [' dizened courtesan'], and she, a *laced mutton*, gave me, a *lost mutton*, nothing for my labour.—*Two G. of V.*, i. 1.

Is he so young a man, and so old a *lifter?* [' thief'; and ' shop-lifter' is still a term in use for one who steals goods from shop-counters].—*Tr. & Cr.*, i. 2.

No, he 's in *Tartar limbo* [' prison,' ' confinement,'] worse than hell.—*Com. of E.*, iv. 2.

I have some of 'em in *Limbo Patrum* [' prison,' ' confinement': the term originating in *Limbus Patrum*, the place where the fathers and patriarchs were supposed to *a*wait the resurrection], and there they are like to dance these three days.—*H. VIII.*, v. 3.

None of these mad mustachio purple-hued *malt-worms* [' ale-topers;' fellows who dip their mustachios so deeply and perpetually in liquor as to stain them purple-red].—1 *H. IV.*, ii. 1.

His face is Lucifer's privy-kitchen, where he doth nothing but roast *malt-worms* [' beer-drinkers'].—2 *H. IV.*, ii. 4.

I think I am as like to *ride the mare* [' come to the gallows'; the two-legged or three-legged mare being a slang name for the gallows].—*Ibid.*, ii. 1.

I will say " marry trap " [' catch who catch can,' ' by Mary, catch me if you can '] with you.—*Merry W.*, i. 1.

I come to her in white, and cry " *Mum* "; she cries, " *Budget* ": and by that we know one another.—That's good too: but what needs either your " *Mum* " or her " *Budget* "? [A cant signal and counter-signal, implying silence and secret intelligence in use among thieves].—*Ibid.*, v. 2.

I went to her in white, and cried " *Mum*," and she cried " *Budget*," as Anne and I had appointed.—*Ibid.*, v. 5.

If you run the *nut-hook's* [' bailiff'; a hooker of thieves] humour on me.—*Ibid.*, i. 1.

Nut-hook, nut-hook, you lie. Come on.—2 *H. IV.*, v. 4.

As the honey of Hybla, my *old lad of the castle* [' roaring boy,' ' roysterer': and Prince Hal applies this term to his boon companion, the fat knight, in reference to the name of " Oldcastle," which Shakespeare originally gave to the character of Sir John Falstaff].—1 *H. IV.*, i. 2.

Let senses rule; the word is, " Pitch and pay " [' pay on delivery, ' pay down at once']; trust none.—*H. V.*, ii. 3.

When you breathe in your watering, they cry " Hem !" and bid you *play it off* [' toss off your drink at a draught'].—1 *H. IV.*, ii. 4.

If a crow help us in, sirrah, we 'll *pluck a crow together* [' have a squabbling-bout,' ' a set-to,' ' a quarrel'].—*Com. of E.*, iii. 1.

Out upon him ! *Prig*, for my life, *prig* [' thief'].—*W. T.*, iv. 2.

> The white sheet bleaching on the hedge, ...
> Doth set my *pugging* [' prigging,' ' thieving,'] tooth on edge.—*Ibid.*, iv. 2 (*Song*).

Thou shalt have a share in our *purchase* ['booty,' 'plunder,' 'stolen goods,'] as I am a true man.—1 *H. IV.*, ii. 1.

They will steal anything, and call it *purchase.*—*H. V.*, iii. 2.

Here's Agamemnon,—an honest fellow enough, and one that loves *quails* ['common women': but though allusion may be made to this sense of the word, as a cant term, in the present passage, we believe, that "loves quails" *may* be used to express 'is fond of quail-fighting,' 'is fond of gambling with quails,' in reference to the ancient practice of matching quails against one another, as cocks were more modernly matched; to which practice Shakespeare alludes in a passage in "Antony and Cleopatra," ii. 3].— *Tr. & Cr.*, v. 1.

What says my bully-*rook* ['rogue,' 'swindler,' 'sharper']?—*Merry W.*, i. 3.

How now, bully-*rook!* . . . tell him, bully-*rook.* . . . What sayest thou, my bully-*rook?*—*Ibid.*, ii. 1.

What saucy merchant was this, that was so full of his *ropery?* ['roguery,' 'ribaldry,' 'impudent banter,' 'abusive joking': the expression originated in the facetious custom of teaching parrots to make allusion to "a rope" (or hanging), as the probable end of those who addressed them].—*R. & Jul.*, ii. 4.

An he begin once, he'll rail in his *rope-tricks* [besides the above meaning, "rope-tricks" is here intended (from its slight similarity in sound) to include the effect of "rhetorics"].—*Tam. of S.*, i. 2.

Sirrah, if they meet not with *Saint Nicholas' clerks* ['thieves,' 'robbers,' 'pickpockets': Saint Nicholas being the patron saint of children and *scholars,* he was said to be tutelary to another race of *clever fellows* and *dexterous gentry*], I'll give thee this neck.—1 *H. IV.*, ii. 1.

Now shall we know if Gadshill have *set a match* ['planned a robbery'].—*Ibid.*, i. 2.

Wouldst thou not be glad to have the niggardly rascally *sheep-biter* ['paltry thief'] come by some notable shame?—*Tw. N.*, ii. 5.

Show your knave's visage, . . . Show your *sheep-biting* face.—*M. for M.*, v. 1.

My revenue is the *silly cheat* ['petty theft'].—*W. T.*, iv. 2.

Slice, I say! pauca, pauca; *slice* ['cut,' 'be off'], I say! that's my humour.— *Merry W.*, i. 1.

It would make a man as mad as a buck, to be so *bought and sold* ['tricked,' 'duped,' 'befooled,' 'outdone'].—*Com. of E.*, iii. 1.

Fly, noble English, you are *bought and sold* ['betrayed,' 'deceived,' 'deluded'].— *John*, v. 4.

Whither, my lord! From *bought and sold* Lord Talbot.—1 *H. VI.*, iv. 4.

For Dickon thy master is *bought and sold.*—*R. III.*, v. 4 (*Scroll*).

Thou art *bought and sold* among those of any wit.—*Tr. & Cr.*, ii. 1.

The boy hath *sold him a bargain* ['made a fool of him'], a goose, that's flat.— *Love's L. L.*, iii. 1.

I know not how they *sold* ['betrayed,' 'defrauded,' 'yielded at too low a price,' 'at too small a cost'] themselves, but thou, like a kind fellow, gavest thyself away gratis.—2 *H. IV.*, iv. 3.

'Tis thou hast *sold* ['betrayed'] me to this novice; . . . to the young Roman boy she hath *sold* me.—*Ant. & C.*, iv. 10.

He hath wronged his honour in marrying the renowned Claudio . . . to a contaminated *stale* ['woman hackneyed in vicious courses'], such a one as Hero.— *M. Ado*, ii. 2.

To link my dear friend to a common *stale.*—*Ibid.*, iv. 1.

No long-staff sixpenny *strikers* ['pickpockets'].—1 *H. IV.*, ii. 1.

He's no swaggerer, hostess; a *tame cheater* ['a petty rogue,' 'a low gamester,' 'a cozener'], i' faith.—2 *H. IV.*, ii. 4.

Every coystril that hither comes inquiring for his *Tib* ['common woman'].— *Per.*, iv. 6.

Peace, good pint-pot! peace, good *tickle-brain!* [this cant term for some kind of strong drink is jocosely applied to Hostess Quickly by Falstaff, as a nick-name].—1 *H. IV.*, ii. 4.

Am I a *woodman* ['a hunter of forbidden game,' 'a pursuer of wanton sports'], ha ?—*Merry W.*, v. 5.

Friar, thou knowest not the duke so well as I do: he's a better *woodman* than thou takest him for.—*M. for M.*, iv. 3.

There are some cant terms, in use when Shakespeare wrote, which designated natives of particular countries famed for dexterous trickery or dissolute manners :—

I will not believe such a *Cataian* [Cataia, or Cathay, was a name for China, whose people have the reputation of being adroit jugglers and the imputation of being dexterous cheats; hence the term " Cataian " became used as a slang term for 'a cheat.' But we believe that Shakespeare included in it the meaning of ' outlandish,' ' far-fetched,' ' extravagant,' ' eccentric '; in the present passage, in reference to Nym's fantastic style of phraseology] though the priest.—*Merry W.* ii. 1.

My lady's a *Cataian* [Sir Toby partly uses this in the sense of 'a rogue,' partly in the sense of 'a strange fantastical creature.'].—*Tw. N.*, ii. 3.

Tell me flatly I am no proud Jack, like Falstaff; but a *Corinthian* [a 'free liver;' Corinth having been notorious for its profligate habits, manners, and people], a lad of mettle.—1 *H. IV.*, ii. 4.

It is thine host, thine *Ephesian* ['jolly companion,' roystering associate']; the term probably included a mixture of 'roguery,' as Ephesus was reputed for its "cozenage" (see the closing speech of act i., " Comedy of Errors"); and we believe moreover that it also included some hint of heterodoxy, judging from the context, "*of the old church*" and "what *pagan*" in the passage we here next cite], calls.—*Merry W.*, iv. 5.

What company?—*Ephesians*, my lord; of the old church.—Sup any women with him?—None, my lord, but old Mistress Quickly, and Mistress Doll Tear-sheet.—What pagan may that be ?—2 *H. IV.*, ii. 2.

I pr'ythee, foolish *Greek* ['merry-maker,' 'frolicsome jester']; the familiar term, a merry grig, is a corruption of 'a merry Greek;' which expression originated in the fact that the Greeks were esteemed a jovial people, and was perhaps partly derived from the Latin *græcari*, to revel, to carouse], depart from me.—*Tw. N.*, iv. 1.

Then she's a *merry Greek* indeed.—*Tr. & Cr.*, i. 2.

A woful Cressid 'mongst the *merry Greeks*.—*Ibid*, iv. 4.

Hector was but a *Trojan* ['thief;' probably originating in a reference to Paris, who stole Helen from her husband, Menelaus] in respect of this . . . unless you play the honest *Trojan*, the poor wench.—*Love's L. L.*, v. 2.

Dost thou thirst, base *Trojan*, to have me fold up Parca's fatal web? . . . Base *Trojan*, thou shalt die.—*H. V.*, v. 1.

Tut ! there are other *Trojans* thou dreamest not of.—1 *H. IV.*, ii. 1.

CHORUSES: INDUCTIONS: PROLOGUES: EPILOGUES.

These are among the dramatic resources used by Shakespeare; but he has introduced them into only a few of his plays :—

Enter TIME, *as Chorus.*

I, that please some, try all; &c.—*W. T.*, iv.

Enter CHORUS *(forming Prologue).*

O for a muse of fire, that would ascend, &c.—*H. V.*, i.

Enter CHORUS.

Now all the youth of England are on fire, &c.—*Ibid.*, ii.

Enter CHORUS.
Thus with imagin'd wing our swift cause flies, &c.—*H. V.*, iii.

Enter CHORUS.
Now entertain conjecture of a time, &c.—*Ibid.*, iv.

Enter CHORUS.
Vouchsafe to those that have not read the story, &c.—*Ibid.*, v.

Enter CHORUS (*forming Epilogue*).
Thus far, with rough and all unable pen, &c.—*Ibid.*, v. 2.

Enter CHORUS (*forming Prologue*).
Two households, both alike in dignity, &c.—*R. & Jul.*, i.

Enter CHORUS.
Now old desire doth in his death-bed lie, &c.—*Ibid.*, i. 5.

Enter GOWER, *as Chorus* (*forming Prologue*).
To sing a song that old was sung, &c.—*Per.*, i.

Enter GOWER, *as Chorus.*
Here have you seen a mighty king, &c.—*Ibid.*, ii.

Enter GOWER, *as Chorus.*
Now sleep yslaked hath the rout, &c.—*Ibid.*, iii.

Enter GOWER, *as Chorus.*
Imagine Pericles arrived at Tyre, &c.—*Ibid.*, iv.

Enter GOWER, *as Chorus.*
Thus time we waste, and longest leagues make short, &c.—*Ibid.*, iv. 4.

Enter GOWER, *as Chorus.*
Marina thus the brothel 'scapes, &c.—*Ibid.*, v.

Enter GOWER, *as Chorus.*
Now our sands are almost run, &c.—*Ibid.*, v. 2.

Enter GOWER, *as Chorus* (*forming Epilogue*).
In Antiochus, and his daughter, you have heard, &c.—*Ibid.*, v. 3.

There is an Induction to the play of "Taming of the Shrew,' consisting of two short scenes, and a brief bit of dialogue :—

INDUCTION.

SCENE I.—*Before an alehouse on a heath.*

Enter HOSTESS *and* SLY.

Sly. I 'll pheeze you, in faith, &c.—*Tam. of S., Induc.* 1.

INDUCTION.

SCENE II.—*A bedchamber in the lord's house.*

SLY *is discovered, with Attendants : some with apparel,* &c.
Sly. For God's sake, a pot of small ale, &c.—*Ibid., Induc.* 2.
First Serv. My lord, you nod ; you do not mind the play.—*Ibid.*, i. 1.

There is an Induction to the historical play of "The Second Part of King Henry IV.," consisting of a speech which forms a kind of Chorus-prologue :—

INDUCTION.

Warkworth.   Before Northumberland's castle.

Enter RUMOUR, *painted full of tongues* .

Open your ears ; for which of you will stop, &c.—2 *H. IV.*, i.

There is a Prologue to the grand drama of " Henry VIII.," and one to
" Troilus and Cressida ":—

PROLOGUE.

I come no more to make you laugh, &c.—*H. VIII.*, i.

PROLOGUE.

In Troy, there lies the scene.   From isles of Greece
The princes orgulous, . . .
. . . and hither am I come
A prologue arm'd, but not in confidence
Of author's pen or actor's voice ; but *suited*
In like conditions as our argument—
To tell you, fair beholders, that our play, &c.—*Tr. & Cr.*, i.

The above words, that we have italicised, show that in this case the
Prologue was clad in armour ; whereas the usual dress worn by the
speaker of a prologue was a suit of black.

There is an incidental prologue (to the interlude of " Pyramus and
Thisbe ") in the course of " A Midsummer Night's Dream " : —

Enter PROLOGUE.

If we offend, it is with our good will, &c.—*Mid. N. D.*, v. 1.

And there is another incidental prologue (to the " Murder of
Gonzago" in the course of " Hamlet ":—

Enter PROLOGUE.

*   *   *   *   *   *

For us, and for our tragedy, &c.—*Hamlet*, iii. 2.

And there are epilogues appended to the following plays :—

EPILOGUE (*spoken by* PROSPERO).

Now my charms are all o'erthrown, &c.—*Temp.*

EPILOGUE (*spoken by* ROSALIND).

It is not the fashion to see the lady the epilogue, &c.—*As You L.*

EPILOGUE (*spoken by a Dancer*).

First, my fear; then my court'sy ; last, my speech, &c.—*2 H. IV.*

EPILOGUE.

'Tis ten to one, this play can never please all, &c.—*H. VIII.*

There are final speeches,* forming a kind of epilogue, to the two
following dramas :—

Puck. If we shadows have offended, &c.—*Mid. N. D.*, v. 2.

King. Let us from point to point. . . .
The king 's a beggar, now the play is done, &c.—*All's W.*, v. 3.

And in the two following, songs are sung that have the effect of an
epilogue :—

SONG.

When daisies pied, and violets blue, &c.—*Love's L. L.*, v. 2.

SONG.

When that I was, and a little tiny boy, &c.—*Tw. N.*, v. 1.

---

* At the close of " Troilus and Cressida " there are some lines that appear somewhat like an intended epilogue of this kind ; but we have recorded our conviction of
their being spurious under the heading, COARSENESSES AND DELICACIES.

CLOSING SCENES: BRIEF SCENES.

It is observable that Shakespeare generally makes the closing scenes of his plays conclude with a speech from one of the leading or most high-ranked characters therein; and that this character (even in his comedies) is invariably a male personage; whereas, in modern dramas (especially comedies) it is almost always a woman character who speaks the final words—what, in theatrical parlance, is called "the tag." Another peculiarity in his closing scenes is the mode in which he winds up the plot or story of a drama in its final scene; sometimes giving the dialogue in such succinct style as shall merely recount points needful to be explained to the audience, but leaving unrecapitulated those already known to them [*See* PASSAGES OF INCOMPLETE EXPLANATION].

Many of his apparently slight and insignificant scenes are worthy of notice as containing indications of his artistic skill in dramatic writing. Certain of these brief scenes are introduced preparatively to a long and important one; as, for example, where two officers of the Capitol enter, "to lay cushions," and prepare for the entrance of the Roman Senators and Tribunes, coming to recognise and reward the military services of Coriolanus against the Volsces. The dialogue between these two attendants, serves admirably to bring forward the view taken of Marcius's haughty and unbending disposition, his claims, his merits, and his chances of attaining the consulship. It commences thus:—

First Off. Come, come, they are almost here. How many stand for consulships?
Sec. Off. Three, they say: but 'tis thought of every one Coriolanus will carry it.
First Off. That's a brave fellow; but he's vengeance proud, and loves not the common people.
Sec. Off. Faith, there have been many great men that have flattered the people, who ne'er loved them; and there be many that they have loved, they know not wherefore, &c., &c.—*Coriol.*, ii. 2.

So likewise the scene where "two or three servants" enter, to prepare a banquet (rear-banquet, or dessert, rather), on board Pompey's galley, when the illustrious guests, Cæsar, Antony, with Lepidus, Enobarbus, and others, have been invited to feast there; the dialogue, with its free discussion of the wine-heated revellers, their unsteady feet, half rendered so by the unaccustomed motion of the vessel, half by the deep potations they have already imbibed, its contempt of the weak yet conceited "third" in the Triumvir—Lepidus, is thoroughly true to nature and highest dramatic art:—

First Serv. Here they'll be, man. Some o' their plants are ill-rooted already; the least wind i' the world will blow them down.
Sec. Serv. Lepidus is high-coloured.
First Serv. They have made him drink alms-drink.
Sec. Serv. As they pinch one another by the disposition, he cries out "No more;" reconciles them to his entreaty, and himself to the drink, &c., &c.—*Ant. & C.*, ii. 7.

Several of Shakespeare's brief scenes (though often omitted in stage representation) are of marked importance to the dramatic evolvement and conduct of the story; and serve significant purpose, moral as well as dramatic, notwithstanding the objections that certain commentators have made to some of these very scenes. So essential are they to the completeness of our great dramatist's design, that he frequently uses them as the " Chorus " was used by the Grecian dramatists—to form an elucidatory comment upon the passing incidents, to denote popular feeling and opinion concerning characters and events, or to carry on the main plot by subsidiary occurrences. In the first of the following examples, it is worthy of remark how Shakespeare has contrived to subtly show the way in which men unconsciously miss valuable opportunities. Had Leonato listened to what his " tedious neighbours had to say to him, he would have been spared his misery in the scene of his daughter's broken-off marriage :—

Leon. What would you with me, honest neighbour ?
Dogberry. Marry, sir, I would have some confidence with you, that decerns you nearly, &c., &c.—*M. Ado*, iii. 5.

By the following short scene, the dramatist not only keeps well before the mind Shylock's unrelenting persecution of the merchant creditor whom he has got within his power, but also shows how impossible it is for the Venetian state legally or expediently to rescue the Christian from the Jew's exaction of the penalty :—

Shylock. Gaoler, look to him : tell not me of mercy ;
This is the fool that lent out money gratis: . . .
Ant. The duke cannot deny the course of law, &c., &c.—*Mer. of V.*, iii. 3.

By the following, Portia (as the young Doctor of Laws) is shown to fulfil, in careful, practical, professional way, the duty of conveying the deed to Shylock for signature ; to receive the ring from her husband which she desired to obtain ; and to desire Gratiano's conducting her clerk to the Jew's house, which affords the opportunity for Nerissa also to secure possession of her husband's ring in a natural manner :—

Portia. Inquire the Jew's house out, give him this deed,
And let him sign it : . . .
Gratiano. Fair sir, you are well o'erta'en :
My lord Bassanio, upon more advice,
Hath sent you here this ring, . . .
Portia. . . . I pray you, show my youth old Shylock's house, &c., &c.
Ibid., iv. 2.

The following is ingeniously calculated to impress upon the audience the fact of the king's absence from England, to denote the rumours of the king's death that have arisen while he is away in Ireland, the vain efforts made by his adherents to preserve allegiance to him, and the dark foreboding with which his downfall is poetically foreshadowed. Dr. Johnson remarks upon this scene that it is " unartfully and irregularly thrust into an improper place," and advises that it should be inserted later on in the play, so as to form the second scene of the third act ; but, to our thinking, the objects of the dramatist, as we have above stated them, are better effected by being introduced at the close of the second act, and thus set apart from the scenes in the third act, where Richard returns to England, and Salisbury joins him with the news of the Welsh defection, than if brought into juxtaposition therewith :—

SCENE IV.—*A camp in Wales.*

Enter SALISBURY, *and a* WELSH CAPTAIN.

Cap. My lord of Salisbury, we have stay'd ten days,
And hardly kept our countrymen together,
And yet we hear no tidings of the king:
Therefore we will disperse ourselves: farewell.
  Sal. Stay yet another day, thou trusty Welshman:
The king reposeth all his confidence in thee.
  Cap. 'Tis thought, the king is dead; we will not stay.
The bay-trees in our country are all wither'd,
And meteors fright the fixed stars of heaven: . . .
  Sal. Ah, Richard, with the eyes of heavy mind
I see thy glory, like a shooting star,
Fall to the base earth from the firmament! &c., &c.—*R. II.*, ii. 4.

The following lets the misgiving of the populace and their discussion of public events be perceived in the most dramatically natural way possible:—

SCENE III.—*London. A street.*

Enter TWO CITIZENS, *meeting.*

First Cit. Good morrow, neighbour: whither away so fast?
  Sec. Cit. I promise you, I scarcely know myself:
Hear you the news abroad?
  First Cit.   Yes—that the king is dead.
  Sec. Cit. Ill news, by'r lady; seldom comes the better:
I fear, I fear, 'twill prove a giddy world.

Enter a THIRD CITIZEN.

Third Cit. Neighbours, God speed! . . .
Doth the news hold of good King Edward's death?
  Sec. Cit. Ay, sir, it is too true; &c., &c.—*R. III.*, ii. 3.

The following, consisting merely of a soliloquy from " a Scrivener," appointed to write out the indictment of Lord Hastings, succinctly depicts the summariness with which the usurper proceeds in putting out of his way those who obstruct his path, and the dismayed clearness though prudent silence with which his course is discerned by lookers-on:—

SCENE VI.—*London. A street.*

Enter a SCRIVENER.

Scriv. Here is the indictment of the good Lord Hastings;
Which in a set hand fairly is engross'd,
That it may be to-day read o'er in Paul's, &c., &c.—*Ibid.*, iii. 6.

The following graphically details the picture of Buckingham's trial and condemnation; together with the public perception of Wolsey's being the originator of this and other state attainders, court disgraces, and removals from royal favour:—

SCENE I.—*London. A street.*

Enter TWO GENTLEMEN, *meeting.*

First Gent. Whither away so fast?
  Sec. Gent.   Oh, God save you!
E'en to the hall, to hear what shall become
Of the great Duke of Buckingham.
  First Gent.   I'll save you
That labour, sir. All's now done, but the ceremony
Of bringing back the prisoner, &c., &c.—*H. VIII.*, ii. 1.

The following, with equal vividness, gives the description of public feeling concerning the divorce between the king and his first queen, Katharine of Arragon, the marriage with Anne Boleyn ; and the gorgeous account of her coronation and great personal beauty, together with allusions to Wolsey's downfall, Gardiner's enmity towards Cranmer, and Thomas Cromwell's advance in royal favour :—

SCENE I.—*A street in Westminster.*

Enter TWO GENTLEMEN, *meeting.*

First Gent. You 're well met once again.
Sec. Gent.   So are you.
First Gent. You come to take your stand here, and behold
The Lady Anne pass from her coronation ? . . .

Enter a THIRD GENTLEMAN.

God save you, sir ! where have you been broiling ?
Third Gent. Among the crowd i' the abbey ; . . .
Sec. Gent.   . . . He of Winchester
Is held no great good lover of the archbishop's,
The virtuous Cranmer, &c. &c.,—*H. VIII.*, iv. 1.

The following is well contrived and inserted, to indicate the insurrectionary condition of Rome, and the auspicious condition of the Volscian State, at the time being ; preparing well the subsequent events in the drama :—

SCENE III.—*A highway between Rome and Antium.*

Enter a ROMAN *and a* VOLSCIAN, *meeting.*

Rom. I know you well, sir, and you know me : your name, I think, is Adrian.
Vols. It is so, sir : truly, I have forgot you.
Rom. I am a Roman ; and my services are, as you are, against them : know you me yet ?
Vols. Nicanor ? No.
Rom. The same, sir, &c. &c.—*Coriol.*, iv. 3.

The following is used by the dramatist as a means of confirming to us the fact of Timon's benevolence and generosity of disposition, and as a means of showing the superficial compassion excited in casual witnesses of social injustices. These three men behold the callous ingratitude with which Timon is treated, they pity his condition, they profess themselves willing to relieve his distress,—*had they been applied to ;* but, as it is, they consider it no business of theirs, make no pause to inquire into the truth of his need, but go on their way with a shrug of the shoulders and a trite axiom upon the prudence of dispensing with pity and suppressing conscience :—

SCENE II.—*Athens. A public place.*

Enter LUCIUS, *with* THREE STRANGERS.

Luc. Who, the Lord Timon ? he is my very good friend, and an honourable gentleman.
First Stran. We know him for no less, though we are but strangers to him, &c., &c.
—*Timon*, iii. 2.

In the following, picturesque description of the natural portents that accompany last night's regicidal act is put into dramatic form and most artistically made part of this grand tragic play ; as also the reports that are current on the events immediately consequent upon the deed that has been done :—

SCENE IV.—*Without the castle.*
Enter ROSSE *and an* OLD MAN.

Old M. Three score and ten I can remember well:
Within the volume of which time I have seen
Hours dreadful, and things strange; but this sore night
Hath trifled former knowings, &c., &c.—*Macb.*, ii. 4.

The following elicits from Dr. Johnson the remark that " it is not easy to assign a reason why a nameless character should be introduced here ; " but we believe that our consummate dramatist did so to give the effect of wide-spread discontent and disaffection, and that this " lord " is but one of many who think thus abhorringly of the usurping " tyrant." This brief but significant scene is excellently calculated to denote Long Time and the steady growth of popular indignation, with determination to obtain rescue from intolerable oppression :—

SCENE VI.—*Forres. A room in the palace.*
Enter LENOX, *and another* LORD.

Len. My former speeches have but hit your thoughts,
Which can interpret farther, &c., &c.,—*Ibid.*, iii. 6.

By the following, Shakespeare contrives to show the influence of passing events upon the mind of Hamlet, as affecting his task of avenging his father's death ; the share they have in urging him to fulfil it promptly, the reasoning they induce, and the resolves they inspire :—

SCENE IV.—*A plain in Denmark.*
Enter FORTINBRAS, *and Forces, marching.*

For. Go, captain; from me greet the Danish king; . . .
Enter HAMLET, ROSENCRANTZ, GUILDENSTERN, &c.

Ham. Good sir, whose powers are these ?
Cap. They are of Norway, sir, &c., &c.,—*Hamlet*, iv. 4.

In the following two brief dialogues—one commencing a scene, and the other concluding a scene—the dramatist introduces current reports that acquaint the audience with coming events essential to the story, but which are not shown in action ; while he gives the concomitant effect of the impression they produce upon the public figuring in the play :—

Edmund. Save thee, Curan.
Curan. And you, sir. I have been with your father, and given him notice that the Duke of Cornwall, and Regan his duchess, will be here with him to-night.
Edmund. How comes that?
Curan. Nay, I know not. You have heard of *the news abroad;* I mean the whispered ones, for they are yet but ear-kissing arguments ?
Edmund. Not I: pray you, what are they ?
Curan. Have you heard of no likely *wars toward,* 'twixt *the Dukes of Cornwall and Albany ?*
Edmund. Not a word.
Curan. You may, then, in time. Fare you well, sir.—*Lear.*, ii. 1.

Gentleman. Holds it true, sir, that *the Duke of Cornwall was so slain?*
Kent. Most certain, sir.
Gentleman. Who is *conductor of his people ?*
Kent. As 'tis said, *the bastard son of Gloster.*
Gentleman. They say, Edgar, his banished son, is with the Earl of Kent in Germany.
Kent. Report is changeable. 'Tis time to look about; *the powers of the kingdom approach apace.*
Gentleman. The arbitrement is like to be bloody. Fare you well, sir.—*Ibid.*, iv. 7.

Occasionally Shakespeare introduces short *contrasting* scenes; where a grotesque character or dialogue immediately precedes a deeply serious or profoundly tragic occurrence. The following picture of rough eagerness and excitement among the people, just before the gorgeous spectacle of the royal christening procession, aids in giving grandeur and solemnity to that pageant :—

SCENE III.—*The palace yard.*
Noise and tumult within. Enter PORTER *and his* MAN.
Porter. You'll leave your noise anon, ye rascals, &c.—*H. VIII.*, v. 3.

The following bout of grinning waggery has been objected to as ill-judged and untimely even by Coleridge, who observes, " It is difficult to understand what effect, whether that of pity or of laughter, Shakespeare intended to produce ; " but, to our mind, the intention was to show how grief and gaiety, pathos and absurdity, sorrow and jesting, elbow each other in life's crowd ; how the calamities of existence fall heavily upon some, while others, standing close beside the grievers, feel no jot of suffering or sympathy. Not only do we fail to perceive the want of harmony here ; we, on the contrary, feel it to be precisely one of those passing discords that produce richest and fullest effect of harmonious contrivance. The footboy Peter's eagerness to have his " merry dump " played to him while the musicians are conveniently in the house, though in the very hour of his young lady's death—the musicians loitering to bandy jokes with the footboy, secure their pay, and get a good dinner ere they go, are not merely in perfect keeping with the Nurse's heartlessness and selfishness in bidding Juliet renounce Romeo for Paris in order to secure her snug place in the rich Capulet's family ; they also serve the purpose of bringing into higher relief the passionate grief of Romeo and his prodigal flinging away of life in order to join her he loves and has lost :—

First Musician. Faith, we may put up our pipes, and be gone. . . . *Enter* PETER.
Peter. Musicians, O, musicians, " Heart's ease, Heart's ease " : Oh, an you will have me live, play " Heart's ease," &c.—*R. & Jul.*, iv. 5.

In the same spirit of effective contrast—true to life and natural course—is the introduction of the following ; and yet it has been strongly denounced, and Coleridge has gone so far as to affirm that it is not Shakespeare's writing. Reluctant as we are to differ with so illustrious an authority in imaginative writing as the author of " The Ancient Mariner " and " Christabel," we cannot help believing that it is not only Shakespeare's composition, but his maturely considered introduction at this point of the tragedy. Firstly, it serves to lengthen out Dramatic Time, which requires that the period from the king's retiring to rest—the dark hours for the commission of the murder—should be supposed to have elapsed ere the now entrance of Macduff to attend upon the king's awakening ; and, secondly, its repulsively coarse humour serves powerfully to contrast, yet harmonise, with the base and gory crime that has been perpetrated. Shakespeare's subtleties of harmony in contrast are among his most marvellous powers ; and we venture to think that this gross joking of the drunken Porter, with Macduff's unconscious joining in the fellow's ribaldry, while the murdered king lies weltering in his blood, and the morning dawn is shedding its approaching light on the foul deed and the filthy talk alike, are among these subtleties:—

> *Porter.* Here's a knocking, indeed! . . .
>   *Enter* MACDUFF *and* LENOX.
> *Macduff.* Was it so late, friend, ere you went to bed,
> That you do lie so late? &c.—*Macb.*, ii. 3.

Again, in the following, how grimly does the earthy gossip of the two grave-digging Clowns—and then the partly material talk, partly mournful moralising, of the prince and his friend concerning the skulls, merging into their almost light interchange of talk with the man who is heaving up the churchyard mould beside the very grave preparing for the woman of Hamlet's love—come in juxtaposition with the advancing funeral train. How it enhances the melancholy of the scene! and what a homily it forms upon humanity and its unconsciousnesses, treading blindly upon the verge of all we hold most sacred and most dear! Surely this was felt and intended by the most consummate of dramatists; and it was not without design that he so ordained these contrasting scenes:—

> *First Clown.* Is she to be buried in Christian burial, that wilfully seeks her own salvation? . . .
>   *Enter* HAMLET *and* HORATIO, &c.—*Hamlet*, v. 1.

Certainly it was not without artistic intention that Shakespeare introduced the following piece of jester's levity immediately before Cassio's gravely anxious appeal, and the subsequent supremely serious scene of tragic interest—that scene which is unsurpassed in all dramatic literature for its skill in the display of human passions worked upon by diabolical insinuation and instigation:—

>   *Enter* CASSIO *and some* MUSICIANS.
> *Cassio.* Masters, play here; . . . *Enter* CLOWN.
> *Clown.* Why, masters, have your instruments, &c.—*Oth.*, iii. 1.

And, in the following, there is the same visible intention of producing contrasted effect; the Clown's rustic obtuseness and grinning familiarity heightening the impression of mingled gorgeousness, voluptuousness, gloom, and imperial will, in the regal Cleopatra's coming death-hour:—

>   *Re-enter* GUARD, *with a* CLOWN *bringing in a basket.*
> *Guard.*   This is the man.
> *Cleo.* Avoid, and leave him.   [*Exit* GUARD.
> Hast thou the pretty worm of Nilus there,
> That kills and pains not?
> *Clown.* Truly, I have him: but I would not be the party that should desire you to touch him, for his biting is immortal; those that do die of it, do seldom or never recover, &c., &c.—*Ant. & C.*, v. 2.

COARSENESSES AND DELICACIES.

There are certain passages of gratuitous coarseness that have been preserved in most editions of Shakespeare's works, as being by possibility his; but we believe, from their irrelevant and *tacked-on* effect, that they are merely excrescences supplied by the actors of those parts wherein they occur; it having formerly been the custom of dramatists to leave passages thus open for filling in at discretion, or as occasion directed. [*See* POINTS LEFT FOR IMPROVISATION.] One of these occurs at the close of " Troilus and Cressida ;" where Pandarus, left by himself, when Troilus has abruptly quitted him, continues the four rhymed lines of his speech with a trashy addition, that wears marvellously the appearance of an interpolation. Our opinion on this point is supported by the fact, that the general diction of the fifth act of this drama bears evident marks of weakness and non-Shakespearian style; as though he had left the concluding act in the manner he had found it written in an earlier drama on this subject, or had permitted the concluding eight scenes (for we believe the first three of act v. to be as certainly Shakespeare's as we doubt the latter ones) to be appended by some other hand approved by the players : or, even, they may have been supplied by the actors themselves. The addition to which we allude is moreover patched on to the previous portion of the speech by a line of introductory prose :—

> Good traders in the flesh, set this in your painted cloths.
>   As many as be here of pander's hall,
>   Your eyes, half out, weep out at Pandar's fall;
>   Or, if you cannot weep, &c., &c.—*Tr. & Cr.*, v. 11.

Another of these passages occurs in the tragedy of " King Lear "; where, after the old king has gone with Kent into the hovel, the Fool utters a speech containing fourteen lines of rhymed ribaldry, which although retained in the folio is omitted in the quartos. This fact, together with the circumstance that the Fool's rhyming occurs *after* Lear has left the stage, suffice to condemn it as spurious : for Shakespeare's Fool utters his half-rambling, half-pertinent morsels for the sake of beguiling his old master's thoughts, and labouring " to outjest his heart-struck injuries "; he does not stay behind to gabble trumpery by himself, addressed solely to the rain and wind :—

> *Fool.* This is a brave night to cool a courtesan. I 'll speak a prophecy ere I go.
>   When priests are more in word than matter;
>   When brewers mar their malt with water;
>   When nobles are, &c., &c.—*Lear*, iii. 2.

We think that wherever there is marked irrelevancy or dramatic purposelessness in gross passages occurring in Shakespeare's plays, these may very confidently be believed to be none of his writing. In several instances where his contemporary playwrights would have made occasion for coarse expression, he has managed to word allusions with comparative decency ; as witness the following two passages. In the first, witty Sir John Falstaff hints at the swarming condition of Wart's ragged garments, thus :—

I cannot put him to a private soldier, that is the leader of *so many thousands.*— 2 *H. IV.,* iii. 2.

And in the second, a similar concomitant of a Bedlam beggar's clothing is thus conveyed :—

Lear. I 'll talk with this same learned Theban.
What is your study?
Edgar. How to prevent the fiend, and *to kill vermin.—Lear,* iii. 4.

As to his delicacies of diction and sentiment, scores might be cited ; but, as single examples, we point to the reverie in " All's Well," iv. 4. and the one in "Winter's Tale," i. 2 [*See* SOLILOQUIES], for proof of what we affirm of his skill and refinement in delineating the mind's reverting to sacredly secret subjects of meditation. Also, we would instance such touches of exquisitely pure feeling and beauty as the following two. In the former, the answer of Leontes, instinct with tender memory of his wife and mysterious attraction towards his unknown daughter, excited by view of that face bearing likeness to the mother's, is singularly in contrast with the gross treatment of the subject in the counterpart passage of the original story whence Shakespeare derived his plot of this play :—

Paulina.   Sir, my liege,
Your eye hath too much youth in 't : not a month
'Fore your queen died, she was more worth such gazes
Than what you look on now.—
Leontes.   I thought of her,
Even in these looks I made.—W. T., v. 1.

In the latter, the poet's skill, subtlety, and delicacy of expression, combined with voluptuous and imaginative description of the highest kind, are unparalleled. By his singular dexterity of writing in the following passage, the words " how dearly they do 't" convey the impression of Iachimo's picturing to himself for a passing moment how exquisitely those lips can kiss ; while the next sentence gives the effect of its being " her breathing" that the lips so "dearly" perform : thus sanctifying and preserving the loveliness beheld by the lawless intruder from the licence of even his very thought :—

How bravely thou becomest thy bed, fresh lily !
And whiter than the sheets ! That I might touch !
But kiss ; one kiss ! *Rubies unparagon'd,*
How dearly they do 't ! 'Tis her breathing that
Perfumes the chamber thus : the flame o' the taper
Bows toward her, and would under-peep her lids
To see the inclosed lights, now canopied
Under these windows, white and azure, lac'd
With blue of heaven's own tinct.—*Cym.,* ii. 2.

COINED WORDS.

Shakespeare, with the right and might of a true poet, and with his peculiar royal privilege as king of all poets, has minted several words that deserve to become current in our language. He coined them for his own special use to express his own special meanings in his own special passages; but they are so expressive and so well framed to be exponents of certain particulars in meanings common to us all, that they deserve to become generally adopted and used:—

> For then the bold and coward,
> The wise and fool, the artist and unread,
> The hard and soft, seem all *affin'd* and kin.—*Tr. & Cr.*, i. 3.

> Now, sir, be judge yourself
> Whether I in any just term am *affin'd*
> To love the Moor.—*Oth.*, i. 1.

> If partially *affin'd*, or leagu'd in office,
> Thou dost deliver more or less than truth,
> Thou art no soldier.—*Ibid.*, ii. 3.

By the condensedly framed word "*affin'd*," Shakespeare expresses, in the first of the above three passages, ' united by affinity;' in the second, ' bound by any claim of affinity;' and in the third, ' swayed by any link of affinity.'

> You, Titus Lartius,
> Must to Corioli back: send us to Rome
> The best, with whom we may *articulate*,
> For their own good and ours.—*Coriol.*, i. 9.

> These things, indeed, you have *articulated*,
> Proclaim'd at market-crosses, read in churches.—1 *H. IV.*, v. 1.

Shakespeare framed for himself the verb " articulate" (from one of the meanings of the Latin word *articulus*, ' an article or condition in a covenant') to express concisely ' enter into articles;' and "articulated," to express ' set forth in articles.'

> You are much more *attask'd* for want of wisdom
> Than prais'd for harmful mildness.—*Lear*, i. 4.

In the above passage, the word " attask'd" succinctly expresses ' taken to task.'

> Or to the dreadful summit of the cliff,
> That *beetles* o'er his base into the sea.—*Hamlet*, i. 4.

" Beetle-brows," to express ' prominent brows,' was a very old epithet; and Shakespeare framed the expressive verb "beetles," to indicate a clift's summit that ' juts out prominently,' that ' projects ' beyond its wave-worn base, like the head of a wooden " beetle " or mallet.

> With *cadent* tears fret channels in her cheeks.—*Lear*, i. 4.

From the Latin word *cadens*, 'falling,' 'trickling,' 'pouring down,' Shakespeare invented the poetical epithet " cadent."

> As, by the same *co-mart*,
> And carriage of the article design'd,
> His fell to Hamlet.—*Hamlet*, i. 1.

Shakespeare framed the word "co-mart," to express 'joint bargains,' 'compact made together,' in the same manner that the words 'co-heiress,' 'co-partner,' &c., are formed, and as he himself formed the word "co-mates" in the following passage:—

> Now, my *co-mates* and brothers in exile.—*As You L.*, ii. 1.
> For government, though high, and low, and lower,
> Put into parts, doth keep in one consent,
> *Congreeing* in a full and natural close,
> Like music.—*H. V.*, i. 2.

By the one word "congreeing," Shakespeare expresses 'agreeing with itself, in all its parts.'

> That, face to face and royal eye to eye,
> You have *congreeted*.—*Ibid.*, v. 2.

The single word "congreeted" expresses 'greeted each other,' 'met together.'

> First, all you peers of Greece, go to my tent;
> There in the full *convive we*.—*Tr. & Cr.*, iv. 5.

Shakespeare frames the above verb to express 'let us be convivial,' 'let us feast together.'

> Yet here she is allow'd her virgin *crants*,
> Her maiden strewments, and the bringing home
> Of bell and burial.—*Hamlet*, v. 1.

Here Shakespeare has anglicised and brought into our language a word which exists in various northern languages, under the form of 'krans,' 'krants,' 'kranz,' and 'crance,' each meaning 'crown' or 'garland.' He has also in the present passage appropriately introduced the custom which prevails in many countries of the north—among the rest, Denmark—of placing on the grave of a maiden the chaplet she wore when in life as token of her virgin condition, together with the strewn flowers emblematical of her purity.

> For my authority bears so *credent* bulk,
> That no particular scandal once can touch,
> But it confounds the breather.—*M. for M.*, iv. 4.

> With what's unreal thou co-active art,
> And fellow'st nothing: then, 'tis very *credent*
> Thou may'st co-join with something.—*W. T.*, i. 2.

> If with too *credent* ear you list his songs.—*Hamlet*, i. 3.

From the Latin participles *credendus*, 'to be believed or trusted,' and *credens*, 'believing,' 'trusting,' Shakespeare fashioned the word 'credent': to express, in the first of the above three passages, 'quality commanding belief or credit'; in the second, 'easily to be believed or credited'; and in the third, 'facilely believing or giving credit.'

> Your wife Octavia, with her modest eyes
> And still conclusion, shall acquire no honour
> *Demuring* upon me.—*Ant. & C.*, iv. 13.

In framing the word "demuring," the poet, with felicitous condensation, expresses, 'looking demurely.'

> The poisonous damp of night *dispunge* upon me.—*Ant. & C.*, iv. 9.

By the single verb " dispunge " is expressed 'discharge as from a spunge.'

> The violence of either grief or joy
> Their own *enactures* with themselves destroy.—*Hamlet*, iii. 2.

This expressive word was fabricated by the poet to designate 'purposes put into action,' ' intentions enacted.'

> Were they not *forc'd* with those that should be ours,
> We might have met them dareful, beard to beard,
> And beat them backward home.—*Macb.*, v. 5.

Shakespeare framed the vigorous word " forc'd " to express ' reinforced,' ' provided with forces'; and yet the emendators have sought to deprive us of it by proposing various substitutions.

> A good sherris-sack hath a twofold operation in it. It ascends me into the brain ; dries me there all the foolish and dull and crudy vapours which environ it, makes it apprehensive, quick, *forgetive*, full of nimble, fiery, and delectable shapes.— 2 *H. IV.*, iv. 3.

This word succinctly expresses ' capable of mentally forging.'

> His heart is *fracted* and corroborate.—*H. V.*, ii. 1.

> And my reliances on his *fracted* dates
> Have smit my credit.—*Timon*, ii. 1.

From the Latin word *fractus*, ' broken,' Shakespeare has fabricated this expression, " fracted."

> When vice makes mercy, mercy 's so extended,
> That for the fault's love is th' offender *friended*.—*M. for M.*, iv. 2.

> Not *friended* by his wish, to your high person
> His will is most malignant.—*H. VIII.*, i. 2.

> Frame yourself
> To orderly solicits, and be *friended*
> With aptness of the season.—*Cym.*, ii. 3.

Shakespeare makes the word " friended " concisely express what is generally conveyed by the word ' befriended.'

> And what so poor a man as Hamlet is
> May do, to express his love and *friending* to you.—*Hamlet*, i. 5.

He makes " friending " imply " friendly feeling.'

> Though the treasure
> Of Nature's *germins* tumble all together.—*Macb.*, iv. 1.

> Crack Nature's moulds, all *germins* spill at once,
> That make ingrateful man !—*Lear*, iii. 2.

He has framed the word " germins " to express ' the principles of germination.'

> He led our powers ;
> Bore the commission of my place and person ;
> The which *immediacy* may well stand up,
> And call itself your brother.—*Lear*, v. 3.

By the word " immediacy " Shakespeare succinctly expresses ' authority immediately derived,' ' representativeship directly delegated and not intermediately obtained.'

> That I some lady trifles have reserv'd,
> *Immoment* toys, things of such dignity
> As we greet modern friends withal.—*Ant. & C.*, v. 2.

Shakespeare coined the word " immoment " to express ' unmomentous,' ' of no moment or importance.' Both of the above-cited words Dr. Johnson denounces ; calling " immediacy " a harsh word, and " immoment " a barbarous word : but we very emphatically dis- agree with the lexicographer's opinion, and venture to think them admirably condensed and significant words, which it would be well to adopt and retain in our language. It appears to us that instead of abjuring felicitously framed expressions because they are unprecedented, we ought, on the contrary, to receive with gratitude the philological inventions of such masters in highest poesy and clearest sense as William Shakespeare, when they frame new and good terms for their own purposes, which will admirably serve ours.

> Yet gives he not till judgment guide his bounty,
> Nor dignifies an *impair* thought with breath.—*Tr. & Cr.*, iv. 5.

From the Latin *impar*, signifying ' unequal,' 'unsuitable,' 'unbe- fitting,' ' unworthy;' from the Latin *imparatus*, signifying ' unpre- pared,' ' unready,' ' perplexed,' ' entangled,' and from the English ' impairing,' as signifying ' injurious,' ' detracting,' Shakespeare has framed the adjective " impair," to express a compound meaning, including the various significations of these derivatives. His contem- poraries used the word " impair " as a substantive ; but Shakespeare made it do duty as an expressive adjective.

> Will all great Neptune's ocean wash this blood
> Clean from my hand ?   No ; this my hand will rather
> The multitudinous seas *incarnardine*,
> Making the green—one red.—*Macb.*, ii. 2.

Shakespeare devised the magnificently poetic verb " incarnardine " from the Italian word *incarnardino*, ' carnation or flesh colour,' to express ' stain carnation-red colour.'

> He grew unto his seat ;
> And to such wondrous doing brought his horse,
> As he had been *incorps'd* and *demi-natur'd*
> With the brave beast.—*Hamlet*, iv. 7.

The word " incorps'd " more compactly expresses ' incorporated,' while " demi-natur'd " poetically suggests the dual formation of the centaur—half-man, half-horse.

> You are born
> To set a form upon that *indigest*,
> Which he hath left so shapeless and so rude.—*John*, v. 7.

> And that your love taught it this alchemy,
> To make of monsters and things *indigest*
> Such cherubins as your sweet self resemble.—*Sonnet* 114.

From the Latin word *indigestus*, ' disordered,' ' confused,' Shake- speare framed the term " indigest," which he uses as a noun, in the first of the above passages, to express ' a mass of confusion or disorder,' ' a chaos or chaotic state' ; and as an adjective, in the second of the above passages, to express ' unformed,' ' shapeless.'

> The heavens themselves, the planets, and this centre,
> Observe degree, priority, and place,
> *Insisture*, course, proportion, season, form,
> Office, and custom, in all line of order.—*Tr. & Cr.*, i. 3.

From the Latin verb *insistere*, 'to stay,' 'stop,' or 'stand still,' Shakespeare framed his word "insisture," to express 'fixed position,' 'appointed situation,' 'steadfast place.'

> As easy may'st thou the *intrenchant* air
> With thy keen sword impress, as make me bleed.—*Macb.*, v. 7.

From the word "trenchant," 'cutting,' Shakespeare has formed the epithet "intrenchant," to express 'incapable of being cut.'

> The diamond—why, 'twas beautiful and hard,
> Whereto his *invis'd* properties did tend.—*Lover's Complaint, Stanza* 31.

The poet formed the word "invis'd" to express 'unseen,' 'invisible.'

> Conspir'd with that *irregulous* devil, Cloten.—*Cym.*, iv. 2.

Shakespeare invented the epithet "irregulous" to express something much more strong than 'irregular'; something that combines the sense of 'disorderly,' 'lawless,' 'licentious,' as well as 'anomalous,' 'mongrel,' 'monstrous'—out of ordinary rule and order in every way.

> But soon that war had end, and the time's state
> Made friends of them, *jointing* their force 'gainst Cæsar.—*Ant. & C.*, i. 2.

Here "jointing" is framed to express 'combining conjointly,' 'joining confederately.'

> At such a point,
> When half to half the world oppos'd, he being
> The *mered* question.—*Ibid.*, iii. 11.

Inasmuch as Shakespeare uses the word "mere" sometimes in the sense of 'absolute,' 'entire,' 'sole,' and sometimes in the sense of 'boundary' or 'limit,' he here forms the word "mered" to express 'limited entirely,' 'confined absolutely.'

> Not Neoptolemus so *mirable*
> (On whose bright crest Fame with her loud'st O-yes
> Cries, "This is he!") could promise to himself
> A thought of added honour torn from Hector.—*Tr. & Cr.*, iv. 5.

From the Latin *mirabilis*, 'wonderful,' 'that which is to be admired at,' or 'marvelled at,' Shakespeare coined for himself the epithet 'mirable.'

> Our discontented counties do revolt;
> Our people quarrel with obedience;
> Swearing allegiance and the love of soul
> To stranger blood, to foreign royalty.
> This inundation of *mistemper'd* humour
> Rests by you only to be qualified.—*John*, v. 1.

> Rebellious subjects, enemies to peace,
> Profaners of this neighbour-stained steel—
> Will they not hear? What, ho! you men, you beasts,
> That quench the fire of your pernicious rage
> With purple fountains issuing from your veins,
> On pain of torture, from those bloody hands
> Throw your *mistemper'd* weapons to the ground.—*R. & Jul.*, i. 1.

In this excellently formed word "mistemper'd," the poet not only gives the effect of 'ill-temper'd,' 'wrathful'; he also gives the effect of 'misguidedly and misdirectedly wrathful'; and he moreover

includes, in the first passage, the additional sense of ' ill-com-
pounded,' and, in the second passage, the additional sense of ' steel-
tempered, but to be used in a bad cause.' [*See* VARIED MEANINGS
COMBINED IN ONE WORD OR SENTENCE.]

> Or—if sour woe delights in fellowship,
> And *needly* will be rank'd with other griefs.—*R. & Jul.*, iii. 2.

Shakespeare has coined the word " needly " to express ' needfully,'
' necessarily ; ' and has used it here in combination with " will be "
as a form of our modern idiom ' needs must be.'

> Earth, yield me roots !
> Who seeks for better of thee, sauce his palate
> With thy most *operant* poison !—*Timon*, iv. 3.
> My *operant* powers their functions leave to do.—*Hamlet*, iii. 2.

Shakespeare constructed the word " operant " as an elegant and
concise form of ' operative,' to express ' actively efficacious.'

> Take but degree away, untune that string,
> And, hark, what discord follows ! each thing meets
> In mere *oppugnancy*.—*Tr. & Cr.*, i. 3.

From the Latin word *oppugnans*, ' resisting,' ' assaulting,' or
' fighting against,' our poet framed the expressive term " oppugnancy,"
to express ' warring opposition.'

> In the most high and *palmy* state of Rome.—*Hamlet*, i. 1.

The palm being the emblem of victory, and the palm being often
mentioned as typical of flourishing (Shakespeare himself, in this very
play, act v., sc. 2, and in "Timon," act v., sc. 1., having passages
which make this allusion), our author here forms the poetical epithet
" palmy " to combinedly express ' victorious and flourishing.'

> As true as steel, as *plantage* to the moon.—*Tr. & Cr.*, iii. 2.

Here the word " plantage" is invented to express plants generally or
collectively, all that is planted, vegetation.

> The *primogenitive* and due of birth.—*Tr. & Cr.*, i. 3.

From the two Latin words *primo*, ' first,' and *genitivus*, ' that which
is born with us,' Shakespeare framed the above word to express
' the claims or right of the first-born.'

> A violet in the youth of *primy* nature.—*Hamlet*, i. 3.

As Shakespeare uses the word " prime " in the sense of ' spring,'
' early bloom,' so here he frames the epithet " primy " to express
' spring-timed,' ' early-blooming.'

> For what, alas ! can these my single arms ?
> What *propugnation* is in one man's valour,
> To stand the push and enmity of those
> This quarrel would excite ?—*Tr. & Cr.*, ii. 2.

From the Latin word *propugnatio*, ' defence,' Shakespeare has
framed the term " propugnation " to express ' power of defence.'

> But once put out thy light,
> Thou cunning'st pattern of excelling nature,
> I know not where is that Promethean heat
> That can thy light *relume*.—*Oth.*, v. 2.

From the Latin, *lumen*, ‘light,’ Shakespeare has invented this elegant verb “ relume,’ to express ‘ re-light,’ ‘ light again.’

> This sight would make him do a desperate turn,
> Yea, curse his better angel from his side,
> And fall to *reprobance.—Oth.*, v. 2.

Shakespeare formed this word, as he formed the words “ arrivance ” and “ iterance ” in the present play [*See* RECURRENCE OF PARTICULAR POINTS], with the termination in “ance” instead of ‘al’ and ‘ ation.’

> This sleep is sound indeed ; this is a sleep,
> That from this golden *rigol* hath divorc’d
> So many English kings.—2 *H. IV.*, iv. 4.

> About the mourning and congealèd face
> Of that black blood a watery *rigol* goes,
> Which seems to weep upon the tainted place.—*Lucrece, Stanza* 250.

From the old Italian word *rigolo*, a small wheel, Shakespeare fashioned the term “ rigol,” to express a ‘ circle ’ or ‘ circlet.’

> Light thickens; and the crow
> Makes wing to the *rooky* wood.—*Macb.*, iii. 2.

The poet has framed the word “rooky ” to express ‘abounding in rooks,’ ‘ with trees in which the rooks build,’ ‘ where there is a rookery.’ This expression has been strangely misunderstood ; while, to our mind, it seems replete with picturesque and self-evident meaning.

> Because that now it lies you on to speak
> To the people; not by your own instruction,
> Nor by the matter which your heart prompts you,
> But with such words that are but *roted* in
> Your tongue, though but bastards, and syllables
> Of no allowance, to your bosom’s truth.—*Coriol.*, iii. 2.

Shakespeare fabricated the condensed word “ roted,” to express ‘ retained by rote,’ ‘ acquired by rote and held ready for conventional utterance.’

> Diana’s lip is not more smooth and *rubious.—Tw. N.*, i. 4.

From the Latin word *rubeus*, ‘ ruddy,’ and from the gem called ‘ ruby,’ Shakespeare devised the exquisite word “ rubious ” to convey the sense of ‘ ruddy,’ ‘ ruby-red.’

> Those happy *smilets*,
> That play’d on her ripe lip, seem’d not to know
> What guests were in her eyes.—*Lear*, iv. 3.

We owe to Shakespeare’s need of an expressive and poetical word in this passage, descriptive of a tender daughter struggling with her tears and striving to retain patient submission amid her sorrow, the beautiful diminutive “ smilets,” which so well designates attempted smiles, half smiles.

> To find a place where all distress is *stel’d.—Lucrece, Stanza* 207.
> Mine eye hath play’d the painter, and hath *stel’d*
> Thy beauty’s form in table of my heart.—*Sonnet* 24.

Shakespeare has fashioned the expressive word “ stel’d ” (partly perhaps in reference to “ stell,” ‘ a fixed place of abode,’ and partly perhaps in reference to " stile," 'an implement used by artists') to imply ' fixed,' ' graven.' [For his usage in this respect, *see* VARIED MEANINGS, &c.]

> The sea, with such a storm as his bare head
> In hell-black night endur'd, would have buoyed up,
> And quench'd the *stellèd* fires.—*Lear*, iii. 7.

From the Latin *stella*, ' star,' and perhaps also in reference to the above-mentioned word " stell," the poet framed the poetical epithet " stellèd," to express ' starry,' ' stationed in the firmament.'

> Forward, not permanent, sweet, not lasting,
> The perfume and *suppliance* of a minute.—*Hamlet*, i. 3.

Shakespeare fabricated the word " suppliance " to express concisely that which is supplied.

> With those legions
> Which I have spoke of, whereunto your levy
> Must be *supplyant*.—*Cym.*, iii. 7.

And the word " supplyant " to condensedly express ' contributive of supplies.'

> And I will never fail beginning nor *supplyment*.—*Ibid.*, iii. 4.

And the word " supplyment " to express ' continued supply.'

> Bring them, I pray thee, with imagin'd speed
> Unto the *Tranect*, to the common ferry
> Which trades to Venice.—*Mer. of V.*, iii. 4.

Shakespeare may have heard the word " Tranect " from some one acquainted with a local peculiarity ; or he may have fashioned it himself either from the Italian *traghetto*, ' ferry,' or from the Latin and Italian *tranare*, to ' swim,' ' sail,' or ' pass over.' Inasmuch as the Italian *tranare* or *trainare* also means to draw or drag, it is possible that the Italian ferry-boat formerly was drawn through the water by means of a process still in use in some places, and which we once saw at Rotterdam, where a ferry-boat was made to traverse the stream, by a man on board laying hold of a rope strained across the canal for the purpose.

> How now! what noise? That spirit 's possess'd with haste
> That wounds the *unsisting* postern with these strokes.—*M. for M.*, iv. 2.

From the Latin *sistere*, ' to stand still,' Shakespeare formed the epithet " unsisting," to express ' unstill,' ' never-resting.' [See his fabrication of the word " insisture," as explained on page 58.]

> Now, by the jealous queen of heaven, that kiss
> I carried from thee, dear; and my true lip
> Hath *virgin'd* it e'er since.—*Coriol.*, v. 3.

It well became Shakespeare, the most passionate and delicate-souled of poets, to invent this expression " virgin'd," as implying ' held sacredly and chastely and exclusively.'

There are some words which Shakespeare has coined for the sake of humorous effect :—

One Bardolph, if your majesty know the man: his face is all *bubukles*, and whelks, and knobs, and flames o' fire.—*H. V.*, iii. 6.

" Bubukles " is facetiously compounded from the French word *bube*, a blotch or sore, and from the word ' buccal ' (pertaining to the cheek ; Latin, *bucca*, the cheek), to signify a cheek-blotch.

If you see this in the map of my microcosm, follows it that I am known well enough too? what harm can your bisson *conspectuities* glean out of this character, if I be known well enough too ?—*Coriol.*, ii. 1.

" Conspectuities " is fabricated from the Latin *conspectus*, ' sight,' ' view.'

His heart is fracted and *corroborate.—H. V.*, ii. 2.

" Corroborate " is Pistol's blunder for some grand word that he intends to match with the choice expression, " fracted "; and he possibly means to say either ' corrodiate ' or ' corollorate.' If he mean to say ' corrodiate,' signifying ' eaten away as by rust,' his mistake would have the doubly comic effect of saying precisely the contrary to what he intends, since " corroborate " really means ' confirmed,' ' strengthened,' ' established '; but if he use " corroborate " for ' corollorate ' (from " corollary," which, besides meaning ' a surplus or crowning quantity,' as used by Shakespeare in the " Tempest," act iv., sc. 1., means also ' a conclusion '), he intends to convey the effect of ' brought to a conclusion,' ' done for.'

You have made fair hands,
You and your crafts ! you have *crafted* fair !—*Coriol.*, iv. 6.

A noun thus fashioned into a verb is not only characteristic of Menenius—who is famous for the jocose fabrication of words—but is a colloquial usage in the English language.

This place is too cold for hell. I 'll *devil-porter* it no farther.—*Macb.*, ii. 3.

He has as many friends as enemies; which friends, sir, as it were, durst not, look you, sir, show themselves, as we term it, his friends whilst he's in *directitude.—Directitude !* What's that ?—*Coriol.*, iv. 5.

The Third Servant, wishing to use a fine long word, and intending to coin some such term as ' discreditude ' or ' dejectitude,' blunders out his grandiloquent " directitude " ; which the First Servant, not comprehending, repeats amazedly and asks the meaning of ; but the Third Servant being at a loss to explain, avoids the inquiry by running on with his harangue.

Lord Angelo *dukes* it well in his absence.—*M. for M.*, iii. 2.

The most sovereign prescription in Galen is but *empiricutic*, and, to this preservative, of no better report than a horse-drench.—*Coriol.*, ii. 1.

Menenius uses " empiricutic " as a droll form of ' empirical.'

He says his name is Master Fer.—Master Fer ! I 'll *fer* him, and firk him, and ferret him.—*H. V.*, iv. 4.

They fought together, but Aufidius got off.—And 'twas time for him too, I 'll warrant him that: an he had stayed by him, I would not have been so *fidiused* for all the chests in Corioli.—*Coriol.*, ii. 1.

Loved me above the measure of a father ;
Nay, *godded* me, indeed.—*Ibid.*, v. 3.

Oh, base *Gongarian* wight !—*Merry W.*, i. 3.

Ancient Pistol's sounding substitution for ' Hungarian '; which was a term of reproach, as the gipsies came from Hungary and Bohemia, and thus it was synonymous with 'vagabond' as well as (punningly) with a hungry, beggarly fellow.

> Dost thou *infamonize* me among potentates?—*Love's L. L.*, v. 2.

Don Armado magniloquently frames the word "infamonize," to express 'defame,' 'render me infamous,'

> You are grand-jurors, are ye? We'll *jure* ye, i' faith.—I *H. IV.*, ii. 2.
>
> He, in good time, must his lieutenant be,
> And I (God bless the mark!), his *Moorship's* ancient.—*Oth.*, i. 1.
>
> It *out-herods* Herod : pray you, avoid it.—*Hamlet*, iii. 2.

Then is there here one Master Caper, at the suit of Master Three-pile the mercer, for some four suits of peach-coloured satin, which now *peaches* him a beggar.—*M. for M.*, iv. 3.

The Clown employs the verb "peaches" as a quibble on the *peach-*coloured satin" and as a familiar form of 'impeaches.'

> How fiery and forward our pedant is!
> Now, for my life, the knave doth court my love.
> *Pedascule*, I'll watch you better yet.—*Tam of S.*, iii. 1.

Hortensio fabricates "pedascule" as a scoffing repetition of "pedant," implying (in Latinised form) that he mentally foots or kicks him with the utmost ignominy.

> Yet heard too much of Phebe's cruelty.—
> She *Phebes* me: mark how the tyrant writes.—*As You L.*, iv. 3.
>
> Thou 'rt an emperor, Cæsar, Keisar, and *Pheezar*.—*Merry W.*, i. 3.

The Host jocularly invents the term "Pheezar" from the verb 'pheeze' (to vex, worry, or harry), in order to denote Falstaff's vexed state of mind and to make a jingle with "Cæsar" and "Keisar."

> Come, Mother Prat; come, give me your hand.—I'll *prat* her. Out of my door, you witch, you rag, you baggage, you polecat, you ronyon! Out, out! I'll conjure you, I'll *fortune-tell* you.—*Ibid.*, iv. 2.
>
> I' faith, sweetheart, methinks now you are in an excellent good *temperality :* your *pulsidge* beats as extraordinarily as heart would desire.—2 *H. IV.*, ii. 4.

Hostess Quickly's word "temperality" gives the effect of a combined or optional meaning of 'temperament' and 'temperature'; while her word 'pulsidge' for 'pulse' aids to convey an impression of fulness that is extremely apt.

> How now, how now, chop-logic! What is this?
> Proud—and I thank you—and, I thank you not;
> And yet not proud: mistress minion, you,
> *Thank* me no *thankings*, nor *proud* me no *prouds*.—*R. & Jul.*, iii. 5.
>
> Take your *vizaments* in that.—*Merry W.*, i. 1.

Sir Hugh Evans's Welsh says, "vizaments," intending to fashion the word 'advisements,' as a term expressive of consideration, circumspection.

There are some words, coined from their expressive sound, which Shakespeare's excellent taste and judgment caused him to adopt in passages where they give spirited effect :—

> For *gnarling* sorrow hath less power to bite
> The man that mocks at it, and sets it light.—*R. II.*, 1. 3.
>
> Thus is the shepherd beaten from thy side,
> And wolves are *gnarling* who shall gnaw thee first.—2 *H. VI.*, iii. 1.

If I go to him, with my armed fist
I 'll *pash* him o'er the face.—*Tr. & Cr.*, ii. 3.

And stands colossus-wise, waving his beam,
Upon the *pashed* corses of the kings.—*Ibid.*, v. 5.

I 'll *potch* at him some way.—*Coriol.*, i. 10.

He 'll go, he says, and *sowle* the porter of Rome gates by the ears.—*Ibid.*, iv. 5.

As young as I am, I have observed these three *swashers.*—*H. V.*, iii. 2.

We 'll have a *swashing* and a martial outside.—*As You L.*, i. 3.

Gregory, remember thy *swashing* blow.—*R. & Jul.*, i. 1.

For she had a tongue with a *tang*,
Would cry to a sailor, " Go hang !"—*Temp.*, ii. 2 (*Song*).

Let thy tongue *tang* arguments of state.—*Tw. N.*, ii. 5 (*Letter*).

And like a dog that is compelled to fight,
Snatch at his master that doth *tarre* him on.—*John*, iv. 1.

Two curs shall tame each other : pride alone
Must *tarre* the mastiffs on, as 'twere their bone.—*Tr. & Cr.*, i. 3.

The nation holds it no sin to *tarre* them to controversy.—*Hamlet*, ii. 2.

It comes to pass oft, that a terrible oath, with a swaggering accent sharply *twanged* off, gives manhood more approbation than ever proof itself would have earned him.— *Tw. N.*, iii. 4.

Sometimes a thousand *twangling* instruments
Will hum about mine ears.—*Temp.*, iii. 2.

While she did call me rascal fiddler
And *twangling* Jack.—*Tam. of S.*, ii. 1.

The exhalations, *whizzing* in the air.—*Jul C.*, ii. 1.

To have a thousand with red burning spits
Come *whizzing* in upon them.—*Lear*, iii. 6.

There are a few peculiar words retained in most editions of Shakespeare, because they are the words printed in the first folio edition, and because they may possibly be the author's original expressions, coined by himself:—

And soberly did mount an *arm-gaunt* steed.—*Ant. & C.*, i. 5.

Upon my secure hour thy uncle stole,
With juice of cursed *hebenon* in a vial,
And in the porches of mine ears did pour
The leperous distilment.—*Hamlet*, i. 5.

You are abus'd, and by some putter-on,
That will be damn'd for 't ; would I knew the villain,
I would *land-damn* him.—*W. T.*, ii. 1.

If these three words be indeed Shakespeare's coinage, they may have been meant by him to signify thus : " Arm-gaunt " may be taken to convey the idea of ' gaunt from long being clad in armed caparisons, and from long bearing an armed rider '; " hebenon " may be accepted as a form of henbane (the oil of which, according to Pliny, disturbs the brain), or of ' ebony ' (which was believed to possess soporific and poisonous qualities) ; and " land-damn " has been supposed to be a mode of succinctly expressing, either ' condemn to quit the land,' or ' doom to the torture of being banked up in earth and left to die.'

COINS.

In Shakespeare's works mention is made of several different coins formerly current; some of which have furnished him with occasion for a play upon the word :—

Noble, or not I for an *angel* [a gold coin, worth about ten shillings].—*M. Ado*, ii. 3.

They have in England a coin, that bears the figure of an angel stamped in gold but that 's insculped upon.—*Mer. of V.*, ii. 7.

This bottle makes an *angel.*—1 *H. IV.*, iv. 2.

She has all the rule of her husband's purse; he hath a legion of *angels*. . . . humour me the *angels.*—*Merry W.*, i. 3.

I had myself twenty *angels* given me this morning; but I defy all *angels.* but in the way of honesty.—*Ibid.*, ii. 2.

Here are the *angels* that you sent for, to deliver you.—*Com. of E.*, iv. 3.

When his fair *angels* would salute my palm.—*John*, ii. 2.

See thou shake the bags of hoarding abbots; imprisoned *angels* set at iberty.—*Ibid.*, iii. 3.

Three or four thousand *chequins* [a coin of Italy, and also of Barbary; its original name, *zecchini*, being derived from *zecca*, a mint. The *zecchino* was a gold coin of Venice, worth about seven or eight shillings] were as pretty a proportion.—*Per.*, iv. 3.

Yet I should bear no *cross* [a coin (of which there were several, various in value) bearing the mark of a cross upon it], if I.—*As You L.*, ii. 4.

He speaks the mere contrary—*crosses* love not him.—*Love's L. L.*, i. 2.

Not a penny; you are too impatient to bear *crosses.*—2 *H. IV.*, i. 2.

I had rather have lost my purse full of *cruzadoes* [Portuguese coins, of which there were three sorts; one with a long cross, one with a short cross, and one with the great cross of Portugal. They were of gold, and varied in value from six shillings and eightpence to nine shillings].—*Oth.*, iii. 4.

You will not pay for the glasses you have burst ?—No, not a *denier* [an old French coin; value, the twelfth part of a *sou*, or halfpenny. It came to be used for expressing the lowest imaginable fraction of money].—*Tam. of S., Induc.* 1.

I 'll not pay a *denier.*—1 *H. IV.*, iii. 3.

My dukedom to a beggarly *denier*, I do mistake.—*R. III.*, i. 2.

When they will not give a *doit* [a small coin, value the eighth part of a penny. Dutch, *duyt*; French, *d'huit*].—*Temp.*, ii. 2.

And take no *doit* of usance for my moneys.—*Mer. of V.*, i. 3.

That *doit* that e'er I wrested from the king.—2 *H. VI.*, iii. 1.

Cushions, leaden spoons, irons of a *doit*, doublets.—*Coriol.*, i. 5.

On a dissension of a *doit*, break out to bitterest enmity.—*Ibid.*, iv. 4.

This morning for ten thousand of your throats I 'd not have given a *doit.*—*Ibid.*, v. 4.

Plain-dealing, which will not cost a man a *doit.*—*Timon*, i. 1.

I cannot be bated one *doit* of a thousand pieces.—*Per.*, iv. 3.

Most monster-like, be shown for poor'st diminutives, for *doits.*—*Ant. & C.*, iv. 10.

A *dollar* [a Dutch and German coin; value from about two shillings and sixpence to four shillings and sixpence. The original name was *thaler*, from *thale*, a dale or valley; the coin having, it is said, been first coined in the valley of St. Joachim]. Dolour comes to him, indeed: you have spoken truer than.—*Temp.*, ii. 1.

To three thousand *dollars* a year.—*M. for M.*, i. 2.

Ten thousand *dollars* to our general use.—*Macb.*, i. 2.

That do prize their hours at a crack'd *drachm !* [A contracted form of *drachma*; which was an old Grecian coin, used also in Rome, worth four sesterces, about sevenpence

There were silver drachmas and brass drachmas; one of the latter probably being here intended.]—*Coriol.*, i. v.

To every several man, seventy-five *drachmas.*—*Jul. C.*, iii. 2.

I had rather coin my heart, and drop my blood for *drachmas.*—*Ibid.*, iv. 3.

No, not so much as a *ducat* [a coin so named from having originally been minted by dukes. A silver ducat was worth about four shillings and sixpence; a gold ducat, nine shillings and sixpence] for delivering your letter.—*Two G. of V.*, i. 1.

But fare thee well; there is a *ducat* for thee.—*Mer. of V.*, ii. 3.

Three thousand *ducats*—well.—*Ibid.*, i. 3.

Be cunning in the working this, and thy fee is a thousand *ducats.*—*M. Ado*, ii. 2.

Who, wanting *gilders* [sometimes spelt '*guilder*'; worth from one shilling and sixpence to two shillings] to redeem their lives.—*Com. of E.*, i. 1.

But that I am bound to Persia, and want *gilders* for my voyage.—*Ibid.*, iv. 1.

A half-fac'd groat [a silver groat worth fourpence with the king's profile on it; the custom previously having been to give the monarch's countenance as a full face] five hundred pounds a-year!—*John*, i. 1.

There is a *groat* to heal your pate.—Me a *groat!* . . . I take thy *groat* in earnest of revenge.—*H. V.*, v. i.

What money is in my purse?—Seven *groats* and twopence.—2 *H. IV.*, i. 2.

As fit as ten *groats* for the hand of an attorney.—*All's W.*, ii. 2.

And here is four *Harry ten shillings* [a coin of this value in the reigns of Henry VII. and Henry VIII., bearing the head of the sovereign upon it; and Shakespeare allows the word "Harry" here to pass for signifying Henry IV.] in *French crowns* [coins stamped with a crown, and worth five shillings] for you.—2 *H. IV.*, iii. 2.

I have lost a seal-ring of my grandfather's worth forty *mark* [a mark was a coin worth thirteen shillings and fourpence].—1 *H. IV.*, iii. 3.

A hundred *mark* is a long one for a poor lone woman.—2 *H. IV.*, ii. 1.

A hundred *marks*, my Kate does put her down.—*Tam. of S.*, v. 2.

Full thirty thousand *marks* of English coin.—*John*, ii. 2.

Of seven *groats* in *mill-sixpences* [coins that were the first milled money made in England, and which were frequently used for counters].—*Merry W.*, i. 1.

Moy [supposed to be a contraction of 'moidore'; a Portuguese coin, worth about twenty-seven shillings] shall not serve; I will have forty *moys;* . . . is that a ton of *moys*?—*H. V.*, iv. 4.

I shall have my eight shillings I won of you at betting?—A *noble* [a coin worth six shillings and eightpence] shalt thou have, and present pay.—*Ibid.*, ii. 1.

Hail *royal* [there was a coin thus called, worth ten shillings] prince!—
Thanks, *noble* peer;
The cheapest of us is ten *groats* too dear.—*R. II.*, v. 5.
Great promotions
Are daily given to ennoble those
That scarce, some two days since, were worth a *noble.*—*R. III.*, i. 3.

Nor thou camest not of the blood *royal*, if thou darest not stand for ten shillings.— 1 *H. IV.*, i. 2.

My lord, there is a *noble*man of the court at door would speak with you: he says he comes from your father.—Give him as much as will make him a *royal* man, and send him back again.—*Ibid.*, ii. 4.

Item bread——*ob.* [the abbreviated form of *obolum*, the Greek word for a small coin; which abbreviation was used in Shakespeare's time as the mode of stating a halfpenny]. Oh, monstrous! but one halfpenny worth of bread.—*Ibid.*, ii. 4.

Sir, for a *quart d'écu* [a French coin, known in England, where it was sometimes spelt 'cardecue.' It means 'quarter of a crown;' and some authorities state it to have been the fourth part of the French *gold* crown, when it was worth eighteenpence; while others say that it was a fourth of the smaller French crown, and worth eightpence] he will sell the fee-simple of his salvation.—*All's W.*, iv. 3.

There's a *quart d'écu* for you.—*All's W.*, v. 2.

And two *Edward shovel-boards* [the broad shillings of Edward VI., used at the game of shovel-board or shuffle-board], that cost me two shillings and twopence a-piece of Yead Miller.—*Merry W.*, i. 1.

Quoit him down, Bardolph, like a *shove-groat shilling.* [At the game of "shove-groat" smooth coins, such as silver groats or shillings, were in great request for playing with; and were named in reference to the game at which they were used.]—*2 H. IV.*, ii. 4.

Here's three *solidares* [believed to be coins, the name of which was originally derived from the Latin, *solidatus*, a soldier in pay] for thee: good boy, wink at me, and say.—*Timon*, iii. 1.

Tester ['sixpence': the original French coin was so called, from its bearing a head —*teste*, or *tête*—upon it] I'll have in pouch, when thou shalt lack.—*Merry W.*, i. 3.

Hold, there's a *tester* for thee.—*2 H. IV.*, iii. 2.

Come on; there is sixpence for you; let's have a song.—There's a *testril* of me too.—*Tw. N.*, ii. 3.

> My face so thin,
> That in mine ear I durst not stick a rose,
> Lest men should say, " Look, where *three-farthings*

[small thin pieces of silver worth this much were coined by Queen Elizabeth, bearing her face and the emblematic rose of England on them; and it was a court mode for fashionable gallants, as well as ladies, to wear a rose stuck behind the ear]
> goes!"—*John*, i. 1.

CORRUPTIONS.

In Shakespeare's plays we meet with several purposed corruptions of words; either to indicate familiar and popular mode of parlance in a contracted form of word, or to mark blundering diction on the part of some ill-educated speaker [*See* PRONUNCIATION], or for the sake of a humorous rhyme, or as producing facetious effect.

I've heard him utter to his son-in-law,
Lord *Aberga'ny* | ' Abergavenny': See ELISIONAL ABBREVIATIONS].—*H. VIII.*, i. 2.

Come apace, good *Audrey* [' Ethelreda']: I will fetch up your goats, *Audrey.* And how, *Audrey?* am I.—*As You L.*, iii. 3.

I think he be, but goodman Puff of *Barson* [' Barston'].—*2 H. IV.*, v. 3.

Slack the *bolins* ['bow-lines'] there! Thou wilt not..—*Per.*, iii. 1.

You have brought her into such a *canaries* ['quandary': which is itself a corruption of the French phrase, *qu'en dirai-je*] . . . could never have brought her to such a *canary* [' quandary'].—*Merry W.*, ii. 2.

Whose club killed Cerberus, that three-headed *canus* [' canis'].—*Love's L. L.*, v. 2.

I will be *cheater* ['escheator'] to them both, and they.—*Merry W.*, i. 3.

Cheater, call you him? I will bar no honest man my house, nor no *cheater;* but I do not love swaggering.—*2 H. IV.*, ii. 4.

I heard say, he was outrun on *Cotsall* [' Cotswold'].—*Merry W.*, i. 1.

The *crowner* [' coroner'] hath set on her, and finds it.—*Hamlet*, v. 1.

Ay, marry, is 't; *crowner's* [' coroner's'] quest law.—*Ibid.*, v. 1.

Or the red-nose innkeeper at *Daintry* * [' Daventry'].—*1 H. IV.*, iv. 2.

---

* It is a moot point whether the corrupt form or the correct form was here used by Shakespeare; as the folio prints the word in this passage, " Dauintry."

By this at *Daintry*, with a puissant troop.—3 *H. VI.*, v. 1.

Can you do it?—*Dexteriously* ['dexterously'], good Madonna.—*Tw. N.*, i. 5.

Why, your *dolphin* ['dauphin'] is not lustier.—*All's W.*, ii. 3.

Pucelle or puzzel, *dolphin* * or dog-fish.—1 *H. VI.*, i. 4.

Dolphin, my boy, my boy, sessa! let him trot by.—*Lear*, iii. 4.

I could play *Ercles* ['Hercules'] rarely, . . . This is *Ercles'* vein, a tyrant's vein.—*Mid. N. D.*, i. 2.

Since my *exion* † ['action'] is entered, and my case.—2 *H. IV.*, ii. 1.

She's as *fartuous* ['virtuous'] a civil modest wife.—*Merry W.*, ii. 2.

Infected with the *fashions* ['farcins' or 'farcy'].—*Tam. of S.*, iii. 2.

I have not seen such a *firago* ['virago'].—*Tw. N.*, iii. 4.

Past cure of the *fives* ['vives'], stark spoiled.—*Tam. of S.*, iii. 2.

Captain *Fluellen* ['Lluellen' or 'Llewellyn'], you must come.—*H. V.*, iii. 2.

When the wind is southerly, I know a hawk from a *handsaw* ['hernshaw'].—*Hamlet*, ii. 2.

The papist, *howsome'er* ['howsoe'er'], their hearts are.—*All's W.*, i. 3.

But he's the very devil *incardinate* ['incarnate'].—*Tw. N.*, v. 1.

Art thou good at these *kickshaws* ['quelque choses'], knight?—*Tw. N.*, i. 3.

And any pretty little tiny *kickshaws*, tell.—2 *H. IV.*, v. 1.

Every *'leven* ['eleven'] wether tods; every tod yields.—*W. T.*, iv. 2.

And, like *Limander* ['Leander'], am I trusty still.—

And I like *Helen* [meaning 'Hero'], till the Fates.—*Mid. N. D.*, v. 1.

And the receipt of reason a *limbeck* ['alembic'] only.—*Macb.*, i. 7.

To the *Lubbar's* ['libbard's' or 'leopard's'], in *Lumbert* ['Lombard'] Street.—2 *H. IV.*, ii. 1.

And how doth the *martlemas* ['Martinmas'], your master?—*Ibid.*, ii. 2.

What *night-rule* [night-revel] now about this haunted grove?—*Mid. N. D.*, iii. 2.

I'll meet thee, Pyramus, at *Ninny's* ['Ninus'] tomb.—*Ibid.*, iii. 1.

Wilt thou at *Ninny's* tomb meet me straightway?—*Ibid.*, v, 1.

How, now, *nuncle!* [uncle] . . . Mark it, *nuncle.*—*Lear*, i. 4.

Swithold ['Saint Withold'] footed thrice the *old* ['wold'].—*Ibid.*, iii. 4 (*Song*).

Burgomasters, great *oneyers* ['ones;' as 'one-ers' in modern familiar phraseology. There seems formerly to have been a fashion of introducing a *y* into a word, for jocular effect; as may be seen in "Yedward," subsequently cited here], such as can hold in.—1 *H. IV.*, ii. 1.

By'rlakin [by our lady kin] a *parlous* ['perilous'] fear.—*Mid. N. D.*, iii. 1.

Thou art in a *parlous* state, shepherd.—*As You L.*, iii. 2.

A *parlous* boy: go to, you are too shrewd.—*R. III.*, ii. 4.

O, 'tis a *parlous* boy; bold, quick, ingenious.—*Ibid.*, iii. 1.

A *parlous* knock; and it cried bitterly.—*R. & Jul.*, i. 3.

Was *parmaceti* ['spermaceti'] for an inward bruise.—1 *H. IV.*, i. 3.

Then he's a rogue and a *passy-measures* ['passamezzo'] pavin: I hate a drunken rogue.—*Tw. N.*, v. i.

If I be ta'en, I'll *peach* ['impeach'] for this.—1 *H. IV.*, ii. 2.

Which now *peaches* ['impeaches'] him a beggar.—*M. for M.*, iv. 3.

---

* In both these two first passages wherein the word "dolphin" is used, it is punningly employed; as the name of the fish so-called, and as the popular corrupted form of "Dauphin."

† That in this same scene Hostess Quickly pronounces "action" correctly is consistent with Shakespeare's mode of making such variations in the diction of imperfect speakers [*See* VARIATIONS]; also "canaries" and "canary" above cited.

God give you good-morrow, master *person* ['parson'].—Master *person*,—quasi pers-on. An if one should be *pierced* [This passage aids in showing how "pers" and "pierce" were often pronounced alike. See "Percy" and "pierce" under PRO-NUNCIATION], which is the one ?—*Love's L. L.,* iv. 2.

And *Phibbus'* ['Phœbus'] car shall shine.—*Mid. N. D.,* i. 2.

But his *phisnomy* ['physiognomy'] is more hotter.—*All's W.,* iv. 5.

They call themselves *saltiers* ['satyrs'], and they.—*W. T.,* iv. 3.

Not *Shafalus* ['Cephalus'] to *Procrus* ['Procris'] was so true.—
As *Shafalus* to *Procrus,* I to you.—*Mid. N. D.,* v. 1.

No; to the *spital* ['hospital'] go.—*H. V.,* ii. 1.

News have I, that my Nell is dead i' the *spital.*—*Ibid.,* v. 1,

She, whom the *spital*-house and ulcerous sores.—*Timon,* iv. 3.

Dost thou *squiny* ['squint'] at me ?—*Lear,* iv. 6.

If he by chance escape your venomed *stuck* ['stock:' from the Italian, 'stoccata'], our purpose may hold there.—*Hamlet,* iv. 7.

And he gives me the *stuck*-in, with such a.—*Tw. N.,* iii. 4.

I *swoonded* ['swooned'] at the sight.—*R. & Jul.,* iii. 2.

To lure this *tassel* ['tiercel' or 'tercel'] -gentle back.—*Ibid.,* ii. 2.

For I am his grace's *tharborough* ['third borough'].—*Love's L. L.,* i. 1.

Thisne, Thisne ['Thisbe'].—Ah, Pyramus.—*Mid. N. D.,* i. 2.

As pale as any clout in the *varsal* ['universal'] world.—*R. & Jul.,* ii. 4.

Take your *vizaments* ['advisements'] in that.—*Merry W.,* i. 1.

Marian Hacket, the fat ale-wife of *Wincot* ['Wilmecote,' or 'Wilnecote'].—*Tam. of S., Induc.* 2.

To countenance William Visor of *Wincot** against.—2 *H. IV.,* v. 1.

Two shilling and twopence a-piece of *Yead* ['Ned' or 'Edward'] Miller, by these gloves.—*Merry W.,* i. 1.

Hear ye, *Yedward* ['Edward'] ; if I tarry.—1 *H. IV.,* i. 2.

In the First Folio, the following passages contain words that are printed so as to afford the possibility that familiar corrupted verbal forms were intended ; but in our editions of Shakespeare's works we have not preserved these corruptions in the text, believing them to have been merely the printer's error, and not the author's originating :—

Take sixpence in earnest of the *berrord* ['bear-ward'].—*M. Ado,* ii. 1

And manacle the *berard* in their chains . . . despite the *bearard* that protects the bear.—2 *H. VI.,* v. 1.

Where is the master, *boson* ['boatswain'].—*Temp.* i., 1.

CROSSING SPEECHES.

In the course of Shakespeare's plays we meet with several instances of dialogue where a speech is made not in sequence with words uttered immediately preceding it; but either in reply to something said a short time before, or in a return to that of which the speaker has been

---

* In this passage the First Folio prints "Woncot"; but it is probable that in both instances the same familiar abbreviation of the village near to Stratford-upon-Avon was intended by Shakespeare.

previously thinking. An extremely natural, and therefore extremely dramatic, effect is thus produced:—

Gonzalo (to ALONZO). Sir, we were talking, that our garments seem now as fresh as when we were *at Tunis* at the marriage of your daughter, who is now queen.
Antonio. And the rarest that e'er came *there.*
Sebastian. Bate, I beseech you, widow Dido.
Antonio. O, widow Dido; ay, widow Dido.
Gonzalo (to ALONZO). Is not, sir, my doublet as fresh as the first day I wore it? I mean, in a sort.
Antonio. That sort was well fished for.
Gonzalo (to ALONZO). When I wore it at your daughter's marriage:
    Alonzo. You cram these words into mine ears, against
The stomach of my sense. *Would I had never*
Married my daughter there !—Temp., ii. 1.

    Ferdinand. Miranda. We wish your peace.   [*Exeunt.*
    Prospero (to ARIEL). Come with a thought. *(To them) I thank you.*
                                     Ibid., iv. 1.

    Duke. No might nor greatness in mortality
Can censure 'scape ; back-wounding calumny
The whitest virtue strikes. What king so strong,
Can tie the gall up in the slanderer's tongue?
But who comes here? [*Enter* ESCALUS, &c.]—*M. for M.,* iii. 2.

    Mariana. Will't please you walk aside?   [*Exit with* ISABELLA.
    Duke. O place and greatness! millions of false eyes
Are stuck upon thee! volumes of report
Run with these false and most contrarious guests
Upon thy doings! thousand escapes of wit
Make thee the father of their idle dream,
And rack thee in their fancies !—Ibid., iv. 1.

It will be perceived that the above two passages, although in different scenes, are but one and the same soliloquy; the second being a resumption of the first, which was broken off by the entrance of Escalus, &c.

    Don John. Sir, they are spoken, and *these things are true.*
    Benedick. This looks not like a nuptial.
    Hero.   *True!* O God!—*M. Ado,* iv. 1.

    Portia.   You must take your chance;
And either not attempt to choose at all,
Or swear before you choose, if you choose wrong
Never to speak to lady afterward
In way of marriage : therefore be advis'd.
    Morocco. Nor will not.—Mer. of V., ii. 1.

Helena. If the living be enemy to the grief, the excess makes it soon mortal.
Bertram. Madam, I desire your holy wishes.
Lafeu. How understand we that ?—All's W., i. 1.

The First Folio (often deplorably erroneous in prefixes) assigns Helena's speech to the Countess, in whose mouth it has no significance ; whereas, in Helena's mouth it is characteristically veiled in expression, yet clear to those who are aware of her secret affection for Bertram,—meaning, 'if the living man I love, dislike me and my grief, its excess will soon kill me.' Lafeu, who is not possessed of her secret, finds her speech enigmatical, and exclaims, "How understand we that ?"

    Lafeu. Lustick, as the Dutchman says . . . why, *he's able to lead her a coranto.*
    Parolles. Mort du vinaigre! Is not this Helen?
    Lafeu. 'Fore God, *I think so.—Ibid.,* ii. 3.

> First Lord. Go, tell the Count Rousillon and my brother,
> We have caught the woodcock, and will keep him muffled
> Till we do hear from them.
>   Second Soldier.   Captain, I will.
>   First Lord. He will betray us all unto ourselves:
> Inform on that.
>   Second Soldier. So I will, sir.—All's W., iv. 1.

The First Lord's words, " Inform on that," have been altered by some commentators, who have not perceived that they are a following up of the previous portion of the speech, and that " he will " is elliptically understood as repeated before "inform." The First Lord is musing upon Parolles' answer to the words previously addressed to him, " haply thou may'st *inform* something to save thy life"; and says he will "inform" on that point—something concerning "ourselves."

>   King Philip. Well could I bear that England had this praise,
> So we could find some pattern of our shame.
> Look, who comes here ! a grave unto a soul ;
> Holding th' eternal spirit, against her will,
> In the vile prison of afflicted breath.
>   *Enter* CONSTANCE.
> I pr'ythee, lady, *go away with me.*
>   Constance. Lo, now ! now see the issue of your peace !
>   King Philip. Patience, good lady ! . . .
> Bind up those tresses. . . .
> Like true, inseparable, faithful loves,
> Sticking together in calamity.
>   Constance. To England, *if you will.*
>   King Philip. Bind up your hairs.—*John*, iii. 4.

The distracted mother's apparently irrelevant speech "to England &c.," is, in fact, a rejoinder to the French king's words addressed to her on her entrance. At the time he uttered them, her thoughts were too much engrossed to notice them; but afterwards—with that curious operation of the memory's ear which gives the echo of a sentence spoken to an absent-minded person many minutes subsequent to its sound—they recur to her, and she answers them in a wild and reckless spirit of despair. By the very repetition of King Philip's words, "Bind up your hairs," this is indicated; as if he would recall her to the point now at issue. Our interpretation of this passage differs from any given by previous commentators; but we think our view shows it in the light of one among many admirable touches whereby the poet has depicted a mind bordering on frenzy in this powerfully affecting scene, as in other scenes in other plays. Moreover, it is in accordance with the mode which, under the present heading of CROSSING SPEECHES, we have shown to be our dramatist's, of allowing a sentence to be spoken in reference to something said some time before in the dialogue. This he has made a special characteristic in one of his speakers, Hotspur, the impetuous-spirited, vehement-spoken man of strong and sudden impulses. Witness the following examples; the first and third of which afford instances of Hotspur's habit, while the second, besides referring to it, shows Prince Henry falling into a similar fashion for the moment himself :—

Lady Percy. Oh, my good lord, why are you thus alone? . . .
Some heavy business hath my lord in hand,
And I must know it, else *he loves me not.*
Hotspur. What, ho!

Enter a SERVANT.

Is Gilliams with the packet gone?
Servant. He is, my lord, an hour ago.
Hotspur. Hath Butler brought those horses . . .
What say'st thou, my lady?
Lady Percy. What is it carries you away? . . .
In faith, I 'll break thy little finger, Harry,
An if thou wilt not tell me all things true.
Hotspur. Away,
Away, you trifler!—*Love ?*—*I love thee not,*
I care not for thee, Kate : this is no world
To play with mammets, and to tilt with lips.—1 *H. IV.*, ii. 3.

Prince Henry. I am now of all humours that have showed themselves humours, since the old days of goodman Adam to the pupil age of this present twelve o'clock at midnight. [FRANCIS *crosses the stage, with wine.*] What 's o'clock, Francis?
Francis. Anon, anon, sir.　　　　　　　　　　　　　　　　　　　　[*Exit.*
Prince Henry. That ever this fellow should have fewer words than a parrot, and yet the son of a woman! His industry is, upstairs and downstairs; his eloquence, the parcel of a reckoning. *I am not yet of Percy's mind,* the Hotspur of the north; he that kills me some six or seven dozen of Scots at a breakfast, washes his hands, and says to his wife, "Fie upon this quiet life! I want work." "Oh, my sweet Harry," says she, "*how many hast thou killed to-day ?*" "Give my roan horse a drench," says he; *and answers, "some fourteen," an hour after*—"a trifle, a trifle."—*Ibid.*, ii. 4.

Douglas. Thou art the king of honour :
No man so potent breathes upon the ground,
But I will beard him.
Hotspur.　　　　　　Do so, *and 'tis well.*

Enter a MESSENGER *with letters.*

What letters hast thou there?　　(*To* DOUGLAS) *I can but thank you.*
　　　　　　　　　　　　　　　　　　　　　　Ibid., iv. 1.

Bardolph. Pray thee, *go down,* good ancient.
Falstaff. Hark thee hither, Mistress Doll.
Pistol. Not I : I tell thee what, Corporal Bardolph.—2 *H. IV.*, ii. 4.

Volumnia. Oh, he is wounded—I thank the gods for 't.
Menenius. So do I too, if it be not too much :—*brings 'a victory in his pocket ?*—the wounds become him.
Volumnia. On 's brows : Menenius, he comes the third time home with the oaken garland.—*Coriol.*, ii. 1.

Coriolanus.　　　　　　　　　　Hear'st thou, Mars.
Aufidius. Name not the god, *thou boy of tears !*
Coriolanus.　　　　　　　　　　　　　　　　Ha!
Aufidius. No more [than a boy of tears].—*Ibid.*, v. 5.

Cassius. No, it is Casca ; *one incorporate*
To our attempts. Am I not stay'd for, Cinna?
Cinna. I am glad on 't. What a fearful night.—*Jul. C.*, i. 3.

Bernardo. Looks it not like the king ? mark it, Horatio.
Horatio. Most like : it harrows me with fear.—*Hamlet*, i. 1.

Horatio. Two nights together. . . . A figure like your father
Arm'd at all points exactly, cap-à-pé,
Appears before them. . . .
Ham. Indeed, indeed, sirs, but this troubles me.
Hold you the watch to-night?
Marcellus. Bernardo.　　　　We do, my lord.

Ham. Arm'd, say you ?
Marcellus. Bernardo. Arm'd, my lord.—*Hamlet,* i. 2.

Horatio. Have after. *To what issue will this come ?*
Marcellus. Something is rotten in the state of Denmark.
Horatio. Heaven will direct it.—Ibid., i. 5.

Polonius. He will come straight . . .
Pray you, *be round with him.*
Hamlet (within). Mother, mother, mother!
Queen.   *I 'll warrant you ;*
Fear me not: withdraw, I hear him coming.—*Ibid.,* iii. 4.

Duke. Whoe'er he be that, in this foul proceeding,
Hath thus beguil'd your daughter of herself,
And you of her, the bloody book of law,
You shall yourself read in the bitter letter,
After your own sense ; yea, though our proper son
Stood in your action.
Brabantio.   Humbly I thank your grace.
Here is the man, this Moor ; whom now, it seems,
Your special mandate, for the state affairs,
Hath hither brought
Duke and Senators. We are very sorry for it.
Duke (to OTHELLO*).* What, in your own part, can you say to this?
Brabantio. [He can say] *Nothing, but* [that] *this is so.—Oth.,* i. 3.

Desdemona. So, get thee gone, good night. *Mine eyes do itch ;*
Doth that bode weeping ?
Emilia.   'Tis neither here nor there.
Desdemona. I have heard it said so [that it does bode weeping].
                                    Ibid., iv. 3.

Iras.   *Royal Egypt !*
Empress !
Charmian. Peace, peace, Iras !
Cleopatra. No more [a queen or empress], *but e'en a woman.*
                               Ant. & C., iv. 13.

Belarius (Aside).   Oh, noble strain !
Oh, worthiness of nature ! . . .
(Aloud) 'Tis the ninth hour o' the morn.
Arviragus.   Brother, farewell.
Imogen. I wish ye sport.
Arviragus. You health. *So please you, sir* [we are ready to attend you].
                                  Cym., iv. 2.

See UNFINISHED SENTENCES for somewhat similar examples of the
kind of naturally and dramatically crossing speeches here instanced.

DEVIATING INTO VARIOUS TENSES.

In the course of narrating an incident that has occurred, Shakespeare
sometimes suddenly deviates into an expression denoting actual time;
so that while the majority of the verbs he uses in the speech or dialogue
are in the past tense, he abruptly introduces a verb in the present tense;
which imparts a spirited effect to the description:—

> I *boarded* the king's ship; now on the beak,
> Now in the waist, the deck, in every cabin,
> I *flam'd* amazement : sometimes *I 'd* divide,
> And burn in many places ; on the topmast,
> The yards, and bowsprit, *would I flame* distinctly,

Then meet, and join.   Jove's lightnings, the precursors
O' the dreadful thunder-claps, more momentary
And sight-outrunning *were* not : the fire, and cracks
Of sulphurous roaring, the most mighty Neptune
Seem to besiege, and *make* his bold waves tremble.—*Temp.*, i. 2.

She *tore* the letter into a thousand halfpence ; *railed* at herself. . . . "I measure him," *says* she, " by my own spirit." . . . Then down upon her knees she *falls, weeps, sobs, beats* her heart, *tears* her hair, *prays, cries,* "Oh, sweet Benedick !"—*M. Ado*, ii. 3.

I have sold all my trumpery ; . . . they *throng* who should buy first, as if my trinkets had been hallowed.—*W. T.*, iv. 3.

Their joy *waded* in tears.   There *was* casting up of eyes, holding up of hands, . . . Our king, . . . *cries,* " Oh, thy mother, thy mother !" then *asks* Bohemia forgiveness, then again *worries* he his daughter with clipping her ; now he *thanks* the old shepherd, which *stands* by.—*Ibid.*, v. 2.

She *lifted* the princess from the earth ; and so *locks* her in embracing, as if she would pin her to her heart.—*Ibid.*, v. 2.

The great supply,
That *was expected* by the Dauphin here,
Are wreck'd *three nights ago* on Goodwin Sands.—*John*, v. 3.

I am a rogue, if I *were* not at half-sword with a dozen of them two hours together. I have 'scaped by miracle. I *am* eight times thrust through the doublet.—1 *H. IV.*, ii. 4.

As we *were sharing*, some six or seven fresh men set upon us—
And *unbound* the rest, and then *come* in the other.—*Ibid.*, ii. 4.

Thrice from the banks of Wye
And sandy-bottom'd Severn *have I sent* him
Bootless home and weather-beaten back.—
Home without boots, and in foul weather too !
How *'scapes* he agues, in the devil's name ?—*Ibid.*, iii. 1.

I have misused the king's press damnably. . . . I *press* me none but good house-holders, yeomen's sons ; *inquire* me out contracted bachelors.—*Ibid.*, iv. 2.

And have the summary of all our griefs,
When time shall serve, to show in articles ;
Which, long ere this, we *offer'd* to the king,
And *might by no suit gain* our audience :
When we *are* wrong'd, and would unfold our griefs,
We *are* denied access unto his person.—2 *H. IV.*, iv. 1.

Suffolk first *died :* and York, all haggled over,
Comes to him, where in gore he *lay* insteep'd,
And *takes* him by the beard ; kisses the gashes
That bloodily *did yawn* upon his face ;
And *cries* aloud, " Tarry, dear cousin Suffolk !
My soul shall thine keep company to heaven ;
Tarry, sweet soul," . . .
Upon these words I *came* and *cheer'd* him up :
He *smil'd* me in the face, *raught* me his hand,
And, with a feeble gripe, *says,* " Dear my lord,
Commend my service to my sovereign."
So *did* he *turn,* and over Suffolk's neck
He *threw* his wounded arm, and *kiss'd* his lips ;
And so, espous'd to death, with blood he *seal'd*
A testament of noble-ending love.—*H. V.*, iv. 6.

The wretched, bloody, and usurping boar,
That *spoil'd* your summer fields and fruitful vines,
Swills your warm blood like wash, and *makes* his trough
In your embowell'd bosoms.—*R. III.*, v. 2.

Before the sun rose he *was harness'd* light,
And to the field *goes* he.—*Tr. & Cr.*, i. 2.

She *came*, and *puts* me her white hand to his cloven chin.—*Tr. & Cr.*, i. 2.

I *saw* him run after a gilded butterfly ; and when he *caught* it, he *let* it go again ; and after it again ; and over and over he *comes*, and up again.—*Coriol.*, i. 3.

> But, *when I came* (some minute ere the time
> Of her awakening), here untimely *lay*
> The noble Paris, and true Romeo, dead.
> *She wakes;* and *I entreated* her come forth
> And bear this work of heaven with patience.—*R. & Jul.*, v. 3.

> And graves *have yawn'd* and *yielded* up their dead ;
> Fierce fiery warriors *fight* upon the clouds,
> In ranks and squadrons and right form of war,
> Which *drizzled* blood upon the Capitol ;
> The noise of battle *hurtled* in the air,
> Horses *did neigh*, and dying men *did groan;*
> And ghosts *did shriek* and squeal about the streets.—*Jul. C.*, ii. 2.

> Two nights together *had* these gentlemen,
> Marcellus and Bernardo . . .
> *Been* thus encounter'd.   A figure like your father,
> Arm'd at all points exactly, cap-à-pé,
> *Appears* before them, and with solemn march
> *Goes slow* and stately by them : thrice he *walk'd*
> By their oppress'd and fear-surprisèd eyes,
> Within his truncheon's length ; whilst they, distill'd
> Almost to jelly with the act of fear,
> *Stand* dumb, and *speak* not to him.   This to me
> In dreadful secrecy impart they did ;
> And I with them the third night *kept* the watch :
> Where, as they had deliver'd, both in time,
> Form of the thing, each word made true and good,
> The apparition *comes*.—*Hamlet*, i. 2.

> Upon our first, he *sent* out to suppress
> His nephew's levies ; which to him *appear'd*
> To be a preparation 'gainst the Polack ;
> But, better look'd into, he truly *found*
> It was against your highness : whereat griev'd—
> That so his sickness, age, and impotence
> Was falsely borne in hand—*sends* out arrests
> On Fortinbras ; which he, in brief, *obeys;*
> *Receives* rebuke from Norway ; and, in fine,
> *Makes* vow before his uncle, never more
> To give th' assay of arms against your majesty.
> Whereon old Norway, overcome with joy,
> *Gives* him three thousand crowns in annual fee.—*Ibid.*, ii. 2.

You *played* once in the university, you *say ?—Ibid.*, iii. 2.

> Three great ones of the city,
> In personal suit to make me his lieutenant,
> *Off-capp'd* to him : . . .
> But he, as loving his own pride and purposes,
> *Evades* them, with a bombast circumstance
> Horribly stuff'd with epithets of war ;
> And, in conclusion,
> *Nonsuits* my mediators ; for, " Certes," *says* he,
> " I have already chose my officer."—*Oth.*, i. 1.

> Then must you speak
> Of one that *lov'd* not wisely, but too well ;
> Of one, not easily jealous, but, being wrought,
> Perplex'd in the extreme ; of one, whose hand,
> Like the base Indian, *threw* a pearl away

> Richer than all his tribe; of one, whose subdu'd eyes,
> Albeit unusèd to the melting mood,
> *Drop* tears as fast as the Arabian trees
> Their medicinal gum.—*Oth.*, v. 2.

> *When I was born :*
> Never were waves nor wind more violent ;
> And from the ladder-tackle *washes* off
> A canvas-climber. " Ha ! " *says* one, " wilt thou ? "
> And with a dropping industry they *skip*
> From stem to stern : the boatswain *whistles*, and
> The master *calls*, and *trebles* their confusion.—*Per.*, iv. 1.

Both Shakespeare's chief narrative poems present numerous instances of this peculiarity in style, besides those afforded in their very opening lines :—

> Even as the sun with purple-colour'd face
> Had ta'en his last leave of the weeping morn,
> Rose-cheek'd Adonis *hied* him to the chase ;
> Hunting he lov'd, but love he laugh'd to scorn :
> Sick-thoughted Venus, *makes* amain unto him,
> And like a bold-fac'd suitor *'gins* to woo him.—*V. & Adon.*, Stanza 1.

> From the besieged Ardea all in post,
> *Borne* by the trustless wings of false desire,
> Lust-breathed Tarquin *leaves* the Roman host,
> And to Collatium *bears* the lightless fire
> Which, in pale embers hid, lurks to aspire.—*Lucrece, Stanza* 1.

In adverting to a future time he allows the speaker to deviate into present tense; thereby giving a forcible and immediate impression to the prediction :—

> Truth *shall* nurse her,
> Holy and heavenly thoughts still counsel her :
> She *shall* be lov'd and fear'd : her own *shall* bless her ;
> Her foes shake like a field of beaten corn,
> And hang their heads with sorrow : good *grows* with her :
> In her days every man *shall* eat in safety,
> Under his own vine, what he plants.—*H. VIII.*, v. 4.

From conditional tense, he permits Cominius—in the heat of martial admiration addressing Marcius—to deviate into future tense, thereby giving more direct and natural effect to the speech:—

> If I *should* tell thee o'er this thy day's work,
> Thou *'lt* not believe thy deeds.—*Coriol.*, i. 9.

Where Silvia and the disguised page, Sebastian, are talking of the supposedly absent Julia, the author allows them to speak of her in the present tense; but suddenly to diverge into the past tense; because, after Silvia's first question, "Is she not passing fair?" the answer throws the subject of inquiry into the condition of a person whose beauty (and almost as if she herself also) had passed away:—

> She *hath been* fairer, madam, than she is :
> *When* she *did think* my master lov'd her well,
> She, in my judgment, *was* as fair as you :
> But since she did neglect her looking-glass,
> And threw her sun-expelling mask away,
> The air hath starv'd the roses in her cheeks,
> And pinch'd the lily tincture of her face,
> That now she is become as black as I.

Therefore Silvia's next question comes with most natural effect :—

> How tall *was* she?—*Two G. of V.*, iv. 4.

Shakespeare has in a few instances used a past tense where ordinarily a present tense is employed :—

> Slaves as ragged as Lazarus in the painted cloth, where the glutton's dogs *licked* his sores.—1 *H. IV.*, iv. 2.

>   What you shall know meantime
> Of this abroad, I shall beseech you, sir,
> To let me be partaker.—
>   Doubt not, sir;
> I *knew** it for my bond.—*Ant. & C.*, i. 4.

> A fire from heaven came, and shrivell'd up
> Their bodies, even to loathing; for they so stunk,
> That all those eyes ador'd them ere their fall,
> Scorn now their hand should give them burial.—
> '*Twas* very strange.—*Per.*, ii. 4.

Very noteworthy is the way in which our poet occasionally uses the word "now" when referring to a past time; thereby giving wonderfully spirited effect to passages of narration :—

> The lioness had torn some flesh away,
> Which all this while had bled; and *now* he fainted,
> And cried, in fainting, upon Rosalind.—*As You L.*, iv. 3.

> Our king, being ready to leap out of himself for joy of his found daughter, as if that joy were *now* become a loss, cries . . . *Now* thanks the old shepherd—*W. T.*, v. 2.

> I sprang not more in joy at first hearing he was a man-child, than *now* in first seeing he had proved himself a man.—*Coriol.*, i. 3.

> Hath *now* this dread and black complexion smear'd
> With heraldry more dismal; head to foot
> *Now* is he total gules.—*Hamlet*, ii. 2.

>   And *now* our cowards
> (Like fragments in hard voyages) became
> The life o' the need . . . ten, chas'd by one,
> Are *now* each one the slaughterman of twenty.—*Cym.*, v. 3.

> And what was first but fear what might be done,
> Grows elder *now*, and cares it be not done.—*Per.*, i. 2.

DISSONANCES.

Shakespeare—remarkable for his harmonious beauty of diction, where musical versification is in keeping with his subject—has certain dissonant effects of expression in passages, where harshness is more consistent and characteristic than smoothness would be. Paulina, hissing out her detestation of Leontes' cruel injustice to his queen, utters a sentence sibilant with ss :—

> What *s*tudied tormen*ts*, tyrant, ha*st* for me?
> What wheel*s*? rack*s*? fire*s*? what flaying? boiling
> In lead*s* or oil*s*? what old or newer torture
> Mu*st* I receive, whose every word de*s*erves
> To ta*s*te of thy mo*st* wor*st*?—*W. T.*, iii. 2.

---

* The effect is thus conveyed of ' I knew it to be my bounden duty, before you asked me to inform you.'

What a capital effect of bluntness is given to King Harry's defiant speech by the rugged little sentence we have italicised in the following lines :—

> They shall have none, I swear, but these my joints,—
> Which, if they have *as I will leave 'em them*,
> Shall yield them little, tell the Constable.—*H. V.*, iv. 3.

And how well consists the close succession of murmuring ss in the following couplet with the image it expresses:—

> Good thing*s* of day begin to droop and drow*s*e ;
> While*s* night'*s* black agent*s* to their prey*s* do rou*s*e.—*Macb.*, iii. 2.

Into Shylock's mouth the poet has put a repetition phrase in the following passage, which gives a sound like the raving bark of the very "dog" he taunts Antonio with having called him:—

> I 'll have my bond ; speak not against *my bond.*
> Thou call'dst me dog before thou hadst a cause ;
> But, since I am a dog, beware my fangs; . . .
> *I 'll have my bond ;* I will not hear thee speak :
> *I 'll have my bond ;* and therefore speak no more. . . .
> I 'll have no speaking ; *I will have my bond.*—*Mer. of V.*, iii. 3.

And, later on, he has put into the same Shylock's mouth the word "Barrabas" (not as spelt in the New Testament, 'Barabbas'), spelt and accented in a mode that imparts a finely snarling effect to the name:—

> These be the Christian husbands! I have a daughter ;
> Would any of the stock of *Barrabas*
> Had been her husband rather than a Christian !—*Ibid*, iv. 1.

In the following, a scornful disgust is thrown into the expression by the tone of words chosen:—

> You shall find there
> A man, who is the abstract of *all faults*
> That *all* men *follow*.—*Ant. & C.*, i. 4.

There is a noteworthy aptness in the next passage, where the iterated checks of "wots what watch" come with as excellent effect of disturbance to the ear, as come the repose and placid cadence of the concluding line with soft effect; each forming a thorough echo to the sense of the respective phrase:—

> But in gross brain little *wots*
> *What watch* the king keeps to maintain the peace,
> *Whose hours the peasant best advantages.*—*H. V.*, iv. 1.

It is worth while to observe how frequently our poet has this kind of unpleasing effect—this dissonant consonance of repeated similar sound— where the word "wot" occurs; also to observe that it accords well with the puzzled impression conveyed by the phrase itself:—

> Anon, I *wot not* by *what* strong escape.—*Com. of E.*, v. 1.
> Than those that walk, and *wot not what* they are.—*Love's L. L.*, i. 1.
> But, my good lord, I *wot not* by *what* power.—*Mid. N. D.*, iv. 1.
> As blanks, benevolences, and I *wot not what :*
> But *what*, o' God's name, doth become of this ?—*R. II.*, ii. 1.

DOUBLE EPITHETS.

Shakespeare occasionally uses more than one epithet descriptive of an object; generally for the sake of giving emphatic effect [*See* Pleonasms], or to denote emotion in the speaker :—

> To be detected with a *jealous rotten* bell-wether.—*Merry W.*, iii. 5.
> For every *pelting petty* officer would use his.—*M. for M.*, i. 2.
> That I should love a *bright particular* star.—*All's W.*, i. 1.
> But such a *headstrong potent* fault it is.—*Tw. N.*, iii. 4.
> Where the warlike Smalus, that *noble honour'd* lord.—*W. T.*, v. 1.
> Rough cradle for such *little pretty* ones !
> *Rude ragged* nurse, *old sullen* playfellow for.—*R. III.*, iv. 1.
> And, when he thinks, *good easy* man, full surely.—*H. VIII.*, ii. 2.
> And sleep in *dull cold* marble, where no mention.—*Ibid.*, iii. 2.
> Thou *idle immaterial* skein of sleave silk.—*Tr. & Cr.*, v. 1.
> To bear with those that say you are *reverend grave* men.—*Coriol.*, ii. 1.
> When you cast your *stinking greasy* caps, in hooting.—*Ibid.*, iv. 6.
> Commend me to thy *honourable virtuous* lord.—*Timon*, iii. 2.
> Pluck the *grave wrinkled* senate from the bench, . . .
> Pluck the lin'd crutch from thy *old limping* sire.—*Ibid.*, iv. 1.
> A *subtle slippery* knave, . . . a *pestilent complete* knave.—*Oth.*, ii. 1.
> One may smell in such a will most *rank foul* disproportion.—*Ibid.*, ii. 3.

He sometimes uses even a triple descriptive epithet :—

> So are those *crisped snaky golden* locks.—*Mer. of V.*, iii. 2.
> A world of *pretty fond adoptious* christendoms.—*All's W.*, i. 1.
> When *holy* and *devout religious* men.—*R. III.*, iii. 7.
> Compassing of his *salt* and most *hidden loose* affection.—*Oth.*, ii. 1.

And in the following passage he has put into the mouth of the peppery Menenius a quadruple epithet :—

> A brace of *unmeriting, proud, violent, testy* magistrates.—*Coriol.*, ii. 1.

In two instances he gives a specimen of heaped-up epithets. The one as a pedantic affectation :—

> After his *undressed, unpolished, uneducated, unpruned, untrained,* or rather, *unlettered,* or ratherest, *unconfirmed* fashion.—*Love's L. L.*, iv. 2.

And the other as an outpouring of indignant scorn :—

> A *base, proud, shallow, beggarly, three-suited, hundred-pound, filthy worsted-stocking* knave; a *lily-livered, action-taking* knave ; a *whoreson, glass-gazing, superserviceable, finical* rogue ; *one-trunk-inheriting* slave.—*Lear*, ii. 2.

It is to be noted that Shakespeare often, as in the above passage, uses an additional epithet with a compound epithet :—

> We must supplant those *rough rug-headed* kerns.—*R. II.*, ii. 1.

In the play from which we have last quoted, there are two passages where some annotators have supposed a compound word is intended ;

but where we believe a double epithet is intended in the first passage, and a double participle in the second :—

> The *sly slow* hours shall not determinate
> The dateless limit of thy dear exile.—*R. II.*, i. 3.
> So, *weeping, smiling*, greet I thee, my earth.—*Ibid.*, iii. 2.

We think that the instances of double epithets used by Shakespeare, as above cited, and the instances of double participle, cited by us as follow, serve to confirm our view :—

> And so in progress to be *hatch'd* and *born.*—*M. for M.*, ii. 2.
> Why should I write this down, that's *riveted*,
> *Screw'd* to my memory ?—*Cym.*, ii. 2.

DRAMATIC LAWS AND ART.

Shakespeare has demonstrated not only that he knew the classical and already existing laws of dramatic art, but that he was also capable of inventing an original code for his own use, and for that of other dramatists who should come after him. His system of dramatic time we have shown at great length, and under a separate heading devoted to that subject [*See* DRAMATIC TIME]; while his contrivance of verisimilitude in dramatic place is also original and ingenious. As an instance of this, we would point out the remarkably numerous scenes into which his drama of " Antony and Cleopatra" is divided, aiding to impart the effect of long time and varied place required for this play, which, historically, extends over a period of ten years, and which demands the alternate display of his characters at Rome, in Egypt, &c. Although in the fifth act there are but two scenes, in the first act of " Antony and Cleopatra" there are five scenes; in the second act, seven scenes ; in the third act, eleven scenes ; and in the fourth act, no fewer than thirteen scenes.

He has various excellent methods of denoting place in his dramas, that serve to keep well before the mind of the spectator the spot where are supposed to transpire the incidents witnessed; and, be it remembered, this was essentially necessary at the time when our great dramatist wrote, there then being none of the modern scenic aids to imagination on the stage where his plays were enacted. He had to give vivacity to their representation, as well as to give life to their composition ; and this he effected by his admirably artistic skill. Sometimes he effects this by poetically picturesque touches, marking the actual presence of the surroundings amid which the speaker is stationed :—

> If by your art, my dearest father, you have
> Put *the wild waters in this roar*, allay them.
> *The sky, it seems*, would pour down stinking pitch,
> But that *the sea, mounting to the welkin's cheek*,
> Dashes the fire out.—*Temp.*, i. 2.
> *How lush and lusty the grass looks ! how green !*—*Ibid.*, ii. 1.
> For me, by *this pale queen of night* I swear.—*Two G. of V.*, iv. 2.

The sun begins to gild the western sky ;
And now it is about the very hour,
That Silvia at Friar Patrick's cell should meet me.—*Two G. of V.*, v. 1.

Whisper her ear, and tell her, *I and Ursula*
Walk in the orchard, and our whole discourse
Is all of her : say that thou overheard'st us ;
And *bid her steal into the pleached bower*,
Where honeysuckles, ripen'd by the sun,
Forbid the sun to enter. . . .
Now, Ursula, when Beatrice doth come,
As we do trace this alley up and down,
Our talk must only be of Benedick. .. .
So angle we for Beatrice ; who *even now*
Is couched in the woodbine coverture.—*M. Ado*, iii. 1.

    And look, the gentle day,
Before the wheels of Phœbus, *round about*
Dapples the drowsy east with spots of grey.—*Ibid.*, v. 2.

Yet you, the murderer, look as bright, as clear
As *yonder Venus in her glimmering sphere.*—*Mid. N. D.*, iii. 2.

Fair Helena ; who more engilds the night
Than *all yon fiery oes and eyes of light.*—*Ibid.*, iii. 2.

My fairy lord, this must be done with haste,
For night's swift dragons cut the clouds full fast,
And *yonder shines Aurora's harbinger.*—*Ibid.*, iii. 2.

Come, sit thee down upon *this flowery bed*,
While I thy amiable cheeks do coy,
And stick musk-roses in thy sleek smooth head,
And kiss thy fair large ears, my gentle joy.—*Ibid.*, iv. 1.

How sweet the moonlight sleeps upon this bank !
Here will we sit, and let the sounds of music
Creep in our ears : soft stillness and the night
Become the touches of sweet harmony.
Sit, Jessica : *look, how the floor of heaven*
Is thick inlaid with patines of bright gold.—*Mer. of V.*, v. 1.

That light we see is burning in my hall.—*Ibid.*, v. 1.

This night methinks is but the daylight sick ;
It looks a little paler : 'tis a day,
Such as the day is when the sun is hid.—*Ibid.*, v. 1.

Well, I 'll end the song. Sirs, cover the while ; the duke will drink *under this tree.*
              As You L., ii. 5.

Stay yet, *look back with me unto the Tower.*
Pity, *you ancient stones*, those tender babes,
Whom envy hath immur'd within *your walls!*
Rough cradle for such little pretty ones !
Rude ragged nurse, old sullen playfellow
For tender princes, use my babies well !
So foolish sorrow *bids your stones farewell.*—*R. III.*, iv. 1.

My prophecy is but half his journey yet ;
For *yonder walls*, that pertly front your town.
Yond' towers, whose wanton tops do buss the clouds,
Must kiss their own feet.—*Tr. & Cr.*, iv. 5.

By all Diana's waiting-women yond',
And by herself, I will not tell you whose.—*Ibid.*, v. 2.

See you yond' coign o' the Capitol—yond' corner-stone ?—*Coriol.*, v. 4.

But, soft ! *what light through yonder window breaks ?*
It is the east, and Juliet is the sun !
Arise, fair sun, and kill the envious moon.—*R. & Jul.*, ii. 2.

O, speak again, bright angel! for *thou art*
As glorious to this night, being o'er my head,
As is a winged messenger of heaven
Unto the white upturned wond'ring eyes
Of mortals, that fall back to gaze on him,
When he bestrides the lazy-pacing clouds,
And sails upon the bosom of the air.—*R. & Jul.*, ii. 2.

The orchard walls are high, and hard to climb,
And the place death, considering who thou art,
If any of my kinsmen find thee here.—
With love's light wings did I o'erperch *these walls.*—*Ibid.*, ii. 2.

Lady, by *yonder blessed moon* I swear,
That *tips with silver all these fruit-tree tops.*— *Ibid.*, ii. 2.

The grey-ey'd morn smiles on the frowning night,
Checkering the eastern clouds with streaks of light;
And flecked darkness like a drunkard reels
From forth day's path and Titan's fiery wheels:
Now, ere the sun advance his burning eye,
The day to cheer, and night's dank dew to dry,
I must up-fill this osier-cage of ours
With baleful weeds and precious-juiced flowers.—*Ibid.*, ii. 3.

Wilt thou be gone? it is not yet near day:
It was the nightingale, and not the lark,
That pierc'd the fearful hollow of thine ear;
Nightly she sings on *yon pomegranate tree:*
Believe me, love, it was the nightingale.—
It was the lark, the herald of the morn,
No nightingale: *look, love, what envious streaks*
Do lace the severing clouds in yonder east:
Night's candles are burnt out, and jocund day
Stands tiptoe on the misty mountain-tops.—*Ibid.*, iii. 5.

I'll say, *yon grey is not the morning's eye,*
'Tis but the pale reflex of Cynthia's brow;
Nor that is not the lark, whose notes do beat
The vaulty heaven so high above our heads.—*Ibid.*, iii. 5.

O, now be gone; *more light and light it grows.*—*Ibid.*, iii. 5.

Give me thy torch, boy: hence, and stand aloof;
Yet put it out, for I would not be seen.
Under *yond' yew-trees* lay thee all along,
Holding thine ear close to the hollow ground;
So shall no foot *upon the churchyard* tread
(*Being loose, unfirm, with digging up of graves*),
But thou shalt hear it.—*Ibid.*, v. 3.

I'll bury thee in a triumphant grave—
A grave? O, no, a lantern, slaughter'd youth;
For *here lies Juliet, and her beauty makes*
This vault a feasting presence full of light.
                    . . . O my love! my wife!
Death, that hath suck'd the honey of thy breath,
Hath had no power yet upon thy beauty:
Thou art not conquer'd; *beauty's ensign yet*
Is crimson in thy lips, and in thy cheeks,
And death's pale flag is not advanced there.—*Ibid.*, v. 3.

What torch is yond', that vainly lends his light
To grubs and eyeless skulls? as I discern,
It burneth in the Capels' monument.—*Ibid.*, v. 3.

As I did sleep under *this yew-tree here,*
I dreamt my master and another fought, . . .
Alack, alack, *what blood is this*, which stains

The stony entrance of this sepulchre ?
What mean *these masterless and gory swords*
To be discolour'd by this place of peace ?—R. & Jul., v. 3.

Let me look back upon thee. O, *thou wall,*
That girdlest in those wolves, dive in the earth,
And fence not Athens. . . . Nothing I'll bear from thee,
But nakedness, thou detestable town !
Take thou that too, with multiplying bans!
Timon will to the woods; where he shall find
Th' unkindest beast more kinder than mankind.
The gods confound (hear me, you good gods all)
The Athenians both within and out *that wall !—Timon.*, iv. 1.

         Why this spade ? this place ?
This slave-like habit ? and these looks of care ?
Thy flatterers yet wear silk, drink wine, lie soft;
Hug their diseas'd perfumes, and have forgot
That ever Timon was. Shame not *these woods*
By putting on the cunning of a carper. . . .
        . . . What, think'st
That the bleak air, thy boisterous chamberlain,
Will put thy shirt on warm ? Will *these moss'd trees*
That have outliv'd the eagle, page thy heels,
And skip when thou point'st out. Will the cold brook,
Candied with ice, caudle thy morning taste,
To cure thy o'ernight's surfeit ?—*Ibid.*, iv. 3.

Here lies the east : doth not the day break here ?—
No.—
O, pardon, sir, it doth ; *and yon grey lines*
That fret the clouds, are messengers of day.—
You shall confess that you are both deceiv'd.
Here, as I point my sword, the sun arises ;
Which is a great way growing on the south,
Weighing the youthful season of the year.
Some two months hence, up higher toward the north
He first presents his fire ; and the high east
Stands, as the Capitol, directly here.—Jul. C., ii. 1.

        Say from whence
You owe this strange intelligence ; or why
Upon *this blasted heath* you stop our way
With such prophetic greeting.—*Macb.*, i. 3.

This castle hath a pleasant seat ; the air
Nimbly and sweetly recommends itself
Unto our gentle senses.—
        This guest of summer,
The temple-haunting martlet, does approve,
By his lov'd mansionry, that the heaven's breath
Smells wooingly here : no jutty, frieze,
Buttress, or coign of vantage, but *this bird*
Hath made his pendent bed and procreant cradle:
Where they most breed and haunt, I have observ'd
The air is delicate.—*Ibid.*, i. 6.

Thou see'st the heavens, as troubled with man's act,
Threaten his bloody stage : by the clock 'tis day,
And yet dark night strangles the travelling lamp :
Is 't night's predominance, or the day's shame,
That darkness does the face of earth entomb,
When living light should kiss it ?—Ibid., ii. 4.

Last night of all,
When *yond' same star*, that 's westward from the pole,

Had made his course to illume that part of heaven
Where now it burns, Marcellus and myself,
The bell then beating one.—*Hamlet,* i. 1.

But, *look, the morn, in russet mantle clad,*
Walks o'er the dew of yon high eastern hill.—*Ibid.,* i. 1.

Blow, winds, and crack your cheeks ! rage ! blow !
You cataracts and hurricanoes, spout
Till you have drench'd our steeples, drown'd the cocks !
You sulphurous and thought-executing fires,
Vaunt-couriers of oak-cleaving thunderbolts,
Singe my white head ! And thou, all-shaking thunder,
Strike flat the thick rotundity o' the world !
Crack nature's moulds, all germins spill at once,
That make ingrateful man ! . . .
Rumble thy bellyful ! spit, fire ! spout, rain !
Nor rain, wind, thunder, fire, are my daughters:
I tax not you, you elements, with unkindness ;
I never gave you kingdom, call'd you children,
You owe me no subscription : then, *let fall*
Your horrible pleasure ; here I stand, your slave,
A poor, infirm, weak, and despis'd old man:
But yet I call you servile ministers,
That will with two pernicious daughters *join*
Your high-engender'd battles 'gainst a head
So old and white as this. O ! O ! 'tis foul !—*Lear,* iii. 2.

           Now, by *yond' marble heaven,*
In the due reverence of a sacred vow,
I here engage my words.—
              Do not rise yet.
Witness, you ever-burning lights above,
You elements that clip us round about,
Witness, that here Iago doth give up
The execution of his wit, hands, heart,
To wrong'd Othello's service !—*Oth.,* iii. 3.

A goodly day not to keep house, with such
Whose roof's as low as ours ! Stoop, boys : *this gate*
Instructs you how to adore the heavens, and bows you
To morning's holy office : the gates of monarchs
Are arch'd so high, that giants may jet through
And keep their impious turbands on, without
Good morrow to the sun. Hail, thou fair heaven !
We house i' the rock, yet use thee not so hardly
As proud livers do.—
           Hail, heaven !—
               Hail, heaven !—
Now for our mountain sport: *up to yon hill :*
Your legs are young; *I'll tread these flats.*—*Cym.,* iii. 3.

           But what is this ?
Here is a path to it ; 'tis some savage hold.—*Ibid.,* iii. 6.

Thou God of *this great vast, rebuke these surges*
Which wash both heaven and hell ; and thou, that hast
Upon the winds command, *bind them in brass,*
Having call'd them from the deep ! O *still*
Thy deafening, dreadful thunders ; gently quench
Thy nimble, sulphurous flashes ! O how, Lychorida,
How does my queen ? *Thou storm, venomously*
Wilt thou spit all thyself ? The seaman's whistle
Is as a whisper in the ears of death,
Unheard.—*Per.,* iii. 1.

In his plots, Shakespeare has a unity of purpose, and a harmony of moral principle, that make his style a special study in this particular alone, besides the countless other perfections marking his dramatic art.

To take the sublime tragedy of "Lear"—as perhaps the most signal example of unity in dramatic plot and ethical purpose—see how he has made the primary story of the filial wickedness of Goneril and Regan with the filial truth of Cordelia towards the old king, reflected by the secondary story of Edmund's treachery and Edgar's fidelity towards their father, Gloster.

Again, in "Timon of Athens" see how the dramatist has contrived to unite the almost episodical events of Alcibiades' career with those of Timon's; and to blend the minor points of the one with the more striking points of the other. In doing this, he has made the originating cause of the military leader's wrath against the Athenian rulers, and the munificent nobleman's hatred towards them, to spring from a similar source—ingratitude.

See how, even in his less grave plays, he has made the subordinate incidents and inculcated lesson a kind of reinforcement of the main events and precept contained therein; as we find this exemplified in his drama of "The Merchant of Venice"; where Portia's fate dependent on the caskets, involving the question of chance and right judgment, is but a harmonious carrying on of the chief points—the mixture of chance and judgment in the legal quirk which saves Antonio's life—the questions of prejudice between castes and faiths, the justice and injustice between Christian and Jew, the malice and pertinacious revenge of Shylock paralleled by the hatred and oppression of Antonio and his Venetian protectors towards the persecuted tribe. And—to adduce but a single instance in evidence of Shakespeare's passages containing coincident dramatic monition—we cite the following speech made by the Second Murderer in "Richard III."; and then the speech made by the usurper himself, upon the same subject—conscience.

Observe how finely the dramatist contrives to make the hireling murderer's temporary qualms—bluntly, nay, coarsely and almost humorously expressed—a kind of rough sketch (at the same time limned with marvellously distinctive characterisation) of that subsequent terrible revealment of the night horrors and agonies that haunt the couch of the royal murderer :—

First Murd. Where's thy conscience now?

Sec. Murd. In the Duke of Gloster's purse.

First Murd. So, when he opens his purse to give us our reward, thy conscience flies out.

Sec. Murd. 'Tis no matter; let it go; there's few or none will entertain it.

First Murd. What if it come to thee again?

Sec. Murd. I'll not meddle with it—it is a dangerous thing, it makes a man a coward: a man cannot steal, but it accuseth him; a man cannot swear, but it checks him; a man cannot lie with his neighbour's wife, but it detects him: 'tis a blushing shame-faced spirit, that mutinies in a man's bosom; it fills one full of obstacles; it made me once restore a purse of gold, that by chance I found; it beggars any man that keeps it : it is turned out of all towns and cities for a dangerous thing ; and every man, that means to live well, endeavours to trust to himself, and live without it.

R. III., i. 4.

K. Rich. Give me another horse—bind up my wounds—
Have mercy, Jesu! Soft! I did but dream.
O, coward conscience, how dost thou afflict me!
The lights burn blue. It is now dead midnight.
Cold fearful drops stand on my trembling flesh.
What! do I fear myself? there's none else by:
Richard loves Richard; that is, I am I.
Is there a murderer here? No—yes, I am:
Then fly. What! from myself? Great reason why;
Lest I revenge. What! myself upon myself!
Alack, I love myself. Wherefore? for any good
That I myself have done unto myself?
O, no! alas, I rather hate myself
For hateful deeds committed by myself!
I am a villain: yet I lie, I am not.
Fool, of thyself speak well: fool, do not flatter.
My conscience hath a thousand several tongues,
And every tongue brings in a several tale,
And every tale condemns me for a villain.
Perjury, perjury, in the high'st degree;
Murder, stern murder, in the dir'st degree;
All several sins, all us'd in each degree,
Throng to the bar, crying all, Guilty! guilty!
I shall despair. There is no creature loves me;
And if I die, no soul shall pity me:
Nay, wherefore should they—since that I myself
Find in myself no pity to myself?
Methought the souls of all that I had murder'd
Came to my tent; and every one did threat
To-morrow's vengeance on the head of Richard.—*R. III.,* v. 3.

Shakespeare has numerous dramatic expedients for introducing certain needful points with easy and natural effect:—

Rosalind. Do you not know I am a woman? when I think, I must speak. Sweet, say on.
Celia. You bring me out. Soft! comes he not here?
Rosalind. 'Tis he, slink by, and note him. 　　　　　[ROSALIND *and* CELIA *retire.*
Enter ORLANDO *and* JAQUES.
　　　　　　　　　　　　　　　　　As You L., iii. 2.

By the above device of making Rosalind and Celia break off their conversation and withdraw while Orlando and Jaques talk together, the dramatist gives an opportunity for a characteristic dialogue between the two latter, and for making the lover avow his passion for his mistress (though unconsciously) in her very presence:—

Orlando. Is 't possible, that on so little acquaintance you should like her? that, but seeing, you should love her? and, loving, woo? and, wooing, she should grant? and will you persèver to enjoy her?—*Ibid.,* v. 2.

This question of Orlando's serves to evoke an explanation of the sudden mutual liking between his brother Oliver and Celia; which else might strike the audience, or readers of the play, as being unnaturally abrupt.

Sly. For God's sake, a pot of small ale. . . .
And once again, a pot o' the smallest ale.—*Tam. of S., Induc.* 2.

Most humorously and appropriately has Shakespeare, by the earnestness and repetition of this call for the weakest of liquors, indicated the thirst that besets the drunkard after his heavy sleep.

> *Countess.* Had you not lately an intent—speak truly—
> To go to Paris?
> *Helena.*   Madam, I had.—*All's W.*, i. 3.

Our author causes the Countess to make this inquiry, because it was necessary that Helena's " intent to go to Paris " should be discussed between them in the present scene for the fartherance of the dramatic action, although there has been no absolute mention previously of the " intent " having come to the Countess's knowledge. [*See* PASSAGES OF INCOMPLETE EXPLANATION.]

> *Countess.* Alas! and would you take the letter of her?
> Might you not know she would do as she has done,
> By sending me a letter?   Read it again.
> *Steward (Reads).* " I am Saint Jaques' pilgrim," &c.—*Ibid.*, iii. 4.

By the lady's desire to hear the letter re-read, the dramatist provides that it shall be heard by the spectators of the play.

> *Viola.* Who governs here?
> *Captain.*   A noble duke, in nature
> As in name.
> *Viola.*   What is his name?
> *Captain.*   Orsino.
> *Viola.* Orsino! I have heard my father name him :
> He was a bachelor then.—*Tw. N.*, i. 2.

This little sentence of Viola's contains one of our dramatist's apparently slight but really subtle touches of artistic contrivance. It lets us into the secret of the original source of this charming heroine's interest in Orsino—her father's mention; while by the single word " bachelor," we are allowed to perceive the peculiar nature of the interest she feels. By this delicate indication of a pre-existing inclination on her part for the count, we are prepared for the circumstance of Viola's at once falling so deeply in love with him, when she comes to know him personally.

> *Sir Toby.* Come hither, knight; come hither, Fabian : we 'll whisper o'er a couplet or two of most sage saws.—*Ibid.*, iii. 4.

Sir Toby's withdrawal apart with the two others affords opportunity for Viola's soliloquy, and gives in a natural manner the effect of their inclination to let the quarrel drop.

> *Florizel.* Hark, Perdita.   [*Taking her aside.*
> (*To* CAMILLO) I 'll hear you by and by.—*W. T.*, iv. 3.

The above device serves a double dramatic purpose. It allows us to perceive how the young prince, seeing that Perdita stands silently—as it were, irresponsively and unassentingly—by while he speaks to Camillo, leads her apart that he may convince her of his own unswerving faith and persuade her to his views ; and it also affords opportunity for Camillo's soliloquy which tells the audience his plan.

> *Camillo.*   My lord,
> Fear none of this. . . . For instance, sir,
> That you may know you shall not want—one word.   [*They talk aside.*
> *Re-enter* AUTOLYCUS.—*Ibid.*, iv. 3.

Very naturally is the lively rogue's soliloquy here introduced, while

Camillo is explaining to the lovers what will be their resources in their wanderings.

> *Florizel.* O Perdita, what have we twain forgot!
> Pray you, a word. [*They converse apart.*]—*W. T.*, iv. 3.

This gives opportunity for Camillo's mention of his intending to inform the king of his son's departure.

> *Poins.* Come, shelter, shelter: *I have removed Falstaff's horse*, and he frets like gummed velvet. . . .
> *Falstaff.* Where's Poins, Hal?
> *P. Henry.* He is walked up to the top of the hill : I 'll go seek him.
> [*Pretends to seek* POINS.
> *Falstaff.* I am accursed to rob in that thief's company: *the rascal hath removed my horse, and tied him I know not where.* . . . *Give me my horse*, you rogues; *give me my horse*, and be hanged! . . .
> *Gadshill.* Case ye, case ye; on with your visors: there's money of the king's *coming down the hill.* . . .
> *P. Henry.* Sirs, *you four shall front them in the narrow lane; Ned Poins and I will walk lower:* if they 'scape from your encounter, then they light on us. . . .
> *Poins.* Sirrah Jack, *thy horse stands behind the hedge: when thou needest him, there thou shalt find him.* . . .
> *First Traveller.* Come, neighbour: the boy *shall lead our horses down the hill;* we 'll walk afoot awhile, and ease our legs. . . .
> *Falstaff.* Come, my masters, let us share, *and then to horse* before day. . . .
> *P. Henry.* Got with much ease. *Now merrily to horse.*—1 *H. IV.*, ii. 2.

How admirably do the above-cited touches set the absolute scene of the Gadshill robbery before our eyes; and how the dramatist has borne in mind the necessity of providing for the fat knight's return to town, by making Poins, after he has had his jest out, tell Sir John where he may find his purloined horse. Shakespeare forgets nothing that may aid dramatic verisimilitude.

> *Falstaff.* Come hither, hostess.   [*Taking her aside.*
> *Enter* GOWER.
> *Chief Justice.* Now, Master Gower, what news?
> *Gower.* The king, my lord, and Henry, Prince of Wales,
> Are near at hand, the rest the paper tells.   [*Gives a letter.*
> *Falstaff.* As I am a gentleman,—
> *Hostess.* Faith, you said so before.
> *Falstaff.* As I am a gentleman : come, no more words of it. . . .
> *Chief Justice.* I have heard better news.
> *Falstaff.* What's the news, my good lord?
> *Chief Justice (to* GOWER). Where lay the king last night?
> *Gower.* At Basingstoke, my lord.
> *Falstaff.* I hope, my lord, all 's well: what is the news, my lord?
> *Chief Justice (to* GOWER). Come all his forces back?
> *Gower.* No; fifteen hundred foot, five hundred horse,
> Are march'd up to my lord of Lancaster,
> Against Northumberland and the archbishop.
> *Falstaff.* Comes the king back from Wales, my noble lord?
> *Chief Justice (to* GOWER). You shall have letters of me presently: come, go along with me, good Master Gower.
> *Falstaff.* My lord !*
> *Chief Justice.* What's the matter?

---

* We seem to actually hear the stentorian roar with which this exclamation is shouted, *compelling* the Lord Chief Justice to attend.

Falstaff. Master Gower, shall I entreat you with me to dinner.

Gower. I must wait upon my good lord here; I thank you, good Sir John.

Chief Justice. Sir John, you loiter here too long, being you are to take soldiers up in counties as you go.

Falstaff. Will you sup with me, Master Gower?

Chief Justice. What foolish master taught you these manners, Sir John?

Falstaff. Master Gower, if they become me not, he was a fool that taught them me. This is the right fencing grace, my lord; tap for tap, and so part fair.—*2 H. IV.*, ii. 2.

The above scene is conceived in the very highest spirit of comedy art. There is first the going apart of Falstaff with Hostess Quickly to pacify her, allowing the entrance of Gower and the Chief Justice's accosting him; then there is the inspection of the letter, while Sir John prevails upon his facile creditor not only to withdraw her action for his debt, but to lend him fresh money; and then comes that capital tilting-bout at cutting each other dead between the Chief Justice and Sir John by steadily not noticing appeal, and as steadily continuing to address the unfortunate third who is present. Of course, Falstaff has decidedly the best of it, and points his successive thrusts with extra sharpness by beginning every one of them with "Master Gower," so that it shall not be mistaken to *whom* he is speaking.

Shallow. I was once of Clement's Inn; where, I think, they will talk of mad Shallow yet.

Silence. You were called lusty Shallow then, cousin.—*Ibid.*, iii. 2.

By this one slight touch the dramatist lets us see that the old justice has so often repeated the bragging accounts of his pranks in his green days and the cognomens they procured him that his cousin Silence knows them by heart.

He jests at scars that never felt a wound.—*R. & Jul.*, ii. 2.

By putting into Romeo's mouth the above comment on Mercutio's dialogue with Benvolio, jesting at love-pangs, which have never been experienced by so light-hearted a fellow as he who thus jests, the dramatist contrives to show us that Romeo has heard his friends calling to him, but that he does not choose to answer them.

> Now, ere the sun advance his burning eye,
> The day to cheer, and night's dank dew to dry,
> I must up-fill this osier cage of ours
> With baleful weeds and precious-juiced flowers.—*Ibid.*, ii. 3.

The gentle friar's occupation prepares dramatically and most naturally for his subsequent knowledge and recommendation of the trance-potion given by him to Juliet.

Timon. Come, bring in all together.　　　　　　*[The banquet brought in.*

Second Lord. All covered dishes!

First Lord. Royal cheer, I warrant you.

Third Lord. Doubt not that, if money and the season can yield it.—*Timon*, iii. 6.

The Second Lord's exclamation is one of Shakespeare's slight but significant touches of dramatic art. By it he draws attention to the point of the guests' anticipation of extra choice fare, and at the same time accounts for the circumstance of their not seeing its real nature until the very moment when the striking effect of its discovery is to be made.

> *Banquo.* Cousins, a word, I pray you.
> *Macbeth (Aside).*   Two truths are told,
> As happy prologues to the swelling act
> Of the imperial theme. *(Aloud)* I thank you, gentlemen.
> *(Aside)* This supernatural soliciting
> Cannot be ill; cannot be good : . . .
> *Banquo.* Look how our partner's rapt.—*Macb.*, i. 3.

The withdrawal apart of Banquo, Rosse, and Angus, admits of
Macbeth's relapsing into that profound reverie upon the witches'
prognostication, which before he had scarcely been able to keep himself
from falling into, even while the royal messengers were addressing
him.

> *Macbeth.* Go bid thy mistress, *when my drink is ready,*
> *She strike upon the bell.* . . .
>   Whiles I threat, he lives :
> Words to the heat of deeds too cold breath gives.   *[A bell rings.*
> I go, and it is done; the bell invites me.
> Hear it not, Duncan ; for it is a knell
> That summons thee to heaven or to hell.   *[Exit.*

> *Enter* LADY MACBETH.

> *Lady Macbeth. That which hath made them drunk hath made me bold ;*
> *What hath quench'd them hath given me fire.* . . .
>   . . . He is about it :
> The doors are open ; and the surfeited grooms
> Do mock their charge with snores : *I have drugg'd their possets,*
> That death and nature do contend about them,
> Whether they live or die.—*Ibid.*, ii. 2.

This point of the antique customary night-draught has been made by
our author to serve three distinct purposes of dramatic art. Macbeth,
wholly engrosed with his intended deed, uses the bell which announces
his night "drink" as the mere signal for his bloody act; Lady Macbeth
swallows her portion as that which shall give her firmness for her task;
while the cup prepared for the already "surfeited grooms" is "drugged"
to make their sleeping through the murder doubly sure.

> *Banquo.*   Look to the lady :
> And *when we have our naked frailties hid,*
> *That suffer in exposure,* let us meet,
> And question this most bloody piece of work,
> To know it farther.—*Ibid.*, ii. 2.

The mention that they will first completely clothe their half-dressed
bodies which risk danger by exposure to the open night-air, serves well
to denote the hasty summons they have had by the ringing of the alarm-
bell, and to indicate the keen northern atmosphere of the castle courtyard
where the scene occurs.

> *First Murderer. The west yet glimmers with some streaks of day :*
> Now spurs the lated traveller apace
> To gain the timely inn ; and near approaches
> The subject of our watch.
> *Third Murderer.*   Hark ! *I hear horses.*
> *Banquo (Within).* Give us a light there, ho !
> *Second Murderer.* Then 'tis he : the rest
> That are within the note of expectation
> Already are i' the court.
> *First Murderer.*   *His horses go about.*

> *Third Murderer.* Almost a mile : *but he does usually,*
> *So all men do, from hence to the palace-gate*
> *Make it their walk.*—*Macb.*, iii. 3.

With vividness do the several touches introduced here set the actual spot before our imagination, and serve to account for Banquo and Fleance being on foot when their attackers lie in wait for them.

> *Marcellus.* Horatio says 'tis but our fantasy,
> And will not let belief take hold of him,
> Touching this dreaded sight, twice seen of us :
> Therefore I have entreated him along
> With us to watch the minutes of this night ;
> That, if again this apparition come,
> He may approve our eyes, and speak to it.
> *Horatio.* Tush, tush, 'twill not appear.—*Hamlet*, i. 1.

This incredulity of Horatio as to the dead king's spirit having appeared is an admirable piece of dramatic contrivance. It forestalls the want of belief that exists among those who read the play or witness its performance; and makes the effect produced upon Horatio's mind, when the spectre actually comes, excite a correspondent impression of reality and awe upon the readers or spectators.

> *Hamlet.* My lord, you played once in the university, you say ?—*Ibid.*, iii. 2.

The prince thus adverts to Polonius's boast as though it were something that the old courtier had just said; while we are allowed to perceive that he has been in the habit of vaunting his having acted in the classical plays which it was the custom for college students to perform.

> *Gloster.* Then, pr'ythee get thee gone : if, for my sake,
> Thou wilt o'ertake us, hence a mile or twain,
> I' the way towards Dover, do it for ancient love ;
> And *bring some covering for this naked soul,*
> Which I 'll entreat to lend me.—*Lear.*, iv. 1.

This request of Gloster's, followed by the old man's compliance with it, serves the dramatic purpose of accounting for Edgar's subsequent appearance in better clothing than his Bedlam beggar's blanket ; and, at the same time, serves the moral purpose of showing Gloster's thought for the unfortunate, elicited by his own misfortunes.

> *Gloster.* Sirrah, naked fellow,—
> *Edgar.* Poor Tom 's a-cold. (*Aside*) I cannot daub it farther.—*Ibid.*, iv. 1.

Very artistically introduced are those few aside-spoken words at the present juncture. They denote the son's grief at his father's calamity, incapacitating him from any longer sustaining his assumed character ; and they bring the Bedlam beggar's jargon to a close at a period of the play when no longer needed.

> *Othello.* Good Michael, look you to the guard to-night.—*Oth.*, ii. 3.

These few words, seemingly insignificant, are of important dramatic use. They give augmented effect to Othello's subsequent anger at Cassio's being betrayed not only into neglect of duty in preserving order, but into breach of order himself ; while they set well before the mind Othello's trust and confidence in Cassio as his chosen officer and his liking for him as a personal friend, calling him by his Christian name, " Michael," which, after the one final impressive appeal (" How comes it, Michael, you are thus forgot ? "), he never again uses.

> *Lepidus.* Here comes the noble Antony.
> *Enter* ANTONY *and* VENTIDIUS.
> *Enobarbus.* And yonder Cæsar.
> *Enter* CÆSAR, MECÆNAS, *and* AGRIPPA.
> *Antony.* If we compose well here, to Parthia :
> Hark you, Ventidius.
> *Cæsar.*　　　　　　I do not know,
> Mecænas ; ask Agrippa.—*Ant. & C.*, ii. 2.

This by-play of the two principals in the approaching interview, each speaking apart with his respective adherent, well marks their assumed indifference, their real displeasure, and their deferring as long as possible the moment of mutual salutation.

> *Queen.* Whiles yet the dew 's on ground, gather those flowers ;
> Make haste : who has the note of them ?
> *First Lady.*　　　　　　　　　I, madam.
> *Queen.* Despatch.　　　　　　　　　[*Exeunt* LADIES.
> Now, master doctor, have you brought those drugs ? . . .
> Doctor, your service for this time is ended ;
> Take your own way.
> *Cornelius* (*Aside*). I do suspect you, madam ;
> But you shall do no harm.
> *Queen* (*to* PISANIO).　　Hark thee, a word.
> *Cornelius* (*Aside*). I do not like her.　She doth think she has
> Strange lingering poisons : I do know her spirit,
> And will not trust one of her malice with
> A drug of such fell nature.　Those she has
> Will stupefy and dull the sense awhile. . . .
> *Queen.* No farther service, doctor,
> Until I send for thee.
> *Cornelius.*　　　　　I humbly take my leave.　　[*Exit.* . . .
> *Queen.* Call my woman : think on my words.　[*Exit* PISANIO. . . .
> 　　　. . . I have given him that
> Which, if he take, shall quite unpeople her
> Of leigers for her sweet ; and which she after,
> Except she bend her humour, shall be assur'd
> To taste of too.
> 　　　*Re-enter* PISANIO *and* LADIES.
> 　　　So, so ; well done, well done :
> The violets, cowslips, and the primroses,
> Bear to my closet.—*Cym.*, i. 6.

It is worthy of observation how the dramatist, in the above little scene, has managed the various points of situation and characteristic indication.　He makes the Queen despatch her ladies for the flowers while she asks the doctor for the deadly drugs which she has bid him compound for her ; introduces Pisanio, that the Queen may speak with him while Cornelius soliloquises on the real nature of the drugs with which he has supplied her, thus letting the audience into the secret of their being harmless ; causes her to dismiss the doctor that she may give the drug to Pisanio ; then sends the latter to call her women while she muses upon the result of her gift, and her farther intentions with regard to more of the same compound.　Especially deserving of notice is the mode in which Shakespeare has employed the incident of flowers culled for medicinal preparations on the present occasion, and on that previously cited from " Romeo and Juliet." In the one, the good old Friar Laurence *himself* gathers them, descanting with kindly enthusiasm on their varied qualities and purposes; in the other, the wicked Queen *bids her ladies* gather them, turning them herself to pernicious account, making them a cloak to her evil designs, and by affecting to busy herself "with the perfumes" and "confections" to be made from them, she screens the "drugs" and "poisonous compounds" in which she secretly deals.

> *Imogen.* Take not away the taper, leave it burning.—*Cym.*, ii. 2.

By this slight touch, the poet provides, with the most natural effect, for the circumstance of Iachimo being able to see all the details of that most exquisite of depicted bed-chambers, and to note them down in aid of his scoundrel design.

> *Imogen.* Thou told'st me, when we came from horse, the place
> Was near at hand.—*Ibid.*, iii. 4.

The above allusion serves to show that the speaker and her faithful attendant have performed the previous portion of their long journey by riding, and have now alighted on account of the more rugged and mountainous district through which their way lies.

> *Arviragus.* I am weak with toil, yet strong in appetite.
> *Guiderius.* There is cold meat i' the cave; we'll browse on that,
> Whilst what we have kill'd be cook'd.—*Ibid.*, iii. 6.

The mention of this " cold meat " is one of the dramatist's well-devised touches to denote the youths' hunter-hunger, also to account for Imogen's finding something to eat when she enters the cave, and for Belarius's exclamation when he looks in and beholds her seated there : " But that *it eats our victuals*, I should think here were a fairy."

> *Cloten. My horse is tied up safe :* out, sword, and to a sore purpose! Fortune, put them into my hand! This is the very description of their meeting-place; and the fellow dares not deceive me.—*Ibid.*, iv. 1.

By making Cloten also refer to his horse, the dramatist maintains the point of travelling on horseback during the earlier portion of the journey, and dismounting when among the Welsh hills.

There are many passages where our dramatist draws special attention to certain points that require to be well impressed upon the notice of the audience or reader.

> *Miranda.*   You have often
> Begun to tell me what I am; but stopp'd,
> And left me to a bootless inquisition,
> Concluding, "Stay; not yet."
> *Prospero.*   *The hour's now come;*
> The very minute bids thee ope thine ear :
> Obey, and *be attentive.* . . . Thy false uncle—
> *Dost thou attend me ?*
> *Miranda.*   Sir, most heedfully.
> *Prospero.* Being once perfected how to grant suits,
> How to deny them, . . . *Thou attend'st not.*
> *Miranda.* O, good sir, I do.
> *Prospero.*   *I pray thee, mark me.* . . .
> *Dost thou hear ?*
> *Miranda.*   Your tale, sir, would cure deafness. . . .

> *Prospero.* . . . *Hear a little farther,*
> And then I 'll bring thee to the present business
> Which now 's upon 's ; without the which this story
> Were most impertinent.—*Temp.*, i. 2.

In the above dialogue Shakespeare, through the occasional reminding words of Prospero to his daughter, bespeaks the unflagging attention of the audience to the narrative which explains the pre-incidents of the dramatic story.

> *Abhorson.* Tell him, he must awake, and that quickly too.
> *Clown.* Pray, Master Barnardine, awake till you are executed, and sleep afterwards.
> *Abhorson.* Go in to him, and fetch him out.
> *Clown.* He is coming, sir, he is coming ; I hear his straw rustle.—*M. for M.*, iv. 3.

By the concluding vivid touch how forcibly we are made to see the caged wild-beast man couching in his lair, with the unwillingness of his keepers to enter his den and fetch him forth.

> *Duke.* Thanks, good Escalus, for thy much goodness.
> *There 's more behind that is more gratulate.* . . .
> . . . *Dear Isabel,*
> *I have a motion much imports your good ;*
> *Whereto if you 'll a willing ear incline,*
> What 's mine is yours, and what is yours is mine.
> So, bring us to our palace ; where we 'll show
> *What 's yet behind, that 's meet you all should know.*—*Ibid.*, v. 1.

This triple reference to the speaker's intention of espousing Isabel is made by way of impressing that intention on the minds of those who see or read the play.

> *Ægeon.* There had she not been long, but she became
> A joyful mother of two goodly sons ;
> And, which was strange, *the one so like the other,*
> *As could not be distinguished but by names.*
> That very hour, and in the self-same inn,
> A poor mean woman was delivered
> Of such a burden, male twins, both alike.
> Those—for their parents were exceeding poor—
> I bought, and brought up to attend my sons. . . .
> My youngest boy, and yet my eldest care,
> At eighteen years became inquisitive
> After his brother ; and importun'd me
> That his attendant—for his case was like,
> Reft of his brother, but *retained his name*—
> Might bear him company in quest of him.—*Com. of E.*, i. 1.

The above particulars are introduced to show that the four boys originally had some distinguishing appellation ; but that afterwards one of each pair of twins, in remembrance of his lost brother, took his name. That the two pair of twins in the play should be named alike was necessary for the dramatic equivoke.

> *Shylock. Three thousand ducats*—well.
> *Bassanio.* Ay, sir, *for three months.*
> *Shylock. For three months*—well.
> *Bassanio. For the which,* as I told you, *Antonio shall be bound.*
> *Shylock. Antonio shall become bound*—well.
> *Bassanio.* May you stead me ? Will you pleasure me ? Shall I know your answer ?
> *Shylock. Three thousand ducats for three months, and Antonio bound.* . . . *Three thousand ducats.* I think I may take *his bond* . . .
> . . . By the near guess of my memory,

> I cannot instantly raise up the gross
> Of full *three thousand ducats*.   What of that ?
> Tubal, a wealthy Hebrew of my tribe,
> Will furnish me.   But soft ! *how many months*
> Do you desire ? . . .
> . . . Ay, ay, *three thousand ducats*.
>   *Antonio.* And *for three months*.
>   *Shylock.* I had forgot :—*three months*.   You told me so.
> *Well then, your bond ;* and let me see,—but hear you ;
> Methought you said you neither lend nor borrow
> Upon advantage. . . .
> *Three thousand ducats*—'tis a good round sum.
> *Three months* from twelve, then let me see the rate—. . .
> Go with me to a notary, seal me there
> Your single bond ; and, in a merry sport,
> If you repay me not on such a day,
> In such a place, such sum or sums as are
> Express'd in the condition, let the forfeit
> Be nominated for an equal pound
> Of your fair flesh, to be cut off and taken
> In what part of your body pleaseth me.—*Mer. of V.*, i. 3.

With consummate dramatic skill has Shakespeare (under the natural semblance of the usurer's hesitation to lend the sum required) kept in view by repetition the *terms* of the loan, and the main circumstance which weighs with Shylock,—the " bond " that Antonio enters into,—while at the same time the Jew takes pains to conceal his own malignant interest in the point.   After letting fall the word, he turns off attention from it, by the words " let me see,—but hear you "; and goes on to speak of another subject.   Then, when he returns to the essential point he mentions it lightly, speaks of a " merry sport "; and afterwards calls it " this merry bond."

> *Salarino.* Antonio hath a ship of rich lading wrecked on the narrow seas ; the Goodwins, *I think, they call the place ;* a very dangerous flat, and fatal, where the carcases of many a tall ship lie buried, as they say.—*Ibid.*, iii. 1.

By making the Italian speaker name the celebrated Goodwin Sands thus dubiously, and advert to its terrible quicksands with a kind of hearsay description, the dramatist keeps strongly present to the mind that the scene of his play is abroad.   For a similar art-purpose he previously (act ii., sc. 7), throws in the words, " they have in *England* a coin that bears the figure of an angel stamped in gold."

> *Portia.*   Take this same letter,
> And use thou all the endeavour of a man
> In speed to Padua : see thou render this
> Into my cousin's hand, Doctor Bellario ;
> And, look, *what notes and garments he doth give thee*,
> Bring them, I pray thee, with imagin'd speed
> Unto the Tranect, to the common ferry
> Which trades to Venice.—*Ibid.*, iii. 4.
>   *Duke. This letter from Bellario* doth commend
> A young and learned doctor to our court.
> Where is he ?
>   *Nerissa.*   He attendeth here hard by,
> To know your answer, whether you'll admit him.
>   *Duke.* With all my heart.   Some three or four of you
> Go give him courteous conduct to this place.
> *Meantime the court shall hear Bellario's letter.*

Clerk (Reads). "Your grace shall understand, that at the receipt of your letter I am very sick: but in the instant that your messenger came, in loving visitation was with me a young doctor of Rome; his name is Balthazar. I acquainted him with the cause in controversy between the Jew and Antonio the merchant: we turned o'er many books together: *he is furnished with my opinion;* which, bettered with his own learning (the greatness whereof I cannot enough commend), comes with him, at my importunity, to fill up your grace's request in my stead. I beseech you, let *his lack of years* be no impediment to let him lack a reverend estimation; for I never knew *so young a body* with so old a head." . . .

> *Portia.* Clerk, *draw a deed of gift.*
> *Shylock.* I pray you, give me leave to go from hence;
> I am not well: *send the deed after me,*
> And I will sign it.—*Mer. of V.,* iv. 1.

> *Portia.* Inquire the Jew's house out, give him *this deed,*
> And let him sign it: we'll away to-night,
> And be a day before our husbands home:
> *This deed* will be well welcome to Lorenzo. —*Ibid.,* iv. 2.

> *Gratiano.* My lord Bassanio gave his ring away
> Unto the judge that begg'd it, and indeed
> Deserv'd it too; and then the boy, his clerk,
> *That took some pains in writing,* he begg'd mine.—*Ibid.,* v. 1.

The above-cited points are all manifestations of artistic skill, whereby the dramatist plausibly explains his heroine's being supplied with the needful documents and apparel by her famous lawyer-cousin for carrying on her design of rescuing her husband's friend from his perilous dilemma; and also Nerissa's being provided with "a deed of gift," which she has but to draw forth from her lawyer-clerk's bag of papers, and copy neatly out for the Jew to sign.

> *Oliver.* Where will the old duke live?
> *Charles.* They say, he is already in the forest of Arden, and a many merry men with him; and there they live like the old Robin Hood *of England.—As You L.,* i. 1.

The same remark applies to the above passage as to the second one from the "Merchant of Venice," previously cited.

> *Celia.* I'll put myself in poor and mean attire,
> And *with a kind of umber smirch my face.—Ibid.,* i. 3.

> *Oliver.* If that an eye may profit by a tongue,
> Then should I know you by description;
> Such garments, and such years: "The boy is fair,
> Of female favour, and bestows himself
> Like a ripe sister: but the woman low,
> And *browner than her brother."—Ibid.,* iv. 3.

By the latter of these passages, the dramatist maintains the truth of the touch contained in the former.

> *First Soldier.* What say you to his expertness in war?
> *Parolles.* Faith, sir, he has led the drum before the English tragedians—to belie him I will not—and more of his soldiership I know not; except, *in that country,* he had the honour to be the officer at *a place there* called Mile-end, to instruct for the doubling of files.—*All's W.,* iv. 3.

By the italicised words, the dramatist reminds us that the scene of the play is laid abroad; thus enabling him to introduce native allusions that otherwise would be misplaced. And so with the next passage quoted:—

> *Sir Toby.* As many lies as will lie in thy sheet of paper, although the sheet were big enough for the bed of Ware *in England,* set 'em down.—*Tw. N.,* iii. 2.

> *Viola.* He nam'd Sebastian : I my brother know
> Yet living in my glass ; even such, and so,
> In favour was my brother : and *he went*
> *Still in this fashion, colour, ornament,*—
> *For him I imitate.*—*Tw. N.*, iii. 4.

This accounts with unforced effect for Viola's being dressed so precisely like her brother as to heighten the natural resemblance between the twins, and cause their being taken for each other during the course of the play.

> *King Richard.* Barkloughly Castle call they this at hand ?
> *Aumerle.* Yea, my lord. *How brooks your grace the air,*
> *After your late tossing on the breaking seas ?*
> *King Richard.* Needs must I like it well : I weep for joy
> To stand upon my kingdom once again.—*R. II.*, iii. 2.

By the poetically worded question put into Aumerle's mouth, the dramatist brings well before the mind that the king has just crossed over from Ireland.

Falstaff. I grant you I was down and out of breath ; and so was he : but we rose both at an instant, and fought a long hour by *Shrewsbury clock.*—1 *H. IV.*, v. 4.

This mention of the church-clock by its name not only gives the humorous effect of pretended exactness to Sir John's account of his exploit, but it serves as a reminder of the site of the scene represented and the celebrated event enacted—the famous battle of Shrewsbury.

If you be not too much cloyed with fat meat, our humble author will continue the story, with Sir John in it, and make you merry with fair Katharine of France : where, for anything I know, Falstaff shall die of a sweat unless already he be killed with your hard opinions ; *for Oldcastle died a martyr, and this is not the man.*— 2 *H. IV.* (*Epilogue*).

This sentence puts the crowning point to the evidence that the character of Falstaff originally bore the name of Oldcastle ; and it testifies how anxious Shakespeare was to mark his having had no intention of associating the character of the witty knight with the heroic sufferer whose name he had at first been given.

> *Porter.* But *this place is too cold* for hell. I 'll devil-porter it no farther.—*Macb.*, ii. 3.
>> *Hamlet. The air bites shrewdly ; it is very cold.*
>> *Horatio. It is a nipping and an eager air.*—*Hamlet*, i. 4.
>> *Lear.* My wits begin to turn.
>> Come on, my boy : how dost, my boy ? *Art cold ?*
>> *I am cold myself.*—*Lear*, iii. 2.
>>> *Edgar.* Through the sharp hawthorn blows *the cold wind.*
>>> H'm ! go to thy cold bed, and warm thee. . . .
>>> . . . Bless thy five wits ! Tom 's *a-cold* ! . . .
> *Fool. This cold night* will turn us all to fools and madmen. . . .
> *Edgar.* Set not thy sweet heart on proud array. Tom 's *a-cold.* . . .
> *Fool.* Now a little fire in a wild field were like an old lecher's heart, a small spark, all the rest on 's body cold.—*Ibid.*, iii. 4.

It is worthy of remark how the allusion to " cold " is used by the dramatist in the above citations from three of his great tragedies, the scene of each of which is laid in a northern climate. In " Macbeth," the locality of the murder—the bleak courtyard of a Scottish thane's castle—is kept in view by the grimly facetious allusion to the bitterness of the nigh put into the Porter's mouth ; in " Hamlet," the platform of the royal Danish fortress-residence, with the shiver of those who come thither, partly arising from chill, partly from awe at the expected apparition ; in " Lear," the repeated reference to the intensity of prevailing " cold " during that night of wandering on the open heath serves well to maintain the effect of inclemency and exposure to the raging storm.

> *Cassio.* 'Fore heaven, an excellent song.
> *Iago. I learned it in England,* where indeed they are most potent in potting.—*Oth.*, ii. 3.

Another of those reminders that the spot where the speaker is, lies abroad.

> *Sec. Gent.* But, pray ye, tell me,
> Is she sole child to the king ?
> *First Gent.* His only child.
> He had two sons—if this be worth your hearing,
> *Mark it*—the eldest of them at three years old,
> I' the swathing clothes the other, from their nursery
> Were stolen ; and to this hour no guess in knowledge
> Which way they went.—*Cym.*, i. 1.

Here the dramatist uses a similar emphatic means of drawing attention to an antecedent point in the story, which we have shown that he employs in an early scene of " The Tempest."

> O Cymbeline ! Heaven and my conscience knows
> Thou didst unjustly banish me : whereon,
> *At three and two years old, I stole these babes ;*
> Thinking to bar thee of succession, as
> Thou reft'st me of my lands.—*Ibid.*, iii. 3.

And by this reminiscent touch Shakespeare again brings before the mind that prevenient particular of the dramatic story which it is needful to remember.

There is another practice of his deserving notice ; it is that he bespeaks attention to purposely insinuating, blundering, affected, or obscure diction, so that it shall not fail of being seen to be intentional on his part :—

> *Launcelot.* The old proverb is very well parted between my master Shylock and you, sir : you have the grace of God, sir, and he hath enough.
> *Bassanio. Thou speak'st it well.*—*Mer. of V.*, ii. 2.

Launcelot Gobbo, alluding to the old proverb, " The grace of God is better than riches," gives a significant pause before the word " enough ; " so that it may imply either ' sufficing wealth ' or the gulp with which he swallows that which forms the diametrically and diabolically opposite extreme to " the grace of God." Bassanio's comment shows that the author meant this to be so understood.

> *Le Beau.* Fair princess, you have lost much good sport.
> *Celia.* Sport ! of what colour ?
> *Le Beau.* What colour, madam ! *how shall I answer you.*—*As You L.*, i. 2.

Celia, in banter of Le Beau's affected pronunciation of the word " sport " (which we may imagine him to pronounce ' spawt ' or ' spot,') asks him the affectedly expressed question, " of what colour ? " for ' of

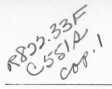
what kind ?' And he, mystified by her words, replies, "How shall I answer you ?"

Helena. I do affect a sorrow, indeed ; but I have it too.
Lafeu. Moderate lamentation is the right of the dead ; excessive grief the enemy to the living.
Helena. If the living be enemy to the grief, the excess makes it soon mortal. . . .
Lafeu. How understand we that ?—*All's W.*, i. 1.

Helena alludes veiledly to her hopeless passion ; and Lafeu, not comprehending her enigmatic language, asks himself in what sense it is to be understood ; the dramatist thereby drawing the attention of the audience to its intended obscurity.

Sir Toby. Will you encounter the house ? my niece is desirous you should enter, if your trade be to her.
Viola. I am bound to your niece, sir ; I mean, she is the list of my voyage.
Sir Toby. Taste your legs, sir : put them to motion.
Viola. My legs do better understand me, sir, *than I understand what you mean* by bidding me taste my legs.—*Tw. N.*, iii. 1.

Viola draws attention to the fashionably euphuistic jargon in which Sir Toby addresses her by showing that it is hardly to be understood, though she humours him by answering him in his own strain of affectation.

Prince Henry. Why, then, your brown bastard is your only drink ; for, look you, Francis, your white canvas doublet will sully : in Barbary, sir, it cannot come to so much.
Francis. What, sir ?—*1 H. IV.*, ii. 4.

The fact that the prince is amusing himself by obfuscating the tapster lad with some of the rambling irrelevance which was one form of jesting rejoinder when Shakespeare wrote, is made obvious by the fellow's bewildered reply.

Bardolph. Away, you whoreson upright rabbit, away !
Page. Away, you rascally Althea's dream, away !
Prince Henry. Instruct us, boy ; what dream, boy ?
Page. Marry, my lord, Althea dreamed she was delivered of a firebrand ; and therefore I call him her dream.
Prince Henry. A crown's worth of *good interpretation :* there it is, boy. [*Giving him money.*]—*2 H. IV.*, ii. 2.

The dramatist marks the blunder in the boy's mythology by the prince's ironical commendation and payment.

Sec. Servant. And he's as like to do 't as any man I can imagine.
Third Servant. Do 't ! he will do 't ; for, look you, sir, he has as many friends as enemies ; which friends, sir, as it were, durst not, look you, sir, show themselves, as we term it, his friends whilst he 's in directitude.
First Servant. Directitude ! *what's that ?*
Third Servant. But when they shall see, sir, his crest up again, and the man in blood, they will out of their burrows, like conies after rain, and revel all with him.—*Coriol.*, iv. 5.

Very pleasantly does the author draw attention to the Third Servant's attempt to coin some such fine long word as 'discreditude' or 'dejectitude,' by making the First Servant interrupt him to ask the meaning of his stumbled-upon version of the intended word ; and still more pleasantly follows up the joke by making the Third Servant avoid any difficulty of explanation, running on with his own harangue instead of noticing his fellow-servant's inquiry.

> *Poet.* You see this confluence, this great flood of visitors.
> I have, in this rough work, shap'd out a man,
> Whom this beneath world doth embrace and hug
> With amplest entertainment: my free drift
> Halts not particularly, but moves itself
> In a wide sea of wax: no levell'd malice
> Infects one comma in the course I hold;
> But flies an eagle flight, bold, and forth on,
> Leaving no tract behind.
> *Pain. How shall I understand you ?*—*Timon*, i. 1.

By the sycophantic painter's demand here thrown in, Shakespeare lets us see his intention of tincturing the poetaster's diction with stilted peculiarity.   [*See* AFFECTED PHRASEOLOGY.]

> *First Player.* But who, oh, who had seen the mobled queen—
> *Hamlet. The "mobled queen ?"*
> *Polonius.* That's good; "mobled queen" is good.—*Hamlet*, ii. 2.

Hamlet's repetition of the epithet " mobled " (which was a form of ' muffled ') serves to show that it is an unusual term, and that it is one to which his correct taste objects, as savouring somewhat of affectation ; while Polonius's remark makes manifest that a commoner taste regards it as a rather select epithet.

> *Guildenstern.* O, my lord, if my duty be too bold, my love is too unmannerly.
> *Hamlet. I do not well understand that.*—*Ibid.*, iii. 2.

The prince's rebuke to the fawning insincerity of the courtier's protestation, aids to impress its hollowness and studied expression upon the audience.

> *Osric.* The king, sir, hath wagered with him six Barbary horses: against the which he has imponed, as I take it, six French rapiers and poniards, with their assigns, as girdle, hangers and so: three of the carriages, in faith, are very dear to fancy, very responsive to the hilts, most delicate carriages, and of very liberal conceit. . . .
> *Hamlet.* . . . Why is this imponed, *as you call it ?*—*Ibid.*, v. 2.

The prince's concluding words serve to mark his raillery of the fine gentleman's mincing pronunciation of " imponed " for ' impawned.'

> *Fool.* Let go thy hold when a great wheel runs down a hill, lest it break thy neck with following it; but the great one that goes up the hill, let him draw thee after. When a wise man gives thee better counsel, give me mine again: *I would have none but knaves follow it*, since a fool gives it.
> That, sir, which serves and seeks for gain,
>   And follows but for form,
> Will pack when it begins to rain,
>   And leave thee in the storm.
> But I will tarry; the fool will stay,
>   And let the wise man fly:
> The knave turns fool that runs away;
>   The fool no knave, perdy.
> *Kent. Where learned you this*, fool ?
> *Fool.* Not i' the stocks, fool.—*Lear*, ii. 4.

By the sentences we have italicised Shakespeare has taken care to denote the bitter and sarcastic irony of the prose " counsel " and of the doggrel jingle of "knave" and "fool" which inculcate the wisdom of deserting a benefactor in his reverses.

> *Dolabella.* Most noble empress, you have heard of me?
> *Cleopatra.* I cannot tell.
> *Dolabella.*   Assuredly, you know me.
> *Cleopatra.* No matter, sir, what I have heard or known.
> You laugh when boys or women tell their dreams:
> Is 't not your trick?
> *Dolabella.*   *I understand not,* madam.
> *Cleopatra.* I dream'd there was an Emperor Antony:—
> O, such another sleep, that I might see
> But such another man!—*Ant. & C.,* v. 2.

Dolabella's words serve to indicate the wild digression of Cleopatra's passionate regret.

Another feature in Shakespeare's dramatic art is the mode in which he makes a scene begin with a sudden reference to a person or persons unnamed, but perfectly understood by the speaker and audience; as, for instance, where the haughty Coriolanus and his equally haughty mother, Volumnia, refer to the objects of their scorn, the commonalty, by a simple pronoun:—

> I muse my mother
> Does not approve me farther, who was wont
> To call *them* woollen vassals, things created
> To buy and sell with groats, . . .
>   . . . lesser had been
> The thwartings of your dispositions, if
> You had not show'd *them* how you were dispos'd
> Ere *they* lack'd power to cross you.—*Coriol.,* iii. 2.

For other passages similar in effect to the above, *see* ABRUPT COMMENCEMENTS.

The dramatist occasionally avoids needless explanation, or needless repetition of points already known to his audience, by such devices as the following:—

> *Baptista.* Whence are you, sir? what may I call your name?
> *Petruchio.* Petruchio is my name; Antonio's son,
> A man well known throughout all Italy.
> *Baptista.* I know him well: you are welcome for his sake.
> *Gremio. Saving your tale,* Petruchio, I pray,
> Let us, that are poor petitioners, speak too.—*Tam. of S.,* ii. 1.

Gremio's interruption prevents the need of Petruchio's repeating to Baptista the circumstance of his father's death, which has already been mentioned.

> *Lysimachus.*   Yet once more
> Let me entreat to know at large the cause
> Of your king's sorrow.
> *Helicanus.*   Sit, sir, I will recount it to you:
> But see, *I am prevented.*—*Per.,* v. 1.

The entrance of Marina is here made to prevent the necessity of Helicanus's recounting that which has been the subject of the previous scenes in the drama.

Sometimes, by the introduction of certain touches, Shakespeare ingeniously imparts an antique effect to the period of the drama in which they occur :—

> Yet, if I knew
> What hoop should hold us stanch, *from edge to edge*
> O' *the world* I would pursue it.—*Ant. & C.*, ii. 2.
>
> Prove this a prosperous day, *the three-nook'd world*
> Shall bear the olive freely.—*Ibid.*, iv. 6.
>
> O sun,
> *Burn the great sphere thou mov'st in!* darkling stand
> The varying shore o' the world.—*Ibid.*, iv. 13.

These three allusions to theories of ancient philosophy give appropriate effect of antiquity: the first referring to the primitive idea conceived of the world, that it was a circular plane or disk, not that it was a sphere or globe, as by modern science it is discovered to be ; the second, to another primitive idea entertained of the world, that it was of triangular form ; and the third, to that tenet of early astronomy, which held that the sun was a planet whirled round the earth by the motion of a solid sphere in which it was fixed.

The dramatist has taken care to emphatically indicate the age of two of his characters ; both of them men of marked intellect, though in each of them intellect is evinced with diametrically opposite effect, by its accompanying moral qualities. They are Hamlet and Iago. In the scene with the grave-digger [*See* DRAMATIC TIME] Hamlet's age is precisely denoted ; while Iago is made to say :—

I have looked upon the world for *four times seven years.*—*Oth.*, i. 3.

Very characteristically and very humorously has Shakespeare, with artistic effect, denoted various samples of intoxication. There is the wild natural animal, the half-savage Caliban, introduced for the first time to the civilised use of fermented liquors ; there is the dogged drunkenness of Barnardine, stultified into brutishness by years of imprisonment without trial ; there is the perpetual fuddled condition of Sir Toby, by birth a gentleman, by habit a sot ; there is the sodden soaking of Silence, who in his cups is stimulated into snatches of songs so long as he can sit upright, but at last is floored and borne to bed ; there are the pot-valiant Horner and the maudlin Peter, plied by their neighbours with drink ; there is Cassio, flustered into feverish mirth and as feverish piety, then into captiousness and quarrelsome irritability, trying ever more and more to maintain his dignity as he feels he is every instant farther losing it ; lastly, there is Lepidus, with solemn pomposity showing off his desire for information on the subject of crocodiles and pyramids, Octavius Cæsar anxious to preserve his wonted coolness and phlegm, Pompey waxing affectionately magnanimous about his "father's house," Enobarbus flushed and prompted to dance, and only the seasoned Antony remaining unaffected by the rousing orgy on board the galley lying near Misenum. We do not quote each of the above examples at full length ; but give the references to the scenes where they may be found as follows :—

Caliban. Freedom, hey-day ! hey-day, freedom ! freedom ! hey-day, freedom !—
Temp., ii. 2.

Stephano. Drink, servant-monster, when I bid thee: *thy eyes are almost set in thy head.* . . . My man-monster hath *drowned his tongue* in sack.—*Temp.*, iii. 2.

Barnardine. Friar, not I: I have been drinking hard all night, and I will have more time to prepare me, or they shall beat out my brains with billets: I will not consent to die this day, that's certain.—*M. for M.*, iv. 3.

Enter Sir Toby Belch.

Olivia. By mine honour, half drunk. What is he at the gate, cousin?
Sir Toby. A gentleman.
Olivia. A gentleman! what gentleman?
Sir Toby. 'Tis a gentleman here—a plague o' these pickle-herrings!—how now, sot?
Clown. Good Sir Toby!
Olivia. Cousin, cousin, how have you come so early by this lethargy?
Sir Toby. Lechery! I defy lechery. There's one at the gate.
Olivia. Ay, marry, what is he?
Sir Toby. Let him be the devil, an he will, I care not: give me faith, say I. Well, it's all one. [*Exit.*]—*Tw. N.*, i. 5.

Enter Sir Toby Belch, *drunk, led by the* Clown.

Duke. How now, gentleman! how is't with you?
Sir Toby. That's all one: he has hurt me, and there's the end on't. Sot, didst see Dick surgeon, sot?
Clown. O, he's drunk, Sir Toby, an hour agone; his eyes were set at eight i' the morning.
Sir Toby. Then he's a rogue, and a passy-measures pavin: I hate a drunken rogue.
Olivia. Away with him! Who hath made this havoc with them?
Sir Andrew. I'll help you, Sir Toby, because we'll be dressed together.
Sir Toby. Will you help? An ass-head, and a coxcomb, and a knave! a thin-faced knave, a gull!
Olivia. Get him to bed, and let his hurt be looked to.—*Ibid.*, v. 1.

Shallow. By the mass, I have drunk too much sack at supper: a good varlet. Now sit down, now sit down: come, cousin.
Silence. Ah, sirrah! quoth-a,—we shall
    (*Singing*) Do nothing but eat, and make good cheer,
        And praise heaven for the merry year;
        When flesh is cheap and females dear,
        And lusty lads roam here and there
          So merrily,
        And ever among so merrily . . .
Falstaff. Carry Master Silence to bed.—*2 H. IV.*, v. 3.

First Neighbour. Here, neighbour Horner, I drink to you in a cup of sack: and fear not, neighbour, you shall do well enough.
Second Neighbour. And here, neighbour, here's a cup of charneco.
Third Neighbour. And here's a pot of good double beer, neighbour: drink and fear not your man.
Horner. Let it come, i' faith, and I'll pledge you all; and a fig for Peter
First 'Prentice. Here, Peter, I drink to thee: and be not afraid.
Second 'Prentice. Be merry, Peter, and fear not thy master: fight for credit of the 'prentices.
Peter. I thank you all: drink, and pray for me, I pray you; for, I think, I have taken my last draught in this world. Here, Robin, an if I die, I give thee my apron: and, Will, thou shalt have my hammer: and here, Tom, take all the money that I have. O Lord, bless me, I pray God! for I am never able to deal with my master, he hath learnt so much fence already.
Salisbury. Come, leave your drinking, and fall to blows. . . .
Horner. Masters, I am come hither, as it were, upon my man's instigation, to prove him a knave, and myself an honest man: and touching the Duke of York, I will take my death, I never meant him any ill, nor the king, nor the queen: and therefore, Peter, have at thee with a downright blow.
York. Despatch: this knave's tongue begins to double.—*2 H. VI.*, ii. 3.

Cassio. 'Fore heaven, they have given me a rouse already.

Montano. Good faith, a little one; not past a pint, as I am a soldier.

Iago. Some wine, ho!

(*Singing*) And let me the canakin, clink, clink; . . .

Cassio. 'Fore heaven, an excellent song.

Iago. I learned it in England, where indeed they are most potent in potting: . . .

Cassio. Is your Englishman so exquisite in his drinking? . . . To the health of our general!

Montano. I am for it, lieutenant; and I'll do you justice.

Iago. O sweet England!

(*Singing*) King Stephen was a worthy peer, . . .

Cassio. Why, this is a more exquisite song than the other.

Iago. Will you hear it again?

Cassio. No; for I hold him to be unworthy of his place, that does those things. Well, heaven's above all; and there be souls must be saved, and there be souls must not be saved.

Iago. It's true, good lieutenant.

Cassio. For mine own part—no offence to the general, nor any man of quality—I hope to be saved.

Iago. And so do I too, lieutenant.

Cassio. Ay, but, by your leave, not before me; the lieutenant is to be saved before the ancient. Let's have no more of this; let's to our affairs. Forgive us our sins! Gentlemen, let's look to our business. Do not think, gentlemen, I am drunk: this is my ancient;—this is my right hand, and this is my left hand: I am not drunk now; I can stand well enough, and speak well enough.

All. Excellent well.

Cassio. Why, very well, then; you must not think, then, that I am drunk.—*Oth.*, ii. 3.

Lepidus. You have strange serpents there.

Antony. Ay, Lepidus.

Lepidus. Your serpent of Egypt is bred, now, of your mud by the operation of your sun: so is your crocodile.

Antony. They are so.

Pompey. Sit—and some wine! A health to Lepidus.

Lepidus. I am not so well as I should be, but I'll ne'er out.

Enobarbus. Not till you have slept; I fear me, you'll be in till then.

Lepidus. Nay, certainly, I have heard, the Ptolemies' pyramises are very goodly things; without contradiction, I have heard that. . . . What manner o' thing is your crocodile?

Antony. It is shaped, sir, like itself: . . .

Lepidus. What colour is it of?

Antony. Of its own colour too.

Lepidus. 'Tis a strange serpent.

Antony. 'Tis so: and the tears of it are wet.

Cæsar. Will this description satisfy him?

Antony. With the health that Pompey gives him, else he is a very epicure. . . .

Pompey.   This health to Lepidus!

Antony. Bear him ashore. I'll pledge it for him, Pompey. . . .

Enobarbus. There's a strong fellow, Menas!

[*Pointing to the Attendant who carries off* Lepidus.

Menas.   Why?

Enobarbus.   He bears

The third part of the world, man, see'st not?

Menas. The third part, then, is drunk: would it were all,

That it might go on wheels!

Enobarbus. Drink thou; increase the reels. . . .

Shall we dance now the Egyptian bacchanals,

And celebrate our drink? . . .

Cæsar. What would you more? Pompey, good night. Good brother,

Let me request you off: our graver business

Frowns at this levity. Gentle lords, let's part;

You see, we have burnt our cheeks : strong Enobarbe
Is weaker than the wine ; and mine own tongue
Splits what it speaks : the wild disguise hath almost
Antick'd us all.   What needs more words ?   Good night.
Good Antony, your hand.
 Pompey.   I 'll try you on the shore.
 Antony. And shall, sir : give 's your hand.
 Pompey.   O Antony,
You have my father's house,—But, what ? we are friends.
Come, down into the boat.
 Enobarbus.   Take heed you fall not.—*Ant. & C.*, ii. 7.

For numerous other resources of Shakespeare's dramatic art *see* the
following headings :—INDICATIONS OF LOOK, GESTURE, &c., INDIRECT
PRAISE OF OTHER CHARACTERS, HISTORIANS' PASSAGES ADOPTED, BRIEF
SCENES, CLOSING SCENES, CHORUSES, and DUMB SHOWS.

DRAMATIC TIME.

One of the most interesting themes for study among Shakespeare's
powers as a play-writer lies in his treatment of Dramatic Time.   In the
first place, he has distinctly stated the usual time of stage duration for
a play's performance :—

Those that come to see
Only a show or two, and so agree
The play may pass, if they be still and willing,
I 'll undertake may see away their shilling
Richly *in two short hours.*—*H. VIII.* (*Prologue*).

The fearful passage of their death-mark'd love,
 And the continuance of their parents' rage,
Which, but their children's end, naught could remove,
 Is now the *two hours'* traffic of our stage.—*R. & Jul.* (*Prologue*).

And he has also manifested his knowledge that a play should generally depict a brief period :—

Our wooing doth not end like an old play ;
Jack hath not Jill : these ladies' courtesy
Might well have made our sport a comedy.—
Come, sir, it wants *a twelvemonth and a day,*
And then 'twill end.—
    That 's too long for a play.—*Love's L. L.*, v. 2.

In the second place, he has shown that he was thoroughly acquainted
with the classical laws* of strictness in Dramatic Time by his plays
of " The Tempest " and " The Comedy of Errors " ; in both of which
the time is accurately preserved within the bounds of visible representation.   This he has taken care to mark with great precision, and
denote as the play proceeds :—

Prospero. What is the time o' the day ?
Ariel.   *Past the mid season.*

---

* We have the authority of Milton (in his Introductory Essay to his " Samson
Agonistes ") for the due length of dramatic time in a play.   He says : " The circum-
scription of time, wherein the whole drama begins and ends, is, according to ancient
rule and best example, within the space of twenty-four hours. "

Prospero. At least two glasses.   The time 'twixt six and now
Must by us both be spent most preciously.—*Temp.*, i. 2.

My father
Is hard at study ; pray now, rest yourself:
He 's safe *for these three hours.*—*Ibid.*, iii. 1.

Now farewell, *till half an hour hence.*—*Ibid.*, iii. 1.

I 'll to my book ;
For yet, *ere supper-time*, must I perform
Much business appertaining.—*Ibid.*, iii. 1.

I 'll yield him thee asleep . . . 'tis a custom with him
I ' the afternoon to sleep.—*Ibid.*, iii. 2.

Within this half-hour will he be asleep.—*Ibid.*, iii. 2.

. . . *How 's the day ?*
Ariel. On the sixth hour ; at which time, my lord,
You said our work should cease.
Prospero.   I did say so,
When first I raised the tempest.—*Ibid.*, v. 1.

How thou hast met us here, who *three hours since*
Were wreck'd upon this shore.—*Ibid.*, v. 1.

What is this maid, with whom thou wast at play ?
Your eld'st acquaintance cannot be *three hours.*—*Ibid.*, v. 1.

The best news is, that we have safely found
Our king and company : the next, our ship—
Which, but *three glasses* since, we gave out split—
Is tight, and yare, and bravely rigg'd, as when
We first put out to sea.—*Ibid.*, v. 1.

Sir, I invite your highness, and your train,
To my poor cell, where you shall take your rest
For this one night ; which, part of it, I 'll waste
With such discourse as, I not doubt, shall make it
Go quick away ; . . . and *in the morn*
I 'll bring you to your ship, and so to Naples.—*Ibid.*, v. 1.

Therefore, by law thou art condemn'd to die.—
Ægeon. Yet this my comfort—when your words are done,
My woes end likewise *with the evening sun.*—*Com. of E.*, i. 1.

Therefore, merchant, I 'll limit thee *this day*,
To seek thy help by beneficial help : . . .
Beg thou, or borrow, to make up the sum,
And live ; if no, then thou art doom'd to die.—*Ibid.*, i. 1.

This very day, a Syracusan merchant
Is apprehended for arrival here ;
And, not being able to buy out his life,
According to the statute of the town,
Dies *ere the weary sun set in the west.*—*Ibid.*, i. 2.

Within this hour it will be dinner-time.—*Ibid.*, i. 2.

Soon *at five o'clock*,
Please you, I 'll meet with you upon the mart.—*Ibid.*, i. 2.

The clock hath strucken twelve upon the bell.—*Ibid.*, i. 2.

Sure, Luciana, *it is two o'clock.*—*Ibid.*, ii. 1.

When spake I such a word ?—
Even now, even here, *not half an hour since.*—*Ibid.*, ii. 2.

In Ephesus I am but *two hours* old.—*Ibid.*, ii. 2.

Come, come, Antipholus, we dine *too late.*—*Ibid.*, ii. 2.

And let us to the Tiger all to dinner ;
And *about evening* come yourself alone
To know the reason of this strange restraint.—*Ibid.*, iii. 1.

I 'll meet you at that place, *some hour hence.—Com. of E.*, iii. 1.
And soon *at supper-time* I 'll visit you,
And then receive my money for the chain.—*Ibid.*, iii. 2.
He had of me a chain : *at five o'clock*
I shall receive the money for the same.—*Ibid.*, iv. 1.
The hour steals on ; I pray you, sir, despatch.
You hear how he importunes me : the chain.—*Ibid.*, iv. 1.
The money that you owe me for the chain.—
I owe you none till I receive the chain.—
You know I gave it you *half an hour since.—Ibid.*, iv. 1.
'Tis time that I were gone : it was *two* ere I left him.—*Ibid.*, iv. 2.
By this, I think, *the dial points at five.—Ibid.*, v. 1.
This day, great duke, she shut the doors upon me,
While she with harlots feasted in my house.—
A grievous fault.   Say, woman, didst thou so ?—
No, my good lord : myself, he, and my sister,
To-day did dine together.—*Ibid.*, v. 1.
Within this hour I was his bondman, sir ;
But he, I thank him, gnaw'd in two my cords.—*Ibid.*, v. i.
Why, here begins *his morning story* right.—*Ibid.*, v. 1.
And all that are assembled in this place,
That by this sympathised *one day*'s error
Have suffer'd wrong, go, keep us company
And we shall make full satisfaction.—*Ibid.*, v. 1.

But in the majority of his plays Shakespeare has substituted for the antique rules of strictness in this particular an original and admirable system of Dramatic Time, which permits his adopting a story that demands scope of period to properly delineate its various incidents, to develop its different characters, and to depict the multiform emotions elicited by successive events and situations.   This system is so ingenious in itself, and is put into operation with so masterly a skill, that it enables the reader or spectator to see a long course of time, or a limited space of time, or even a simultaneous progress of protracted time and current time both together, without a violation of probability or injury to naturalness of effect.   The critics who first pointed out this system of combined long and short time in Shakespeare's dramatic art as being invented and practised by him were the Rev. N. J. Halpin and Professor Wilson, in November, 1849, each gentleman laying claim to having made the discovery by his own separate perception from study of the subject : and certain is it, that every fresh and minute examination of Shakespeare's process in managing Dramatic Time proves that this discovery is a veritable elucidation of the scheme upon which he worked.   He made fresh laws in Art for himself; and regulated his method of procedure according to their ordination, with equal ease and might of power. Where, as in his great tragedy of " Othello," the passion demanded prompt action with immediate despatch, he allows the spectator to behold but a few hours' space between the conception of wrong and the fulfilment of vengeance; but where, also, the impression of long-wedded faith and happiness destroyed by iniquitous suggestion demanded protracted period, he permits the spectator to imagine that many days, weeks, months have elapsed between the arrival of the married pair in Cyprus and the final murder of Desdemona by her husband.

So in other of his dramas, where the appropriateness of stage representation or the exigencies of hurried act and feeling require acceleration, impetus, and rapid movement, he conveys the effect of brief time; while where latitude for a needed series of passing occurrences is no less imperative, he contrives to produce the sense of lengthened time. The means by which he establishes these two impressions— sometimes by stated mention of particular hours or epochs, sometimes by casual allusion, sometimes by vaguely worded inference, but always of set purpose and with admirably effectual fulfilment of intended object —will be made obvious by the collected citations here given; which shall first denote the traces of Short Time and then the traces of Long Time in each play, so as to illustrate the dramatist's motives and plan with regard to both. Thus, in "The Two Gentlemen of Verona," Shakespeare having to give the effect of a passage in the lives of two young men which is placed before the eyes of an audience at a single sitting, he contrives to impart the idea of swift progress of time by various touches indicative of haste and immediate action; but having also to represent sufficient space for the several journeys from Verona to Milan, the sojourn there, and the subsequent adventures of the heroes and their ladies, he has thrown in such hints of lengthened time as shall serve this purpose:—

Saw you my master?—
But now he parted hence, to embark for Milan.—
Twenty to one, then, he *is shipp'd already.—Two G. of V.*, i. 1.
Madam, *dinner is ready*, and *your father stays.—Ibid.*, i. 2.
No more of stay; to-morrow thou must go.—Ibid., i. 3.
Sir Proteus, your father calls for you:
He is in haste; therefore, I pray you, go.—*Ibid.*, i. 3.
Why muse you, sir? *'tis dinner-time.—Ibid.*, ii. 1.
Launce, *away, away, aboard!* thy master is shipp'd, and *thou art to post after* with oars.—*Ibid.*, ii. 3.
I'll send him hither to you *presently.**—*Ibid.*, ii. 4.
I must unto the road, to disembark
Some necessaries that I needs must use;
And then I'll *presently* attend you.—
Will you *make haste?*—
I will.—*Ibid.*, ii. 4.
This night he meaneth with a corded ladder
To climb celestial Silvia's chamber-window;
Myself in counsel, his competitor.
Now, *presently*, I'll give her father notice
Of their disguising and pretended flight.—*Ibid.*, ii. 6.
Love, *lend me wings to make my purpose swift*,
As thou hast lent me wit to plot this drift.—*Ibid.*, ii. 6.
For which the youthful lover now is gone,
And *this way comes he with it presently.—Ibid.*, iii. 1.
Sir Valentine, *whither away so fast?—Ibid.*, iii. 1.
Advise me where I may have such a ladder.—
When would you use it? pray, sir, tell me that.—
This very night; for love is like a child,
That longs for every thing that he can come by.—
By seven o'clock I'll get you such a ladder.—*Ibid.*, iii. 1.

---

* " Presently," meaning ' immediately.'

Be gone! I will not hear thy vain excuse;
But, as thou lov'st thy life, *make speed* from hence.—*Two G. of V.*, iii. 1.

Run, boy; *run, run*, and seek him out.—*Ibid.*, iii. 1.

The time now serves not to expostulate :
Come, I 'll convey thee through the city-gate.—*Ibid.*, iii. 1.

I pray thee, Launce, an if thou see'st my boy,
Bid him make haste, and meet me at the north gate.—
Go, sirrah, find him out. *Come*, Valentine.—*Ibid.*, iii. 1.

Thou must *run* to him, for thou hast stayed so long, that *going will scarce serve the turn.*—*Ibid.*, iii. 1.

Let us into the city *presently*,
To sort some gentlemen well skill'd in music.—
About it, gentlemen. . . . *Even now about it.*—*Ibid.*, iii. 2.

Madam, good *even* to your ladyship.—*Ibid.*, iv. 2.

By *this pale queen of night* I swear.—*Ibid.*, iv. 2.

This is the hour that Madam Silvia
Entreated me to call, and know her mind.—*Ibid.*, iv. 3.

Sir Eglamour, a thousand times *good morrow.*—*Ibid.*, iv. 3.

I am *thus early* come, to know what service
It is your pleasure to command me in.—*Ibid.*, iv. 3.

When will you go ?—
　　　　　　　　This evening coming.—*Ibid.*, iv. 3.

Go *presently*, and take this ring with thee.—*Ibid.*, iv. 4.

The sun begins to gild the *western* sky ;
And *now it is about the very hour*
That Silvia at Friar Patrick's cell should meet me.
　　*　　　*　　　*　　　*　　　*　　　*
See, where she comes ! Lady, a happy *evening.*—
Amen, amen ! *go on*, good Eglamour,
Out at the postern by the abbey-wall :
I fear I am attended by some spies.—
Fear not : the forest is not three leagues off;
If we recover that, we are sure enough.—*Ibid.*, v. 1.

Therefore, I pray you, *stand not to discourse*,
But mount you presently. . . .
Despatch, sweet gentlemen, *and follow me.*—*Ibid.*, v. 2.

So far, Short Time : now comes Long Time :—

To Milan let me hear from thee *by letters*,
Of thy success in love, and *what news else*
Betideth here in absence of thy friend ;
And I likewise *will visit thee in mine.*—*Ibid.*, i. 1.

Nor need'st thou much importune me to that
Whereon *this month* I have been hammering.—*Ibid.*, i. 3.

　　　　　　　　He writes
How happily he lives, how well belov'd,
And *daily graced by the emperor ;*
Wishing me with him, partner of his fortune.—*Ibid.*, i. 3.

You *were wont*, when you laugh'd, to crow like a cock ; when you walk'd, to walk like one of the lions ; when you fasted, it was presently after dinner ; when you look'd sadly, it was for want of money : and *now you are* metamorphosed with a mistress.—*Ibid.*, ii. 1.

She that you gaze on so, *as she sits at supper ?*—*Ibid.*, ii. 1.

For *often* have you writ to her ; and she, in modesty,
Or else *for want of idle time*, could not again reply.—*Ibid.*, ii. 1.

Here is my hand for my true constancy;
And *when that hour o'erslips me in the day*
Wherein I sigh not, Julia, for thy sake,
The next ensuing hour some foul mischance
Torment me for my love's forgetfulness.—*Two G. of V.*, ii. 2.

Ay, Proteus, but *that life is alter'd now* :
I have done penance for contemning love ;
Whose high imperious thoughts have punish'd me
With bitter fasts, with penitential groans,
With *nightly* tears, and *daily* heart-sore sighs.—*Ibid.*, ii. 4.

This love of theirs myself have *often* seen,
Haply, when they have judg'd me fast asleep ;
And *oftentimes* have purpos'd to forbid
Sir Valentine her company, and my court.—*Ibid.*, iii. 1.

I *nightly* lodge her in an upper tower.—*Ibid.*, iii. 1.

Since his exile she hath despis'd me most.—*Ibid.*, iii. 2.

Whence came you ?—
From Milan.—
Have you long sojourned there ?—
Some sixteen months.—*Ibid.*, iv. 1.

But, host, doth this Sir Proteus, that we talk on,
Often resort unto this gentlewoman ?—*Ibid.*, iv. 2.

For *I have heard him say, a thousand times,*
His Julia gave it him at his departure.—*Ibid.*, iv. 4.

To think upon her woes, I do protest,
That I have wept *a hundred several times.*—*Ibid.*, iv. 4.

O thou, that dost inhabit in my breast,
Leave not the mansion *so long* tenantless,
Lest, growing ruinous, the building fall,
And leave no memory of what it was !
Repair me with thy presence, Silvia !—*Ibid.*, v. 4.

In his play of " The Merry Wives of Windsor," the author had to confine its time within the limits of natural and visible transaction before the spectators' eyes, and yet to allow time for the various tricks played off by the two merry dames upon their obese wooer: he has accordingly managed to imply current actual time together with several days' time in his own ingenious method :—

Come, we have *a hot venison pasty to dinner* : come, gentlemen, I hope we shall drink down all unkindness.—*Merry W.*, i. 1.

The dinner is on the table ; my father desires your worships' company. . . . *I will not be absence at the grace.* . . . *The dinner attends you, sir.* . . . I may not go in without your worship : *they will not sit, till you come.* . . . I pray you, sir, *walk in.* . . . Come, gentle Master Slender, *come ; we stay for you.* . . . Come, come. . . . Come on, sir.—*Ibid.*, i. 1.

I pray you, be gone. I will make an end of my dinner ; there's pippins and cheese to come.—*Ibid.*, i. 2.

I have writ me a letter to her ; here another to Page's wife, who *even now* gave me good eyes too.—*Ibid.*, i. 3.

My humour *shall not cool* : I will incense Page to deal with poison.—*Ibid.*, i. 3.

We'll have a posset for 't *soon at night*, in faith, at the latter end of a seacoal fire.—*Ibid.*, i. 4.

Well, I shall see her *to-day*. . . . if thou see'st her *before me, commend me.* . . . Well, farewell ; *I am in great haste now.*—*Ibid.*, i. 4.

Will you go, Mistress Page ?—Have with you.   You'll *come to dinner*, George ?—*Ibid.*, ii. 1.

Give your worship *good-morrow.—Good-morrow*, good wife.—*Merry W.*, ii. 2.

Her husband will be absence from his house *between ten and eleven.—Ten and eleven?*—Ay, forsooth. . . . *Ten and eleven.* . . . I will not fail her.—*Ibid.*, ii. 2.

He hath sent your worship a *morning's* draught of sack.—*Ibid.*, ii. 2.

I shall be with her *between ten and eleven.* . . . Come you to me *at night;* you shall know how I speed.—*Ibid.*, ii. 2.

Eleven o'clock the hour: I will prevent this, detect my wife, be revenged on Falstaff, and laugh at Page. *I will about it; better three hours too soon, than a minute too late.—Ibid.*, ii. 2.

Vat is de clock, Jack?—*'Tis past the hour*, sir, that Sir Hugh promised to come.—*Ibid.*, ii. 3.

The clock gives me my cue, and my assurance bids me search: there I shall find Falstaff.—*Ibid.*, iii. 2.

I have good cheer at home; and *I pray you all to go with me.*—I must excuse myself, Master Ford.—And so must I, sir: we have *appointed to dine* with Mistress Anne.—*Ibid.*, iii. 2.

I beseech you, heartily, *some of you go home with me to dinner:* besides your cheer, you shall have sport.—*Ibid.*, iii. 2.

Well, *I promised you a dinner; come, come, walk in the Park;* I pray you, pardon me.—*Ibid.*, iii. 3.

I pray thee, once *to-night* give my sweet Nan this ring.—*Ibid.*, iii. 4.

Her husband goes *this morning* a-birding: she desires you once more to come to her *between eight and nine.—Ibid.*, iii. 5.

Between nine and ten, sayest thou?—*Eight and nine*, sir.—Well, *be gone:* I will not miss her.—*Ibid.*, iii. 5.

Her husband is *this morning* gone a-birding: I have received from her another embassy of meeting; *'twixt eight and nine is the hour*, Master Brook.—*'Tis past eight* already, sir.—Is it? I will then address me to my appointment. *Come to me at your convenient leisure*, and you shall know how I speed.—*Ibid.*, iii. 5.

Is he at Master Ford's already, thinkest thou?—Sure, *he is by this*, or *will be presently.* . . . Mistress Ford desires you *to come suddenly.—Ibid.*, iv. 1.

Get you home, boy. Come, *we stay too long.—Ibid.*, iv. 1.

But are you sure of your husband now?—*He's a-birding*, sweet Sir John.—*Ibid.*, iv. 2.

To-night at Herne's oak, *just 'twixt twelve and one*,
Must my sweet Nan present the fairy queen.—*Ibid.*, iv. 6.

And here it rests—that you'll procure the vicar
To stay for me at church *'twixt twelve and one.—Ibid.*, iv. 6.

The matter will be known *to-night*, or never. Be you in the Park *about midnight.* at Herne's oak, and you shall see wonders.—*Ibid.*, v. 1.

I am in haste; go along with me: I'll tell you all, Master Brook. . . . *follow me:* I'll tell you strange things of this knave Ford; on whom *to-night* I will be revenged . . . *follow: strange things in hand*, Master Brook: *follow.—Ibid.*, v. 1.

Come, come; we'll couch i' the Castle ditch, till we see the light of our fairies. . . . *It hath struck ten o'clock.*—The night is dark.—*Ibid.*, v. 2.

Where is Nan now, and her troop of fairies? . . . They are all couched in a pit hard by Herne's oak, with obscured lights; which, at the very instant of Falstaff's and our meeting, they will at once display *to the night.* . . . *The hour draws on:* to the oak, to the oak!—*Ibid.*, v. 3.

Trib, trib, fairies: *come:* . . . *follow me into the pit;* . . . come, come; *trib, trib.*—*Ibid.*, v. 4.

The Windsor bell hath *struck twelve; the minute draws on.—Ibid.*, v. 5.

Away! disperse! But *till 'tis one o'clock*,
Our dance of custom round about the oak
Of Herne the hunter, let us not forget.—*Ibid.*, v. 5.

Yet be cheerful, knight: thou shalt eat a posset *to-night* at my house.—*Ibid.*, v. 5.

> Good husband, *let us every one go home*,
> And laugh this sport o'er by a country fire ;
> Sir John and all.—
>   Let it be so.   Sir John,
> To Master Brook you yet shall hold your word ;
> For he, *to-night*, shall lie with Mistress Ford.—*Merry W.*, v. 5.

Then, Long Time :—

Let 's be revenged on him : let 's appoint him a meeting ; give him a show of comfort in his suit ; and *lead him on with a fine-baited delay*, till he hath pawned his horses to mine host of the Garter.—*Ibid.*, ii. 1.

I 'll give you a pottle of burnt sack to give me recourse to him, and tell him my name is Brook ; only for a jest.—My hand, bully : thou shalt have *egress and regress ;* said I well ? and thy name shall be Brook.—*Ibid.*, ii. 1.

She bade me tell your worship, that her husband is seldom from home ; but, she hopes, *there will come a time.*—*Ibid.*, ii. 2.

We have *lingered about a match* between Anne Page and my cousin Slender, and this day we shall have our answer.—*Ibid.*, iii. 2.

Let him be sent for *to-morrow, eight o'clock*, to have amends.—*Ibid.*, iii. 3.

I do invite you *to-morrow morning* to my house to breakfast : after, we 'll a-birding together.—*Ibid.*, iii. 3.

I pray you now, remembrance *to-morrow* on the lousy knave, mine host.—*Ibid.*, iii. 3.

> You wrong me, sir, *thus still to haunt my house :*
> I told you, sir, my daughter is dispos'd of.—*Ibid.*, iii. 4.

I was at her house the hour she appointed me.—And sped you, sir ?—Very ill-favouredly. . . . they conveyed me into a buck-basket.—*Ibid.*, iii. 5.

There was one conveyed out of my house *yesterday* in this basket.—*Ibid.*, iv. 2.

>   Let our wives
> *Yet once again*, to make us public sport,
> Appoint a meeting with this fat old fellow,
> Where we may take him, and disgrace him for it.—
> There is no better way than that they spoke of.—
> How ? to send him word they 'll meet him in the Park *at midnight ?*—*Ibid.*, iv. 4.

> And ask him why, *that hour of fairy revel*,
> In their so sacred paths he dares to tread
> In shape profane. . . . and *in that time*
> Shall Master Slender steal my Nan away.—*Ibid.*, iv. 4.

Went you not to her *yesterday*, sir, as you told me you had appointed ?—I went to her, Master Brook, like a poor old man : but I came from her, Master Brook, like a poor old woman.—*Ibid.*, v. 1.

As Shakespeare had to denote in his grandly moral drama of " Measure for Measure" speedy retribution for sin committed, together with sufficient space for the supposed period of the duke's absence, during which he may duly watch the conduct of Angelo in the administration of justice, the Dramatic Time is managed with peculiar skill in the introduction of coexistent accelerating touches, and retarding touches.

First, for the accelerating touches :—

Claudio to prison ! 'tis not so.—
Nay, but I know 'tis so : I saw him arrested ; saw him carried away ; and, which is more, *within these three days* his head is to be chopped off.—*M. for M.*, i. 2.

This may be : he promised to meet me *two hours since*, and he was ever precise in promise-keeping-—*Ibid.*, i. 2.

Here comes Signior Claudio, led by the provost to prison.—*Ibid.*, i. 2.

The *new* deputy now for the duke,—
Whether it be the fault and glimpse of *newness*,
Or whether that the body public be
A horse whereon the governor doth ride,
Who, *newly* in the seat, . . . but this *new* governor
Awakes me all the enrolled penalties.
        . . . and, for a name,
Now puts the drowsy and neglected act
Freshly on me.—*M. for M.*, i. 3.
Send after the duke, and appeal to him.—
I have done so, but *he's not to be found.*—*Ibid.*, i. 3.
This day my sister should the cloister enter,
And there receive her approbation:
Acquaint her with the danger of my state;
Implore her, in my voice, that she make friends
To the strict deputy; bid herself assay him.—*Ibid.*, i. 3.
I'll to her. . . . *within two hours.*—*Ibid.*, i. 3.
        He *arrests* him on it;
And *follows close* the rigour of the statute,
To make him an example. . . . Has censur'd him
Already ; and, as I hear, the provost *hath*
A warrant for his execution.—*Ibid.*, i. 5.
        Go to Lord Angelo,
And let him learn to know, when maidens sue,
Men give like gods. . . . But *speedily.*—*Ibid.*, i. 5.
        Sir, he must die.
    . . . See that Claudio
Be executed *by nine to-morrow morning.*
Bring him his confessor, let him be prepar'd;
For *that's the utmost of his pilgrimage.*—*Ibid.*, ii. 1.

What's o'clock, think you?—*Eleven*, sir.—I pray you home *to dinner* with me.—*Ibid.*, ii. 1.

Is it your will Claudio shall die *to-morrow ?*—
Did I not tell thee, yea? hadst thou not order?—*Ibid.*, ii. 2.
Here is the sister of the man condemn'd
Desires access to you.—*Ibid.*, ii. 2.
He's sentenc'd ; 'tis too late.—*Ibid.*, ii. 2.
        He must die *to-morrow.*—
To-morrow ? O, that's sudden ! Spare him, spare him !
He's not prepar'd for death.—*Ibid.*, ii. 2.
When must he die ?—
        As I do think, *to-morrow.*—*Ibid.*, ii. 3.
Your partner, as I hear, *must die to-morrow,*
And I am going with instruction to him.— . . .
Must die to-morrow.—*Ibid.*, ii. 3.
To sue to live, I find I seek to die ;
And, seeking death, find life: *let it come on.*—*Ibid.*, iii. 1.
Lord Angelo, having affairs to heaven,
Intends you for his *swift* embassador,
Where you shall be an everlasting leiger:
Therefore, your best appointment *make with speed :*
To-morrow you set on.—*Ibid.*, iii. 1.
        This night's the time
That I should do what I abhor to name,
Or else thou diest *to-morrow.*—*Ibid.*, iii. 1.
Be ready, Claudio, for your death *to-morrow.*—*Ibid.*, iii. 1.

Therefore *prepare yourself to death.* Do not satisfy your resolution with hopes that are fallible: *to-morrow you must die ;* go to your knees, and *make ready.*—*Ibid.*, iii. 1.

How will you do to content this substitute, and to save your brother?—I am *now going* to resolve him.—*M. for M.*, iii. 1.

Haste you speedily to Angelo: if *for this night* he entreat you to his bed, give him promise of satisfaction. *I will presently* to St. Luke's: there, at the moated grange, resides this dejected Mariana. *At* that place call upon me; and *despatch* with Angelo, that it may be *quickly.*—*Ibid.*, iii. 1.

Provost, my brother Angelo will not be altered; Claudio *must die to-morrow*: let him be furnished with divines, and have all charitable preparation. . . .—This friar hath been with him, and advised him for the entertainment of death.—*Good even*, good father.—*Ibid.*, iii. 2.

And *now is he resolved to die.*—*Ibid.*, iii. 2.

With Angelo *to-night* shall lie
His old betrothed, but despis'd.—*Ibid.*, iii. 2.

Hath anybody inquired for me here *to-day? Much upon this time* have I promised here to meet.—You have not been inquired after: *I have sat here all day.*—*Ibid.*, iv. 1.

There have I made my promise *on the heavy
Middle of the night* to call upon him.—*Ibid.*, iv. 1.

I shall attend your leisure: *but make haste;
The vaporous night approaches.*—*Ibid.*, iv. 1.

To-morrow morning are to die Claudio and Barnardine.—*Ibid.*, iv. 2.

Sirrah, here's a fellow will help you *to-morrow*, in your execution.—*Ibid.*, iv. 2.

You, sirrah, provide your block and your axe *to-morrow four o'clock.*—*Ibid.*, iv. 2.

Look, *here's the warrant*, Claudio, for thy death:
'Tis now dead midnight, and *by eight to-morrow*
Thou must be made immortal.—*Ibid.*, iv. 2.

Who call'd here of late?—
None, *since the curfew rung.*—
Not Isabel?—
No.—
They will, then, *ere 't be long.*—*Ibid.*, iv. 2.

There he must stay *until the officer
Arise* to let him in: *he is call'd up.*—
Have you no countermand for Claudio yet,
But he must die to-morrow?—
None, sir, none.—
As near the dawning, provost, *as it is*,
You shall hear more *ere morning.*—*Ibid.*, iv. 2.

This is his lordship's man.—
And *here comes* Claudio's pardon.—
My lord hath sent you *this note; . . . Good morrow; for*, as I take it, *it is almost day.*—*Ibid.*, iv. 2.

Whatsoever you may hear to the contrary, let Claudio be executed *by four of the clock;* and, *in the afternoon*, Barnardine. For my better satisfaction, let me have Claudio's head sent me *by five.*—*Ibid.*, iv. 2.

What is that Barnardine, who is to be executed *in the afternoon?*—*Ibid.*, iv. 2.

Let this Barnardine be *this morning* executed, and his head borne to Angelo.—*Ibid.*, iv. 2.

The contents of *this* is the return of the duke: you shall anon over-read it at your pleasure; where you shall find, *within these two days he will be here.* This is a thing that Angelo knows not; for he *this very day* receives letters of strange tenor; . . . *Look, the unfolding star calls up the shepherd.* . . . Call your executioner, and *off with Barnardine's head*: I will give him *present shrift*, and advise him for a better place. . . . Come away; *it is almost clear dawn.*—*Ibid.*, iv. 2.

Master Barnardine! *You must rise and be hanged, . . .* You must be so good, sir, *to rise and be put to death.*—*Ibid.*, iv. 3.

Away! I am sleepy.—Tell him *he must awake, and that quickly too.*—*Ibid.*, iv. 3.

Is the axe upon the block, sirrah ?—*Very ready*, sir.—*M. for M.*, iv. 3.

I would desire you *to clap into your prayers ;* for, look you, *the warrant's come.* . . .
Here comes your ghostly father : do we jest now, think you ?— . . . I will not consent
to die *this day*, that 's certain. . . . I will not die *to-day* for any man's persuasion. . . .
After him, fellows ; *bring him to the block.*—*Ibid.*, iv. 3.

Here in the prison, father,
There died *this morning* of a cruel fever
One Ragozine.—*Ibid.*, iv. 3.

O, 'tis an accident that heaven provides !
Despatch it presently : the hour draws on
Prefix'd by Angelo.   See this be done,
And sent according to command ; . . .
This shall be done, good father, *presently.*
But Barnardine *must die this afternoon.*—*Ibid.*, iv. 3.

Ere twice the sun hath made his journal greeting
To th' under generation, you shall find
Your safety manifested.—
I am your free dependant.—
Quick, despatch, and send the head to Angelo.
Now will I write letters to Angelo—
The provost, he shall bear them—whose contents
Shall witness to him *I am near at home.*—*Ibid.*, iv. 3.

Here is the head ; I 'll carry it myself.—
Convenient is it.   *Make a swift return ;*
. . . *I 'll make all speed.*—*Ibid.*, iv. 3.

Good morning to you, fair and gracious daughter.—
The better, given me by so holy a man.
Hath yet the deputy sent my brother's pardon ?—
He hath releas'd him, Isabel, from the world :
His head is off, and sent to Angelo.—*Ibid.*, iv. 3.

The duke *comes home to-morrow ;* nay, dry your eyes !
One of our convent, and his confessor,
Gives me this instance : *already he hath carried*
Notice to Escalus and Angelo ;
Who *do prepare to meet him* at the gates,
There to give up their power.—*Ibid.*, iv. 3.

This letter then to Friar Peter give ;
'Tis that he sent me of the duke's return :
Say, by this token, I desire his company
At Mariana's house *to-night.*—*Ibid.*, iv. 3.

And why should we
Proclaim it *in an hour before his entering*,
That if any crave redress. . . . Let it be proclaim'd :
Betimes i' the morn I 'll call you at your house. . . .
Good night.—*Ibid.*, iv. 4.

Go, *call at* Flavius' house,
And tell him where I stay : *give the like notice*
To Valentinus, Rowland, and to Crassus,
And bid them bring the trumpets to the gate ;
But *send me Flavius first.*—
It shall be speeded well.—
I thank thee, Varrius ; *thou hast made good haste :*
Come, we will walk.   There 's other of our friends
Will greet us here anon.—*Ibid.*, iv. 5.

Come, I have found you out a stand most fit,
Where you may have such vantage on the duke,
He shall not pass you.   *Twice have the trumpets sounded ;*
The generous and gravest citizens
Have hent the gates, and *very near upon*
The duke is entering : therefore hence, away.—*Ibid.*, iv. 6.

And I did yield to him : but *the next morn betimes,*
His purpose surfeiting, *he sends a warrant*
For my poor brother's head.—*M. for M.,* v. 1.

But yesternight, my lord, she and that friar,
I saw them at the prison.—*Ibid.,* v. 1.

But Tuesday night last gone, in's garden house,
He knew me as a wife.—*Ibid.,* v. i.

Let my trial be mine own confession :
Immediate sentence then, *and sequent death,*
Is all the grace I beg.—
> Come hither, Mariana.

Say, wast thou e'er contracted to this woman ;—
I was my lord.—
Go take her hence, and *marry her instantly.*
Do you the office, friar ; which consummate,
Return him here again.—*Ibid.,* v. 1.

It was the *swift celerity* of his death,
Which I did think with slower foot came on,
That brain'd my purpose.—*Ibid.,* v. 1.

We do condemn thee to the very block
Where Claudio stoop'd to death, and *with like haste.*
Away with him !—*Ibid.,* v. 1.

Secondly, for the retarding touches :—

> We shall write to you,
> *As time and our concernings shall importune,*
> How it goes with us ; and do look to know
> What doth befall you here.—*Ibid.,* i. 1.

I have deliver'd to Lord Angelo
(A man of stricture and firm abstinence)
My absolute power and place here in Vienna,
And he supposes me *travell'd to Poland.*—*Ibid.,* i. 4.

I will bethink me: *come again to-morrow.**
. . . Well; *come to me to-morrow.*—
> *At what hour to-morrow*

Shall I attend your lordship ?—
> *At any time 'fore noon.*—*Ibid.,* ii. 2.

> What ! do I love her,
That I desire to *hear her speak again,*
And feast upon her eyes ?—*Ibid.,* ii. 2.

> *Answer me to-morrow,*
Or, by the affection that now guides me most,
I 'll prove a tyrant to him.—*Ibid.,* ii. 4.

How much is the good duke deceived in Angelo ! *If ever he return,* and I can speak to him, I will open.—*Ibid.,* iii. 1.

Much please the absent duke, *if peradventure he shall ever return* to have hearing of this business.—*Ibid.,* iii. 1.

What news, friar, of the duke ?—
I know none. Can you tell me of any ?—
Some say, *he is with the Emperor of Russia ;* other some, *he is in Rome.* . . . Lord Angelo dukes it well in his absence.—*Ibid.,* iii. 2.

---

* It is noticeable with what art-skill Shakespeare uses even *the same word* with accelerating or retarding force of effect, according to his purpose. In this play he uses the word " to-morrow " in certain passages to hasten on the action and time ; whereas in the present passage he employs the word " to-morrow " as a means of *putting off to another day* the answer which Angelo is to give Isabella in her suit for her brother, and thereby deferring Claudio's execution long beyond the period first appointed for its taking place.

> Here comes a man of comfort, whose advice
> Hath *often* still'd my brawling discontent.—*M. for M.*, iv. 1.

> Yet, I believe, there comes
> No countermand; *no such example have we.*—*Ibid.*, iv. 2.

Lord Angelo, belike thinking me remiss in mine office, awakens me with this *unwonted* putting on; methinks strangely, for *he hath not used it before.*—*Ibid.*, iv. 2.

His friends still wrought reprieves for him: and, indeed, his fact, *till now in the government of Lord Angelo*, came not to an undoubtful proof.—*Ibid.*, iv. 2.

To make you understand this in a manifested effect, I crave but *four days' respite;* for the which you are to do me both a present and a dangerous courtesy.—Pray, sir, in what?—In the *delaying death.*—*Ibid.*, iv. 2.

Every letter he hath writ hath disvouched other.—*Ibid.*, iv. 4.

> My business in this state
> Made me *a looker-on* here in Vienna,
> Where *I have seen corruption boil and bubble,*
> *Till it o'errun the stew:* laws for all faults,
> But *faults so countenanc'd, that the strong statutes*
> Stand like *the forfeits in a barber's shop,*
> As much in mock as mark.—*Ibid.*, v. 1.

In his charming comedy of "Much Ado about Nothing" the dramatist—having to convey the effect of a passing occurrence in the life of a young count eager for the arrival of his wedding-day, together with the machinations of an evil-doer to prevent the marriage from taking place, and the plottings of friends to bring about a union between a lady and gentleman who have a liking for each other nothwithstanding their habitual wit-combats—has contrived to give blended brief and protracted time throughout its scenes. The indications of brief time are:—

I learn in this letter, that Don Pedro of Arragon comes *this night* to Messina.—He is *very near by this:* he was *not three leagues off* when I left him.—*M. Ado*, i. 1.

Don Pedro is approached.—*Ibid.*, i. 1.

Tell him *I will not fail him at supper;* for indeed he hath made great preparation.—*Ibid.*, i. 1.

> I know we shall have revelling *to-night:*
> I will assume thy part in some disguise. . . .
> *In practice let us put it presently.*—*Ibid.*, i. 1.

How now, brother! where is my cousin, your son? Hath he provided this music? —*He is very busy about it.*—*Ibid.*, i. 2.

That he loved my niece your daughter, and meant to acknowledge it *this night* in a dance; and, if he found her accordant, he meant *to take the present time by the top,* and *instantly* break with you of it.—*Ibid.*, i. 2.

Go you with me, and I will use your skill. Good cousin, have a care *this busy time.*—*Ibid.*, i. 2.

I came yonder from a great supper: . . . *Let us to the great supper.*—*Ibid.*, i. 3.

Was not Count John *here at supper?*—*Ibid.*, ii. 1.

The revellers are entering, brother.—*Ibid.*, ii. 1.

And he swore *he would marry her to-night.*—*Ibid.*, ii. 1.

Go, then; *find me a meet hour* to draw Don Pedro and the Count Claudio alone.—*Ibid.*, ii. 2.

I will *presently go* learn their day of marriage.—*Ibid.*, ii. 2.

> How still *the evening is,*
> As hush'd on purpose to grace harmony!—*Ibid.*, ii. 3.

My lord, will you walk ? *dinner* is ready.*—*M. Ado*, ii. 3.

Let us send her *to call him in to dinner.*—*Ibid.*, ii. 3.

Against my will, I am sent to *bid you come in to dinner.*—*Ibid.*, ii. 3.

> When are you married, madam ?—
> Why, every day *to-morrow.* Come, go in :
> I 'll show thee some attires ; and have thy counsel,
> Which is the best to furnish me *to-morrow.*—*Ibid.*, iii. 1.

I do but stay till your marriage be consummate, and then go I toward Arragon.— *Ibid.*, iii. 2.

Hero and Margaret have *by this* played their parts with Beatrice.—*Ibid.*, iii. 2.

Means your lordship *to be married to-morrow ?*—You know he does.—*Ibid.*, iii. 2.

Go but with me *to-night*, you shall see her chamber-window entered, even *the night before her wedding-day :* if you love her then, *to-morrow wed her.*—*Ibid.*, iii. 2.

If I see anything *to-night* why I should not *marry her to-morrow*, in the congregation, where I should wed, there will I shame her.—*Ibid.*, iii. 2.

Bear it coldly *but till midnight*, and let the issue show itself.—*Ibid.*, iii. 2.

Let us sit here upon the church-bench *till two*, and then all to bed. One word more, honest neighbours. I pray you, watch about Signior Leonato's door ; for *the wedding being to-morrow*, there is a great coil *to-night.*—*Ibid.*, iii. 3.

I have *to-night* wooed Margaret, the lady Hero's gentlewoman, by the name of Hero. —*Ibid.*, iii. 3.

Good Ursula, *wake* my cousin Beatrice, and *desire her to rise.*—*Ibid.*, iii. 4.

Good morrow, coz.—*Good morrow*, sweet Hero.—*Ibid.*, iii. 4.

'Tis almost five o'clock, cousin ; *'tis time you were ready.*—*Ibid.*, iii. 4.

Madam, withdraw : the prince, the count, Signior Benedick, Don John, and all the gallants of the town, *are come to fetch you to church.*—*Help to dress me, good coz, good Meg, good Ursula.*—*Ibid.*, iii. 4.

Brief, I pray you ; for you see *it is a busy time with me.*—*Ibid.*, iii. 5.

Take their examination yourself, and bring it me : *I am now in great haste*, as may appear unto you.—*Ibid.*, iii. 5.

My lord, *they stay for you to give your daughter to her husband.*—*I 'll wait upon them : I am ready.*—*Ibid.*, iii. 5.

Come, Friar Francis, *be brief ;* only to the plain form of marriage, and you shall recount their particular duties afterwards.—*Ibid.*, iv. 1.

> What man was he talk'd with you *yesternight*
> Out at your window, *betwixt twelve and one ?*—*Ibid.*, iv. 1.

> Myself, my brother, and this grieved count,
> Did see her, hear her, *at that hour last night*,
> Talk with a ruffian at her chamber-window.—*Ibid.*, iv. i.

> Lady, were you her bedfellow *last night ?*—
> No, truly not ; although, until *last night*,
> I have this twelvemonth been her bedfellow.—*Ibid.*, iv. 1.

>   O, my father !
> Prove you that any man with me convers'd
> At hours unmeet, or that I *yesternight*
> Maintain'd the change of words with any creature,
> Refuse me, hate me, torture me to death.—*Ibid.*, iv. 1.

---

* Although the word " dinner " is here used, it seems more probable that " supper " was meant ; because at the commencement of the scene " evening " is mentioned, and in Shakespeare's time the usual hour for dinner was about mid-day, while supper was the evening meal. Nevertheless, it is true that " evening " was the term formerly used to express any time after twelve o'clock in the day ; and therefore it is possible that the period of the present scene is intended to be somewhere after noon, in which case the word " dinner " is correct.

Prince John is *this morning* secretly stolen away: Hero was in this manner accused; in this very manner refused; and, upon the grief of this, suddenly died.—*M. Ado*, iv. 2.

> *Here come* the prince and Claudio *hastily*.—
> Good den, good den.—
>   Good day to both of you.—
> Hear you, my lords,—
>   *We have some haste*, Leonato.—
> *Some haste*, my lord !   Well, fare you well, my lord :
> Are you *so hasty now* ?   Well, all is one.—*Ibid.*, v. 1.

Come, bring away the plaintiffs : *by this time* our sexton hath reformed Signior Leonato of the matter. . . . *Here comes* master Signior Leonato, and the sexton too. —*Ibid.*, v. 1.

> Hang her an epitaph upon her tomb,
> And sing it to her bones—*sing it to-night :*
> *To-morrow morning come you to my house ;*
> And since you could not be my son-in-law,
> Be yet my nephew.—*Ibid.*, v. 1.

> *To-morrow*, then, *I will expect your coming ;*
> *To-night* I take my leave.—*Ibid.*, v. 1.

> *Until to-morrow morning*, lords, farewell.—
> Farewell, my lords: *we look for you to-morrow.*
> We will not fail.—
>   *To-night I'll mourn* with Hero.—*Ibid.*, v. 1.

Claudio undergoes my challenge ; and either I must *shortly hear from him*, or I will subscribe him a coward.—*Ibid.*, v. 2.

Madam, *you must come to your uncle.* Yonder 's old coil at home : it is proved, my lady Hero hath been falsely accused, the prince and Claudio mightily abused; and Don John is the author of all, who is fled and gone. *Will you come presently ?*— *Ibid.*, v. 2.

> Now, unto thy bones *good night !*
> Yearly will I do this rite.—
> *Good morrow*, masters ; *put your torches out :*
> The wolves have prey'd ; and look, the *gentle day*,
> *Before the wheels of Phœbus, round about*
> *Dapples the drowsy east with spots of grey.*
> Thanks to you all, and leave us : fare you well.—
> *Good morrow*, masters : each his several way.—
> Come, let us hence, and put on other *weeds ;*
> *And then to Leonato's we will go.*—
> *And Hymen now with luckier issue speeds,*
> Than this, for whom we rendered up this woe.—*Ibid.*, v. 3

> The prince and Claudio promis'd *by this hour*
> To visit me.—*Ibid.*, v. 4.

> But, for my will, my will is, your good will
> May stand with ours, *this day to be conjoin'd*
> In the state of honourable marriage.—*Ibid.*, v. 4.

> *Good-morrow* to this fair assembly.—
> *Good-morrow*, prince ; *good-morrow*, Claudio :
> *We here attend you.* Are you yet determin'd
> *To-day to marry with my brother's daughter ?*—
> I 'll hold my mind, were she an Ethiop.—
> *Call her forth*, brother : *here 's the friar ready.*
> Let 's have a dance ere we are married. . . . We 'll have dancing afterwards.—*First, of my word ; therefore, play, music !*—*Ibid.*, v. 4.

> My lord, your brother John *is ta'en in flight,*
> *And brought* with armed men *back to Messina.*—
> Think not on him till to-morrow. . . . *Strike up, pipers !*--*Ibid.*, v. 4.

The indications of protracted time are :—

My dear friend Leonato hath invited you all. I tell him *we shall stay here at least a month ;* and he heartily prays some occasion may detain us longer.—*M. Ado,* i. 1.

Here, Claudio, I have wooed in thy name, and fair Hero is won : I have broke with her father, and, his good will obtained, *name the day of marriage,* and God give thee joy !—*Ibid.,* ii. 1.

Count Claudio, when mean you to go to church ?—To-morrow, my lord: Time goes on crutches till love have all his rites.—*Not till Monday,* my dear son, *which is hence a just seven-night ;* and a time too brief, too, *to have all things answer my mind.* —Come, you shake the head at *so long a breathing :* but, I warrant thee, Claudio *the time shall not go dully* by us. I will, *in the interim, undertake one of Hercules' labours ;* which is, to bring Signior Benedick and the lady Beatrice into a mountain of affection, the one with the other. I would fain have it a match ; and I doubt not but to fashion it, if you three will but minister such assistance as I shall give you direction.—My lord, I am for you, though it cost me *ten nights' watchings.*—*Ibid.,* ii. 1.

They will scarcely believe this without trial: *offer them instances ;* which shall bear no less likelihood than to see me at her chamber-window ; hear me call Margaret, Hero ; hear Margaret term me Claudio ; and bring them to see this *the very night before the intended wedding ;* for *in the meantime* I will so fashion the matter that Hero shall be absent.—*Ibid.,* ii. 2.

I have known, when there was no music with him but the drum and the fife ; and *now* had he rather hear the tabor and the pipe: *I have known, when* he would have walked ten mile afoot to see a good armour ; and *now* will he *lie ten nights awake,* carving the fashion of a new doublet.—*Ibid.,* ii. 3.

Get us some excellent music ; for *to-morrow night* we would have it at the lady Hero's chamber-window.—*Ibid.,* ii. 3.

Come hither, Leonato : what was it *you told me of to-day,* that your niece Beatrice was in love with Signior Benedick ?—*Ibid.,* ii. 3.

Why, what effects of passion shows she ?— . . . What effects, my lord ? *She will sit you—you heard my daughter tell you how.*—*Ibid.,* ii. 3.

" Shall I," says she, " that have *so oft* encountered him with scorn, write to him that I love him ? "—This says she now when she is beginning to write to him ; for *she'll be up twenty times a night* and *there will she sit* till she have writ a sheet of paper : my daughter tells us all.—*Ibid.,* ii. 3.

The ecstasy hath so much overborne her, that *my daughter is sometime afeard* she will do a desperate outrage to herself.—*Ibid.,* ii. 3.

Hero thinks surely she will die ; for she says *she will die if he love her not ; and she will die, ere she make her love known ; and she will die if he woo her, rather than she will bate one breath of her accustomed* crossness.—*Ibid.,* ii. 3.

Well, I am sorry for your niece. Shall we go seek Benedick, and tell him of her love ?—Never tell him, my lord : let her *wear it out* with good counsel.—*Ibid.,* ii. 3.

> Who hath, indeed, most like a liberal villain,
> Confess'd the vile encounters *they have had*
> *A thousand times* in secret.—*Ibid.,* iv. 1.

I'll tell thee how Beatrice praised thy wit *the other day.* . . . he swore a thing to me *on Monday night,* which he forswore *on Tuesday morning.* . . . Thus did she, *an hour together,* trans-shape thy particular virtues : yet *at last* she concluded with a sigh, thou wast the properest man in Italy.—*Ibid.,* v. 1.

I pray thee now, tell me, for which of my bad parts didst thou *first fall in love* with me ?—For them all together: . . . But for which of my good parts did you *first suffer love* for me ?—*Ibid.,* v. 2.

The author of " Love's Labour's Lost " had to indicate the visit of a French princess and her train at the court of Navarre, together with a sojourn of sufficient length to admit of the king and his lords falling in love with her and her ladies, courting them by divers interviews and entertainments.   The effects of quickly passing time are thus thrown in :—

> When, spite of cormorant devouring Time,
> *Th' endeavour of this present breath* may buy
> That honour which shall bate his scythe's keen edge,
> And make us heirs of all eternity.—*Love's L. L.*, i. 1.
>
> Our *late edict* shall strongly stand in force.—*Ibid.*, i. 1.
>
> Your oaths are past ; and *now subscribe your names.*—*Ibid.*, i. 1.
>
>   *Here comes in embassy*
> The French king's daughter with yourself to speak.—*Ibid.*, i. 1.

Betook myself to walk.   The time when ?   *About the sixth hour ;* when beasts most graze, birds best peck, and *men sit down to that nourishment which is called supper :* so much for the time when.—*Ibid.*, i. 1 (*Letter*).

Did you hear *the proclamation* [that which has been before mentioned as " our late edict."] ?—*Ibid.*, i. 1.

> *Now*, madam, *summon up your dearest spirits :*
> Consider whom the king your father sends ;
> To whom he sends ; and what's his embassy.—*Ibid.*, ii. 1.
>
> Tell him, the daughter of the king of France,
> On serious business, *craving quick despatch,*
> Importunes personal conference with his grace :
> *Haste, signify so much.*—*Ibid.*, ii. 1.
>
> *Here comes Boyet.*—
>   Now, what admittance, lord ?—
> Navarre had notice of your fair approach ;
> And he and his competitors in oath
> *Were all address'd to meet you,* gentle lady,
> *Before I came.* . . .
> *Here comes Navarre.*—*Ibid.*, ii. 1.
>
> Vouchsafe to read the purpose of my coming,
> And *suddenly resolve me in my suit.*—*Ibid.*, ii. 1.
>
> If my observation, which very seldom lies,
> By the heart's still rhetoric disclos'd with eyes,
> Deceive me not now, *Navarre is infected.*—
> With what ?—
> With that which we lovers entitle, affected.—
> Your reason ?—
> Why, all his behaviours did make their retire
> To the court of his eye, peeping thorough desire :
> His heart, like an agate, with your print impress'd,
> Proud with his form, in his eye pride express'd :
> His tongue, *all impatient* to speak, not to see,
> *Did stumble in haste* in his eyesight to be ;
> All senses to that sense did make their repair,
> To feel only looking on fairest of fair.—*Ibid.*, ii. 1.

Take this key, give enlargement to the swain, *bring him festinately* hither.*—*Ibid.*, iii. 1.

> O, stay, slave ; I must employ thee :
> As thou wilt win my favour, good my knave,
> Do one thing for me that I shall entreat.—
> When would you have it done, sir ?—
> O, *this afternoon.*— . . .
> I will come to your worship to-morrow morning.—
> *It must be done this afternoon.*   Hark, slave,
> It is but this,—
> *The princess comes to hunt here in the park,*

---

* " Festinately " ; that is, speedily.

> And in her train there is a gentle lady ;
> When tongues speak sweetly, then they name her name,
> And Rosaline they call her : ask for her ;
> And to her white hand see thou do commend
> This seal'd-up counsel.   There's thy guerdon ; go.—*Love's L. L.*, iii. 1.
> Well, lords, *to-day* we shall have our despatch : . . .
> Then, forester, my friend, where is the bush
> That we must stand and play the murderer in ?—
> Hereby, upon the edge of yonder coppice ;
> A stand where you may make the fairest shoot.— . . .
> But, come, the bow : *now* mercy goes to kill,
> And shooting well is then accounted ill.—*Ibid.*, iv. 1.
> God give you *good-morrow*, master person.—*Ibid.*, iv. 2.

I do dine to-day at the father's of a certain pupil of mine.—*Ibid.*, iv. 2.

Away ! *the gentles are at their game*, and we will to our recreation.—*Ibid.*, iv. 2.

> Shall we resolve to woo these girls of France ?—
> And win them too : therefore let us devise
> Some entertainment for them in their tents.—
> *First, from the park let us conduct them thither ;*
> Then, homeward, every man attach the hand
> Of his fair mistress.   *In the afternoon*
> We will with some strange pastime solace them,
> Such as *the shortness of the time* can shape ;
> For revels, dances, masks, and merry hours,
> Forerun fair Love, strewing her way with flowers.—
> Away, away ! *no time shall be omitted,*
> *That will be time,* and may by us be fitted.—*Ibid.*, iv. 3.

Your reasons *at dinner* have been sharp and sententious. . . . I did converse *this quondam day* with a companion of the king's.—*Ibid.*, v. 1.

It is the king's most sweet pleasure and affection, to congratulate the princess at her pavilion in *the posteriors of this day*, which the rude multitude call *the afternoon*.
                                                                    Ibid., v. 1.

> Madam, and pretty mistresses, give ear :
> *Immediately they will again be here*
> In their own shapes.— . . .
> Will they return ?—
>   They will, they will. . . .
> Therefore change favours ; and, when they repair,
> Blow like sweet roses in the summer air. . . .
> Ladies, withdraw : *the gallants are at hand.*—
> *Whip to our tents, as roes run over land.*—*Ibid.*, v. 2.
> We have had pastimes here, and pleasant game :
> A mess of Russians *left us but of late.*—*Ibid.*, v. 2.
> We four, indeed, confronted were with four
> In Russian habit : here they stay'd *an hour,*
> *And talk'd apace ;* and in that hour, my lord,
> They did not bless us with one happy word.—*Ibid.*, v. 2.
> Boyet, *prepare ; I will away to-night.*—
> Madam, not so ; I do beseech you, stay.—
> *Prepare, I say.*—*Ibid.*, v. 2.

The effects of more slowly passing time are thus introduced :—

> You three, Biron, Dumain, and Longaville,
> Have sworn *for three years' term* to live with me,
> My fellow-scholars, and to keep those statutes
> That are recorded in this schedule here.— . . .
> I am resolved : 'tis but a *three years' fast :*
> The mind shall banquet though the body pine.— . . .
> So much, dear liege, I have already sworn,
> That is, *to live and study here three years.*—*Ibid.*, i. 1.

I only swore to study with your grace,
And *stay here in your court for three years' space.—Love's L. L.,* i. 1.

Yet confident I 'll keep to what I swore,
And *bide the penance of each three years' day.—Ibid.,* i. 1.

" Item, if any man be seen to talk with a woman *within the term of three years,* he shall endure such public shame as the rest of the court can possibly devise."—*Ibid.,* i. 1.

Necessity will make us all forsworn,
Three thousand times within this three years' space.—Ibid., i. 1.

I will pronounce your sentence: you shall fast *a week* with bran and water.—I had rather pray *a month* with mutton and porridge.—*Ibid.,* i. 1.

The duke's pleasure is, that you keep Costard safe: and you must let him take no delight, nor no penance; but a' must fast *three days a week.—Ibid.,* i. 2.

Navarre hath made a vow,
Till painful study shall out-wear three years,
No woman may approach his silent court :
Therefore *to us seem'th it a needful course,*
Before we enter his forbidden gates,
To know his pleasure.—Ibid., ii. 1.

Boyet, you can produce acquittances
For such a sum, from special officers
Of Charles his father.—
Satisfy me so.—
So please your grace *the packet is not come,*
Where that and other specialties are bound :
To-morrow you shall have a sight of them.—
It shall suffice me : at which interview,
All liberal reason I will yield unto.
Meantime, receive such welcome at my hand
As honour, without breach of honour, may
Make tender of to thy true worthiness :
You may not come, fair princess, in my gates ;
But here without, you shall be so receiv'd
As you shall deem yourself lodg'd in my heart,
Though so denied fair harbour in my house.
Your own good thoughts excuse me, and farewell :
To-morrow shall we visit you again.—Ibid., ii. 1.

On Saturday we will return to France.—*Ibid.,* iv. 1.

Thou hast mistaken his letter. . . . Here, sweet, put up this : 'twill be thine *another day.—Ibid.,* iv. 1.

That same Biron *I 'll torture ere I go.—Ibid.,* v. 2.

We came to visit you ; *and purpose now*
To lead you to our court.—Ibid., v. 2.

O, you have liv'd in desolation here,
Unseen, unvisited, much to our shame.—
Not so, my lord ; it is not so, I swear ;
We have had pastimes here and pleasant game.—Ibid., v. 2.

For your sakes *have we neglected time,*
Play'd foul play with our oaths : your beauty, ladies,
Hath much deform'd us, fashioning our humours
Even to the opposed end of our intents.—Ibid., v. 2.

The " Midsummer Night's Dream " affords a curious instance of the ingenuity with which its author contrives to give two distinct sets of Dramatic Time in the same play. Its title, and the chief impression it produces, allows a single night of summer fanciful incident to be supposed as the period which this lovely drama depicts ; whereas it

also embraces the interval that elapses between the opening speech of
Theseus and the concluding benediction on his nuptials, an interval of
four days. This interval is expressly stated in the outset of the play.
There is mention of the appointed meeting in the wood being fixed to
take place on the night of the day following that when the play begins;
the various adventures in the wood succeed each other: and yet, so
artistically is the corresponding hastening process simultaneously
maintained, that no violence is done to our sense of veritableness
when in the course of the first scene of the fourth act we find that the
morning of the nuptials has arrived, and in the next scene learn that
the ceremony has actually been performed. The four days seem
naturally to have passed, even while we seem to have beheld but a
sole night of midsummer dreamy doings in fairy-land. The poet casts
his own magic spell over us; and we accept the four days or one night
as equally possible, just as he wills. The means he uses are these: by
swift hints :—

> Our queen and all her elves *come here anon.*—
> The king *doth keep his revels here to-night.*—*Mid. N. D.,* ii. 1.
>
> Ill met *by moonlight,* proud Titania.—*Ibid.,* ii. 2.
>
> Well, go thy way: *thou shalt not from this grove,*
> *Till I torment thee* for this injury.—*Ibid.,* ii. 2.
>
> Where is Lysander, and fair Hermia? . . .
> Thou told'st me *they were stol'n into this wood;*
> *And here am I.*—*Ibid.,* ii. 2.
>
> Fare thee well, nymph: *ere he do leave this grove,*
> *Thou shalt fly him, and he shall seek thy love.*—*Ibid.,* ii. 2.
>
> I know a bank where the wild thyme blows,
> Where oxlips, and the nodding violet grows;
> Quite over-canopied with luscious woodbine,
> With sweet musk-roses, and with eglantine:
> *There sleeps Titania some time of the night,*
> Lull'd in these flowers with dances and delight. . . .
> And *with the juice of this I'll streak her eyes,*
> And make her full of hateful fantasies.
> Take thou some of it, and seek through this grove:
> A sweet Athenian lady is in love
> With a disdainful youth: *anoint his eyes;*
> But do it when the next thing he espies
> May be the lady: . . .
> And *look thou meet me ere the first cock crow.*—*Ibid.,* ii. 2.
>
> Come, *now a roundel and a fairy song;*
> Then, *for the third part of a minute, hence;*—
>   . . . *Sing me now asleep;*
> Then to your offices, and let me rest.—*Ibid.,* ii. 3.
>
> What thou see'st when thou dost wake,
>   [*Squeezes the flower on* Titania's *eyelids.*
> Do it for thy true love take;
> Love and languish for his sake:
> Be it ounce, or cat, or bear,
> Pard, or boar with bristled hair,
> In thy eye that shall appear
> *When thou wak'st,* it is thy dear.
> Wake when some vile thing is near.—*Ibid.,* ii. 3.
>
> Fair love, you faint with wandering in the wood;
> And, to speak troth, I have forgot our way:

We'll rest us, Hermia, if you think it good,
And tarry for the comfort of the day.—
Be it so, Lysander : find you out a bed ;
For *I upon this bank will rest my head.*—*Mid. N. D.*, ii. 3.

        And, *good night*, sweet friend.
Thy love ne'er alter till thy sweet life end !—
Amen, amen, to that fair prayer, say I ;
And then end life, when I end loyalty !
Here is my bed : sleep give thee all his rest !—
With half that wish the wisher's eyes be press'd !　　　　[*They sleep.*
        Ibid., ii. 3.

Night and silence ! who is here ?
Weeds of Athens he doth wear :
This is he, my master said,
Despised the Athenian maid ;
And here the maiden, sleeping sound,
On the dank and dirty ground ;
Pretty soul ! she durst not lie
Near this lack-love, this kill-courtesy.
Churl, upon thy eyes I throw
      [*Squeezes the flower on* LYSANDER'S *eyelids.*
All the power this charm doth owe.
When thou wak'st, let love forbid
Sleep his seat on thy eyelid :
So awake when I am gone,
For *I must now to Oberon.*—*Ibid.*, ii. 3.

Are we all met ?—
Pat, pat ; and here's a marvellous convenient place for our rehearsal.　This green
plot shall be our stage, this hawthorn brake our 'tiring-house.—*Ibid.*, iii. 1.

    Titania (waking). What angel *wakes me* from my flowery bed ?—
        Ibid., iii. 1.

I pray thee, gentle mortal, sing again :
Mine ear is much enamour'd of thy note ;
So is mine eye enthralled to thy shape ;
And thy fair virtue's force perforce doth move me,
On the first view, to say, to swear, I love thee.—*Ibid.*, iii. 1.

My mistress with a monster *is in love.* . . .
I led them on in this distracted fear,
And left sweet Pyramus translated there :
When in that moment (so it came to pass)
Titania *wak'd and straightway lov'd an ass.*—
This falls out better than I could devise.
But hast thou yet latch'd the Athenian's eyes
With the love-juice, as I did bid thee do ?—
I took him sleeping : *that is finish'd too.*—*Ibid.*, iii. 2.

About the wood go swifter than the wind,
And Helena of Athens look thou find : . . .
By some illusion see thou bring her here :
I 'll charm his eyes against she do appear.—
I go, I go ; look how I go—
Swifter than arrow from the Tartar's bow.—
    Flower of this purple dye,
    Hit with Cupid's archery,
        [*Squeezes the flower on* DEMETRIUS'S *eyelids.*
    Sink in apple of his eye.—*Ibid.*, iii. 2.

Am I not Hermia ?　Are not you Lysander ?
I am as fair now, as I was erewhile.
Since night, you lov'd me ; yet *since night* you left me.—*Ibid.*, iii. 2.

      In love unto Demetrius,
I told him of your stealth unto this wood,

He follow'd you ; for love, *I follow'd him ;*
But he hath chid me hence, and threaten'd me
To strike me, spurn me, nay, to kill me too:
And *now*, so you will let me quiet go,
To Athens will I bear my folly back,
And follow you no farther : *let me go.—Mid. N. D.*, iii. 2.

Now follow, if thou dar'st, *to try whose right*,
Of thine or mine, *is most in Helena.—*
Follow? nay, *I'll go with thee, cheek by jole.—Ibid.*, iii. 2.

Hie therefore, Robin, overcast the night ; . . .
And from each other look thou lead them thus,
Till o'er their brows death-counterfeiting sleep
With leaden legs and batty wings doth creep :
Then crush this herb into Lysander's eye ;
Whose liquor hath this virtuous property,
To take from thence all error with his might,
And make his eyeballs roll with wonted sight.
When they next wake, all this derision
Shall seem a dream and fruitless vision ;
And back to Athens shall the lovers wend,
With league, whose date till death shall never end.
Whiles I in this affair do thee employ,
I'll to my queen and beg her Indian boy ;
And then I will her charmed eye release
From monster's view, and all things shall be peace.—
My fairy lord, *this must be done with haste*,
For *night's swift dragons cut the clouds full fast*,
And yonder shines Aurora's harbinger ;
               . . . *haste ; make no delay :*
We may effect this business yet ere day.—Ibid., iii. 2.

The villain is much lighter-heel'd than I :
I follow'd fast, but faster he did fly ;
That fallen am I in dark uneven way,
And here will rest me. *(Lies down.)* Come, thou gentle day !—
          . . . Faintness constraineth me
To measure out my length on this cold bed.
By day's approach look to be visited.—   [*Lies down and sleeps.*
          . . . *Shine, comforts, from the east*,
That I may back to Athens, *by daylight*,
From these that my poor company detest :
And sleep, that sometimes shuts up sorrow's eye,
Steal me awhile from mine own company.—   [*Lies down and sleeps.*
Here will I rest me *till the break of day.—*   [*Lies down and sleeps.*
          On the ground sleep sound :
          I'll apply to your eye,
             Gentle lover, remedy.
                         [*Squeezing the herb on* LYSANDER'S *eyelids.*
When thou wak'st thou tak'st
True delight in the sight
Of thy former lady's eye :
And the country proverb known,
That every man should take his own,
  In your waking shall be shown.—Ibid., iii. 2.

And, gentle Puck, take this transformèd scalp
From off the head of this Athenian swain ;
That he, awaking when the other do,
May all to Athens back again repair,
And think no more of *this night's* accidents,
But as the fierce vexation of a dream.
But *first* I will release the fairy queen.

Be, as thou wast wont to be;
> [*Touching her eyelids with a herb.*

See, as thou wast wont to see:
Dian's bud o'er Cupid's flower
Hath such force and blessed power.
Now, my Titania; *wake you, my sweet queen.*—Mid. N. D., iv. 1.

   Come, my queen, take hands with me,
And rock the ground whereon these sleepers be.
Now thou and I are new in amity,
And will to-morrow midnight solemnly
Dance in Duke Theseus' house triumphantly:
And bless it to all fair prosperity.
There shall the pairs of faithful lovers be
Wedded, with Theseus, all in jollity.—
   Fairy king, attend, and mark:
   I do hear *the morning lark.*—
   Then, my queen, in silence sad,
   Trip we after the night's shade:
   We the globe can compass soon,
   Swifter than the wandering moon.—
   Come, my lord; and *in our flight,*
   Tell me how it came *this night,*
   That I sleeping here was found
   With these mortals on the ground.—*Ibid.*, iv. 1.

Go, one of you, find out the forester;
For *now our observation is perform'd;*
And since *we have the vaward of the day,*
My love shall hear the music of my hounds:
Uncouple in the western valley; let them go;
Despatch, I say, and find the forester.—*Ibid.*, iv. 1.

   But, soft! what nymphs are these?—
My lord, this is my daughter here asleep;
And this, Lysander; this Demetrius is;
This Helena, old Nedar's Helena:
I wonder of their being together.—
No doubt they *rose up early* to observe
The rite of May; and, hearing our intent,
Came here in grace of our solemnity.
But speak, Egeus; *is not this the day*
That Hermia should give answer of her choice?—
It is, my lord.—
Go, bid the huntsmen *wake them* with their horns.
> [*Exit an attendant. Horns and shout within.* LYSANDER,
> DEMETRIUS, HERMIA, *and* HELENA, *awake and start up.*

Good-morrow, friends. Saint Valentine is past:
Begin these woodbirds but to couple now?—*Ibid.*, iv. 1.

Egeus, I will overbear your will;
For, *in the temple, by and by* with us,
These couples shall eternally be knit:
And, *for the morning now is something worn,*
Our purpos'd hunting shall be set aside.
Away with us to Athens: three and three,
We'll hold a feast in great solemnity.—*Ibid.*, iv. 1.

   Are you sure
That we are awake? It seems to me
That yet we sleep, we dream. Do not you think
The duke *was here,* and *bid us follow him?*—
Yea; and my father.—
   And Hippolyta.—
And he did bid us follow to the temple.—

Why then, *we are awake : let's follow him ;*
And by the way let us recount our dreams.—*Mid. N. D.,* iv. 1.

Masters, *the duke is coming from the temple,* and *there is two or three lords and ladies more married.*—*Ibid.,* iv. 2.

The duke hath dined. Get your apparel together, good strings to your beards, new ribbons to your pumps; *meet presently at the palace;* every man look o'er his part; for the short and the long is, our play is preferred. . . . *No more words: away! go; away!*—*Ibid.,* iv. 2.

'Tis strange, my Theseus, that these lovers speak of.—
More strange than true.— . . .
But all *the story of the night* told over,
And all their minds transfigur'd so together,
More witnesseth than fancy's images,
And grows to something of great constancy;
But, howsoever, strange and admirable.—
Here come the lovers, full of joy and mirth.
Joy, gentle friends! joy and fresh days of love,
Accompany your hearts. . . .
Come now, what masks, what dances shall we have,
To wear away *this long age of three hours,*
Between our after-supper and bedtime?—*Ibid.,* v. 1.

The iron tougue of midnight hath told twelve :
Lovers, to bed; *'tis almost fairy time.*—*Ibid.,* v. 1.

Now it is the time of night,
    That the graves, all gaping wide,
Every one lets forth his sprite,
    In the churchway paths to glide;
And we fairies, *that do run*
    By the triple Hecate's team,
From the presence of the sun,
    Following darkness like a dream,
Now are frolic :—*Ibid.,* v. 1.

Now, until the break of day,
Through this house each fairy stray. . . .
Trip away; make no stay;
Meet me all *by break of day.*—*Ibid.,* v. 1.

If we shadows have offended,
Think but this (and all is mended),
That you have but slumber'd here,
While these visions did appear.
And this weak and idle theme,
No more yielding but a dream. . . .
So *good night unto you all.*—*Ibid.,* v. 1.

And now by slow hints :—

Now, fair Hippolyta, our nuptial hour
Draws on apace; *four happy days* bring in
Another moon: but, oh, methinks, *how slow*
This old moon wanes ! She *lingers my desires,*
Like to a stepdame, or a dowager,
Long withering out a young man's revenue.—
Four days will quickly steep themselves in nights;
Four nights will quickly dream away the time;
And then the moon, like to a silver bow
New bent in heaven, shall behold the night
Of our solemnities.—*Ibid.,* i. 1.

Take time to pause; and, *by the next new* moon
(The sealing-day betwixt my love and me
For everlasting bond of fellowship),

Upon that day either prepare to die
For disobedience to your father's will,
Or else to wed Demetrius.—*Mid. N. D.*, i. 1.

Demetrius, and Egeus, go along:
*I must employ you in some business
Against our nuptial;* and confer with you
Of something nearly that concerns yourselves.—*Ibid.*, i. 1.

If thou lov'st me, then,
Steal forth thy father's house *to-morrow night;*
And in the wood, a league without the town, . . .
There will I stay for thee.— . . .
In that same place thou hast appointed me,
To-morrow truly will I meet thee.—*Ibid.*, i. 1.

Helen, to you our minds we will unfold:
To-morrow night, when Phœbe doth behold
Her silver visage in the wat'ry glass,
Decking with liquid pearl the bladed grass
(A time that lovers' flights doth still conceal),
Through Athens' gates have we devised to steal.—
And in the wood, where often you and I
Upon faint primrose-beds were wont to lie,
Emptying our bosoms of their counsel sweet,
There my Lysander and myself shall meet; . . .
Keep word, Lysander: we must starve our sight
From lovers' food *till morrow deep midnight.*—*Ibid.*, i. 1.

I will go tell him of fair Hermia's flight:
Then to the wood will he, *to-morrow night*,
Pursue her.—*Ibid.*, i. 1.

Here is the scroll of every man's name, which is thought fit, through all Athens, to play in our interlude before the duke and duchess *on his wedding-day at night.*—*Ibid.*, i. 2.

But, masters, here are your parts: and I am to entreat you, request you, and desire you, to con them *by to-morrow night;* and meet me in the palace wood, a mile without the town, by moonlight; there will we rehearse.—*Ibid.*, i. 2.

How long within this wood intend you stay?—
Perchance *till after Theseus' wedding-day.*—*Ibid.*, ii. 2.

Doth the moon shine that night we play our play?—
A calendar, a calendar! look in the almanack; find out moonshine, find out moonshine.—
Yes, it doth shine *that night.*—*Ibid.*, iii. 1.

A crew of patches, rude mechanicals,
That work for bread upon Athenian stalls,
Were met together to rehearse a play,
Intended for great Theseus' nuptial day.—*Ibid.*, iii. 2.

The play of " The Merchant of Venice " furnishes notable instances of Shakespeare's system of dual Dramatic Time: he having given the impression of rapidly passing time, occupied in the transit to and from Venice and Belmont—an inconsiderable distance, as he has taken care incidentally to mark—and also the impression of sufficient length of time for the expiration of the date when the forfeiture in the bond becomes due. The skill with which the dramatist contrives to dwell upon the period of " three months " as that for which the money is required that Antonio signs the bond for, fixing that period fully in the mind of the hearer or reader ere making the Jew substitute a vaguely stated period by the words, " if you repay me not *on such a day* "—the mode in which Shakespeare sways the imagination to believe that this vaguely stated period transpires while only a brief period is actually shown to transpire—form part of his admirable system, as original in invention as it is perfect in its carrying out. First, we have the abbreviating process :—

> *Good-morrow*, my good lords.—
> Good signiors both, when shall we laugh ? Say, when ? . . .
> My Lord Bassanio, since you have found Antonio,
> We two will leave you : but, *at dinner-time*,
> I pray you, have in mind where we must meet.—*Mer. of V.*, i. 1.

> Come, good Lorenzo.   Fare ye well, awhile :
> I 'll end my exhortation *after dinner*.—
> Well, we will leave you, then, *till dinner-time*.—*Ibid.*, i. 1.

> Well ; tell me now, what lady is the same
> To whom you swore a secret pilgrimage,
> That you *to-day* promis'd to tell me of ?—*Ibid.*, i. 1.

> Go, *presently inquire*, and so will I,
> Where money is ; and I no question make,
> To have it of my trust, or for my sake.—*Ibid.*, i. 1.

The four strangers seek for you, madam, *to take their leave :* and *there is a forerunner come from a fifth*, the Prince of Morocco ; who brings word, the prince his master *will be here to-night*.— . . . Come, Nerissa.   Sirrah, go before.   *Whiles we shut the gate upon one wooer, another knocks at the door.*—*Ibid.*, 1. 2.

May I speak with Antonio ?—If it please you *to dine* with us.—*Ibid.*, i. 3.

> Then *meet me forthwith at the notary's*.
> Give him direction for this merry bond ;
> And *I will go and purse the ducats straight !*
> I 'll to my house, left in the fearful guard
> Of an unthrifty knave ; and *presently*
> I will be with you.—
>   *Hie thee*, gentle Jew.—*Ibid.*, i. 3.

>   *Come, bring me unto my chance.*—
> First, forward to the temple : *after dinner*
> *Your hazard shall be made.*—*Ibid.*, ii. 1.

You may do so ; but *let it be so hasted, that supper be ready at farthest by five of the clock.*   See these letters delivered ; put the liveries to making ; and desire Gratiano *to come anon to my lodging.*—*Ibid.*, ii. 2.

>   Thou hast obtain'd thy suit :
> Shylock, thy master, *spoke with me this day*,
> And hath preferr'd thee, if it be preferment,
> To leave a rich Jew's service, to become
> The follower of so poor a gentleman.—*Ibid.*, ii. 2.

> These things bought, and orderly bestow'd,
> *Return in haste*, for *I do feast to-night*
> My best esteem'd acquaintance : *hie thee*, go.—*Ibid.*, ii. 2.

> Nay, but *I bar to-night ;* you shall not gage me
> *By what we do to-night.*—
>   No, that were pity :
> I would entreat you rather to put on
> Your boldest suit of mirth, for we have friends
> That purpose merriment.   But, fare you well ;
> I have some business.—
> And I must to Lorenzo and the rest :
> But *we will visit you at supper-time.*—*Ibid.*, ii. 2.

> And, Launcelot, *soon at supper* shalt thou see
> Lorenzo, who is thy new master's guest.—*Ibid.*, ii. 3.

Nay, we will *slink away in supper-time*,
Disguise us at my lodging, and return
All in an hour. . . .
'Tis now but four o'clock : we have *two hours*
To furnish us.—*Mer. of V.*, ii. 4.

Whither goest thou ?—
Marry, sir, to bid my old master, the Jew, *to sup to-night* with my new master, the
Christian.—*Ibid.*, ii. 4.

Gentlemen,
Will you prepare for this mask to-night ?
I am provided of a torch-bearer.—
Ay, marry, *I'll be gone about it straight.*—
And so will I.—
⠀⠀⠀⠀⠀⠀⠀⠀Meet me and Gratiano
At Gratiano's lodging *some hour hence. . . .*
Fair Jessica shall be my torch-bearer.—*Ibid.*, ii. 4.

I am bid forth to supper, Jessica :
⠀⠀⠀⠀⠀⠀. . . I am right loath to go :
There is some ill a-brewing towards my rest,
For I did dream of money-bags to-night.—
⠀⠀⠀⠀⠀⠀⠀⠀. . . By Jacob's staff, I swear
I have no mind of *feasting forth to-night :*
But I will go. . . .
⠀⠀⠀⠀⠀⠀. . . Well, Jessica, go in :
Perhaps I will return immediately.—Ibid., ii. 5.

This is the pent-house under which Lorenzo
Desir'd us to make stand.—
⠀⠀⠀⠀⠀⠀⠀⠀⠀*His hour is almost past.*—
And it is marvel he outdwells his hour,
For lovers ever run before the clock.—*Ibid.*, ii. 6.

⠀⠀⠀⠀⠀⠀⠀⠀So are you, sweet,
Even in the lovely garnish of a boy.
But come at once ;
For the close night doth play the runaway,
And we are stay'd for at Bassanio's feast.—
I will make fast the doors, and gild myself
With some more ducats, and *be with you straight. . . .*
What, *art thou come ? On, gentlemen ; away !*
Our masking mates by this time for us stay.—Ibid., ii. 6.

Fie, fie, Gratiano ! where are all the rest ?
'Tis nine o'clock ; our friends all stay for you.
No mask to-night : the wind is come about ;
Bassanio presently will go aboard :
I have sent twenty out to seek for you.—
I am glad on 't : I desire no more delight
Than *to be under sail and gone to-night.—Ibid.*, ii. 6.

Portia, *adieu. I have too griev'd a heart*
To take a tedious leave : thus lovers part.—Ibid., ii. 7.

Why, man, *I saw Bassanio under sail :*
With him is Gratiano gone along ;
And in their ship, I 'm sure, Lorenzo is not.—
The villain Jew *with outcries rais'd the duke ;*
Who went with him to search Bassanio's ship.—
He came too late, the ship was under sail :
But there the duke was given to understand
That *in a gondola were seen together*
Lorenzo and his amorous Jessica.
Besides Antonio certified the duke,
They were not with Bassanio in his ship.—*Ibid.*, ii. 8.

Quick, quick, I pray thee ; draw the curtain straight :
The Prince of Arragon *hath ta'en his oath,*
And comes to his election presently.—
Behold, there stand the caskets, noble prince:
If you choose that wherein I am contain'd,
Straight shall our nuptial rites be solemniz'd ;
But if you fail, *without more speech,* my lord,
You must be gone from hence immediately.—*Mer. of V.,* ii. 9.

Give me a key for this,
And *instantly unlock my fortunes here.* . . .
Sweet, *adieu.* I 'll keep my oath,
Patiently to bear my wroth. . . .
Come, draw the curtain, Nerissa. . . .
Madam, there is alighted at your gate
A young Venetian, one that comes before
To signify the approaching of his lord ;
. . . Yet I have not seen
So likely an embassador of love. . . .
Come, come, Nerissa ; *for I long to see*
Quick Cupid's post, that comes so mannerly.—*Ibid.,* ii. 9.

Let me choose ;
For, as I am, I live upon the rack.—*Ibid.,* iii. 2.

My eyes, my lord, *can look as swift as yours :*
You saw the mistress, I beheld the maid :
You lov'd, I lov'd ; for intermission
No more pertains to me, my lord, than you.
Your fortune stood upon the caskets there ;
And so did mine too, as the matter falls.—*Ibid.,* iii. 2.

Lorenzo and Salanio, *welcome hither ;*
If that *the youth of my new interest here*
Have power to bid you welcome.—*Ibid.,* iii. 2.

First, go with me to church and call me wife,
And *then away to Venice to your friend ;*
. . . *Come, away !*
For *you shall hence upon your wedding-day* . . .
O love, *despatch all business,* and *be gone !*—
Since I have your good leave to go away,
I will make haste : but, till I come again,
No bed shall e'er be guilty of my stay,
Nor rest be interposer 'twixt us twain.—*Ibid.,* iii. 2.

These griefs and losses have so bated me,
That *I shall hardly spare a pound of flesh*
To-morrow to my bloody creditor.—*Ibid.,* iii. 3.

Take this same letter,
And *use thou all the endeavour of a man*
In speed to Padua : see thou render this
Into my cousin's hand, Doctor Bellario ;
And, look, what notes and garments he doth give thee,
Bring them, I pray thee, *with imagin'd speed*
Unto the Tranect, to the common ferry
Which trades to Venice. *Waste no time in words,*
But get thee gone : I shall be there before thee. —
Madam, *I go with all convenient speed.*—*Ibid.,* iii. 4.

But, *come, I 'll tell thee all my whole device*
When I am in my coach, which stays for us
At the park gate ; and therefore *haste away,*
For *we must measure twenty miles to-day.*—*Ibid.,* iii. 4.

Go in, sirrah; bid them *prepare for dinner.*—That is done, sir; they have all stomachs.—Goodly lord, what a wit-snapper are you! then, bid them *prepare dinner.*— That is done too, sir ; only, cover is the word.— . . . Go to thy fellows; *bid them cover the table, serve in the meat, and we will come in to dinner.—Mer. of V.*, iii. 5.

> Nay, but ask my opinion, too, of that.—
> I will anon : *first let us go to dinner.— Ibid.*, iii. 5.

> Go one, and call the Jew into the court.—
> *He's ready at the door : he comes*, my lord.—*Ibid.*, iv. 1.

> Therefore, I do beseech you,
> Make no more offers, use no farther means,
> But, *with all brief and plain conveniency,*
> *Let me have judgment*, and the Jew his will.—*Ibid.*, iv. 1.

> Upon my power I may dismiss this court,
> *Unless Bellario*, a learned doctor,
> Whom I have sent for to determine this,
> *Come here to-day.*—
> My lord, *here stays without*
> *A messenger with letters from the doctor,*
> *New come from Padua.*—
> Bring us the letters; *call the messenger.*—*Ibid.*, iv. 1.

> *This letter from Bellario* doth commend
> A young and learned doctor to our court. . . .

" Your grace shall understand, that *at the receipt of your letter I am very sick :* but *in the instant that your messenger came*, in loving visitation was with me a young doctor. . . . I acquainted him with the cause in controversy between the Jew and Antonio the merchant: we turned o'er many books together: he is furnished with my opinion ; which, bettered with his own learning (the greatness whereof I cannot enough commend), *comes with him, at my importunity, to fill up your grace's request in my stead.*" . . . And here, *I take it, is the doctor come.* Give me your hand. Came you from old Bellario ?—

> I did, my lord.—
> You are welcome : *take your place.*—*Ibid.*, iv. 1.

> Sir, I entreat you *home with me to dinner.*—
> I humbly do desire your grace of pardon :
> *I must away this night toward Padua,*
> And *it is meet I presently set forth.* . . .
> Most worthy gentleman, I and my friend
> *Have by your wisdom been this day acquitted*
> *Of grievous penalties.*—*Ibid.*, iv. 1.

> Go, Gratiano, *run and overtake him ;*
> Give him the ring ; and bring him, if thou canst,
> Unto Antonio's house: *away ! make haste.*
> Come, you and I *will thither presently ;*
> And *in the morning early will we both*
> *Fly toward Belmont :* come, Antonio.—*Ibid.*, iv. 1.

> Inquire the Jew's house out, give him this deed,
> And let him sign it : *we 'll away to-night,*
> *And be a day before our husbands home.* . . .
> Fair sir, *you are well o'erta'en :*
> My lord Bassanio, upon more advice,
> Hath sent you here this ring ; and *doth entreat*
> *Your company at dinner.*—
> That cannot be. . . .
> *Away ! make haste :* thou know'st where I will tarry.—*Ibid.*, iv. 2.

> The moon shines bright : *in such a night as this,*
> When the sweet wind did gently kiss the trees,
> And they did make no noise—in such a night. . .
> *Who comes so fast in silence of the night ?*—*Ibid.*, v. 1

My mistress will *before the break of day*
Be here at Belmont.— . . .
　　　　　　　　. . . *My master will be here ere morning.*
Sweet soul, let's in, and there expect their coming.
And yet no matter : *why should we go in?*
My friend Stephano, signify, I pray you,
Within the house, *your mistress is at hand ;*
And bring your music forth into the air.
How sweet the moonlight sleeps upon this bank !
Here will we sit, and let the sounds of music
Creep in our ears : soft stillness *and the night*
Become the touches of sweet harmony.—*Mer of V.*, v. 1.

Dear lady, *welcome home.*—
We have been praying for our husbands' welfare,
Which speed, we hope, the better for our words.
Are they return'd ?—
　　　　　　　　Madam, they are not yet ;
But there is come a messenger before,
To signify their coming. . . .
Your husband is at hand ; I hear his trumpet.—*Ibid.*, v. 1.

This night, methinks, is but the daylight sick ;
It looks a little paler . . .
　　　　. . . *You are welcome home*, my lord.—*Ibid.*, v. 1.

And pardon me, my gentle Gratiano ;
For that same scrubbed boy, the doctor's clerk,
In lieu of this *last night* did lie with me.—*Ibid.*, v. 1.

Here is a letter, read it at your leisure ;
It comes from Padua, from Bellario :
There you shall find that Portia was the doctor ;
Nerissa there, her clerk : Lorenzo here
Shall witness *I set forth as soon as you,*
And even but now return'd ; I have not yet
Enter'd my house.—*Ibid.*, v. 1.

　　　　　　　　It is almost morning,
And yet I am sure you are not satisfied
Of these events at full.—*Ibid.*, v. 1.

Or *go to bed now, being two hours to-day.*—*Ibid.*, v. 1.

Then comes the prolonging process :—

Three thousand ducats; well.—Ay, sir, *for three months.*—*For three months ;* well. . . .
three thousand ducats *for three months*, and Antonio bound.—*Ibid.*, i. 3.

But soft ! *how many months* do you desire ?—*Ibid.*, i. 3.

And *for three months.*—I had forgot : *three months*, you told me so.—*Ibid.*, i. 3.

　　　　Three months from twelve, then let me see the rate.—*Ibid.*, i. 3.

Go with me to a notary, seal me there
Your single bond ; and, in a merry sport,
If you repay me not *on such a day,*
In such a place, such sum or sums as are
Express'd in the condition, let the forfeit
Be nominated for an equal pound
Of your fair flesh.—*Ibid.*, i. 3.

Why, fear not, man ; I will not forfeit it :
Within these two months—that's a month before
This bond expires—I do expect return
Of thrice three times the value of this bond.—*Ibid.*, i. 3.

My ships come home *a month before the day.*—*Ibid.*, i. 3.

Let good Antonio *look he keep his day,*
Or he shall pay for this.—

Marry, well remember'd.
I reasoned with a Frenchman *yesterday*,
Who told me—in the narrow seas that part
The French and English, there miscarrièd
A vessel of our country, richly fraught;
I thought upon Antonio when he told me;
And wish'd in silence that it were not his.—*Mer. of V.*, ii. 8.

I saw Bassanio and Antonio part;
Bassanio told him he would make some speed
Of his return: he answer'd, " Do not so;
Slubber not business for my sake, Bassanio,
But *stay the very riping of the time;*
And for the Jew's bond which he hath of me,
Let it not enter in your mind of love."—*Ibid.*, ii. 8.

What news on the Rialto?—Why, *yet it lives there unchecked*, that Antonio hath a ship of rich lading wrecked on the narrow seas.—*Ibid.*, iii. 1.

Do you hear whether Antonio have had any loss at sea or no?—There I have another bad match: a bankrupt, who *dare scarce show his head on the Rialto;* a beggar, that *was used to come so smug upon the mart:* let him look to his bond.—*Ibid.*, iii. 1.

How now, Tubal! *What news from Genoa? hast thou found my daughter?—I often came where I did hear of her, but cannot find her.—* . . . Would she were hears'd at my foot, and the ducats in her coffin! *No news of them?* Why, so: *and I know not what's spent in the search:* Why thou—loss upon loss! the thief gone with so much, *and so much to find the thief;* and no satisfaction, no revenge: nor no ill luck stirring but what lights o' my shoulders. . . .—Yes, other men have ill luck too. Antonio, *as I heard in Genoa,*—What, what, what? ill luck, ill luck?—Hath an argosy cast away, coming from Tripolis.—I thank God! I thank God! Is it true, is it true?—I spoke with some of the sailors that escaped the wreck.—I thank thee, good Tubal. Good news, good news! ha! ha! *Where? in Genoa?—Your daughter spent in Genoa,* as I heard, *one night fourscore ducats. . . . There came divers of Antonio's creditors in my company to Venice,* that swear he cannot choose but break. . . . *One of them showed me a ring, that he had of your daughter* for a monkey. . . . But Antonio is certainly undone.—Nay, that's true, that's very true. Go, Tubal, fee me an officer; *bespeak him a fortnight before.* I will have the heart of him, if he forfeit.—*Ibid.*, iii. 1.

I pray you, *tarry: pause a day or two*
Before you hazard; for, in choosing wrong,
I lose your company; therefore, *forbear awhile.* . . .
I would detain you here some month or two,
Before you venture for me. . . .
I speak too long; but *'tis to peize the time,*
To eke it, and to draw it out in length,
To stay you from election.—*Ibid.*, iii. 2.

He plies the duke at morning and at night;
And doth impeach the freedom of the state,
If they deny him justice: twenty merchants,
The duke himself, and the magnificoes
Of greatest port, *have all persuaded with him;*
But none can drive him from the envious plea
Of forfeiture, of justice, and his bond.—
When I was with him, I have heard him swear,
To Tubal, and to Chus, his countrymen,
That he would rather have Antonio's flesh
Than twenty times the value of the sum
That he did owe him.—*Ibid.*, iii. 2.

My ships have all miscarried, *my creditors grow cruel, my estate is very low, my bond to the Jew is forfeit;* and since in paying it, it is impossible I should live, all debts are cleared between you and I, if I might see you at my death. Notwithstanding, use your pleasure: if your love do not persuade you to come, let not my letter.—*Ibid.*, iii. 2.

Gaoler, look to him : tell not me of mercy. . . .
Gaoler, look to him.—
　　　　　　　　Hear me yet, good Shylock.—
I 'll have my bond; speak not against my bond :
I have sworn an oath that I will have my bond. . . .
The duke shall grant me justice.　I do wonder,
Thou naughty gaoler, that thou art so fond
To come abroad with him at his request.—
I pray thee, hear me speak.—
I 'll have my bond; I will not hear thee speak :
I 'll have my bond ; and therefore speak no more.
I 'll not be made a soft and dull-ey'd fool,
To shake the head, *relent*, and sigh, *and yield*
To Christian intercessors.　Follow not ;
I 'll have no speaking : I will have my bond.—*Mer. of V.*, iii. 3.

Lorenzo, *I commit into your hands*
The husbandry and manage of my house,
Until my lord's return : for mine own part,
I have toward heaven breath'd a secret vow
To live in prayer and contemplation,
Only attended by Nerissa here,
Until her husband and my lord's return :
There is a monastery two miles off,
And there we will abide.—Ibid., iii. 4.

My people do already know my mind,
And will acknowledge you and Jessica
In place of lord Bassanio and myself.
So fare you well, till we shall meet again.—
Fair thoughts and happy hours attend on you !—Ibid., iii. 4.

Shylock, the world thinks, and I think so too,
That thou but lead'st this fashion of thy malice
To the last hour of act ; and then, 'tis thought,
Thou 'lt show thy mercy and remorse, more strange
Than is thy strange apparent cruelty ;
And where thou now exact'st the penalty
(Which is a pound of this poor merchant's flesh),
Thou wilt not only loose the forfeiture,
But, touch'd with human gentleness and love,
Forgive a moiety of the principal ;
Glancing an eye of pity on *his losses*,
That have of late so huddled on his back,
Enow to press a royal merchant down.—*Ibid.*, iv. 1.

I pray you, is my master yet return'd ?—
He is not, nor *we have not heard from him.—Ibid.*, v. 1.

In the enchanting sylvan drama of " As You Like It," Shakespeare
has combined the effect of a transitory scene of romantic life with the
effect of enough space of time to allow a vision of an indefinite number
of days, weeks—what you will—passing before the imagination as
spent in that most perfect of poetical woods, the Forest of Arden.　To
give the effect of transitoriness befitting the few hours wherein a play
is performed, he gives many more hints of short time than of long
time ; and he aids this by the introduction of abruptness in event and
promptness in action—having no fewer than four cases of love at first
sight (Orlando and Rosalind, Oliver and Celia, Phœbe and Ganymede,
Touchstone and Audrey), together with the sudden conversion of the
usurping duke, related in the last scene of the play.　The numerous
hints of Short Time are these:—

Was not Charles, the duke's wrestler, here to speak with me?—So please you, *he is here at the door, and importunes access to you.*—Call him in. 'Twill be a good way; and *to-morrow the wrestling is.*—*Good-morrow* to your worship. . . . *You wrestle to-morrow* before the new duke?—Marry, do I, sir; . . . *To-morrow,* sir, *I wrestle* for my credit.—*As You L.,* i. 1.

If he *come to-morrow,* I'll give him his payment. . . . *it shall not be so long ; this wrestler shall clear all :* nothing remains but that I kindle the boy thither; *which now I'll go about.*—*Ibid.,* i. 1.

Shall we see this wrestling, cousin?—You must, if you stay here; *for here is the place appointed for the wrestling, and they are ready to perform it.*—*Yonder, sure, they are coming :* let us now stay and see it.—*Ibid.,* i. 2.

Is it possible, *on such a sudden, you should fall into so strong a liking with old Sir Rowland's youngest son ?*—*Ibid.,* i. 3.

Look, here comes the duke.—With his eyes full of anger.
    Mistress, *despatch you with your safest haste,*
    And get you from our court.—*Ibid.,* i. 3.

          You, niece, provide yourself:
If you outstay the time, upon mine honour,
And in the greatness of my word, you die.—*Ibid.,* i. 3.

            Let's away,
And get our jewels and our wealth together ;
Devise the fittest time and safest way
To hide us from pursuit that will be made
After my flight. Now go we in content
To liberty, and not to banishment.—*Ibid.,* i. 3.

The melancholy Jaques grieves at that, . . .
To-day my lord of Amiens and myself
Did steal behind him, as he lay along
Under an oak. . . .—Show me the place :
I love to cope him in these sullen fits,
For then he's full of matter.—
I'll bring you to him straight.—*Ibid.,* ii. 1.

The ladies, her attendants of her chamber,
Saw her a-bed; and, *in the morning early,*
They found the bed untreasur'd of their mistress.—
. . . She believes, wherever they are gone,
That youth is surely in their company.—
Send to his brother ; fetch that gallant hither :
If he be absent, bring his brother to me;
I'll make him find him : *do this suddenly :
And let not search and inquisition quail
To bring again these foolish runaways.*—*Ibid.,* ii. 2.

Why would you be so fond to overcome
The bony priser of the humorous duke?
Your praise is come too swiftly home before you.—*Ibid.,* ii. 3.

Your brother . . .
Hath heard your praises; and *this night he means
To burn the lodging were you use to lie,
And you within it.*—*Ibid.,* ii. 3.

Why, whither, Adam, wouldst thou have me go?—
No matter whither, so you come not here.—
    . . . *Come thy ways ; we'll go along together ;*
And ere we have thy youthful wages spent,
We'll light upon some settled low content.—
Master, go on, and I will follow thee
To the last gasp, with truth and loyalty.—*Ibid.,* ii. 3.

Now am I in Arden ; the more fool I.—*Ibid.,* ii. 4.

Good even to you, friend.—
And to you, gentle sir, and to you all.—*As You L.*, ii. 4.

Assuredly, the thing is to be sold:
Go with me : if you like, upon report,
The soil, the profit, and this kind of life,
I will your very faithful feeder be,
And buy it with your gold right suddenly.—Ibid., ii. 4.

Well, I 'll end the song. Sirs, *cover the while ; the duke will drink under this tree.*
He hath been all *this day* to look you.—And I have been all *this day* to avoid him.—
Ibid., ii. 5.

For my sake be comfortable; hold death awhile at the arm's end: *I will here be
with thee presently ;* and if I bring thee not something to eat, I will give thee leave to
die : but if thou diest before I come, thou art a mocker of my labour.   Well said!
thou lookest cheerly; *and I 'll be with thee quickly.—Ibid.*, ii. 6.

My lord, *he is but even now gone hence :*
Here was he merry, hearing of a song. . . .
Go, seek him : tell him I would speak with him.—
He saves my labour *by his own approach.—Ibid.*, ii. 7.

" *Good-morrow*, fool," quoth I.   " No, sir," quoth he,
" Call me not fool till Heaven hath sent me fortune : "
And then he drew a dial from his poke,
And, looking on it with lack-lustre eye,
Says very wisely, " *It is ten o'clock :*
Thus may we see," quoth he, " how the world wags :
'*Tis but an hour ago since it was nine ;
And after one hour more 'twill be eleven ;*
And so, from hour to hour,we ripe and ripe,
And then, from hour to hour, we rot and rot ;
And thereby hangs a tale.—*Ibid.*, ii. 7.

Then, *but forbear your food a little while,*
Whiles, like a doe, I go to find my fawn,
And give it food.   There is an old poor man,
Who after me hath many a weary step
Limp'd in pure love : *till he be first suffic'd,*
Oppress'd with two weak evils, age and hunger,
I will not touch a bit.—
                    Go find him out,
And we will nothing waste till you return.—Ibid., ii. 7.

Welcome.   Set down your venerable burden,
And let him feed.—
                    I thank you most for him. . . .
Welcome ; fall to.—Ibid., ii. 7.

More villain thou.   Well, push him out of doors ;
And let my officers of such a nature
Make an extent upon his house and lands :
Do this expediently, and turn him going.—Ibid., iii. 1.

I pray you, *what is 't o'clock ?* You should ask me, what time o' day: there's no clock
in the forest.—*Ibid.*, iii. 2.

My cote . . . *Go with me to it,* and I 'll show it you : and, by the way, you shall tell
me where in the forest you live. *Will you go ?*—With all my heart, good youth.—Nay,
you must call me Rosalind. *Come, sister, will you go ?—Ibid.*, iii. 2.

Come apace, good Audrey ; I will fetch up your goats, Audrey. And how, Audrey ?
Am I the man yet ? Doth my simple feature content you ? . . . *I am here with thee
and thy goats,* as the most capricious poet, honest Ovid, was among the Goths.—
Ibid., iii. 3.

Be it as it may be, *I will marry thee :* and to that end, I have been with Sir Oliver
Mar-text, the vicar of the next village ; who *hath promised to meet me in this place of
the forest, and to couple us* . . . *Here comes Sir Oliver.* Sir Oliver Mar-text, you are

well met: *will you despatch us here under this tree*, or shall we go with you to your chapel?—Is there none here to give the woman? . . . She must be given, or the marriage is not lawful.—*Proceed, proceed:* I 'll give her.—*Good even*, good Master What-ye-call 't: . . . *even a toy in hand here*, sir: nay, pray, be covered.— *Will you be married, motley?*—*As You L.*, iii. 3.

Why did he swear *he would come this morning*, and comes not?—*Ibid.*, iii. 4.

> If you will see a pageant truly play'd,
> Between the pale complexion of true love
> And the red glow of scorn and proud disdain,
> *Go hence a little*, and I shall conduct you,
> If you will mark it.—
>   *O come, let us remove:*
> The sight of lovers feedeth those in love.
> *Bring us to this sight.*—*Ibid.*, iii. 4.

> Dead shepherd, *now I find* thy saw of might,—
> " Who ever lov'd that lov'd not *at first sight?* "—*Ibid.*, iii. 5.

> I 'll write to him a very taunting letter,
> And thou shalt bear it: wilt thou, Silvius?—
> Phœbe, *with all my heart*.—
>   *I 'll write it straight.*—*Ibid.*, iii. 5.

Good day, and happiness, dear Rosalind! . . .

Why, how now, Orlando! where have you been all this while? You a lover? An you serve me such another trick, never come in my sight more.—My fair Rosalind, *I come within an hour of my promise*.—Break an hour's promise in love! He that will divide a minute into a thousand parts, and break but a part of the thousandth part of a minute in the affairs of love, it may be said of him, that Cupid hath clapped him o' the shoulder, but I 'll warrant him heart-whole.—*Ibid.*, iv. 1.

Come, woo me, woo me; for now I am in a holiday humour, and like enough to consent.—*Ibid.*, iv. 1.

For these two hours, Rosalind, I will leave thee.—Alas, dear love! *I cannot lack thee two hours*.—I must attend the duke at dinner: *by two o'clock I will be with thee again*.— . . . *Two o'clock is your hour?* . . . If you break one jot of your promise, or *come one minute behind your hour*, I will think you the most pathetical break-promise.—*Ibid.*, iv. 1.

I 'll tell thee, Aliena, *I cannot be out of the sight of Orlando:* I 'll go find a shadow, and *sigh till he come*.—*Ibid.*, iv. 1.

How say you now? *Is it not past two o'clock?* and here much Orlando! . . . Look, *who comes here?*—

> My errand is to you, fair youth;
> My gentle *Phœbe did bid me give you this:*   [*Giving a letter.*
> I know not the contents. . . .

Well, *go your way to her*, . . . If you be a true lover, *hence, and not a word;* for *here comes more company.*—

> Good morrow, fair ones: pray you, if you know
> Where in the purlieus of this forest stands
> A sheepcote, fenc'd about with olive-trees?—
> West of this place, down in the neighbour bottom: . . .
> But *at this hour* the house doth keep itself;
> There's none within. . . .
> *When last the young Orlando parted from you,*
> *He left a promise to return again*
> *Within an hour.*—*Ibid.*, iv. 3.

> *In brief, he led me to the gentle duke,*
> Who gave me fresh array and entertainment,
> Committing me unto my brother's love;
> *Who led me instantly unto his cave,*
> There stripp'd himself, and here upon his arm
> The lioness had torn some flesh away,
> Which all this time had bled; and now he fainted,
> And cried, in fainting, upon Rosalind.

> *Brief*, I recover'd him, bound up his wound ;
> And, *after some small space*, being strong at heart,
> *He sent me hither*, stranger as I am,
> *To tell this story, that you might excuse*
> *His broken promise.*—*As You L.*, iv. 3.

Pray you, draw homewards. Good sir, *go with us.*—*That will I, for I must bear answer back* how you excuse my brother, Rosalind.— . . . *Will you go ?*—*Ibid.*, iv. 3.

Good even, Audrey.—God ye *good even*, William.—And *good even* to you, sir.—*Good even*, gentle friend.—*Ibid.*, v. 1.

Therefore tremble, and *depart.*—Do, good William.—God rest you merry, sir.—Our master and mistress seek you ; *come, away, away !*—*Trip, Audrey ; trip, Audrey. I attend, I attend.*—*Ibid.*, v. 1.

Is 't possible, that *on so little acquaintance you should like her ?* that, *but seeing, you should love her ?* and, *loving, woo ?* and, *wooing, she should grant ?* and will you persèver to enjoy her ?—Neither call the giddiness of it in question, the poverty of her, *the small acquaintance, my sudden wooing,* nor *her sudden consenting ;* but say with me, I love Aliena ; say with her, that she loves me ; *consent with both,* that we may enjoy each other ; it shall be to your good ; for my father's house, and all the revenue that was old Sir Rowland's *will I estate upon you, and here live and die a* shepherd.—*You have my consent. Let your wedding be to-morrow :* thither will I invite the duke, and all his contented followers. *Go you and prepare Aliena ;* for look you, *here comes my Rosalind.*—*Ibid.*, v. 2.

There was never anything so sudden, but the fight of two rams, and Cæsar's thrasonical brag of—" I came, saw, and overcame :" for your brother and my sister *no sooner met, but they looked ; no sooner looked, but they loved ; no sooner loved, but they sighed ; no sooner sighed, but they asked one another the reason ; no sooner knew the reason, but they sought the remedy : and in these degrees have they made a pair of stairs to marriage, which they will climb incontinent. . . . They shall be married to-morrow,* and I will bid the duke to the nuptial.—*Ibid.*, v. 2.

By so much the more shall I *to-morrow* be at the height of heart-heaviness, by how much I shall think my brother happy in having what he wishes for.—Why, then, *to-morrow* I cannot serve your turn for Rosalind ?—I can live no longer by thinking.— I will weary you, then, no longer with idle talking. . . . If you do love Rosalind so near the heart as your gesture cries it out, *when your brother marries Aliena, shall you marry her :* . . . it is not impossible to me, if it appear not inconvenient to you, *to set her before your eyes to-morrow.* . . . Therefore, put you in your best array, bid your friends ; for *if you will be married to-morrow,* you shall ; and to Rosalind, if you will. —*Ibid.*, v. 2.

To-morrow meet me all together. I will marry you, if ever I marry woman, and *I 'll be married to-morrow :* I will satisfy you, if ever I satisfied man, and *you shall be married to-morrow :* I will content you, if what pleases you contents you, and *you shall be married to-morrow.*—*Ibid.*, v. 2.

To-morrow is the joyful day, Audrey ; *to-morrow will we be married.*—*Ibid.*, v. 3.

> I have promis'd to make all this matter even.
> Keep you your word, O duke, to give your daughter ;
> You yours, Orlando, to receive his daughter :
> Keep your word, Phœbe, that you 'll marry me,
> Or else, refusing me, to wed this shepherd :
> Keep your word, Silvius, that you 'll marry her,
> If she refuse me : *and from hence I go,*
> *To make these doubts all even.*—*Ibid.*, v. 4.

> *Here's eight that must take hands,*
> *To join in Hymen's bands.* . . .
> Whiles a wedlock-hymn we sing,
> Feed yourselves with questioning ;
> *That reason wonder may diminish,*
> *How thus we met, and these things finish.*—*Ibid.*, v. 4.

And to the skirts of this wild wood he came ;
Where, *meeting with an old religious man,*

> *After some question with him, was converted*
> *Both from his enterprise and from the world ;*
> His crown bequeathing to his banish'd brother,
> And all their lands restor'd to them again,
> That were with him exiled.—*As You L.*, v. 4.

> *Proceed, proceed :* we will begin these rites,
> As we do trust they'll end, in true delights.—*Ibid.*, v. 4.

The hints of Long Time are these:—

There's no news at the court, sir, but *the old news :* that is the old duke is banished by his younger brother, the new duke. . . . Where will the old duke live ?—They say, he is already in the forest of Arden, and a many merry men with him; and *there they live* like the old Robin Hood of England : they say, *many young gentlemen flock to him every day*, and *fleet the time carelessly*, as they did in the golden world.—*Ibid.*, i. 1.

> But I can tell you, that *of late* this duke
> Hath ta'en displeasure 'gainst his gentle niece,
> Grounded upon no other argument,
> But that *the people praise her for her virtues*,
> *And pity her for her good father's sake.*—*Ibid.*, i. 2.

> *Within these ten days* if that thou be'st found
> So near our public court as twenty miles,
> Thou diest for it.—*Ibid.*, i. 3.

> Ay, Celia ; we stay'd her for your sake,
> Else had she with her father rang'd along.—
> I did not *then* entreat to have her stay ;
> It was your pleasure, and your own remorse :
> *I was too young that time* to value her ;
> But now I know her : if she be a traitor,
> Why so am I ; we still have slept together ;
> Rose at an instant, learn'd, play'd, eat together ;
> And wheresoe'er we went, like Juno's swans,
> Still we went coupled and inseparable.—*Ibid.*, i. 3.

> I pray thee, if it stand with honesty,
> Buy thou the cottage, pasture, and the flock,
> And thou shalt have to pay for it of us.—
> And we will mend thy wages. *I like this place,*
> *And willingly could waste my time in it.*—*Ibid.*, ii. 4.

I'll give you a verse to this note, that I made *yesterday* in despite of my invention.— *Ibid.*, ii. 5.

> Find out thy brother, wheresoe'er he is ;
> Seek him with candle ; bring him dead or living,
> *Within this twelvemonth*, or turn thou no more
> To seek a living in our territory.—*Ibid.*, iii. 1.

And *how like you this shepherd's life*, Master Touchstone ?—*Ibid.*, iii. 2.

Is it a man ?—And *a chain, that you once wore*, about his neck. Change you colour ?—*Ibid.*, iii. 2.

But doth he know that I am in this forest, and in man's apparel ? *Looks he as freshly as he did the day he wrestled ?*—*Ibid.*, iii. 2.

Where dwell you, pretty youth ?—With this shepherdess, my sister ; *here in the skirts of the forest*, like fringe upon a petticoat.—*Ibid.*, iii. 2.

There is a man *haunts the forest*, that abuses our young plants with carving Rosalind on their barks.—*Ibid.*, iii. 2.

I would cure you, if you would but call me Rosalind, and *come every day to my cote*, and woo me.—*Ibid.*, iii. 2.

He attends here on the duke your father.—I met the duke *yesterday*, and had much question with him.—*Ibid.*, iii. 4.

> Mistress and master, *you have oft inquir'd*
> After the shepherd that complain'd of love.—*Ibid.*, iii. 4.

And *he hath bought the cottage and the bounds*
That the old carlot once was master of.—*As You L.*, iii. 5.

O, *I have heard him speak of that same brother.*—*Ibid.*, iv. 3.

We shall find a time, Audrey; *patience,* gentle Audrey.—*Ibid.*, v. 1.

My lord, *the first time that I ever saw him,*
Methought he was a brother to your daughter.—*Ibid.*, v. 4.

The Dramatic Time in "The Taming of the Shrew" is so managed as to give the duly brief effect of a play witnessed at a sitting by Kit Sly, the tinker; who, in the Induction, is brought, drunk and fast asleep, by a nobleman's freak to the luxurious mansion where he is persuaded he is its proprietor, and has a comedy performed to divert him. But while this duly brief effect is given, the no less requisite protracted effect is presented that may allow of the needful space for Petruchio to work the cure of his shrewish bride. Accordingly, the effect of brevity is produced by such touches as the following:—

I pray, sir, tell me, is it possible
That *love should of a sudden take such hold?*—*Tam. of S.*, i. 1.

Tranio, *at once*
Uncase thee; take my colour'd hat and cloak:
When Biondello comes, he waits on thee.—*Ibid.*, i. 1.

I come to wive it wealthily in Padua;
If wealthily, then happily in Padua.— . . .
I can, Petruchio, help thee to a wife
With wealth enough, and young, and beauteous;
Brought up as best becomes a gentlewoman:
Her only fault (and that is faults enough)
Is, that she is intolerable curst,
And shrewd, and froward; . . .—
Hortensio, peace! thou know'st not gold's effect:
Tell me her father's name, *and 'tis enough;*
For I will board her, though she chide as loud
As thunder. . . .
I will not sleep, Hortensio, *till I see her.*—*Ibid.*, i. 2.

Now shall my friend Petruchio *do me grace;*
And offer me, disguis'd in sober robes,
To old Baptista as a schoolmaster
Well seen in music, to instruct Bianca;
That so I may, by this device, at least
Have leave and leisure to make love to her.—*Ibid.*, i. 2.

Trow you *whither I am going?* To Baptista Minola.
I promis'd to inquire carefully
About a schoolmaster for the fair Bianca:
And, by good fortune, I have lighted well
On this young man; for learning and behaviour
Fit for her turn; well read in poetry,
And other books.—*Ibid.*, i. 2.

Please ye we may contrive *this afternoon.*—*Ibid.*, i. 2.

I am a gentleman of Verona, sir,
That—hearing of her beauty and her wit,
Her affability and bashful modesty,
Her wondrous qualities and mild behaviour—
Am bold to show myself a forward guest
Within your house, to make mine eye the witness
Of that report which I so oft have heard.—*Ibid.*, ii. 1.

Pardon me, sir, the boldness is mine own;
That, being a stranger in this city here,

Do make myself a suitor to your daughter,
Unto Bianca, fair and virtuous.—*Tam. of S.,* ii. 1.

Sirrah, *lead these gentlemen*
To my daughters; and tell them both,
These are their tutors: bid them use them well.
We will go walk a little in the orchard,
And then to dinner. You are passing welcome,
And so I pray you all to think yourselves.—
Signior Baptista, *my business asketh haste,*
And every day I cannot come to woo.—*Ibid.,* ii. 1.

Signior Petruchio, will you go with us,
Or shall I send my daughter Kate to you?—
I pray you do; I will attend her here,
And woo her with some spirit when she comes. . . .
If she deny to wed, *I 'll crave the day*
When I shall ask the banns, and when be married.
But here she comes; and now, Petruchio, *speak.*
Good-morrow, Kate; for that 's your name, I hear.—*Ibid.,* ii. 1.

And therefore, *setting all this chat aside,*
Thus in plain terms: *your father hath consented*
That you shall be my wife; your dowry 'greed on;
And, will you, nill you, I will marry you. . . .
Here comes your father: never make denial;
I must and will have Katharine to my wife.—
Now, Signior Petruchio, how speed you with my daughter?--
How but well, sir? how but well? . . .
                . . . We have 'greed so well together,
That upon Sunday is the wedding-day.—*Ibid.,* ii. 1.

Give me thy hand, Kate: I will unto Venice,
To buy apparel 'gainst the wedding-day.
Provide the feast, father, and bid the guests;
I will be sure, my Katharine shall be fine.—
I know not what to say: but *give me your hands;*
God send you joy, Petruchio! 'tis a match.—
                . . . *Sunday comes apace:*
We will have rings, and things, and fine array;
And, kiss me, Kate, *we will be married o' Sunday.*—
Was ever match clapp'd up so suddenly?—*Ibid.,* ii. 1.

But now, Baptista, *to your younger daughter:*
Now is the day we long have look'd for:
I am your neighbour, and was suitor first.—*Ibid.,* ii. 1.

Fiddler, forbear; you grow too forward, sir:
Have you *so soon* forgot the entertainment
Her sister Katharine welcom'd you withal?—
. . . When in music we have *spent an hour,*
Your lecture shall have leisure for as much.—*Ibid.,* iii. 1.

Mistress, your father prays you leave your books,
And help to dress your sister's chamber up:
You know, *to-morrow is the wedding-day.*—
Farewell, sweet masters both; *I must be gone.*—
'Faith, mistress, *then I have no cause to stay.*—*Ibid.,* iii. 1.

Signior Lucentio, *this is the 'pointed day*
That Katharine and Petruchio should be married.—*Ibid.,* iii. 2.

Why, sir, you know *this is your wedding-day.*—*Ibid.,* iii. 2.

But where is Kate? *I stay too long from her:*
The morning wears, 'tis time we were at church. . . .
. . . What a fool am I to chat with you,
When I should bid good-morrow to my bride,
And seal the title with a lovely kiss.—*Ibid.,* iii. 2.

Were it not that my fellow schoolmaster
Doth watch Bianca's steps so narrowly,
'Twere good, methinks, *to steal our marriage ;*
Which once perform'd let all the world say no,
I'll keep mine own, despite of all the world.—*Tam. of S.*, iii. 2.

That, at the parting, all the church did echo :
And *I*, seeing this, *came thence for very shame ;*
And after me, I know, *the rout is coming.*
Such a mad marriage never was before :
Hark, hark ! I hear the minstrels play.—
Gentlemen and friends, I thank you for your pains :
I know *you think to dine with me to-day*,
And have prepared great store of wedding cheer ;
But so it is, *my haste doth call me hence*,
And therefore here I mean to take my leave.—
Is 't possible you will away to-night ?—
I must away to-day before night come. . . .
Dine with my father, drink a health to me ;
For I must hence ; and farewell to you all.—
Let us entreat you stay till after dinner.—
It may not be—
              Let me entreat you.—
It cannot be.—*Ibid.*, iii. 2.

But for my bonny Kate, *she must with me.*
          . . . Grumio,
Draw forth thy weapon, we 're beset with thieves ;
Rescue thy mistress, if thou be a man.
Fear not, sweet wench, they shall not touch thee, Kate :
I 'll buckler thee against a million.—
Nay, *let them go*, a couple of quiet ones.—
Went they not quickly, I should die with laughing.—*Ibid.*, iii. 2.

Is my master and his wife coming, Grumio ?—
O, ay, Curtis, *ay ;* and therefore fire, fire ; cast on no water . . . the carpets laid,
and everything in order ?—
All ready. . . . All things is ready. How near is our master ?—*E'en at hand,
alighted by this ;* and therefore be not—Cock's passion, silence ! *I hear my master.*—
Where be these knaves ? What, no man at door, to hold my stirrup, nor to take my
horse ! . . . *Go, rascals, go, and fetch my supper in.* . . . Sit down, Kate, and
welcome.—*Ibid.*, iv. 1.

What 's this, mutton ?—
              Ay.—
                     Who brought it ?—
                              I.—
'Tis burnt ; and so is all the meat.
What dogs are these ! Where is the rascal cook ?
How durst you, villains, bring it from the dresser,
And *serve it thus to me* that love it not ?
There, *take it to you*, trenchers, cups, and all : . . .
I tell thee, Kate, 'twas burnt and dried away : . . .
And better 'twere, that both of us did fast,
Since, of ourselves, ourselves are choleric,
Than feed it with such over-roasted flesh.
Be patient ; to-morrow 't shall be mended,
And, *for this night*, we 'll fast for company :
Come, I will bring thee to thy bridal chamber.—*Ibid.*, iv. 1.

Away, away ! for he is coming hither.— . . .
She eat no meat to-day, nor none shall eat ;
Last night she slept not, *nor to-night she shall not.*—*Ibid.*, iv. 1.

Quick proceeders, marry!   Now, tell me, I pray,
You that durst swear that your mistress Bianca
Lov'd none in the world so well as Lucentio.—*Tam. of S.*, iv. 2.

Signior Lucentio,
Here is my hand, *and here I firmly vow*
Never to woo her more ; but do forswear her, . . .—
And here I take the like unfeigned oath,
Never to marry with her, though she would entreat: . . .—
For me, that I may surely keep mine oath,
I will be married to a wealthy widow,
Ere three days pass. . . .—Then *we are rid of Licio*.—
I' faith, he'll have a lusty widow now,
That shall be woo'd and wedded in a day.—*Ibid.*, iv. 2.

Kate, *eat apace; and now*, my honey love,
Will we return unto thy father's house. . . .
What, *hast thou din'd ?* The tailor stays thy leisure.—*Ibid.*, iv. 3.

We will hence forthwith
To feast and sport us at thy father's house.
Go, call my men, and let us straight to him;
And bring our horses unto Long-lane end;
There will we mount, and thither walk on foot.
Let's see; I think *'tis now some seven o'clock,*
And well we come there by dinner-time.—
I dare assure you, sir, *'tis almost two;*
And *'twill be supper-time ere you come there.*—
It shall be seven, ere I go to horse.—*Ibid.*, iv. 3.

I told him that your father was at Venice
And that *you look'd for him this day* in Padua.—
Here comes Baptista. . . .
Signior Baptista, *you are happily met.*
Sir, *this is the gentleman I told you of.* . . .

My son Lucentio
Made me acquainted with a weighty cause
Of love between your daughter and himself. . . .

. . . *To stay him not too long,*
I am content, in a good father's care,
To have him match'd; and, if you please to like
No worse than I, upon some good agreement,
Me shall you find ready and willing
With one consent to have her so bestow'd. . . .

. . . If you say no more than this,
That like a father you will deal with him,
And pass my daughter a sufficient dower,
The match is made, and all is done:
Your son shall have my daughter with consent.—*Ibid.*, iv. 4.

Then at my lodging, an it like you:
There doth my father lie; and there, *this night*,
We'll pass the business privately and well.
Send for your daughter by your servant here;
My boy *shall fetch the scrivener presently.*
The worst is this—that, *at so slender warning*,
You're like to have a thin and slender pittance.—
It likes me well.   Cambio, *hie you home,*
And bid Bianca make her ready straight;
And, if you will, tell what hath happen'd—
Lucentio's father is arriv'd in Padua,
And how she's like to be Lucentio's wife.—
I pray the gods she may with all my heart!—
Dally not with the gods, but get thee gone.
Signior Baptista, *shall I lead the way?* . . .—
I follow you.—*Ibid.*, iv. 4.

His daughter *is to be brought by you to the supper.*—And then ?—The old priest at St. Luke is at your command at all hours.—And what of all this ?—I cannot tell ; expect they are busied about a counterfeit assurance : take you assurance of her *cum privilegio ad imprimendum solum; to the chuich : take the priest, clerk, and some sufficient* honest witnesses. If this be not what you look for, *I have no more to say.* . . . *I cannot tarry :* I knew a wench *married in an afternoon as she went to the garden for parsley* to stuff a rabbit ; and so may you, sir ; and so, adieu, sir. My master hath appointed me to go to St. Luke's, *to bid the priest be ready to come against you come* with your appendix.—*I may, and will,* if she be so contented : . . . *I 'll roundly go about her.*—*Tam. of S.,* iv. 4.

Come on, o' God's name ; *once more toward our father's.*—*Ibid.,* iv. 5.

Softly and *swiftly,* sir, *for the priest is ready.*—*I fly,* Biondello : but they may chance to need thee at home ; therefore leave us.—Nay, faith, I 'll see the church o' your back ; and then *come back to my master as soon* as I can. . . . Sir, *here 's the door, this is Lucentio's house :* my father's bears more toward the market-place ; *thither must I,* and *here I leave you,* sir.—*Ibid.,* v. 1.

I have seen them in the church together : God send 'em good shipping !—*Ibid.,* v. 1.

> Bianca's love
> Made me exchange my state with Tranio,
> While he did bear my countenance in the town ;
> *And happily I have arriv'd at the last*
> *Unto the wished haven of my bliss.*—*Ibid.,* v. 1.

> My fair Bianca, bid my father welcome,
> While I with self-same kindness welcome thine.
> Brother Petruchio, sister Katharina—
> And thou Hortensio, with thy loving widow—
> *Feast with the best, and welcome to my house.*—*Ibid.,* v. 2.

> Now fair befall thee, good Petruchio !
> The wager thou hast won ; and I will add
> Unto their losses twenty-thousand crowns ;
> Another dowry to another daughter,
> *For she is chang'd,* as she had never been.—*Ibid.,* v. 2.

> *Come,* Kate, *we 'll to bed.*
> We three are married, but you two are sped.
> 'Twas I won the wager, though you hit the white ;
> And, being a winner, God give you *good night.*—*Ibid.,* v. 2.

While, on the contrary, the effect of prolongation is produced by such touches as those that follow :—

> Here let us breathe, and haply *institute*
> *A course of learning and ingenious studies.*
> . . . *for the time I study,*
> Virtue, and that part of philosophy
> Will I apply, that treats of happiness
> By virtue specially to be achiev'd.
> Tell me thy mind ; for I have Pisa left,
> And am to Padua come, as he that leaves
> A shallow plash, to plunge him in the deep,
> And *with satiety* seeks to quench his thirst.—*Ibid.,* i. 1.

> If Biondello now were come ashore,
> We could at once put us in readiness ;
> And *take a lodging fit to entertain*
> *Such friends as time in Padua shall beget.*—*Ibid.,* i. 1.

> For who shall bear your part
> And be in Padua here Vincentio's son ;
> *Keep house, and ply his book ; welcome his friends ;*
> *Visit his countrymen, and banquet them ?*— . . .
> Thou shalt be master, Tranio, in my stead,
> *Keep house, and port, and servants, as I should.*—*Ibid.,* i. 1.

On Sunday next, you know,
My daughter Katharine is to be married :
Now, *on the Sunday following*, shall Bianca
Be bride to you, if you make this assurance.—*Tam. of S.*, ii. 1.

Travel you far on, or are you at the farthest ?—
Sir, at the farthest *for a week or two :*
But then up farther, and as far as Rome,
And so to Tripoli, if God lend me life.—*Ibid.*, iv. 2.

And in my house you shall be friendly lodged :
        . . . *So shall you stay*
Till you have done your business in the city : . . .
My father is here *look'd for every day*,
To pass assurance of a dower in marriage
'Twixt me and one Baptista's daughter here.—*Ibid.*, iv. 2.

But I, who never knew how to entreat,
Am starv'd for meat, giddy for lack of sleep ;
With oaths kept waking, and with brawling fed.—*Ibid.*, iv. 3.

Tailor, *I'll pay thee for thy gown to-morrow.*—*Ibid.*, iv. 3.

        Sirs, let 't alone,
I will not go to-day ; and ere I do,
It shall be what o'clock I say it is.—*Ibid.*, iv. 3.

At last, though long, our jarring notes agree.—*Ibid.*, v. 2.

In " All's Well that Ends Well " Shakespeare had to reconcile the concentrated space of time fit for a drama with the protracted space of time demanded by the exigencies of the story ; and he has done this through the medium of alternately introduced intimations of speedily current time and of long lapses of time. The former far surpass the latter in number ; giving such admirably accelerating effect to the passage of time, that insensibly we glide over each successive period, and they all melt into distance as things gone by while we feel but the force of present and actual moments. First for the accelerating intimations, which induce the belief in speedily current and actual time :—

In delivering my son from me, I bury a second husband.—
And I, *in going*, madam, weep o'er my father's death anew: *but I must attend his majesty's command.*—*All's W.*, i. 1.

        'Twas pretty, though a plague,
To see him every hour: . . .
But now he 's gone, and my idolatrous fancy
Must sanctify his relics. Who comes here ?
One that goes with him.—*Ibid.*, i. 1.

The king's disease—*my project* may deceive me,
But my intents are fix'd, and will not leave me.—*Ibid.*, i. 1.

        What 's he *comes here ?*—
It is the Count Rousillon, my good lord,
Young Bertram. . . . *Welcome*, count ;
My son 's no dearer.—
        Thank your majesty.—*Ibid.*, i. 2.

Madam, *I was very late more near her* than, I think, she wished me: alone she was, and did communicate to herself, her own words to her own ears; she thought, I dare vow for her, they touched not any stranger sense. Her matter was, she loved your son : . . . this she delivered in the most bitter touch of sorrow, that e'er I heard virgin exclaim in : which I held *my duty speedily to acquaint you withal.*—*Ibid.*, i. 3.

        Had you not lately an intent, speak truly, *to go to Paris ?*—
Madam, *I had.*—*Ibid.*, i. 3.

> Would your honour
> But give me leave to try success, I 'd venture
> The well-lost life of mine on his grace's cure,
> *By such a day and hour.— . . .*
> Why, Helen, thou shalt have my leave, and love,
> Means, and attendants, and my loving greetings
> To those of mine in court : . . .
> *Be gone to-morrow.—All's W.,* i. 3.

> What her is this ?—
> Why, Doctor She ; my lord, *there 's one arriv'd*
> If you will see her.—*Ibid.,* ii. 1.

> And, hearing your high majesty is touch'd
> With that malignant cause, wherein the honour
> Of my dear father's gift stands chief in power,
> *I come to tender it.—Ibid.,* ii. 1.

> Art thou so confident ?   Within what space
> Hop'st thou my cure ?—
> The greatest grace lending grace,
> *Ere twice the horses of the sun shall bring*
> *Their fiery torcher his diurnal ring ;*
> *Ere twice in murk and occidental damp*
> *Moist Hesperus hath quench'd his sleepy lamp ;*
> *Or four and twenty times the pilot's glass*
> *Hath told the thievish minutes how they pass ;*
> *What is infirm from your sound parts shall fly,*
> *Health shall live free, and sickness freely die.—Ibid.,* ii. 1.

> Sweet practiser, thy physic I will try,
> That ministers thine own death, if I die.—
> *If I break time,* or flinch in property
> Of what I spoke, unpitied let me die.—*Ibid.,* ii. 1.

> I know my business is but to the court.— . . .
> An end, sir : to your business.   Give Helen this,
> And urge her to a present answer back. . . .
> *I am there before my legs.—Haste you again.—Ibid.,* ii. 2.

Here comes the king.—Lustick, as the Dutchman says : I 'll like a maid the better
whilst I have a tooth in my head : why, he is able to lead her a coranto.— . . .

> Go, call before me all the lords in court.
> Sit, *my preserver,* by thy patient's side ;
> And with this healthful hand, *whose banish'd sense*
> *Thou hast repeal'd,* a second time receive
> The confirm of my promis'd gift.—*Ibid.,* ii. 3.

> I dare not say, I take you ; but *I give*
> *Me, and my service, ever whilst I live,*
> *Into your guiding power.   This is the man.—*
> Why, then, young Bertram, take her; *she 's thy wife.—Ibid.,* ii. 3.

> Take her by the hand,
> And tell her she is thine : to whom I promise
> A counterpoise ; if not to thy estate,
> A balance more replete.—
> *I take her hand.—*
> Good fortune, and the favour of the king,
> Smile upon this contract ; *whose ceremony*
> *Shall seem expedient on the now-born brief,*
> *And be perform'd to-night.—Ibid.,* ii. 3.

> O my Parolles, *they have married me !—Ibid.,* ii. 3.

> To the war !—
> It shall be so : *I 'll send her to my house,*
> *Acquaint my mother with my hate to her,*
> *And wherefore I am fled ; write to the king*

That which I durst not speak : his present gift
Shall furnish me to those Italian fields
Where noble fellows strike: . . .
Go with me to my chamber, and advise me.
I'll send her straight away : to-morrow
I'll to the wars, she to her single sorrow.— . . .
Therefore *away, and leave her ; bravely go.*—*All's W.,* ii. 3.

Madam, *my lord will go away to-night ;*—
          . . . What's his will else ?—
That you will take your instant leave o' the king,
And make this haste as your own good proceeding, . . .
That *having this obtain'd, you presently*
Attend his farther pleasure.—*Ibid.,* ii. 4.

Is she gone to the king ?—*She is.*—*Will she away to-night ?*—*As you 'll have her.*
I have writ my letters, casketed my treasure,
Given order for our horses ; and to-night,
When I should take possession of the bride,
End ere I do begin.— *Ibid.,* ii. 5.

I have, sir, as I was commanded from you,
Spoke with the king, and have procur'd his leave
For present parting ; . . . —*This drives me to entreat you,*
That presently you take your way for home ; . . .
My haste is very great : farewell ; hie home. . . .
I pray you, stay not, but in haste to horse.—
I shall not break your bidding, good my lord.— . . .
Away ! and for our flight.—*Ibid.,* ii. 5.

                    You know your places well ;
When better fall, for your avails they fell :
To-morrow to the field.—*Ibid.,* iii. 1.

                    Towards Florence is he ?—
Ay, madam.—
                    And to be a soldier ?—
Such is his noble purpose . . .—
          . . . Return you thither ?—
Ay, madam, *with the swiftest wing of speed.*— *Ibid.,* iii. 2.

                    I will be gone ;
My being here it is that holds thee hence :
Shall I stay here to do 't ? no, no, although
The air of paradise did fan the house,
And angels offic'd all : *I will be gone,*
That pitiful rumour may report *my flight,*
To consolate thine ear. *Come, night ; end, day !*
For with the dark, poor thief, *I 'll steal away.*—*Ibid.,* iii. 2.

                    This very day,
Great Mars, I put myself into thy file.—*Ibid.,* iii. 3.

If I had given you this at *overnight,*
She might have been o'erta'en ; and yet she writes,
Pursuit would be but vain.—
          . . . *Write, write,* Rinaldo,
To this unworthy husband of his wife ; . . .
Despatch the most convenient messenger :
When, haply, he shall hear that she is gone,
He will return ; and hope I may, that she,
Hearing so much, *will speed her foot again,*
Led hither by pure love.—*Ibid.,* iii. 4.

The troop is past. Come, pilgrim, I will bring you
Where you shall host ; of enjoin'd penitents
There 's four or five, to great Saint Jaques bound,
Already at my house.—

I humbly thank you:
Please it this matron and this gentle maid
To eat with us to-night, the charge and thanking
Shall be for me. . . .
. . . *We'll take your offer kindly.—All's W.*, iii. 5.

By the hand of a soldier *I will undertake it.—But you must not now slumber in it.—I'll about it this evening:* and *I will presently* pen down my dilemmas, encourage myself in my certainty, put myself into my mortal preparation; and, *by midnight,* look to hear farther from me.—*Ibid.*, iii. 6.

We have almost embossed him;—*you shall see his fall to-night*; . . . when his disguise and he is parted, tell me what a sprat you shall find him; *which you shall see this very night.* . . .—*Now will I lead you* to the house, *and show you the lass I spoke of.—Ibid.*, iii. 6.

Why, then, *to-night*
Let us assay our plot; . . .
But let's about it.—Ibid., iii. 7.

But couch, ho! *here he comes, to beguile two hours in* a sleep, *and then to return* and swear the lies he forges.—*Ten o'clock: within these three hours 'twill be time enough to go home.—Ibid.*, iv. 1.

Go, tell the Count Rousillon, and my brother,
We have caught the woodcock, and will keep him muffled
Till we do hear from them.—*Ibid.*, iv. 1.

When midnight comes, knock at my chamber-window: . . .
When you have conquer'd my yet maiden bed,
Remain there but an hour, nor speak to me:
My reasons are most strong. . . .
And on your finger, *in the night*, I'll put
Another ring.—*Ibid.*, iv. 2.

You have not given him his mother's letter?—*I have deliver'd it an hour since.* . . . He hath perverted a young gentlewoman here in Florence, of a most chaste renown; and *this night* he fleshes his will in the spoil of her honour. . . . *We shall not then have his company to-night?—Not till after midnight; for he is dieted to his hour.—That approaches apace.—Ibid.*, iv. 3.

Where's your master?—He met the duke in the street, sir, of whom he hath taken a solemn leave: *his lordship will next morning for France.—Ibid.*, iv. 3.

How now, my lord! is't not *after midnight?—I have to-night despatch'd sixteen businesses, a month's length a-piece, by an abstract of success:* I have congé'd with the duke, done my adieu with his nearest; buried a wife, mourned for her; writ to my lady mother *I am returning;* entertained my convoy; *and between these main parcels of despatch, effected many nicer needs:* the last was the greatest, but that I have not ended yet.—If the business be of any difficulty, and *this morning your departure hence, it requires haste* of your lordship.—I mean, the business is not ended, as fearing to hear of it hereafter. But shall we have this dialogue between the fool and the soldier? *Come, bring forth this counterfeit model.* . . .—*Bring him forth: he has sat i' the stocks all night.—Ibid.*, iv. 3.

So, look about you: know you any here?—*Good-morrow*, noble captain. . . . Captain, what greeting will you to my lord Lafeu? *I am for France.* . . . Fare you well, sir; *I am for France too:* we shall speak of you there.— . . . *I'll after them.—Ibid.*, iv. 3.

His grace is at Marseilles; *to which place*
We have convenient convoy. You must know,
I am supposed dead: the army breaking,
My husband hies him home; where, heaven aiding,
And by the leave of my good lord the king,
We'll be before our welcome.—Ibid., iv. 4.

But with the word, the time will bring on summer,
When briers shall have leaves as well as thorns,
And be as sweet as sharp. *We must away;*
Our waggon is prepar'd, and time revives us.—*Ibid.*, iv. 4.

Your daughter-in-law had been alive *at this hour and your son here at home.*—*All's W.,* iv. 5.

And I was about to tell you, since I heard of the good lady's death, and that my lord, your son, *was upon his return home,* I moved the king, my master, to speak in the behalf of my daughter; . . . How does your ladyship like it?—With very much content, my lord; and I wish it happily effected.—*His highness comes post from Marseilles,* of as able body as when he numbered thirty: *he will be here to-morrow.* . . .—It rejoices me, *that I hope I shall see him ere I die.* I have letters *that my son will be here to-night:* I shall beseech your lordship to remain with me till they meet together. . . . O madam, *yonder's my lord your son.* . . . *Let us go see your son, I pray you: I long to talk with* the young noble soldier.—*Ibid.,* iv. 5.

> But *this exceeding posting, day and night,*
> Must wear your spirits low; we cannot help it:
> But *since you have made the days and nights as one,*
> To wear your gentle limbs in my affairs,
> Be bold you do so grow in my requital,
> As nothing can unroot you. *In happy time,*
> This man may help me to his majesty's ear.
>   . . . I do beseech you, sir,
> *Since you are like to see the king before me,*
> Commend the paper to his gracious hand, . . .
> *I will come after you, with what good speed*
> *Our means will make us means.*—
>   This I 'll do for you.—
> And you shall find yourself to be well thank'd,
> Whate'er falls more. *We must to horse again:*
> *Go, go, provide.*—*Ibid.,* v. 1.

The king's coming; I know by his trumpets. Sirrah, inquire farther after me; I had talk of you *last night.*—*Ibid.,* v. 2.

> We lost a jewel of her; and our esteem
> Was made much poorer by it: but your son,
> As mad in folly, lack'd the sense to know
> Her estimation home.—
>   *'Tis past,* my liege;
> And I beseech your majesty to make it
> Natural rebellion, done i' the blaze of youth: . . .
>   . . . Well, *call him hither;*
> *We are reconcil'd, and the first view shall kill*
> *All repetition.*—*Ibid.,* v. 3.
> Not one word more of the consumed time.
> *Let's take the instant by the forward top;*
> For we are old, and *on our quick'st decrees*
> *Th' inaudible and noiseless foot of time*
> *Steals ere we can effect them.*—*Ibid.,* v. 3.
> *Send forth your amorous token for fair Maudlin:*
> *The main consents are had;* and here we 'll stay
> To see our widower's second marriage-day.—*Ibid.,* v. 3.
>   His name 's Parolles.—
> *I saw the man to-day,* if man he be.—
> Find him, and *bring him hither.*—*Ibid.,* v. 3.
> *To prison with her: and away with him.*
> Unless thou tell'st me where thou hadst this ring,
> *Thou diest within this hour.*—*Ibid.,* v. 3.

Next, for the protractive intimations:—

Little Helen, farewell: *if I can remember thee,* I will think of thee at court . . . farewell. *When thou hast leisure,* say thy prayers; when thou hast done, *remember thy friends: get thee a good husband,* and use him as he uses thee: so, farewell.—*Ibid.,* i. 1.

'Tis our hope, sir,
After well-enter'd soldiers, to return
And find your grace in health.—
No, no, it cannot be; and yet my heart
Will not confess he owes the malady
That doth my life besiege. *Farewell, young lords;*
Whether I live or die, be you the sons
Of worthy Frenchmen.—*All's W.,* ii. 1.

'Twill be two days ere I shall see you; so,
I leave you to your wisdom.—*Ibid.,* ii. 5.

Go thou toward home; where I will never come,
Whilst I can shake my sword, or hear the drum.—*Ibid.,* ii. 5.

But I am sure, the younger of our nature,
That surfeit on their ease, *will day by day*
Come here for physic.—
                    Welcome shall they be.—*Ibid.,* iii. 1.

Let me see what he writes, and *when he means to come.*—*Ibid.,* iii. 2.

                    Where is my son, I pray you?
Madam, *he's gone to serve the Duke of Florence:*
We met him thitherward; for thence we came,
And, *after some despatch in hand at court,*
Thither we bend again.—*Ibid.,* iii. 2.

                    You are welcome, gentlemen.
I will entreat you, *when you see my son,*
To tell him that his sword can never win
The honour that he loses.—*Ibid.,* iii. 2.

                    Every night he comes
With musics of all sorts, and songs compos'd
To her unworthiness: it nothing steads us,
To chide him from our eaves; *for he persists,*
As if his life lay on 't.—*Ibid.,* iii. 7.

Sir, his wife, *some two months since fled from his house:* her pretence is *a pilgrimage*
to Saint Jaques le Grand; which holy undertaking, with most austere sanctimony, she
accomplished; and, there residing, the tenderness of her nature became as a prey to her
grief; in fine, made a groan of her last breath; and now she sings in heaven.—
Ibid., iv. 3.

One of the greatest in the Christian world
Shall be my surety; . . .
Time was I did him a desired office,
Dear almost as his life.—*Ibid.,* iv. 4.

In " Twelfth Night " Shakespeare has contrived to give the requisite
effect of the due limits within which a drama should be preserved,
together with the effect of sufficient space for the events of the story
to take place naturally, by manifold touches of Short Time and a few
touches of Long Time.   The manifold touches of Short Time are
these :—

Who governs here?—
                    A noble duke, in nature
As in name.—
                    What is his name?—
                                        Orsino.—
Orsino! I have heard my father name him:
He was a bachelor then.—
And so is now, or was so very late; . . .
                    . . . *I'll serve this duke:*
Thou shalt present me . . .
                    . . . I thank thee: *lead me on.*—*Tw. N.,* i. 2.

> Cesario,
> Thou know'st no less but all; I have unclasp'd
> To thee the book even of my secret soul:
> Therefore, good youth, *address thy gait unto her;*
> *Be not denied access, stand at her doors,*
> And tell them, there thy fixed foot shall grow
> Till thou have audience.— . . .
> Say I do speak with her, my lord, what then?—
> O then unfold the passion of my love. . . .
> . . . *I'll do my best*
> *To woo your lady.*—*Tw. N.*, i. 4.

Madam, *there is at the gate a young gentleman much desires to speak with you.* . . . Who of my people hold him in delay?—Sir Toby, madam, your kinsman.—Fetch him off, I pray you. . . . By mine honour, half drunk. . . . Cousin, cousin, *how have you come so early by this lethargy?*— . . . Madam, *yond' young fellow swears he will speak with you.* . . . *Let him approach* . . . give me my veil: come, throw it o'er my face. We'll once more hear Orsino's embassy.—*Ibid.*, i. 5.

I heard you were saucy at my gates; and allowed your approach, rather to wonder at you than to hear you. If you be not mad, *be gone;* if you have reason, *be brief:* . . . *Will you hoist sail,* sir? *here lies your way.*—No, good swabber; I am to hull here *a little longer.*—*Ibid.*, i. 5.

> *Get you to your lord;*
> I cannot love him: let him send no more;
> *Unless, perchance, you come to me again,*
> To tell me how he takes it. *Fare you well:*
> . . . *Farewell*, fair cruelty.—*Ibid.*, i. 5.

> . . . *Not too fast:* soft, soft!
> Unless the master were the man. How now!
> *Even so quickly may one catch the plague?*
> Methinks I feel this youth's perfections,
> With an invisible and subtle stealth,
> To creep in at mine eyes.—*Ibid.*, i. 5.

> *Run after that same peevish messenger,*
> The county's man: he left this ring behind him,
> Would I, or not: tell him I'll none of it.
> Desire him not to flatter with his lord,
> Nor hold him up with hopes; I am not for him:
> *If that the youth will come this way to-morrow,*
> I'll give him reasons for't. *Hie, thee*, Malvolio.—*Ibid.*, i. 5.

Will you stay no longer? nor will you not that I go with you?—By your patience, no. . . . *Fare ye well at once:* . . . *I am bound to the Count Orsino's court: farewell.*—
> The gentleness of all the gods go with thee!
> I have many enemies in Orsino's court,
> Else would I *very shortly see thee there:*
> But, come what may, I do adore thee so,
> That danger shall seem sport, and *I will go.*—*Ibid.*, ii. 1.

Were not you *even now* with the Countess Olivia?—*Even now*, sir; *on a moderate pace I have since arrived but hither.*—*Ibid.*, ii. 2.

Approach, Sir Andrew: *not to be a-bed after midnight is to be up betimes;* and *diluculo surgere*, thou know'st,— . . . *to be up after midnight, and to go to bed then, is early:* so that, *to go to bed after midnight, is to go to bed betimes..*—*Ibid.*, ii. 3.

Shall we *rouse the night-owl* in a catch that will draw three souls out of one weaver? . . .—What a caterwauling do you keep here! If my lady have not *called up* her steward, Malvolio, and bid him turn you out of doors, never trust me. . . .—My masters, are you mad? or what are you? Have you no wit, manners, nor honesty, but to gabble like tinkers *at this time of night?*—*Ibid.*, ii. 3.

Sweet Sir Toby, *be patient for to-night:* since the youth of the count's *was to-day with my lady*, she is much out of quiet. For Monsieur Malvolio, let me alone with him: if I do not gull him into a nayword, and make him a common recreation, do not think I have wit enough to lie straight in my bed: . . . *For this night*, to bed, and dream on the event. Farewell.—*Good-night*, Penthesilea. . . . Come, come; I 'll go burn some sack, *'tis too late to go to bed now :* come, knight; come, knight.— *Tw. N.*, ii. 3.

> Give me some music: now, *good-morrow*, friends:
> Now, good Cesario, but that piece of song,
> That old and antique song, *we heard last night :* . . .

He is not here, so please your lordship, that should sing it.—Who was it?—Feste, the jester, my lord; a fool that the lady Olivia's father took much delight in: *he is about* the house.—*Seek him out: and play the tune the while.* . . . O, fellow, *come, the song we had last night.* . . . *Are you ready*, sir?—*Ay, pr'ythee, sing.*—*Ibid.*, ii. 4.

> *Once more*, Cesario,
> *Get thee to yond' same sovereign cruelty :*
> Tell her, my love, more noble than the world,
> Prizes not quantity of dirty lands. . . .—
> Sir, *shall I to this lady ?*—
>   Ay, that 's the theme.
> *To her in haste ;* give her this jewel; say,
> My love can give no place, bide no denay.—*Ibid.*, ii. 4.

Get ye all three into the box-tree: *Malvolio's coming down this walk :* he has been yonder i' the sun, practising behaviour to his own shadow *this half-hour.*—*Ibid.*, ii. 5.

> *I saw thee late at the Count Orsino's.*—*Ibid.*, iii. 1.

You 're servant to the Count Orsino, youth. . . .—Madam, *I come to whet your gentle thoughts on his behalf.*—*Ibid.*, iii. 1.

> The clock upbraids me with the waste of time. . . .
> There lies your way, due west. . . .
> Yet come again ; for thou perhaps may'st move
> That heart, which now abhors, to like his love.—*Ibid.*, iii. 1.

Challenge me the count's youth to fight with him ; . . .—Will either of you bear me a challenge to him?—*Go, write it in a martial hand.* . . . Go, *about it.* . . . *About it.*—*Ibid.*, iii. 2.

Look, where the youngest wren of nine comes.—If you desire the spleen, and will laugh yourselves into stitches, *follow me.* Yond' gull Malvolio is turned heathen, a very renegado; for there is no Christian, that means to be saved by believing rightly, can ever believe such impossible passages of grossness. *He 's in yellow stockings.*— And cross-gartered?—Most villainously. . . . *Come, bring us, bring us where he is.*— *Ibid.*, iii. 2.

> *I could not stay behind you :* my desire,
> More sharp than filed steel, *did spur me forth ;* . . .—
> *Shall we go see* the reliques of this town ?—
> To-morrow, sir: *best first go see* your lodging.—
> I am not weary, and 'tis long *to night :*
> I pray you, let us satisfy our eyes
> With the memorials and the things of fame
> That do renown this city. . . .—
> It doth not fit me. Hold, sir, here 's my purse.
> In the south suburbs, at the Elephant,
> Is best to lodge: *I will bespeak our diet,*
> *Whiles you beguile the time* and feed your knowledge
> With viewing of the town ; . . .—
> I 'll be your purse-bearer, and *leave you for an hour.*—*Ibid.*, iii. 3.

> *I have sent after him :* he says he 'll come:
> How shall I feast him ? What bestow of him ? . . .

Madam, *the young gentleman of the Count Orsino's is returned:* I could hardly entreat him back : *he attends your ladyship's pleasure.*—*I 'll come to him.*—*Ibid.*, iii. 4.

Come, we 'll have him in a dark room, and bound. My niece *is already in the belief* that he 's mad.—*Ibid.*, iii. 4.

Here's the challenge, read it : . . .—If this letter move him not, his legs cannot : I 'll give 't him.—You may have very fit occasion for 't : *he is now* in some commerce with my lady, and *will by-and-by depart*.—*Go*, Sir Andrew ; *scout me for him at the corner of the orchard*, like a bum-bailie : *so soon as ever thou seest him*, draw ; and, as thou drawest, swear horrible ; . . . *Away !* . . .—*Here he comes* with your niece : give them way, till he take leave, and *presently after him*.—*Tw. N.*, iii. 4.

That defence thou hast, betake thee to 't ; . . . dismount thy tuck ; *be yare in thy preparation*, for thy assailant is quick, skilful, and deadly.—*Ibid.*, iii. 4.

Signior Fabian, *stay you by this gentleman till my return*. . . .—*Will you walk towards him ?* I will make your peace with him, if I can.—*Ibid.*, iii. 4.

Nay, I pr'ythee, put on this gown and this beard ; make him believe thou art Sir Topas, the curate : *do it quickly ;* I 'll call Sir Toby the whilst. . . .—*To him*, Sir Topas.—What ho ! I say, peace in this prison ! . . .—Who calls there ?—Sir Topas, the curate, *who comes to visit* Malvolio the lunatic.—*Ibid.*, iv. 2.

I would we were well rid of this knavery. If he may be conveniently delivered, I would he were, . . . *Come by-and-by to my chamber.*—*Ibid.*, iv. 2.

Good fool, some ink, paper, and light ; and *convey what I will set down to my lady :* it shall advantage thee more than ever the bearing of letter did.—I will help you to 't . . . I pr'ythee, be gone.—*I am gone, sir ; and anon, sir, I 'll be with you again, in a trice.*—*Ibid.*, iv. 2.

> Where 's Antonio, then ?
> *I could not find him at the Elephant :*
> *Yet there he was, and there I found this credit,*
> That he did range the town to seek me out.
> His counsel *now* might do me golden service.—*Ibid.*, iv. 3.

> But *here the lady comes.*—
> Blame not *this haste* of mine. If you mean well,
> *Now go with me and with this holy man*
> *Into the chantry by :* there, before him,
> And underneath that consecrated roof,
> *Plight me the full assurance of your faith ;*
> That my most jealous and too doubtful soul
> May live at peace : he shall conceal it,
> Whiles you are willing it shall come to note,
> What time we will our celebration keep,
> According to my birth. What do you say ?—
> I 'll follow this good man, and go with you ;
> And, having sworn truth, ever will be true.—
> *Then lead the way, good father.*— *Ibid.*, iv. 3.

If you will *let your lady know I am here to speak with her*, and *bring her along with you*, it may awake my bounty farther.—Marry, sir, lullaby to your bounty *till I come again. I go, sir* . . . let your bounty take a nap, *I will awake it anon.*—*Here comes the man*, sir, that did rescue me.—*Ibid.*, v. 1.

> Denied me mine own purse,
> Which I had recommended to his use
> *Not half an hour before.*—
> How can this be ?—
> *When came he to this town ?*—*To-day*, my lord.—*Ibid.*, v. 1.

Hast thou forgot thyself ? *Is it so long ?*
Call forth the holy father. . . .
. . . O, welcome, father !
Father, I charge thee, by thy reverence,
Here to unfold (though *lately* we intended
To keep in darkness, what occasion *now*
Reveals before 'tis ripe) what thou dost know
Hath *newly* pass'd between this youth and me.—
A contract of eternal bond of love,
Confirm'd by mutual joinder of your hands,

> Attested by the holy close of lips,
> Strengthen'd by interchangement of your rings;
> And all the ceremony of this compact
> Seal'd in my function, by my testimony:
> *Since when, my watch hath told me, toward my grave*
> *I have travell'd but two hours.—Tw. N.*, v. 1.

He has hurt me, and there's the end on 't. Sot, didst see Dick surgeon, sot?—O, he's drunk, Sir Toby, *an hour agone;* his eyes were set *at eight i' the morning.—Ibid.*, v. 1.

> Pardon me, sweet one, even for *the vows*
> *We made each other but so late ago.—Ibid.*, v. 1.

> Antonio! O, my dear Antonio!
> *How have the hours rack'd and tortur'd me,*
> *Since I have lost thee!—Ibid.*, v. 1.

Fetch Malvolio hither: . . . how does he, sirrah?—Truly, madam, he holds Belzebub at the stave's end, as well as a man in his case may do: *he has here writ a letter to you; I should have given it you to-day morning;* but as a madman's epistles are no gospels, so it skills not much when they are delivered.—*Ibid.*, v. 1.

> My lord, so please you, these things farther thought on,
> To think me as well a sister as a wife,
> *One day shall crown the alliance on 't,* so please you,
> *Here at my house,* and at my proper cost.—
> Madam, I am most apt t' embrace your offer.—*Ibid.*, v. 1.

>   Good madam, hear me speak;
> And let no quarrel, nor no brawl to come,
> Taint the condition of *this present hour,*
> Which I have wonder'd at.—*Ibid.*, v. 1.

The few touches of Long Time are these:—

Sir Toby, you must come in earlier *o' nights:* your cousin, my lady, takes great exceptions to your ill hours. . . . That quaffing and drinking will undo you: *I heard my lady talk of it yesterday;* and of a foolish knight, *that you brought in one night* here to be her wooer.—*Ibid.*, i. 3.

I 'll ride home to-morrow, Sir Toby . . . 'Faith, *I 'll home to-morrow*, Sir Toby: your niece will not be seen; or, if she be, it 's four to one she 'll none of me: the count himself, here hard by, woos her.—She 'll none o' the count. . . . Tut, there 's life in 't, man.—*I 'll stay a month longer.—Ibid.*, i. 3.

If the duke continue these favours towards you, Cesario, you are like to be much advanced: *he hath known you but three days,* and already you are no stranger.—*Ibid.*, i. 4.

> *O time thou must untangle this, not I;*
> It is too hard a knot for me t' untie!—*Ibid.*, ii. 2.

Thou wast in very gracious fooling *last night.—Ibid.*, ii. 3.

>   I did send,
> *After the last enchantment you did here,*
> A ring in chase of you.—*Ibid.*, iii. 1.

> With the same 'haviour that your passion bears,
> *Go on my master's griefs.* . . .
> . . . I beseech you, *come again to-morrow* . . .
> Well, *come again to-morrow.—Ibid.*, iii. 4.

> When came he to this town?
> To-day, my lord; and *for three months before*
> (No interim, not a minute's vacancy)
> *Both day and night did we keep company.*
>   . . . Fellow, thy words are madness:
> *Three months this youth hath tended upon me.—Ibid.*, v. 1.

> I 'll bring you to a captain in this town,
> Where lie my maiden weeds; by whose gentle help

I was preserv'd, to serve this noble count.
All the occurrence of my fortune since
Hath been between this lady and this lord. . . .—
Boy, *thou hast said to me a thousand times,*
Thou never shouldst love woman like to me. . . .—
The captain that *did bring me first on shore*
Hath my maid's garments: he *upon some action*
Is now in durance, at Malvolio's suit.—*Tw. N.*, v. 1.

In "King John," as in all Shakespeare's historical dramas, the author had to indicate a long period of action so managed as to appear but the brief summary which "may" (to use his own words) "be digested in a play": and he accordingly gives a profusion of denotements of rapidly passing and actually current time, while he sparingly inserts such reminders of longer lapses of time as are absolutely needful for historical event. The imagination of those who witness or read his chronicle plays is held spell-bound; accepting with perfect good faith the illusory and double Dramatic Time which the dramatist conjures up by his "so potent" art.

The detailed instances (amounting to nearly two thousand) in Shakespeare's English historical plays were originally written out by us; but on due consideration, for the sake of condensity, we have cancelled the portion of manuscript containing them; contenting ourselves with merely calling our readers' notice to the mode in which the Dramatic Time is managed in the "Third Part of King Henry VI., forming one of the many internal evidences (to our mind) that it contains proving it to be almost, if not entirely, the work of Shakespeare's own hand. Not only are the indications of Short Time more numerous than those of Long Time; but even these latter are touched by such concomitant hints of hurried action that the effect of brevity and compression are subtly conveyed in just the requisite manner to condense the various alternations of fortune and vicissitudes of success that occurred during the tragical period known as "the wars of the Roses" in English history into the apparent space befitting a five-act drama. Traceable throughout is that skill by which illusory speed and real slowness, illusory length and real haste, are so blended as to produce upon the imagination of the reader or spectator an acquiescence in the veritableness of the represented Dramatic Time. Also, we take occasion to point out the artistic manner in which Dramatic Time is conducted throughout the long third scene in the fifth act of "King Richard III."; which commences with allusion to the setting sun, goes on with sequential references to "supper-time" and "nine o'clock," to the stealing on of the hours, to the approach of night, to the reaching "midnight," intermingled with frequent anticipations of "to-morrow"; then to the announcement of dawn and cock-crow time, with the advance of morning; and finally to the setting in of day, bringing on that animated summons to immediate attack: all together conducing to impress the imagination with the thorough naturalness whereby the time has sped from overnight to next day before the very eyes of the spectator. Moreover, we would call special attention to the masterly touches by which the Dramatic Time is

managed in "King Henry VIII.," so as to compress within due limits
the salient events of that interesting reign. So skilfully are the occurrences summed and made to appear actually passing or already past,
that we feel no difficulty in believing them to transpire within the
requisitely brief period of a drama.

We now proceed to the rest of our elucidation of the subject by cited
passages.

The long-sustained and continuously waged war during the siege of
Troy demanded of Shakespeare, in his adoption of "Troilus and Cressida" as theme for a play, very peculiar treatment of its Dramatic Time.
He has therefore given many needful indications of Long Time, while
he has given even to those of Short Time a certain impression of
maintained action. For instance, in adverting to the fight, he has
frequently introduced the expression "*to-day*": which, while it gives
the effect of actual contest, also conveys the impression of an each day
renewed contest ; thus inducing the belief in the going-on of the ten
years' war, at the same time that he condenses it into the bounds of
a five-act drama. First, then, for these instances of Short Time : he
begins, in his Prologue, by claiming to plunge into the midst of the
long-continued war between the Greeks and Trojans ; but he proceeds
by giving the denotements of present and passing time in the manner
we have above stated :—

> In Troy, there lies the scene. From isles of Greece
> The princes orgulous, their high blood chaf'd,
> *Have to the port of Athens sent their ships,*
>   . . . *from th' Athenian bay*
> *Put forth toward Phrygia: and their vow is made*
> *To ransack Troy,* . . .
> *To Tenedos they come ;*
> And the deep-drawing barks *do there disgorge*
> Their warlike fraughtage: *now* on Dardan plains
> The fresh and yet unbruised Greeks *do pitch*
> *Their brave pavilions:* . . .
> *Now expectation*, tickling skittish spirits,
> On one and other side, Trojan and Greek,
> *Sets all on hazard :* and hither am I come
> A prologue arm'd, . . .
> To tell you, fair beholders, that *our play*
> *Leaps o'er the vaunt and firstlings of those broils,*
> *Beginning in the middle ; starting thence away*
> *To what may be digested in a play.*—*Tr. & Cr.* (*Prologue*).

>   I tell thee, *I am mad*
> *In Cressid's love :* . . .
> What news, Æneas, from the field *to-day ?*—
> That Paris is returned home, and hurt. . . .
> Hark, what good sport is out of town *to-day !* . . .—
> But to the sport abroad ; are you bound thither ?—
> *In all swift haste.*—
> *Come, go we, then, together.*—*Ibid.*, i. 1.

>   Hector, whose patience
> Is as a virtue fix'd, *to-day* was mov'd :
> He chid Andromache, and struck his armourer
> And, like as there were husbandry in war,
> *Before the sun rose*, he was harness'd light,
> And to the field goes he . . .

Good morrow, uncle Pandarus.—*Good morrow*, cousin Cressid: what do you talk of? *Good morrow*, Alexander. How do you, cousin? When were you at Ilium?— *This morning*, uncle.—What were you talking of when I came? *Was Hector armed and gone, ere ye came to Ilium? Helen was not up*, was she?—Hector was gone; but *Helen was not up.*—E'en so: Hector was stirring *early*. . . .

Hark! they are coming from the field ; shall we stand up here, and see them, as they pass toward Ilium? . . . Yonder comes Paris, yonder comes Paris. . . . Who said he came hurt home *to-day?* he's not hurt. . . . That's Helenus: I think he went not forth *to-day.* . . . Sir, *my lord would instantly speak with you.*—Where?—At your own house; there he unarms him.—Good boy, *tell him I come.*—*Tr. & Cr.*, i. 2.

> Speak frankly as the wind;
> *It is not Agamemnon's sleeping hour:*
> *That thou shalt know*, Trojan, *he is awake,*
> *He tells thee so himself.* . . .—
> Now, Ulysses, I begin to relish thy advice;
> And *I will give a taste of it forthwith*
> To Agamemnon: *go we to him straight.*—*Ibid.*, i. 3.

> Achilles bids me say, he is much sorry,
> If any thing more than your sport and pleasure
> Did move your greatness, and this noble state,
> *To call upon him;* he hopes it is no other,
> But, for your health and your digestion sake—
> An *after-dinner's* breath.—*Ibid.*, ii. 3.

He desires you, that if the king call for him *at supper*, you will make his excuse.— . . . What exploit's in hand? *Where sups he to-night?* . . . You must not know *where he sups*. . . . Sweet lord, who's a-field to-day?—Hector, Deiphobus, Helenus, Antenor, and all the gallantry of Troy: I would fain have armed *to-day*, but my Nell would not have it so. . . . I long to hear how they sped *to-day*. . . . *They're come from field: let us to Priam's hall, to greet the warriors.*—*Ibid.*, iii. 1.

> O, be thou my Charon,
> *And give me swift transportance* to those fields
> Where I may wallow in the lily beds
> Propos'd for the deserver! O gentle Pandarus,
> *From Cupid's shoulder pluck his painted wings,*
> *And fly with me to Cressid!*—

Walk here i' the orchard; *I'll bring her straight.* . . . She's making her ready; *she'll come straight:* . . . *I'll fetch her.* . . . *Here she is now:* . . . *Come in, come in: I'll go get a fire.*—*Will you walk in*, my lord? . . . *Will you walk in*, my lord?—*Ibid.*, iii. 2.

> Now, *princes*, for the service I have done you,
> *Th' advantage of the time prompts me aloud*
> To call for recompense.—*Ibid.*, iii. 3.

Good day, good day.—. . . *Good morrow*, Ajax.—Ha?—*Good morrow.*—*Ibid.*, iii. 3

> *Good morrow* lord Æneas. . . .—In humane gentleness,
> *Welcome to Troy, now*, by Anchises' life,
> *Welcome indeed!* . . .
> What business, lord, *so early?*—
> I was sent for to the king; but why, I know not.—
> *His purpose meets you:* 'twas to bring this Greek
> To Calchas' house; and there to render him,
> For the freed Antenor, the fair Cressid:
> Let's have your company; or, if you please,
> *Haste there before us:* I constantly do think
> (Or, rather, call my thought a certain knowledge)
> My brother Troilus *lodges there to-night:*
> *Rouse him*, and give him note of our approach, . . .
> . . . *On, lord*, we'll follow you.—
> *Good morrow*, all.—*Ibid.*, iv. 1.

> Dear, trouble not yourself: *the morn is cold.*
> Then, sweet my lord, *I'll call mine uncle down;*
> He shall unbolt the gates—

Trouble him not ;
To bed, to bed : . . . Good morrow, then.
Pr'ythee now to bed. . . . but that *the busy day,*
Wak'd by the lark, hath rous'd the ribald crows,
And dreaming *night* will hide our joys no longer,
I would not from thee.—
                Night hath been too brief.—
Beshrew the witch ! with venomous wights she stays,
As tediously as hell ; *but flies the grasps of love,*
With wings more momentary-swift than thought. . . .
Hast not slept *to-night ?* . . .
Good morrow, lord, good morrow.—
Who 's there ? my lord Æneas ! By my troth,
I knew you not : what news with you *so early ?* . . .
My lord, *I scarce have leisure to salute you,*
My matter is so rash : there is at hand
Paris your brother, and Deiphobus,
The Grecian Diomed, and our Antenor
Deliver'd to us : and for him, *forthwith,*
Ere the first sacrifice, within this hour,
We must give up to Diómedes' hand
The lady Cressida. . . .
They are at hand, and ready to effect it . . .
Thou must be gone, wench, thou must be gone : thou art changed for Antenor : thou must to thy father, and be gone from Troilus.—*Tr. & Cr.*, iv. 2.

It is great morning ; and the hour prefix'd
Of her delivery to this valiant Greek
Comes fast upon : good my brother Troilus,
Tell you the lady what she is to do,
And haste her to the purpose.—
                Walk into her house ;
I 'll bring her to the Grecian presently.—*Ibid.*, iv. 3.

My lord, *is the lady ready ?*—
Hark ! you are call'd : some say, *the Genius so*
Cries, " Come ! " to him that instantly must die.—
Bid them have patience ; *she shall come anon.* . . .
Welcome, Sir Diomed ! *here is the lady*
Which for Antenor we deliver you.—*Ibid.*, iv. 4.

Hark ! Hector's trumpet.—
                How have we spent *this morning !*
'Tis Troilus' fault : *come, come, to field with him.*—
Let us make ready straight.—
Yea, *with a bridegroom's fresh alacrity,*
Let us address to tend on Hector's heels :
The glory of our Troy doth *this day* lie
On his fair worth and single chivalry.—*Ibid.*, iv. 4.

Here art thou in appointment fresh and fair,
Anticipating time with starting courage.
Give with thy trumpet a loud note to Troy,
Thou dreadful Ajax ; . . .
No trumpet answers.—
                'Tis but early days.— . . .
The Trojans' trumpet.—
                Yonder comes the troop.—
. . . as you and lord Æneas
Consent upon the order of their fight,
So be it ; either to the uttermost,
Or else a breath : . . .
They are oppos'd already.— . . .
They are in action.—

Now, Ajax, hold thine own !—
        Hector, thou sleep'st
Awake thee ! . . . Princes, enough, so please you . . .
To-night all friends.—
Thy hand upon that match.—
First, all you peers of Greece, *go to my tent ;*
There in the full convive we. . . .
There Diomed *doth feast with him to-night.—Tr. & Cr.*, iv. 5.
I 'll heat his blood with Greekish wine *to-night*. . . .
Come, come, Thersites, help to trim my tent ;
This night in banqueting must all be spent.
Away, Patroclus !— . ..
So now, fair Prince of Troy, *I bid good night.*
Ajax commands the guard to tend on you.—
Thanks, and *good night*, to the Greeks' general.—
Good night, my lord.—
     Good night, sweet lord Menelaus. — . . .
Good night and welcome, both at once, to those
That go or tarry.—
      Good night. —
Old Nestor tarries ; and you too, Diomed,
Keep Hector company an hour or two.—
I cannot, lord ; I have important business,
The tide whereof is now. Good night, great Hector.—
  . . . And so, *good night.*—
Come, come, enter my tent.—Ibid., v. 1.
What, *are you up here ?* ho ! speak.—
Who calls ?—
Diomed. Calchas, I think. Where 's your daughter ? —
She comes to you.— . . .
Good night.— . . .
No, no, good night : I 'll be your fool no more.— . . .
And so, good night.— . . .
Good night : I pr'ythee, come. . . .
    . . . *Cressid was here but now.* . . .—
I have been seeking you this hour, my lord :
Hector, *by this, is arming him in Troy ;*
Ajax, your guard, stays to conduct you home.—
Have with you, prince. . . .
I 'll bring you to the gates.—Ibid., v. 2.
Unarm, unarm, and do not fight *to-day*.—
You train me to offend you ; get you in :
By all the everlasting gods, I 'll go !—
My dreams will, sure, prove ominous to the day. . . .
    . . . *Ho ! bid my trumpet sound !* . . .
How now, young man ! mean'st thou to fight *to-day ?* . .
Unarm thee, go ; and doubt thou not, brave boy,
I 'll stand *to-day* for thee, and me, and Troy. . . .
Troilus, I would not have you fight *to-day.*— . . .
    . . . and I myself
Am like a prophet suddenly enrapt,
To tell thee that *this day* is ominous :
Therefore, come back.—
     Æneas is a-field ;
And I do stand engag'd to many Greeks,
Even in the faith of valour, to appear
This morning to them. . . .
Go in, and cheer the town : *we 'll forth and fight ;*
Do deeds worth praise, and tell you them at night.— . . .
They are at it, hark ! Proud Diomed, believe,
I come to lose my arm, or win my sleeve.—*Ibid.*, v. 3.

Now they are clapper-clawing one another ; I 'll go look on. . . . and *now* is the cur
Ajax prouder than the cur Achilles, and will not arm *to-day*—*Tr. & Cr.,* v. 4.

>   Ajax hath lost a friend,
> And foams at mouth, and *he is arm'd, and at it,*
> Roaring for Troilus ; who hath done *to-day*
> Mad and fantastic execution.—*Ibid.,* v. 5.

>   Fate, hear me what I say !
> I reck not though I end my life *to-day.*—*Ibid.,* v. 6.

> *Now is my day's work done ;* I 'll take good breath :
> Rest, sword ; thou hast thy fill of blood and death.—
> Look, Hector, how *the sun begins to set ;*
> How *ugly night comes breathing at his heels :*
> *Even with the vail and dark'ning of the sun,*
> *To close the day up, Hector's life is done.*— . . .
> *The dragon wing of night o'erspreads the earth,*
> And, stickler-like, the armies separates.—*Ibid.,* v. 9.

> Stand, ho ! yet are we masters of the field :
> Never go home ; *here starve we out the night.*—
> *Hector is slain.*—
>   Hector ! The gods forbid !—
> *He 's dead ;* and at the murderer's horse's tail,
> In beastly sort, dragg'd through the shameful field.—*Ibid.,* v. 11.

And here are the denotements of Long Time :—

> *At Priam's table do I sit ;*
> *And when fair Cressid comes into my thoughts*—
> So, traitor ! When she comes ! *When is she thence ?*—
Well, she looked *yesternight* fairer than ever I saw her look, or any woman else. . . .
I would somebody had heard her talk *yesterday,* as I did. . . . She 's a fool to stay
behind her father ; let her to the Greeks, and so I 'll tell her *the next time I see her.* . . .
>   . . . Helen must needs be fair,
> When with your blood you *daily* paint her thus. . . .
> I cannot come to Cressid but by Pandar ;
> And he 's as tetchy to be woo'd to woo,
> As she is stubborn-chaste *against all suit.*—*Ibid.,* i. 1.

They say, he *yesterday* coped Hector in the battle, and struck him down ; the disdain
and shame whereof have *ever since* kept Hector fasting and waking. . . . She came to
him *th' other day* into the compassed window. . . . Well, cousin, I told you a thing
yesterday ; think on 't.—*Ibid.,* i. 2.

> *Words, vows, gifts, tears, and love's full sacrifice,*
> *He offers* in another's enterprise :
> But more in Troilus thousand fold I see
> Than in the glass of Pandar's praise may be ;
> *Yet hold I off.*—*Ibid,* i. 2.

> Nor, princes, is it matter new to us,
> That we come short of our suppose so far,
> That *after seven years' siege,* yet Troy walls stand.—*Ibid.,* i. 3.

>   With him, Patroclus,
> Upon a lazy bed, *the livelong day*
> Breaks scurril jests ;
> And with ridiculous and awkward action
> (Which, slanderer, he imitation calls)
> He pageants us. *Sometime,* great Agamemnon,
> Thy topless deputation he puts on, . . .—
> Ajax *is grown* self-will'd ; and bears his head
> In such a rein, in full as proud a place
> As broad Achilles ; *keeps his tent like him ;*
> *Makes factious feasts ; rails on our state of war,*
> Bold as an oracle ; *and sets Thersites*

(A slave whose gall coins slander like a mint)
To match us in comparisons with dirt.—*Tr. & Cr.*, i. 3.

And will *to-morrow* with his trumpet call,
Mid-way between your tents and walls of Troy,
To rouse a Grecian that is true in love.—*Ibid.*, i. 3.

Thou grumblest and railest *every hour* on Achilles, . . .—
This, sir, is proclaimed through all our host :
That Hector, by the fifth hour of the sun,
Will, with a trumpet, 'twixt our tents and Troy,
To-morrow morning call some knight to arms.—*Ibid.*, ii. 1.

After so many hours, lives, speeches spent,
Thus once again says Nestor from the Greeks.—*Ibid.*, ii. 2.

Achilles will not to the field *to-morrow.* . . .
Fresh kings are come to Troy *to-morrow.*—*Ibid.*, ii. 3.

Prince Troilus, *I have lov'd you night and day*
For many weary months.—*Ibid.*, iii. 2.

I have abandon'd Troy, left my possession,
Incurr'd a traitor's name ; *expos'd myself,*
From certain and possess'd conveniences,
To doubtful fortunes ; sequestering from me all
That time, acquaintance, custom, and condition
Made tame and most familiar to my nature. . .
You have a Trojan prisoner, call'd Antenor,
Yesterday took : Troy holds him very dear.
Oft have you (often have you thanks therefore)
Desir'd my Cressid in right great exchange,
Whom Troy hath still denied.—*Ibid.*, iii. 3.

Withal, bring word if Hector will *to-morrow*
Be answer'd in his challenge. . . .
    . . . Now shall we see *to-morrow*—
An act that very chance doth throw upon him—
Ajax renown'd. . . .
He must fight singly *to-morrow* with Hector. . . . If *to-morrow* be a fair day, by
eleven o'clock it will go one way or other.—*Ibid.*, iii. 3.

You told how Diomed, *a whole week by days,*
Did haunt you in the field.—
      Health to you, valiant sir,
During all question of the gentle truce. . . .
     . . . let him die,
With every joint a wound, and that *to-morrow !*—*Ibid.*, iv. 1.

I will corrupt the Grecian sentinels,
To give thee *nightly visitation.*—*Ibid.*, iv. 4.

I have, thou gallant Trojan, *seen thee oft,*
Labouring for destiny, make cruel way
Through ranks of Greekish youth.—*Ibid.*, iv. 5.

You may have *every day* enough of Hector,
If you have stomach.—*Ibid.*, iv. 5.

     I am thwarted quite
From my great purpose in *to-morrow's* battle.—*Ibid.*, v. 1.

I will not meet with you *to-morrow night.* . . .
To-morrow will I wear it on my helm.—*Ibid.*, v. 2.

The spirited style in which the chief occurrences in the career of
Coriolanus are condensed into the limits of a tragedy by Shakespeare's art in contriving the Dramatic Time of his play bearing the
name of its Roman hero, is worthy of close examination and high
admiration. So spirited is it, that the imagination is hurried away

into full credence of the requisite brevity of the period needed for naturally witnessing a stage representation ; while only the absolutely demanded hints of Long Time are brought in here and there as the drama proceeds. First, for the passages indicative of Short Time :—

First, you know, *Caius Marcius is chief enemy to the people.*—We know 't, we know 't. —*Let us kill him,* and we 'll have corn at our own price. Is 't a verdict *?—No more talking on 't ; let it be done : away, away !* . . . Where 's Caius Marcius ?—Here : what 's the matter ?—*The news is, sir, the Volsces are in arms.*—*Coriol.,* i. 1.

> *Our army 's in the field :*
> We never yet made doubt but *Rome was ready*
> *To answer us.*—*Ibid.,* i. 2.

Madam, the lady Valeria *is come to visit you.*— . . . My ladies both, *good day* to you. . . . *Come, lay aside your stitchery ;* I must have you play the idle huswife with me *this afternoon.* . . . In truth, la, go with me ; and I 'll tell you excellent news of your husband. . . . there came news from him *last night.* . . . Thus it is: *the Volsces have an army forth ; against whom Cominius the general is gone,* with one part of our Roman power : your lord, and Titus Lartius, *are set down before their city Corioli ; they nothing doubt prevailing, and to make it brief wars.*—*Ibid.,* i. 3.

> The citizens of Corioli *have issued,*
> *And given to Lartius and to Marcius battle :*
> I saw our party to their trenches driven,
> And then I came away.—
> > . . . How long is 't since ?—
> *Above an hour,* my lord.—
> *'Tis not a mile ; briefly we heard their drums :*
> How couldst thou in a mile confound an hour,
> And bring thy news so late ?—
> > *Spies of the Volsces*
> *Held me in chase,* that I was forc'd to wheel
> Three or four miles about ; *else had I, sir,*
> *Half an hour since brought my report.*—*Ibid.,* i. 6.

> I do beseech you
> > . . . by the vows
> We have made to endure friends, *that you directly*
> *Set me against Aufidius and his Antiates ;*
> *And that you not delay the present, but,*
> *Filling the air with swords advanc'd and darts,*
> *We prove this very hour.*—*Ibid.,* i. 6.

> *Within these three hours,* Tullus,
> *Alone I fought in your Corioli walls,*
> And made what work I pleas'd.—*Ibid.,* i. 8.

> If I should tell thee o'er thy *this day's work,*
> Thou 'lt not believe thy deeds : . . .
> > . . . from *this time,*
> For what he did before Corioli, call him,
> With all th' applause and clamour of the host,
> CAIUS MARCIUS CORIOLANUS. . . .
> > . . . Go we to our tent :
> The blood upon your visage dries ; *'tis time*
> *It should be look'd to ;* come.—*Ibid.,* i. 9.

> *The town is ta'en !* . . . Go you to the city ;
> Learn how 'tis held ; and what they are that must
> Be hostages for Rome.—
> > Will not you go ?—
> *I am attended at the cypress grove :* I pray you
> ('Tis south the city mills), *bring me word thither*
> How the world goes, that to the pace of it
> *I may spur on my journey.*—*Ibid.,* i. 10.

The augurer tells me we shall have news *to-night*. . . . How now, my as fair as noble ladies (and the moon, were she earthly, no nobler), *whither do you follow your eyes so fast ?*—Honourable Menenius, *my boy Marcius approaches ; for the love of Juno, let us go.*— . . . Hoo! *Marcius coming home !* . . . I will make my very house reel *to-night.—Coriol.*, ii. 1.

Come, come, they are almost here. . . . *Make way, they are coming.*— . . .
Therefore, please you,
Most reverend and grave elders, to desire
The present consul, and last general
In our well-found successes, to report
A little of that worthy work perform'd
By Caius Marcius Coriolanus; *whom
We meet here*, both to thank, and to remember
With honours like himself. . . .
The senate, Coriolanus, *are well pleas'd
To make thee consul.—Ibid.*, ii. 2.

Here he comes, and in the gown of humility : . . .—Pray you now, if it may stand with the tune of your voices that I may be consul, *I have here the customary gown.—* . . .
*You have stood your limitation ; and the tribunes
Endue you with the people's voice :* remains
That, in th' official marks invested, you
Anon do meet the senate.—
Is this done ?—
The custom of request *you have discharg'd :
The people do admit you ;* and are summon'd
To meet anon, upon your approbation. . . .
May I change these garments ?—
You may, sir.—
That I 'll straight do ; and, knowing myself again,
Repair to the senate-house.— . . .
He has it now ; and, by his looks, methinks,
'Tis warm at his heart.— . . .
Get you hence instantly ; and tell those friends,
They have chose a consul that will from them take
Their liberties : . . . *To the Capitol,
Come :* we 'll be there before the stream o' the people.—*Ibid.*, ii. 3.

Tullus Aufidius, then, *had made new head ?*—
He had, my lord ; *and that it was which caus'd
Our swifter composition.—Ibid.*, iii. 1.
*He has spoken like a traitor, and shall answer
As traitors do.* . . .
Go, call the people ; in whose name, myself
Attach thee as a traitorous innovator,
A foe to the public weal : *obey, I charge thee,
And follow to thine answer.—* . . .
. . . *Lay hands upon him,*
And bear him to the rock.— . . .
. . . *Will you hence,
Before the tag return ?* whose rage doth rend
Like interrupted waters, and o'erbear
What they are us'd to bear.—
Pray you, be gone.— . . .
. . . Nay, come away. . . .
. . . *Speak briefly*, then ;
*For we are peremptory to despatch
This viperous traitor :* to eject him hence,
Were but one danger ; and to keep him here,
Our certain death : therefore *it is decreed
He dies to-night.—* . . . *We 'll hear no more.
Pursue him to his house, and pluck him thence.—Ibid.*, iii. 1.

What, will he come ?—
                              He's coming.— . . .
Well, *here he comes.— . . . We,*
Even from this instant, banish him our city ;
In peril of precipitation
From off the rock Tarpeian. . . .
It shall be so, it shall be so ; let him away : he's banish'd, and it shall be so. . . .
The people's enemy is gone, is gone !—Our enemy is banish'd ! he is gone ! hoo ! hoo !—
Go see him out at gates, and follow him,
As he hath follow'd you, with all despite ; . . .
Come, come, let us see him out at gates, come ;
The gods preserve our noble tribunes ! *Come.—Coriol.,* iii. 3.

Come, leave your tears ; *a brief farewell :* the beast
With many heads butts me away. . . .
          . . . bring me but out at gate.
Come, my sweet wife, my dearest mother, and
My friends of noble touch ; when I am forth,
Bid me farewell, and smile.—Ibid., iv. 1.

            You'll sup with me ?—
Anger's my meat ; I sup upon myself,
And so shall starve with feeding. *Come, let's go.—Ibid.,* iv. 2.

I shall, *between this and supper,* tell you most strange things from Rome; all tending
to the good of their adversaries. Have you an army ready, say you ?—A most royal
one ; the centurions and their charges, distinctly billeted, *already in the entertainment,*
and to be on foot at an hour's warning.—*I am joyful to hear of their readiness,* and am
the man, I think, that shall *set them in present action. . . .* Well, *let us go together.—*
Ibid., iv. 3.

A goodly city *is this Antium. . . .* Direct me, if it be your will,
Where great Aufidius lies : is he in Antium ?—
He is, and feasts the nobles of the state
At his house *this night.—*
                          Which is his house, beseech you ?—
This, here, before you.— . . . I'll enter : if he slay me,
He does fair justice ; if he give me way,
I'll do his country service.—*Ibid.,* iv. 4.

The cruelty and envy of the people,
Permitted by our dastard nobles, who
Have all forsook me, hath devour'd the rest ;
And suffer'd me by the voice of slaves to be
Whoop'd out of Rome. *Now, this extremity*
Hath brought me to thy hearth : not out of hope,
Mistake me not, to save my life ; . . .
          . . . but in mere spite,
To be full quit of those my banishers,
Stand I before thee here. . . .
                    . . . O, come, go in,
And take our friendly senators by the hands ;
Who now are here, taking their leaves of me,
Who am prepar'd against your territories,
Though not for Rome itself. *. . . But come in :*
Let me commend thee first to those that shall
Say " yea " to thy desires. A thousand welcomes !
And more a friend than e'er an enemy ;
Yet, Marcius, that was much. Your hand ; *most welcome !—*
Here's a strange alteration ! . . . He is so made on here within, as if he were son
and heir to Mars ; set at upper end o' the table ; no question asked him by any of the
senators, but they stand bald before him : our general himself makes a mistress of
him ; sanctifies himself with 's hand, and turns up the white o' the eye to his discourse.
But the bottom of the news is, our general is cut i' the middle, and but one half of what
he was yesterday ; for the other has half, by the entreaty and grant of the whole table.

He 'll go, he says, and sowle the porter of Rome gates by the ears : he will mow down all before him, and leave his passage polled.— . . . But when goes this forward ?— *To-morrow ; to-day ; presently ; you shall have the drum struck up this afternoon : 'tis, as it were, a parcel of their feast, and to be executed ere they wipe their lips.*— . . . They are rising, they are rising.—In, in, in, in !—*Coriol.*, iv. 5.

> that Marcius,
> *Join'd with Aufidius, leads a power 'gainst Rome,*
> And vows revenge as spacious as between
> The young'st and oldest thing. . . .
> *A fearful army, led by Caius Marcius,*
> *Associated with Aufidius, rages*
> *Upon our territories ; and have already*
> *O'erborne their way, consum'd with fire, and took*
> *What lay before them.*— . . . Here come the clusters.
> . . . You are they
> That made the air unwholesome, when you cast
> Your stinking greasy caps, in hooting at
> Coriolanus' exile. *Now he's coming ;*
> And not a hair upon a soldier's head,
> Which will not prove a whip : as many coxcombs,
> As you threw caps up, will he tumble down,
> And pay you for your voices.—*Ibid.*, iv. 6.

> So that *all hope is vain,*
> Unless his noble mother, and his wife ;
> Who, as I hear, mean to solicit him
> For mercy to his country. *Therefore, let's hence,*
> *And with our fair entreaties haste them on.*—*Ibid.*, v. 1.

> I am an officer of state, and *come*
> To speak with Coriolanus.—

Has he *dined*, canst thou tell ? for I would not speak with him till *after dinner*. . . . *Away !*—How ! *Away !*— . . . *Be gone.* Mine ears against your suits are stronger than your gates against my forces. . . . *Another word*, Menenius, *I will not hear thee speak.*— . . . I say to you, as I was said to, *Away !*—*Ibid.*, v. 2.

> Ha ! what shout is this ?
> *Shall I be tempted to infringe my vow*
> *In the same time 'tis made ? I will not.*— . . .
> You have said you will not grant us anything ;
> For we have nothing else to ask, but that
> Which you *deny already :* yet we will ask :
> That, if you fail in our request, the blame
> May hang upon your hardness . . .
> . . . *He turns away :*
> *Down, ladies ; let us shame him with our knees.*
> To his surname, Coriolanus, 'longs more pride,
> Than pity to our prayers. *Down : an end ;*
> *This is the last : so we will home to Rome,*
> *And die among our neighbours.* . . . *Come, let us go :* . . .
> . . . *Yet give us our despatch :* . . .
> . . . O mother, mother !
> *What have you done ?* . . . O my mother ! mother ! O !
> *You have won a happy victory to Rome ;*
> *But, for your son*—believe it, O, beli ve it—
> *Most dangerously you have with him prevail'd,*
> *If not most mortal to him.* But let it come. . . .
> *Come, enter with us.* Ladies, you deserve
> To have a temple built you : all the swords
> In Italy, and her confederate arms,
> Could not have made *this peace.*—*Ibid.*, v. 3.

Is 't possible that *so short a time* can alter the condition of a man ?—There is difference between a grub and a butterfly ; yet your butterfly was a grub. This

Mārcius *is grown from man to dragon: he has wings;* he's more than a creeping thing. . . . *Mark what mercy his mother shall bring from him:* there is no more mercy in him, than there is milk in a male tiger; that shall our poor city find. . . .

> *Good news, good news; the ladies have prevail'd,*
> *The Volscians are dislodg'd, and Marcius gone:*
> *A merrier day* did never yet greet Rome,
> No, not the expulsion of the Tarquins. . . .
>   . . . Why, *hark you!*
> The trumpets, sackbuts, psalteries, and fifes,
> Tabors, and cymbals, and the shouting Romans,
> Make the sun dance. *Hark you!*—
>   This is good news:
> *I will go meet the ladies.* . . . You have pray'd well *to-day:*
> *This morning* for ten thousand of your throats
> I'd not have given a doit. *Hark, how they joy!*— . . .
>   . . . *They are near the city?*—
> *Almost at point to enter.*—
>   *We will meet them,*
> And help the joy.—
>   *Enter the* LADIES, *&c.*
> *Behold our patroness,* the life of Rome! . . .
>   . . . Welcome, ladies, welcome.—*Coriol.,* v. 4.

> Go tell the lords of the city, *I am here:*
> Deliver them this paper: *having read it,*
> *Bid them repair to the market-place;* where I,
> Even in theirs and in the commons' ears,
> Will vouch the truth of it. . . . *Despatch.*— . . .
> *Your native town you enter'd like a post,*
> *And had no welcomes home; but he returns,*
> *Splitting the air with noise.*— . . . *Say no more:*
> *Here come the lords.* . . .
> *He approaches:* you shall hear him.—
> Hail, lords! *I am return'd your soldier;* . . .
>   . . . *We have made peace,*
> With no less honour to the Antiates,
> Than shame to the Romans.— . . .
> You lords and heads of the state, perfidiously
> *He has betray'd your business, and given up,*
> *For certain drops of salt, your city Rome*
> (*I say your city*) *to his wife and mother;*
> *Breaking his oath and resolution, like*
> *A twist of rotten silk.* . . .
>   . . . O Tullus!
> *Thou hast done a deed* whereat valour will weep.—
>   . . . *Bear from hence his body.*—*Ibid.,* v. 5.

And, secondly, for the passages indicative of Long Time:—

Indeed, no, by your patience; I will not over the threshold *till my lord return from the wars.*—*Ibid.,* i. 3.

>   He is *retir'd to Antium.*
> Spoke he of me?—
>   He did, my lord.—
>   How? what?—
> *How often he had met you,* sword to sword;
> That of all things upon the earth he hated
> Your person most; that he would pawn his fortunes
> To hopeless restitution, so he might
> Be call'd your vanquisher.—
>   *At Antium lives he?*—
> *At Antium.*—

I wish I had a cause *to seek him there,*
To oppose his hatred fully.—Coriol., iii. 1.

Whither wilt thou go ? Take good Cominius
With thee awhile : determine on some course,
More than a wild exposure to each chance
That starts i' the way before thee.— . . .
I'll follow thee a month, devise with thee
Where thou shalt rest, that thou may'st hear of us,
And we of thee ; so, if the time thrust forth
A cause for thy repeal, we shall not send
O'er the vast world to seek a single man ;
And lose advantage, which doth ever cool
I' the absence of the needer.—
                                Fare ye well :
Thou hast years upon thee, and thou art too full
Of the war's surfeits, to *go rove* with one
That 's yet unbruised. . . .
While I remain above the ground, you shall
Hear from me still ; and never of me aught
But what is like me formerly.— . . .
If I could shake off but one seven years
From these old arms and legs, by the good gods,
I'd with thee every foot.—Ibid., iv. 1.

                        Thou hast beat me out
Twelve several times, and I have nightly since
Dreamt of encounters 'twixt thyself and me ;
We have been down together in my sleep,
Unbuckling helms, fisting each other's throat,
And waked half dead with nothing.—*Ibid.*, iv. 5.

We hear not of him, neither need we fear him ;
His remedies are tame i' the present peace
And quietness o' the people, which before
Were in wild hurry. Here do we make his friends
Blush that the world goes well ; who rather had,
Though themselves did suffer by 't, *behold*
Dissentious numbers pestering streets, than see
Our tradesmen singing in their shops, and going
About their functions friendly.—
We stood to 't in good time. Is this Menenius ?—
'Tis he, 'tis he. O, *he is grown most kind*
Of late. Hail, sir !—
                        Hail to you both.—
Your Coriolanus is not much miss'd,
But with his friends : *the commonwealth doth stand ;*
And so would do, were he more angry at it.—
All 's well ; and might have been much better, if
He could have temporis'd.—
                        Where is he, hear you ?—
Nay, I hear nothing : his mother and his wife
Hear nothing from him.— . . .
This is a happier and more comely time
Than when these fellows ran about the streets,
Crying confusion.—Ibid., iv. 6.
                        You are they
That made the air unwholesome, when you cast
Your stinking greasy caps, in hooting at
Coriolanus' exile. . . .
*I ever said we were i' the wrong when we banish'd him.—*So did we all.—*Ibid.*, iv. 6.
                He bears himself more proudlier,
Even to my person, *than I thought he would*

When first I did embrace him : . . .
All places yield to him ere he sits down ;
And the nobility of Rome are his.—*Coriol.*, iv. 7.
We will before the walls of Rome *to-morrow*
Set down our host . . .
　　　　　　　　. . . O, a kiss
Long as my exile, sweet as my revenge !
Now, by the jealous queen of heaven, that kiss
I carried from thee, dear ; and my true lip
Hath virgin'd it *e'er since.*—*Ibid.*, v. 3.
　　　　　　　I rais'd him, and I pawn'd
Mine honour for his truth : who being so heighten'd,
He water'd his new plants with dews of flattery,
Seducing so my friends ; . . . he came unto my hearth ;
Presented to my knife his throat : I took him ;
Made him joint-servant with me ; *gave him way*
In all his own desires ; nay, *let him choose*
Out of my files, his projects to accomplish,
My best and freshest men ; serv'd his designments
In mine own person ; holp to reap the fame
Which he did end all his.—*Ibid.*, v. 5.

If you have writ your annals true, 'tis there,
That, like an eagle in a dove-cote, *I*
Flutter'd your Volscians in Corioli.—*Ibid.*, v. 5.

In " Timon of Athens " there is sufficient length of time implied to allow of the events which precede, accompany, and close the reverse of fortune which befalls the hero ; but yet, while this is the case, the Dramatic Time is so managed that they seem to occur within the space which comes beneath the possible ken of spectators sitting at a play. By Shakespeare's system of simultaneously introduced Short Time and Long Time, this dramatic illusion is effected.

Here are the passages introducing Short Time :—

Good day, sir.— . . . When comes your book forth ?—
Upon the heels of my presentment, sir.— . . .
How this lord is follow'd !—
The senators of Athens : happy man !—
Look, more !
You see this confluence, this great flood of visitors. . . .
You see how all conditions, how all minds
(As well of glib and slippery creatures, as
Of grave and austere quality) *tender down*
Their services to lord Timon. . . .
　　　　　　　. . . *Imprison'd is he*, say you ?—
Ay, my good lord : five talents is his debt.
　　　　　　. . . I 'll pay the debt, and free him. . . .
Commend me to him : I will send his ransom ;
And, *being enfranchis'd*, bid him come to me.— . . .
Vouchsafe my labour, and long live your lordship !—
I thank you ; you shall hear from me anon :
Go not away. What have you there, my friend ?—
A piece of painting, *which I do beseech*
Your lordship to accept.—
　　　　　　　　Painting is welcome. . . .
　　　　　　　. . . I like your work ;
And you shall find I like it : wait attendance
Till you hear farther from me. . . . give me your hand ;
We must needs dine together.— . . .
Good morrow to thee, gentle Apemantus. . . .

Wilt dine with me, Apemantus?— . . .
What trumpet's that?—
　　　　　　'Tis Alcibiades, and
Some twenty horse, all of companionship.—
Pray, entertain them; give them guide to us.
You must needs dine with me: go not you hence,
Till I have thank'd you: when dinner's done,
Show me this piece. . . .
What time o' day is 't, Apemantus?— . . .
Time to be honest. . . .
Thou art going to lord Timon's feast?—
Ay, to see meat fill knaves, and wine heat fools.
　　　　　　. . . *Come, shall we in,*
And taste lord Timon's bounty? . . .
I 'll keep you company.—Timon, i. 1.

You have done our pleasures much grace, fair ladies,
Set a fashion on our entertainment, . . .
Ladies, *there is an idle banquet*
Attends you: please you to dispose yourselves.—
Most thankfully, my lord. . . .
Where be our men?—
Here, my lord, in readiness.—
Our horses!— . . .
　　　　　　Lights, more lights!—
　　　　　　　　The best of happiness,
Honour, and fortunes, keep with you, lord Timon!—
Ready for his friends. [*Exeunt* ALCIBIADES, LORDS, *&c.—Ibid.,* i. 2.

　　　　　　　　Caphis, ho!
Caphis, I say!—
　　　　　　Here, sir, what is your pleasure?—
Get on your cloak, and haste you to lord Timon;
Importune him for moneys; be not ceas'd
With slight denial. . . . *Get you gone.—*
I go, sir.—Ibid., ii. 1.

I must be round with him, *now he comes from hunting.*
Fie, fie, fie, fie!—
　　　　　　Good even, Varro: what,
You come for money?—
　　　　　　Is 't not your business too?—
It is: and yours too, Isidore?—
　　　　　　　It is so.—
Would we were all discharg'd!—
　　　　　　I fear it.—
Here comes the lord.—
So soon as dinner's done, we 'll forth again.— . . .
He humbly prays your speedy payment.—
If you did know, my lord, my master's wants,— . . .
And I am sent expressly to your lordship.—
Give me breath.
I do beseech you, good my lords, keep on;
I 'll wait upon you instantly. Come hither: pray you,
How goes the world, *that I am thus encounter'd*
With clamorous accounts of date-broke bonds,
And the detention of long-since-due debts,
Against my honour?—
　　　　　　Please you, gentlemen
The time is unagreeable to this business:
Your importunacy cease till *after dinner;*
That I may make his lordship understand
Wherefore you are not paid.—

                              Do so, my friends.
See them well entertain'd.—
                          Pray, draw near. . . .
Pray you, walk near : I 'll speak with you anon. . . .
          . . . My dear-lov'd lord,
Though *you hear now* (too late !), *yet now 's a time—*
The greatest of your having lacks a half
To pay your present debts.— . . .
            . . . The future comes apace.— . . .
And *in some sort, these wants of mine are crown'd,*
That I account them blessings ; *for by these*
Shall I try friends : you shall perceive how you
Mistake my fortunes ; I am wealthy in my friends.
Within there ! Flaminius ! Servilius !—
My lord ? my lord ?—
I will despatch you severally : you, to lord Lucius: to lord Lucullus you; *I hunted with his honour to-day ;* you, to Sempronius: commend me to their loves; and, I am proud, say, that *my occasions have found time to use them toward a supply of money.* . . . Go you, sir, to the senators . . . *bid them send o' the instant a thousand talents to me.—*
                    I have been bold
(For that I knew it the most general way)
To them to use your signet and your name ;
But they do shake their heads, and I am here
No richer in return.—Timon, ii. 2.

*I have told my lord of you; he is coming down to you.—*I thank you, sir.—*Here 's my lord.—*One of lord Timon's men ? a gift, I warrant. Why, this hits right; I dreamt of a silver basin and ewer *to-night.* . . . what hast thou there under thy cloak, pretty Flaminius ?—'Faith, nothing but an empty box, sir, which, in my lord's behalf, I come to entreat your honour to supply; who, *having great and instant occasion to use fifty talents, hath sent to your lordship to furnish him, nothing doubting your present assistance therein* . . . *this is no time to lend money,* especially upon bare friendship.— . . . Has friendship such a faint and milky heart, *it turns in less than two nights ?* . . . this slave unto his honour *has my lord's meat in him.—Ibid.,* iii. 1.

I can tell you one thing, my lord, and which I hear from common rumours,—*now lord Timon's happy hours are done and past, and his estate shrinks from him.—* . . . *not long ago, one of his men was with the lord Lucullus, to borrow so many talents ;* nay, urged extremely for't, and showed what necessity belonged to't, and yet *was denied.—* . . . And *what has he sent now ? He has only sent his present occasion now,* my lord: *requesting your lordship to supply his instant use with so many talents.—Ibid.,* iii. 2.

This was my lord's best hope ; *now all are fled,*
Save the gods only : *now his friends are dead.—Ibid.,* iii. 3.
Well met ; *good morrow,* Titus and Hortensius.— . . .
One business does command us all ; for mine
Is money.—
            So is theirs and ours.—
                          And sir Philotus too !—
Good day at once.—
                    Welcome, good brother.—
What do you think the hour ?—
                          Labouring for *nine.—*
So much ?—
            Is not my lord seen yet ?—
                          Not yet.—
I wonder on 't ; he was wont to shine at seven.—
Ay, but *but the days are waxed shorter with him.* . . .
Pray, is my lord ready to come forth ?— . . . O, *here 's Servilius ; now we shall know some answer.—*If I might beseech you, gentlemen, *to repair some other hour,* I should derive much from't ; . . . Go, *bid all my friends again,* . . . *I'll once more feast the rascals.—Ibid.,* iii. 4.

We are for law: *he dies;* urge it no more,
On height of our displeasure: friend or brother,
He forfeits his own blood that spills another.—
     . . . And, not to swell our spirit,
He shall be executed presently.—Timon, iii. 5.

  The *good time of day* to you, sir.— . . . *He hath sent me an earnest inviting.*—
. . . *Here he comes.*— . . . Gentlemen, *our dinner* will not recompense this long stay:
feast your ears with the music awhile, if they will fare so harshly o' the trumpet's
sound; *we shall to't presently*— . . . *Alcibiades is banished.*— . . . *Will you draw
near?—I 'll tell you more anon. Here 's a noble feast toward.*— . . . *Each man to his
stool, with that spur as he would to the lip of his mistress:* your diet shall be in all
places alike. *Make not a city feast of it, to let the meat cool ere we can agree upon the
first place: sit, sit.* . . . *Uncover, dogs, and lap.* . . .
     May you a better feast never behold,
     You knot of mouth-friends! smoke and lukewarm water
     Is your perfection. *This is Timon's last.* . . .
     *Burn, house! sink, Athens! henceforth hated be
     Of Timon, man, and all humanity!* . . .
     Let's make no stay.—Ibid., iii. 6.

      *Nothing I 'll bear from thee,
    But nakedness, thou detestable town!*
    Take thou that too, with multiplying bans!
    Timon will to the woods.—Ibid., iv. 1.

      *Such a house broke!
   So noble a master fallen! All gone!* and not
   One friend to take his fortune by the arm,
   And go along with him!— . . . More of our fellows.—
   All broken implements of a ruin'd house.— . . .
      . . . Good fellows all,
   The latest of my wealth I 'll share amongst you. . . .
      . . . Alas, kind lord!
   *He 's flung in rage from this ingrateful seat
   Of monstrous friends;* nor has he with him to
   Supply his life, or that which can command it.
   I 'll follow, and inquire him out.—Ibid., iv. 2.

     Therefore, be abhorr'd
   All feasts, societies, and throngs of men!
   His semblable, yea, himself, Timon disdains:
   Destruction fang mankind! *Earth, yield me roots!*
       What is here?
   Gold? yellow, glittering, precious gold? No, gods,
   I am no idle votarist. *Roots, you clear heavens!*—
      . . . *What art thou there?* . . .
   What is thy name? Is man so hateful to thee,
   That art thyself a man?—
   I am Misanthropos, and hate mankind.
     . . . *There 's gold to pay thy soldiers:*
   Make large confusion; *and, thy fury spent,
   Confounded be thyself! Speak not, be gone.*— . . .
   Strike up the drum towards Athens! Farewell, Timon.—Ibid., iv. 3.

I am sick of this false world; and will love naught
But even the mere necessities upon 't.
Then, Timon, presently prepare thy grave.—Ibid., iv. 3.

      Rascal thieves,
Here 's gold. . . . Love not yourselves; *away!*
Rob one another. *There 's more gold:* cut throats;
All that you meet are thieves. *To Athens go.—Ibid.*, iv. 3.

Oh, you gods!
Is yond' despised and ruinous man my lord? . . .

He has caught me in his eye : I will present
My honest grief unto him ; and as my lord,
Still serve him with my life.   My dearest master !—
Away ! what art thou ?— . . .
An honest poor servant of yours.—
       . . . Thou singly honest man,
Here take : the gods, out of my misery,
Have sent thee treasure, *go,* live rich and happy ; . . .
And so, *farewell,* and thrive.—
                 O let me stay,
And comfort you, my master.—
                 If thou hat'st curses,
Stay not ; fly, whilst thou 'rt bless'd and free.—Timon, iv. 3.

Hail, worthy Timon !— . . .
We are hither come to offer you our service.— . . .
Hence, *pack !* there 's gold ; ye came for gold, ye slaves :
You have done work for me, there 's payment : *hence !—Ibid.,* v. 1.

               Bring us to his cave :
It is our part, and promise to the Athenians,
To speak with Timon.— . . . *Bring us to him,*
And chance it as it may.—
               Here is his cave,
Peace and content be here !   Lord Timon ! Timon !
Look out and speak to friends : th' Athenians,
By two of their most reverend senate, greet thee :
Speak to them, noble Timon.—
Thou sun, that comfort'st, burn ! *speak, and be hang'd :*
         . . . *So soon we shall drive back*
Of Alcibiades th' approaches wild ;
Who, like a boar too savage, doth root up
His country's peace.— . . .
         . . . *Stay not, all 's in vain.—*
Why, I was writing of my epitaph ;
It will be seen to-morrow : my long sickness
Of health and living *now begins to mend,*
And nothing brings me all things.—Ibid., v. 2.

           His expedition promises
Present approach.—
We stand much hazard, if they bring not Timon.—*Ibid.,* v. 3.

Sound to this coward and lascivious town
Our terrible approach.— . . . *Now the time is flush,*
When crouching marrow, in the bearer strong,
Cries of itself, " No more."— . . .
       . . . Then, dear countryman,
Bring in thy ranks, but leave without thy rage :
Spare thy Athenian cradle.— . . .
Descend, and open your uncharged ports :
Those enemies of Timon's and mine own,
Whom you yourselves shall set out for reproof,
Fall, and no more. . . .—
       . . . 'Tis most nobly spoken.—
Descend, and keep your words.—
My noble general, *Timon is dead.—Ibid.,* v. 5.

And here are the passages introducing Long Time :—

Please you, my lord, that honourable gentleman, lord Lucullus, *entreats your company to-morrow to hunt with him.—Ibid.,* i. 2.

       And late, five thousand ; to Varro and to Isidore
       He owes nine thousand ; *besides my former sum,*

Which makes it five and twenty. *Still in motion*
Of raging waste? It cannot hold; it will not.—*Timon*, ii. 1.

Go to my steward.—
Please it your lordship, *he hath put me off*
To the succession of new days this month. . . .—
I pr'ythee *but repair to me next morning.*— . . .
'*Twas due* on forfeiture, my lord, *six weeks*
And past.—
   Your steward puts me off, my lord.—*Ibid.*, ii. 2.

       Ventidius lately
Buried his father; by whose death, he's stepp'd
Into a great estate: *when he was poor,*
Imprison'd, and in scarcity of friends,
I clear'd him with five talents.—*Ibid.*, ii. 2.

We banish thee for ever.— . . .
If, *after two days' shine*, Athens contain thee,
Attend our weightier judgment. . . .—
   . . . Banishment!
It comes not ill; I hate not to be banish'd;
It is a cause worthy my spleen and fury,
That I may strike at Athens. I'll cheer up
My discontented troops, and lay for hearts.—*Ibid.*, iii. 5.

I think this honourable lord did but try us *this other day.*— . . . I am e'en sick of shame, that *when your lordship this other day sent to me*, I was so unfortunate a beggar.— . . . *He gave me a jewel the other day*, and now he has beat it out of my hat. —*Ibid.*, iii. 6.

I have heard in some sort of thy miseries.—
Thou saw'st them, *when I had prosperity.*—
I see them now; *then was a blessed time.*—*Ibid.*, iv. 3.

Thy flatterers yet wear silk, drink wine, lie soft;
Hug their diseas'd perfumes, *and have forgot*
That ever Timon was. . . .
Where liest o' nights, Timon?—
     Under that's above me.—*Ibid.*, iv. 3.

   Have you forgot me, sir?—
Why dost thou ask that? *I have forgot all men:*
Then, if thou grant'st thou'rt a man, *I have forgot thee.*—*Ibid.*, iv. 3.

Does *the rumour* hold for true, that he is so full of gold?—Certain: Alcibiades *reports it;* Phrynia and Timandra had gold of him: he likewise enriched poor straggling soldiers with great quantity. '*Tis said*, he gave unto his steward a mighty sum.— . . . You are honest men: *you have heard* that I have gold; I am sure you have: speak truth; you are honest men.—*So it is said*, my noble lord.—*Ibid.*, v. 1.

     O, forget
What we are sorry for ourselves in thee.
The senators with one consent of love
Entreat thee back to Athens.—*Ibid.*, v. 2.

When thy first griefs were but a mere conceit,
Ere thou hadst power, or we had cause of fear,
We sent to thee.— . . . So did we woo
Transformed Timon to our city's love
By humble message and by promis'd means:
   . . . *Nor are they living*
Who were the motives that you first went out;
Shame, that they wanted cunning in excess,
Hath broke their hearts.—*Ibid.*, v. 5.

The Dramatic Time is managed so ingeniously by Shakespeare in the play of " Julius Cæsar," as to allow of long intervals elapsing insensibly and gliding by almost unperceived. He has so contrived the indications of Short Time and Long Time to be blended, during the progress of the first, second, and third acts, that we pass from the period at which the drama opens—the Ides (or 13th) of February, when the feast of Lupercal was celebrated—to the Ides (or 15th) of March, while we seem to have beheld but the transition of some few hours. Similarly, during the fourth and fifth acts, the events that followed upon the assassination of Julius Cæsar are made to succeed each other with such imperceptible tokens of ever-advancing time, that we find ourselves arrived at their close with no sense of undue length in dramatic period.

By keeping well before the spectator the presence of night, super-vening upon afternoon and evening, and then the gradual approach of dawn, of morning, and of day, the dramatist has magically contrived to bring on the date of Cæsar's death in the third act, even while linking it subtly with the very date on which the dictator was offered and refused the crown of Rome in the first act; so that a whole month is *illusorily* passed, while but the passing from one day to the next is *actually* accounted for.

These are the betokenings of Short Time :—

Hence ! home, you idle creatures get you home:
Is this a holiday ? What ! know you not,
Being mechanical, you ought not walk
Upon *a labouring day* without the sign
Of your profession ? . . .
But wherefore art thou not in thy shop *to-day ?*
Why dost thou lead these men about the streets ?—
. . . *We make holiday, to see Cæsar, and to rejoice in his triumph.*— . .
And *do you now* put on your best attire ?
And *do you now* cull out a holiday ?
And *do you now* strew flowers in his way,
That comes in triumph over Pompey's blood ?
Be gone ! Run to your houses . . .
You know *it is the feast of Lupercal.—Jul. C.*, i. 1.

The games are done, and Cæsar is returning.—
As they pass by, pluck Casca by the sleeve ;
And he will, after his sour fashion, tell you
What hath proceeded worthy note to-day.— . . .
Ay, Casca ; tell us *what hath chanc'd to-day*, . . .

Why, *there was a crown offered him :* and being offered him, he put it by with the back of his hand, thus; and then the people fell a-shouting.— . . . Will you *sup with me to-night*, Casca?—No, I am promised forth.— . . . For this time I will leave you . . .

. . . *I will this night*,
In several hands, *in at his window throw*,
As if they came from several citizens,
Writings, all tending to the great opinion
That Rome holds of his name ; wherein obscurely
Cæsar's ambition shall be glanced at.—*Ibid.*, i. 2.

Good even, Casca, *brought you Cæsar home ?*
Why are you breathless ? and why stare you so ?—
. . . *never till to-night, never till now*,
Did I go through a tempest dropping fire.— . . .
Good night, then, Casca : this disturbed sky
Is not to walk in.— . . . Cassius, *what night is this !*
A very pleasing night to honest men.—

> *. . . I have walk'd about the streets,*
> *Submitting me unto the perilous night, . . .*
> Now could I, Casca, name to thee a man
> Most like *this dreadful night, . . .*
> And I do know, *by this,* they stay for me
> In Pompey's porch: for now, *this fearful night,*
> There is no stir or walking in the streets.— . . .
>   *. . . What a fearful night is this!—*
>   *. . . Take this paper,*
> *And look you lay it in the prætor's chair,*
> *Where Brutus may but find it; and throw this*
> *In at his window.—* . . . Well, I will hie
> *And so bestow these papers as you bade me.—*
> That done, repair to Pompey's theatre.
> Come, Casca, you and I will, yet, ere day,
> See Brutus at his house. . . . Let us go,
> For it is after midnight; and, ere day,
> We will awake him, and be sure of him.—*Jul. C.,* i. 3.

> I cannot, by the progress of the stars,
> Give guess *how near to day.* Lucius, I say!
> I would it were my fault to sleep so soundly. . . .
> Get me a taper in my study, Lucius:
> When it is lighted, come and call me here.— . . .
> The taper burneth in your closet, sir.
> Searching the window for a flint, I found
> This paper, thus seal'd up; and, I am sure,
> *It did not lie there when I went to bed.—*
> *Get you to bed again; it is not day.*
> *Is not to-morrow,* boy, *the ides of March?—* . . .
> Sir, 'tis your brother Cassius at the door,
> Who doth desire to see you.—
>   Is he alone?—
> No, sir, there are more with him.— . . .
>   *. . . O conspiracy,*
> Sham'st thou to show thy dangerous brow *by night,*
> When evils are most free?— . . .
> *Good morrow,* Brutus; do we trouble you?—
> *I have been up this hour; awake, all night.—*
>   *. . . They are all welcome.*
> What watchful cares do interpose themselves
> Betwixt your eyes and *night?—*
> Shall I entreat a word?—
> Here lies the east: doth not the day break here?—
> No.—
> O, pardon, sir, it doth; and *yon grey lines*
> *That fret the clouds are messengers of day.—*
>   *. . . The clock hath stricken three.—*
> 'Tis time to part.—
>   But it is doubtful yet,
> *Whether Cæsar will come forth to-day,* or no: . . .
> *The unaccustom'd terror of this night,*
> And the persuasion of his augurers,
> May hold him *from the Capitol to-day.—* . . .
> Let me work;
> For I can give his humour the true bent,
> And I will bring him to the Capitol.—
> Nay, we will all of us be there to fetch him.—
> *By the eighth hour.—* . . .
> *The morning comes upon us:* we'll leave you, Brutus.— . . .
> And so, *good morrow* to you every one. . . .
> Portia, what mean you? *Wherefore rise you now?*

It is not for your health thus to commit
Your weak condition to the raw cold *morning*.—
Nor for yours neither.   You 've ungently, Brutus,
Stole from my bed : and *yesternight, at supper,*
You suddenly arose, and walk'd about,
Musing and sighing, with your arms across; . . .—
            . . . Good Portia, *go to bed*.—
Is Brutus sick, and is it physical
To walk unbraced, and suck up the humours
Of the dank *morning ?*   What, is Brutus sick,
And will he steal out of his wholesome bed,
To dare the vile contagion of the *night*,
            . . . and what men *to-night*
Have had resort to you ;— . . .
Hark, hark ! one knocks : Portia, go in awhile ;
And by-and-by thy bosom shall partake
The secrets of my heart. . . .
Leave me with haste.— . . .
Vouchsafe *good morrow* from a feeble tongue.—
            . . . What it is, my Caius,
I shall unfold to thee, as we are going
To whom it must be done.—
                    Set on your foot ;
And, with a heart new fir'd, I follow you,
To do I know not what : but it sufficeth
That Brutus leads me on.—
                    Follow me, then.—*Jul. C*., ii. 1.

Nor heaven nor earth have been at peace to-night :
Thrice hath Calphurnia in her sleep cried out,
" Help, ho ! They murder Cæsar!" who 's within ?—
My lord.—
Go bid the priests *do present sacrifice,*
And bring me their opinions of success.—
I will, my lord.—
What mean you, Cæsar?   Think you to walk forth ?
You shall not stir out of your house *to-day*.—
            . . . What say the augurers ?—
They would not have you to stir forth *to-day*.— . . .
Cæsar should be a beast without a heart,
If he should stay at home *to-day* for fear.— . . .
Do not go forth *to-day*. . . .
We 'll send Mark Antony to the senate-house ;
And he shall say you are not well *to-day*.— . . .
Cæsar, all hail !   *Good morrow*, worthy Cæsar:
I come to fetch you to the senate-house.—
And you are come in very happy time
To bear my greeting to the senators,
And tell them that *I will not come to-day*. . . .
Calphurnia here, my wife, stays me at home :
She dreamt *to-night* she saw my statua,
Which, like a fountain with a hundred spouts,
Did run pure blood . . . and on her knee
Hath begg'd that I will *stay at home to-day*. . . .
            . . . The senate have concluded
To give, this day, a crown to mighty Cæsar.— . . .
How foolish do your fears seem *now*, Calphurnia !
I am ashamed I did yield to them.
Give me my robe, for I will go :
And look where Publius *is come to fetch me*.—
Good morrow, Cæsar.—
            Welcome, Publius.

What, Brutus, *are you stirr'd so early too ?*
Good morrow, Casca. . . .
What is 't o'clock ?—
                Cæsar, *'tis strucken eight.*— . . .
See ! Antony, *that revels long o' nights,*
Is notwithstanding up. Good morrow, Antony.—
So to most noble Cæsar.—
             Bid them prepare within :
I am to blame to be thus waited for.
Now, Cinna : now, Metellus : what, Trebonius !
I have an hour's talk in store for you ;
Remember that you call on me to-day.—*Jul. C.,* ii. 2.

Here will I stand till Cæsar pass along,
And as a suitor will I give him this.—*Ibid.,* ii. 3.

I pr'ythee, boy, *run to the senate-house ;*
Stay not to answer me, but *get thee gone.* . . .
I would have had thee there, and here again,
Ere I can tell thee what thou shouldst do there. . . .
What is 't o'clock ?—
          About the ninth hour, lady.—
Is Cæsar yet gone to the Capitol ?—
Madam, not yet : *I go to take my stand,*
To see him pass on to the Capitol. . . .
Good morrow to you. Here the street is narrow : . . .
I 'll get me to a place more void, and there
Speak to great Cæsar as he comes along.— . . .
Run, Lucius, and commend me to my lord ;
Say I am merry : *come to me again,*
And bring me word what he doth say to thee.—*Ibid.,* ii. 4.

The ides of March are come.—
Ay, Cæsar ; but not gone.—
Hail, Cæsar ! Read this schedule. . . .
Delay not, Cæsar ; *read it instantly.*— . . .
I wish *your enterprise to-day* may thrive.— . . .
He wish'd *to-day our enterprise might thrive.*— . . .
Trebonius *knows his time ; for, look you,* Brutus,
He draws Mark Antony out of the way.—
Where is Metellus Cimber ? *Let him go,*
And presently prefer his suit to Cæsar.—
He is address'd : press near and second him.—
Casca, *you are the first that rears your hand.*—
Are we all ready ?— . . .
Speak, hands, for me !—
Et tu, Brute ? Then fall, Cæsar !—*Ibid.,* iii. 1.

Here comes Antony. Welcome, Mark Antony.—
O mighty Cæsar ! dost thou lie so low ?
Are all thy conquests, glories, triumphs, spoils,
Shrunk to this little measure ? Fare thee well.
I know not, gentlemen, what you intend,
Who else must be let blood, who else is rank :
If I myself, *there is no hour so fit*
As Cæsar's death's hour. . . .
           That 's all I seek :
And am moreover suitor *that I may*
Produce his body to the market-place ;
And in the pulpit, as becomes a friend,
Speak in the order of his funeral.—
You shall, Mark Antony. . . .
I will myself into the pulpit first. . . .
Prepare the body, then, and follow us.— . . .

You serve Octavius Cæsar, do you not?—
I do, Mark Antony.—
Cæsar did write for him to come to Rome.—
He did receive his letters, and is coming.— . . .
. . . Is thy master coming?—
He lies to-night within seven leagues of Rome.—
Post back with speed, and tell him what hath chanc'd.—*Jul. C.*, iii. 1.

The noble Brutus is ascended: silence! . . .
I have done no more to Cæsar, than you shall do to Brutus.   The question of his
death is enrolled in the Capitol. . . . *Here comes his body, mourned by Mark Antony.*
. . . Friends, Romans, countrymen, lend me your ears; *I come to bury Cæsar, not to
praise him.* . . .
*But yesterday, the word of Cæsar might
Have stood against the world: now, lies he there,*
And none so poor to do him reverence. . . .
But *here's a parchment with the seal of Cæsar*—
I found it in his closet—*'tis his will*:
Let but the commons hear this testament.— . . .
We'll hear the will: read it, Mark Antony.—
The will, the will! we will hear Cæsar's will.— . . .
*Read the will; we'll hear it, Antony;
You shall read us the will, Cæsar's will.*— . . .
The will! the testament!—
They were villains, murderers: *the will! read the will.*— . . .
Most noble Cæsar! *we'll revenge his death.*— . . .
*Now let it work: mischief, thou art afoot,
Take thou what course thou wilt.*   How now, fellow!—
Sir, *Octavius is already come to Rome.*—
Where is he?—
He and Lepidus are at Cæsar's house.—
And *thither will I straight* to visit him:
He comes upon a wish.— . . .
I heard him say, *Brutus and Cassius
Are rid like madmen through the gates of Rome.*—*Ibid.*, iii. 2.

I dreamt to-night that I did feast with Cæsar.— . . .
Answer every man directly.—*Ay, and briefly.*— . . .
Proceed; directly.— . . . *Tear him, tear him!*
Come, brands, ho! firebrands!   *To Brutus', to Cassius'; burn all: some to Decius'
house, and some to Casca's; some to Ligarius': away, go!*—*Ibid.*, iii. 3.

These many, then, shall die; their names are prick'd.—
. . . And *now*, Octavius,
Listen great things: *Brutus and Cassius
Are levying powers: we must straight make head:*
Therefore let our alliance be combin'd,
Our best friends made, and our best means stretch'd out;
And *let us presently go sit in council.*—*Ibid.*, iv. 1.

Stand, ho!—
Give the word, ho! and stand.—
What now, Lucilius! *is Cassius near?*—
*He is at hand; and Pindarus is come
To do you salutation from his master.*—
. . . if he be *at hand*,
I shall be satisfied.—
I do not doubt
But that *my noble master will appear
Such as he is*, full of regard and honour.—
. . . Comes his army on?—
They mean *this night* in Sardis to be quarter'd;
*The greater part, the horse in general,
Are come with Cassius.*—

　　　　　　　　　　Hark ! he is arriv'd :
March gently on to meet him.—*Jul. C.*, iv. 2.
In such a time as this, it is not meet
That every nice offence should bear his comment.— . . .
　　　　　　. . . shall we *now*
Contaminate our fingers with base bribes,
And sell the mighty space of our large honours
For so much trash as may be grasped thus ? . . .
　　　　　　. . . from *this day* forth,
I 'll use you for my mirth.—*Ibid.*, iv. 3.
Lucilius and Titinius, bid the commanders
Prepare to lodge their companies *to-night*.—
And come yourselves, and bring Messala with you,
Immediately to us.— . . .
No man bears sorrow better.　*Portia is dead.*—
Ha ! Portia.—
She is dead.— . . .
Now sit we close about this taper here,
And call in question our necessities.— . . .
　　　　　. . . I have here received letters,
That *young Octavius and Mark Antony*
Come down upon us with a mighty power,
Bending their expedition toward Philippi. . .
Well, *to our work alive.*　What do you think
Of *marching to Philippi presently ?* . . .
Our legions are brim-full, our cause is ripe.— . . .
　　　　　. . . Then, with your will, *go on ;*
We 'll along ourselves, and meet them at Philippi.
The deep of night is crept upon our talk,
And nature must obey necessity ;
Which we will niggard with a little rest.
There is no more to say ?—
　　　　　　　　No more.　*Good night ;*
Early to-morrow will we rise, and hence.—
Lucius, my gown.　Farewell, good Messala :
Good night, Titinius : noble, noble Cassius,
Good night, and good repose.—
　　　　　　　　O my dear brother !
This was an ill beginning of the *night :* . . .
Good night, my lord.—
　　　　　　Good night, good brother.—
Good night, lord Brutus.— . . .
　　　　　. . . Gentle knave, *good night ;*
I will not do thee so much wrong to wake thee :
If thou dost nod, thou break'st thy instrument ;
I 'll take it from thee ; and, good boy, *good night.* . . .
Go and commend me to my brother Cassius ;
Bid him set on his powers betimes before,
And we will follow.—*Ibid.*, iv. 3.
Now, Antony, our hopes are answered :
You said, the enemy would not come down,
But keep the hills and upper regions ;
It proves not so : *their battles are at hand ;*
They mean to warn us at Philippi here,
Answering before we do demand of them.— . . .
　　　　　. . . *Prepare you, generals :*
The enemy comes on in gallant show ;
Their bloody sign of battle is hung out,
And something to be done immediately.— . . .
Flatterers !　Now, Brutus, thank yourself :
This tongue had not offended so *to-day*,

If Cassius might have ruled.— . . .
Defiance, traitors, hurl we in your teeth :
If you dare fight to-day, come to the field ;
If not, when you have stomachs.—
Why, now, blow wind, swell billow, and swim bark !
The storm is up and all is on the hazard. . . .
This is my birthday ; as this very day
Was Cassius born. . . .
Coming from Sardis on our former ensign
Two mighty eagles fell ; and there they perch'd,
Gorging and feeding from our soldiers' hands ;
Who to Philippi here escorted us :
This morning are they fled away and gone ; . . .
        . . . Now, most noble Brutus,
The gods *to-day* stand friendly, that we may,
Lovers in peace, lead on our days to age ! . . .
If we do lose this battle, *then is this*
The very last time we shall speak together : . . .—
        . . . But *this same day*
Must end that work the ides of March begun . . .
        . . . O, that a man might know
The end of this day's business, ere it come !
But it sufficeth, that the day will end,
And then the end is known. *Come, ho ! away !*—*Jul. C.,* v. 1.

Ride, ride, Messala, ride, and give these bills
Unto the legions on the other side :
Let them set on at once ; for I perceive
But cold demeanour in Octavius' wing,
And *sudden push gives them the overthrow.*
Ride, ride, Messala : let them all come down.—*Ibid.,* v. 2.

Fly farther off, my lord, *fly farther off ;*
Mark Antony is in your tents, my lord :
Fly, therefore, noble Cassius, *fly far off.*— . . .
Mount thou my horse, and *hide thy spurs in him,*
Till he have brought thee *up to yonder troops,*
And here again ; that I may rest assur'd
Whether yond' troops are friend or enemy.—
I will be here again, even with a thought.— . . .
This day I breathed first : time is come round,
And where I did begin, there I shall end ;
My life is run his compass. . . .
        . . . Cæsar, *thou art reveng'd,*   [*Dies.*
Even with the sword that kill'd thee.—
But Cassius is no more. O setting sun,
As in thy red rays thou dost sink to-night,
So in his red blood Cassius' day is set :
The sun of Rome is set ! our day is gone. . . .
        . . . Brutus, *come apace,*
And see how I regarded Caius Cassius.— . . .
        . . . Lucilius, come ;
And come, young Cato ; let us to the field :
Labeo and Flavius, *set our battles on :*
'Tis three o'clock ; and, Romans, yet *ere night*
We shall try fortune in a second fight.—*Ibid.,* v. 3.

Statilius show'd the torch-light ; but, my lord,
He came not back : he is or ta'en or slain.— . . .
The ghost of Cæsar hath appear'd to me
Two several times by night—at Sardis once,
And, *this last night, here in Philippi fields :*
I know my hour is come. . . .

Our enemies have beat us to the pit :
It is more worthy to leap in ourselves,
Than tarry till they push us. . . .
I shall have glory by *this losing day*,
More than Octavius and Mark Antony
By this vile conquest shall attain unto.
So, *fare you well at once ;* for Brutus' tongue
Hath almost ended his life's history :
Night hangs upon mine eyes; my bones would rest,
That have but labour'd to attain *this hour*. . . .
Hold, then, my sword, and turn away thy face,
While I do run upon it. Wilt thou, Strato ?—
Give me your hand first : fare you well, my lord.—
Farewell, good Strato. *Cæsar, now be still :*
I kill'd not thee with half so good a will.—
> [*He runs on his sword, and dies.*
> . . . Brutus only overcame himself,
And no man else hath honour by his death.— . . .
According to his virtue let us use him,
With all respect and rites of burial.
Within my tent his bones *to-night* shall lie,
Most like a soldier, order'd honourably.
So, *call the field to rest :* and *let 's away*,
To part the glories of *this happy day.—Jul. C.*, v. 5.

And these are the betokenings of Long Time :—

Beware the ides of March.—
> What man is that ?—
A soothsayer bids you *beware the ides of March.—*
Set him before me ; let me see his face.—
Fellow, come from the throng ; look upon Cæsar.—
What say'st thou to me now ? speak once again.—
Beware the ides of March.—Ibid., i. 2.

> What you have said,
I will consider ; what you have to say,
I will with patience hear ; and *find a time*
Both meet to hear and answer such high things.—*Ibid.*, i. 2.

Will you dine with me to-morrow ? . . .
To-morrow, if you please to speak with me,
I will come home to you ; or, if you will,
Come home to me, and I will wait for you.—
I will do so : *till then*, think of the world.—*Ibid.*, i. 2.

Comes Cæsar to the Capitol *to-morrow ?*—
He doth ; for he did bid Antonius
Send word to you, *he would be there to-morrow.*— . . .
Indeed, they say, the senators *to-morrow*
Mean to establish Cæsar as a king.—*Ibid.*, i. 3.

Such instigations have been *often* dropp'd
Where I have took them up.—*Ibid.*, ii. 1.

You all did see that *on the Lupercal*
I thrice presented him a kingly crown,
Which he did thrice refuse : was this ambition ?
Yet Brutus says he was ambitious.—*Ibid.*, iii. 2.

Let me tell you, Cassius, you yourself
Are much condemn'd to have an itching palm ;
To *sell and mart your offices for gold*
To undeservers. . . .
Remember March, the ides of March remember :
Did not great Julius bleed for justice' sake ?— . . .

When Cæsar liv'd, he durst not thus have mov'd me.—
　　　　　　　. . . *I did send to you*
For certain sums of gold, *which you denied me ;*
　　　　　　　. . . *I did send*
To you for gold to pay my legions,
Which you denied me : was that done like Cassius ?
Should I have answer'd Caius Cassius so ?—. . .
　　　　　　　. . . *I denied you not.—*
You did.—
　　　　I did not : he was but a fool
That brought my answer back.—Jul. C., iv. 3.
The enemy increaseth *every day.—Ibid.,* iv. 3.
Speak to me what thou art.—
　　　　　　　Thy evil spirit, Brutus.—
Why com'st thou ?—
To tell thee *thou shalt see me at Philippi.—*
Well, *then I shall see thee again ?—*
　　　　　　　Ay, at Philippi.—
Why, *I will see thee at Philippi, then.—Ibid.,* iv. 3.
Villains, *you did not so, when your vile daggers*
Hack'd one another in the sides of Cæsar.—Ibid., v. 1.

Very artistically is the Dramatic Time in the tragedy of " Macbeth" managed, so as to give the needful scope for naturally proceeding events, and yet so as to bring them within the limits of a witnessed performance. Especially noteworthy is the skilful mode in which the time is treated during the second act ; when we pass from midnight, through the dark hours of that darker deed, unto the approach of dawn, the breaking of the morning, the advent of day and the discovery of the murder that has been perpetrated—all gradually and most plausibly brought on. Then, on the very heel of that event, are ushered in fresh occurrences—the burial of the dead king, the flight of his sons and natural successors, the investiture of the new monarch and regicide—all anticipating and preparing for the troublous reign and long period of national suffering that supervene ; so that the mind admits the apparently protracted time necessary for these, even while witnessing but the lapse of three concluding dramatic acts. And first, for the tokens of Brief Time :—

When shall we three meet again
In thunder, lightning, or in rain ?—
When the hurly-burly 's done,
When the battle 's lost and won.—
That will be ere the set of sun.—
Where the place ?—
　　　　　　　Upon the heath.—
There to meet with Macbeth.—Macb., i. 1.
Who comes here ?—
　　　　　　　The worthy thane of Rosse.—
What a haste looks through his eyes ! . . .
No more that thane of Cawdor shall deceive
Our bosom interest : *go, pronounce his present death,*
And with his former title greet Macbeth.—
I 'll see it done.—Ibid., i. 2.

A drum, a drum !
Macbeth doth come.— . . .
So foul and fair a day I have not seen. . . .

> . . . Who 's here ?—
> *The king hath happily receiv'd, Macbeth,*
> *The news of thy success.* . . . *As thick as tale,*
> *Came post with post ;* and every one did bear
> Thy praises in his kingdom's great defence,
> And pour'd them down before him.—
> 　　　　　　　　　　　　*We are sent*
> *To give thee, from our royal master, thanks ;—* . . .
> And, for an earnest of a greater honour,
> *He bade me, from him, call thee thane of Cawdor :—* . . .
> 　　　. . . *Let us toward the king.*
> 　　　　　. . . *Come, friends.*—Macb., i. 3.

> O worthiest cousin ! . . . *Welcome hither :*
> 　　　. . . *From hence to Inverness,*
> And bind us farther to you.— . . .
> *I 'll be myself the harbinger, and make joyful*
> *The hearing of my wife with your approach ;*
> *So, humbly take my leave.* . . .
> 　　　　　　. . . *Let us after him,*
> *Whose care is gone before to bid us welcome.*—Ibid., i. 4.

" *They met me in the day of success ;* and I have learned by the perfectest report, they have more in them than mortal knowledge. When I turn'd in desire to question them farther, they made themselves air, into which they vanished. *Whiles I stood rapt in the wonder of it, came missives from the king, who all-hailed me, ' Thane of Cawdor ' ; by which title, before, these weird sisters saluted me.*" . . .

> *Glamis thou art, and Cawdor ;* and shalt be
> What thou art promis'd : . . . *Hie thee hither,*
> That I may pour my spirits in thine ear ;— . . .
> The king comes here to-night.—
> 　　　　　　　　Thou 'rt mad to say it :
> *Is not thy master with him ?* who, wer 't so,
> Would have inform'd for preparation.—
> So please you, it is true : *our thane is coming :*
> *One of my fellows had the speed of him ;*
> *Who, almost dead for breath, had scarcely more*
> *Than would make up his message.*— . . .
> 　　　. . . Great Glamis ! worthy Cawdor !
> Greater than both, by the all-hail hereafter !
> Thy letters have *transported me beyond*
> *This ignorant present, and I feel now*
> *The future in the instant.*—
> 　　　　　　　My dearest love,
> Duncan comes here to-night.—
> 　　　　　　　And when goes hence ?—
> To-morrow, as he purposes.—
> 　　　　　　　*O, never*
> *Shall sun that morrow see !* . . .
> 　　　　. . . *He that 's coming*
> *Must be provided for :* and you shall *put*
> *This night's great business into my despatch*—Ibid., i. 5.

> Where 's the thane of Cawdor ?
> *We cours'd him at the heels, and had a purpose*
> *To be his purveyor : but he rides well ;*
> *And his great love, sharp as his spur, hath holp him*
> *To his home before us.* Fair and noble hostess,
> *We are your guest to-night*—Ibid., i. 6.

> If it were done when 'tis done, then *'twere well*
> *It were done quickly.*— . . .
> *He has almost supp'd :* why have you left the chamber ?

> . . . *When Duncan is asleep*
> (*Whereto the rather shall his day's hard journey*
> *Soundly invite him*), *his two chamberlains*
> Will I with wine and wassail so convince.— . . .
>   . . . *I am settled, and bend up*
> *Each corporal agent to this terrible feat.*
> *Away, and mock the time with fairest show.*—*Macb.*, i. 7.

> *How goes the night*, boy?—
> *The moon is down; I have not heard the clock.*—
> *And she goes down at twelve.*—
>   *I take't, 'tis later*, sir.— . . .
> What, sir, *not yet at rest? The king's a-bed.* . . .
> Go *bid thy mistress, when my drink is ready,*
> *She strike upon the bell,   Get thee to bed* . . .
>   . . . *Now o'er the one half world*
> *Nature seems dead, and wicked dreams abuse*
> *The curtain'd sleep.* . . . Thou sure and firm-set earth,
> Hear not my steps, which way they walk, for fear
> Thy very stones prate of my whereabout,
> And *take the present horror from the time,*
> *Which now suits with it.   Whiles I threat, he lives:*
> *Words to the heat of deeds too cold breath gives.*
> *I go, and it is done; the bell invites me.*
> Hear it not, Duncan; for *it is a knell*
> *That summons thee to heaven or to hell.*—*Ibid.*, ii. 1.

> *It was the owl that shriek'd, the fatal bellman,*
> *Which gives the stern'st good-night.   He is about it:*
> The doors are open. . . .—
> *I have done the deed.*— . . .
>   . . . *I hear a knocking*
> At the south entry: *retire we to our chamber:*
> A little water clears us of this deed: . . .
> *Get on your night-gown, lest occasion call us,*
> *And show us to be watchers.*— . . .
> *Wake Duncan with thy knocking! I would thou couldst!*—*Ibid.*, ii. 2.

Here's a knocking, indeed! . . . *Knock, knock;* never at quiet! What are you? . . .
Anon, anon! I pray you, remember the porter.—
Was it so late, friend, *ere you went to bed, that you do lie so late?*—'Faith, sir, *we*
were carousing till the second cock: . . .—I believe, drink gave thee the lie *last night.*
. . . Is thy master stirring?
> *Our knocking has awak'd him; here he comes.*—
> *Good morrow*, noble sir.—
>   *Good morrow*, both.
> *Is the king stirring*, worthy thane?—
>   Not yet.—
> He did command me *to call timely on him:*
> *I have almost slipp'd the hour.*— . . .
> *Goes the king hence to-day?*—
>   He does: he did appoint so.—
> *The night has been unruly:* . . . the obscure bird
> Clamour'd *the livelong night.*— . . .
>   . . . *'Twas a rough night.*— . . .
> Approach the chamber, and destroy your sight
> With a new Gorgon: do not bid me speak;
> See, and then speak yourselves.   *Awake, awake!*—.
>   . . . *O Banquo, Banquo,*
> *Our royal master's murder'd!*— . . .
> Had I but died *an hour before this chance,*
> I had liv'd a blessed time; for, *from this instant,*
> There's nothing serious in mortality. . . .

Your royal father's murder'd.—
                 O, by whom ?—
Those of his chamber, as it seem'd, had done 't : . . .—
O, yet I do repent me of *my fury*,
That I did kill them.—
              Wherefore did you so ?—
Who can be wise, amaz'd, temperate, and furious,
Loyal and neutral, *in a moment ?* No man :
The expedition of my violent love
Out-run the pauser reason. . . .
      . . . Let's briefly put on manly readiness,
And meet i' the hall together.— . . .
         . . . Let's not consort with them :
             . . . I'll to England.—
To Ireland, I : our separated fortune
Shall keep us both the safer : . . .—
           . . . Therefore, to horse ;
And let us not be dainty of leave-taking,
But shift away.—*Macb.*, ii. 3.
               I have seen
Hours dreadful, and things strange ; but *this sore night*
Hath trifled former knowings.— . . .
            . . . by the clock 'tis day,
And yet dark night strangles the travelling lamp :
Is 't night's predominance, or the day's shame,
That darkness does the face of earth entomb,
When living light should kiss it ?— . . .
Is 't known who did this more than bloody deed ?— . . .
Malcolm and Donalbain, the king's two sons,
Are stol'n away and fled ; which puts upon them
Suspicion of the deed.— . . . Then, *'tis most like,*
The sovereignty will fall upon Macbeth.—
He is already nam'd ; and gone to Scone
To be invested.—
           Where is Duncan's body ?—
Carried to Colme-kill,
The sacred storehouse of his predecessors,
And guardian of their bones.—*Ibid.*, ii. 4.

Thou hast it now—king, Cawdor, Glamis, all,
As the weird women promis'd.— . . .
To-night we hold a solemn supper, sir,
And I 'll request your presence. . . .
Ride you this afternoon ?—
Ay, my good lord.—
We should have else desir'd your good advice, . . .
In *this day's* council ; . . .
Is 't far you ride ?—
As far, my lord, as will *fill up the time*
'Twixt this and supper : go not my horse the better,
I must become a borrower of the night
For a dark hour or twain.—
             Fail not our feast.
      . . . Hie you to horse : adieu,
Till you return at night. Goes Fleance with you ?—
Ay, my good lord : *our time does call upon us.*—
I wish your horses swift, and sure of foot ;
And *so I do commend you to their backs.*
Farewell.
Let every man be master of his time
Till seven at night ; to make society
The sweeter welcome, we will keep ourself

Till supper-time alone : while then, God be with you.—
                    . . . *Within this hour, at most,*
I will advise you where to plant yourselves ;
Acquaint you with the perfect spy o' the time,
The moment on 't ; for 't must be done to-night, . . .
Fleance his son, that keeps him company,
Whose absence is no less material to me
Than is his father's, *must embrace the fate*
Of that dark hour. . . .
It is concluded : Banquo, thy soul's flight,
If it find heaven, must find it out to-night.—*Macb.*, iii. 1.

Is Banquo gone from court ?—
Ay, madam, *but returns again to-night.*— . . .
Gentle my lord, sleek o'er your rugged looks ;
Be bright and jovial *among your guests to-night.*— . . .
                    . . . *Ere the bat hath flown*
His cloister'd flight ; ere, to black Hecate's summons,
The shard-borne beetle, with his drowsy hums,
Hath rung night's yawning peal, there shall be done
A deed of dreadful note.— . . .
                    . . . *Come, seeling night,*
Scarf up the tender eye of pitiful day ;
And with thy bloody and invisible hand
Cancel and tear to pieces that great bond
Which keeps me pale !   Light thickens ; and *the crow*
Makes wing to the rooky wood :
Good things of day begin to droop and drowse ;
Whiles night's black agents to their preys do rouse.—*Ibid.*, iii. 2.

The west yet glimmers with some streaks of day :
Now spurs the lated traveller apace,
To gain the timely inn ; and near approaches
The subject of our watch.— . . .
It will be rain *to-night.*—
                    Let it come down.—
O, treachery !   *Fly, good Fleance, fly, fly, fly !*
Thou may'st revenge.—*Ibid.*, iii. 3.

You know your own degrees, sit down : at first
And last, the hearty welcome.— . . .
                    . . . There 's blood upon thy face.—
'Tis Banquo's, then.—
'Tis better thee without than he within.
Is he despatch'd ?—
My lord, *his throat is cut ; that I did for him.*
        . . . Most royal sir, *Fleance is 'scap'd.*—
            . . . *At once, good night :*
Stand not upon the order of your going,
But go at once.—
                    Good night ; and better health
Attend his majesty !—
                    A kind good night to all !—
                . . . *What is the night ?*—
Almost at odds with morning, which is which.—*Ibid.*, iii. 4.

            This night I 'll spend
Unto a dismal and a fatal end :
Great business must be wrought ere noon : . . .
Hark ! I am call'd ; my little spirit, see,
Sits in a foggy cloud, and stays for me.—
Come, let's make haste ; she 'll soon be back again.—*Ibid.*, iii. 5.

                    Let *this pernicious hour*
Stand aye accursed in the calendar !

Come in! without there! . . .
I did hear
The galloping of horse: who was 't came by?—
'Tis two or three, my lord, that bring you word,
Macduff is fled to England.— . . .
Time, thou anticipat'st my dread exploits:
The flighty purpose never is o'ertook,
Unless the deed go with it: from this moment,
The very firstlings of my heart shall be
The firstlings of my hand. And even now,
To crown my thoughts with acts, be it thought and done:
The castle of Macduff I will surprise;
Seize upon Fife; give to the edge o' the sword
His wife, his babes, and all unfortunate souls
That trace him in his line. No boasting like a fool;
This deed I'll do before this purpose cool.—Macb., iv. 1.

He has killed me, mother:
Run away, I pray you!—Ibid., iv. 2.

What I am truly,
Is thine, and my poor country's, to command:
Whither, indeed, before thy here-approach,
Old Siward, with ten thousand warlike men,
Already at a point, was setting forth:
Now we'll together.— . . .
When I came hither to transport the tidings,
Which I have heavily borne, *there ran a rumour*
Of many worthy fellows that were out;
Which was to my belief witness'd the rather,
For that *I saw the tyrant's power a-foot:*
Now is the time of help; your eye in Scotland
Would create soldiers, make our women fight,
To doff their dire distresses.—
Be it their comfort,
We are coming thither: gracious England hath
Lent us good Siward and ten thousand men.— . . .
Your castle is surpris'd; your wife and babes
Savagely slaughter'd.— . . .
. . . Gentle Heavens,
Cut short all intermission; front to front,
Bring thou this fiend of Scotland and myself;
Within my sword's length, set him; if he 'scape,
Heaven forgive him too!—
This tune goes manly.—
Come, go we to the king; our power is ready;
Our lack is nothing but our leave: Macbeth
Is ripe for shaking, and the powers above
Put on their instruments.—Ibid., iv. 3.

Lo you, here she comes! This is her very guise; and, upon my life, fast asleep.
Observe her; stand close.— . . . Will she go now to bed?—Directly.— . . . Good
night.— . . . Good night, good doctor.—*Ibid.,* v. 1.

The English power is near, led on by Malcolm,
His uncle Siward, and the good Macduff:— . . .
. . . Near Birnam wood
Shall we well meet them; that way are they coming.— . . .
. . . What does the tyrant?—
Great Dunsinane he strongly fortifies:— . . .
. . . Now does he feel
His secret murders sticking on his hands;
Now minutely revolts upbraid his faith-breach:
Those he commands move only in command,

Nothing in love : now does he feel his title
Hang loose about him, like a giant's robe
Upon a dwarfish thief.—*Macb.*, v. 2.

Give me my armour.—
                                'Tis not needed yet.—
I'll put it on.
Send out more horses, skirr the country round ;
Hang those that talk of fear.   *Give me mine armour.* . . .
Come, put mine armour on ; give me my staff :
Seyton, *send out.*   Doctor, *the thanes fly from me.*
Come, sir, despatch. . . . *Pull't off, I say.*
            . . . *Bring it after me.*—*Ibid.*, v. 3.

Cousins, *I hope the days are near at hand*
That chambers will be safe.—
                                We doubt it nothing.—
What wood is this before us ?—
                                The wood of Birnam.—
      . . . *The time approaches,*
That will with due decision make us know
What we shall say we have, and what we owe. . . .
Towards which, *advance the war.*—*Ibid.*, v. 4.

The queen my lord is dead.—
She should have died hereafter ;
There would have been a time for such a word.
To-morrow, and to-morrow, and to-morrow,
Creeps in this petty pace from day to day,
To the last syllable of recorded time ;
And *all our yesterdays have lighted fools*
The way to dusty death.   Out, out, brief candle !
Life's but a walking shadow ; a poor player,
That struts and frets his hour upon the stage,
And then is heard no more. . . .
Thou com'st to use thy tongue ; *thy story, quickly.*— . . .
As I did stand my watch upon the hill,
I look'd toward Birnam, and anon, methought,
The wood began to move.—
                                Liar and slave !—
Let me endure your wrath, if 't be not so :
Within this three mile *may you see it coming ;*
I say, a moving grove.— . . .
                  . . . and *now a wood*
Comes toward Dunsinane.   Arm, arm, and out !—*Ibid.*, v. 5.

Do we but find the tyrant's power *to-night,*
Let us be beaten, if we cannot fight.—*Ibid.*, v. 6.

They have tied me to a stake ; I cannot fly,
But, bear-like, I must fight the course.— . . .
This way, my lord ; *the castle's gently render'd ;*
The tyrant's people on both sides do fight ;
The noble thanes do bravely in the war ;
The day almost itself professes yours,
And little is to do.—
So great a day as this is cheaply bought.—
Macduff is missing, and your noble son.—
Your son, my lord, has paid a soldier's debt ; . . .
            . . . *like a man he died.*—
                  Then he is dead ?—
Ay, and brought off the field.— . . .
And so, God be with him !   Here comes newer comfort.—
Hail, king ! for so thou art : behold, where stands
The usurper's cursed head : . . .—

> *So, thanks to all at once, and to each one,*
> *Whom we invite to see us crown'd at Scone.—Macb.*, v. 7.

And, secondly, for the tokens of Lengthened Time :—

> *I dreamt last night of the three weird sisters ;*
> To you they have show'd some truth.—
>
>   I think not of them:
> Yet, *when we can entreat an hour to serve,*
> *We would spend it in some words upon that business,*
> *If you would grant the time.—*
>
>   *At your kind'st leisure.—Ibid.*, ii. 1.
>
>   *On Tuesday last,*
> A falcon, towering in her pride of place,
> Was by a mousing owl hawked at, and killed.— . . .
>
>   . . . *Will you to Scone ?—*
> No, cousin, I 'll to Fife.—
>
>   Well, I will thither.—
> Well, *may you see things well done there.—Ibid.*, ii. 4.
>
>   *We 'll take to-morrow.* . . .
> *We hear, our bloody cousins are bestow'd*
> *In England and in Ireland ;* not confessing
> Their cruel parricide, *filling their hearers*
> *With strange invention : but of that to-morrow ;*
> *When, therewithal, we shall have cause of state*
> *Craving us jointly.* . . .
>
>   . . . He chid the sisters,
> *When first they put the name of king upon me,*
> And bade them speak to him. . . .
> *Was it not yesterday we spoke together ?—*
> *It was,* so please your highness.— . . .
> I did so ; and went farther, which is now
> Our point of *second meeting.—Ibid.*, iii. 1.
>
> But let the frame of things disjoint,
> Both the worlds suffer,
> Ere we will eat our meal in fear, and sleep
> In the affliction of these terrible dreams
> *That shake us nightly.—Ibid.*, iii. 2.
>
> There the grown serpent lies : *the worm, that 's fled,*
> *Hath nature that in time will venom breed,*
> No teeth for the present. Get thee gone : *to-morrow*
> *We 'll hear, ourselves, again.—* . . .
> This is the very painting of your fear ;
> This is the air-drawn dagger, *which, you said,*
> *Led you to Duncan.—* . . .
> How say'st thou, that Macduff denies his person
> At our great bidding ?—
>
>   Did you send to him, sir ?—
> I hear it by the way ; but I will send :
> *There 's not a one of them, but in his house*
> *I keep a servant fee'd. I will to-morrow*
> (And betimes I will) *to the weird sisters :*
> More shall they speak ; for now I am bent to know,
> By the worst means, the worst. For mine own good,
> All causes shall give way : *I am in blood*
> *Stept in so far, that, should I wade no more,*
> *Returning were as tedious as go o'er :*
> Strange things I have in head, that will to hand ;
> Which must be acted ere they may be scann'd.—*Ibid.*, iii. 4.
>
>   *How did you dare*
>   *To trade and traffic with Macbeth*
>   *In riddles and affairs of death ;*

And I, the mistress of your charms,
The close contriver of all harms,
Was never call'd to bear my part,
Or show the glory of our art? . . .
But make amends now: get you gone,
And *at the pit of Acheron*
Meet me i' the morning: thither he
Will come to know his destiny:
Your vessels and your spells provide,
Your charms, and every thing beside.—*Macb.*, iii. 5.

My former speeches have but hit your thoughts,
Which can interpret farther: only, I say,
Things have been strangely borne.   *The gracious Duncan*
Was pitied of Macbeth: marry, he was dead:
And the right-valiant Banquo walk'd too late;
Whom, you may say, if 't please you, Fleance kill'd,
For *Fleance fled:* . . .
But, peace! for from broad words, and 'cause he fail'd
His presence at the tyrant's feast, *I hear,*
Macduff lives in disgrace: sir, can you tell
Where he bestows himself?—
                                        The son of Duncan,
From whom this tyrant holds the due of birth,
Lives in the English court; and is receiv'd
Of the most pious Edward with such grace,
That the malevolence of fortune nothing
Takes from his high respect: thither Macduff
Is gone to pray the holy king, upon his aid
To wake Northumberland and warlike Siward:
That, by the help of these (with Him above
To ratify the work), *we may again*
Give to our tables meat, sleep to our nights;
Free from our feasts and banquets bloody knives;
Do faithful homage, and receive free honours;
All which we pine for now: and this report
Hath so exasperate the king, that he
Prepares for some attempt of war.—
                                        Sent he to Macduff?—
He did.—*Ibid.*, iii. 6.

What had he done to make him fly the land?—
You must have patience, madam.—
                                        He had none:
His flight was madness. . . .
            . . . *to leave his wife, to leave his babes,*
His mansion, and his titles, in a place
From whence himself does fly?— . . .
                    . . . for your husband,
He is noble, wise, judicious, and best knows
The fits o' the season.   I dare not speak much farther:
But *cruel are the times, when we are traitors,*
And do not know ourselves; when we hold rumour
From what we fear, yet know not what we fear,
But float upon a wild and violent sea,
Each way and move.—*Ibid.*, iv. 2.

                    Each new morn
New widows howl, new orphans cry: new sorrows
Strike heaven on the face, that it resounds
As if it felt with Scotland, and yell'd out
Like syllable of dolour.—

What I believe, I 'll wail;
What know, believe; and *what I can redress,*
As I shall find the time to friend, I will.
What you have spoke, it may be so perchance.
This tyrant, whose sole name blisters our tongues,
Was once thought honest: you have lov'd him well;
He hath not touch'd you yet. . . .
Why in that rawness left you wife and child
(Those precious motives, those strong knots of love)
Without leave-taking ?— . . .
    . . . *Bleed, bleed, poor country !*
Great tyranny, lay thou thy basis sure,
For goodness dares not check thee ! wear thou thy wrongs,
The title is affeer'd !— . . .
I think our country sinks beneath the yoke;
It weeps, it bleeds; and each new day a gash
Is added to her wounds: I think, withal,
There would be hands uplifted in my right;
And here, from gracious England, have I offer
Of goodly thousands.— . . .
    . . . O nation miserable!
With an untitled tyrant, bloody-sceptr'd,
When shalt thou see thy wholesome days again,
Since that the truest issue of thy throne
By his own interdiction stands accurs'd,
And does blaspheme his breed ?— . . .
    . . . Devilish Macbeth
By many of these trains hath sought to win me
Into his power; and modest wisdom plucks me
From over-credulous haste. . . .
A most miraculous work in this good king:
Which often, since my here remain in England,
I have seen him do.— . . .
Stands Scotland where it did ?—
       Alas, poor country,
Almost afraid to know itself! It cannot
Be call'd our mother, but our grave, where nothing,
But who knows nothing, is once seen to smile;
Where sighs, and groans, and shrieks that rent the air,
Are made, not mark'd; where violent sorrow seems
A modern ecstasy: the dead man's knell
Is there scarce ask'd for who; and good men's lives
Expire before the flowers in their caps,
Dying or ere they sicken.— . . .
    . . . *What is the newest grief ?—*
That of an hour's age doth hiss the speaker;
Each minute teems a new one.— . . .
. . . *They were well at peace, when I did leave them.*—Macb., iv. 3.

I have two nights watched with you, but can perceive no truth in your report. *When was it she last walked ?*—Since his majesty went into the field, I have seen her rise from her bed, throw her night-gown upon her, unlock her closet, take forth paper, fold it, write upon it, read it, afterwards seal it, and again return to bed; yet all this while in a most fast sleep.— . . . In this slumbery agitation, besides her walking and other actual performances, *what, at any time, have you heard her say ?* . . . How came she by that light ?—Why, it stood by her: *she has light by her continually;* 'tis her command. . . . *It is an accustomed action with her, to seem thus washing her hands:* I have known her continue in this a quarter of an hour.— . . . The Thane of Fife *had a wife; where is she now ?* . . . I tell you yet again, Banquo 's buried; he cannot come out on 's grave.— . . . Foul whisperings are abroad: unnatural deeds do breed unnatural troubles.—*Ibid.*, v. 1. .

I have liv'd long enough : *my way of life*
Is fallen into the sear, the yellow leaf;
And that which should accompany old age,
As honour, love, obedience, troops of friends,
I must not look to have ; but, in their stead,
Curses, not loud, but deep, mouth-honour, breath
Which the poor heart would fain deny, and dare not.—*Macb.*, v. 3.

We learn no other but the confident tyrant
Keeps still in Dunsinane, and will endure
Our setting down before't.—Ibid., v. 4.

In "Hamlet" the Dramatic Time is very peculiarly treated, and deserves particular investigation. Not only are there in this play unusually numerous indications of Long Time, but the lapses of time *previous to the commencement of the drama itself* are denoted with a significance that require attention being paid to them as part of the systematised timing therein marked. Witness, the allusions to the occasions whereon the Ghost has appeared before to those who see it in the first scene ; witness the references to the interval that has elapsed since the death of Hamlet's father ; those to the period of the prince's attachment to Ophelia ; those to his friendship for Horatio ; those to his predilection for the players ; and those to his boyish affection towards the court-jester Yorick, which latter point serves to confirm the dramatist's intimation of the age he intends his hero to be at the period of the play. By way of counteracting a too protracted effect from these many indications of Long Time, Shakespeare has not failed to accompany most of them by subtle concomitant touches of speed ; as for instance, where he introduces the embassage to Norway, the departure of Laertes to France, the sending Hamlet to England, he has taken care to word them in such terms as shall convey the impression of swift occurrence and rapidly passing events. Moreover, he has availed himself of the expedient of *vagueness in stated period* on more than one occasion during this play ; as, where Horatio and the officers on watch are recounting the incident of the Ghost appearing to them : the former saying it stayed "while one with moderate haste might tell a hundred," and the two latter rejoining "Longer, longer." Likewise, where the prince, Horatio, and the officers are awaiting the apparition, the brief opening dialogue—"I think it lacks of twelve.—No, it is struck.— Indeed ? I heard it not"—serves at once to draw attention to the hour, and yet leave it unprecisely decided. Also, where Hamlet, under shelter of the incoherency natural to his assumed madness, alludes to his father's death as having taken place "within these *two hours;*" and replies to Ophelia's corrected statement of "Nay, 'tis *twice two months,* my lord," by answering "O heavens ! die *two months* ago, and not forgotten yet ?" Then, too, by his own skilful mode of keeping perpetually reiterated tokens of Present Time and Short Time well before the mind, Shakespeare has effectually epitomised the incidents of even this eventful drama into such bounds as shall seem those of feasibly beheld transaction ; and here are collected the said tokens :—

You come most carefully upon your hour.—
'Tis now struck twelve ; get thee to bed, Francisco.—
Well, *good night.*

If you do meet Horatio and Marcellus,
The rivals of my watch, *bid them make haste.*—
I think I hear them.   Stand, ho! who is there?— . . .
Give you good night.— . . .
What, has this thing appear'd again *to-night?* . . .
Therefore I have entreated him along
With us to watch *the minutes of this night.* . . .
Peace! break thee off; look, where it comes again!— . .
What art thou, that usurp'st *this time of night.* . . .
Thus, twice before, and *just at this dead hour,*
With martial stalk hath he gone by our watch.— . . .
          . . . Our last king,
Whose image *even but now* appear'd to us. . . .
But, soft, behold! lo, where it comes again! . . .
'Tis gone.— . . .
It was about to speak, *when the cock crew.*—
And then it started, like a guilty thing
Upon a fearful summons.   I have heard,
The cock, that is the trumpet to the morn,
Doth with his lofty and shrill-sounding throat
Awake the god of day.— . . .
It faded on the crowing of the cock.— . . .
But, *look, the morn, in russet mantle clad,*
Walks o'er the dew of yon high eastern hill.
Break we our watch up: and, by my advice,
Let us impart *what we have seen to-night*
Unto young Hamlet.— . . .
Let's do't, I pray; and I *this morning* know
Where we shall find him most conveniently.—*Hamlet,* i. 1.

Now for ourself, and for this time of meeting:
Thus much the business is: *we have here writ*
To Norway . . . and *we here despatch*
You, good Cornelius, and you, Voltimand,
For bearers of this greeting to old Norway;* . . .
Farewell; and let your haste commend your duty. . . .
Take thy fair hour, Laertes, time be thine,
And thy best graces spend it at thy will! . . .
No jocund health that Denmark drinks *to-day,*
But the great cannon to the clouds shall tell;— . . .
          . . . That it should come to this!—
But two months dead!* nay, *not so much, not two:*
          . . . and yet *within a month.* . . .
A little month; or ere those shoes were old
With which she follow'd my poor father's body,
Like Niobe, all tears; why she, even she—
O God! a beast, that wants discourse of reason,
Would have mourn'd longer—married with mine uncle,
          . . . *within a month;*
Ere yet the salt of most unrighteous tears
Had left the flushing in her galled eyes,
She married.   *O, most wicked speed, to post*
With such dexterity to incestuous sheets.—*Ibid.,* i. 2.

I am very glad to see you.   *Good even,* sir . . .
But what is your affair in Elsinore?— . . .
My lord, I came to see your father's funeral.—
I pray thee, do not mock me, fellow-student;

---

* Be it observed, that the indications of Short and Long Time are so blended, in such passages as the above, that we have to enter them under both heads.   Very satisfactory proof, surely, that all this systematic duplicate marking of Dramatic Time is thoroughly *intentional* on the part of our great author.

I think, it was to see my mother's wedding.—
Indeed, my lord, *it followed hard upon.* . . .
My lord, I think I saw him yesternight.—
Saw who ?—
My lord, the king your father.— . . .
Hold you the watch to-night ?—
                              We do, my lord.—
                    . . . Stay'd it long ?—
While one with moderate haste might tell a hundred.—
Longer, longer.—
Not when I saw it.— . . .
                    I will watch to-night ; . . .
And whatsoever else *shall hap to-night,*
Give it an understanding, but no tongue ;
I will requite your loves.   So, fare you well :
Upon the platform, *'twixt eleven and twelve,*
I'll visit you . . .
              . . . *Would the night were come !—Hamlet,* i. 2.

My necessaries are embark'd : farewell ; . . .
I stay too long : but here my father comes.— . . .
Yet here, Laertes ! *aboard, aboard, for shame !*
The wind sits in the shoulder of your sail,
And you are stay'd for.   There, my blessing with you !— . . .
Most humbly do I take my leave, my lord.—
The time invites you ; go, your servants tend.—Ibid., i. 3.

What hour now ?—
              I think it lacks of twelve.—
No, it is struck.—
Indeed ? I heard it not : *then it draws near the season*
Wherein the spirit held his wont to walk.
What does this mean, my lord ?—
The king doth wake *to-night,* and takes his rouse. . . .
              . . . *Look, my lord ! it comes !* . . .
                    What may this mean,
That thou, dead corse, again, in complete steel,
Revisit'st thus *the glimpses of the moon,*
Making *night* hideous.—*Ibid.,* i. 4.

                    My hour is almost come,
When I to sulphurous and tormenting flames
Must render up myself. . . .
But, soft ! *methinks I scent the morning air ;*
Brief let me be. . . . *Fare thee well at once,*
The glow-worm shows the matin to be near,
And 'gins to pale his uneffectual fire :
Adieu, adieu ! Hamlet, remember me.— . . .
Never make known *what you have seen to-night.—Ibid.,* i.

My lord, *as I was sewing in my chamber,*
Lord Hamlet, with his doublet all unbrac'd ;
              . . . *he comes before me.*
              . . . *that done, he lets me go :*
And, with his head over his shoulder turn'd,
He seem'd to find his way without his eyes ;
For out o' doors he went without their help,
And, to the last, bended their light on me.—
Come, go with me : I will go seek the king.
              . . . *That hath made him mad.—*
              . . . *Come, go we to the king :*
This must be known.—Ibid., ii. 1.

Welcome, dear Rosencrantz and Guildenstern !
Moreover that we much did long to see you,

The need we have to use you did provoke
Our hasty sending.— . . .
And I beseech you *instantly to visit*
My too much changed son. Go, some of you,
And bring these gentlemen where Hamlet is.— . . .
Th' embassadors from Norway, my good lord,
Are joyfully returned.— . . .
And I do think . . . *that I have found*
The very cause of Hamlet's lunacy.—
O speak of that; that do I long to hear.—
Give first admittance to th' embassadors :
My news shall be the fruit to that great feast.—
Thyself do grace to them, and *bring them in.—* . . .
Go to your rest; *at night we 'll feast together :*
Most welcome home.—Hamlet, ii. 2.

But, look, where sadly the poor wretch comes reading.—
Away, I do beseech you, both away :
I 'll board him presently. O, give me leave.
How does my good lord Hamlet ?— . . .
 I will leave him, *and suddenly contrive the means of meeting between him and my daughter.* . . . You go to seek the lord Hamlet; *there he is.—* . . . How dost thou, Guildenstern ? Ah, Rosencrantz ! Good lads, how do ye both ? . . . what have you, my good friends, deserved at the hands of fortune, that she *sends you to prison hither ?* . . . But, in the beaten way of friendship, *what make you at Elsinore ?* . . . I know the good king and queen *have sent for you.—* . . . *We were sent for.* . . . To think, my lord, if you delight not in man, what lenten entertainment the players shall receive from you : we coted them on the way; and *hither are they coming, to offer you service.—* . . . *There are the players.—* . . . *The actors are come hither*, my lord.— . . . *look, where my abridgement comes. You are welcome, masters ; welcome, all : I am glad to see thee well : welcome, good friends* . . . *we 'll have a speech straight : come, give us a taste of your quality ; come, a passionate speech.* . . . 'Tis well; I 'll have thee speak out the rest *soon.* Good my lord, *will you see the players well bestowed ?* . . . *Take them in.—Come, sirs.—Follow that lord ;* and look you mock him not. My good friends, *I 'll leave you till to-night : you are welcome to Elsinore.* . . . *I 'll have these players play something like the murder of my father, before mine uncle : I 'll observe his looks ; I 'll tent him to the quick ; if he but blench, I know my course.—Ibid.*, ii. 2.

Did he receive you well ?—
Most like a gentleman.— . . .
Madam, it so fell out, that *certain players*
We o'er-raught on the way : of these we told him ;
And there did seem in him a kind of joy
To hear of it : *they are about the court ;*
And, as I think, *they have already order*
This night to play before him.— . . .
 . . . *we have closely sent for Hamlet hither,*
That he, as 'twere by accident, may here
Affront Ophelia.— . . .
Ophelia, walk you here. Gracious, so please you,
We will bestow ourselves. . . .
I hear him coming : let 's withdraw, my lord.—
                 . . . How now, Ophelia !
You need not tell us what lord Hamlet said ;
We heard it all. My lord, do as you please ;
But, if you hold it fit, *after the play,*
Let his queen mother all alone entreat him
To show his grief : let her be round with him ;
And I 'll be plac'd, so please you, *in the ear*
Of all their conference.— . . . *It shall be so.—Ibid.*, iii. 1.
 How now, my lord ! *will the king hear this piece of work ?—And the queen, too, and that presently.—Bid the players make haste. Will you two help to hasten them ?— We will, my lord.—What ho, Horatio !—Here, sweet lord, at your service —* . . .

*There is a play to-night before the king. . . . They are coming to the play; I must
be idle: get you a place . . . Be the players ready?—Ay, my lord.—* . . . *The king
rises.—What, frighted with false fire! How fares my lord?—Give o'er the play.—*
. . . *She desires to speak with you in her closet, ere you go to bed.—We shall
obey, were she ten times our mother.—* . . . *My lord, the queen would speak with you,
and presently.—* . . . *Then will I come to my mother by-and-by.—* . . . *I will say so.—
By-and-by is easily said.*　Leave me, friends.

> 'Tis now the very witching time of night,
> When churchyards yawn, and hell itself breathes out
> Contagion to this world: *now could I drink hot blood,*
> *And do such bitter business as the day*
> *Would quake to look on.　Soft! now to my mother.—Hamlet,* iii. 2.

> My lord, *he's going to his mother's closet:*
> Behind the arras I'll convey myself,
> *To hear the process; . . .* Fare you well, my liege:
> I'll call upon you *ere you go to bed,*
> And tell you what I know.— . . .
> *Now might I do it pat, now he is praying;*
> *And now I'll do't.—Ibid.,* iii. 3.

> *He will come straight. . . . I'll silence me e'en here.*
> Pray you, be round with him.—
> Fear me not: withdraw, *I hear him coming.—*
> *Now, mother, what's the matter? . . .*
> *How now! a rat?　Dead, for a ducat, dead!—*
> *Oh, I am slain!— . . .*
> Why, *look you there! look, how it steals away!*
> *My father, in his habit as he liv'd!*
> *Look, where he goes, even now, out at the portal! . . .*
> *Good night: but go not to my uncle's bed;*
> 　　　　*. . . Refrain to-night. . . .*
> 　　*. . . Once more, good night:*
> 　　　　*. . . For this same lord,*
> *I do repent. . . . So again, good night.—Ibid.,* iii. 4.

> Ah, my good lord, *what have I seen to-night!—*
> What, Gertrude?　How does Hamlet?—
> Mad as the sea and wind.— . . . *Where is he gone?—*
> *To draw apart the body he hath kill'd:— . . .*
> *The sun no sooner shall the mountains touch,*
> *But we will ship him hence. . . .*
> *Go seek him out; speak fair, and bring the body*
> *Into the chapel.　I pray you, haste in this.*
> Come, Gertrude, *we'll call up our wisest friends;*
> *And let them know, both what we mean to do,*
> *And what's untimely done.—Ibid.,* iv. 1.

*I have sent to seek him, and to find the body. . . . Now, Hamlet, where's Polonius?—
At supper.—At supper!　Where?—Not where he eats, but where he is eaten: a
certain convocation of politic worms are e'en at him . . . if you find him not within
this month, you shall nose him as you go upstairs into the lobby.—Go seek him there.—
He will stay till you come.—*

> Hamlet, this deed, for thine especial safety,— . . .
> 　　　　*. . . must send thee hence*
> *With fiery quickness: therefore prepare thyself;*
> *The bark is ready, and the wind at help,*
> *Th' associates tend, and everything is bent*
> For England.— . . . *Come, for England!—*
> *Follow him at foot; tempt him with speed aboard;*
> *Delay it not; I'll have him hence to-night:*
> *Away; for everything is seal'd and done,*
> *That else leans on th' affair: pray you, make haste.—Ibid.,* iv. 3.

So, *captain, from me greet the Danish king;*
Tell him that, by his licence, Fortinbras
Claims the conveyance of a promis'd march
O'er his kingdom. You know the rendezvous. . . .
. . . *Will't please you go*, my lord?—
I'll be with you straight. Go a little before.
How all occasions do inform against me,
And spur my dull revenge !—Hamlet, iv. 4.

I will not speak with her.—
She is importunate; indeed, distract:
Her mood will needs be pitied.— . . .
Let her come in.— . . .
Come, my coach !   Good night, ladies; good night, sweet ladies; good night; good
night.—

Follow her close; give her good watch, I pray you.—
. . . *Save yourself*, my lord:
The ocean, overpeering of his list,
Eats not the flats with more impetuous haste
Than young Laertes, in a riotous head,
O'erbears your officers. . . .
The doors are broke.—
Where is this king ?—Ibid., iv. 5.

Now must your conscience my acquittance seal. . . .
. . . Letters, my lord, from Hamlet:—
. . . Laertes, you shall hear them. . . .
" High and mighty, you shall know *I am set naked on your kingdom.* To-morrow
shall I beg leave to see your kingly eyes; when I shall, first asking your pardon there-
unto, recount the occasions of *my sudden and more strange return."—* . . .
. . . How now, sweet queen !—
One woe doth tread upon another's heel,
So fast they follow : your sister's drown'd, Laertes.—Ibid., iv. 7.

Is she to be buried in Christian burial that wilfully seeks her own salvation ?—I tell
thee *she is; and therefore make her grave straight.—* . . .
But soft ! but soft ! aside; *here comes the king,*
The queen, the courtiers: who is that they follow
And with such maimed rites ? . . .
. . . *What ! the fair Ophelia !*
. . . Dost thou *come here* to whine?
To outface me with leaping in her grave?
Be buried quick with her, and so will I.— . . .
I pray you, good Horatio, wait upon him.
Strengthen your patience in *our last night's speech;*
We'll put the matter to the present push.
Good Gertrude, set some w tch over your son.
This grave shall have a living monument;
An hour of quiet shortly shall we see.—Ibid., v. 1.

Your lordship is right welcome back to Denmark. . . . But, my lord, his majesty
bade me signify to you, that *he has laid a great wager on your head* . . . *here is newly*
come to court Laertes; . . . *the king, sir, hath laid, that in a dozen passes between*
yourself and him, he shall not exceed you three hits: he hath laid, on twelve for nine;
and it would come to immediate trial, if your lordship would vouchsafe the answer.—
. . . *Let the foils be brought, the gentleman willing, and the king hold his purpose,*
I will win for him if I can.— . . . My lord, his majesty commended him to you by
young Osric, who brings back to him, that you attend him in the hall: he sends to
know *if your pleasure hold to play with Laertes,* or that you will take longer time.—
I am constant to my purposes; they follow the king's pleasure: if his fitness speaks,
mine is ready; now, or whensoever, provided I be so able as now.—*The king and*
queen and all are coming down.—In happy time.— . . . *Give them the foils,* young
Osric. . . . *Come, begin;* and you, the judges, bear a wary eye.—*Come on, sir.—*
Come, my lord.— . . . *They bleed on both sides.* How is it, my lord.—How is it,

Laertes ?—Why, as a woodcock to mine own springe, Osric; *I am justly killed with mine own treachery.*—How does the queen ?—She swoons to see them bleed.—No, no, the drink, the drink,—O, my dear Hamlet! The drink, the drink ! *I am poisoned.*— . . . The king, the king's to blame.—The point envenom'd too!—*then, venom, to thy work.* 　　　　　　　　　　　　　　　　　　　　　　　　　　　[*Stabs the king.*— . . .

> 　　　　　　. . . Oh, *I die,* Horatio;
> 　　　　　　. . . *The rest is silence.*— 　　　　　　　　　　　　　　　[*Dies.*
> *Now cracks a noble heart : good night,* sweet prince;
> And flights of angels sing thee to thy rest !
> *Why does the drum come hither ?*—
> *Where is this sight ?*—
> 　　　　　　. . . *The sight is dismal;*
> *And our affairs from England come too late :*
> *The ears are senseless that should give us hearing,*
> *To tell him his commandment is fulfill'd,*
> *That Rosencrantz and Guildenstern are dead :*— . . .
> But *since, so jump upon this bloody question,*
> *You from the Polack wars, and you from England,*
> *Are here arriv'd,* give order that these bodies
> High on a stage be placed to the view ;
> And let me speak to the yet unknowing world,
> How these things came about.— . . .
> 　　　　　. . . *Let us haste to hear it.*—*Hamlet,* v. 2.

While, on the other hand, here are the tokens of Long Time, which, in this play, are so unusually numerous ; although at the same time, as we have already observed, they are adroitly tinctured with marks of transitoriness :—

> Has this thing appear'd *again* to-night ?—
> I have seen nothing.—
> Horatio says 'tis but our fantasy,
> And will not let belief take hold of him
> Touching this dreaded sight, *twice seen of us :* . . .
> . . . if *again* this apparition come.— . . .
> 　　　　　　. . . Sit down awhile ;
> And let us *once again* assail your ears,
> That are so fortified against our story,
> What we *two nights have seen.*—
> 　　　　　　　　　　Well, sit we down
> And let us hear Bernardo speak of this.—
> *Last night of all,*
> When yond' same star that 's westward from the pole
> Had made his course to illume that part of heaven
> Where now it burns, Marcellus and myself,
> *The bell then beating one,*— . . .
> Thus *twice before,* and just at this dead hour
> *With martial stalk hath he gone by our watch.*— .
> . . . Sit down and tell me, he that knows,
> Why this same strict and most observant watch
> *So nightly toils* the subject of the land ;
> And why *such daily cast of brazen cannon,*
> And foreign mart for implements of war ;
> Why *such impress of shipwrights, whose sore task*
> Does not divide the Sunday from the week ;
> What might be toward, that this sweaty haste
> *Doth make the night joint labourer with the day.*—*Ibid.,* i. 1.
> 　　　　　　　We here despatch
> You, good Cornelius, and you, Voltimand,
> For *bearers of this greeting to old Norway :* . . .
> What wouldst thou have, Laertes ?—

My dread lord,
Your leave and favour *to return to France;*
From whence though willingly I came to Denmark,
To show my duty in your coronation;
Yet now, I must confess, that duty done,
My thoughts and wishes bend again toward France,
And bow them to your gracious leave and pardon.—
Have you your father's leave?   What says Polonius?—
He hath, my lord, *wrung from me my slow leave*
By laboursome petition; and, at last,
Upon his will I seal'd my hard consent:
I do beseech you, give him leave to go.—
Take thy fair hour, Laertes; *time be thine,*
And thy best graces spend it at thy will!—*Hamlet,* i. 2.

But *two months* dead! . . .
. . . and yet, within *a month,* . . .
A little *month.* . . . within *a month:* . . .
She married.—*Ibid.,* i. 2.

And what make you *from Wittenberg,* Horatio? . . .
But what, in faith, make you *from Wittenberg?* . . .
We'll teach you to drink deep ere you depart.— . . .
Two nights together had these gentlemen,
Marcellus and Bernardo, on their watch,
In the dead vast and middle of the night,
Been thus encounter'd.   A figure like your father,
Arm'd at all points exactly, cap-a-pé,
Appears before them, and with solemn march
Goes slow and stately by them: thrice he walk'd
By their oppress'd and fear-surprised eyes,
Within his truncheon's length; whilst they, distill'd
Almost to jelly with the act of fear,
Stand dumb, and speak not to him.   *This to me*
In dreadful secrecy impart they did;
And I with them the third night kept watch.—*Ibid.,* i. 2.

And, sister, *as the winds give benefit,*
And convoy is assistant, do not sleep,
But *let me hear from you.*—*Ibid.,* i. 3.

'Tis told me, *he hath very oft of late*
Given private time to you; and you yourself
Have of your audience been most free and bounteous:—
He hath, my lord, *of late made many tenders*
Of his affection to me.— . . .
. . . *From this time,*
Be somewhat scanter of your maiden presence,
Set your entreatments at a higher rate
Than a command to parley. . . .
I would not, in plain terms, *from this time forth,*
Have you so slander any moment's leisure,
As to give words or talk with the lord Hamlet.—*Ibid.,* i. 3.

But tell
Why thy canoniz'd bones, *hears'd in death,*
Have burst their cerements; why the sepulchre,
Wherein we saw thee quietly inurn'd,
Hath op'd his ponderous and marble jaws,
To cast thee up again!—*Ibid.,* i. 4.

As I, perchance, *hereafter* shall think meet
To put an antic disposition on,
That you, *at such times* seeing me, never shall . . .
. . . note
That you know aught of me.—*Ibid.,* i. 5.

Inquire me first what Danskers are in Paris;
And how, and who, what means, and where they keep,
What company, at what expense; and finding,
By this encompassment and drift of question,
That they do know my son, come you more nearer
Than your particular demands will touch it. . . .
He closes thus: " I know the gentleman;
I saw him yesterday, or t' other day,
Or then, or then, with such, or such."—*Hamlet,* ii. 1.

What, *have you given him any hard words of late ?*—
No, my good lord; but, *as you did command,*
I did repel his letters, and denied
His access to me.—*Ibid.,* ii. 1.

                                      I entreat you both,
That, being of so young days brought up with him,
And since so neighbour'd to his youth and humour,
That you vouchsafe your rest here in our court
Some little time: so by your companies
To draw him on to pleasures, and to gather,
So much as from occasion you may glean,
Whether aught, to us unknown, afflicts him thus.—
                          . . . If it will please you
To show us so much gentry and goodwill,
As to expend your time with us awhile,
For the supply and profit of our hope,
Your visitation shall receive such thanks
As fits a king's remembrance.—*Ibid.,* ii. 2.

                He sent out to suppress
His nephew's levies; which to him appear'd
To be a preparation 'gainst the Polack;
But, better look'd into, he truly found
It was against your highness: whereat griev'd—
That so his sickness, age, and impotence,
Was falsely borne in hand—*sends out arrests*
On Fortinbras; *which he,* in brief, *obeys;*
Receives rebuke from Norway; and in fine,
Makes vow before his uncle, never more
To give th' assay of arms against your majesty.—*Ibid.,* ii. 2.

This, in obedience, hath my daughter shown me:
And more above, hath *his solicitings,*
As they fell out by time, by means and place,
All given to mine ear. . . .
            . . . And then I precepts gave her,
That *she should lock herself from his resort,*
Admit no messengers, receive no tokens.
Which done, she took the fruits of my advice;
And he, repulsed (a short tale to make),
Fell into a sadness; then into a fast;
Thence to a watch; thence into a weakness;
Thence to a lightness; and by this declension,
Into the madness wherein now he raves,
And all we wail for.— . . .
You know, *sometimes he walks four hours together*
Here in the lobby.—
                So he does, indeed.—
At such a time I 'll loose my daughter to him:
Be you and I behind an arras then;
Mark the encounter.—*Ibid.,* ii. 2.

How pregnant *sometimes* his replies are!— . . . *I have of late* (but wherefore I know
not) *lost all my mirth, forgone all custom of exercises.*—*Ibid.,* ii. 2.

What players are they?—Even those *you were wont to take delight in*, the tragedians of the city.—How chances it they travel? their residence, both in reputation and profit, was better both ways.—I think, their inhibition comes by the means of *the late innovation*.—Do they hold the same estimation *they did when I was in the city?*— . . . 'Faith, *there has been much to do on both sides;* and the nation holds it no sin to tarre them to controversy: there was, *for a while*, no money bid for argument, unless the poet and the player went to cuffs in the question.— . . . It is not very strange; for my uncle is king of Denmark, and those that would make mows at him *while my father lived*, give twenty, forty, fifty, a hundred ducats a-piece for his picture in little. . . . O, my old friend! *Thy face is valanced since I saw thee last;* comest thou to beard me in Denmark? What! my young lady and mistress! By 'r lady, *your ladyship is nearer heaven*, than when I saw you last, *by the altitude of a chopine.* Pray Heaven, *your voice*, like a piece of uncurrent gold, *be not cracked within the ring.* . . . *I heard thee speak a speech once, but it was never acted; or, if it was, not above once; for the play, I remember, pleased not the million;* 'twas caviare to the general: but it was (as I received it, and others, whose judgments in such matters cried in the top of mine) an excellent play; well digested in the scenes, set down with as much modesty as cunning. *I remember*, one said. . . . one speech in it *I chiefly loved . . . if it live in your memory*, begin at this line.—*Hamlet*, ii. 2.

We 'll hear a play *to-morrow*. . . . We 'll have it *to-morrow night.*—*Ibid.*, ii. 2.

<blockquote>

      It cannot be
But I am pigeon-liver'd, and lack gall
To make oppression bitter; or, *ere this*,
I should have fatted all the region kites
With this slave's offal.—*Ibid.*, ii. 2.

</blockquote>

<blockquote>

How does your honour *for this many a day?*— . . .
My lord, I have remembrances of yours,
That I have longed long to re-deliver;
I pray you, now, receive them.—
         No, not I;
I never gave you aught.—
My honour'd lord, *I know right well you did;*
And, with them, words of so sweet breath compos'd,
As made the things more rich: their perfume lost,
Take these again; for, to the noble mind,
Rich gifts wax poor when givers prove unkind.— . . .

</blockquote>

. . . *I did love you once.—* Indeed, my lord, *you made me believe so.—You should not have believed me.* . . . *I loved you not.—I was the more deceived.*—

<blockquote>

O what a noble mind is here o'erthrown!
The courtier's, soldier's, scholar's, eye, tongue, sword:
Th' expectancy and rose of the fair state,
The glass of fashion, and the mould of form,
Th' observ'd of all observers, quite, quite down!
And I, of ladies most deject and wretched;
That suck'd the honey of his music vows,
Now see that noble and most sovereign reason,
Like sweet bells jangled, out of tune and harsh;
That unmatch'd form and feature of blown youth,
Blasted with ecstasy. O, woe is me!
To have seen what I have seen, see what I see!—*Ibid.*, iii. 1.

</blockquote>

<blockquote>

      There 's something in his soul,
O'er which his melancholy *sits on brood;*
And I do doubt, *the hatch, and the disclose,*
Will be some danger: which to prevent,
I have in quick determination
Thus set it down: he shall with speed *to England,*
For the demand of our neglected tribute;
Haply, *the seas, and countries different,*
With variable objects, shall expel
This something settled matter in his heart;

</blockquote>

Whereon his brains *still beating*, puts him thus
From fashion of himself.   What think you on 't ?—
It shall do well : but yet do I believe,
The origin and commencement of his grief
Sprung from neglected love . . .
          . . . If she find him not,
To England send him.—*Hamlet*, iii. 1.

Since my dear soul was mistress of her choice,
And could of men distinguish, her election
Hath seal'd thee for herself : for thou hast been
As one, in suffering all, that suffers nothing ;
A man that fortune's buffets and rewards
Hast ta'en with equal thanks.—*Ibid.*, iii. 2.

Look you, how cheerfully my mother looks, and my father died within these two hours.—Nay, *'tis twice two months*, my lord.—So *long ?* Nay, then, let the devil wear black, for I 'll have a suit of sables.   O heavens ! die *two months* ago, and not forgotten yet—*Ibid.*, iii. 2.

                    Therefore prepare you ;
I your commission will forthwith despatch,
And *he to England shall along with you :*
The terms of our estate may not endure
Hazard so dangerous, as doth *hourly grow*
Out of his lunacies.—
               We will ourselves provide.— . . .
Arm you, I pray you, to this speedy *voyage.*—*Ibid.*, iii. 3.

Up, sword ; and *know thou a more horrid hent :*
When he is drunk, asleep, or in his rage. . . .
This physic but prolongs thy sickly days.—*Ibid.*, iii. 3.

Do you not come *your tardy son to chide,*
That, *laps'd in time and passion, lets go by*
Th' important acting of your dread command ?
O say !—
Do not forget : this visitation
Is but to whet thy almost blunted purpose.—*Ibid.*, iii. 4.

                    Refrain to-night ;
And that *shall lend a kind of easiness*
To the next abstinence : the next more easy ;
For use almost can change the stamp of nature,
And master the devil. . . .
I must to England ; you know that ?—
                         Alack,
I had forgot : 'tis so concluded on.—
There 's letters sealed : and my two schoolfellows,
Whom I will trust as I will adders fang'd,
They bear the mandate ; they must sweep my way,
And marshal me to knavery.   Let it work ;
For 'tis the sport, to have the engineer
Hoist with his own petar : and it shall go hard
But *I will delve one yard below their mines*
And blow them at the moon.—*Ibid.*, iii. 4.

Alas, how shall this bloody deed be answer'd ?
It will be laid to us, whose providence
Should have kept short, restrain'd, and out of haunt,
This mad young man.—*Ibid.*, iv. 1.

How dangerous is it, that *this man goes loose !* . . .
This sudden sending him away must seem
Deliberate pause : diseases, *desperate grown,*
By desperate appliance are reliev'd. . . .
And, England, if my love thou hold'st at aught . . .

> *. . . thou may'st not coldly set*
> *Our sovereign process ;* which imports at full,
> *By letters conjuring to that effect,*
> The present death of Hamlet.—*Hamlet,* iv. 3.
> *We go to gain a little patch of ground.—Ibid.,* iv. 4.
>   I do not know
> Why *yet I live to say, " This thing 's to do."—Ibid.,* iv. 4.
> *How long hath she been thus ?—* . . .
>   *. . . It springs*
> *All from her father's death.* . . .
>   *. . . First, her father slain :*
> *Next, your son gone ;* and he most violent author
> Of his own just remove : *the people muddied,*
> *Thick and unwholesome in their thoughts and whispers,*
> *For good Polonius' death ;* and we have done but greenly,
> In hugger-mugger *to inter him : poor Ophelia*
> *Divided from herself and her fair judgment,* . . .
> *Last,* and as much containing as all these,
> *Her brother is in secret come from France ;*
> *Feeds on his wonder, keeps himself in clouds,*
> *And wants not buzzers to infect his ear*
> *With pestilent speeches of his father's death.—Ibid.,* iv. 5.

I would give you some violets, but they withered all *when my father died.—Ibid.,* iv. 5.

What are they that would speak with me ?—-Sailors, sir : they say *they have letters for you.*—Let them come in. I do not know *from what part of the world I should be greeted, if not from lord Hamlet.—* . . . *There 's a letter for you, sir ; it comes from the embassador that was bound for England.—*. . . *" Ere we were two days old at sea,* a pirate of very warlike appointment gave us chase. Finding ourselves too slow of sail, we put on a compelled valour : in the grapple I boarded them : on the instant they got clear of our ship : so I alone *became their prisoner. They have dealt with me* like thieves of mercy. . . . Rosencrantz and Guildenstern *hold their course for England."—Ibid.,* iv. 6.

> *You have been talk'd of since your travel much,*
> And that in Hamlet's hearing, for a quality
> Wherein, they say, you shine. . . .
>   *. . . Two months since,*
> Here was a gentleman of Normandy.— . . .
> *I know him well :* . . .—
> He made confession of you ;
> *And gave you such a masterly report,*
> For art and exercise in your defence,
> And for your rapier most especially,
> That he cried out, 'twould be a sight indeed,
> If one could match you. . . .
>   . . . this report of his
> Did Hamlet so envenom with his envy,
> That he could nothing do but *wish and beg*
> *Your sudden coming o'er,* to play with you. . . .
> *Hamlet, returned, shall know you are come home :*
> *We 'll put on those shall praise your excellence,*
> And set a double varnish on the fame
> The Frenchman gave you. . . .
>   *. . . Let's farther think of this ;*
> *Weigh what convenience both of time and means*
> May fit us to our shape.—*Ibid.,* iv. 7.

By the Lord, Horatio, *these three years* I have taken note of it. . . . *How long hast thou been a grave-maker ?.*—Of all the days i' the year, *I came to 't that day our last king Hamlet overcame Fortinbras.—How long is that since ?—* . . . *It was the very day that young Hamlet was born ;* he that is mad, and *sent into England.* . . . *I have been sexton here,* man and boy, *thirty years.—Ibid.,* v. 1.

This skull hath lain yon i' the earth three and twenty years.—Whose was it?— . . .
This same skull, sir, was Yorick's skull, the king's jester.— . . . Alas, poor Yorick!
I knew him, Horatio: a fellow of infinite jest, of most excellent fancy: *he hath borne*
me on his back a thousand times; and now, how abhorred in my imagination it is! my
gorge rises at it. Here hung those lips, *that I have kissed I know not how oft.*
—*Hamlet,* v. 1.

Now, *the next day*
Was our sea-fight; and *what to this was sequent*
Thou know'st already.—*Ibid.,* v. 2.

You will lose this wager, my lord.—I do not think so: *since he went into France, I*
have been in continual practice.—*Ibid.,* v. 2.

The imagination is so impressed with that one single appalling
night of tempest, distress, and wrong, in the play of " King Lear,"
that all other time seems merged in those few terrible hours; nevertheless, the dramatist has so contrived the marking of the Dramatic Time
in this sublime tragedy as to afford space for the plausible advance of
its various incidents. By a few carefully introduced touches, for
instance, he lets the lapse of time be just sufficiently perceived to allow
natural progress from the opening of the play to the period when
Goneril's first outrage against her old father breaks out in the suggested dismissal of part of his train of a hundred knights; and, again,
from this point to the arrival of Lear at Gloster's castle. The former
is indicated by the old king's exclamation, " What! fifty of my
followers at a clap! *Within a fortnight!* "—while the latter is so
arranged as to be hurried on with the effect of rapid transit, and yet by
a passing, vaguely worded expression of Kent's a simultaneous illusory
effect of Longer Time is given, where he says to Oswald, " *Is it two*
days since I tripped up thy heels, and beat thee, before the king? "
In the same ingenious way is a whole day suffered to elapse before the
very eyes of the audience, during the fourth scene of the second act, by
means of the artful introduction of such phrases as " the night before,"
" to-night," " good morrow; " then the coming in of Cornwall and
Regan; then the arrival of Goneril, followed by the cruel debate of the
two unnatural daughters as to how their father shall henceforth reside
with them, maimed of his faithful adherents; and, lastly, the expressions, " the night comes on," and " 'tis a wild night," which usher in
the one tremendous night which engrosses our chief attention; so that
we find ourselves wafted from one night to the next without the
slightest shock to our sense of verisimilitude. Here follow the collection of Short Time denotements:—

We have *this hour* a constant will to publish
Our daughters' several dowers . . .
. . . Tell me, my daughters
(Since *now we will divest us, both of rule,*
Interest of territory, cares of state),
Which of you, shall we say, doth love us most?
That we our largest bounty may extend
Where nature doth with merit challenge.—*Lear,* i. 1.

This is most strange,
That she, who *even but now* was your best object,
The argument of your praise, balm of your age,
The best, the dearest, should *in this trice of time*

Commit a thing so monstrous, to dismantle
So many folds of favour.—*Lear*, i. 1.

I think our father *will hence to-night.—Ibid.*, i. 1.

Kent banish'd thus ! And France in choler parted !
And the king *gone to-night !* subscribed his power !
Confin'd to exhibition ! *All this done*
Upon the gad !—Ibid., i. 2.

I will place you where you shall hear us confer of this, and by an auricular assurance have your satisfaction; and that *without any farther delay than this very evening.—Ibid.*, i. 2.

And let his knights have colder looks among you ;
What grows of it, no matter; advise your fellows so :
I would breed from hence occasions, and I shall,
That I may speak: *I'll write straight to my sister,*
To hold my course. Prepare for dinner.—Ibid., i. 3.

Let me not stay a jot for dinner; go get it ready. How now ! what art thou ? . . . Follow me; thou shalt serve me: if I like thee no worse *after dinner*, I will not part from thee yet. *Dinner, ho, dinner !* . . .

What, *have you writ that letter to my sister ?—*
Ay, madam.—
Take you some company, and *away to horse :*
Inform her full of my particular fear;
And thereto add such reasons of your own,
As may compact it more. *Get you gone ;*
And hasten your return.—Ibid., i. 4.

Go you before to Gloster with these letters. Acquaint my daughter no farther with anything you know than comes from her demand out of the letter. *If your diligence be not speedy, I shall be there before you.—I will not sleep*, my lord, *till I have delivered your letter.—* . . . *Be my horses ready ?—*Thy asses *are gone about 'em.—* . . . How now ! *Are the horses ready ?—Ready*, my lord.—*Come, boy.—Ibid.*, i. 5.

I have been with your father, and given him notice that the Duke of Cornwall and Regan his duchess *will be here with him to-night.—* . . .
The duke be here to-night ? The better ! Best !
. . . O sir, fly this place ;
Intelligence is given where you are hid ;
You have *now the good advantage of the night :*
Have you not spoken 'gainst the Duke of Cornwall ?
He's coming hither ; now, i' the night, i' the haste,
And Regan with him.— . . .
. . . The noble duke my master,
My worthy arch and patron, *comes to-night :* . . .
Hark, the duke's trumpets ! I know not why he comes.— . . .
How now, my noble friend ! *Since I came hither*
(*Which I can call but now*) I have heard strange news.— . . .
Was he not companion with the riotous knights
That tend upon my father ? . . .
I have *this present evening* from my sister
Been well inform'd of them.— . . .
You know not why we came to visit you,
Thus out of season, *threading dark-ey'd night :* . . .
Our father he hath writ, so hath our sister,
Of differences, which I best thought it fit
To answer from our home ; the several messengers
From hence attend despatch.—*Ibid.*, ii. 1.

Good dawning to thee, friend : art of this house ? . . . *Is it two days since* I tripped up thy heels, and beat thee, before the king ? . . . *You come with letters against the king.* . . . *The messengers from our sister and the king.* . . .
It pleased the king, his master, *very late,*
To strike at me, upon his misconstruction ;

When he, compact, and flattering his displeasure,
Tripp'd me behind.— . . .

. . . Fetch forth the stocks !
As I have life and honour, *there shall he sit till noon.*—
Till noon! till night, my lord ; *and all night too.* . . .
Give you *good-morrow !* . . .
Approach, thou beacon to this under globe,
That by thy comfortable beams I may
Peruse this letter. . . .

. . . Fortune, *good night.*—*Lear*, ii. 2.

As I learn'd,
The night before there was no purpose then
Of this remove.— . . .

. . . My lord, *when at their home*
I did commend your highness' letters to them,
Ere I was risen from the place that show'd
My duty kneeling, came there a reeking post,
Stew'd in his haste, half breathless, panting forth
From Goneril, his mistress, salutations ;
Deliver'd letters, spite of intermission,
Which presently they read : on whose contents,
They summon'd up their meiny, straight took horse ;
Commanded me to follow.— . . .
Deny to speak with me ? They are sick ? they are weary ?
They have travell'd hard to-night ? Mere fetches ; . . .
Go, tell the duke and 's wife I 'd speak with them,
Now, presently ; bid them come forth and hear me,
Or at their chamber-door I 'll beat the drum
Till it cry sleep to death. . . .
Good morrow to you both.— . . .

. . . What trumpet 's that ?—
I know 't, my sister's : this approves her letter,
That she would soon be here.— . . .
The king is in high rage.—

Whither is he going ?—
He calls to horse ; but will I know not whither. . . .
Alack, *the night comes on*, and the bleak winds
Do sorely ruffle ; for many miles about
There 's scarce a bush.— . . .
Shut up your doors, my lord ; *'tis a wild night.*—*Ibid.*, ii. 4.

This night, wherein the cub-drawn bear would crouch,
The lion and the belly-pinched wolf
Keep their fur dry, *unbonneted he runs*,
And bids what will take all.—*Ibid.*, iii. 1.

Good nuncle, in ; and ask thy daughters' blessing: *here's a night pities neither wise
men nor fools.*— . . .
Alas ! sir, are you here ? things that love night,
Love not *such nights as these :* the wrathful skies
Gallow the very wanderers of the dark,
And make them keep their caves . . .

. . . Alack, bare-headed !
Gracious my lord, *hard by here is a hovel ;*
Some friendship will it lend you 'gainst the tempest ;
Repose you there ;— . . .

. . . Come, *bring us to this hovel.*—*Ibid.*, iii. 2.

I have received a letter this night ; 'tis dangerous to be spoken ; I have locked the
letter in my closet . . . we must incline to the king: *I will seek him, and privily
relieve him :* . . .
This courtesy, forbid thee, *shall the duke
Instantly know ;* and of that letter too.—*Ibid.*, iii. 3.

Here is the place, my lord; good my lord, enter:
The tyranny of the open night's too rough
For nature to endure.— . . .
                            In such a night
To shut me out! Pour on, I will endure:—
In such a night as this! . . .
This cold night will turn us all to fools and madmen.— . . . *'Tis a naughty night
to swim in.*— . . . This is the foul fiend Flibbertigibbet: *he begins at curfew, and
walks till the first cock.*— . . .
                    Though their injunction be to bar my doors,
                    And let *this tyrannous night* take hold upon you,
                    Yet have I ventur'd to come seek you out,
                    And bring you where both fire and food is ready. . . .
                            . . . I had a son,
                    Now outlaw'd from my blood; he sought my life,
                    But lately, very late; I lov'd him, friend,
                    No father his son dearer: true to tell thee,
                    The grief hath craz'd my wits. *What a night's this!—Lear*, iii. 4.

I will have my revenge, *ere I depart his house.—Ibid.*, iii. 5.

Here is better than the open air; take it thankfully. I will piece out the comfort
with what addition I can: *I will not be long from you.—Now, good my lord, lie here,
and rest awhile.*—Make no noise, make no noise; draw the curtains: so, so, so: *we'll
go to supper i' the morning:* so, so, so.— . . .
                    I have o'erheard a plot of death upon him:
                    There is a litter ready; lay him in 't,
                    And drive towards Dover, friend, where thou shalt meet
                    Both welcome and protection. *Take up thy master:*
                    If thou shouldst dally half an hour, his life,
                    With thine, and all that offer to defend him,
                    Stand in assured loss: *take up, take up;*
                    And follow me, that will to some provision
                    Give thee quick conduct.— . . .
                    What will hap more *to-night*, safe 'scape the king!—*Ibid.*, iii. 6.

Post speedily to my lord your husband; show him this letter: *the army of France is
landed.* Seek out the traitor Gloster.—Hang him *instantly.*—Pluck out his eyes.—
. . . *Advise the duke*, where you are going, *to a most festinate preparation:* we are
bound to the like. *Our posts shall be swift and intelligent betwixt us. Farewell, dear
sister; farewell, my lord of Gloster.* How now! where's the king?—
                    My lord of Gloster hath convey'd him hence:
                    Some five or six and thirty of his knights,
                    Hot questrists after him, met him at gate;
                    Who, with some other of the lord's dependants,
                    Are gone with him toward Dover. . . .
                            . . . *Get horses for your mistress.* . . .
                    Come, sir, *what letters had you late from France?* . . .
                    And what confederacy have you with *the traitors
                    Late footed in the kingdom?*—
                    To whose hands have you sent the lunatic king?
                    Speak.— . . .
                    The sea, with such a storm as his bare head
                    In hell-black night endured, would have buoy'd up,
                    And quench'd the stelled fires:
                    Yet, poor old heart, he holp the heavens to rain.— . . .
                    I have receiv'd a hurt: follow me, lady.
                    *Turn out that eyeless villain; throw this slave
                    Upon the dunghill.* Regan, *I bleed apace:*
                    Untimely comes this hurt: give me your arm.—*Ibid.*, iii. 7.

I' the last night's storm I such a fellow saw;
Which made me think a man a worm.—*Ibid.*, iv. 1.

Well, sir, *the poor distress'd Lear's in the town.—Ibid.*, iv. 3.

Alack, 'tis he: why, *he was met even now*
As mad as the vex'd sea. . . .
      . . . A century send forth;
Search every acre in the high-grown field,
And *bring him to our eye . . . seek, seek for him;* . . .
     . . . News, madam;
The British powers are marching hitherward.—
'Tis known before; our preparation stands
In expectation of them.—Lear, iv. 4.

'Tis time to look about; the powers of the kingdom approach apace.—The arbitrement is like to be bloody. Fare you well, sir.—My point and period will be throughly wrought, or well or ill, as *this day's battle's* fought.—*Ibid.,* iv. 7.

Sir, you have shown *to-day* your valiant strain,
And fortune led you well: *you have the captives*
Who were the opposites of this day's strife:— . . .
     . . . Sir, *I thought it fit*
To send the old and miserable king
To some retention, and appointed guard;
   . . . *With him I sent the queen.—Ibid.,* v. 3.

Never (O fault!) reveal'd myself unto him,
Until some half-hour past, when I was arm'd.—*Ibid.,* v. 3.

I pant for life: some good I mean to do,
Despite of mine own nature. *Quickly send—*
Be brief in it—to the castle; for my writ
Is on the life of Lear, and on Cordelia:
Nay, send in time.—
     Run, run, oh, run! . . .
   . . . *Haste thee, for thy life.—*
    . . . *She's gone for ever!*
I know when one is dead, and when one lives;
She's dead as earth.— . . .
   . . . Look on her—look—her lips—
Look there, look there!—[*Dies.*]—*Ibid.,* v. 3.

And here follow the collection of Long Time denotements :—

Ourself, *by monthly course,*
With reservation of a hundred knights,
By you to be sustain'd, *shall our abode*
Make with you by due turns.—Ibid., i. 1.

Five days we do allot thee, for provision
To shield thee from diseases of the world;
And, *on the sixth,* to turn thy hated back
Upon our kingdom: if *on the tenth day* following
Thy banish'd trunk be found in our dominions,
The moment is thy death. . . .
Time shall unfold what plighted cunning hides:
Who cover faults, at last shame them derides.
Well may you prosper!— . . .

I think our father will hence to-night.—That's most certain, and with you; *next month* with us.—*Ibid.,* i. 1.

I am thinking, brother, of a prediction I read *the other day,* what should follow these eclipses. . . . Come, come, *when saw you my father last?—The night gone by.*—Spake you with him?—Ay, *two hours together.—* . . . Bethink yourself, wherein you may have offended him: and at my entreaty forbear his presence till *some little time* hath qualified the heat of his displeasure.—*Ibid.,* i. 2.

By day and night he wrongs me; *every hour*
He flashes into one gross crime or other,
That sets us all at odds: I 'll not endure it:
His knights *grow riotous,* and himself upbraids us
On every trifle.—*Ibid.,* i. 3.

I have perceived a most faint neglect *of late;* which I have rather blamed as mine own jealous curiosity, than as a very pretence and purpose of unkindness: I will look farther into 't. But where 's my fool ? I have not seen him *this two days.—Since my young lady's going into France,* sir, *the fool hath much pined away.*— . . . When were you wont to be so full of songs, sirrah ?—I have used it, nuncle, *ever since* thou madest thy daughters thy mothers.— . . . How now, daughter ! what makes that frontlet on ? Methinks you are too much *of late* i' the frown.— . . .

> Not only, sir, this your all-licens'd fool,
> But other of your insolent retinue
> Do *hourly* carp and quarrel ; breaking forth
> In rank and not-to-be-endured riots. . . .
> I would you would make use of your good wisdom,
> Whereof I know you are fraught ; and put away
> These dispositions, which *of late* transform you
> From what you rightly are. . . .
> This admiration, sir, is much o' the favour
> Of other *your new pranks.*— . . .
> What ! fifty of my followers at a clap !
> *Within a fortnight !*—Lear, i. 4.

Have you heard of no likely wars toward, 'twixt the dukes of Cornwall and Albany ? ―Not a word.—*You may, then, in time.*—*Ibid.,* ii. 1.

> Thy half o' the kingdom *hast thou not forgot,*
> Wherein I thee endow'd.— . . .
> If, *till the expiration of your month,*
> *You will return and sojourn with my sister,*
> Dismissing half your train, *come then to me.*—Ibid., ii. 4.

>   *What hath been seen,*
> *Either in snuffs and packings of the dukes ;*
> *Or the hard rein which both of them have borne*
> *Against the old kind king ;* or something deeper,
> Whereof perchance these are but furnishings;
> But, true it is, from France there comes a power
> Into this scatter'd kingdom ; who already,
> Wise in our negligence, have secret feet
> In some of our best ports, and are at point
> To show their open banner. Now to you :
> *If on my credit you dare build so far*
> *To make your speed to Dover,* you shall find
> Some that will thank you, making just report
> Of how unnatural and bemadding sorrow
> The king hath cause to plain.—*Ibid.,* iii. 1.

These injuries the king now bears *will be revenged home ; there is part of a power already footed.*—Ibid., iii. 3.

> There is a litter ready ; lay him in 't,
> And *drive towards Dover,* friend, *where thou shalt meet*
> *Both welcome and protection.*—Ibid., iii. 6.

Go thrust him out at gates, and *let him smell his way to Dover.*

> Let 's follow the old earl, and *get the Bedlam*
> *To lead him where he would.*—Ibid., iii. 7.

>   If, for my sake,
> Thou wilt o'ertake us, *hence a mile or twain,*
> *I' the way toward Dover,* do it for ancient love ;
> And bring some covering for this naked soul,
> Whom I 'll entreat to lead me. . . .

Know'st thou the way to Dover ?—Both stile and gate, horseway and footpath. . . . Dost thou know Dover?—Ay, master.—

> There is a cliff, whose high and bending head
> Looks fearfully in the confined deep :
> *Bring me but to the very brim of it,*

And I'll repair the misery thou dost bear,
With something rich about me: from that place
I shall no leading need.—
>Give me thy arm:
Poor Tom *shall lead thee.—Lear*, iv. 1.

Welcome, my lord: I marvel our mild husband
Not met us on the way. Now, where's your master?—
Madam, within; but never man *so chang'd.*
I told him *of the army that was landed ;*
He smil'd at it; I told him *you were coming ;*
His answer was, "The worse"; *of Gloster's treachery,*
And of the loyal service of his son,
When I inform'd him, then he call'd me sot,
And told me I had turn'd the wrong side out:
What most he should dislike, seems pleasant to him;
What like, offensive.— . . .
>. . . Back, Edmund, to my brother;
Hasten his musters, and conduct his powers :
I must change arms at home, and give the distaff
Into my husband's hands. This trusty servant
Shall pass between us : ere long you are like to hear,
If you dare venture in your own behalf,
A mistress's command. . . .
France spreads his banners in our noiseless land ;
With plumed helm thy slayer begins threats.—Ibid., iv. 2.

Why *the King of France is so suddenly gone back,* know you the reason?—
Something he left imperfect in the state,
Which since his coming forth is thought of ; which
Imports to the kingdom so much fear and danger,
That *his personal return* was most requir'd
And necessary.—
Whom hath he *left behind him* general?—*Ibid.,* iv. 3.

Our troops set forth to-morrow : stay with us ;
The ways are dangerous.—*Ibid.,* iv. 5.

When the rain came to wet me once, and the wind to make me chatter ; when the thunder would not peace at my bidding ; there I found them, there I smelt them out.—
Ibid., iv. 6.

>Be better suited:
These weeds are memories of those worser hours ;
I pr'ythee, put them off.—*Ibid.,* iv. 7.

>All the skill I have
Remembers not these garments; nor *I know not*
Where I did lodge last night,—Ibid., iv. 7.

Shakespeare has, in his supreme tragedy of "Othello," given perhaps the most noted instance of his peculiar system of Dramatic Time. In conformity with the requisites of succinct dramatic representation, which demand that such brief period should appear as may be naturally beheld at one sitting, and in conformity with the hurry of passion and rapid action suitable to the subject here treated, he has given the effect of but one afternoon, night, next day, between the arrival in Cyprus and the murder of Desdemona ; but, concomitantly, in order to satisfy the mind, which requires a certain lapse of time from the bridal unto the conviction of broken wedded faith, the poet has given an illusory impression of a much longer space between the arrival in Cyprus and the fulfilment of Othello's vengeance. Traced minutely, we find but a few hours actually accounted for ; yet, traced minutely, we likewise find hints of lengthened sojourn and successive event, which imply not only many hours, but many days and weeks. So occultly is this managed by the author, that the apparent inconsistency puzzled his earlier commentators, and subjected him to their accusation of forgetfulness, oversight, discrepancy, neglect of rules, indifference to rules, disdain of laws, or ignorance of laws ; far from this, however, he has shown himself not only observant of rules and conversant with laws as they existed by classical precedent, but also capable of framing rules and ordaining laws by virtue of his own authority and his own creative genius. The seeming incongruity is a deliberate system of coexistent Long and Short Time to suit the purposes of Dramatic Art ; and admirably has Shakespeare devised and fulfilled this system. In Othello, the vestiges of Short Time are the following :—

> If 't be your pleasure and most wise consent
> (As partly, I find, it is) that your fair daughter,
> *At this odd-even and dull watch o' the night,*
> Transported, with no worse nor better guard,
> But with a knave of common hire, a gondolier,
> To the gross clasps of a lascivious Moor. . . .
>   . . . Get weapons, ho !
> And *raise some special officers of the night.—Oth.,* i. 1.
>
> *The goodness of the night upon you,* friends !
> What is the news ?—
>   The duke does greet you, general ;
> And *he requires your haste-post-haste appearance,*
> *Even on the instant.—*
>   What is the matter, think you ?—
> Something from Cyprus, as I may divine :
> *It is a business of some heat : the galleys*
> *Have sent a dozen sequent messengers*
> *This very night at one another's heels ;*
> *And many of the consuls, rais'd and met,*
> *Are at the duke's already : you have been hotly call'd for ;*
> When, being not at your lodging to be found,
> *The senate hath sent about three several quests,*
> *To search you out.—*
>   'Tis well I am found by you.
> I will but spend a word here in the house,
> And go with you.—
>   Ancient, what makes he here ?—
> 'Faith, he *to-night* hath boarded a land carrack. . . .
>   . . . How ! the duke in council !
> *In this time of the night !—Ibid.,* i. 2.
>
>   Welcome, gentle signior ;
> We lack'd your counsel and your help *to-night.* . . .
>   . . . *Th' affair cries haste,*
> *And speed must answer it.—*
> *You must away to-night.—*
>   *With all my heart.—*
> *At nine i' the morning here we 'll meet again.* . . .
> *Good night to every one.—* . . .
> Come, Desdemona ; *I have but an hour*
> *Of love, of worldly matters and direction,*
> *To spend with thee : we must obey the time.—* . . .

Where shall we meet i' the morning ?—At my lodging.—*I 'll be with thee betimes.—*
Ibid., i. 3.

News, lads! *our wars are done.*
The desperate tempest hath so bang'd the Turks,
That their designment halts: a noble ship of Venice
Hath seen a wreck and sufferance
On most part of their fleet.—
How! is this true?—
　　　　　　　　　The ship is here put in,
A Veronessa; *Michael Cassio,*
Lieutenant to the warlike Moor Othello,
Is come on shore. . . .
For *every minute is expectancy*
Of more arrivance.— . . .
The riches of the ship is come on shore !
Ye men of Cyprus, let her have your knees.
Hail to thee, lady!— . . .
　　The Moor ! I know his trumpet.—'Tis truly so.—*Let's meet him, and receive him.—*
Lo, where he comes ! . . .
　　　　　　　Come, Desdemona.
　　Once more, *well met at Cyprus.—Oth.,* ii. 1.

　　The lieutenant to-night watches on the court of guard : . . . Watch you to-night;
for the command, I'll lay't upon you: Cassio knows you not: I'll not be far from
you: do you find some occasion to anger Cassio.—*Ibid.,* ii. 1.

　　It is Othello's pleasure, our noble and valiant general, that, upon *certain tidings now
arrived,* importing the mere perdition of the Turkish fleet, every man put himself into
triumph; . . . for, besides these beneficial news, *it is the celebration of his nuptial. . . .*
there is full liberty of feasting, *from this present hour of five, till the bell have told
eleven.—Ibid.,* ii. 2.
　　Good Michael, look you to the guard to-night. . . .
　　Michael, *good night ; to-morrow with your earliest*
　　Let me have speech with you. . . .
　　Good night.—
　　Welcome, Iago: *We must to the watch.—Not this hour,* lieutenant; *'tis not yet ten
o'clock.* Our general cast us *thus early* for the love of his Desdemona; whom let
us not therefore blame. . . . Come, lieutenant, I have a stoop of wine; and here
without are a brace of Cyprus gallants, that would fain have a measure to the health
of black Othello.—Not *to-night,* good Iago: I have very poor and unhappy brains for
drinking. . . . I have drunk but one cup *to-night,* and that was craftily qualified too,
and, behold, what innovation it makes here.— . . . What, man! *'tis a night of revels :*
the gallants desire it.—Where are they?—Here at the door; I pray you, call them in.
—I'll do't; but it dislikes me.—
　　　　　If I can fasten but one cup upon him,
　　　　　With that which he hath drunk *to-night* already,
　　　　　He'll be as full of quarrel and offence
　　　　　As my young mistress' dog.　Now, my sick fool, Roderigo,
　　　　　Whom love has turned almost the wrong side out,
　　　　　To Desdemona hath *to-night* carous'd
　　　　　Potations pottle deep; and he's to watch:
　　　　　Three lads of Cyprus . . .
　　　　　Have I *to-night* fluster'd with flowing cups,
　　　　　And they watch too.— . . .
　　　　　'Fore heaven, *they have given me a rouse already.—* . . .
　　　　　Speak, who began this? on thy love I charge thee. -
　　　　　I do not know: *friends all but now, even now,*
　　　　　In quarter, and in terms bride and groom
　　　　　Devesting them for bed *; and then, but now*
　　　　　(As if some planet had unwitted men),
　　　　　Swords out, and tilting one at other's breast,
　　　　　In opposition bloody.— . . .
　　　　　　　　　. . . nor know I aught
　　　　　By me that's said or done amiss *this night ;—* . . .
　　　　　　　　　. . . What, in a town of war,
　　　　　Yet wild, the people's hearts brimful of fear,

To manage private and domestic quarrel,
In night, and on the court and guard of safety!—
        . . . I return'd, the rather
For that I heard the clink and fall of swords,
And Cassio high in oath; which till *to-night*
I ne'er might say before. When I came back
(*For this was brief*) I found them close together,
At blow and thrust; even as again they were
When you yourself did part them.— . . .
Betimes in the morning, I will beseech the virtuous Desdemona to undertake for me:
I am desperate of my fortunes, if they check me here.—You are in the right. *Good
night,* lieutenant; I must to the watch.—*Good night,* honest Iago.— . . . I have been
to-night exceedingly well cudgelled— . . .
        . . . By the mass, *'tis morning;*
Pleasure and action make the hours seem short.—*Oth.,* ii. 3.

Masters, play here; I will content your pains;
Something that's brief; and *bid good morrow,* general.— . . .
. . . If the gentlewoman that attends the general's wife *be stirring,* tell her there's
one Cassio entreats her a little favour of speech: wilt thou ao this?—*She is stirring,*
sir.— . . . In happy time, Iago.—
You have not been a-bed, then?—
Why, no; *the day had broke*
Before we parted. I have made bold, Iago,
To send in to your wife: my suit to her
Is, that she will to virtuous Desdemona
Procure me some access.—
        I'll send her to you presently;— . . .
Good morrow, good lieutenant;—*Ibid.,* iii. 1.
These letters give, Iago, to the pilot;
And, by him, do my duties to the senate:
That done, I will be walking on the works;
Repair there to me.—Ibid., iii. 2.

Be thou assur'd, good Cassio, I will do
All my abilities in thy behalf.— . . .
Madam, *here comes my lord.*— . . .
How now, my lord!
I have been talking with a suitor here,
A man that languishes in your displeasure.—
        . . . Went he hence now?—
Ay, sooth; so humbled,
That he hath left part of his grief with me,
To suffer with him. *Good love, call him back.*—
Not *now,* sweet Desdemona.—*Ibid.,* iii. 3.

I heard thee say but now, thou lik'dst not that,
When Cassio left my wife: what didst not like?—*Ibid.,* iii. 3.
        How now, my dear Othello!
Your dinner and the generous islanders
By you invited, do attend your presence.—
I am to blame.—
Why is your speech so faint? are you not well?—
I have a pain upon my forehead here.—
Faith, that's with watching; 'twill away again;
Let me but bind it hard, *within this hour*
It will be well.—*Ibid.,* iii. 3.

What will you give me now for that same handkerchief?
. . . *She let it drop by negligence, and to th' advantage,*
I, being here, took't up. Look, here it is.— . . .
I will in Cassio's lodging lose this napkin,
And let him find it . . .
        . . . *such a handkerchief.*

(I am sure it was your wife's) *did I to-day*
See Cassio wipe his beard with.— . . .
        . . . Look here, Iago;
All my fond love thus do I blow to heaven: 'tis gone.
Arise, black vengeance, from thy hollow hell!
Yield up, O love, thy crown and hearted throne
To tyrannous hate! . . .
        . . . I will withdraw,
To furnish me with some swift means of death
For the fair devil.—*Oth.*, iii. 3.

I pray you bring me on the way a little;
And say if I shall *see you soon at night.*—
'Tis but a little way that I can bring you;
For I attend here: but *I 'll see you soon.*—*Ibid.*, iii. 4.

What did you mean by *that same handkerchief you gave me even now?* . . . An you 'll *come to supper to-night;* you may;— . . . *Will you sup there?*—Faith, *I intend so.*—*Ibid.*, iv. 1.

Ay, let her rot, and perish, and be damned *to-night.* . . . Get me some poison, Iago; *this night.* . . . *this night*, Iago.—Do it not with poison, *strangle her in her bed.* . . . And for Cassio—let me be his undertaker: you shall hear more *by midnight.*—*Ibid.*, iv. 1.

And, sir, *to-night*,
I do entreat that we may sup together:
You are welcome, sir, to Cyprus.—*Ibid.*, iv. 1.

        Pr'ythee, *to-night*
Lay on my bed my wedding sheets. . . .
Hark, how *these instruments summon to supper!*
The messengers of Venice stay the meat: . . .
Roderigo, if thou hast that in thee indeed, which I have greater reason to believe *now* than ever—I mean, purpose, courage, and valour—*this night* show it: if thou the next night following enjoy not Desdemona, take me from this world with treachery
. He *sups to-night* with a harlotry, and thither will I go to him: he knows not yet of his honourable fortune. If you will watch his going thence—which I will fashion to fall out *between twelve and one*—you may take him at your pleasure: I will be near to second your attempt, and he shall fall between us. . . . *It is now high supper-time*, *and the night grows to waste: about it.*—*Ibid.*, iv. 2.

        Madam, *good night;* I humbly thank your ladyship.—
        Your honour is most welcome.—
                Will you walk, sir?

O,—Desdemona,—
My lord?
Get you to bed on the instant; I will be returned forthwith.— . . .
I have laid those sheets you bade me on the bed.—
All 's one. Good father! how foolish are our minds!
If I do die before thee, pr'ythee, shroud me
In one of those same sheets.— . . .
        . . . That song, *to-night*,
Will not go from my mind. . . .
So, get thee gone; *good night.* . . .
Good night, good night.—*Ibid.*, iv. 3.

Here, stand behind this bulk; *straight will he come:*
Wear thy good rapier bare, and put it home:
Quick, quick; fear nothing; I 'll be at thy elbow.—
        . . . Villain, *thou diest!*—
        Minion, *your dear lies dead*,
And your unblest fate hies.— . . .
Two or three groan: *it is a heavy night:* . . .
Cassio *hath here been set on in the dark*
By Roderigo, and fellows that are 'scaped:

He's almost slain, and Roderigo dead.— . . .
Go know of Cassio *where he supp'd to-night.*
What, do you shake at that ?—
He supp'd at my house; but I therefore shake not.— . . .
Emilia, *run you to the citadel,*
And tell my lord and lady what hath happ'd.
Will you go on, I pray? *This is the night*
That either makes me, or fordoes me quite.—*Oth.*, v. 1.

Have you pray'd to-night, Desdemona ?—
                                        Ay, my lord.—
If you bethink yourself of any crime,
Unreconcil'd as yet to heaven and grace,
Solicit for it straight.— . . .
            . . . *thou 'rt on thy death-bed.—*
Ay, but not yet to die.—
                    Yes, presently;
Therefore confess thee freely of thy sin; . . .—
Kill me to-morrow; let me live *to-night.—*
Nay, if you strive,—
                But half-an-hour !—
                                Being done,
There is no pause.—
                But while I say one prayer !—
It is too late.—   [*Smothers her.* . . .
My wife! my wife! what wife? *I have no wife.*
Oh, insupportable ! *O heavy hour!* . . .
I kiss'd thee, ere I kill'd thee : no way but this,
Killing myself, to die upon a kiss.—[*Dies.*]—*Ibid.*, v. 2.

While, on the other hand, the vestiges of Long Time are the
following :—

So that, dear lords, if I be left behind,
A moth of peace, *and he go to the war,*
The rites for which I love him are bereft me,
And I *a heavy interim shall support*
By his dear absence. Let me go with him.— . . .
Adieu, brave Moor ! *use Desdemona well.—*
Look to her, Moor, if thou hast eyes to see :
She has deceiv'd her father, *and may thee.—*
My life upon her faith ! Honest Iago,
My Desdemona must I leave to thee :
I pr'ythee, *let thy wife attend on her;*
And bring them after in the best advantage.—Ibid., i. 3.

        How, how ? Let 's see:
After some time, to abuse Othello's ear
That he is too familiar with his wife.—*Ibid.*, i. 3.

        The Moor himself 's at sea,
And is in full commission here for Cyprus.— . . .
The divine Desdemona.—
                What is she ?—
She that I spake of, our great captain's captain,
Left in the conduct of the bold Iago;
Whose footing here anticipates our thoughts,
A *se'nnight's* speed.—*Ibid.*, ii. 1.

        Good love, call him back.—
Not now, sweet Desdemona; *some other time.—*
But shall 't be shortly ?—
                The sooner, sweet, for you.—
Shall 't be to-night at supper ?—
                No, not to-night.—

> *To-morrow, dinner,* then ?—
>   *I shall not dine at home ;*
> *I meet the captains at the citadel.—*
> Why, then, *to-morrow night ; or Tuesday morn ;*
> *On Tuesday noon, or night ; on Wednesday morn :*
> I pr'ythee, name the time; but let it not
> Exceed *three days.—Oth.,* iii. 3.

> I am glad I have found this napkin :
> This was her first remembrance from the Moor :
> My wayward husband *hath a hundred times*
> *Woo'd me to steal it ;* but she so loves the token—
> For he conjur'd her she should ever keep it—
> That *she reserves it evermore about her,*
> *To kiss and talk to.—* . . .
> What handkerchief !—
> Why, that the Moor first gave to Desdemona ;
> That *which so often you did bid me steal.—Ibid.,* iii. 3.

> What sense had I of *her stolen hours* of lust ?
> I saw 't not, thought it not, it harm'd not me :
> *I slept the next night well,* was free and merry ;
> I found not Cassio's kisses on her lips.—*Ibid.,* iii. 3.

>   I lay with Cassio *lately ;*
> And, being troubled with a raging tooth,
> I could not sleep.
> There are a kind of men so loose of soul,
> That in their sleeps will mutter their affairs :
> One of this kind is Cassio : . . .
> Have you not *sometimes seen* a handkerchief,
> Spotted with strawberries, in your wife's hand ?— . . .
> Within these *three days* let me hear thee say
> That Cassio 's not alive.—*Ibid.,* iii. 3.

> Is not this man jealous ?—
> *I ne'er saw this before.—* . . .
> *'Tis not a year or two shows us a man.—Ibid.,* iii. 4.

> How now, good Cassio ! *what 's the news with you ?—*
> Madam, *my former suit :** I do beseech you,
> That by your virtuous means I may again
> Exist, and be a member of his love,
> Whom I, with all the office of my heart,
> Entirely honour : I would not be delay'd.—
>   . . . Alas, thrice-gentle Cassio !
> My advocation is not now in tune ;
> My lord is not my lord ; *nor should I know him,*
> *Were he in favour, as in humour, altered.*
>   . . . *Something, sure, of state—*
> *Either from Venice, or some unhatch'd practice*
> *Made demonstrable here in Cyprus to him—*
> Hath puddled his clear spirit . . .
>   . . . Nay, we must think men are not gods,
> *Nor of them look for such observances*
> *As fit the bridal !—Ibid.,* iii. 3.

---

* It is in this brief scene that so much lapse of time is *implied ;* for Cassio speaks of his " former suit," and Desdemona sends for him to inform him of the progress she has made in her advocacy on his behalf, although there is no absolutely stated interval since she begged Othello to let Cassio come and plead for recall, and her husband refused to allow this return to be made either " to-night," " to-morrow," or within the next " three days." So systematically is Long Time *implied,* while Short Time is *preserved,* that it is impossible not to believe in this having been the author's thorough intention and artistic plan.

And I was going to your lodging, Cassio.
What! keep a week away? seven days and nights?
Eight score eight hours? and lovers' absent hours,
More tedious than the dial eight score times?
O weary reckoning!—
     Pardon me, Bianca:
I have *this while* with leaden thoughts been press'd;
But I shall, in a more continuate time,
Strike off *this score of absence.* Sweet Bianca,
Take me this work out.—
    O Cassio! whence came this?
This is some token from *a newer friend:*
To the felt absence, now, I feel a cause:
Is 't come to this? Well, well.—*Oth.,* iii. 4.

My lord is fallen into an epilepsy:
This is his second fit; *he had one yesterday.—Ibid.,* iv. 1.

For I will make him tell the tale anew,
Where, how, how oft, how long ago, and when
He hath, and is again to cope your wife.—*Ibid.,* iv. 1.

She was here even now; *she haunts me in every place.* I was, *the other day,* talking
on the sea-bank with certain Venetians; and thither comes this bauble.—*Ibid.,* iv. 1

   May be, the letter mov'd him;
For, as I think, they do command him home,
Deputing Cassio in his government.— . . .
Is this the noble Moor whom our full senate
Call all-in-all sufficient? this the noble nature
Whom passion could not shake? whose solid virtue
The shot of accident, nor dart of chance,
Could neither graze nor pierce?—
     He is much chang'd.—
  . . . What, strike his wife!
   . . . *Is it his use?—Ibid.,* iv. 1.

You have seen nothing, then?—
Nor ever heard, nor ever did suspect.— . . .
What, *did they never* whisper?—
    Never, my lord.—
Nor send you out of the way?—
    Never.—
To fetch her fan, her gloves, her mask, nor nothing?—
Never, my lord.—*Ibid.,* iv. 2.

Lay on my bed *my wedding sheets.—Ibid.,* iv. 2.

   Who *keeps her company?*
What place? what time? what form? what likelihood?— . . .
If e'er my will did trespass 'gainst his love,
Either in discourse of thought or actual deed;
Or that mine eyes, mine ears, or any sense,
Delighted them in any other form;
Or that I do not yet, and ever did,
And ever will,—though he do shake me off
To beggarly divorcement—*love him dearly,*
Comfort forswear me!—*Ibid.,* iv. 2.

Every day thou daff'st me with some device, Iago; and rather, as it seems to me
now, keepest from me all conveniency than suppliest me with the least advantage of
hope. I will, indeed, *no longer* endure it; nor am I yet persuaded to put up in peace
what already I have foolishly suffered.—Ibid., iv. 2.

'Tis pitiful; but yet Iago knows
That she with Cassio hath the act of shame
A thousand times committed.—*Ibid.,* v. 2.

> That handkerchief thou speak'st of
> I found by fortune, and did give my husband ;
> For *often*, with a solemn earnestness,
> More than, indeed, belong'd to such a trifle,
> *He begg'd of me to steal it.—Oth.,* v. 2.

In Shakespeare's masterpiece of historic dramatic composition, "Antony and Cleopatra," he has boldly taken a period that spans a whole decade ; and yet has so subjected it to his power of compression as to make it appear plausibly transpiring within the ken of stage representation. Ten historical years elapsed between the epoch of Fulvia's death and that of Marc Antony's and Cleopatra's ; while the dramatist has placed the announcement of the former at the opening of his drama, and the occurrence of the latter at its close, without violating our sense of natural time-progress. He has done this by means of systematically given dual Dramatic Time—concurrent Short Time and Long Time ; and, moreover, he has enhanced the illusory effect of each, by giving to each latent minglings of its opposite. In the indications of Long Time there are coexistent traces of brevity, and in the indications of Short Time there are coexistent touches of protraction. He has so involved Long Time with hints of Short Time, and Short Time with hints of Long Time, that he has left vague and unstated precise time of any kind ; he has merely denoted certain epochs while referring to passing incidents, and has marked periods by allusion to successive events. By an artistic undefinedness he has managed to produce a magically definite impression of natural dramatic course ; and the ten historical years melt before our eyes into the five theatrical acts by the might of Shakespeare's playwright art. First, we enumerate the indications of Short Time, in which are mingled with present progress hints of other and prolonged time :—

> Nay, but *this dotage of our general's*
> O'erflows the measure: those his goodly eyes,
> That o'er the files and musters of the war
> Have glow'd like plated Mars, *now bend, now turn,*
> *The office and devotion of their view*
> *Upon a tawny front.—* . . .
> *News,* my good lord, *from Rome.—* . . .
> Now, for the love of Love and her soft hours,
> Let's not confound the time with conference harsh ;
> *There's not a minute of our lives should stretch*
> *Without some pleasure now.* What sport to-night ?—
> Hear the ambassadors.— . . .
> No messenger ; but thine, and all alone,
> *To-night we'll wander through the streets,* and note
> The qualities of people. *Come, my queen ;*
> *Last night you did desire it.—Ant. & C.,* i. 1.

> *Bring in the banquet quickly ;* wine enough
> Cleopatra's health to drink. . . .

We'll know all our fortunes.—*Mine, and most of our fortunes, to-night, shall be— drunk to bed.—Ibid.,* i. 2.

> Fulvia thy wife is dead.—
>   Where died she ?—
> In Sicyon :— . . .
> *There's a great spirit gone.* . . .
> I must from this enchanting queen break off :
> Ten thousand harms, more than the ills I know,

My idleness doth hatch. Ho, Enobarbus!—
What's your pleasure, sir?—
I must with haste from hence. . . . Fulvia is dead. . . .
         . . . Let our officers
Have notice what we purpose. I shall break
The cause of our expedience to the queen,
And get her love to part. For not alone
The death of Fulvia, with more urgent touches,
Do strongly speak to us ; but the letters, too,
Of many our contriving friends in Rome
Petition us at home . . .
         . . . Say, our pleasure,
To such whose place is under us, requires
Our quick remove from hence.—Ant. & C., i. 2.
         By the fire
That quickens Nilus' slime, *I go from hence*
Thy soldier, servant ; making peace, or war,
As thou affect'st . . . *Let us go. Come ;*
Our separation so abides, and flies,
That thou, residing here, go'st yet with me,
And I, *hence fleeting*, here remain with thee.
Away !—Ibid., i. 3.
         Here comes
The noble Antony.—
         And yonder Cæsar.— . . .
Welcome to Rome.— . . .
         . . . Great Mark Antony
Is now a widower. . . .
To hold you in perpetual amity,
To make you brothers, and to knit your hearts
With an unslipping knot, *take Antony*
Octavia to his wife : . . . By this marriage,
All little jealousies, *which now seem great,*
And all great fears, *which now import their dangers,*
Would then be nothing : truths would be but tales,
Where now half tales be truths.— . . .
         . . . Let me have thy hand :
Farther this act of grace ; and from *this hour*,
The heart of brothers govern in our loves,
And sway our great designs !— . . .
         . . . Time calls upon us :
Of us must Pompey presently be sought,
Or else he seeks out us.— . . .
         . . . Haste we for it :
Yet, ere we put ourselves in arms, *despatch we*
The business we have talk'd of.—
         With most gladness ;
And do invite you to my sister's view,
Whither straight I 'll lead you.—Ibid., ii. 2.
Good night, sir. . . . *Good night*, dear lady.
Good night, sir.—
         Good night.— . . .
. . . though *I make this marriage* for my peace,
I' the east my pleasure lies.—*Ibid.,* ii. 3.
Trouble yourselves no farther : *pray you hasten*
Your generals after.—
         Sir, *Mark Antony*
Will e'en but kiss Octavia, and we 'll follow.—Ibid., ii. 4.
Madam, *he 's married to Octavia. . . .*
I, *that do bring the news*, made not the match.—*Ibid.,* ii. 5.

You have made me offer
Of Sicily, Sardinia; and I must
Rid all the sea of pirates; then to send
Measures of wheat to Rome: this 'greed upon,
To part with unhack'd edges, and bear back
Our targes undinted.—
              That's our offer.—
                        Know then,
I came before you here, a man *prepar'd*
To take this offer.— . . .
          . . . *Well met here.*—
I hope so, Lepidus. *Thus we are agreed;*
I crave, our composition may be written,
And seal'd between us.—
                  That's the next to do.—
We'll feast each other, ere we part; and let's
Draw lots who shall begin. . . .
          . . . How far'st thou, soldier?—
                                Well;
And well am like to do; for, I perceive,
Four feasts are toward.— . . .
Aboard my galley I invite you all:
Will you lead, lords ?—
                  Show us the way, sir.—
                              Come.— . . .

We came hither to fight with you.—For my part, I am sorry it is turned to a drinking. Pompey doth *this day* laugh away his fortune. . . . *Come, sir, will you aboard ?* I have a health for you.—I shall take it, sir: we have used our throats in Egypt.— *Come, let's away.—Ant. & C.,* ii. 6.

This is not yet an Alexandrian feast.—
It ripens towards it. Strike the vessels, ho!
Here is to Cæsar! . . . Be a child o' *the time.*—
Possess it, I'll make answer: but I had rather fast
From all four days, than drink so much *in one.*—
Ha, my brave Emperor!
Shall we dance now the Egyptian Bacchanals,
And celebrate our drink?— . . .
What would you more? Pompey, *good night.*
. . . What needs more words? *Good night.—Ibid.,* ii. 7.

Now, darting Parthia, art thou struck; and now
Pleas'd fortune does of Marcus Crassus' death
Make me revenger. Bear the king's son's body
Before our army. Thy Pacorus, Orodes,
Pays this for Marcus Crassus.— . . .
              . . . Thou wilt write to Antony?—
                  . . . *Where is he now?*
He purposeth to Athens: whither, *with what haste*
The weight we must convey with us will permit,
We shall appear before him. On, there; pass along.—*Ibid.,* iii. 1.

What, *are the brothers parted?*—
They have despatched with Pompey; he is gone;
The other three are sealing. Octavia weeps
To part from Rome; Cæsar is sad. . . .   [*Trumpet sounds.*
This is to horse. Adieu, noble Agrippa.— . . .
Farewell, my dearest sister, fare thee well.—Ibid., iii. 2.

There's strange news come, sir.—What, man?—*Cæsar and Lepidus have made wars upon Pompey.*— . . .
                  Where's Antony?—
He's walking in the garden—thus; and spurns
The rush that lies before him; cries "Fool, Lepidus!"

And threats the throat of that his officer
That murder'd Pompey.—

      Our great navy 's rigged.—
For Italy and Cæsar. More, Domitius;
My lord desires you presently : my news
I might have told hereafter.—

        'Twill be naught :
But let it be. *Bring me to Antony.*—
Come, sir.—*Ant. & C.*, iii. 5.

         Lastly, he frets
That Lepidus of the triumvirate
Should be depos'd ; and, being, that we detain
All his revenue.—

      Sir, this should be answer'd.—
'Tis done already, and the messenger gone.—*Ibid.*, iii. 6.

Hail, Cæsar, and my lord! hail, most dear Cæsar !— . . .
Why have you stol'n upon us *thus ? you come not*
Like Cæsar's sister; the wife of Antony
Should have an army for an usher : . . .

     . . . but *you are come*
A market-maid to Rome.— . . .

       Good my lord,
To come thus was I not constrain'd, but did it
On my free will. My lord, Mark Antony,
Hearing that you prepar'd for war, acquainted
My griev'd ear withal ; whereon, I begg'd
His pardon for return.—

     Which soon he granted. .
Where is he now ?—

      My lord, in Athens.—
No, my most wronged sister; *Cleopatra*
Hath nodded him to her. . . .

    . . . *Welcome to Rome ;*
Nothing more dear to me. *You are abus'd*
Beyond the mark of thought : and the high gods,
To do you justice, make their ministers
Of us and those that love you. Best of comfort ;
And ever welcome to us.—*Ibid.*, iii. 6.

Your presence needs must puzzle Antony ;
Take from his heart, take from his brain, from 's time,
What should not then be spar'd. *He is already*
Traduc'd for levity ; and 'tis said in Rome
That Photinus a eunuch, and your maids,
Manage *this war.*— . . .

    . . . Is it not strange, Canidius,
That from Tarentum and Brundusium
He could *so quickly cut the Ionian sea,*
And take in Toryne ? You have heard on 't, sweet ? — . . .
The news is true, my lord; *he is descried ;*
Cæsar has taken Toryne.—
Can he be there in person ? 'tis impossible . . .

     . . . *we 'll to our ship.*
Away, my Thetis !— . . .

     . . . *This speed of Cæsar's*
Carries beyond belief.— . . .
The emperor calls Canidius.—
With news the time 's with labour ; and throes forth,
Each minute, some.—*Ibid.*, iii. 7.

Set we our squadrons on yon side o 'the hill,
In eye of Cæsar's battle ; from which place

We may the number of the ships behold,
And so proceed accordingly.—
Naught, naught, all naught! I can behold no longer:
The Antoniad, the Egyptian admiral,
With all their sixty, fly, and turn the rudder:
To see't mine eyes are blasted.— . . .
     . . . Yon ribald-rid nag of Egypt—
Whom leprosy o'ertake!—*i' the midst o' the fight*
When vantage like a pair of twins appear'd,
Both as the same, or rather ours the elder,
The brize upon her, like a cow in June,
Hoists sails and flies.—
      That I beheld:
Mine eyes did sicken at the sight, and could not
Endure a farther view.—
       She once being loof'd,
The noble ruin of her magic, Antony,
Claps on his sea-wing, and, like a doting mallard,
Leaving the fight in height, flies after her.— . . .
O, he has given example for our flight,
Most grossly, by his own!—
Ay, are you thereabouts? Why, then, *good night*
Indeed.—
Towards Peloponnesus are they fled.—
'Tis easy to 't; and there I will attend
What farther comes.—
     To Cæsar will I render
My legions and my horse: six kings already
Show me the way of yielding.—Ant. & C., iii. 8.

Let him appear that's come from Antony.
   . . . *Approach and speak.* . . .
      For Antony
I have no ears to his request. The queen
Of audience, nor desire, shall fail; so she
From Egypt drive her all-disgraced friend,
Or take his life there: this if she perform,
She shall not sue unheard. *So to them both.—*
Fortune pursue thee!—
     Bring him through the bands.—
To try thy eloquence, now 'tis time: despatch:
From Antony win Cleopatra.— . . .
     . . . *Cæsar, I go.—Ibid.,* iii. 10.

    I dare him, therefore,
To lay his gay comparisons apart,
And answer me declin'd, sword against sword,
Ourselves alone. I'll write it: follow me.—Ibid., iii. 11.

    A messenger from Cæsar. . . .
     Admit him, sir. . . .
      . . . *Cæsar's will?—*
Hear it apart.—
    None but friends: *say boldly.—*
     . . . Most kind messenger,
Say to great Cæsar this; tell him, I am prompt
To lay my crown at's feet, and there to kneel. . . .
    . . . *Take hence this Jack, and whip him.—*
    . . . *Tug him away: being whipp'd,*
Bring him again: this Jack of Cæsar's shall
Bear us an errand to him. . . .
Is he whipp'd?—
    Soundly, my lord.— . . .

        . . . Get thee back to Cæsar,
Tell him thy entertainment : look, thou say
He makes me angry with him ; for he seems
Proud and disdainful, harping on *what I am,*
Not what he knew I was : he makes me angry ;
And *at this time* most easy 'tis to do 't.—*Ant. & C.*, iii. 11.

                 Come,
Let's have one other gaudy night : call to me
All my sad captains ; fill our bowls ; *once more*
Let's mock the midnight bell.—
                It is my birthday :
I had thought to have held it poor ; but, since my lord
Is Antony again, I will be Cleopatra.—
We will yet do well.—
Call all his noble captains to my lord.—
Do so, we 'll speak to them ; *and to-night I 'll force*
The wine peep through their scars. Come on, my queen ;
There 's sap in 't yet. . . .
              . . . I will seek
Some way to leave him.—Ibid., iii. 11.

He calls me boy ; and chides, as he had power
To beat me out of Egypt ; *my messenger*
He hath whipp'd with rods ; dares me to personal combat,
Cæsar to Antony : let the old ruffian know,
I have many other ways to die ; *meantime,*
Laugh at his challenge.—Ibid., iv. 1.

He will not fight with me, Domitius.— . . .
Call forth my household servants : *let's to-night*
Be bounteous at our meal. . . .
Well, my good fellows, *wait on me to-night :*
Scant not my cups . . .
             . . . Tend me to-night ;
Maybe, it is the period of your duty : . . .
Tend me to-night two hours, I ask no more. . . .
           . . . My hearty friends,
You take me in too dolorous a sense ;
For I spake to you for your comfort ; did desire you
To burn this night with torches. . . .
           . . . Let's to supper, come,
And drown consideration.—*Ibid.*, iv. 2.

Brother, *good night : to-morrow is the day.—*
It will determine one way. . . . *Good night to you.—*
Well, sir, *good night.—*
Soldiers, have careful watch.—
And you. *Good night, good night.—Ibid.*, iv. 3.

Eros ! mine armour, Eros !—
             Sleep a little.—
No, my chuck. *Eros, come ; mine armour, Eros !*
Come, good fellow, put mine iron on :
If fortune be not ours *to-day*, it is
Because we brave her : *come :—* . . .
Thou fumblest, Eros ; and my queen 's a squire
More tight at this than thou : *despatch.* O love,
That thou couldst see *my wars to-day*, and knew'st
The royal occupation ! thou shouldst see
A workman in 't. *Good morrow to thee ; welcome :*
Thou look'st like him that knows a warlike charge :
To business that we love *we rise betime,*
And go to 't with delight.—

A thousand, sir,
Early though 't be, have on their riveted trim,
And at the port expect you.—
The morn is fair.   Good morrow, general.—
Good morrow, general.—
                    'Tis well blown, lads ;
This morning, like the spirit of a youth
That means to be of note, *begins betimes.—Ant. & C.,* iv. 4.

The gods make *this a happy day* to Antony !— . . .
The kings that have revolted, and the soldier
That has this morning left thee, would have still
Follow'd thy heels.—
                    Who's gone this morning ?—
                                        Who !

One ever near thee : *call for Enobarbus,*
He shall not hear thee ; or from Cæsar's camp
Say, " I am none of thine."—
                    What say'st thou ? —
                                        Sir,

He is with Cæsar.—
                    Sir, his chests and treasure
He has not with him.—
                    Is he gone ?—
                                Most certain.—
Go, Eros, send his treasure after ; do it ;
Detain no jot, I charge thee: . . . *despatch.—Ibid.,* iv. 5.

Go forth, Agrippa, and begin the fight :—
                    . . . *Antony*
Is come into the field.— . . .
                    . . . Enobarbus, *Antony*
Hath after thee sent all thy treasure, with
His bounty overplus: the messenger
Came on my guard ; and *at thy tent is now*
Unloading of his mules.— . . .
                            . . . O Antony,
Thou mine of bounty, how wouldst thou have paid
My better service, when my turpitude
Thou dost so crown with gold !   *This blows my heart :*
If swift thought break it not, a swifter mean
Shall outstrike thought ; but thought will do 't, I feel.
I fight against thee ! No: *I will go seek*
Some ditch wherein to die.—Ibid., iv. 6.

We have beat him to his camp : run one before,
And let the queen know of our gests.   To-morrow,
Before the sun shall see us, we 'll spill the blood
That has to-day escap'd. . . .
                    . . . *he hath fought to-day*
As if a god, in hate of mankind, had
Destroy'd in such a shape. . . .
Had our great palace the capacity
To camp this host, *we all would sup together,*
And drink carouses to the next day's fate,
Which promises royal peril.—*Ibid.,* iv. 8.

If we be not reliev'd *within this hour,*
We must return to the court of guard : *the night*
Is shiny ; and, they say, we must embattle
By the second hour i' the morn.—
                            This last day was
A shrewd one to us.—
                    O bear me witness, *night,—* . . .

The poisonous damp *of night* dispunge upon me,
That life, a very rebel to my will,
May hang no longer on me. . . .
O Antony! O Antony!—   [*Dies.*
The hand of death hath raught him. *Hark! the drums
Demurely wake the sleepers.* Let us bear him
To the court of guard; he is of note: *our hour
Is fully out.*—*Ant. & C.,* iv. 9.

Their preparation is *to-day* by sea:
We please them not by land. . . .
                      . . . *All is lost!
My fleet hath yielded to the foe; and yonder
They cast their caps up,* and carouse together
Like friends long lost. . . .
O sun! thy uprise shall I see no more:
*Fortune and Antony part here; even here
Do we shake hands. All come to this?* . . .
                      . . . *Betray'd I am;*
O this false soul of Egypt! . . .
To the young Roman boy she hath sold me, and I fall
Under this plot; she dies for 't. Eros, ho!—*Ibid.,* iv. 10.

                      *To the monument!
There lock yourself,* and send him word you are dead.—*Ibid.,* iv. 11.

                  She render'd life,
Thy name so buried in her.—
                      Dead, then —?
                              Dead.—
Unarm, Eros; *the long day's task is done,*
And we must sleep. . . . *Off, pluck off:* . . .
              . . . *Apace, Eros, apace.*
No more a soldier: bruised pieces, go;
You have been nobly borne. From me awhile.   [*Exit* EROS.
I will o'ertake thee, Cleopatra, and
Weep for my pardon. *So it must be, for now
All length is torture.* . . .
Eros! I come, my queen. Eros! . . . Come, Eros! Eros!—
What would my lord?— . . .
                  . . . Thou art sworn, Eros,
That, when the exigent should come (*which now
Is come indeed*), when I should see behind me
The inevitable prosecution of
Disgrace and horror, that on my command,
Thou then wouldst kill me: do 't; *the time is come.—* . . .
Why, there, then: [*Falls on his sword.*] *Thus do I escape* the sorrow
Of Antony's death.—   [*Dies.*
                  . . . *I will be
A bridegroom in my death, and run into 't
As to a lover's bed.* Come, then; and, Eros,
Thy master dies thy scholar: *to do thus*
I learn'd of thee.—   [*Falls on his sword.* . . .
I have done my work, ill, friends: O, make an end
Of what I have begun.—
                  *The star is fallen.—
And time is at his period.—* . . .
Bear me, good friends, where Cleopatra bides;
'Tis the last service that I shall command you.— . . .
              . . . *Most heavy day!*—*Ibid.,* iv. 12.

              How now! is he dead?
His death's upon him, but not dead.
Look out o' the other side your monument;

His guards have brought him thither.— . . .
I am dying, Egypt, dying.— . . .
　　　　　. . . *come, come, Antony*—
Help me, my women—we must draw thee up :
Assist, good friends.—
　　　　　　O quick, or I am gone.—
　　　　　. . . *Now my spirit is going ;*
I can no more.—
　　　　　Noblest of men, woo't die ? . . .
　　　　　　. . . *Oh, see, my women,*　　[ANTONY *dies.*
The crown o' the earth doth melt : my lord ! . . .
　　　　　　. . . is it sin
To rush into the secret house of death,
Ere death dare come to us ? . . .
　　　　　. . . Ah, women, women, look,
Our lamp is spent, it's out !　Good sirs, take heart:
We'll bury him ; and then, *what's brave, what's noble,*
Let's do it after the high Roman fashion,
And make death proud to take us.　Come, away :
This case of that huge spirit now is cold.—Ant. & C., iv. 13.

I say, O Cæsar, Antony is dead. . . .
　　　　　. . . *He is dead, Cæsar ;*— . . .
The business of this man looks out of him ;
We'll hear him what he says.　Whence are you ?—
A poor Egyptian yet.　The queen my mistress,
Confin'd in all she has, her monument,
Of thy intents desires instruction.—Ibid., v. 1.

Cæsar sends greeting to the queen of Egypt. . . .
O Cleopatra ! *thou art taken, queen !*—
Quick, quick, good hands.—　　　　　[*Drawing a dagger.*
　　　　Hold, worthy lady, hold !　[*Disarms her.*
Do not yourself such wrong.— . . .
Make way there !　Cæsar !—
Which is the queen of Egypt ?—
It is the emperor, madam.— . . .
My master, and my lord !—
　　　　　　Not so.　*Adieu.*--
He words me, girls, he words me, that I should not
Be noble to myself; but, hark thee, Charmian.—
Finish, good lady ; *the bright day is done,*
And we are for the dark.—
　　　　　Hie thee again:
I have spoke already, and it is provided ;
Go, *put it to the haste.* . . .
Show me, my women, like a queen : go fetch
My best attires ; *I am again for Cydnus,*
To meet Mark Antony ; sirrah Iras, go.
Now, noble Charmian, *we'll despatch indeed.*— . . .
　　　　　. . . *Here is a rural fellow*
That will not be denied your highness' presence :
He brings you figs.—
Let him come in.　What poor an instrument
May do a noble deed !　*he brings me liberty.*
My resolution's plac'd, and I have nothing
Of woman in me : *now* from head to foot
I am marble-constant ; *now* the fleeting moon
No planet is of mine.— . . .
Hast thou the pretty worm of Nilus there,
That kills and pains not ?—
Truly, I have him :— . . .
Well, *get thee gone ; farewell.*—

Yes, *forsooth:* I wish you joy of the worm.—
Give me my robe, put on my crown ; *I have*
Immortal longings in me: now no more
The juice of Egypt's grape shall moist this lip
Yare, yare, good Iras, quick. Methinks I hear
Antony call; I see him rouse himself
To praise my noble act ; I hear him mock
The luck of Cæsar, which the gods give men
To excuse their after wrath : *husband, I come: . . .*
If she first meet the curled Antony
He 'll make demand of her, and spend that kiss
Which is my heaven to have. *Come, thou mortal wretch,*
With thy sharp teeth this knot intrinsicate
Of life at once untie : poor venomous fool,
Be angry, and despatch. . . .
O Antony! Nay, I will take thee too.   *[Applying another asp.*
What should I stay,—   *[Falls on a bed, and dies.*
In this wild world? so fare thee well.
Now boast thee, death, in thy possession lies
A lass unparallel'd.— . . .
How goes it here ?—
                     All dead.—
                         Cæsar, thy thoughts
Touch their effects in this : *thyself art coming*
To see perform'd the dreaded act, which thou
So sought'st to hinder. . . .
O sir, you are too sure an augurer;
That you did fear is done.—
                     Bravest at the last ;
She levell'd at our purposes, *and, being royal,*
Took her own way.—Ant. & C., v. 2.

And next, we enumerate the indications of Long Time, which are
tinctured with hints of curtness :—

                 I am full sorry
That he approves the common liar, who
Thus speaks of him at Rome : *but I will hope*
Of better deeds to-morrow.—Ibid., i. 1.

                     From Alexandria˙
This is the news: *he fishes, drinks, and wastes*
The lamps of night in revel :— . . .
                     Here 's more news.—
Thy biddings have been done ; *and every hour,*
Most noble Cæsar, *shalt thou have report*
How 'tis abroad. Pompey is strong at sea ;
And it appears he is belov'd of those
That only have fear'd Cæsar : to the ports
The discontents repair, and men's reports
Give him much wrong'd.— . . .
                     Cæsar, I bring thee word,
Menecrates and Menas, famous pirates,
Make the sea serve them, which they ear and wound
With keels of every kind ; many hot inroads
They make in Italy.— . . .
                     . . . Antony,
Leave thy lascivious wassails. . . .
Let his shames quickly
Drive him to Rome.— . . .
                     . . . To-morrow, Cæsar,
I shall be furnish'd to inform you rightly
Both what by sea and land I can be able

To front this present time.—
                              Till which encounter,
It is my business too.   Farewell.—
Farewell, my lord : *what you shall know meantime*
Of stirs abroad, I shall beseech you, sir,
To let me be partaker.—*Ant. & C.*, i. 4.

Give me to drink mandragora.—
                              Why, madam ?—
That I might sleep out *this great gap of time,*
My Antony is away.— . . .
Where think'st thou he is now ?   Stands he, or sits he ?
Or does he walk ? or is he on his horse ?
                    . . . *He's speaking now,*
Or, murmuring, " *Where's my serpent of old Nile ?* "
For so he calls me. . . .
How goes it with my brave Mark Antony ?—
Last thing he did, dear queen,
He kiss'd—the last of many doubled kisses—
This orient pearl. . . . " Good friend," quoth he,
" Say *the firm Roman to greet Egypt sends*
This treasure of an oyster ; at whose foot,
To mend the petty present, *I will piece*
Her opulent throne with kingdoms ; all the east,
Say thou, *shall call her mistress.*"— . . .
          . . . What, *was he sad or merry ?*—
Like to the time o' the year between the extremes
Of hot and cold, *he was nor sad nor merry.*—
          . . . He was not merry,
Which seem'd to tell them *his remembrance lay*
In Egypt with his joy ; . . . Met'st thou *my posts ?*—
Ay, madam, *twenty several messengers :*
Why do you send so thick ?—
                              Who's born *that day*
When I forget to send to Antony
Shall die a beggar . . .
Get me ink and paper ;
He shall have every day a several greeting,
Or I'll unpeople Egypt.—*Ibid.*, i. 5.

                              Mark Antony
In Egypt sits at dinner, and will make
No wars without doors : Cæsar gets money where
He loses hearts : Lepidus flatters both.— . . .
          . . . *Cæsar and Lepidus*
Are in the field : a mighty strength they carry.—
Where have you this ? 'tis false.—
                              From Silvius, sir.—
He dreams : I know *they are in Rome* together
Looking for Antony.— . . .
Mark Antony is every hour in Rome
Expected : since he went from Egypt, 'tis
A space for farther travel.—*Ibid.*, ii. 1.

                              I wrote to you,
When rioting in Alexandria ; you
Did pocket up my letters, and with taunts
Did gibe my missive out of audience.—
                              Sir,
He fell upon me ere admitted : *then*
Three kings I had newly feasted, and did want
Of what I was i' the morning : but, *next day*
I told him of myself ; which was as much

As to have ask'd him pardon.— . . .
To lend me arms and aid when I requir'd them,
The which you both denied.—
     Neglected, rather ;
And then, *when poison'd hours had bound me up*
From mine own knowledge. . . .
I did not think to draw my sword 'gainst Pompey ;
For *he hath laid strange courtesies and great*
Of late upon me.—Ant. & C., ii. 2.

You stayed well by it in Egypt.—Ay, sir ; *we did sleep day out of countenance, and made the night light with drinking.—Eight wild boars roasted whole at a breakfast, and but twelve persons there ;* is this true ?—This was but as a fly by an eagle : *we had much more monstrous matter of feast, which worthily deserved noting.—* . . .
Good Enobarbus, *make yourself my guest*
Whilst you abide here.—Ibid., ii. 2.

The world and my great office will sometimes
Divide me from your bosom.—
     All which time
Before the gods my knee shall bow my prayers
To them for you. . . .
Now, sirrah, you do wish yourself in Egypt ?—
Would I had never *come from thence*, nor you
Thither !—
   If you can, your reason ?—
       I see it in
My motion, have it not in my tongue : but yet
Hie you to Egypt again.— . . .
    . . . *I will to Egypt.—Ibid.*, ii. 3.

     We shall,
As I conceive *the journey*, be at the Mount
Before you, Lepidus.—
     Your way is shorter ;
My purposes do draw me much about :
You 'll win two days upon me.—Ibid., ii. 4.

    That time— O times !—
I laugh'd him out of patience ; and *that night*
I laugh'd him into patience ; and *next morn*,
Ere the ninth hour, I drunk him to his bed ;
Then, put my tires and mantles on him, whilst
I wore his sword Philippan. *O, from Italy !*
Ram thou thy fruitful tidings in mine ears,
That *long time* have been barren.—*Ibid.*, ii. 5.

    Since I saw you last,
There is a change upon you.—Ibid., ii. 6,

    Sister, *prove such a wife*
As my thoughts make thee, and as my farthest band
Shall pass on thy approof. . . .
    . . . No, sweet Octavia,
You shall hear from me still ; the time shall not
Out-go my thinking on you.—Ibid., iii. 2.

    Madam, *in Rome*
I look'd her in the face ; and saw her led
Between her brother and Mark Antony.— . . .
I will employ thee back again : I find thee
Most fit for business : go make thee ready ;
Our *letters* are prepar'd.—*Ibid.*, iii. 3.

Nay, nay, Octavia, not only that—
That were excusable, that, *and thousands more*
Of semblable import—but *he hath wag'd*

New wars 'gainst Pompey. . . .
         . . . But, as you requested,
Yourself shall go between us : the meantime, lady,
I 'll raise the preparation of a war. . . .
         . . . *Provide your going;*
Choose your own company, and command what cost
Your heart has mind to—*Ant. & C.*, iii. 4.

Contemning Rome, *he has done all this, and more,*
In Alexandria : here 's the manner of it :
I' the market-place, on a tribunal silvered,
Cleopatra and himself in chairs of gold
Were publicly enthron'd : . . . she
In the habiliments of the goddess Isis
That day appear'd ; and *oft before* gave audience,
As 'tis reported, so.—*Ibid.*, iii. 6.

         We should have met you
By sea and land ; supplying every stage
With an augmented greeting.— . . .
         . . . who now are *levying*
The kings o' the earth for war : he hath assembled
Bocchus, the king of Lybia ; Archelaus,
Of Cappadocia ; Philadelphos, king
Of Paphlagonia ; the Thracian king, Adallas ;
King Malchus of Arabia ; king of Pont ;
Herod of Jewry ; Mithridates, king
Of Comagene ; Polemon and Amyntas,
The kings of Mede and Lycaonia,
With a more larger list of sceptres. . . .
Your letters did withhold our breaking forth ;
Till we perceiv'd, both how you were wrong led,
And we in negligent danger. Cheer your heart :
Be you not troubled with the time, which drives
O'er your content these strong necessities ;
But *let determin'd things to destiny*
Hold unbewail'd their way.—*Ibid.*, iii. 6.

         Now I must
To the young man send humble treaties, dodge
And palter in the shifts of lowness, who
With half the bulk o' the world play'd as I pleas'd,
Making and marring fortunes.—*Ibid.*, iii. 9.

Lord of his fortunes he salutes thee, and
Requires *to live in Egypt :* which not granted,
He lessens his requests ; and to thee sues
To let him breathe between the heavens and earth,
A private man in Athens : this for him.
Next, Cleopatra does confess thy greatness ;
Submits her to thy might ; and of thee craves
The circle of the Ptolemies for her heirs,
Now hazarded to thy grace.—*Ibid.*, iii. 10.

If from the field I shall *return once more*
To kiss these lips, I will appear in blood ;
I and my sword will earn our chronicle : . . .
I will be treble-sinew'd, hearted, breath'd,
And fight maliciously : for *when mine hours*
Were nice and lucky, men did ransom lives
Of me for jests ; but now I 'll set my teeth,
And send to darkness all that stop me.—*Ibid.*, iii. 11.

         Let our best heads
Know that *to-morrow the last of many battles*
We mean to fight : within our files there are,

Of those that serv'd Mark Antony but late,
Enough to fetch him in.—*Ant. & C.,* iv. 1.

         To-morrow, soldier,
By sea and land I 'll fight : or I will live,
Or bathe my dying honour in the blood
Shall make it live again. . . .
         . . . *perchance to-morrow*
You 'll serve another master. I look on you,
As one that takes his leave. . . .
         . . . Know, my hearts,
I hope well of to-morrow ; and will lead you,
Where rather I 'll expect victorious life,
Than death and honour.—*Ibid.,* iv. 2.

Would thou and those thy scars *had once prevail'd*
To make me fight at land !—*Ibid.,* iv. 5.

Alexas did revolt ; and went to Jewry on
Affairs of Antony ; there did persuade
Great Herod to incline himself to Cæsar,
And leave his master, Antony : for this pains
Cæsar hath hang'd him. *Canidius, and the rest*
That fell away, have entertainment, but
No honourable trust.—*Ibid.,* iv. 6.

I *made these wars* for Egypt ; and the queen—
Whose heart I thought I had, for she had mine ;
Which, whilst it was mine, had annex'd unto 't
A million more, now lost—she, Eros, has
Pack'd cards with Cæsar, and false-play'd my glory
Unto an enemy's triumph.—*Ibid.,* iv. 12.

        Cæsar through Syria
Intends his journey ; and, within three days,
You with your children will he send before.—*Ibid.,* v. 2.

The shiftings of the various localities wherein the incidents in the play of Cymbeline occur—now in Britain and now in Italy, sometimes in Cymbeline's palace, anon near Milford Haven, sometimes before the Welsh cave, and anon in Rome—demanded such an adjustment of Dramatic Time as should allow naturally for change of place while giving the effect of stage concentration. Shakespeare has accordingly thrown in touches of rapidity, whenever he has introduced transition, that produce the impression of speedily achieved removal. Thus, he uses such phrases as " straight away for Britain," and " away to Britain post I in this design ; " tending to convey the idea of ease and swiftness, which operate upon the imagination, and induce it to accept as readily passed such mentioned space and interim. The mind, too, is repeatedly kept fixed upon present and current time, so as to preserve dramatic succinctness and impart unity of effect throughout. The grand secret of Shakespeare's dominion in Dramatic Art is unity of impression ; he invariably produces unity of impression, however he may subject the respective unities of time and place to his own ordinances.

Here, then, are the passages indicative of Short Time, which maintain present and current transaction in the mind :—

His daughter, and the heir of 's kingdom, whom
He purpos'd to his wife's sole son (a widow
That late he married) hath referr'd herself
Unto a poor but worthy gentleman : *she 's wedded ;*

Her husband banish'd ; she imprison'd : all
Is outward sorrow.—Cym., i. 1.

I will from hence to-day.—
                                        You know the peril.
I'll fetch a turn about the garden, pitying
The pangs of barr'd affections ; though the king
Hath charg'd you should not speak together. . . .
                . . . *Be brief, I pray you :*
If the king come, I shall incur I know not
How much of his displeasure.— . . .
                . . . Should we be taking leave
As long a term as yet we have to live,
The loathness to depart would grow. *Adieu !* . . .
                . . . *Alack, the king !—*
Thou basest thing, *avoid ! hence, from my sight !*
If after this command thou fraught the court
With thy unworthiness, thou diest: away !
Thou 'rt poison to my blood.—
                                        The gods protect you !
And bless the good remainders of the court !
I am gone.—   [*Exit. . . .*
                . . . *Why came you from your master ?—*
On his command : *he would not suffer me*
To bring him to the haven : left these notes
Of what commands I should be subject to,
When 't pleas'd you to employ me.— . . .
                . . . *About some half-hour hence,*
I pray you, speak with me: *you shall at least*
Go see my lord aboard : for this time leave me.—*Ibid.,* i. 2.

                        What was the last
That he spake to thee ? . . .
And that was all ?—
                        No, madam; for *so long*
As he could make me with this eye or ear
Distinguish him from others, he did keep
The deck, with glove, or hat, or handkerchief,
Still waving, as the fits and stir of 's mind
Could best express *how slow his soul sail'd on,*
How swift his ship.—Ibid., i. 4.

Here comes the Briton : let him be so entertained amongst you as suits, with
gentlemen of your knowing, to a stranger of his quality.— . . . *Let there be covenants*
drawn between us : my mistress exceeds in goodness the hugeness of your unworthy
thinking : *I dare you to this match : here's my ring.*—I will have it no lay.—By the
gods, *it is one.—* . . . *Your hand ; a covenant :* we will have these things set down by
lawful counsel, and *straight away* for Britain, *lest the bargain should catch cold and*
starve : I will fetch my gold, and have our two wagers recorded.—Agreed.—*Ibid.,* i. 5.

Whiles yet the dew's on ground, gather those flowers ;
Make haste : who has the note of them ?—
                                        I, madam.—
Despatch.—Ibid., i. 6.

Madam, a noble gentleman of Rome,
Comes from my lord with letters.—. . .
                . . . Thanks, good sir :
You are kindly welcome. . . .
                . . . I will keep them
In my bedchamber.—
                        They are in a trunk,
Attended by my men ; I will make bold
To send them to you, only for *this night ;*

> *I must aboard to-morrow.—* . . .
> But not away to-morrow!—
> > O, *I must*, madam:
> Therefore I shall beseech you, if you please
> To greet your lord with writing, *do't to-night.—Cym.*, i. 7.

Did you hear of a stranger, *that's come to court to-night?* . . . *There's an Italian come;* and, 'tis thought, one of Leonatus' friends.— . . . Come, I'll go see this Italian *what I have lost to-day at bowls, I'll win to-night of him.—Ibid.*, ii. 1.

> *What hour is it?—*
> > *Almost midnight, madam.—*
> *I have read three hours*, then: mine eyes are weak:
> Fold down the leaf where I have left: *to bed:*
> Take not away the taper, leave it burning;
> And if thou canst awake *by four o' the clock,*
> I pr'ythee, call me. *Sleep hath seized me wholly.*
> To your protection I commend me, gods!
> From fairies, and the tempters *of the night,*
> Guard me, beseech ye!
> > [*Sleeps.* IACHIMO *comes from the trunk*
> *O sleep*, thou ape of death, *lie dull upon her!*
> And be her sense but as a monument,
> Thus in a chapel lying! *Come off, come off;* [*Taking off her bracelet.*]
> . . . *She hath been reading late*
> The tale of Tereus; here the leaf's turned down,
> Where Philomel gave up. *I have enough:*
> *To the trunk again*, and shut the spring of it.
> *Swift, swift, you dragons of the night, that dawning*
> May bare the raven's eye! I lodge in fear;
> Though this a heavenly angel, hell is here.
> *One, two, three—*[*Clock strikes*]*—time, time.—Ibid.*, ii. 2.

It's almost morning, is't not?*—Day*, my lord.*—I would this music would come.* . . . *Come on, tune:* . . . So, *get you gone.* . . . *Here comes the king.—*I am glad I was up so late; for that's the reason I was up *so early:* he cannot choose but take this service I have done, fatherly. *Good morrow* to your majesty.— . . .

> So like you, sir, the embassadors from Rome;
> The one is Caius Lucius.—
> > A worthy fellow,
> Albeit *he comes on angry purpose now;*
> > . . . Our dear son,
> When you have *given good morning* to your mistress,
> Attend the queen and us;— . . .
> *If she be up*, I'll speak with her; if not
> Let her lie still and dream. *By your leave, ho!—*
> > What's your lordship's pleasure?—
> Your lady's person: *is she ready?—* . . .
> *Good morrow*, fairest: sister, your sweet hand.—
> *Good morrow*, sir. . . .
> > How now, Pisanio! . . .
> To Dorothy my woman *hie thee presently.* . . .
> > *Go bid my woman*
> *Search for a jewel, that too casually*
> *Hath left mine arm:* it was thy master's; 'shrew me
> If I would lose it for a revenue
> Of any king's in Europe. *I do think*
> *I saw't this morning:* confident I am
> *Last night 'twas on mine arm.—Ibid.*, ii. 3.
> > *By this, your king*
> *Hath heard of great Augustus:* Caius Lucius
> *Will do's commission throughly:* . . .
> > *. . . See! Iachimo!—*

The swiftest harts have posted you by land ;
And winds of all the corners kiss'd your sails,
To make your vessel nimble.—
　　　　　　　　　　　　　　Welcome, sir.—
I hope *the briefness of your answer made*
The speediness of your return.— . . .
　　　　　　　　　　　. . . *I now*
Profess myself the winner of her honour,
Together with your ring.—Cym., ii. 4.

Now say, what would Augustus Cæsar with us ?— . . .
　　　　　　　　　　　. . . *War and confusion*
In Cæsar's name pronounce I 'gainst thee : look
For fury not to be resisted. *Thus defied,*
I thank thee for myself.—Ibid., iii. 1.

　　　　　　　　　　　Leonatus !
Oh, master ! *what a strange infection*
Is fallen into thy ear ! . . .
Thy mind to her is now as low as were
Thy fortunes. How ! *that I should murder her ?*
　　　. . . [*Reading.*] "Do't: the letter
That I have sent her by her own command
Shall give thee opportunity"— . . .
Madam, *here is a letter* from my lord.—
　　　　　　　　　　. . You good gods,
Let *what is-here contain'd* relish of love. . . .
Oh, for a horse with wings ! Hear'st thou, Pisanio ?
He is at Milford-Haven : read. . . .
　　　. . . I have heard of riding wagers,
Where horses have been nimbler than the sands
That run i' the clock's behalf : but this is foolery :
Go bid my woman feign a sickness ; say
She 'll home to her father : and provide me presently
A riding suit, no costlier than would fit
A franklin's housewife.—
　　　　　　　　　Madam, you 're best consider.—
I see before me, man : nor here, nor here,
Nor what ensues, but have a fog in them,
That I cannot look through. *Away, I pr'ythee ;*
Do as I bid thee : there 's no more to say ;
Accessible is none but Milford way.—Ibid., iii. 2.

A goodly day not to keep house, with such
Whose roof 's as low as ours ! Stoop, boys : this gate
Instructs you how to adore the heavens, and bows
You to *morning's* holy office : the gates of monarchs
Are arch'd so high, that giants may jet through
And keep their impious turbands on, without
Good morrow to the sun. Hail, thou fair heaven ! . . .
Now for our mountain sport : up to yon hill :
Your legs are young ; I 'll tread these flats. . . .
　　　. . . But, *up to the mountains !*
This is not hunter's language : *he that strikes*
The venison first, shall be the lord o' the feast. . . .
　　　. . . Hark, *the game is rous'd !* . . .
　　　. . . *The game is up.—Ibid.,* iii. 3.

Thou told'st me, when we came from horse, *the place*
Was near at hand : ne'er long'd my mother so
To see me first, *as I have now :* Pisanio ! man !
Where is Posthumus ? . . .
Why tender'st thou that paper to me. . . .
　　　　　. . . *My husband's hand !*

        . . . *Speak, man :* thy tongue
May take off some extremity, which to read
Would be even mortal to me.— . . .
What shall I need to draw my sword? *the paper*
Hath cut her throat already. . . .
            . . . Nay, *be brief :*
I see into thy end, and am almost
A man already.—
        First, make yourself but like one.
For thinking this, I have already fit
('Tis in my cloak-bag) doublet, hat, hose, all
That answer to them.— . . .
        . . . *Pr'ythee, away :*
There 's more to be consider'd; but we 'll even
All that good time will give us : this attempt
I 'm soldier to, and will abide it with
A prince's courage. *Away, I pr'ythee.—*
Well, madam, *we must take a short farewell,*
Lest, being miss'd, I be suspected of
Your carriage from the court. My noble mistress,
Here is a box ; I had it from the queen :
What 's in 't is precious ; if you are sick at sea,
Or stomach-qualm'd at land, a dram of this
Will drive away distemper. *To some shade,*
*And fit you to your manhoo*d.—*Cym.,* iii. 4.

My emperor hath wrote; *I must from hence.—* . . .
Where is our daughter? She hath not appear'd
Before the Roman, nor to us hath tender'd
The duty of the day . . . *call her before us ;—* . . .
        . . . Please you, sir,
Her chambers are all lock'd ; and there 's no answer
That will be given to the loud'st of noise we make.—
      . . . *'Tis certain she is fled.*
Go in and cheer the king : he rages, none
Dare come about him.—
         All the better : *may*
This night forestal him of the coming day !— . . .
Who is here? What! are you packing, sirrah ?
Come hither : ah, you precious pander ! Villain,
Where is thy lady ? In a word ; or else
Thou art straightway with the fiends.—Ibid., iii. 5.

        But, *what is this ?*
Here is a path to 't : *'tis some savage hold :*
   . . . Ho! No answer? then *I 'll enter.—* . . .
You, Polydore, *have prov'd best woodman,* and
Are master of the feast.— . . .
Good masters, harm me not :
Before I enter'd here, I call'd ; and thought
To have begg'd or bought what I have took : . . .
     . . . *Here 's money for my meat ;*
I would have left it on the board, so soon
As I had made my meal ; and parted
With prayers for the provider.— . . .
      . . . Pr'ythee, fair youth,
Think us no churls, nor measure our good minds
By this rude place we live in. Well encounter'd !
'Tis almost night : you shall have better cheer
Ere you depart ; and thanks to stay and eat it.
Boys, bid him welcome. . . .
Boys, *we 'll go dress our hunt. Fair youth, come in :*
Discourse is heavy, fasting : when we have *supp'd,*
We 'll mannerly demand thee of thy story.—*Ibid.,* iii. 6.

I am near to the place where they should meet, if Pisanio have mapped it truly. . . . Posthumus, *thy head, which now is growing upon thy shoulders, shall within this hour be off; thy mistress enforced; thy garments cut to pieces before thy face; and all this done, spurn her home to her father;* . . . *My horse is tied up safe: out, sword, and to a sore purpose!*—*Cym.,* iv. 1.

> *You are not well:* remain here in the cave;
> We'll come to you after hunting. . . .
> *'Tis the ninth hour o' the morn.*— . . .
>   . . . Pisanio,
> *I'll now taste of thy drug.*— . . .
>   . . . *To the field, to the field!*
> We'll leave you for this time; go in, and rest.—
> *We'll not be long away.*—
> *It is great morning. Come, away!* who's there?—
> *I cannot find those runagates;* that villain
> Hath mock'd me: I am faint.—
>   Those runagates!
> Means he not us? I partly know him; 'tis
> Cloten, the son o' the queen.— . . .
> He is but one: you and my brother search
> What companies are near: *pray you away;*
> Let me alone with him.— . . .
>   . . . What hast thou done?—
> I am perfect what: *cut off one Cloten's head,*
> Son to the queen, after his own report;— . . .
>   . . . I had no mind
> To hunt *this day:* the boy Fidele's sickness
> Did make my way long forth.— . . .
> We'll hunt no more *to-day,* nor seek for danger
> Where there's no profit. *I pr'ythee, to our rock;*
> You and Fidele play the cooks: I'll stay
> Till hasty Polydore return, and *bring him*
> *To dinner presently.* . . .
>   . . . My ingenious instrument!
> Hark, Polydore, it sounds! but what occasion
> Hath Cadwal now to give it motion? Hark!—
> Is he at home?—
>   *He went hence even now.* . . .
>   . . . Look, here he comes,
> *And brings the dire occasion in his arms*
> Of what we blame him for!—
>   *The bird is dead,*
> That we have made so much on. . . .
>   . . . *Let us bury him,*
> And not protract with admiration what
> Is now due debt. *To the grave.* . . .
> *We have done our obsequies: come, lay him down.*—
> Here's a few flowers; but *'bout midnight more:*— . . .
> I have gone *all night.* . . .
> *Last night* the very gods show'd me a vision.—*Ibid.,* iv. 2.
>
> The Roman legions, all from Gallia drawn,
> *Are landed on your coast.* . . .
>   . . . come more, *for more you're ready.*—*Ibid.,* iv. 3.
>
>   *I am brought hither*
> Among the Italian gentry, and to fight
> Against my lady's kingdom.—*Ibid.,* v. 1.
>
> *It is a day turn'd strangely:* or betimes
> Let's reinforce, or fly.—*Ibid.,* v. 2.
>
> *To-day* how many would have given their honours
> To have sav'd their carcases!—*Ibid.,* v. 3.

You shall not *now* be stolen, *you have locks upon you.*— . . . *Knock off his manacles ;
bring your prisoner to the king.—Cym.,* v. 4.

>   'Tis now the time
> To ask of whence you are ; report it.— . . .
>   . . . I must report
> *The queen is dead.*— . . .
> Why did you throw your wedded lady from you ?
> Think that you are upon a rock ; *and now*
> *Throw me again.*— . . .
> *Here are your sons again ;*— . . .
>   . . . The vision
> Which I made known to Lucius ere the stroke
> Of this yet scarce-cold battle, *at this instant*
> *Is full accomplish'd.—Ibid.,* v. 5.

While, on the other hand, here are the passages of Long Time,
which mention transition, yet which convey the idea of speedy
passing :—

> You must be gone ;
> And *I shall here abide the hourly shot*
> *Of angry eyes.*— . . .
>   . . . *I will remain*
> *The loyal'st husband* that did e'er plight troth :
> *My residence in Rome at one Philario's ;*
>   . . . *thither write,* my queen.—*Ibid.,* i. 2.
>   Away with her,
> And *pen her up* . . .
>   . . . *let her languish*
> *A drop of blood a day ;* and, being aged,
> Die of this folly !—*Ibid.,* i. 2.
> *When shall we hear from him ?*—
>   Be assur'd, madam,
> *With his next vantage.*— . . .
>   . . . ere I could tell him
> *How I would think on him, at certain hours,*
> Such thoughts and such ; or I could make him swear
> *The shes of Italy should not betray*
> *Mine interest and his honour ;* or have charg'd him,
> *At the sixth hour of morn, at noon, at midnight,*
> *To encounter me with orisons, for then*
> *I am in heaven for him.—Ibid.,* i. 4.

But how comes it, *he is to sojourn with you ?*— . . . How worthy he is, *I will leave to
appear hereafter.*— . . . thus far you shall answer : if you *make your voyage* upon her,
and give me directly to understand you have prevail'd, I am no farther your enemy.—
. . . we will have these things set down by lawful counsel, and straight away *for
Britain.—Ibid.,* i. 5.

> *Weeps she still,* say'st thou ? Dost thou think, *in time*
> She will not quench, and let instructions enter
> Where folly now possesses ?—*Ibid.,* i. 6.
>
> A father cruel, and a step-dame false ;
> A foolish suitor to a wedded lady,
> *That hath her husband banished ;*— . . .
> Madam, a noble gentleman of Rome,
> Comes from my lord *with letters.*— . . .
> *Continues well* my lord ? his health, ' beseech you ?—
> Well, madam.—
> Is he *dispos'd to mirth ?* I hope he is.—
> Exceeding pleasant ; none a stranger there
> So merry and so gamesome : *he is call'd*
> The Briton reveller.—

When he was here,
He did incline to sadness ; and *oft-times*
Not knowing why.—
    I never saw him sad. . . .
   . . . join gripes with hands
Made hard with hourly falsehood.— . . .
      My lord, I fear,
Hath forgot Britain.— . . .
     . . . *From Gallia*
I cross'd the seas on purpose, and on promise
To see your grace.—*Cym.,* i. 7.

   Alas, poor princess,
Thou divine Imogen, *what thou endur'st !*
Betwixt a father by thy stepdame govern'd ;
A mother *hourly coining plots ;* a wooer
More hateful than the foul expulsion is
Of thy dear husband.—*Ibid.,* ii. 1.

I am advised to give her music *o' mornings.* . . .
The exile of her minion is too new ;
She hath not yet forgot him : *some more time*
Must wear the print of his remembrance out,
And then she 's yours.— . . .
So like you, sir, embassadors *from Rome.*—*Ibid.,* ii. 3.

  What means do you make to him ?—
Not any ; but *abide the change of time ;*
Quake in the present winter's state, and wish
That warmer days would come.— . . .
Was Caius Lucius in the Britain court
When you were there ?—
     He was expected then,
But not approached.—
I 'll make a journey twice as far, to enjoy
A second night of such sweet shortness which
Was mine in Britain.—*Ibid.,* ii. 4.

His majesty bids you welcome. *Make pastime with us a day or two, or longer :*
if you seek us afterwards in other terms, you shall find us in our salt-water girdle.—
Ibid., iii. 1.

Madam, here is *a letter from my lord.*— . . .
    . . . read, and tell me
How far 'tis thither. If one of mean affairs
May plod it in a week, why may not I
Glide thither in a day ? Then, true Pisanio
(*Who long'st, like me, to see thy lord*). . . .
    . . . Say, and speak thick,
    . . . how far it is
To this same blessed Milford. . . .
    . . . But, first of all,
How we may steal from hence ; and, *for the gap*
That we shall make in time, from our hence-going
And our return, to excuse. . . .
How many score of miles may we well ride
'Twixt hour and hour ?—
     One score twixt sun and sun,
Madam, 's enough for you, and too much too.—
Why, one that rode to 's execution, man,
Could never go *so slow.*—*Ibid.,* iii. 2.

False to his bed ! What is it to be false ?
To lie in watch there, and to think on him ?
To weep 'twixt clock and clock ? if sleep charge nature,
To break it with a fearful dream of him,

And cry myself awake ? that 's false to his bed,
Is it ?
     . . . O, gracious lady,
Since I receiv'd command to do this business,
I have not slept one wink.— . . .
      . . . Wherefore, then
Didst undertake it ? Why hast thou abus'd
So many miles with a pretence ? this place ?
Mine action, and thine own ? our horses' labour ?
The time inviting thee ? the perturb'd court,
For *my being absent ;* whereunto I never
Purpose return ? *Why hast thou gone so far,*
To be unbent, when thou hast ta'en thy stand,
Th' elected deer before thee ?—
      But to win time.
To lose so bad employment. . . .
I 'll give but notice you are dead, and *send him*
Some bloody sign of it ; for 'tis commanded
I should do so : *you shall be miss'd at court,*
And that will well confirm it.—
      Why, good fellow,
What shall I do the while ? where bide ? how live ?—
      . . . Th' embassador,
Lucius the Roman, *comes to Milford-Haven*
To-morrow ; now, if you could wear a mind
Dark as your fortune is, and but disguise
That which, to appear itself, must not yet be
But by self-danger, *you should tread a course*
Pretty and full of view ; yea, haply, *near*
The residence of Posthumus—so nigh, at least,
That though his actions were not visible, yet
Report should render him hourly to your ear,
As truly as he moves.— . . .
     . . . 'fore noble Lucius
Present yourself, *desire his service,* . . .
      . . . *Your means abroad,*
You have me, rich ; and *I will never fail*
Beginning nor supplyment. . . .
     . . . We must take a short farewell,
Lest, being miss'd, I be suspected of
Your carriage from the court. My noble mistress,
Here is a box ; I had it from the queen :
What 's in 't is precious ; *if you are sick at sea,*
Or stomach-qualm'd at land, a dram of this
Will drive away distemper.—*Cym.,* iii. 4.

My emperor hath *wrote ;* I must from hence ;
      . . . I desire of you
A conduct over-land to Milford-Haven. . . .
    . . . Your hand, my lord.—
Receive it friendly ; but *from this time forth*
I wear it as your enemy.—
      Sir, *the event*
Is yet to name the winner : fare you well.—
Leave not the worthy Lucius, good my lords,
Till he have cross'd the Severn.—*Ibid.,* iii. 5.

Since the exile of Posthumus, most retir'd
Hath her life been ; the cure whereof, my lord,
'Tis time must do . . . *when last I went to visit her,*
She pray'd me to excuse her keeping close ;
Whereto constrain'd by her infirmity,
She should that duty leave unpaid to you

Which *daily* she was bound to proffer: this
She wish'd me to make known ; but our great court
Made me *to blame in memory.*—
                          Her doors lock'd ?
Not seen of late ?— . . .
That man of hers, Pisanio, her old servant,
I have not seen these two days.— . . .
How can she be with him? *When was she miss'd ?*
He is in Rome.— . . .
She's far enough ; and what he learns by this,
May prove his travel, not her danger.— . . .
I'll write to my lord she's dead. O Imogen!
Safe may'st thou wander, safe return again!— . . .
  Hast any of thy late master's garments in thy possession ?—I have, my lord, at my lodging, the same suit he wore *when he took leave of my lady and mistress.—* . . . *Meet thee at Milford-Haven! . . . Even there, thou villain Posthumus, will I kill thee. . . .* She said *upon a time* (the bitterness of it I now belch from my heart) that she held the very garment of Posthumus in more respect than my noble and natural person . . . *to the court I'll knock her back, foot her home again. . . . How long is't since she went to Milford-Haven ?—She can scarce be there yet.—Cym.*, iii. 5.

I see, a man's life is a tedious one :
I have tir'd myself; and *for two nights together*
Have made the ground my bed. I should be sick,
But that my resolution helps me. *Milford,*
When from the mountain-top Pisanio show'd thee,
Thou wast within a ken : O Jove ! I think
Foundations fly the wretched.—*Ibid.*, iii. 6.

To them the legions garrisoned in Gallia,
      . . . Have *cross'd the sea ; attending*
You here at Milford-Haven with your ships :
They are in readiness.—
                     But what *from Rome ?—*
The senate hath stirr'd up the confiners
And gentlemen of Italy; most willing spirits,
That promise noble service : and they come
Under the conduct of bold Iachimo,
Sienna's brother.—
               When expect you them ?—
With the next benefit o' the wind.—Ibid., iv. 2.

A fever with the absence of her son ;
A madness, of which her life's in danger.— . . .
               . . . for my mistress,
I nothing know *where she remains, why gone,*
Nor when she purposes return.— . . .
The day that she was missing he was here :—
               The time is troublesome.
We'll slip you for a season ; but our jealousy
Does yet depend.— . . .
I heard no letter from my master, since
I wrote him Imogen was slain : 'tis strange :
Nor hear I from my mistress, who did promise
To yield me often tidings ; neither know I
What is betid to Cloten ; but remain
Perplex'd in all. . . .
These present wars shall find I love my country. . . .
All other doubts, *by time let them be cleared.—Ibid.*, iv. 3.

Upon a time (unhappy was the clock
That struck the hour !), *it was in Rome* (accursed
The mansion where !), *'twas at a feast. . . .*
               . . . the good Posthumus,

. . . . sitting sadly,
Hearing us praise our loves of Italy . . .
. . . He, true knight,
No lesser of her honour confident
Than I did truly find her, stakes this ring;
. . . Away *to Britain*
Post I in this design: well may you, sir,
Remember me at court; where I was taught
Of your chaste daughter the wide difference
'Twixt amorous and villanous . . . .
And, to be brief, my practice so prevail'd,
That *I return'd* with simular proof enough
To make the noble Leonatus mad.—*Cym.*, v. 5.

but *her son*
Is gone, we know not how, nor where.—
My lord,
Now fear is from me, I 'll speak troth. Lord Cloten,
Upon my lady's missing, came to me
With his sword drawn; foam'd at the mouth, and swore,
If I discover'd not *which way she was gone,*
It was my instant death. By accident,
I had a feign'd letter of my master's
Then in my pocket; which directed him
To seek her on the mountains near to Milford.—*Ibid.*, v. 5.

Did you e'er meet?—
Ay, my good lord.—
And at first meeting lov'd;
Continu'd so, until we thought he died.— . . .
. . . *Where? how liv'd you?*
And when came you to serve our Roman captive?
How parted with your brothers? how first met them?
Why fled you from the court? and whither? These
And your three motives to the battle, with
I know not how much more, should be demanded;
And *all the other by-dependencies,*
From chance to chance: but nor the time nor place
Will serve our long inter'gatories.—*Ibid.*, v. 5.

In Shakespeare's four Chorus-Plays he has availed himself of the means supplied by the intervention of a Chorus for stating certain gaps of time necessary to be understood by the audience; as, more modernly, the French dramatists have intimated different periods in the same drama by styling such dramas " pièces à deux époques," and the English dramatists have done by announcing that an interval [of so many days, weeks, months, or years, as the case may be] is supposed to take place between the acts. But though, in common with other playwriters of his own time, Shakespeare has, in these four plays, introduced the machinery of a Chorus, he has not failed also to introduce his own system of dual Dramatic Time; interfusing simultaneous Short Time and Long Time during the progress of the acts and scenes. In " The Winter's Tale " he has brought in " Time, as Chorus," at the commencement of act iv., by way of marking the interval of " sixteen years " which has elapsed between the desertion of the infant Perdita by Antigonus at her father's command and her betrothal to Florizel when she appears as queen of the sheep-shearing festival; yet he has likewise indicated the progress of time in other passages of this play.

First, then, for the enumeration of those passages which indicate Short Time :—

If you shall chance, Camillo, to visit Bohemia, on the like occasion whereon my services *are now on foot.*—*W. T.*, i. 1.

Stay your thanks awhile,

And pay them when you part.—

Sir, *that's to-morrow*. . . .

. . . *No longer stay.*—

One seven-night longer.—

Very sooth, to-morrow. . . .

. . . *Is he won yet ?*—

He'll stay, my lord.— . . .

. . . If you would seek us,

We are yours i' the garden. . . .

Here comes Bohemia.— . . .

Good day, Camillo.— . . .

The king hath on him such a countenance,
As he had lost some province, and a region
Lov'd as he loves himself: *even now I met him*
With customary compliment ; when he,
Wafting his eyes to the contrary, and falling
A lip of much contempt, *speeds from me.* . . .

. . . Mark my counsel,

Which must be even as swiftly followed as
I mean to utter it. . . .

I am appointed him to murder you.—

By whom, Camillo ?—

By the king.—

For what ?—

He thinks, nay, with all confidence he swears,
As he had seen 't, or been an instrument
To vice you to 't, *that you have touch'd his queen*
Forbiddenly.— . . .
If, therefore, you dare trust my honesty—
That lies inclosed in this trunk, which you
Shall bear along impawn'd—*away to-night.*
Your followers I will whisper to the business ;
And will, by twos and threes, at several posterns
Clear them o' the city : for myself, I 'll put
My fortunes to your service, which are here
By this discovery lost. *Be not uncertain ;* . . .

. . . *Give me thy hand :*

Be pilot to me, and thy places shall
Still neighbour mine. *My ships are ready, and*
My people did expect my hence departure
Two days ago. . . .

. . . *Come, Camillo ;*

I will respect thee as a father, if
Thou bear'st my life off hence : *let us avoid.*—
It is in mine authority to command
The keys of all the posterns : *please your highness*
To take the urgent hour : come, sir, away !—*Ibid.*, i. 2.

The queen, your mother, *rounds apace.* . . .

. . . *Come, sir, now*

I am for you again : pray you, *sit by us,*
And tell's a tale.—

Merry or sad shall 't be ?—

As merry as you will.—

A sad tale 's best *for winter*.

I have one of sprites and goblins.—

> *Let's have that, good sir.*
Come on ; sit down : come on. . . .
> *. . . Nay, come, sit down ; then on.*—W. T., ii. 1.
Was he met there ? his train ? Camillo with him ?—
Behind the tuft of pines I met them ; never
*Saw I men so scour on their way : I ey'd them
Even to their ships.*— . . .
> *. . . I have said
She's an adult'ress ; I have said with whom :
More, she's a traitor ; and Camillo is
A federary with her.* . . .
> *. . . Away with her to prison !* . . .
> *. . . Camillo's flight,*
Added to their familiarity, . . .
> *. . . doth push on this proceeding.*—Ibid., ii. 1.
> On her frights and griefs
(Which never tender lady hath borne greater),
She is, something before her time, deliver'd.— . . .
Commend my best obedience to the queen :
If she dares trust me with her little babe,
*I'll show't the king, and undertake to be
Her advocate* to the loud'st.— . . .
> *I'll presently
Acquaint the queen of your most noble offer ;*
Who, *but to-day,* hammer'd of this design.—Ibid., ii. 2.
How does the boy ?—
> He took good rest *to-night ;* . . .
Madam, he hath not slept *to-night ;* commanded
None should come at him.—
> Not so hot, good sir :
I come to bring him sleep. . . . I
Do come with words as med'cinal as true,
Honest as either, *to purge him of that humour
That presses him from sleep.* . . .
> *. . . I say, I come
From your good queen.*— *. . . The good queen,*
For she is good, *hath brought you forth a daughter ;
Here 'tis ;* commends it to your blessing.— . . .
My child ? *away with't !* even thou, that hast
A heart so tender o'er it, *take it hence,
And see it instantly consum'd with fire ;*
Even thou, and none but thou. *Take it up straight :
Within this hour bring me word 'tis done.* . . .
I am a feather for each wind that blows : . . .
> *. . . But, be it ; let it live :
It shall not neither. . . . We enjoin thee,*
As thou art liegeman to us, that thou carry
This female bastard hence. . . . Take it up.—
*I swear to do this, though a present death
Had been more merciful. Come on, poor babe :* . . .
Poor thing, condemn'd to loss ! . . .
> *. . .* Please your highness, *posts,*
From those you sent to the oracle, *are come*
An hour since : *Cleomenes and Dion,
Being well arriv'd* from Delphos, *are both landed,
Hasting to the court.*—
> So please you, sir, *their speed
Hath been beyond account.*—
> *. . . 'Tis good speed ;* foretells
The great Apollo *suddenly* will have
The truth of this appear. *Prepare you, lords ;*

Summon a session, that we may arraign
Our most disloyal lady.—*W. T.*, ii. 3.

This sessions (to our great grief, we pronounce)
Even pushes 'gainst our heart; the party tried,
The daughter of a king, our wife, and one,
Of us too much belov'd. . . .
Produce the prisoner . . .
Read the indictment. . . .
                    . . . for behold me,—
A fellow of the royal bed, which owe
A moiety of the throne, a great king's daughter,
The mother to a hopeful prince, *here standing*
To prate and talk for life and honour 'fore
Who please to come and hear.— . . .
                    . . . lastly, *hurried*
Here to this place, i' the open air, *before*
I have got strength of limit. . . .
Hast thou read truth ?—
                    Ay, my lord; *even so*
As it is here set down.—
There is no truth at all i' the oracle:
The sessions shall proceed: this is mere falsehood.—
My lord the king, the king !— . . .
The prince your son, with mere conceit and fear
Of the queen's speed, is gone.—
                    How ! gone !—
                              Is dead.— . . .
This news is mortal to the queen : look down,
And *see what death is doing.*—
                    Take her hence :
Her heart is but o'ercharged; she will recover:
I have too much believ'd mine own suspicion :
Beseech you, tenderly apply to her
Some remedies for life.— . . .
                    . . . *The queen, the queen,*
The sweet'st, dear'st creature 's dead.—*Ibid.*, iii. 2.

Thou art perfect, then, *our ship hath touch'd upon*
The deserts of Bohemia ?—
                    Ay, my lord; and fear
We have landed in ill time: the skies look grimly,
And threaten present blusters.   In my conscience,
The heavens with *that we have in hand* are angry,
And frown upon us.—
Their sacred wills be done !   *Go, get aboard ;*
Look to thy bark: *I 'll not be long before*
I call upon thee.—
Make your best haste ; and go not
Too far i' the land: 'tis like to be loud weather;
Besides, this place is famous for the creatures
Of prey that keep upon 't.—
                    Go thou away :
I 'll follow instantly.—
                    I am glad at heart
To be so rid o' the business.—
                    Come, poor babe :
                    . . . Blossom, speed thee well !
There lie ; and there thy character : there these ;
Which may, if fortune please, both breed thee, pretty,
And still rest thine.   *The storm begins.* . . .
                    . . . *Farewell !*
The day frowns more and more ; thou art like to have

A lullaby too rough : I never saw
The heavens so dim by day. A savage clamour !
Well may I get aboard ! This is the chase :
I am gone for ever.—W. T., iii. 3.
Name of mercy ! when was this, boy ?—

Now, now ; I have not winked since I saw these sights : the men are not yet cold under water, nor the bear half dined on the gentleman, he 's at it now.— . . . Thou met'st with things dying, *I with things new born. Here 's a sight for thee ;* . . . home, home, the next way . . . let my sheep go: *come, good boy, the next way home.—Go you the next way with your findings. I 'll go see* if the bear be gone from the gentleman, and how much he hath eaten . . . if there be any of him left, *I 'll bury it.—* . . . *'Tis a lucky day,* boy, and we 'll do good deeds on 't.—*Ibid.,* iii. 3.

Now take upon me, in the name of Time,
To use my wings. Impute it not a crime
To me or *my swift passage, that I slide*
O'er sixteen years, and leave the growth untried
Of that wide gap ; since it is in my power
To o'erthrow law, and in one self-born hour
To plant and o'erwhelm custom. . . .
                    . . . Your patience this allowing,
I turn my glass, and give my scene such growing,
As you had slept between. . . .
                    . . . *imagine me,*
Gentle spectators, *that I now may be*
In fair Bohemia ; and remember well,
I mentioned a son o' the king's, *which Florizel*
I now name to you ; and with speed so pace
To speak of Perdita.—Ibid., iv. (*Chorus*).

The penitent king, my master, *hath sent for me ;* to whose feeling sorrows I might be some allay, or I o'erween to think so, which is *another spur to my departure.—*As thou lovest me, Camillo, wipe not out the rest of thy services *by leaving me now.—Ibid.,* iv. 1.

I have served prince Florizel. . . . *but now I am out of service.—Ibid.,* iv. 2.

                    This your sheep-shearing
Is as a meeting of the petty gods,
And you the queen on 't.— . . .
                    . . . *See, your guests approach :* . . .
Fie, daughter ! when my old wife liv'd, *upon*
This day she was both pantler, butler, cook ;
Both dame and servant. . . .
                    . . . You are retir'd,
As if you were a feasted one, and not
The hostess of the meeting: *pray you, bid*
These unknown friends to us welcome. . . .
                    . . . *Come on,*
And bid us welcome to your sheep-shearing,
As your good flock shall prosper.—
                    Sir, welcome :
It is my father's will, I should take on me
The hostess-ship o' the day : you 're welcome, sir. . . .
          . . . Sir, the year growing ancient—
Not yet on summer's death, nor on the birth
Of trembling winter—the fairest flowers o' the season
Are our carnations. . . .
Let 's see these four threes of herdsmen . . . *let them come in, but quickly now.—*
Why, *they stay at door, sir.—* . . . *'Tis time to part them.*
          . . . *Take hands, a bargain !* . . .
                    . . . *Come on,*
Contract us 'fore these witnesses.—
                    Come, your hand ;

And, daughter, yours.— . . .
Mark our contract.—
                    Mark your divorce, young sir. . . .
                         . . . Undone, undone!
If I might die within this hour, I have liv'd
To die when I desire.— . . .
          . . . Gracious my lord,
You know your father's temper: at this time
He will allow no speech.— . . .
    For the outside of thy poverty, *we must make an exchange; therefore discase thee
instantly*, . . . and change garments with this gentleman. . . . Nay, *pr'ythee,
despatch; the gentleman is half flayed already.*— . . . *Despatch, I pr'ythee.*— . . .
Unbuckle, unbuckle.
          Fortunate mistress—let my prophecy
Come home to ye!—you must retire yourself
Into some covert: *take your sweetheart's hat
And pluck it o'er your brows; muffle your face!
Dismantle you, and, as you can, disliken
The truth of your own seeming; that you may*
(For I do fear eyes over) *to shipboard
Get undescried.* . . .
*What I do next, shall be to tell the king
Of this escape*, and whither they are bound;
Wherein, my hope is, I shall so prevail
To force him after: in whose company
I shall review Sicilia, for whose sight
I have a woman's longing.—
                    Fortune speed us!
Thus we set on, Camillo, *to the sea-side.*—
The swifter speed the better.— . . .
    The prince himself is about a piece of iniquity, stealing away from his father. . . .
There lies such secrets in this fardel and box, which none must know but the king;
and *which he shall know within this hour*, if I may come to the speech of him. . . .
Tell me (for you seem to be honest plain men) what you have to the king; being
something gently considered, *I'll bring you where he is aboard.*—W. T., iv. 3.

          What were more holy
Than to rejoice the former queen is well?
What holier than—for royalty's repair,
For present comfort, and for future good—
To bless the bed of majesty again
With a sweet fellow to't?— . . .
               . . . Had our prince
(Jewel of children) seen *this hour*, he had pair'd
Well with this lord.— . . .
               . . . By his command
Have I here touch'd Sicilia, and from him
Give you all greetings, that a king, at ffiend,
Can send his brother.— . . .
               . . . Please you, great sir,
*Bohemia greets you from himself by me;
Desires you to attach his son*, who has
(His dignity and duty both cast off)
Fled from his father, from his hopes, and with
A shepherd's daughter.—
               Where's Bohemia? Speak.—
Here in your city; I now came from him: . . .
He's with the king your father.—
                    Who? Camillo?—
Camillo, sir; I spake with him; *who now
Has these poor men in question.*— . . .
               . . . *I will to your father:*

Your honour not o'erthrown by your desires,
I 'm friend to them and you: *upon which errand*
I now go toward him.—W. T., v. i.

Beseech you, sir, *were you present at this relation?—I was by at the opening of the*
fardel, heard the old shepherd deliver the manner how he found it. . . . *Here comes a*
gentleman that happily knows more. The news, Rogero?—Nothing but bonfires: *the*
oracle is fulfilled; the king's daughter is found: such a deal of wonder is broken out
within this hour, that ballad-makers cannot be able to express it. *Here comes the lady*
Paulina's steward: he can deliver you more. How goes it now, sir?— . . . *Did you*
see the meeting of the two kings?—No.—Then have you lost a sight, which was to be
seen, cannot be spoken of. . . . *Are they returned to the court?*—No: the princess
hearing of her mother's statue, which is in the keeping of Paulina . . . *thither with*
all greediness of affection are they gone; and there they intend to sup.— . . . *Shall we*
thither, and with our company piece the rejoicing?—Who would be thence that has
the benefit of access? every wink of an eye, some new grace will be born: our absence
makes us unthrifty to our knowledge. *Let's along.*— . . . *Here come those* I have
done good to against my will, and *already appearing in the blossoms of their fortune.*—
. . . I know *you are now,* sir, a gentleman born.—Ay, and have been so any time
these four hours.— . . . Hark! the kings and the princes, our kindred, *are going to*
see the queen's picture.—Ibid., v. 2.

> *That you have vouchsaf'd*
> With your crown'd brother, and these your contracted
> Heirs of your kingdoms, *my poor house to visit,*
> It is a surplus of your grace, which never
> My life may last to answer.— . . .
> . . . *we came*
> To see the statue of our queen:— . . .
> . . . *here it is: prepare*
> To see the life as lively mock'd, as ever
> Still sleep mock'd death: *behold! and say, 'tis well.*— . . .
> . . . But yet, Paulina,
> Hermione was not so much wrinkled, nothing
> So aged *as this seems.*—
> Oh, not by much.—
> So much the more our carver's excellence;
> Which *lets go by* some sixteen years, and makes her
> As she liv'd now.—
> *As now* she might have done
> So much to my good comfort, *as it is*
> *Now piercing to my soul.* Oh, thus she stood,
> Even with such life of majesty (warm life,
> *As now it coldly stands*), when first I woo'd her
> . . . Lady,
> Dear queen, that ended when I but began,
> *Give me that hand of yours to kiss.*—
> Oh, patience!
> *The statue is but newly fix'd, the colour's*
> *Not dry.* . . . Either forbear,
> *Quit presently the chapel, or resolve you*
> *For more amazement.* If you can behold it,
> *I 'll make the statue move indeed, descend,*
> *And take you by the hand.* . . .
> . . . *Music, awake her; strike!*
> 'Tis time; descend; be stone no more; approach;
> *Strike all that look upon with marvel.* Come;
> *I 'll fill your grave up: stir; nay, come away;*
> *Bequeath to death your numbness, for from him*
> *Dear life redeems you.* You perceive, she stirs.— . . .
> . . . *Oh, she's warm!*
> If this be magic, let it be an art
> Lawful as eating.—

She embraces him.—
She hangs about his neck :
If she pertain to life, let her speak too.—
　　　　　. . . *Mark a little while.*
Please you to interpose, fair madam : kneel,
And pray your mother's blessing.　Turn, good lady ;
Our Perdita is found. . . .
　　　　　. . . Oh, peace, Paulina !
Thou shouldst a husband take by my consent,
As I by thine, a wife : this is a match,
And made between 's by vows.　*Thou hast found mine ;*
　　　　　. . . *I 'll not seek far*
(For him, I partly know his mind) *to find thee*
An honourable husband.　Come, Camillo,
And take her by the hand, whose worth and honesty
Is richly noted, *and here justified*
By us, a pair of kings.　*Let 's from this place. . . .*
　　　　　. . . *hastily lead away.—W. T.,* v. 3.

And secondly, for the enumeration of those passages which indicate
Long Time :—

If you shall chance, Camillo, *to visit Bohemia,* . . . you shall see, as I have said,
great difference betwixt our Bohemia and your Sicilia.—I think, *this coming summer,*
the King of Sicilia means to pay Bohemia the visitation which he justly owes him.—
Ibid., i. 1.

Nine changes of the watery star have been
The shepherd's note, since we have left our throne
Without a burden. . . .
　　　　　. . . No longer stay.—
One seven-night longer.—
　　　　　Very sooth, to-morrow.—
Yet of your royal presence I 'll adventure
The borrow of a week.　When at Bohemia
You take my lord, I 'll give him my commission,
To let him there a month behind the gest
Prefix'd for 's parting. . . .
　　　　　. . . I think, most understand
Bohemia stays here longer.—
　　　　　Ha ?—
　　　　　　Stays here longer.—Ibid., i. 2.

　　　　　We shall
Present our services to a fine new prince,
One of these days ; and then you 'd wanton with us,
If we would have you.—
　　　　　She is spread *of late*
Into a goodly bulk : good time encounter her !—*Ibid.,* ii. 1.

　　　　　How will this grieve you,
When you shall come to clearer knowledge, that
You thus have publish'd me. . . .
I must be patient *till the heavens look*
With an aspect more favourable.—Ibid., ii. 1.

　　　　　I have despatch'd in post
To sacred Delphos, to Apollo's temple,
Cleomenes and Dion, whom you know
Of stuff'd sufficiency : now, *from the oracle*
They will bring all.—Ibid., ii. 1.

Nor night, nor day, no rest : it is but weakness
To bear the matter thus—mere weakness. . . .
Conceiving the dishonour of his mother,
He straight *declin'd, droop'd, took it deeply,*

Fasten'd and fix'd the shame on 't in himself,
Threw off his spirit, his appetite, his sleep,
And downright languish'd . . .
      . . . let him be,
Until a time serve.—W. T., ii. 3.
      We enjoin thee,
As thou art liegeman to us, that thou carry
This female bastard hence ; and that thou *bear it*
To some remote and desert place, quite out
Of our dominions.—Ibid., ii. 3.
     Twenty-three days
They have been absent.—Ibid., ii. 3.
     If the event o' *the journey*
Prove as successful to the queen—oh, be 't so !—
As it hath been to us rare, pleasant, speedy,
The time is worth the use on 't.—Ibid., iii. 1.

You here shall swear upon this sword of justice,
That you, Cleomenes and Dion, *have*
Been both at Delphos ; and from thence have brought
This seal'd-up oracle, by the hand deliver'd
Of great Apollo's priest ; and that, *since then,*
You have not dar'd to break the holy seal,
Nor read the secrets in 't.—*Ibid.,* iii. 2.
     Once a day I 'll visit
The chapel where they lie ; and tears shed there
Shall be my recreation : *so long as nature*·
Will bear up with this exercise, so long
I daily vow to use it.—Ibid., iii. 2.
     If such thing be, thy mother
Appear'd to me last night ; for ne'er was dream
So like a waking.—*Ibid.,* iii. 3.
     Impute it not a crime
To me or my swift passage, that I slide
O'er *sixteen years,* and leave the growth untried
Of *that wide gap.—Ibid.,* iv. (*Chorus*).

It is *fifteen years* since I saw my country, . . . It is *three days* since I saw the
prince.—*Ibid.,* iv. 1.

I have served Prince Florizel, and, *in my time,* wore three-pile.—*Ibid.,* iv. 2.
     I bless *the time*
When my good falcon made her flight across
Thy father's ground.— . . .
     . . . He says he loves my daughter :
I think so too ; for never gaz'd the moon
Upon the water, *as he 'll stand, and read,*
As 'twere, my daughter's eyes.— . . .
How often have I told you 'twould be thus !
How often said my dignity would last
But till 'twere known !— . . .
As you have *ever been* my father's honour'd friend,
When he shall miss me (as, in faith, I mean not
To see him any more), cast your good counsels
Upon his passion : let myself and fortune
Tug *for the time to come.—* . . .
     . . . Now were I happy, if
His going I could frame to serve my turn ;
Save him from danger, do him love and honour ;
Purchase *the sight again of dear Sicilia,*
And that unhappy king, my master, whom
I so much thirst to see. . . .

. . . Have you thought on
Any place whereto you 'll go ?—
　　　　　　　　　　　　Not any yet :— . . .
　　　　　. . . *Make for Sicilia;*
And there present yourself and your fair princess
(For so, I see, she must be) '*fore Leontes.* . . .
Nay, but *my letters, by this means being there*
So soon as you arrive, shall clear that doubt.—*W. T.,* iv. 3.
For has not the divine Apollo said,
Is 't not the tenour of his oracle,
That king Leontes shall not have an heir,
Till his lost child be found ?—Ibid., v. 1.
She came from Libya.—
　　　　　　　　　Where the warlike Smalus,
That noble honour'd lord, is fear'd and lov'd ?—
Most royal sir, from thence ; from him, whose daughter
His tears proclaim'd his, parting with her : *thence*
(A prosperous south wind friendly) *we have cross'd*
To execute the charge my father gave me,
For visiting your highness : my best train
I have from your Sicilian shores dismiss'd ;
Who *for Bohemia bend,* to signify
Not only my success in Libya, sir,
But my arrival, and my wife's, in safety
Here where we are.—
　　　　　　　　　The blessed gods
Purge all infection from our air, *whilst you*
Do climate here !—Ibid., v. 1.
　　　　　　　　　Meets he on the way
The father of this seeming lady, and
Her brother, *having both their country quitted*
With this young prince.—
　　　　　　　　　Camillo has betray'd me ;
Whose honour and whose honesty, till now,
Endur'd all weathers.—Ibid., v. i.

The princess, hearing of her mother's statue, which is in the keeping of Paulina—
a piece *many years in doing,* and now newly performed by that rare Italian master,
Julio Romano.— . . . I thought she had some great matter there in hand ; for she hath
privately *twice or thrice a day, ever since the death of Hermione,* visited that removed
house.— *Ibid.,* v. 2.

I brought the old man and his son aboard the prince ; told him I heard them talk of
a fardel, and I know not what : but he *at that time,* over-fond of the shepherd's
daughter (so he then took her to be), who began to be much sea-sick, and himself little
better, *extremity of weather continuing,* this mystery remained undiscovered.— . . . You
are well met, sir. You denied to fight with me *this other day,* because I was no gentleman born.—*Ibid.,* v. 2.

Hermione was not *so much wrinkled,* nothing
So aged as this seems.—
　　　　　　　　　Oh, not by much.—
So much the more our carver's excellence ;
Which lets go by *some sixteen years,* and makes her
As she liv'd now.— . . .
　　　　　　　　　. . . Oh, thus she stood,
Even with such life of majesty (warm life,
As now it coldly stands), *when first I woo'd her !* . . .
　　　　　　　　　　　　. . . Lady,
Dear queen, *that ended when I but began,*
Give me that hand of yours to kiss.— . . .
My lord, your sorrow was too sore laid on,
Which *sixteen winters* cannot blow away,

So many summers dry: scarce any joy
Did ever *so long* live; no sorrow
But kill'd itself much sooner.— . . .
         . . . Nay, present your hand:
When she was young, you woo'd her; now, *in age*,
Is she become the suitor.— . . .
Ay, and make it manifest *where she has liv'd*,
Or how stolen from the dead.— . . .
         . . . Tell me, mine own,
Where hast thou been preserv'd ? where liv'd ? how found
Thy father's court? for thou shalt hear, that I—
Knowing by Paulina that the oracle
Gave hope thou wast in being—*have preserv'd*
Myself to see the issue.— . . .
         . . . I saw her,
As I thought, dead; and have in vain, *said many*
A prayer upon her grave. . . .
         . . . Good Paulina,
Lead us from hence; where we may leisurely
Each one demand, and answer to *his part*
Perform'd in this wide gap of time, since first
We were dissever'd.—*W. T.*, v. 3.

In his magnificent chronicle-drama of "Henry V.," Shakespeare has not only introduced a Chorus at the commencement of each act and at the close of the play as epilogue, serving to mark the progress of time and the variation of place in the historic story; but he has also given many passages indicative of Dramatic Time, on his own system of concurrent or alternate rapidity and slowness in these denotements. To begin with those of swiftly passing and actually present time:—

For 'tis your thoughts that now must deck our kings,
Carry them here and there; *jumping o'er times*,
Turning th' accomplishment of many years
Into an hour-glass.—*H. V.*, i. (*Chorus*).

My lord, I 'll tell you; *that self bill is urg'd*,
Which in the eleventh year of the last king's reign
Was like, and had indeed against us pass'd,
But that the scambling and unquiet time
Did push it out of farther question.—
But how, my lord, shall we resist it now?— . . .
The king is full of grace and fair regard.—
And a true lover of the holy church.—
The courses of his youth promis'd it not.— . . .
         . . . *We are blessed in the change.*— . . .
         . . . But my good lord,
How now for mitigation of this bill
Urg'd by the commons ? Doth his majesty
Incline to it or no?—
         He seems indifferent ;
Or, rather, swaying more upon our part,
Than cherishing th' exhibiters against us:
For *I have made an offer* to his majesty—
Upon our spiritual convocation,
And *in regard of causes now in hand*,
Which I have open'd to his grace at large,
As touching France—to give a greater sum
Than ever at one time the clergy yet
Did to his predecessors part withal.—
How did this offer seem receiv'd, my lord?—

With good acceptance of his majesty;
Save that there was not time enough to hear.— . . .
What was th' impediment that broke this off?—
The French embassador upon that instant
Crav'd audience; and the hour, I think, is come
To give him hearing: is it four o'clock?—
It is.—
Then go we in, to know his embassy.—*H. V.*, i. 1.

This was a merry message.—
We hope to make the sender blush at it.
Therefore, my lords, *omit no happy hour*
That may give fartherance to our expedition;
For *we have now no thought in us* but France,
Save those to God, *that run before our business.*
Therefore, let our proportions for these wars
Be soon collected, and all things thought upon
That may with reasonable swiftness add
More feathers to our wings.—*Ibid.*, i. 2.

Now all the youth of England are on fire, . . .
Now thrive the armourers, and honour's thought
Reigns solely in the breast of every man.
They sell the pasture now to buy the horse;
Following the mirror of all Christian kings,
With winged heels, as English Mercuries:
For now sits Expectation in the air; . . .
Linger your patience on; and *well digest*
Th' abuse of distance, while we force a play.
The sum is paid; the traitors are agreed;
The king is set from London; and the scene
Is now transported, gentles, *to Southampton,—*
There is the playhouse now, there must you sit:
And thence to France *shall we convey you safe,*
And bring you back, clearing the narrow seas
To give you gentle pass.—*Ibid.*, ii. (*Chorus*).

Well met, Corporal Nym.—*Good morrow*, Lieutenant Bardolph.—What, are Ancient
Pistol and you friends yet? . . . *I will bestow a breakfast to make you friends;* and
we'll be all three sworn brothers to France. . . . It is certain, corporal, that *he is
married to Nell Quickly:* and, certainly, she did you wrong; for you were troth-plight
to her. . . . Here comes Ancient Pistol and his wife; good corporal, be patient here.
— . . . Mine host Pistol, you must come to my master—and you, hostess—*he is very
sick*, and would to bed. . . . 'faith *he's very ill.*— . . . *The king has killed his heart.*
Good husband, *come home presently.* . . . As ever you came of women, *come in quickly
to Sir John.* Ah, poor heart! he is so shaked of a burning quotidian tertian, that it is
most lamentable to behold. *Sweet men, come to him.*—*Ibid.*, ii. 1.

Now sits the wind fair, and we will aboard. . . .
Who are the late commissioners?—
I one, my lord:
Your highness bade me ask for it *to-day.*—
So did you me, my liege.—
And me, my royal sovereign.—
Then, Richard, Earl of Cambridge, there is yours;
There yours, Lord Scroop of Masham; and, sir knight,
Grey of Northumberland, this same is yours;
Read them; and know, I know your worthiness. . . .
We will aboard to-night. Why, how now, gentlemen
What see you in those papers, that you lose
So much complexion?— . . .
          . . . *I do confess my fault;*
And do submit me to your highness' mercy.—
          . . . Their faults are open:

Arrest them to the answer of the law ;— . . .
Never did faithful subject more rejoice
At the discovery of most dangerous treason,
Than I do *at this hour joy o'er myself ;*
Prevented from a damned enterprise :
My fault, but not my body, pardon, sovereign.—
God quit you in his mercy ! hear your sentence.
      . . . *Get you therefore hence,*
Poor miserable wretches, *to your death :*
The taste whereof, God, of his mercy, give you
Patience to endure, and true repentance
Of all your dear offences ! *Bear them hence.*
Now, lords, for France ; . . .
Since God so graciously *hath brought to light*
This dangerous treason, lurking in our way
To hinder our beginnings, we doubt not now
But every rub is smoothed on our way.
Then forth, dear countrymen : let us deliver
Our puissance into the hand of God,
Putting it straight in expedition.
Cheerly to sea ; the signs of war advance —*H. V.*, ii. 2.

      . . . For *Falstaff he is dead,*
And we must yearn therefore.— . . .
Shall we shog ? the king will be gone from Southampton.—
Come, let 's away.—*Ibid.*, ii. 3.

Thus come the English with full power upon us ; . . .
Therefore the dukes of Berry, and of Bretagne,
Of Brabant and of Orleans, *shall make forth,*
And you, prince Dauphin, *with all swift despatch.—* . . .
Despatch us with all speed, lest that our king
Come here himself to question our delay ;
For *he is footed in this land already.—*
You shall be soon despatch'd with fair conditions :
A night is but small breath and little pause
To answer matters of this consequence.—*Ibid.*, ii. 4.

Thus with imagin'd speed our swift scene flies,
In motion of no less celerity
Than that of thought. Suppose that you have seen
The well-appointed king at Hampton pier
Embark his royalty ; and his brave fleet
With silken streamers the young Phœbus fanning :
Play with your fancies. . . .
      . . . *Follow, follow !*
Grapple your minds to sternage of this navy ; . . .
Work, work your thoughts, and therein see a siege ;
Behold the ordnance on their carriages,
With fatal mouths gaping on girded Harfleur.
Suppose, th' embassador from the French comes back ;
Tells Harry that the king doth offer him
Katharine his daughter ; and, with her, to dowry,
Some petty and unprofitable dukedoms.
The offer likes not : and the nimble gunner
With linstock now the devilish cannon touches,
And down goes all before them.—Ibid., iii. (*Chorus*).

I see you stand like greyhounds in the slips,
Straining upon the start. The game 's afoot :
Follow your spirit ; and, upon this charge,
Cry—God for Harry ! England ! and Saint George !—*Ibid.*, iii. 1.

I say, *gude day*, Captain Fluellen.—*God-den* to your worship, goot Captain Jamy.—
How now, Captain Macmorris ! have you quit the mines ? have the pioneers given

o'er?— . . . *the work ish give over, the trumpet sound the retreat* . . . *the day is hot*, and the weather, and the wars, and the king, and the dukes: it is no time to discourse.–
. . . *The town sounds a parley.—H. V.*, iii. 2.

> Our expectation hath *this day* an end:
> The Dauphin, whom of succour we entreated,
> Returns us, that his powers are not yet ready
> To raise so great a siege.   Therefore, dread king,
> *We yield our town and lives to thy soft mercy.*
> Enter our gates; dispose of us and ours;
> For we no longer are defensible.—
> Open your gates.   Come, uncle Exeter,
> *Go you and enter Harfleur.* . . .
> *To-night in Harfleur* will we be your guest.—*Ibid.*, iii. 3.

> 'Tis certain, *he hath passed the river Somme.* . . .
> Where is Montjoy, the herald?   *Speed him hence:*
> *Let him greet England with our sharp defiance.*
> *Up, princes! and, with spirit of honour, edg'd*
> *More sharper than your swords, hie to the field!—* . . .
>   . . . *haste on Montjoy;*
> And let him say to England, that we send
> To know what willing ransom he will give. . . .
> *Now forth, lord constable, and princes all,*
> *And quickly bring us word of England's fall.—Ibid.*, iii. 5.

> I hope they will not *come upon us now.—*
> We are in God's hand, brother, not in theirs;
> March to the bridge; *it now draws toward night:*
> Beyond the river we'll encamp ourselves;
> And on to-morrow bid them march away.—*Ibid.*, iii. 6.

Tut! I have the best armour of the world. *Would it were day!—* . . . *Will it never be morning?—* . . . *What a long night is this!—* . . . the armour that I saw in your tent *to-night*, are those stars, or suns, upon it?— . . . *Will it never be day?* I will trot to-morrow a mile, and my way shall be paved with English faces.—I will not say so, for fear I should be faced out of my way: but *I would it were morning;* for I would fain be about the ears of the English.— . . . *'Tis midnight; I'll go arm myself.—The Dauphin longs for morning.—* . . . My lord high constable, *the English lie within fifteen hundred paces of your tents.—* . . . *Would it were day!* Alas, poor Harry of England! he longs not *for the dawning*, as we do.— . . . *Now is it time to arm: come, shall we about it?—*

>   It is now two o'clock.—*Ibid.*, iii. 7.

> *Now entertain conjecture of a time,*
> *When creeping murmur, and the poring dark,*
> *Fills the wide vessel of the universe.*
> *From camp to camp, through the foul womb of night,*
> *The hum of either army stilly sounds,* . . .
> Steed threatens steed, in high and boastful neighs
> Piercing *the night's dull ear;* and from the tents,
> The armourers, accomplishing the knights,
> With busy hammers closing rivets up,
> *Give dreadful note of preparation.*
> *The country cocks do crow, the clocks do toll,*
> *And the third hour of drowsy morning name.*
> Proud of their numbers, and secure in soul,
> The confident and over-lusty French
> Do the low-rated English play at dice;
> *And chide the cripple tardy-gaited night.* . . .
>   . . . The poor condemned English,
> Like sacrifices, by their watchful fires
> Sit patiently, and inly ruminate
> *The morning's danger.* . . .
>   . . . Oh, now, who will behold

The royal captain of this ruin'd band,
Walking from watch to watch, from tent to tent,
Let him cry, " Praise and glory on his head !"
For forth he goes and visits all his host;
Bids them good morrow with a modest smile. . . .
Nor doth he dedicate one jot of colour
Unto *the weary and all-watched night;* . . .
Behold, as may unworthiness define,
A little touch of Harry in the night:
And so our scene must to the battle fly.—*H. V.*, iv. (*Chorus*).

Good morrow, brother Bedford. . . .
. . . Our bad neighbour *makes us early stirrers.* . . .
Good morrow, old Sir Thomas Erpingham :
A good soft pillow for that good white head
Were better than a churlish turf of France.—
Not so, my liege : *this lodging* likes me better,
Since I may say, " Now lie I like a king."— . . .
Lend me thy cloak, Sir Thomas. Brothers both,
Commend me to the princes in our camp;
Do my good-morrow to them ; and, anon,
Desire them all to my pavilion.—*Ibid.*, iv. 1.

Brother John Bates, *is not that the morning which breaks yonder ?*—I think it be : but we have no great cause to desire *the approach of day.*—*We see yonder the beginning of the day*, but I think we shall never see the end of it. . . . I believe, *as cold a night as 'tis*, he could wish himself in Thames up to the neck.

. . . . Not *to-day*, O Lord,
O, not *to-day*, think not upon the fault
My father made in compassing the crown ! . . .
. . . Ay,
I know thy errand, I will go with thee :
The day, my friends, and all things stay for me.—*Ibid.*, iv. 1.

The sun doth gild our armour ; up, my lords !— . . .
The English are embattled, you French peers.—
To horse, you gallant princes ! straight to horse ! . . .
There is not work enough for all our hands;
Scarce blood enough in all their sickly veins,
To give each naked curtle-axe a stain,
That our French gallants shall *to-day* draw out. . . .
Why do you stay so long, my lords of France ?
Yon island carrions, desperate of their bones,
Ill-favour'dly become *the morning field.*— . . .
I stay but for my guard : *on, to the field !*
I will the banner from a trumpet take,
And use it for my haste. Come, come away !
The sun is high, and we outwear the day.—*Ibid.*, iv. 2.

Farewell, kind lord; *fight valiantly to-day :*
And yet I do thee wrong to mind thee of it,
For thou art fram'd of the firm truth of valour— . . .
. . . O that we *now* had here
But one ten-thousand of those men in England
That do no work *to-day !*— . . .
This day is called the feast of Crispian :
He that outlives *this day*, and comes safe home,
Will stand a-tiptoe when *this day* is nam'd,
And rouse him at the name of Crispian.
He that shall live *this day*, and see old age,
Will yearly on the vigil feast his neighbours. . . .
And Crispin Crispian shall ne'er go by,
From *this day* to the ending of the world,
But we in it shall be remembered ;

We few, we happy few, we band of brothers;
For he, *to-day* that sheds his blood with me,
Shall be my brother; be he ne'er so vile,
This day shall gentle his condition.— . . .
My sovereign lord, *bestow yourself with speed ;*
The French are bravely in their battles set,
And will with all expedience charge on us.—
All things are ready, if our minds be so.—
Perish the man whose mind is backward now !— . . .
Once more *I come to know of thee*, King Harry,
If for thy ransom thou wilt now compound,
Before thy most assured overthrow.— . . .
    . . . Who hath sent thee *now ?*—
The Constable of France.— . . .
A many of our bodies shall, no doubt,
Find native graves; upon the which, I trust,
Shall witness live in brass of *this day's work*. . . .
And my poor soldiers tell me, yet *ere night*
They 'll be in fresher robes; or they will pluck
The gay new coats o'er the French soldiers' heads,
And turn them out of service. If they do this—
As, if God please, they shall—*my ransom then*
Will soon be levied. . . .
    . . . *Now, soldiers, march away:*
And how thou pleasest, God, *dispose the day.—H. V.*, iv. 3.

Well have we done, thrice valiant countrymen:
But all 's not done; yet keep the French the field.—
The Duke of York commends him to your majesty.—
Lives he, good uncle ? thrice *within this hour*
I saw him down; thrice up again, and fighting.—*Ibid.*, iv. 6.

Here comes the herald of the French, my liege.—
His eyes are humbler than they us'd to be.—. . . .
I come to thee for charitable licence,
That we may wander o'er this bloody field
To book our dead, and then to bury them.— . . .
    . . . I tell thee truly, herald,
I know not if the day be ours or no ;
For yet a many of your horsemen peer
And gallop o'er the field.—
      The day is yours.—
Praised be God, and not our strength for it !
What is this castle call'd that stands hard by ?—
They call it Agincourt.—
Then call we this the field of Agincourt,
Fought on the day of Crispin Crispianus.— . . .
Bring me just notice of the numbers dead
On both our parts. *Call yonder fellow hither.—*
Soldier, you must come to the king.—
Soldier, why wear'st thou that glove in thy cap ?—
An 't please your majesty, 'tis the gage of one that I should fight withal, if he be
alive.—An Englishman ?—An 't please your majesty, a rascal that swaggered with
me last night.—*Ibid.*, iv. 7.

Captain, I beseech you now, *come apace to the king:* . . . Sir, know you this glove ?
—Know the glove ! I know the glove is a glove.—I know this; and *thus I challenge it*
[*Strikes him.*]— . . . My liege, this was my glove; here is the fellow of it ; and he
that I gave it to in change promised to wear it in his cap; I promised to strike him,
if he did; I met this man with my glove in his cap, and *I have been as good as my*
word.— . . . Give me thy glove, soldier: look, here is the fellow of it. 'Twas I,
indeed, thou promisedst to strike; and thou hast given me most bitter terms.— . . .
Your majesty came not like yourself; you appeared to me but as a common man;

witness *the night,* your garments, your lowliness . . . therefore, I beseech your highness, pardon me.—

> *Here, uncle Exeter, fill this glove with crowns,*
> *And give it to this fellow.* Keep it, fellow;
> And wear it for an honour in thy cap. . . .
> *Now, herald, are the dead number'd?—*
> *Here is the number of the slaughter'd French.—* . . .
> *Where is the number of our English dead?* . . .
> . . . When, without stratagem,
> But *in plain shock and even play of battle,*
> Was ever known *so great and little loss*
> On one part and on th' other? Take it, God,
> For it is none but thine! . . .
> *Come, go we in procession to the village.* . . .
> *Do we all holy rites:*
> *Let there be sung* NON NOBIS *and* TE DEUM;
> *The dead with charity inclos'd in clay.*—*H. V.,* iv. 8.

> Now we bear the king
> Toward Calais: *grant him there; there seen,*
> *Heave him away upon your winged thoughts*
> *Athwart the sea.* Behold, the English beach
> *Pales in the flood with men, with wives, and boys,*
> Whose shouts and claps outvoice the deep-mouth'd sea,
> Which, *like a mighty whiffler 'fore the king,*
> *Seems to prepare his way: so let him land;*
> *And solemnly see him set on to London.*
> *So swift a pace hath thought, that even now*
> *You may imagine him upon Blackheath.* . . .
> . . . *now behold,*
> *In the quick forge and working-house of thought,*
> How London doth pour out her citizens!
> . . . *Now in London place him;*
> . . . *and omit*
> All the occurences, whatever chanc'd,
> Till *Harry's back-return again to France:*
> *There must we bring him; and myself have play'd*
> *The interim, by remembering you 'tis past.*
> *Then brook abridgment; and your eyes advance,*
> *After your thoughts, straight back again to France.*—*Ibid.,* v. (*Chorus*).

Nay, that's right; but why wear you your leek *to-day?* Saint Davy's day is past.— . . . Why *here he comes,* swelling like a turkey-cock.— . . . You called me yesterday mountain-squire; but I will make you *to-day* a squire of low degree. *I pray you, fall to:* if you can mock a leek, you can eat a leek.— . . . Quiet thy cudgel; *thou dost see I eat.*—. . . . News have I that my Nell *is dead* i' the spital.—*Ibid.,* v. 1.

> *Peace to this meeting, wherefore we are met!*
> Unto our brother France, and to our sister,
> Health and *fair time of day!* . . .
> So happy be the issue, brother England,
> *Of this good day and of this gracious meeting,*
> *As we are now glad to behold your eyes;* . . .
> The venom of such looks, we fairly hope,
> Have lost their quality: and *that this day*
> *Shall change all griefs and quarrels into love.—* . . .
> . . . Fair Katharine and most fair!
> Will you vouchsafe to teach a soldier terms
> Such as will enter at a lady's ear,
> And *plead his love-suit to her gentle heart?* . . .

Canst thou love me?—I cannot tell.—Can any of your neighbours tell, Kate? I'll ask them. Come, I know, thou lovest me: and *at night,* when you come into your closet, you 'll question this gentlewoman about me: . . . *Come, your answer* in broken music, for thy voice is music, and thy English broken; therefore, queen of all, Katharine, break thy mind to me in broken English—*wilt thou have me ?*—Dat is, as it shall please de roy mon père.—Nay, it will please him well, Kate, it shall please him, Kate.—*Den it shall also content me.*—*Upon that I kiss your hand, and I call you my queen.*— . . . *Here comes your father.*— . . . *Shall Kate be my wife ?*—So please you.—. . . *The king hath granted every article; his daughter first; and then, in sequel, all*, according to their firm proposed natures.— . . . *Now, welcome, Kate : and bear me witness all, that here I kiss her as my sovereign queen.*—H. V., v. 2.

> Thus far, with rough and all unable pen,
>   Our bending author hath pursu'd the story;
> In little room confining mighty men,
>   *Mangling by starts the full course of their glory.*
> Small time, but, in that small, most greatly liv'd
>   This star of England.—*Ibid.*, v. (*Chorus*).

Now to follow with those of more slowly passing and longer time :—

> *When we have match'd our rackets to these balls,*
> *We will, in France, by God's grace, play a set,*
> Shall strike his father's crown into the hazard. . . .
> Tell you the Dauphin, I am coming on,
> *To venge me as I may*, and to put forth
> My rightful hand in a well-hallow'd cause. . . .
> For we have now no thought in us *but France*,
> Save those to God, that run before our business,
> Therefore let our proportions for *these wars*
> Be soon collected. . . .
> *We 'll chide this Dauphin at his father's door.*—*Ibid.*, i. 2.

> *Linger your patience on ;* and well digest
> Th' abuse of distance, while we force a play . . .
> The king is set *from London ;* and the scene
> Is now transported, gentles, *to Southampton.* . . .
> And thence *to France* shall we convey you safe.—*Ibid.*, ii. (*Chorus*).

> For us, *we will consider of this farther :*
> *To-morrow shall you bear our full intent*
> *Back to our brother England.* . . .
> *To-morrow shall you know our mind at full.*—*Ibid.*, ii. 4.

> Suppose, that you have seen
> The well-appointed king *at Hampton pier*
> *Embark his royalty.* . . .
> For so appears this fleet majestical,
> *Holding due course for Harfleur.*—*Ibid.*, iii. (*Chorus*).

Bardolph *stole a lute-case, bore it twelve leagues, and sold it for three halfpence.* Nym and Bardolph are sworn brothers in filching; and *in Calais they stole a fire-shovel.*—*Ibid.*, iii. 2.

> *The winter coming on, and sickness growing*
> *Upon our soldiers, we will retire to Calais.*
> To-night in Harfleur will we be your guest;
> *To-morrow for the march are we addrest.*—*Ibid.*, iii. 3.

We give express charge, that *in our marches through the country*, there be nothing compelled from the villages. . . .

> . . . Tell thy king, *I do not seek him now ;*
> *But could be willing to march on to Calais*
> Without impeachment. . . .
> *My people are with sickness much enfeebled ;*
> *My numbers lessen'd.*—*Ibid.*, iii. 6.

> Tell him, I 'll knock his leek about his pate,
> *Upon Saint David's day.*— . . .

If ever thou come to me and say, after to-morrow, " This is my glove," by this hand, I will take thee a box on the ear.—*Ibid.*, iv. 1.

Our gayness and our gilt are all besmirch'd
With rainy marching in the painful field;
There's not a piece of feather in our host
(Good argument, I hope, we will not fly),
And time hath worn us into slovenry.—H. V., iv. 3.

I was not angry *since I came to France*
Until this instant.—*Ibid.,* iv. 7.

We'll then to Calais; and to England then;
Where ne'er *from France* arriv'd more happy men.—*Ibid.,* iv. 8

I humbly pray them to admit th' excuse
Of time, of numbers, and due course of things,
Which cannot *in their huge and proper life*
Be here presented.   Now we bear the king
Toward Calais: . . .
            . . . Behold, *the English beach.* . . .
            . . . See him set on *to London.* . . .
            . . . imagine him *upon Blackheath;* . . .
How *London* doth pour out her citizens . . .
            . . . in *London* place him.
(As yet the lamentation of the French
Invites *the king of England's stay at home;*
The emperor's coming in behalf of France,
To order peace between them) ; and omit
All the occurrences, whatever chanc'd,
Till Harry's back-return again to France: . . .
                . . . and your eyes advance,
After your thoughts, straight back again *to France.—Ibid.,* v. *(Chorus).*

Why wear you your leek to-day? *Saint Davy's day* is past.— . . . He is come to
me, and prings me pread and salt *yesterday,* look you, and bid me eat my leek. . . .
You called me *yesterday* mountain-squire.— . . . I have seen you gleeking and galling
at this gentleman *twice or thrice.*— . . . *Old I do wax; and from my weary limbs honour
is cudgelled.* . . . *To England will I steal.—Ibid.,* v. 1.

The Dramatic Time in "Romeo and Juliet" extends over four days :
the day of the brawl with which the play opens and of the feast on that
same night at Capulet's house ; the day on which the youthful hero and
heroine are married to each other by Friar Laurence, on which Mercutio
and Tybalt are killed, and on which old Capulet promises his daughter
to County Paris for a wife; the day when at dawn Romeo leaves Verona
for Mantua, when the parents announce to Juliet that she is to have
Paris for her husband, and when she obtains the sleeping-potion, taking
it that same night; and, finally, the day on which Romeo hears of Juliet's
death, returning in all haste to swallow poison and die beside her that
very night.   The lapse of these four days is ingeniously notified by the
dramatist with sufficient distinctness to give verisimilitude in space for
action ; and yet, he so contrives to give speedy effect by touches of
brief time, that the whole seems to transpire naturally within the usual
stage " two hours."   He has introduced a Chorus in this play, as prologue and as close to the first act ; but farther indications of Dramatic
Time lie scattered through various passages of this most exquisite
love-drama.   Firstly, for those of Short Time :—

The fearful passage of their death-mark'd love,
   And the continuance of their parents' rage,
Which, but their children's end, naught could remove,
   Is now the two hours' traffic of our stage.—R. & Jul., i.
                                          (Chorus prologue).

For this time, all the rest depart away:
You, Capulet, shall along with me;
And, Montague, come you *this afternoon*,
To know our farther pleasure in this case.— . . .
Who set this ancient quarrel *new abroach ?*
Speak, nephew, were you by when it began ?—
Here were the servants of your adversary,
And yours, *close fighting ere I did approach:*
I drew to part them : in the instant came
The fiery Tybalt, with his sword prepar'd. . . .
While we were interchanging thrusts and blows,
Came more and more, and fought on part and part,
Till the prince came, who parted either part.—
Oh, where is Romeo *? saw you him to-day ?*
Right glad I am he was not at this fray.—
Madam, *an hour before the worshipp'd sun*
Peer'd forth the golden window of the east,
A troubled mind drave me to walk abroad; . . .
So early walking did I see your son . . .
See, where he comes : so please you, step aside;
I 'll know his grievance, or be much denied. . . .
Good morrow, cousin.—
                          Is the day so young ?—
But new struck nine.— . . .
Where shall we dine ? O me! *what fray was here ?*
Yet tell me not, for I have heard it all.—R. & Jul., i. 1.
But *Montague is bound as well as I,*
In penalty alike;— . . .
But *now*, my lord, *what say you to my suit ?—*
But saying o'er what I have said before :
My child is yet a stranger to the world,
She hath not seen the change of fourteen years. . . .
But woo her, gentle Paris, get her heart,
My will to her consent is but a part. . . .
This night I hold an old accustom'd feast,
Whereto I have invited many a guest, . . .
At my poor house look to behold *this night*
Earth-treading stars, . . .
                          . . . even such delight
Among fresh female buds shall you *this night*
Inherit at my house; hear all, all see,
And like her most, whose merit most shall be: . . .
Come, go with me. *Go, sirrah*, trudge about
Through fair Verona; find those persons out
Whose names are written there, *and to them say,*
My house and welcome on their pleasure stay.— . .
                          . . . *Good-den*, good fellow.—
God gi' good-den. . . .
A fair assembly: whither should they come ?—Up.—Whither ?—*To supper ;* to our
house.—Whose house ?—My master's.— . . .
At this same ancient feast of Capulet's
Sups the fair Rosaline, whom thou so lov'st ;
With all the admired beauties of Verona:
Go thither. . . .
I 'll go along, no such sight to be shown,
But to rejoice in splendour of mine own.—*Ibid.*, i. 2.
The valiant Paris seeks you for his love.— . . .
What say you ? can you love the gentleman ?
This night you shall behold him at our feast ;
Read o'er the volume of young Paris' face,
And find delight writ there with beauty's pen.— . . .

Madam, *the guests are come, supper served up, you called, my young lady asked for,*
the nurse cursed in the pantry, and everything in extremity. I must hence to wait; I
beseech you, follow straight.—

> *We follow thee. Juliet, the County stays.—R. & Jul.*, i. 3.
>
> *I dreamt a dream to-night —* . . .
> *Supper is done, and we shall come too late.—*
> I fear, too early: for my mind misgives
> Some consequence, yet hanging in the stars,
> Shall bitterly begin his fearful date
> With *this night's revels.* . . .
> But He, that hath the steerage of my course,
> Direct my sail! *On, lusty gentlemen.—Ibid.*, i. 4.
>
> *You are welcome, gentlemen! Come, musicians, play.*
> *A hall, a hall! give room! and foot it girls.* . . .
> *What lady is that*, which doth enrich the hand
> Of yonder knight?— . . .
> The measure done, I'll watch her place of stand,
> And, touching hers, make blessed my rude hand.
> Did my heart love till *now?* forswear it, sight!
> For I ne'er saw true beauty till *this night.—* . . .
> Uncle, this is a Montague, our foe;
> A villain, that is hither come in spite,
> To scorn at our solemnity *this night.—* . . .
>   . . . *Is she a Capulet?*
> O dear account! *my life is my foe's debt.—*
> *Away, begone!* the sport is at the best.—
> Ay, so I fear; the more is my unrest.—
> Nay, gentlemen, *prepare not to be gone;*
> *We have a trifling banquet towards.*
> *Is it e'en so? Why, then, I thank you all;*
> I thank you, honest gentlemen; *good night.*
> *More torches there! Come on, then, let's to bed.*
> Ah, sirrah, by my fay, *it waxes late:*
> *I'll to my rest.—*
> Come hither, nurse. . . .
> *What's he that follows there, that would not dance?—*
> I know not.—
> *Go, ask his name:* if he be married,
> My grave is like to be my wedding-bed.—
> *His name is Romeo, and a Montague;*
> *The only son of your great enemy.—*
> *My only love sprung from my only hate!*
> *Too early seen unknown, and known too late!—* . . .
> *Come, let's away; the strangers are all gone.—Ibid.*, i. 5.
>
> *Now old desire doth in his death-bed lie,*
>   *And young affection gapes to be his heir;*
> That fair, for which love groan'd for, and would die,
>   With tender Juliet, *is now not fair.*
> *Now Romeo is belov'd, and loves again.—Ibid.*, i. (*Chorus*).
>
> Come, he hath hid himself among these trees,
> To be consorted with the humorous *night:—* . . .
> Romeo, *good night:* I'll to my truckle-bed;—*Ibid.*, ii. 1.
>
> *What light through yonder window breaks?*
> *It is the east, and Juliet is the sun!*
> *Arise, fair sun, and kill the envious moon.* . . .
> O, speak again, bright angel! for thou art
> As glorious to *this night*, being o'er my head,
> As is a winged messenger of heaven.— . . .
> What man art thou, that, thus bescreen'd *in night*,
> So stumblest on my counsel?—

I have *night's* cloak to hide me from their sight.— . . .
Thou know'st the mask of *night* is on my face,
Else would a maiden blush bepaint my cheek,
For that which thou hast heard me speak *to-night*. . .
      . . . therefore, pardon me ;
And not impute this yielding to light love,
Which the dark *night* hath so discovered.— . . .
Well, do not swear : although I joy in thee,
I have no joy of this contract *to-night :* . . .
      . . . Sweet, *good night !* . . .
Good night, good night ! as sweet repose and rest
Come to thy heart, as that within my breast !—
O, wilt thou leave me so unsatisfied ?—
What satisfaction canst thou have *to-night ?*— . . .
O blessed, blessed *night !* I am afeard,
Being in *night*, all this is but a dream.— . . .
Three words, dear Romeo, and *good night indeed.* . . .
A thousand times *good night !*— . . .
How silver-sweet sound lovers' tongues *by night.*— . . .
'Tis almost morning ; I would have thee gone : . . .
Good night, good night ! parting is such sweet sorrow,
That I shall say good night, till it be morrow.— . . .
Hence will I to my ghostly father's cell,
His help to crave, and my dear hap to tell.—*R. & Jul,*, ii. 2.

The grey-ey'd morn smiles on the frowning night,
Checkering the eastern clouds with streaks of light ;
And flecked darkness like a drunkard reels
From forth day's path and Titan's fiery wheels ;
Now, ere the sun advance his burning eye,
The day to cheer and night's dank dew to dry,
I must up-fill this osier cage of ours
With baleful weeds and precious-juiced flowers.— . . .
Good morrow, father !—
       Benedicite !
What early tongue so sweet saluteth me ?
Young son, it argues a distemper'd head,
So soon to bid good morrow to thy bed : . . .
Therefore thy *earliness* doth me assure
Thou art uprous'd by some distemperature ;
Or if not so, then here I hit it right,
Our Romeo hath not been in bed to-night.— . . .
Then plainly know, *my heart's dear love is set*
On the fair daughter of rich Capulet :
As mine on hers, so hers is set on mine ;
And all combin'd save what thou must combine
By holy marriage : when, and where, and how,
We met, we woo'd, and made exchange of vow,
I 'll tell thee as we pass ; but this I pray,
That thou consent to marry us to-day.—
Holy Saint Francis ! what a change is here !
Is Rosaline, whom thou didst love so dear,
So soon forsaken ?— . . .
I pray thee, chide not : *she, whom I love now,*
Doth grace for grace and love for love allow ;
The other did not so. . . .
O, let us hence ; I stand on sudden haste.—*Ibid.*, ii. 3.

Where the devil should this Romeo be ?
Came he not home to-night ?—
Not to his father's ; I spoke with his man.—
Ah, that same pale hard-hearted wench, that Rosaline,

Torments him so, that he will sure run mad.—
Tybalt, the kinsman of old Capulet,
Hath sent a letter to his father's house.—
A challenge, on my life.— . . .
Here comes Romeo, here comes Romeo.— . . .

Signior Romeo, *bon jour!* there's a French salutation to your French slop. *You gave us the counterfeit fairly last night.—Good morrow to you both.—* . . . Why *is not this better now than groaning for love?* now art thou sociable, now art thou Romeo; now art thou what thou art, by art as well as by nature.— . . . *God ye good morrow,* gentlemen.—God ye good-den, fair gentlewoman.—Is it good-den ?—'Tis no less, I tell you; for the bawdy hand of the dial is on the prick of *noon.* . . . Romeo, will you come to your father's? we'll *to dinner* thither.—I will follow you.— . . . Pray you, sir, a word: and as I told you, *my young lady bade me inquire you out;—* . . . Bid her devise some means to come to shrift *this afternoon; and there she shall at Friar Laurence' cell be shriv'd and married.—* . . . *This afternoon, sir? well, she shall be there.—*

> And stay, good nurse, behind the abbey-wall:
> *Within this hour* my man shall be with thee,
> And bring thee cords made like a tackled stair;
> Which to the high top-gallant of my joy
> Must be my convoy *in the secret night.—R. & Jul.*, ii. 4.

> *The clock struck nine when I did send the nurse;*
> *In half an hour she promis'd to return.*
> Perchance she cannot meet him: that's not so. . . .
> *Now is the sun upon the highmost hill*
> *Of this day's journey; and from nine to twelve*
> *Is three long hours*, yet she is not come. . . .
> *O God, she comes!   O honey nurse, what news?*
> *Hast thou met him?* . . .
> *Now, good sweet nurse,* . . .
> *Nay, come, I pray thee, speak; good, good nurse, speak.—* . . .
>   . . . What, *have you dined* at home?—
> *No, no;* but all this did I know before.
> *What says he of our marriage? what of that?* . . .
> *Sweet, sweet, sweet nurse, tell me, what says my love?* . . .
> Here's such a coil!   *Come, what says Romeo?—*
> Have you got leave *to go to shrift to-day?—*
> I have.—
> *Then hie you hence to Friar Laurence' cell,*
> *There stays a husband to make you a wife:* . . .
> *Hie you to church; I must another way,*
> *To fetch a ladder*, by the which your love
> Must climb a bird's nest *soon, when it is dark:*
> I am the drudge, and toil in your delight;
> But you shall bear the burden *soon at night.*
> *Go; I'll to dinner; hie you to the cell.—*
> *Hie to high fortune! honest nurse, farewell.—Ibid.*, ii. 5.

> So smile the heavens upon *this holy act*,
> That after-hours with sorrow chide us not!— . . .
> *Do thou but close our hands with holy words.* . . .
> *Here comes the lady:* O, so light a foot
> Will ne'er wear out the everlasting flint.— . . .
> *Good even* to my ghostly confessor.— . . .
> *Come, come with me, and we will make short work;*
> For, by your leaves, you shall not stay alone,
> Till *holy Church incorporate two in one.—Ibid.*, ii. 6.

> I pray thee, good Mercutio, let's retire:
> *The day is hot*, the Capulets abroad,
> And, if we meet, we shall not 'scape a brawl. . . .
> By my head, *here come the Capulets.—*

By my heel, I care not.—
Follow me close, for I will speak to them.
Gentlemen, *good-den :* a word with one of you.— . . .
This gentleman, the prince's near ally,
My very friend, *hath got his mortal hurt*
In my behalf; my reputation stain'd
With Tybalt's slander ; Tybalt, *that an hour*
Hath been my kinsman :— . . .
O Romeo, Romeo, *brave Mercutio's dead !*— . . .
This day's black fate on more days doth depend ;
This but begins the woe, others must end.—
Here comes the furious Tybalt back again.—
Alive ! in triumph ! and Mercutio slain !
Away to heaven, respective lenity,
And *fire-ey'd fury be my conduct now !*— . . .
Romeo, away, begone !
The citizens are up, and Tybalt slain :
Stand not amaz'd : the prince will doom thee death,
If thou art taken : *hence, be gone, away !*— . . .
Romeo slew him, he slew Mercutio ;
Who now the price of his dear blood doth owe ?—
Not Romeo, prince, he was Mercutio's friend ;
His fault concludes but what the law should end,
The life of Tybalt.—
　　　　　　　　And for that offence,
Immediately we do exile him hence. . . .
　　. . . *let Romeo hence in haste,*
Else, when he's found, that hour is his last.—*R. & Jul.*, iii. 1.
Gallop apace, you fiery-footed steeds,
Towards Phœbus' mansion : such a waggoner
As Phaeton would whip you to the west,
And bring in cloudy night immediately. . . .
　　　　　　　. . . *Come, civil night,* . . .
Come, night ; come, Romeo, come, thou day in night ; . . .
Come, gentle night ; come, loving, black-brow'd night,
Give me my Romeo. . . .
　　　　　. . . *So tedious is this day,*
As is the night before some festival
To an impatient child, that hath new robes,
And may not wear them.　*O, here comes my nurse,*
And she brings news. . . .
Now, nurse, what news ?　What hast thou there ? *the cords*
That Romeo bade thee fetch ?—
　　　　　　　　Ay, ay, the cords.—
Ah me, *what news ?* why dost thou wring thy hands?—
Ah well-a-day ! *he's dead, he's dead, he's dead !*— . . .
Tybalt is gone, and Romeo banish'd ;
Romeo, that kill'd him, he is banish'd.— . . .
Shall I speak ill of him that is my husband ?
Ah, poor my lord, what tongue shall smooth thy name,
When I, *thy three-hours wife*, have mangled it ?— . . .
Hie to your chamber : I'll find Romeo
To comfort you : I wot well where he is.
Hark ye, *your Romeo will be here at night :*
I'll to him ; he is hid at Laurence' cell.—*Ibid.*, iii. 2.
Romeo, come forth ; come forth, thou fearful man.— . . .
Father, what news ? what is the prince's doom ?— . . .
Not body's death, but body's banishment—. . . .
'Tis torture, and not mercy : . . .
Wert thou as young as I, Juliet thy love,
An hour but married, Tybalt murdered,

Doting like me, and like me banished,
Then might'st thou speak.— ...
I come from Lady Juliet.—

Welcome, then.—
O holy friar, O, tell me, holy friar,
Where is my lady's lord, where's Romeo ?—
There on the ground, with his own tears made drunk.— ...
What, rouse thee, man ! thy Juliet is alive,
For whose dear sake thou wast but lately dead;
There art thou happy. ...
Go, get thee to thy love, as was decreed,
Ascend her chamber, hence and comfort her :
But look thou stay not till the watch be set,
For then thou canst not pass to Mantua ; ...
Go before, nurse : commend me to thy lady ;
And bid her hasten all the house to bed,
Which heavy sorrow makes them apt unto:
Romeo is coming.— ...
Here, sir, a ring she bid me give you, sir.
Hie you, make haste, for it grows very late.—
How well my comfort is reviv'd by this !—
Go hence ; good night ; and here stands all your state:
Either be gone before the watch be set,
Or by the break of day disguis'd from hence : ...
Give me thy hand ; 'tis late : farewell ; good night.—R. & Jul., iii. 3.

Things have fallen out, sir, so unluckily,
That *we have had no time to move our daughter :* ...
'Tis very late, she'll not come down to-night :
I promise you, but for your company,
I would have been a-bed an hour ago.—
These times of woe afford no time to woo.
Madam, *good night :* commend me to your daughter.—
I will, and *know her mind early to-morrow ;*
To-night, she's mew'd up to her heaviness.— ...
Wife, *go you to her ere you go to bed ;*
Acquaint her here of my son Paris' love ;
And bid her, mark you me, on Wednesday next—
But, soft ! *What day is this ?—*

Monday, my lord.—
Monday ! ha, ha ! Well, Wednesday is *too soon ;*
O' Thursday let it be ; o' Thursday, tell her,
She shall be married to this noble earl.
Will you be ready ? Do you like this haste ? ...

... what say you to Thursday ?—
My lord, I would that Thursday were to-morrow.—
Well, *get you gone :* o' Thursday be it, then.
Go you to Juliet ere you go to bed,
Prepare her, wife, against this wedding-day.
Farewell, my lord. Light to my chamber, ho !
Afore me, *it is so very late, that we*
May call it early by-and-by ; good night.—Ibid., iii. 4.

Wilt thou be gone ? It is not yet near day :
It was the nightingale, and not the lark,
That pierc'd the fearful hollow of thine ear.— ...
It was the lark, the herald of the morn,
No nightingale; *look, love, what envious streaks*
Do lace the severing clouds in yonder east ;
Night's candles are burnt out, and jocund day
Stands tiptoe on the misty mountain-tops.
I must be gone and live, or stay and die.—
Yon light is not daylight, I know it, I :

It is some meteor that the sun exhales,
To be to thee *this night* a torch-bearer.— . . .
I 'll say *yon grey* is not the morning's eye. . . .
How is 't, my soul ? let 's talk, it is not day.—
It is, it is—hie hence, be gone, away ! . . .
Oh, now be gone; more light and light it grows. — . . .
Madam !—

       Nurse ?—
Your lady mother 's coming to your chamber :
The day is broke : be wary, look about.—
Then, window, *let day in*, and let life out.
Farewell, farewell ! one kiss, and I 'll descend.—
Art thou gone so ? my lord, my love, my friend !— . . .
Ho, daughter ! *are you up ?*
Who is 't that calls ? is it my lady mother ?
Is she not down so late, or up so early ?
What unaccustom'd cause procures her hither ?— . . .
Now, by Saint Peter's church, and Peter too,
He shall not make me there a joyful bride.
I wonder at this haste ; that I must wed
Ere he, that should be husband, comes to woo :
I pray you, tell my lord and father, madam,
I will not marry yet.— . . .
Here comes your father ; tell him so yourself.— . . .
Go in ; and tell my lady I am gone,
Having displeas'd my father, *to Laurence' cell,*
To make confession, and to be absolv'd. . . .
I 'll to the friar, to know his remedy.—R. & Jul., iii. 5.

On Thursday, sir ? *the time is very short.*—
My father Capulet will have it so ;
And I am nothing slow to slack his haste.— . . .
Now do you know the reason of *this haste.*—
I would I knew not why it should be slow'd.
Look, sir, *here comes the lady towards my cell.*— . . .
Are you at leisure, holy father, now ;
Or shall I come to you at evening mass ?—
My leisure serves me, pensive daughter, now.— . . .
Oh, shut the door ! and when thou hast done so,
Come weep with me ; past hope, past cure, past help !—
Ah, Juliet, *I already know thy grief.*— . . .
Give me some present counsel.— . . .
Hold, then ; *go home, be merry, give consent*
To marry Paris. . . .
Take thou this phial, being then in bed,
And this distilled liquor drink thou off :
When, presently, through all thy veins shall run
A drowsy humour. . . .
Now, when the bridegroom in the morning comes
To rouse thee from thy bed, *there art thou dead.* . . .
Hold ; get you gone, be strong and prosperous
In this resolve : I 'll send a friar with speed
To Mantua, with my letters to thy lord.—
Love, give me strength ! and strength shall help afford.
Farewell, dear father !—Ibid., iv. 1.

What, *is my daughter gone to Friar Laurence ?*—
Ay, forsooth. . . .
See, where she comes from shrift with merry look.—
How now, my headstrong ! where have you been gadding ?—
Where I have learn'd me to repent the sin
Of disobedient opposition
To you and your behests ;— . . .

Send for the County; go tell him of this:
I'll have this knot knit up to-morrow morning.— . . .
Nurse, will you go with me into my closet,
To help me sort such needful ornaments
As you think fit *to furnish me to-morrow?—*
No, not till Thursday; there is time enough.—
Go, nurse, go with her: we'll to church to-morrow.—
We shall be short in our provision:
'Tis now near night.—
                 Tush, I will stir about,
And all things shall be well, I warrant thee, wife:
Go thou to Juliet, help to deck up her;
I'll not to bed to-night; let me alone;
I'll play the housewife for this once. What, ho!
They are all forth: well, I will walk myself
To County Paris, to prepare him up
Against to-morrow.—*R. & Jul.*, iv. 2.

Ay, those attires are best: but, gentle nurse,
I pray thee, *leave me to myself to-night;— . . .*
What, are you busy, ho? need you my help?—
No, madam; *we have cull'd such necessaries*
As are behoveful for our state to-morrow:
So please you, *let me now be left alone,*
And let the nurse this night sit up with you;
For, I am sure, you have your hands full all,
In this so sudden business.—
                 Good night:
Get thee to bed, and rest; for thou hast need.—
Farewell! God knows when we shall meet again. . . .
Come, phial.
What if this mixture do not work at all?
Shall I be married, then, to-morrow morning?
No, no; this shall forbid it: lie thou there. . . .
Romeo, I come! this do I drink to thee.—Ibid., iv. 3.

Come, stir, stir, stir; the second cock hath crow'd,
The curfew bell hath rung, 'tis three o'clock:— . . .
Get you to bed; 'faith, you'll be sick to-morrow
For this night's watching.— . . .
       . . . *Good faith, 'tis day:*
The County will be here with music straight,
For so he said he would: *I hear him near.*
Nurse! Wife! what, ho! what, nurse, I say!
Go waken Juliet, go and trim her up;
I'll go and chat with Paris; hie, make haste,
Make haste; the bridegroom he is come already:
Make haste, I say.—Ibid., iv. 4.

Mistress! what, mistress! Juliet! fast, I warrant her, she. . . .
I must needs wake you: Lady! lady! lady!
Alas! alas! Help! help! *my lady's dead!— . . .*
What noise is here?—
             O lamentable day!—
What is the matter?—
          Look, look! O heavy day!— . . .
For shame! *bring Juliet forth; her lord is come.—*
She's dead, deceas'd, she's dead; alack the day!—
Alack the day! she's dead, she's dead, she's dead!— . . .
Come, is the bride ready to go to church?—
Ready to go, but never to return:
O son, *the night before thy wedding-day*
Hath death lain with thy wife: *there she lies.— . . .*

Have I thought long to see *this morning's face,*
And doth it give me such a sight as this?—
Accurs'd, unhappy, wretched, hateful day!
Most miserable hour.— . . .
Dry up your tears, and stick your rosemary
On this fair corse; and, as the custom is,
In all her best array bear her to church: . . .
. . . *every one prepare*
To follow this fair corse unto her grave.— . . .

O, play me some merry dump, to comfort me.—Not a dump we; 'tis no time to play now.— . . . Come, we'll in here; tarry for the mourners; and stay dinner.—*R. & Jul.,* iv. 5.

If I may trust the flattering truth of sleep,
My dreams presage some joyful news at hand:
My bosom's lord sits lightly in his throne;
And *all this day* an unaccustom'd spirit
Lifts me above the ground with cheerful thoughts. . . .
News from Verona! How now, Balthazar!
Dost thou not bring me letters from the friar?
How doth my lady?— . . .
Her body sleeps in Capels' monument,
And her immortal part with angels lives.
I saw her laid low in her kindred's vault,
And presently took post to tell it you.— . . .
. . . *Get me ink and paper,*
And hire post-horses; I will hence to-night.— . . .
. . . *Get thee gone,*
And hire those horses; I'll be with thee straight.
Well, Juliet, I will lie with thee to-night.
Let's see for means: O mischief, thou art swift
To enter in the thoughts of desperate men!
I do remember an apothecary—
And hereabouts he dwells— . . .
What, ho! apothecary!—
Who calls so loud?—
Come hither, man. I see that thou art poor;
Hold, there is forty ducats: *let me have*
A dram of poison. . . .
Come, cordial, and not poison, go with me
To Juliet's grave; for there I must use thee.—Ibid., v. 1.

Get me an iron crow, and bring it straight
Unto my cell.—
Brother, I'll go and bring it thee.—
Now must I to the monument alone;
Within this three hours will fair Juliet wake.—Ibid., v. 2.

What cursed foot wanders this way *to-night,*
To cross my obsequies and true love's rite?
What, with a torch? muffle me, night, awhile.—
Give me that mattock and the wrenching iron.
Hold, take this letter; *early in the morning*
See thou deliver it to my lord and father. . . .
Wilt thou provoke me? *then have at thee, boy!—*
O Lord! *they fight! I will go call the watch.—*
Oh, *I am slain!—* . . .
Here's to my love! O true apothecary!
Thy drugs are quick. Thus with a kiss I die.—
Saint Francis be my speed! how oft *to-night*
Have my old feet stumbled at graves. . . .
It burneth in the Capels' monument.—
It doth so, holy sir; and there's my master,

One that you love.—
　　　Who is it?—
　　　　　Romeo.—
How long hath he been there?—
　　　　Full half an hour.— . . .
Romeo! O, pale! Who else? what, Paris too?
And steep'd in blood? *Ah, what an unkind hour*
Is guilty of this lamentable chance!
The lady stirs. . . . *Lady, come from that nest*
Of death, contagion, and unnatural sleep:
A greater Power than we can contradict
Hath thwarted our intents: come, come away:
Thy husband in thy bosom there lies dead;
And Paris too: come, I'll dispose of thee
Among a sisterhood of holy nuns;
Stay not to question, for the watch is coming;
Come, go, good Juliet. I dare no longer stay.—
Go, get thee hence, for I will not away.
What's here? a cup, clos'd in my true love's hand?
Poison, I see, hath been his timeless end:
O churl! drink all, and leave *no friendly drop,*
To help me after? I will kiss thy lips;
Haply, some poison yet doth hang on them,
To make me die with a restorative.
Thy lips are warm!—
Lead, boy; which way?—
Yea, noise? *then I'll be brief. O happy dagger!*
This is thy sheath; there rest, and let me die.— . . .
Pitiful sight; here lies the County slain;
And Juliet bleeding; *warm, and newly dead,*
Who here hath lain these two days buried.
Go tell the prince—run to the Capulets—
Raise up the Montagues.— . . .
What misadventure is *so early up,*
That calls our person *from our morning's rest?—* . . .
Sovereign, here lies the County Paris slain;
And Romeo dead; and Juliet, dead before,
Warm and new killed.— . . .
Come, Montague; for thou art early up,
To see thy son and heir more early down.—
Alas, my liege, *my wife is dead to-night.—* . . .
　　　　　. . . I writ to Romeo,
That he should hither come *as this dire night,*
To help to take her from her borrow'd grave,
Being the time the potion's force should cease. . . .
　　　　　. . . Then, all alone,
At the prefixed hour of her waking,
Came I to take her from her kindred's vault.— . . .
I brought my master news of Juliet's death;
And then in post he came from Mantua,
To this same place, to this same monument.
This letter he early bid me give his father.— . . .
A glooming peace *this morning* with it brings;
The sun, for sorrow, *will not show his head.—R. & Jul.,* v. 3.

And, secondly, for those of Long Time:—

The fearful passage of their death-mark'd love,
　And the continuance of their parents' rage,
Which, but their children's end, naught could remove,
　Is now the two hours' traffic of our stage.—*Ibid.,* i. (*Chorus prologue*).
But passion lends them power, *time means, to meet.—Ibid.,* i. (*Chorus*).

If that thy bent of love be honourable,
Thy purpose marriage, *send me word to-morrow*
By one that I 'll procure to come to thee,
Where, and what time, thou wilt perform the rite. . . .
To-morrow will I send.— . . .
                    . . . *At what o'clock to-morrow*
Shall I send to thee?—
                    At the hour of nine.—
I will not fail: 'tis twenty years till then.—*R. & Jul.*, ii. 2.

I anger her *sometimes*, and tell her that Paris is the properer man.—*Ibid.*, ii, 4.

                    To Mantua ;
Where thou shalt live, till we can find a time
To blaze your marriage, reconcile your friends,
Beg pardon of the prince, and call thee back
With twenty hundred thousand times more joy
Than thou went'st forth in lamentation. . . .
Sojourn in Mantua ; I 'll find out your man,
And *he shall signify from time to time*
Every good hap to you that chances here.—*Ibid.*, iii. 3.

And bid her, mark you me, *on Wednesday next.* . . .
                    . . . Well, *Wednesday* is too soon ;
O' Thursday let it be : o' Thursday tell her,
She shall be married to this noble earl. . . .
                    . . . what say you to *Thursday ?—*
My lord, I would that *Thursday* were to-morrow.—
Well, get you gone : *o' Thursday be it, then.*—*Ibid.*, iii. 4.

To be to thee this night a torch-bearer,
And light thee *on thy way to Mantua.* . . .
I must hear from thee every day in the hour,
For in a minute there are many days :
Oh, by this count I shall be much in years,
Ere I again behold my Romeo.—
Farewell ! I will omit *no opportunity*
That may convey my greetings, love, to thee.—*Ibid.*, iii. 5.

Evermore weeping for your cousin's death ?
What, wilt thou wash him from his grave with tears ? . . .
                    . . . *I 'll send to one in Mantua,*
Where that same banish'd runagate doth live,
Shall give him such an unaccustom'd dram,
That he shall soon keep Tybalt company.—*Ibid.*, iii. 5.

                    Early *next Thursday* morn,
The gallant, young, and noble gentleman,
The County Paris, at Saint Peter's Church,
Shall happily make thee there a joyful bride.— . . .
But fettle your fine joints *'gainst Thursday next,*
To go with Paris to Saint Peter's Church. . . .
I tell thee what, get thee to church *o' Thursday,*
Or never after look me in the face. . . .
Thursday is near ;— . . .
Delay this marriage for a month, a week. . . .
Is it more sin to wish me thus forsworn,
Or to dispraise my lord with that same tongue
Which she hath praised him with above compare
So many thousand times ?—Ibid., iii. 5.

On Thursday, sir? the time is very short.— . . .
That may be, must be, love, *on Thursday next.* . . .
Juliet, *on Thursday* early will I rouse you :
Till then, adieu ; and keep this holy kiss.— . . .
I hear thou must, and nothing may prorogue it,

On Thursday next be married to this County.— . . .
    . . . *Wednesday is to-morrow ;*
To-morrow night look that thou lie alone. . . .
And *in this borrow'd likeness of shrunk death*
Thou shalt continue two and forty hours,
And then awake as from a pleasant sleep. . . .
In the meantime, against thou shalt awake,
Shall Romeo *by my letters* know our drift ;
And hither shall he come : and he and I
Will watch thy waking, *and that very night*
Shall Romeo bear thee hence to Mantua.—*R. & Jul.*, iv. 1.

No, not till Thursday ; there is time enough.—*Ibid.*, iv. 2.

      How now, Balthazar !
Dost thou not *bring me letters from the friar ?* . . .
I do *remember* an apothecary—
And hereabouts he dwells—*which late I noted.* . . .
As I remember, this should be the house.—*Ibid.*, v. 1.

Welcome *from Mantua :* What says Romeo?
Or, if his mind be writ, give me *his letter.*—
Going to find a bare-foot brother out,
One of our order, to associate me,
Here in this city visiting the sick,
And finding him, the searchers of the town,
Suspecting that we both were in a house
Where the infectious pestilence did reign,
Seal'd up the doors, and would not let us forth ;
So that my speed to Mantua there was stay'd.—*Ibid.*, v. 2.

What said my man, when my betossed soul
Did not attend him *as we rode ?*—*Ibid.*, v. 3.

And Juliet bleeding ; warm, and newly dead,
Who here *hath lain these two days buried.*—*Ibid.*, v. 3.

   Meantime I writ to Romeo. . . .
But he which bore my letter, Friar John,
Was stay'd by accident ; and yesternight
Return'd my letter back.—*Ibid.*, v. 3.

I brought my master news of Juliet's death ;
And then in post *he came from Mantua,*
To this same place, to this same monument.—*Ibid.*, v. 3.

In his drama of " Pericles," besides introducing Gower as Chorus at occasional intervals to mark the progress of the story, and denote the lapses of time that take place at certain stages of it, Shakespeare has strewed amid the scenes some passages indicative of Dramatic Time, both short and long. But those of Short Time are generally such as notify periods arrived or past, and incidents happening or having occurred. The passages conveying the effect of Short Time are the following :—

Young prince of Tyre, you have at large receiv'd
The danger of the task you undertake.—
I have, Antiochus.— . . .
Scorning advice, read the conclusion, then ;
Which read and not expounded, 'tis decreed,
As these before thee, thou thyself shalt bleed.— . . .
Like a bold champion, I assume the lists,
Nor ask advice of any other thought
But faithfulness and courage.—   [*Reads the riddle.* . . .
   . . . *Your time's expir'd :*
Either expound now, or receive your sentence.— . . .

. . . He has found the meaning :
But I will gloze with him. . . .
He hath found the meaning, for the which we mean
To have his head. . . .
Thaliard behold, *here's poison, and here's gold ;*
We hate the prince of Tyre, and *thou must kill him :* . . .
Let your breath cool yourself, telling your haste.—
My lord, *prince Pericles is fled.—*
                              As thou
Wilt live, *fly after* . . . ne'er return,
Unless thou say, " Prince Pericles is dead."—*Per.,* i. 1.

So, *this is Tyre, and this the court. Here must I kill king Pericles* . . . Hush !
here come the lords of Tyre.— . . . *Lord Thaliard from Antiochus is welcome.—*
From him I come,
With message unto princely Pericles ;
But, *since my landing, I have understood*
Your lord hath betook himself to unknown travels,
My message must return from whence it came.—*Ibid.,* i. 3.

We have heard your miseries as far as Tyre,
And seen the desolation of your streets :
Nor come we to add sorrow to your tears,
But to relieve them of their heavy load.— . . .
Your grace is welcome to our town and us.—
Which welcome we'll accept.—Ibid., i. 4.

          The good in conversation
          (To whom I give my benison)
          Is still at Tharsus.—Ibid., ii. (*Chorus*).

Hark you, sir ; do you know where you are ?—Not well.—Why, I'll tell you : *this
is called Pentapolis, and our king, the good Simonides.—*. . . *How far is his court
distant from this shore?—*Marry, sir, *half-a-day's journey :* and I'll tell you, he hath a
fair daughter, and *to-morrow is her birthday ;* and there are princes and knights come
from all parts of the world, to just and tourney for her love.—Were my fortunes equal
to my desires, I could wish to make one there.—
          . . . *My shipwreck now's no ill,*
          Since I have here my father's gift in's will.—
          What mean you, sir ?—
          To beg of you, kind friends, this coat of worth. . . .
          And that you'd guide me to your sovereign's court,
          Where with it I may appear a gentleman ;— . . .
          Why, wilt thou tourney for the lady ?—
          I'll show the virtue I have borne in arms.—
Why, *do ye take it ;* and the gods give thee good on't !— . . . *and I'll bring thee to
the court myself.—*
          Then honour be but a goal to my will,
          This day I'll rise, or else add ill to ill.—*Ibid.,* ii. 1.

          Are the knights ready to begin the triumph ?—
          They are, my liege.— . . .
          'Tis now your honour, daughter, to explain
          The labour of each knight in his device.— . . .
          And what's the sixth and last, the which the knight himself
          With such a graceful courtesy deliver'd ?—
          He seems to be a stranger ; but his present is
          A wither'd branch, that's only green at top ;
          The motto, " In hac spe vivo."— . . .
          He well may be a stranger, for *he comes*
          To an honour'd triumph strangely furnished.—
          And on set purpose let his armour rust
          Until this day, to scour it in the dust.— . . .
          But stay, *the knights are coming :* we'll withdraw
          Into the gallery.—*Ibid.,* ii. 2.

Prepare for mirth, for mirth becomes a feast :
You are princes and my guests.—
    But you, my knight and guest ;
To whom this wreath of victory I give,
And crown you king of this day's happiness.— . . .
      . . . *Come, queen o' the feast*
(*For, daughter, so you are*), *here take your place :*
Marshal the rest, as they deserve their grace.— . . .
      . . . *he desires to know of you,*
Of whence you are, your name and parentage.—
A gentleman of Tyre (my name, Pericles ;
My education been in arts and arms),
Who, looking for adventures in the world,
Was by the rough seas reft of ships and men,
And, *after shipwreck, driven upon this shore.*— . . .
Come, gentlemen, we sit too long on trifles,
And waste the time which looks for other revels.
Even in your armours, as you are address'd,
Will very well become a soldier's dance.— . . .
      . . . Unclasp, unclasp ;
Thanks, gentlemen, to all ; *all have done well,*
But you the best. Pages and lights to conduct
These knights unto their several lodgings ! Yours, sir,
We have given order to be next our own.—
I am at your grace's pleasure.—
Princes, *it is too late to talk of love ;*
And that's the mark I know you level at :
Therefore, *each one betake him to his rest ;*
To-morrow, all for speeding do their best.—*Per.*, ii. 3.

Even in the height and pride of all his glory,
When he was seated, and his daughter with him,
In a chariot of inestimable value,
A fire from heaven came and shrivelled up
Their bodies, even to loathing.—*Ibid.*, ii. 4.

        Lord Helicane, a word.—
With me ? and welcome. *Happy day,* my lords.—
Know, that *our griefs are risen to the top,*
And now at length they overflow their banks.—*Ibid.*, ii. 4.

Good morrow to the good Simonides.— . . .
Though loath to bid farewell, we take our leaves.—
So, *they're well despatched : now to my daughter's letter :*
She tells me here, she'll wed the stranger knight,
Or never more to view nor day nor light.
'Tis well, mistress ; *your choice agrees with mine.* . . .
Well, I commend her choice ;
And *will no longer have it be delay'd.*
Soft ! *here he comes :* I must dissemble it.— . . .
      . . . *I am beholden to you,*
For your sweet music this last night.— . . .
What do you think of my daughter, sir ?—
As of a most virtuous princess.— . . .
Here comes my daughter. . . .
Therefore, hear you, mistress ; either frame
Your will to mine—and you, sir, hear you,
Either be rul'd by me, *or I'll make you*—
Man and wife : nay, come, your hands
And lips must seal it too. . . .
It pleaseth me so well, *that I will see you wed ;*
Then, with what haste you can, get you to bed.—*Ibid.*, ii. 5.

Now sleep yslaked hath the rout ;
No din but snores the house about,
Made louder by the o'erfed breast
Of *this most pompous marriage-feast.*
The cat, with eyne of burning coal,
Now couches 'fore the mouse's hole : . . .
Hymen hath brought the bride to bed,
Where, by the loss of maidenhead,
A babe is moulded.   Be attent;
And time that is so briefly spent,
With your fine fancies quaintly eche :
What 's dumb in show, I 'll plain with speech. . . .
To the court of King Simonides
Are letters brought. . . .
      . . . *The sum of this,*
Brought hither to Pentapolis,
Yravished the regions round. . . .
Brief, he must hence depart to Tyre :
His queen, with child, makes her desire
(Which who shall cross?) *along to go :*
Omit we all their dole and woe :
Lychorida, her nurse, she takes,
And so to sea. . . .
The lady shrieks, and, well-a-near
Does fall in travail with her fear : . . .
In your imaginat'on hold
This stage the ship, upon whose deck
The sea-tost Pericles appears to speak.—*Per.,* iii. (*Chorus*).
          Lucina, O,
Divinest patroness, and midwife gentle
To those that cry by night, *convey thy deity*
Aboard our dancing boat ; make swift the pangs
Of my queen's travails !   Now, Lychorida !—
Here is a thing too young for such a place,
Who, if it had conceit, would die, as I
Am like to do: *take in your arms this piece*
Of your dead queen. . . .
Here 's all that is left living of your queen,
A little daughter.— . . .
For *thou 'rt the rudeliest welcome to this world,*
That e'er was prince's child. . . .
Sir, *your queen must overboard :* the sea works high, the wind is loud, and will not
lie till the ship be cleared of the dead . . . therefore *briefly yield her ; for she must*
overboard straight.—*As you think meet.*   Most wretched queen !—*Here she lies, sir.*—
A terrible child-bed hast thou had, my dear ;
No light, no fire : the unfriendly elements
Forgot thee utterly ; *nor have I time*
To give thee hallow'd to thy grave, but straight
Must cast thee, scarcely coffin'd, in the ooze ; . . .
            . . . *Hie thee, whiles I say*
A priestly farewell to her : suddenly, woman.— . . .
Mariner, say *what coast is this ?*—*We are near Tharsus.*—*Thither, gentle mariner,*
alter thy course for Tyre.   When canst thou reach it ?—*By break of day,* if the wind
cease.—O, *make for Tharsus.*   There will I visit Cleon, for the babe cannot hold out
to Tyrus: there I 'll leave it at careful nursing.   *Go thy ways, good mariner : I 'll*
bring the body presently.—*Ibid.,* iii. 1.
It has been a turbulent and stormy night.—
I have been in many ; *but such a night as this,*
Till now, I ne'er endur'd.— . . .
            . . . *Good morrow,* sir.—
Good morrow to your lordship.—

Gentlemen,
Why do you stir so early ?— . . .
That is the cause we trouble you *so early ;* . . .
But I much marvel that your lordship, having
Rich tire about you, *should at these early hours*
Shake off the golden slumber of repose.— . . .'
. . . Sir, *even now*
Did the sea toss upon our shore this chest :— . . .
. . . *Wrench it open straight :* . . .
. . . *What 's here ? a corse ?—*
. . . *This chanc'd to-night.—*
Most likely, sir.—
Nay, *certainly to-night ;*
For look, how fresh she looks !
This queen will live : nature awakes ; a warmth
Breathes out of her : she hath not been entranc'd
Above five hours : see how she 'gins to blow
Into life's flower again ! . . .
. . . Hush, gentle neighbours !
Lend me your hands ; to the next chamber bear her.
Get linen : *now* this matter must be look'd to,
For her relapse is mortal. *Come, come ;*
And Æsculapius guide us !—*Per.*, iii. 2.

Most honour'd Cleon, *I must needs be gone ;* . . .
. . . *My gentle babe Marina* (whom,
For she was born at sea, I have nam'd so) *here*
I charge your charity withal, and leave her
The infant of your care. . . . *So I take my leave.—Ibid.*, iii. 3.

But since king Pericles,
My wedded lord, I ne'er shall see again,
A vestal livery will I take me to.— . . .
Madam, if this you purpose as you speak,
Diana's temple is not distant far,
Where you may 'bide until your date expire.—*Ibid.*, iii. 4.

Imagine Pericles arriv'd at Tyre,
Welcom'd and settled to his own desire.
His woful queen we leave at Ephesus,
Unto Diana there a votaress.
Now to Marina bend your mind,
Whom our fast-growing scene must find
At Tharsus. . . .
Lychorida, our nurse, is dead :
And cursed Dionyza hath
The pregnant instrument of wrath
Prest for this blow. The unborn event
I do commend to your content :
Only *I carry winged time*
Post on the lame feet of my rhyme ;
Which never could I so convey,
Unless your thought went on my way.
Dionyza doth appear,
With Leonine, a murderer.—Ibid., iv. (*Chorus*).

Thy oath remember ; *thou hast sworn to do 't :*
'Tis but a blow, which never shall be known.
Thou canst not do a thing i' the world so soon,
To yield thee so much profit.— . . .
I will do 't ; but yet she is a goodly creature.—
. . . *Here*
She comes weeping for her only mistress' death. . . .
Walk with Leonine ; the air is quick there,

And it pierces and sharpens the stomach. *Come,*
Leonine, take her by the arm, walk with her. . . .
Come, come, I know 'tis good for you.
Walk half an hour, Leonine, at the least :
Remember what I have said.— . . .
If you require a little space for prayer,
I grant it ; pray ; but be not tedious,
For the gods are quick of ear, and I am sworn
To do my work with haste. . . .
                   . . . *I am sworn,*
And will despatch.— . . .
A prize ! a prize !—
            Half-part, mates, half-part.
Come, let 's have her aboard suddenly.—*Per.,* iv. 1.

These roguing thieves serve the great pirate Valdes ;
And *they have seized Marina. Let her go :*
There 's no hope she 'll return. *I 'll swear she 's dead,*
And thrown into the sea.—*Ibid.,* iv. 2.

Come your ways. . . . What 's her price, Boult ?—I cannot be bated one doit of a thousand pieces.—*Well, follow me, my masters, you shall have your money presently. Wife, take her in ;* . . .

Alack, that Leonine was so slack, so slow !
He should have struck, not spoke ; or that these pirates
(Not enough barbarous) had not o'erboard thrown me
For to seek my mother !— . . .
You are lit into my hands, where you are like to live.—
            The more my fault,
To 'scape his hands where I was like to die.—*Ibid.,* iv. 3.

                   O villain Leonine !
Whom thou hast poison'd too. . . .
               . . . What canst thou say,
When noble Pericles shall demand his child ?—
That she is dead.—*Ibid.,* iv. 4.

Thus time we waste, and longest leagues *make short ;*
Sail seas in cockles, have an wish but for 't : . . .
Well-sailing ships, and bounteous winds, *have brought*
This king to Tharsus (think this pilot thought ;
So with his steerage shall your thoughts grow on),
To fetch his daughter home, who first is gone . . .
And Pericles, in sorrow all devour'd,
With sighs shot through, and biggest tears o'ershow'r'd,
Leaves Tharsus, and again embarks. . . .
            . . . *our scene must play*
His daughter's woe and heavy well-a-day,
In her unholy service. Patience, then,
And think you now are all in Mitylen.—*Ibid.,* iv. 4 (*Chorus*).

Well, *I had rather than twice the worth of her, she had ne'er come here.*— . . . *Here comes the lord Lysimachus, disguised.*— . . . *Come, we will leave his honour and her together. Go thy ways.*— . . .

               . . . I did not think
Thou couldst have spoke so well ; ne'er dream'd thou couldst.
Had I brought hither a corrupted mind,
Thy speech had alter'd it. Hold, here 's gold for thee :
Persever in that clear way thou goest,
And the gods strengthen thee !—. . .
              . . . That the gods
Would safely deliver me from this place !
Here, here 's gold for thee.
If that thy master would gain by me,
Proclaim that I can sing, weave, sew, and dance,

With other virtues, which I 'll keep from boast;
And *I will undertake all these to teach.*
I doubt not but this populous city will
Yield many scholars.— . . .
Well, I will see what I can do for thee : if I can place thee, I will.—Per., iv. 6.

*Marina thus the brothel 'scapes, and chances
Into an honest house,* our story says. . . .
. . . *Here we her place ;*
And to her father turn our thoughts again,
Where we left him, on the sea. We there him lost ;
Whence, driven before the winds, *he is arrived
Here where his daughter dwells ; and on this coast
Suppose him now at anchor.* The city striv'd
God Neptune's annual feast to keep : from whence
Lysimachus, our Tyrian ship espies,
His banners sable, trimmed with rich expense ;
And to him in his barge with fervour hies.—Ibid., v. (*Chorus*).

Sir, *there's a barge put off from Mitylene,
And in it is Lysimachus, the governor,
Who craves to come aboard. What is your will ?
That he have his.—* . . .
I am the governor of this place you lie before.—
Sir, *our vessel is of Tyre, in it the king.—*. . .
Sir, *we have a maid in Mitylene, I durst wager,
Would win some words of him.—* . . .
. . . Oh, *here is
The lady that I sent for. Welcome, fair one !—*. . .
. . . Sir, *I will use
My utmost skill in his recovery,
Provided
That none but I and my companion maid
Be suffer'd to come near him.—*
Come, let us leave her ;
And the gods make her prosperous !—
Now, blessing on thee ! rise ; *thou art my child.—Ibid.,* v. 1.

My temple stands in Ephesus ; *hie thee thither,
And do upon mine altar sacrifice.—Ibid.,* v. 2.

*Now our sands are almost run ;
More a little, and then dumb.*
This, as my last boon, give me—
For such kindness must relieve me—
That you aptly will suppose
What pageantry, what feats, what shows,
What minstrelsy, and pretty din,
The regent made in Mitylin,
To greet the king. So he thriv'd,
That *he is promis'd to be wiv'd
To fair Marina ;* but in no wise
Till he had done his sacrifice,
As Dian bade ; whereto being bound,
*The interim, pray you, all confound.
In feather'd briefness sails are fill'd,
And wishes fall out as they 're will'd.
At Ephesus, the temple see,
Our king, and all his company.
That he can hither come so soon,
Is by your fancy's thankful boon.—Ibid.,* v. 2 (*Chorus*).

Hail Dian ! to perform thy just command,
I here confess myself the king of Tyre.— . . .
Noble sir,

If you have told Diana's altar true,
This is your wife.— . . .
            . . . *Oh, come, be buried*
A second time within these arms.—
                        My heart
Leaps to be gone into my mother's bosom.—
Look, who kneels here! Flesh of thy flesh, Thaisa ;
Thy burden at sea, and call'd Marina,
For she was yielded there.—
                    Bless'd and mine own !— . . .
                . . . *Thaisa,*
This prince, the fair-betrothed of your daughter
Shall marry her at Pentapolis.—*Per.*, v. 3.

And the passages denoting Long Time are the following:—

            Not an hour,
In the day's glorious walk, or peaceful night
(The tomb where grief should sleep), *can breed me quiet.*
Here pleasures court mine eyes, and mine eyes shun them ;
And danger, which I fear'd, is *at Antioch,*
Whose arm seems far too short to hit me here:
Yet neither pleasure's art can joy my spirits,
Nor yet *the other's distance* comfort me.— . . .
Therefore, my lord, *go travel for a while,*
Till that his rage and anger be forgot,
Or till the Destinies do cut his thread of life.— . . .
Tyre, I now look from thee, then, and *to Tharsus*
Intend my travel, where I'll hear from thee ;
And by whose letters I'll dispose myself.—Ibid., i. 2.
                    He's gone *to travel.—* . . .
Your lord hath *betook himself to unknown travels.—Ibid.*, i. 3.

    Good Helicane hath stay'd at home,
    Not to eat honey like a drone
    From others' labours; for *though he strive*
    To killen bad, keep good alive ;
    And, to fulfil his prince' desire,
    Sends word of all that haps in Tyre.—Ibid., ii. (*Chorus*).

A gentleman of Tyre . . .
Who, *looking for adventures in the world,*
Was by the rough seas reft of ships and men.—*Ibid.*, ii. 3.

A twelvemonth longer, let me entreat you
To forbear the absence of your king;
If in which time expir'd, he not return,
I shall with aged patience bear your yoke.—*Ibid.*, ii. 4.

    By many a dearn and painful perch
    Of Pericles the careful search,
    By the four opposing coigns,
    Which the world together joins,
    Is made with all due diligence
    That horse, and sail, and high expense,
    Can stead the guest.—*Ibid.*, iii. (*Chorus*).

My *twelve months* are expir'd and Tyrus stands
In a litigious peace.—*Ibid.*, iii. 3.
                    Beseeching you
To give her princely training, that she may
Be manner'd as she is born. . . .
        . . . *Till she be married*, madam,
By bright Diana, whom we honour, *all*
Unscissar'd shall this hair of mine remain.—Ibid., iii. 3.

But since King Pericles,
My wedded lord, *I ne'er shall see again*,
A vestal livery will I take me to,
And never more have joy.— . . .
Diana's temple is not distant far,
Where you may 'bide until your date expire.—Per., iii. 4.

At Tharsus, and *by Cleon train'd*
In music, letters; . . .
                    . . . this maid
Hight Philoten : and it is said
For certain in our story, *she*
Would ever with Marina be.—Ibid., iv. (*Chorus*).

                    We every day
Expect him here : when he shall come, and find
Our paragon to all reports thus blasted,
He will repent *the breadth of his great voyage.* . . .
                    . . . *I saw you lately*
When you caught hurt in parting two that fought.—*Ibid.*, iv. 1.

        We wept after her hearse,
And even yet we mourn : her monument
Is almost finish'd.—Ibid., iv. 4.

Thus time we waste, and *longest leagues* make short;
Sail seas in cockles, have an wish but for 't ;
Making (to take your imagination)
From bourn to bourn, region to region.
By you being pardon'd, we commit no crime
To use one language, in *each several clime*
Where our scenes seem to live. . . .
                    . . . Pericles
Is now *again thwarting the wayward seas.* . . .
Old Escanes, whom Helicanus late
Advanc'd in time to great and high estate,
Is left to govern. . . .
                    . . . He swears
Never to wash his face, nor cut his hairs :
He puts on sackcloth, and to sea.—*Ibid.*, iv. 4 (*Chorus*).

Our vessel is of Tyre, in it the king ;
A man, who *for this three months hath not spoken*
To any one, nor taken sustenance,
But to prorogue his grief.– *Ibid.*, v. 1.

My temple stands in Ephesus ; hie thee thither.— . . .
My purpose was *for Tharsus*, there to strike
The inhospitable Cleon : but I am
For other service first ; *toward Ephesus*
Turn our blown sails.—Ibid., v. 2.

        What pageantry, what feats, what shows,
        What minstrelsy, and pretty din,
        The regent made in Mitylin,
        To greet the king.—Ibid., v. 2 (*Chorus*).

                    She at Tharsus
Was nurs'd with Cleon : whom at fourteen years
He sought to murder ; but her better stars
Brought her to Mitylene. . . .
And what this fourteen years no razor touch'd,
To grace thy marriage-day, I 'll beautify.—Ibid., v. 3.

Shakespeare occasionally has passages of what may be called Blended
Time ; that is to say, passages where effects of Long and Short Time

are so interfusedly given that he conveys a blended impression of both in the same sentence:—

> *My purpose was not to have seen you here;*
> *But meeting with Solanio by the way,*
> He did entreat me, past all saying nay,
> *To come with him along.—Mer. of V.,* iii. 2.

> *I have despatch'd in post*
> *To sacred Delphos, to Apollo's temple,*
> Cleomenes and Dion.—*W. T.,* ii. 1.

Whose loss of his most precious queen and children, are even now to be afresh lamented.—Ibid., iv. 1.

> How far is it, my lord, to *Berkley* now?—
> Believe me, noble lord,
> I am a stranger *here in Glo'stershire*
> *These high, wild hills, and rough uneven ways,*
> *Draw out our miles, and make them wearisome;*
> And yet your fair discourse hath been as sugar,
> *Making the hard way sweet and delectable.*
> But I bethink me, *what a weary way*
> *From Ravenspurg to Cotswold will be found*
> In Ross and Willoughby, wanting your company,
> Which, I protest, *hath very much beguil'd*
> *The tediousness and process of my travel.—R. II.,* ii. 3.

> Nor shall we need his help *these fourteen days.* . . .
> *A shorter time shall send me to you, lords:*
> *And in my conduct shall your ladies come;*
> *From whom you now must steal, and take no leave.—*1 *H. IV.,* iii. 1.

> How now, good Blunt! *thy looks are full of speed.—*
> *So hath the business that I come to speak of.*
> *Lord Mortimer of Scotland hath sent word,*
> *That Douglas and the English rebels met,*
> *The eleventh of this month at Shrewsbury.—* . . .
> *The Earl of Westmoreland set forth to-day;*
> With him my son, Lord John of Lancaster;
> *For this advertisement is five days old;*
> *On Wednesday next, Harry, you shall set forward;*
> *On Thursday we ourselves will march:*
> *Our meeting is at Bridgnorth: and, Harry, you*
> *Shall march through Glo'stershire;* by which account,
> Our business valued, *some twelve days hence*
> *Our general forces at Bridgnorth shall meet.*
> *Our hands are full of business: let's away;*
> *Advantage feeds him fat, while men delay.—Ibid.,* iii. 2.

> Therefore, my lords, *omit no happy hour*
> *That may give fartherance to our expedition;*
> *For we have now no thought in us but France,*
> *Save those to God, that run before our business.*
> *Therefore, let our proportions for these wars*
> *Be soon collected, and all things thought upon,*
> *That may with reasonable swiftness add*
> *More feathers to our wings; for, God before,*
> *We'll chide this Dauphin at his father's door.*
> *Therefore, let every man now task his thought,*
> *That this fair action may on foot be brought.—H. V.,* i. 2.

> You are they
> *That made the air unwholesome, when you cast*
> *Your stinking greasy caps, in hooting at*
> Coriolanus' exile. Now he's coming.—*Coriol.,* iv. 6.

Thursday is near.—R. & Jul., iii. 5.

On Thursday, sir? the time is very short.—Ibid., iv. 1.

Sir, *March is wasted fourteen days.—Jul. C.*, ii. 1.

                Some holy angel
Fly to the court of England, and unfold
His message ere he come; that a swift blessing
May soon return to this our suffering country
Under a hand accurs'd!—Macb., iii. 6.

              We here despatch
You, good Cornelius, and you, Voltimand,
For bearers of this greeting to old Norway.—Hamlet, i. 2.

How weary, stale, flat, and unprofitable
Seem to me all the uses of this world! . . .
    . . . *That it should come to this!*
But two months dead; nay, not so much, not two:
      . . . *and yet, within a month* . . .
A little month; or ere those shoes were old
With which she follow'd my poor father's body,
Like Niobe, all tears; why she, even she—
O God! a beast, that wants discourse of reason,
Would have *mourn'd longer—married with mine uncle,*
          . . . *within a month;*
Ere yet the salt of most unrighteous tears
Had left the flushing in her galled eyes,
She married. O, most wicked speed, to post
With such dexterity to incestuous sheets!—Ibid., i. 2.

He shall with speed to England.—Ibid., iii. 1.

             Therefore, prepare you;
I your commission will forthwith despatch,
And he to England shall along with you.—Ibid., iii. 3.

It must be shortly known to him from England,
What is the issue of the business there.—Ibid., v. 2.

The exile of her minion is too new;
She hath not yet forgot him: some more time
Must wear the print of his remembrance out,
And then she's yours.—Cym., ii. 3.

Lucius hath wrote already to the emperor
How it goes there. It fits us, therefore, ripely
Our chariots and our horsemen be in readiness:
The powers that he already hath in Gallia
Will soon be drawn to head, from whence he moves
His war for Britain.—Ibid., iii. 5.

DUMB SHOWS.

Into his own plays Shakespeare has sparingly introduced this kind of dramatic resource; for by a passage in one of his tragedies he has testified how poorly he thought of it as a mere attraction to the illiterate portion of the audience, who were incapable of appreciating good dialogue, and therefore preferred something that appealed merely to the eye:—

The groundlings;* who, for the most part, are capable of nothing but inexplicable *dumb shows* and noise.—*Hamlet*, iii. 2.

---

* Thus called because they occupied the 'ground' or 'pit' of the theatre.

So "inexplicable" were most of these "dumb shows"—when left merely to their self-denoting demonstration unaided by verbal explanation—that they were usually accompanied by some kind of "Prologue," or "Chorus," who *explained* to the audience that which these shows were intended to represent; just as the "motions" or "puppet-shows," then in vogue, had a showman who *interpreted* the meaning of his exhibition to its spectators. This particular is denoted by the following passage, where Speed, observing Silvia approach and Valentine advance to meet her, likens the lady to a well-dressed figure or doll, and his master to a showman or interpreter who will supply her with speech by opening dialogue:—

Oh, excellent *motion!* Oh, exceeding *puppet!* now will he *interpret* to her.—*Two G. of V.*, ii. 1.

Tokens of the practice of having a prologue or chorus to explain a dumb show, and an interpreter to explain a puppet-show, are also to be traced in some of the following passages that enumerate the Dumb Shows occurring in Shakespeare's plays :—

Enter PYRAMUS *and* THISBE, WALL, MOONSHINE, *and* LION, *as in dumb show.*
> *Prologue.* Gentles, perchance you wonder at this show;
> But wonder on, till truth make all things plain.
> This man is Pyramus, if you would know;
> This beauteous lady Thisby is, &c.—*Mid. N. D.*, v. 1.

The Vision.*—*Enter, solemnly tripping one after another, six Personages, clad in white robes, wearing on their heads garlands of bays, and golden vizards on their faces; branches of bays, or palm, in their hands. They first congee unto her, then dance; and, at certain changes, the first two hold a spare garland over her head; at which, the other four make reverend court'sies: then, the two that held the garland deliver the same to the other next two, who observe the same order in their changes, and holding the garland over her head: which done, they deliver the same garland to the last two, who likewise observe the same order: at which (as it were by inspiration) she makes in her sleep signs of rejoicing, and holdeth up her hands to heaven: and so in their dancing they vanish, carrying the garland with them. The music continues.—H. VIII.*, iv. 2.

Trumpets sound. The Dumb Show enters.

Enter a King and a Queen, very lovingly; the Queen embracing him. She kneels, and makes show of protestation unto him. He takes her up, and declines his head upon her neck: lays him down upon a bank of flowers: she, seeing him asleep, leaves him. Anon comes in a fellow, takes off his crown, kisses it, and pours poison in the king's ears, and exit. The Queen returns, finds the King dead, and makes passionate action. The Poisoner, with some two or three mutes, comes in again, seeming to lament with her. The dead body is carried away. The Poisoner wooes the Queen with gifts: she seems loath and unwilling awhile; but in the end accepts his love. [*Exeunt.*
Ophelia. What means this, my lord? . . . *Belike, this show imports the argument of the play.*

Enter PROLOGUE.

Hamlet. We shall know by this fellow. . . .
Ophelia. Will he tell us what this show meant?

---

* Strictly, this "Vision" does not perhaps come under the denomination of a Dumb Show; but rather under that of a pageant, with which the play of Henry VIII. abounds. [*See* STAGE DIRECTIONS AND ENTRANCES; also, RECURRENCE OF PARTICULAR POINTS.]

Hamlet. Ay. . . .. This is one Lucianus, nephew to the king.
Ophelia. You are as good as a chorus, my lord.
Hamlet. I could *interpret* between you and your love, if I could see the *puppets*
dallying.—*Hamlet,* iii. 2.

Enter CYMBELINE,* *attended;* BELARIUS, GUIDERIUS, ARVIRAGUS, PISANIO, *and Roman*
   Captives. The Captains present POSTHUMUS *to* CYMBELINE, *who delivers him over*
   to a Gaoler; after which all go out.—Cym., v. 3.

*Ente*r GOWER, *as Chorus.*

   Here have you seen a mighty king. . . .
   But *tidings to the contrary*
   Are brought your eyes; what need speak I ?

DUMB SHOW.

Enter, from one side, PERICLES, *talking with* CLEON; *their trains with them. Enter,*
   from the other side, a Gentleman, with a letter to PERICLES; *who shows the letter*
   to CLEON; *then gives the messenger a reward, and knights him. Exeunt* PERICLES,
   CLEON, *&c., severally.—Per.,* ii. *(Gower).*

Enter GOWER, *as Chorus.*

   Now sleep yslaked hath the rout. . . .
   What's dumb in show, I'll plain with speech.

DUMB SHOW.

Enter, from one side, PERICLES *and* SIMONIDES, *with Attendants; a Messenger meets*
   them, kneels, and gives PERICLES *a letter: he shows it to* SIMONIDES; *the lords*
   kneel to PERICLES. *Then, enter* THAISA *with child, and* LYCHORIDA : SIMONIDES
   shows his daughter the letter; she rejoices: she and PERICLES *take leave of her*
   father, and depart with LYCHORIDA *and their Attendants. Then, exeunt*
   SIMONIDES *and the rest.—Ibid.,* iii. *(Gower).*

Enter GOWER, *as Chorus, before the monument of* MARINA *at Tharsus.*

   Thus time we waste, and longest leagues make short. . . .
   Like motes and shadows see them move awhile;
   Your ears unto your eyes I'll reconcile.

DUMB SHOW.

Enter, from one side, PERICLES *with his Train;* CLEON *and* DIONYZA *from the other.*
   CLEON *shows* PERICLES *the tomb of* MARINA; *whereat* PERICLES *makes lamenta-*
   tion, puts on sackcloth, and in a mighty passion departs. Exeunt the rest.—
   Ibid., iv. 4. *(Gower).*

ELDER: ELDEST: OLD: OLDER: OLDEST.

Shakespeare occasionally uses these words with a signification that
includes much more than mere reference to age and time; and we
think that it is the overlooking this point which has occasioned commentators to imperfectly comprehend a passage where the word "elder"
occurs, and to propose changing the expression there. If the following
various modes in which Shakespeare employs these words, and the

---

* This indicates a Dumb Show; yet it is hardly more than one of the stage directions
already given in the present Act. [*See* STAGE DIRECTIONS AND ENTRANCES.] As we
have shown, by the instances now cited, Dumb Shows generally occurred at the commencement of a scene; rarely, as in this instance, at the close of a scene.

inclusive sense he assigns to them, be examined, we believe it will be perceived that "elder" is the expression he used in the passage from "Cymbeline," v. 1. :—

> 'Tis very true: O wise and upright judge!
> How much more *elder*

['sage,' 'experienced,' 'mature in judgment,' as well as 'older,' 'more advanced in age or years']

> art thou than thy looks !—*Mer. of V.*, iv. 1.

> My gracious lord, I tender you my service,
> Such as it is, being tender, raw, and young,
> Which *elder days*

['a more advanced time'; when I shall be less "raw" and 'more experienced,' as well as 'older']

> shall ripen and confirm
> To more approved service and desert.—*R. II.*, ii. 3.

> As dissolute, as desperate; yet, through both
> I see some sparkles of a better hope,
> Which elder days

['a more advanced time'; when he shall be 'sager' as well as 'older']

> may happily bring forth.—*Ibid.*, v. 3.

> Danger knows full well
> That Cæsar is more dangerous than he:
> We are two lions litter'd in one day,
> And I the *elder*

['the more potent and mighty,' as well as 'the first born']

> and more terrible.—*Jul. C.*, ii. 2.

> I said an *elder*

['more experienced, from being older and from having had longer practice'*]

> soldier, not a better.—*Ibid.*, iv. 3.

> But in my terms of honour
> I stand aloof; and will no reconcilement,
> Till by some *elder*

[of higher authority, of superior responsibility, in questions of punctilio]

> masters, of known honour,
> I have a voice and precedent of peace,
> To keep my name ungor'd.—*Hamlet*, v. 2.

> When vantage like a pair of twins appear'd
> Both as the same, or rather ours the *elder*.

['better,' 'superior,' as well as 'older' or 'first born'].—*Ant. & C.*, iii. 8.

> Behold divineness no *elder*

['superior,' 'more exalted;' no 'older' or 'more dignified' and 'reverend']

> than a boy !—*Cym.*, iii. 6.

> You snatch some hence for little faults; that's love
> To have them fall no more: you some permit
> To second ills with ills, each *elder*†

[ill deed committed by one grown older in a course of ill-doing, more experienced in evil, more hardened in guilt, more confirmed in sin ; 'more hardened,' 'more confirmed,' 'of larger growth']

> worse,
> And make them dread it, to the doers' thrift.—*Ibid.*, v. 1.

---

* The exact words Cassius had previously used were, " I am a soldier, I, *older in practice*, abler than yourself to make conditions;" but the retorts between the friends here, during their quarrel, serve to show that "older" implies something of "better," 'superior,' 'more skilled and practised.'

† This is the passage (alluded to by us at the beginning of the present heading) where previous commentators have suspected error in the word "elder"; but which we believe to have been the word here used by Shakespeare.

Then it is thus: the passions of the mind,
That have their first conception by mis-dread,
Have after-nourishment and life by care:
And what was first but fear what might be done,
Grows *elder*
['larger,' 'stronger,' 'more confirmed,' 'more established,' and 'more advanced in
time,' 'having attained to a later period']
> now, and cares it be not done.—*Per.*, i. 2.

What is this maid, with whom thou wast at play?
Your *eld'st* ['oldest,' 'longest in time']
> acquaintance cannot be three hours.—*Temp.*, v. 1.

My youngest boy, and yet my *eldest*
['most important,' 'most urgent,' 'most pressing,' 'first needing attention']
> care.—*Com. of E.*, i. 1.

It hath the primal *eldest*
['earliest elicited,' 'first occurring,' and 'strongest,' 'most heavy']
> curse upon 't—
A brother's murder!—*Hamlet*, iii. 3.

Shakespeare sometimes uses "old" to express 'mature,' 'well-skilled,' 'proficient':—

His years but young, but his experience *old*.—*Two G. of V.*, ii. 4.

Had you been as wise as bold,
Young in limbs, in judgment *old*.—*Mer. of V.*, ii. 7 (*Scroll*).

I never knew so young a body with so *old* a head.—*Ibid.*, iv. 1 (*Letter*).

I am only *old* in judgment and understanding.—*2 H. IV.*, i. 2.

Sometimes to express 'well-practised,' 'long-accustomed':—

Is he so young a man, and so *old* a lifter?—*Tr. & Cr.*, i. 2.

Sometimes to express 'former,' 'bygone':—

And dallies with the innocence of love,
Like the *old* age.—*Tw. N.*, ii. 4.

Since the *old* days of goodman Adam to the pupil age of this present twelve o'clock
at midnight.—*1 H. IV.*, ii. 4.

Now *old* desire doth in his death-bed lie.—*R. & Jul.*, i. 5 (*Chorus*).
This is the *old* man still.—*Timon*, iii. 6.

O, my *old* friend! Thy face is valanced since I saw thee last.—*Hamlet*, ii. 2.

Sometimes to express 'long-standing,' 'long-established,' 'long-used':—

What *old*, or newer torture must I receive.—*W. T.*, iii. 2.

What, *old* acquaintance! could not all this flesh.—*1 H. IV.*, v. 4.

This is the *old* fashion; you two never meet, but you fall.—*2 H. IV.*, ii. 4.

Insisting on the *old* prerogative and power.—*Coriol.*, iii. 3.

Sometimes to express 'before-used,' 'stale,' 'worn-out':—

That is an *old* device; and it was play'd when I.—*Mid. N. D.*, v. 1.

Our *old* ling and our Isbels o' the country are nothing like your *old* ling and your
Isbels o' the court.—*All's W.*, iii. 2.

How your fooling grows *old*, and people dislike it.—*Tw. N.*, i. 5.

Musty seeds, remnants of packthread, and *old* cakes of roses.—*R. & Jul.*, v. 1.

These are *old* fond paradoxes, to make fools laugh.—*Oth.*, ii. 1.

Sometimes to express 'confirmed,' 'well-known':—

This news is *old* enough, yet it is every day's news.—*M. for M.*, iii. 2.

There's no news at court, sir, but the *old* news.—*As You L.*, i. 1.

This is *old :* what is the success ?—*Ant. & C.,* iii. 5.

Sometimes to express 'inveterate,' 'long-continued' :—

Yet I have a trick of the *old* rage.—*Love's L. L.,* v. 2.

Sometimes to express 'practised,' 'hardened' :—

Doth she not think me an *old* murderer.—*R. & Jul.,* iii. 3.

Sometimes to express 'original,' 'pristine' :—

Virtue cannot so inoculate our *old* stock, but we shall relish of it.—*Ham.,* iii. 1.
Be jointed to the *old* stock, and freshly grow.—*Cym.,* v. 4. and 5 (*Scroll*).

Sometimes to express 'confirmed,' 'genuine' :—

This borrow'd passion stands for true *old* woe.—*Per.,* iv. 4 (*Gower*).

Sometimes as an epithet expressive of familiarity :—

If the *old* fantastical duke of dark corners had.—*M. for M.,* iv. 3.
One that *old* Frederick, your father, loves.—*As You L.,* i. 2.
The priest was good enough, for all the *old* gentleman's saying.—*Ibid.,* v. 1.
How now, *old* lad ?—Welcome, you.—*Tam. of S.,* iv. 1.
Well, go thy ways, *old* lad ; for thou shalt ha 't.—*Ibid.,* v. 2.

And he frequently uses " old " in a sense it formerly bore of 'excessive,' 'extraordinary,' 'abounding,' 'outrageous' :—

I 'll rack thee with *old* cramps, fill all thy bones.—*Temp.,* i. 2.
Here will be an *old* abusing of God's patience.—*Merry W.,* i. 4.
Yonder 's *old* coil at home : it is proved.—*M. Ado.,* v. 2.
We shall have *old* swearing that they did give.—*Mer. of V.* iv. 2.

Master, master ! *Old* news, and such news as you have never heard of !—Is it new and old too ? how may that be ?—*Tam. of S.,* iii. 2.

By the mass, here will be *old* utis : it will be.—2 *H. IV.,* ii. 4.

If a man were porter of hell-gate, he should have *old* turning the key.—*Macb.,* ii. 3.

He occasionally uses " older " to express 'longer accustomed,' 'more experienced,' 'more confirmed,' 'more proficient':—

I am a soldier, I, *older* in practice, abler than yourself
To make conditions.—*Jul. C.,* iv. 3.

An *older* and a better soldier none
That Christendom gives out.—*Macb.,* iv. 3.

And, in the following passage, he uses " oldest " to express 'most long-practised,' 'most long-known':—

Rob, murder, and commit the *oldest* sins the newest kind of way ?—2 *H. IV.,* iv. 4.

ELISIONAL ABBREVIATIONS.

Shakespeare uses elisional abbreviations of various kinds. He sometimes employs 'a for 'he,' in familiar or humorous dialogue. He occasionally has an apostrophe before a substantive to express 'the':—

Pray heartily he be at '*palace.*—*W. T.,* iv. 3.
Who knocks so loud at '*door ?*—2 *H. IV.,* ii. 4.
A dozen captains stay at '*door* for you.—*Ibid.,* ii. 4.

Sometimes an apostrophe after a word to express ' is ':—

> Words against me! *This'* a good friar belike!—*M. for M.*, v. 1.
> Why, *this'* a heavy chance ' twixt him and you.—*Tam. of S.*, i. 2.
> *This'* a good block.—*Lear*, iv. 6.
> Since *Leonatus'* false.—*Cym.*, iii. 6.

Sometimes an apostrophe after a noun in the singular, to express its plural:—

> Made thee more profit
> Than other *princess'* can, that have more time
> For vainer hours, and tutors not so careful.—*Temp.*, i. 2.
> A thousand of his people butchered;
> Upon whose dead *corse'* there was such misuse.—1 *H. IV.*, i. 1.

Sometimes an apostrophe after a noun or a proper name, instead of the more usual 's, to mark the possessive case:—

> Sits on his *horse'* back at mine *hostess'* door.—*John*, ii. 1.
> The bodies shall be dragged at my *horse'* heels.—2 *H. VI.*, iv. 3.
> Our *mistress'* sorrows we were pitying.—*H. VIII.*, ii. 3.
> And to fulfil his *prince'* desire.—*Per.*, ii. (*Gower*).
> Go, call at *Flavius'* house.—*M. for M.*, iv. 5.
> By the fire that quickens *Nilus'* slime.—*Ant. & C.*, i. 3.

He occasionally gives 'd for ' would ':—

> We '*d** jump the life to come.—*Macb.*, i. 7.

Sometimes he gives ha' for ' have ':—

> Will you *ha'* the truth on 't ?—*Hamlet*, v. 1.

Sometimes ha't for ' have it ':—

> Sir, I pray you, let me *ha't.*—*Coriol.*, ii. 3.

In a few instances it 's for ' it is '; instead of the more usual abbreviation, 'tis (of which, of course, Shakespeare has numerous examples needless to cite):—

> *It 's* supper-time, my lord; *it 's* nine o'clock.—*R. III.*, v. 3.
> And *it 's* come to pass, this tractable obedience is a slave.—*H. VIII.*, i. 2.
> The hey-day in the blood is tame, *it 's* humble.—*Hamlet*, iii. 4.
> *It 's* true, good lieutenant.—*Oth.*, ii. 3.
> Yet still *it 's* strange
> What Cloten 's being here to us portends.—*Cym.*, iv. 2.

Sometimes 'll for ' will ':—

> I '*ll* put a girdle round the earth
> In forty minutes.—*Mid. N. D.*, ii. 2.
> I '*ll* give him my commission.—*W. T.*, i. 2.
> We '*ll* fit the kid-fox with a pennyworth.—*M. Ado*, ii. 3.
> We '*ll* thwack him hence with distaffs.—*W. T.*, i. 2.

Sometimes o' for ' of ':—

> We, poor unfledg'd,
> Have never wing'd from view *o'* the nest.—*Cym.*, iii. 3.

Sometimes o' for ' off '.—

> You i' the camlet, get up *o'* the rail.—*H. VIII.*, v. 3.

---

* Printed in the 1623 Folio, *Wee 'ld.*

Sometimes o' for ' on ' :—

> Cupid hath clapp'd him *o*' the shoulder.—*As You L.*, iv. 1.
>
> O' Thursday let it be : *o*' Thursday, tell her.—*R. & Jul.*, iii. 4.

Sometimes 'r for ' our' :—

> By '*r* lady, sir, and some dogs will catch well.—*Tw. N.*, ii. 3.
>
> By '*r* lakin, I can go no farther, sir.—*Temp.*, iii. 3.

In some instances, he uses 's for ' has' :—

> For he '*s* a spirit of persuasion.—*Temp.*, ii. 1.
>
> He '*s* walk'd the way of nature.—*2 H. IV.*, v. 2.

In one instance, Shakespeare uses 's for ' he is' :—

> Though he be painted one way like a Gorgon,
> The other way '*s* a Mars.—*Ant. & C.*, ii. 5.

In some instances, he uses 's for ' his' :—

> But Tuesday night last gone, in '*s* garden-house,
> He knew me as a wife.—*M. for M.*, v. 1.
>
> To let him there a month behind the gest
> Prefix'd for '*s* parting.—*W. T.*, i. 2.
>
> Neither the king, nor '*s* heirs,
> (Tell you the duke) shall prosper.—*H. VIII.*, i. 2.
>
> One hand on his dagger,
> Another spread on '*s* breast.—*Ibid.*, i. 2.
>
> He hath a witchcraft
> Over the king in '*s* tongue.—*Ibid.*, iii. 2.
>
> The master-cord on '*s* heart !—*Ibid.*, iii. 2.
>
> There is a mutiny in '*s* mind.—*Ibid.*, iii. 2.

A plague upon Antenor ! I would they had broke '*s* neck !—*Tr. & Cr.*, iv. 2.

> Will he swagger himself out on '*s* own eyes ?—*Ibid.*, v. 2.

On '*s* brows ; Menenius, he comes the third time home with the oaken garland.—*Coriol.*, ii. 1.

> Death, that dark spirit, in '*s* nervy arm doth lie.—*Ibid.*, ii. 1.
>
> A curse begin at very root on '*s* heart,
> That is not glad to see thee !—*Ibid.*, ii. 1.
>
> That to '*s* power he would have made them mules.—*Ibid.*, ii. 1.
>
> He had rather venture all his limbs for honour,
> Than one on '*s* ears to hear it.—*Ibid.*, ii. 2.
>
> He would not flatter Neptune for his trident,
> Or Jove for '*s* power to thunder.—*Ibid.*, iii. 1.
>
> Tie leaden pounds to '*s* heels.—*Ibid.*, iii. 1.
>
> Sanctifies himself with '*s* hand.—*Ibid.*, iv. 5.
>
> Banquo '*s* buried ; he cannot come out on '*s* grave.—*Macb.*, v. 1.
>
> There are no tongues else for '*s* turn.—*Hamlet*, v. 2.
>
> If a man's brains were in '*s* heels.—*Lear*, i. 5.

Why one's nose stands in the middle on '*s* face ?—No.—Why, to keep one's eyes of either side '*s* nose.—*Ibid.*, i. 5.

> Go, tell the duke and '*s* wife I 'd speak with them.—*Ibid.*, ii. 4.
>
> His daughter, and the heir of '*s* kingdom.—*Cym.*, i. 1.
>
> And in '*s* spring became a harvest.—*Ibid.*, i. 1.
>
> Still waving, as the fits and stirs of '*s* mind
> Could best express how slow his soul sail'd on,
> How swift his ship.—*Ibid.*, i. 4.

Caius Lucius
Will do 's commission throughly.—*Cym.*, ii. 4.
Why, one that rode to 's execution, man,
Could never go so slow.—*Ibid.*, iii. 2.
And thus I set my foot on 's neck.—*Ibid.*, iii. 3.
I know the shape of 's leg.—*Ibid.*, iv. 2.
In doing this for 's country.—*Ibid.*, v. 3.
Your death has eyes in 's head, then.—*Ibid.*, v. 4.
I cut off 's head.—*Ibid.*, v. 5.
Since I have here my father's gift in 's will.—*Per.*, ii. 1.

In other instances, he uses 's for ' is ' :—

And then I 'll bring thee to the present business
Which now 's upon 's.—*Temp.*, i. 2.
Consider whom the king your father sends ;
To whom he sends ; and what 's his embassy.—*Love's L. L.*, ii. 1.
A woman 's general ; what should we fear ?—*3 H. VI.*, i. 2.
And high note 's
Ta'en of your many virtues.—*H. VIII.*, ii. 3.
His heart 's his mouth ;
What his breast forges, that his tongue must vent.—*Coriol.*, iii. 1.
One score 'twixt sun and sun,
Madam 's enough for you, and too much too.—*Cym.*, iii. 2.
Nor know not
What air 's from home.—*Ibid.*, iii. 3,
There 's livers out of Britain.—*Ibid.*, iii. 4
My shipwreck now 's no ill.—*Per.*, ii. 1.
Were more than you expect, or more than 's fit.—*Ibid.*, ii. 3.
Nay, how absolute she 's in 't —*Ibid.*, ii. 5.

On one occasion, he uses 's to express ' is as ' :—

Thou art the best o' the cut-throats : yet he 's good
That did the like for Fleance.—*Macb.*, iii. 4.

He also uses 's elliptically, for ' which is ' :—

Where liest o' nights, Timon ?—Under that 's above me.—*Timon*, iv. 3.

Likewise elliptically, for ' who is ' :—

Thou speak'st like him 's untutor'd to repeat.—*Per.*, i. 4.

In other cases he employs 's ' for us ' :—

The present business
Which now 's upon 's.—*Temp.*, i. 2.
We 'll part the time between 's then.—*W. T.*, i. 2.
We are yours i' the garden : shall 's attend you there ?—*Ibid.*, i. 2.
Many thousand on 's
Have the disease, and feel 't not.—*Ibid.*, i. 2.
Pray you, sit by us,
And tell 's a tale.—*Ibid.*, ii. 1.
This is a match,
And made between 's by vows.—*Ibid.*, v. 3.
And let 's away to London.—*3 H. VI.*, v. 5.
And then let 's dream
Who's best in favour.—*H. VIII.*, i. 4.
Shall 's to the Capitol ?—*Coriol.*, iv. 6.
Yet do not
Upbraid 's with our distress.—*Ibid.*, v. 1.

If he covetously reserve it, how shall 's get it ?—*Timon*, iv. 3.

Kind gentlemen, let 's go see poor Cassio dress'd.—*Oth.*, v. i.

Say, where shall 's lay him ?—*Cym.*, iv. 2.

Where we have liv'd ; and so extort from 's that
Which we have done.—*Ibid.*, iv. 4.

Shall 's have a play of this ?—*Ibid*, v. 5.

                We will die all three,
But I will prove that two on 's are as good
As I have given out him.—*Ibid.*, v. 5.

In one passage he uses 'st for 'hast' :—

                I 'll say, thou 'st gold :
Thou wilt be throng'd to shortly.—*Timon*, iv. 3.

He frequently uses 't for ' it ' :—

                There 's something in 't,*
More than my father's skill.—*All's W.*, i. 3.

There is something in 't that stings his nature.—*Ibid.*, iv. 3.

              There 's something in 't
That is deceivable.—*Tw. N.*, iv. 3.

One day shall crown the alliance on 't, so please you.—*Ibid.*, v. 1.

              This tempest,
Dashing the garment of this peace, aboded
The sudden breach on 't.—*H. VIII.*, i. 1.

              Is it therefore
Th' embassador is silenc'd ?—
              Marry, is 't.—*Ibid.*, i. 1.

Induce you to the question on 't ?—*Ibid.*, ii. 4.

Bearing a state of mighty moment in 't.—*Ibid.*, ii. 4.

              And, I fear,
Thou play'dst most foully for 't.—*Macb.*, iii. 1.

Will you ha' the truth on 't ?—*Hamlet*, v. 1.

Since the true life on 't was.—*Cym.*, ii. 4.

              If 't be summer news,
Smile to 't before.—*Ibid.*, iii. 4.

              I' the world's volume
Our Britain seems as of it, but not in 't.—*Ibid.*, iii. 4.

These flowers are like the pleasures of the world ;
This bloody man, the care on 't.—*Ibid.*, iv. 2.

Bid the captains look to 't.—*Ibid.*, iv. 2.

              I have belied a lady,
The princess of this country, and the air on 't
Revengingly enfeebles me.—*Ibid.*, v. 2.

Augustus lives to think on 't.—*Ibid.*, v. 5.

How absolute she 's in 't.—*Per.*, ii. 5.

              Now the good gods
Throw their best eyes upon 't !—*Ibid.*, iii. 1.

Unscissar'd shall this hair of mine remain,
Though I show ill in 't.—*Ibid.*, iii. 3.

---

  * In the present passage " in 't " (printed distinctly thus in the Folio, in all the three passages where this abbreviation occurs) was proposed by Hanmer to be altered to ' hints '; an alteration adopted by Warburton and by some other editors since. But the original expression, " there 's something in 't," is twice again used by Shakespeare (once in this very play) ; whereas he never uses ' hint ' as a verb, always as a noun.

There is one instance of Shakespeare's using "you 're" to express 'you were,' instead of the more ordinary meaning 'you are'; of which latter abbreviation there are, of course, in his works many instances that need not be cited :—

> Madam, *you 're* best consider.—*Cym.*, iii. 2.

And an instance of "thou 'rt" for 'thou wert,' not 'thou art':—

> Fetch us in fuel; and be quick, *thou 'rt* best.—*Temp.*, ii. 2.

There are some words which Shakespeare sometimes elisionally abbreviates :—

> The kitchen malkin pins
> Her richest lockram *'bout* [about] her reechy neck.—*Coriol.*, ii. 1.
> Here 's a few flowers; but *'bout* [about] midnight, more.—*Cym.*, iv. 2.
> 'Twould *'braid* [upbraid] yourself too near for me to tell it.—*Per.*, i. 1.
> Thou shalt *'by* [aby] this dear.—*Mid. N. D.*, iii. 2.
> What *'cerns* [concerns] it you if I wear pearl and gold.—*Tam. of S.*, v. 1.
> That no man *'counts* [accounts] of her beauty.—*Two G. of V.*, ii. 1.
> Murder, stern murder, in the *dir'st* [direst] degree.—*R. III.*, v. 3.
> As he, being *'drest* [address] to some oration.—*Tr. & Cr.*, i. 3.
> Your *eld'st* [eldest] acquaintance cannot be three hours.—*Temp.*, v. 1.
> As, let 'em [them] have their rights, they 're ever forward.—*H. VIII.*, iv. 1.
> The farced title running *'fore* [before] the king.—*H. V.*, iv. 1.
> But fettle your fine joints *'gainst* [against] Thursday next.—*R. & Jul.*, iii. 5.
> Some say, that ever *'gainst* [against] that season comes.—*Hamlet*, i. 1.
> The din of war *'gan* [began] pierce his ready sense.—*Coriol.*, ii. 2.
> I *'gin* [begin] to be a-weary of the sun.—*Macb.*, v. 5.
> Now *'gins* [begins] to bite the spirits.—*Temp.*, iii. 3.
> Perjury, perjury, in the *high'st* [highest] degree.—*R. III.*, v. 3.
> If you are *learn'd*, [learned] be not as common fools.—*Coriol.*, iii. 1.
> All this coil is *'long* [along] of you.—*Mid. N. D.*, iii. 2.
> By law of nature and of nations, *'long* [belong]
> To him and to his heirs.—*H. V.*, ii. 4.
> With such austerity as *'longeth* [belongeth] to a father.—*Tam. of S.*, iv. 4.
> It is an honour *'longing* [belonging] to our house.—*All's W.*, iv. 2.
> No ceremony that to great ones *'longs* [belongs].—*M. for M.*, ii. 2.
> Lay me stark *nak'd* [naked], and let the water-flies
> Blow me into abhorring!—*Ant. & C.*, v. 2.
> That I have *'nointed* [anointed] an Athenian's eyes.—*Mid. N. D.*, iii. 2.
> I 'll bring him the best *'parel* [apparel] that I have.—*Lear*, iv. 1.
> I 'll give thee, ere I leave thee, so much money,
> To warrant thee, as I am *'rested* [arrested] for.—*Com. of E.*, iv. 4.

The man, sir, that, when gentlemen are tired, gives them a fob, and *'rests* [arrests] them.—*Ibid.*, iv. 3.

> Of all *'say'd* [assayed] yet, may'st thou prove prosperous!
> Of all *'say'd* [assayed] yet, I wish thee happiness!—*Per.*, i. 1.
> That *'scuse* [excuse] serves many men to save their gifts.—*Mer. of V.*, iv. 1.
> Search for a jewel, that too casually
> Hath left mine arm: it was thy master's; *'shrew* [beshrew] me,
> If I would lose it for a revenue
> Of any king's in Europe.—*Cym.*, ii. 3.

And *'stablish* [establish] quietness on every side.—1 *H. VI.*, v. 1.

Unto her
He gave the *'stablishment* [establishment] of Egypt.—*Ant. & C.*, iii. 6.

The most oppórtune place, the *strong'st* [strongest] suggestion.—*Temp.*, iv. 1.

By looking back what I have left behind
'Stroy'd [destroyed] in dishonour.—*Ant. & C.*, iii. 9.

'Tide [betide] life, *'tide* [betide] death, I come without delay.—*Mid. N. D.*, v. 1.

Of all the men i' the world
I would have *'voided* [avoided] thee.—*Coriol.*, iv. 5.

Thou speakest wiser than thou art *'ware* [aware] of.—Nay, I shall ne'er be *'ware* [aware] of mine own wit, till I break my shins against it.—*As You L.*, ii. 4.

'Ware [beware] pencils, ho !—*Love's L. L.*, v. 2.

The bull has the game: *'ware* [beware] horns, ho !—*Tr. & Cr.*, v. 8.

*Whe'r** [whether] thou be'st he or no.—*Temp.*, v. 1.

Good sir, say *whe'r* [whether] you 'll answer me or no.—*Com. of E.*, iv. 1.

And gape at *wid'st* [widest] to glut him.—*Temp.*, i. 1.

He has elisionally abbreviated forms, that are in popular.use, of some proper names :—

Oh, my lord *Aberga'ny* [Abergavenny], fare you well !—*H. VIII.*, i. 1.

Maud, Bridget, Marian, Cicely, Gillian, *Jen'* [Jenny] !—*Com. of E.*, iii. 1.

ELLIPSES OF COMPARISON.

Shakespeare has several passages of comparison and similitude, where the mode of expression is very elliptical :—

Oh, gentle Proteus, Love's a mighty lord,
And hath so humbled me, as, I confess,
There is no woe [comparable] to his correction,
Nor [in comparison] to his service no such joy on earth !—*Two G. of V.*, ii. 4.

All I can is nothing [in comparison] to her [merit].—*Ibid.*, ii. 4.

He is then a giant [as compared] to an ape : but then is an ape a doctor [as compared] to such a man.—*M. Ado*, v. 1.

And much too little of that good I saw
Is my report [compared] to his great worthiness.—*Love's L. L.*, ii. 1.

This third, dull lead, with warning all as blunt [as the lead is dull].—*Mer. of V.*, ii. 7.

I would she were as lying a gossip in that as [any gossip who] ever knapped ginger.
—*Ibid.*, iii. 1.

She's a lamb, a dove, a fool [compared] to him.—*Tam. of S.*, iii. 2.

I 'd give bay Curtal and his furniture,
My mouth no more were broken than these boys' [mouths are broken].—*All's W.*, ii. 3.

War is no strife [compared] to the dark house and the detested wife.—*Ibid.*, ii. 3.

I will devise a death as cruel for thee
As thou art tender [compared] to 't.—*W. T.*, iv. 3.

O'ershine you as much as the full moon doth the cinders of the element, which show like pins' heads [as compared] to her.—2 *H. IV.*, iv. 3.

Unto whose grace our passion is as subject
As are our wretches fetter'd in our prisons [subject to our grace].—*H. V.*, i. 2.

---

* The Folio generally misprints this abbreviation ' where '; but in the passage we have cited from " The Comedy of Errors," the Folio prints " whe'r."

If he be perjur'd, see you now, his reputation is as arrant a villain and a jack-sauce, as ever [was the reputation of any villain who with] his plack shoe trod upon Got's ground and his earth.—*H. V.,* iv. 7.

No way [comparable] to that, for weakness, which she enter'd.—1. *H. VI.,* iii. 2.

These are petty faults [compared] to faults unknown,
Which time will bring to light in smooth Duke Humphrey.—2 *H. VI.,* iii. 1.

Her hand,
In whose comparison all whites are ink,
Writing their own reproach; [compared] to whose soft seizure
The cygnet's down is harsh.—*Tr. & Cr.,* i. 1.

And in such indexes, although small pricks
[Compared] To their subsequent volumes.—*Ibid.,* i. 3.

They call him Troilus; and on him erect
A second hope, as fairly built as [is their first on] Hector.—*Ibid.,* iv. 5.

The most sovereign prescription in Galen is but empiricutic, and, [compared] to this preservative, of no better report than a horse-drench.—*Coriol.,* ii. 1.

But with such words that are but roted in
Your tongue, though but bastards and syllables
Of no allowance, [compared] to your bosom's truth.—*Ibid.,* iii. 2.

He no more remembers his mother now than an eight-year old horse [remembers its mare mother].—*Ibid.,* v. 4.

These flaws and starts (impostors [as compared] to true fear) would well become a woman's story.—*Macb.,* iii. 4.

So excellent a king; that was [compared] to this,
Hyperion [compared] to a satyr.—*Hamlet,* i. 2.

The apparition comes: I knew your father;
These hands are not more like [each other, than this apparition was like your father].—*Ibid.,* i. 2.

The harlot's cheek, beautied with plastering art,
Is not more ugly [compared] to the thing that helps it,
Than is my deed [compared] to my most painted word.—*Ibid.,* iii. 1.

An eye like [that of *] Mars, to threaten and command;
A station like [that of] the herald Mercury.—*Ibid.,* iii. 4.

Your Dane, your German . . . are nothing [compared] to your English.—*Oth.,* ii. 3.

His faults, in him, [appear the more evident from contrast with his many excellent qualities, and] seem as the spots of heaven, more fiery by night's blackness.—*Ant. & C.,* i. 4.

To be called into a huge sphere, and not to be seen to move in't, [is as sorry a blank as] are the holes where eyes should be, which pitifully disaster the cheeks.—*Ibid.,* ii. 7.

Thy mind [compared] to her [noble nature] is now as low as were thy fortunes [in comparison with her rank].—*Cym.,* iii. 2.

[There is] No life [comparable] to ours.—*Ibid.,* iii. 3.

One sand another not more resembles [than he does] that sweet rosy lad who died, and was Fidele.—*Ibid.,* v. 5.

ELLIPTICAL STYLE.

One of the striking peculiarities of Shakespeare's style is the elliptical mode in which he permits a word or words to be understood in certain sentences; a practice which not only imparts great succinctness and condensation of effect to his diction, but which affords

---

* *See* ELLIPTICAL STYLE for several passages where 'that of' is understood in the sentence.

that prompt impression which is so greatly the dramatist's object to produce upon his hearers. By here presenting in collective juxta-position, as well as alphabetically, the various passages of ellipsis that occur in his writings, and by grouping together those particular ellipses which afford precisely similar examples of understood words, means are given of comparing certain of his speeches hitherto considered obscure with those which are less so; thus making the latter an aid to elucidate the former. In citing these various passages, we place between brackets the words that are to be elliptically under-stood in each phrase :—

Hold [a] little faith, though thou hast too much fear.—*Tw. N.*, v. 1.

With good advice and [a] little medicine.—2 *H. IV.*, iii. 1.

But, as it were, in [a] sort or limitation.—*Coriol.*, ii. 1.

It would not seem too dear [a price to pay].—*All's W.*, iii. 7.

That seems [about] to speak things strange.—*Macb.*, i. 2.

Construe the times, [according] to their necessities.—2 *H. IV.*, iv. 1.

If I do vow a [n act of] friendship, I'll perform it.—*Oth.*, iii. 3.

Became [adopted as] the accents of the valiant.—2 *H. IV.*, ii. 3.

[Ah, how] unsafe [is ours] the while, that we must.—*Macb.*, iii. 2.

Ay that I do; and [all we Shallows*] have done any time these.—*Merry W.*, i. 1.

When I have deck'd the sea . . . [and] under my burden groan'd.—*Temp.*, i. 2.

That make their wills their law, [and] have some unhappy.—*Two G. of V.*, v. 4.

Lodowick and Gratii, two hundred [and] fifty each.—*All's W.*, iv. 3.

The year of our redemption four hundred [and] twenty-six.—*H. V.*, i. 2.

Thy conceit is soaking, [and] will draw in.—*W. T.*, i. 2.

'Tis good speed; [and] foretells [that] the great Apollo.—*Ibid.*, ii. 3.

A sight which was to be seen, [and] cannot be [duly] spoken of.—*Ibid.*, v. 2.

Eight tall ships, [and] three thousand men of war.—*R. II.*, ii. 1.

Whose soldier now, [and] under whose blessed cross we are.—1 *H. IV.*, i. 1.

Must deck our kings, [and] carry them here and there.—*H. V.*, i. (*Chorus*).

Jumping o'er times, [and] turning th' accomplishment of.—*Ibid.*, i. (*Chorus*).

By that you love the dearest in this world, [and] as you wish.—*H. VIII.*, iii. 2.

A scourge to her enemies, [and] you have been a rod to.—*Coriol.*, ii. 3.

Pawn me to this your honour, [and] she is his.—*Timon*, i. 1.

Treason can but peep to what it would, [and] acts little of his will.—*Hamlet*, iv. 5.

Antony sent to her, [and] invited her to supper.—*Ant. & C.*, ii. 2.

Preserv'd the Britons, [and] was the Roman's bane.—*Cym.*, v. 3.

Are now reviv'd, [and] to the majestic cedar join'd.—*Ibid.*, v. 5.

Fall away like water from ye, [and are] never found again.—*H. VIII.*, ii. 1.

We'll be all three sworn brothers [and go] to France.—*H. V.*, ii. 1.

It is no other but the main [and obvious cause].—*Hamlet*, ii. 2.

[And to be of] less noble mind than she, which by her death.—*Ant. & C.*, iv. 12.

Can dearly witness, [and who are] yet freshly pitied.—*H. VIII.*, v. 2.

Were but one danger; and to keep him here [another—] your certain death.—*Coriol.*, iii. 1.

One's Junius Brutus, [another's] Sicinius Velutus.—*Ibid.*, i. 1.

More exquisite than [any] lady, [than all] ladies, [than all] woman [-kind].—*Cym.*, iii. 5.

What earthly name [appended] to interrogatories can.—*John*, i. iii.

---

* This ellipsis is put into the mouth of Justice Shallow for the sake of humorously blundering effect.

Right worthy [are] you [of] priority.—*Coriol*, i. 1.

King Lear hath lost, he and his daughter [are] ta'en.—*Lear*, v. 2.

Whither [are you] bound ?—*Cym.*, iii. 6.

Bellona's bridegroom, lapp'd in [armour of] proof.—*Macb.*, i. 2.

Made such a sinner of his memory [as] to credit his own lie.—*Temp.*, i. 2.

May serve [as] a nursery to our gentry.—*All's W.*, i. 2.

So stain our judgment . . . [as] to prostitute our . . . [as] to esteem a.—*Ibid.*, ii. 1.

I will be so much a sinner [as] to be a double-dealer.—*Tw. N.*, v. 1.

So unsettled [as] to appoint myself in this vexation.—*W. T.*, i. 2.

But [as] it does fulfil my vow, I needs must.—*Ibid.*, iv. 3.

Do not prove me so ; [as] yet, I am none.—*John*, iv. 3.

Fool me not so much [as] to [let me] bear it tamely.—*Lear*, ii. 4.

Whom hath he left behind him [as] general ?—*Ibid.*, iv. 3.

But [as] since my landing I have understood.—*Per.*, i. 3.

Leav'st the kingly couch [as full of disquiet as] a watch-case.—2 *H. IV.*, iii. 1.

Were as pretty a proportion [as need be] to live quietly [with], and so give over [our present occupation].—*Per.*, iv. 3.

Heaven me such usage send [as that I may] not [have] to pick bad from bad, but [if—I must have bad usage—that I may] by bad [usage] mend !—*Oth.*, iv. 3.

With thought of such affections [as then glowed within you]—*W. T.*, v. 1.

I will not say, thou shalt be so well master'd [as thou wert] ; but, be sure, no less belov'd [than thou wert].—*Cym.*, iv. 2.

I was too young [at] that time to value her.—*As You L.*, i. 3.

Ne'er mother rejoic'd [at] deliverance more.—*Cym.*, v. 5.

How may likeness [be] made in crimes . . . to draw.—*M. for M.*, iii. 2.

And the owner of it [be] blest.—*Mid. N. D.*, v. 2.

And yet [be] the son of a woman !—1 *H. IV.*, ii. 4.

But not [be] remember'd in thy epitaph !—*Ibid.*, v. 4.

I cannot put him to [be] a private soldier.—2 *H. IV.*, iii. 2.

You see how soon the day [became] o'ercast.—*R. III.*, iii. 2.

To prepare this body, like to them, to what I must [become].—*Per.*, i. 1.

But Heaven hath [been] pleas'd to have it so.—*Hamlet*, iii. 4.

All places yield to him ere he sits down [before them].—*Coriol.*, iv. 7.

Myself in counsel, [being] his competitor.—*Two G. of V.*, ii. 6.

If fortune thy foe were not, nature [being] thy friend.—*Merry W.*, iii. 3.

After [being] well-enter'd soldiers, to return.—*All's W.*, ii. 1.

Of [being] here and everywhere.—*Tw. N.*, v. 1.

Which, [being] of a weak and niggardly projection.—*H. V.*, ii. 4.

You having lands, and [being] bless'd with beauteous wives.—*R. III.*, v. 3.

You [being] a brother of us, it fits we thus proceed.—*H. VIII.*, v. 1.

And [being] found—despatch [is the word]—*Lear*, iii. 1.

[Being] commended to our master, not to us.—*Per.*, i. 3.

Swear against [being moved by] objects [likely to inspire relenting].—*Timon*, iv. 3.

But [being possess'd of] riches fineless is [being] as poor as.—*Oth.*, iii. 3.

In which your pain [bestow] that way, I 'll this.—*Lear*, iii. 1.

[Between] whom [and myself], though in general part we.—*Timon*, v. 3.

It is without me, as within me ; not imagin'd, [but] felt.—*Cym.*, iv. 2.

Counterpoise, [by] a full third part, the charges.—*Coriol.*, v. 5.

The fame which he did end [by making] all his.—*Ibid.*, v. 5.

To punish me with [causing] this [man's death], and [to punish] this [man] with [causing] me [to kill him].—*Hamlet*, iii. 4.

I dare not [come down out of the monument], dear,—*Ant. & C.*, iv. 13.

She [coming] from whom we all were sea-swallow'd.—*Temp.*, ii. 1.

Took the Phœnix and her fraught [coming] from Candy.—*Tw. N.*, v. 1.

I must speak with him [coming] from the pridge.—*Hen. V.*, iii. 6.

Ere [coming to] a determinate resolution.—*H. VIII.*, ii. 4.

Never, before this happy child, did I get anything [comparable with it].—*Ibid.*, v. 4.

Will give you that [death] like beasts, which you shun beastly, and may save [yourselves from] but to look back in frown.—*Cym.*, v. 3.

Therefore pardon me; and [do] not impute this yielding to.—*R. & Jul.*, ii. 2.

I am not bound to [do] that [which even] all slaves are free to [do or not to do].— *Oth.*, iii. 3.

If in which time expir'd he [do] not return.—*Per.*, ii. 4.

Nor [do I] fear to lose it, thy safety being the motive.—*Lear*, i. 1.

But mock, [do you] bestow your su'd-for tongues?—*Coriol.*, ii. 3.

No more [does] my grief, in such a precious loss.—*Tr. & Cr.*, iv. 4.

But [doom'd] to be still hot summer's tanlings.—*Cym.*, iv. 4.

Since we saw [each other] in France.—*H. VIII.*, i. 1.

When shall we see [each other] again?—*Tr. & Cr.*, iv. 4.

When shall we see [each other] again?—*Cym.*, i. 2.

You and I have known [each other], sir.—*Ant. & C.*, ii. 6.

[Even] thieves are not judg'd but they are by to hear.—*R. II.*, iv. 1.

Not worshipp'd with [even] a waxen epitaph.—*H. V.*, i. 2.

Had Henry [even] got an empire by his marriage.—2 *H. VI.*, i. 1.

[Even] i' the presence he would say untruths.—*H. VIII.*, iv. 2.

I shall forestall thee, lord Ulysses, [even] thou!—*Tr. & Cr.*, iv. 5.

But that I loved Rome [even] more [than I loved Cæsar].—*Jul. C.*, iii. 2.

That might [even] to half a soul and to a notion craz'd.—*Macb.*, iii. 1.

Blood hath been shed ere now [even] i' the olden time.—*Ibid.*, iii. 4.

[Even] a good and virtuous nature may recoil.—*Ibid.*, iv. 3.

Their dear causes would . . . excite [even] the mortified man.—*Ibid.*, v. 2.

For [even] madness would not err.—*Hamlet*, iii. 4.

[Even] eyes without feeling, feeling without sight.—*Ibid.*, iii. 4.

Through tatter'd clothes [even] small vices do appear.—*Lear*, iv. 6.

That were the most, [even] if he should husband you.—*Ibid.*, v. 3.

I never knew [even] a Florentine more kind and honest.—*Oth.*, iii. 1.

Might stick the small'st opinion on [even] my least misuse.—*Ibid.*, iv. 2.

The honour's sacred . . . [even] supposing that I lack'd it.—*Ant. & C.*, ii. 2.

[Even] the seven-fold shield of Ajax cannot keep.—*Ibid.*, iv. 12.

The temple of Virtue was she; yea, and [even] she herself.—*Cym.*, v. 5.

Evil that might annoy [even but so much as] my finger.—*H. V.*, ii. 2.

Usurpers, tyrants, and what [ever] 's worse [than these].—*As You L.*, ii. 1.

Here they shall not lie, for [fear of] catching cold.—*Two G. of V.*, i. 2.

This peace is [fit for] nothing, but to rust iron.—*Coriol.*, iv. 5.

[For] me, poor man, my library was dukedom large enough.—*Temp.*, i 2.

[For] whose thankless natures . . . not all the whips.—*Timon*, v. 1.

More than I could frame employment [for].—*Ibid.*, iv. 3.

The cardinal instantly will find employment [for].—*H. VIII.*, ii. 1.

What restraint and grievance the law . . . will give him cable [for].—*Oth.*, i. 2.

As I will kneel to him with thanks [for].—*Ant. & C.*, v. 2.

Had that was well worth watching [for].—*Cym.*, ii. 4.

This point [for] which now you censure him.—*M. for M.*, ii. 1.

Fear you his tyrannous passion more, alas, than [for] the queen's life?—*W. T.*, ii. 3.

And beg [for] thy pardon ere he do accuse thee.—*R. II.*, v. 2.

If any fear lesser [for] his person than [he fears] an ill report.—*Coriol.*, i. 6.

What doth her beauty serve [for], but as a note.—*R. & Jul.*, i. 1.

And touch thy instrument [for] a strain or two.—*Jul. C.*, iv. 3.

Do not fear [for] our person : there 's such divinity doth.—*Hamlet*, iv. 5.

She wish'd that Heaven had made [for] her such a man.—*Oth.*, i. 3.

He hath been search'd [for] among the dead and living.—*Cym.*, v. 5.

Now, [for an explanation of] what mov'd me to 't, I will.—*H. VIII.*, ii. 4.

[For the sake] of charity, what kin are you to me ?—*Tw. N.*, v. 1.

Than you shall find cause [for them] in Cæsar.—*Ant. & C.*, v. 2.

To sweep the dust [from] behind the door.—*Mid. N. D.*, v. 2.

I 'd [go] with thee every foot [of the way].—*Coriol.*, iv. 1.

[Go and inquire] again ; and bring me word how 'tis with her.—*Cym.*, iv. 3.

As if that [god], whatsoever god [he may be], who leads him.—*Coriol.*, ii. 1.

Towards Florence is he [gone] ?—*All's W.*, iii. 2.

All [good wishes] to you.—*Timon*, i. 2.

He was expected then, but [had] not [yet] approach'd.—*Cym.*, iii. 4.

My education [has] been in arts and arms.—*Per.*, ii. 3.

Sorrow would [have] solace, and mine age would [have] rest.—*2 H. VI.*, ii. 3.

And flies [have] fled under shade.—*Tr. & Cr.*, i. 3.

We should by this . . . [have] found it so.—*Coriol.*, iv. 6.

[He] bequeathed me by will . . . and, as thou sayest, [he] charged my brother, on his blessing, to breed me well.—*As You L.*, i. 1.

[He] whose hap shall be to have her will not.—*Tam. of S.*, i. 2.

They call him Doricles ; and [he] boasts himself to have.—*W. T.*, iv. 3.

And [he] vaulted with such ease into his seat.—*1 H. IV.*, iv. 1.

How does the king ?—Madam, [he] sleeps still.—*Lear*, iv. 7.

And [he] will, no doubt, be found.—*Cym.*, iv. 3.

[He is] my lord of Kent : remember him hereafter.—*Lear*, i. 1.

[He is ever] ready for his friends.—*Timon*, i. 2.

Her hedges [heretofore] even-pleach'd, like prisoners.—*H. V.*, v. 2.

And now our [heretofore] cowards . . . became the life o' the need.—*Cym.*, v. 3.

To have them recompens'd as [highly as they are] thought on.—*W. T.*, iv. 3.

Daring [himself as] an opposite to every danger.—*R. III.*, v. 4.

To repair [hither] some other hour, I should derive.—*Timon*, iii. 4.

Derived from the ancient [house of] Capulet.—*All's W.*, v. 3.

[How] grace [ought] to stand, and [how] virtue [ought to] go.—*M. for M.*, iii. 2.

Ay, Timon, and [I] have cause.—*Timon*, iv. 3.

Make the wars against my stomach, [I] having alike your cause ?—*Ant. & C.*, ii. 2.

And [I] do invite you to my sister's view.—*Ibid.*, ii. 2.

Not any ; but [I] abide the change of time.—*Cym.*, ii. 4.

Bless'd [I] pray [that] you [may] be.—*Ibid.*, v. 5.

[I] being down, [he] insulted, railed, and put.—*Lear*, ii. 2.

[I] having more man than wit about me, drew.—*Ibid.*, ii. 4.

[I] who with half the bulk o' the world play'd as I pleas'd.—*Ant. & C.*, iii. 9.

[I am] gone, sir : farewell.—*Lear*, iv. 6.

[I am] a gentleman of Tyre, my name [is] Pericles.—*Per.*, ii. 3.

Now, [I care for] no discourse, except it be of love.—*Two G. of V.*, ii. 4.

My lord, [I drink to you] in [all the truth of my] heart.—*Timon*, i. 2.

[I had] best draw my sword.—*Cym.*, iii. 6.

Even [I might call thee] daughter, [for] welcome [art thou] in no less degree [than a daughter].—*As You L.*, v. 4.

Or [I must practise] this [deceit upon him], or [I must] perish [by his fury].—
Cym., iii. 5.

I know not why, nor wherefore [I should feel impelled] to say, live, boy.—Ibid., v. 5.

As [if] the year had found some months asleep.—2 H. IV., iv. 4.

As [if] they had seen me with these hangman's hands.—Macb., ii. 2.

As [if] some fly had tickl'd slumber, not as [if it were] death's dart.—Cym., iv. 2.

'Tis as [it] I should entreat you [to] wear your gloves.—Oth., iii. 3.

[It] within thine eyes sat twenty thousand deaths.—Coriol., iii. 3.

Youth becomes as [if it were] aged.—M. for M., iii. 1.

[If there should] come more, for more you're ready.—Cym., iv. 3.

But, [if thou] be refus'd, let the white death sit.—All's W., ii. 3.

As [if to] bid me tell my tale in express words.—John, iv. 2.

Norfolk, [in] so far as [it is] to mine enemy [that I swear, I too will keep all this].—
R. II., i. 3.

Unless [in] his noble mother and his wife.—Coriol., v. 1.

And [in addition] to that dauntless temper of his.—Macb., iii. 1.

[In proof] that Norfolk lies, here do I throw down this.—R. II., iv. 1.

I will do [in proportion to] my good will, sir.—2 H. IV., iii. 2.

Since you came too late [in respect] of our intent.—R. III., iii. 5.

I am not [in truth] what I am [in appearance].—Oth., i. 1.

And rear it in the place [in which] your father's stands.—3 H. VI., ii. 6.

Turning dispiteous [intention to] torture out of door.—John, iv. 1.

Contenteth me, and [is] worth a monarchy.—2 H. VI., iv. 10.

The which to leave [is] a thousand-fold more bitter than.—H. VIII., ii. 3.

[Is] all come to this? The hearts that spaniel'd me.—Ant. & C., iv. 10.

The falcon [is as good] as the tercel.—Tr. & Cr., iii. 2.

Why, then, [is it that] your fears . . . should move you to.—John, iv. 2.

To love [it] concerneth us to add her father's liking.—Tam of S., iii. 2.

Were [it] I alone [who had] to pass [through] the difficulties.—Tr. & Cr., ii. 2.

For him [it] shall fly out of itself.—Coriol., i. 10.

Tell me in sadness, who is [it] that you love?—R. & Jul., i. 1.

But [it] flies an eagle flight.—Timon, i. 1.

I'd exchange [it] for this one wish.—Ibid., iv. 3.

Like a bold flood o'erbear [it].—Coriol., iv. 5.

That nothing can allay [it].—John, iii. 1.

[It] shall not be long but I'll be here again.—Macb., iv. 2.

As [it is] in the [estimation of the] prizer.—Tr. & Cr., ii. 2.

But [it is requisite] to support him after.—Timon, i. 1.

The element itself, till [it shall have known] seven years' heat.—Tw. N., i. 1.

Take them away: [keep] good guard, until their.—Lear, v. 3.

[Let] those enemies of Timon's . . . fall, and no more.—Timon, v. 5.

Which [let it be] often [repeated].—Coriol., iii. 2.

[Let me] to the trunk again, and shut the spring of it.—Cym., ii. 2.

But [let me remember] my design, to note the chamber.—Ibid., ii. 2.

Which [letter, he] failing [to have], periods his comfort.—Timon, i. 1.

Else, surely, his [loan] had equall'd [your master's loan].—Ibid., iii. 4.

And [make him] write to her a love-line.—All's W., ii. 1.

For one to say a soldier lies, is stabbing [matter].—Oth., iii. 4.

When we hold rumour from what we fear [may threaten us], yet know not what we
[ought justly to] fear.—Macb., iv. 2.

My mind misgives [me] some consequence, yet hanging.—R. & Jul., i. 4.

Fetch me the handkerchief: my mind misgives [me].—Oth., iii. 4.

That I might do you service, so good as you have done [me].—*Ant. & C.*, iv. 2.

Unarm [me], Eros; the long day's task is done.—*Ibid.*, iv. 12.

By reflection, by [means of] some other things [than itself].—*Jul. C.*, i. 2.

The king enacts more wonders than a [mere mortal] man [could be expected to perform].—*R. III.*, v. 4.

I profess myself her adorer, not [merely] her friend.—*Cym.*, i. 5.

So much fairer and [more] spotless shall mine innocence appear.—*H. VIII.*, iii. 2.

The enemies of Cæsar shall say this [much.]—*Jul. C.*, iii. 1.

In despite of [my disinclination for] mirth, [I] mean to be merry.—*Com. of E.*, iii. 1.

Not [needing] to know what we speak one to another.—*All's W.*, iv. 1.

So his familiars to his [now] buried fortunes slink all away [from him].—*Timon*, iv. 2.

[O] that [there] may blow no sneaping winds at home.—*W. T.*, i. 2.

The ways you have for [obtaining] dignities.—*H. VIII.*, iii. 2.

Who wins me by that means I told you [of].—*Mer. of V.*, ii. 1.

The great'st infection that e'er was heard or read [of].—*W. T.*, i. 2.

[Of] what an honest man should have, he has nothing.—*All's W.*, iv. 3.

And I did never ask it [of] you again.—*John*, iv. 1.

We, at the height [of our advantage], are ready to decline.—*Jul. C.*, iv. 3.

As not to know the language [of the land] I have liv'd in.—*H. VIII.*, iii. 1.

Execution of the rest [of the offices pertaining to a king].—*Lear*, i. 1.

You 're a gentleman of mine own way [of thinking in religious opinion].—*H. VIII.*, v. 1.

Some haunted by the ghosts [of those whom] they have depos'd.—*R. II.*, iii. 2.

Those occasions [of which] at Eltham Place I told your majesty.—*1 H. VI.*, iii. 1.

I bid for you [offering my liking in exchange for yours], as I do buy [by paying money in exchange for what I purchase].—*Cym.*, iii. 6.

To die upon the bed my father died [on].—*W. T.*, iv. 3.

As well appeareth by the cause you come [on].—*R. II.*, i. 1.

To be exalted [on a level] with the threatening clouds.—*Jul. C.*, i. 3.

Not [only] what is dangerous present, but the loss of.—*Coriol.*, iii. 2.

And not [only] your knowledge [and] your personal pain.—*Per.*, iii. 2.

Tybalt, that [only] an hour hath been my kinsman.—*R. & Jul.*, iii. 1.

To-morrow with your earliest [opportunity] let me have speech with you—*Oth.*, ii. 3.

Let us address [ourselves] to tend on Hector's heels.—*Tr. & Cr.*, iv. 4.

If savage, take [payment for what I need] or lend [it me from kindliness].—*Cym.*, iii. 6.

On [peril of incurring the] height of our displeasure.—*Timon*, iii. 5.

There be [persons], an if they might [divulge].—*Hamlet*, i. 5.

There 's something in 't [persuades me], more than . . . that his.—*All's W.*, i. 3.

Avoid your accusation : [pretending that] he made trial of you.—*M. for M.*, iii. 1.

For this [recrimination] is [apart] from the present [consideration].—*Ant. & C.*, ii. 6.

Who haply may misconstrue us in [regard to] him.—*R. III.*, iii. 5.

I am [representing], in this [appeal], your wife.—*Coriol.*, iii. 2.

Which [risk] to defeat, I must produce my power.—*All's W.*, ii. 3.

But for the [sake of] the general [community].—*Jul. C.*, ii. 1.

We could, an if we would [say].—*Hamlet*, i. 5.

She shall not sue unheard. So [say] to them both.—*Ant. & C.*, iii. 10.

Our fears do make us [seem] traitors.—*Macb.*, iv. 2.

And lack gall to make oppression [seem] bitter [to me].—*Hamlet*, ii. 2.

Make your wantonness [seem] your ignorance.—*Ibid.*, iii. 1.

Did make my way [seem] long [when I went] forth.— *Cym.*, iv. 2.

To-morrow, they made Britain [seem like] India.—*H. VIII.*, i. 1.

Most like I did, for I was [seemingly] dead.—*Cym.*, v. 5.

Yet all this while [she was] in a most fast sleep.—*Macb.*, v. 1.

The better that your lordship [should] please to ask.—*R. III.*, iii. 2.

As faults [should be] from seeming, free!—*M. for M.*, iii. 2.

That your fair daughter . . . [should be] transported . . . to the gross.—*Oth.*, i. 1.

When our actions do not [show us to be traitors].—*Macb.*, iv. 2.

Nor shall appear [so] in Sicilia.—*W. T.*, iv. 3.

Do not [so] stain the even virtue of our enterprise . . . [as] to think* that or our cause or our performance.—*Jul. C.*, ii. 1.

So much differ, and we [still] alive that liv'd [then]?—*Timon*, iii. 1.

Rather than [such as betoken] envy [towards] you.—*Coriol.*, iii. 3.

No time shall be omitted that will be [sufficient] time.—*Love's L. L.*, iv. 3.

[Supposing] he says he'll come; how shall I feast him?—*Tw. N.*, iii. 4.

Where is thy lady? [tell me] in a word, or else.—*Cym.*, iii. 5.

One sand another not more resembles [than he does] that sweet rosy lad who died.—*Ibid.*, v. 5.

And a soul [than which there is] none better in my kingdom.—*H. VIII.*, v. 1.

Morn to the lark, less welcome [than you are to us].—*Cym.*, iii. 6.

If thou engrossest all the griefs [that] are thine.—*All's W.*, iii. 2.

Good Heaven! [that] these nobles should such stomachs bear.—1 *H. VI.*, i. 3.

Direct mine arms [that] I may embrace his neck.—*Ibid.*, ii. 5.

Or I fall into the trap [that] is laid for me.—*H. VIII.*, v. 1.

This morning see [that] you do appear before them.—*Ibid.*, v. 1.

My mind gave me [that] in seeking tales and informations.—*Ibid.*, v. 2.

[That] heaven ever laid up to make parents happy.—*Ibid.*, v. 4.

He [that] last ask'd the question.—*Timon*, ii. 2.

What should I do, [that] I do not?—*Ant. & C.*, i. 3.

The preparation of a war [that] shall stain [that of] your brother.—*Ibid.*, iii. 4.

To you . . . he commands [that] his absolute commission [shall be given].—*Cym.*, iii. 7.

An issue I might propagate [that] are arms to princes.—*Per.*, i. 2.

Scorn now [that] their hand should give them burial.—*Ibid.*, ii. 4.

Ay, for [that half which comes to] the state—not for [that half which comes to] Antonio.—*Mer. of V.*, iv. i.

[That he] hath commanded to-morrow morning to the.—*H. VIII.*, v. i.

And [that I] do now not basely die, not cowardly.—*Ant. & C.*, iv. 13.

In a word, [that I might be] but even now worth this.—*Mer. of V.*, i. 1.

When thou canst get the ring [that is] upon my finger.—*All's W.*, iii. 2.

[That is your] question: [now comes my answer] why an hour.—*M. Ado*, v. 2.

Black and fearful on [that of] the opposer.—*All's W.*, iii. 1.

A sense as cold as is [that of] a dead man's nose.—*W. T.*, ii. 1.

A name so slight . . . as [that of] the Pope.—*John*, iii. 1.

Than I am made by [that of] my young lord and [by] thee.—*R. III.*, i. 2.

The loss you have is but [that of] a son being king.—*Ibid.*, iv. 4.

She praised his complexion above [that of] Paris.—*Tr. & Cr.*, i. 2.

The sound of Marcius' tongue from [that of] every meaner man ['s].—*Coriol.*, i. 6.

Your master's confidence was above [that of] mine.—*Timon*, iii. 4.

He forfeits his own blood that spills [that of] another.—*Ibid.*, iii. 5.

---

* This phrase may be thus elliptically constructed; or "to think" may be used for 'by thinking.'

With my two daughters' dowers digest [that of] the third.—*Lear*, i. 1.

On the life of Lear, and on [that of] Cordelia.—*Ibid.*, v. 3.

The office opposite to [that of] Saint Peter.—*Oth.*, iv. 2.

His soldiership is twice [that of] the other twain.—*Ant. & C.*, ii. 1.

And be her sense but as [that of] a monument.—*Cym.*, ii. 2.

A power [that proved to be] much smaller than the.—2 *H. IV.*, i. 3.

Saw you anything more [that was] wonderful?—*Jul. C.*, i. 3.

[That was in] my salad days . . . ['twas to be] cold in judgment.—*Ant. & C.*, i. 5.

[That you are] sent by the king your father to greet him.—*W. T.*, iv. 3.

'Tis [the] love I bear thy glories [that] makes me speak.—3 *H. VI.*, ii. 1.

Holy oil, Edward [the] Confessor's crown.—*H. VIII.*, iv. 1.

[The] reason [is], because they then less need one another.—*Coriol.*, iv. 5.

Not that I loved Cæsar [the] less [though I killed him].—*Jul. C.*, iii. 2.

[The] Graces [are] her subjects, and her thoughts [are] the king of every virtue [that] gives renown to men!—*Per.*, i. 1.

The moist star . . . was sick almost to [the condition in which it will be at] Doomsday with eclipse.—*Hamlet*, i. 1.

[The conviction of] thy truth and integrity is rooted in us.—*H. VIII.*, v. 1.

You undergo [the difficulty of proving] too strict a paradox.—*Timon*, iii. 5.

In speaking, not to incur [the imputation of] the last.—*R. III.*, iii. 7.

For [the murder of] this same lord, I do repent.—*Hamlet*, iii. 4.

At [the price of] a few drops of women's rheum.—*Coriol.*, v. 5.

Have [the right to deliver] their free voices: [and] Rome.—*H. VIII.*, ii. 2.

As here by [the side of] Cæsar, and by you [to be] cut off.—*Jul. C.*, iii. 1.

This is [the summons] to [betake ourselves to our] horse.—*Ant. & C.*, iii. 2.

Unless you call [the width of] three fingers [in fat] on the ribs bare.—1 *H. IV.*, iv. 3.

Or, timely knowing [them], the remedy is then born.—*Cym.*, i. 7.

Because [then] she will not be annoy'd with suitors.—*Tam. of S.*, i. 1.

And [there] wants [now nothing] but nomination.—*R. III.*, iii. 4.

Meanwhile [there] must be an earnest motion made.—*H. VIII.*, ii. 4.

In sweet music [there] is such art.—*Ibid.*, iii. 1 (*Song*).

[There] remains that, in th' official marks invested, you.—*Coriol.*, ii. 3.

In cities [there are] mutinies; in countries [there is] discord; in palaces [there is] treason; and the bond [is] cracked.—*Lear*, i. 2.

To this hour [there is] no guess in knowledge which way they went.—*Cym.*, i. 1.

Hold, [there is] my hand: be factious for redress.—*Jul. C.*, i. 3.

Like our strange garments, [they] cleave not to their mould.—*Macb.*, i. 3.

I may not be too forward, lest, [this] being seen, thy brother.—*R. III.*, v. 3.

Go on: [this is] right royal.—*Ant. & C.*, iii. 11.

Thou wast the cause, and [this was thy] most accurs'd effect.—*R. III.*, i. 2.

There be [those] that can rule Naples as well as he that sleeps.—*Temp.*, ii. 1.

[Those] who were below him he us'd as creatures.—*All's W.*, i. 2.

There are [those] that dare; and I myself have ventur'd.—*H. VIII.*, v. 1.

[Thou] shalt see, thy other daughter will use thee kindly.—*Lear*, i. 5.

And, [through] Jove's accord, [there is] nothing so full of heart [as they are].—*Tr. & Cr.*, i. 3.

Must intimate [thy possession of] skill infinite, or [thy being] monstrous desperate.—*All's W.*, ii. 1.

And [' tis] held for certain the king will venture.—*H. VIII.*, ii. 1.

You 'll find ['tis] a most unfit time to disturb him.—*Ibid.*, ii. 2.

And ['tis] not wholesome to our cause.—*Ibid.*, iii. 2.

And ['tis] fear'd she 'll with the labour end.—*Ibid.* v. 1.

And ['tis] not ever [that] the justice and the truth.—*H. VIII.*, v. 1.

I know this cannot be.—['Tis] not possible.—*Coriol.*, iv. 6.

['Tis] fit I [should go to] meet them.—*Timon*, v. 1.

Yet ['tis] better [to be] thus, and [by myself] known to be contemn'd.—*Lear*, iv. 1.

['Tis] riotous madness, to be entangled with.—*Ant. & C.*, i. 3.

['Tis] a fever with the absence of her son.—*Cym.*, iv. 3.

For, ['tis a chance great as the stake of] heaven to earth.—1 *H. IV.*, v. 2.

Dar'st with thy . . . [to] make pale our cheek.—*R. II.*, ii. 1.

Wish'd him on the barren mountains [to] starve.—1 *H. IV.*, i. 3.

Is that letter, I caus'd you [to] write, yet sent away?—*H. VIII.*, iv. 2.

And struck him on [to] his knee.—*Coriol.*, ii. 2.

The prince will doom thee [to] death, if thou art taken.—*R. & Jul.*, iii. 1.

Listening [to] their fear, I could not say amen.—*Macb.*, ii. 2.

[To] which . . . this sword of mine shall give them instant way.—*Lear*, v. 3.

Go, charge Agrippa [to] plant those that have revolted.—*Ant. & C.*, iv. 6.

But not the form of what he should attend [to].—1 *H. IV.*, i. 3.

And the very ports they blow [to].—*Macb.*, i. 3.

All lovers swear more performance than they are able [to achieve].—*Tr. & Cr.*, iii. 2.

Have not transformed him [to an] ape.—2 *H. IV.*, ii. 2.

Until I know this [to be] sure uncertainty.—*Com. of E.*, ii. 2.

Would suffer her poor knight [to be] surprised.—*All's W.*, i. 3.

I take these wise men . . . [to be] no better than the.—*Tw. N.*, i. 5.

That slander, sir, is found [to be] a truth now.—*H. VIII.*, ii. 1.

I know my life [to be] so even.—*Ibid.*, iii. 1.

I know you [to be] wise, religious.—*Ibid.*, v. 1.

Where thou hast feign'd him [to be] a worthy fellow.—*Timon*, i. 1.

Men's reports give him [to be] much wrong'd.—*Ant. & C.*, i. 4.

Must seem [to be the result of] deliberate pause.—*Hamlet*, iv. 3.

'Tis [to deserve] to be chid as we rate boys.—*Ant. & C.*, i. 4.

Which should perceive nothing but love from us [to each other].—*Jul. C.*, iv. 2.

As [to those of] infants [which are] empty of all thought.—*Tr. & Cr.*, iv. 2.

May be wrought from that [to which] it is dispos'd.—*Jul. C.*, i. 2.

Did you assay [to win] him to any pastime?—*Hamlet*, iii. 1.

Doth seem [to wish] to have thee crown'd withal.—*Macb.*, i. 5.

Why, either were you [too] ignorant to see't, or, seeing it.—*Coriol.*, ii. 3.

As well appeareth by the cause you come [upon].—*R. II.*, i. 1.

Oh, that I had him . . . to use my lawful sword [upon].—*Coriol.*, v. 5.

These deeds must not be thought [upon] after these ways.—*Macb.*, ii. 2.

That, if you fail [us] in our request, the blame may.—*Coriol.*, v. 3.

Fear'd gods, [vouchsafe me] a part of it!—*Cym.*, iv. 2.

I have no farther [want] with you.—*Coriol.*, ii. 3.

May complain of [want of] good breeding.—*As You L.*, iii. 2.

Am starv'd for [want of] meat, giddy for lack of sleep.—*Tam. of S.*, iv. 3.

Who are sick for [want of] breathing and exploit.—*All's W.*, i. 2.

Which then our [want of] leisure would not let us hear.—*R. II.*, i. 1.

Out of work and cold for [want of] action.—*H. V.*, i. 2.

The [want of] leisure and the fearful time cuts off.—*R. III.*, v. 3.

The [want of] leisure and enforcement of the time.—*Ibid.*, v. 3.

Fear not our [want of] care, sir.—*Coriol.*, i. 7.

If you suspect my [want of] husbandry or [my] falsehood.—*Timon*, ii. 2.

Who, almost dead for [want of] breath.—*Macb.*, i. 5.

I was at point to sink for [want of] food.—*Cym.*, iii. 6.

'Gainst whose shore [we] riding, her fortunes.—*Per.*, v. 3.

And, as [well as] you can, disliken the truth of.—*W. T.*, iv. 3.

I would my horse had the speed of your tongue, and [were] so good.—*M. Ado*, i. 1.

I feel [what] my master's passion [will be]!—*Timon*, iii. 1.

[What] say you, sir?—*Cym.*, iv. 2.

At many leisures [when] I propos'd [to do so].—*Timon*, ii. 2.

At many times [when] I brought in my accounts [and] laid.—*Ibid.*, ii. 2.

Yet now's a time, [when] the greatest of your having lacks a half.—*Ibid.*, ii. 2.

True ornament [whereby] to know a holy man.—*R. III.*, iii. 7.

Seeks not to find that [which] her search implies.—*All's W.*, i. 3.

The reason [which] mov'd these warlike lords to this.—1 *H. VI.*, ii. 5.

These our ships, [which] you happily may think are.—*Per.*, i. 4.

That all those eyes [which] ador'd them ere their fall.—*Ibid.*, ii. 4.

This ornament, [which] makes me look dismal.— *Ibid.*, iv. 3.

I am nothing slow [which, if I were, might tend] to slack his haste.—*R. & Jul.*, iv.

The imposition clear'd, [which is] hereditary ours.—*W. T.*, i. 2.

Strain'd from that fair use [which is natural to it].—*R. & Jul.*, ii. 3.

Those only have fear'd Cæsar [while seeming attach'd to him].—*Ant. & C.*, i. 3.

She lov'd me well [who] deliver'd it to me.—*Two G. of V.*, iv. 4.

[Who] has a most weak *pia mater*.—*Tw. N.*, i. 5.

[Who] have sold their fortunes at their native homes.—*John*, ii. 1.

The hate of those [who] love not the king.—*R. II.*, ii. 2.

And join'st with them [who] will be thy slaughter-men.—1 *H. VI.*, iii. 3.

Happy; and so are all [who] are near her.—*H. VIII.*, iv. 1.

Cranmer will find a friend [who] will not shrink from him.—*Ibid.*, iv. 1.

Those men [who] blush not in actions blacker than.—*Per.*, i. 1.

Those [who own] that [they] would mischief me [if they could] than those that do [injure me while professing friendship].—*Timon*, iv. 3.

That father [who was] lost, lost his.—*Hamlet*, i. 2.

Declare the cause [why] my father.—1 *H. VI.*, ii. 5.

My residence in Rome [will be] at one Philario's.—*Cym.*, i. 2.

Much more, and [with] much more cause.—*H. V.*, v. (*Chorus*).

Let us once again assail your ears . . . [with] what we.—*Hamlet*, i. 1.

And what mighty magic . . . I won his daughter [with].—*Oth.*, i. 3.

I can be able to front this present time [with].—*Ant. & C.*, i. 4.

Are partners [with him] in the business.—*Cym.*, i. 7.

This creature's no such [wonderful] thing.—*Ant. & C.*, iii. 3.

Return them [word, that] we are ready.—*Per.*, ii. 2.

Our scouts have found the adventure [would be] very easy.—3 *H. VI.*, iv. 2.

He [would have] waved indifferently 'twixt doing.—*Coriol.*, ii. 2.

Makes her as she [would have looked had she] liv'd now.—*W. T.*, v. 3.

Which he said was precious and [would prove] cordial to me.—*Cym.*, iv. 2.

Let's go see poor Cassio ['s wound] dress'd.—*Oth.*, v. 1.

And [yet] you will rather show our general louts.—*Coriol.*, iii. 2.

Tempt him not so too far; I wish [you would] forbear.—*Ant. & C.*, i. 3.

To satisfy [your just wrath] . . . take no stricter render of me than my all.—*Cym.*, v. 4.

He often allows a word in one part of a sentence to be elliptically understood as *repeated* in another part of the same sentence, or even in another part of the same dialogue :—

We must receive him *according* to the honour of his sender ; and towards himself, [according to] his goodness forespent on us, we must extend our notice.—*Cym.*, ii. 3.

You *advise* me well.—I protest [I *advise* you], in the sincerity.—*Oth.*, ii. 3.

And, when we fall, we answer others' merits in our name, [*and*] are therefore to be pitied.—*Ant. & C.*, v. 2.

And crickets sing at the oven's mouth, [*and*] are the blither for their drouth.—*Per.*, iii. (*Gower*).

Thoughts *are* no subjects; intents [*are*] but merely thoughts.—*M. for M.*, v. 1.

They *are* taught their manage, and to that end riders [*are*] dearly hired.—*As You L.*, i. 1.

Where are now your fortunes ! Shipwreck'd upon a kingdom, where [*are*] no pity, no friends, no hope; [*where*] no kindred weep for me.—*H. VIII.*, iii. 1.

They *are* actions that a man might play: but I have that within which passeth show ; these [*are*] but.—*Hamlet*, i. 2.

But [*as*] justly *as* you have exceeded all promise.—*As You L.*, i. 2.

Man's life is [*as*] cheap *as* beast's.—*Lear*, ii. 4.

I hold you but [*as*] a subject of this war, not *as* a brother.—*Ibid.*, v. 3.

Not for such an end [*as*] thou seek'st *as* base *as* strange.—*Cym.*, i. 7.

Which are [*as*] often the sadness of parting, *as* the procuring.—*Ibid.*, v. 4.

Love goes toward love, *as schoolboys* [go] from their books; but love from love, [*as schoolboys* go] toward school with.—*R. & Jul.*, ii. 2.

Against mine honour *aught*, my bond to wedlock, or my love and duty, [*aught*] against your sacred person.—*H. VIII.*, ii. 4.

What he might *be*—if, what he might [*be*], he is not.—*Oth.*, iv. 1.

Either *be gone* before the watch be set, or [*be gone*] by the break of day.—*R. & Jul.*, iii. 3.

Do you know, and dare not *be intelligent* to me ? 'Tis thereabouts ; for, to yourself, what you do know, you must [*be intelligent*].—*W. T.*, i. 2.

Or *by* pronouncing of some doubtful phrase . . . or [*by*] such ambiguous giving out, to note that you know.—*Hamlet*, i. 5.

Your colt's tooth is not *cast yet*.—No, my lord ; nor shall not [*be cast yet*], while I have a stump.—*H. VIII.*, i. 3.

A merrier *day* did never yet greet Rome, no not the [*day* of the] expulsion of the Tarquins —*Coriol.*, v. 4.

Should be *depos'd ;* and, being [*depos'd*], that we detain.—*Ant. & C.*, iii. 6.

You *do* not understand yourself so clearly as it behoves my daughter and your honour [*to do*].—*Hamlet*, i. 3.

What they *do* delay, they [*do*] not deny.—*Ant. & C.*, ii. 1.

Rights by rights fouler [*do fail*] strengths by strengths *do fail*.—*Coriol.*, iv. 7.

One fire *drives out* one fire ; one nail [*drives out*] one nail.—*Ibid.*, iv. 7.

As fire *drives out* fire, so pity [*drives out*] pity.—*Jul. C.*, iii. 1.

May you a better *feast* never behold. . . . This is Timon's last [*feast*].—*Timon*, iii. 6.

Not nature, to whom all sores lay siege, can bear great *fortune*, but by contempt of nature. Raise me this beggar [to *fortune*], and deny 't that lord.—*Ibid.*, iv. 3.

And I have *found* Demetrius like a [*found*] jewel.—*Mid. N. D.*, iv. 1.

As lying a *gossip* in that as [any *gossip* who] ever knapped ginger.—*Mer. of V.*, iii. 1.

The worm, that 's fled, *hath* nature that in time will venom breed, [but *hath*] no teeth for the present.—*Macb.*, iii. 4.

I *have* dined with him, and told him on 't ; and [*have*] come again to supper to him.—*Timon*, iii. 1.

And *have* an hour of hearing; and, by 'r lady, [*have* it] held current music too.—*H. VIII.*, i. 3.

He will not hear, till [*he*] feel.—*Timon*, ii. 2.

For that *he has* . . . envied against the people . . . as now at last [*he has*] given hostile strokes.—*Coriol.*, iii. 3.

He was then of a crescent note; [*he was*] expected to prove.—*Cym.*, i. 5.

He will betray us all unto ourselves: [*he will*] inform on that.—*All's W.*, iv. 1.

I 'll willingly to *him* ; to gain [*him*] his colour.—*Cym.*, iv. 2.

I love him not, nor hate him not; and yet [*I*] have more cause.—*As You L.*, iii. 5.

I am yet unknown to woman; [*I*] never was forsworn; [*I*] scarcely *have* coveted what was mine own ; at no time [*have I*] broke my faith; [*I*] would not betray the devil to his fellow; and [*I*] delight no less in.—*Macb.*, iv. 3.

Have *I*, my lord? [*I*] assure you, my good liege.—*Hamlet*, ii. 2.

I had my father's signet in my purse. . . . [*I*] folded the writ up in form of the other; [*I*] subscrib'd it; [*I*] gave 't the impression; [and *I*] plac'd it safely.—*Ibid.*, v. 2.

While *I* to this hard house . . . which even but now, [*I*] demanding after you, denied me to come in.—*Lear*, iii. 2.

I see it in my motion, [*I*] have it not in my tongue.—*Ant. & C.*, ii. 3.

I am not made of stone, but [*I am*] penetrable to your kind entreaties.—*R. III.*, iii. 7.

I am joyful to hear of their readiness . . . and [*I am*] most glad of your company.—*Coriol.*, iv. 3.

I bleed, sir; but [*I am*] not kill'd.—*I am* not sorry neither.—*Oth.*, v. 2.

Art thou *proud* yet? Ay, [*I am proud*] that *I am* not thee.—I [*am proud*] that I was no prodigal.—I [*am proud*], that I am one now.—*Timon*, iv. 3.

I am sorry to see you ta'en from liberty, [and *I am sorry*] to look on the business present.—*H. VIII.*, i. 1.

I would not prize them without her love; for her [*I would*] employ them all.—*W. T.*, iv. 3.

If my actions *were* tried by every tongue, [*if*] every eye saw them, [*if*] envy and base opinion [*were*] set against them.—*H. VIII.*, iii. 1.

If you do wrongfully seize Hereford's rights, [*if you do*] call in the letters-patents that he hath.—*R. II.*, ii. 1.

What, i' the storm ? i' the night? Let pity not be believ'd [*in*] !—*Lear*, iv. 3.

Persever *in* that clear way [*in which*] thou goest.—*Per.*, iv. 6.

Have ever won more *in their* officer than [*in their* own] person.—*Ant. & C.*, iii. 1,

He 's disposed as [*is*] the hateful raven: . . . for he 's inclin'd as *is* the rav'nous wolf.—*2 H. VI.*, iii. 1.

In that he *is* a fox, by nature prov'd [to be] *an enemy* to the flock . . . as Humphrey [*is*] prov'd by reasons [to be *an enemy*] to my liege.—*Ibid.*, iii. 1.

So hers *is* set on mine ; and all [*is*] combin'd.—*R. & Jul.*, ii. 3.

Their bloody sign of battle *is* hung out, and something [*is*] to be done.—*Jul. C.*, v. 1.

That lady *is* not now living; or this gentleman's opinion [*is*], by this, worn out.—*Cym.*, i. 5.

Though this [*is*] a heavenly angel, hell *is* here.—*Ibid.*, ii. 2.

Her face [*is*] the book of praises, where *is* read.—*Per.*, i. 1.

That Cranmer *is* return'd with welcome, [and *is*] install'd Lord Archbishop of Canterbury.—*H. VIII.*, iii. 2.

No port *is* free ; no place [*is* there], that guard.—*Lear*, ii. 3.

Ever shall [*it*] in safety rest,
And the owner of *it* [be] blest.—*Mid. N. D.*, v. 2.

If *it* be denied, [*it*] will much impeach the justice.—*Mer. of V.*, iii. 3.

Had *it* stretched so far, [*it*] would have made nature immortal.—*All's W.*, i. 1.

Be [*it*] what *it* is, the action of my life is like *it*.—*Cym.*, v. 4.

Nurses are not the fates, to foster *it*, nor ever to preserve [*it*].—*Per.*, iv. 4.

Noted and most *known* [to be *known*] to youth and liberty.—*Hamlet*, ii. 1.

Passion *lends them* power, time [*lends them*] means to meet.—*R. & Jul.*, i. 5 (*Chorus*).

Therefore, [*let*] all hearts in love use their own tongues ; *let* every eye negotiate for itself.—*M. Ado*, ii. 1.

Let four captains bear Hamlet . . . and, for his passage, [*let*] the soldiers' music.— *Hamlet*, v. 2.

Ne'er *long'd* my mother so to see me first, as I have [*long'd*] now.—*Cym.*, iii. 4.

Little are we beholden to your *love*, and little [was this *love*] look'd for at your helping hands.—*R. II.*, iv. 1.

Is, of a king, become a banish'd *man*, and forc'd to live in Scotland a forlorn [*man*].—*3 H. VI.*, iii. 3.

And *may* direct his course as [*may*] please himself.—*R. III.*, ii. 2.

That none of you *may* live his natural age, but by some unlook'd accident [*may* be] cut off.—*Ibid.*, i. 3.

My relief *must* not be toss'd and turn'd to me in words, but [*must*] find supply immediate.—*Timon*, ii. 1.

Yet I *must* not, for certain friends that are both his and mine, whose loves I may not drop, but [*must*] wail.—*Macb.*, iii. 1.

Your presence *needs must* puzzle Antony : [*needs must*] take from his heart, take from his brain.—*Ant. & C.*, iii. 7.

The tadpole, the wall-*newt* and the water [-*newt*].—*Lear*, iii. 4.

I do not know what *kind* of my *obedience* I should tender ; more than my all [of *obedience*] is [as] nothing [compared with that which is due].—*H. VIII.*, ii. 3.

When you have push'd out [*of*] your gates the very defender *of* them.—*Coriol.*, v. 2.

Of thy deep duty more impression show than [*of*] that of common sons.—*Ibid.*, v. 3.

What you shall know meantime *of* stirs abroad, I shall beseech you, sir, to let me be partaker [*of*].—*Ant. & C.*, i. 4.

Vast confusion waits—as doth a raven *on* a sick-fallen beast—[*on*] the imminent decay of wrested pomp.—*John*, iv. 3.

On him erect a second hope, as fairly built as [*on*] Hector.—*Tr. & Cr.*, iv. 5.

And have prevail'd as much *on* him, as [*on*] you.—*R. III.*, i. 1.

[*On*] whom heavens, in justice, both *on* her and hers, have laid most heavy hand.— *Cym.*, v. 5.

Thy sight, which should make *our eyes* flow with joy, *hearts* dance with comforts, constrains them [*our eyes* to] weep, and [*our hearts* to] shake with fear and sorrow.— *Coriol.*, v. 3.

Pass no farther.—Ha ! what is that ?—It will be dangerous to go on : [*pass*] no farther.—*Ibid.*, iii. 1.

My next poor *petition* is . . . The last [*petition*] is.—*H. VIII.*, iv. 2.

Thou hast not half the *power* to do me harm as I have [*power* to] endure to be hurt.—*Oth.*, v. 2.

He *puts* on sackcloth, and [*puts*] to sea.—*Per.*, iv. 4 (*Gower*).

Hereditary, *rather* than purchas'd ; what he cannot change, [*rather*] than what he chooses.—*Ant. & C.*, i. 4.

She shows a body *rather* than a life ; a statue, [*rather*] than a breather.—*Ibid.*, iii. 3.

Have you an army *ready*, say you?—A most royal one . . . *already* in the entertainment, and [*ready*] to be on foot.—*Coriol.*, iv. 3.

They smart to hear themselves *remembered*.—Should they not [be *remember'd*], well might they fester.—*Ibid.*, i. 9.

Say that Marcius *return* me, as Cominius is return'd, unheard ; what then ? [*Say that* I *return*] but as a discontented friend, grief-shot with his.—*Ibid.*, v. 1.

To know our enemies' minds, we'd *rip* their hearts ; [to *rip*] their papers, is more lawful.—*Lear*, iv. 6.

But thought *'s* the slave of life, and life [*'s*] time's fool.—1 *H. IV.*, v. 4.

So *seem*, as if you were inspir'd to do those duties which you tender to her; ⌊make it *seem*] that you in all obey her.—*Cym.*, ii. 3.

Haply, you shall not *see me* more: or if [you do *see me*, you will *see me*] a mangled shadow.—*Ant. & C.*, iv. 2.

No simple man that *sees* this jarring discord . . . but [*sees*] that it doth presage some ill event.—1 *H. VI.*, iv. 1.

Hubert *shall* be your man, [and *shall*] attend on you.—*John*, iii. 3.

When I *shall* dwell with worms, and my poor name [*shall* be] banish'd.—*H. VIII.*, iv. 2.

I nothing know where *she* remains, why [*she* is] gone.—*Cym.*, iv. 3.

Here is four Harry ten *shillings* in French crowns for you. . . . you shall have forty [*shillings*], sir.—2 *H. IV.*, iii. 2.

Should be as holy as severe; [*should be* a] pattern in himself.—*M. for M.*, iii. 2.

When service *should* in my old limbs lie lame, and unregarded age [*should* be] in corners thrown.—*As You L.*, ii. 3.

Of any power to expel *sickness*, but prolong his hour [of *sickness*].—*Timon*, iii. 1.

Why did you *suffer* Iachimo . . . and [*suffer* Posthumus] to become the geck and scorn o' the other's villany?—*Cym.*, v. 4.

Which, *taken at the flood*, leads on to fortune; omitted [to be *taken at the flood*], all the voyage of.—*Jul. C.*, iv. 3.

That you may, fair lady, perceive [*that*] I speak sincerely, and [*that*] high note's ta'en of your many virtues.—*H. VIII.*, ii. 3.

The feast is sold *that* is not often vouch'd, while 'tis a making, [*that*] 'tis given with welcome.—*Macb.*, iii. 4.

I, *that* please some, try all; [*that* am] both joy and terror.—*W. T.*, iv. (*Chorus*).

'Tis not my profit *that does lead* mine honour; [but] mine honour [*that does lead*] it.—*Ant. & C.*, ii. 7.

What thing is it *that I* never did see man die! [*that I*] scarce ever look'd on blood, . . . [*that I*] never bestrid a horse.—*Cym.*, iv. 4.

[*The*] last thing he did, dear queen, he kiss'd—*the* last of many doubled kisses—this orient pearl.—*Ant. & C.*, i. 5.

This might be *the pate of* a politician. . . . This might be [*the pate of*] my lord such-a-one.—*Hamlet*, v. 1.

I pray *thee*, loving wife, and [*thee*,] gentle daughter.—2 *H. IV.*, ii. 3.

If *they* should speak, [*they*] would almost damn those ears.—*Mer. of V.*, i. 1.

For *they* wear themselves in the cap of the time, there [*they*] do muster true gait, eat, speak, and move.—*All's W.*, ii. 1.

That . . . my accusers, be [*they*] what *they* will.—*H. VIII.*, v. 2.

They ne'er cared for us yet: [*they*] suffer us to famish . . . [*they*] make edicts . . . [*they*] repeal daily . . . and [*they*] provide.—*Coriol.*, i. 1.

And *they* within our power, [*they*] shall never see.—*Lear*, v. 1.

It was she first told me *thou* wast mad; then [*thou*] cam'st in smiling.—*Tw. N.*, v. 1.

Be *thou* a spirit of health or goblin damn'd, [whether *thou*] bring with thee airs from heaven or.—*Hamlet*, i. 4.

Thou that beget'st him that did thee beget; *thou* that wast born at sea. . . . *Thou* ·_ast been godlike perfect) [*thou*] the heir of kingdoms.—*Per.*, v. 1.

Or perform my bidding, or *thou liv'st* in woe; do 't and [*thou liv'st*] happy.—*Ibid.*, v. 2.

For with [the *tidings* of] her death that *tidings* came.—*Jul. C.*, iv. 3.

Thy false uncle—Dost thou attend me?—Sir, most heedfully.—[*Thy false uncle*] being once perfected.—*Temp.*, i. 2.

And be *thy wife* (if any be so mad [as to become *thy wife*]).—*R. III.*, iv. 1.

If you knew *to* whom you show this honour, [*to*] how true a gentleman you send relief, [*to*] how dear a lover.—*Mer. of V.*, iii. 4.

Bid him repair *to* us *to* Ely House *to* see [*to*] this business.—*R. II.*, ii. 1.

There needs no ghost, my lord, [*to*] come from the grave *to* tell us this.—*Hamlet*, i. 5.

Better [*to be*] thus, and known *to be* contemn'd than still [*to be*] contemn'd.— *Lear*, iv. 1.

To be acknowledg'd, madam, is [*to be*] o'erpaid.—*Ibid.*, iv. 7

I have much *to do* [*to do* anything] but *to* go hang my head.—*Oth.*, iv. 3.

Best of comfort [*to us*] ; and ever welcome *to us*.—*Ant. & C.*, iii. 6.

Prove *true*, imagination, oh, prove *true !* . . . oh, if it prove [*true*], tempests are kind.—*Tw. N.*, iii. 4.

To die *upon* the bed my father died [*upon*].—*W. T.*, iv. 3.

Was by the rough seas reft of ships and men, *and*, after shipwreck, driven . . . [*was*] bereft of ships and men, [*and*], cast on this shore.—*Per.*, ii. 3.

You are as *welcome*, worthy sir, as I have words to bid you [*welcome* with].— *Cym.*, i. 7.

'*Twere* a paper *lost*, as offer'd mercy [that *were lost*] is.—*Ibid.*, i. 3.

To make the truth appear *where it* seems hid, and hide the false [*where it*] seems true.—*M. for M.*, v. 1.

Lucius, *who 's* that [*who*] knocks ?—*Jul. C.*, ii. 1.

From Cordelia, *who* hath most fortunately been inform'd of my obscured course; and [*who*] shall find time.—*Lear*, ii. 2.

But myself, *who had* the world as my confectionary ; [*who had*] the mouths, the tongues, the eyes.—*Timon*, iv. 3.

Who would not *wish* to be from wealth exempt, since riches point to misery and contempt ? *Who would* be so mock'd with glory ? or [*who would wish*] to live but in a dream of friendship ? [*who would wish*] to have his pomp, and all what state compounds, but only painted.—*Timon*, iv. 3.

My inch of taper *will* be burnt and done, and blindfold death [*will*] not let me see my son.—*R. II.*, i. 3.

A vulgar comment *will be* made of it, and that [*will be*] supposed by the common rout.—*Com. of E.*, iii. 1.

Whose repetition *will be* dogg'd with curses ; whose chronicle [*will be*] thus writ.— *Coriol.*, v. 3.

Unless you undertake that *with* me, [*with*] which *with* as much safety you might answer him.—*Tw. N.*, iii. 4.

Had I but serv'd my God *with* half the zeal [*with* which] I serv'd my king.— *H. VIII.*, iii. 2.

With patience more than savages could suffer [*with*].—*Ant. & C.*, i. 4.

Your eye in Scotland *would* create soldiers, [and *would*] make our women fight.— *Macb.*, iv. 3.

Thou *wouldst have* plung'd thyself in general riot ; [*wouldst have*] melted down thy youth . . . and never [*wouldst have*] learn'd the icy precepts of respect, but [*wouldst have*] follow'd.—*Timon*, iv. 3.

You must be so too, if [*you*] heed me.—*Temp.*, ii. 1.

And leave *you* hindmost ; or . . . [*you*] lie there for pavement.- -*Tr. & Cr.*, iii. 3.

Perchance some single vantages *you* took, when my indisposition put *you* back ; and that unaptness [*you*] made your minister.—*Timon*, ii. 2.

As *you* are old and reverend, [*you*] should be wise.—*Lear*, i. 4.

Your high self . . . *you have* obscur'd with a swain's wearing ; and me, poor lowly maid, [*you have*] most goddess-like prank'd up.—*W. T.*, iv. 3.

In Antiochus and his daughter *you have* heard . . . in Pericles, his queen, and daughter [*you have*] seen.—*Per.*, v. 3 (*Gower*).

Beseech *your highness*, give us better credit . . . and beseech [*your highness*] so to esteem of us.—*W. T.*, ii. 3.

He even has passages where a word or phrase gives a somewhat similar word or phrase to be elliptically understood in the sentence :—

You are darken'd in this *action*, sir, even by your own [*act*].—*Coriol.*, iv. 7.

This shall make our purpose [*appear*] necessary, and not envious : which so *appearing* to the common eyes.—*Jul. C.*, ii. 1.

Pale and *bloodless*, [the *blood*] being all descended.—2 *H. VI.*, iii. 2.

They of Rome are enter'd in our *counsels*, and know . . . what ever [proposals made in *council*] have been thought on.—*Coriol.*, i. 2.

I cannot *make you* what amends I would, therefore accept such kindness as I can [*do you*].—*R. III.*, iv. 4.

> Had I been thief-stolen,

As my two brothers, [*I had been*] happy !—*Cym.*, i. 7.

Your *imprisonment* shall not be long; I will deliver you, or else lie [*in prison*] for you.—*R. III.*, i. 1.

I died for hope [of *lending thee aid*] ere I could *lend thee aid*.—*Ibid.*, v. 3.

Out of his noble nature, [and *out of the*] zeal and obedience.—*H. VIII.*, iii. 1.

Press not a falling man *too far !* 'tis virtue [to forbear from *pressing him too far*].—*Ibid.*, iii. 2.

I have no spur to prick the *sides* of my intent, but only vaulting ambition, which o'erleaps itself, and falls on the other [*side*].—*Macb.*, i. 7.

Thanks, fortune, yet. . . . and [*I thank* thee] though it was mine own.—*Per.*, ii. 1.

I abhor *this* dilatory sloth and [*these*] tricks of Rome.—*H. VIII.*, ii. 4.

And how [*they live* there], and who [*they are*], what means [*they have*] and where *they keep.*—*Hamlet*, ii. 1.

As we are going [*to those*] to whom it must be done.—*Jul. C.*, ii. 1.

Will you ha' the *truth* on't ? . . . Why, there thou say'st [*true*].—*Hamlet*, v. 1.

What makes this change ?—[*What is*] the matter ?—*Coriol.*, iii. 1.

Nor has he *with* him [*wherewith*] to supply his life.—*Timon.*, iv. 2.

Occasionally he has passages where a verb in one form gives the same verb in another form to be elliptically understood [*See* VERBS PECULIARLY USED] :—

Your uncle York *is* join'd with Bolingbroke ; and all your northern castles [*are*] yielded up, and all your southern gentlemen [*are*] in arms.—*R. II.*, iii. 2.

Now *is* the winter of our discontent made. . . . and all the clouds, that lower'd upon our house, [*are*] in the deep.—*R. III.*, i. 1.

So much *is* my poverty of spirit, so mighty and so many [*are*] my defects.—*Ibid.*, iii. 7.

Thy Clarence he *is* dead. . . . Vaughan, Grey, [*are*] untimely smother'd.—*Ibid.*, iv. 4.

The queen *is* comfortless, and we [*are*] forgetful.—*H. VIII.*, ii. 4.

It *is*, as the air, invulnerable, and our vain blows [*are*] malicious.—*Hamlet*, i. 1.

There *is* no shuffling, . . . and we ourselves [*are*] compell'd.—*Ibid.*, iii. 3.

Am I not witch'd like her ? or [*art*] thou not false like him ?—2 *H. VI.*, iii. 2.

Which ever has [*been*] and ever shall *be* growing.—*H. VIII.*, iii. 2.

That [I] am, have [*been*], and will *be.*—*Ibid.*, iii. 2.

That means not [to *be*], hath not [*been*], or *is* not in love ! If then one *is*, or hath [*been*], or means to *be.*—*Tr. & Cr.*, i. 3.

When he hath [*coped*], and is again to *cope* your wife.—*Oth.*, iv. 1.

Than you have [*deserv'd*] or will *deserve* at my hand.—*All's W.*, ii. 5,

The sum of all I can [*disclose*], I have *disclos'd.*—*R. III.*, ii. 4.

Dismay'd not this our captains, Macbeth and Banquo ?—Yes ; as sparrows [*dismay*] eagles, or the hare [*dismays*] the lion.—*Macb.*, i. 2.

That what he will [*do*], he *does ;* and *does* so much.—*Tr. & Cr.*, v. 5.

What can you say to *draw* a third more opulent than your sisters [have *drawn*] ?— *Lear*, i. 1.

Love *goes* toward love, as schoolboys [*go*] from their books; but love ⌊*goes*⌋ from love, [as schoolboys *go*] toward school.—*R. & Jul.*, ii. 2.

The Earl of Worcester *hath* broke his staff . . . and all the household servants [*have*] fled with him.—*R. II.*, ii. 2.

She *hath* not given so many good words breath as for her Greeks and Trojans [*have*] suffer'd death.—*Tr. & Cr.*, iv. 1.

Your eyes *are* lode-stars; and your tongue's sweet air [*is*] more.—*Mid. N. D.*, i. 1.

Our tears *are* not yet brew'd.—Nor [*is*] our strong sorrow.—*Macb.*, ii. 3.

Thou *art* the midwife to my woe, and Bolingbroke [*is*] my.—*R. II.*, ii. 2.

This might *be* my lord such-a-one . . . and now [*is*] my lady Worm's.—*Hamlet*, v. 1.

Jove *knows* what man thou might'st have made; but I [*know*], thou diedst, a most rare boy, of melancholy!—*Cym.*, iv. 2.

She was *belov'd*, she *lov'd*; she is [*belov'd*], and doth [*love*].—*Tr. & Cr.*, iv. 5.

He *loves* me well, and I have given him reasons [to *love* me].—*Jul. C.*, ii. 1.

At first meeting *lov'd*; continu'd so [*loving* him] until we.—*Cym.*, v. 5.

Was like [to *pass*], and had indeed against us *pass'd!*—*H. V.*, i. 1.

Do you not *think* he *thinks* himself a better man than I am?—No question [that he does *think* so].—*Tr. & Cr.*, ii. 3.

Bloodily *were* butcher'd, and I myself [*was*] secure in.—*R. III.*, iii. 5.

Ajax *was* here the voluntary, and you [*were*] as under.—*Tr. & Cr.*, ii. 1.

He occasionally has a form of question where the word "not" is elliptically understood:—

But [why should we *not*] rather follow our forceful instigation?—*W. T.*, ii. 1.

Nay, gave [I *not*] notice he was from thence discharg'd?—*H. VIII.*, ii. 4.

Or at least [have *not* been] strangely neglected?—*Ibid.*, iii. 2.

At what ease might [*not*] corrupt minds procure knaves as corrupt to swear against you?—*Ibid.*, v. 1.

What heart receives [*not*] from hence the conquering part, to steel a strong opinion to themselves?—*Tr. & Cr.*, i. 3.

Who knows if one of her women, being corrupted, hath [*not*] stolen it from her?—*Cym.*, ii. 4.

For farther instances of Shakespeare's elliptical style, *see* ELLIPSES OF COMPARISON, ELLIPTICALLY USED WORDS, and PECULIAR CONSTRUCTION.

ELLIPTICALLY USED WORDS.

Shakespeare frequently uses single words with largely elliptical and inclusive force. He sometimes employs nouns elliptically:—

Much *attribute* [attributed merit] he hath.—*Tr. & Cr.*, ii. 3.

A night is but small *breath* [breathing time] and little pause.—*H. V.*, ii. 4.

But that my *coat* [under-coat of mail armour] is better.—*Oth.*, v. 1.

I can make no *collection* [collective deduction] of it.—*Cym.*, v. 5.

He gave you all the *duties* [qualities duly belonging to] of a man.—1 *H. IV.*, v. 2.

I am much asham'd of my *exchange* [of woman's for man's clothes].—*Mer. of V.*, ii. .

Hath borne his *faculties* [of royalty, sovereign powers] so meek.—*Macb.*, i. 7.

The native mightiness and [power decreed to him by] *fate* of him.—*H. V.*, ii. 4.

He is a man, setting his *fate* [the misfortune of appearing criminal fated to befal him, and the fiery temper decreed him by fate] aside, of comely virtues.—*Timon*, iii. 5.

The [remission of the] *forfeit*, sov'reign, of my servant's life.—*R. III.*, ii. 1.

What [act of] *friendship* may I do thee?—*Timon*, iv. 3.

If I do vow a [n act of] *friendship*, I'll perform it.—*Oth.*, iii. 3.

Have for the *gilt* [gold coin] of France (oh, guilt indeed!).—*H. V.*, ii. (*Chorus*).

If I were not at *half-sword* [half a sword's length] with a dozen.—1 *H. IV.*, ii. 4.

'Tis now your *honour* [honourable task], daughter, to explain.—*Per.*, ii. 2.

Our *imputation* [imputed excellence] shall be oddly pois'd.—*Tr. & Cr.*, i. 3.

In the *imputation* [imputed excellence] laid on him by them, in his meed he's un-fellowed.—*Hamlet*, v. 2.

Which then our [want of] *leisure* would not let us hear.—*R. II.*, i. 1.

The [want of] *leisure* and the fearful time cuts off.—*R. III.*, v. 3.

For now all *length* [of endurance and existence] is torture.—*Ant. & C.*, iv. 12.

It is no other but the *main* [and obvious cause].—*Hamlet*, ii. 2.

We answer others' *merits* [deeds meriting reprobation and punishment] in our name, are therefore to be pitied.—*Ant. & C.*, v. 2.

That man might ne'er be wretched for his *mind* [high-mindedness, liberality of spirit].—*Timon*, i. 2.

The night-mare and her *nine-fold* [nine-numbered foals].—*Lear*, iii. 4.

Swear against *objects* [likely to inspire relenting].—*Timon*, iv. 3.

One that feeds on *objects* [of pursuit], arts, and imitations.—*Jul. C.*, iv. 1.

That woman that cannot make her fault her husband's *occasion* [occasioning; to be occasioned by her husband].—*As You L.*, iv. 1.

And nature, stronger than his just *occasion* [the resentment occasioned by his brother], made him.—*Ibid.*, iv. 3.

May one be pardon'd, and retain the *offence* [the gain for which the offence was committed]?—*Hamlet*, iii. 3.

And prologue to the *omen* [ominous event] coming on.—*Ibid.*, i. 1.

Pride, haughtiness, *opinion* [opiniatedness; the arrogance of inordinate self-opinion], and disdain.—1 *H. IV.*, iii. 1.

Smoke and lukewarm water is your *perfection* [perfect image or resemblance].—*Timon*, iii. 6.

What [the royal] *presence* must not know.—*R. II.*, i. 3.

The grass whereon thou tread'st the *presence* [-chamber] strew'd.—*Ibid.*, i. 3.

The two great cardinals wait in the *presence* [-chamber].—*H. VIII.*, iii. 1.

I' the [royal] *presence* he would say untruths.—*Ibid.*, iv. 2.

This [royal] *presence* knows, and you must needs have heard.—*Hamlet*, v. 2.

I'll make division of my *present* [store of money] with you.—*Tw. N.*, iii. 4.

In her sex, her years, *profession* [of that which she is able to perform], wisdom, and constancy, hath amaz'd me.—*All's W.*, ii. 1.

His *remedies* [chances of remedying his downfall] are tame.—*Coriol.*, iv. 6.

If they set down before us, for the *remove* [the removal of them] bring up your army.—*Ibid.*, i. 2.

Reason and *respect* [to consequences] make livers pale, and lustihood deject.—*Tr. & Cr.*, ii. 2.

The icy precepts of *respect* [to prudence and decorum].—*Timon*, iv. 3.

'Tis worse than murder, to do upon [that which should command] *respect* such violent outrage.—*Lear*, ii. 4.

In thy *reverence* [time of life when reverence is due] and thy chair days, thus to die in ruffian battle?—2 *H. VI.*, v. 2.

Say that *right* [righteous vengeance] for *right* [righteous vengeance] hath dimm'd your infant morn.—*R. III.*, iv. 4.

Drove us to seek out this *head of safety* [collective force whereby we hope to gain safety].—1 *H. IV.*, iv. 3.

He hath a wisdom that doth guide his valour
To act in *safety* [moral safety, righteous precaution].—*Macb.*, iii. 1.

Thou shalt see an answerable *sequestration* [from each other].—*Oth.*, i. 3.

The *severals* [several particulars] and unhidden passages.—*H. V.*, i. 1.

Are you yet to your own *souls* ['welfare] so blind.—*R. III.*, i. 4.

As you are a king, speak in your [royal] *state*.—2 *H. IV.*, v. 2.

Where it shall mingle with the *state* [majestic state, statèliness] of floods.— *2 H. IV.*, v. 2.

To make them instruments of fear and warning
Unto some monstrous *state* [of things, affairs, or events].—*Jul. C.*, i. 3.

Lest example breed, by his *sufferance** [suffering him to go unpunished], more of such a kind.—*H. V.*, ii. 2.

But God be thanked for prevention ;
[At] which I in *sufferance* [suffering death] heartily will rejoice.—*Ibid.*, ii. 2.

Persuade me rather to be slave and sumpter [*sumpter*-mule]
To this detested groom.—*Lear*, ii. 4.

The *sweet* [sweetest portion] o' the year.—*W. T.*, iv. 2 (*Song*).

The *sweet* [sweetest portion] of the night.—*2 H. IV.*, v. 3.

Turning dispiteous [purpose to] *torture* out of door !—*John*, iv. 1.

Throw away respect, *tradition* [traditional observance], form, and ceremonious duty.
—*R. II.*, iii. 2.

We must supplant those rough rug-headed kerns,
Which live like *venom* [venomous reptiles], where no *venom* [venomous reptiles], else.—*Ibid.*, ii. 1.

You 're a gentleman of mine own *way* [of thinking in religious questions] ; I know you wise.—*H. VIII.*, v. 1.

Why then, you princes, do you with cheeks abash'd behold our *works* [the inadequate amount of what we have done.]—*Tr. & Cr.*, i. 3.

There are some technical terms, used by Shakespeare, where the names of implements, instruments, weapons, &c., are employed for their bearers or users :—

Bring up the *brown bills* [brown-bill-bearers].—*Lear*, iv. 6.

The *drum* [drummer] your honour hears marcheth from Warwick.—*3 H. VI.*, v. 1.

There is an *ensign* [ensign-bearer] there at the pridge.—*H. V.*, iii. 6.

This *ensign*† [ensign-bearer] here of mine was turning back;
I slew the coward, and did take it from him.—*Jul. C.*, v. 3.

I have procured thee, Jack, a charge of *foot* [foot-soldiers].—
I would it had been of *horse* [horse-soldiers].—*1 H. IV.*, iii. 3.

Consisting equally of *horse* [horse-soldiers] and *foot* [foot-soldiers]. . . .
Shall have the leading of the *foot* and *horse*. . . .
Shall be well winged with our chiefest *horse*.—*R. III.*, v. 3.

The general of our *horse* thou art.—*All's W.*, iii. 3.

'Tis Alcibiades, and some twenty *horse* [horsemen].—*Timon*, i. 1.

The armipotent Mars, of *lances* [lancemen] the almighty.—*Love's L. L.*, v. 2.

And turn our impress'd *lances*† in our eyes,
Which do command them.—*Lear*, v. 3.

Where is the *post* that came from valiant Oxford ?—*3 H. VI.*, v. 1.

Thou shalt be my lieutenant, monster, or my *standard* [standard-bearer].—Your lieutenant, if you list; he 's no *standard* [punningly; one prevented by liquor from standing upright].—*Temp.*, iii. 2.

Thou, *trumpet* [trumpeter], there 's my purse. Now crack thy lungs, and split thy brazen pipe.—*Tr. & Cr.*, iv. 5.

Shakespeare often employs adjectives elliptically :—

To take advantage of *the* ABSENT *time* [the time when the King is absent], and fright our native peace.—*R. II.*, ii. 3.

---

* In Shakespeare's time this word as well as " suffer " and " suffered," were used with much force of ellipsis ; and it will be seen by passages subsequently here cited that he thus employed them.

† In both the above passages to which this note refers, the terms being used for the weapons and their bearers, allows the poet to employ the word (" ensign " in the first passage, " lances " in the second) in its double sense.

May seem as shy, as grave, as just, as *absolute* [absolutely meritorious, completely excellent] as angels.—*M. for M.*, v. 1.

It is a most *absolute* and excellent horse.—*H. V.*, iii. 7.

Therefore, most *absolute* sir, if thou wilt have the.—*Coriol.*, iv. 5.

This Philoten contends in skill with *absolute* Marina.—*Per.*, iv. (*Gower*).

And the will dotes, that is *attributive* [of excellence or merit]
To what infectiously itself affects,
Without some image of the affected merit.—*Tr. & Cr.*, ii. 2.

It was a *bare* [bare-faced, unblushing] petition of a state
To one whom they had punish'd.—*Coriol.*, v. 1.

When *better* [better men, officers superior to yourselves in rank] fall, for your avails they fell.—*All's W.*, iii. 1.

Too *ceremonious* [observant of ceremonial forms] and traditional [scrupulous in respecting traditional privilege].—*R. III.*, iii. 1.

Thou visible God, that solder'st CLOSE *impossibilities* [things that seem impossible to be brought close together] and mak'st them kiss!—*Timon*, iv. 3.

Go to thy COLD *bed* [bed to which one goes being cold; bed feeling cold at first plunge into it], and warm thee.—*Tam. of S., Induc.* 1.

Go to thy *cold bed*, and warm thee.—*Lear*, iii. 4.

COMMON *pleasures* [pleasures to be enjoyed by you all in common], to walk abroad, and recreate yourselves.—*Jul. C.*, iii. 2.

Wherein the CUB-DRAWN *bear* [the bear whose dugs are drawn by its cubs] would couch.—*Lear*, iii. 1.

What too CURIOUS *dreg* [dreg too curiously, carefully, or scrupulously seen] espies my sweet lady in the fountain of our love?—*Tr. & Cr.*, iii. 2.

Plots have I laid, inductions *dangerous* [leading to dangerous consequences], by drunken prophecies, libels, and dreams.—*R. III.*, i. 1.

To-morrow with your *earliest* [opportunity], let me have speech with you.—*Oth.*, ii. 3.

But, for those EARTHLY *faults* [faults committed against earthly laws], I quit them all.—*M. for M.*, v. 1.

That's a perilous shot out of an *elder* [elder-wood] gun.—*H. V.*, iv. 1.

[At] *First* he was a noble servant to them.—*Coriol.*, iv. 7.

Upon our *first* [appeal, or remonstrance], he sent out to suppress.—*Hamlet*, ii. 2.

FREE *lords* [lords free to utter your opinion; free to speak plainly and free to act decisively], cold snow melts with the sun's.—*2 H. VI.*, iii. 1.

And to deliver, like *free* [free-spoken] and honest men.—*H. VIII.*, iii. 1.

Do faithful homage, and receive FREE *honours* [honours free from pollution in the hand that confers them, free from taint of servility in us that accept them, and free from fear and constraint in their possession].—*Macb.*, iii. 6.

And hold her *free* [free from blame, pure, and chaste].—*Oth.*, iii. 3.

You know my father left me some prescriptions
Of rare and prov'd effects, such as his reading
And manifest experience had collected
For GENERAL *sovereignty* [sovereign remedies in various cases].—*All's W.*, i. 3.

I have been bold (for that I knew the most *general* [generally comprehensive, collectively effectual] way) to them to use your signet and your name.—*Timon*, ii. 2.

There's more behind that is more *gratulate* [subject of congratulation].—*M. for M.*, v. 1.

Thy praises in *his kingdom's* GREAT* *defence* [defending so greatly his great kingdom].—*Macb.*, i. 3.

The other lords, like lions wanting food,
Do rush upon us as *their* HUNGRY *prey* [the prey for which they are hungry].—*1 H. VI.*, i. 2.

---

* It will be perceived how some of the epithets here quoted—as, "great," "ignorant," "learned," "solemn"—have not only elliptical but duplicate effect in these passages.

And every man hence to *his* IDLE *bed* [the bed where he may lie idle].—*Jul. C.*, ii. 1.

Thy letters have transported me beyond
This IGNORANT *present*, [this present moment unacquainted with the existence of that which hereafter will exist] and I feel now
The future in the instant.—*Macb.*, i. 5.

What IGNORANT* *sin have I committed* [What senseless sin have I ignorantly committed].—*Oth.*, iv. 2.

More than the *instant* [instantly levied, suddenly raised] army we can make, might stop our countryman.—*Coriol.*, v. 1.

My strange and self-abuse is *the* INITIATIVE *fear* [the fear that attends the initiative steps in guilt], that wants hard use: we are yet but young in deed. —*Macb.*, iii. 4.

Do you know, and dare not be *intelligent* [conveyant of intelligence, explicit] to me ?—*W. T.*, i. 2.

Which are to France the spies and speculations
Intelligent [conveying intelligence, giving information] of our state.—*Lear*, iii. 1.

This is the letter he spoke of, which approves him an *intelligent* [intelligent of events, and communicating intelligence of them] party to the advantages of France.—*Ibid.*, iii. 5.

Our posts shall be swift and *intelligent* [conveyant of intelligence] betwixt us.—*Ibid.*, iii. 7.

A single voice; and that not pass'd me but *by* LEARNED *approbation* of the judges [by the ascertained approbation of the learned judges].—*H. VIII.*, i. 2.

In the porches of mine ears did pour *the* LEPEROUS *distilment* [the distilment causing leprosy].—*Hamlet*, i. 5.

Strew me over with MAIDEN *flowers* [such flowers as are used in burying maidens], that all the world.—*H. VIII.*, iv. 2.

Sorrow were ever raz'd, and testy wrath
Could never be *her* MILD *companion* [the companion of her mildness].—*Per.*, i. 1.

Garnish'd and deck'd in MODEST* *complement* [accomplishment or complete excellence modestly displayed].—*H. V.*, ii. 2.

If these men have defeated the law and outrun NATIVE *punishment* [punishment naturally theirs, punishment to which they are born if they offend, and punishment in their native land].—*Ibid.*, iv. 1.

And we *in* NEGLIGENT *danger* [in danger of being negligent, in danger from negligence].—*Ant. & C.*, iii. 6.

This shows you are above,
You justicers, that these *our* NETHER *crimes* [the crimes of us here below, the crimes of us in this nether world] so speedily can venge !—*Lear*, iv. 2.

To sing a song that *old* [of old, in olden times] was sung.— *Per.*, i. (*Gower*).

Are at point to show their *open* [openly displayed, as well as unfurled] banner.—*Lear*, iii. 1.

The tyranny of *the* OPEN *night's* [night in the open air is] too rough for nature to endure.—*Ibid.*, iii. 4.

A PARTIAL *slander* [an imputation of partiality] sought I to avoid.—*R. II.*, i. 3.

We should think ourselves for ever *perfect* [perfectly contented, perfect in content].—*Timon*, i. 2.

Go together, *you* PRECIOUS *winners all* [you who have gained what is so precious to you all].—*W. T.*, v. 3.

My love admits no qualifying dross;
No more my grief, *in such a* PRECIOUS *loss* [in the loss of that which is so precious].—*Tr. & Cr.*, iv. 4.

There hangs a vaporous drop *profound* [possessed of profoundly occult properties].—*Macb.*, iii. 5.

His subject am I not, *nor here* PROVINCIAL [nor accountable to the jurisdiction of this province].—*M. for M.*, v. 1.

---

* It is to be observed, that in many of these elliptically used adjectives, Shakespeare employs an epithet not as a means of qualifying the object named, but as a means of elliptically conveying particulars connected therewith.

That may with REASONABLE *swiftness* [the swiftness of reasoning thought, and all the swiftness that can be reasonably expected or hoped].—*H. V.*, i. 2.

To have seen much, and to have nothing, is to have RICH *eyes* [eyes that have beheld many valuable things] and poor hands.—*As You L.*, iv. 1.

Whose beauty did astonish the survey of RICHEST *eyes* [eyes that had seen the largest number of beautiful women].—*All's W.*, v. 3.

First, if all obstacles were cut away,
And that my path were even to the crown,
As *the* RIPE *revenue* [that which comes to me in right of greater maturity in age and judgment] and due of birth.—*R. III.*, iii. 7.

Were our ROYAL *faiths* [faiths due to regal authority, faiths towards the king] martyrs in love.—*2 H. IV.*, iv. 1.

Have shown at full their ROYAL [loyally disposed, allegiant, faithful towards the king] minds.—*H. VIII.*, iv. 1.

The venom'd vengeance ride upon our swords ;
Spur them to RUTHFUL *work* [deeds that in their result produce ruth or pity], rein them from ruth.—*Tr. & Cr.*, v. 3.

Away with SCRUPULOUS *wit* [policy that too scrupulously weighs chances] ! now arms must rule.—*3 H. VI.*, iv. 7.

What other bond than SECRET *Romans* [Romans secretly united in a mutual cause]. —*Jul. C.*, ii. 1.

Upon my SECURE *hour* [hour of fancied security] thy uncle stole.—*Hamlet*, i. 5.

To lip a wanton in a SECURE *couch* [couch fancied to be secure from dishonour], and to suppose her chaste.—*Oth.*, iv. 1.

You have some SICK *offence* [offensive thought causing mental sickness] within your mind.—*Jul. C.*, ii. 1.

If you 'll bestow a *small* [quantity, portion, or amount] (of what you have little) patience awhile.—*Coriol.*, i. 1.

Although before *the* SOLEMN *priest I have sworn* [the solemn priest I have solemnly sworn], I will not bed her.—*All's W.*, ii. 3.

Dismiss'd me thus, with his SPEECHLESS *hand* [hand waved in silence, hand signing to me without accompanying speech].—*Coriol.*, v. 1.

I wot not by what STRONG *escape* [escape effected by strength], he broke from those that had the guard of him.—*Com. of E.*, v. 1.

Whose death 's, indeed, the *strongest* [strongest probability, most probable] in our censure.—*Per.*, ii. 4.

The better arm you to the SUDDEN *time* [time of sudden changes that will take place in affairs after the king's death].—*John*, v. 6.

Are there not men in your ward *sufficient* [of sufficient capacity, sufficingly competent] to serve it ? . . . . the names of some six or seven, the most *sufficient* of your parish.—*M. for M.*, ii. 1.

My meaning, in saying he is a good man, is to have you understand me, that he is *sufficient* [sufficiently competent to pay, sufficient in money credit] . . . the man is, notwithstanding, *sufficient.*—*Mer. of V.*, i. 3.

You 'll never meet a more *sufficient* [competent, well-qualified] man.—*Oth.*, iii. 4.

Is this the noble Moor whom our full senate call all-in-all *sufficient* [of complete excellence, completely qualified] ?—*Ibid.*, iv. 1.

With sunken rock and *sumless* [not to be summed, that cannot be computed] treasuries.—*H. V.*, i. 2.

Let the *superfluous* [endowed with superfluity, possessed of superabundance] and lust-dieted man.—*Lear*, iv. 1.

That he can hither come so soon,
Is by your fancy's *thankful* [thankfully received] boon.—*Per.*, v. 2 (*Gower*).

All my treasury is yet but UNFELT *thanks* [thanks not felt in any effect by those to whom the thanks are paid, instead of not felt by him who mentions them].—*R. II.*, ii. 3.

Beshrew the witch ! with VENOMOUS *wights* [persons who deal in nocturnal magic, those who secretly concoct poison] she stays as tediously as hell.—*Tr. & Cr.*, iv. 2.

Yet here she is allowed her VIRGIN *crants* [garlands, chaplets, coronals, or wreaths customary for a virgin], her MAIDEN *strewments* [flower-strewings usual for a maiden's grave], and the bringing home of bell and burial.—*Hamlet*, v. 1.

Oppress'd with two WEAK *evils* [evils causing weakness], age and hunger.—*As You L.*, ii. 7.

Is my lord well, that he doth speak so *wide* [of the truth, as well as of delicacy and propriety]?—*M. Ado.*, iv. 1.

No, no; no such matter; you are *wide* [of the truth, of the mark]: come, your disposer is sick.—*Tr. & Cr.*, iii. 1.

Still, still, far *wide* [of rationality, of his senses].—*Lear*, iv. 7.

Pyrrhus at Priam drives; in rage, strikes *wide* [of his mark].—*Hamlet*, ii. 2.

And with those hands, that grasp'd the heaviest club, subdue *my* WORTHIEST *self* [myself, worthiest of destruction].—*Ant. & C.*, iv. 10.

Several of the above-cited elliptically used words have been suspected of error by previous commentators, because Shakespeare's peculiar style in this particular has not been sufficiently discerned; but we think the number of passages we have here brought together, demonstrating his frequent practice of thus employing words, will suffice to confirm future commentators in the correctness of many expressions supposed to have been misprinted. While on the subject of our poet's elliptically used adjectives, we take occasion to remark upon the numerous choicely expressive epithets, containing largely inclusive meaning as well as vivid significance, that he uses; of which the following are but a few:—

Bind fast his *corky* [dry, rigid; like the bark of a cork-tree] arms.—*Lear*, iii. 7.

> Not all these, laid in bed majestical,
> Can sleep so soundly as the wretched slave,
> Who, with a body fill'd, and vacant mind,
> Gets him to rest cramm'd with DISTRESSFUL *bread*,

[the bread of distress, the food of penury and misery, sorry fare; as well as bread distressfully earned].—*H. V.*, iv. 1.

> We need no grave to sweeten honesty:
> There's not a grain of it the face to sweeten
> Of the whole *dungy* [foul, rank-smelling] earth.—*W. T.*, ii. 1.

> Kingdoms are clay: our *dungy* [gross, material] earth alike
> Feeds beast as man.—*Ant. & C.*, i. 1.

Ned, pr'ythee, come out of that *fat* [fulsome with reeking hogsheads of beer, with coarse men and women, and with the frequent presence of unctuous Sir John Falstaff] room.—*1 H. IV.*, ii. 4.

And thou, *fresh* piece of excellent witchcraft . . . kisses the hands of your *fresh* princess [this epithet, twice applied to Perdita, serves to set her before us in her clear complexioned, clear-souled purity and brightness; with the bloom of a country maiden's cheek and the white temples of the born princess].—*W. T.*, iv. 3.

> But man, proud man,
> Dress'd in a little brief authority—
> Most ignorant of what he's most assured,
> His *glassy* essence

[that essential nature of man which is like glass from its faculty to reflect the image of others in its own, and from its fragility and liability to injury or destruction].—*M. for M.*, ii. 2.

A *glooming* [besides the effect of gloomy and sad, this word gives the sense of lowering, overcast by the heavens] peace this morning with it brings.—*R. & Jul.*, v. 3.

A good *lenten* [used in reference to the season of Lent, when fasting and abstinence are observed, this word implies meagre, spare, dry, stinted; in reference to the clown's answer it implies not only brief, but scant and bare of wit, precisely what the saucy Maria intends to convey] answer: I can tell thee.—*Tw. N.*, i. 5.

For if the French be lords of this *loud* [a monosyllable of four letters, thus used by a master-poet, sets before our imagination the uproar of battle—the drums and tramplings and trumpetings and shoutings and groanings of an engagement] day, he means to recompense.—*John*, v. 4.

Peace is a very apoplexy, lethargy; *mulled* [suggesting the idea of softness and drowsy quality; as that of wine warmed, spiced, and sweetened] deaf, sleepy, insensible.—*Coriol.*, iv. 5.

How doth that *royal* [this epithet, thus appended, conveys the idea not only of noble, illustrious, exalted; it arouses recollection of those magnates of commerce, those princes of the mercantile world—such as our own Sir Thomas Gresham, whose popular title was "the royal merchant"—for whom Italy in her Venice and Genoa, England in her London and Liverpool, have been famous] merchant, good Antonio?—*Mer. of V.*, iii. 2.

Your son was misled with a snipt-taffeta fellow there, whose villanous saffron would have made all the *unbaked* and *doughy* [besides indicating the raw and pasty character of idle young fellows, these epithets include reference to the practice of putting "saffron" into pastry; and thus morally as well as personally complete the metaphor, by implying that Parolles leavened his associates with his vices and imbued their nature with the ugly colour of his own, after inducing them to adopt his absurd fashions in attire] youth of a nation in his colour.—*All's W.*, iv. 5.

A *whitely* [the very epithet for Biron to use, when—unwilling to allow Rosaline to be *fair*—he involuntarily expresses the effect of a brilliant complexion looking almost white—certainly, dazzling—in contrast with her black eyebrows, eyelashes, and hair] wanton with a velvet brow, with two pitch-balls stuck in her face for eyes.—*Love's L. L.*, iii. 1.

Shakespeare uses a few adverbs elliptically:—

Hark! the drums *demurely* [with the solemnly measured beat, the gravely regulated sound that summons sleeping soldiers to wake and prepare themselves for a second day's fighting after a first that has just before been described "as a shrewd one to us"] wake the sleepers.—*Ant. & C.*, iv. 9.

That thou commend it *strangely* [as a stranger, as an alien born] to some place, where chance.—*W. T.*, ii. 3.

So thou the garland wear'st *successively* [by right of succession].—*2 H. IV.*, iv. 4.

He uses many verbs elliptically:—

Unless my sins ABUSE *my divination* [cause* me to be abused, or deceived, in my divination. See "brav'd," "disdain," "dumbs," "laming," "pines," "think," here cited].—*Cym.*, iv. 2.

Let us *address* [ourselves] to tend on Hector's heels.—*Tr. & Cr.*, iv. 4.

Call thyself sister, for I *aim* [at] thee.—*Com. of E.*, iii. 2.

Virtue, and that part of philosophy
Will I *apply* [my mind to], that treats of happiness.—*Tam. of S.*, i. 1.

One of our order, to *associate* [with] me.—*R. & Jul.*, v. 2.

He should have *brav'd* [caused to be brave or glorious] the east an hour ago.—*R. III.*, v. 3.

The most opportune place, the strong'st suggestion our worser genius *can†* [make, or present to us].—*Temp.*, iv. 1.

For what, alas, *can* [do, effect, avail] these my single arms?—*Tr. & Cr.*, ii. 2.

I've seen myself, and serv'd against, the French,
And they *can* [do] well on horseback.—*Hamlet*, iv. 7.

---

* In Shakespeare's time several verbs were used with the words "cause to" or "cause to be" elliptically understood. In Chapman's Homer's "Hymn to Apollo," we find:—
"And made the sea-trod ship *arrive them* [cause them to arrive] near the grapeful Crissa."

† This word was sometimes used by the old writers with the elliptical force of 'can do'; and Chaucer even uses "could" for 'could do' or 'knew well how to do': "It followed well she *coulde* good." This is line 524 of "The Book of the Duchess," or "Dream of Chaucer," in Charles Cowden Clarke's "RICHES OF CHAUCER."

What *can* [do, effect, avail] man's wisdom in the restoring his bereaved sense ?—
Lear, iv. 4.

> And when
> With wild wood-leaves and weeds I have strew'd his grave,
> And on it said a century of prayers,
> Such as I *can* [am able to do], twice o'er, I 'll weep.—*Cym.*, iv. 2.

He shall be interr'd, as soldiers *can* [are able to do].—*Ibid.*, iv. 2.

> Let the priest in surplice white,
> That defunctive music *can* [is able to perform],
> Be the death-divining swan,
> Lest the requiem lack his right.—*Phœnix & Turtle, Stanza* 4.

What a full fortune does the thick-lips owe,
If he can *carry 't* [away, off, or through. *See* IDIOMS for other instances of " carry "
used elliptically] thus !—*Oth.*, i. 1.

> Your prattling nurse
> Into a rapture lets her baby cry
> While she *chats* him [over : gossips about him].—*Coriol.*, ii. 1.

The reverent care I bear unto my lord
Made me *collect* [collectively perceive to exist] these dangers in the duke.—
2 *H. VI.*, iii. 1.

Ajax shall *cope* [with] the best.—*Tr. & Cr.*, ii. 3.

> Yet am I noble as the adversary
> I come to *cope* [withal].—*Lear*, v. 3.

Which might *deprive* [you of] your sovereignty of reason.—*Hamlet*, i. 5.

> Wherefore should I
> Stand in the plague of custom, and permit
> The curiosity of nations to *deprive* me [of inheritance].—*Lear*, i. 2.

That longer you *desire* the court [should delay its proceedings].—*H. VIII.*, ii. 4.

I will *discharge* [the debt to] thee ere I go.—*Com. of E.*, iv. 4.

She did DISDAIN *my child* [cause my child to be disdained], and stood between her
and her fortunes.—*Per.*, iv. 4.

Deep clerks she *dumbs* [causes to be silent, or to remain as if dumb] ; and with her
neeld composes.—*Ibid.*, v. (*Gower*).

A good leg will *fall* [away; shrink, dwindle] ; a straight back will stoop ; a black
beard will turn white.—*H. V.*, v. 2.

And makes Diana's rangers FALSE *themselves* [be false to themselves, play themselves false], yield up their deer to.—*Cym.*, ii. 3.

Go : I 'll *hold* [to my engagement, keep my appointment].—*M. W.*, v. 1.

To be thus *jaded* [treated as jades] by a piece of scarlet.—*H. VIII.*, iii. 2.

The ne'er-yet-beaten horse of Parthia
We have *jaded* [driven like jades] out o' the field.—*Ant. & C.*, iii. 1.

For feature, *laming* [causing to seem lame or deformed in comparison] the shrine of
Venus.—*Cym.*, v. 5.

You bade me ban, and will you bid me *leave* [off ; cease, desist] ?—2 *H. VI.*, iii. 2.

Here, there, and every where, he *leaves* [them dead] and takes.—*Tr. & Cr.*, v. 5.

As common as the stairs *that* MOUNT *the Capitol* [by which the Capitol is mounted].
—*Cym.*, i. 7.

Whose influence if now I court not, but *omit* [to court], my fortunes will ever after
droop.—*Temp.*, i. 2.

Therefore OMIT *him not* [omit not to propitiate him] ; blunt not his love, nor lose
the good.—2 *H. IV.*, iv. 4.

To see great Pompey *pass* [through, or along] the streets of Rome.—*Jul. C.*, i. 1.

Though well we may not *pass* [judgment, or sentence] upon his life without the
form of justice.—*Lear*, iii. 7.

The jury, *passing* [judgment, or sentence] on the prisoner's life, may in the sworn twelve have a thief or two . . . what know the laws that thieves do *pass* on thieves? —*M. for M.*, ii. 1.

Disturb him not, let him *pass* [away; die] peacefully.—*2 H. VI.*, iii. 3.

Thus might he *pass* [away; expire, die], indeed: yet he revives.—*Lear*, iv. 6.

When the thunder would not [hold its] *peace* at my bidding.—*Ibid.*, iv. 6.

Where shivering cold and sickness PINES *the clime* [render the climate such as to cause pining away or languishing].—*R. II.*, v. 1.

What unaccustomed cause PROCURES *her* [presence] hither?—*R. & Jul.*, iii. 5.

So we were *quit* [from; free from, away from] here.—*H. V.*, iv. 1.

Takes no account how things go from him; nor RESUMES * *no care* [takes no recapitulatory care, no summing-up care] of what is to continue.—*Timon*, ii. 2.

RETURN *them* [answer; give them notice in return], we are ready; and our daughter.—*Per.*, ii. 2.

Or we are Romans, and will give you that
Like beasts, which you shun beastly, and may
Save [yourselves from] but to look back in frown.—*Cym.*, v. 3.

Since last we *saw* [each other] in France.—*H. VIII.*, i. 1.

When shall we *see* [each other] again?—*Tr. & Cr.*, iv. 4.

Oh, the gods! when shall we *see* [each other] again?—*Cym.*, i. 2.

To Ely House to *see* [to] this business.—*R. II.*, ii. 1.

We'll not commend what we intend to *sell* [dearly].—*Tr. & Cr.*, iv. 1.

Thou may'st not coldly *set* [a rate upon; estimate, reckon, value] our sovereign process.—*Hamlet*, iv. 4.

It SIGNS *well* [is a good sign; it augurs well] does it not?—*Ant. & C.*, iv. 3.

I'll SILENCE *me e'en here* [I'll silently station myself even here]. Pray you, be round with him.—*Hamlet*, iii. 4.

Sit, gods, upon your thrones, *and smile* [derisively, in derision] at Troy!— *Tr. & Cr.*, v. 11.

Showing, we would not *spare* Heaven [spare Heaven our offence, refrain from offending Heaven. *See* VARIED MEANINGS, &c., for a sentence where Shakespeare uses "spare" with much inclusive force] as we love it, but as we stand in fear.—*M. for M.*, ii. 3.

Than to *suffer* the flesh-fly [to] blow my mouth.—*Temp.*, iii. 1.

That would *suffer* her poor knight [to be] surprised.—*All's W.*, i. 3.

What! will you not *suffer* me [to strike her]? Nay.—*Tam. of S.*, ii. 1.

Now 'tis the spring, and weeds are shallow-rooted;
Suffer them now [to remain undisturbed], and they'll o'ergrow the garden.— 2 *H. VI.*, iii. 1.

My duty cannot *suffer* [me] to obey in all.—*Lear*, iii. 4.

With patience more than savages could *suffer* [with].—*Ant. & C.*, i. 4.

I see men's judgments are
A parcel of their fortunes; and things outward
Do draw the inward quality after them,
To *suffer* [abatement, diminution, deterioration, or declension] all alike.—*Ibid.*, iii. 11.

First let them try themselves. So did your son;
He was *so* SUFFER'D [suffer'd to do so]: so came I.—*2 H. IV.*, ii. 3.

Lest, being *suffer'd* [to remain] in that harmful slumber.—*2 H. VI.*, iii. 2.

Who, being SUFFER'D *with* [to remain within reach of] the bear's fell paw.—*Ibid.*, v. 1.

A little fire is quickly trodden out;
Which, being *suffer'd* [to remain unextinguished], rivers cannot quench.— 3 *H. VI.*, iv. 8.

If anything that's civil, speak; if savage,
Take [payment for what I need] or *lend* [it me from kindliness].—*Cym.*, iii. 6.

---

* It appears to us that Shakespeare here uses the verb "resumes" with a meaning similar to the one in which the French employ their word "résumé," as signifying 'recapitulation,' 'summary,' or 'summing-up.'

You shall enjoy them—everything set off
That might so much as THINK *you* [cause you to be thought] enemies.—*2 H.IV.*, iv. 1.

Marcius, 'tis true that you have lately *told* [foretold, predicted to] us.—*Coriol.*, i. 1.

For I have ever *verified* [affirmed the excellence of, averred the merit of] my friends (of whom he's chief).—*Ibid.*, v. 2.

Upon which better part our prayers come in,
If thou VOUCHSAFE *them* [vouchsafe to accept them on the conditions stated].—*John*, iii. 1.

Vouchsafe [to accept] my labour, and long live your lordship!—*Timon*, i. 1.

Vouchsafe [to accept or receive] good morrow from a feeble tongue.—*Jul. C.*, ii. 1.

But say, this *weed* [out] her love from Valentine.—*Two G. of V.*, iii. 2.

To *weed* [out] my vice, and let his grow.—*M. for M.*, iii. 2.

To *weed* [out] this wormwood from your fruitful brain.—*Love's L. L.*, v. 2.

Shakespeare has used several participles elliptically:—

I am as *well* ACQUAINTED [well off for acquaintances] here as I was in our house of profession.—*M. for M.*, iv. 3.

But your favour is well *appeared* [made to appear; manifested, shown, denoted] by your tongue.—*Coriol.*, iv. 3.

If you are *arm'd* [with moral strength] to do, as sworn to do.—*Love's L. L.*, i. 1.

And am [morally] *arm'd* to suffer, with a quietness of spirit.—*Mer. of V.*, iv. 1.

But little: I am [morally] *arm'd* and well prepar'd.—*Ibid.*, iv. i.

Glad am I that your highness is so [morally] *arm'd*
To bear the tidings of calamity.—*R. II.*, iii. 2.

The quality of mercy . . . is *twice* BLESSED [doubly endowed with the power of blessing]—it blesseth him that gives, and him that takes.—*Mer. of V.*, iv. 1.

Ere the bat hath flown his CLOISTER'D *flight* [flight which is taken round and round through cloisters].—*Macb.*, iii. 2.

When he *compact* [for 'compacted'; joined in a compact with him], and flattering his displeasure.—*Lear*, ii. 2.

And what says *my* CONCEAL'D *lady* [my lady, whose being mine, together with our marriage which made her mine, is concealed from the world] to our cancell'd love.—*R. & Jul.*, iii. 3.

That, unless a man were *cursed* [under a curse], I.—*Tr. & Cr.*, v. 3.

That, sons at perfect age, and fathers *declin'd* [in age], the father should be as ward to the son.—*Lear*, i. 2.

And answer me *declin'd* [in age and power], sword against sword, ourselves alone.—*Ant. & C.*, iii. 11.

Hath drawn him from *his own* DETERMINED *aid* [that aid which he himself had determined to lend].—*John*, ii. 2.

I pray you see *him presently* DISCHARG'D [that my debt to him be immediately discharged].—*Com. of E.*, iv. 1.

Would *we were all* DISCHARG'D [that all the debts owing to us were discharged].—*Timon*, ii. 2.

Because *we'll be* DRESSED [have our wounds dressed] together.—*Tw. N.*, v. 1.

Let's go see poor *Cassio* DRESS'D [Cassio's wounds dressed].—*Oth.*, v. 1.

Leak'd is our barque;
And we, poor mates, stand on the DYING *deck* [deck crowded with men expecting death] hearing the.—*Timon*, iv. 2.

When you were more *endear'd* [dearly pledged, engaged by more dear motives] to it than now.—*2 H. IV.*, ii. 3.

The *fated* [fate-ordaining.] sky gives us free scope.—*All's W.*, i. 1.

Thus ornament is but the *guiled* [full of guile, beguiling] shore to a most dangerous sea.—*Mer. of V.*, iii. 2.

Or like a creature native and *indu'd* [endowed with qualities that fitted her, gifted with powers that qualified her] unto that element.—*Hamlet*, iv. 7.

Must not be shed by such *a* JADED *groom* [a groom fit only to wait upon jades, or wretched horses].—2 *H. VI.*, iv. 1.

He is gracious, if he be *observ'd* [treated with due observance].—2 *H. IV.*, iv. 4.

Before the primest creature that's *paragon'd* [cited as a paragon] o' the world.—*H. VIII.*, ii. 4.

That man—*how dearly ever* PARTED [however favourably endowed with good parts, however well gifted].—*Tr. & Cr.*, iii. 3.

Prayers from PRESERVED *souls* [souls preserved from mundane temptations], from fasting maids.—*M. for M.*, ii. 2.

Things of like value, differing in the owners, are PRIZED *by their masters* [are rated according to the esteem in which their possessor is held].—*Timon*, i. 1.

Where ladies shall be frighted, and, gladly *quak'd* [caused to quake, made to tremble], hear more.—*Coriol.*, i. 9.

The base o' the mount is RANK'D *with all deserts* [occupied by ranks of men of various degrees in merit], all kind of.—*Timon*, i. 1.

With Tarquin's RAVISHING *strides* [strides of a ravisher], towards his design moves like a ghost.—*Macb.*, ii. 1.

Yet, by *reputing* [spreading the reputation] of his high descent.—2 *H. VI.*, iii. 1.

Best you *saf'd* [safely conveyed] the bringer out of the host.—*Ant. & C.*, iv. 6.

Thy tooth is not so keen, because thou art not *seen* [to be an unnatural injustice and cruelty, as "man's ingratitude" is].—*As You L.*, ii. 7 (*Song*).

Wounding SUPPOSED *peace* [peace supposed to exist, peace not really subsisting]: all these bold fears.—2 *H. IV.*, iv. 4.

My THRICE-DRIVEN *bed of down* [bed made of feathers which have been driven by a fan, to separate the downier portions from the coarser portions].—*Oth.*, i. 3.

Sixth part of each? A TREMBLING *contribution!* [contribution that may well cause trembling].—*H. VIII.*, i. 2.

The TWINN'D *stones* [stones as like one another as twins] upon the NUMBER'D *beach* [beach composed of numbers]?—*Cym.*, i. 7.

And leave itself *unfurnish'd* [unsupplied with the other eye—its fellow, its companion, its partner. In our poet's time, "unfurnished" was used to signify 'unmatched,' unprovided with that which forms the pair].—*Mer. of V.*, iii. 2.

All by the name of dogs: *the* VALU'D *file* [the file or list where dogs valuable for particular qualities are entered: including also the meaning of the file in which dogs have their several qualities valued, described, and specially stated: thus using the word "valu'd" so as to combine its senses of 'esteemed' and 'estimated'] distinguishes the swift, the slow, the subtle.—*Macb.*, iii. 1.

Whereon th' imperious flood hath left *a* WITNESS'D *usurpation* [traces that bear witness to its usurpation].—2 *H. IV.*, i. 1.

So rare a *wonder'd* [wondrously gifted] father and a wife, make this place Paradise.—*Temp.*, iv. 1.

More longing, wavering, sooner lost and *worn* [away or out] than women's are.—*Tw. N.*, ii. 4.

These few days' wonder will be quickly *worn* [out; passed away, effaced, obliterated].—2 *H. VI.*, ii. 4.

The imminent decay of WRESTED *pomp* [pomp that has been wrested from its rightful owner].—*John*, iv. 3.

And Shakespeare sometimes uses pronouns elliptically [*See* RE-LATIVELY USED PRONOUNS]:—

A gift that Heaven gives *for* HIM [for his behoof, for his advantage], which buys a place next.—*H. VIII.*, i. 1.

It doth much content me to hear *him* [that he is] so inclin'd.—*Hamlet*, iii. 1.

He does deny him, *in respect of* HIS [as respects his own fortune, in proportion to that which he himself possesses], what charitable men afford to beggars.—*Timon*, iii. 2.

Say, Voltimand, *what* [news] from our brother Norway ?—*Hamlet*, ii. 2.

I met a courier, one mine ancient friend ;
Whom [between whom and myself], though in general part we were opposed,
Yet our old love made a particular force,
And made us speak like friends.—*Timon*, v. 2.

Shakespeare sometimes employs the word " along " elliptically :—

Bear not *along* [with thee] the clogging burden.—*R. II.*, i. 3.

I 'll entreat you written to bear *along* [with you].—*All's W.*, iii. 2.

He brings the mayor *along* [with him].—*R. III.*, iii. 5.

Will you *along* [with us] ?—*Coriol.*, ii. 3.

Speak the word *along* [the ranks].—*Jul. C.*, iv. 2.

Gallus, go you *along* [with him].—*Ant. & C.*, v. 1.

He uses the word " for " with large elliptical force :—

Yet here they shall not lie *for* [fear of] catching cold.—*Two G. of V.*, i. 2.

For [fear of] going on death's net.—*Per.*, i. 1.

For [fear of] blunting the fine point of seldom pleasure.—*Sonnet* 52.

The duke cannot deny the course of law,
For [the sake of] the commodity that strangers have
With us in Venice.—*Mer. of V.*, iii. 3.

I know no personal cause to spurn at him,
But *for* [the sake of] the general.—*Jul. C.*, ii. 1.

Patience, good sir, even *for* [the sake of] this charge.—*Per.*, iii. 1.

Am starv'd *for* [want of] meat.—*Tam. of S.*, iv. 3.

A nursery to our gentry, who are sick
For [want of] breathing and exploit.—*All's W.*, i. 2.

All out of work, and cold *for* [want of] action.—*H. V.*, i. 2.

Who, almost dead *for* [want of] breath.—*Macb.*, i. 5.

To prepare the ways you have *for* [procuring] dignities.—*H. VIII.*, iii. 2.

That I should purchase the day before *for* [the amount of] a little part, and undo a great deal of honour !—*Timon*, iii. 2.

Would half my wealth would buy this *for* [the amount of] a lie !—*Coriol.*, iv. 6.

Men did ransom lives of me [in repayment] *for* jests.—*Ant. & C.*, iii. 11.

So bad a prayer as his was never yet [a precursor] *for* sleep.—*Ibid.*, iv. 9.

One way or other, she is [fit] *for* a king.—3 *H. VI.*, iii. 2.

A hilding [fit] *for* a livery.—*Cym.*, ii. 3.

Bring in our daughter, clothed like a bride,
[Fit] *For* the embracements even of Jove himself.—*Per.*, i. 1.

More of thee merited than a band of Clotens
Had ever scar *for* [entitling them to claim].—*Cym.*, v. 5.

He also occasionally uses " from " elliptically :—

She [coming, or, on our way] *from* whom we all were sea-swallowed, though some cast again.—*Temp.*, ii. 1.

I have, sir, as I was commanded [by the messenger who came] *from* you, spoke with the king.—*All's W.*, ii. 5.

Orsino, this is that Antonio
That took the Phœnix and her fraught [coming, or, on her way] *from* Candy.—*Tw. N.*, v. 1.

The king is coming; and I must speak with him [coming, or, on my way] *from* the pridge.—*H. V.*, iii. 6.

The seven-fold shield of Ajax cannot keep [in]
The battery [proceeding, or, that comes] *from* my heart.   Oh, cleave my sides !
Heart, once be stronger than thy continent,
Crack thy frail case.—*Ant. & C.*, iv. 12.

He liv'd [free] *from* all attainder of suspect.—*R. III.*, iii. 5.

Will this hold, think you ?—Signior Iachimo will not [withdraw, or, retract] *from* it.—*Cym.*, i. 5.

The noise is round about us.—Let us [withdraw, or, move away] *from* it.—*Ibid.*, iv. 4.

[Go, or, be away] *From* me awhile.—*Ant. & C.*, iv. 12.

In the following two passages " no " is used with elliptical force :—

How might she tongue me!   Yet reason dares her *no.*—*M. for M.*, iv. 4.

" Dares her no " implying ' bids her not dare to do it.'

How tastes it ? is it bitter ? forty pence, *no.*—*H. VIII.*, ii. 3.

" Forty pence, no " implying ' I 'll wager forty pence that it is not.'
Shakespeare occasionally uses the word "none" with much elliptical
force of effect, and with such inclusive signification that some commentators have either missed his meaning, or proposed alteration in the
phrases wherein it occurs.   For instance, the phrase in the first of the
two following passages has been explained to mean ' none else would
be so simple ' ; whereas, we think, if the context be duly considered,
our interpretation will be found to be the right one :—

For, without you were so simple, *none else would* [no one would perceive these love-
tokens in you but myself].—*Two G. of V.*, ii. 1.

Some rise by sin, and some by virtue fall :
Some run from brakes of vice, and *answer none* [' without having to answer for any
vicious courses '] ;
And some condemned for a fault alone.—*M. for M.*, ii. 1.

EMPHASIS.

There are several passages in Shakespeare's plays where a word must
be emphasised in order to develop the full meaning of the sentence.
He, as a writer for the stage and a thorough master of declamation,
knew the effect produced by this, and the force therein contained ; and
consequently his practice should be borne in mind for the due comprehension of certain phrases, such as the following :—

Will 't hold ? will 't hold ?—It *does :* but time will—and so—I do conceive.—
Timon, iii. 6.

> We 'll consecrate the steps that Ajax makes
> When they go *from* Achilles.—*Tr. & Cr.*, ii. 3.
> They know your grace hath cause and means and might :
> So *hath* your highness ; never king of England
> Had nobles richer and more loyal subjects.—*H. V.*, i. 2.
> *Her* love is not the hare that I do hunt.—*As You L.*, iv. 3.
> Put up thy gold : go on—*here 's* gold—go on.—*Timon*, iv. 3.
> Go, counsellor ;
> Thou and my bosom henceforth shall be twain.
> I 'll to the friar, to know *his* remedy.—*R. & Jul.*, iii. 5.

O, stand up bless'd!
Whilst, with no softer cushion than the flint,
I kneel before *thee ;* and unproperly
Show duty, as mistaken all this while
Between the child and parent.—*Coriol,* v. 3.
　　　　　　　　　　　　　Dost thou think
I 'll grace thee with that robbery, thy stol'n name
Coriolanus in Corioli ?—*Ibid.,* v. 5.
Am *I* like such a fellow ?—*R. & Jul.,* iii. 1.
Thou canst not say *I* did it.—*Macb.,* iii. 4.

In the above line, as in some others, Shakespeare has actually emphasised a monosyllable where the rhythmical accent does not, strictly speaking, lie ; thus producing doubly impressive effect.

Why with some *little* train, my lord of Buckingham ?—*R. III.,* ii. 2
Nay, but hear me.—Nay but hear *me.—W. T.,* iv. 3.
What, art thou angry, Pandarus ? what, with *me ?—Tr. & Cr.,* i. 1.
What, with *me* too, Thersites ?—*Ibid.,* ii. 1.

Who 's there ?—
Nay, answer *me :* stand, and unfold yourself.—*Hamlet,* i. 1.

Oh, will you eat no grapes, my royal fox ?
Yes, but you will, *my* noble grapes, an if
My royal fox could reach them.—*All's W.,* ii. 1.

Now, Jove, in his next commodity of hair send thee a beard!—By my troth, I 'll tell thee—I am almost sick for one; though I would not have it grow on *my* chin.—*Tw. N.,* iii. 1.

Look to your babe, my lord ; 'tis yours :— . . .
My child ? away with 't !—*W. T.,* ii. 3.

Thou say'st the king grows mad ; I 'll tell thee, friend,
I am almost mad myself: I had a son,
Now outlaw'd from my blood; he sought my life . . .
The grief hath craz'd *my* wits.—*Lear,* iii. 4.

You know me by my habit.—Well, then, I know thee ; what shall I know *of* thee ?—My master's mind.—*H. V.,* iii. 6.
　　　　　　　　　　　　Unto bad causes swear
Such creatures as men doubt: but do not stain
The even virtue of *our* enterprise.—*Jul. C.,* ii. 1.

Say, if thou 'dst rather hear it from *our* mouths,
Or from our masters' ?—*Macb.,* iv. 1.

Shall we see this wrestling, cousin ?—*As You L.,* i. 2.

Mark Antony *shall* say I am not well ;
And, for thy humour, I *will* stay at home.
Here 's Decius Brutus, *he* shall tell them so.—*Jul. C.,* ii. 2.

Be bright and jovial among your guests to-night.—
So *shall* I, love ; and so, I pray, be *you.—Macb.,* iii. 2.

He that will give good words to *thee,* will flatter
Beneath abhorring.—*Coriol.,* i. 1.

I sell *thee* poison, thou hast sold me none.—*R. & Jul.,* v. 1.

Howbeit they would hold up this salique law
To bar your highness claiming from the female ;
And rather choose to hide them in a net,
Than amply to imbar *their* crooked titles
Usurp'd from you and your progenitors.—*H. V.,* i. 2.

Why should I play the Roman fool, and die
On mine own sword ?　Whiles I see lives, the gashes
Do better upon *them.—Macb.,* v. 7.

There are verier knaves desire to live, for all he be a Roman : and there be some of *them* too, that die against their wills; so should I, if I were one.—*Cym.*, v. 4.

I 'll graff it with you, and then I shall graff it with a medlar: *then* it will be the earliest fruit i' the country.—*As You L.*, iii. 2.

And oft 'tis seen, the wicked prize itself
Buys out the law : but 'tis not so above ;
There is no shuffling,—*there* the action lies
In his true nature.—*Hamlet*, iii. 3.

I shall, king Harry : and so, fare thee well:
Thou never shalt hear herald any more.—
I fear, *thou 'lt* once more come again for ransom.—*H. V.*, iv. 3.

Thy half o' the kingdom hast *thou* not forgot,
Wherein I thee endow'd.—*Lear*, ii. 4.

Nor none of thee, thou pale and common drudge
'Tween man and man ; but thou, thou meagre lead,
Which rather threatenest than dost promise aught,
Thy paleness moves me more than eloquence. —*Mer. of V.*, iii. 2.

With a true heart
And brother-love I do it.—
And let Heaven
Witness, how dear I hold this confirmation.—
Good man, those joyful tears show *thy* true heart.—*H. VIII.*, v. 2.

Was 't you that did so oft contrive to kill him ?—
'*Twas* I ; but '*tis* not I : I do not shame
To tell you what I was, since my conversion
So sweetly tastes, being the thing I am.—*As You L.*, iv. 3.

How many be there of them ?—Some eight, or ten.—
Zounds ! will they not rob *us ?*—1 *H. IV.*, ii. 2.

What is the matter,
That being pass'd for consul with full voice,
I am so dishonour'd that the very hour
You take it off again ?—
Answer to *us.*—*Coriol.*, iii. 3.

The thane of Cawdor lives : why do you dress me
In borrow'd robes ?—
Who *was* the thane, lives yet ;
But under heavy judgment bears that life
Which he deserves to lose.—*Macb.*, i. 3.

This *was* your husband : look you now, what follows:
Here *is* your husband.—*Hamlet*, iii. 4.

And he 's as like to do 't as any man I can imagine.—
Do 't ! he *will* do 't.—*Coriol.*, iv. 5.

Why, Sir John, do you think, though we would have thrust virtue out of our hearts by the head and shoulders, and have given ourselves without scruple to hell, that ever the devil could have made *you* our delight ?—*Merry W.*, v. 5.

No, I 'll none of *you.*—Why, my sweet lord ?—You 'll kiss me hard, and speak to me as if I were a baby still. I love *you* better.—*W. T.*, ii. 1.

There 's for *you*, Patroclus.—*Tr. & Cr.*, ii. 1.

Pray get you out.—Away !—Away ! Get *you* away.—*Coriol.*, iv. 5.

Welcome, Publius.
What ! Brutus, are *you* stirr'd so early too ?—*Jul. C.*, ii. 2.

His private arbours, and new-planted orchards,
On this side Tiber ; he hath left them *you*,
And to your heirs for ever.—*Ibid.*, iii. 2.

My lord, I have news to tell you.—
My lord, I have news to tell *you.*—*Hamlet*, ii. 2.

A great deal of *your* wit, too, lies in your sinews.—*Tr. & Cr.*, ii. 1.

Your good voice, sir; what say you?—*Coriol.*, ii. 3.

ENIGMATICAL PHRASEOLOGY,

Shakespeare sometimes makes his personages express themselves obscurely or ambiguously for the sake of characteristic effect. Into Helena's mouth he has put markedly veiled language; denoting the struggles of a secret passion to conceal itself, with the occasional irrepressible betrayals of its existence, taking the shape of enigmatical sentences and hinted meanings :—

Helena. I do affect a sorrow, indeed; but I have it too.—*All's W.*, i. 1.

While giving the effect of a reply to the Countess's reproof, these words really signify, 'I allow my sorrow to pass for regret at my father's death; but I have it really for my inauspicious love, and for Bertram's approaching departure.'

Helena. If the living be enemy to the grief, the excess makes it soon mortal [*See* CROSSING SPEECHES for our explanation of this speech].—*Ibid.*, i. 1.

> *Helena.* Not my virginity yet.
> There shall your master have a thousand loves,
> A mother, and a mistress, and a friend,
> A phœnix, captain, and an enemy,
> A guide, a goddess, and a sovereign,
> A counsellor, a traitress, and a dear;
> His humble ambition, proud humility,
> His jarring concord, and his discord dulcet,
> His faith, his sweet disaster; with a world
> Of pretty, fond, adoptious christendoms,
> That blinking Cupid gossips. Now shall he—
> I know not what he shall :—God send him well !—
> The court's a learning-place; and he is one—
> *Parolles.* What one, i' faith?
> *Helena.* That I wish well.—*Ibid.*, i. 1.

By her words "the court's a learning-place" Helena implies that the word "*there*" at the commencement of her riddle-like speech, refers to "the court"; whereas we believe her word "there" signifies, her own maiden self dedicated in fulness of affection to him she loves, even though he should never accept the gift.

> *Countess.* What's the matter,
> That this distemper'd messenger of wet,
> The many-colour'd Iris, rounds thine eye?
> Why—that you are my daughter?
> *Helena.* That I am not.—*Ibid.*, i. 3.

By these four monosyllables Helena, while seeming to regret that she is only the Countess's daughter by affection, really deplores that she is not her daughter by marriage with her son.

> *Helena.* Why, then, to-night
> Let us assay our plot; which, if it speed,
> Is wicked meaning in a lawful deed,
> And lawful meaning in a lawful act;
> Where both not sin, and yet a sinful fact.—*Ibid.*, iii. 7.

Helena thus, with characteristically enigmatic words, declares that her husband intending wickedly will act lawfully; that she will intend lawfully and act lawfully; and that they both will commit no sin, while seeming to do so. At a subsequent point of the play, Helena again uses characteristically veiled language, delicate in expression, yet fervid in feeling and imagination [*See* SOLILOQUIES for the passage commencing " But, O, strange men "] ; and there is another instance cited under the same heading [*See* SOLILOQUIES for the passage commencing " Affection ! thy intention stabs the centre"] which contains example of our poet's peculiar power of writing forcible meaning in the most shrouded language.

> *Duke.* Thou dost speak masterly :
> My life upon 't, young though thou art, thine eye
> Hath stay'd upon some favour that it loves ;—
> Hath it not, boy ?
> *Viola.* A little, by your favour.—*Tw. N.*, ii. 4.

This reply, seemingly signifying ' a little, by your leave,' hiddenly expresses ' I have suffered mine eye to rest upon your own countenance (or " favour ") at moments when your not perceiving me has favoured my looking upon you.'

> *Duke.* But died thy sister of her love, my boy ?
> *Viola.* I am all the daughters of my father's house,
> And all the brothers too ; and yet I know not.—*Ibid.*, ii. 4.

Here the gentle girl-page answers so as to convey the effect of her averring that there are no female survivors in her family, and that she has no brother living, while she really owns herself to be the only daughter of her father and disclaims being his son.

> *Olivia.* Stay : I pr'ythee, tell me what thou think'st of me.
> *Viola.* That you do think you are not what you are.
> *Olivia.* If I think so, I think the same of you.
> *Viola.* Then think you right : I am not what I am.
> *Olivia.* I would you were as I would have you be !
> *Viola.* Would it be better, madam, than I am,
> I wish it might ; for now I am your fool. . . .
> By innocence I swear, and by my youth,
> I have one heart, one bosom, and one truth—
> And that no woman has ; nor never none
> Shall mistress be of it, save I alone.—*Ibid.*, iii. 1

In the whole of this dialogue, Viola charmingly reveals to us, who are in her secret, her womanhood, while she merely seems, to Olivia, confessing her inability to return the lady's avowed preference.

> *Portia.* I pray you, tarry : pause a day or two
> Before you hazard ; for, in choosing wrong,
> I lose your company : therefore, forbear awhile.
> There 's something tells me (but it is not love),
> I would not lose you ; and you know yourself,
> Hate counsels not in such a quality.
> But lest you should not understand me well
> (And yet a maiden hath no tongue but thought),
> I would detain you here some month or two,
> Before you venture for me.   I could teach you
> How to choose right, but then I am forsworn ;
> So will I never be : so may you miss me ;
> But if you do, you 'll make me wish a sin,
> That I had been forsworn.   Beshrew your eyes,
> They have o'erlook'd me, and divided me ;
> One half of me is yours, the other half yours—

> Mine own, I would say ; but if mine, then yours,
> And so all yours !   O, these naughty times
> Put bars between the owners and their rights !
> And so, though yours, not yours.—*Mer. of V.*, iii. 2.

Bewitchingly true is this speech to womanly nature in its grace and archness: disclaiming love, yet letting love be seen in every phrase of playful riddling half-confession.

> *Lady Capulet.* Evermore weeping for your cousin's death ? . . .
> *Juliet.* Yet let me weep for such a feeling loss.
> *Lady Capulet.* So shall you feel the loss, but not the friend
> Which you weep for.
> *Juliet.*   Feeling so the loss,
> I cannot choose but ever weep the friend.
> *Lady Capulet.* Well, girl, thou weep'st not so much for his death,
> As that the villain lives which slaughter'd him.
> *Juliet.* What villain, madam ?
> *Lady Capulet.*   That same villain, Romeo.
> *Juliet.* Villain and he be many miles asunder.
> God pardon him ! I do, with all my heart ;
> And yet no man, like he, doth grieve my heart.
> *Lady Capulet.* That is, because the traitor murderer lives.
> *Juliet.* Ay, madam, from the reach of these my hands :
> Would none but I might venge my cousin's death !
> *Lady Capulet.* We will have vengeance for it, fear thou not :
> Then weep no more.   I 'll send one to Mantua —
> Where that same banish'd runagate doth live—
> Shall give him such an unaccustom'd dram,
> That he shall soon keep Tybalt company :
> And then, I hope, thou wilt be satisfied.
> *Juliet.* Indeed, I never shall be satisfied
> With Romeo, till I behold him—dead—
> Is my poor heart so for a kinsman vex'd :
> Madam, if you could find out but a man
> To bear a poison, I would temper it ;
> That Romeo should, upon receipt thereof,
> Soon sleep in quiet.   O, how my heart abhors
> To hear him nam'd—and cannot come to him,
> To wreak the love I bore my cousin Tybalt
> Upon his body that hath slaughter'd him !—*R. & Jul.*, iii. 5.

These shifts and evasions of speech are ·precisely such as a young Italian girl, brought up in fear of her parents rather than in loving confidence with them, would instinctively use, when pressed to desperation by a passion of love and grief.

> *Fool.* For you trow, nuncle,
> The hedge-sparrow fed the cuckoo so long,
> That it had its head bit off by its young.
> So out went the candle, and we were left darkling.—*Lear*, i. 4.

> *Fool.* Winter 's not gone yet, if the wild geese fly that way.
>   Fathers that wear rags
>   Do make their children blind ;
>   But fathers that bear bags
>   Shall see their children kind.
>   Fortune, that arrant whore,
>   Ne'er turns the key to the poor.

But, for all this, thou shalt have as many dolours for thy daughter as thou canst tell in a year.—*Ibid.*, ii. 4.

Fool.—We 'll set thee to school to an ant, to teach thee there's no labouring i' the winter. All that follow their noses are led by their eyes, but blind men ; and there 's not a nose among twenty but can smell him that's stinking. Let go thy hold when a great wheel runs down a hill, lest it break thy neck with following it ; but the great one that goes up the hill, let him draw thee after. When a wise man gives thee better counsel, give me mine again : I would have none but knaves follow it, since a fool gives it.

> That sir which serves and seeks for gain,
>   And follows but for form,
> Will pack when it begins to rain,
>   And leave thee in the storm.
> But I will tarry; the fool will stay,
>   And let the wise man fly :
> The knave turns fool that runs away ;
>   The fool no knave, perdy.—*Lear*, ii. 4.

By such scraps of figuratively enigmatic sarcasm and worldly-wise precept, Lear's Fool marks his sense of his old master's ill-usage. In the last of the three above-cited passages, the line "the knave turns fool that runs away" has been thought erroneous by some commentators ; who propose that "knave" and "fool" should be transposed. But we think that Shakespeare, in his own noble philosophy, here affirms that the cunning rogue who deserts his benefactor in the time of reverse, from motives of prudence, shows himself fool as well as knave—moral miscalculator as well as moral coward.

Occasionally, for the sake of characteristic effect, Shakespeare gives purposely confused or obscure diction [*See* PECULIAR CONSTRUCTION] :—

> *Edmund.* In wisdom, I should ask thy name ;
> But, since thy outside looks so fair and warlike,
> And that thy tongue some 'say of breeding breathes,
> What safe and nicely I might well delay
> By rule of knighthood, I disdain and spurn :
> Back do I toss these treasons to thy head ;
> With the hell-hated lie o'erwhelm thy heart ;
> Which—for they yet glance by, and scarcely bruise—
> This sword of mine shall give them instant way,
> Where they shall rest for ever.—*Ibid.*, v. 3.

The above speech is worded in just that incoherent manner which would characterise a man enraged at finding himself denounced as a villain, and conscious that he is one ; while the following speech is couched in exactly such inexplicit terms, such half-expressed, half-suppressed suggestions, as serve to whet his hearer's desire to hear more :—

> *Iago.*   I do beseech you—
> Though I perchance am vicious in my guess,
> As, I confess, it is my nature's plague
> To spy into abuses, and oft my jealousy
> Shapes faults that are not—that your wisdom yet,
> From one that so imperfectly conceits,
> Would take no notice ; nor build yourself a trouble
> Out of his scattering and unsure observance.
> It were not for your quiet nor your good,
> Nor for my manhood, honesty, or wisdom,
> To let you know my thoughts.—*Oth.*, iii. 3.

A remarkable instance of a speech overlaid with confusing casuistical intervolvments and specious argumentation, for the purpose of sophistically perplexing the mind of the person addressed, is cited at

full under our heading of REPEATED WORDS.   It is the speech beginning
thus :—

> So mak'st thou faith an enemy to faith ; &c.—*John*, iii. 1.

Shakespeare puts a riddling speech of purposedly obscure expression
into the Danish prince's mouth, where he is seeking to puzzle and
mislead the two courtierly spies, Rosencrantz and Guildenstern :—

> *Rosencrantz.* My lord, you must tell us where the body is, and go with us to the king.
> *Hamlet.* The body is with the king, but the king is not with the body.   The king is
> a thing—
> *Guildenstern.* A thing, my lord !
> *Hamlet.* Of nothing : bring me to him.—*Hamlet*, iv. 2.

Our interpretation of the above riddle is—'Materiality and corporeal
grossness characterise the king ; but the king has no real or virtuous
substance, no genuine matter in him : he is a thing of naught, a mere
worthless nonentity.'

> Here come I from my princely general
> To know your griefs; to tell you from his grace,
> That he will give you audience ; and wherein
> It shall appear that your demands are just,
> You shall enjoy them—everything set off
> That might so much as think you enemies.—2 *H. IV.*, iv. 1.

The concluding phrase of the last-cited speech is so ambiguously
expressed as to bear several interpretations; therein precisely serving
the purpose of the speaker.   It may mean 'everything set apart, cast
out, thrown forth, acquitted, excluded, or excepted, that might so much
as cause you to be thought enemies'; or may mean, 'everything counterbalanced, rendered account for, or yielded retribution for, that might so
much as cause you to be thought enemies.'

> *Romeo. Alas ! that love, whose view is muffled still,*
> *Should, without eyes, see pathways to his will !*
> Where shall we dine?   Oh, me !   What fray was here?
> Yet tell me not, for I have heard it all.
> *Here's much to do with hate, but more with love.*—*R. & Jul.*, i. 1.

The two sentences we have italicised in the above-quoted passage
are spoken by Romeo in enigmatical fashion, according to his then
mood.   The first sentence comprises double meaning; and signifies not
only, 'Alas! that the blind god should be able to shoot so surely!' but
also, 'Alas! that love, notwithstanding its muffled sight, should be
able blindfold to find its way to its object!'

The second sentence also includes two meanings; that the fray has
much to do with the hate between the rival houses, yet affects him
more, inasmuch as his Rosaline is a member of the Capulet family;*
and likewise that while the fray exhibits the animosity which divides
the two factions, it at the same time denotes the anxious affection felt
on his account by his father and by his friend Benvolio.

> *Antony.* You do mistake your business; my brother never
> Did urge me in his act; I did inquire it;
> And have my learning from some true reports,
> That drew their swords with you.   Did he not rather
> Discredit my authority with yours;

---

* This point is traceable from the list of guests invited to Capulet's ball.

> And make the wars alike against my stomach,
> Having alike your cause? Of this my letters
> Before did satisfy you. If you'll patch a quarrel,
> As matter whole you have to make it with,
> It must not be with this.—*Ant. & C.,* ii. 2.

The concluding sentence means, 'If you wish to botch up a quarrel, as you have whole and sound matter to make it good with, you must not use such flimsy stuff as this.' The speaker purposely uses equivocal phraseology here; Antony allowing Cæsar to understand either. 'If you desire to pick a quarrel with me, you could find stronger ground for basing it upon than these frivolous causes of complaint,' or, 'If you wish to make up the quarrel between us, you have better means of doing so than by ripping up these trivial grievances.'

Justice, and your father's wrath, should he take me in his dominion, could not be so cruel to me, as you, oh, the dearest of creatures, would even renew me with your eyes. —*Cym.,* iii. 2 (*Letter*).

The phraseology of this sentence is purposely obscure and enigmatical, and conveys a double idea. One is intended by the writer of the letter to be obvious to the person addressed—his wife ; ' could not so cruelly wound but that the sight of you could cure and revive me ! ' the other is perceptible to the reader of the play ; 'could not be so cruel to me as you have been ' [in the supposed wrong that Imogen has done Posthumus].

In the last-cited passage, and in the one from " Romeo and Juliet," where the heroine says, "I never shall be satisfied with Romeo, till I behold him—dead—is my poor heart," &c., there are instances of ambiguous or duplicate meaning given to a sentence by peculiar or wrong punctuation ; so in the following passage, a similar effect is similarly produced :—

> *Prologue.* If we offend, it is with our good will.
> That you should think, we come not to offend,
> But with good will. To show our simple skill,
> That is the true beginning of our end.
> Consider, then, we come but in despite.
> We do not come as minding to content you,
> Our true intent is. All for your delight,
> We are not here. That you should here repent you,
> The actors are at hand; and, by their show,
> You shall know all, that you are like to know.—*Mid. N. D.,* v. 1.

In the following passage, Shakespeare has given us a specimen of a speech, humorously obscure and confused ; where the speaker gets bewildered and entangled in an attempt at lucid explanation :—

Bardolph. Sir, pardon ; a soldier is better accommodated than with a wife.

Shallow. It is well said, in faith, sir ; and it is well said indeed too. Better accommodated ! it is good ; yea, indeed is it : good phrases are surely, and ever were, very commendable. Accommodated ! it comes of *accommodo :* very good ; a good phrase.

Bardolph. Pardon me, sir ; I have heard the word. Phrase, call you it ? By this good day, I know not the phrase ; but I will maintain the word with my sword to be a soldierlike word, and a word of exceeding good command, by heaven. Accommodated ; that is, when a man is, as they say, accommodated ; or, when a man is—being— whereby—he may be thought to be accommodated ; which is an excellent thing.— 2 *H. IV.,* iii. 2.

FAMILIAR AND HOMELY EXPRESSIONS.

In many passages, Shakespeare uses words and phrases of the most simple description; so much so, that they have been denounced as too plain, too common, too undignified for the demands of poetic diction: but we think that in every case where objection has been thus taken, the word or phrase which our poet has employed, will be found, upon due examination and reflection, to have peculiar fitness; either by reason of its appropriate simplicity, its characteristic effect, or its dramatic purpose—all of which render it, in its way, poetical:—

Be of good cheer, youth: you a man? you lack a man's heart.—I do so, I confess it. Ah! sirrah, *a body* would think this was well counterfeited: I pray you, tell your brother how well I counterfeited. Heigh-ho!—*As You L.*, iv. 3.

Nor heaven peep through the *blanket* of the dark,
To cry, "Hold, hold!"—*Macb.*, i. 5.

Your commendations, madam, get from her tears.—
'Tis the best *brine* a maiden can *season* her praise in.—*All's W.*, i. 1.

Jesu Maria, what a deal of *brine*
Hath wash'd thy sallow cheeks for Rosaline!
How much salt water thrown away in waste,
To *season* love, that of it doth not taste!—-*R. & Jul.*, ii. 3.

But for our gentlemen,
The common file (a plague! tribunes for them!),
The mouse ne'er shunn'd the cat as they did *budge*
From rascals worse than they.—*Coriol.*, i. 6.

He that's coming
Must be provided for: and you shall put
This night's great *business* into my despatch.—*Macb.*, i. 5.

We will proceed no farther in this *business.*—*Ibid.*, i. 7.

Masking the *business* from the common eye,
For sundry weighty reasons.—*Ibid.*, iii. 1.

Here burns my *candle* out—ay, here it dies,
Which, whiles it lasted, gave king Henry light.—3 *H. VI.*, ii. 6.

Out, out, brief *candle!*
Life's but a walking shadow.—*Macb.*, v. 5.

For, by these blessed *candles* of the night.—*Mer. of V.*, v. 1.

Night's *candles* are burnt out, and jocund day
Stands tiptoe on the misty mountain-tops.—*R. & Jul.*, iii. 5.

There's husbandry in heaven,
Their *candles* are all out.—*Macb.*, ii. 1.

Full thirty times hath Phœbus' cart* gone round
Neptune's salt wash and Tellus' orbed ground.—*Hamlet*, iii. 2.

Thou hast never in thy life
Show'd thy dear mother any courtesy;
When she (poor hen), fond of no second brood,
Has *cluck'd* thee to the wars, and safely home,
Loaden with honour.—*Coriol.*, v. 3.

Is this a dagger which I see before me,
The handle toward my hand? Come, let me *clutch* thee:
I have thee not, and yet I see thee still.—*Macb.*, ii. 1.

What! will the line stretch out to the *crack* of doom?—*Ibid.*, iv. 1.

I say, O Cæsar, Antony is dead.—
The breaking of so great a thing should make

---

* "Cart" was formerly sometimes used for 'car' or 'chariot.'

> A greater *crack :* the round world
> Should have shook lions into civil streets,
> And citizens to their dens.—*Ant. & C.,* v. 1.

> The fire, and *cracks*
> Of sulphurous roaring, the most mighty Neptune
> Seem to besiege, and make his bold waves tremble,
> Yea, his dread trident shake.—*Temp.,* i. 2.

> If I say sooth, I must report they were
> As cannons overcharg'd with double *cracks.*—*Macb.,* i. 2.

> Confederates
> (So *dry* he was for sway) with the King of Naples
> To give him annual tribute, do him homage.—*Temp.,* i. 2.

> But I remember, when the fight was done,
> When I was *dry* with rage and extreme toil,
> Breathless and faint, leaning upon my sword,
> Came there a certain lord, neat, trimly dress'd
> Fresh as a bridegroom.—1 *H. IV.,* i. 3.

> Visit by night your lady's chamber-window
> With some sweet consort; to their instruments
> Tune a deploring *dump ;** the night's dead silence
> Will well become such sweet complaining grievance.—*Two G. of V.,* iii. 2.

> Come, thick night,
> And pall thee in the *dunnest* smoke of hell.—*Macb.,* i. 5.

" Dunnest " has been stigmatised as a *mean* epithet ; to our thinking it is full of poetic truth and impressiveness, conveying the effect of darkest and grimmest colour.

> To-morrow, and to-morrow, and to-morrow,
> Creeps in this petty pace from day to day,
> To the last syllable of recorded time;
> And all our yesterdays have lighted fools
> The way to *dusty* death.—*Ibid.,* v. 5.

> Before he should thus stoop to the herd, but that
> The violent *fit o' the time* craves it as physic
> For the whole estate, I would put mine armour on,
> Which I can scarcely bear.—*Coriol.,* iii. 2.

> But, for your husband,
> He is noble, wise, judicious, and best knows
> The *fits o' the season.*—*Macb.,* iv. 2.

> Cold, cold, my *girl!*
> Even like thy chastity.—*Oth.,* v. 2.

> Who would fardels bear,
> To *grunt* and *sweat* under a weary life.—*Hamlet,* iii. 1.

Hark, in thine ear : change places ; and, *handy-dandy*, which is the justice, which is the thief?—*Lear,* iv. 6.

His incensement at this moment is so implacable, that satisfaction can be none but by pangs of death and sepulchre : *hob, nob,* is his word ; give 't or take 't.—*Tw. N.,* iii. 4.

Losses, that have of late so *huddled* on his back.—*Mer. of V.,* iv. 1.

Huddling jest upon jest, with such impossible conveyance upon me.—*M. Ado,* ii. 1.

> The people muddied,
> Thick and unwholesome in their thoughts and whispers,
> For good Polonius' death ; and we have done but greenly,
> In *hugger-mugger* to inter him.—*Hamlet,* iv. 5.

That skull had a tongue in it, and could sing once: how the knave *jowls* it to the ground, as if it were Cain's jaw-bone, that did the first murder.—*Ibid.,* v. 1.

---

* Originally a grave term for a melancholy strain or ditty.

'Twixt my extremes and me this bloody *knife*
Shall play the umpire.—*R. & Jul.*, iv. 1.

Come thick night,
And pall thee in the dunnest smoke of hell,
That my keen *knife* see not the wound it makes.—*Macb.*, i. 5.

By the clock, 'tis day,
And yet dark night strangles the travelling *lamp*.—*Ibid.*, ii. 4.

He fishes, drinks, and wastes
The *lamps* of night in revel.—*Ant. & C.*, i. 4.

Let the great gods,
That keep this dreadful *pother* o'er our heads,
Find out their enemies now.—*Lear*, iii. 2.

Something, sure, of state,—
Either from Venice, or some unhatch'd practice
Made demonstrable here in Cyprus to him,—
Hath *puddled* his clear spirit.—*Oth.*, iii. 4.

O, from Italy!
*Ram** thou thy fruitful tidings in mine ears,
That long time have been barren.—*Ant. & C.*, ii. 4.

Since God so graciously hath brought to light
This dangerous treason, lurking in our way
To hinder our beginnings, we doubt not now
But every *rub* is smoothed on our way.—*H. V.*, ii. 2.

To die,—to sleep;—
To sleep! perchance to dream;—ay, there's the *rub*.—*Hamlet*, iii. 1.

Madam, we'll play at bowls—
'Twill make me think the world is full of *rubs*,
And that my fortune runs against the bias.—*R. II.*, iii. 4.

His captain's heart,
Which in the *scuffles* of great fights hath burst
The buckles on his breast.—*Ant. & C.*, i. 1.

Will you *shog* off? I would have you solus.—*H. V.*, ii. 1.

Shall we *shog?* the king will be gone from Southampton.—*Ibid.*, ii. 3.

Slubber not business for my sake, Bassanio.—*Mer of V.*, ii. 8.

You must therefore be content to *slubber* the gloss of your new fortunes with this more stubborn and boisterous expedition.—*Oth.*, i. 3.

Why, that's my bawcock. What, hast *smutch'd* thy nose?
They say, it is a copy out of mine.—*W. T.*,.i. 2.

His faults, in him, seem as the *spots* of heaven,
More fiery by night's blackness.—*Ant. & C.*, i. 4.

For I can here disarm thee with this *stick*,
And make thy weapon drop.—*Temp.*, i. 2.

Nature wants *stuff*
To vie strange forms with fancy; yet, to imagine
An Antony, were nature's piece 'gainst fancy,
Condemning shadows quite.—*Ant. & C.*, v. 2

I'do not think
So fair an outward, and such *stuff* within,
Endows a man but he.—*Cym.*, i. 1.

And with some sweet oblivious antidote
Cleanse the *stuff'd* bosom of that perilous *stuff*
Which weighs upon the heart.—*Macb.*, v. 3.

---

* "Ram" was objected to by Ritson, in this passage, as "a *vulgar* word"; and he proposed to substitute 'rain.' But "ram" is a strong and forcible word; just the word for Cleopatra to use; and therefore Shakespeare put it most characteristically into her mouth.

Steevens proposed to change " stuff'd " here to ' foul,' saying that the ear " must be shocked by the recurrence of so harsh a word." But we know that Shakespeare frequently gave repetitions of similar words in the same sentence [*See* REPEATED WORDS]; and as for its being a harsh word, see how Shakespeare uses " stuff" and " stuff'd " in the passages here collectively cited, where he evidently considers them expressive epithets, and nowise harsh or wanting in poetic dignity. See, too, how he uses " stuff'd " for physical oppression, where he makes Beatrice say:—

> I am *stuff'd*, cousin, I cannot smell.—*M. Ado*, iii. 4.

To our thinking, the very iteration of " stuff'd" and " stuff" in the present line, serves to give it the effect of stifling over-burdened sensation which it describes.

> I have despatch'd in post
> To sacred Delphos, to Apollo's temple,
> Cleomenes and Dion, whom you know
> Of *stuff'd* sufficiency.— *W. T.*, ii. 1.

> So noble a master fall'n ! All gone ! and not
> One friend to *take his fortune by the arm*,
> And go along with him.—*Timon*, iv. 2.

> I will to Venice ; Sunday comes apace :
> We will have rings, and *things*, and fine array.—*Tam. of S.*, ii. 1.

> And now, my honey love,
> Will we return unto thy father's house,
> And revel it as bravely as the best,
> With silken coats, and caps, and golden rings,
> With ruffs, and cuffs, and farthingales, and *things ;*
> With scarfs, and fans, and double change of bravery,
> With amber bracelets, beads, and all this knavery.—*Ibid.*, iv. 3.

Johnson pronounces "things," in this last passage, to be "a poor word"; adding, "perhaps the author had not another that would rhyme." Without dwelling upon the absurdity of fancying Shakespeare at a loss for a rhyming word, we think that the one he uses in both the above-cited passages a thoroughly apt term. It is put into Petruchio's mouth as a sarcastic employment of the word much favoured by the female sex when talking rapturously of inexpressibly charming finery, which they are in the habit of summing up as "lovely *things*." In the same spirit of sarcasm, Petruchio immediately after uses the word "knavery," to imply the trumpery, frippery, and trickery of ornament.

> Admir'd Miranda !
> Indeed, the *top* of admiration ; worth
> What 's dearest to the world !—*Temp.*, iii. 1.

> How would you be,
> If He, which is the *top* of judgment, should
> But judge you as you are ?—*M. for M.*, ii. 2.

> This shower, blown up by tempest of the soul,
> Startles mine eyes, and makes me more amaz'd
> Than had I seen the vaulty *top* of heaven
> Figur'd quite o'er with burning meteors.—*John*, v. 2.

> What is this,
> That rises like the issue of a king,
> And wears upon his baby brow the round
> And *top* of sovereignty ?—*Macb.*, iv. 1.

All the stor'd vengeances of Heaven fall
On her ingrateful *top !* strike her young bones,
You taking airs, with lameness!—*Lear*, ii. 4.

Didst thou but know the inly *touch* of love,
Thou wouldst as soon go kindle fire with snow,
As seek to quench the fire of love with words.—*Two G. of V.*, ii. 7.

This she delivered in the most bitter *touch* of sorrow
That e'er I heard virgin exclaim in.—*All's W.*, i. 3.

But I perceive in you so excellent a *touch* of modesty, that you will not extort from me what I am willing to keep in.—*Tw. N.*, ii. 1.

One *touch* of nature makes the whole world kin.—*Tr. & Cr.*, iii. 3.

　　　　　　　　　　He loves us not;
He wants the natural *touch ;* for the poor wren,
The most diminutive of birds, will fight,
Her young ones in the nest, against the owl.—*Macb.*, iv. 2.

I am senseless of your wrath ; a *touch* more rare
Subdues all pangs, all fears.—*Cym.*, i. 2.

　　　　　　　　　Thou 'lt come no more,
Never, never, never, never, never !
Pray you, *undo this button :*—thank you, sir.—*Lear*, v. 3.

Now, how dost thou look now ? O, ill-starr'd *wench !*
Pale as thy *smock !* when we shall meet at compt,
This look of thine will hurl my soul from heaven,
And fiends will snatch at it.—*Oth.*, v. 2.

If you will have it in showing, you shall read it in—*What do ye call* there.—*All's W.*, ii. 3.

Good even, good Master *What-do-ye-call't :* how do you, sir? You are very well met.—*As You L.*, iii. 3.

Madam, an hour before the worshipp'd sun
Peer'd forth the golden *window* of the east.—*R. & Jul.*, i. 1.

Then, Jupiter, thou king of gods . . .
Thy crystal *window* ope ; look out.—*Cym.*, v. 4.

In the following passages, Shakespeare uses " ne'er " and " never " in an idiom which, when he wrote, was thought merely a familiarism and no vulgarism, as it is at present :—

I 'll be damned for *never a king's son* in Christendom.—*1 H. IV.*, i. 2.
There is *ne'er a king* in Christendom could be better.—*Ibid.*, ii. 1.
I think there 's *never a man* in Christendom can.—*R. III.*, iii. 4.
There 's *ne'er a villain* dwelling in all Denmark.—*Hamlet*, i. 5.

HISTORIANS' PASSAGES ADOPTED.

Shakespeare, as the greatest of all dramatists, and especially as a writer of historical dramas, well knew the value of going directly to the historians' pages for details, and even of adopting from them actual portions best suited to his purpose. He was evidently a diligent reader of the old chronicles of his own country, and a careful studier of Sir Thomas North's translation of Plutarch ; for he has not only given the vivid colouring of verisimilitude which deriving from authentic sources imparts to dramatic and poetic composition, but he has, in many instances, taken absolute passages from these prose narrations, and put them into his own glowing verse diction. Some among the most noteworthy of these adopted passages and accurately introduced points we here collect to show with what judgment our author worked in this respect, as in so many others, to render his writings perfect in composition and style. The following are derived from Holinshed's " Chronicles ":—

> *Captain.* 'Tis thought the king is dead; we will not stay.
> *The bay-trees in our country all are wither'd,*
> And meteors fright the fixed stars of heaven ;
> The pale-fac'd moon looks bloody on the earth,
> And lean-look'd prophets whisper fearful change ;
> Rich men look sad, and ruffians dance and leap—
> The one in fear to lose what they enjoy,
> The other to enjoy by rage and war :
> These signs forerun the death or fall of kings.—*R. II.*, ii. 4.
>
> *Bolingbroke.* In God's name, I 'll ascend the regal throne.
> *Bishop of Carlisle.* Marry, God forbid !
> Worst in this royal presence may I speak,
> Yet best beseeming me to speak the truth.
> Would God, that any in this noble presence
> Were enough noble to be upright judge
> Of noble Richard ! &c.

[*See* the whole speech; which, with the incident that follows, of the bishop's arrest, is transcribed with faithful closeness from Holinshed's narration].—*Ibid.*, iv. 1.

> *Archbishop of York.* What is this forest call'd ?
> *Hastings.* 'Tis *Gaultree Forest,* an 't shall please your grace.—*2 H. IV.*, iv. 1.
>
> *King Henry IV.* Doth any name particular belong
> Unto the lodging where I first did swoon ?
> *Warwick.* 'Tis call'd *Jerusalem,* my noble lord.
> *King Henry.* Laud be to God ! even *there my life must end.*
> *It hath been prophesied to me many years,*
> *I should not die but in Jerusalem ;*
> Which vainly I suppos'd the Holy Land :
> But, bear me to that chamber ; *there I 'll lie ;*
> *In that Jerusalem shall Harry die.*—*Ibid.*, iv. 4.
>
> *King Henry V.* No! How might a prince of my great hopes forget
> So great indignities you laid upon me ?
> What ! *rate, rebuke,* and roughly *send to prison*
> *The immediate heir of England !* Was this easy ?
> May this be wash'd in Lethe, and forgotten ?
> *Chief Justice.* I then did use the person of your father ;
> The image of his power lay then in me :
> And, in the administration of his law,
> Whiles I was busy for the commonwealth,
> Your highness pleased to forget my place,
> The majesty and power of law and justice,
> The image of the king whom I presented,
> And *struck me in my very seat of judgement ;*
> *Whereon, as an offender to your father,*
> *I gave bold way to my authority,*
> *And did commit you, &c., &c.*—*Ibid.*, v. 2.
>
> *Archbishop of Canterbury.* My lord, I 'll tell you—*that self bill is urg'd,*
> *Which in the eleventh year of the last king's reign*
> *Was like, and had indeed against us pass'd,*
> But that the scambling and unquiet time
> Did push it out of farther question.
> *Bishop of Ely.* But how, my lord, shall we resist it now ?
> *Canterbury.* It must be thought on. If it pass against us,
> We lose the better half of our possession :
> For all the temporal lands, which men devout

By testament have given to the Church,
Would they strip from us; being valu'd thus,—
As much as would maintain, to the king's honour,
Full fifteen earls and fifteen hundred knights,
Six thousand and two hundred good esquires;
And, to relief of lazars and weak age,
Of indigent faint souls past corporal toil,
A hundred almshouses, right well supplied;
And to the coffers of the king beside,
A thousand pounds by the year: thus runs the bill.—*H. V.*, i. 1.

Canterbury. Then hear me, gracious sovereign, and you peers,
That owe yourselves, your lives, and services
To this imperial throne. *There is no bar*
To make against your highness' claim to France
But this, which they produce from Pharamond,—
In terram Salicam mulieres ne succedant,
"No woman shall succeed in Salique land;"
Which Salique land the French unjustly gloze
To be the realm of France, and Pharamond
The founder of this law and female bar.
Yet their own authors, &c., &c.—Ibid., i. 2.

Bedford. The king hath note of all that they intend,
By interception which they dream not of.
Exeter. Nay, but *the man that was his bedfellow,*
Whom he hath dull'd and cloy'd with gracious favours—
That he should, for a foreign purse, so sell
His sovereign's life to death and treachery!—*Ibid.,* ii. 2.

King Henry. Here, Fluellen; wear thou this favour for me, and stick it in thy cap *when Alençon and myself were down together,* I plucked this glove from his helm.—*Ibid.,* iv. 7.

King Henry. Do we all holy rites:
Let there be sung Non nobis and Te Deum;
The dead with charity enclos'd in clay:
And then to Calais; and to England then;
Where ne'er from France arriv'd more happy men.—*Ibid.,* iv. 8.

You may imagine him upon Blackheath;
Where that *his lords desire him to have borne*
His bruised helmet and his bended sword
Before him through the city: he forbids it,
Being free from vainness aud self-glorious pride;
Giving full trophy, signal, and ostent,
Quite from himself to God.—Ibid., v. (*Chorus*).

Cade. So, sirs: now go some and *pull down the Savoy*; others, to the inns of court; down with them all.
Dick. I have a suit unto your lordship.
Cade. Be it a lordship, thou shalt have it for that word.
Dick. Only *that the laws of England may come out of your mouth.* . . .
Cade. I have thought upon it, it shall be so. Away, burn all the records of the realm; *my mouth shall be the parliament of England.*—*2 H. VI.,* iv. 7.

In the above passage, two incidents recorded by Holinshed as occurring in Wat Tyler's rebellion are here made use of by the dramatist as taking place during Cade's insurrection.

Edward. Dazzle mine eyes, or do I see *three suns?*
Richard. Three glorious suns, each one a perfect sun;
Not separated with the racking clouds,
But sever'd in a pale clear-shining sky.
See, see! they join, embrace, and seem to kiss,
As if they vow'd some league inviolable:
Now are they but one lamp, one light, one sun.

Edward. 'Tis wondrous strange, the like yet never heard of.
I think it cites us, brother, to the field—
That we, the sons of brave Plantagenet,
Each one already blazing by our meeds,
Should, notwithstanding, join our lights together,
And overshine the earth, as this the world.
Whate'er it bodes, *henceforward will I bear*
Upon my target three fair shining suns.—3 *H. VI.,* ii. 1.

King Henry VI. My Lord of Somerset, what youth is that,
Of whom you seem to have so tender care?
Somerset. My liege, it is young Henry, Earl of Richmond.
King Henry. Come hither, England's hope.   [*Lays his hand on his head.*
                                          If secret powers
Suggest but truth to my divining thoughts,
This pretty lad will prove our country's bliss.
His looks are full of peaceful majesty;
His head by nature fram'd to wear a crown,
His hand to wield a sceptre; and himself
Likely in time to bless a regal throne.
Make much of him, my lords; for this is he
Must help you more than you are hurt by me.—*Ibid.,* iv. 7.

Buckingham. . . . Me seemeth good, that, with some little train,
Forthwith *from Ludlow* the young prince be fet
Hither to London, to be crown'd our king.—*R. III.,* ii. 2.

Buckingham. . . . For we to-morrow *hold divided councils,*
Wherein thyself shalt highly be employ'd.—*Ibid.,* iii. 1.

Messenger. . . . Besides, he says there are *two councils held;*
And that may be determin'd at the one
Which may make you and him to rue at th' other. . . .
Hastings. . . . Bid him not fear *the separated councils.* . . .
Stanley. . . . You may jest on, but, by the holy rood,
I do not like *these several councils,* I.—*Ibid.,* iii. 2.

Gloster. . . . My lord of Ely, when I was last in Holborn,
I saw good strawberries in your garden there:
I do beseech you send for some of them.—*Ibid.,* iii. 4.

Hastings. . . . *Three times to-day my foot-cloth horse did stumble,*
And started, when he look'd upon the Tower,
As loath to bear me to the slaughter-house.—*Ibid.,* iii. 4.

Buckingham. Will not King Richard let me speak with him?—*Ibid.,* v. 1.
Buckingham.   Every man,
After *the hideous storm that follow'd,* was
A thing inspir'd; and, not consulting, broke
Into a general prophecy—that this tempest,
Dashing the garment of this peace, aboded
The sudden breach on 't.—*H. VIII.,* i. 1.

Queen Katharine. Sir, I desire you, do me right and justice;
And to bestow your pity on me: for
I am a most poor woman, and a stranger,
Born out of your dominions, &c., &c. [See whole speech].—*Ibid.,* ii. 4.

Lady Macbeth. . . . When Duncan is asleep
(Whereto the rather shall his day's hard journey
Soundly invite him), *his two chamberlains*
Will I with wine and wassail so convince,
That memory, the warder of the brain,
Shall be a fume, and the receipt of reason
A limbeck only: when in swinish sleep
Their drenched natures lie as in a death,
What cannot you and I perform upon
Th' unguarded Duncan? *What not put upon*

His *spongy officers, who shall bear the guilt
Of our great quell?*—Macb., i. 7.

　Lennox. The night has been unruly : where we lay
Our *chimneys were blown down ;* and, as they say,
*Lamentings heard i' the air ; strange screams of death ;
And prophesying, with accents terrible,
Of dire combustion and confus'd events
New hatch'd to the woeful time : the obscure bird
Clamour'd the livelong night :* some say, *the earth
Was feverous and did shake.*—Ibid., ii. 3.

　Old Man. Threescore and ten I can remember well :
Within the volume of which time I have seen
Hours dreadful and things strange ; but *this sore night
Hath trifled former knowings.*
　Rosse.　　　　　　　　　　Ah, good father,
Thou seest the heavens, as troubled with man's act,
Threaten his bloody stage; *by the clock 'tis day,
And yet dark night strangles the travelling lamp :*
Is 't night's predominance, or the day's shame,
That *darkness does the face of earth entomb,
When living light should kiss it ?*
　Old Man.　　　　　　　　'Tis unnatural,
Even like the deed that's done.　On Tuesday last,
*A falcon, towering in her pride of place,
Was by a mousing owl hawk'd at and kill'd.*
　Rosse. And Duncan's *horses* (a thing most strange and certain),
Beauteous and swift, the minions of their race,
*Turn'd wild in nature, broke their stalls, flung out,
Contending 'gainst obedience, as they would make
War with mankind.*
　Old Man.　　　　　'Tis said *they eat each other.*
　Rosse. They did so—to the amazement of mine eyes,
That look'd upon 't.—Ibid., ii. 4.

The incident of the "two chamberlains" and the portents that
attended the regicidal deed, are recorded by the old chronicler as oc-
curing when King Duff was murdered ; but the dramatist ingeniously
employs these striking particulars as accompanying the midnight
assassination of King Duncan.

　Queen . . . The fam'd *Cassibelan, who was once at point—
Oh, giglot fortune !—to master Cæsar's sword,
Made Lud's town with rejoicing fires bright,
And Britons strut with courage.*—Cym., iii. 1.

The poet has here assigned to Cassibelan an exploit which, according
to the old chronicle, was achieved by his brother Nennius.

　Cym. . . . *Our ancestor was that Mulmutius which
Ordain'd our laws*—whose use the sword of Cæsar
Hath too much mangled ; whose repair and franchise
Shall, by the power we hold, be our good deed ;
Though Rome be therefore angry ; *Mulmutius made our laws,
Who was the first of Britain which did put
His brows within a golden crown, and call'd
Himself a king.*—Ibid., iii. 1.

　Cym.　　　　　　　　　　Thou art welcome, Caius.
*Thy Cæsar knighted me ; my youth I spent
Much under him ; of him I gather'd honour.*—Ibid., iii. 1.

　Posthumus. . . . *the king himself
Of his wings destitute, the army broken,*

> *And but the backs of Britons seen, all flying*
> *Through a strait lane, &c., &c.—Cym., v. 3.*

See the whole of this portion of the dialogue; which gives a spirited version of a description found in Holinshed's "History of Scotland," narrating the incident of the Roman army being stopped in a narrow lane by three persons, and stating that these three brave persons were the Hays, father and two sons. The dramatist avails himself of the historian's recorded event, by attributing it to three of the personages in his noble drama of "Cymbeline."

In his Roman plays, Shakespeare has drawn largely from the picturesque pages of Plutarch; transferring some of the eloquent passages therefrom almost verbatim into his own scenes, while giving them poetic form and colour:

> *Coriolanus. My name is Caius Marcius, who hath done*
> *To thee particularly, and to all the Volsces,*
> *Great hurt and mischief : thereto witness may*
> *My surname, Coriolanus: &c., &c.—Coriol., iv. 5.*
>
> *Volumnia. Should we be silent and not speak, our raiment*
> *And state of bodies would bewray what life*
> *We have led since thy exile, &c., &c.—Ibid., v. 3.*
>
> *Casca. A common slave* (you know him well by sight)
> *Held up his left hand, which did flame and burn*
> *Like twenty torches join'd ; and yet his hand,*
> *Not sensible of fire, remain'd unscorch'd, &c., &c.—Jul. C., i. 3.*
>
> *Cæsar. . . .* What say the augurers ?
> *Servant.* They would not have you to stir forth to-day.
> Plucking the entrails of an offering forth,
> *They could not find a heart within the beast.—Ibid., ii. 2.*

As an instance of our dramatist's skill in selecting, arranging, and appropriately adapting the materials he employed, it is to be observed that the ominous circumstances preceding the death of Cæsar, introduced by Shakespeare in act i., sc. 3, and the incident of the soothsayers finding no heart in the beast they sacrificed, introduced by Shakespeare in act ii., sc. 2, are recorded in one and the same passage by Plutarch.

> *Brutus. . . .* With this she fell distract,
> And, her attendants absent, *swallow'd fire.—Ibid., iv. 3.*
>
> *Cæsar.*   Antony,
> Leave thy lascivious wassails. *When thou once*
> *Wast beaten from Modena, where thou slew'st*
> *Hirtius and Pansa, consuls, at thy heel*
> *Did famine follow, &c., &c.—Ant. & C., i. 4.*
>
> *Mecænas. Eight wild boars roasted whole at a breakfast,* and but twelve persons
> there; is this true ?—*Ibid., ii. 2.*
>
> *Enobarbus.* I will tell you.
> *The barge she sat in, like a burnish'd throne,*
> *Burn'd on the water: &c., &c.—Ibid., ii. 2.*
>
> *Soothsayer.* Cæsar's.
> Therefore, O Antony, *stay not by his side :*
> *Thy demon—that thy spirit which keeps thee—is*
> *Noble, courageous, high, unmatchable,*
> *Where Cæsar's is not ; but, near him, thy angel*
> *Becomes a Fear, as being o'erpower'd : therefore·*
> *Make space enough between you.*

> *Antony.*   Speak this no more.
> *Soothsayer.* To none but thee ; no more, but when to thee.
> *If thou dost play with him at any game,*
> *Thou art sure to lose ; and, of that natural luck,*
> *He beats thee 'gainst the odds : thy lustre thickens,*
> *When he shines by :* I say again, *thy spirit*
> *Is all afraid to govern thee near him ;*
> *But, he away, 'tis noble.*
>   *Antony* . . . Be it art or hap,
> He hath spoken true : *the very dice obey him ;*
> *And, in our sports, my better cunning faints*
> *Under his chance : if we draw lots, he speeds ;*
> *His cocks do win the battle still of mine,*
> *When it is all to naught ; and his quails ever*
> *Beat mine, inhoop'd, at odds.*—*Ant. & C.,* ii. 3.

>   *Charmian.*   'Twas merry when
> You wager'd on your angling; *when your diver*
> *Did hang a salt-fish on his hook, which he*
> *With fervency drew up.*—*Ibid.,* ii. 5.

>   *Pompey.* Then so much have I heard :
> And I have heard : *Apollodorus carried* . . .
> *A certain queen to Cæsar in a mattress.*—*Ibid.,* ii. 5.

>   *Cæsar.* Contemning Rome, he has done all this, and more,
> In Alexandria : here 's the manner of it :—
> *I' the market-place, on a tribunal silver'd,*
> *Cleopatra and himself in chairs of gold*
> *Were publicly enthron'd : &c., &c.*—*Ibid.,* iii. 6.

We have selected the following passages as being among the many
that show his mode of employing historical truths, and moulding them
to dramatic purpose, and his admirable manner of taking merest hints
from original sources, while making them his own by judicious
adaptation, alteration, and improvement :—

>   *Arthur.* God shall forgive you Cœur-de-Lion's death
> The rather that you give his offspring life,
> Shadowing their right under your wings of war :
> I give you welcome with a powerless hand,
> But with a heart full of unstained love.—*John,* ii. 1.

Historic fact showed Prince Arthur to be older than the dramatist
represents him to be ; but Shakespeare knew that the pathos of the
story would be heightened by his making the boy a child of tender
years.

The poet found justification for his causing the boy to speak with a
grace and propriety seldom distinguishing children of his age from a
record made by Froissart in his " Chronicles "; where he describes the
conduct of the Princess of France, then " a yonge childe of eyght yere
of age."

>   *Groom.* I was a poor groom of thy stable, king,
> When thou wert king; who, travelling towards York,
> With much ado, at length have gotten leave
> To look upon my sometimes royal master's face.
> Oh, how it yearn'd my heart, when I beheld,
> In London streets, that coronation-day,
> When Bolingbroke road on roan Barbary !
> That horse that thou so often hast bestrid,
> That horse that I so carefully have dress'd !
>   *King Richard.* Rode he on Barbary ? &c., &c.—*R. II.,* v. 5.

Froissart relates an anecdote of a favorite greyhound that belonged to King Richard, and fawned upon him exclusively; till once, the dog left the King and leapt upon the Duke of Lancaster with the same shows of fondness that he formerly showed only to the King; a piece of canine fickleness that, it is said, struck Richard keenly. Probably it was this anecdote that suggested to Shakespeare the incident which he has so affectingly introduced, judiciously changing the animal from a dog to a horse.

> *Cassius.* Ha, ha! how vilely doth this cynic rhyme!—*Jul. C.,* iv. 3.

In North's Plutarch the intruder upon Brutus and Cassius is represented to be "a cynic philosopher;" but the dramatist, with appropriate effect, makes him one of those cynical professional rhymesters that used to follow the camp in ancient wars (such as Thersites in "Troilus and Cressida"), serving to amuse the idler hours of the leaders, to celebrate in doggrel their feats, and occasionally to administer biting sarcasms and rebukes.

> *Paulina.*   Sir, my liege,
> Your eye hath too much youth in't: not a month
> 'Fore your queen died, she was more worth such gazes
> Than what you look on now.
> *Leontes.*   I thought of her,
> Even in these looks I made.—*W. T.,* v. 1.

The conduct of the plot at this juncture of the story in the original source, whence Shakespeare derived the groundwork of his drama of "The Winter's Tale" (Robert Greene's novel of "Pandosto: the Triumph of Time"; afterwards entitled "The History of Dorastus and Fawnia"), is of so coarse a character, as to raise still higher our admiration of Shakespeare's exquisite treatment of the subject, by reason of his supreme tact and taste in adaptation.

> *First Gentleman.* But I much marvel that your lordship, having
> Rich tire about you, should at these early hours
> Shake off the golden slumber of repose.—*Per.,* iii. 2.

Instead of a physician, as in the original (the "Gesta Romanorum") Shakespeare makes Cerimon a nobleman who dedicates his wealth and leisure to the study of physic and to the relief of his suffering fellow-creatures; thereby reading the lesson of benevolent opulence and wisdom preferring a life of active utility to one of ease and self-indulgence.

> *Pericles.* . . . Didst thou not say, when I did push thee back,
> (Which was when I perceived thee), that thou cam'st
> From good descending?—*Ibid.,* v. 1.

The dramatist, with his usual sense of delicate propriety, makes the King put his daughter aside with a gesture of impatient rejection, instead of following the original; which describes Pericles as *striking* the unknown maiden when she first accosts him.

As evidence of the consummate skill with which Shakespeare invented characters from faintest indications, we would mention that his choice full-length picture of the "humorous patrician," Menenius Agrippa, had no more marked origin than a brief sentence in North's Plutarch, which relates that "The senate being afeard of their departure, did send unto them certaine of *the pleasantest old men*, and the most acceptable to the people among them. Of those Menenius Agrippa was he who was sent for chiefe man of the message from the senate. He, after many good perswasions and gentle requests made to the people on behalfe of the senate, knit up his oration in the end with a notable tale, in this manner: that on a time all the members of man's body did rebell against the belly, complaining of it," &c. Similarly the dramatist's fine portraiture of Domitius Enobarbus, with its spirited delineation and profoundly touching close, grew from these few lines in North's Plutarch:—" He dealt very friendly and courteously with Domitius, and against Cleopatra's mind. For he being sick of an ague when he went and tooke a little boate to go unto Cæsar's campe, Antonius was very sorie for it, but *yet he sent after him all his cariage, traine, and men:* and the same Domitius, *as though he gave him to understand that he repented his open treason, died immediately after.*"

Shakespeare has registered the names of certain historically mentioned brave men "in the bead-roll of eternal fame," by allusion to them in his chronicle-plays:—

> Where is the number of our English dead?—
> Edward the Duke of York, the Earl of Suffolk,
> Sir Richard Ketly, Davy Gam, Esquire.—*H. V.*, iv. 8.

> But get you to Smithfield, and gather head,
> And thither I will send you Matthew Gough.—*2 H. VI.*, iv. 5.

> Sir Walter Herbert, a renowned soldier;
> Sir Gilbert Talbot, Sir William Stanley;
> Oxford, redoubted Pembroke, Sir James Blunt,
> And Rice ap Thomas, with a valiant crew.—*R. III.*, iv. 5.

There are some inaccuracies found in Shakespeare that are attributable to the original sources whence he derived his historical plots or incidents [*See* ALLEGED ANACHRONISMS, &c.]:—

> Also King Lewis the Tenth [Ninth],
> Who was sole heir to the usurper Capet.—*H. V.*, i. 2.

IDIOMS.

Shakespeare, the most vigorous writer of English that ever set pen to paper, abounds in idiomatic phrases. He uses several idioms that were in use when he wrote, but which have either fallen into disuse or have become slightly modified in expression; and he uses others that are still in familiar use among us. He employs several idioms similar in sense, but variously worded; and several similarly worded idioms, but with various significations. It will be obvious that there is difficulty in classifying the examples collected under the present heading; and still more difficulty—nay, impossibility—in placing them alphabetically. The utmost that can be done is to collect, under the general denomination of IDIOMS, such phrases as are usually understood to rank as idiomatic expressions; and this we have done to the best of our power.

And bring them after *in the best advantage* ['in the most advantageous manner'].—*Oth.*, i. 3.

Yes, a dozen; and as many *to the vantage* ['over and above,' 'in addition to them '].—*Oth.*, iv. 3.

My fortunes every way as fairly rank'd (if not *with vantage*) ['additionally so,' 'more so'] as Demetrius'.—*Mid. N. D.*, i. 1.

Go, bid thy master well *advise himself* ['reflect,' 'consider'].—*H. V.*, iii. 6.

Have you nothing said upon his party 'gainst the duke of Albany? *Advise yourself* ['recollect yourself,' 'bethink yourself,' 'reflect,' 'consider'].—*Lear*, ii. 1.

You go *against the hair* ['against the grain,' 'contrary to the nature or quality'] of your professions.—*Merry W.*, ii. 3.

He is melancholy without cause, and merry *against the hair* ['contrary to the nature of mirth'].—*Tr. & Cr.*, i. 2.

Thou desirest me to stop in my tale *against the hair* ['contrary to the spirit of jesting'].—*R. & Jul.*, ii. 4.

Made you *against the grain* [the more usual idiom: 'contrary to your inclination'] to voice him consul.—*Coriol.*, ii. 3.

This is for all ['once for all,' 'I tell you this as your guidance for the future'].—*Hamlet*, i. 3.

And all the madness is ['what makes me feel more mad, or vexed, is'] he cheers them up too.—*Timon*, i. 2.

You are *such another!* ['such an extraordinary creature'].—*Tr. & Cr.*, i. 2.

The falcon *as the tercel* ['is as good as the tercel'].—*Ibid.*, iii. 2.

As who should say ['as one who should say'].—*R. II.*, v. 4.

That's *as much to say as* [old form of 'as much as to say'], I wear not motley in my brain.—*Tw. N.*, i. 5.

Which is *as much to say as*—let the magistrates.—*2 H. VI.*, iv. 2.

That's *as much as to say* [here Shakespeare uses the more usual form of this idiom] —Can she so? . . . That's *as much as to say*—bastard virtues.—*Two G. of V.*, iii. 1.

Say ['supposing'], this were death.—*Temp.*, i. 2.

Say, I do speak with her, my lord, what then?—*Tw. N.*, i. 4.

Say that some lady, as, perhaps, there is.—*Ibid.*, ii. 4.

Say that Marcius return me, as Cominius is return'd.—*Coriol.*, v. 1.

Why, *say*, they are vile and false.—*Oth.*, iii. 3.

Or, *say*, they strike us, or scant our former having.—*Ibid.*, iv. 3.

Say, this becomes him . . . yet must Antony.—*Ant. & C.*, i. 4.

Ha! *I have said* [similar to the Italian idiom, *Basta!* 'enough,' 'I say no more,' let it suffice'].   Be gone.—*Henry VIII.*, v. 1.

My wife kill'd too?—*I have said.*—Be comforted.—*Macb.*, iv. 3.

Give me particulars.—*I have said.*—*Ant. & C.*, i. 2.

Make me not offended in your distrust.—*I have said.*—*Ibid.*, iii. 2.

You have said ['you have had your say'], sir.—*Two G. of V.*, ii. 4.

You have said; but whether wisely or no, let the forest judge.—*As You L.*, iii. 2.

You have said, sir.   To see this age!   A sentence is but.—*Tw. N.*, iii. 1.

You have said, sir.   We looked not for Mark Antony here.—*Ant. & C.*, ii. 6.

I had rather chop this hand off *at a blow* ['at one single stroke'].—*3 H. VI.*, v. 1.

What fifty of my followers, *at a clap?* ['all at once,' 'suddenly'].—*Lear*, i. 4.

Ten masts *at each* ['each placed at the end of each'] make not the altitude.—*Ibid.*, iv. 6.

May worthy Troilus be half *attached with* ['possessed by,' 'seized with,' 'overpowered by'] that which here his passion doth express.—*Tr. & Cr.*, v. 2.

No, faith, die *by attorney* ['by deputy,' 'by proxy'].—*As You L.*, iv. 1.

I, *by attorney* ['as deputed by her'] bless thee from thy mother.—*R. III.*, v. 3.

And there *awake God's gentle-sleeping peace* ['arouse divine patience, and convert it into avenging wrath'].—*Ibid.*, i. 3.

In the mildness of your sleepy thoughts, which here we *waken* ['rouse into energy'] to our country's good.—*R. III.*, iii. 7.

We will not *wake your patience* ['rouse your patience, and convert it into wrath'].—*M. Ado*, v. 1.

If none, *awake your dangerous lenity* ['arouse your perilous forbearance, and convert it into more judicious severity'].—*Coriol.*, iii. 1.

And *extort a poor soul's patience* ['force a poor soul's patience into wrath'], all to make your sport.—*Mid. N. D.*, iii. 2.

She *never could away with me* ['never could bear me'].—Never, never; she would always say she *could not abide* ['could not endure'] Master Shallow.—*2 H. IV.*, iii. 2.

'A *could never abide* carnation.—*H. V.*, ii. 3.

Why he *cannot abide* a gaping pig.—*Mer. of V.*, iv. 1.

Nay, *I do bear a brain* ['I have my wits about me,' 'I have a good memory'].—*R. & Jul.*, i. 3.

O, there has been much *throwing about of brains* ['wit-contest,' 'sharp argument on both sides'].—*Hamlet*, ii. 2.

Cudgel thy brains ['puzzle thy wits'] no more about it.—*Ibid.*, v. 1.

And let us *knog our prains together* ['lay our heads together,' 'debate together'] to be revenge on this same.—*Merry W.*, iii. 1.

I see them *lay their heads together* ['consult together'], to surprise me.—*2 H. VI.*, iv. 8.

What! *Bear her in hand* ['beguile her on by false appearance of good-will'] until they come to take hands.—*M. Ado*, iv. 1.

I tell you, sir, *she bears me fair in hand* ['she gives me fair encouragement'].—*Tam. of S.*, iv. 2.

To *bear a gentleman in hand* ['lure a gentleman on with false expectation'], and then stand upon security!—*2 H. IV.*, i. 2.

Your daughter, whom she *bore in hand to love* ['beguiled under an appearance of love'] with such integrity.—*Cym.*, v. 5.

How you were *borne in hand* ['led on by false expectations'], how cross'd.—*Macb.*, iii. 1.

Was falsely *borne in hand* ['deluded, beguiled by pretexts'].—*Hamlet*, ii. 2.

Cæsar doth *bear me hard* ['bear a hard opinion of me,' 'bear me ill-will,' 'bear me a grudge'].—*Jul. C.*, i. 3.

Caius Ligarius doth *bear Cæsar hard.*—*Ibid.*, ii. 1.

I do beseech ye, if you *bear me hard.*—*Ibid.*, iii. 1.

To *bear a hard opinion* of his truth.—*Two G. of V.*, ii. 7.

As we'll direct her how 'tis best to *bear it* ['carry the matter,' 'conduct the affair'].—*All's W.*, iii. 7.

But *bear it* ['conduct yourselves,' 'demean yourselves'] as our Roman actors do.—*Jul. C.*, ii. 1.

And, for turning away, let summer *bear it out* ['enable me to endure it'].—*Tw. N.*, i. 5.

I hope your warrant will *bear out* ['authorise,' 'exonerate you in,' 'bear you harmless through'] the deed.—*John*, iv. 1.

If I cannot once or twice in a quarter *bear out* ['uphold,' 'support,' 'carry through,' 'justify,' 'vindicate'] a knave against an honest man, I have but very little credit with your worship.—*2 H. IV.*, v. 1.

To *bear up* ['have fortitude'] against what should ensue.—*Temp.*, i. 2.

Therefore *bear up* ['keep up your courage'], and board 'em.—*Ibid.*, iii. 2.

So long as nature will *bear up with* ['sustain'] this exercise, so long I daily vow to use it.—*W. T.*, iii. 2.

I pray you, *bear with* ['be patient with'] me; I can go no farther.—For my part, I had rather *bear with* you.—*As You L.*, ii. 4.

And though I must be content to *bear with* [' be tolerant with '] those that say you are reverend grave men.—*Coriol.*, ii. 1.

Tell him his pranks have been too broad to *bear with* ['be tolerated'].—*Hamlet*, iii. 4.

A woman that *bears all down* [' carries all before her,' ' overcomes every obstacle '] with her brain.—*Cym.*, ii. 1.

He *bears him* ['presumes'] on the place's privilege.—1 *H. VI.*, ii. 4.

We might have met them dareful, *beard to beard* [' in close opposition'], and beat them backward home.—*Macb.*, v. 5.

This naughty man shall *face to face* ['confrontingly'] be brought to Margaret.—*M. Ado*, v. 1.

And fighting *foot to foot* [' in close opposition '].—*Ant. & C.*, iii. 7.

In single opposition, *hand to hand* [' in close fight '].—1 *H. IV.*, i. 3.

Set *limb to limb* ['*limb in comparison with limb*'], and thou art far the lesser.—2 *H. VI.* iv. 10.

Sir John, you loiter here too long, *being* [' since '] you are to take soldiers up in counties as you go.—2 *H. IV.*, ii. 1.

Being that I flow in grief, the smallest twine may lead me.—*M. Ado*, iv. 1.

Be it so [' supposing that,' ' if it prove that '] she will not here before your grace consent to marry with Demetrius.—*Mid N. D.*, i. 1.

The multitude, *beside themselves* [' out of their wits,' ' bereft of their senses'] with fear.—*Jul. C.*, iii. 1.

To put him quite *beside his patience* [' out of patience '].—1 *H. IV.*, iii. 1.

Quite *beside the government of patience!* [' beyond the control of self-restraint '].—*Cym.*, ii. 4.

Very many have been *beside their wit* [' out of their wits,' ' out of their senses '].—*M. Ado*, v. 1.

How fell you *beside your five wits?* [' out of your wits '].—*Tw. N.*, iv. 2.

For mine 's *beyond beyond* [' out of all reckoning,' ' past expression '].—*Cym.*, iii. 2.

You *look beyond him* [' overshoot the mark in estimating him,' ' misjudge him '] quite: the prince but studies.—2 *H. IV.*, iv. 4.

The king has *gone beyond me* [' outwitted me,' ' out-generaled me,' ' outstepped me in politic proceeding'].—*H. VIII.*, iii. 2.

Which *went beyond* [' outstepped,' ' exceeded,' ' surpassed'] all man's endeavours.—*Ibid.*, iii. 2.

If she *went before* [' surpassed,' ' excelled '] others I have seen, as that diamond outlustres many.—*Cym.*, i. 5.

If I would think my heart *out of thinking* [' beyond the power of thinking'].—*M. Ado*, iii. 4.

But that a joy *past joy* [' beyond all usual joys,' ' surpassing most joys'] calls out on me.—*R. & Jul.*, iii. 3.

The king will *bid you battle* [' challenge you to battle,' ' engage you in battle'] presently.—1 *H. IV.*, v. 2.

Issue forth, and *bid them battle* straight.—3 *H. VI.*, i. 2.

Shall cross the seas, and *bid false Edward battle*.—*Ibid.*, iii. 3.

Issue out again and *bid us battle* . . . force enough to *bid his brother battle* . . . and *bid thee battle*, Edward.—*Ibid.*, v. 2.

And means to *give you battle* presently.—1 *H. VI.*, v. 2.

He hath *bid me to* [' invited me to'] a calf's head and a capon.—*M. Ado*, v. 1.

To *bid my old master*, the Jew, *to sup to-night* with my new master, the Christian.—*Mer. of V.*, ii. 4.

I am *bid forth to supper*, Jessica.—*Ibid.*, ii. 5.

I will *bid the duke to the nuptial*.—*As You L.*, v. 2.

Their love is not so great, Hortensio, but we may *blow our nails* [' remain baffled,' kick our heels,' ' go whistle '] together.—*Tam. of S.*, i. 1.

And Dick the shepherd *blows his nail* ['blows his finger-ends to give them warmth' and (acording to the idiom formerly so used) 'remains baffled,' 'passes away vexatiously idle time': equivalent to the more modern idiomatic phrase, 'kicks his heels,' 'goes whistle'].—*Love's L. L.*, v. 2 (*Song*).

What time the shepherd, *blowing of his nails,*
Can neither call it perfect day nor night.—3 *H. VI.*, ii. 5.

For it is you have *blown this coal* ['kindled this spark of discord'] betwixt my lord and me . . . you charge me that I have *blown this coal ;* I do deny it.—*H. VIII.*, ii. 4.

Then vail your stomachs, for it is *no boot* ['no use,' 'of no avail,' 'profitless,' 'fruitless'].—*Tam. of S.*, v. 2.

Norfolk, throw down ; we bid ; there is *no boot.—R. II.*, i. 1.

Then talk no more of flight, it is *no boot.*—1 *H. VI.*, iv. 6

Grace *to boot* ['in addition to my own wit,' 'in aid of my self-defence'].—*W. T.*, i. 2.

Now, by my sceptre, and my soul *to boot* ['in addition, as well'].—1 *H. IV.*, iii. 2.

With all appliances and means *to boot.*—2 *H. IV.*, iii. 1.

This, and Saint George *to boot.—R. III.*, v. 3.

Helen, to change, would give an eye *to boot.—Tr. & Cr.*, i. 2.

And the rich East *to boot.—Macb.*, iv. 3.

Thou hast thy mistress still—*to boot*, my son.—*Cym.,* 1. 6.

Horse-hairs, and calves'-guts, nor the voice of unpaved eunuch *to boot,* can never amend.—*Ibid.*, ii. 3.

All curses madded Hecuba gave the Greeks,
And mine *to boot*, be darted on thee!—*Ibid.*, iv. 2.

Hearty thanks: the bounty and the benison of heaven *to boot, and boot !* ['over and above,' 'moreover, and still moreover'].—*Lear*, iv. 6.

My gravity . . . could I, *with boot*, ['advantageously,' 'with profit'] change for an idle plume.—*M. for M.*, ii. 4.

You, to your rights ; *with boot* ['with extra advantages'] and such additions as your honours have more than merited.—*Lear*, v. 3.

Young York he is *but boot* ['only makeweight,' 'merely an additional advantage given in to form an equivalent'].—*R. III.*, iv. 4.

I shall not *break your bidding* ['disobey your commands'].—*All's W.*, ii. 5.

Then thou canst not *break her* ['break her in,' 'instruct her in playing'] to the lute ?—*Tam. of S.*, ii. 1.

If he break ['if he fail to pay'], thou may'st with better face exact the penalty.—*Mer. of V.*, i. 3.

If he should *break his day* ['fail in paying on the day agreed,' 'commit a breach of contract'].—*Ibid.*, i. 3.

Well, I'll *break in* ['effect forcible entrance'], go borrow me a crow. . . . If by strong hand you offer to *break in.—Com. of E.*, iii. 1.

To *break within* the bloody house of life.—*John*, iv. 2.

Boyet, you can carve ; *break up* [an idiom formerly used for 'cutting up' when applied to cooked poultry, and for 'opening' or 'breaking the seal,' when applied to letters ; "a capon" being a gallant technicality for a love-letter, as the French word *poulet* was a term for a *billet-doux*] this capon.—*Love's L. L.*, iv. i.

Break up ['break open'] the gates.—1 *H. VI.*, i. 3.

Break up ['dissolve,' 'dismiss'] the court.—*H. VIII.*, ii. 4.

Now will we *break with* ['disclose the matter to'] him.—*Two G. of V.*, i. 3.

I am to *break with* ['disclose to,' 'communicate to'] thee of some affairs.—*Ibid.*, iii. 1.

And I will *break with* ['impart the matter to'] her, and with her father.—*M. Ado*, i. 1.

And instantly *break with* you of it.—*Ibid.*, i. 2.

And hath withdrawn her father to *break with* him about it.—*Ibid.*, ii. 1.

For my life, to *break with* him about Beatrice.—*Ibid.*, iii. 2.

Break with your wives of your departure hence.—1 *H. IV.*, iii. 1.

Let us not *break with* him ; for he will never follow.—*Jul. C.*, ii. 1.

We have appointed to dine with mistress Anne, and I would not *break with* ['fail in our engagement with'] her for more money that I 'll speak of.—*Merry W.*, iii. 2.

It cannot be the Volsces dare *break with* ['come to a rupture with,' 'quarrel with'] us.—*Coriol.*, iv. 6.

I 'll be with you, niece, by-and-by.—*To bring*, uncle ['I 'll bring as good as I get,' 'I 'll be even with you'].—*Tr. & Cr.*, i. 2.

You *bring me out* ['put me out,' 'interrupt me,' 'disconcert me'].—*As You L.*, iii. 2.

They do not mark me, and that *brings me out* ['puts me out'].—*Love's L. L.*, v. 2.

I 'll *bring you* ['escort you,' 'accompany you'] thither.—*M. Ado*, iii. 2.

We will *bring you* on your way.—*Love's L. L.*, v. 2.

How far *brought you* ['did you accompany'] high Hereford on his way?—*R. II.*, i. 4.

You either fear his humour, or my negligence, that you *call in question* ['put into doubt,' 'express a doubt of'] the continuance of his love.—*Tw. N.*, i. 4.

In this I do not *call* your faith *in question*.—*Tr. & Cr.*, iv. 4.

Now sit we close about this taper here,
And *call in question* ['discuss the question of,' 'take in review,' 'bring forward for consideration'] our necessities.—*Jul. C.*, iv. 3.

His means of death, his obscure funeral. . . .
Cry to be heard, as 'twere from heaven to earth,
That I must *call 't in question* ['challenge it,' 'make it subject of inquiry,' 'demand explanation of it'].—*Hamlet*, iv. 5.

Full surfeits and the dryness of his bones
Call on him ['call him to account,' 'take him to task,' 'call him to a reckoning,' 'cite him to pay'] for 't.—*Ant. & C.*, i. 4.

'Tis not due yet; I would be loath to pay him before his day. What need I be so forward with him that *calls not on me*? ['calls me not to a reckoning,' 'cites me not to pay'].—*1 H. IV.*, v. 1.

A very serious business *calls on him* ['demands his attention'].—*All's W.*, ii. 4.

But that a joy past joy *calls out on me* ['summons me'].—*R. & Jul.*, iii. 3.

I am bound to *call upon you* ['summon you,' 'cite you to appear'].—*M. for M.*, iii. 2.

May be, I will *call upon you* ['summon you'] anon.—*Ibid.*, iv. 1.

Speak not you to him, till we *call upon you* ['appeal to you'].—*Ibid.*, v. 1.

I 'll *call upon you* ['summon you'] straight: abide within.—*Macb.*, iii. 1.

Our time does *call upon us* ['summon us away'].—*Ibid.*, iii. 1.

This, and what needful else that *calls upon us* ['demands our attention'], by the grace of Grace, we will perform.—*Ibid.*, v. 7.

Time *calls upon us* ['requires us to hasten'].—*Ant. & C.*, ii. 2.

I 'll *call to you* ['call at your house,' 'come to your house'].—*Timon*, i. 2.

He 'll *call you to* ['summon you to'] so hot an answer of it.—*H. V.*, ii. 4.

How far *is 't call'd* ['is it reckoned'] to Forres?—*Macb.*, i. 3.

I 'll give you a remuneration: why, *it carries it* ['it carries the day,' 'it surpasses,' 'it transcends'].—*Love's L. L.*, iii. 1.

It must be a very plausive invention that *carries it* ['suffices,' 'avails'] . . . yet slight ones will not *carry it* ['avail,' 'suffice'].—*All's W.*, iv. 1.

Are you all resolved to give your voices? But that 's no matter; the greater part *carries it* ['prevails,' 'gains the day'].—*Coriol.*, ii. 3.

He will *carry 't*, he will *carry 't* ['succeed,' 'prevail']; *'tis in his buttons* ['it is in him to do it,' 'he is quite capable of such a thing,' ''tis within his compass']; he will *carry 't*.—*Merry W.*, iii. 2.

Shall pride *carry 't?* ['prevail,' 'triumph,' 'get the day'].—*Tr. & Cr.*, ii. 3.

O, he would miss it, rather than *carry it* ['gain,' 'win,' 'succeed,' 'prevail'] but by the suit o' the gentry.—*Coriol.*, ii. 1.

'Tis thought of every one Coriolanus will *carry it*.—*Ibid.*, ii. 2.

If there be
Such valour in the bearing, what make we

Abroad ?   Why then, women are more valiant, That stay at home, if bearing *carry it* ['get the palm,' 'rank first,' 'have highest merit ascribed '].—*Timon*, iii. 5.

A la stoccata *carries it away* ['gets the better,' 'triumphs '].—*R. & Jul.*, iii. 1.

Do the boys *carry it away* ['get the upper hand,' 'prevail '].—*Hamlet*, ii. 2.

He 'd *carry it so* ['manage it so,' 'contrive it so'] to make the sceptre his —*H. VIII.*, i. 2.

And *carry it so* ['conduct the matter so '], as I have set it down.—*Lear*, v. 3.

We may *carry it thus* ['go on at this rate '], for our pleasure and his penance, till our very pastime, tired out.—*Tw. N.*, iii. 4.

Shall the elephant Ajax *carry it thus* ['domineer in this way '] ?   He beats me, and I rail at him.—*Tr. & Cr.*, ii. 3.

What a full fortune does the thick-lips owe, if he can *carry 't thus* ['succeed thus ']. —*Oth.*, i. 1.

If case ['if the case be that,' 'in case '] some one of you would fly from us.—3 *H. VI.*, v. 4.

He is not valiant.—Thou liest, most ignorant monster: I am *in case* ['in a condition,' 'in a frame of mind,' 'in the mood,'] to justle a constable.—*Temp.*, iii. 2.

I 'll break my staff, bury it *certain fathoms* ['an unspecified depth '] in the earth.—*Ibid.*, v. 1.

Till some *certain shot* ['unspecified money '] be paid.—*Two G. of V.*, ii. 5.

Sent my peasant home for *certain ducats* ['unspecified amount of ducats ']: he with none return'd.—*Com. of E.*, v. 1.

I did send to you for *certain sums* ['unspecified amount '] of gold, which you denied me.—*Jul. C.*, iv. 3.

They take the flow o' the Nile by *certain scales* ['unspecified measurement '] i' the pyramid.—*Ant. & C.*, ii. 7.

And *certain stars* ['unspecified number '] shot madly from their spheres, to hear the sea-maid's music.—*Mid. N. D.*, ii. 2.

A hue and cry hath follow'd *certain men* ['unspecified number '] into this house.—1 *H. IV.*, ii. 4.

To borrow *so many* ['unspecified number '] talents.—*Timon*, iii. 2.

Beyond all manner of *so much* ['unspecified amount'] I love you.—*Lear*, i. 1.

He 's very wild ; addicted *so and so* ['unspecified vices '].—*Hamlet*, ii. 1.

Such and such ['unspecified kind and number'] pictures.—*Cym.*, ii. 2.

There is no *certain princess* ['unnamed, but understood'] that appears.—*Love's L. L.*, iv. 3.

A lodg'd hate and *a certain loathing* ['specially felt, but left undefined'] I bear Antonio.—*Mer. of V.*, iv. 1.

Of *a certain knight* ['alluded to as an instance '], that swore.—*As You L.*, i. 2.

A certain queen ['particularly meant, but left unnamed '] to Cæsar in a mattress.—*Ant. & C.*, ii. 6.

I know thou *canst not choose* ['cannot do otherwise,' 'cannot avoid doing so '].—*Temp.*, i. 2.

Yond same cloud *cannot choose* but fall by pailfuls.—*Ibid.*, ii. 2.

I *cannot choose* but pity her.—*Two G. of V.*, iv. 4.

That *cannot choose* but amaze him.—*Merry W.*, v. 3.

That swear he *cannot choose* but break.—*Mer. of V.*, iii. 1.

Such an affection, which *cannot choose* but branch now.—*W. T.*, i. 1.

It *cannot choose* but be a noble plot.—1 *H. IV.*, i. 3.

Which *cannot choose* but bring him quickly on.—*Ibid.*, v. 2.

Cannot choose but they must blab.—*Oth.*, iv. 1.

This is *clean kam* ['quite beside the purpose,' 'quite irrelevant'].—Merely awry : when he did love his country.—*Coriol.*, iii. 1.

But men may construe things after their fashion,
Clean from the purpose ['quite apart from the drift'] of the things themselves — *Jul. C.*, i. 3.

A pox of drowning thyself! it is *clean out of the way* ['quite out of the question,' 'quite beside the purpose'].—*Oth.*, i. 3.

What *colour for* ['appearance of reason for,' 'pretext for'] my visitation shall I hold up before him?—*W. T.*, iv. 3.

But yet we want *a colour for* ['a show of justice for,' 'an appearance of justice for'] his death.—*2 H. VI.*, iii. 1.

It is no matter, if I do halt; I have the wars *for my colour* ['for my excuse,' 'my pretext'], and my pension shall seem the more reasonable.—*2 H. IV.*, i. 2.

Under pretence to see the queen his aunt
(For 'twas indeed *his colour* ['his pretext,' 'his ostensible motive'], but he came
To whisper Wolsey), here makes visitation.—*H. VIII.*, i. 1.

Cæsar's ambition . . . *against all colour* ['contrary to all show of right,' 'without any ostensible right'], here did put the yoke on us.—*Cym.*, iii. 1.

Since the quarrel will *bear no colour* ['possess no plausibility,' 'give no appearance of being just'] for the thing he is.—*Jul. C.*, ii. 1.

Seek *no colour* ['no pretext,' 'no pretended cause'] for your going, but bid farewell and go.—*Ant. & C.*, i. 3.

This must be *patched with cloth of any colour* ['set to rights by any plausible excuse'].—*Coriol.*, iii. 1.

There is a kind of confession in your looks, which your modesties have not craft enough *to colour* ['to cover by a show of specious meaning'].—*Hamlet*, ii. 2.

That show of such an exercise *may colour* ['give an appearance of ostensible motive for'] your loneliness.—*Ibid.*, iii. 1.

Under *the colour of* ['the pretence of'] commending him.—*Two G. of V.*, iv. 2.

Under *the colour of* his usual game.—*3 H. VI.*, iv. 5.

Under whose colours ['in whose service'] he had fought so long.—*R. II.*, iv. 1.

Those that weep . . . *under her colours* ['on her behalf,' 'on her side,' 'as her partisans'], are wonderfully to extend him.—*Cym.*, i. 5.

How might we see Falstaff bestow himself to-night *in his true colours* ['according to his veritable disposition,' 'without any show of being better than he is'].—*2 H. IV.*, ii. 2.

He that is well hanged in this world needs to *fear no colours* ['dread no threats or danger, under whatever aspect they may approach'] . . . I can tell thee where that saying was born, of, I *fear no colours* ['fear no foe, under whatever colours he may fight'] . . . In the wars.—*Tw. N.*, i. 5.

I do *fear colourable colours* ['mistrust plausible appearances'].—*Love's L. L.*, iv. 2.

Here's such ado to make no stain a stain,
As *passes colouring* ['exceeds all specious pretence'].—*W. T.*, ii. 2.

Who deserved so long a breeding as his white beard *came to* ['amounted to,' 'gave token of meriting'] in doing this.—*Cym.*, v. 3.

For more than blushing *comes to* ['amounts to'].—*H. VIII.*, ii. 3.

Superfluity *comes sooner by* ['sooner attains'] white hairs; but competency lives longer.—*Mer. of V.*, i. 2.

The stone's too hard to *come by* ['attain'].—*Cym.*, ii. 4.

On the expectation of plenty: *come in time* ['be in time,' 'come early'].—*Macb.*, ii. 3.

Nay, for a need, thus far *come near my person* ['touch upon what personally regards me']; tell them, when that my mother.—*R. III.*, iii. 5.

She that makes dainty, she, I 'll swear, hath corns; am I *come near you* ['piqued you,' 'touched upon a susceptible point'] now?—*R. & Jul.*, i. 5.

How he *comes o'er us* ['taunts us,' 'twits us'] with our wilder days.—*H. V.*, i. 2.

Lord Longaville said, I *came o'er* ['overcame,' 'overpowered'] his heart;
And trow you what he called me?—Qualm, perhaps.—*Love's L. L.*, v. 2.

I have turned away my other guests; they must *come off* ['come down with the cash,' 'pay handsomely']. I 'll sauce them.—*Merry W.*, iv. 3.

This *comes off well* ['is well delivered or expressed'] here's a wise officer.—*M. for M.*, ii. 1.

This *comes off well* ['is admirably done,' 'is capitally executed'; including the technicality of art 'comes out well,' 'is well brought into relief'] and excellent.—*Timon*, i. 1.

Now, this overdone, or *come tardy off* ['inefficiently performed'], though it make the unskilful laugh, cannot but make the judicious grieve.—*Hamlet*, iii. 2.

As, *i' the contrary* ['on the contrary,' 'on the other hand'], the foulness is the punishment.—*H. VIII.*, iii. 2.

I do not find that thou dealest justly with me.—
What *in the contrary* ? ['on the contrary,' 'that is the contrary'].—*Oth.*, iv. 2.

The king's attorney, *on the contrary* ['on the other side'], urg'd on the examinations, proofs, confessions of.—*H. VIII.*, ii. 1.

I have to show *to the contrary* ['proving the reverse'] . . . I could show you *to the contrary*.—*Merry W.*, ii. 1.

Whatever you may hear *to the contrary* ['in opposition to this'] let Claudio be executed by four of the clock.—*M. for M.*, iv. 2 (*Note*).

Yet our power shall *do a courtesy to* ['comply with,' 'gratify,' 'confer a favour upon'] our wrath.—*Lear*, iii. 7.

Now this mask was *cried* ['proclaimed,' 'pronounced'] incomparable.—*H. VIII.*, i. 1.

Came to my tent, and *cried on* ['proclaimed,' 'announced'] victory.—*R. III.*, v. 3.

This quarry *cries on* ['proclaims,' 'announces'] havoc.—*Hamlet*, v. 2.

Whose noise is this that *cries on* ['cries out,' 'proclaims'] murder ?—*Oth.*, v. 1.

Why, who *cries out on* ['denounces,' 'exclaims against'] pride,
That can therein tax any private party ?—*As You L.*, ii. 7.

His mangled Myrmidons, that, noseless, handless, hack'd and chipp'd, come to him, *crying on* ['exclaiming against'] Hector.—*Tr. & Cr.*, v. 5.

Cried I aim ? * ['have I spoken encouragingly ?'] said I well ?—*Merry W.*, ii. 3.

And to these violent proceedings all my neighbours shall *cry aim* ['give encouragement,' 'applaud,' 'approve'].—*Ibid.*, iii. 2.

It ill beseems this presence to *cry aim*
To these ill-tuned repetitions.—*John*, ii. 1.

Now, if you can blush, and *cry guilty* ['confess yourself guilty,' 'plead guilty'], cardinal.—*H. VIII.*, iii. 2.

Shall of a corse *cry woe* ['lament,' 'exclaim wofully'].—*Lear*, iii. 2.

And *cry* these dreadful summoners *grace* ['beseech grace of,' 'supplicate for mercy from'].—*Ibid.*, iii. 2.

I cry thee mercy ['I beg thy pardon,' 'I crave thy forgiveness or forbearance'], then, for I did think, that thou hadst.—*R. III.*, i. 3.

Cry the man mercy ; love him; take his offer.—*As You L.*, iii. 5.

O, *cry you mercy*, sir ; I have mistook.—*Two G. of V.*, v. 4.

Give me audience for awhile.—*I cry you mercy.*—1 *H. IV.*, i. 3.

Good master secretary, *I cry your honour mercy.*—*H. VIII.*, v. 2.

And, by that destiny, to perform an act,
Whereof what 's past is prologue; what to come,
In yours and my *discharge* ['enacting,' 'performance'].—*Temp.*, ii. 1.

I will *discharge it* ['enact it,' 'perform it'] in either your straw-colour beard, your orange-tawny beard.—*Mid. N. D.*, i. 2.

---

* The folio misprints this, 'Cride-game ;' but the passages above cited (one of which occurs in the same play) of the expression "Cry aim," warrant the supposition that a similar phrase was here used by Shakespeare.

Not a man in all Athens able to *discharge Pyramus* ['enact or perform the part of Pyramus'] but he.—*Mid. N. D.*, iv. 2.

It would have been a fine tragedy: and so it is, truly; and very notably *discharged* ['enacted,' 'performed'].—*Ibid.*, v. 1.

I pray you, *see him presently discharg'd* ['see that my debt to him be immediately discharged'].—*Com. of E.*, iv. 1.

Would *we were all discharg'd !* ['that all the debts owing to us were discharged']. —*Timon*, ii. 2.

Ay, ay, farewell; *thy office is discharg'd* ['thou hast discharged thine office'].— *2 H. VI.*, ii. 4.

Heaven shall be brib'd to *do him justice* ['see him righted,' 'accord him right'] and revenge on you.—*John*, ii. 1.

Thy arm may *do thee justice* ['achieve justice for thee'].—*Lear*, v. 3.

To the health of our general!—I am for it, lieutenant; and I'll *do you justice* ['respond to you heartily'].—*Oth.*, ii. 3.

And the high gods, to *do you justice* ['see justice done you,' 'see you righted'], make their ministers of us.—*Ant. & C.*, iii. 6.

Let us be jocund: will you troll the catch you taught me, but while-ere?—At thy request, monster, I will *do reason, any reason* ['do rightly,' 'do justice to your request,' 'do what is reasonable, anything in reason'].—*Temp.*, iii. 2.

I shall *do that that is reason.* . . . I will do it as shall become one that would *do reason* ['act rightly, justly, reasonably'].—*Merry W.*, i. 1.

And *do him right* ['act justly by him'] that, answering one foul wrong, lives not to act another.—*M. for M.*, ii. 2.

If it *do him right*, then he hath wrong'd himself.—*As You L.*, ii. 7.

Do me right ['respond to my challenge,' 'give me satisfaction'], or I will protest your cowardice.—*M. Ado*, v. 1.

Why, now you have *done me right* ['responded to me heartily']. *Do me right.* ['pledge me, drink foot to foot with me, do justice to my toast'].—*2 H. IV.*, v. 3.

My lord, *in heart* ['I drink to you in all heartiness,' 'I pledge you with all my heart']; and let the health go round.—*Timon*, i. 2.

Cup us ['let us pledge each other in brimming cups'], till the world go round, *cup us*, till the world go round!—*Ant. & C.*, ii. 7 *(Song)*.

Come and *crush a cup of wine* ['toss off a glass of wine,' 'drain a goblet of wine']. —*R. & Jul.*, i. 2.

Which the rather we shall be *bless'd to do* * ['glad to do,' 'happy to do'], if he remember a kinder value.—*Coriol.*, ii. 2.

Blessed are clouds *to do* as such clouds do!—*Love's L. L.*, v. 2.

And then we shall be *blessed to do* your pleasure.—*John*, iii. 1.

Do your best wills, and make me *bless'd to obey !*—*Cym.*, v. 1.

And then, I grant, we put a sting in him,
That at his will he may *do danger* ['do harm,' 'do mischief'] with.—*Jul. C.*, ii. 1.

The neglecting it may *do much danger* ['produce much mischief,' 'work much harm'].—*R. & Jul.*, v. 2.

Take time to *do him dead* ['kill him,' 'put him to death'].—*3 H. VI.*, i. 4.

Done to death ['put to death,' 'killed'] by slanderous tongues.—*M. Ado*, v. 3 *(Scroll)*.

Unless false Suffolk straight be *done to death.*—*2 H. VI.*, iii. 2.

By the stern lord Clifford *done to death.*—*3 H. VI.*, ii. 1.

To bar my master's heirs in true descent,
Heaven knows I *will not do it to the death* ['I will maintain till death my resolve not to do it,' or 'I will not do it, were my refusal to cause my death'].—*R. III.*, iii. 2.

---

* In this passage the word "bless'd" has been variously altered by various emendators; but we think that the three other passages here cited and collected together, where Shakespeare has used the same idiom, serve to prove that in the present instance it is the one he employed.

He that hath a will to *die by himself* ['die by his own hands'] fears it not from another.—*Coriol.*, v. 2.

I'll *die on him* ['risk dying by his sword'] that says so, but yourself.—*Two G. of V.*, ii. 4.

To *die upon the hand* ['die by the hand'] I love so well.—*Mid. N. D.*, ii. 2.

When he shall hear she *died upon his words* ['died in consequence of his words'] the idea of her life shall sweetly.—*M. Ado*, iv. 1.

One that no persuasion can *do good upon* ['produce impression upon,' 'avail with']. —1 *H. IV.*, iii. 1.

Well he may chance to *do some good on her* ['produce some impression upon her']. —*R. & Jul.*, iv. 2.

Who can *do good on him?* ['produce beneficial impression upon him']— *M. for M.*, iv. 2.

Faith, there has been *much to do* ['much ado, much fuss'] on both sides.— *Hamlet*, ii. 2.

To have so *much to do* to bring him in!—*Oth.*, iii. 3.

I have *much to do*, but to go hang my head.—*Ibid.*, iv. 3.

They fell sick and died—I *could not do withal* ['could not help it']; then I'll repent, and wish.—*Mer. of V.*, iii. 4.

A piece many years *in doing* ['in course of execution'], and now newly performed by that rare Italian master.—*W. T.*, v. 2.

How have you done ['how have you been,' 'how has your health gone on'] since last we saw in France?—*H. VIII.*, i. 1.

But *'tis doubt* ['' 'tis doubtful,' 'it is to be doubted'], when time shall call him home . . . whether our kinsman.—*R. II.*, i. 4.

Depress'd he is already; and depos'd, *'tis doubt*, he will be.—*Ibid.*, iii. 4.

We'll *draw cuts* ['draw lots,' 'decide by chance'] for the senior: till then lead thou first.—*Com. of E.*, v. 1.

If we *draw lots*, he speeds.—*Ant. & C.*, ii. 3.

That man and wife *draw lots*, who first shall die.—*Per.*, i. 4.

As he *drains his draughts* of Rhenish *down* ['swills,' 'swallows,' 'drinks'].— *Hamlet*, i. 4.

Well drawn ['well drained, or drunk off at a draught,' 'well swigged or swilled'; (modern) 'well pulled'], monster, in good sooth.—*Temp.*, ii. 2.

The lines of my body are as *well drawn* ['well designed,' 'well moulded'] as his.— *Cym.*, iv. 1.

Why *are you drawn?* ['are your swords drawn'] Wherefore this ghastly looking? —*Temp.*, ii. 1.

O well-a-day, lady, if *he be not drawn!* ['his sword be not drawn'].—*H. V.*, ii. 1.

What, *art thou drawn* ['is thy sword drawn'] among these. . . .
What, *drawn*, and talk of peace!—*R. & Jul.*, i. 1.

I never come into any room in a tap-house, but I am *drawn in* ['taken in,' 'duped,' 'befooled,' 'tricked'].—*M. for M.*, ii. 1.

Shall *draw him on* ['lure him on,' 'beguile him'] to his confusion.—*Macb.*, iii. 5.

So by your companies to *draw him on* ['beguile him,' 'induce him,' 'persuade him'] to pleasures, and to gather.—*Hamlet*, ii. 2.

Draw ['draw to,' 'close'] the curtains.—*Mer. of V.*, ii. 7.

Come, *draw* the curtain, Nerissa.—*Ibid.*, ii. 9.

Do not *draw* the curtain . . . I'll *draw* the curtain . . . Shall I *draw* the curtain? —*W. T.*, v. 3.

Make no noise; *draw* the curtains: so, so, so.—*Lear*, iii. 6.

Quick, quick, I pray thee; *draw* ['draw back,' 'draw aside'] the curtain straight: the prince of Arragon.—*Mer. of V.*, ii. 9.

We will *draw* the curtain, and show you the picture.—*Tw. N.*, i. 5.

Draws a curtain, that shows the ignorant a kind of.—1 *H. IV.*, iv. 1.

Come, *draw* the curtain, and let's see your picture.—*Tr. & Cr.*, iii. 2.

For an end ['to this end,' 'for this purpose'], we must suggest the people in what hatred he still hath held them.—*Coriol.*, ii. 1.

A slave, that *still an end* ['perpetually,' 'never-endingly'] turns me to shame.— *Two G. of V.*, iv. 4.

But, to *make an end* ['conclude my story'] of the ship.—*W. T.*, iii. 3.

Without an oath, I'll *make an end on't* ['conclude the song'].—*Hamlet*, iv. 5.

My lord, and I have *made an end* ['come to the end of all his money']: I have no more to reckon, he to spend.—*Timon*, iii. 4.

O, *make an end* ['complete,' 'finish'] of what I have begun.—*Ant. & C.*, iv. 12.

He'd *make an end of* ['destroy'] thy posterity.—*Coriol.*, iv. 2.

They say, he *made a good end* ['died peacefully'].—*Hamlet*, iv. 5.

My hair be fixed *on end* ['upright'], as one distract.—*2 H. VI.*, iii. 2.

My hair doth stand *on end* to hear her curses.—*R. III.*, i. 3.

And each particular hair to stand *on end*, like quills.—*Hamlet*, i. 5.

Your bedded hair . . . starts up, and stands *on end*.—*Ibid.*, iii. 4.

The cardinal *is the end* ['is the ultimate cause,' 'is at the bottom'] of this.— *H. VIII.*, ii. 1.

The fame which he did *end all his* ['end by making all his,' 'in the end, make all his'].—*Coriol.*, v. 5.

There's in him stuff that *puts him to these ends* ['inspires him with using these means'].—*H. VIII.*, i. 1.

And when I did correct him for his fault the other day, he did vow upon his knees he would *be even with me* ['give me as good as he got,' 'have his revenge.' *See* "to bring," previously cited under the present heading].—*2 H. VI.*, i. 3.

He nods at us, as who should say, I'll *be even with you* ['be revenged on you'].— *Ibid.*, iv. 7.

I will *be even with thee*, doubt it not.—*Ant. & C.*, iii. 7.

We shall not spend a large expense of time,
Before we reckon with your several loves
And *make us even with you* ['acquit the debt we owe you'].—*Macb.*, v. 7.

Till *I am even'd with him* ['have my reprisal with him'], wife for wife.—*Oth.*, ii. 1.

That *I can match her* ['be even with her,' 'give her as good as she brings,' 'equal her in contest'].—*Mid. N. D.*, iii. 2.

My father is here look'd for *every day* ['at any moment,' 'very soon'].— *Tam. of S.*, iv. 2.

I *every day* expect an embassage from my.—*R. III.*, ii. 1.

We *every day* expect him here.—*Per.*, iv. 1.

Why, *every day** ['ever after,' 'evermore,' 'always,'] to-morrow.—*M. Ado*, iii. 1.

For the rain it raineth *every day* ['constantly,' 'perpetually'].—*Tw. N.*, v. 1 (*Song*).

Though the rain it raineth *every day*.—*Lear*, iii. 2 (*Song*).

Every day, some sailor's wife, the masters of some merchant.—*Temp.*, ii. 1.

Many young gentlemen flock to him *every day*.—*As You L.*, i. 1.

Hearing how that *every day* men of great worth resorted to this forest.—*Ibid.*, v. 4.

> First, it was usual with him, *every day*
> It would infect his speech.—*H. VIII.*, i. 2.

This news is old enough, yet it is *every day's* ['ordinary,' 'common,' 'modern,' 'usual'].—*M. for M.*, iii. 2.

---

* In many editions this passage is printed with a break between "day" and "to-morrow;" but in the Folio it is printed as we give it in the text; and we believe that the speaker (Hero) means to say, 'Why, to-morrow I shall be ever after married,' in sportive reply to Ursula's asking "When *are* you married?" instead of, 'When *are* you to be married?'

You may have *every day* ['any day,' 'whenever you please'] enough of Hector.—*Tr. & Cr.*, iv. 5.

Do not you know my lady's foot by the squire? ['have you not the length of my lady's foot,' 'do you not know her humour exactly'] and *laugh upon the apple of her eye?* ['laugh in accordance with her directing glance'].—*Love's L. L.*, v. 2.

We shall express our duty *in his eye* ['in his presence'; this was according to a state formula used in Shakespeare's time].—*Hamlet*, iv. 4.

Hop in his walks, and *gambol in his eyes* ['frolic in his sight'].—*Mid. N. D.*, iii. 1.

Her gentlewomen . . . *tended her i' the eyes* ['waited upon her looks,' 'attended in her sight'], and made their bends adornings.—*Ant. & C.*, ii. 2.

I am now *so far in offence* ['so deeply in disgrace from having offended'] with my niece.—*Tw. N.*, iv. 2.

I am *so far already in* ['so deeply indebted already for'] your gifts.—*Timon*, i. 2.

All fast? ['all the doors fastened'] what means this? Ho!—*H. VIII.*, v. 2.

The gates *made fast!* ['fastened']—3 *H. VI.*, iv. 7.

I will *make fast* ['fasten'] the doors.—*Mer. of V.*, ii. 6.

Now, Montague, *sit fast* ['remain where thou art,' 'be firm,' 'stand fast']; I seek for thee.—3 *H. VI.*, v. 2.

Stand fast; we have as many friends as enemies.—*Coriol.*, iii. 1.

Stand fast ['remain firm,' 'be constant'], good fate, to his hanging!—*Temp.*, i. 1.

O, Lewis, *stand fast!* the devil tempts thee here.—*John*, iii. 1.

If you'll *stand fast*, we'll beat them to.—*Coriol.*, i. 4.

Stand fast ['remain firmly united here'] together, lest some.—*Jul. C.*, iii. 1.

There is *no fear in him* ['no danger,' 'nothing for us to fear in him']; let him not die.—*Jul. C.*, ii. 1.

I promise you, *I fear you* ['I fear for you'].—*Mer. of V.*, iii. 5.

You shall not need to *fear me* ['fear for me'].—*All's W.*, iii. 5.

His physicians *fear him* ['fear for him'] mightily.—*R. III.*, i. 1.

Let him go, Gertrude; do not *fear our person* ['fear for our person'].—*Hamlet*, iv. 5.

He was much *fear'd* ['feared for'] by his physicians.—1 *H. IV.*, iv. 1.

Would we were all discharg'd! I *fear it* ['fear that we shall not be discharged,' or 'paid'].—*Timon*, ii. 2.

We must away all night.—Tut, never *fear me* ['fear my not doing as I ought to do'].—1 *H. IV.*, iv. 2.

Fear not that ['fear not but I'll do that'], I warrant thee.—2 *H. VI.*, iv. 3.

How! turn thy back, and run?—*Fear me not* ['do not fear but that I shall do what I ought to do'].—*R. & Jul.*, i. 1.

O, *fear me not* ['do not fear that I shall do what I ought not to do'].—*Hamlet*, i. 3.

Be not familiar with her.—*Fear me not.*—*Lear*, v. 1.

Fear not our care ['fear not our want of care'], sir.—*Coriol.*, i. 7.

And *of their feather* ['of their kind,' 'of their sort'] many more proud birds.—3 *H. VI.*, ii. 1.

Both of you are birds *of self-same feather* ['of similar kind'].—*Ibid.*, iii. 3.

I am not *of that feather* ['of that kind'], to shake off my friend.—*Timon*, i. 1.

E'en a crow *o' the same nest* ['of the same kind'].—*All's W.*, iv. 3.

A bird *of my tongue* ['of my mode of speech'] is better than a beast of yours.—*M. Ado*, i. 1.

The composition that your valour and fear makes in you is a virtue *of a good wing* ['strong in flight'].—*All's W.*, i. 1.

My purpose is, indeed, a horse *of that colour* ['of that kind,' 'of that species'].—*Tw. N.*, ii. 3.

Sport? *Of what colour?* ['of what sort'].—*As You L.*, i. 2.

As boys and women are, for the most part, cattle *of this colour* ['of this kind'].—*Ibid.*, iii. 2.

This is a fellow *of the self-same colour* ['of the same kind'] our sister speaks of.— *Lear*, ii. 2.

Not that our heads are some brown, some black, some auburn, some bald, but that our wits are *so diversely coloured* ['of such different kinds'].—*Coriol.*, ii. 3.

Curses all Eve's daughters, *of what complexion* ['of what kind,' 'of what character'] soever.—*Merry W.*, iv. 2.

What kind of woman is 't ?—*Of your complexion* ['of your general appearance'].— *Tw. N.*, ii. 4.

Should she fancy, it should be one *of my complexion* ['of my general appearance'].— —*Ibid.*, ii. 5.

Belike this is a man *of that quirk* ['addicted to such whims,' 'of that kind of disposition'].—*Ibid.*, iii. 4.

I will show myself *highly fed* ['well trained,' 'well brought up,' 'well educated,' 'superiorly bred'; and (punningly) 'pampered,' 'nourished with dainties and tit-bits'] and lowly taught.*—*All's W.*, ii. 2.

A good knave, i' faith, and *well fed* ['well trained,' 'well taught his tricks of word-catching as a professional jester'].—*Ibid.*, ii. 4.

In what he did profess, *well found* † ['well versed,' 'well grounded in the knowledge of,' 'thoroughly skilled'].—*Ibid.*, ii. 1.

The present consul, and last general,
In our *well-found* ['favourably received,' 'approvingly accepted'] successes, to report a little of that worthy work.—*Coriol.*, ii. 2.

As a schoolmaster *well seen* ['well versed,' 'skilled,' 'practised,' or 'grounded'] in music, to instruct Bianca.—*Tam. of S.*, i. 2.

I believe, it is *a fetch of warrant* ['a warrantable contrivance,' 'an allowable trick or stratagem'].—*Hamlet*, ii. 1.

And, like a shifted wind unto a sail,
It makes the course of thoughts to *fetch about* ['veer,' 'turn about,' 'change direction'].—*John*, iv. 2.

Till tongues *fetch breath* ['take breath,' 'pause for an instant'] that may proclaim them louder.—*Per.*, i. 4.

Hark, how hard he *fetches breath* ['breathes,' 'snores'].—1 *H. IV.*, ii. 4.

She does so blush, and *fetches her wind* ['breathes,' 'pants,' 'gasps'] so short, as if she were frayed with a sprite . . . she *fetches her breath* as short as a new-ta'en sparrow.—*Tr. & Cr.*, iii. 2.

And his own letter, the honourable board of council out, must *fetch him in* ['must bring him in,' 'must include him whom'] he papers.—*H. VIII.*, i. 1.

Within our files there are, of those that serv'd Mark Antony but late, enough to *fetch him in* ['take him,' 'capture him,' 'defeat him'].—*Ant. & C.*, iv. 1.

Might break out, and swear he'd *fetch us in* ['take us,' 'capture us,' 'defeat us'].— *Cym.*, 4. 2.

You speak this to *fetch me in* ['entrap me,' 'take advantage of me.' *See* "drawn in" previously cited], my lord.—*M. Ado*, i. 1.

Let's *fetch him off* ['rescue him,' 'get him back'], or make remain alike. —*Coriol.*, i. 4.

Let him *fetch off* ['rescue,' 'redeem,' 'bring back'] his drum.—*All's W.*, iii. 6.

And will *fetch off* ['take off,' 'murder'] Bohemia for 't.—*W. T.*, i. 2.

---

* The clown uses "lowly taught" (for the sake of antithesis) in the sense of 'taught to be humble, deferential, or respectful.'

† "Well found" in this passage has been interpreted by some commentators to mean the same as "well-found" in "Coriolanus"; but we believe that Shakespeare here used "well found" in a kindred sense with the idiom (usual in his time) of "well seen," which he employs in "The Taming of the Shrew," act i., sc. 2; though, in Shakespeare's inclusive mode of using words, he may have intended the expression to include both significations, inasmuch as both perfectly suit the present passage.

As I return, I will *fetch off* ['bring away with me': with the included meaning of 'entrap,' 'ensnare,' 'take advantage of'] these justices.—2 *H. IV.*, iii. 2.

I'll *fetch a turn* ['take a turn'] about the garden.—*Cym.*, i. 2.

Youthful and unhandled colts *fetching mad bounds* ['taking wild leaps'], bellowing, and neighing loud.—*Mer. of V.*, v. i.

In the soldier is *flat* ['downright,' 'absolute'] blasphemy.—*M. for M.*, ii. 2.

The *flat* ['downright,' 'out and out'] transgression of a schoolboy.—*M. Ado*, ii. 1.

A goose, that's *flat* ['positive,' 'certain'].—*Love's L. L.*, iii. 1.

I'll not march through Coventry with them, that's *flat* ['sure,' 'positive'].— 1 *H. IV.*, iv. 2.

Should dying men *flatter with* ['flatter'] those that live?—*R. II.*, ii. 1.

None of these rogues and cowards, but Ajax *is their fool* ['is a fool to them,' 'is a fool in comparison with them for courage'].—*Lear*, ii. 2.

Now this mask was cried incomparable; and the ensuing night *made it a fool and beggar* ['made it seem poor and contemptible in comparison with the succeeding one']. —*H. VIII.*, i. 1.

What is he for a fool ['what kind of fool is he'] that betroths himself.— *M. Ado*, i. 2.

Out, fool! *I forgive thee for a witch* ['I acquit thee of being a witch,' 'I'll warrant thee for being no witch'].—*Ant. & C.*, i. 2.

Well, sir, in brief, the gown is *not for me* ['not to be purchased by me,' 'not to my taste'].—*Tam. of S.*, iv. 3.

Well, a horn *for my money* ['is the instrument to my taste'], when all's done.— *M. Ado*, ii. 3.

The wars *for my money* ['are what best please me,' 'are most to my taste'].— *Coriol.*, iv. 5.

I'll take the ghost's word *for a thousand pound* ['staking a thousand pounds on its truth'].—*Hamlet*, iii. 2.

How now! a rat? Dead, *for a ducat* ['staking a ducat that I have hit him'], dead! —*Ibid.*, iii. 4.

For and ['and eke,' 'and also'], a shrouding sheet.—*Ibid.*, v. 1 (*Song*).

Forbear me ['leave me,' 'withdraw'].—*Ant. & C.*, i. 2.

Forbear me ['cease speaking and leave me'] till anon.—*Ibid.*, ii. 7.

We must *forbear* ['break off our conversation and withdraw']; here comes the gentleman.—*Cym.*, i. 1.

Your oath once broke, you *force not* ['care not,' 'regard not,' 'lay no stress upon,' 'pay no heed'] to forswear.—*Love's L. L.*, v. 2.

For me, I *force not* ['heed not,' 'regard not,' 'care not for'] argument a straw, since that my case is past the help of law.—*Lucrece, Stanza* 146.

We must *of force* ['of course,' 'of necessity,' 'necessarily'] dispense with this decree.—*Love's L. L.*, i. 1.

That, when he wak'd, *of force* she must be ey'd.—*Mid. N. D.*, iii. 2.

But *of force* must yield to such inevitable shame.—*Mer. of V.*, iv. 1.

Dear sir, *of force* I must attempt you farther.—*Ibid.*, iv. 1.

Who, *of force*, must know the royal fool thou cop'st with.—*W. T.*, iv. 3.

Will this content you, Kate?—It must, *of force.*—1 *H. IV.*, ii. 3.

Good reasons must, *of force*, give place to better.—*Jul. C.*, iv. 3.

Those occasions, uncle, were *of force* ['of weight,' 'momentous,' 'availing']: there-fore, my loving lords.—1 *H. VI.*, iii. 1.

And lo, where George of Clarence sweeps along, *Of force* ['provided with forces,' 'with strength,' 'efficiently and availingly sup-ported'] enough to bid his brother battle.—3 *H. VI.*, v. 1.

And, *force perforce*, ['in spite of resistance,' 'strength for strength,' 'force pitted against force'] keep Stephen Langton.—*John*, iii. 1.

Was, *force perforce*, compell'd to banish him.—2 *H. IV.*, iv. 1.

As, *force perforce*, the age will pour it in.—*2 H. IV.*, iv. 4.

And, *force perforce*, I 'll make him yield the crown.—*2 H. VI.*, i. 1.

And require my dukedom of thee, which, *perforce* [' of necessity,' ' inevitably '], I know, thou must restore.—*Temp.*, v. 1.

Your health, the which, if you give o'er to stormy passion, must *perforce* decay.— *1 H. IV.*, i. 1.

I must *perforce* compound with mistful eyes.—*H. V.*, iv. 6.

Perforce must wither . . . humanity must *perforce* prey on itself, like monsters of the deep.—*Lear*, iv. 2.

He rush'd into my house, and took *perforce* [' by compulsion,' ' by violence '] my ring away.—*Com. of E.*, iv. 3.

And take *perforce* my husband from the abbess.—*Ibid.*, v. 1.

What he hath taken away from thy father *perforce*.—*As You L.*, i. 2.

Betroth'd, and would have married her *perforce*.—*R. & Jul.*, v. 3.

And from him give you all greetings that a king, *at friend* [' at amity,' ' on terms of friendship '], can send his brother.—*W. T.*, v. 1.

I know that we shall have him well *to friend* [' to be our friend,' ' for friend '].— *Jul. C.*, iii. 1.

As I shall find the time *to friend* [' befriend me,' ' be favourable or propitious to me '].—*Macb.*, iv. 3.

Had I admittance, and opportunity *to friend* [' to be my friend,' ' to befriend me '].— *Cym.*, i. 5.

To crave the French king's sister *to wife* [' as a wife '] for Edward.—*3 H. VI.*, iii. 1.

A woman that lord Brutus took *to wife*.—*Jul. C.*, ii. 1.

With dirge in marriage . . . taken *to wife* .—*Hamlet*, i. 2.

Is Warwick *friends with* [' on friendly terms with '] Margaret ?—*3 H. VI.*, iv. 1.

Friends am I with [' I am friendly towards '] you all.—*Jul. C.*, iii. 1.

The noble gentleman *gave up the ghost* [' expired '].—*3 H. VI.*, ii. 3.

Our army lies, ready to *give up the ghost* [' expire '].—*Jul. C.*, v. 1.

These news would cause him once more *yield the ghost*.—*1 H. VI.*, i. 1.

And often did I strive to *yield the ghost*.—*R. III.*, i. 4.

I 'll grow a talker *for this gear* [' for the sake of this that has just been mentioned '].— *Mer. of V.*, i. 1.

She 's a good wench *for this gear* [' for the sake of this that I have been mentioning '].—*Ibid.*, ii. 2.

But I will *remedy this gear* [' settle this business,' ' redress this affair '] ere long.— *2 H. IV.*, iii. 1.

Will this gear ne'er be mended ? [' is there no remedy for this matter '].— *Tr. & Cr.*, i. 1.

An she be not, *she has the mends in her own hands* [' she must find the remedy in her own patience,' ' she must bear it as well as she can '].—*Ibid.*, i. 1.

If they *get ground* [' gain advance '] and vantage of the king.—*2 H. IV.*, ii. 3.

I should *get ground* [' gain advantage '] of your fair mistress.—*Cym.*, i. 5.

And I will strive with things impossible;

Yea, *get the better* [' conquer,' ' get the upper hand '] of them.—*Jul. C.*, ii. 1.

Should so *get the start of* [' prevail over,' ' rise above,' ' go beyond '] the majestic world, and bear the palm alone.—*Ibid.*, i. 2.

Some *get within him* [' get within his guard,' ' close with him ']; take his sword away.—*Com. of E.*, v. 1.

And to offer to *get your living* [' gain your bread '] by the.—*As You L.*, iii. 2.

Buy food, and *get thyself in flesh* [' grow fatter '].—*R. & Jul.*, v. 1.

Get thee gone [' be gone,' ' go '], and hire those horses.—*Ibid.*, v. 1.

Stay not to answer me, but *get thee gone*.—*Jul. C.*, ii. 4.

Get you gone; and hasten your return.—*Lear*, i. 4.

He added to your having—*gave you some ground* ['allowed you to advance upon him,' 'let you gain some advantage over him'].—*Cym.*, ii. 3.

As proper a man as ever went on four legs cannot make him *give ground* ['flinch,' 'draw back,' 'allow advantage to be taken'].—*Temp.*, ii. 2.

Give ground ['recede a little'], if you see him furious.—*Tw. N.*, iii. 4.

Their points being broken . . . Began to *give me ground*: but I followed me close, came in.—*1 H. IV.*, ii. 4.

Richard cried, "Charge! and *give no foot of ground!*" ['do not recede a single foot'].—*3 H. VI.*, i. 4.

Giving no ground ['giving no advantage,' 'yielding no jot'] unto the house of York.—*Ibid.*, ii. 6.

If he come to-morrow, I'll *give him his payment* ['pay him out,' 'give him a settler,' 'do for him'].—*As You L.*, i. 1.

I'll make them pay; I'll *sauce them.* . . . I'll *sauce them* ['treat them to a heavy reckoning'].—*Merry W.*, iv. 3.

As fast as she answers thee with frowning looks, I'll *sauce her* ['treat her to a bespattering'] with bitter words.—*As You L.*, iii. 5.

Why, then, the devil *give him good of it!* ['give him the benefit of it,' 'give him advantage from it'].—*Mer. of V.*, iv. 1.

Much good dich thy good heart ['much good may it do thy good heart'], Apemantus! —*Timon*, i. 2.

After this process, to *give her the avaunt* ['give her dismissal,' 'bid her begone'].— *H. VIII.*, ii. 3.

Nay, *give me not the boots* ['don't mock me' 'don't pretend to give me advantage']. —*Two G. of V.*, i. 1.

I *give thee the bucklers* ['give thee the honours of the contest,' 'I yield,' 'I own myself defeated'].—*M. Ado*, v. 2.

What will you *give* us? No money, on my faith; but *the gleek* ['to give the gleek' meant 'to tip one a gibe,' 'to fling one a jest'], I will *give you the minstrel* ['twit you with being a minstrel'].—Then will I *give you the serving-creature* ['twit you with being a servant'].—*R. & Jul.*, iv. 5.

Give me your hands ['give me your applause,' 'clap your hands'] if we be friends.— *Mid. N. D.*, v. 2.

Will he *give you the nod?* ['give you a careless salutation,' 'cut you,' 'call you, by inference, a noddy,' 'treat you as a simpleton,' 'imply that he will have nothing to do with you'].—*Tr. & Cr.*, i. 2.

I say, *she did nod;* and you ask me if *she did nod;* and I say, I. And that set together, is,—*noddy.*—*Two G. of V.*, i. 1.

Give me the lie ['call me liar,' 'taunt me with being a liar'], do; and try whether I am not now a gentleman born.—*W. T.*, v. 2.

Who would *give a bird the lie*, though he cry.—*Mid. N. D.*, iii. 1.

Give me the lie another time.—I did not *give the lie*.—*Temp.*, iii. 2.

And, *giving him the lie*, leaves him.—I believe, drink *gave thee the lie* [punningly: 'laid thee on the floor' and 'made thee lie long and late'].—*Macb.*, ii. 3.

Give me your favour ['forgive me,' 'pardon my inattention,' 'give me your favourable construction,' 'give me your indulgence'].—*Ibid.*, i. 3.

Give me pardon ['I beg your pardon,' 'pardon me,' 'excuse me'], sir; if, sir, you come with news from the court.—*2 H. IV.*, v. 3.

Yet I can *give you inkling* ['give you a hint,' 'give you a glimpse'] of an ensuing evil.—*H. VIII.*, ii. 1.

They have *had inkling* ['had a hint or glimpse'] this fortnight what we intend to do.—*Coriol.*, i. 1.

If he *give me way* ['give way to me,' 'give me my way,' 'give me a hearing'] I'll do his country service.—*Ibid.*, iv. 4.

Shall we *give o'er* ['give up,' 'cease our efforts'] and drown?—*Temp.*, i. 1.

Let her remain; but I'll ne'er *give o'er*.—*Cym.*, ii. 3.

You scorn to believe me; 'twere best I did *give o'er.—Per.*, v. 1.

Have the pioneers *given o'er ?—H. V.*, iii. 2.

Who, half through, *gives o'er*, and leaves his.—2 *H. IV.*, i. 3.

Give 't not o'er so: to him again, entreat him.—*M. for M.*, ii. 2.

Send her another; never *give her o'er* ['cease your efforts to obtain her,' 'give her up'].—*Two G. of V.*, iii. 1.

These vows are Hermia's: will you *give her o'er ?* . . . now you *give her o'er* ['give her up'].—*Mid. N. D.*, iii. 2.

The visitor will not *give him o'er* ['cease importuning him,' 'refrain from remonstrating with him'] so.—*Temp.*, ii. 1.

Master Fenton, talk not to me; my mind is heavy: I will *give over* ['give up,' 'yield hope of'] all.—*Merry W.*, iv. 6.

To live quietly, and so *give over.*—Why, to *give over* ['give up business,' 'cease from earning'], I pray you ?—*Per.*, iv. 3.

To embrace your own safety, and *give over* ['relinquish'] this attempt.—*As You L.*, i. 2.

I will *give over* ['cease'] my suit, and repent.—*Oth.*, iv. 2.

To *give you over* ['leave you,' 'quit you'] at this first encounter, unless you will accompany me thither.—*Tam. of S.*, i. 2.

But thou art altogether *given over* ['given up as hopeless,' 'reprobate,' 'lost to grace,' 'abandoned to wickedness,' 'forsaken'].—1 *H. IV.*, iii. 3.

I have *given over* ['ceased,' 'given up urging'], I will speak no more.—2 *H. IV.*, ii. 3.

My crown I should *give off* ['yield,' 'resign,' 'give up'].—*John*, v. 1.

Follow the noise so far as we have quarter;
Let 's see how it will *give off* ['give over,' 'leave off'],—*Ant. & C.*, iv. 3.

I thought ye would never have *given out* ['given up,' 'yielded,' 'surrendered,' 'resigned'] these arms till you had recovered your ancient freedom.—2 *H. VI.*, iv. 8.

Two on 's are as good as I have *given out* ['proclaimed,' 'asserted'] him.—*Cym.*, v. 5.

'Tis *given out* ['reported,' 'asserted'], that, sleeping in mine orchard, a serpent stung me.—*Hamlet*, i. 5.

This is the monkey's own *giving out* ['reporting,' 'proclaiming']: she is persuaded I will marry her.—*Oth.*, iv. 1.

The duke is virtuous, mild, and too *well given* ['well disposed,' 'well inclined'] to dream on evil, or to work my downfall.—2 *H. VI.*, iii. 1.

He 's not dangerous, he is a noble Roman, and *well given.*—*Jul. C.*, i. 2.

An he had been cannibally *given* ['inclined,' 'disposed'], he might have broiled and eaten him too.—*Coriol.*, iv. 5.

If she had been a woman cardinally* *given.*—*M. for M.*, ii, 2.

If that man should be lewdly *given*, he deceiveth me.—1 *H. IV.*, ii. 4.

A very honest woman, but something *given* ['apt,' 'prone,' 'subject,' 'liable,' 'inclined'] to lie.—*Ant. & C.*, v. 2.

Lord, lord, how this world is *given* to lying!—1 *H. IV.*, v. 4.

Lord, lord, how *subject* we old men are to this vice of lying!—2 *H. IV.*, iii. 2.

I am not *prone* to weeping, as our sex commonly are.—*W. T.*, ii. 1.

And as *prone* to mischief as able to perform 't.—*H. VIII.*, i. 1.

O world, how *apt* the poor are to be proud!—*Tw. N.*, iii. 1.

Yet if my name were *liable* to fear.—*Jul. C.*, i. 2.

For he is *given* ['addicted'] to sports, to wildness, and much company.—*Ibid.*, ii. 1.

And lovers are *given* to poetry.—*As You L.*, iii. 3.

---

* "Cardinally" is constable Elbow's blunder for 'carnally;' there being double humour in the substituted word, since it suggests the 'cardinal virtues,' instead of the sins he proceeds to enumerate.

If thou wert any way *given* to virtue.—1 *H. IV.*, iii. 3.

And *given* unto the house of York *such head* ['given such power, such dominion,' and 'given such licence, such freedom from restraint'; this latter included sense is in accordance with the idiomatic phrase, 'to give a horse his head,' signifying 'to let him have his own way'].—3 *H. VI.*, i. 1.

Fellow, *give place* ['begone,' 'leave the place']; here is no longer stay.—*R. II.*, v. 5.

Give place ['give up thy place to me,' 'yield thy place']: by heaven, thou shalt rule no more o'er him whom.—3 *H. VI.*, v. i.

Sirrah, *give place* ['make way,' 'make room,' 'stand back'].—*Jul. C.*, iii. 1.

Give us the place alone ['leave us alone,' 'withdraw']: we will hear this divinity.—*Tw. N.*, i. 5.

But in what habit will you *go along ?* ['go on your way,' 'travel'].—*Two G. of V.*, ii. 7.

Come, *go along* ['go away,' 'be gone']; my wife is coming.—*Com. of E.*, iv. 4.

Demetrius and Egeus, *go along* ['go with me'].—*Mid. N. D.*, i. 1.

Come, *go along* ['go with us'], and see the truth.—*Tam. of S.*, iv. 5.

Widow, *go you along* ['go with us']: lords, use.—3 *H. VI.*, iii. 2.

Huntsman, what say'st thou? wilt thou *go along ?*—*Ibid.*, iv. 5.

Soft! I will *go along* ['go with you'].—*R. & Jul.*, i. 1.

I 'll *go along*, no such sight to be shown, but to.—*Ibid.*, i. 2.

Gallus, *go you along* ['go with him'].—*Ant. & C.*, v. 1.

Good Metellus, *go along by him* ['go by the way of his house,' 'go round by his house'].—*Jul. C.*, ii. 1.

If that thy gentry, Britain, *go before* ['excel']
This lout, as he exceeds our lords.—*Cym.*, v. 2.

I was then a young traveller; rather shunned to *go even with* ['acquiesce with,' 'form my own conduct upon,' 'accede to'] what I heard, than in my every action to be guided by others' experiences.—*Ibid.*, i. 5.

Were you a woman, as the rest *goes even* ['accords,' 'coheres,' 'coincides,' 'is smoothly consistent'], I should.—*Tw. N.*, v. 1.

In what key shall a man take you, to *go in the song* ['sing correctly with you,' 'speak in the same tune'].—*M. Ado*, i. 1.

It shall go hard ['things shall come to a bad pass with me,' 'matters shall be difficult indeed'], but I 'll prove it by another.—*Two G. of V.*, i. 1.

And *it shall go hard*, but I will better the instruction.—*Mer. of V.*, iii. 1.

It shall go hard, if Cambio go without her.—*Tam. of S.*, iv. 4.

And *it shall go hard*, but I will delve one yard below their mines.—*Hamlet*, iii. 4.

If law, authority, and power deny not,
It will go hard ['it will come to a difficult pass,' 'it will fall out fatally'] with poor Antonio.—*Mer. of V.*, iii. 2.

When a man's servant shall play the cur with him, look you, *it goes hard* ['it is a hard case'].—*Two G. of V.*, iv. 4.

My life, sir! how, I pray? for *that goes hard* ['that would be a hard case'].—*Tam. of S.*, iv. 2.

What, not an oath? nay then, *the world goes hard* ['it is a hard case,' 'it comes to a fine pass'], when Clifford cannot spare his friends an oath —3 *H. VI.*, ii. 6.

There is an old tale *goes* ['current'] that Herne the hunter.—*Merry W.*, iv. 4.

I do presume, sir, that you are not fall'n
From the report that *goes* ['is current'] upon your goodness.—*All's W.*, v. 1.

The story then *goes false* ['is falsely reported'], you threw it him out of a casement.—*Ibid.*, v. 3.

What was his cause of anger ?—*The noise goes* ['the report is,' 'it is said,' 'they say'], this: there is among.—*Tr. & Cr.*, i. 2.

At least *the whisper goes* so.—*Hamlet*, i. 1.

The cry goes, that you shall marry her.—*Oth.*, iv. 1.

Thus it goes ['thus it runs,' 'this is its tenor'].—*As You L.*, ii. 5.

A passing merry one, and *goes to the tune* ['is set to the tune,' 'is adapted to the tune'] of "Two Maids."—*W. T.*, iv. 3.

Who goes there ['who is that passing by'], ha ?—*Tam. of S.*, i. 2.

Who goes there ?—A friend.—*H. V.*, iv. 1.

Who goes there ?—Stay, or thou diest.—*3 H. VI.*, iv. 3.

What's he that goes there ?—Falstaff, an't please.—*2 H. IV.*, i. 2.

We shall write to you . . . *how it goes with us* ['how we are going on,' 'what is happening to us'].—*M. for M.*, i. 1.

Lucius hath wrote already to the emperor
How it goes ['what is going on' or 'occurring'] here.—*Cym.*, iii. 5.

How goes it ['what is going on,' 'what is happening'] now, sir ?—*W. T.*, v. 2.

Be not a niggard of your speech : *how goes it ?*—When I came hither.—*Macb.*, iv. 3.

How goes it here ?—All dead.—*Ant. & C.*, v. 2.

How goes it ['how is all going on'] with my brave Mark Antony ?—*Ibid.*, i. 5.

How goes it now ? he looks gentler than he did.—*Oth.*, iv. 3.

Bring me word *how 'tis with her* ['how she is,' 'how she is going on']. A fever with the absence of her son.—*Cym.*, iv. 3.

Tell me, *how goes the world ?* ['what is there going on,' 'what news is there abroad']. —*Tam. of S.*, iv. 1.

I have not seen you long : *how goes the world ?*—*Timon*, i. 1.

How goes the world, sir, now ?—*Macb.*, ii. 4.

How goes the world with thee ? ['how art thou going on'].—*R. III.*, iii. 2.

How goes the world ['how comes this,' 'what is the matter'], that I am thus encounter'd with clamorous demands.—*Timon*, ii. 2.

Thus *goes every one to the world* ['everybody gets married'] but I, and I am sunburned.—*M. Ado.*, ii. 1.

I hope it is no dishonest desire, to desire to be *a woman of the world* ['a married woman'].—*As You L.*, v. 3.

Her beauty and her brain *go not together* ['are not matched,' 'are not on a par'].— *Cym.*, i. 2.

Go to ['have done,' 'be quiet,' 'enough'] ; carry this.—*Temp.*, iv. 1.

To pray for her ! *Go to* ['well, well,' 'even so,' 'be it so'].—*Love's L. L.*, iii. 1.
[*See* OATHS, EXCLAMATIONS, &c.]

'Tis not ten years gone ['ten years have not elapsed,' 'it is not ten years ago'] since Richard.—*2 H. IV.*, iii. 1.

'Tis not four days gone, since I heard thence.—*Coriol.*, i. 2.

O, he's drunk, Sir Toby, *an hour agone*.—*Tw. N.*, v. 1.

For *long agone* I have forgot to court.—*Two G. of V.*, iii. 1.

Master, I have *gone thorough* ['bid high,' 'gone thoroughly to work in the price I have offered'] for this piece.—*Per.*, iv. 3.

Would have bought me lights *as good cheap* ['as cheap,' 'as good a bargain'] at the dearest chandler's.—*1 H. IV.*, iii. 3.

That's Antenor : he has a shrewd wit, I can tell you ; and he's a man *good enough* [used as "rather" is sometimes jocosely used, to express 'very good,' 'excellent'].— *Tr. &. Cr.*, i. 2.

I have no exquisite reason for't, but I have reason *good enough* ['perfectly sufficing'].—*Tw. N.*, ii. 3.

'Faith, the priest was *good enough*, for all the.—*As You L.*, v. 1.

I do not say, thwack our general ; but he was always *good enough* ['a match,' 'a more than sufficient equal'] for him.—*Coriol.*, iv. 5.

Sir, I know that *well enough* ['perfectly well,' 'thoroughly'].—*Two G. of V.*, ii. 1.

I know you *well enough* . . . you know him *well enough*.—*M. Ado.*, ii. 1.

And the stony-hearted villains know it *well enough*.—*1 H. IV.*, ii. 2.

Go to ; I know you *well enough.*—1 *H. IV.*, iii. 3.

Menenius, you are known *well enough* too . . . if I be known *well enough* too ?—Come, sir, come, we know you *well enough.*—*Coriol.*, ii. 1.

The knight 's in admirable fooling.—Ay, he does *well enough* [' capitally,' ' excellently well '], if he be disposed.—*Tw. N.*, ii. 3.

And fear not, neighbour, you shall do *well enough.*—2 *H. VI.*, ii. 3.

I am not drunk now; I can stand *well enough*, and speak *well enough.*—*Oth.*, ii. 3.

Cry " lost," and so *good night !* [' farewell to us '].—*W. T.*, i. 2.

If he fall in, *good night !* [' farewell to him,' ' he 's done for '] or sink, or swim.—1 *H. IV.*, i. 3.

Why, then, *good night* [' farewell to our success,' ' our cause is lost '], indeed.—*Ant. & C.*, iii. 8.

And that the spoil *got on* [' gained from '] the Antiates.—*Coriol.*, iii. 3.

My queen and Eros have, by their brave instruction, *got upon me* [' gained in advance of me,' ' forestalled me in securing '] a nobleness in record.—*Ant. & C.*, iv. 12.

It is *great morning* [' broad day '] ; and the hour.—*Tr. & Cr.*, iv. 3.

It is now *high supper-time* [' high time for supper,' ' fully supper-time '], and the night grows to waste.—*Oth.*, iv. 2.

And therefore 'tis *high time* [' fully time '] that I were hence.—*Com. of E.*, iii. 2.

So I will not rest till I have run *some ground* [' a good distance,' ' a long way '].—*Mer. of V.*, ii. 2.

I will run *as far as God has any ground** [' as far as the land extends,' ' to the sea-shore '].—*Ibid.*, ii. 2.

I will ride, *as far as land will let me*, by your side.—*R. II.*, i. 3.

My father did something smack, something *grow to* [' lean towards ' (' knavery ' or ' dishonesty,' understood), ' incline that way,' ' approach near to ']—he had a kind of taste.—*Mer. of V.*, ii. 2.

They that my trust must *grow to* [' cleave to,' cling to,' ' rely upon'], live not here.—*H. VIII.*, iii. 1.

I grow to you [' I embrace you closely,' ' I clasp you in fervent friendship '].—*All's W.*, ii. 1.

I lay aside that which *grows to me !* [' belongs to me,' ' pertains to me,' ' is a part of me ']. If thou gettest any leave of me.—2 *H. IV.*, i. 2.

Then read the names of the actors; and so *grow to a point* [' come to the point,' ' come to the matter in hand '].—*Mid. N. D.*, i. 2.

Touch you the sourest points with sweetest terms,
Nor curstness *grow to the matter* [' come near the subject,' ' mingle in our discussion '].—*Ant. & C.*, ii. 2.

If matters *grow to your liking* [' proceed,' ' turn out,' ' happen, as you could wish '].—*Merry W.*, i. 1.

Your husband 's here *at hand* [' close by,' ' near '].—*Ibid.*, iii. 3.

All books of love, see that *at any hand* [' at any rate,' ' at all events,' ' on any account '] . . . not her that chides, sir, *at any hand*, I pray.—*Tam. of S.*, i. 2.

Let him fetch off his drum *in any hand* [' in any case,' ' at any rate,' ' at all events '].—*All's W.*, iii. 6.

Else shall you not *have any hand at all about* [' have anything to do with,' ' take any part in '] his funeral.—*Jul. C.*, iii. 1.

Have you received no promise of satisfaction *at her hands?* [' from her '].—*Merry W.*, ii. 2.

Tell him so yourself, and see how he will take it *at your hands* [' from you '].—*R. & Jul.*, iii. 5.

Deserved *at the hands of* [' from '] Fortune.—*Hamlet*, ii. 2.

---

* The dramatist with felicitously humorous effect puts this expression into the mouth of one born in Venice ; where there is a very limited amount of ground.

Therefore, *of all hands* ['on all hands,' 'on all sides,' 'on every account,' 'in every respect'] must we be forsworn.—*Love's L. L.*, iv. 3.

That covenants may be kept *on either hand* ['on both sides'].—*Tam. of S.*, ii. 1.

Before, behind thee, and *on every hand*,
Enwheel thee round.—*Oth.*, ii. 1.

If promises be kept *on every hand.*—1 *H. IV.*, iii. 2.

He is as tall a man *of his hands* ['of his height,' 'of his size'] as any is between this and his head.—*Merry W.*, i. 4.

That I am a proper fellow *of my hands:* and those.—2 *H. IV.*, ii. 2.

Thou art a tall fellow *of thy hands* . . . thou art no tall fellow *of thy hands* . . . I would thou wouldst be a tall fellow *of thy hands.*—*W. T.*, v. 2.

You have *made fair hands* ['done a fine piece of mischief,' 'made a pretty mess'], you and your crafts.—*Coriol.*, iv. 6.

You have *made good work*, you and your apron-men. . . . You have *made good work*, you and your cry!—*Ibid.*, iv. 6.

Ye have *made a fine hand*, fellows.—*H. VIII.*, v. 3.

Change places; and *handy-dandy**['which hand is which hand,' 'which is the right hand and which is the left,' 'which is right and which is wrong'], which is the justice, which is the thief?'—*Lear*, iv. 6.

Stay, stand apart; I know not *which is which* ['the one from the other'].—*Com. of. E.*, v. 1.

Read me the superscription of these letters: I know not *which is which.*—*Timon*, ii. 2.

Hob, nob ['have it, or have it not,' 'hit or miss'] is his word; give 't or take 't.—*Tw. N.*, iii. 4.

But, *hit or miss* ['succeed or not succeed'] our project's life this shape of sense assumes.—*Tr. & Cr.*, i. 3.

When these mutualities so marshal the way, *hard at hand* ['hard by,' 'close by,' 'very near,' 'immediately'] comes the master and main exercise.—*Oth.*, ii. 1.

Be ready here *hard by* ['close by,' 'near at hand'] in the brewhouse.—*Merry W.*, iii. 3.

Where is he?—He attendeth here *hard by.*—*Mer. of V.*, iv. 1.

If you will know my house, 'tis at the tuft of olives, here *hard by.*—*As You L.*, iii. 5.

The count himself, here *hard by*, woos her.—*Tw. N.*, i. 3.

Well have you heard, but something *hard of hearing* ['deafly,' indistinctly,' 'inaccurately heard'].—*Tam. of S.*, ii. 1.

Indeed, my lord, it follow'd *hard upon* ['quickly,' 'soon after'].—*Hamlet*, i. 2.

I have been *drinking hard* ['drinking to excess,' 'toping'] all night, and I will have more time.—*M. for M.*, iv. 3.

They call *drinking deep*, dyeing scarlet.—1 *H. IV.*, ii. 4.

Say, you ne'er had done 't,
(*Harp on that* ['dwell on that,' 'repeat that'] still) but by our.—*Coriol.*, ii. 3.

O, gracious duke, *harp not on that;* nor do not.—*M. for M.*, v. 1.

Harp not on that string, madam; that is past.—*Harp on it* still shall I till heart-strings break.—*R. III.*, iv. 4.

Still *harping on* ['dwelling on,' 'recurring to'] my daughter.—*Hamlet*, ii. 2.

Harping on what I am, not what he knew I was.—*Ant. & C.*, iii. 11.

Have after ['let us follow'].—*Hamlet*, i. 4.

Have at you ['here goes,' 'I'm ready to try my success against you,' 'I'll have an onset with you'] for a bitter jest or two!—*Tam. of S.*, v. 2.

Have to ['I will go to,' 'I will try my success with'] my widow!—*Ibid.*, iv. 5.

Ha' to ['here's to,' 'I drink to'] thee, lad.—*Ibid.*, v. 2.

---

* The name of an old game for children; where the hands and places of the players are rapidly interchanged, and success depends upon guessing which is which.

Have through ['here goes, to make my way through'] the very midst of you!—
2 *H. VI.*, iv. 8.

Have with you ['I'm ready to go with you'], mine host.—*Merry W.*, ii. 1.

When I have laid proud Athens *on a heap* ['in a heap,' 'in ruins,' 'in the dust'].
—*Timon*, iv. 3.

There were drawn *upon a heap* ['in a heap,' 'in a cluster,' 'in a crowd'] a hundred
ghastly women.—*Jul. C.*, i. 3.

Let us, *on heaps* ['in heaps,' 'in numbers'], go offer up our lives.—*H. V.*, iv. 5.

Catarrhs, *loads* ['quantities,' 'lots,' 'plenty,' 'a great deal'] o' gravel i' the back,
lethargies, cold palsies.—*Tr. & Cr.*, v. 1.

If I had a monopoly out, they would have part on 't, and *loads* ['a great quantity,'
'a large amount'] too.—*Lear*, i. 4.

All men's honours lie like *one lump* ['a mass,' 'a heap'] before him, to be fashion'd
into what pitch he pleases.—*H. VIII.*, ii. 2.

And then we may deliver our supplications *in the quill* ['all together,' 'all collectively,' 'all in a body,' 'all in a cluster,' 'all in a crowd,' 'all in a heap'].—2 *H. VI.*, 1. 3.

Since you do *take it*, love, *so much at heart* ['think so seriously about it,' 'fret so
much about it'].—*Mer. of V.*, v. 1.

An you speak ill of the devil, how he *takes it at heart* ['takes it to heart,' 'frets at it,'
'is vexed at it'].—*Tw. N.*, iii. 4.

With all my heart ['I heartily consent'], so thou canst get a wife.—*Mer. of V.*, iii. 2.

For if the Jew do cut but deep enough,
I'll pay it instantly *with all my heart* ['heartily,' 'right willingly,' 'most readily;'
and (punningly) 'with the whole of my heart,' 'with all the blood in my heart'].
—*Ibid.*, iv. 1.

And forgave him *with all their hearts* ['right heartily'].—*Jul. C.*, i. 2.

Bid her *have good heart* ['take courage.' 'be of good cheer'].—*Ant. & C.*, v. i.

Well, then, *take a good heart*, and counterfeit to be a man.—*As You L.*, iv. 3.

Good sirs, *take heart:* we'll bury him.—*Ant. & C.*, iv. 13.

Now I have *taken heart* ['taken courage,' 'roused myself'], thou vanishest.—
Jul. C., iv. 3.

Cheer your heart ['be cheerful'] : be you not troubled.—*Ant. & C.*, iii. 6.

Be of good cheer ['take heart,' 'take courage'], youth.—*As You L.*, iv. 3.

I pr'ythee, lady, *have a better cheer* ['be more cheerful,' 'entertain a better hope'].—
All's W., iii. 2.

And *out of heart* ['discouragedly,' 'despondently'], master . . . and *out of heart*
you love her, being *out of heart* ['discouraged,' 'despondent,' 'dejected'] that you
cannot enjoy her.—*Love's L. L.*, iii. 1.

I shall be *out of heart* ['discouraged,' 'hopeless'] shortly, and then I.—1 *H. IV.*, iii. 3.

Well, Petruchio, this has *put me in heart* ['given me courage, 'encouraged me'].—
Tam. of S., iv. 5.

My lord, *in heart* ['in all heartiness I pledge you, I drink to you'] ; and let the
health go round.—*Timon*, i. 2.

But *goes thy heart with this ?* ['do you speak this from your heart,' 'does this accord
with thy heart's feeling'].—*Lear*, i. 1.

I have tremor cordis on me, *my heart dances* ['my heart trembles' or 'quivers,' 'my
heart is agitated'] ; but not for joy—not joy.—*W. T.*, i. 2.

Make our eyes flow with joy, *hearts dance* ['hearts leap up,' 'bound'] with comforts
—*Coriol.*, v. 3.

He has it now; and by his looks, methinks,
'*Tis warm at his heart* ['it gladdens his heart,' 'it makes his heart glow'].—*Ibid.*, ii. 3.

This gentle and unforc'd accord of Hamlet
Sits smiling to my heart ['delights' or 'rejoices my heart'].—*Hamlet*, i. 2.

My bosom's lord sits lightly in his throne ['my heart feels light and happy'].—
R. & Jul., v. 1.

Crack my clear voice with sobs, and *break my heart* ['exhaust myself,' 'destroy myself'] with sounding Troilus.—*Tr. & Cr.*, iv. 2.

To *break the heart of* ['grieve,' 'deject'] generosity,
And make bold power look pale.—*Coriol.*, i. 1.

Wilt *break my heart?* ['destroy me,' 'kill me with grief'].—*Lear*, iii. 4.

No, no, *my heart will burst* ['will break'], an if I speak;
And I will speak, that so *my heart may burst.*—*3 H. VI.*, v. 5.

Then *burst his mighty heart* ['his mighty heart broke'].—*Jul. C.*, iii. 2.

O, that *my heart would burst!* . . . his flaw'd *heart . . . burst* smilingly.—*Lear*, v. 3.

Your *heart is burst*, you have lost half your soul.—*Oth.*, i. 1.

Why, that contempt will *kill the speaker's heart* ['grievously discourage'].—*Love's L. L.*, v. 2.

He was furnished like a hunter.—O, ominous! he comes to *kill my heart* [punningly: 'destroy my hart,' 'and capture my heart,' 'vanquish my heart'].—*As You L.*, iii. 2.

To take on me to keep and *kill thy heart* ['pain,' 'destroy by anguish'].—*R. II.*, v. 1.

The king has *killed his heart* ['broken his heart,' 'destroyed him by anguish'].—*H. V.*, ii. 2.

Offer me no money, I pray you; that *kills my heart* ['grieves me poignantly'].—*W. T.*, iv. 2.

Ah, Joan, this *kills thy father's heart* outright!—*1 H. VI.*, v. 4.

Set not thy sweet *heart on* ['do not love absorbingly'] proud array.—*Lear*, iii. 4.

I'll *prove it on thy heart* ['fight with thee in proof of my words'].—*Ibid.*, v. 3.

Are bent to *prove upon thy heart* . . . thou liest.—*Ibid.*, v. 3.

Do, *an thou darest for thy heart* ['if you can find it in your heart,' or 'in your power'] —*2 H. IV.*, ii. 4.

Cannot take two from twenty, *for his heart* ['cannot find it in his heart' or 'in his power'].—*Cym.*, ii. 1.

That it would have *done a man's heart good* .['rejoiced a man'] to see.—*2 H. IV.*, iii. 2.

By God's lid, it *does one's heart good* ['rejoices one'].—*Tr. & Cr.*, i. 2.

Why, this will *do Helen's heart good now* ['rejoice Helen'], ha!—*Ibid.*, i. 2.

From heart of very heart ['from my inmost heart'], great Hector, welcome.—*Ibid.*, iv. 5.

In my heart's core, ay, in *my heart of heart* ['my inmost heart'], as I do thee.—*Hamlet*, iii. 2.

You may ride's with one soft kiss a thousand furlongs, ere with spur *we heat an acre* ['we run an acre's course' or 'race'].—*W. T.*, i. 2.

He will drive you out of your revenge, and turn all to a merriment, if you *take not the heat* ['do not get the start of him,' 'get ahead of him,' 'run in before him': also including the sense of 'strike not while the iron is hot,' 'pursue not your advantage immediately,' 'act not promptly'].—*2 H. IV.*, ii. 4.

We must do something, and i' the heat ['we must strike while the iron is hot,' 'we must hit on some plan, and act promptly'].—*Lear*, i. 1.

And the best quarrels, *in the heat* ['in the first warmth of temper' or 'impulse'] are curs'd by those that feel their sharpness.—*Ibid.*, v. 3.

Not *in this heat* ['in this warmth of temper'], sir, now.—*Coriol.*, iii. 1.

It is a business of *some heat* ['of some pressure,' 'requiring some speedy and immediate attention'].—*Oth.*, i. 3.

I *hold it* ['reckon it,' 'consider it,' 'esteem it'] a sin to match.—*M. Ado*, ii. 1.

I *hold it* the more knavery to conceal it.—*W. T.*, iv. 3.

Hold it a fashion, and a toy in blood.—*Hamlet*, i. 3.

I once did *hold it*, as our statists do, a baseness to write fair.—*Ibid.*, v. 2.

Burgomasters and great oneyers, such as can *hold in* ['restrain themselves,' 'refrain,' 'preserve sedateness'].—*1 H. IV.*, ii. 1.

If there be more, more woeful, *hold it in* ['refrain from saying it,' ' keep it unsaid '].—
Lear, v. 3.

Yet *hold I off* ['remain coy,' 'maintain my reserve']. Women are angels, wooing:
things won are done.—*Tr. & Cr.*, i. 2.

That unassailable *holds on* ['maintains,' 'keeps up,' 'preserves'] his rank, unshak'd
of motion.—*Jul. C.*, iii. 1.

Well said, brazen-face, *hold it out* ['keep up your pretence of immaculacy,' 'persist
in your assertion of innocence'].—*Merry W.*, iv. 2.

Till my tale be heard, and *hold no longer out* ['no longer keep up the semblance
of virtue'].—*M. for M.*, v. 1.

Can any face of brass *hold longer out* ?—*Love's L. L.*, v. 2.

She would not *hold out enemy* ['be inimical,' 'preserve enmity'] for ever, for giving
it to me.—*Mer. of V.*, iv. 1.

I will *hold friends* ['keep friends,' 'keep on friendly terms,' 'preserve amity'] with
you, lady.—*M. Ado*, i. 1.

Now happy he, whose cloak and cincture can *hold out* ['wear through,' 'sustain']
this tempest.—*John*, iv. 3.

All Kent hath yielded; nothing there *holds out* ['keeps up resistance,' 'remains
firm'] but Dover castle.—*Ibid.*, v. 1.

Hold out my horse ['let the strength of my horse last out,' 'or suffice'], and I will
first be there.—*R. II.*, ii. 1.

No, no, he cannot long *hold out* ['sustain,' 'go through'] these pangs.—*2 H. IV.*,
iv. 4.

Else ne'er could they *hold out* ['keep on,' 'persist,' 'persevere in resistance'] so as
they do.—*1 H. VI.*, i. 2.

Mine eyes cannot *hold out water* ['keep from tears,' 'refrain from shedding tears'],
methinks.—*Timon*, i. 2.

For the babe cannot *hold out* ['bear the fatigue,' 'sustain the voyage'] to Tyrus.—
Per., iii. 1.

And *hold your own* ['keep up your consequence,' 'maintain your position'], in any
case, with such austerity as.—*Tam. of S.*, iv. 4.

Doth she *hold her own well* ? ['wear well,' 'keep her good looks'].—*2 H. IV.*, iii. 2.

Now, Ajax, *hold thine own* ! ['fight firmly,' 'keep up your reputation for being a
good fighter'].—*Tr. & Cr.*, iv. 5.

For women's fear and love *hold quantity* ['are of equal amount,' 'have parity,' 'are
on a par'].—*Hamlet*, iii. 2.

Things base and vile, *holding no quantity* ['possessing no intrinsic merit,' 'having
no equal worth with the person estimating them'], love can transpose to form and
dignity.—*Mid. N. D.*, i. 1.

With such powers as might *hold sortance* ['keep rank,' 'accord,' 'be suitable'] with
his quality.—*2 H. IV.*, iv. 1.

Hold you there ['keep in that frame of mind']: farewell.—*M. for M.*, iii. 1.

There rest ['remain in that state of mind']. Your partner.—*Ibid.*, ii. 3.

Our purpose may *hold there* ['succeed by that means'].—*Hamlet*, iv. 7.

Dost thou *hold there* ['keep to that same story'] still ?—*Ant. & C.*, ii. 5.

He hath ta'en the infection: *hold it up* ['maintain the same ground,' 'pursue the
same course,' 'go on with more of the same story'].—*M. Ado*, ii. 3.

Wink at each other ; *hold the sweet jest up*.—*Mid. N. D.*, iii. 2.

It lies much in your *holding up* ['carrying out the idea,' 'fulfilling the scheme '].—
M. for M., iii. 1.

Thou sayest well, and *it holds well* ['it is carried out farther,' 'it is farther confirmed'] too.—*1 H. IV.*, i. 2.

'Tis said, he *holds you well* ['much esteems you,' 'looks upon you favourably'] ; and
will be led, at your request.—*Tr. & Cr.*, ii. 3.

He *holds me well* ['thinks favourably of me'] ; the better.—*Oth.*, i. 3.

Thou told'st me thou didst *hold him in thy hate* [' hate him ' |.—*Oth.*, i. 1.

If thou didst ever *hold me in thy heart* [' hold me dear,' ' love me '].—*Hamlet*, v. 2.

My course, which *holds not colour* [' consists not,' ' suits not,' ' matches not '] with the time.—*All's W.*, ii. 5.

O, the father ! how he *holds his countenance !* [' keeps a serious face '].—1 *H. IV.*, ii. 4.

Here comes Baptista : *set your countenance* [' keep a steady look '].—*Tam. of S.*, iv. 4.

Look, what thy soul *holds dear* [' loves,' ' prizes '], imagine it.—*R. II.*, i. 3.

Life every man *holds dear ;* but the dear man
Holds honour far more *precious dear* than life.—*Tr. & Cr.*, v. 3.

I *hold* your dainties *cheap* [' think little of,' ' set small store by '], sir, and your welcome *dear.*—*Com. of E.*, iii. 1.

And *hold* their manhoods *cheap* [' think poorly of,' ' despise '].—*H. V.*, iv. 3.

Now humble as the ripest mulberry, that will not *hold the handling* [' bear rough touching '].—*Coriol.*, iii. 2.

A rotten case *abides no handling* [' bears no inspection,' ' examination,' ' testing '].—2 *H. IV.*, iv. 1.

And would not *hold taking* [' bear touching '], I doubt me.—*Timon*, i. 2.

What, must I *hold a candle to* [' betray,' ' expose '] my shames ?—*Mer. of V.*, ii. 6.

Thy affections, which do *hold a wing* [' take a course,' ' pursue a path '] quite from the flight of all thy ancestors.—1 *H. IV.*, iii. 2.

And the remembrancer of her, to *hold the hand fast* [' to keep her pledged faith '] to her lord.—*Cym.*, i. 6.

The fellow has a deal of that too much,
Which *holds him much to have* [' upholds him much in general opinion,' or ' avails him well to possess '].—*All's W.*, iii. 2.

I *hold you a penny* [' bet you a penny,' ' lay you a penny '].—*Tam. of S.*, iii. 2.

At the duke's oak we meet.—Enough ; *hold or cut bow-strings* [' I will keep my appointment, or you may cut my bow-strings ' : a form of pledge for meeting among archers, which passed into common use].—*Mid. N. D.*, i. 2.

Or I 'll find a Marshalsea shall *hold ye play* [' keep you amused,' ' keep you engaged '] these two months.—*H. VIII.*, v. 3.

And *hold our lives in mercy* [' have our lives at his mercy,' ' in his power '].—*Lear*, i. 4.

If e'er thou stand *at mercy of my sword* [' within my power '].—*Tr. & Cr.*, iv. 4.

For him, and in his right, we *hold this town* [' keep possession of this town,' ' keep this town armed and defended '].—*John*, ii. 1.

For he that *holds his kingdom* [' keeps possession of his kingdom,' ' retains his kingdom '] *holds the law* [' has power over,' or ' controls the law '].—*Ibid.*, iii. 1.

It *holds current* [' remains uncontradicted,' ' holds good '] that I told you yesternight.—1 *H. IV.*, ii. 1.

Doth the news hold [' is the news confirmed '] of good King Edward's death ?—*R. III.*, ii. 3.

Does the rumour *hold for true* [' prove true '], that he is so full of gold ?—*Timon*, v. 1.

For God's sake, *hold your hands* [' forbear to strike '].—*Com. of E.*, i. 2.

Nay, by your leave, *hold your hands.*—*All's W.*, iv. 3.

Good now, *hold thy tongue* [' be silent '].—*Com. of E.*, iv. 4.

Come, sing; and you that will not, *hold your tongues.*—*As You L.*, ii. 5.

Yet, Pucelle, *hold thy peace.*—1 *H. VI.*, iii. 2.

Hold your peaces !—Good my lord.—*W. T.*, ii. 1.

Defy them, then, or else *hold close thy lips.*—3 *H. VI.*, ii. 2.

And to the head of Angelo *accuse him home and home* [' accuse him thoroughly,' ' fully,' ' expose him completely '].—*M. for M.*, iv. 3.

Mend, and *charge home* [' attack fiercely to the utmost '], or, by the fires of heaven, I 'll.—*Coriol.*, i. 4.

He *charges home* [' makes fierce onslaught upon '] my unprovided body.—*Lear*, ii. 1.

In this point *charge him home* [' tax him severely and searchingly '].—*Coriol.*, iii. 3.

That *confirms it home* [' confirms it perfectly ']: this is Pisanio's deed.—*Cym.*, iv. 2.

Lack'd the sense to *know her estimation home* [' know her merit fully '].—*All's W.*, v. 3.

Look, you *lay home to him* [' rate him unsparingly ']: tell him his pranks.—*Hamlet*, iii. 4.

All my services you have *paid home* [' rewarded amply '].—*W. T.*, v. 3.

Till he hath found a time to *pay us home* [' pay us out,' ' revenge himself upon us fully '].—*1 H. IV.*, i. 3.

But I will *punish home* [' avenge thoroughly ']: No, I will weep no more.—*Lear*, iii. 4.

Wear thy good rapier bare, and *put it home* [' thrust fatally and surely '].—*Oth.*, v. 1.

No farther halting : *satisfy me home* [' confess openly '] what is become of her.—*Cym.*, iii. 5.

He *speaks home* [' tells plain truths '], madam : you may relish him.—*Oth.*, ii. 1.

Let me say, I cannot *speak him home* [' do him thorough justice '].—*Coriol.*, ii. 2.

Speak to me home [' tell me frankly and candidly '], mince not the general tongue.—*Ant. & C.*, i. 2.

Who may, in th' ambush of my name, *strike home* [' smite penally '], and yet my nature never.—*M. for M.*, i. 4.

Fortune's blows, when most *struck home* [' severely smiting '], being gentle wounded, craves a noble cunning.—*Coriol.*, iv. 1.

I 'll warrant she 'll *tax him home* [' accuse him severely and searchingly '].—*Hamlet*, iii. 3.

You have *told them home* [' rated them unsparingly '].—*Coriol.*, iv. 2.

That, *trusted home* [' relied upon fully,' ' believed in its fullest extent '], might yet enkindle you unto the crown.—*Macb.*, i. 3.

He hath *eaten me out of house and home* [' ruined me by his extravagance ']; he hath put all my substance.—*2 H. IV.*, ii. 1.

Like horses *hot at hand* [' full of fire when led by the hand '], make gallant show and promise.—*Jul. C.*, iv. 2.

Nay, 'twill be *this hour* [' an hour at least '] ere I have done weeping.—*Two G. of V.*, ii. 3.

We have done but greenly, *in hugger-mugger* [' in secret,' ' stealthily,' ' clandestinely '] to inter him.—*Hamlet*, iv. 5.

Beldam, I think we watch'd you *at an inch* [' at the very moment,' ' in the very nick of time,' ' to a nicety '].—*2 H. VI.*, i. 4.

And make him *by inch-meal* [' inch by inch,' ' an inch at a time '] a disease!—*Temp.*, ii. 2.

O, that I had her here, to tear her *limb-meal !* [' a limb at a time,' ' limb by limb,' ' limb from limb '].—*Cym.*, ii. 4.

Take the bonds along with you, and *have the dates in compt* [' take account of the dates '].—*Timon*, ii. 1.

Have theirs, themselves, and what is theirs, *in compt* [' in trust,' ' as that which is to be accounted for '] to make.—*Macb.*, i. 6.

I 'll give you a verse to this note, that I made yesterday *in despite of* [' in a struggle with,' ' in spite of my tardy,' or ' poor '] invention.—*As You L.*, ii. 5.

In spite of [' notwithstanding,' ' contrary to,' ' against the wish of '] your heart, I think.—*M. Ado*, v. 2.

To fashion this false sport *in spite of me* [' to spite me,' ' to vex me '].—*Mid. N. D.*, iii. 2.

And sleep *in spite of* [' notwithstanding the '] thunder.—*Macb.*, iv. 1.

O'erbearing interruption, *spite of* [' in defiance of,' ' against the will of '] France ?—*John*, iii. 4.

I love thee so, that, *maugre* [' in spite of,' ' notwithstanding '] all thy pride, nor wit, nor reason, can my passion hide.—*Tw. N.*, iii. 1.

I protest—*maugre* thy strength, youth, place, and eminence,
Despite thy victor sword and fire-new fortune,
Thy valour and thy heart—thou art a traitor.—*Lear*, v. 3.

But that the poor monster's *in drink* ['drunk,' 'intoxicated'].—*Temp.*, ii. 2.

But yet I slew him manfully, *in fight* ['while fighting'].—*Two G. of V.*, iv. 1.

That's a fault that water will mend.—No, sir, 'tis *in grain* ['dyed of a fast or fixed colour,' 'stained indelibly']; Noah's flood could not do it.—*Com. of E.*, iii. 2.

'Tis *in grain*, sir, 'twill endure wind and weather.—*Tw. N.*, i. 5.

The quintessence of every sprite Heaven would *in little* ['in miniature,' 'in abstract,' 'epitomised'] show.—*As You L.*, iii. 2 (*Verses*).

A hundred ducats apiece for his picture *in little*.—*Hamlet*, ii. 2.

This day was view'd *in open* ['openly,' 'publicly'] as his queen.—*H. VIII.*, iii. 2.

I fear me thou wilt give away thyself *in paper* ['in securities,' 'in bonds'] shortly.—*Timon*, i. 2.

To London, all *in post* ['in post-haste,' 'at utmost speed']; and, as I guess, to make a bloody supper in the Tower.—3 *H. VI.*, v. 5.

All this I speak *in print* ['literally,' 'exactly'], for *in print* ['in printed form,' 'in type'] I found it.—*Two G. of V.*, ii. 1.

I will do it, sir, *in print* ['literally,' 'accurately,' 'faithfully,' 'punctually'].—*Love's L. L.*, iii. 1.

Oh, sir, we quarrel *in print* ['according to printed form,' 'methodically,' 'systematically'], by the book.—*As You L.*, v. 4.

I love a ballad *in print* ['printed,' 'in printed form'], a'-life; for then we are sure they are true.—*W. T.*, iv. 3.

We must speak *by the card* ['accurately,' 'correctly,' 'precisely,' 'according to the rule laid down in the register, calendar, or card of etiquette'], or equivocation will undo us.—*Hamlet*, v. 1.

Tell me *in sadness* ['seriously,' 'sedately'], who is that you love.—*R. & Jul.*, i. 1.

Now, *in good sadness* ['in all seriousness,' 'seriously speaking'].—*Tam. of S.*, v. 2.

Or, *in sooth* ['in truth,' 'truly'], I would Master Fenton had her.—*Merry W.*, iii. 4.

Well drawn, monster, *in good sooth* ['in all truth,' 'truly,' 'indeed'].—*Temp.*, ii. 2.

Good troth, you do me wrong—*good troth*, you do.—*Mid. N. D.*, ii. 3.

Sooth, when I was young, and handed love as you do.—*W. T.*, iv. 3.

And, *sooth to say*, in countenance somewhat doth resemble you.—*Tam. of S.*, iv. 2.

Very sooth, to-morrow.—*W. T.*, i. 2.

Yet, *good deed*, Leontes, I love thee not a jar o' the clock behind.—*Ibid.*, i. 2.

I may not, *verily*.—*Verily! . . . Verily* you shall not go: a lady's *verily* is as potent as a lord's . . . by your dread *verily*, one of them you shall be.—*Ibid.*, i. 2.

In truth, sir, and she is pretty, and honest.—*Merry W.*, i. 4.

In good truth, the poet makes a most excellent description of it.—*H. V.*, iii. 6.

O, that I knew he were but *in by the week!* ['really engaged to me,' 'really my servant:' the phrase was formerly used when hiring attendants or labourers; and the lady-speaker uses it of her suitor, because 'servant' was sometimes employed for lover or wooer].—*Love's L. L.*, v. 2.

Let the music *knock it* ['strike up,' 'sound out'].—*H. VIII.*, i. 4.

Her offence must be of such unnatural degree, *that monsters it* ['as to be monstrous,' 'as to assume the proportions of a monster'], or your.—*Lear*, i. 1.

I hope *it is not so low with him* ['affairs are not at such low ebb with him,' 'he is not so badly off'] as he made it seem in the trial of his several friends.—*Timon*, iii. 6.

We'll *keep no great ado* ['make no great fuss,' 'have not much ceremony'], a friend or two.—*R. & Jul.*, iii. 4.

I pr'ythee, tell me, doth he *keep his bed?* ['remain in bed']—1 *H. IV.*, iv. 1.

Other slow arts entirely *keep the brain* ['possess the brain,' 'occupy the brain'].—*Love's L. L.*, iv. 3.

You mar our labour : *keep your cabins* ['remain in your cabins '].—*Temp.*, i. 1.

If of life you *keep a care* ['take heed,' 'preserve the desire '],
Shake off slumber, and beware.—*Ibid.*, ii. 1 (*Song*).

Did ever dragon *keep so fair a cave ?* ['dwell in so fair a cave ']—*R. & Jul.*, iii. 2.

And make them *keep their caves* ['remain in their caves '].—*Lear*, iii. 2.

He 's much out of health. and *keeps his chamber* ['remains in,' 'is confined to his chamber '].—Many do *keep their chambers*, are not sick.—*Timon*, iii. 4.

How hard it is for women to *keep counsel* ['preserve secrecy,' 'keep a secret '].—*Jul. C.*, ii. 4.

Two may *keep counsel*, putting one away ?—*R. & Jul.*, ii. 4.

I can *keep honest counsel* ['keep honest secrets '].—*Lear*, i. 4.

I pray you, turn the key, and *keep our counsel* ['keep our secret '].—*Oth.*, iv. 2.

I will, at the least, *keep your counsel* ['keep your secret '].—*Merry W.*, iv. 6.

Keep your fellows' counsels and your own ['be discreet, all of you ']; and good night.—*M. Ado*, iii. 3.

He did *keep the deck* ['remain on deck '].—*Cym.*, i. 4.

Keep the door ['guard the door ']. O thou vile king.—*Hamlet*, iv. 5.

Dromio, *keep the gate* ['stay at the gate, to prevent any one entering '].—*Com. of E.*, ii. 2.

But *keep the hills* ['remain upon the hills '] and upper regions.—*Jul. C.*, v. 1.

Keep house ['be at the head of the household '], and ply his book . . .
Keep house, and port, and servants, as I should.—*Tam. of S.*, i. 1.

A goodly day not to *keep house* ['remain indoors '], with such.—*Cym.*, iii. 3.

I may call him my master, look you, for I *keep his house* ['take care of his house,' 'am his housekeeper '].—*Merry W.*, i. 4.

Who cannot keep his wealth must *keep his house* ['stay at home,' 'remain indoors'].—*Timon*, iii. 3.

You will turn good husband now, Pompey ; you will *keep the house.*—*M. for M.*, iii. 2.

If he would not *keep so good a house* ['maintain so expensive a household '].—*Timon*, iii. 1.

But at this hour the house *doth keep itself* ['takes care of itself']; there 's none within.—*As You L.*, iv. 3.

And I 'll *keep London* ['take possession of London,' 'keep guard over London '] with my soldiers.—3 *H. VI.*, i. 1.

Shall we disturb him, since he *keeps no mean ?* ['observes no moderation in his talk,' 'keeps no measure in his conversation '].—1 *H. VI.*, i. 2.

But *keeps the pridge* ['retains possession of,' 'maintains his position on,' 'militarily occupies the bridge '] most valiantly.—*H. V.*, iii. 6.

The Earl of Pembroke *keeps his regiment* ['remains with his regiment'].—*R. III.*, v. 3.

You would swear directly their very noses had been counsellors to Pepin or Clotharius, they *keep state so* ['bear themselves with such stateliness,' 'behave so pompously '].—*H. VIII.*, i. 3.

That would have brook'd the eternal devil to *keep his state* ['reign,' 'have dominion '] in Rome as easily as a king.—*Jul. C.*, i. 3.

But tell the Dauphin I will *keep my state* ['behave right royally ']; be like a king, and show my sail of greatness.—*H. V.*, i. 2.

Our hostess *keeps her state* ['remains in her seat of state ']; but, in best time, we will require her welcome.—*Macb.*, iii. 4.

Keeps his tent ['remains in his tent '] like him.—*Tr. & Cr.*, i. 3.

Who *keeps the tent* ['remains in his tent '] now ?—*Ibid.*, v. 1.

If we lose the field, we cannot *keep the town* ['maintain military possession of the town '].—*Coriol.*, i. 7.

To sit and *keep the turn of tippling* ['drink foot to foot,' 'have an equal drinking-bout '] with a slave.—*Ant. & C.*, i. 4.

Like peasant foot-boys do they *keep the walls* [' remain within the protection of the walls '], and dare not take up arms.—1 *H. VI.*, iii. 2.

And thou this day hadst *kept thy chair* [' retained possession of thy throne'] in peace.—3 *H. VI.*, ii. 6.

This blessed day ever in France shall be *kept festival* [' kept as a holiday'].— *John*, iii. 1.

Had all your quarters been so safely *kept* [' guarded,' ' defended,' ' watched '], as that whereof I had the government.—1 *H. VI.*, ii. 1.

I have not *kept my square* [' preserved decorum,' ' lived in an orderly manner,' ' maintained a regular course']; but that to come shall all be done by the rule.— *Ant. & C.*, ii. 3.

I am too blunt and saucy: *here's my knee* [' I'll kneel to thee '].—*Cym.*, v. 5.

Well, *here is my leg* [' I make my obeisance or salutation '].—1 *H. IV.*, ii. 4.

He that cannot *make a leg* [' make a bow,' ' make an obeisance '], put off's cap, kiss his hand.—*All's W.*, ii. 2.

You *make a leg*, and Bolingbroke says ay.—*R. II.*, iii. 3.

He'll *lay about him* [' fight well,' ' strike manfully '] to-day.—*Tr. & Cr.*, i. 2.

And *lay apart* [' put aside,' ' give up '] the borrow'd glories.—*H. V.*, ii. 4.

Would the nobility *lay aside* [' put by,' ' suspend '] their ruth.—*Coriol.*, i. 1.

Lay by [' put aside,' ' cease '] all nicety and prolixious blushes.—*M. for M.*, ii. 4.

Got with swearing, " *Lay by* " [' stand and deliver'; and, punningly, ' put by,' ' save up money'] and spent with crying, " Bring in."—1 *H. IV.*, i. 2.

Hung their heads, and then *lay by* [' remained still '].—*H. VIII.*, iii. 1 (*Song*).

And *lay for* [' lay myself out for,' ' endeavour to win,' ' strive to gain '] hearts.— *Timon*, iii. 5.

I see them *lay their heads together* [' consult together '], to surprise me.—2 *H. VI.*, iv. 8.

All of you have *laid your heads together* [' schemed,' ' plotted '] . . . to make away. —*Ibid.*, iii. 1.

I could *lay on* [' deal blows '] like a butcher.—*H. V.*, v. 2.

Lay on [' strike hard '], Macduff; and damn'd be he that first.—*Macb.*, v. 7.

If thou count'st it shame, *lay it on me* [' impute it to me,' ' lay it to my charge '].— *Tam. of S.*, iv. 3.

I would I could see this taborer! *he lays it on* [' he plays famously,' ' he gives us enough of his music '].—*Temp.*, iii. 2.

My father hath made her mistress of the feast, and she *lays it on* [' is profuse in her outlay '].—*W. T.*, iv. 2.

There's *laying on* [' dealing blows,' ' hearty fighting '].—*Tr. & Cr.*, i. 2.

Will you give me money, captain?—*Lay out, lay out* [' spend freely,' ' disburse lavishly '].—1 *H. IV.*, iv. 2.

Let it alone [' leave it untouched '], thou fool.—*Temp.*, iv. 1.

Ah, *let be, let be* [' let it alone,' ' leave off'].—*Ant. & C.*, iv. 4.

Let go [' be still,' ' press the point no farther '].—*Coriol.*, iii. 2.

Let go [' leave your hold ']; by heaven, I'll have it.—*Hamlet*, v. 2.

I *had as lief* [' am as willing '] you would tell me of.—*Merry W.*, iii. 1.

Warm slaves, as *had as lief* [' would as willingly '] hear the devil as a drum.— 1 *H. IV.*, iv. 2.

Nothing but heart's sorrow and a *clear life* [' pure life,' ' sinless life,' ' reformed life'] ensuing.—*Temp.*, iii. 3.

If grace had bless'd thee with a *fairer life* [' more virtuous life '].—*R. III.*, iv. 4.

So, with *good life* [' life-like enactment,' ' spirited performance or acting'] and observation strange.—*Temp.*, iii. 3.

Defend your reputation, or bid farewell to your *good life* [' character for honesty and virtuous conduct '] for ever.—*Merry W.*, iii. 3.

In respect of itself, it is *a good life* ['a pleasant life,' 'an agreeable mode of life'] ; but in respect that it is.—*As You L.*, iii. 2.

Would you have a love-song, or a song of *good life ?* ['virtuous conduct,' 'decorous behaviour'] . . . I care not for *good life.*—*Tw. N.*, ii. 3.

I know *my life so even* ['my life to be so uniformly virtuous, so consistently moral'].—*H. VIII.*, iii. 1.

His life was gentle ['his life was gracious, virtuous, well-bred, that of a gentleman, purely moral and good'].—*Jul. C.*, v. 5.

He hath a daily beauty in his life ['he has a grace and good estimation in his life'] that makes me ugly.—*Oth.*, v. 1.

Tut, *there's life in't* ['there is a hopeful element in it,'], man.—*Tw. N.*, i. 3.

Then *there's life in't* ['there is still a chance,' 'there is hope still'].—*Lear*, iv. 6.

There's sap in't yet ['there is vitality in it still,' 'our cause is not yet wholly without hope'].—*Ant. & C.*, iii. 11.

Cousin Hereford, *upon pain of life* ['on penalty of losing your life'], till twice five summers have enrich'd our fields.—*R. II.*, i. 3.

Kent, *on thy life* ['as thou valuest thy life'], no more !—*Lear*, i. 1.

Haste thee, *for thy life* ['as thou regardest life'].—*Ibid.*, v. 3.

To such a part, which never I shall discharge *to the life* ['with lifelike verisimilitude].—*Coriol.*, iii. 2.

And give them repetition *to the life* ['with lifelike precision of truth,' 'with vitality of perfect resemblance'].—*Per.*, v. 2.

This lodging *likes me* ['pleases me'] better, since I.—*H. V.*, iv. 1.

Which *likes me better* than to wish us one.—*Ibid.*, iv. 3.

The offer *likes not* ['does not please'].—*Ibid.*, iii. (*Chorus*).

Hold *little faith* ['a little faith,' 'some little faith'], though.—*Tw. N.*, v. 1.

But the mustard is too hot *a little* ['rather.' *See* "Good enough" cited previously under this heading.—*Tam. of S.*, iv. 3.

I would prick your guts *a little* ['rather ;' implying 'a good deal'].—*H. V.*, ii. 1.

When thou seest him, *a little* ['somewhat ;' implying 'emphatically,' 'witness my obedience'].—*Cym.*, iii. 4.

In Nature's infinite book of secrecy *a little* ['somewhat considerably'] I can read.—*Ant. & C.*, i. 2.

Yet come *a little* ['for a short time,' 'for a brief space'] . . . Get me some wine, and let me speak *a little* . . . .—*Ibid.*, iv. 13.

Let me speak *a little* ['for a short space ;' but implying 'very effectually']. This youth that you see here.—*Tw. N.*, iii. 4.

I am hush'd until our city be afire,
And then I'll speak *a little* ['very much to the purpose,' 'with concentrated force and import'].—*Coriol.*, v. 3.

That teacheth tricks *eleven and twenty long* ['to the amount of thirty-one'].—*Tam. of S.*, iv. 2.

A play there is, my lord, some ten words *long* ['hardly more than ten words in length'].—*Mid. N. D.*, v. 1.

I have been dear to him, lad—*some two thousand strong* ['to the tune of two thousand pounds,' 'to the amount of about two thousand pounds'] or so.—*Tw. N.*, iii. 2.

The Earl of Westmoreland, *seven thousand strong* ['with a force of seven thousand men'], is marching hitherwards.—1 *H. IV.*, iv. 1.

They say, the bishop and Northumberland are *fifty thousand strong* ['fifty thousand soldiers in strength,' 'have a force of fifty thousand men'].—2 *H. IV.*, iii. 1.

Unless you call *three fingers on the ribs* ['the width of three fingers in fat upon the ribs'] bare.—1 *H. IV.*, iv. 2.

These keep seeming and savour *all the winter long* ['all through the winter,' 'all the length of the winter'].—*W. T.*, iv. 3.

This bird of dawning singeth *all night long.*—*Hamlet*, i. 1.

And there live we *as merry as the day is long* ['merry from morning till night,' 'merry all through the day'].—*M. Ado*, i. 1.

I should be *as merry as the day is long.*—*John*, iv. 1.

He loves your wife; *there's the short and the long* ['there is the whole truth of the matter'].—*Merry W.*, ii. 1.

That sal I surely do, *that is the breff and the long.*—*H. V.*, iii. 2.

And fought *a long hour* ['a full hour,' 'more than an hour,' 'a tedious hour'] by Shrewsbury clock.—*1 H. IV.*, v. 4.

A hundred mark is *a long one* ['a heavy one;' implying 'a heavy loan,' 'a large sum'] for a poor lone woman to bear.—*2 H. IV.*, ii. 1.

Farewell, *a long farewell* ['a final farewell,' 'an eternal farewell'], to all my greatness!—*H. VIII.*, iii. 2.

You're *a made old man* ['a man whose fortune's made,' 'a fortunate old man']: if the sins of your youth are forgiven.—*W. T.*, iii. 3.

If our sport had gone forward, we had all been *made men* ['men whose fortunes were made'].—*Mid. N. D.*, iv. 2.

And *thinks himself made* ['thinks himself most fortunate'] in the unchaste composition.—*All's W.*, iv. 3.

As *I am made* ['my fortune's made,' 'my position is made'] without him, so I'll stand, if the king please —*H. VIII.*, ii. 2.

If it prove lawful prize, *he's made* ['his fortune is made'] for ever.—*Oth.*, i. 2.

There's enough to *make us all* ['make the fortunes of us all'] —*1 H. IV.*, ii. 2.

This is the night that either *makes me* ['makes my fortune,' 'ensures my success'], or fordoes me quite.—*Oth.*, v. 1.

And *what they made* ['what they did'] there, I know not.—*Merry W.*, ii. 1.

What made your master ['what did your master do'] in this place?—*R. & Jul.*, v. 3.

But *what make you here?* ['what do you do here' 'what causes you to be here'].—*Merry W.*, iv. 2.

What make you from home? ['what causes you to be away from home'].—*Oth.*, iii. 4.

Foul wrinkled witch, *what mak'st thou* ['what dost thou,' 'what causest thou to be'] in my sight?—*R. III.*, i. 3.

One that *made means* ['contrived,' 'took surreptitious measures'] to come by what he hath.—*Ibid.*, v. 3.

There was never yet fair woman, but she *made mouths* ['made grimaces,' 'practised captivating looks'] in a glass.—*Lear*, iii. 2.

Makes mouths at ['mocks at,' 'defies'] the invisible event.—*Hamlet*, iv. 4.

He is *so made on* ['made so much of,' 'so idolised'] here within.—*Coriol.*, iv. 5.

The bird is dead, that we have *made so much on* ['cherished so dearly,' 'petted so much'].—*Cym.*, iv. 2.

I will *make much of* ['set much store by'] your voices.—*Coriol.*, ii. 3.

Be comfortable to my mother, your mistress, and *make much of her* ['cherish her well,' 'take good care of her'].—*All's W.*, i. 1.

Make much of him ['prize him dearly,' 'take good care of him'], my lords; for this is he, must help you more.—*3 H. VI.*, iv. 6.

And *make as much of me* ['regard me as devotedly'], as when.—*Ant. & C.*, iv. 2.

What *faults he made* ['faults he committed'] before.—*Coriol.*, v. 5.

Had you been as I took you for, I *made no offence* ['committed no offence'].—*H. V.*, iv. 8.

What offence hath this man *made you* ['done you,' 'offered you,' 'committed against you'].—*M. for M.*, iii. 2.

Towards him I made ['I went towards him']; but he.—*R. & Jul.*, i. 1.

Seeing this goodly vessel ride before us, *I made to it* ['I came to it,' 'I directed my course towards it'].—*Per.*, v. 1.

With horsemen, that *make to him* ['speed to him,' 'hie to him,' 'hurry to him'] on the spur.—*Jul. C.*, v. 3.

Look, how he *makes to* ['approaches,' 'goes toward'] Cæsar.—*Jul. C.*, iii. 1.

They 've left their barge, and landed ; and *hither make* ['approach,' 'come hither'].—*H. VIII.*, i. 4.

A portly sail of ships *make hitherward* ['approach,' 'direct their course hither'].—*Per.*, i. 4.

Are *making hither* ['directing their course hither'] with all due expedience.—*R. II.*, ii. 1.

Make after ['hasten after'] him, poison his delight.—*Oth.*, i. 1.

Albeit considerations infinite do *make against it* ['tell against it,' 'make it ineligible'].—*1 H. IV.*, v. 1.

As the time and place doth *make against me* ['tell against me,' 'bear evidence against me'].—*R. & Jul.*, v. 3.

There is no bar to *make against* ['form an impediment to'] your highness' claim to France.—*H. V.*, i. 2.

And what beside may *make against* ['prejudice,' 'injure'] the house of Lancaster.—*3 H. VI.*, ii. 1.

Desperation is all the policy, strength, and defence, that Rome can *make against* ['muster against,' 'bring against'] them.—*Coriol.*, iv. 6.

Which *makes much against* ['detracts from,' 'tells against'] my manhood, if I should take from another's pocket.—*H. V.*, iii. 2.

Foreslow no longer; *make we hence amain* ['let us hasten away'].—*3 H. VI.*, ii. 3.

Two ships from far *making amain* ['hastening,' 'coming swiftly'] to us.—*Com. of E.*, i. 1.

If we do now *make our atonement* ['take a conciliatory course'], well, our peace will like a broken limb united.—*2 H. IV.*, iv. 1.

He desires to *make atonement* ['effect a reconciliation,' 'bring about an agreement'] between the Duke of Gloster and.—*R. III.*, i. 3.

To *make atonements* ['effect reconciliations' or 'agreements'] and compromises between you.—*Merry W.*, i. 1.

It may be judged I *made the duke away* ['killed the duke'].—*2 H. VI.*, iii. 2.

O joy, e'en *made away* ['dispersed,' 'dissolved,' 'drowned in tears'], ere it can be born!—*Timon*, i. 2.

And all to *make away* ['destroy,' 'put an end to'] my guiltless life.—*2 H. VI.*, iii. 1.

One of them is hereabout, and cannot *make away* ['get away,' 'get off,' 'escape'].—*Oth.*, v. 1.

I kill thee, *make thee away* ['destroy thee,' 'murder thee'].—*As You L.*, v. 1.

And thine ignorance *makes thee away* ['destroys thee'].—*All's W.*, i. 1.

I was too strict to *make mine own away* ['destroy' or 'ruin my own offspring'].—*R. II.*, i. 3.

Hence ! *make your best of it* ['bear it as well as you can,' 'do the best you may with it,' and 'make the best of your way away,' 'be off as quickly as you can'].—*Tam. of S.*, iv. 3.

Let 's *make the best of it* ['put the best construction we can upon this deed,' 'give the best version we can of it'].—*Coriol.*, v. 5.

And thou that art his mate, *make boot* ['make profit,' 'make your advantage'] of this.—*2 H. VI.*, iv. 1.

Give him no breath, but now *make boot* of his distraction.—*Ant. & C.*, iv. 1.

She that *makes dainty* ['hesitates,' 'is coy,' 'squeamishly refuses'], she, I 'll swear, hath corns.—*R. & Jul.*, i. 5.

And he that stands upon a slippery place,
Makes nice ['squeamishly refuses to take advantage'] of no vile hold to stay him up.—*John*, iii. 4.

She *makes it strange* ['affects coyness,' 'pretends aversion'] ; but she would be best pleased.—*Two G. of V.*, i. 2.

Make the doors ['make the doors fast' (*See* "Make fast," previously cited), 'fasten the doors'] upon a woman's wit.—*As You L.*, iv. 1.

At this time *the doors are made* ['the doors are fastened'] against you.— *Com. of E.*, iii. 1.

He's a god or a painter; for he *makes faces* [punningly, 'creates countenances, 'limns countenances,' and 'makes grimaces'].—*Love's L. L.*, v. 2.

Shame itself! why do you *make such faces?* ['twist your face into such contortions,' 'look so grimly'].—*Macb.*, iii. 4.

If the drink you give me touch my palate adversely, I *make a crooked face* ['pull a wry face,' 'make a grimace'] at it . . . if you chance to be pinched with the colic, you *make faces* ['make wry faces,' or 'grimaces'] like mummers.—*Coriol.*, ii. 1.

But by *the fair weather that you make yourself* ['the conciliation that you practise']: it is needful that.—*M. Ado*, i. 3.

But I must *make fair weather* ['practise conciliation'] yet awhile, till Henry be more weak.—2 *H. VI.*, v. 1.

He sits in his state, as a thing *made for* ['framed to represent'] Alexander.— *Coriol.*, v. 4.

Make for ['direct your course to,' 'repair to'] Sicilia; and there present yourself.— *W. T.*, iv. 3.

He *makes for* ['shapes his course towards'] England.—*R. III.*, iv. 4.

Therefore the dukes of Berry and of Bretagne . . . . shall *make forth* ['set out,' 'depart'], and you.—*H. V.*, ii. 4.

Make forth ['march forward,' 'advance']; the generals.—*Jul. C.*, v. i.

The bow is bent and drawn, *make from* ['get out of the way of,' 'stand clear of,' 'hasten away from'] the shaft.—*Lear*, i. 1.

Get posts and letters, and *make friends* ['collect friends,' 'gather together those who are friendly to our cause'].—2 *H. IV.*, i. 1.

For those you *make friends* ['win into friendship with you,' 'treat as friends'], and give your hearts to.—*H. VIII.*, ii. 1.

I pray you, *make us friends* ['establish a friendly relation between us']; I will pursue the amity.—*All's W.*, ii. 5.

Since this bar in law *makes us friends* ['produces friendship between us'], it shall be so far forth.—*Tam. of S.*, i. 1.

Which since we cannot do to *make you friends* ['render you friendly to each other'], be ready, as your lives.—*R. II.*, i. 1.

Our best friends *made* ['secured,' 'attached firmly to us'], and our best means stretch'd out.—*Jul. C.*, iv. 1.

And all thy friends—which thou must *make thy friends* ['secure in friendly bonds,' 'attach firmly,' 'strengthen into friendly adherents']—have but their stings.— 2 *H. IV.*, iv. 4.

The poor advanc'd *makes friends of enemies* ['turns enemies into friends']. And hitherto doth love on fortune tend.—*Hamlet*, iii. 2.

This I *made good* ['rendered obvious,' 'verified,' 'proved'] to you in our last conference.—*Macb.*, iii. 1.

Our potency *made good* ['established,' 'proved,' 'testified'], take thy reward.— *Lear*, i. 1.

Saw'st thou not, boy, how Silver *made it good* ['recovered the lost scent,' 're-established the track of the game'] at the hedge corner, in the coldest fault?—*Tam. of S.*, *Induc.* 1.

Made good ['rendered impassable,' 'firmly blocked up,' 'resolutely defended'] the passage, cried to those that fled.—*Cym.*, v. 3.

What I told you then, I hope I shall have leisure to *make good* ['confirm,' 'fulfil,' 'realise'].—*Com. of E.*, v. i.

This letter doth *make good* ['confirm,' 'prove true'] the friar's words.— *R. & Jul.*, v. 3.

Here to *make good* ['confirm,' 'maintain,' 'uphold'] the boisterous late appeal . . . My body shall *make good* upon this earth.—*R. II.*, i. 1.

Take convenient numbers to *make good* ['defend,' 'hold sure possession of'] the city.—*Coriol.*, i. 5.

I will *make it good* ['confirm my words,' 'back my accusation'] how you dare, with what you dare, and when you dare.—*M. Ado*, v. 1.

Shall be their father's bail. . . . I'll warrant they'll *make it good* ['support it,' 'ratify it'].—2 *H. VI.*, v. 1.

Hector . . . shall *make it good* ['uphold his challenge'].—*Tr. & Cr.*, i. 3.

Make that good ['prove that assertion,' 'explain that saying'].—*Tw. N.*, i. 5.

If he *make this good* ['verify this eulogy of him'], he is.—*Two G. of V.*, ii. 4.

What power is in Agrippa, if I would say, "Agrippa, be it so," to *make this good* ['substantiate this proposal'].—*Ant. & C.*, ii. 2.

Then go with me, to *make the matter good* ['put the plan in practice,' 'carry out our scheme'].—*Tam. of S.*, iv. 2.

Three times hath Henry Bolingbroke *made head* ['raised a hostile force,' 'risen in rebellion'] against my power.—1 *H. IV.*, iii. 1.

When Tarquin *made a head* for Rome, he fought.—*Coriol.*, ii. 2.

Tullus Aufidius, then, had *made new head?*—*Ibid.*, iii. 1.

Let us *make head* ['raise a hostile force,' 'rise in rebellion'].—2 *H. IV.*, i. 1.

We must straight *make head.*—*Jul. C.*, iv. 1.

If we, without his help, can *make a head* to push.—1 *H. IV.*, iv. 1.

In time, may *make some stronger head* ['offer a more rebellious opposition,' 'rise into rebellion'].—*Cym.*, iv. 2.

Making another head ['raising a fresh force'] to fight again.—3 *H. VI.*, ii. 1.

And all indign and base adversities
Make head ['muster hostilely'] against my estimation!—*Oth.*, i. 3.

Make holiday ['revel festively,' 'play instead of work'].—*Temp.*, iv. 1.

But, indeed, sir, we *make holiday*, to see Cæsar.—*Jul. C.*, i. 1.

In which time I will *make a lip* ['look scornfully,' or 'mockingly'] at the physician. —*Coriol.*, ii. 1.

And *make and mar* ['fulfil and frustrate'] the foolish fates.—*Mid. N. D.*, i. 2.

It makes him, and it mars him ['it inspirits him,' 'and it dispirits him']; it sets him on, and it takes him off.—*Macb.*, ii. 3.

It makes us, or it mars us ['it gives us complete success, or it discomfits us entirely']; think on that.—*Oth.*, v. 1.

I'll *make one* ['take a part'] in a dance, or so.—*Love's L. L.*, v. 1.

To *make one* ['be one'] among these wooers.—*Tam. of S.*, i. 1.

Lucentio shall *make one*, though Paris came.—*Ibid.*, i. 2.

I'll *make one* ['be of the party'] too.—*Tw. N.*, ii. 5.

Where thou wilt, lad, I'll *make one*. . . . Hal, wilt thou *make one?*—1 *H. IV.*, i. 2.

I could wish to *make one* ['be one of the combatants'] there.—*Per.*, ii. 1.

I shall *make two* ['be a second'] in the company.—*Merry W.*, iii. 3.

I will plant you two, and let the fool *make a third* ['be a third in this party'], where he shall find the letter.—*Tw. N.*, ii. 3.

There's two of you; the devil *make a third* ['may form a third of the same description'].—2 *H. VI.*, iii. 2.

Seven of my people, with an obedient start, *make out* ['hasten out of the room'] for him.—*Tw. N.*, ii. 5.

You are a merry gamester, my lord Sands.—Yes, if I *make my play* ['succeed in my play,' 'win my game'].—*H. VIII.*, i. 4.

Every way *makes my game** ['ensures my success,' 'wins the stake I play for,' 'suits my purpose'].—*Oth.*, v. 1.

---

* "Game" is the word in the Quarto reading of this passage; 'gaine' in the First and Second Folio, and 'gain' in the Third Folio.

Made prize and purchase of ['took captive and secured'] his wanton eye.— *R. III.*, iii. 7.

Cæsar's no merchant, to *make prize* ['take account,' 'reckon up,' 'chaffer'] with you of things that.—*Ant. & C.*, v. 2.

Let 's fetch him off, or *make remain* ['remain,' 'stay'] alike.—*Coriol.*, i. 4.

That to our sister you do *make return* ['return,' 'go back'].—*Lear*, ii. 4.

To *make road* ['make an inroad,' 'march hostilely'] upon us again.—*Coriol.*, iii. 1.

Or a part to *tear a cat in*, to *make all split* ['rant and roar'].—*Mid. N. D.*, i. 2.

Is it your will to *make a stale of me* ['offer me as a stale bargain,' 'put me into the awkward dilemna of being offered to the first bidder'] amongst these mates.—*Tam. of S.*, i. 1.

Had he none else to *make a stale* ['make a dupe of,' 'make a stalking-horse of'] but me ?—3 *H. VI.*, iii. 3.

This is the pent-house under which Lorenzo desir'd us to *make stand* ['stand,' 'take up our stand'].—*Mer. of V.*, ii. 6.

Doth *make a stand at* ['resolve upon,' 'decide upon,' 'fix upon'] what your highness will.—*John*, iv. 2.

In this covert will we *make our stand* ['take up our stand'].—3 *H. VI.*, iii. 1.

Therefore I 'll *make him sure* ['make sure of him,' 'make sure work with him']; yea, and I 'll swear I killed him.—1 *H. IV.*, v. 4.

If I can get him within my pistol's length,
I 'll *make him sure.*—*Per.*, i. 1.

Of late *made many tenders of* ['frequently proffered,' 'often professed'] his affection to me.—*Hamlet*, i. 3.

If she should *make tender of* ['proffer,' 'offer,' 'profess'] her love, 'tis very possible he 'll scorn it.—*M. Ado*, ii. 3.

May *make tender of* to thy true worthiness.—*Love's L. L.*, ii. 1.

And show'd thou *mak'st some tender of* ['hast some loving regard for,' 'holdest in some tenderness'] my life,—1 *H. IV.*, v. 4.

All other circumstances *made up* ['being confirmatory'] to the deed.—*W. T.*, ii. 1.

Sent before my time into this breathing world, scarce half *made up* ['formed,' 'framed'].—*R. III.*, i. 1.

Being scarce *made up* ['grown,' 'arrived'], I mean, to man, he had not apprehension of.—*Cym.*, iv. 2.

Each syllable that breath *made up* ['formed,' 'gave utterance to'] between them.— *Oth.*, iv. 2.

Remain assur'd that he's a *made up* ['consummate,' 'complete,' 'accomplished,' 'finished'] villain.—*Timon*, v. 1.

Will *make up full clear* ['fully clear up,' 'make fully and clearly apparent'], whensoever he 's convented.—*M. for M.*, v. 1.

As strongly as words could *make up* ['constitute'] vows.—*Ibid.*, v. 1.

Beg thou, or borrow, to *make up* ['complete,' 'raise in full'] the sum.— *Com. of E.*, i. 1.

Two of both kinds *make up* ['amount to'] four.—*Mid. N. D.*, iii. 2.

That you three fools lack'd me fool, to *make up* ['complete,' 'fulfil the complement of'] the mess.—*Love's L. L.*, iv. 3.

O, ay, *make up* ['make out the full meaning of'] that.—*Tw. N.*, ii. 5.

Philip, *make up* ['bring up your forces'] : my mother is assail'd.—*John*, iii. 2.

I beseech your majesty, *make up*, lest your retirement do amaze your friends . . . *Make up* to Clifton : I 'll to Sir Nicholas.—1 *H. IV.*, v. 4.

The sands are number'd that *make up* ['sum up'] my life.—3 *H. VI.*, i. 4.

He *makes up* ['designs,' 'appoints the names on,' 'selects those who are to be on'] the file of all the gentry.—*H. VIII.*, i. 1.

Than to *make up* ['form,' 'come to'] a free determination.—*Tr. & Cr.*, ii. 2.

Could not, with all their quantity of love,
Make up [' amount to '] my sum.—*Hamlet*, v. 1.

Election *makes not up* [' cannot come to a decision '] on such conditions.—*Lear*, i. 1.

The gods *make up* [' confer an equivalent for '] the rest upon you !—*Per.*, iii. 3.

This bottle *makes an angel* [' amounts to an angel of money '] that I have already spent for you.—1 *H. IV.*, iv. 2.

While I *make way* [' hasten away '] from hence to save my life.—*Tam. of S.*, i. 1.

Make way [' give me room to pass '], unruly woman !—*R. II.*, v. 2.

This might have been prevented, and *made whole* [' set to rights,' ' adjusted '], with very easy arguments of love.—*John*, i. 1.

For their own credit sake, *make all whole* [' settle matters duly,' ' adjust all difficulties,' ' put matters straight '].—1 *H. IV.*, ii. 1.

You shall *make it whole* [' restore it to good and harmonious condition '] again ; you shall piece it out with a piece of.—*Tr. & Cr.*, iii. 1.

A piece of work that will *make sick men whole* [' restore sick men to health,' ' render sick men well '].—*Jul. C.*, ii. 1.

That *no manner person* [' no kind of person,' ' no person whatever '] have any time recourse unto the princes.—*R. III.*, iii. 5.

I think your highness *saw this many a day* [' has seen for this period of many days ']. —*H. VIII.*, v. 2.

Many a time and often [' very many times and frequently.' *See* PLEONASMS] I have dined with him.—*Timon*, iii. 1.

Done. The wager ?—A laughter.—*A match* [' agreed '].—*Temp.*, ii. 1.

You shall have it, worthy sir.—*A match* [' agreed ; ' and, punningly, ' a pair '] there is in all two worthy voices begged.—*Coriol.*, ii. 3.

Or I 'll *cry a match* [' affirm that I have won the race '].—*R. & Jul.*, ii. 4.

I vill teach a scurvy Jack-a-nape priest to *meddle or make* [' interfere and make mischief '].—*Merry W.*, i. 4.

The less you *meddle or make* [' interfere,' ' have to do '] with them, why, the more is for your honesty.—*M. Ado*, iii. 3.

I 'll not *meddle nor make* [' mix myself up,' ' interfere '] no farther.—*Tr. & Cr.*, i. 1.

Spirit, we must prepare to *meet with* [' counteract,' ' defeat by opposing measures '] Caliban.—*Temp.*, iv. 1.

That Falstaff at that oak shall *meet with* [' come according to assignation with '] us. —*Merry W.*, iv. 2.

How rarely does it *meet with* [' accord with,' ' consist with '] this time's guise, when man was wished to love his enemies !—*Timon*, iv. 3.

Me seemeth [' it appears to me '] good, that, with some. —*R. III.*, ii. 2.

Methinks [' I think,' ' it seems to me '] he hath no drowning mark.—*Temp.*, i. 1.

My loving greetings to *those of mine* [' those who belong to me,' ' my relations,' ' my kinsfolk '] in court.—*All's W.*, i. 3.

A gentleman *of mine* [' belonging to my retinue '] I have despatched with letters. —*R. II.*, iii. 1.

O God, I fear, thy justice will take hold
On me, and you, and *mine* [' those who belong or are related to me '], and yours, for this.—*R. III.*, ii. 1.

That you shall all repent the loss of *mine* [' my relatives,' 'my kinsmen '].—*R. & Jul.*, iii. 1.

Look, here comes one, a gentlewoman *of mine* [' under my charge, care, or jurisdiction '].—*M. for M.*, ii. 3.

But, as 'tis, we *cannot miss* [' cannot do without '] him.—*Temp.*, i. 2.

Your free undertaking *cannot miss* [' cannot fail to have '] a thriving issue.—*W. T.*, ii. 2.

He *misses not* [' does not err,' ' does not mistake '] much.—*Temp.*, ii. 2.

Who might be your mother ? [This phrase, in reference to a beauty's " *mother*," appears to us to contain some idiomatic scoff, the point of which was known at the time when Shakespeare wrote ; but which it is difficult to ascertain at present. *See* our next-quoted passage, in support of our belief].—*As You L.*, iii. 5.

Some jay of Italy, *whose mother was her painting* ['the producer of whose beauty was her rouged face,' 'whose sole origin of comeliness was her painted complexion'; also including the scoff we believe to be involved in our precedingly quoted passage. *See*, moreover, the two following passages].—*Cym.*, iii. 4.

Nor *thy tailor*, rascal, *who is thy grandfather : he made those clothes, which*, as it seems, *make thee.—Ibid.*, iv. 2.

You cowardly rascal, nature disclaims in thee : *a tailor made thee.—Lear*, ii. 2.

Why, I said nothing.—*Mum* ['be silent,' 'silence'], then, and no more.—*Temp.*, iii. 2.

Speak not you to him, till we call upon you.—*Mum* ['I am silent,' ' I will be silent'].— *M. for M.*, v. 1.

I will hold my tongue ; so your face bids me, though you say nothing. *Mum, mum.—Lear*, i. 4.

The citizens *are mum* ['are silent'], say not a word.—*R. III.*, iii. 7.

That's as much as to say, bastard virtues ; that, indeed, know not their fathers, and therefore *have no names* ['are illegitimate'].—*Two G. of V.*, iii. 1.

Then, belike, my children shall *have no names* ['be illegitimate'].—*Ant. & C.*, i. 2.

Thy issue blurr'd with *nameless* ['illegitimate'] bastardy.—*Lucrece, Stanza* 75.

I have cases of buckram *for the nonce* ['for the occasion,' 'for the emergency'], to immask our noted outward garments.—1 *H. IV.*, i. 2.

This is a riddling merchant *for the nonce* ['for the occasion,' 'now'].—1 *H. VI.*, ii. 3.

I 'll have prepar'd him a chalice *for the nonce* ['for that occasion,' 'for the special purpose '].—*Hamlet*, iv. 7.

By seven *o'clock* ['of the clock,' ' on the clock '] I 'll get.—*Two G. of V.*, iii. 1.

I pray *what is 't o'clock* ['what is the time by the clock '].—*As You L.*, iii. 2.

Eighty odd ['eighty and some more'] years of sorrow.—*R. III.*, iv. 1.

Of wounds *two dozen odd* ['two dozen and more'].—*Coriol.*, ii. 3.

Every tod yields—*pound and odd shilling* ['a pound and some shillings over, or more'].—*W. T.*, iv. 2.

Three hundred and odd ['three hundred and some more'] pounds.—1 *H. IV.*, iv. 2.

A fortnight, *and odd days* ['and some days more '].—*R. & Jul.*, i. 3.

The fox, the ape, and the humble-bee
Were still *at odds* ['forming an odd number ;' and, punningly, 'at variance with each other'], being but three.—*Love's L. L.*, iii. 1.

I do not know that Englishman alive, with whom my soul is any jot *at odds* ['at outs,' ' out of favour,' 'unagreed,' 'in quarrel'].—*R. III.*, ii. 1.

And pity 'tis you liv'd *at odds* so long.—*R. & Jul.*, i. 2.

What is the night ?—Almost *at odds* ['at an even question,' 'at a moot point,' 'at an uncertain period'] with morning, which is which.—*Macb.*, iii. 1.

Every hour he flashes into one gross crime or other, that sets us all *at odds* ['at variance,' 'in opposition to each other,' 'in disorder,' 'in confusion'].—*Lear*, i. 3.

His quails ever beat mine, inhoop'd, *at odds* ['when pitted against each other,' and 'when there is a more than even wager pending'].—*Ant. & C.*, ii. 3.

I shall win *at the odds* ['even if there be an unequal bet laid on my winning'] . . . your grace hath *laid the odds* ['laid a more than even wager '] . . . we have therefore *odds* [' the advantage on our side '].—*Hamlet*, v. 2.

Is *at most odds* ['most at variance,' 'most out of keeping'] with his own gravity and patience that ever you saw.—*Merry W.*, iii. 1.

The odds is [' it is more than an even chance'], that we scarce are men, and you are gods.—*Cym.*, v. 2.

But now *'tis odds* ['there is an inequality of chances'] beyond arithmetic.— *Coriol.*, iii. 1.

And, of that natural luck, he beats thee *'gainst the odds* ['against all probabilities of superior advantage in unequal betting '].—*Ant. & C.*, ii. 3.

Hold, sir, or *I'll throw your dagger o'er the house* ['I'll attack you recklessly, furiously'].—*Tw. N.*, iv. 1.

That *I have shot mine arrow o'er the house* ['I have made a reckless aim,' 'I have behaved too regardlessly'].—*Hamlet*, v. 2.

Nor with such free and friendly conference,
As he hath us'd *of old* ['formerly,' 'in former times'].—*Jul. C.*, iv. 2.

Even for that our love *of old*, I pray thee, hold thou.—*Ibid.*, v. 5.

For those *of old*, and the late dignities heap'd up.—*Macb.*, i. 6.

Three talents *on the present* ['on the moment,' 'on the nail,' 'in present payment']; in future, all.—*Timon*, i. 1.

But *that's all one* ['that is of no consequence'], if he be.—*Two G. of V.*, iii. 1.

But, I warrant you, *all is one* ['it is of no consequence,' 'it is no matter'] with her.—*Merry W.*, ii. 2.

Must needs be granted to be much *at one* ['of one rate of goodness,' 'upon a par'].—*H. V.*, v. 2.

I would we were all *of one mind* ['of the same way of thinking,' 'of the same opinion'], and *one mind* good.—*Cym.*, v. 4.

Both our inventions meet and *jump in one* ['accord together,' 'prove one and the same'].—*Tam. of S.*, i. 1.

Whose mind and mine, I know, in that *are one* ['are the same,' 'are agreed'].—*Lear*, i. 3.

I met a courier, *one mine ancient friend* ['an old friend of mine,' 'one of my old friends.' See ITALIAN IDIOM].—*Timon*, v. 3.

Motley's *the only wear* ['the best,' 'the most excellent,' 'the chief thing for wearing']. . . . *It is my only suit.*—*As You L.*, ii. 7.

Glasses, glasses, is *the only drinking* ['the best for drinking from'].—*2 H. IV.*, ii. 1.

He is the *only* ['chiefest,' 'highest in excellence'] man in Italy.—*M. Ado*, iii. 1.

Your worm is your *only* ['choicest'] emperor for diet.—*Hamlet*, iv. 3.

Here she comes weeping for her *only* ['chief,' 'principal'] mistress' death.—*Per.*, iv. 1.

Thou wast not *out* ['completely'] three years old.—*Temp.*, i. 2.

Could speak thee *out* ['completely,' 'thoroughly'].—*H. VIII.*, ii. 4.

Thou hast beat me *out* ['out and out,' 'thoroughly'] twelve several times.—*Coriol.*, iv. 5.

Very good orators, when they are *out* ['put out,' 'disconcerted'], they will spit.—*As You L.*, iv. 1.

When the butt is *out* ['empty,' 'exhausted'], we will drink water.—*Temp.*, iii. 2.

The limit of your lives is *out* ['expired'].—*R. III.*, iii. 3.

On the catastrophe and heel of pastime,
When it was *out* ['over,' 'at an end,' 'concluded'].—*All's W.*, i. 2.

Why dost thou not speak, Elbow?— He cannot, sir, *he's out at elbow* ['he has a threadbare coat;' and, punningly, 'he is startled and put out by this peremptory repetition of his name'].—*M. for M.*, ii. 1.

Well, sirs, I am almost *out at heels* ['penniless,' 'ragged,' 'ill-shod'].—*Merry W.*, i. 3.

The poor jade is wrung in the withers *out of all cess* ['out of all measure,' 'beyond reckoning,' 'excessively'].—*1 H. IV.*, ii. 1.

He loved her *out of all nick* ['beyond all means of reckoning'].—*Two G. of V.*, iv. 2.

And yet again, wonderful, and after that, *out of all whooping!* ['beyond the loudest exclamations of amazement'].—*As You L.*, iii. 2.

Should have kept short, restrain'd, and *out of haunt* ['out of company,' 'apart from general concourse or society'].—*Hamlet*, iv. 1.

And I paid nothing for it neither, but was *paid* ['paid out,' 'served out,' 'beaten'] for my learning.—*Merry W.*, iv. 5.

Two, I am sure, I have *paid* . . . seven of the eleven I *paid*.—*1 H. IV.*, ii. 4.

I have *paid* Percy, I have made him sure.—*Ibid.*, v. 3.

I am *paid* ['punished,' 'made to suffer'] for 't now.—*Ant. & C.*, ii. 5.

Here's that, I warrant you, will *pay them* ['pay them out'] all.—*Com. of E.*, iv. 2.

Swore he would *pay him again* ['serve him out,' 'give him like for like'] when he was able.—*Mer. of V.*, i. 2.

Or he shall *pay* ['suffer severely'] for this.—*Ibid.*, ii. 8.

If this prove true they'll *pay* for 't.—*W. T.*, ii. 1.

If we prevail, their heads shall *pay* ['pay the penalty'] for it.—*R. II.*, iii. 2.

You *pay* him ['punish him,' 'pay him out'] then !—*H. V.*, iv. 1.

He *pays you* ['retaliates upon you,' 'pitches into you'] as surely as your feet hit the ground they step on.—*Tw. N.*, iii. 4.

Pardon me ['forgive me'] wife. Henceforth do what thou wilt.—*Merry W.*, iv. 4.

Oh, sir, *pardon me !* ['excuse me'].*—*Ant. & C.*, iv. 12.

Your graces find me here *part of a housewife* ['somewhat of a housewife,' 'in some measure a housewife'].—*H. VIII.*, iii. 1.

As 'twere *in love's particular* ['from a motive of particular affection'], be more to me, your friend, than any.—*Ibid.*, iii. 2.

Who lov'd him *in a most dear particular* ['with a most particular affection']—*Coriol.*, v. 1.

Yet our old love *made a particular force* ['acted with special effect,' 'gave the motive of private feeling'].—*Timon*, v. 3.

Nor does the ministration and required office *on my particular* ['as regards me in particular,' 'in my own person,' 'in me personally'].—*All's W.*, ii. 5.

As far *as touches my particular* ['as regards myself'].—*Tr. & Cr.*, ii. 2.

My more particular ['my own more personal motive'], and that which most with you should safe my going, is Fulvia's death.—*Ant. & C.*, i. 3.

Of him, that, *his particular to foresee* ['having an eye to his own private interest'], smells from the general weal.—*Timon*, iv. 3.

Yet I wish, sir (I mean, *for your particular* ['for your own sake'].—*Coriol.*, iv. 7.

Forgive me *in thine own particular* ['as regards thyself,' 'in thine own person']; but let the world.—*Ant. & C.*, iv. 9.

For his particular ['as far as himself is concerned'], I 'll receive him gladly, but not one follower.—*Lear*, ii. 4.

As for these silken-coated slaves, *I pass not* ['I care not,' 'I heed not,' 'I pay no regard to them.' *See* "Force not," previously cited].—*2 H. VI.*, iv. 2.

Though well we may not *pass upon* ['pass judgment upon,' 'pass sentence upon,' 'decide condemningly upon'] his life without the form of justice, yet our power shall do.—*Lear*, iii. 7.

The jury, *passing on* ['passing judgment on,' 'passing sentence on'] the prisoner's life, may . . . . what know the laws that thieves do *pass on* ['pass sentence on'] thieves?—*M. for M.*, ii. 1.

The women so cried and shriek'd at it, that *it passed* ['it exceeded all belief,' 'it was beyond imagination'].—*Merry W.*, i. 1.

And all the rest so laughed, that *it passed*.—*Tr. & Cr.*, i. 2.

A most incomparable man . . . *he passes* ['he surpasses,' 'he excels,' 'he exceeds the ordinary race of men'].—*Timon*, i. 1.

Why, *this passes !* ['this exceeds belief,' 'this goes beyond the bounds of credibility']. . . . *This passes !*—*Merry W.*, iv. 2.

'Tis *passing good* ['excellent']: I pr'ythee let me have it.—*Tam. of S.*, iv. 3.

The which he loved *passing well* ['extremely'] . . . a daughter that I love *passing well*.—*Hamlet*, ii. 2.

A maiden battle, then? O, *I perceive you* ['I understand your meaning,' 'I perceive your drift'].—*Tr. & Cr.*, iv. 5.

---

* *See* "Richard II.," v. 3, for a passage in illustration of these two modes of using "pardon me"; where York says:—

"Speak it in French, king; say, *pardonnez moi*."

Nay, *conceive me, conceive me* ['comprehend what I mean'], sweet coz; what I do, is to pleasure you, coz.—*Merry W.*, i. 1.

I cannot conceive you ['I do not understand your meaning'].—*Lear*, i. 1.

Tut, a pin! ['pooh, nonsense!' 'pshaw, this is trifling!'] this shall be answered —*Merry W.*, i. 1.

Pho, pho! come, *tell a pin* ['you are talking nonsense,' 'you are trifling']: you are forsworn.—*Tr. & Cr.*, v. 2.

No matter for the dish, sir.—No, indeed, sir, *not of a pin* ['it does not signify a jot,' 'it is no matter in the least'].—*M. for M.*, ii. 1.

I would not *care a pin* ['care the least,' 'care the most trifling amount'] if the other three were in.—*Love's L. L.*, iv. 3.

Yet here's one *in place* ['now present'] I cannot pardon.—*M. for M.*, v. 1.

As firmly as yourself were still *in place* ['there present'].—*Tam. of S.*, i. 2.

When yet you were *in place* ['in worldly position'], and in account, nothing so strong and fortunate as I.—1 *H. IV.*, v. 1.

An I had thee *in place where* ['in a spot where we might fight it out,' 'in a fitting spot'], thou shouldst know it.—*Tam. of S.*, iv. 3.

Ay, or very falsely *pocket up* ['receive,' 'accept for true'] his report.—*Temp.*, ii. 1.

Let me *pocket up* ['put in my pocket,' 'hide away'] my pedler's excrement.—*W. T.*, iv. 3.

You did *pocket up* ['put away unread'] my letters.—*Ant. & C.*, ii. 2.

Well, ruffian, I must *pocket up* ['put up with,' 'bear,' 'brook,' 'endure'] these wrongs because.—*John*, iii. 1.

You will not *pocket up* wrong.—1 *H. IV.*, iii. 3.

If I should take from another's pocket, to put into mine; for it is plain *pocketing up of wrongs* ['putting up with injuries,' and, punningly, 'putting stolen goods into one's pocket']—*H. V.*, iii. 2.

Bequeathed me by will but *poor a thousand crowns* ['a mere thousand crowns.' *See* ITALIAN IDIOM].—*As You L.*, i. 1.

A hundred upon *poor four of us* ['merely four of us'].—1 *H. IV.*, ii. 4.

Ah, *poor our sex* ['our poor sex'], this fault in us I find.—*Tr. & Cr.*, v. 1.

Ah, *poor, my lord* ['my poor lord'], what tongue shall smooth?—*R. & Jul.*, iii. 2.

What *poor an instrument* ['how poor an instrument,' 'what a poor instrument'] may do a noble deed!—*Ant. & C.*, v. 2.

See, they have shut him in.—*To the pot* ['gone to pot,' 'gone to perdition'], I warrant him.—*Coriol.*, i. 4.

She is now the wife of Marcus Antonius.—*Pray you* [similar to 'I beg your pardon?' used to imply, 'Did I understand you rightly?' or 'What did you say?'], sir?—'Tis true—*Ant. & C.*, ii. 6.

I do not like thy look, *I promise thee* ['I can assure thee'].—*M. Ado*, iv. 2.

Not by my consent, *I promise you* ['I assure you'].—*Merry W.*, iii. 2.

Will you sup with me to-night, Casca?—No, I am *promised forth* ['engaged to go out,' 'under a promise to visit elsewhere'].—*Jul. C.*, i. 2.

And all my pains is *sorted to no proof* ['proved of no avail,' 'tended to no purpose,' 'met with no approval'].—*Tam. of S.*, iv. 3.

But *to the purpose* ['let us proceed at once to the point in question']—*Two G. of V.*, iv. 1.

And my misgiving still falls shrewdly *to the purpose* ['apt in its drift,' 'appositely,' 'correct in its aim'].—*Jul. C.*, iii. 1.

What should we say, my lord?—Why, anything—but *to the purpose* ['straight-forwardly,' 'with directness and truth'].—*Hamlet*, ii. 2.

Since, of two usuries, the merriest was *put down* ['suppressed'], and the worser allowed by order of law a furred gown.—*M. for M.*, iii. 2.

You have *put him down* ['silenced him,' 'snubbed him,' 'mortified and quashed him,' 'subdued him'], lady, you have *put him down*.—*M. Ado*, ii. 1.

Mark now, how a plain tale shall *put you down* ['confute you] —1 *H. IV.*, ii. 4.

To seek to *put me down* ['depose me'], and reign thyself.—3 *H. VI.*, i. 1.

It is best *put finger in the eye* ['whimper,' 'cry like a baby'], an she knew why.— *Tam. of S.*, i. 1.

No longer will I be a fool, to *put the finger in the eye*, and weep.—*Com. of E.*, ii. 2.

Put in ['cut in,' ' go forward,' 'make your claim,' ' present your bill '] now, Titus.— *Timon*, iii. 4.

The ship is here *put in* ['entered the port,' ' sailed into the harbour '].—*Oth.*, ii. 1.

Who *put* unluckily *into* ['sailed into '] this bay.—*Com. of E.*, v. 1.

I see, lady, the gentleman is *not in your books* ['not in your favour,' ' not in your good graces '].—*M. Ado*, i. 1.

O, *put me in thy books* ['take me into your good graces '].—*Tam. of S.*, ii. 1.

He hath *ta'en you newly into his grace* ['taken you lately into his favour '].— *M. Ado*, i. 3.

Will you be *put in mind* ['reminded'] of his blind fortune.—*Coriol.*, v. 5.

I am thus bold to *put your grace in mind* ['remind your grace '] of what you promis'd me.—*R. III.*, iv. 2.

I 'll *put it in proof* ['put it to the proof,' ' put it in practice '].—*Lear.*, iv. 6.

Go, *put it to the haste* ['put it into speedy execution,' ' do it quickly '].—*Ant. & C.*, v. 2.

As common bruit doth *put it* ['represent it '].—*Timon*, v. 2.

I do repent me that I *put it* ['suggested it '] to you.—*Oth.*, iii. 3.

I will show you such a necessity in his death, that you shall think yourself bound to *put it* ['inflict it '] on him.—*Ibid.*, iv. 2.

I *put you o'er* ['refer you'] to heaven, and to my mother.—*John*, i. 1.

Even here I will *put off* ['give up,' ' yield,' ' discard '] my hope.—*Temp.*, iii. 3.

Yet I cannot *put off* ['alter,' ' reverse '] my opinion so easily.—*Merry W.*, ii. 1.

But *puts it off* ['defers it '] to a compell'd restraint.—*All's W.*, ii. 4.

Finely *put off !* ['shot, as a telling retort,' ' thrust, as a parrying rejoinder ']. . . . Finely *put on* ['urged, as a final home-blow']. . . . Finely *put on*, indeed !—*Love's L. L.*, iv. 1.

Put off ['lay aside,' ' cease '] your maiden blushes.—*H. V.*, v. 2.

Have *put off* ['discarded,' ' discharged '] the spinsters, carders, fullers, weavers, who, unfit for other life, compell'd.—*H. VIII.*, i. 2.

He hath sent me an earnest inviting, which many my near occasions did urge me to *put off* ['decline,' ' waive,' ' excuse myself from accepting '].—*Timon*, iii. 6.

Puts him off ['foils him,' ' baffles him,' ' snubs him,' ' parries his attack '], slights him, with " Whoop, do me no harm, good man."—*W. T.*, iv. 3.

That thus you should proceed to *put me off* ['repudiate me,' ' divorce me,' ' put me away '], and take your good grace from me ?—*H. VIII.*, ii. 4.

He hath *put me off* ['postponed me,' ' prorogued me,' ' deferred me '] to the suc- cession of new days this month. . . . Your steward *puts me off*, my lord.—*Timon*, ii. 2.

Ay, and the targets, to *put off* ['avert,' ' protect from '] the shame.—*Per.*, i. 1.

There 's a barge *put off from* ['left the harbour of,' ' left the shore of '] Mitylene.— *Ibid.*, v. 1.

Let me cut the cable : and, when we are *put off* ['away from the harbour,' ' away from the land '], fall to their throats.—*Ant. & C.*, ii. 7.

What place make you special, when you *put off* ['dismiss'] that with such contempt ? . . . He may easily *put it off* ['dismiss a subject,' ' parry an attack,' ' carry a matter off coolly '] at court : he that cannot make a leg, *put off 's* ['take off'] his cap, kiss his hand ; . . . O Lord, sir ! there 's a simple *putting-off* ['means of parrying an attack,' ' carrying off a matter coolly '].—*All's W.*, ii. 2.

Try your penitence, if it be sound, or hollowly *put on* ['assumed '].—*M. for M.*, ii. 3.

Which he will *put on us* ['cram us with,' ' force upon us '], as pigeons feed their young.—*As You L.*, i. 2.

And the powers above *put on* ['urge forward,' 'incite'] their instruments.—*Macb.*, iv. 3.

If it be so (as so 'tis *put on* ['suggested to,' 'hinted to'] mé).—*Hamlet*, i. 3.

And there *put on* ['impute to'] him what forgeries.—*Ibid.*, ii. 1.

Devils will the blackest sins *put on* ['instigate'].—*Oth.*, ii. 3.

Say, you ne'er had done 't (harp on that still) but by our *putting-on* ['instigation,' 'incitement'].—*Coriol.*, ii. 3.

Than in *putting on* ['assuming,' 'wearing'] the mere form.—*Oth.*, ii. 1.

You are abus'd, and by some *putter-on* ['instigator,' 'inciter,' 'suggester'], that will be damn'd for 't.—*W. T.*, ii. 1.

As *putter-on* ['instigator and imposer,'] of these exactions.—*H. VIII.*, i. 2.

What not *put upon* ['impute to,' 'lay to the charge of'] his spungy officers, who shall bear the guilt.—*Macb.*, i. 7.

And *put upon him* ['assumed,' 'gave himself the airs of'] such a deal of man, that worthied him.—*Lear*, ii. 2.

You *put me* ['compel me,' 'force me'] to forget a lady's manners.—*Cym.*, ii. 3.

And *put us* ['compel us,' 'constrain us'] to our answer.—*Ibid.*, iv. 2.

Then she *puts you to* ['brings you,' 'causes you to make'] entreaty, and there begins new mattter.—*As You L.*, iv. 1.

I shall now *put you* ['test you,' 'try you'] to the height of your breeding.—*All's W.*, ii. 2.

You have *put me now to* ['set me now to enact,' 'induced me now to perform'] such a part.—*Coriol.*, iii. 2.

Let him *put me to my purgation* ['put me to the test,' 'bring me to my proof'].—*As You L.*, v. 4.

For me to *put him to his purgation* ['bring him to book,' 'cleanse his impurities'] would, perhaps, plunge him.—*Hamlet*, iii. 2.

O gentle lady, do not *put me to 't* ['set me this task'].—*Oth.*, ii. 1.

Mark Antony *put me to* ['drove me to,' 'excited me to,' 'roused me to'] some impatience.—*Ant. & C.*, ii. 6.

The traitor lives, the true man's *put to death* ['killed'].—*R. II.*, v. 3.

Our treasure seiz'd, our soldiers *put to flight* ['made to fly'].—*3 H. VI.*, iii. 3.

Had hoisted sail, and *put to sea* ['gone out to sea'] to-day.—*Com. of E.*, v. 1.

I am *put to sea* with her, whom here I cannot hold.—*W. T.*, iv. 3.

To take his brother here, and *put him to the sword* ['kill him, murder him'].—*As You L.*, v. 3.

Peace . . . should not . . . in . . . France, *put up* ['raise again'] her lovely visage ?—*H. V.*, v. 2.

Had not your man *put up* ['sent up in flight,' 'started from its cover'] the fowl so suddenly, we had had more sport.—*2 H. VI.*, ii. 1.

Show thy valour, and *put up* ['sheathe'] your sword . . . pry'thee, *put up* ['sheathe thy sword'].—*H. V.*, ii. 1.

Put up ['put in thy pocket'] thy gold.—*Timon*, iv. 3.

Why so earnestly seek you to *put up* ['conceal,' 'hide away'] that letter.—*Lear*, i. 2.

'Faith, we may *put up* ['put away in their cases'] our pipes.—*R. & Jul.*, iv. 5.

Nor am I yet persuaded, to *put up* ['put up with,' 'brook,' 'endure'] in peace what already I have foolishly suffered.—*Oth.*, iv. 2.

It is, *in contempt of question* ['without doubt,' 'indisputably'] her hand.—*Tw. N.*, ii. 5.

As I subscribe not that, nor any other,
But *in the loss of question* ['losing sight of the question,' 'merely for the sake of argument']—that you, his sister.—*M. for M.*, ii. 4.

This haste was *hot in question* ['the subject of warm debate'],
And many limits of the charge set down but yesternight.—*1 H. IV.*, i. 1.

'Tis the way to *call hers*, exquisite, *in question more* ['to make her beauty the more a subject of admiration.' *See* "Call in question," previously cited].—*R. & Jul.*, i. 1.

For those earthly faults, *I quit them all* ['I acquit you of them all'].—*M. for M.*, v. 1.

Hortensio will be *quit with* ['even with '] thee by changing.—*T. of S.*, iii. 1.

To quit their grief ['to parallel their grief,' 'to render an equivalent for their grief,' 'to requite their grief'], tell thou the lamentable tale of me.—*R. II.*, v. 1.

I think thou art *quit for that* ['free of blame on that score'].—*2 H. IV.*, ii. 4.

He that dies this year is *quit for* ['exempt for,' 'unliable for'] the next.—*Ibid.*, iii. 2.

So we were *quit here* ['safe away from here,' 'free from danger here'].—*H. V.*, iv. 1.

To be *full quit of* ['fully even with,' 'fully revenged upon'] those my banishers, stand I before thee here.—*Coriol.*, iv. 5.

I am quit ['I am quit of thee,' 'I am rid of thee'].—*Timon*, iv. 3.

Draw; seem to defend yourself; now '*quit you well* ['acquit yourself well'].—*Lear*, ii. 1.

Took such sorrow, that he *quit being* ['left life,' 'died '].—*Cym.*, i. 1.

Being ignorant to whom it goes, I writ *at random* ['at hap-hazard,' 'without special direction'], very doubtfully.—*Two G. of V.*, ii. 1.

You being then, *if you be remembered* ['if you remember'], cracking the stones. . . . I telling you then, *if you be remembered.*—*M. for M.*, ii. 1.

Not so sharp as friend *remember'd not* ['remembering not'].—*As You L.*, ii. 7 (*Song*).

Now *I am remember'd* ['I remember'], scorn'd at me.—*Ibid.*, iii. 5.

If you be remember'd ['if you remember'] I did not bid you.—*Tam. of S.*, iv. 3.

If your majesty *is remembered of it* ['remember it'].—*H. V.*, iv. 7.

If I had *been remember'd* ['remembered it,' 'thought of it'], I could have given my uncle's grace a flout.—*R. III.*, ii. 4.

I have remember'd me ['I have bethought me,' 'now I think of it'], thou shalt hear our counsel.—*R. & Jul.*, i. 3.

I am now going to *resolve him* ['assure him'], I had rather my brother die by the law, than my son should.—*M. for M.*, iii. 1.

What, master, read you? first *resolve me that* ['solve me that point,' 'settle that question'].—*Tam. of S.*, iv. 2.

May it please your highness to *resolve me* ['settle the point for me,' 'decide my case'] now.—*3 H. VI.*, iii. 2.

Why, then *resolve me* ['give me your decision,' 'satisfy me definitely'], whether you will or no.—*R. III.*, iv. 2.

Resolve thee ['be resolved,' 'be resolute,' 'be decided'], Richard; claim the English crown.—*3 H. VI.*, i. 1.

I will *resolve you* ['give you my decision'] herein presently.—*R. III.*, iv. 2.

My letter will *resolve him of my mind* ['inform him of my decision,' 'let him know my resolution'].—*R. III.*, iv. 5.

He was a man; this, *in respect* ['respectively speaking,' 'comparatively speaking'], a child.—*3 H. VI.*, v. 5.

Where many *of the best respect* ['of the highest respectability'] in Rome.—*Jul. C.*, i. 2.

Thou art a fellow *of a good respect* ['of much respectability'].—*Ibid.*, v. 5.

So it be new, *there's no respect* ['it is of no consequence,' 'there is no regard or consideration paid to'] how vile.—*R. II.*, ii. 1.

And away with *the rest* ['the remainder'].—*Temp.*, iv. 1.

Who are *the rest?* ['the others'].—*Love's L. L.*, ii. 1.

The rest ['the other physicians'] have worn me out.—*All's W.*, i. 2.

Thanks, sir; *all the rest is mute* ['for anything beyond "thanks" I am silent'].—*Ibid.*, ii. 3.

Were you a woman, as *the rest* ['the other evidence'] goes even, I should my tears let fall.—*Tw. N.*, v. 1.

The name, and all the additions to a king;
The sway, revenue, execution of *the rest* ['the other offices which remain for a king to perform'].—*Lear*, i. 1.

As I have *set up my rest* ['made up my mind,' 'determined,' 'resolved'] to run away.—*Mer. of V.*, ii. 2.

Since you *set up your rest* ['make up your mind,' 'determine'] 'gainst remedy.—*All's W.*, ii. 1.

The County Paris hath *set up his rest* ['made up his mind,' 'resolved'] that you shall rest but little.—*R. & Jul.*, iv. 5.

Here will I *set up my everlasting rest* ['finally make up my mind for death'; and, with a play upon the phrase, 'remain for ever at peace'].—*Ibid.*, v. 3.

He that *sets up his rest* ['makes up his mind'] to do more exploits with his mace than a morris-pike.—*Com. of E.*, iv. 3.

I will do as I may: that is *my rest* ['the point of my resolve,' 'my determination'], —*H. V.*, ii. 1.

And longing (*saving your honour's reverence* ['with respect be it said,' 'begging your honour's pardon for the freedom of saying so']) for stewed prunes, sir.—*M. for M.*, ii. 1.

Such a one as a man may not speak of, without he say, *sir-reverence.*—*Com. of E.*, iii. 2.

I think you would have me say, *saving your reverence.*—*M. Ado*, iii. 4.

By the fiend, who, *saving your reverence*, is the devil himself. . . .

. . . His master and he (*saving your worship's reverence*) are scarce.—*Mer. of V.*, ii. 2.

But that he is (*saving your reverence*) a whoremaster.—*1 H. IV.*, ii. 4.

Draw thee from the mire of this (*save reverence*) love.—*R. & Jul.*, i. 4.

The rather (*saving reverence of the word*) for 'tis said.—*Cym.*, iv. 1.

Madam, be still,—*with reverence may I say*; for every word you.—*2 H. VI.*, iii. 2.

And care not who they sting *in his revenge* ['in revenge for him'].—*Ibid.*, iii. 2.

On safe-guard ['with a guard to protect him'] he came to me.—*Coriol.*, iii. 1.

Deliver him *to safety* ['to safe-keeping,' 'into custody']; and return.—*John*, iv. 2.

Hold him *in safety* ['in custody'], till the Prince come.—*R. & Jul.*, v. 3.

He hath the jewel of my life *in hold* ['in keeping,' 'in custody'].—*Tam. of S.*, i. 2.

How sayest thou ['what wilt thou say, when I tell thee'], that my master is become a notable lover?.—*Two G. of V.*, ii. 5.

My brother Jaques he keeps *at school* ['at college,' 'an academical student'], and report speaks goldenly.—*As You L.*, i. 1.

In going back *to school* ['to college,' 'to be a student'] in Wittenberg.—*Hamlet*, i. 2.

You will *set cock-a-whoop!* ['play the blusterer,' 'be bumptious,' 'be crowing,' 'be hectoring'], you'll be the man!—*R. & Jul.*, i. 5.

King Cophetua *set eye upon* ['saw'] the pernicious.—*Love's L. L.*, iv. 1 (*Letter*).

Now *set the teeth* ['clench the teeth, in token of firm will'], and stretch.—*H. V.*, iii. 1.

He did so *set his teeth*, and tear it.—*Coriol.*, i. 3.

And that would *set my teeth nothing on edge* ['not give my teeth nearly so much the sensation of grinding each other in desperation at hearing a discordant noise'], nothing so much as.—*1 H. IV.*, iii. 1.

Doth *set my pugging tooth on edge* ['whet my appetite for stealing,' 'sharpen my hunger for theft'].—*W. T.*, iv. 2 (*Song*).

Well, I'll *set you forth* ['show you up,' 'describe you finely'].—*Mer. of V.*, iii. 5.

Nay, I'll *tickle ye* ['touch you up,' 'show you up,' 'represent you finely'] for a young prince.—*1 H. IV.*, ii. 4.

We'll *set thee to school* ['send thee or put thee to school'] to an ant.—*Lear*, ii. 4.

I think you *set nothing by* ['think nothing of,' 'count as nothing'] a bloody coxcomb.—*Tw. N.*, v. 1.

Love *set on* ['placed on thy head'] thy horns.—*Merry W.*, v. 5.

To-morrow you *set on* ['set forth,' 'set out on your journey'].—*M. for M.*, iii. 1.

That that I did, I was *set on* ['instigated,' 'incited,' 'egged on'] to do't by Sir Toby.—*Tw. N.*, v. 1.

Now—Esperance!—Percy!—and *set on* ['make the onslaught'].—*1 H. IV.*, v. 2.

Cassio hath here been *set on* ['attacked'] in the dark.—*Oth.*, v. 1.

Labeo and Flavius, *set our battles on* ['lead our battalions on, forward, to the attack'].—*Jul. C.*, v. 3.

Set on your foot ['lead the way,' 'hasten forward,' 'put the best foot forwards'] and . . . I follow you.—*Jul. C.*, ii. 1.

Bid him *set on* ['set forward,' 'set out with,' 'send onwards'] his powers betimes before, and we will follow.—*Ibid.*, iv. 3.

So were there a patch *set on* ['placed on'] learning, to see him.—*Love's L, L.*, iv. 2.

Your wrongs do *set a scandal on* ['put or fix a scandal on'] my sex.—*Mid. N. D.*, ii. 2.

And *set me on the proof* ['put me to the proof.]—*Timon*, ii. 2.

No sooner achieved, but we'll *set upon* ['attack'] them.—1 *H. IV.*, i. 2.

We four *set upon* ['attacked'] some dozen . . . some six or seven fresh men *set upon* us.—*Ibid.*, ii. 4.

You shall enjoy them, everything *set off* ['set apart,' 'cast out,' 'thrown forth,' 'acquitted,' 'excluded,' 'excepted,' or 'counterbalanced,' 'rendered account for,' 'yielded retribution for'; the speaker purposely using an ambiguous expression in order to delude his hearers]—2 *H. IV.*, iv. 1.

This present enterprise *set off his head* ['not reckoned against him,' 'not set down to his account'], I do not think.—1 *H. IV.*, v. i.

That it is place which lessens and *sets off* ['displays to advantage,' 'gives favourable effect to'].—*Cym.*, iii. 3.

He hath a kind of honour *sets him off* ['adorns him,' 'embellishes him'], more than a mortal seeming.—*Ibid.*, i. 7.

Put thee into my service for any other reason than to *set me off* ['show me up,' 'make my size the more apparent'], why, then, I have no judgment.—2 *H. IV.*, i. 2.

When they were ready to *set out* ['depart,' 'set forth'] for London.—*H. VIII.*, ii. 2.

Whom you yourselves shall *set out* ['set apart,' 'point out'] for reproof.—*Timon*, v. 5.

I heard a bird so sing ['it is whispered abroad,' 'it is a current report'], whose music, to my thinking, pleas'd.—2 *H. IV.*, v. 5.

I sing but after you ['I speak but in your tune,' 'I do but follow the cue that you have given me,' 'I do but accord with your own words, or with what you have yourself said'].—*Ant. & C.*, i. 5.

Come, in what key shall a man take you, to *go in the song?* ['to accord with your opinion,' 'to speak in the same tune with you'].—*M. Ado*, i. 1.

O'er which his melancholy *sits on brood* ['broods,' 'dwells moodily'].—*Hamlet*, iii. 1.

E'er since *sits on his horseback* ['sits on horseback'] at.—*John*, ii. 1.

Whate'er he be, *it skills not much* ['it signifies little,' 'it matters not much.' *See* "Force not," previously cited], we'll fit him.—*Tam. of S.*, iii. 2.

So *it skills not* much when they are delivered.—*Tw. N.*, v. 1.

It skills not greatly who impugns our doom.—2 *H. VI.*, iii. 1.

Yet *'tis greater skill* ['it is more to the purpose,' 'more effectual,' 'of greater force'] in a true hate to pray.—*Cym.*, ii. 5.

It boots not ['it is of no use,' 'of no avail'] to complain.—*R. II.*, iii. 4.

It needs not, nor *it boots thee not*, proud queen.—3 *H. VI.*, i. 4.

It boots not to resist both wind and tide.—*Ibid.*, iv. 3.

He smells April and May ['he smells of spring-time,' 'he has an air of sweetness and floweriness about him'].—*Merry W.*, iii. 2.

A beggar, though she *smelt brown bread and garlic* ['smelt of coarse food,' 'had an unsavoury smell about her'].—*M. for M.*, iii. 2.

And boys, with women's voices, strive to *speak big* ['speak loud,' 'speak in a manly tone,' 'speak blusteringly'].—*R. II.*, iii. 2.

She has brown hair, and *speaks small* ['speaks softly'], like a woman.—*Merry W.*, i. 1.

And you may *speak as small* ['speak as softly'] as you will.—*Mid. N. D.*, i. 2.

He *speaks plain cannon* ['speaks like cannonading']—fire and smoke and bounce.—*John*, ii. 2.

I *speak to thee plain soldier* ['speak to thee as a plain soldier'].—*H. V.*, v. 2.

Didst *speak him fair?* ['did you speak to him gently and unreprovingly']— *om. of E.*, iv. 2.

Could he not *speak them fair* ['speak persuasively, unprovokingly']?—*Coriol.*, iii. 1.

You *speak him far* [' speak of him in largely praising terms,' 'with wide latitude of encomium'].—*Cym.*, i. 1.

Is my lord well, that he doth *speak so wide?* [' speak so wide of the truth,' 'far from the truth,' and 'so wide of, or far from, delicacy and propriety'].—*M. Ado*, iv: 1.

Speak within door [' speak not so loud as to be heard outside the house,' 'keep your tongue within bounds'].— *Oth.*, iv. 2.

He *speaks holiday* [' speaks finely,' 'in such terms as befit a festival,' 'with more than usual refinement'].—*Merry W.*, iii. 2.

He *speaks nothing but madman* [' speaks only mad stuff'].—*Tw. N.*, i. 5.

An he do nothing but *speak nothing* [' talk meaningless rubbish'], he shall be nothing here.—*2 H. IV.*, ii. 4.

Gratiano *speaks an infinite deal of nothing*, more than.—*Mer. of V.*, i. 1.

Drunk? and *speak parrot?* [' talk without sense, like a parrot'].—*Oth.*, ii. 3.

She *speaks poniards* [' speaks cuttingly,' 'sharply'] and every word stabs.—*M. Ado*, ii. 1.

Why, these are very *crotchets that he speaks* [whimsical repetitions of the words "note," "notes," and "noting"].—*Ibid.*, ii. 3.

To *speak puling* [' speak in a whining tone'], like a beggar at Hallowmas.—*Two G. of V.*, ii. 1.

Speak sad brow and true maid [' speak with a serious face and like a truth-telling maiden'].—*As You L.*, iii. 2.

Do you *speak in the sick tune?* [' in the tone of a sick person'].—*M. Ado*, iii. 4.

He *speaks the common tongue* [' uses the ordinary language,' 'repeats the general report'], which all men speak with him.—*Timon*, i. 1.

Speak to the business [' come at once to the matter in hand'], master secretary.— *H. VIII.*, v. 2.

I stand on fire: *come to the matter* [' come at once to the point in question'].—*Cym.*, v. 5.

When you *speak best unto the purpose* [' speak most appositely,' 'most efficiently'], it is not worth.—*Coriol.*, ii. 1.

For now I *speak to some purpose* [' speak with a serious meaning'].—*As You L.*, v. 2.

Thou never *spok'st to better purpose* [' more judiciously,' 'more effectively']. . . . But once before I *spoke to the purpose*: when?—*W. T.*, i. 2.

Lord Angelo is precise; *stands at a guard with envy* [' defies envy or detraction'].— *M. for M.*, i. 4.

And *stand the buffet* [' exchange blows'] with knaves that smell of sweat.— *Ant. & C.*, i. 4.

I *stand wholly for you* [' I am entirely in your favour'].—*Merry W.*, iii. 2.

Thou that *stand'st so for* [' art so stanch a partisan for'] Posthumus.—*Cym.*, iii. 5.

When he *did stand for* [' was candidate for the office of'] consul.—*Coriol.*, v. 5.

When Marcius *stood for* [' was a partisan for'] Rome.—*Ibid.*, iv. 6.

Stand good father to me [' be a kind father to me,' 'be favourable to me and to my suit'].—*Tam of S.*, iv. 4.

Stand my good lord [' befriend me,' 'be propitious to me'].—*2 H. IV.*, iv. 3.

Good master corporate Bardolph, *stand my friend.*—*Ibid.*, iii. 2.

Standing your friendly lord [' being your befriending advocate'].—*Coriol.*, ii. 3.

And make him *good friend* [' befriending advocate'] to the people.—*Ibid.*, ii. 3.

We'll be thy *good masters* [' befriending patrons,' 'benefactors'].—*W. T.*, v. 2.

I would be *good to thee* [' befriend thee'].—*Timon*, i. 2.

She's my good lady [' she is my good friend,' 'she befriends me': employed ironically in this passage].—*Cym.*, ii. 3.

He is my good lord [' he is my patron,' 'my benefactor'].—*All's W.*, ii. 3.

My hopes, not surfeited to death, *stand in bold cure* [' remain in confident expectation of being fulfilled'].—*Oth.*, ii. 1.

This rest might yet have balm'd thy broken senses,
Which, if convenience will not allow,
Stand in hard cure [' risk remaining unhealed'].—*Lear*, iii. 6.

His life, with thine . . . . *stand in assured loss* ['are exposed to sure peril '].—*Lear*, iii. 6.

Wherefore should I *stand in the plague of custom* ['remain, like a plague-smitten creature, set apart by custom '].—*Ibid.*, ii. 2.

Stands in attainder of ['remains convicted of,' 'remains disgraced with'] eternal shame.—*Love's L. L.*, i. 1.

My life *stands in the level* ['lies at the mercy'] of your dreams, which I 'll lay down. —*W. T.*, iii. 2.

The help of one *stands me in little stead* ['is of small use to me'].—1 *H. VI.*, iv. 6.

You *stand within his danger* ['are in his power as his debtor,' 'are liable to his exaction of payment on infliction of penalty, and are in danger of his vindictive measures'], do you not?—*Mer. of V.*, iv. 1.

Nor *stands it safe* ['is it safe'] with us, to let.—*Hamlet*, iii. 3.

Stand no more off ['repel me no longer,' 'remain no longer aloof'],
But give thyself unto my sick desires.—*All's W.*, iv. 2.

Though the truth of it *stands off* ['stands out,' 'shows forth prominently and distinctively'] as gross as black from white.—*H. V.*, ii. 2.

Your skill shall, like a star i' the darkest night,
Stick fiery *off* indeed.—*Hamlet*, v. 2.

This *comes off* well and excellent.—*Timon*, i. 1.

In these times you *stand on* ['attach much importance to'] distance, your passes, stoccadoes, and I know not what.—*Merry W.*, ii. 1.

The good I *stand on* ['rely upon'] is my truth and honesty.—*H. VIII.*, v. 1.

To *stand on* ['wait for,' 'dally with,' 'insist on using'] more mechanic compliment. —*Ant. & C.*, iv. 4.

Who *stand so much on* ['attach so much importance to,' 'stickle so much for'; and, punningly, 'stand up on'] the new form, that they cannot sit at ease on the old bench. —*R. & Jul.*, ii. 4.

Why, brother, wherefore *stand you on* ['lose time insisting upon'] nice points?—3 *H. VI.*, iv. 7.

And do not *stand on* quillets how to slay him.—2 *H. IV.*, iii. 1.

That *stands on* tricks whem I am undisposed.—*Com. of E.*, i. 2.

If that thy valour *stand on* ['is punctilious on the score of'] sympathy, there is my gage.—*R. II.*, iv. 1.

I *stand on* ['it behoves me to use'] sudden haste.—*R. & Jul.*, ii. 3.

And then *stand upon* ['insist upon'] security! . . . then they must *stand upon* security.—2 *H. IV.*, i. 2.

What conditions we shall *stand upon*? ['insist upon'].—*Ibid.*, iv. 1.

'Tis but the time, and drawing days out, that men *stand upon* ['are anxious for,' 'attach importance to'].—*Jul. C.*, iii. 1.

The sore terms we *stand upon* ['are on,' 'exist on'] with the gods.—*Per.*, iv. 3.

You *stand upon* ['are punctilious about'] your honour!—*Merry W.*, ii. 2.

And *stands upon* ['prides himself upon'] the honour of his birth.—1 *H. VI.*, ii. 4.

We *stand upon our manners* ['we are on our good behaviour,' 'we are anxious to show that we know how to behave'].—*W. T.*, iv. 3.

Stand not upon ['be not punctilious as to'] the order of your going, but go at once.—*Macb.*, iii. 4.

And *stand upon* ['insist upon having'] my common part.—*Coriol.*, i. 9.

Do not *stand upon 't* ['insist upon the point '].—*Ibid.*, ii. 3.

This fellow *doth not stand upon* ['is not particular about'] points.—*Mid. N. D.*, v. 1.

Consider how it *stands upon* ['affects,' 'concerns'] my credit.—*Com. of E.*, iv. 1.

Does it not, think'st thee, *stand me now upon* ['now behove me'] . . .
To quit him with this arm?—*Hamlet*, v. 2.

Because that now *it lies you on* ['it behoves you,' 'it is incumbent on you'] to speak to the people.—*Coriol.*, iii. 2.

For my state *stands on me* ['makes it incumbent on me,' 'requires me'] to defend, not to debate.—*Lear*, v. 1.

It *stands your grace upon* ['behoves your grace'] to do him right.—*R. II.*, ii. 3.

For *it stands me much upon* ['it is very important to me,' 'it concerns me nearly'] to stop all hopes.—*R. III.*, iv. 2.

It only *stands our lives upon* ['behoves us as we value our lives,' 'is needful for the sake of our lives'] to use our strongest hands.—*Ant. & C.*, ii. 1.

When articles, too nicely urg'd, be *stood on* ['insisted on'].—*H. V.*, v. 2.

I never *stood on* ['attached much importance to'] ceremonies, yet now they fright me.—*Jul. C.*, ii. 2.

For once we *stood up* ['made a stand,' 'contended,' 'asserted our rights,' 'showed fight'] about the corn.—*Coriol.*, ii. 3.

Or else it *stood upon* ['depended upon'] the choice of friends.—*Mid. N. D.*, i. 1.

You that *stood so much upon* ['insisted so much upon,' 'contended so much for'] the voice of occupation.—*Coriol.*, iv. 6.

Now for the rebels, which *stand out* ['continue in contumacy'] in Ireland.—*R. II.*, i. 4.

You have of late *stood out* ['maintained opposition'] against your brother.—*M. Ado*, i. 3.

Most of our city did: only myself *stood out* ['refused concession'].—*Tw. N.*, iii. 3.

That so *stood out* ['remained refractory'] against the holy church.—*John*, v. 2.

Makes him *stand to* ['remain firm to his purpose,' 'stick to his intention'], and not *stand to*.—*Macb.*, ii. 3.

'Tis he.—*Stand to 't* ['abide by your purpose'].—*Ibid.*, iii. 3.

Now, I 'll *stand to it* ['maintain'], the pancakes were naught.—*As You L.*, i. 2.

An thy mind *stand to 't* |'keep steady,' 'adhere,' 'remain in the same mood'], boy, steal away bravely.—*All's W.*, ii. 1.

And yet you will *stand to it* ['stick to the same story,' 'maintain it to be truth']; you will not pocket up wrong.—1 *H. IV.*, iii. 3.

Is 't a lusty yeoman? will he *stand to 't?* ['remain firm to his duty,' 'fulfil his office'].—2 *H. IV.*, ii. 1.

I beseech you, *stand to me* ['stand my friend,' 'befriend me'].—*Ibid.*, ii. 1.

I 'll back with you; and pray you, *stand to me* ['remain constant to me'] in this cause.—*Coriol.*, v. 3.

Or let us *stand to* ['abide by,' 'preserve'] our authority, or let us lose it.—*Ibid.*, iii. 1.

And call them pillars that will *stand to* ['abide by,' 'remain firm to'] us.—3 *H. VI.*, ii. 3.

Will speak more in a minute, than he will *stand to* ['stick to,' 'be true to,' 'fulfil,' 'make good'] in a month.—*R. & Jul.*, ii. 4.

To this point I stand ['I stick to this point,' 'I remain firm on this point'].—*Hamlet*, iv. 5.

Sir John *stands to* ['keeps,' 'abides by'] his word.—1 *H. IV.*, i. 2.

You speak not like yourself; who ever yet have *stood to* ['adhered to,' 'held by,' 'upheld'] charity.—*H. VIII.*, ii. 4.

We *stood to 't* ['remained firm'] in good time.—*Coriol.*, iv. 6.

I pray thee, if it *stand with* ['accord with,' 'be consistent with'] honesty,
Buy thou the cottage, pasture, and the flock.—*As You L.*, ii. 4.

For I *stay dinner* ['remain to dine'] there.—*R. III.*, iii. 2.

Tarry for the mourners, and *stay dinner.*—*R. & Jul.*, iv. 5.

The messengers of Venice *stay the meat* ['await the meal,' 'are waiting for the repast'].—*Oth.*, iv. 2.

Our throats are sentenced, and *stay upon* ['wait but for'] execution.—*Coriol.*, v. 4.

Worthy Macbeth, we *stay upon* your leisure.—*Macb.*, i. 3.

Be the players ready?—Ay, my lord; they *stay upon your patience* ['await your pleasure'].—*Hamlet*, iii. 2.

He *stays upon your will* [' awaits your willingness to see him '].—*Ant. & C.*, i. 2.

This creature's *no such thing* [' no such great things,' ' no such wonderful beauty '].—*Ibid.*, iii. 3.

With devotion's visage, and pious action, we do *sugar o'er* [' sweeten,' ' give a sweet appearance to '] the devil himself.—*Hamlet*, iii. 1.

And I am *sun-burned*, [' unattractive,' ' plain-looking,' ' not fair,' ' unlovely '].—*M. Ado*, ii. 1.

The Grecian dames are *sun-burned*, and not worth the.—*Tr. & Cr.*, i. 3.

Whose face *is not worth sun-burning* [' cannot be made plainer than it is naturally'].—*H. V.*, v. 2.

That am *with Phœbus' amorous pinches black* [' sun-burned,' ' dark-complexioned,' implying ' not fair,' ' not lovely '].—*Ant. & C.*, i. 5.

There did this perjur'd goldsmith *swear me down* [' browbeat me, by falsely swearing '] that I this day of him receiv'd.—*Com. of E.*, v. 1.

Lest the device *take air* [' get wind,' ' become breathed about,' ' become generally known'; and, punningly and figuratively, ' be exposed to the air '], and taint.—*Tw. N.*, iii. 4.

Be brisk awhile, and the longer liver *take all* [' be the winner,' ' have the best of it '].—*R. & Jul.*, i. 5.

And bids what will *take all*.—*Lear*, iii. 1.

My lord, you *take us even at the best* [' make the best of us,' ' accept us in the most favourable manner '].—*Timon*, i. 2.

Tell him Timon speaks it . . . and let him *take 't at worst* [' take it offensively,' ' take affront at it '].—*Ibid.*, v. 2.

I think affliction may subdue the cheek,
But not *take in* [' subdue,' ' overcome '] the mind.—*W. T.*, iv. 3.

Take in [' conquer,' ' defeat,' ' vanquish'] that kingdom, and enfranchise that —*Ant. & C.*, i. 1.

When he hath mus'd of *taking* kingdoms *in* [' conquering '].—*Ibid.*, iii. 11.

Take in [' reef,' ' contract,' ' reduce,' ' lessen '] the top-sail.—*Temp.*, i. 1.

And swore, with his own single hand he'd *take us in* [' capture us,' ' defeat us.' *See* " Fetch us in," previously cited].—*Cym.*, iv. 2.

Though I *take thee in* [' encounter thee in '] the king's company.—*H. V.*, iv. 1.

I will *take thee a box on the ear* [' give thee a box on the ear '].—*Ibid.*, iv. 1.

I have sworn to *take him a box o' the ear*.—*Ibid.*, iv. 7.

Take him on the costard [' strike him on the head '].—*R. III.*, i. 4.

For Heaven's sake, *take a house* [' take refuge in some holy house,' ' take sanctuary '].—*Com. of E.*, v. 1.

And your brother York, have *taken sanctuary* [' taken refuge under a consecrated roof '].—*R. III.*, iii. 1.

Cudgel you, and make you *take the hatch* [' leap over the half-door,' ' escape hastily '].—*John*, v. 1.

Come, Warwick, *take the time* [' take the opportunity '].—3 *H. VI.*, v. 1.

Every fairy *take his gait* [' take his way '].—*Mid. N. D.*, v. 2.

Let him *take his haste** [' make haste,' ' hasten.' *See* " Put it to the haste," previously cited], come hither.—*Timon*, v. 2.

Make your soonest haste [' hasten,' ' use despatch '].—*Ant. & C.*, iii. 4.

What *a taking was he in* [' a fright, flurry, fluster, or pucker, he was in '] when your husband asked what was in the basket.—*Merry W.*, iii. 3.

---

* The word " haste " has been suspected of error in this passage, and has been altered by some emendators; but the other instances here cited of similar idioms used by Shakespeare serve to show that it is his expression ; and, moreover, the parallel passage in North's Plutarch, whence Shakespeare evidently derived the groundwork for this play, aids in proving that " haste " is right.

You 'll mar the light by *taking it in snuff* ['taking it in anger,' 'taking offence at it']. —*Love's L. L.*, v. 2.

Who therewith angry, when it next came there, *took it in snuff*.—1 *H. IV.*, i. 3.

Marina's life seeks to *take off* ['destroy.' *See* "Fetch off," previously cited] by treason's knife.—*Per.*, iv. (*Gower*).

The deep damnation of his *taking-off* ['destruction,' 'murder,' 'assassination'].— *Macb.*, i. 7.

Let her, who would be rid of him, devise his speedy *taking-off*.—*Lear*, v. 1.

Seem to break loose; *take on* ['make pretence'], as you would follow; but yet come not.—*Mid. N. D.*, iii. 2.

It is my father's will, I should *take on me* ['assume,' 'undertake'] the hostess-ship o' the day.—*W. T.*, iv. 3.

'Twere no good part, to *take on me* to keep and kill thy heart.—*R. II.*, v. 1.

He *takes on him* to understand so much.—*Tw. N.*, i. 5.

If you will *take it on you* to assist him, it shall redeem.—*M. for M.*, iv. 2.

'Tis like you 'll prove a jolly surly groom,
That *take it on you* ['behave yourself,' 'conduct yourself'] at the first so roundly.— *Tam. of S.*, iii. 2.

You must *take Thisby on you* ['undertake to play the part of Thisbe'].— *Mid. N. D.*, i. 2.

One that *takes upon him* ['undertakes'] to be a dog indeed . . . to *take a fault upon me* ['be answerable for a fault,' 'acknowledge having committed a fault'] that he did. —*Two G. of V.*, iv. 4.

If this young gentleman have done offence, I *take the fault on me*.—*Tw. N.*, iii. 4.

She *takes upon her* ['behaves herself,' 'bears herself'] bravely at first dash.— 1 *H. VI.*, i. 2.

You must either be directed by some that *take upon them* ['undertake'] to know; or *take upon yourself* ['undertake to comprehend'] that, which I am sure you do not know.—*Cym.*, v. 4.

And *take upon command* ['take at your own disposal,' 'take according to your own pleasure'] what help we have.—*As You L.*, ii. 7.

She does so *take on with* ['chide,' 'scold,' 'rate at'] her men.—*Merry W.*, iii. 5.

He so *takes on* ['angrily complains'] yonder with my husband.—*Ibid.*, iv. 2.

How will my mother, for a father's death, *take on with* ['lamentingly rave at'] me, and ne'er be satisfied.—3 *H. VI.*, ii. 5.

Do: I 'll *take the sacrament on 't* ['take the sacrament as witness to my oath with regard to the truth of it'].—*All's W.*, iv. 3.

You shall not only *take the sacrament* to bury mine intents.—*R. II.*, iv. 1.

Takes on the point of honour ['pledges his honour,' 'takes the onus or responsibility upon his own honour'] to support so dissolute a crew.—*Ibid.*, v. 3.

They *take it already upon their salvation* ['already pledge their salvation'] that though I be but Prince of Wales.—1 *H. IV.*, ii. 4.

For, *take 't of my soul* ['I 'll pledge my soul upon it,' or 'I speak it from my soul'], my lord leans wondrously to discontent.—*Timon*, iii. 4.

I 'll *take it upon my death* ['take the risk of death as witness to my oath'], I gave him this wound in the thigh.—1 *H. IV.*, v. 1.

I will *take my death*, I never meant him any ill.—2 *H. VI.*, ii. 3.

And *took it on his death*, that this, my mother's son.—*John*, i. 1.

I *took 't upon mine honour* thou hadst it not.—*Merry W.*, ii. 2.

Therefore *this order hath Baptista ta'en* ['Baptista has taken these measures,' 'Baptista has provided'] that none.—*Tam. of S.*, i. 2.

There is order ta'en for you ['there have been measures taken for your disposal,' 'there has been provision made for you'].—*R. II.*, v. 1.

Honest Iago hath *ta'en order for 't* ['taken means to effect it,' 'made provision to secure its being done'].—*Oth.*, v. 2.

If your worship will *take order* ['take remedial measures'] for the drabs and the knaves —*M. for M.*, ii. 1.

Whilst to *take order* for the wrongs I went.—*Com. of E.*, v. 1.

I 'll *order take* ['take secure measures'] my mother shall not hear.—*All's W.*, iv. 2.

And I will *take such order* ['take such measures'], that thy friends shall ring for thee.—2 *H. IV.*, iii. 2.

Whilst I *take order* ['take due measures'] for mine own affairs.—2 *H. VI.*, iii. 1.

I will *take order* ['provide,' 'arrange'] for her keeping close.—*R. III.*, iv. 2.

Some one *take order* Buckingham be brought to Salisbury.—*Ibid.*, iv. 4.

I were unmannerly, to *take you out* ['select you as my partner in the dance and lead you forth to dance '], and not to kiss you.—*H. VIII.*, i. 4.

I 'll have the work *ta'en out* ['copied'], and give 't Iago.—*Oth.*, iii. 3.

Sweet Bianca, *take me this work out* ['copy this work for me']. . . . I like the work well : ere it be demanded (as like enough it will), I 'd have it copied.—*Ibid.*, iii. 4.

I must *take out* ['copy'] the work! . . . This is some minx's token, and I must *take out* the work! . . . I 'll *take out* no work on 't.—*Ibid.*, iv. 1.

Take your patience to you ['summon your patience to your aid'], and I 'll say nothing.—*W. T.*, iii. 2.

You must *take your patience to you.*—*H. VIII.*, v. 1.

I pray you, sir, *take patience :* I have hope.—*Lear*, ii. 4.

And never cried, "*Have patience*, good people!"—*As You L.*, iii. 2.

Pray you, *use your patience :* in good time.—*Merry W.*, iii. 1.

By your patience ['by your leave'], no.—*Tw. N.*, ii. 1.

Pray you, *be ever known to patience* ['still preserve your patience'].—*Ant. & C.*, iii. 6.

There cannot be those numberless offences 'gainst me, that I cannot *take peace with* ['take peacefully,' 'take with resignation and forgiveness'].—*H. VIII.*, ii. 1.

With my vex'd spirits I cannot *take a truce* ['pacify,' 'reduce to order or quietude']. —*John*, iii. 1.

Could not *take truce with* ['pacify'] the unruly spleen of Tybalt.—*R. & Jul.*, iii. 1.

The seas and winds (old wranglers) *took a truce* ['made temporary peace'], and did him service.—*Tr. & Cr.*, ii. 2.

Your majesty *takes no scorn* ['does not scorn'] to wear the leek upon Saint Tavy's day.—*H. V.*, iv. 7.

And *take foul scorn* ['think it foul scorn'] to fawn on him.—1 *H. VI.*, iv. 4.

Be not *ta'en tardy* ['caught loitering,' 'captured when too late for escape'] by unwise delay.—*R. III.*, iv. 1.

If he love Cæsar, all that he can do
Is to himself—*take thought* ['become pensive,' 'turn melancholy'], and die for Cæsar.—*Jul. C.*, ii. 1.

But we 'll *take to-morrow* ['use to-morrow,' 'employ or appropriate to-morrow'].—*Macb.*, iii. 1.

And how was that *ta'en up?* ['made up,' 'settled,' 'accommodated'].—*As You L.*, v. 4.

I knew when seven justices could not *take up* ['settle'] a quarrel.—*Ibid.*, v. 4.

I have his horse to *take up* the quarrel.—*Tw. N.*, iii. 4.

Good Brabantio *take up* ['accept reconciledly,' 'receive as settled'] this mangled matter at the best.—*Oth.*, i. 3.

I will *take up* ['cap,' 'put a crowning to'] that with.—*H. V.*, iii. 7.

I will *cap* ['take up,' 'put a climax to'], that proverb with, there is flattery in friendship.—*Ibid.*, iii. 7.

Perforce, a third must *take up* ['take in hand,' 'cope with'] us.—2 *H. IV.*, i. 3.

I could myself *take up* a brace of the best of them.—*Coriol.*, iii. 1.

Being you are to *take* soldiers *up* ['enlist,' 'raise,' 'levy'] in counties as you go.— 2 *H. IV.*, ii. 1.

You have *taken up* ['raised,' 'levied'], under the counterfeited zeal of God, the subjects of his substitute, my father,—*Ibid.*, iv. 2.

Good my sovereign, *take up* ['check,' 'rebuke'] the English short.—*H. V.*, ii. 4.

I was *taken up* ['chidden,' 'snubbed'] for laying them down.—*Two G. of V.*, i. 2.

Yet art thou good for nothing but *taking up* ['twitting,' 'taunting']; and that thou 'rt scarce worth.—*All's W.*, ii. 3.

And *take up* ['obtain on credit'; and, punningly, 'pick up'] commodities upon our bills?—2 *H. VI.*, iv. 7.

We are like to prove a goodly commodity, being *taken up* ['obtained on credit'; and, punningly, 'arrested,' 'apprehended'] of these men's bills.—*M. Ado*, iii. 3.

If a man is thorough with them in honest *taking up* ['obtaining goods on credit'], then they must stand upon security.—2 *H. IV.*, i. 2.

Can with his very bulk *take up* ['absorb,' 'impede,' 'intercept'] the rays o' the beneficial sun.—*H. VIII.*, i. 1.

And schoolboys' tears *take up* ['impede,' 'blear'] the glasses of my sight!—*Coriol.*, iii. 2.

How it rages, how it *takes up* ['swallows up,' 'submerges'] the shore!—*W. T.*, iii. 3.

They three were *taken up* ['saved from the water,' 'rescued'] by fishermen of Corinth.—*Com. of E.*, i. 1.

I would your grace would *take me with you* ['let me understand you,' 'suffer my comprehension to accompany your meaning'].—1 *H. IV.*, ii. 4.

Soft! *take me with you, take me with you*, wife.—*R. & Jul.*, iii. 5.

Whatsoe'er he is, he 's *bravely taken here* ['received as a brave man here,' 'admitted here to be a brave man'].—*All's W.*, iii. 5.

Nay, *task me to my word* ['put my word to the test'].—1 *H. IV.*, iv. 1.

Else I should *tell him well** ['tell him flatly,' 'tell him plainly,' 'rate him well,' 'call him to account,' 'tell him his own,' 'tell him a piece of my mind'], i 'faith, I should.—*Timon*, i. 2.

Why, then I 'll *tell her plain*, she sings as sweetly.—*Tam. of S.*, ii. 1.

I was about to speak, and *tell him plainly*, the self-same sun.—*W. T.*, iv. 3.

I mind to *tell him plainly* what I think.—3 *H. VI.*, iv. 1.

And *tell me flatly* I am no proud Jack.—1 *H. IV.*, ii. 4.

He *tells me flatly*, there is no mercy for me in Heaven.—*Mer. of V.*, iii. 5.

If I find a hole in his coat, I will *tell him my mind*.—*H. V.*, iii. 6.

And yet, in some respects, I grant I cannot go,—*I cannot tell* ['I cannot say,' 'I cannot tell what to make of it'; and, punningly, 'I cannot pass current,' 'I cannot reckon as good money'].—2 *H. IV.*, i. 2.

I cannot tell: ['I know not what to think of it,' 'I cannot say how it may be'] the world is grown so bad.—*R. III.*, i. 3.

Whose life 's *as tender to me* ['as precious to me'] as my soul.—*Two G. of V.*, v. 4.

And show'd thou *mak'st some tender of my life* ['hast some loving regard for my life'], in this fair rescue thou hast brought.—1 *H. IV.*, v. 4.

By my life, I do; which I *tender dearly* ['prize highly'], though I say I am a magician.—*As You L.*, v. 2.

If any friend will pay the sum for him,
He shall not die, *so much we tender him* ['so highly do we value him'].—*Com. of E.*, v. 1.

I *tender so* ['am so affectionately anxious for'] the safety of my liege.—2 *H. VI.*, iii. 1.

And so betide to me, *as well I tender you* ['as carefully I endeavour to preserve you,' and 'as faithfully I am attached to you'], and all of yours!—*R. III.*, ii. 4.

If . . . I *tender not* ['do not tenderly love'] thy beauteous princely daughter!—*Ibid.*, iv. 4.

You *tender more* ['have more regard for'] your person's honour than your high profession spiritual.—*H. VIII.*, ii. 4.

---

* Following the punctuation of the First Folio (altered by some emendators), we believe this phrase to be meant by Shakespeare as a similar idiom to those of which we give the six following examples,—"tell her plain," &c.

Tender yourself more dearly ['pay more regard to what is due to yourself'], or, . . . you'll *tender me a fool* ['show me how you befool yourself with this tenderness'].—*Hamlet*, i. 3.

For thine especial safety, which *we do tender* ['we are as affectionately anxious for'], as we dearly grieve for that.—*Ibid.*, iv. 3.

Ay, *are you thereabouts?* ['is that your way of thinking,' 'is that your opinion']. Why, then, good night, indeed.—*Ant. & C.*, iii. 8.

Do you know, and dare not be intelligent to me? *'Tis thereabouts* ['that is about the truth of it'].—*W. T.*, i. 2.

How a score of ewes now?—*Thereafter as they be* ['that's according to what they may turn out to be in goodness'].—2 *H. IV.*, iii. 2.

O, ho, *are you there with me?* ['are you on the tack of trying to delude me,' 'are you trying to catch me with that plea'].—*Lear*, iv. 6.

They're here with me ['they are detecting me,' 'they are pointing me out as a deceived husband'] already [*See* INDICATIONS OF CONDUCT AND GESTURE, &c.].—*W. T.*, i. 2.

I know Anne's mind; *that's neither here nor there* ['no matter for that,' 'let that pass,' 'that is nothing to the purpose,' 'that is of no consequence.' *See* "That's all one" previously cited].—*Merry W.*, i. 4.

Doth that bode weeping?—*'Tis neither here nor there* ['it signifies nothing particular, any way'].—*Oth.*, iv. 3.

The one as long as th' other: *'tis pity of him* ['tis to be regretted for him'].—*Ibid.*, ii. 3.

'Tis pity of him.—Let his shames quickly drive.—*Ant. & C.*, i. 4.

Good faith, *it is such another* ['she is such a whimsical'] Nan; but, I detest, an honest maid.—*Merry W.*, i. 4.

'Tis such another fitchew! marry, a perfumed one.—*Oth.*, iv. 1.

Welcome; *fall to* ['begin eating'].—*As You L.*, ii. 7.

Well said, Hal! *to it* ['go at it,' 'fight away'], Hal!—1 *H. IV.*, v. 4.

And *to't they go* ['they begin fighting'] like lightning.—*R. & Jul.*, iii. 1.

To't ['begin guessing'] again, come . . . Marry, now I can tell.—*To't.*—Mass, I cannot tell.—*Hamlet*, v. 1.

The clown shall make those laugh whose lungs are *tickled o' the sere* [there was an old idiom thus worded which signified 'easily excited to mirth,' and the present passage may be taken in this sense; otherwise, the entire phrase seems to us to mean 'shall make even those laugh whose lungs are *troubled with dryness*'].—*Ibid.*, ii. 2.

Come what come may, *time and the hour* ['the epoch destined to witness a special event.' *See* PLEONASMS] runs through the roughest day.—*Macb.*, i. 3.

And I, *to blame* ['very blameably,' 'deserving blame'], have held him here too long. —*Com. of E.*, iv. 1.

My thanks are *too dear a halfpenny* ['too dear a halfpenny-worth,' 'too dear by a halfpenny,' 'too dear at a halfpenny'].—*Hamlet*, ii. 2.

He held them *sixpence all too dear* ['too dear at sixpence'].—*Oth.*, ii. 3 (*Song*).

There is, sir, an aiery of children, little eyases, that *cry out on the top of question* ['challenge applause beyond appeal'; and, punningly, 'pipe out their parts at the top of their shrill infantine voices'] and are most.—*Hamlet*, ii. 2.

As I received it, and others, whose judgments in such matters *cried in the top of mine* ['were of higher authority than mine,' 'were more beyond appeal than mine'].—*Ibid.*, ii. 2.

If He, which is *the top of judgment* ['the supreme in judgment'], should but judge you as you are.—*M. for M.*, ii. 2.

Admir'd Miranda! Indeed, *the top of admiration* ['the supreme point of admiration,' 'the crowning height of admiration'].—*Temp.*, iii. 1.

To amplify too much, would make much more, and *top extremity* ['surpass the extreme of sorrow'].—*Lear*, v. 3.

So far he *topp'd my thought* ['surpassed my imagination'], that I, in forgery of shapes and tricks, came short of what he did.—*Hamlet*, iv. 7.

But like to groves, *being topp'd* [' being pruned,' ' cut,' ' lopped'], they higher rise.—*Per.*, i. 4.

And *topping all others* [' surpassing every one else '] in boasting.—*Coriol.*, ii. 1.

Which to do, *trebles thee o'er* [' will make thee thrice as great as thou wert before'].—*Temp.*, ii. 1.

Hast thou, spirit, performed *to point* [' punctiliously,' ' exactly '] the tempest that I bade thee?—*Ibid.*, i. 2.

On a trice [' in a trice,' ' in the third of a moment,' ' ere one could count three '], so please you, even in a dream, were we divided from them.—*Ibid.*, v. 1.

It sums up thousands *in a trice.—Cym.*, v. 4.

Where we, *in all her trim* [' in trimmest condition,' ' in readiest order for sailing'], freshly beheld our royal, good, and gallant ship.—*Temp.*, v. 1.

The ship is *in her trim* ; the merry wind blows fair.—*Com. of E.*, iv. 1.

But, by the mass, our hearts are *in the trim* [' in the right cue or mood,' ' in a state of alert readiness'].—*H. V.*, iv. 3.

They come like sacrifices *in their trim* [' thus preparedly decked up'], and to the fire-ey'd maid of smoky war.—1 *H. IV.*, iv. 1.

O, *this is trim* [' this is nice,' ' agreeable,' ' pleasant '].—*Tr. & Cr.*, iv. 5.

Thus has he . . . only got *the tune of the time* [' the prevailing key-note of fashionable jargon '], and outward habit.—*Hamlet*, v. 2.

If it be aught *to the old tune* [' to the same purpose as of old or formerly '], my lord, it is as fat and fulsome.—*Tw. N.*, v. i.

Went it not so?—*To the self-same tune and words* [' to that identical purport and announcement '].—*Macb.*, i. 3.

This tune [' this tone of thinking and speaking'] goes manly.—*Ibid.*, iv. 3.

He is not *in this tune* [' in this mood'], is he?—*Tr. & Cr.*, iii. 3.

Who sometime, *in his better tune* [' in his saner mood,' ' in his more harmonious frame of mind'], remembers what we.—*Lear*, iv. 3.

My advocation is *not now in tune* [' not now in accordance with his mood'].—*Oth.*, iii. 4.

And let him *ply his music* [' go on to what tune he pleases,' ' conduct himself in any style and at any rate he chooses '].—*Hamlet*, ii. 1.

Gentle my lord, *turn back* [' return and hear me '].—*M. for M.*, ii. 2.

Turn thee back [' return '], and tell thy king.—*H. V.*, iii. 6.

We *turn not back* [' do not return '] the silks upon the merchant.—*Tr. & Cr.*, ii. 2.

Turn back [' return '], dull earth, and find thy centre out.—*R. & Jul.*, ii. 1.

Cassius or Cæsar never shall *turn back* * [' return '],
For I will slay myself.—*Jul. C.*, iii. 1.

If he be chaste, the flame will back descend,
And *turn him to* [' occasion him,' ' give him '] no pain.—*Merry W.*, v. 5.

The which shall *turn you to* [' occasion you'] no farther harm than so much loss of time.—*Coriol.*, iii. 1.

Oh, my heart bleeds to think o' the teen that I have *turn'd you to* [' occasioned you,' ' caused you'].—*Temp.*, i. 2.

And all the trouble thou hast *turn'd me to* [' caused me,' ' given me '].—3 *H. VI.*, v. 5.

A slave that still an end *turns me to* [' causes me,' ' brings me'] shame.—*Two G. of V.*, iv. 4.

If the rest of my fortunes *turn Turk* [' experience a sudden reverse,' ' become adverse'] with me.—*Hamlet*, iii. 2.

Well, an you be not *turned Turk* [' become a thorough apostate to your creed that no man is worthy of being your husband,' ' changed your mind entirely'].—*M. Ado*, iii. 4.

---

* Malone and others alter " or " to ' on ' in this passage, affirming that " turn back " cannot be taken in the sense of ' return ; ' but we think that the four preceding instances we have cited, serve to show that Shakespeare does occasionally use the expression " turn back " to signify ' return.'

Not so, sir; *under correction* ['by your leave,' 'with your permission be it spoken,' 'subject to your setting to rights, if I am wrong'], sir, I hope, it is not so . . . *under correction*, sir, we know.—*Love's L. L.*, v. 2.

Under your good correction, I have seen, when, after execution.—*M. for M.*, ii. 2.

Look you, *under your correction*, there is not many.—*H. V.*, iii. 2.

Under the correction ['while I disclaim, or deprecate the imputation'] of bragging, be it spoken, I should quickly.—*Ibid.*, v. 2.

What we will do, we do *upon command* ['under orders,' 'by authority given'].—*R. III.*, i. 4. [*See* "Take *upon command*," previously cited.]

Let your highness *command upon me* ['command me,' 'lay commands upon me'] ; to the which my duties.—*Macb.*, iii. 1.

By his great authority ;
Which often hath no less prevail'd than so,
On your command ['by your own orders'].—*W. T.*, ii. 1.

Have you nothing said *upon his party* ['on his side,' 'on his behalf,' 'as a partisan of his'] 'gainst the duke.—*Lear*, ii. 1.

The fit is momentary; *upon a thought* ['as quick as thought,' 'with the speed of thought'] he will be well again.—*Macb.*, iii. 4.

Come *with a thought!* . . . Ariel, come!—*Temp.*, iv. 1.

And, *with a thought*, seven of the eleven I paid.—1 *H. IV.*, ii. 4.

He comes *upon a wish* ['immediately on my wish,' 'just as I have been wishing for him'].—*Jul. C.*, iii. 2.

All this done *upon the gad!* ['upon the spur of the moment'].—*Lear*, i. 2.

With horsemen, that make to him *on the spur* ['as fast as their steeds, hastened by spurring, can go'].—*Jul. C.*, v. 3.

Or *look upon* ['face,' 'confront,' 'meet face to face'] our Britons.—*Cym.*, ii. 4.

To deliver his head *in the view* ['to the sight'] of Angelo.—*M. for M.*, iv. 2.

And *in the view* ['in the sight'] of the shepherd.—*W. T.*, v. 2.

Here, *in the view* of men, I will unfold some causes of.—*R. II.*, iii. 1.

Fetch hither Richard, that *in common view* ['in sight of every one'] he may surrender.—*Ibid.*, iv. 1.

In the view ['in sight,' 'in the presence'] of many lords, resign'd the crown.—3 *H. VI.*, i. 1.

In view ['in the sight'] of Trojans and of Greeks.—*Tr. & Cr.*, i. 3.

Alas, that love, so gentle *in his view* ['in his appearance'],
Should be so tyrannous and rough in proof!—*R. & Jul.*, i. 1.

They lie *in view* ['within sight'] ; but have not spoke as yet.—*Coriol.*, i. 4.

The enemy's *in view*; draw up your powers.—*Lear*, v. 1.

Even with this I lost *fair England's view* ['sight of fair England'].—2 *H. VI.*, iii. 2.

And do invite you to *my sister's view* ['the sight or presence of my sister'], whither straight I'll lead you.—*Ant. & C.*, ii. 2.

You should tread a course pretty and *full of view* ['full of promising aspect,' 'full of means of observation,' and 'full in view.' *See* Varied Meanings combined in One Word or Sentence].—*Cym.*, iii. 4.

I'll show it you : and, *by the way* ['as we go along thither'], you shall tell me where in the forest you live.—*As You L.*, iii. 2.

For, *by the way*, I'll sort occasion, as index.—*R. III.*, ii. 2.

And *by the way* possess thee what she is.—*Tr. & Cr.*, iv. 4.

This, *by the way* ['by-the-bye,' 'meantime'], I let you understand.—*Tam. of S.*, iv. 2.

And one that is your friend, I can tell you that *by the way* ['moreover'].—*Merry W.*, i. 4.

We come not *by the way* ['by means'] of accusation, to taint that honour.—*H. VIII.*, iii. 1.

I hear it *by the way* ['by indirect means,' 'by side-wind information,' 'by a surreptitious course'].—*Macb.*, iii. 4.

Come your ways, come your ways ['come along,' 'come hither with me'].—*Tr. & Cr.*, iii. 2.

Look to 't, I charge you : *come your ways.—Hamlet*, i. 3.

Well, *go thy way* [' go along with thee,' 'pursue thine own way']: thou shalt not from this grove, till I.—*Mid. N. D.*, ii. 2.

Well, *go thy way* [' be off with thee,' ' be gone,' 'I give thee thy way'] ; if Sir Toby would leave drinking, thou.—*Tw. N.*, i. 5.

Go thy way ['go on thine own way,' 'thou know'st well what thou 'rt about']. Hector ! There 's a brave man . . . *Go thy way*, Troilus, *go thy way* !—*Tr. & Cr.*, i. 2.

Go thy ways, wench ; serve God.—*R. & Jul.*, ii. 5.

Say'st thou so, old Jack ; *go thy ways* ; I 'll make more of thy old body than I have done.—*Merry W.*, ii. 2.

Go thy ways, old Jack ; die when thou wilt, if manhood, good manhood, be not forgot.—*1 H. IV.*, ii. 4.

Ay, *go your ways, go your ways* [' go away,' 'go along with you']: I knew.—*As You L.*, iv. 1.

God amend us, God amend ! we are much *out o' the way* ['strayed from rectitude, or the right path '].—*Love's L. L.*, iv. 3.

He draws Mark Antony *out of the way* ['apart,' ' away'].—*Jul. C.*, iii. 1.

A pox of drowning thyself ! it is clean *out of the way* ['out of the question, ' away from the purpose '].—*Oth.*, i. 3.

I 'll devise a mean to draw the Moor *out of the way* [' apart,' ' away'], that your converse and business.—*Ibid.*, iii. 1.

Is 't lost ? is 't gone ? speak, is it *out o' the way?* [' mislaid '].—*Ibid.*, iii. 4.

But at fourscore it is *too late a week* [' too late a period of time,' 'too late an epoch,' 'too late by at least a week.' *See* "Too dear a halfpenny," previously cited].—*As You L.*, ii. 3.

She 'll burn *a week longer* [' at least a week longer,' 'a good portion of time longer'] than the whole world.—*Com. of E.*, iii. 2.

Well be with you ['I wish you well,' 'good wishes to you'], gentlemen !—*Hamlet*, ii. 2.

If the sins of your youth are forgiven you, *you 're well to live* ['you will live well,' ' you will be fortunate to live '].—*W. T.*, iii. 3.

Well said ! [' well done '] thou look'st cheerly.—*As You L.*, ii. 6.

Spread, Davy ; spread, Davy : *well said*, Davy.—*2 H. IV.*, v. 3.

Well said, my hearts !—*R. & Jul.*, i. 5.

Come, give me that : this way ; *well said.—Ant. & C.*, iv. 4.

What said he ? How looked he ? *Wherein went he ?* [' In what clothes was he dressed].—*As You L.*, iii. 2.

And he *went still in this fashion* [' was always dressed in this style'], colour. ornament.—*Tw. N.*, iii. 4.

Jove sometime *went disguis'd* [' was disguisedly attired'], and why not I ?—*2 H. VI.*, iv. 1.

Never lack'd gold, and yet *went never gay* [' never dressed gaily '].—*Oth.*, ii. 1.

And thane of Cawdor too ; *went it not so ?* [' did not the prediction run thus'].—*Macb.*, i. 3.

When three or four of his blind brothers *went to it* [' were killed,' 'went to death,' ' went to destruction '].—*Two G. of V.*, iv. 4.

He shall conceal it,
Whiles you are willing it shall come to note,
What time [' at which time,' ' when '] we will our celebration keep.—*Tw. N.*, iv. 3.

An thou canst not smile *as the wind sits* [' according to the mood that pleases thy superiors '], thou 'lt catch cold.—*Lear*, i. 4.

Is 't possible? *Sits the wind in that corner ?* [' does the air of her favour blow in that direction,' ' is this the state of affairs '].—*M. Ado*, ii. 3.

Though my reason *sits in the wind against me* ['blows me in the contrary direction,' 'advises me to a different course'].—*Ant. & C.*, iii. 8.

There is something in the wind ['there is something going forward,' 'there is something adverse threatening'], that we cannot get in.—*Com of E.*, iii. 1.

By this same coxcomb that *we have i' the wind* ['we have got the wind of,' 'got the upper hand of'; also, 'we have got scent of,' 'on whose track we are'].— *All's W.*, iii. 6.

He knows the game: how true he *keeps the wind !* ['maintains the advantage he has gained,' 'pursues the track he is on'].—3 *H. VI.*, iii. 2.

Why do you go about to *recover the wind of me ?* ['take advantage of me'].— *Hamlet*, iii. 2.

It keeps *on the windy side* ['on the safe side,' 'on the side protected from the wind,' 'on the advantageous side'] of care.—*M. Ado*, ii. 1.

Still you keep *o' the windy side* of the law: good.—*Tw. N.*, iii. 4.

Brown, madam: and her forehead *as low as she would wish it* ['lower than she could wish it to be'].—*Ant. & C.*, iii. 3.

So will you *wish on me* ['invoke curses upon me'], when the rash mood is on.— *Lear*, ii. 4.

O, *a good wish upon you !* ['may you have your wish'].—*As You L.*, i. 3.

Exceeding those that I can *wish upon thee* ['invoke upon thee'].—*R. III* , i. 3.

I will *wish him* ['recommend him'] to her father.—*Tam of S.*, i. 1.

I would not *wish them to* ['aspire after for them,' 'desire for them'] a fairer death. —*Macb.*, v. 7.

When man was *wish'd to* ['enjoined to,' 'desired to'] love his enemies !—*Timon*, iv. 3.

Bringeth sensible regreets—*to wit* ['that is to say,' 'be it known'], (besides commends, and courteous breath), gifts of rich value!—*Mer. of V.*, ii. 9.

Diest; or, *to wit*, I kill thee, make thee away.—*As You L.*, v. 1.

To wit, no female should be inheritrix in Salique land.—*H. V.*, i. 2.

To wit, an indigested and deformed lump.—3 *H. VI.*, v. 6.

But 'tis *no wit* ['unwise'] to go —*R. & Jul.*, i. 4.

Witness ['as may be attested by'] our too much memorable shame, when Cressy battle.—*H. V.*, ii. 4.

You appeared to me but as a common man; *witness* the night, your garments, your lowliness.—*Ibid.*, iv. 8.

Witness the hole you made in Cæsar's heart.—*Jul. C.*, v. i.

Witness this army, of such mass and charge.—*Hamlet*, iv. 4.

Woe, woe are we ['most grieved are we.' *See* OATHS, EXCLAMATIONS, &c.], sir, you may not live to wear.—*Ant. & C.*, iv. 12.

Hob, nob, *is his word* ['is his decree']; give 't or take 't.—*Tw. N.*, iii. 4.

That is done too, sir; only cover *is the word* ['the determined fact,' 'the decreed thing,' 'the definitive sentence'].—*Mer. of V.*, iii. 5.

Slaying *is the word ;* it is a deed in fashion.—*Jul. C.*, v. 5.

If they suffer our departure, death's *the word.*—*Ant. & C.*, i. 2.

Hanging *is the word*, sir; if you be ready for that.—*Cym.*, v. 4.

Pardon's *the word* to all.—*Ibid.*, v. 5.

Coupe le gorge! That *is the word.* I thee defy again.—*H. V.*, ii. 1.

The word is, " Pitch and pay "; trust none.—*Ibid.*, ii. 3.

The word is, mildly: pray you, let us go.—*Coriol.*, iii. 2.

Now have I *done a good day's work* ['accomplished a good deed.' *See* " Made good work," previously cited].—*R. III.*, ii. 1.

How earnestly are you *set a' work* ['urged to act'], and how ill requited!— *Tr. & Cr.*, v. 11.

My son profits nothing *in the world* ['whatever'] at his book.—*Merry W.*, iv. 1.

I do nothing *in the world* but lie.—*Love's L. L.*, iv. 3.

And it is nothing, nothing *in the world.—Mid. N. D.,* v. 1.

He hath no interest in me *in the world.—As You L.,* v. i.

I will choose mine heir from forth the beggars *of the world* ['in chief,' 'in especial,' 'paramount,' 'most notorious '].—*Timon,* i. 1.

The beauty *of the world !* the paragon of animals !—*Hamlet,* ii. 2.

I therefore apprehend and do attach thee, for an abuser *of the world* ['pre-eminent,' 'unparalleled'; and also implying ' of mankind,' 'of the public '], a practiser of arts inhibited.—*Oth.,* i. 2. [*See* "A woman *of the world,*" previously cited, for an idiom formerly in use.]

Seeming ! I will *write against it* ['denounce it,' 'protest against it '].—*M. Ado,* iv. 1.

I 'll *write against them* ['denounce them,' 'protest against them '], detest them, curse them.—*Cym.,* ii. 5.

I 'd give bay Curtal and his furniture,
My mouth were no more broken than these boys',
And *writ as little beard* ['subscribed or confessed to owning as little beard,' 'gave tokens of possessing as little beard '].—*All's W.,* ii. 3.

I must tell thee, sirrah, I *write man* ['give evidence of the right to be called a man,' 'show that I am worthy to be styled a man,' 'proclaim myself to be a man ']; to which title age cannot bring thee.—*Ibid.,* ii. 3.

Observe his inclination *in yourself* ['in your own person,' 'by your own observations '].—*Hamlet,* ii. 1.

Shakespeare uses some idiomatic terms of number :—

A brace of ['two '] draymen bid God speed him well.—*R. II.,* i. 4.

And I . . have lost *a brace of* kinsmen.—*R. & Jul.,* v. 3.

I have not *a case of* ['three '] lives.—*H. V.,* iii. 2.

A couple ['two '] of Ford's knaves, his hinds.—*Merry W.,* iii. 5.

Have ta'en *a couple of* as arrant knaves as any in Messina.—*M. Ado,* iii. 5.

I am sworn brother to *a leash of* ['three '] drawers.—1 *H. IV.,* ii. 4.

That you three fools lack'd me, fool, to make up *the mess* ['the four '].—*Love's L. L.,* iv. 3.

A mess of ['four '] Russians left us but of late.—*Ibid.,* v. 2.

Where are your *mess of* ['four '] sons to back you now.—3 *H. VI.,* i. 4.

Here comes *a pair of* ['two '] very strange beasts.—*As You L.,* v. 4.

Here justified by us, *a pair of* kings.—*W. T.,* v. 3.

Made *a pair of* ['a set of,' 'a flight of'] stairs to marriage.—*As You L.,* v. 2.

And *a pair of* ['a set of'] stocks in the town ?—*Com. of E.,* iii. 1.

I 'll make a fat *pair of* ['set of'] gallows.—1 *H. IV.,* ii. 1.

Than the length and breadth of *a pair of* ['a set of'] indentures?—*Hamlet,* v. 1.

I yet am unprovided of *a pair of* ['a set of'] bases . . . thou shalt have my best gown to make thee *a pair.—Per.,* ii. 1.

Shakespeare uses several idioms of elliptical expression :—

[Be gone] *about it :* you know where to find me.—2 *H. IV.,* i. 2.

[Hasten] *after,* Aumerle ! Mount thee.—*R. II.,* v. 2.

And he to England shall [go] *along* with you.—*Hamlet,* iii. 3.

Thou shalt not [go] *back,* till I have borne.—*Jul. C.,* iii. 1.

Let Romeo [depart] *hence* in haste.—*R. & Jul.,* iii. 1.

Early to-morrow will we rise, and [go] *hence.—Jul. C.,* iv. 3.

I will [go] *from hence* to-day.—*Cym.,* i. 2.

Say she 'll [go] *home* to her father.—*Cym.,* iii. 2.

I 'll [go] through Glo'stershire.—2 *H. IV.,* iv 3.

I 'll [go] to the king, my master, that is dead.—*Ibid.,* v. 2.

I 'll not [go] to Rome, *I 'll* [go] back with you.—*Coriol.,* v. 3.

Menas, *I 'll not* [go] on shore.—*Ant. & C.,* ii. 7.

I'll willingly [go] to him: to gain his colour.—*Cym.*, iv. 2.

By this sun that shines, *I'll* [go] thither.—*Ibid.*, iv. 4.

I'll [have] no more drumming; a plague of all drums!—*All's W.*, iv. 3.

I'll [have] no swaggerers . . . no, *I'll* [have] no swaggerers.—2 *H. IV.*, ii. 4.

No; *I'll* [have] no Anne Bullens for him.—*H. VIII.*, iii. 2.

No, *I'll* [have] nothing; for if I should be brib'd too.—*Timon*, i. 2.

[Let us go] *in* to my tent, the air is raw and cold.—*R. III.*, v. 3.

Shall we [go] *in?* I'll keep you company.—*Timon*, i. 1.

Good nuncle [go], *in*, and ask thy daughter's blessing.—*Lear*, iii. 2.

Thither I *must* [go], although against my will.—*Com. of E.*, iv. 1.

You *must* [fight] no more.—*Tr. & Cr.*, iv. 5.

I *must* [go] to England; you know that?—*Hamlet*, iii. 4.

I *must* [go] to the watch.—*Oth.*, ii. 3.

On mine own accord I'll [go] *off*.—*W. T.*, ii. 3.

[Go] *on*, Bardolph; lead the men away.—2 *H. IV.*, iii. 2.

I will [go] *on* with my speech in your praise.—*Tw. N.*, i. 5.

Or shall we [go] *on*, and not depend on you?—*Jul. C.*, iii. 1.

Please it your grace, [go] *on* to the state affairs.—*Oth.*, i. 3.

Thither *shall it* [go], then: and happily may.—*John*, v. 7.

[Away, be gone] *to* the church: take the priest.—*Tam. of S.*, iv. 4.

[Let us proceed] *to* this gear—the sooner the better.—2 *H. VI.*, i. 4.

Achilles will not [go] *to* the field to-morrow.—*Tr. & Cr.*, ii. 3.

Pray you, let's [go] *to* him.—*Coriol.*, iii. 1.

Let's [go] *to* our affairs. Forgive us our sins!—*Oth.*, ii. 3.

If you have any music that may not be heard, [set] *to*'t again.—*Ibid.*, iii. 1.

If we compose well here [we will undertake the expedition], *to* Parthia.—*Ant. & C.*, ii. 2.

He shall [go] *to* Parthia.—*Ibid.*, ii. 3.

He purposeth [to go] *to* Athens: whither, with what haste.—*Ibid.*, iii. 1.

[Go] *to* the sea-side straightway: I will possess you.—*Ibid.*, iii. 9.

[Go] *to* him again: tell him he wears the rose of youth.—*Ibid.*, iii. 11.

[Hasten] *to* the monument! . . . *To* the monument! . . . *To* the monument!—*Ibid.*, iv. 11.

[Let me repair] *to* the trunk again, and shut the spring of it.—*Cym.*, ii. 2.

[Betake you] *to* some shade, and fit you to your manhood.—*Ibid.*, iii. 4.

Pray, sir, [let us go] *to* the army: I and my brother.—*Ibid.*, iv. 4.

Now [let me turn] *to* my daughter's letter.—*Per.*, ii. 5.

What, shall we [go] *toward* the Tower?—*R. III.*, iii. 2.

Let us [go] *toward* the king.—*Macb.*, i. 3.

But [be gone], *up* to the mountains!—*Cym.*, iii. 3.

Bid them all home; he's gone, and *we'll* [go] no farther.—*Coriol.*, iv. 2.

Now *we'll* [go] together; and the chance of goodness.—*Macb.*, iv. 3.

Sons, *we'll* [go] higher to the mountains.—*Cym.*, iv. 4.

Soft, soft! *we'll* [have] no defence.—*Ibid.*, iii. 4.

His lordship *will* [depart] next morning for France.—*All's W.*, iv. 3.

We *will* [go] ourself in person to this war.—*R. II.*, i. 4.

We *will not* [move] from the helm to sit and weep.—3 *H. VI.*, v. 4.

Why, then, *will I* [fight] no more.—*Tr. & Cr.*, iv. 5.

Where's Hector? I *will* [have, or fight with] none but Hector.—*Ibid.*, v. 5.

I *will not* [go] out of doors . . . I *will not* [go] over the threshold . . . indeed, I *will not* [go] forth.—*Coriol.*, i. 3.

Nay, your wit *will not* [issue] so soon out as another man's will—'tis strongly wedged up in a block-head —*Ibid.*, ii. 3.

I *will* [go] to-morrow (and betimes I *will* [go]) to the.—*Macb.*, iii. 4.

He calls to horse ; but *will* [go] I know not whither.—*Lear*, ii. 4.

I will [go] *with* you to the court.—2 *H. IV.*, iii. 2.

By the good gods, I'd [go] *with* thee every foot.—*Coriol.*, iv. 1.

I mean, Master Slender, what *would you* [have] with me ?—Truly, for mine own part, *I would* [have] little or nothing with you.—*Merry W.*, iii. 4.

Now, say, Chatillon, what *would France* [have] with us ?—*John*, i. 1.

He is very sick, and *would* [go] to bed.—*H. V.*, ii. 1.

There's something more *would* [proceed] out of thee; what say'st ?—*H. VIII.*, i. 2.

Now say, what *would Augustus Cæsar* [have] with us ?—*Cym.*, iii. 1.

Where's Troilus ?—What *wouldst thou ?* [have with him].—*Tr. & Cr.*, v. 6.

IMPERATIVE MOOD: SUBJUNCTIVE MOOD.

Shakespeare occasionally uses both these moods very elliptically; allowing one or more words to be understood in the sentence thus constructed. Witness the following passages where he employs the imperative mood :—

But, be it [so] ; let it live: it shall not neither.—*W. T.*, ii. 3.

Love they to live ['let them love to live'] that love and honour have.—*R. II.*, ii. 1.

Hold out my horse ['let but my horse hold out'], and I will first be there.—*Ibid.*, ii. 1.

[May] thy ignominy sleep with thee in the grave,
But not [be] remember'd in thy epitaph !—1 *H. IV.*, v. 4.

Now bind my brows with iron ; and [let] approach
The ragged'st hour that time and spite dare bring,
To frown upon th' enrag'd Northumberland.—2 *H. IV.*, i. 1.

Yet [let] Heavens have glory for this victory !—1 *H. VI.*, iii. 2.

Dismay not ['be not dismayed'], princes, at this accident.—*Ibid.*, iii. 3.

Before young Talbot from old Talbot fly,
[Let] the coward horse that bears me fall and die !—*Ibid.*, iv. 6.

[Let it] sort how it will, I shall have gold for all.—2 *H. VI.*, i. 2.

Ask what thou wilt : [would] that I had said and done !—*Ibid.*, i. 4.

[May] such hope have all the line of John of Gaunt !—3 *H. VI.*, i. 1.

This day, [let] no man think he has business at his house.—*H. VIII.*, v. 4.

Know the whole world ['be it known to the whole world'] he is as valiant.—*Tr. & Cr.*, ii. 3.

Appear it ['let it appear'] to your mind that.—*Ibid.*, iii. 3.

[Let] what [ever] may be sworn by, both divine and human, seal what I end withal! —*Coriol.*, iii. 1.

Wash they ['let them wash'] his wounds with tears.—*R. & Jul.*, iii. 2.

Henceforth [let there] be no feast, whereat a villain's not.—*Timon*, iii. 6.

[Would] that the whole life of Athens were in this !—*Ibid.*, iv. 3.

[Let] those enemies of Timon's, and mine own,
Whom you yourselves shall set out for reproof,
Fall, and no more.—*Ibid.*, v. 5.

If I know this, know ['be it known to'] all the world besides, that.—*Jul. C.*, i. 3.

Now know you ['be it known to you'], Casca, I have mov'd.—*Ibid.*, i. 3.

[May] the gods to-day stand friendly, that we may,
Lovers in peace, lead on our days to age !—*Ibid.*, v. 1.

Therefore our everlasting farewell [let us] take.—*Ibid.*, v. 1.

And [may] the chance of goodness be like our warranted quarrel !—*Macb.*, iv. 3.

[Let] the soldiers' music and the rites of war
Speak loudly for him.—*Hamlet*, v. 2.

Answer my life ['let my life answer for'] my judgment.—*Lear*, i. 1.

[Let] what will hap more to-night, safe 'scape the king ['may the king escape safely'].—*Ibid.*, iii. 6.

Oh, my dear father! [may] Restoration hang thy medicine on my lips.—*Ibid.*, iv. 7.

But [may] all the charms of love, salt Cleopatra, soften thy wan'd lip!—*Ant. & C.*, ii. 1.

To make you brothers, and to knit your hearts
With an unslipping knot, take Antony ['let Antony take'] Octavia to his wife.—*Ibid.*, ii. 2.

And never fly off our loves again ['never let our loves fly off again']!—*Ibid.*, ii. 2.

Haste we for it ['let us haste for it'] : yet, ere we put ourselves in arms, despatch we ['let us despatch'] the business we have talk'd of.—*Ibid.*, ii. 2.

Lie they ['let them lie'] upon thy hand, and be undone by 'em!—*Ibid.*, ii. 5.

[Would] that he and Cæsar might determine this great war in single fight!—*Ibid.*, iv. 4.

This mortal house I'll ruin, do Cæsar what he can ['let Cæsar do what he can'].—*Ibid.*, v. 2.

[May] no exorciser harm thee!—*Cym.*, iv. 2 (*Song*).

[Let] to write and read be henceforth treacherous!—*Ibid.*, iv. 2.

[Let] the hazard therefore due fall on me.—*Ibid.*, iv. 4.

[Let] every villain be call'd Posthumus Leonatus.—*Ibid.*, v. 5.

Quiet and gentle [be] thy conditions! . . . Happy what follows ['may what follows be happy']! . . . Now [may] the good gods throw their best eyes upon it!—*Per.*, iii. 1.

And witness the following passages where he employs the subjunctive mood :—

Prove it so ['if it should prove so'], let fortune pay the due for it, not I.—*Mer. of V.*, iii. 2.

Live thou ['if thou live'], I live.—*Ibid.*, iii. 2.

Oh, if it prove [true], tempests are kind.—*Tw. N.*, iii. 4.

[Though] his youth [be] in flood, I'll prove this truth with my three drops of blood.—*Tr. & Cr.*, i. 3.

[If I] live a thousand years, I shall not find myself so apt to die.—*Jul. C.*, iii. 1.

Prove this ['if this should prove'] a prosperous day.—*Ant. & C.*, iv. 6.

Live Roderigo ['if Roderigo live'], he calls me to a restitution.—*Oth.*, v. 1.

In the following passage, Shakespeare uses the imperative mood somewhat peculiarly :—

Let your highness command upon me.—*Macb.*, iii. 1.

And, in the following, transposedly :—

Now, mild may be thy life ['may thy life be mild']!—*Per.*, iii. 1.

INDICATIONS OF CONDUCT, LOOK, AND GESTURE.

Several of these are to be found in Shakespeare's plays; like a true dramatist, accompanying and illustrating, by denotements of action and appearance, certain passages of his dialogue. Some among them denote a glance or a gesture on the part of the person speaking :—

Ariel. . . . The king's son have I landed by himself;
Whom I left cooling of the air with sighs
In an odd angle of the isle, and sitting,
His arms *in this sad knot* [*Mimickingly folding his own arms across his breast*].—*Temp.*, i. 2.

Antonio. . . . Whom I, with this obedient steel, three inches of it,
Can lay to bed for ever; whiles you, *doing thus* [*Making a thrust, expressive of stabbing*],
To the perpetual wink for aye might put
This ancient morsel, this Sir Prudence.—*Ibid.*, ii. 1.

Gobbo. . . . Lord, worshipped might he be! *What a beard hast thou got!* [*Laying his hand on the back of* LAUNCELOT'S *head, as the lad kneels beside him; and mistaking its shock of hair for a beard*].—*Mer. of V.*, ii. 2.

Leontes.   Didst perceive it?
[*Aside*] They'r: *here with me* [*Making the sign vulgarly used for stigmatising a deceived husband*] already; whispering, rounding, "Sicilia is a so-forth."—*W. T.*, i. 2.

Leontes. I thought of her, even *in these looks I made* [*Gazing upon* PERDITA, *his unknown daughter*].—*Ibid.*, v. 1.

Faulconbridge. . . . But, mother, I am not Sir Robert's son;
I have disclaim'd Sir Robert and my land;
Legitimation, name, and all is gone:
Then, good my mother, let me know my father—
Some proper man, I hope: *who was it, mother* [*Throwing his arm round her, and dropping his voice to a winning tone*].—*John*, i. 1.

King Richard. I weep for joy, to stand upon my kingdom once again.
Dear earth, *I do salute thee with my hand,*
Though rebels wound thee with their horses' hoofs:
As a long parted mother with her child,
Plays fondly with her tears and smiles, in meeting;
So, weeping, smiling, greet I thee, my earth,
And *do thee favour with my royal hands* [*Laying his hand as in caressing benediction on the earth*].—*R. II.*, iii. 2.

Aumerle. Some honest Christian trust me with a gage:
That Norfolk lies, *here do I throw down this* [*Throwing down a hood:* which, Holinshed records, was borrowed from a by-stander].—*Ibid.*, iv. 1.

Falstaff. . . . Oh, it is much that a lie with a slight oath, and a jest *with a sad brow* [this shows that Falstaff occasionally enhanced some of his jokes by uttering them with a grave face and a quiet dry manner; though we may be sure that others he delivered with a loud laugh, and *all*, with a twinkle of his eye that spoke volumes in archness and roguery of meaning: and it is pleasant to have this indication from Shakespeare's own hand of his Falstaff's manner], will do with a fellow that never had the ache in his shoulders! Oh, you shall see him laugh till his face be like a wet cloak ill laid up!—*2 H. IV.*, v. 1.

Pistol. . . . Sir John, thy tender lambkin now is king;
Harry the Fifth's the man. I speak the truth:
When Pistol lies, *do this* [making a contemptuous gesture indicative of insult; usually performed by placing the thumb between the fore and middle finger]; and *fig me*, like the bragging Spaniard.—*Ibid.*, v. 3.

Williams. Sir, know you *this glove* [*Showing the glove he has received overnight from the king*]?
Fluellen. Know the glove! I know the glove is a glove.
Williams. I know *this* [*Pointing to the glove worn in* FLUELLEN'S *cap*]; and *thus I challenge it* [*Strikes* FLUELLEN].—*H. V.*, iv. 8.

King Henry. Give me thy glove, soldier [*Pointing to the glove worn by* WILLIAMS, *and given to him by the king overnight*]: *look here is the fellow of it* [*Producing his own other glove that he had retained when he gave one to* WILLIAMS].—*Ibid.*, iv. 8.

Suffolk. Look on my George [*Showing the insignia of the order, which he wears beneath his disguise*]. I am a gentleman: rate me at what thou wilt, thou shalt be paid.—*2 H. VI.*, iv. 1.

Warwick. . . . *There's thy reward* [*Giving the messenger a gratuity*], *be gone.—*
3 *H. VI.*, iii. 3.

Clarence. Father of Warwick, know you *what this means ?* [*Taking the red rose out
of his hat, and flinging it at* WARWICK.] Look here, I *throw my infamy at thee.—*
Ibid., v. 1.

Gloster. . . . This shoulder was ordain'd so thick, to heave ;
And heave it shall some weight, or break my back :
Work *thou* [*Pointing to his own head*] the way, and *that* [*Pointing to his own hand*]
shall execute.—*Ibid.*, v. 7.

Menenius. Take my cap [*Flinging up his cap*], Jupiter, and I thank thee. Hoo !
Marcius coming home !—*Coriol.*, ii. 1.

Third Citizen. He said he had wounds, which he could show in private ; and with
his hat, *thus waving it in scorn* [*Mimicking the action described*], " I would be consul,"
says he : " aged custom, but by your voices, will not so permit me ; your voices therefore " : when we granted that, *here was* [*Making a gesture of waving off scornfully*],
" I thank you for your voices—thank you—your most sweet voices : now you have
left your voices, I have no farther with you."—Was not this mockery ?—*Coriol.*, ii. 3.

Volumnia. I pr'ythee now, my son, go to them, *with this bonnet* [*Pointing to her son's
bonnet*] in thy hand ; and *thus far having stretched it* [*Stretching out her arm as if with
a cap held off in salutation*], *here be with them* [*Making continuous signs of courteous
inclination of the body and head*], thy knee bussing the stones (for in such business
action is eloquence, and the eyes of the ignorant more learned than the ears), waving
thy head, *which often, thus* [*Still continuing her prompted gestures*], correcting thy
stout heart, now humble as the ripest mulberry that will not hold the handling.—
Ibid., iii. 2.

Samson. Nay, as they dare. *I will bite my thumb at them ;* which is a disgrace to
them, if they bear it [*Bites his thumb at* ABRAHAM *and* BALTHASAR, *as they enter :* this
was a contemptuous gesture, made by putting the thumb-nail into the mouth, and
letting it slip from the teeth with a jerk and a slight noise ; which was considered a
desperate insult, and an excellent mode of beginning a quarrel].—*R. & Jul.*, i. 1.

Gregory [*Aside to* SAMSON]. Say—better : *here comes one of my master's kinsmen*
[*Looking towards the quarter whence* TYBALT *approaches*].—*Ibid.*, i. 1.

Timon. . . . Nothing I'll bear from thee
But nakedness, thou detestable town !
Take thou that too [*Successively throwing portions of his dress back in the direction
of Athens, towards which he looks as he goes*], with multiplying bans.—*Timon*, iv. 1.

Timon. Away, thou tedious rogue. *I am sorry I shall lose a stone by thee* [*Throwing
a stone at* APEMANTUS].—*Ibid.*, iv. 3.

Hamlet. . . . Remember thee ! Ay, thou poor ghost, while memory holds a seat in
this distracted globe [*Putting his hand to his head*].—*Hamlet*, i. 5.

Hamlet. . . . That you, at such times seeing me, never shall, *with arms encumber'd
thus, or this head-shake* [*Making the gestures described*], or by pronouncing.—*Ibid.*, i. 5.

Voltimand. . . . With an entreaty, *herein farther shown* [*Giving a paper*], that it
might please you to.—*Ibid.*, ii. 2.

Polonius. . . . I have a daughter—have, while she is mime—who, in her duty and
obedience, mark, *hath given me this* [*Producing* HAMLET'S *letter to* OPHELIA].—
Ibid., ii. 2.

Polonius. Take this from this [*Pointing to his head and to his shoulder*] if this be
otherwise.—*Ibid.*, ii. 2.

Polonius. Ophelia, walk you here. . . . *Read on this book* [*Giving her a prayer-book*] ;
that show of such an exercise may colour your loneliness.—*Ibid.*, iii. 1.

Laertes. . . . Adieu, my lord : I have a speech of fire, that fain would blaze, but
that *this folly douts it* [*Passing his hand across his moistened eyes*].—*Ibid.*, iv. 7.

King. Stay ; give me to drink. Hamlet, *this pearl is thine* [*Pretending to place a
pearl in the cup, and dropping a poisonous drug therein*] ; *here's to thy health* [*Drinking
from another cup*].—*Ibid.*, v. 2.

Kent. . . . Approach, thou beacon to this under globe,
That by thy comfortable beams *I may*
Peruse this letter [*Drawing forth a letter, and attempting to read it by the still imper-*
fect light of coming dawn].—*Lear*, ii. 2.

Lear. . . . *Off, off, you lendings! come, unbutton here* [*Tearing off his clothes*].—
Ibid., iii. 4.

Goneril. . . . *Wear this* [*Giving* EDMUND, *a favour*], spare speech;
Decline your head [*Bending over* EDMUND, *and kissing him, while affecting to whisper*
with him] : *this kiss, if it durst speak, would stretch thy spirits up.*—*Ibid.*, iv. 2.

Regan. . . . If you do find him, pray you, *give him this* [*Placing some ring or token*
in OSWALD's *care, to convey to* EDMUND].—*Ibid.*, iv. 5.

Edmund. Come hither, captain; hark. *Take thou this note* [*Giving the paper that*
contains the warrant for the execution of LEAR *and* CORDELIA]; *go.*—*Ibid.*, v. 3.

Othello. . . . I cannot speak enough of this content;
It stops me here; it is too much of joy:
And this, and this [*Giving* DESDEMONA *repeated kisses*], the greatest discords be,
That e'er our hearts shall make!—*Oth.*, ii. 1.

Othello. . . . Look here, Iago; *all my fond love thus do I blow to heaven* [*Making*
sign of discarding from his heart its passion of grief and affection]: 'tis gone.—
Ibid., iii. 3.

Othello. . . . Now, by yond' marble heaven, *in the due reverence of a sacred vow, I*
here engage my words.   [*Kneeling.*
        Iago. Do not rise yet.   [*Kneeling also.*
        Witness, you ever-burning lights above,
        You elements that clip us round about,—
        Witness that here Iago doth give up
        The execution of his wit, hands, heart,
        To wrong'd Othello's service.—*Ibid.*, iii. 3.

Cassio. . . . And, by this hand, *she falls me thus about my neck* [*Throwing his arm*
over IAGO's *shoulder*]—
Othello. Crying "O dear Cassio!" as it were, *his gesture imports it.*—*Ibid.*, iv. 1.

Lodovico. The duke and senators of Venice greet you.   [*Giving* OTHELLO *a packet.*
Othello. I kiss the instrument of their pleasures [*Taking the packet with an air of*
deference, opening it, and beginning to read it].—*Ibid.*, iv. 1.

Othello. Devil!   [*Striking* DESDEMONA.
Desdemona. I have not deserv'd this.
        Lodovico. My lord, this would not be believ'd in Venice,
        Though I should swear I saw it : 'tis very much . . .
    . . . What, *strike his wife?*—*Ibid.*, iv. 1.

Othello. We have done our course; *there's money for your pains* [*Throws a purse*
towards EMILIA] : I pray you, turn the key, and keep our counsel.—*Ibid.*, iv. 2.

Desdemona. . . . *Here I kneel* [*Kneeling*]: if e'er my will did trespass 'gainst his love
. . . comfort forswear me!—*Ibid.*, iv. 2.

Iras. There's a palm [*Holding forth her hand*] presages chastity, if nothing else.—
Ant. & C., i. 2.

Second Messenger. In Sicyon: her length of sickness, with what else more serious
importeth thee to know, *this bears* [*Presenting a letter*].—*Ibid.*, i. 2.

Cæsar. Sit.
Antony. Sit, sir.
Cæsar. Nay, then— [*Taking his seat*].—*Ibid.*, ii. 2.

Cæsar's words have been differently interpreted here, by other
commentators, but we believe them to be an indication that he gives
way to Antony's request that he will be seated, and that they are
tantamount to—' Nay, then, if you will have it so, I consent.'

Cæsar. . . . Let me request you off: our graver business
Frowns at this levity.   Gentle lords, let's part;
You see, we have burnt our cheeks: strong Enobarbe
Is weaker than the wine; and *mine own tongue*
Splits what it speaks [*Pronouncing thickly and inarticulately*]: the wild disguise hath
almost antick'd us all.—*Ant. & C.*, ii. 7.

Enobarbus. Hoo! says 'a.   There's my cap [*Flinging up his cap*].—*Ibid.*, ii. 7.

Charmian. . . . Now boast thee, death, in thy possession lies a lass unparallel'd.
Downy windows, close [*Closing* CLEOPATRA'S *eyelids*]; and golden Phœbus never he
beheld of eyes again so royal!   *Your crown's awry; I'll mend it* [*Adjusts the diadem
upon* CLEOPATRA'S *head*], and then play.—*Ibid.*, v. 2.

Iachimo. . . . *Come off, come off* [*Detaching the bracelet from* IMOGEN'S *arm*]; as
slippery, as the Gordian knot was hard!   'Tis mine.—*Cym.*, ii. 2.

Imogen. . . . *Give colour to my pale cheek with thy blood* [*Laying her face upon the
breast of the corse which she believes to be that of her husband*], that we the horrider
may seem to those which chance to find us.   O my lord, my lord!—*Ibid.*, iv. 2.

Cerimon. Your master will be dead ere you return;
There's nothing can be minister'd to nature
That can recover him.   *Give this to the 'pothecary* [*Giving the servant a prescription to
be made up;* for the behoof of the servant himself, who may be supposed to have
received some bruise or injury during the shipwreck in which his master has been
injured past help], and tell me how it works.—*Per.*, iii. 2.

Thaisa.   Now I know you better,
When we with tears parted Pentapolis,
The king my father gave you *such a ring* [*Pointing to the ring upon* PERICLES' *finger*].
Pericles. This, this: no more, you gods!—*Ibid.*, v. 3.

Others denote look or gesture in the person addressed :—

Celia. And a chain, that you once wore, about his neck.   *Change you colour?*—
As You L., iii. 2.

> *Countess.*   Nay, a mother:
> Why not a mother?   when I said a mother,
> *Methought you saw a serpent: what's in mother,*
> *That you start at it?* . .
> God's mercy, maiden!   *does it curd thy blood,*
> To say, I am thy mother?   What's the matter,
> *That this distemper'd messenger of wet,*
> *The many-colour'd Iris, rounds thine eye?* . . .
> Heaven shield, you mean it not!   daughter, and mother,
> *So strive upon your pulse.   What! pale again?* . . .
> But tell me then, 'tis so; for, look, *thy cheeks*
> *Confess it th' one to th' other;* and *thine eyes*
> *See it so grossly shown in thy behaviours,*
> *That in their kind they speak it.*—*All's W.*, i. 3.

Olivia. God comfort thee!   *Why dost thou smile so, and kiss thy hand so oft?*—
Tw. N., iii. 4.

Leontes. . . . What!   *look upon my brother:* both your pardons,
That e'er I put between your holy looks
My ill suspicion.—*W. T.*, v. 3.

Those few subtly introduced words serve to show that Hermione
keeps her face sensitively averted from Polixenes, until her husband
thus penitently avows his former unworthy misconstructions.

> *Constance.* . . . What dost thou mean by *shaking of thy head?*
> Why dost thou *look so sadly on my son?*
> What means *that hand upon that breast of thine?*
> Why *holds thine eye that lamentable rheum,*
> Like a proud river peering o'er his bounds?
> Be *these sad signs* confirmers of thy words?—*John*, iii. 1.

> *Lady Percy.* Then should you be nothing but musical;
> For you are altogether governed by humours.
> *Lie still, ye thief,* and hear the lady sing in Welsh.
> *Hotspur.* I had rather hear Lady, my brach, howl in Irish.
> *Lady Percy. Wouldst thou have thy head broken ?*
> *Hotspur.* No.
> *Lady Percy. Then be still.*—1 *H. IV.,* iii. 1.

Excellently the above serves to show the by-play of Hotspur's characteristic restlessness ; which here takes the form of half impudent conjugal caress, half impatient military petulance at the music.

> *Northumberland.* How doth my son and brother ?
> *Thou tremblest ; and the whiteness in thy cheek*
> *Is apter than thy tongue to tell thy errand.*
> *Even such a man, so faint, so spiritless,*
> *So dull, so dead in look, so woe-begone,*
> Drew Priam's curtain in the dead of night,
> And would have told him, half his Troy was burn'd . . .
> I see *a strange confession in thine eye :*
> *Thou shak'st thy head,* and hold'st it fear, or sin,
> To speak a truth.—2 *H. IV.,* i. 1.

> *Clarence. Thy voice is thunder, but thy looks are humble.*
> *First Murderer.* My voice is now the king's, my looks mine own.
> *Clarence. How darkly and how deadly dost thou speak !*
> *Your eyes do menace me : why look you pale ?*
> Who sent you hither ? Wherefore do you come ?—*R. III.,* i. 4.

King Richard. . . . My lord of Surrey, *why look you so sad ?*—*Ibid.,* v. 3.

Capulet. . . . How now ! *a conduit, girl ?* What, *still in tears ?*
> *Evermore showering ?* . . . Out, you *green-sickness*
> Carrion ! out, you baggage ! you *tallow-face !*—*R. & Jul.,* iii. 5.

> *Balthasar.* I do beseech you, sir, have patience ;
> *Your looks are pale and wild,* and do import
> Some misadventure.—*Ibid.,* v. 1.

> *Lady Macbeth.* . . . *Your face,* my thane, *is as a book where men*
> *May read strange matters :* to beguile the time,
> Look like the time ; bear welcome in your eye,
> Your hand, your tongue ; look like the innocent flower,
> But be the serpent under it. . . . *Only look up clear;*
> To alter favour ever is to fear.—*Macb.,* i. 5.

Lennox. Here, my good lord. *What is 't that moves your highness ?*—*Ibid*, iii. 4.

> *Lady Macbeth.* . . . Shame itself!
> *Why do you make such faces ?* When all 's done,
> You look but on a stool.
> *Macbeth.* Pr'ythee, see there ! behold ! look ! lo ! how say you ?
> Why, what care I ? If *thou canst nod,* speak too. . . .
> Thou hast no speculation in *those eyes*
> *Which thou dost glare with !*—*Ibid.,* iii. 4.

> *Malcolm.*   Merciful Heaven !
> What, man ! *ne'er pull your hat upon your brows ;*
> Give sorrow words : *the grief that does not speak*
> Whispers the o'erfraught heart, and bids it break.—*Ibid.,* iv. 3.

> *Macbeth.* . . . The devil damn thee black, thou *cream-fac'd* loon !
> Where got'st thou *that goose look ?* . . .
> Go, prick thy face, and *over-red thy fear,*
> Thou lily-liver'd boy. What soldiers, patch *?*
> Death of thy soul ! *those linen cheeks of thine*
> Are counsellors to fear. What soldiers, *whey-face ?*—*Ibid.,* v. 3.

Othello. . . . And *didst contract and purse thy brow together.*
As if thou then hadst shut up in thy brain
Some horrible conceit.—*Oth.*, iii. 3.

Iago. I see, *this hath a little dash'd your spirits.* . . .
. . . but, *I do see you are mov'd.—Ibid.*, iii. 3.

Desdemona. Alas, the heavy day! *Why do you weep?*
Am I the occasion of *these tears*, my lord?—*Ibid.*, iv. 2.

Iago. Do not weep, do not weep: alas, the day!—*Ibid.*, iv. 2.

Iago. What, *look you pale?* . . . *Look you pale*, mistress? . . .
Nay, *if you stare*, we shall hear more anon. . . .
What, *do you shake at that?*

Bianca. He supp'd at my house; but I therefore shake not.—*Ibid.*, v. 1.

Desdemona. And yet I fear you; for you are fatal then,
When *your eyes roll so.* . . .
Alas! why *gnaw you so your nether lip?*
Some bloody passion *shakes your very frame.—Ibid.*, v. 2.

Emilia. Nay, *lay thee down and roar;*
For thou hast kill'd the sweetest innocent,
That e'er did lift up eye.—*Ibid.*, v. 2.

Gratiano. Fie! *your sword upon a woman!—Ibid.*, v. 2.

Othello. Now, how dost thou look now? O ill-starr'd wench!
Pale as thy smock! when we shall meet at compt,
This look of thine will hurl my soul from heaven.—*Ibid.*, v. 2.

Pisanio. Madam, a noble gentleman from Rome,
Comes from my lord with letters.
Iachimo.   *Change you, madam?*
The worthy Leonatus is in safety,
And greets your highness dearly.—*Cym.*, i. 7.

Cymbeline.   *Thou weep'st and speak'st.*
The service that you three have done is more
Unlike than this thou tell'st.—*Ibid.*, v. 5.

Marina. I said, my lord, if you did but know my parentage, *you would not do me violence.—Per.*, v. 1.

Others denote look or gesture in the person spoken of :—

Countess. . . . *Her eye is sick on 't:* I observe her now.—*All's W.*, i. 3.

Maria. He's coming, madam; but *in very strange manner.*
He is, sure, possessed, madam.
Olivia. Why what's the matter? does he rave?
Maria. No, madam, *he does nothing but smile.—Tw. N.*, iii. 4.

Paulina. Music, awake her; strike!
'Tis time; descend; be stone no more; approach;
Strike all that look upon with marvel . . .
                 . . . You perceive, *she stirs.* . . .
                 . . . Nay, present your hand:
When she was young, you woo'd her; now, in age,
Is she become the suitor. . . .
Polixenes. She embraces him.
Camillo. She hangs about his neck.—W. T., v. 3.

Falstaff. . . . That thou art my son, I have partly thy mother's word, partly my own opinion; but chiefly, *a villanous trick of thine eye, and a foolish hanging of thy nether lip*, that doth warrant me.—1 *H. IV.*, ii. 4.

Northumberland. Yea, *this man's brow*, like to a title-leaf,
Foretells the nature of a tragic volume:
So looks the strond, whereon th' imperious flood
Hath left a witness'd usurpation.—2 H. IV., i. 1.

Lady Percy. . . . And *speaking thick*, which nature made his blemish,
Became the accents of the valiant.—*Ibid.*, ii. 3.

Falstaff. Carry Master Silence to bed.—Ibid., v. 3.

Catesby. The king is angry: see, *he gnaws his lip.—R. III.*, iv. 2.

King Richard. Saw'st thou the *melancholy* lord Northumberland?—*Ibid.*, v. 3.

Agamennon. Is not yond' Diomed, with Calchas' daughter?

Ulysses. 'Tis he, I ken *the manner of his gait;*
He rises on the toe : that spirit of his
In aspiration lifts him from the earth.—*Tr. & Cr.*, iv. 5.

Brutus. I will do so : but, look you, Cassius,
The angry spot doth glow on Cæsar's brow,
And all the rest look like a chidden train :
Calphurnia's cheek is pale ; and *Cicero*
Looks with such ferret and such fiery eyes,
As we have seen him in the Capitol,
Being cross'd in conference by some senators.—*Jul. C.*, i. 2.

Cæsar. . . . Yond' Cassius *has a lean and hungry look ;*
He thinks too much : such men are dangerous. . . .
Seldom he smiles ; and smiles in such a sort
As if he mock'd himself, and scorn'd his spirit
That could be mov'd to smile at any thing.—Ibid., i. 2.

Othello. Look, how he laughs already ! . . .
Now he denies it faintly, and laughs it out. . . .
Now he importunes him to tell it o'er. . . .
So, so, so, so: *they laugh that win.* . . .
Iago beckons me ; now he begins the story.—Oth., iv. 1.

Iago. . . . Do you perceive *the gastness of her eye ?* . . .
Behold her well; I pray you, look upon her:
Do you see, gentlemen ? nay, *guiltiness will speak*
Though tongues were out of use.—Oth., v. 1.

First Servant. Here they 'll be, man. *Some o' their plants are ill-rooted already ;*
the *least wind i' the world will blow them down.*
Second Servant. Lepidus is high-coloured.—Ant. & C., ii. 7.

Belarius. I cannot tell : long is it since I saw him,
But time hath nothing blurr'd those lines of favour
Which then he wore ; *the snatches in his voice,*
And burst of speaking, were as his : I am absolute
'Twas very Cloten.—*Cym.*, iv. 2.

Pericles. Look, who kneels here ! Flesh of thy flesh, Thaisa,
Thy burden at the sea, and called Marina.—*Per.*, v. 3.

Occasionally, there are indications of look or gesture in the person spoken of, though addressed in the second person :—

Iago (Aside). He takes her by the palm : ay, *well said, whisper :* with as little a web as this will I ensnare as great a fly as Cassio. Ay, *smile upon her,* do ; I will gyve thee in thine own courtship. *You say true ; 'tis so, indeed :* if *such tricks as these* strip you out of your lieutenantry, it had been better you had not *kissed your three fingers so oft,* *which now again you are most apt to play the sir in.* Very good ; *well kissed ! an excellent courtesy !* 'tis so indeed. *Yet again your fingers to your lips ?—Oth.*, ii. 1.

Guiderius. Oh, *sweetest, fairest lily !*
My brother *wears thee not the one half so well*
As when thou grew'st thyself.—Cym., iv. 2.

In the two following passages we have indication of a peculiar gesture denoting hearty relish of something heard :—

One *rubb'd his elbow*, thus, and fleer'd, and swore,
A better speech was never spoke before.—*Love's L. L.*, v. 2.

To face the garment of rebellion
With some fine colour, that may please the eye
Of fickle changelings, and poor discontents,
Which gape, and *rub the elbow*, at the news
Of hurly-burly innovation.—1 *H. IV.*, v. 1.

In the following two passages there are indications of peculiar dress, badge, or other distinctive peculiarity, marking persons who approach ; and recognized before the wearers come near enough for their identity to be clearly discerned :—

Here comes *two of the house of the Montagues.*—R. & Jul.,* i. 1.
Macduff.   See, who comes here ?
Malcolm. My countryman ; but yet I know him not.—Macb., iv. 3.

By the Scottish tartan dress worn by Rosse, the prince recognizes him for a compatriot ; but does not know him individually until he comes close.

In the following passage, the dramatist draws attention to the change of manner in Edgar when he drops the Bedlam beggar's diction, and assumes one which he may pass off afterwards as that of " some fiend " supposed to have possessed " Poor Tom " :—

> *Gloster. . . . Methinks thy voice is alter'd ; and thou speak'st*
> *In better phrase and matter than thou didst.—Lear,* iv. 6.

INDIRECT PRAISE OF CHARACTER.

Shakespeare has an adroit way of putting description and praise of character into the mouths of other personages in the drama ; and sometimes, with enhanced effect, into the mouth of a person unfriendly to the one involuntarily or reluctantly praised. The dramatist himself has a passage illustrative of this point :—

> But what the repining enemy commends,
> That breath fame blows ; that praise, sole pure, transcends.—*Tr. & Cr.,* i. 3.
>   *Angelo. . . .* What's this, what's this ? Is this her fault or mine ?
> The tempter or the tempted, who sins most, ha ?
> *Not she ; nor doth she tempt : but it is I,*
> *That, lying by the violet in the sun,*
> *Do, as the carrion does, not as the flower,*
> *Corrupt with virtuous season.—M. for M.,* ii. 2.

Don Pedro. And Benedick is not the unhopefullest husband that I know. Thus far can I praise him ; *he is of a noble strain, of approved valour, and confirmed honesty.—M. Ado,* ii. 1.

Oliver. . . . I hope I shall see an end of him ; for my soul, yet I know not why, hates nothing more than he. Yet *he's gentle ; never schooled, and yet learned ; full of noble device ; of all sorts enchantingly beloved.—As You L.,* i. 1.

> *Polixenes. This is the prettiest low-born lass that ever*
> *Ran on the green sward : nothing she does or seems*
> *But smacks of something greater than herself,*
> *Too noble for this place.—W. T.,* iv. 3.
>   *Florizel.*   Old sir, *I know*
> *She prizes not such trifles as these are :*
> *The gifts she looks from me are pack'd and lock'd*
> *Up in my heart.—Ibid.,* iv. 3.

---

* The Montague faction wore a token in their hats, to distinguish them from their rivals, the Capulets.

Iago. . . . *The Moor is of a free and open nature*
That thinks men honest that but seem to be so.—*Oth.*, i. 3.

Iago. . . . *The Moor*—howbeit I endure him not—
Is of a constant, loving, noble nature.—*Ibid.*, ii. 1.

Cassio. *She's a most exquisite lady.*
Iago. And I'll warrant her, full of game.
Cassio. Indeed, *she is a most fresh and delicate creature.*
Iago. What an eye she has; methinks it sounds a parley of provocation.
Cassio. *An inviting eye; and yet methinks right modest.*
Iago. And when she speaks, is it not an alarum to love?
Cassio. *She is, indeed, perfection.*—*Ibid.*, ii. 3.

Iago. . . . *She is of so free, so kind, so apt, so blessed a disposition, that she holds it a vice in her goodness, not to do more than she is requested.* . . . *'Tis most easy the inclining Desdemona to subdue in any honest suit: she's framed as fruitful as the free elements.*—*Ibid.*, ii. 3.

Othello. . . . *O, the world hath not a sweeter creature: she might lie by an emperor's side, and command him tasks.* . . . *So delicate with her needle! An admirable musician!* O, *she will sing the savageness out of a bear! Of so high and plenteous wit and invention!* . . . *And then of so gentle a condition!*—*Ibid.*, iv. 1.

Othello.   Come, swear it, damn thyself;
Lest, *being like one of Heaven*, the devils themselves
Should fear to seize thee. . . . O thou weed,
Who art so lovely fair, and smell'st so sweet,
That the sense aches at thee. . . .
Was *this fair paper*, this most goodly book,
Made to write whore upon?—*Ibid.*, iv. 2.

Belarius. . . . This youth, howe'er distress'd, *appears he hath had Good ancestors.*
Arviragus. *How angel-like he sings!*
Guiderius. But his neat cookery! *he cut our roots in characters, And sauc'd our broths, as Juno had been sick, And he her dieter.*
Arviragus.   Nobly he yokes
A smiling with a sigh,—*as if the sigh Was that it was, for not being such a smile;*
The smile mocking the sigh, that it would fly
From *so divine a temple*, to commix
With winds that sailors rail at.—*Cym.*, iv. 2.

Posthumus. . . .   Gods! if you
Should have ta'en vengeance on my faults, I never
Had liv'd to put on this: so had you saved
The noble Imogen to repent: and struck
Me, wretch, more worth your vengeance. . . . So I'll die
For thee, Imogen! *even for whom my life Is, every breath, a death.*—*Ibid.*, v. 1.

Lucius. . . . This one thing only
I will entreat: my boy, a Briton born,
Let him be ransom'd: never master had
A page *so kind, so duteous, diligent, So tender over his occasions, true, So feat, so nurse-like: let his virtue* join
With my request.—*Ibid.*, v. 5.

Arviragus.   One sand another
Not more resembles that *sweet rosy lad*
Who died, and was Fidele.   What think you?
Guiderius. The same dead thing alive.
Belarius. Peace, peace; see farther; he eyes us not; forbear;
Creatures may be alike: *were't he, I am sure He would have spoke to us.*—*Ibid.*, v. 5.

Iachimo. . . .   the good Posthumus
(What should I say ? *he was too good* to be
Where ill men were ; *and was the best of all*
Amongst the rar'st of good ones). . . . This Posthumus
(*Most like a noble lord in love*, and one
That had a royal lover) took his hint ;
And, not dispraising whom we prais'd (*therein*
He was as calm as virtue), he began
His mistress' picture . . . He, *true knight*,
No lesser of her honour confident
Than I did truly find her, stakes this ring ;
And would so, had it been a carbuncle
Of Phœbus' wheel ; and might so safely, had it
Been all the worth of his car.   Away to Britain
Post I in this design : well may you, sir,
Remember me at court ; *where I was taught*,
Of your chaste daughter, the wide difference
'Twixt amorous and villanous. . . .
. . . I return'd with simular proof enough
To make *the noble Leonatus* mad.—*Cym.*, v. 5.

IRONICAL PHRASES.

Shakespeare has some sentences of irony, or ironically expressed :—

Words against me !   *This' a good friar, belike.*—*M. for M.*, v. 1.

Good Master Mustard-seed, *I know your patience well.*—*Mid. N. D.*, iii. 1.

He knows me, as the blind man knows the cuckoo,
By the bad voice.—*Mer. of V.*, v. 1.

Thou tell 'st me there is murder in mine eye :
'Tis pretty, sure, and *very probable*,
That eyes—that are the frail'st and softest things,
Who shut their coward gates on atomies—
Should be call'd tyrants, butchers, murderers !—*As You L.*, iii. 5.

Your gifts are so good, here 's none will hold you.—*Tam. of S.*, i. 1.

Here's no knavery ! see, to beguile the old folks, how the young folks lay their heads together.—*Ibid.*, i. 2.

I play the noble housewife with the time,
To entertain it so merrily with a fool.—*All's W.*, ii. 2.

There was excellent command—to charge in with our horse upon our own wings, and to rend our own soldiers !—*Ibid.*, iii. 6.

What wisdom stirs amongst you ?   Come, sir.—*W. T.*, ii. 1.

I know how much an ounce.—*Very wisely*, puppies !—*Ibid.*, iv. 3.

Bullets on this town.—*O, prudent discipline !*—*John*, ii. 2.

Here's a good world !   Knew you of *this fair work ?*—*Ibid.*, iv. 3.

Well you deserve : they well deserve to have,
That know the strong'st and surest way to get.—*R. II.*, iii. 3.

There 's honour for you !   *Here's no vanity !*—1 *H. IV.*, v. 3.

Ay, or *more than we should seek after ; for we know enough, if we know we are the king's subjects ; if his cause be wrong, our obedience to the king wipes the crime of it out of us.*—*H. V.*, iv. 1.

I will never trust his word after.—*You pay him then !   That's a perilous shot* out of an elder gun, that a poor and a private displeasure can do against a monarch !—*Ibid.*, iv. 1.

Injurious duke, that threat'st where is no cause.—
True, madam, none at all : what call you this ?—2 *H. VI.*, i. 4.

'Tis meet that lucky ruler be employ'd ;
Witness the fortune he hath had in France.—*2 H. VI.*, iii. 1.

Full well hath Clifford played the orator,
Inferring arguments of mighty force.—*3 H. VI.*, ii. 2.

Here's a good world the while ! Who is so gross,
That cannot see this palpable device ?—*R. III.*, iii. 6.

A proper title of a peace; and purchas'd
At a superfluous rate !—*H. VIII.*, i. 1.

Our count-cardinal has done this, and *'tis well ; for worthy Wolsey, who cannot err,*
he did it.—*Ibid.*, i. 1.

With *all their honourable points of ignorance*
Pertaining thereunto (as fights and fireworks ;
Abusing better men than they can be,
Out of *a foreign wisdom*).—*Ibid.*, i. 3.

How *holily* he works in all his business !
And with what zeal ! . . .
. . . And is not this course *pious ?*—*Ibid.*, ii. 2.

This priest has no pride in him.—Not to speak of.—*Ibid.*, ii. 2.

Follow your envious courses, men of malice ;
You have Christian warrant for them.—*Ibid.*, iii. 2.

Whilst *your great goodness, out of holy pity,*
Absolv'd him with an axe.—*Ibid.*, iii. 2.

Yes, that *goodness,*
Of gleaning all the lands' wealth into one,
Into your own hands, cardinal, by extortion ;
The *goodness* of your intercepted packets,
You writ to the pope, against the king : your *goodness,*
Since you provoke me, shall be most notorious.—*Ibid.*, iii. 2.

Tied all the kingdom : *simony was fair play.*—*Ibid.*, iv. 2.

You are always my good friend ; if your will pass,
I shall both find your lordship judge and juror,
You are so merciful.—*Ibid.*, v. 2.

Where are these porters,
These lazy knaves ? *Ye have made a fine hand,* fellows :
There's a *trim* rabble let in : are all these
Your faithful friends o' the suburbs ? *We shall have*
Great store of room, no doubt, left for the ladies,
When they pass back from the christening.—*Ibid.*, v. 3.

Care for us ! *True, indeed !* they ne'er cared for us yet.—*Coriol.*, i. 1.

That envied his receipt : even so most *fitly*
As you malign our senators for that
They are not such as you.—*Ibid.*, i. 1.

Take my prayers with you.
I would the gods had nothing else to do,
But to confirm my curses.—*Ibid.*, iv. 2.

Now, sir, is your name Menenius ?—
'Tis a spell, you see, of much power : you know the way home again.—*Do you hear*
how we are shent for keeping your greatness back ?—*Ibid.*, v. 2.

But, an you will not wed, *I 'll pardon you.*—*R. & Jul.*, iii. 5.

Flow this way ! *A brave fellow ! he keeps his tides well.*—*Timon*, i. 2.

I feel my master's passion ! *this slave*
Unto his honour has my master's meat in him.—*Ibid.*, iii. 1.

O *proper* stuff !
This is the very painting of your fear.—*Macb.*, iii. 4.

Who cannot want the thought, how monstrous
It was for Malcolm and for Donalbain
To kill their gracious father? damned fact!
How it did *grieve* Macbeth! did he not straight,
In *pious* rage, the two delinquents tear,
That were the slaves of drink, and thralls of sleep?
Was not that *nobly* done? Ay, and *wisely* too.--*Macb.*, iii. 6.

That I essentially am not in madness,
But mad in craft. *'Twere good, you let him know;*
For who, that's but a queen, fair, sober, wise,
Would from a paddock, from a bat, a gib,
Such dear concernings hide? who would do so?
No, *in despite of sense and secrecy,*
Unpeg the basket on the house's top,
Let the birds fly, and, like the famous ape,
To try conclusions, in the basket creep,
And break your own neck down.—*Hamlet*, iii. 4.

This is the excellent foppery of the world, that, when we are sick in fortune (often the surfeit of our own behaviour), we make guilty of our disasters, the sun, the moon, and the stars : as if we were villains by necessity.—*Lear*, i. 2.

I 'll not be struck, my lord.—*Nor tripped neither*, you base football-player.—*Ibid* , i. 4.

'Tis politic and safe to let him keep
At point a hundred knights : yes, that, on every dream,
Each buz, each fancy, each complaint, dislike,
He may enguard his dotage with their powers,
And hold our lives in mercy.—*Ibid.*, i. 4.

    Got praises of the king
For him attempting who was self-subdu'd ;
And, *in the fleshment of this dread exploit,*
Drew on me here again.—*Ibid.*, ii. 2.

A woman's shape doth shield thee.—
Marry, your *manhood* now !—*Ibid.*, iv. 2.

'Tis meet I should be us'd so, very meet.
How have I been behav'd, that he might stick
The small'st opinion on my least misuse ?—*Oth.*, iv. 2.

Your mother too : *she's my good lady ;* and will conceive,
I hope, but the worst of me.—*Cym.*, ii. 3.

    This is her honour !
Let it be granted you have seen all this (and praise
Be given to your remembrance), the description
Of what is in her chamber nothing saves
The wager you have laid.—*Ibid.*, ii. 4.

And he has some sentences spoken as what might be said, or suggested to be said :—

That shall not be much amiss: yet, as the matter now stands, he will avoid your accusation ; *he made trial of you only.*—*M. for M.*, iii. 1.

    And we understand him well,
How he comes o'er us with our wilder days,
Not measuring what use we made of them.
We never valu'd this poor seat of England ;
And therefore, living hence, did give ourself
To barbarous licence ; as 'tis ever common
That men are merriest when they are from home.—*H. V.*, i. 2.

I will go meet them : and, my lord Æneas,
We met by chance ; you did not find me here.—*Tr. & Cr.*, iv. 2.

<blockquote>
This is some fellow,
Who, having been prais'd for bluntness, doth affect
A saucy roughness, and constrains the garb
Quite from his nature: <i>he cannot flatter, he—</i>
An honest mind and plain—he must speak truth !
An they will take it, so ; if not, he 's plain.—Lear, ii. 2.
</blockquote>

<blockquote>
See where he is, who 's with him, what he does :
I did not send you : if you find him sad,
Say I am dancing: if in mirth, report
That I am sudden sick.—<i>Ant. & C.</i>, i. 3.
</blockquote>

<blockquote>
Then was the time for words: no going then :
Eternity was in our lips and eyes,
Bliss in our brows' bent ; none our parts so poor,
But was a race of heaven : they are so still,
Or thou, the greatest soldier of the world,
Art turn'd the greatest liar.—<i>Ibid.</i>, i. 3.
</blockquote>

<blockquote>
Cæsar? Why, <i>he 's the Jupiter of men.</i>—
What 's Antony? <i>The god of Jupiter.</i>—
Spake you of Cæsar? Hoo! <i>the nonpareil !</i>—
O Antony ! Oh, thou Arabian bird !—
Would you praise Cæsar, say, " Cæsar "—go no farther.—
Indeed, he plied them both with excellent praises.—
But he loves Cæsar best ;—yet he loves Antony:
Hoo! <i>hearts, tongues, figures, scribes, bards, poets, cannot</i>
Think, speak, cast, write, sing, number—hoo !—
His love to Antony. But as for Cæsar,
Kneel down, kneel down, and wonder.—<i>Ibid.</i>, iii. 2.
</blockquote>

<blockquote>
                Lo, here she comes.
I am ignorant in what I am commanded.—Cym., iii. 2.
</blockquote>

<blockquote>
                Some jay of Italy,
Whose mother was her painting, hath betray'd him:
Poor I am stale, a garment out of fashion ;
And, for I am richer than to hang by the walls,
I must be ripp'd :—to pieces with me !—Ibid., iii. 4.
</blockquote>

In the following passages Shakespeare has some ironical compliments, or complimentary expressions mockingly applied :—

How now, <i>noble Pompey !</i> . . . Adieu, <i>trusty Pompey.</i>—<i>M. for M.</i>, iii. 2.

Princes and counties ! <i>surely, a princely testimony, a goodly count, Count Confect ; a sweet gallant, surely !</i>—<i>M. Ado</i>, iv. 1.

O noble fool ! A worthy fool ! Motley 's the only wear.—As You L., ii. 7.

And art, indeed, the most comparative, rascallest, <i>sweet young prince.</i>—1 <i>H. IV.</i>, i. 2.

How now, <i>my sweet creature of bombast !</i>—<i>Ibid.</i>, ii. 4.

O, <i>my sweet beef</i>, I must still be good angel to thee.—<i>Ibid.</i>, iii. 3.

Well said, i' faith, Wart; thou 'rt <i>a good scab.</i>—2 <i>H. IV.</i>, iii. 2.

<blockquote>
Before we met, or that a stroke was given,
Like to <i>a trusty squire</i>, did run away.—1 <i>H. VI.</i>, iv. 1.
</blockquote>

Yet <i>god Achilles</i> still cries, " Excellent ! "—<i>Tr. & Cr.</i>, i. 3.

<blockquote>
Good night, sweet lord Menelaus.—
Sweet draught : sweet, quoth'a ! sweet sink, sweet sewer.—Ibid., v. 1.
</blockquote>

<blockquote>
That there should be small love 'mongst these <i>sweet knaves,</i>
And all this courtesy !—<i>Timon</i>, i. 1.
</blockquote>

'Tis <i>a noble Lepidus.</i>—A <i>very fine one.</i>—<i>Ant. & C.</i>, iii. 2.

<blockquote>
Still going? This is a lord ! <i>O noble misery,</i>
To be i' the field, and ask, what news, of me !—<i>Cym.</i>, v. 3.
</blockquote>

And in the following passage he has an ironical simile :—

<blockquote>
That 's done ; as near as the extremest ends
Of parallels ; <i>as like as Vulcan and his wife.</i>—<i>Tr. & Cr.</i>, i. 3.
</blockquote>

ITALIAN IDIOM.

Shakespeare occasionally uses a peculiar idiomatic phraseology similar to that employed in the Italian language. He sometimes thus transposes the adjective and the pronoun in a phrase :—

Dear my brother, let him that was the cause.—*W. T.*, v. 3.
Then, *dear my* liege, mine honour let me try.—*R. II.*, i. 1.
Dear my lord, make me acquainted with your cause of grief.—*Jul. C.*, ii. 1.
Dear my lord, be not familiar with her.—*Lear*, v. 1.
Dread my lord, your leave and favour to return.—*Hamlet*, i. 2.
Gentle my lord, you scarce can right me thoroughly then.—*W. T.*, ii. 1.
Gentle my lord, sleek o'er your rugged looks.—*Macb.*, iii. 2.
Good my lord, give me thy favour still.—*Temp.*, iv. 1.
Here, *good my* glass, take this for telling true.—*Love's L. L.*, iv. 1.
Good my mouse of virtue, answer me.—*Tw. N.*, i. 5.
Then, *good my* mother, let me know my father.—*John*, i. 1.
Thanks, *good my* countryman.—*H. V.*, iv. 7.
The Countess of Richmond, *good my* lord of Stanley.—*R. III.*, i. 3.
Good my brother Tròilus, tell you the lady.—*Tr. & Cr.*, iv. 3.
I beg of you to know me, *good my* lord.—*Timon*, iv. 3.
But, *good my* brother, do not, as some.—*Hamlet*, i. 3.
Good my liege,—Peace, Kent!—*Lear*, i. 1.
Do, *good my* friend. In happy time, Iago.—*Oth.*, iii. 1.
Good my liege, the day that she was missing.—*Cym.*, iv. 3.
Good my lord of Rome, call forth your soothsayer.—*Ibid.*, v. 5.
Gracious my lord, you know your father's temper.—*W. T.*, iv. 3.
Gracious my lord, hard by here is a hovel.—*Lear*, iii. 2.
Accept it and wear it, *kind my* lord.—*Timon*, i. 2.
Ah, *poor my* lord, what tongue shall smooth thy name.—*R. & Jul.*, iii. 2.
I pray thee, Rosalind, *sweet my* coz, be merry.—*As You L.*, i. 2.
O, *sweet my* mother, cast me not away!—*R. & Jul.*, iii. 5.

Sometimes he thus transposes the noun and the pronoun :

You *brother mine*, that entertain'd ambition.—*Temp.*, v. 1.
O *mistress mine*, where are you roaming ?—*Tw: N.*, ii. 3 (*Song*).
Lady mine, proceed.—*H. VIII.*, i. 2.

Sometimes he thus uses a demonstrative pronoun and a possessive pronoun together :—

Notwithstanding *that your* bond of duty.—*Ibid.*, iii. 2.
Handlest in thy discourse, oh, *that her* hand,
In whose comparison all whites are ink.—*Tr. & Cr.*, i. 1.
Thou know'st that we two went to school together:
Even for *that our* love of old, I pray thee.—*Jul. C.*, v. 5.
Thy demon—*that thy* spirit which keeps thee—is
Noble, courageous, high, unmatchable.—*Ant. & C.*, ii. 3.
And threats the throat of *that his* officer
That murder'd Pompey.—*Ibid.*, iii. 5.
Draw *that thy* honest sword, which thou hast worn.—*Ibid.*, iv. 12.
Praise her but for *this her* without-door form.—*W. T.*, ii. 1.
This your sheep-shearing is as a meeting.—*Ibid.*, iv. 2.
This your air of France hath blown that vice in me.—*H. V.*, iii. 6.

If I should tell thee o'er *this thy* day's work.—*Coriol.*, i. 9.
Trebonius doth desire you to o'er-read,
At your best leisure, *this his* humble suit.—*Jul. C.*, iii. 1.
No ; *this my* hand will rather the multitudinous seas incarnadine,—*Macb.*, ii. 2.
May soon return to *this our* suffering country.—*Ibid.*, iii. 6.
Forgive me *this my* virtue ; for in the fatness.—*Hamlet*, iii. 4.
And *this her* son cannot take two from twenty.—*Cym.*, ii. 1.
These your unusual weeds.—*W. T.*, iv. 2.
And *those our* droplets which from niggard nature fall.—*Timon*, v. 5.
Do you misdoubt this sword, and *these my* wounds ?—*Ant. & C.*, iii. 7.
To be full quit of *those my* banishers.—*Coriol.*, iv. 5.
Of half that worth as *those your* swords, made rich.—*Jul. C.*, iii. 1.
Would thou, and *those thy* scars, had once prevail'd.—*Ant. & C.*, iv. 5.
In feeding them with *those my* former fortunes.—*Ibid.*, iv. 13.

Sometimes he thus uses the word " so " :—

You, that have turn'd off a first *so* noble wife.—*All's W.*, v. 3.
From whose *so* many weights of baseness cannot
A dram of worth be drawn.—*Cym.*, iii. 5.
Who may, haply, be a little angry for my *so* rough usage.—*Ibid.*, iv. 1.

Sometimes he thus uses the word " one " :—

I met a courier, *one* mine ancient friend.—*Timon*, v. 2.
And he is *one* the truest manner'd.—*Cym.*, i. 7.

Sometimes, thus, the word " other " :—

Is much o' the favour of *other* your new pranks.—*Lear*, i. 4.

Sometimes, thus, the word " some " :—

That I have said to *some* my standers-by.—*Tr. & Cr.*, iv. 5.

Sometimes, thus, the word " every " :—

Single I'll resolve you . . . of *every* these happen'd accidents.—*Temp.*, v. 1.

Sometimes, thus, the word " many " :—

An earnest inviting, which *many* my near occasions did urge me to put off.—*Timon*,
iii. 6.

Sometimes, thus, the word " poor " :—

Bequeathed me by will but *poor* a thousand crowns, and, as thou sayest, charged my
brother.—*As You L.*, i. 1.
Ah ! *poor* our sex ! this fault in us I find.—*Tr. & Cr.*, v. 2.
Ah ! *poor* my lord ! what tongue shall smooth thy name.—*R. & Jul.*, iii. 2.
What *poor* an instrument may do a noble deed !—*Ant. & C.*, v. 2.

It will be perceived that the Italians, in such phrases as *caro mio
fratello, signora mia, quella sua mano, questa mia mano, uno mio antico
amico, povero nostro sesso,* use precisely similar idiomatic forms of
phraseology to some among those which we have here collected as used
by Shakespeare.

ITERATED WORDS.

Shakespeare occasionally employs an iterated word or short phrase
with excellent effect, to express various impulses, moods or conditions
of feeling, and, sometimes, to express earnestness :—

> I have done nothing but in care of *thee*
> (Of *thee*, my dear one! *thee*, my daughter!).—*Temp.*, i. 2.

Come, *woo me, woo me;** for now I am in a holiday humour, and like enough to consent. What would you say to me now, an I were your *very very* Rosalind.—*As You L.*, iv. 1.

> There is no tongue that moves, *none, none* i' the world,
> So soon as yours, could move me.—*W. T.*, i. 2.

> Good *Hubert, Hubert, Hubert*, throw thine eye
> On yond' young boy.—*John*, iii. 3.

> This land of such *dear* souls, this *dear, dear* land,
> *Dear* for her reputation through the world.—*R. II.*, ii. 1.

>   *Not to-day*, O Lord,
> Oh, *not to-day*, think not upon the fault,
> My father made in compassing the crown!—*H. V.*, iv. 1.

> A very *little little* let us do, and all is done.—*Ibid.*, iv. 2.

> *Gods, gods!* 'tis strange, that from their cold'st neglect
> My love should kindle to inflam'd respect.—*Lear*, i. 1.

> These are portents; but yet, *I hope, I hope*,
> They do not point on me.—*Oth.*, v. 2.

> The Jove of power make me, *most weak, most weak*,
> Your reconciler!—*Ant. & C.*, iii. 4.

> Even to thy pure and *most most* loving breast.—*Sonnet* cx.

Sometimes to express eagerness or impatience:—

What, what, what? ill luck? ill luck? . . . *Is it true? is it true?*—*Mer. of V.*, iii. 1.

Possess us, possess us; tell us something of him.—*Tw. N.*, ii. 3.

Go, *after, after*, cousin Buckingham.— *R. III.*, iii. 5.

How now, how now! what say the citizens?—*Ibid.*, iii. 7.

What, what, what? let's partake, . . . *Wherefore? wherefore?* . . .
They are rising, they are rising. In, in, in, in.—*Coriol.*, iv. 5.

Nay, come, I pray thee, speak; *good, good* nurse, speak. . . .
Sweet, sweet, sweet nurse, tell me, what says my love?—*R. & Jul.*, ii. 5.

Bind him, I say.—*Hard, hard.* O filthy traitor!—*Lear*, iii. 7.

O well-divided disposition! *Note him*,
Note him, good Charmian, 'tis the man; but *note him.*—*Ant. & C.*, i. 5.

Go *hang*, sir, *hang!* Tell me of that? away!—*Ibid.*, ii. 7.

But *why, why, why?* . . . Well, *is it, is it?*—*Ibid.*, iii. 7.

Sometimes to express exultation:—

Freedom, hey-day! hey-day, freedom! freedom! hey-day, freedom!.—*Temp.*, ii. 2.

I thank God! I thank God! . . . *Good news, good news!* . . . *I am very glad of it:* I'll plague him; I'll torture him: *I am glad of it.* . . . Nay, *that's true, that's very true.*—*Mer. of V.*, iii. 1.

Sometimes to express vehement emotion:—

Why, *there, there, there, there!* a diamond gone, cost me two thousand ducats in Frankfort.—*Ibid.*, iii. 1.

You are *forsworn, forsworn* . . . *Arm, arm*, you Heavens, against these perjur'd kings. . . . *Hear me!* O, *hear me!* . . . *War! war!* no peace! peace is to me a war!—*John*, iii. 1.

Lo, *now! now* see the issue of your peace! . . . *Death, death:* O, amiable lovely *death!* . . . I am not mad; *too well, too well* I feel the different plague of each calamity.—*Ibid.*, iii. 4.

---

* In this passage there is the assumed playful manner thinly veiling the real earnestness beneath.

> *It is the cause, it is the cause,* my soul—
> Let me not name it to you, you chaste stars !—
> *It is the cause.* Yet I 'll not shed her blood.—*Oth.*, v. 2.

> *'Twill out, 'twill out :* I hold my peace, sir ? no ;
> I 'll be in speaking liberal as the air :
> Let heaven, and men, and devils, let them *all,*
> *All, all,* cry shame against me, yet I 'll speak.—*Ibid.*, v. 2.

> By Heaven, *I do not, I do not,* gentlemen.—*Ibid.*, v. 2.

Sometimes to express passionate emotion :—

> *Instance, O instance!* strong as Pluto's gates ;
> Cressid is mine, tied with the bonds of Heaven :
> *Instance, O instance!* strong as Heaven itself ;
> The bonds of Heaven are slipp'd, dissolv'd, and loos'd.—*Tr. & Cr.*, v. 2.

> For fear of that, I still will stay with thee ;
> And never from this palace of dim night
> Depart again : *here, here* will I remain
> With worms that are thy chambermaids ; oh, *here*
> Will I set up my everlasting rest.—*R. & Jul.*, v. 3.

Sometimes to express mournful emotion :—

> *To-day, to-day,* unhappy day too late,
> O'erthrows thy joys, friends, fortune, and thy state.—*R. II.*, iii. 2.

> *Too well, too well,* thou tell'st a tale so ill.—*Ibid.*, iii. 2.

> And my large kingdom for *a little grave,*
> *A little little grave,* an obscure *grave.*—*Ibid.*, iii. 3.

> *To-morrow, and to-morrow, and to-morrow,*
> Creeps in this petty pace from day to day,
> To the last syllable of recorded time ;
> And all our yesterdays have lighted fools
> The way to dusty death. *Out, out,* brief candle !—*Macb.*, v. 5.

> O that this *too too* solid flesh would melt,
> Thaw, and resolve itself into a dew ! . . . *O God ! O God !*
> How weary, stale, flat, and unprofitable
> Seem to me all the uses of this world !
> *Fie on 't ! O fie !* 'tis an unweeded garden
> That grows to seed.—*Hamlet*, i. 2.

You cannot, sir, take from me anything that I will more willingly part withal—
except my life, except my life, except my life.—*Ibid.*, ii. 2.

> How is 't ? Feel you your legs ? You stand.—
> *Too well, too well.*—*Lear*, iv. 6.

> *Still, still,* far wide.—*Ibid.*, iv. 7.

> I am *dying,* Egypt, *dying.*—*Ant. & C.*, iv. 13.

Sometimes to express passionate regret and anguish :*—

> *Stars, stars,* and all eyes else dead coals !—*W. T.*, v. 1.

> *O God ! O God !* that e'er this tongue of mine,
> That laid the sentence of dread banishment
> On yond' proud man, should take it off again
> With words of sooth !—*R. II.*, iii. 3.

> *Howl, howl, howl, howl !* O, you are men of stones. . . .

No, *no, no* life ! . . . Thou 'lt come no more, *never, never, never, never, never !*—
Lear, v. 3.

---

* As Milton does in the exquisite two lines from " Lycidas " :—
   " But, O the heavy change, *now thou art gone,*
   Now thou art gone, and never must return ! "

O my dear *Cassio !* my sweet *Cassio !*
O *Cassio, Cassio, Cassio !* . . .
Alas, he faints ! O *Cassio, Cassio, Cassio !—Oth.,* v. 1.
O *fool ! fool ! fool !—Ibid.,* v. 2.

                    O Posthumus ! alas,
Where is thy head ? *where's that ?* Ah me ! *where's that ?*
Pisanio might have kill'd thee at the heart,
And left this head on.—*Cym.,* iv. 2.

Sometimes to express solemn feeling :—

More needs she the divine than the physician :
God, God forgive us all !—*Macb.,* v. 1.

Sometimes to express bitter feeling :—

Down, down I come ; like glistering Phaeton,
Wanting the manage of unruly jades.
In the *base court ? Base court,* where kings grow base,
To come at traitors' calls, and do them grace.
In the *base court ?* Come *down ? Down,* court, *down,* king !—*R. II.,* iii. 3.

Sometimes to express sarcastic emphasis :—

But from the inward motion to deliver
Sweet, sweet, sweet poison for the age's tooth.—*John,* i. 1.
Up, cousin, *up ;* your heart is *up,* I know.—*R. II.,* iii. 3.
My lord, my lord, I am a simple woman.—*H. VIII.,* ii. 4.
My tables—meet it is I set it down,
That one may *smile,* and *smile,* and be a villain.—*Hamlet,* i. 5.

Sometimes to express ironical affirmation :—

We are not safe, Clarence ; *we are not safe.—R. III.,* i. 1.
But I shall live, my lord, to give them thanks,
That were the cause of my imprisonment.—
No doubt, no doubt : and so shall Clarence too.—*Ibid.,* i. 1.

Sometimes to express emphatic and impressive affirmation :—

Richard yet lives, hell's black intelligencer ;
Only reserv'd their factor, to buy souls,
And send them thither : but *at hand, at hand,*
Ensues his piteous and unpitied end.—*Ibid.,* iv. 4.
Perjury, perjury, in the highest *degree ;*
Murder, stern *murder,* in the dir'st *degree ;*
All several sins, all us'd in each *degree,*
Throng to the bar, crying all—*Guilty ! guilty !—Ibid.,* v. 3.

Sometimes used to express desperation :—

Naught, naught, all *naught !* I can behold no longer :
The Antoniad, the Egyptian admiral,
With all their sixty, fly, and turn the rudder :
To see 't mine eyes are blasted.—*Ant. & C.,* iii. 8.

Sometimes to express awe :—

But *never till* to-night, *never till* now,
Did I go through a tempest dropping fire.—*Jul. C.,* i. 3.

If thou hast any sound, or use of voice,
Speak to me . . . speak to me . . . O, *speak ! . . . speak of it :* stay, and *speak !*
—*Hamlet,* i. 1.

Sometimes to express agitation :—

My lord *the king, the king !—W. T.,* iii. 2.

Now, now, I have not winked since I saw these sights.—*Ibid.,* iii. 3.

I know not, madam : 'tis *too bad, too bad.—Lear*, ii. 1.
Why, why is this? think'st thou I 'd make a life of jealousy.—*Oth.*, iii. 3.
I see, this hath a little dash'd your spirits.—
Not a jot, not a jot.—Ibid., iii. 3.

Sometimes to express sobbing :—

                        O lords,
When I have said, cry woe ! *the queen, the queen,*
The sweet'st, dear'st creature 's dead.—*W. T.*, iii. 2.
            Do not laugh at me ;
For, as I am a man, I think this lady
To be my child Cordelia.—
                And so *I am, I am.* . . .
You have some cause, they have not.—
            No cause, no cause.—Lear, iv. 7.

Sometimes to express ebbing breath, in dying :—

Do you see this? *Look* on her—*look*—her lips—
Look there, look there !—[*Dies.*]—*Ibid.*, v. 3.
In speaking as I think, *I die—I die.* —[*Dies.*]—*Oth.*, v. 2.
A master-leaver and a fugitive.
O Antony ! O Antony !—[*Dies.*]—*Ant. & C.*, iv. 9.

Sometimes to express physical impressions :—

           Now, now, now, now ;
Pull off my boots : *harder, harder :* so.—*Lear*, iv. 6.

Sometimes to express wildness of manner :—

What do you read, my lord ?
Words, words, words.—Hamlet, ii. 2.
How does your honour for this many a day ?—
I humbly thank you ; *well, well, well.—Ibid.*, iii. 1.
Mother, mother, mother !—*Ibid.*, iii. 4.
On him, on him ! Look you, how pale he glares !—*Ibid.*, iii. 4.
Why, *look* you there ! *look*, how it steals away !
My father, in his habit as he liv'd !
Look, where he goes, even now, out at the portal !—*Ibid.*, iii. 4.

Sometimes as an impressive exclamation :—

List, list, O, list ! If thou didst ever thy dear father love.—*Ibid.*, i. 3.
O, horrible ! *O horrible* ! most *horrible.—Ibid.*, i. 5.

Sometimes in pathetic appeal :—

Show you sweet Cæsar's wounds, *poor poor* dumb mouths,
And bid them speak for me.—*Jul. C.*, iii. 2.

Sometimes in pacifying denial or remonstrance :—

Have you heard any imputation to the contrary ?—
Oh, *no, no, no, no ;* my meaning in saying he is a good man, is to have you under-
stand me that he is sufficient.—*Mer. of V.*, i. 3.
Now the red pestilence strike all trades in Rome,
And occupations perish !—
What, what, what ! I shall be lov'd when I am lack'd.—*Coriol.*, iv. 1.

Sometimes in petulant contradiction :—

Why, here 's no crab ; and therefore look not sour.—
There is, there is.—Tam. of S., ii. 1.
He is elder.—
Pardon me, pardon me.—Tr. & Cr., i. 2.

Sometimes in pottering inquiry :—

> *What's that, what's that?* . . . What do you talk of ? . . .
> What were you talking of when I came ?—*Tr. & Cr.*, i. 2.

Sometimes, and admirably, as a characteristic of garrulous senility :—

Justice Shallow. That he will not: *'tis your fault, 'tis your fault : 'tis a good dog.*
. . . Sir, *he's a good dog,* and *a fair dog;* can there be more said ? *He's good, and
fair.*—*Merry W.*, i. 1.

He hath wrong'd me, Master Page. . . . *He hath wrong'd me;* indeed, *he hath; at a
word, he hath;* believe me, Robert Shallow, Esquire, saith, *he is wronged.*—*Ibid.*, i. 1.

Nay, *conceive me, conceive me,* sweet coz.—*Ibid.*, i. 1.

'Tis the heart, Master Page; *'tis here, 'tis here.*—*Ibid.*, ii. 1.

Marry, *I thank you* for it; *I thank you* for that good comfort.—*Ibid.*, iii. 4.

Indeed, Master Ford, this is not well, *indeed.*—*Ibid.*, iv. 2.

*Justice Shallow. Come on, come on, come on, sir; give me your hand, sir, give me
your hand, sir.*—2 *H. IV.*, iii. 2.

The same, Sir John, *the very same* . . . and *the very same* day did I fight with one
Sampson Stockfish.—*Ibid.*, iii. 2.

Certain, 'tis *certain; very sure, very sure : death,* as the Psalmist saith, *is certain
to all; all* shall die . . . *Death is certain* . . . *Dead! See, see!* he drew a good
bow;—and *dead!* he shot a fine shoot : . . . *Dead!* . . . And is old Double *dead!—
Ibid.*, iii. 2.

It is well said, in faith, sir; and *it is well said indeed,* too. Better accommodated!
it is good; yea, *indeed, is it :* . . . very *good; a good* phrase.—*Ibid.*, iii. 2.

Give me your good hand, give me your worship's good hand : by my troth, you look
well, and bear your years very *well :* welcome, *good* Sir John.—*Ibid.*, iii. 2.

*Where's the roll? where's the roll? where's the roll? Let me see, let me see, let me
see : so, so, so, so.* Yea, marry, sir: *Ralph Mouldy! let them* appear as I call; *let
them do so, let them do so. Let me see; where is Mouldy?*—*Ibid.*, iii. 2.

Very singular good! In faith, *well said,* Sir John; *very well said.*—*Ibid.*, iii. 2.

Ha, ha, ha! *you can do it,* sir; *you can do it.*—*Ibid.*, iii. 2.

Nay, she must *be old;* she cannot choose but *be old;* certain *she's old.*—*Ibid.*, iii. 2.

That we have, that we have, that we have; in faith, Sir John, *we have :* our watchword was, "Hem, boys!" *Come, let's to dinner; come, let's to dinner.* O the days
that we have seen! *Come, come.*—*Ibid.*, iii. 2.

*I will not excuse you; you shall not be excused; excuses shall not be admitted; there
is no excuse shall serve; you shall not be excused.* Why, *Davy!* . . . *Davy, Davy,
Davy, Davy,*—*let me see, Davy; let me see, Davy; let me see :* yea, marry, *William
Cook,* bid him come hither. *Sir John, you shall not be excused.* . . . With red wheat,
Davy. But for *William Cook.* . . . Let it be cast, and paid. *Sir John, you shall not
be excused* . . . any pretty little tiny kickshaws, tell *William Cook* . . . Yea, *Davy,*
I will *use him well :* a friend i' the court is better than a penny in purse. *Use his men
well, Davy.* . . . Where are you, *Sir John? Come, come, come,* off with your boots.
. . . *Come, Sir John.*—*Ibid.*, v. 1.

Barren, barren, barren; beggars all, beggars all, Sir John : marry, good air. *Spread,
Davy; spread, Davy :* well said, *Davy.* . . . *A good varlet, a good varlet, a very good
varlet,* Sir John. By the mass, I have drunk too much sack at supper : *a good varlet.
Now sit down, now sit down :* come, cousin. . . . *Be merry,* Master Bardolph; and my
little soldier there, *be merry* . . . Honest Bardolph, *welcome :* if thou wantest anything,
and wilt not call, beshrew thy heart. *Welcome,* my little tiny thief; and *welcome,*
indeed, too. . . . Lack nothing: *be merry.*—*Ibid.*, v. 3.

It doth so.— . . . *it doth so.—* . . . *It doth, it doth, it doth.**— . . . It is most
certain.— . . . 'Tis so, indeed.—*Ibid.*, v. 5.

---

* The Quarto assigns the three speeches of Shallow, "It doth so," &c., to Pistol;
while the Folio corrects the error in the first instance, though leaving it in the two
latter. But we think the mere *iteration* suffices to prove that all three speeches belong
to Shallow.

Sometimes as producing humorous effect :—

There is not a white hair on your face, but should have his effect of gravity.—
His effect of *gravy, gravy, gravy.—2 H. IV.,* i. 2.
A pick-axe, and *a spade, a spade.—Hamlet,* v. 1 (*Song*).

Sometimes to express graceful and undulating motion :—

> When you do dance, I wish you
> A wave o' the sea, that you might ever do
> Nothing but that; move *still, still* so,
> And own no other function.—*W. T.,* iv. 3.

Occasionally Shakespeare iterates a word, with the addition of an emphatic epithet :—

> Madam, you have done me *wrong, notorious wrong.—Tw. N.,* v. 1.
> And *him*—O *wondrous him !* O miracle of men !—*2 H. IV.,* ii. 3.
> The third day comes a *frost,* a *killing frost.—H. VIII.,* iii. 2.
> What you have charg'd me with, that have I done ;
> And *more, much more ;* the time will bring it out.—*Lear,* v. 3.
> This hand, whose *touch,* whose *every touch.—Cym.,* i. 7.

IT SEEMS.

Shakespeare uses this phrase, and a few similar phrases, in a somewhat peculiar manner ; sufficiently so to testify that the original reading of the First Folio, in the passage below cited from " Romeo and Juliet," is as the author wrote it, and consequently should be retained in the text.　The editor of the Second Folio substituted the words "her beauty" for " it seems she " ; and since then many editors have adopted the substitution, although there is not the slightest known authority for its having been Shakespeare's writing.　Whereas we now collect together several passages in which he uses phrases so closely resembling " it seems she," that we think there can be no doubt these were the words he here employed :—

> Oh, she doth teach the torches to burn bright !
> *It seems she* hangs upon the cheek of night
> Like a rich jewel in an Ethiop's ear ;
> Beauty too rich for use, for earth too dear !—*R. & Jul.,* i. 5.
> The sky, *it seems,* would pour down stinking pitch,
> But that the sea, mounting to the welkin's cheek,
> Dashes the fire out.—*Temp.,* i. 2.
> *It seems,*his sleeps were hinder'd by thy railing :
> And therefore comes it, that his head is light.—*Com. of E.,* v. 1.
> *It seems* * it is as proper to our age
> To cast beyond ourselves in our opinions,
> As it is common for the younger sort
> To lack discretion.—*Hamlet,* ii. 1.
> *It seems* not meet, nor wholesome to my place,
> To be produc'd (as, if I stay, I shall)
> Against the Moor.—*Oth.,* i. 1.

---

* This is the reading of the Folio, while the Quartos give ' By Heaven　instead of " It seems."

Inform us of thy fortunes; for *it seems*
They crave to be demanded.—*Cym.*, iv. 2.

There might you have beheld one joy crown another, so, and in such manner, that, *it seemed*, sorrow wept to take leave of them—for their joy waded in tears.—*W. T.*, v. 2.

And now and then an ample tear trill'd down
Her delicate cheek : *it seem'd* she was a queen
Over her passion ; who, most rebel-like,
Sought to be king o'er her.—*Lear*, iv. 3.

Ay, madam, it is common.—
                    If it be,
Why *seems it* so particular with thee ?—*Hamlet*, i. 2.

What a haste looks through his eyes ! so should he look
That seems to speak things strange.—*Macb.*, i. 2.

Nothing she does or seems but smacks of something greater than herself.—*W. T.*, iv. 3.

All that impedes thee from the golden round,
Which fate and metaphysical aid *doth seem*
To have thee crown'd withal.—*Macb.*, i. 5.

Plant those that have revolted in the van,
That Antony *may seem to spend* his fury upon himself.—*Ant. & C.*, iv. 6.

                    Wherein our dearest friend
Prejudicates the business, and *would seem*
To have us make denial.—*All's W.*, i. 2.

You would play upon me ; you *would seem to know* my
Stops ; you would pluck out the heart of my mystery.—*Hamlet*, iii. 2.

How courtesy *would seem to cover* sin,
When what is done is like a hypocrite,
The which is good in nothing but in sight.—*Per.*, i. 1.

She is stirring, sir ; if she will stir hither, *I shall seem to notify* unto her.—*Oth.*, iii. 1.

An it shall please you to break up this, *it shall seem to signify.*—*Mer. of V.*, ii. 4.

Write me a prologue ; and let the prologue *seem to say.*—*Mid. N. D.*, iii. 1.

JESTING.

There are a few peculiar and whimsical modes of jesting to be met with in Shakespeare, which we here point out. One is an irrelevancy in jesting; where the fun consists in a mad waggery of darting off upon a track wholly disconnected with the conversation then going on :—

Art thou wise ?—

Ay, sir, I have a pretty wit.—

Why, thou sayest well. I do now remember a saying—" The fool doth think he is wise ; but the wise man knows himself to be a fool." *The heathen philosopher, when he had a desire to eat a grape, would open his lips when he put it into his mouth ; meaning thereby, that grapes were made to eat, and lips to open.* You do love this maid ?—

I do, sir.—

Give me your hand. Art thou learned ?—

No, sir.—

Then learn this of me : to have, is to have ; *for it is a figure in rhetoric, that drink, being poured out of a cup into a glass, by filling the one doth empty the other ; for all your writers do consent, that ipse is he :* now, you are not ipse, for I am he.—

Which he, sir ?—

He, sir, that must marry this woman.—*As You L.*, v. 1.

In sooth, thou wast in very gracious fooling last night, *when thou spokest of Pigro-gromitus, of the Vapians passing the equinoctial of Queubus :* 'twas very good, i' faith. I sent thee sixpence for thy leman : hadst it ?—

I did impeticos thy gratillity; *for Malvolio's nose is no whipstock : my lady has a white hand, and the Myrmidons are no bottle-ale houses.—Tw. N.,* ii. 3.

Bonos dies, Sir Toby : *for, as the old hermit of Prague, that never saw pen and ink, very wittily said to a niece of king Gorboduc, " That, that is, is ;" so I, being master parson, am master parson ; for, what is that, but that ? and is, but is ?—Ibid.,* iv. 2.

By the lord, thou sayest true, lad. *And is not my hostess of the tavern a sweet wench ?—*

As the honey of Hybla, my old lad of the castle. *And is not a buff jerkin a most sweet robe of durance ?—*

How now, how now, mad wag ! what, in thy quips, and thy quiddities ? What a plague have I to do with a buff jerkin ?—Why, what a pox have I to do with my hostess of the tavern ?—*1 H. IV.,* i. 2.

Wilt thou rob this leathern-jerkin, crystal-button, nott-pated, agate-ring, puke-stocking, caddis-garter, smooth-tongue, Spanish-pouch,—

O lord, sir, who do you mean ?—

Why then, your brown bastard is your only drink ; for, look you, Francis, your white canvas doublet will sully : in Barbary, sir, it cannot come to so much.—

What, sir ?—*Ibid.,* ii. 4.

> Take thou some new infection to thy eye,
> And the rank poison of the old will die.—
> *Your plantain leaf is excellent for that.—*
> For what, I pray thee ?—
> *For your broken shin.—R. & Jul.,* i. 2.

Another fashionable form of jesting, when Shakespeare wrote, was the asserting palpable absurdities ; such as the following—affirming that the blind god is a quick seer, and the blacksmith god is a good carpenter :—

But speak you this with a sad brow ? or do you play the flouting Jack, *to tell us Cupid is a good hare-finder, and Vulcan a rare carpenter ?—M. Ado,* i. 1.

Another was the propounding riddle-like questions :—

What was a month old at Cain's birth, that's not five weeks old as yet ?—Love's L. L., iv. 2.

What is he, that builds stronger than either the mason, the shipwright, or the carpenter ?—Hamlet, v. 1.

Another was the giving gravely hoaxing answers to foolish questions :—

What manner o' thing is your crocodile ?—

It is shaped, sir, like itself ; and it is as broad as it hath breadth ; it is just so high as it is, and moves with its own organs ; it lives by that which nourisheth it ; and the elements once out of it, it transmigrates.—

What colour is it of ?—

Of its own colour too.—

'Tis a strange serpent.—

'Tis so : and the tears of it are wet.—Ant. & C., ii. 7.

He gives more than one specimen of quibbling jesting on the subject of late orgies and early rising :—

Approach, Sir Andrew : *not to be a-bed after midnight is to be up betimes ;* and *diluculo surgere,* thou know'st,—

Nay, by my troth, I know not ; but I know, to be up ate, is to be up late.—

A false conclusion : I hate it as an unfilled can. *To be up after midnight, and to go to bed then, is early ; so that, to go to bed after midnight, is to go to bed betimes.—Tw. N.,* ii. 3.

I am glad I was up so late ; for that's the reason I was up so early.—Cym., ii. 3.

There is a quaintly worded jest that Shakespeare has twice indulged in, with slight variation :—

An honest, willing, kind fellow, as ever servant shall come in house withal ; and, I warrant you, no tell-tale, nor no breed-bate: *his worst fault is, that he is given to prayer ; he is something peevish that way : but nobody but has his fault.*—Merry *W.*, i. 4.

Every man has his fault, and honesty is his.—Timon, iii. 1.

He has several jesting passages of blundering speech :—

I am the dog ;—no, the dog is himself, and I am the dog,—O, the dog is me, and I am myself : ay, so, so.—*Two G. of V.*, ii. 3.

I am the poor duke's constable, and my name is Elbow.—*M. for M.*, ii. 1.

But *we are the poor duke's officers.*—M. *Ado*, iii. 5.

You must understand he goes but *to see a noise that he heard*, and is to come again. —*Mid. N. D.*, iii. 1.

The eye of man hath not heard, the ear of man hath not seen, man's hand is not able to taste, his tongue to conceive, nor his heart to report, what my dream was.—*Ibid.*, iv. 1.

I am famished in his service ; *you may tell every finger I have with my ribs.*— Mer. *of V.*, ii. 2.

It was not for nothing that my nose fell a-bleeding on Black Monday last at six o'clock i' the morning, *falling out that year on Ash-Wednesday was four year in the afternoon.—Ibid.*, ii. 5.

For the table, sir, *it shall be served in ; for the meat, sir, it shall be covered.— Ibid.*, iii. 5.

Petruchio is coming, in a new hat and an old jerkin ; a pair of old breeches thrice turned ; a pair of boots that have been candle-cases, one buckled, another laced ; an old rusty sword ta'en out of the town armoury, with a broken hilt, and chapeless ; *with two broken points.*—Tam. of S.*, iii. 2.

Grumio, my horse !—

Ay, sir, they be ready : *the oats have eaten the horses.—Ibid.*, iii. 2.

'Twere as good a deed as *to drink when a man's a-hungry*, to challenge him to the field.—*Tw. N.*, ii. 3.

Here 's another ballad, of a fish, that appeared upon the coast, on Wednesday *the fourscore of April, forty thousand fathom above water*, and sang this ballad.— *W. T.*, iv. 3.

Hast thou never an eye in thy head ? canst not hear ?—1 *H. IV.*, ii. 1.

It is written, that *the shoemaker should meddle with his yard, and the tailor with his last, the fisher with his pencil, and the painter with his nets.*—R. & *Jul.*, i. 2.

Sirrah, if *thou wouldst not be a villain, but do me true service, undergo those employments wherein I should have cause to use thee with a serious industry—that is, what villany soe'er I bid thee do, to perform it directly and truly—I would think thee an honest man.—Cym.*, iii. 5.

And, in the following passage, Shakespeare gives us an example of a joke that was in vogue when he wrote,†—of translating Latin sentences into English with an entirely different meaning from the original:—

Hac ibat, as I told you before,—*Simois*, I am Lucentio, *hic est*, son unto Vincentio of Pisa,—*Sigeia tellus*, disguised thus to get your love ;—*Hic steterat*, and that Lucentio that comes a-wooing,—*Priami*, is my man Tranio,—*regia*, bearing my port,—*celsa senis*, that we might beguile the old pantaloon.—*Tam. of S.*, iii. 1.

---

* These " points," apparently referring to the sword, refer to the dress ; being tagged strings or laces formerly used to attach the upper part of the suit to the lower.

† Chaucer also turns it to excellently humorous effect in his story of " The Cock and the Fox," where sly Master Chanticleer thus befools his Madame Partelote :—

> For all so siker, as ' *In principio*
> *Mulier est hominis confusio*,'
> (Madam, the sentence of this Latin is,
> ' Woman is mannés joy and mannés bliss ').

LEGAL PHRASES.

Shakespeare has introduced so many of these into his works, that some persons have supposed he must at one time of his life have been a lawyer; but when we remember that he was on familiar terms with the Thomas Greenes, father and son, who were attorneys at Stratford-upon-Avon, and that he probably spent many an hour in their office, we think his acquiring an intimate acquaintance with legal terms is fully accounted for. To a mind like Shakespeare's the acquisition of knowledge of all sorts was like inhaling the air he breathed—a sheer vital necessity; he could no more help the one than the other, and both he turned to best account. Numerous and accurate as are the legal terms used by Shakespeare, they are not more numerous or more accurate than many other special technical expressions employed by him, giving vigour and lifelike animation to his style; for whatever he heard and learned, he stored in the treasure of his wisdom, and reproduced it refined and embellished when he needed it in illustration or elucidation of the philosophy in his dramas. Not only was Shakespeare friendly with the Greene family; he met many a law-student and lawyer among his London associates; and from these also he doubtless collected many of the following legal phrases that he has so profusely introduced :—

Belike that now she hath *enfranchis'd* them,
Upon some *other pawn for fealty.*—*Two G. of V.*, ii. 4.

Who writes himself *armigero*, in any *bill, warrant, quittance*, or *obligation, armigero.*
—*Merry W.*, i. 1.

Why, I'll *exhibit a bill in parliament for the putting down* of men.—*Ibid.*, ii. 1.

If the devil have him not *in fee-simple, with fine and recovery*, he will never, I think, in the way of waste.—*Ibid.*, iv. 2.

Our city's institutions, and the *terms*
For common justice, you're as pregnant in
As art and practice hath enriched any
That we remember.—*M. for M.*, i. 1.

Or I'll have mine *action of battery* on thee.—
If he took you a box o' th' ear, you might have your *action of slander* too.—
Ibid., ii. 1.

May he not do it by *fine and recovery* ?—*Com. of E.*, ii. 2.

May it please your grace, Antipholus, my husband—
Whom I made lord of me and all I had,
At your important *letters*—this ill day
A most outrageous fit of madness took him.—*Ibid.*, v. 1.

The manner of it is, I was *taken with the manner.*—*Love's L. L.*, i. 1.

Sole imperator and great general
Of trotting *paritors.*—*Ibid.*, iii. 1.

What *present* hast thou there ?—*Ibid.*, iv. 3.

I beg the ancient privilege in Athens—
As she is mine, I may dispose of her:
Which shall be either to this gentleman,
Or to her death, according to our law
Immediately provided in that case.—*Mid. N. D.*, i. 1.

Go with me to a notary, *seal* me there
Your *single bond.* . . .
If he should *break his day*, what should I gain
By the exaction of the forfeiture ?—*Mer. of V.*, i. 3.

Let good Antonio look he *keep his day*,
Or he shall pay for this.—*Mer. of V.*, ii. 8.

So please my lord the duke, and all the court,
To quit the fine for one half of his goods;
I am content, so he will let me have
The other half *in use*, to render it,
Upon his death, unto the gentleman
That lately stole his daughter.—*Ibid.*, iv. 1.

And *charge us there upon inter'gatories*,
And we will *answer all things faithfully.*—*Ibid.*, v. 1.

Three proper young men, of excellent growth and presence.—With *bills* on their necks ;—"*Be it known unto all men by these presents.*"—*As You L.*, i. 2.

And let my officers of such a nature
Make an extent upon his house and lands.—*Ibid.*, iii. 1.

And say, you would *present her at the leet*,
Because she brought stone jugs, and no *seal'd quarts.*—
Tam. of S., *Induc.* 2.

And, *for that dowry*, I 'll *assure her of*
Her *widowhood**—be it that she survive me—
In *all my lands and leases whatsoever.*—*Ibid.*, ii. 1.

My father is here look'd for every day,
To *pass assurance of a dower in marriage*
'Twixt me and one Baptista's daughter here.—*Ibid.*, iv. 2.

We 'll *pass* the business privately and well.
Send for your daughter by your servant here ;
My boy shall fetch the scrivener presently.—*Ibid.*, iv. 4.

But I must attend his majesty's command, to whom I am now *in ward*, evermore in subjection.—*All's W.*, i. 1.

I have a desire to hold my acquaintance with thee, or rather my knowledge, that I may say, *in the default*, he is a man I know.—*Ibid.*, ii. 3.

Sir, for a quart d'écu he will sell the *fee-simple* of his salvation, the inheritance of it; and *cut the entail from all remainders*, and *a perpetual succession* for it perpetually.—*Ibid.*, iv. 3.

I will buy me a son-in-law in a fair, and *toll* for this: I 'll none of him.—*Ibid.*, v. 3.

Your cousin, my lady, takes great exceptions to your ill hours.—Why let her *except before excepted.*—*Tw. N.*, i. 3.

We will bring the device to the bar, and crown thee for a *finder of madmen.*—*Ibid.*, iii. 4.

Let thy fair wisdom, not thy passion, sway
In this uncivil and unjust *extent*
Against thy peace.—*Ibid.*, iv. 1.

Force me to keep you *as a prisoner*,
Not like a guest ; *so you shall pay your fees*
When you depart, and save your thanks.—*W. T.*, i. 2.

Your most obedient counsellor ; yet that dares
Less appear so, in *comforting* your evils,
Than such as most seem yours.—*Ibid.*, ii. 3.

Your worship had like to have given us one, if you had not *taken* yourself *with the manner.*—*Ibid.*, iv. 3.

If that shepherd be not *in hand-fast*, let him fly.—*Ibid.*, iv. 3.

There might you have beheld one joy crown another, *so, and in such manner*, that it seemed sorrow wept to take leave of them—for their joy waded in tears.—*Ibid.*, v. 2.

Upon thy cheek lay I this zealous kiss,
As seal to this indenture of my love.—*John*, ii. 1.

---

* " Widowhood " is here used for ' right as a widow,' or ' widow's jointure.

And lay aside my high blood's royalty,
Which fear, not reverence, makes thee to *except.—R. II.*, i. 1.

If you do wrongfully seize Hereford's rights,
Call in the letters-patents that he hath
By his *attorneys-general* to *sue*
His livery, and deny his offer'd *homage*,
You pluck a thousand dangers on your head.—*Ibid.*, ii. 1.

'Tis *in reversion* that I do *possess.—Ibid.*, ii. 2.

Whilst you have fed upon my signories,
Dispark'd my parks, and fell'd my forest-woods.—*Ibid.*, iii. 1.

Thou stolest a cup of sack eighteen years ago, and wert *taken with the manner*, and ever since thou hast blushed extempore.—1 *H. IV.*, ii. 4.

An *the indentures be drawn*, I'll away. . . . By this our *book is drawn ;* we will but *seal*, and then to horse.—*Ibid.*, iii. 1.

Grew a companion to the common streets,
Enfeoff'd himself to popularity.—*Ibid.*, iii. 2.

He came but to be Duke of Lancaster,
To *sue his livery*, and beg his peace.—*Ibid.*, iv. 3.

To *punish you by the heels* would amend the attention of your ears. . . . Your lordship may minister the potion of *imprisonment* to me in respect of poverty.— 2 *H. IV.*, i. 2.

Marry, sir, thus ; those *precepts* cannot be *served.—Ibid.*, v. i.

I will devise matter enough out of this Shallow to keep Prince Harry in continual laughter the wearing out of six fashions (which is four *terms*, or two *actions*), and he shall laugh.—*Ibid.*, v. 1.

Either accept the title thou usurp'st,
Of benefit proceeding from our king.—1 *H. VI.*, v. 4.

Nay, he can make *obligations*, and write court-hand.—2 *H. VI.*, iv. 2.

And, *contrary to the king, his crown, and dignity*, thou hast built a paper-mill.— *Ibid.*, iv. 7.

Here's the lord of the soil come to seize me for *a stray*, for entering his *fee-simple* without leave.—*Ibid.*, iv. 10.

Master lieutenant, now that God and friends
Have shaken Edward from the regal seat,
And turn'd my captive state to liberty,
My fear to hope, my sorrows unto joys—
At our enlargement what are thy due fees ?—3 *H. VI.*, iv. 6.

Windy *attorneys* to their *client* woes,
Airy *succeeders* of *intestate* joys !—*R. III.*, iv. 4.

Tell me what state, what dignity, what honour,
Canst thou *demise* to any child of mine ?—*Ibid.*, iv. 4.

It shall be therefore bootless that *longer you desire the court.—H. VIII.*, ii. 4.

You are mine enemy ; and *make my challenge*,
You shall not be my judge : . . .
I utterly *abhor*, yea, from my soul
Refuse you for my judge.—*Ibid.*, ii. 4.

To confirm his goodness, tied it by *letters-patents.—Ibid.*, iii. 2.

That therefore such *a writ be su'd against you ;*
To forfeit all your goods, lands, tenements,
Chattels, and whatsoever, and to be
Out of the king's protection.—Ibid., iii. 2.

How now ! a kiss *in fee-farm.—Tr. & Cr.*, iii. 2.

What, billing again ?   Here's—" *In witness whereof the parties interchangeably.*"— *Ibid.*, iii. 2.

And the rivelled *fee-simple* of the tetter.—*Ibid.*, v. 1.

To beg of Hob and Dick, that do appear,
Their needless *vouches ?*—*Coriol.*, ii. 3.

An I were so apt to quarrel as thou art, any man should buy the *fee-simple* of my life for an hour and a quarter.—*R. & Jul.*, iii. 1.

The rest of your *fees*,* oh, gods—the senators of Athens, together with the common lag of people—what is amiss in them, you gods, make suitable for destruction.—*Timon*, iii. 6.

> Thou know'st that Banquo, and his Fleance, lives.—
> But in them nature's *copy's* not eterne.—*Macb.*, iii. 2.
>
> Cancel and tear to pieces that great *bond*
> Which keeps me pale!—*Ibid.*, iii. 2.
>
> But yet I'll make assurance *double* sure,
> And take a *bond* of fate: thou shalt not live.—*Ibid.*, iv. 1.
>
> Wear thou thy wrongs, the title is *affeer'd!*—*Ibid.*, iv. 3.
>
> What concern they?
> The general cause? or is it a *fee-grief*
> Due to some single breast?—*Ibid.*, iv. 3.
>
> All those his lands which he stood *seiz'd of.*—*Hamlet*, i. 1.
>
> Gives him three thousand crowns *in annual fee.*—*Ibid.*, ii. 2.
>
> Nor will it yield to Norway or the Pole
> A ranker rate, should it be *sold in fee.*—*Ibid.*, iv. 4.

If I drown myself wittingly, it argues an act: and *an act hath three branches;* it is to act, to do, and to perform: argal, she drowned herself wittingly.—*Ibid.*, v. 1.

Why may not that be the skull of a lawyer? Where be his quiddits now, his *quillets*, his *cases*, his *tenures*, and his tricks? Why does he suffer this rude knave now to knock him about the sconce with a dirty shovel, and will not tell him of his *action of battery?* H'm! This fellow might be in's time a great buyer of land, with his *statutes*, his *recognizances*, his *fines*, his *double vouchers*, his *recoveries:* is this the fine of his *fines*, and the recovery of his *recoveries*, to have his fine pate full of fine dirt? will his *vouchers* vouch him no more of his *purchases*, and *double* ones too, than the length and breadth of a pair of *indentures?* The very *conveyances* of his lands will hardly lie in this box: and must the *inheritor* himself have no more, ha?—*Ibid.*, v. 1.

> And cry these dreadful *summoners* grace.—*Lear*, iii. 2.

No, *they cannot touch me for coining; I am the king himself.*—*Ibid.*, iv. 6.

> And, in conclusion, *nonsuits* my mediators.—*Oth.*, i. 1.
>
> For thy *solicitor* shall rather die,
> Than give thy *cause* away.—*Ibid.*, iii. 3.
>
> Who has a breast so pure,
> But some uncleanly apprehensions
> Keep *leets* and *law-days*, and *in session* sit
> With meditations lawful?—*Ibid.*, iii. 3.

Where's Fulvia's *process?* Cæsar's, I would say? both?—*Ant. & C.*, i. 1.

> Labienus
> (This is stiff news) hath, with his Parthian force,
> *Extended* Asia from Euphrates.—*Ibid.*, i. 2.
>
> But my full heart remains *in use* with you.—*Ibid.*, i. 3.

Upon his own *appeal*, seizes him: so the poor third is up, till death enlarge his confine.—*Ibid.*, iii. 5.

> A conqueror that will *pray in aid* for kindness,
> Where he for grace is kneel'd to.—*Ibid.*, v. 2.
>
> Here's a *voucher*, stronger than ever law could make.—*Cym.*, ii. 2.
>
> Senseless bauble, art thou a *feodary* for this act.—*Ibid.*, iii. 2.
>
> But when the heart's *attorney* once is mute,
> The *client* breaks, as desperate in his suit —*V. & Adon.*, Stanza 56.

---

* "Fees" is here used in its legal and feudal sense of all tenements that are held by any acknowledgment of superiority to a higher lord; and is applied by the poet to the senators and commoners of Athens, as creatures who hold their existence by sufferance of the gods.

Which purchase if thou make, for fear of slips,
Set thy *seal-manual* on my wax-red lips.—*V. & Adon., Stanza* 86.

Say *for non-payment* that *the debt should double.*—*Ibid.,* 87.

Her *pleading* hath deserv'd a greater *fee.*—*Ibid.,* 102.

Dim *register* and *notary* of shame !—*Lucrece, Stanza* 110.

To trembling *clients* be you mediators:
For me I force not argument a straw,
Since that my *case is past the help of law.*—*Ibid.,* 146.

My bloody judge forbade my tongue to speak:
No rightful *plea* might plead for justice there.—*Ibid.,* 236.

The deep vexation of his inward soul
Hath *serv'd* a dumb *arrest* upon his tongue.—*Ibid.,* 255.

So should that beauty which you *hold in lease*
Find no *determination.*—*Sonnet* 13.

And summer's *lease* hath all *too short a date.*—*Ibid.,* 18.

When to *the sessions* ot sweet silent thought
I *summon* up remembrance of things past.—*Ibid.,* 30.

Thy *adverse party* is thy *advocate,*
And 'gainst myself *a lawful plea commence :*
Such civil war is in my love and hate,
That I an *accessory* needs must be
To that sweet thief which sourly robs from me.—*Ibid.,* 35.

But *the defendant* doth that *plea* deny,
And says in him thy fair appearance lies.
To *'cide this title* is *impannelled*
A *quest* of thoughts, all *tenants* to the heart ;
And by their *verdict* is determined
The clear eye's moiety, and the dear heart's part.—*Ibid.,* 46.

How with this rage shall beauty *hold a plea,*
Whose *action* is no stronger than a flower ?—*Ibid.,* 65.

But be contented: when that fell *arrest*
Without all bail shall carry me away.—*Ibid.,* 74.

Upon thy part I can set down a story
Of faults conceal'd, wherein I am *attainted.*—*Ibid.,* 88.

Which works on leases of short-number'd hours.—*Ibid.,* 124.

Hence, thou *suborn'd informer !* a true soul,
When most *impeach'd* stands least in thy controul.—*Ibid.,* 125.

And I myself am *mortgag'd* to thy will,
Myself I 'll *forfeit,* so that other mine
Thou wilt restore, to be my comfort still. . . .
He learn'd but, *surety*-like, to write for me,
Under that bond that him as fast doth bind.
The *statute* of thy beauty thou wilt take,
Thou usurer, that putt'st forth all to use,
And *sue* a friend, came *debtor* for my sake.—*Ibid.,* 134.

Why so large *cost,* having *so short a lease,*
Dost thou upon thy fading mansion spend ?—*Ibid.,* 146.

My woful self, that did in freedom stand,
And was my own *fee-simple* (not in part).—*A Lover's Comp., Stanza* 21.

Shakespeare has introduced a few Latin law terms in the course of his dramas :—

Take you assurance of her, *cum privilegio ad imprimendum solùm :* to the church ; take the priest.—*Tam. of S.,* iv. 4.

> Men shall hold of me *in capite.*—2 *H. VI.,* iv. 7.
>
> They may, *cum privilegio,* wear away
> The lag end of their lewdness, and be laugh'd at.—*H. VIII.,* i. 3.
>
> Fall into the compass of a *præmunire.*—*Ibid.,* iii. 2.

He has also used a few terms derived from old French legal expressions :—

> Crier Hobgoblin, make the fairy *o-yes* [*oyez,* 'hear ye '].—*Merry W.,* v. 5.
>
> Some tricks, some *quillets* [*qu'il est,* 'that it is'; which phrase formed the commencement of allegations in law proceedings], how to cheat the devil.—*Love's L. L.,* iv. 3.
>
> But in these nice sharp *quillets* of the law,
> Good faith, I am no wiser than a daw.—1 *H. VI.,* ii. 4.
>
> This precious book of love, this unbound lover,
> To beautify him, only lacks *a cover* [in double reference to the cover of a book, and to the legal term ' coverture,' which signifies marriage subsistent. The term is legally applied to a woman's marriage; and comes from the old French law-term, *femme couverte,* meaning a woman sheltered by marriage under her husband].—*R. & Jul.,* i. 3.

LETTERS, WRITTEN PARTLY IN VERSE, PARTLY IN PROSE.

This seems to have been a fashion in Shakespeare's time, especially for amatory epistles ; since he has given us more than one example of them. Probably, therefore, the line beginning the first letter quoted below was intended to be a portion of its prose commencement, as there is no line corresponding in rhyme therewith ; while the verse continuation is in rhymed lines, and the conclusion returns again to prose :—

> Dian, the count 's a fool, and full of gold.— . . .
> When he swears oaths, bid him drop gold, and take it,
>   After he scores, he never pays the score ;
> Half won is match well made ; match, and well make it ;
>   He ne'er pays after debts, take it before ;
> And say a soldier, Dian, told thee this ;
> Men are to mell with, boys are not to kiss ;
> For count of this, the count 's a fool, I know it,
> Who pays before, but not when he does owe it.
>   Thine, as he vowed to thee in thine ear,
>   PAROLLES.—*All's W.,* iv. 3.

To the unknown beloved, this, and my good wishes. . . .

>   Jove knows, I love :
>   But who ?
>   Lips do not move ;
>   No man must know. . . .
>   I may command where I adore ;
>   But silence, like a Lucrece knife,
>   With bloodless stroke my heart doth gore :
>   M, O, A, I, doth sway my life. . . .

If this fall into thy hand, revolve. In my stars I am above thee ; but be not afraid of greatness ; some are born great, some achieve greatness, and some have, &c.—*Tw. N.,* ii. 5.

To the celestial, and my soul's idol, the most beautified Ophelia. . . . In her excellent white bosom, these. . . .

> Doubt thou the stars are fire ;
> Doubt that the sun doth move ;
> Doubt truth to be a liar ;
> But never doubt I love.

O dear Ophelia, I am ill at these numbers ; I have not art to reckon my groans : but that I love thee best, O most best, believe it.   Adieu.

Thine evermore, most dear lady, whilst this machine is to him, HAMLET.— *Hamlet,* ii. 2.

LOVE EXAGGERATIONS.

Shakespeare has in various passages shown the exaggerated phrases and hyperbolical expressions that lovers affect and permit themselves to use :—

> It is thyself, mine own self's better part,
> *Mine eye's clear eye, my dear heart's dearer heart,*
> *My food, my fortune, and my sweet hope's aim,*
> *My sole earth's heaven, and my heaven's claim.—Com. of E.,* iii. 2.

For I will be *horribly in love* with her.—*M. Ado,* ii. 3.

The rather, gentle princess, because *I love thee cruelly.—H. V.,* v. 2.

> Nor never woo in rhyme, like a blind harper's song !
> *Taffeta phrases, silken terms precise,*
> *Three pil'd hyperboles, spruce affectation,*
> *Figures pedantical.—Love's L. L.,* v. 2.

> And thou, thrice-crowned queen of night, survey
> With thy chaste eye, from thy pale sphere above,
> Thy huntress' name, *that my full life doth sway.—*
> *As You L.,* iii. 2 *(Verses).*

M, O, A, I, *doth sway my life.—Tw. N.,* ii. 5 *(Verses).*

> There shall your master have a thousand loves,
> A mother, and a mistress, and a friend,
> *A phœnix, captain, and an enemy,*
> *A guide, a goddess, and a sovereign,*
> *A counsellor, a traitress, and a dear ;*
> *His humble ambition, proud humility,*
> *His jarring concord, and his discord dulcet,*
> *His faith, his sweet disaster ;* with *a world*
> *Of pretty, fond, adoptious christendoms,*
> *That blinking Cupid gossips.—All's W.,* i. 1.

> A *traitor* you do look like ; but such *traitors*
> His majesty seldom fears.—*Ibid.,* ii. 1.

With him, *the mortal Venus, the heart-blood of beauty, love's invisible soul.* . . . Helen.—*Tr. & Cr.,* iii. 1. .

> To bed, to bed : sleep *kill* those pretty eyes,
> And give as soft attachment to thy senses
> As infants empty of all thought.—*Ibid.,* iv. 2.

> Why, then, oh, *brawling love !* oh, *loving hate !*
> Oh, *anything, of nothing first create !*
> Oh, *heavy lightness ! serious vanity !*
> *Mis-shapen chaos of well-seeming forms !*
> *Feather of lead, bright smoke, cold fire, sick health !*
> *Still-waking sleep, that is not what it is !*
> This love feel I, that feel no love in this. . . .
> *Love is a smoke rais'd with the fume of sighs ;*

> *Being purg'd, a fire sparkling in lovers' eyes;*
> *Being vex'd a sea nourish'd with lovers' tears:*
> What is it else ? *a madness most discreet,*
> *A choking gall, and a preserving sweet.*—R. & Jul., i. 1.
> At my poor house look to behold this night
> *Earth-treading stars that make dark heaven light.*—Ibid., i. 2.
> Oh, *serpent heart, hid with a flowering face !*
> Did ever dragon keep so fair a cave ?
> *Beautiful tyrant ! fiend angelical !*
> *Dove-feather'd raven ! wolfish-ravening lamb !*
> *Despised substance of divinest show !*
> *Just opposite to what thou justly seem'st,*
> *A damned saint, an honourable villain !*
> O, nature ! what hadst thou to do in hell,
> When thou didst *bower the spirit of a fiend*
> *In mortal paradise of such sweet flesh ?*
> *Was ever book containing such vile matter,*
> *So fairly bound ?*   O, *that deceit should dwell*
> *In such a gorgeous palace !*—Ibid., iii. 2.
> Oh, *my fair warrior !*—Oth., ii. 1.
> I was (unhandsome *warrior* as I am)
> Arraigning his unkindness with my soul.—Ibid., iii. 4.

In this last-cited passage, the dramatist causes Desdemona to make touching allusion to her husband's having previously called her "warrior"; which was a title frequently given by amorous gallants to their lady-loves, in deprecation of their supposed cruelty and antagonism, and which is applied by Othello to his bride-wife, in allusion to her refusing (in act i., sc. 3) to "be left behind, a moth of peace, and he go to the war."

In the first passage from "All's Well" and in the first and third passage from "Romeo and Juliet" above quoted, we have specimens of those rapturous tirades which it was formerly the mode, in poetic or romantic language, to lavish upon love and the object of affection; full of fanciful antitheses, whimsically opposite attributes, and half-reproachful, half-admiring epithets, expressive of the mingled torment and joy belonging to this sovereign passion.

MODE OF ADDRESS OR SALUTATION.

Our dramatist employs certain courteous phrases of address, salutation, or rejoinder, in special form. As commencement of address in rejoinder :—

Sir, my lord, I could do this.—W. T., i. 2.

Sir, my gracious lord, to chide at your.—Ibid., iv. 3.

As an address of recognition on meeting :—

Welcome, from Egypt, sir.—Half the heart of Cæsar, *worthy Mecænas ! my honourable friend, Agrippa !*—Good Enobarbus !—Ant. & C., ii. 2.

Accosting, by one who enters :—

With all my heart, gentlemen, both : and how fare you ?—Timon, iii. 6.

Brutus, my lord !—Jul. C., ii. 1.

Phrase of courtesy, in passing before some one :—

> Lead you on :
> Follow, Cominius ; we must follow you ;
> Right worthy you priority.—*Noble Marcius !*—*Coriol.*, i. 1.

Elliptical form of address :—

> [I say] *to you all three,*
> The senators alone of this great world.—*Ant. & C.*, ii. 6.

Elliptical phrase, announcing an entrance :—

> [Here] she [comes] *and the duke her husband.*—*Lear*, v. 1.

Elliptical phrases of acquiescence :—

> Who's there ? my woman Helen ?—*Please you, madam.*—*Cym.*, ii. 2.
> 'Tis the ninth hour o' the morn . . .
> . . . *So please you, sir.*—*Ibid.*, iv. 2.

Elliptical phrase, spoken in polite rejoinder :—

Welcome to Rome.—Thank you.—Sit.—Sit, sir.—*Nay then*—[since you will have
it so, I take my seat first].—*Ant. & C.*, ii. 2.

Affected *double* style of address :—

> *Good sparks and lustrous*, a word, *good metals.*—*All's W.*, ii. 1.

Reply to one who salutes on entering :—

> My ladies both, good day to you.—
> *Sweet madam.*—*Coriol.*, i. 3.
> Save you, worthy general !
> *With all my heart, sir.*—*Oth.*, iv. 1.

Reply to one who salutes on departing :—

> Now fare you well, good sir.—*With all my heart.*—*Lear*, iv. 6.

Salutation to some one taking leave :—

> I 'll to the king,
> And say I spoke with you.—*My honour'd lord.*—*H. VIII.*, ii. 3.

Salutation from some one taking leave :—

God be with you ; fare you well.—*Good my lord !*—*Hamlet*, ii. 1.
You are welcome to Elsinore.—*Good my lord !*—*Ibid.*, ii. 2.

Mutual amenities between a host and his departing friends :—

> *We are so virtuously bound,*—
> 　　　　　　*And so*
> *Am I to you.*—*So infinitely endear'd,*—
> *All to you.*　Lights, more lights !—
> 　　　　　　*The best of happiness,*
> *Honour, and fortunes, keep with you, lord Timon !*—
> *Ready for his friends.*—*Timon*, i. 2.

Salutation in reply to one who is drinking and wishing good health :—

> The queen carouses to thy fortune, Hamlet.—
> *Good madam !*—*Hamlet*, v. 2.

Salutation of pledging while drinking [*See* IDIOMS] :—

> My lord, in heart ; and let the health go round.—*Timon*, i. 2.

Said in reply to one who is speaking laudatorily :—

> Horatio, thou art e'en as just a man
> As e'er my conversation cop'd withal.—
> *O, my dear lord.*—*Hamlet*, iii. 2.

Peculiar phrase of distinctive announcement :—

Pompey the Great,—*Your servant, and Costard.—Love's L. L.*, v. 2.

We talk of young Master Launcelot.—*Your worship's friend, and Launcelot, sir.—Mer. of V.*, ii. 1.

Shakespeare occasionally makes a speaker allude to himself in the third person :—

> Twelve years since, Miranda, twelve years since,
> *Thy father* was the Duke of Milan.—*Temp.*, i. 2.

And what news else betideth here in absence of *thy friend.—Two G. of V.*, i. 1.

> My heart assures me, that *the Earl of Warwick*
> Shall one day make the Duke of York a king. . . .
> *Richard* shall live to make the Earl of Warwick.—2 *H. VI.*, ii. 2.

Whenever *Buckingham* doth turn his hate upon your grace. —*R. III.*, ii. 1.

And dare be bold to weep for *Buckingham* . . . and, if he speak of *Buckingham,* pray, tell him you met *him.—H. VIII.*, ii. 1.

> More ready to cry out, " Who knows what follows ? "
> Than *Hector* is.—*Tr. & Cr.*, ii. 2.

Ne'er speak or think that *Timon's* fortunes 'mong his friends.—*Timon*, ii. 2.

When *Marcus Brutus* grows so covetous.—*Jul. C.*, iv. 3.

On *Cassius*, for *Cassius* is aweary of the world . . . better than ever thou lov'dst *Cassius.—Ibid.*, iv. 3.

If *Cassius* might have rul'd . . . this very day was *Cassius* born.—*Ibid.*, v. 1.

And what so poor a man as *Hamlet* is may do.—*Hamlet*, i. 5.

Who calls on *Hamlet?—Ibid.*, iv. 2.

> Was 't *Hamlet* wrong'd Laertes ? Never *Hamlet :*
> If *Hamlet* from *himself* be ta'en away,
> And, when *he* 's not *himself*, does wrong Laertes,
> Then *Hamlet* does it not ; *Hamlet* denies it.
> Who does it then ? *His* madness : if 't be so,
> *Hamlet* is of the faction that is wrong'd ;
> *His* madness is poor *Hamlet's* enemy.—*Ibid.*, v. 2.
> *The queen* carouses to thy fortune, Hamlet.—*Ibid.*, v. 2.

And he occasionally makes a speaker use the third person in mentioning one who is present :—

> It lies as sightly on the back of *him.—John*, ii. 1.
>   . . . was that done like *Cassius?*
> Should I have answer'd *Caius Cassius* so ?—*Jul. C.*, iv. 3.
> To be but mirth and laughter to his *Brutus.—Ibid.*, iv. 3.
> And *my poor fool* is hang'd !—*Lear*, v. 3.
> Why did *he* marry Fulvia, and not love her?
> I 'll seem the fool I am not ; *Antony*
> Will be himself.—But stirr'd by *Cleopatra.—Ant. & C.*, i. 1.
> Great *Mark Antony* is now a widower.—*Ibid.*, ii. 2.

Occasionally he causes a speaker to change the person in reference to the same object during the same sentence :—

> My loving lord *Dumain* [3rd person] is mortified:
> The grosser manner of these world's delights
> *He* [3rd person] throws upon the gross world's baser slaves :
> To love, to wealth, to pomp, *I* [1st person] pine and die,
> With all these living in philosophy.—*Love's L. L.*, i. 1.

O *Cæsar* [2nd person], read mine first ; for mine 's a suit
That touches *Cæsar* [3rd person] nearer: read it, great *Cæsar* [2nd person].—*Jul. C.*, iii. 1.

Good now, sit down [2nd person], and tell me, *he* [3rd person] that knows, why this same strict and most.—*Hamlet*, i. 1.

And occasionally he makes a speaker address in the second person some one who is not present :—

Why blame *you* me to love *you ?*—Whom do you speak to, "Why blame you me to love you ? "—To her that is not here, nor doth not hear.—*As You L.*, v. 2.

My learn'd and well-beloved servant, *Cranmer*,
Pry'thee, return ! with *thy* approach, I know.—*H. VIII.*, ii. 4.

And, *thou great-siz'd coward*,
No space of earth shall sunder our two hates :
I 'll haunt *thee* like a wicked conscience still.—*Tr. & Cr.*, v. 11.

Five times, *Marcius*,
I have fought with *thee ;* so often hast *thou* beat me.—*Coriol.*, i. 10.

Come, *Antony*, and young *Octavius*, come,
Revenge *yourselves* alone on Cassius.—*Jul. C.*, iv. 3.

Thou hast one daughter,
Who redeems nature from the general curse.—*Lear*, iv. 6.

Antony,
Leave *thy* lascivious wassails. When *thou* once
Wast beaten from Modena, where *thou* slew'st
Hirtius and Pansa, consuls, at *thy* heel
Did famine follow, &c., &c. [to the end of speech].—*Ant. & C.*, i. 4.

Wherefore write *you* not
What monsters her accuse ? *Leonatus !*
O *master !* what a strange infection
Is fallen into *thy* ear ! &c., &c.—*Cym.*, iii. 2.

Pisanio, I 'll now taste of *thy* drug.—*Ibid.*, iv. 2.

Would, *Polydore*, *thou* hadst not done 't ! though valour
Becomes *thee* well enough.—
. . . *Polydore*,
I love *thee* brotherly ; but envy much
Thou hast robb'd me.—*Ibid.*, iv. 2.

And, in the following passage, he causes a speaker to apostrophise the absent and the present together :—

What have *you* done ?
Tigers, not daughters, what have *you* perform'd ?
A father, and a gracious aged man,
Whose reverence the head-lugg'd bear would lick,
Most barbarous, most degenerate ! have *you* madded.
Could my good brother suffer *you* to do it ?—*Lear*, iv. 2.

MUSICAL TERMS.

So frequent and so apt is Shakespeare's use of musical terms and his introduction of them into various passages of his works, that he might as well be supposed to have been a musician as a lawyer [*See* LEGAL PHRASES] ; but we believe that his knowledge of musical terms no more proves him to have been a practical musician than his acquaintance with legal expressions shows him to have practised the law. From professional men in both pursuits, he was able—with his capacity for gathering whatever might turn to profit in his art as poet and dramatist—to acquire even the large amount of familiarity with the several technicalities in each vocation that he has displayed. He has more than once introduced some of the Guidonian names for the notes in the musical scale—ut, re, mi, fa, sol, la, si :—

> *Ut, re, sol, la, mi, fa.* Under pardon, sir.—*Love's L. L.*, iv. 2.
>
> I 'll try how you can *sol, fa*, and sing it.—*Tam. of S.*, i. 2.
>
> A *re*, to plead Hortensio's passion,
> B *mi*, Bianca, take him for thy lord,
> C *fa ut*, that loves with all affection ;
> D *sol re*, one cliff, two notes have I :
> E *la mi*, show pity, or I die.—*Ibid.*, iii. 1 (*Gamut*).
>
> I 'll *re* you, I 'll *fa* you ; do you note me ?—
> An you *re* us and *fa* us, you note us.—*R. & Jul.*, iv. 5.

These eclipses do portend these divisions ! *fa, sol, la, mi.*—*Lear*, i. 2.

He uses some of the terms belonging to musical notation :—

One *cliff*, two *notes* have I.—*Tam. of S.*, iii. 1.

And any man may sing her, if he can take her *cliff;* she 's *noted.*—*Tr. & Cr.*, v. 2.

> As peace should still her wheaten garland wear,
> And stand a *comma** 'tween their amities.—*Hamlet*, v. 2.
>
> Do it in *notes.*—Note this before my *notes*,
> There 's not a *note* of mine that 's worth the noting.—
> Why these are very *crotchets* that he speaks ;
> Note, notes, forsooth, and, *nōthing†.*—*M. Ado*, ii. 3.

No hearing, no feeling, but my sir's song, and admiring the *nōthing†* of it.—*W. T.*, iv. 3.

I will carry no *crotchets.*—*R. & Jul.*, iv. 5.

Rests me his *minim rest*, one, two, and the third in.—*Ibid.*, ii. 4.

To teach you *gamut.* . . . I am past my *gamut* long ago.—Yet read the *gamut* of Hortensio.—*Gamut* I am, the ground of all accord. . . . Call you this *gamut ?*—*Tam. of S.*, iii. 1.

He uses several terms pertaining to musical instruments :—

It is a vice in her ears, which *horse-hairs* and *calves'-guts.*—*Cym.*, ii. 3.

What say you, Simon *Catling ?*—*R. & Jul.*, iv. 5.

Unless the fiddler Apollo get his sinews to make *catlings* on.—*Tr. & Cr.*, iii. 3.

The devil rides upon a *fiddle-stick.*—1 *H. IV.*, ii. 4.

An thou make minstrels of us, look to hear nothing but discords: here 's my *fiddle-stick.*—*R. & Jul.*, iii. 1.

Call me what instrument you will, though you can *fret* me, you cannot play upon me.—*Hamlet*, iii. 2.

> Why, no ; for she hath broke the lute to me.
> I did but tell her she mistook her *frets*,
> And bow'd her hand to teach her fingering ;
> When, with a most impatient devilish spirit,
> "*Frets*, call you these ?" quoth she; "I 'll fume with them."—
> > *Tam. of S.*, ii. 1.

---

* Some commentators have supposed that the word "comma" here means the smallest point in punctuation ; but, considering the context of the whole passage, we think it is not so likely that he used a term in *punctuation*, as a term referring to *concord*. "Comma" is employed by theoretical musicians to express 'the least of all the sensible intervals in music,' showing the exact proportion between *concords*. Tuners of organs and pianofortes use the word "comma" thus to the present day. We believe that Shakespeare used "comma" here to express a link of amicably harmonious connection.

† Shakespeare was evidently so tickled with this pun, that he could not resist repeating the play upon the word between nothing (sounded with a long o) and noting.

How oft, when thou, my music, music play'st,
Upon that blessed wood whose motion sounds
With thy sweet fingers, when thou gently sway'st
The wiry concord that mine ear confounds,
Do I envy those *jacks* that nimble leap
To kiss the tender inward of thy hand . . .
Since *jacks* so happy are in this,
Give them thy fingers, me thy lips to kiss.—*Sonnet* 128.

Nay, but his jesting spirit; which is now crept into a *lute-string*, and now governed by *stops*.—*M. Ado*, iii. 2.

The winds did sing it to me; and the thunder,
That deep and dreadful *organ-pipe*, pronounc'd
The name of Prosper: it did base my trespass.—*Temp.*, iii. 3.

I am the cygnet to this pale faint swan,
Who chants a doleful hymn to his own death,
And from the *organ-pipe* of frailty sings
His soul and body to their lasting rest.—*John*, v. 7.

O, you are well tun'd now!
But I 'll set down the *pegs* that make this music,
As honest as I am.—*Oth.*, ii. 1.

Open your ears; for which of you will *stop*
The vent of hearing when loud Rumour speaks? . . .
. . . Rumour is a pipe
Blown by surmises, jealousies, conjectures;
And of so easy and so plain a *stop*,
That the blunt monster with uncounted heads,
The still-discordant wavering multitude,
Can play upon it.—*2 H. IV.* (*Induc.*)

That they are not a pipe for fortune's finger
To sound what *stop* she pleases.—*Hamlet*, iii. 2.

Look you, these are the *stops* . . . you would play upon me; you would seem to know my *stops*.—*Ibid.*, iii. 2.

Govern these *ventages* with your finger and thumb.—*Ibid.*, iii. 2.

Such to-be-pitied and *o'er-wrested* seeming
He acts thy greatness in.—*Tr. & Cr.*, i. 3.

But this Antenor,
I know, is such a *wrest* in their affairs,
That their negotiations all must slack,
Wanting his manage.—*Ibid.*, iii. 3.

He makes mention of several musical instruments :—

And others, when the *bag-pipe* sings i' the nose . . . why he, a swollen *bag-pipe*.—*Mer. of V.*, iv. 1.

No, the *bag-pipe* could not move you.—*W. T.*, iv. 3.

Yea, or the drone of a Lincolnshire *bag-pipe*.—*1 H. IV.*, i. 2.

He that went, like a *base-viol*, in a case of leather.—*Com. of E.*, iv. 3.

What is this?—A *cittern* head.—*Love's L. L.*, v. 2.

I have known, when there was no music with him but the *drum* and the *fife*; and now had he rather hear the *tabor* and the *pipe*.—*M. Ado*, ii. 3.

And when you hear the *drum*,
And the vile squeaking of the wry-neck'd *fife*.—*Mer. of V.*, ii. 5.

Farewell the neighing steed, and the shrill *trump*,
The spirit-stirring *drum*, the ear-piercing *fife*.—*Oth.*, iii. 3.

The oars were silver, which to the tune of *flutes* kept stroke.—*Ant. & C.*, ii. 2.

These *drums!* these *trumpets*, *flutes!* what!—*Ibid.*, ii. 7.

His word is more than the miraculous *harp*.—*Temp.*, ii. 1.

To be sung by an Athenian eunuch to the *harp*.—*Mid. N. D.*, v. 1.

The case of a treble *hautboy* was a mansion for him.—2 *H. IV.*, iii. 2.

For Orpheus' *lute* was strung with poets' sinews.—*Two G. of V.*, iii. 2.

For God defend the *lute* should be like the case!—*M. Ado*, ii. 1.

As sweet and musical as bright Apollo's *lute*, strung with his hair.—*Love's L. L.*, iv. 3.

Take you the *lute ;* and you the set of books.—*Tam. of S.*, ii. 1.

Or an old lion, or a lover's *lute.*—1 *H. IV.*, i. 2.

> Sung by a fair queen in a summer's bower,
> With ravishing division, to her *lute.*—*Ibid.*, iii. 1.

And, like thee, Nero, play on the *lute*, beholding the towns burn.—1 *H. VI.*, i. 4.

> He capers nimbly in a lady's chamber,
> To the lascivious pleasing of a *lute.*—*R. III.*, i. 1.

Take thy *lute*, wench. . . . Orpheus with his *lute.*—*H. VIII.*, iii. 1.

Or when to the *lute* she sung.—*Per.*, iv. (*Gower*).

Upon the *lute* doth ravish . . . that Phœbus' *lute*, the queen of music, makes.—*Pass. Pil.*, Stanza 6.

Pretty! What say you, Hugh *Rebeck* ?—*R. & Jul.*, iv. 5.

Indeed he hath played on his prologue like a child on a *recorder.*—*Mid. N. D.*, v. 1.

Come, some music! come, the *recorders!* . . . Oh, the *recorders :* let me see one.—*Hamlet*, iii. 2.

> The *trumpets, sackbuts, psalteries*, and *fifes*,
> *Tabors*, and *cymbals*, and the shouting Romans,
> Make the sun dance. Hark you!—*Coriol.*, v. 4.

Then I beat my *tabor ;* at which like.—*Temp.*, iv. 1.

Or I will play on the *tabor* to the worthies.—*Love's L. L.*, v. 1.

Dost thou live by thy *tabor ?* . . . or, the church
Stands by thy *tabor*, if thy *tabor* stands by the church.—*Tw. N.*, iii. 1.

You would never dance again after a *tabor* and *pipe.*—*W. T.*, iv. 3.

The shepherd knows not thunder from a *tabor*, more.—*Coriol.*, i. 6.

Beat loud the *tabourines*, let the *trumpets* blow.—*Tr. & Cr.*, iv. 5.

Make mingle with our rattling *tabourines.*—*Ant. & C.*, iv. 8.

> And now my tongue's use is to me no more,
> Than an unstring'd *viol*, or a *harp.*—*R. II.*, i. 3.

You 're a fair *viol*, and your sense the strings.—*Per.*, i. 1.

He plays o' the *viol-de-gamboys*, and speaks three or four languages word for word without book.—*Tw. N.*, i. 3.

He uses several terms for tunes, or pieces of music :—

Will you troll the *catch* you taught me. . . . This is the tune of our *catch*, played by the picture.—*Temp.*, iii. 2.

Now let 's have a *catch.* . . . Shall we rouse the night-owl in a *catch.* . . . I am dog at a *catch.* . . . Let our *catch* be, " Thou knave."—*Tw. N.*, ii. 3.

We did keep time in our *catches.*—*Ibid.*, ii. 3.

Makes Welsh as sweet as *ditties* highly penn'd.—1 *H. IV.*, iii. 1.

The *ditty* does remember my drown'd father.—*Temp.*, i. 2.

And this *ditty*, after me, sing, and dance it.—*Mid. N. D.*, v. 2.

Though there was no great matter in the *ditty.*—*As You L.*, v. 3.

I framed to the harp many an English *ditty.*—1 *H. IV.*, iii. 1.

For she doth welcome daylight with her *ditty.*—*Pass. Pil.*, Stanza 11.

And there sung the dolefull'st *ditty.*—*Ibid.*, 15.

To their instruments tune a deploring *dump.*—*Two G. of V.*, iii. 2.

Play me some merry *dump*, to comfort me.—Not a *dump* we ; 'tis no time to play now.—*R. & Jul.*, iv. 5.

> Sing no more *ditties*, sing no mo
> Of *dumps* so dull and heavy.—*M. Ado*, ii. 3 (*Song*).

An old hat and "the humour of forty *fancies*" pricked in 't for a feather.—*Tam. of S.*, iii. 2.

And sung those tunes to the overscutched huswives that he heard the carman whistle, and sware they were his *fancies* or his *good-nights.*—*2 H. IV.*, iii. 2.

And profound Solomon tuning a *jig.*—*Love's L. L.*, iv. 3.

He 's for a *jig*, or a tale of bawdry, or he sleeps.—*Hamlet*, ii. 2.

All my merry *jigs* are quite forgot.—*Pass. Pil.*, Stanza 13.

Pull'd the poor wretch from her melodious *lay* to.—*Hamlet*, iv. 7.

Let the bird of loudest *lay.*—*Phœnix & Turtle*, Stanza 1.

That she will light to listen to the *lays.*—*2 H. VI.*, i. 3.

She dances as goddess-like to her admired *lays.*—*Per.*, v. (*Gower*).

Melodious birds sing *madrigals.*—*Merry W.*, iii. 1 (*Song*).

Come, now, a *roundel*, and a fairy song.—*Mid. N. D.*, ii. 3.

He employs some technicalities of musical execution :—

And bow'd her hand to teach her *fingering.*—*Tam. of S.*, ii. 1.

Madam, before you touch the instrument,
To learn the order of my *fingering.*—*Ibid.*, iii. 1.

Come, on, tune : if you can penetrate her with your *fingering*, so.—*Cym.*, ii. 3.

Govern these ventages with your finger and thumb.—*Hamlet*, iii. 2.

A sound, but not in *government.*—*Mid. N. D.*, v. 1.

And to the nightingale's complaining notes
Tune my distresses, and *record* my woes.—*Two G. of V.*, v. 4.

Made the night-bird mute, that still *records* with moan.—*Per.*, iv. (*Gower*).

Will you *troll* the catch you taught me.—*Temp.*, iii. 2.

And *turn* his merry note unto the sweet bird's throat.—*As You L.*, ii. 5 (*Song*).

Let 's *tune*, and to it lustily a while.—*Two G. of V.*, iv. 2.

How? *out of tune* on the strings.—Not so ; but yet *so false*, that he grieves my very heart-strings.—*Ibid.*, iv. 2.

It is *too sharp*. . . . Nay, now you are *too flat.*—*Ibid.*, ii. 1.

It is the lark that sings so *out of tune.*—*R. & Jul.*, iii. 5.

Like sweet bells jangled, *out of tune* and harsh.—*Hamlet*, iii. 1.

And scald rhymers ballad us *out o' tune.*—*Ant. & C.*, v. 2.

His lecture will be done, ere you have *tuned.*—*Tam. of S.*, iii. 1.

Though there was no great matter in the ditty, yet the note was very *untuneable.*—You are deceived, sir ; we *kept time*, we *lost not our time.*—*As You L.*, v. 3.

We did *keep time*, sir, in our catches . . . *out o' time*, sir ? ye lie.—*Tw. N.*, ii. 3.

Still *virginalling* on his palm.—*W. T.*, i. 2.

And several technicalities of musical nomenclature :—

'Tis now in tune.—All but the *base.*—The *base* is right.—*Tam. of S.*, iii. 1.

I have sounded the very *base* string of humility.—*1 H. IV.*, ii. 4.

Is there any one else longs to see this *broken music.**—*As You L.*, i. 2.

Come, your answer in *broken music.*—*H. V.*, v. 2.

Fair prince, here is good *broken music.*—*Tr. & Cr.*, iii. 1.

And boding screech-owls make the *concert* full !—*2 H. VI.*, iii. 2.

Visit by night your lady's chamber-window with some sweet *consort.*—*Two G. of V.*, iii. 2.

Consort ! what, dost thou make us minstrels ? an thou make minstrels of us, look to hear nothing but *discords*. . . . Zounds, *consort !*—*R. & Jul.*, iii. 1.

I never heard so musical a *discord*, such sweet thunder.—*Mid. N. D.*, iv. 1.

How shall we find the *concord* of this *discord* ?—*Ibid.*, v. 1.

---

* "Broken music" was an old English technicality for music performed on stringed instruments.

And chattering pies in dismal *discord* sung.—3 *H. VI.*, v. 6.

And mar the *concord* with too harsh a *descant.—Two G. of V.*, i. 2.

For on that *ground* I 'll make a holy *descant.—R. III.*, iii. 7.

Sung . . . with ravishing *division* to her lute.—1 *H. IV.*, iii. 1.

Some say the lark makes sweet *division.—R. & Jul.*, iii. 5.

Well said, my lord ! well, you say so *in fits.—Tr. & Cr.*, iii. 1.

In what key shall a man take you, *to go in the song ?—M. Ado*, i. 1.

Both warbling of one song, both *in one key.—Mid. N. D.*, iii. 2.

And with an accent *tun'd in self-same key.—Tr. & Cr.*, i. 3.

There wanteth but a *mean* to fill your song.—

The *mean* is drown'd with your unruly *base.—Two G. of V.*, i. 2.

Nay, he can sing a *mean* most meanly.—*Love's L. L.*, v. 2.

They are most of them *means* and *bases.—W. T.*, iv. 2.

The *choir*, with all the choicest *music* of the kingdom.—*H. VIII.*, iv. 1.

Bid the *music* leave, they are harsh and heavy to me.—*Ibid.*, iv. 2.

What music is this ?—I do but partly know, sir : it is *music in parts.—Tr. & Cr.*, iii. 1.

My lessons make no *music in three parts.—Tam. of S.*, iii. 1.

See if thou canst find out Sneak's *noise ;* Mistress Tear-sheet would fain hear some music.—2 *H. IV.*, ii. 4.

The *plain-song* cuckoo gray.—*Mid. N. D.*, iii. 1 (*Song*).

That is the very *plain-song* of it.—The *plain-song* is.—*H. V.*, iii. 2.

May bring his *plain-song*, and have an hour of hearing.—*H. VIII.*, i. 3.

He fights as you sing *prick-song, keeps time.—R. & Jul.*, ii. 4.

More than light airs, and *recollected terms.—Tw. N.*, ii. 4.

But *screw* your courage to the *sticking-place.—Macb.*, i. 7.

Three-man songmen all, and very good ones.—*W. T.*, iv. 2.

O fie ! the *treble* jars.—*Tam. of S.*, iii. 1.

In the following passage, Shakespeare uses a word that has been supposed to be the commencement of some song ; but we rather believe " Concolinel " to be a few syllables strung together by the dramatist to express warbling, or humming a tune,—as ' la li ra,' ' fal, lal, lal, la,' or ' fol de rol lol ' are used :—

Warble, child ; make passionate my sense of hearing.—*Concolinel.*—Sweet air !—*Love's L. L.*, iii. 1.

Shakespeare alludes to and employs some of the burdens formerly introduced into songs :—

With such delicate burdens of " *dildos* " and " *fadings*," " jump her and thump her."—*W. T.*, iv. 3.

Ding-dong. Hark, now I hear them—*ding-dong, bell.—Temp.*, i. 2 (*Song*).

Let us all ring fancy's knell ;
I 'll begin it, *ding-dong, bell.*
Ding-dong, bell.—Mer. of V., iii. 2 (*Song*).

Heigh, ho ! sing, heigh, ho ! unto the green holly ;
Most friendship is feigning, most loving mere folly :
Then heigh, ho ! the holly !—As You L., ii. 7 (*Song*).

Philomel, with melody,
Sing in our sweet lullaby ;
Lulla, lulla, lullaby ; lulla, lulla, lullaby.—Mid. N. D., ii. 3 (*Song*).

Then, *lullaby*, the learned man hath got the lady gay ;
For now my song is ended.—*Pass. Pil., Stanza* 12.

Converting all your sounds of woe
Into *Hey, nonny, nonny.—M. Ado*, ii. 3.

> *With a hey, and a ho, and a hey nonino.—As You L.*, v. 3.
> They bore him bare-fac'd on the bier ;
> *Hey non nonny, nonny, hey nonny.—Hamlet*, iv. 5 *(Song)*.
> Says *suum, mun, nonny.—Lear*, iii. 4.

He has expressed some birds' notes by written words :—

> Hark, hark ! I hear
> The strain of strutting chanticleer
> Cry, *Cock-a-doodle-doo.—Temp.*, i. 2 *(Song)*.
> Save the nightingale alone . . .
> " Fie, fie, fie," now would she cry ;
> " *Tereu, Tereu !* " by-and-by.—*Pass. Pil.*, *Stanza* 15.
> The lark, that *tirra-lirra* chants.—*W. T.*, iv. 2 *(Song)*.
> Then nightly sings the staring owl,
> *To-who ; tu-whit, to-who*, a merry note.—*Love's L. L.*, v. 2 *(Song)*.

He employs some of the technical terms for certain musical flourishes on bugles or hunting-horns, and on trumpets :—

> Hunting thee hence with *hunt's up* to the day.—*R. & Jul.*, iii. 5.
> And then to sigh, as 'twere *the mort o' the deer.—W. T.*, i. 2.

But that I will have a *recheat* winded in my forehead, or hang my bugle in an invisible baldrick.—*M. Ado*, i. 1.

> *Sennet.*   Enter to the Parliament, KING HENRY.—2 *H. VI.*, iii. 1.
> *Sennet.*   The Lords come forward.—3 *H. VI.*, i. 1.
> Trumpets, *sennet*, and cornets.   Enter two VERGERS.—*H. VIII.*, ii: 4.

A *sennet* sounded.   Enter CÆSAR, ANTONY, LEPIDUS, POMPEY, &c.—*Ant. & C.*, ii. 7.

> A *tucket* sounds.—*Mer. of V.*, v. 1.
> *Tucket* within.—*Lear*, ii. 1.
> *Tucket* within.—*Ibid.*, ii. 1, and ii. 4.
> Then let the trumpets sound the *tucket-sonance.—H. V.*, iv. 2.

Shakespeare makes more than one allusion to the custom of illustrious personages being preceded, when they arrive, by a peculiar flourish on the trumpet :—

> Your husband is at hand ; *I hear his trumpet.—Mer. of V.*, v. 1.
> And *even there, methinks an angel spake : ***
> Look, where the holy legate comes apace.—*John*, v. 2
> *What lusty trumpet thus doth summon us ?—Ibid.*, v. 2.
> *What trumpet ?* look, Menelaus.—From Troy.—*Tr. & Cr.*, i. 3.
> *What trumpet 's that ?*—'Tis Alcibiades.—*Timon*, i. 1.
> *Hark, the duke's trumpets !* I know not why he comes.—*Lear*, ii. 1.
> *What trumpet 's that ?*—I know 't—my sister's : this approves her letter,
> That she would soon be here.—*Ibid.*, ii. 4.
> The Moor ! *I know his trumpet.—Oth.*, ii. 1.
> *What trumpet is that same ?*—Something from Venice, sure.—*Ibid.*, iv. 1.

And also to the custom of players, or performers in a masque, being preceded on arrival by a flourish of trumpets :—

> *The trumpets sound :* be mask'd ; *the maskers come.—Love's L. L.*, v. 2.

---

* We believe these words to indicate that a trumpet sounds, heralding the approach of Pandulph, the Pope's legate ; as " what lusty trumpet," &c., announces the approach of Faulconbridge.

Sirrah, go *see what trumpet 'tis that sounds :*
Belike, some noble gentleman that means,
Travelling some journey, to repose him here.
How now ! who is it ?—An it please your honour,
Players that offer service to your lordship.—Tam. of S., Induc. i.
[*Flourish of trumpets within.*]—*There are the players.—Hamlet*, ii. 2.

Shakespeare, in the following passage, makes allusion to a celebrated musician of his time :—

Dowland to thee is dear, whose heavenly touch
Upon the lute doth ravish human sense.—*Pass. Pil., Stanza* 6.

And, in the following passages, he points out persons of particular callings said to be specially addicted to music :—

Shall we rouse the night-owl in a catch, that will draw three souls out of one *weaver ?—Tw. N.*, ii. 3.

Do ye make an alehouse of my lady's house that ye squeak out your *coziers'* catches. —*Ibid.*, ii. 3.

I would I were a *weaver;* I could sing psalms or anything.—1 *H. IV.*, ii. 4.

I will not sing.—'Tis the next way to turn *tailor*, or be redbreast teacher.—*Ibid.*, iii. 1.

OATHS, EXCLAMATIONS, &c.

The variety and extreme appropriateness of the oaths, exclamations, interjections, ejaculations, imprecations, adjurations, and forms of asseveration used by Shakespeare are especially interesting as a study in dramatic fitness and philological resource. Most characteristically does he put different invocations or exclamatory phrases into the mouths of certain of his characters :—

Grace go with you! *Benedicite !—M. for M.*, ii. 3.
Good-morrow, father.—
　　　　　　Benedicite !—R. & Jul., ii. 3.

The above expression of combined blessing and salutation the dramatist assigns, in the first instance, to the benignant friar-duke, and, in the second instance, to the benevolent Friar Laurence.

God's *bread !* it makes me mad.—*Ibid.*, iii. 5.

The above solemn expression is uttered by the irate old Capulet, as we hear it used, to this day, by Italian quarrellers in Italian form— "*per l' Ostia.*"

Jesu Maria ! what a deal of brine hath wash'd.—*Ibid.*, ii. 3.

The dramatist, with marked propriety, gives the above exclamation to an Italian friar, as it is one exclusively belonging to Catholic countries. It is a contracted form of *Jesu-Mariæ*, ' Jesus of Mary,' or ' Jesus the son of Mary.'

Holy Saint Francis ! what a change is here!—*Ibid.*, ii. 3.
Saint Francis be my speed ! how oft to-night have my.—*Ibid.*, v. 3.

It will at once be perceived how aptly the above exclamations are uttered by a *Franciscan* friar.

Saint Denis be my speed !—H. V., v. 2.
*Saint Denis bless this happy stratagem !—*1 *H. VI.*, iii. 2.

In the first of the above two instances Harry of England invokes the patron saint of France to aid him in his attempts to woo in French; and, in the second, Charles, the French Dauphin, asks a blessing from the patron saint of his native land.

> This proves that thou canst not read.—
> Come, fool, come: try me in thy paper.—
> There; and *Saint Nicholas be thy speed!*—*Two G. of V.*, iii. 1.

Launce asks for his fellow-servant's assistance in reading from " St. Nicholas," because he was the patron saint of children and scholars.

> Yes, *by Saint Patrick*, but there is, Horatio.—*Hamlet*, i. 5.

This saint being the patron saint of Ireland, and Ireland having been in ancient times a famed seat of learning whence the whole northern world derived their erudition, there is peculiar fitness in making the studious Danish Prince use this form of affirmation,

> Now, *by Saint Paul*, this news is bad indeed.—*R. III.*, i. 1.
> Or, *by Saint Paul*, I 'll make a corse of him that disobeys! . . .
> Or, *by Saint Paul*, I 'll strike thee to my foot.—*Ibid.*, i. 2.
> *By holy Paul*, they love his grace but lightly.—*Ibid.*, i. 3.
> Now, *by Saint Paul I swear*, I will not dine until I.—*Ibid.*, iii. 4.
> *By the Apostle Paul*, shadows to-night have struck.—*Ibid.*, v. 3.

Shakespeare makes Richard six times swear thus, " Paul " being by tradition the saint habitually invoked by that monarch.

> All 's one. *Good father!* how foolish are our minds!—*Oth.*, iv. 3.

Into the mouth of " the gentle Desdemona " is this gently reliant aspiration most aptly placed.

> *Name of mercy!* when was this, boy ?—*W. T.*, iii. 3.

It is the old shepherd who uses the above simply beautiful adjuration.

> *By my christendom,*
> So I were out of prison, and kept sheep,
> I should be as merry as the day is long.—*John*, iv. 1.

On the lips of poor little Prince Arthur the above phrase has an infantinely pious effect, thoroughly natural and touching.

> Now, *by two-headed Janus*, Nature hath fram'd strange.—*Mer. of V.*, i. 1.
> *By Janus*, I think no.—*Oth.*, i. 2.

In the former of the above two passages it is Salarino, in the latter Iago (both Venetians), who use this oath; and it is still an Italian habit to use mythological names in adjuration.

> *Gods, gods!* 'tis strange, that from their cold'st neglect.—*Lear*, i. 1.
> *O gods!* who is 't can say, I am at the worst.—*Ibid.*, iv. 1.
> *O gods!* he has the stamp of Marcius!—*Coriol.*, iv. 1.
> *O gods and goddesses!* these flowers are like the.—*Cym.*, iv. 2.
> *By the gods*, it is one.—*Ibid.*, i. 5.
> *The gods!* it smites me beneath the fall I have.—*Ant. & C.*, v. 2.
> *O the gods!* what 's the matter ?—*Tr. & Cr.*, iv. 2.
> *O me, the gods!* you must not speak of that.—*Coriol.*, ii. 3.
> *O the blest gods!* so will you wish on me, when.—*Lear*, ii. 4.
> *O the good gods!*—Nay, that is certain.—*Ant. & C.*, v. 2.

> *Ye gods*, it doth amaze me, a man of such.—*Jul. C.*, i. 2.
> *O ye gods*, render me worthy of this noble wife!—*Ibid.*, ii. 1.

In all the above passages " gods " is put thus plurally and appropriately into the mouths of those who lived in pagan times.

> *What may be sworn by, both divine and human,*
> *Seal what I end withal!*—*Coriol.*, iii. 1.

This form of attestation is peculiarly well given to Coriolanus, since we are informed that the Romans swore by what was human as well as divine ; by their head, by their eyes, by the dead bones and ashes of their parents, &c.

> *Pluto and hell!* all hurt behind!—*Ibid.*, i. 4.

It is the same Coriolanus who employs the above appropriately heathen execration.

> Welcome to Troy ! now, *by Anchises' life,*
> Welcome, indeed ! *By Venus' hand I swear,*
> No man alive can love, in such a sort.—*Tr. & Cr.*, iv. 1.

Æneas first swears by his father Anchises' life, which was so dear to him that when Troy was burning and the old man was too infirm to fly, the son took his parent on his shoulders and bore him safely away ; and, secondly, by the hand of the goddess (his reputed mother), which had received a wound from Diomed when she took part in one of the encounters during the Trojan war.

> To prove to you that Helen loves him—she came, and puts me her white hand to his cloven chin,—
> *Juno have mercy!* how came it cloven ?—
> Why, you know, 'tis dimpled.—*Ibid.*, i. 2.

Cressida, pretending to take her uncle's expression of " cloven chin " as involving a charge of bodily defect, deprecates the power of " Juno," in her attribute of presiding goddess of childbirth.

> My boy Marcius approaches ; *for the love of Juno*, let's go.—*Coriol.*, ii. 1.

Volumnia, as a proud Roman mother, naturally invokes the name of the matron-goddess.

> *By Juno*, that is queen
> Of marriage, all the viands that I eat
> Do seem unsavoury, wishing him my meat.—*Per.*, ii. 3.

This is said aside by Thaisa, when falling in love with Pericles, at the banquet.

> *O Jupiter!* how weary are my spirits !—*As You L.*, ii. 4.

> *O most gentle Jupiter!* what tedious homily of love have you wearied your parishioners withal.—*Ibid.*, iii. 2.

In both the above passages, Rosalind invokes " Jupiter " as the god of good spirits ; in which capacity, and under his name of 'Jove,' he gave origin to the word 'jovial.'

> *By Jupiter*, I had it from her arm.—
> Hark you, he swears ; *by Jupiter* he swears.
> 'Tis true ;—nay, keep the ring—'tis true.—*Cym.*, ii. 4.

Thus making Posthumus impressed by the solemnity of the oath, when Iachimo swears " by Jupiter," is most characteristic ; for, besides that swearing by the father of gods and men was held to be among the most binding of all vows, it is naturally of peculiar strength to Posthumus, who (as we find from a passage in act v., sc. 4) was born under Jove's own star, and who was married in Jove's own temple.

> *By the fire that quickens Nilus' slime*, I go from hence.—*Ant. & C.*, i. 3.
> *Moon and stars!* Whip him.—*Ibid.*, iii. 11.

Mark Antony's use of the two above-quoted oaths is as characteristic of Roman usage as Coriolanus's form of attestation ("What may be sworn by, both divine and human"), which we have previously given and commented upon.

> *Apollo, perfect me in the characters!*—*Per.*, iii. 2.
> Come, come; and *Æsculapius guide us!*—*Ibid.*, iii. 2.

Appropriately is the learned and benevolent Cerimon made, in the first of the above two passages, to invoke the aid of the god of letters and erudition, when about to read the scroll which may be written in an unknown language, and, in the second, to implore succour of the god of medicine, when essaying to avert "relapse" from befalling the just-rescued Thaisa.

> *O, dear Diana*, where am I? where's my lord.—*Ibid.*, iii. 2.

The dramatist's putting this invocation into Thaisa's mouth on her first awakening from her trance is subtly appropriate: her calling upon the virgin goddess's name serves to suggest, the young princess so few months a wife, that her maiden appeals for divine aid spring most naturally to her lips, and also serve to aptly usher in the subsequent dedication of herself, as a votaress in Diana's temple.

Shakespeare frequently employs some of the minor oaths that were in vogue when he wrote, taking the place of more sacred forms of adjuration:—

> *By day and night*, he's traitor to the height.—*H. VIII.*, i. 2.
> *O day and night*, but this is wondrous strange!—*Hamlet*, i. 5.
> *By this good day*, I know not the phrase.—*2 H. IV.*, iii. 2.
> But, in defence, *by mercy*, 'tis most just.—*Timon*, iii. 5.
> *By these ten bones*, my lords, he did speak.—*2 H. VI.*, i. 3.
> So I do still, *by these pickers and stealers.*—*Hamlet*, iii. 2.
> *By this hand*, I will supplant some of your teeth.—*Temp.*, iii. 2.
> *By this hand*, they are scoundrels and substractors.—*Tw. N.*, i. 3.
>> *By these gloves*, did he . . . *by these gloves* . . .
>> *By these gloves*, then, 'twas he.——*Merry W.*, i. 1.
> *By this hat*, then, he in the red face had it.—*Ibid.*, i. 1.
> Seven, *by these hilts*, or I am a villain else.—*1 H. IV.*, ii. 4.
> Now, *by my sword*, I will kill all his coats.—*Ibid.*, v. 3.
> Now, *by my sword*, well hast thou fought to-day.—*2 H. VI.*, v. 3.
> *By this sword*, he that makes the first thrust, I'll kill him; *by this sword*, I will.—Sword is an oath, and oaths must have their course.—*H. V.*, ii. 1.
> *By my troth*, and *in good earnest*, and *so God mend me*, and by all pretty oaths that are not dangerous.—*As You L.*, iv. 1.
> *By my troth*, I would not undertake her.—*Tw. N.*, i. 3.
> *By my troth*, the fool has an excellent breast.—*Ibid.*, ii. 3.
> *By yea and nay*, sir, then I swore in jest.—*Love's L. L.*, i. 1.

By yea and nay, sir, I dare say, my cousin.—*2 H. IV.*, iii. 2.

Sir, I thank you; *by yea and no*, I do.—*Merry W.*, i. 1.

By yea and no, I think the 'oman is a witch.—*Ibid.*, iv. 2.

No, I thank you, *forsooth*, heartily; I am very well. . . . I am not a-hungry, I thank you, *forsooth.—Ibid.*, i. 1.

No, no, *forsooth;* I dare not, for my life.—*Tam. of S.*, iv. 3.

No, *sooth*, sir: my determinate voyage is.—*Tw. N.*, ii. 1.

In sooth, thou wast in very gracious fooling.—*Ibid.*, ii. 3.

Well drawn, monster, *in good sooth.—Temp.*, ii. 2.

Very sooth, to-morrow.—*W. T.*, i. 2.

For the heavens, he shows me where the bachelors sit.—*M. Ado*, ii. 1.

For the heavens, rouse up a brave mind.—*Mer. of V.*, ii. 2.

No notes of sally, *for the heavens*, sweet brother.—*Tr. & Cr.*, v. 3.

And he often uses petty oaths that were corruptions of serious ones:—

Bodykins [God's body] Master Page, though I now.—*Merry W.*, ii. 3.

God's bodikins [God's body], man, much better.—*Hamlet*, ii. 2.

By cock [by God], they are to blame.—*Ibid.*, iv. 5 (*Song*).

By cock and pye [by God and Pie*], you shall not choose.—*Merry W.*, i. 1.

By cock and pye, sir, you shall not away to-night.—*2 H. IV.*, v. 1.

Cock's passion [God's passion], silence! I hear my master.—*Tam. of S.*, iv. 1.

Cox' my passion [God's passion]! give me your hand.—*All's W.*, v. 1.

By my fay [by my faith], a goodly nap.—*Tam. of S., Induc.* 2.

By my fay, it waxes late: I'll to my rest.—*R. & Jul.*, i. 5.

For, *by my fay*, I cannot reason.—*Hamlet*, ii. 2.

By Gis [Jesus], and by Saint Charity.—*Ibid.*, iv. 5 (*Song*).

By God's sonties [Saints: in old language, 'saunctes'], 'twill be.—*Mer. of V.*, ii. 2.

Ay, by *gogs-wouns* [God's wounds]! quoth he.—*Tam. of S.*, iii. 2.

By my *halidom* [holy-dom; or holiness], I was fast asleep.—*Two G. of V.*, iv. 2.

By my *holidame* [Holy Dame; or Blessed Lady], here comes.—*Tam. of S.*, v. 2.

Now, by my *hood* [manhood; or knighthood], a Gentile.—*Mer. of V.*, ii. 6.

By 'r lady [by our Lady], sir, and some dogs.—*Tw. N.*, ii. 3.

And, *by 'r lady*, held current music too.—*H. VIII.*, i. 3.

By 'r lakin [by our Lady], I can go no farther.—*Temp.*, iii. 3.

By 'r lakin, a parlous fear.—*Mid. N. D.*, iii. 1.

Ay, my good lord.—*I 'fecks* [In faith]? Why, that's my.—*W. T.*, i. 2.

Yea, *marry* [by Mary], that's the eftest way.—*M. Ado*, iv. 2.

Marry, so I mean, sweet Katharine.—*Tam. of S.*, ii. 1.

Od's body [God's body], the turkeys in my pannier.—*1 H. IV.*, ii. 1.

Od's heartlings [God's heart], that's a pretty jest, indeed!—*Merry W.*, iii. 4.

Od's lifelings [God's life], here he is!—*Tw. N.*, v. 1.

Od's my little life [God's life]! I think she means.—*As You L.*, iii. 5.

Od's me [God's blessing be upon me; or God save me]! Qu'ai-je oublié? dere is some simples in my closet.—*Merry W.*, i. 4.

Because they say, *od's nouns* [God's wounds].—*Ibid.*, iv. 1.

Od's pittikins [God's pity]! can it be six miles yet?—*Cym.*, iv. 2.

Od's plessed will [God's blessed will]! I will not be.—*Merry W.*, i. 1

Od's my will [God's will]! her love is not the.—*As You L.*, iv. 3.

Perdy [French: par Dieu], your doors were lock'd.—*Com. of E.*, iv. 4.

My lady is unkind, *perdy.—Tw. N.*, iv. 2.

---

* "Pie," was the familiar English name given to the book which ordained the manner of saying and solemnizing the offices of the Roman Catholic church.

Yea, in thy maw, *perdy.—H. V.*, ii. 1.

Why, then, belike, he likes it not, *perdy.—Hamlet*, iii. 2.

The fool no knave, *perdy.—Lear*, ii. 4.

'*Sblood* [God's blood]! I 'll not bear my own flesh.—1 *H. IV.*, ii. 2.

'*Sblood*, my lord, they are false.— *Ibid.*, ii. 4.

'*Sblood*, I would my face were in your belly.—*Ibid.*, iii. 3.

'*Sfoot* [God's foot], I 'll learn to conjure and raise devils.—*Tr. & Cr.*, ii. 3.

'*Slid* [God's eye-lid : or God's lid, possibly in allusion to the *cover* of the vessel containing the Host], 'tis but venturing.—*Merry W.*, iii. 4.

'*Slid*, I 'll after him again, and beat him.—*Tw. N.*, iii. 4.

'*Slight* [God's light], I could so beat the rogue!—*Ibid.*, ii. 5.

'*Slight*, will you make an ass o' me?—*Ibid.*, iii. 2.

'*Swounds* [God's wounds], show me what thou 'lt do.—*Hamlet*, v. 1.

Zounds [God's wounds], will they not rob us?—1 *H. IV.*, ii. 2.

Zounds ! an I were now by this rascal.—*Ibid.*, ii. 3.

Zounds ! ye fat paunch, an ye call me coward.—*Ibid.*, ii. 4.

In the following three passages Shakespeare satirises various peculiarities of his time, in connection with oaths and oath-taking. In the first, he satirises a silly fashion of using some special much-hacked oath :—

I pray you, sir, are you a courtier?—

O Lord, sir ! . . . that loves you.—*O Lord*, sir ! . . . this homely meat.—*O Lord*, sir ! . . . &c., &c.—*All's W.*, ii. 2.

In the second, he satirises aristocratic objection to plebeian and paltry oaths :—

Not mine, *in good sooth.*—

Not yours, *in good sooth !* 'Heart, you swear like a comfit-maker's wife ! " Not you, *in good sooth :* " and, " *As true as I live*," and, " *As God shall mend me ;* " and, " *As sure as day ;* " and giv'st such sarcenet surety for thy oaths, as if thou never walk'dst farther than Finsbury. Swear me, Kate, like a lady as thou art, a good mouth-filling oath ; and leave " in sooth," and such protest of pepper gingerbread, to velvet-guards and Sunday citizens.—1 *H. IV.*, iii. 1.

And in the third, he satirises those blustering personages who affect a habit of swearing as a mark of gentility :—

When *a gentleman is disposed to swear*, it is not for any standers-by to curtail his oaths, ha ?—*Cym.*, ii. 1.

In several passages Shakespeare characteristically introduces French oaths :—

Dr. Caius. O *diable ! diable !* vat is in my closet?—*Merry W.*, i. 4.

Dr. Caius. Diable ! Jack Rugby, mine host de Jarretière.—*Ibid.*, iii. 1.

Constable of France. O *diable !—H. V.*, iv. 5.

Princess Katharine. O *bon Dieu !—Ibid.*, v. 2.

Constable of France. Dieu de batailles ! where have they.—*Ibid.*, iii. 5.

Dauphin. O *Dieu vivant !* shall a few.—*Ibid.*, iii. 5.

French Soldier. O *Seigneur Dieu !—Ibid.*, iv. 4.

Duke of Orleans. O *Seigneur !—Ibid.*, iv. 5.

> *Earl of Warwick.* Anjou and Maine ! myself did win them both ;
> Those provinces these arms of mine did conquer :
> And are the cities, that I got with wounds,
> Deliver'd up again with peaceful words ?
> *Mort Dieu !—*2 *H. VI.*, i. 1.

Duke of Bourbon. Mort de ma vie ! if they march.—*H. V.*, iii. 5.

Dauphin. Mort de ma vie ! all is confounded, all.—*H. V.,* iv. 5.
Parolles. Mort du vinaigre ! is not this Helen?—*All's W.,* ii. 3.

Shakespeare employs very many peculiar ejaculations and impre-cations :—

On a day,—*alack the day !*—*Love's L. L.,* iv. 3 (*Verses*).
Alack the heavy day ! that I have worn so.—*R. II.,* iv. 1.
Alas the day ! I know not.—*Merry W.,* iv. 2.
Alas the day ! what good could they pretend ?—*Macb.,* ii. 4.
Alas the day ! I never gave him cause.—*Oth.,* iii. 4.
O *well-a-day,* Mistress Ford !—*Merry W.,* iii. 3.
O *well-a-day,* lady, if he be not drawn !—*H. V.,* ii. 1.
Ah *well-a-day !* he 's dead, he 's dead.—*R. & Jul.,* iii. 2.
O *well-a-day,* that ever I was born !—*Ibid.,* iv. 5.
When, *well-a-day,* we could scarce help ourselves.—*Per.,* ii. 1.
The lady shrieks, and, *well-a-near !* does fall.—*Ibid.,* iii. (*Gower*).
O, *woe the day !*—No harm.—*Temp.,* i. 2.
But, *alas the while !* If Hercules and Lichas.—*Mer. of V.,* ii. 1.
Woe the while ! O, cut my lace.—*W. T.,* iii. 2.
But, *woe the while !* our fathers' minds are dead.—*Jul. C.,* i. 3.
God help the while ! a bad world, I say.—1 *H. IV.,* ii. 4.
Ay, sir, it is too true; *God help the while !*—*R. III.,* ii. 3.
Three foot of it doth hold: *bad world the while !*—*John,* iv. 2.
Here 's a good world the while ! Who is so gross.—*R. III.,* iii. 6.
Lord help us! *it is a world to see !*—*M. Ado,* iii. 5.
Alas, and woe !—*Ant. & C.,* iv. 12.
Loop to hang a doubt on; or *woe upon thy life !*—*Oth.,* iii. 3.
I am *woe for 't,* sir.—*Temp.,* v. 1.

> Ah, *woe is me for* Gloster, wretched man !—
> *Be woe for me,* more wretched than he is.—2 *H. VI.,* iii. 2.

O, *woe is me !* To have seen what I have seen.—*Hamlet,* iii. 1.
'Fore me, I speak in respect.—*All's W.,* ii. 3.
'Fore me, this fellow speaks !—*Coriol.,* i. 1.
Afore me, it is so very late, that we.—*R. & Jul.,* iii. 4.
Now, *afore me,* a handsome fellow !—*Per.,* ii. 1.
Before me, she 's a good wench.—*Tw. N.,* ii. 3.
Before me ! look where she comes.—*Oth.,* iv. 1.
'Fore Heaven, an excellent song.—*Ibid.,* ii. 3.
'Fore God, you have here a goodly dwelling.—2 *H. IV.,* v. 3.
Now, *afore God,* I am so vexed, that every.—*R. & Jul.,* ii. 4.
Now, *afore God,* this reverend holy friar.—*Ibid.,* iv. 2.
For, *God before,* we 'll chide this Dauphin.—*H. V.,* i. 2.
Yet, *God before,* tell him we will come on.—*Ibid.,* iii. 6.
Ah me, unhappy ! To be a queen.—2 *H. VI.,* iii. 2.
Where is thy head ? where 's that ? *Ah me !* where 's that ?—*Cym.,* iv. 2.
O *me !* the word choose !—*Mer. of V.,* i. 2.
Body o' me, where is it ?—*H. VIII.,* v. 2.
God's me [*See* " Od's me," previously explained], my horse.—1 *H. IV.,* ii. 3.
I' the name of me,—O, help me, help me !—*W. T.,* iv. 2.
Who (*God bless the mark !*) is a kind of devil.—*Mer. of V.,* ii. 2.
And I (*God bless the mark !*) his Moorship's ancient.—*Oth.,* i. 1.
Of guns and drums and wounds (*God save the mark !*)—1 *H. IV.,* i. 3.

I saw the wound, I saw it with mine eyes,
(*God save the mark!*) here on his manly breast.—*R. & Jul.*, iii. 2.
For lovers, lacking (*God warn us!*) matter, the cleanliest.—*As You L.*, iv. 1.
Well, *God 'ield you!* They say the owl was a.—*Hamlet*, iv. 5.
God 'ild you, for your last company.—*As You L.*, iii. 3.
God 'ild you, sir, I desire you of the like.—*Ibid.*, v. 4.
How you shall bid *God yield us* for your pains.—*Macb.*, i. 6.
Heaven shield, my mother play'd my father fair!—*M. for M.*, iii. 1.
To bring in (*God shield us!*) a lion among ladies.—*Mid. N. D.*, iii. 1.
God shield, you mean it not!—*All's W.*, i. 3.
God shield, I should disturb devotion!—*R. & Jul.*, iv. 1.
God-a-mercy, old heart, thou speak'st cheerfully.—*H. V.*, iv. 1.
God for his mercy! what a tide of woes.—*R. II.*, ii. 2.
God for his mercy, what treachery is here!—*Ibid.*, v. 2.
O, *I cry you mercy;* you are the singer.—*R. & Jul.*, iv. 5.
Cry you mercy, I took you for a joint-stool.—*Lear*, iii. 6.
Grace to boot! Of this make no conclusion.—*W. T.*, i. 2.
This, and *Saint George to boot!* What think'st thou—*R. III.*, v. 3.

> *The bounty and benison of Heaven*
> *To boot, and boot!*—*Lear*, iv. 6.

> Now, *by the death of Him that died for all*,
> These counties were the keys of Normandy.—*2 H. VI.*, i. 1.

Nay, *by the mass*, that he did not.—*Merry W.*, iv. 2.
But, *by the mass*, our hearts are in the trim.—*H. V.*, iv. 3.
'*Mass*, thou lov'dst plums well, that wouldst venture so.—*2 H. VI.*, ii. 1.
To 't.—*Mass*, I cannot tell.—Cudgel thy brains no more.—*Hamlet*, v. 1.
An early stirrer, *by the rood*.—*2 H. IV.*, iii. 2.
Nay, *by the rood*, she could have run.—*R. & Jul.*, i. 3.
No, *by the rood*, not so: you are the queen.—*Hamlet*, iii. 4.
But, *by the holy rood*, I do not like these.—*R. III.*, iii. 2.
Good my complexion! dost thou think.—*As You L.*, iii. 2.
O, *a good wish upon you!* you will try in time.—*Ibid.*, i. 3.
We must give folks leave to prate: *what the good year!*—*Merry W.*, i. 4.
What the good year, my lord! why are you.—*M. Ado*, ii. 3.
What the good year! one must bear.—*2 H. IV.*, ii. 4.
What the good year! do you think I would.—*Ibid.*, ii. 4.
What o' devil's name, tailor, call'st thou this?—*Tam. of S.*, iv. 3.
What the devil should move me to undertake.—*All's W.*, iv. 1.
I cannot tell *what the dickens* his name is.—*Merry W.*, iii. 2.
What a plague means my niece, to take.—*Tw. N.*, i. 3.
What a plague have I to do with a buff jerkin?—*H. IV.*, i. 2.
What a plague mean ye to colt me thus?—*Ibid.*, ii. 2.
What a plague call you him?—*Ibid.*, ii. 4.
What the vengeance, could he not speak them fair?—*Coriol.*, iii. 1.
But *what though?* Courage!—*As You L.*, iii. 3.
The bull has the game! '*ware horns, ho!*—*Tr. & Cr.*, v. 8.
'*Ware pencils, ho!* let me not die your debtor.—*Love's L. L.*, v. 2.
The gods rebuke me, but it is tidings to wash.—*Ant. & C.*, v. 1.
Would I might be dead, if I in thought felt not.—*Two G. of V.*, iv. 4.
Would I were dead, but that, methinks, already.—*W. T.*, v. 3.
Would I were dead! if God's good will were so.—*3 H. VI.*, ii. 5.
Ay, or else *I would I might be hanged*, la.—*Merry W.*, i. 1.

Would I were hanged, la, else.—*Merry W.*, v. 5.

Would I were hanged, but I thought there was.—*Coriol.*, iv. 5.

But *I 'll be hang'd*, sir, if he wear your livery.—*R. & Jul.*, iii. 1.

I will be hang'd, if some eternal villain.—*Oth.*, iv. 2.

Beshrew me, but you have a quick wit.—*Two G. of V.*, i. 1.

Beshrew me, but I love her heartily.—*Mer. of V.*, ii. 6.

Beshrew my heart, but I pity the man.—*Mid. N. D.*, v. 1.

Beshrew my soul, but I do love the favour.—*John*, v. 4.

Beshrew him for it ! How comes this trick upon him !—*Oth.*, iv. 2.

Beshrew his hand, I scarce could understand it.—*Com. of E.*, ii. 1.

Beshrew thee, cousin, which didst lead me.—*R. II.*, iii. 2.

Beshrew your eyes, they have o'erlook'd me.—*Mer. of V.*, iii. 2.

Beshrew the witch ! with venomous wights.—*Tr. & Cr.*, iv. 2.

'Shrew me, if I would lose it for a revenue.—*Cym.*, ii. 3.

'Shrew my heart, you never spoke what did.—*W. T.*, i. 2.

Ha ! *bots on 't*, 'tis come at last.—*Per.*, ii. 1.

Plague on 't, an I thought he had been valiant.—*Tw. N.*, iii. 4.

Pox on 't, I 'll not meddle with him.—*Ibid.*, iii. 4.

A pox on 't, let it go ; 'tis but a drum.—*All's W.*, iii. 6.

A murrain on 't ! I took this for silver.—*Coriol.*, i. 5.

A murrain on your monster, and *the devil take your fingers !*—*Temp.*, iii. 2.

A red murrain o' thy jade's tricks !—*Tr. & Cr.*, ii. 1.

The red plague rid you, for learning me your language !—*Temp.*, i. 2.

Now the red pestilence strike all trades in Rome.—*Coriol.*, iv. 1.

Come away, or I 'll fetch thee *with a wannion.*—*Per.*, ii. 1.

Here 's packing, *with a witness*, to deceive us all !—*Tam. of S.*, v. 1.

In several passages Shakespeare shows how " Jove " was often used by Christians; and even, sometimes, side by side with "God" or "Lord":—

> Why, all the souls that were, were forfeit once ;
> And *He* that might the vantage best have took,
> Found out the remedy. How would you be,
> If *He*, which is the top of judgment, should
> But judge you as you are ? . . .
> Could great men thunder
> As *Jove* himself does, *Jove* would ne'er be quiet.—*M. for M.*, ii. 2.

By *Jove !* I always took three threes for nine.—

O *Lord !* sir, it were pity you should get your living by reckoning, sir.—How much is it ?—O *Lord !*—*Love's L. L.*, v. 2.

> What is not holy, that we swear not by,
> But take *the Highest* to witness : then, pray you, tell me
> If I should swear by *Jove's* great attributes.—*All's W.*, iv. 2.

> But it is *Jove's* doing, and *Jove* make me thankful ! . . .

Well, *Jove*, not I, is the doer of this, and he is to be thanked. . . . Pray *God*, he be not bewitched !—*Tw. N.*, iii. 4.

Jove bless thee, master *parson.*—*Ibid.*, iv. 2.

God save thy grace, King Hal ! . . . *God* save thee, my sweet boy ! . . . My king ; my *Jove !* I speak to thee.—*2 H. IV.*, v. 5.

> He wills you, in the name of *God Almighty*,
> That you divest yourself. . . .
> Therefore in fierce tempest is he coming,
> In thunder and in earthquake, like a *Jove ;* . . .
> And bids you, in the bowels of *the Lord*,
> Deliver up the crown.—*H. V.*, ii. 4.

God's will! I pray thee, wish not one man more.
By *Jove*, I am not covetous for gold. . . .
God's peace! I would not lose so great an honour.—*H. V.*, iv. 3.

If I do not leave you all as dead as a door-nail, I pray *God* I may never eat grass more. . . . I beseech *Jove* on my knees, thou mayest be turned to hobnails.—2 *H. VI.*, iv. 10.

Great *Jove*, Othello guard, and swell his sail with. . . .
Hail to thee, lady! *and the grace of Heaven*,
Before, behind thee, and on every hand,
Enwheel thee round!—*Oth.*, ii. 1.

By Heaven, he echoes me. . . . *By Heaven*, I'll know thy thoughts. . . . And, O you mortal engines, whose rude throats *th' immortal Jove's* dread clamours counterfeit. . . . Or, *by the worth of mine immortal* soul, thou hadst been better have been born a dog.—*Ibid.*, iii. 3.

O *Jove*, I think
*Foundations** fly the wretched; such, I mean,
Where they should be reliev'd.—*Cym.*, iii. 6.

Shakespeare uses various interjections, with various force of effect, to express different feelings :—

Ah [earnestly], how much might the man deserve of me that would right her!—*M. Ado*, iv. 1.

Ah [persuasively], Gaunt, his blood was thine!—*R. II.*, i. 2.

Ah [cajolingly], you sweet little rogue, you! . . . *Ah*, rogue! i' faith, I love thee . . . *ah*, villain!—2 *H. IV.*, ii. 4.

Ah, ah! [sighing] why sigh you so profoundly?—*Tr. & Cr.*, iv. 2.

Ah [lamentingly], sir! *ah*, sir! Well, death's the end of all.—*R. & Jul.*, iii. 3.

Ah, ha! [exultingly] does she so?—*Tw. N.*, iii. 4.

Cries, *ah, ha!* [one of the forms of diabolical address and diabolical ejaculation, in the old stage mysteries] to the devil.—*Ibid.*, iv. 2 (*Song*).

Alack [compunctiously], what trouble was I then to you!—*Temp.*, i. 2.

Alack [mournfully], and what shall good old York there see,
But empty lodgings and unfurnish'd walls.—*R. II.*, i. 2.

Alack [earnestly], there lies more peril in thine eye.—*R. & Jul.*, ii. 2.

No, no; *alack* [deprecatingly], there's other work in hand.—*Cym.*, v. 5.

He is a proper man's picture; but, *alas* [playfully deploring], who can converse with a dumb show?—*Mer. of V.*, i. 2.

Yonder they lie; the poor old man, their father, making such pitiful dole over them, that all the beholders take his part with weeping.—*Alas!* [sympathisingly].—*As You L.*, i. 2.

Alas [regretfully], I have shown too much the rashness of a woman!—*W. T.*, iii. 2.

Alas [pityingly], poor Richard! where rode he the while?—*R. II.*, v. 2.

Alas [in sorrow and alarm], he's mad!—*Hamlet*, iii. 4.

Alas [submissively], what ignorant sin have I committed?—*Oth.*, iv. 2.

Go to; *away!* [in dismissal].—*Temp.*, v. 1.

Away, you rogue, *away!* [gruffly] I am sleepy.—*M. for M.*, iv. 3.

Away, away! [in haste] no time shall be omitted.—*Love's L. L.*, iv. 3.

Away [loathingly], you Ethiop!—*Mid. N. D.*, iii. 2.

Away, away [scornfully], mad ass! his name is Lucentio.—*Tam. of S.*, v. 1.

Away, you whoreson upright rabbit, *away!* [testily].—2 *H. IV.*, ii. 2.

Pray, get you out.—*Away!* [haughtily].—*Coriol.*, iv. 5.

---

* "Foundations" is here used, in a general sense, for edifices or dwelling-places; also, in a particular sense, with reference to establishments (usually *religious* ones) where a revenue was settled for charitable purposes, and where alms and relief were given.

Hath denied my access to thee.—*Away !* [repulsingly].—*Coriol.*, v. 2.

In sooth you are to blame.—*Away !* [wrathfully].—*Oth.*, iii. 4.

O Desdemona ! *Away ! away ! away !* [in agony of weeping].—*Ibid.*, iv. 2.

Instance, briefly; *come* [patronisingly], instance. . . . A better instance, I say ; *come*. . . . A more sounder instance ; *come*.—*As You L.*, iii. 2.

Come [authoritatively], I charge you both go with me. . . .
. . . *Come, come*, you she knight-errant, *come*.—*1 H. IV.*, v. 4.

Come, you rogue, *come* [defiantly], bring me to justice.—
Ay, *come*, you starved bloodhound ! . . . *Come*, you thin thing ! *come*, you rascal !—
Ibid., v. 4.

Come [soothingly], enough.—*Coriol.*, iii. 1.

O heavenly powers.—*Come* [commandingly], hold your peace.—*Oth.*, v. 2.

Come [dictatorially], I 'll to my chamber.—*Cym.*, i. 3.

Come [with arrogant condescension], I 'll go see this Italian.—*Ibid.*, ii. 1.

*Come** [insolently], there 's no more tribute to be paid.—*Ibid.*, iii. 1.

Come on, come on [scoffingly: more as we now use " come, come "], you are pictures out of doors, bells in your parlours.—*Oth.*, ii. 1.

Come on [encouragingly], assay.—*Ibid.*, ii. 1.

Come on [dictatorially], tune : if you can penetrate.—*Cym.*, ii. 3.

Come, come [impatiently] ; sans compliment, what news abroad ?—*John*, v. 6.

Come, come [encouragingly], what need you blush ?—*Tr. & Cr.*, iii. 2.

Come, come [hurryingly], they are almost here.—*Coriol.*, ii. 2.

Come, come [remonstratively], you have been too rough.—*Ibid.*, iii. 2.

Cry, *Fie* [blamingly] upon my grave !—*W. T.*, iii. 2.

Fie [chidingly], daughter ! when my old wife liv'd.—*Ibid.*, iv. 3.

Fie ! [perspiringly] this is hot weather.—*2 H. IV.*, iii. 2.

Fie [denyingly], there is no such man ; it is impossible.—*Oth.*, iv. 2.

Fie, fie ! [self-reprovingly] no thought of him.—*W. T.*, ii. 3.

> I must be round with him, now he comes from hunting :
> *Fie, fie, fie, fie !* [reprobatingly].—*Timon*, ii. 2.

Fie, fie, fie ! [partly deploringly, partly reprovingly].—*Coriol.*, iv. 2.

See you here, sir ?—*O fie, fie, fie !* [reproachfully].—*Ant. & C.*, iii. 9.

I was last chidden for being too slow.—*Go to* [rebukingly], sir.—*Two G. of V.*, ii. 1.

But for you—well, *go to* [implying an unspoken compliment].—*Merry W.*, i. 4.

Have I encompassed you ? *go to* [exultingly] ; via !—*Ibid.*, ii. 2.

Go to [repressively], sir ; you weigh equally.—*M. for M.*, iv. 2.

And one that knows the law, *go to* [boastfully] ; and a rich fellow enough, *go to*.—
M. Ado, iv. 2.

> And I to sigh for her ! to watch for her !
> To pray for her. *Go to* [vexedly conceding] ; it is a plague
> That Cupid will impose for my neglect of his.—*Love's L. L.*, iii. 1.

> Well, then, it now appears you need my help :
> *Go to* [affirmatively], then ; you come to me.—*Mer. of V.*, 1. 3.

I shall have good fortune ! *Go to* [self-congratulatorily], here 's a simple line of life !
— *Ibid.*, ii. 2.

You must begin, " Will you, Orlando,' —*Go to* [playfully consenting] .
Will you, Orlando, have to wife this Rosalind ?—*As You L.*, iv. 1.

Fear not, Baptista ; we will content you, *go to* [reassuringly].—*Tam. of S.*, v. 1.

This is hard and undeserved measure, my lord.—*Go to* [contemptuously], sir ; you were beaten in Italy for picking a.—*All's W.*, ii. 3.

---

* It is worthy of remark that the dramatist has made this word " come," a characteristically repeated expression in the mouth of the vulgar blusterer, Cloten.

Though you are a fool and a knave, you shall eat; *go to* [relentingly], follow.—*All's W.*, v. 2.

Is this your promise? *go to* [chidingly], hold your tongue.—*John*, iv. 1.

Nay, rather let me have it, as you are a false thief.—*Go to* [waggishly]; homo is a common name to all men.—1 *H. IV.*, ii, 1.

Go to [in bantering assent]; I stand the push of your one thing that you will tell. —2 *H. IV.*, ii. 2.

There are other men fitter to go out than I.—*Go to* [contradictingly]; peace, Mouldy! you shall go.—*Ibid.*, iii. 2.

Go to [consentingly]; stand aside . . . you shall have forty, sir.—*Go to*, stand aside.—*Ibid.*, iii. 2.

I would you would, Master Shallow.—*Go to* [conclusively]; I have spoke at a word. Fare you well.—*Ibid.*, iii. 2.

Ye are too bold: *go to* [frowningly]; I'll make ye know.—*H. VIII.*, ii. 2.

An her hair were not somewhat darker than Helen's (well, *go to* [petulantly]), there were no more comparison.—*Tr. & Cr.*, i. 1.

Go to [agreeingly], a bargain made: seal it, seal it.—*Ibid.*, iii. 2.

No, truly, sir; not a penny.—*Go to* [insistingly], I say, you shall.—*R. & Jul.*, ii. 4.

Go to [sarcastically]: perchance some single vantages you took.—*Timon*, ii. 2.

Abler than yourself to make conditions.—
Go to [scornfully]; you are not, Cassius.—*Jul. C.*, iv. 3.

I'll be with thee betimes.—*Go to* [approvingly]; farewell. . . . I'll sell all my land. —*Go to;* farewell: put money enough in your purse.—*Oth.*, i. 3.

And so she did.—Why, *go to* [insidiously], then.—*Ibid.*, iii. 3.

Is't come to this? Well, well.—*Go to* [angrily], woman!
Throw your vile guesses in the devil's teeth.—*Ibid.*, iii. 4.

Go to [in bitterly ironical encouragement]; well said, well said.—*Ibid.*, iv. 1.

Pr'ythee, come; will you?—*Go to* [consentingly], say no more.—*Ibid.*, iv. 1.

You are a fool; *go to* [silencingly].—*Ibid.*, iv. 2.

Well; *go to* [sneeringly]; very well.—Very well! *go to*!
I cannot go to, man; nor 'tis not very well.—*Ibid.*, iv. 2.

With Cassio, mistress. *Go to* [imperatively], charm your tongue.—*Ibid.*, v. 2.

Therefore speak no more.—*Go to* [scoffingly obedient], then; your considerate stone.—*Ant. & C.*, ii. 2.

Good madam, hear me.—Well, *go to* [with suppressed irritation], I will; but there's no goodness in thy face.—*Ibid.*, ii. 5.

She died by foul play.—O, *go to* [with sorrowful and reluctant acquiescence]. Well, well,
Of all the faults beneath the Heavens, the gods
Do like this worst.—*Per.*, iv. 4.

Go to, go to [displeasedly]: no matter for the dish, sir.—*M. for M.*, ii. 1.

Go to, go to [soothingly]; peace, peace! we must deal gently with him.— *Tw. N.*, iii. 4.

Go to, go to [in riddance], thou art a foolish fellow:
Let me be clear of thee.—*Ibid.*, iv. 1.

I serve thee not.—Well, *go to, go to* [fretfully].—*Tr. & Cr.*, ii. 1.

Go to, sweet queen, *go to* [pacifyingly].—*Ibid.*, iii. 1.

The falcon as the tercel, for all the ducks i' the river: *go to, go to* [rallyingly and vauntingly].—*Ibid.*, iii. 2.

Go to, go to [censuringly]; you have known what you should not.—*Macb.*, v. 1.

Ay, fashion you may call it; *go to, go to* [disdainfully].—*Hamlet*, i. 3.

Where is the fellow? Half afeard to come.—*Go to, go to* [waving aside the excuse]. Come hither, sir.—*Ant. & C.*, iii. 3.

Ha [blusteringly], thou mountain foreigner!—*Merry W.*, i. 1.

Ha [inquiringly], what say'st thou, Silvius?—*As You L.*, iii. 3.

Ha [chucklingly], it was a merry night.—2 *H. IV.*, iii. 2.

Ha [patronisingly], cousin Silence, that thou hadst seen that that this knight and I have seen !—*Ibid.*, iii. 2.

Ha [vauntingly], Sir John, said I well ?—*Ibid.*, iii. 3.

Ha ? [carelessly] no, no, i' faith ; thou singest well enough.—*M. Ado*, ii. 3.

" Some are born great,"—*Ha ?* [perplexedly].—*Tw. N.*, iii. 4.

Richard !—*Ha ?* [reply as if to a call]—I call thee not.—*R. III.*, i. 1.

Who is there, *ha ?* [angrily] . . . Who am I, *ha ?* . . . Is this an hour for temporal affairs, *ha ?*—*H. VIII.*, ii. 2.

Good-morrow, Ajax.—*Ha ?* [with a cutting stare] Good-morrow.—Ay, and good next day too.—[*Exit.*]—*Tr. & Cr.*, iii. 3.

Who does me this, *ha ?* [in bitter self-questioning].—*Hamlet*, ii. 2.

It is a common thing.—*Ha ?* [sharply].—*Oth.*, iii. 3.

Ha ! [threateningly] o' my life, if I were young again, the sword should end it.—*Merry W.*, i. 1.

The prince's fool ! *Ha !* [vexedly] it may be I go under that title, because I am merry.—*M. Ado*, ii. 1.

Ha ! [ponderingly] " Against my will I am sent to bid you come in to dinner "—there 's a double meaning in that.—*Ibid.*, ii. 3.

Kill Claudio.—*Ha !* [refusingly] not for the wide world.—*Ibid.*, iv. 1.

> Do but hear me, sir.—Ha ! [vehemently] I 'll tell thee what ;
> Thou art damn'd as black.—*John*, iv. 3.

And dout them with superfluous courage, *ha !* [excitedly].—*H. V.*, iv. 2.

Ha ! [irefully] durst the traitor breathe out so proud words ?—3 *H. VI.*, iv. 1.

> To win her, all the world to nothing !
> Ha ! [vauntingly].—*R. III.*, i. 2.

> The king cried, ha ! [sternly] at this.—Now God incense him,
> And let him cry, ha ! louder !—*H. VIII.*, iii. 2.

Ha ! [impetuously] Canterbury ?—Ay, my good lord.—*Ibid.*, v. 1.

Avoid the gallery. *Ha !* [imperiously] I have said. Be gone ! What !—*Ibid.*, v. 1.

Ha ! [in angry surprise] 'Tis he indeed.—*Ibid.*, v. 1.

Pass no farther.—*Ha !* [indignantly] what is that ?—*Coriol.*, iii. 1.

Ha ! [in grieved surprise] banishment ? be merciful, say death.—*R. & Jul.*, iii. 3.

What hands are here ! *Ha !* [shudderingly] they pluck out mine eyes !—*Macb.*, ii. 2.

> Cordelia, Cordelia ! stay a little. *Ha !* [passionately eager listening]
> What is 't thou say'st ? Her voice was ever soft.—*Lear*, v. 3.

Ha ! [pretendedly awakened suspicion] I like not that.—*Oth.*, iii. 3.

> You cannot, if my heart were in your hand ;
> Nor shall not, whilst 'tis in my custody.—
> Ha ! [furiously].—*Ibid.*, iii. 3.

> Then, would to heaven that I had never seen it !
> Ha ! [with ireful suspicion] wherefore ?—*Ibid.*, iii. 4.

Help, master, help ! here 's a fish hangs in the net. . . . *Ha !* [heavily].—*Per.*, ii. 1.

Ha, ha ! [wondering laughter], What things are these, my lord Antonio ? Will money buy them ?—*Temp.*, v. 1.

You 'll ne'er be good, nor suffer others.—*Ha, ha !* [bantering laughter] Alas, poor wretch ! . . . You smile, and mock me, as if I meant naughtily.—*Ha, ha !*—*Tr. & Cr.*, iv. 2.

> What day is this ?—Monday, my lord.—
> Monday ! ha, ha ! [slight surprise] Well, Wednesday is too soon ;
> O' Thursday let it be.—*R. & Jul.*, iii. 4.

Ha, ha ! [scoffing laughter] how vilely doth this cynic rhyme.—*Jul. C.*, iv. 3.

Ha, ha ! [bitter laughter] are you honest ?—*Hamlet*, iii. 1.

Ha ! ha ! [outburst of passion] false to me ?—*Oth.*, iii. 3.

Ha, ha! [expression of tedium]   Give me to drink mandragora.—*Ant. & C.,* i. 5.

Ha, ha, ha! [senile laughter] most excellent, i' faith! . . . *Ha, ha, ha!* you can do it, sir; you can do it.—*2 H. IV.,* iii. 2.

She gives it out that you shall marry her: do you intend it?—*Ha, ha, ha!* [mocking laughter] . . . bear some charity to my wit; do not think it so unwholesome. *Ha, ha, ha!* . . . so hales and pulls me: *ha, ha ha!* [laughter of levity].—*Oth.,* iv. 1.

How now!   Interjections?   Why then, some of laughing, as, *ha, ha, he!* [careless laughter].—*M. Ado,* iv. 1.

Doth turn oh! oh! to *ha! ha! he!* [happy laughter].—*Tr. & Cr.,* iii. 1 (*Song*).

What harmony is this? my good friends, *hark!* [calling attention to supernatural music].—*Temp.,* iii. 3.

Hark! [the anxious listening for possible sounds by those engaged in a guilty deed] Peace! it was the owl that shriek'd. . . . *Hark!* I laid their daggers ready; he could not miss them. . . . *Hark!* Who lies in the second chamber? . . . *Hark!* more knocking.—*Macb.,* ii. 2.

Yet here's a spot.—*Hark!* [listening to the murmured accents of a sleep-walker] she speaks: I will set down what comes from her.—*Ibid.,* v. 1.

Hark! [listening to an imagined noise] who is it that knocks?—It is the wind.—*Oth.,* iv. 2.

O, help!—*Hark!* [listening to a wounded person's call] . . . Nobody come? then I shall bleed to death.—*Hark!*—*Ibid.,* v. 1.

My ingenious instrument!

Hark [calling attention to a musical summons], Polydore, it sounds! . . . *Hark!*—*Cym.,* iv. 2.

Heigh [a cheering shout], my hearts! cheerly, cheerly.—*Temp.,* i. 1.

My lord, my lord!—*Heigh! heigh!* [a jeering shout] the devil rides upon a fiddlestick: what's the matter?—*1 H. IV.,* ii. 4.

By my troth, I am exceeding ill: *heigh-ho!* [a languishing sigh].—*M. Ado,* iii. 4.

How well I counterfeited.   *Heigh-ho!* [a gasp, after recovering from a swoon]   This was not counterfeit.—*As You L.,* iv. 3.

Heigh-ho! [a yawn]   An 't be not four by the day, I 'll be hanged: Charles' wain is over the new chimney.—*1 H. IV.,* ii. 1.

Heigh-ho! [an affected sigh]   In love, i' faith, to the very tip of the nose.—*Tr. & Cr.,* iii. 1.

Hem them away.—I would try, if I could cry *hem* [clearing the throat, in suppression of uneasiness of spirit], and have him.—*As You L.,* i. 3.

There 's a man, niece! *Hem!* [clearing the throat, to attract attention!]   Brave Troilus! the prince of chivalry!—*Tr. & Cr.,* i. 2.

Cough, or cry *hem* [clearing the throat, as a token of warning], if any body come.—*Oth.,* iv. 2.

Freedom, *hey-day!* [in hilarity] *hey-day,* freedom! freedom! *hey-day,* freedom!—*Temp.,* ii. 2.

Hey-day! [in impatient disdain], a riddle! neither good nor bad!—*R. III.,* iv. 4.

Hey-day! [in astonishment] spirits and fires!—*Tr. & Cr.,* v. 1.

Hey-day! [in contemptuous surprise] what a sweep of vanity comes this way! They dance!—*Timon,* i. 2.

H'm * [in moody reverie],—ha! is this a vision? is this a dream? do I sleep? Master Ford, awake!—*Merry W.,* iii. 5.

I cried, "*H'm*" [in suppressed impatience], and "Well, go to," but mark'd him not.—*1 H. IV.,* iii. 1.

Jove bless great Ajax.—*H'm!* [in mimicry of a self-absorbed bully]—I come from the worthy Achilles,—Ha!—Who most humbly desires you to invite Hector to his tent,—*H'm!*—And to procure safe conduct from Agamemnon.—*Tr. & Cr.,* iii. 3.

---

* In the Folio this exclamation is sometimes spelt 'Hum' and sometimes 'Humh.'

Must he needs trouble me in 't, *h'm !* [grumblingly] 'bove all others ? . . . And does he send to me ? Three ? *H'm !—Timon*, iii. 3.

The heaviest sound that ever yet they heard.—*H'm !* [in suppressed emotion] I guess at it.—*Macb.*, iv. 3.

H'm ! [reflectively] this fellow might be in 's time.—*Hamlet*, v. 1.

H'm ! [in grieved amazement] Conspiracy !—*Lear*, i. 2.

H'm ! [shiveringly] go to thy cold bed, and warm thee.—*Ibid.*, iii. 4.

If you say so, I hope you will not kill me.—*H'm !* [unwilling to reply]—And yet I fear you.—*Oth.*, v. 2.

Not her danger.—*H'm !* [reading over the letter to himself] . . . sirrah, is this letter true ?—*Cym.*, iii. 5.

Hail, sir ! my lord, lend ear.—*H'm !* [absently] ha ?—*Per.*, v. 1.

I pray you, leave me.—*Ho !* [bantering expostulation] now you strike like the blind man.—*M. Ado*, ii. 1.

What noise there, *ho ?* [angry inquiry].—*W. T.*, ii. 3.

Who 's there ? speak, *ho !* [military challenge of inquiry] speak quickly, or I shoot. —*John*, v. 6.

All fast ? What means this ? *Ho !* [authoritative summons] Who waits there ? Sure, you know me.—*H. VIII.*, v. 2.

Ho ! [impatient call] bid my trumpet sound !—*Tr. & Cr.*, v. 3.

What, are you busy, *ho ?* [kindly inquiry].—*R. & Jul.*, i. 3.

Stand, *ho !* [sentinels' challenge] Who is there ?—*Hamlet*, i. 1.

The guard, *ho !* [wounded summons]—O, despatch me !—*Ant. & C.*, iv. 12.

> *Ho !* [attemptedly loud summons] Who 's there ?
> If anything that 's civil, speak ; if savage,
> Take, or lend. *Ho !* No answer ? Then I 'll enter.—*Cym.*, iii. 6.

Sweet lady, *ho, ho* [fantastical smiling].—*Tw. N.*, iii. 4.

Ho, ho [cynical laughter], confess'd it ! hang'd it, have you not ? . . . *Ho, ho !* I laugh to think that babe a bastard.—*Timon*, i. 2.

Ho, ho, ho ! [the written form of the mocking laugh ascribed to Puck in the old ballads describing his pranks] Coward, why com'st thou not ?—*Mid. N. D.*, iii. 2.

Ho, ho, ho ! [forced laugh] Now, the witch take me, if I meant it thus ! Grace grow where those drops fall !—*Ant. & C.*, iv. 2.

What ho ! [calling to one within a cave] slave ! Caliban !—*Temp.*, i. 2.

What ho ! [neighbourly call] gossip Ford ! *what ho !—Merry W.*, iv. 2.

What ho ! [call for admission at a prison-entrance] Peace here ; grace and good company !—*M. for M.*, iii. 1.

What ho ! what ho ! what ho ! [sailorly call].—*Oth.*, i. 3.

Whoa, ho, hoa !—Hilloa ! loa ! [rustic shouting]—What ! art so near ?—*W. T.*, iii. 2.

Whoo ! ho ! ho ! [blubbering] father Page !—*Merry W.*, v. 5.

Hoo ! [joyful shout] Marcius coming home.—*Coriol.*, ii. 1.

Our enemy is banish'd ! he is gone ! *Hoo ! hoo !* [plebeian shout].—*Ibid.*, iii. 3.

Hoo ! [roistering shout] Says 'a ! There 's my cap !—*Hoo !* Noble captain, come.—*Ant. & C.*, ii. 7.

Spake you of Cæsar ? *Hoo !* [laudatory shout] the nonpareil ! . . . yet he loves Antony : *Hoo !* hearts, tongues, figures, scribes, bards, poets, cannot think, speak, cast, write, sing, number—*hoo !*—his love to Antony.—*Ibid.*, iii. 2.

There, *hold* [giving back a letter]: I will not look upon.—*Two G. of V.*, iv. 4.

Hold [tendering his commission], therefore, Angelo.—*M. for M.*, i. 1.

Hold ! [interposing] hurt him not, for God's sake !—*Com. of E.*, v. 1.

Hold [giving money], there 's expenses for thee.—*Tw. N.*, iii. 1.

Hold [parting combatants], Toby ! on thy life, I charge thee, *hold !—Ibid.*, iv. 1.

Hold [giving a weapon], Wart, traverse.—*2 H. IV.*, iii. 2.

Hold [giving keys], take these keys, and fetch more spices.—*R. & Jul.*, iv. 4.

Hold [giving his hand], my hand : be factious for redress.—*Jul. C.*, i. 3.

Hold [bidding his heart not break], my heart !—*Hamlet*, i. 5.

Holla [calling to a servant], within ! sirrah, lead these.—*Tam. of S.*, ii. 1.

Holla ! [calling, in the dark] Bernardo !—*Hamlet*, i. 1.

Holla ! [a command, in the dark] stand there !—*Oth.*, i. 2.

Holla, holla ! [scornful denial] That eye that told you so look'd but a-squint.—*Lear*, v. 3.

How ! [surprised inquiry] the best ?   What wert thou.—*Temp.*, i. 2.

How ! [angry inquiry] away with that audacious lady.—*W. T.*, ii. 3.

How ! [astonishment] not your own desire !—*Coriol.*, ii. 3.

It is not lost ; but what an if it were ?   *How !* [wrath].—*Oth.*, iii. 3.

Why, *how now !* [cheerful inquiry] do you speak in the sick tune ?—*M. Ado*, iii. 4.

Why, *how now* [poutingly], Orlando ! where have you been all this while ?   You a lover !—*As You L.*, iv. 1.

My lady would not lose him for more than I 'll say.—*How now* [rebukingly] mistress !—*Tw. N.*, iii. 4.

Why, *how now* [roaring inquiry], my bawcock, how dost thou, chuck ?—*Ibid.*, iii. 4.

How now [arousingly], fair shepherd ! your heart is full of something that does take your mind from feasting.—*W. T.*, iv. 3.

Why, *how now* [remonstratingly], general ! no more of that. . . . *How now*, my lord !—*Oth.*, iii. 3.

How now [half surprised, half humouring her], my sweet Bianca ! *how now, how now !*—*Ibid.*, iv. 1.

And I thank you always with my heart, *la* [in senile affirmation] ; with my heart.—*Merry W.*, i. 1.

Ay, or else I would I might be hanged, *la* [in flabby affirmation].—*Ibid.*, i. 1.

Truly, I will not go first ; truly, *la* [foolishly insisting] ; I will not do you that wrong. . . . You do yourself wrong, indeed, *la.*—*Ibid.*, i. 1.

This is all, indeed, *la* [lying affirmation].—*Ibid.*, i. 4.

Surely, I think you have charms, *la* [waggish affirmation] ; yes, in truth.—*Ibid.*, ii. 2.

I 'll make the best in Gloucestershire know on 't ; would I were hanged, *la* [flabbily threatening], else.—*Ibid.*, v. 5.

As ever his plack shoe trod upon Got's ground and his earth, in my conscience, *la* [pepperily affirmative].—*H. V.*, iv. 7.

Nay, that shall not serve your turn ; that shall it not, in truth, *la* [pettishly affirmative].—*Tr. & Cr.*, iii. 1.

In faith, I will, *la* [coquettishly affirmative] ; never trust me else.—*Ibid.*, v. 2.

Indeed, *la* [earnestly affirmative], 'tis a noble child.—*Coriol.*, i. 3.

In truth, *la* [persuasively insisting], go with me.—*Ibid.*, i. 3.

Indeed, *la* [artlessly affirmative], without an oath, I 'll make an end on 't.—*Hamlet*, iv. 5.

Sooth, *la* [blandishingly affirmative], I 'll help.—*Ant. & C.*, iv. 4.

Believe me, *la* [innocently affirmative], I never kill'd a mouse, nor hurt a fly.—*Per.*, iv. 1.

Hath sent to your lordship to furnish him, nothing doubting your present assistance therein.—*La, la, la, la,* [hypocritical sympathy], nothing doubting, says he ? alas, good lord !—*Timon*, iii. 1.

La you ! [pretended amazement] an you speak iN of the devil, how he takes it at heart !—*Tw. N.*, iii. 4.

Lo [calling attention to a particular point in narration], what befel ! he threw his eye aside, and, mark, what object.—*As You L.*, iv. 3.

Lo [calling attention to pretended circumstance], how hollow the fiend speaks within him !—*Tw. N.*, iii. 4.

The love I bore your queen,—*lo* [self-rebukingly], fool again ! I 'll speak of her no more.—*W. T.*, iii. 3.

Lo! [despondently] this is all : nay, yet depart not so.—*R. II.*, i. 2.

Lo, lo, lo, lo [jeeringly admiring], what modicums of wit he utters !—*Tr. & Cr.*, ii. 1.

Lo thee! [as a signal to strike the desired blow].—*Ant. & C.*, iv. 12.

Why, *lo you now* [in playful surprise], I have spoke to the purpose twice.—*W. T.*, i. 2.

Lo you now ! [helplessly] you hear : when she will take.—*Ibid.*, ii. 3.

Lord [in girlish amazement], how it looks about !—*Temp.*, i. 2.

Lord! [sportively] I could not endure a husband with.—*M. Ado*, ii. 1.

Lord [jeeringly], how wise you are !—*Love's L. L.*, i. 2.

Lord [scornfully], what fools these mortals be !—*Mid. N. D.*, iii. 2.

Lord [rustic wonder], how art thou changed !—*Mer. of V.*, ii. 2.

Lord ! [female scorn at womanly submission] let me never have a cause to sigh till I be brought to such a silly pass !—*Tam of S.*, v. 2.

Lord [vexation], how we lose our pains !—*All's W.*, v. 1.

Lord [placid content], who would live turmoiled in the court.—*2 H. VI.*, iv. 10.

Lord [complaining], how my head aches !—*R. & Jul.*, ii. 5.

Lord ! [a sudden snatch of solemnity] we know what we are, but we know not what we may be.—*Hamlet*, iv. 5.

Lord, lord ! [pertly] to see what folly reigns in us.—*Two G. of V.*, i. 2.

Lord, lord ! [waggishly] your worship 's a wanton !—*Merry W.*, ii. 2.

Lord, lord! [conceitedly] how the ladies and I have put him down !—*Love's L. L.*, iv. 1.

Lord, lord [impudent denunciation of falsehood by a liar], how this world is given to lying.—*1 H. IV.*, v. 4.

Lord, lord [pretended deploring of falsehood], how subject we old men are to this vice of lying !—*2 H. IV.*, iii. 2.

Lord, lord ! [garrulous gladness] she will be a joyful woman. . . .

Lord, lord ! [garrulous praise] when 'twas a little prating thing.—*R. & Jul.*, ii. 4.

O Lord [mockingly], he will hang upon him like.—*M. Ado*, i. 1.

No, no ; *O lord!* [pert contradiction] sir, no.—*Love's L. L.*, i. 2.

O Lord [abject pleading], sir, let me live, or let me see.—*All's W.*, iv. 3.

How, now, mistress !—*O Lord !* [pretendedly startled].—*Tw. N.*, iii. 4.

O Lord ! [in mental anguish] my boy, my Arthur.—*John*, iii. 2.

O Lord ! [blaringly] good my lord captain,—what, dost thou roar before thou art pricked ?—*O Lord*, sir, I am a.—*2 H. IV.*, iii. 2.

Not to-day, *O Lord !* [in earnest supplication] O, not to-day, think not upon the fault my father made.—*H. V.*, iv. 1.

O Lord ! [in troubled narration of a dream] methought what pain it was to drown ! what dreadful noise.—*R. III.*, i. 4.

O Lord ! [in pained surprise] why look'st thou sad ?—*R. & Jul.*, ii. 5.

O Lord ! [sanctimoniously] I could have stayed here all the night, to hear good counsel : O, what learning is.—*Ibid.*, iii. 3.

O Lord [in alarm], they fight ! I will go call the watch.—*Ibid.*, v. 3.

O lord, lord ! [playfully] it is a hard matter for.—*As You L.*, iii. 2.

Do not torment me : *O!* [growlingly] . . . The spirit torments me : *O !*—*Temp.*, ii. 2.

O ! [ardently] she is ten times more gentle than her father 's crabbed . . . but you. *O you !* so perfect.—*Ibid.*, iii. 1.

O ! [supplicatorily] think on that ; and mercy then will.—*M. for M.*, ii. 2.

O ! [fervently] were it but my life, I 'd throw it down.—*Ibid.*, iii. 1.

O [furiously], I will to him, and pluck out his eyes !—*Ibid.*, iv. 3.

O [narratively], when she had writ it. . . . *O*, she tore the letter into a thousand half-pence.—*M. Ado*, ii. 3.

O [sarcastically], that woman that cannot make her fault.—*As You L.*, iv. 1.

But, *O* [amorous reflection], how bitter a thing it is.—*As You L.*, v. 2.

O [disdainfully], sir, I will not be so hard-hearted.—*Tw. N.*, i. 5.

O ! [in pretended pain] good sir, tenderly, *O !*—*W. T.*, iv. 2.

It is my lady; *O* [enamoured transport], it is my love ! *O*, that she knew she were ! . . . *O*, that I were a glove upon that hand. . . . *O*, speak again, bright angel ! . . . *O* Romeo, Romeo ! . . . *O*, be some other name ! . . . *O* gentle Romeo, if thou dost love, pronounce it faithfully. . . . *O*, swear not by the moon, th' inconstant moon. . . . *O*, wilt thou leave me so unsatisfied ? . . . *O* blessed, blessed night ! . . . *O*, for a falconer's voice, to lure this tassel-gentle back again !—*R. & Jul.*, ii. 2.

O ! [impassioned dread] by this count I shall be much in years ere I again behold my Romeo. . . . *O*, think'st thou we shall ever meet again ?—*Ibid.*, iii. 5.

Well, then—sustain me : *O !* [ready to sink].—*Ant. & C.*, iii. 9.

O [passionate remorse], bear me witness, night. . . . Be witness to me, *O* thou blessed moon ! . . . *O* sovereign mistress of true melancholy ! . . . *O* Antony ! nobler than my revolt is infamous, forgive me. . . . *O* Antony ! *O* Antony !—*Ibid.*, iv. 9.

O [jocular consolation], of this contradiction you shall now be quit. *O*, the charity of a penny cord !—*Cym.*, v. 4.

O, O, 'tis foul ! [passionate complaint]—*Lear*, iii. 2.

O ! O ! O ! [a man's agony of weeping] Nay, lay thee down and roar ; for thou hast kill'd the sweetest innocent. . . . *O* Desdemona ! Desdemona ! dead ! *O ! O ! O !*—*Oth.*, v. 2.

These lovers cry—*Oh ! oh !* [mockery of weeping] they die ! . . . Doth turn *oh ! oh !* to ha ! ha ! he ! . . . *Oh ! oh !* a while, but ha ! ha ! ha ! *Oh ! oh !* groans out for ha ! ha ! ha !—*Tr. & Cr.*, iii. 1 (*Song*).

Oh, oh, oh ! [Falstaffian roar at being burnt by the fairies' tapers].—*Merry W.*, v. 5.

All the perfumes of Arabia will not sweeten this little hand. *Oh, oh, oh !* [profound sigh of remorse].—*Macb.*, v. 1.

O, ho [vauntingly], monster ! we know what belongs to a frippery.—*Temp.*, iv. 1.

O, ho ! [exultingly] do you come near me now ?—*Tw. N.*, iii. 4.

O, ho ! [a cry of wandering wits]—Nay, but Ophelia.—*Hamlet*, iv. 5.

O, ho [cunning of insanity], are you there with me ?—*Lear*, iv. 6.

O, ho ! [detectingly] I know the riddle.—*Ibid.*, v. 1.

O ho, O ho ! [savage defiance] would it had been done !—*Temp.*, i. 2.

O heaven ! [flabby ecstasy] this is Mistress Anne Page.—*Merry W.*, i. 1.

O heaven ! [paternal grief] How got she out ?—*Oth.*, i. 1.

O heavens ! [agitation] why does my blood thus muster to my heart ?—*M. for M.*, ii. 4.

I am asham'd ; *O heavens'!* [affectation of modesty] what have I done ?—*Tr. & Cr.*, iii. 2.

O heavens ! [bitterly ironical] die two months ago, and not forgotten yet ?—*Hamlet*, iii. 2.

O heavens ! [hypocritical regret] that this treason were not.—*Lear*, iii. 5.

O heavens ! O heavens ! [a burst of wifely weeping].—*Coriol.*, iv. 1.

Soft [bespeaking attention], sir : one word more.—*Temp.*, i. 2.

Soft ! [enjoining silence] comes he not here ?—*As You L.*, iii. 2.

Soft ! [self-imposed attention] and the impressure her Lucrece. . . . *Soft !* here follows prose.—*Tw. N.*, ii. 5.

Not too fast : *soft, soft* [self-checking].—*Ibid.*, i. 5.

Come, here's my heart : something's afore't : *Soft, soft !* [bidding wait a moment] we'll no defence.—*Cym.*, iii. 4.

Shakespeare employs some exclamations that are formed from expressive sound :—

Oh, well flown, bird !—i' the clout, i' the clout : *hewgh !* [the old king's whistle in imitation of the falconer's call to the hawk, and of the twang of the arrow through the air].—*Lear*, iv. 6.

Pur! [Edgar, in his assumption of Poor Tom's rambling jargon, mimics the noise made by the animal he names] the cat is grey.—*Lear*, iii. 6.

We did keep time, sir, in our catches. *Sneck up!* [a scoffing interjection, equivalent to 'go, hang!'—put into the boozing Sir Toby's mouth, as having the effect of a hiccup].—*Tw. N.*, ii. 3.

Whew! [Falstaff's vexed mockery of the thieves' whistle] A plague upon you all! Give me my horse.—1 *H. IV.*, ii. 2.

Shakespeare makes use of several exclamations, technically or otherwise specially employed :—

That woman, who cried out "*Clubs!*" [the cry used in ancient London to summon constabulary aid, or to rally the city apprentices] when I might see from far.—*H. VIII.*, v. 3.

Clubs, bills, and partisans! strike.—*R. & Jul.*, i. 1.

Oh, *esperance!* [the motto and battle-cry of the Percy family].—1 *H. IV.*, ii. 3.

Now, *Esperance!* Percy! and set on.—*Ibid.*, v. 2.

A hall, a hall! [the exclamation formerly used when it was needful to clear a space in a crowded assembly] give room!—*R. & Jul.*, i. 5.

Halloo, halloo, loo, loo! [a cry used in hare-hunting].—*Lear*, iii. 4.

Cry, *havock* [the word used in war as a declaration that no quarter should be given], kings! back to the stained field.—*John*, ii. 2.

Do not cry *havock*, where you should but hunt.—*Coriol.*, iii. 1.

Cry, "*havock!*" and let slip the dogs of war.—*Jul. C.*, iii. 1.

This quarry cries on *havock*.—*Hamlet*, v. 2.

Hey [cry of the chase, to encourage the hounds], Mountain, *hey!*— Silver! *there it goes!* Silver!—Fury, Fury! *there* Tyrant, *there!* hark, hark!—*Temp.*, iv. 1.

Illo, ho, ho! my lord!—*Hillo, ho, ho, boy!* [the call used by falconers to the hawk, when they would have it descend from the air to them] come, bird, come.—*Hamlet*, i. 5.

To cry, "*Hold, hold!*" [the phrase formally and solemnly used when parting combatants or forbidding an assault].—*Macb.*, i. 5.

Hold, for your lives!—*Hold, hold*, lieutenant!. . . . *Hold!* the general speaks to you, *hold*, for shame!—*Oth.*, ii. 3.

Hold, hold, hold, hold!—My noble masters.—*Coriol.*, v. 5.

Cry, *holla!* [a term of the riding-school; whereby the horse was checked or stopped] to thy tongue, I pry'thee; it curvets most unseasonably.—*As You L.*, iii. 2.

Kill, kill, kill, kill, kill [the word given formerly in the army, when an onset was made upon the enemy] him!—*Coriol.*, v. 5.

> And when I have stolen upon these sons-in-law,
> Then, *kill, kill, kill, kill, kill, kill.*—*Lear*, iv. 6.

Now, bull! now, dog! '*Loo*, Paris, '*loo!* [a cry used at bull-baiting] now, my double-henned sparrow! '*loo*, Paris, '*loo!* The bull has the game: 'ware horns, ho!—*Tr. & Cr.*, v. 8.

Peace!—Hear the crier! [Faulconbridge likens Austria's exclamation of "*Peace!*" to the proclamation, "Silence!" made by criers in courts of justice].—*John*, ii. 1.

> It is his highness' pleasure that the queen
> Appear in person here in court. *Silence!*—*W. T.*, iii. 2.

Saint Denis [the battle-cry of France] to *Saint Cupid!* [the battle-cry playfully adopted by the French Princess].—*Love's L. L.*, v. 2.

Between Saint Denis and *Saint George* [the battle-cry of England].—*H. V.*, v. 2.

So-ho, so-ho! [the cry, in hunting the hare, when the game is perceived]—What see'st thou?—*Two G. of V.*, iii. 1.

So-ho!—What hast thou found?—No hare, sir.—*R. & Jul.*, ii. 4.

And "*tailor*" [an exclamation used when any one slipped from a seat and fell backwards: conjectured to have been because a person so stumbling falls as a tailor squats upon his board] cries, and falls into a cough.—*Mid. N. D.*, ii. 1.

Yoke you like draught oxen, and make you plough up the war.—What, what?—Yes, good sooth : *to*, Achilles ! *to*, Ajax ! *to !* [the expression of urging used by ploughmen to their cattle].—*Tr. & Cr.*, ii. 1.

O, *well flown, bird!* [the falconer's expression when the hawk was successful in its flight].—*Lear*, iv. 6.

There lies your way, due west.—Then *westward-ho !* [this, and its counterpart exclamation, 'eastward-ho !' were the cries with which the Thames watermen offered to convey passengers in their boats either towards the city or the contrary quarter of London].—*Tw. N.*, iii. 1.

Shakespeare uses some exclamations derived from foreign sources :—

Adieu, good Monsieur Melancholy.—*As You L.*, iii. 2.

With no less religion than if thou wert indeed my Rosalind : so, *adieu*.—*Ibid.*, iv. 1.

Once more, *adieu ;* the rest let sorrow say.—*R. II.*, v. 1.

Adieu !—Nay, stay a little : were you but riding forth to air yourself, such parting were too petty.—*Cym.*, i. 2.

Baccare ! you are marvellous forward.—*Tam of S.*, ii. 1.

I will not change my horse with any that treads but on four pasterns.   *Ça, ha !* He bounds from the earth, as if his entrails were hairs.—*H. V.*, iii. 7.

Coragio ! bully-monster, *coragio !*—*Temp.*, v. 1.

Bravely, *coragio !*—*All's W.*, ii. 5.

Diablo, ho! the town will rise.—*Oth.*, ii. 3.

" Steal," foh ! a *fico* for the phrase!—*Merry W.*, i. 3.

Die, and *figo* for thy friendship!—*H. V.*, iii. 6.

The *figo* for thee, then !—*Ibid.*, iv. 1.

> *Gramercies*, Tranio, well dost thou advise. . . .
> *Gramercies*, lad ; go forward.—*Tam of S.*, i. 1.

Gramercies, good fool: how does your mistress ?—*Timon*, ii. 2.

Gramercy : wouldst thou aught with me ?—*Mer. of V.*, ii. 2.

Gramercy, fellow.   There, drink that for me.—*R. III.*, iii. 2.

Good ! *Gramercy.*—*Timon*, ii. 2.

Good master page, sit.   *Proface !*—*2 H. IV.*, v. 3.

Rivo ! says the drunkard.—*1 H. IV.*, ii. 4.

Let the world slide : *sessa !*—*Tam. of S.*, *Induc.* 1.

Sessa ! let him trot by.—*Lear*, iii. 4.

Sessa ! Come, march to wakes and fairs.—*Ibid.*, iii. 6.

Have I encompassed you ? go to, *via !*—*Merry W.*, ii. 2.

Via, goodman Dull ! thou hast spoken no word.—*Love's L. L.*, v. 1.

Cried, " *Via !* we will do 't, come what will come."—*Ibid.*, v. 2.

" *Via !*" says the fiend ; " away ! " says the fiend.—*Mer. of V.*, ii. 2.

Via ! les eaux et la terre.—*H. V.*, iv. 2.

Why, *Via !* to London will we march amain.—*3 H. VI.*, ii. 1.

> I see them lording it in London streets,
> Crying " *Villiago !*" unto all they meet.—*2 H. VI.*, iv. 8.

And he introduces one English oath corrupted by French pronunciation :—

By *gar*, it is a shallenge . . . by *gar*, I vill cut.—*Merry W.*, i. 4.

He also uses some peculiar adjurations :—

But, *for all our loves*, first let them try.—*2 H. IV.*, ii. 3.

Would desire you to send her your little page of *all loves*.—*Merry W.*, ii. 2.

Speak, of *all loves !*—*Mid. N. D.*, ii. 3.

Of charity, what kin are you to me ?—*Tw. N.*, v. 1.

Sweet saint, *for charity*, be not so curst.—*R. III.*, i. 2.

Also, some peculiar asseverations :—

And yet to win her, *all the world to nothing !—R. III.,* i. 2.
And *all the world to nothing*, that he dares ne'er come back.—*R. & Jul.,* iii. 5.
For, *heaven to earth*, some of us never shall a second time.—*1 H. IV.,* v. 2.
    And of his friends there, *it is lots to blanks*,
    My name hath touch'd your ears.—*Coriol.,* v. 2.
Master, *for my hand*, both our inventions meet.—*Tam. of S.,* i. 1.
Not to tremble : *my life for yours.—Mid. N. D.,* iii. 1.

Also, some exclamations of salutation :—

Hail, mortal !—*Hail ! Hail ! Hail !—Ibid.,* iii. 1.
All hail, great master ! grave sir ! *hail !—Temp.,* i. 2.
Cæsar, *all hail !* good morrow, worthy Cæsar.—*Jul. C.,* ii. 2.
All hail, Macbeth ! *hail to thee,* thane of Glamis !—*Macb.,* i. 3.
*Hail to your lordship !—*I am glad to see you well.—*Hamlet,* i. 2.
*Hail to your grace !—*I am glad to see your highness.—*Lear,* ii. 4.
God-den to your worship, goot Captain Jamy.—*H. V.,* iii. 2.
O, *God ye good den.—*May not one speak ?—*R. & Jul.,* iii. 5.
God ye good morrow, gentlemen.—*God ye good den.—Ibid.,* ii. 4.
God give you good-morrow, master person.—*Love's L. L.,* iv. 2.
Good den, brother.—*M. Ado,* iii. 2.
Good even, Varro.—*Timon,* ii. 2.
Good day and happiness, dear Rosalind !—*As You L.,* iv. 1.
Till he have cross'd the Severn. *Happiness.—Cym.,* iii. 5.
Sir Proteus, *save you !* Saw you my master ?—*Two G. of V.,* i. 1.
Save thee, friend, and thy music.—*Tw. N.,* iii. 1.
Save you, sir.—And you.—*Coriol.,* iv. 4.
Save thee, Curan.—And you, sir.—*Lear,* ii. 1.

He has some passionately emotional exclamations, of singularly simple and concentrated force in expression :—

Is it even so? *then I defy you, stars !—R. & Jul.,* v. 1.
Death of thy soul ! those linen cheeks of thine.—*Macb.,* v. 3.
My breath and blood ! Fiery ? the fiery duke ?—*Lear,* ii. 4.
Death on my state ! wherefore should he sit here ?—*Ibid.,* ii. 4.
    Howl, howl, howl, howl ! O, you are men of stones :
    Had I your tongues and eyes, I 'd use them so
    That Heaven's vault should crack. *She 's gone for ever !*
    I know when one is dead, and when one lives ;
    She 's dead as earth !—Ibid., v. 3.

He has also given us a specimen of the meaningless exclamations (such as, ' My mare, God save her ! ' and ' My sow, God bless her ! ') sometimes formerly used :—

    If I spar'd any
    That had a head to hit. . . .
    Let me ne'er hope to see a chine again ;
    And that I would not for *a cow, God save her !—H. VIII.,* v. 3.

Also, specimens of elliptical exclamations :—

Women ! *Help Heaven !* [' Heaven help them ! '] men their creation mar
In profiting by them.—*M. for M.,* ii. 4.
God help [them], poor souls, how idly do they talk !—*Com. of E.,* iv. 4.
Now, *the Lord help* [me] ! they vex me past my patience !—*H. VIII.,* ii. 4.

He uses some interjections of denunciation :—

"*Aroint thee*, witch ! " the rump-fed ronyon cries.—*Macb.*, i. 3.

And, *aroint thee*, witch, *aroint thee.*—*Lear*, iii. 4 (*Song*).

Rogues, hence, *avaunt !* vanish like hailstones.—*Merry W.*, i. 3.

Avaunt, thou witch !　Come, Dromio, let us go.—*Com. of E.*, iv. 3.

Avaunt, perplexity !　What shall we do if they return.—*Love's L. L.*, v. 2.

Avaunt, thou hateful villain, get thee gone !—*John*, iv. 3.

You hunt-counter, hence ! *avaunt !*—*2 H. IV.*, i. 2.

You dogs ! *avaunt*, you cullions !—*H. V.*, iii. 2.

Avaunt, thou dreadful minister of hell !—*R. III.*, i. 2.

Avaunt ! and quit my sight ! let the earth hide thee.—*Macb.*, iii. 4.

Avaunt, you curs !—*Lear*, iii. 6.

Avaunt ! be gone ! thou hast set me on the rack.—*Oth.*, iii. 3.

Hence, *avaunt !*—*Ibid.*, v. 1.

Ah, thou spell ! *Avaunt !*—*Ant. & C.*, iv. 10.

Avaunt, thou damned door-keeper !—*Per.*, iv. 6.

> Satan, *avoid !* I charge thee, tempt me not ! . . .
> *Avoid thee*, fiend !—*Com. of E.*, iv. 3.

False fiend, *avoid !*—*2 H. VI.*, i. 4.

Thou basest thing, *avoid !* hence, from my sight !—*Cym.*, i. 2.

Out, devil ! I remember them too well.—*R. III.*, i. 3.

Out, rascal dogs !—*Timon*, v. 1.

Out on thee, rude man !—*John*, i. 1.

Out upon you ! what a man are you.—*R. & Jul.*, ii. 4.

And some interjections of disgust :—

> And fall a-cursing, like a very drab, a scullion !
> Fie upon 't ! *foh !*—*Hamlet*, ii. 2.

Foh ! one may smell in such a will most rank.—*Oth.*, iii. 3.

As I ? *foh !* fie upon thee !—*Ibid.*, v. 1.

And smelt so ? *pah !*—*Hamlet*, v. 1.

Fie, fie, fie ! *pah, pah !* Give me an ounce of civet, good apothecary, to sweeten my imagination.—*Lear*, iv. 6.

And some of contempt, disparagement, slighting rejection, or lightly waiving a subject :—

> She is full of most blessed condition.—
> *Blessed figs' end . . . blessed pudding !*—*Oth.*, ii. 1.

Should be ! should *buz !*—*Tam. of S.*, ii. 1.

The actors are come hither, my lord.—*Buz, buz !*—*Hamlet*, ii. 2.

What, with two points on your shoulder ? *Much !*—*2 H. IV.*, ii. 4.

I promise you, my lord, you mov'd me much.—*Much !*—*Timon*, i. 2.

Is it not past two o'clock ? and here *much* Orlando !—*As You L.*, iv. 3.

> I 'll tell you what,—*Pho, pho !* come, tell a pin : . . .
> Guardian ! why, Greek !—*Pho, pho !* adieu ; you palter.—*Tr. & Cr.*, v. 2.

Pish !—*Pish* for thee, Iceland dog !—*H. V.*, ii. 1.

The incorporate conclusion : *pish !*—*Oth.*, ii. 1.

It is not words that shake me thus : *pish !*—*Ibid.*, iv. 1.

Shakespeare also uses an old form of the above expression ; which was sometimes spelt " push " :—

And made a *push* at chance and sufferance.—*M. Ado*, v. 1.

> Know you the quality of lord Timon's fury ?—
> *Push !* did you see my cap ?—*Timon*, iii. 6.

Affection ! *pooh !* you speak like a green girl.—*Hamlet*, i. 3.

The gods grant them true !—True ! *pow wow.*—*Coriol.*, ii. 1.

Tilly-fally, Sir John, never tell me.—*2 H. IV.*, ii. 4.

Am I not of her blood ? *Tilly-vally*, lady.—*Tw. N.*, ii. 3.

Tush ! I may as well say the fool's the fool.—*M. Ado*, iii. 3.

Tush, that's a wooden thing ! . . . *Tush*, women have been captivate ere now.— 1 *H. VI.*, v. 3.

Tush, my good lord, this superficial tale.—*Ibid.*, v. 5.

'Tis now near night.—*Tush !* I will stir about.—*R. & Jul.*, iv. 2.

Some misadventure.—*Tush !* thou art deceiv'd.—*Ibid.*, v. 1.

That they combine not there.—*Tush, tush !*—*Coriol.*, iii. 2.

Tush, tush, 'twill not appear.—*Hamlet*, i. 1.

Tut, a pin ! this shall be answered.—*Merry W.*, i. 1.

Tut, never fear me : I am as vigilant as.—*1 H. IV.*, iv. 2.

Tut ! I have the best armour of the world.—*H. V.*, iii. 7.

Tut ! that's a foolish observation.—*3 H. VI.*, ii. 6.

Tut, tut ! grace me no grace, nor uncle me.—*R. II.*, ii. 3.

Tut, tut ! here is a mannerly forbearance.—*1 H. VI.*, ii. 4.

Tut, tut, my lord, we will not stand to prate.—*R. III.*, i. 3.

In the following passage Shakespeare uses the English equivalent to the Italian exclamation, "Buona notte!" uttered to express a desperate resignation, when a cause or a game is lost :—

If he fall in, *good night !* or sink or swim.—*1 H. IV.*, i. 3.

He sometimes uses expressive interjections that denote particular moods of mind or condition of body :—

Tom's a-cold,—Oh, *do de, do de, do de* [to denote teeth chattering and shivering]. Bless thee from whirlwinds star-blasting, and taking !—*Lear*, iii. 4.

Dogs leap the hatch, and all are fled. *Do de, de, de.*—*Ibid.*, iii. 6.

Fe, fe, fe, fe ! [to denote heat and flurry]. Ma foi, il fait fort chaud. Je m'en vais à la cour.—*Merry W.*, i. 4.

Nay, an you get it, you shall get it by running. *Sa, sa, sa, sa,* [uttered by one running off].—*Ibid.*, iv. 6.

Sola, sola ! [shouted out by one excitedly running].—*Love's L. L.*, iv. 1.

Sola, sola ! wo ha, ho ! *sola, sola !*—Who calls ?—*Sola !* did you see Master Lorenzo and Mistress Lorenzo ? *Sola, sola !*—Leave hollaing, man : here.—*Sola !* where ? where ?—*Mer. of V.*, v. 1.

Sit down, Kate, and welcome. *Soud, soud, soud, soud !* [to denote fatigue, heat, and impatience. Shakespeare, like his great rival in comedy-writing, Molière, took the pains to invent and write down such kind of expressive interjections].—*Tam. of S.*, iv. 1.

In the following passage our dramatist has employed interjections descriptively, with excellent effect :—

He would manage you his piece thus : and he would about, and about, and come you in, and come you in : " *rah, tah, tah*," would he say ; " *bounce*," would he say ; and away again.—*2 H. IV.*, iii. 2.

Sometimes he gives interjections used avertively or deprecatingly :—

Ah, *let be, let be !* thou art the armourer of my heart.—*Ant. & C.*, iv. 4.

From the mire of this (*save reverence*) love.—*R. & Jul.*, i. 4.

And which gifts (*saving your mincing*) the capacity.—*H. VIII.*, ii. 3.

The fiend, who, *saving your reverence*, is the devil himself.—*Mer. of V.*, ii. 2.

Such a one as a man may not speak of, without he say *sir-reverence* [an old corrupted form of ' save reverence '].—*Com. of E.*, iii. 2.

To bring in (*God shield us !*) a lion among ladies.—*Mid. N. D.*, iii. 1.
God shield, you mean it not !—*All's W.*, i. 3.
God shield, I should disturb devotion !—*R. & Jul.*, iv. 1.

Sometimes he gives interjections used defiantly or mockingly :—

Do, do.—Thou stool for a witch !—Ay, *do, do ;* thou sodden-witted lord ! . . . *do,* rudeness ; *do,* camel ; *do, do.*—*Tr. & Cr.*, ii. 1.
Now the pledge ; *now, now, now.*—*Ibid.*, v. 2.
Thou hast a fine forehead.—Ay, *you may, you may.*—*Ibid.*, iii. 1.
You are never without your tricks: *you may, you may.*—*Coriol.*, ii. 3.

In the following passage he uses an interjection sarcastically :—

Still going ? *This is a lord !* O, noble misery, to be.—*Cym.*, v. 3.

Sometimes he uses an interjection insistingl :—

Ay, *good now*, love, love, nothing but love.—*Tr. & Cr.*, iii. 1.
Good now, sit down, and tell me.—*Hamlet*, i. 1.

Sometimes, dissentingly :—

Take good Cominius with thee. . . . *O the gods !*—*Coriol.*, iv. 1.

And sometimes, deprecatingly :—

Hadst thou foxship to banish him . . . *O blessed heavens !*—*Ibid.*, iv. 2.

PARADOXICAL PHRASEOLOGY.

There are some of Shakespeare's passages which are written with so much of paradox in their style, as to possess that startling effect of quaintness and almost humour, which characterises the " Irish bull." These passages occur in his serious as well as in his comic plays ; because the great dramatist well knew that the human mind, in its emotional moods—whether grave or gay—is apt to deal with, and even to express itself, in strained forms of whimsical idea and imagery :—

I *am gone*, though I *am here.*—*M. Ado*, iv. 1.
I must tell thee, sirrah, I write *man ; to which title age cannot bring thee.*—*All's W.*, ii. 3.
If thou 'lt see a thing *to talk on when thou art dead* and rotten, come hither.—*W. T.*, iii. 3.

> Great king, *within this coffin I present*
> *Thy buried fear.*—*R. II.*, v. 6.
> And *all thy friends—which thou must make thy friends—*
> Have but their stings and teeth newly ta'en out.—2 *H. IV.*, iv. 4.
> Their wounded steeds
> Fret fetlock deep in gore, and with wild rage
> Yerk out their armed heels at their dead masters,
> *Killing them twice.*—*H. V.*, iv. 7.
> Sword, I will hallow thee for this thy deed,
> And *hang* thee o'er my tomb when I am dead.*—2 *H. VI.*, iv. 10.
> And *dead men's cries do fill the empty air.*—*Ibid.*, v. 2.
> Well, lords, *we have not got that which we have.*—*Ibid.*, v. 3.
> Nor no one here ; for *curses never pass*
> *The lips of those that breathe them in the air.*—*R. III.*, i. 3.

---

* " And hang thee " is a boldly poetical ellipsis for ' And have thee hanged.'

Then, *taking him from thence that is not there,*
You break no privilege nor charter there.—*R. III.*, iii. 1.
Richard except, those whom we fight against
Had rather have us win than him they follow.—*Ibid.*, v. 3.

I do not know
What kind of my obedience I should tender ;
More than my all is nothing.—*H. VIII.*, ii. 3.

You shames of Rome ! you herd of—boils and plagues
Plaster you o'er ; *that you may be abhorr'd* *
Farther than seen, and one infect another
Against the wind a mile !—*Coriol.*, i. 4.

We have power in ourselves to do it, but it is a power that we have no power to do.—
Ibid., ii. 3.

Would I were hanged, but *I thought there was more in him than I could think.*—
Ibid., iv. 5.

I would not be a Roman, of all nations ; I had as lief be a condemned man.—
Ibid., iv. 5.

That we did, we did for the best ; and *though we willingly consented to his banishment*
yet it was against our will.—*Ibid.*, iv. 6.

She speaks, yet she says nothing : what of that ?
Her eye discourses, I will answer it.—*R. & Jul.*, ii. 2.
Thou know'st *the mask of night is on my face,*
Else would a maiden blush bepaint my cheek
For that which thou hast heard me speak to-night.—*Ibid.*, ii. 2.

At what o'clock *to-morrow*
Shall I send to thee ?—At the hour of nine.—
I will not fail : *'tis twenty years till then.*—*Ibid.*, ii. 2.
Now, *when the bridegroom in the morning comes*
To rouse thee from thy bed, *there art thou dead.*—*Ibid.*, iv. 1.

It tutors nature : artificial strife
Lives in these touches, *livelier than life.*—*Timon*, i. 1.

Leak'd is our bark ;
And we, poor mates, stand on *the dying deck,*
Hearing the surges threat : we must all part
Into this *sea of air.*—*Ibid.*, iv. 2.

If thou hadst not been born the worst of men,
Thou hadst been a knave and flatterer.—*Ibid.*, iv. 3.

Cowards *die many times before their deaths !*
The valiant never taste of death but once.—*Jul. C.*, ii. 2.

We are two lions *litter'd in one day,*
And *I the elder*† and more terrible.—*Ibid.*, ii. 2.

My thought, whose murder yet is but fantastical,
Shakes so my single state of man, that function
Is smother'd in surmise *;* and *nothing is*
But what is not.—*Macb.*, i. 3.

More is thy due than more than all can pay.—*Ibid.*, i. 4.

If it were done when 'tis done, then 'twere well
It were done quickly.—*Ibid.*, i. 7.

Father'd he is, and yet he's fatherless.—*Ibid.*, iv. 2.

The queen that bore thee
Oftener upon her knees than on her feet,
Died every day she liv'd.—*Ibid.*, iv. 3.

---

* Here " abhorr'd " is, with poetic licence, employed for 'smelt abhorringly.'
† For an explanation of Shakespeare's peculiar and inclusive mode of employing the word " elder," *See* ELDER, &c., and PECULIAR USE OF WORDS.

The poet adopted the foregoing expression from Scripture: "I protest by your rejoicing, which I have in Christ Jesus our Lord, *I die daily.*"—1. *Cor.*, xv. 31.

> What you have charg'd me with, that have I done;
> And more, much more; the time will bring it out:
> *'Tis past, and so am I.*—*Lear*, v. 3.
>
> *I must be cruel, only to be kind.*—*Hamlet*, iii. 4.
>
> Whip me such *honest knaves.*—*Oth.*, i. 1.
>
> For when my outward action doth demonstrate
> The native act and figure of my heart
> In compliment extern, 'tis not long after
> But I will wear my heart upon my sleeve
> For daws to peck at: *I am not what I am.*—*Ibid.*, i. 1.
>
> Her honour is an essence that's not seen;
> *They have it very oft, that have it not.*—*Ibid.*, iv. 1.
>
> Where is this rash and most unfortunate man?—
> *That's he that was Othello ;—here I am.*—*Ibid.*, v. 2.
>
> What our contempts do often hurl from us,
> We wish it ours again; the present pleasure,
> By revolution lowering, does become,
> The opposite of itself: *she's good, being gone.*—*Ant. & C.*, i. 2.
>
> I am his fortune's vassal, and *I send him*
> *The greatness he has got.*—*Ibid.*, v. 2.
>
> *Wherein I am false I am honest ; not true, to be true.*—*Cym.*, iv. 3.
>
> So I'll die
> For thee, O Imogen, even for whom *my life*
> *Is, every breath, a death.*—*Ibid.*, v. 1.
>
> O Imogen! *I'll speak to thee in silence.*—*Ibid.*, v. 4.
>
> What think you?—*The same dead thing alive.*—*Ibid.*, v. 5.
>
> By thine own tongue thou art condemn'd, and must
> Endure our law: *thou art dead.*—*Ibid.*, v. 5.
>
> Yon sometime famous princes, like thyself,
> Drawn by report, adventurous by desire,
> *Tell thee, with speechless tongues* and semblance pale,
> That, without covering, save yon field of stars,
> Here they stand martyrs, slain in Cupid's wars;
> And *with dead cheeks advise thee* to desist.—*Per.*, i. 1.
>
> Those that much covet are with gain so fond,
> *That what they have not, that which they possess,*
> *They scatter and unloose it from their bond,*
> And so, by hoping more, they have but less;
> Or, gaining more, the profit of excess
> Is but to surfeit, and such griefs sustain,
> That *they prove bankrupt in this poor-rich gain.*—*Lucrece, Stanza* 20.

PARAPHRASES.

Shakespeare occasionally uses a paraphrase, or a periphrastic form of expression. Sometimes seriously, with graceful effect; and sometimes playfully or humorously, with exaggerated effect :—

I with *the morning's love* ['Cephalus:' of whom Aurora was enamoured] have oft made sport.—*Mid. N. D.*, iii. 2.

> Holla your name to the reverberate hills,
> And make *the babbling gossip of the air* [' Echo']
> Cry out, Olivia !—*Tw. N.*, i. 5.

Fare ye well at once: my bosom is full of kindness; and I am yet *so near the manners of my mother* [' so nearly betrayed into shedding womanish tears'] that, upon the least occasion more, mine eyes will tell tales of me.—*Ibid.*, ii. 1.

And *all my mother came into mine eyes* [' all the womanly emotion in my nature sprang to mine eyes'], and gave me up to tears.—*H. V.*, iv. 6.

And embraced, as it were, from *the ends of opposed winds* [' the quarters whence the four winds blow,' ' east to west, north to south,' ' opposite regions'].—*W. T.*, i. 1.

And my name yok'd with *his that did betray the Best !* [' Judas Iscariot's'].—*Ibid.*, i. 2.

And stop this *gap of breath* [' mouth '] with fulsome dust.—*John*, iii. 4.

Now, now, you *stars that move in your right spheres* [' nobles who revolted, but have now returned to your allegiance '].—*Ibid.*, v. 7.

> His face thou hast, for even so look'd he,
> *Accomplish'd with the number of thy hours* [' when he was of thy age '].—*R. II.*, ii. 1.

> Ten thousand bloody crowns of mothers' sons
> Shall ill become *the flower of England's face* [' the flowery face of England's soil : ' including the idea of the ' flower of England's youth,' ' the finest and choicest young men of England '].—*Ibid.*, iii. 3.

> I can speak English, lord, as well as you ;
> For I was train'd up in the English court;
> Where, being but young, I framed to the harp
> Many an English ditty, lovely well,
> And *gave the tongue a helpful ornament* [' gave the language the aiding ornament of versification,' by writing poetry].—1 *H. IV.*, iii. 1.

I understand thy looks: *that pretty Welsh* [' those speaking tears'] which thou pour'st down from *these swelling heavens* [' these blue eyes swollen with weeping '] I am too perfect in.—*Ibid.*, iii. 1.

> They come like sacrifices in their trim,
> And to *the fire-ey'd maid of smoky war* [' the goddess Bellona'], all hot and bleeding, will we offer them.—*Ibid.*, iv. 2.

Though *it discolours the complexion of my greatness* [' it makes my princehood blush '] to acknowledge it.—2 *H. IV.*, ii. 2.

And the examples *of every minute's instance* [' that every minute produces or brings forth '].—*Ibid.*, iv. 1.

And consecrate *commotion's bitter edge* [' the sword of bitter contention and rebellion '].—*Ibid.*, iv. 1.

And I, in the clear sky of fame, o'ershine you as much as the full moon doth *the cinders of the element* [' the stars '], which show like pins' heads to her.—*Ibid.*, iv. 3.

> Nay, more, to spurn at your most royal image,
> And *mock your workings in a second body* [' set at naught your decrees as carried out in the person of a deputed representative '].—*Ibid.*, v. 2.

Go, *clear thy crystals* [' dry thine eyes '].—*H. V.*, ii. 3.

Say, if my father *render fair return* [' send back a favourable answer '], it is against my will.—*Ibid.*, ii. 4.

Thus with *imagin'd wing* [' the wing of imagination '] our swift scene flies in motion of no less celerity than that of thought.—*Ibid.*, iii. (*Chorus*).

Bring them, I pray thee, with *imagin'd speed* [' the speed of imagination '] unto the Tranect, to the common ferry.—*Mer. of V.*, iii. 4.

> Small time, but, in that small, most greatly liv'd
> *This star of England* [' Henry V.'].—*H. V.*, v. 2 (*Chorus*).

> And stood against them as *the hope of Troy* [' Hector ']
> Against the Greeks that would have enter'd Troy.—3 *H. VI.*, ii. 1.

I pass'd, methought, *the melancholy flood* ['the river Styx']
With *that grim ferry-man* ['Charon'] which poets write of,
Unto the kingdom of perpetual night.—*R. III.*, i. 4.

Why, then *the thing of courage* ['the tiger'], as rous'd with rage, with rage doth sympathise.—*Tr. & Cr.*, i. 3.

For that will physic *the great Myrmidon* ['Achilles'].—*Ibid.*, i. 3.

Come, *draw this curtain, and let's see your picture* ['put back your veil, and let us behold your face'].—*Ibid.*, iii. 2.

But we will *draw the curtain, and show you the picture* ['put back my veil, and let you see my face'].—*Tw. N.*, i. 5.

By all *Diana's waiting-women* ['the stars, attendant upon the crescent moon'] yond', and by herself.—*Tr. & Cr.*, v. 2.

When with his *Amazonian chin* ['chin with no more beard upon it than an Amazon's chin,' 'unbearded chin'] he drove the bristled lips before him.—*Coriol.*, ii. 2.

Here I clip *the anvil of my sword* ['that body upon which I have heretofore laid as heavy blows as those which a smith lays upon an anvil']; and do contest as hotly.— *Ibid.*, iv. 5.

Now, by *the jealous queen of heaven* ['Juno'], that kiss I carried from thee, dear.— *Ibid.*, v. 3.

Turn back, *dull earth* ['the earthly part of me,' 'my body,' 'the corporeal and material portion of me'], and find thy centre out.—*R. & Jul.*, ii. 1.

> O blessed breeding sun, draw from the earth
> Rotten humidity; below *thy sister's orb* ['the moon']
> Infect the air !—*Timon*, iv. 3.

And, but in the plainer and simpler kind of people, *the deed of saying* ['the fulfilment of protestation'] is quite out of use.—*Ibid.*, v. 1.

Till that *Bellona's bridegroom* ['Macbeth ; worthy to be matched with the goddess of war'], *lapp'd in proof* ['incased in armour of proof'], *confronted him with self-comparisons* ['met him with competitive strokes equal to his own'].—*Macb.*, i. 2.

> The wind-shak'd surge, with high and monstrous mane,
> Seems to cast water on *the burning bear* ['the Great Bear constellation'],
> And quench *the guards of th' ever-fixed pole* ['the star Arctophylax, guarding the polar or North Star and the Great Bear'].—*Oth.*, ii. 1.

Even then *this forked plague* ['this penalty of horns'] is fated to us when we do quicken.—*Ibid.*, iii. 3.

Now canopied under these *windows* ['eyelids,' 'eyes,' 'casements'], white and azure, lac'd with blue of heaven's own tinct.—*Cym.*, ii. 2.

> The roses in thy lips and cheeks shall fade
> To paly ashes; thy *eyes' windows* ['eyelids'] fall.—*R. & Jul.*, iv. 1.

And makes *Diana's rangers* ['virgin ladies'] false themselves.—*Cym.*, ii. 3.

> This *mortal house* ['body,' 'perishable frame'] I'll ruin,
> Do Cæsar what he can.—*Ant. & C.*, v. 2.

He bears a tempest, which his *mortal vessel* ['his frail body'] tears, and yet he rides it out.—*Per.*, v. 4 (*Gower*).

Celestial Dian, *goddess argentine* ['deity of the silver moon'] I will obey thee.— *Ibid.*, v. 2.

PARENTHESES.

It is noteworthy that Shakespeare's parentheses are frequently of very condensed significance, containing much earnestness and wisdom put into extremely small space :—

> If powers divine
> Behold our human actions (*as they do*),
> I doubt not then, but innocence shall make
> False accusation blush.—*W. T.*, iii. 2.

Force should be right ; or rather, right and wrong
(*Between whose endless jar justice resides*)
Should lose their names, and so should justice too.—*Tr. & Cr.*, i. 3.

Rashly (*and prais'd be rashness for it : let us know,
Our indiscretion sometimes serves us well,
When our deep plots do pall : and that should teach us
There 's a divinity that shapes our ends,
Rough-hew them how we will.—That is most certain.—*)
Up from my cabin,
My sea-gown scarf'd about me, in the dark
Groped I to find out them : had my desire.—*Hamlet*, v. 2.

Led him, begg'd for him, sav'd him from despair ;
Never (*O fault !*) revealed myself unto him.—*Lear*, v. 3.

But when we in our viciousness grow hard
(*Oh, misery on 't !*), the wise gods seel our eyes.—*Ant. & C.*, iii. 11.

                You do seem to know
Something of me, or what concerns me : pray you
(*Since doubting things go ill often hurts more
Than to be sure they do ; for certainties
Either are past remedies, or, timely knowing,
The remedy then born*) discover to me
What both you spur and stop.—*Cym.*, i. 7.

How should I be reveng'd ? If this be true—
*As I have such a heart that both mine ears
Must not in haste abuse*—if it be true,
How should I be reveng'd ?—*Ibid.*, i. 7.

Shakespeare occasionally uses a peculiar form of construction in a parenthetical sentence ; so that the parenthesis is much intermingled with the context :—

              Have not you seen, Camillo
(But that 's past doubt—you have, or your eye-glass
Is thicker than a cuckold's horn), or heard
(For, to a vision so apparent, rumour
Cannot be mute), or thought (for cogitation
Resides not in that man *that does not think*),
My wife is slippery ?—*W. T.*, i. 2.

No more such wives : therefore, no wife : one worse,
And better us'd, would make her sainted spirit
Again possess her corse, and *on this stage*
(Where we offenders now *appear*), soul-vex'd,
Begin, " And why to me ? "—*Ibid.*, v. 1.

In the above passage the First Folio prints ' And begin ' instead of " Begin, And ; " which is Capell's correction, adopted by Steevens and others. We have also adopted it as being probable ; but we by no means feel sure that, after all, the right reading in this speech is attained.

If you 'll bestow *a small* (*of what you have little*) patience awhile, you 'll hear the belly's answer.—*Coriol.*, i. 1.

' Amount ' is elliptically understood after " small," and " of " is understood as repeated after " little."

PARTICULAR NAMES.

There are two names, a man's name and a woman's name, which have always struck us as revealing something of Shakespeare's own life-history, since he has twice employed each; and, in both instances, he has given the particular name to a particular kind of character. In the first instance, he has given the name " Antonio " to the *generous and devoted friend* of Bassanio in the " Merchant of Venice "; and also to the enthusiastic sea-captain who is the *generous and devoted friend* of Sebastian in " Twelfth Night." [*See* APPRECIATION OF FRIENDSHIP, &c.] Antonio the royal merchant, in his worshipping attachment to the young lord Bassanio, and Antonio the noble-natured sea-captain, in his self-dedication to the patrician youth Sebastian, appear to us to mirror Shakespeare's own adoring sentiment towards the unnamed object of his friendship in the " Sonnets." Both these impersonations of manly fondness for an idolised young friend—both these embodiments of modest merit merging itself into passionate admiration of a chosen ideal—both these dramatic characters, named alike " Antonio," have long impressed us as being creations wherein the author put himself and his own strength of affection into delineated form. In the second instance, he has given the name " Rosaline " to the brilliant-complexioned beauty with dark eyes and hair in " Love's Labour's Lost "; and to the brilliant-complexioned beauty with dark eyes and hair in " Romeo and Juliet ": while both these " Rosalines " bear strong resemblance to the unnamed brilliant-complexioned beauty with dark eyes and hair who figures in the Sonnets. The following passages, thus brought together under one view, will serve to manifest the evident points of similitude :—

> A *whitely** wanton with a *velvet brow*,
> With *two pitch balls* stuck in her face *for eyes.—Love's L. L.*, iii. 1.

> By heaven, thy love is *black as ebony.*—
> Is *ebony like her?* oh, wood divine. . . .
> No face is fair that is not full *so black.* . . .
> Devils soonest tempt, resembling spirits of light.
> Oh, *if in black my lady's brows be deckt*,
> It *mourns* that painting and usurping hair
> Should ravish doters with a false aspect!
> And therefore is she born *to make black fair.*
> Her favour turns the fashions of the days,
> For native blood is counted painting now;
> And therefore red, that would avoid dispraise,
> Paints itself *black, to imitate her brow.* . . .—*Ibid.*, iv. 3.
> I 'll prove her fair, or talk till doomsday here.—*Ibid.*, iv. 3.

> Ah! that same *pale hard-hearted* wench,† that Rosaline,
> Torments him so, that he will sure run mad. . . .

Alas! poor Romeo, he is already dead! stabbed with *a white wench's black eye.*†— *R. & Jul.*, ii. 4.

---

* This word (misprinted ' whitly' in the Folio) appears to us to be the very epithet to express a complexion that looks *fair*, almost *white*, and certainly *dazzling*, in contrast with black eyes, eyebrows, eyelashes, and hair.

† This conjunction of " pale " and " white " with " black," appears to us to be in unison with the word " whitely " conjunctively with " velvet " and " pitch," previously. Epithets of seeming disparagement; but, thus combined, implying beautiful contrast.

In the old age *black* was not counted fair,
Or if it were, it bore not beauty's name;
But *now is black beauty's successive heir.* . . .
Therefore *my mistress' eyes are raven black ;*
Her eyes so suited, as they mourners seem
At such, who, not born fair, no beauty lack,
Slandering creation with a false esteem :
Yet *so they mourn, becoming of their woe,*
That every tongue says, beauty should look so.—Sonnet 127.
If hairs be wires, *black* wires grow on her head. . . .
And yet, by heaven, *I think my love as rare*
As any she belied with false compare.—*Ibid.* 130.
Thy black is fairest in my judgment's place.—*Ibid.* 131.
Thine eyes I love, and they, as pitying me,
Knowing thy heart torments me with disdain,
Have put on *black*, and *loving mourners be*,
Looking with pretty ruth upon my pain.
And truly not the morning sun of heaven
Better becomes the grey cheeks of the east,
Nor that full star that ushers in the even
Doth half that glory to the sober west,
As *those two mourning eyes become thy face :*
O, let it, then, as well beseem thy heart
To mourn for me, *since mourning doth thee grace*,
And suit thy pity like in every part.
Then will I swear beauty herself is black,
And all they foul that thy complexion lack.—*Ibid.* 132.

The name, " Falstaff," now indelibly associated with all that is most witty, most humorous, most epicurean, and most irresistibly pleasant in dramatic delineation, was not the name originally bestowed by Shakespeare on Prince Hal's companion, the fat knight who figures in the " Merry Wives," in the First and Second Parts of " King Henry IV.," and (by mention) in " King Henry V." There exists internal evidence that the character was first called by its author " Sir John Oldcastle " ; but as that was the name of a heroic martyr known to history, Shakespeare renamed his immortal creation, and called him " Sir John Falstaff." See the introductory notes to the First and Second Parts of " King Henry IV.," and notes 41, i., and 94, v., to the " Second Part of King Henry IV." in our "Annotated Edition of Shakespeare," published by Messrs. Cassell and Co., for the details of this evidence. We have some idea that as one of the characteristics of " Sir John Falstaff " is a luxurious regard to his own safety, almost amounting to lack of bravery, the author may have fabricated this name from that of " Sir John *Fastolfe*," the recreant knight in the " First Part of King Henry VI."—a notorious coward.

In the invention of several names given to certain of his men characters, Shakespeare has imparted significant effect to their respective appropriation :—

Sir Andrew Ague-cheek [the lank-witted knight in]—*Tw. N.*
Abhorson [the prison hangman and executioner in]—*M. for M.*
Ariel [the aerial and airy sprite in]—*Temp.*
Autolycus [the mercurial-natured and Mercury-propensitied rogue in]—*W. T.*
Sir Toby Belch [the burly toper in]—*Tw. N.*
Borachio [the dissolute ' wine-skin ' of a fellow in]—*M. Ado.*

Young Charbon the Puritan and old Poysam the Papist [the first the French word for ' coal ' or ' charcoal,' in allusion to the eternal fires with which the Puritan preachers menaced their hearers; the second, a corruption of the French word *poisson*, in allusion to the fish eaten by Papists on fast-days].—*All's W.*, i. 3.

Costard [the ruddy apple-faced and round apple-headed rustic in]—*Love's L. L.*

Dogberry [the officer of the watch who has " always been called a merciful man ; " but who deems himself an exemplar of legal severity : to whom Shakespeare has given one of the names of the cornelian cherry-tree, the fruit of which is remarkably austere ; and who figures in]—*M. Ado.*

Dull [the doltish constable in]—*Love's L. L.*

Feste [the festive-spirited jester in]—*Tw. N.*

Froth [the empty-headed " foolish gentleman " in]—*M for M.*

Gadshill [the highwayman on the famous road near Rochester in]—1 *H. IV.*

Old Gobbo [the blind old hobbler, probably intended to be also a ' hunchback,' as this Italian name implies, in]—*Mer. of V.*

Did not goodwife *Keech* [a lump of fat rolled up by butchers ready for the chandlers], the butcher's wife, come in.—2 *H. IV.*, ii. 1.

Lafeu [the fiery old French nobleman in]—*All's W.*

Lavatch [probably a corruption of the French word *lavage*, a familiar term for ' slop,' ' puddle,' ' washiness ': the muddy-principled Clown who has " no mind to Isbel " since he was at court, who stops his nose when accosted by one who has been " muddied in fortune's mood," and who figures in]—*Ibid.*

Le Beau [the fine-gentleman courtier in]—*As You L.*

Marcus Luccicos* [the Greek soldier of Cyprus, or Estradiot, inquired for by the Duke in]—*Oth.*, i. 3.

Malvolio [the ill-willed steward, " sick of self-love," in]—*Tw. N.*

Moth [the little page who flutters round that tall tallow-candle and shining light of fantasticalness, his master, Don Adriano de Armado, in]—*Love's L. L.*

Neighbour Mugs [the yawning First Carrier who, by his " an 't were not as good a deed as drink," is fond of lingering over his mug of ale, and who pudders about the inn yard in]—1 *H. IV.*

Nym [the pickpocket " coney-catching rascal " in]—*M. W.* and *H. V.*

Oswald [a name of Saxon origin, signifying ' house-ruler,' or ' major-domo ' ; and given to the feudally faithful steward of Goneril, in]—*Lear.*

Parolles [the wordy braggart in]—*All's W.*

Pinch [the schoolmaster and conjuror, described as " a hungry, lean-fac'd villain, a mere anatomy . . . a needy, hollow-ey'd, sharp-looking wretch, a living dead man," in]—*Com of E.*, v. 1.

Pistol [the ever-recoiling, sharp-snapping, noisy swaggerer, in]—*M. W.*, 1 and 2 *H. IV.*, and *H. V.*

Proteus [the fickle, unstable, changeable lover in]—*Two G. of V.*

Puff of Barson [puffed off by Silence, as greater than " one of the greatest men in the realm," in]—2 *H. IV.*, v. 3.

Shallow [the un-deep justice, believing himself to be of unfathomable profundity, in] —*Merry W.* and 2 *H. IV.*

Silence [the taciturn justice, prone admirer of Shallow, in]—2 *H. IV.*

Slender [limp and attenuated worshipper of his " Cousin Shallow " and of " sweet Anne Page," in]—*Merry W.*

Simple [the simpleton servant to simpleton Master Slender, in]—*Ibid.*

Sly [the cunning tinker, who shirks paying his reckoning, and sticks fast to " a pot of small ale," in]—*Tam. of S. (Induc.)*

Master Surecard [for whom Sir John Falstaff mistakes Master Silence].— 2 *H. IV.*, iii. 2.

---

* This is the form of name given by both Folio and Quarto edition of our poet; though Capell and others alter it to ' Lucchese.'

Touchstone [the faithful cheerful-hearted jester, whose attachment is tested by following his lady mistress into exile].—*As You L.*

Verges [a corruption of 'verjuice,' which is made from crab-apples : "a good old man," and "honest as the skin between his brows " ; but who fancies he emulates his " partner," Dogberry in official austerity and crabbedness, and clinches his hardest-to-swallow assertions of being " the malefactors," &c., with a sapless " Nay, that's certain "].—*M. Ado.*

Shakespeare has also given some expressive names to some of his women characters :—

Cordelia [the cordial daughter of the wilful and ill-used old king ; who hoards in her heart her filial love, till she pours it forth in the hour of her father's distress].—*Lear.*

Diana [the chaste evader of Bertram's illicit suit].—*All's W.*

Marina [the princess " born at sea "].—*Per.*

Miranda [the " admired " of Prince Ferdinand].—*Temp.*

Patience [the gentle waiting-gentlewoman of Queen Katharine].—*H. VIII.*

Perdita [the " lost " daughter of Leontes and Hermione].—*W. T.*

Viola [the sweet lady in page's weeds, like the modest violet lurking beneath the hedge-side grass and wild-flowers.]—*Tw. N.*

Jane Nightwork [the flaunting " bona-roba," who " heard the chimes at midnight " with Falstaff and Shallow " in the Windmill in Saint George's Fields "].—*2 H. IV.*

Mistress Overdone [the old hardworker in loathliest trade].—*M. for M.*

Hostess Quickly [the active landlady of the Boar's Head tavern in Eastcheap].—*1* and *2 H. IV.* and *H. V.*

Mistress Quickly [the pottering busy-body of Windsor; probably the spinster sister of Hostess Quickly].—*Merry W.*

Doll Tear-sheet [the rantipole companion of Sir John Falstaff and his associates].—*2 H. IV.*

The dramatist has given several groups of characteristic names :—

Here 's young Master *Rash.* . . . Then is there here one Master *Caper*, at the suit of Master *Three-pile* the mercer. . . . Young *Dizzy*, and young Master *Deep-vow*, and Master *Copper-spur*, and Master *Starve-lackey* . . . and young *Drop-heir* that killed lusty *Pudding*, and Master *Forthright* the tilter and brave Master *Shoe-tie* the great traveller, and wild *Half-can* that stabbed *Pots* [the set of lawless young scamps and scapegraces met by the Clown in prison].—*M. for M.*, iv. 3.

Peter Quince, the carpenter ; *Snug*, the joiner ; *Nick Bottom*, the weaver ; *Francis Flute*, the bellow's-mender ; *Tom Snout*, the tinker ; *Robin Starveling*, the tailor [the "hempen-homespuns," the " rude-mechanicals " who enact the interlude before Duke Theseus and his court].—*Mid. N. D.*

Peas-blossom, *Cobweb*, *Moth*, and *Mustard-seed* [the fairy-attendants upon Queen Titania].—*Ibid.*

Fang and *Snare* [the sheriffs' officers in]—*2 H. IV.*

Little *John Doit* of Staffordshire, and *black George Bare*, and *Francis Pickbone*, and *Will Squele*, a Cotswold man,—you had not four such swinge-bucklers in all the inns of court again [the four riotous provincial associates of Master Shallow in his mad metropolitan career of former London days].—*2 H. IV.*, iii. 2.

Mouldy, *Shadow*, *Wart*, *Feeble* and *Bull-calf* [the raw recruits provided by Justice Shallow for selection by Falstaff].—*Ibid.*

Simon Catling, *Hugh Rebeck*, and *James Soundpost* [" the musicians " bantered by Peter. *See* MUSICAL TERMS].—*R. & Jul.*, iv. 5.

Shakespeare has some dramatically adopted names :—

Aliena [the name adopted by Princess Celia, when she goes with her cousin into exile, voluntarily alienating herself from her father].—*As You L.*, i. 3.

Cesario [the name adopted by Viola, when passing as a youth].—*Tw. N.*, i. 4.

Richard du Champ [the name given by Imogen to her supposed dead master].—
Cym., iv. 2.

Fidele [the name given by Imogen as her own, when she is met by Belarius and her brothers, disguised as a boy, in their cave].—*Ibid.*, iii. 6.

Ganymede [the name assumed by Rosalind when going into exile, dressed as a young lad].—*As You L.*, i, 3.

Lodowick [the name taken by Duke Vincentio, when he is in the garb of a friar].—*M. for M.*, v. 1.

Roderigo [the name temporarily assumed by Sebastian after shipwreck].—*Tw. N.*, ii. 1.

Sebastian [the name under which Julia engages herself to Proteus as his page].—*Two G. of V.*, iv. 4.

Sir Topas [the name adopted by Feste the clown, when he presents himself to Malvolio as the curate fetched to visit the steward in his imputed madness. There is peculiar propriety in this name ; inasmuch as among the alleged properties of precious stones, the *topaz* was believed to possess the virtue of curing insanity].—*Tw. N.*, iv. 2.

In the following instance, Shakespeare uses the same name for two different personages in one play ; for a suitor of Julia in Verona, and for the faithful friend of Silvia in Milan :—

What think'st thou of the fair *Sir Eglamour ?*—*Two G. of V.*, i. 2.

Sir Eglamour, a thousand times good morrow.—*Ibid.*, iv. 3.

In the following instance, Shakespeare gave duplicate names, Antipholus and Dromio, to the two pair of twins, for the sake of the dramatic *équivoque* maintained throughout the play ; but the passages here quoted impart naturalness to the circumstance by showing that originally the four boys had some distinguishing appellation, though subsequently one of each pair of twins, in remembrance of his lost brother, takes his name :—

A joyful mother of two goodly sons ;
And, which was strange, the one so like the other,
As *could not be distinguish'd but by names.*—*Com. of E.*, i. 1.
That his attendant—for his case was like,
Reft of his brother, but retain'd his name—
Might bear him company in the quest of him.—*Ibid.*, i. 1.

In two plays, Shakespeare has made use of a name slightly varied :—

What think'st thou of the rich *Mercatio ?*—*Two G. of V.*, i. 2.

Peace, peace, *Mercutio*, peace!—*R. & Jul.*, i. 4.

And in two plays, he has used the same name (according to Italian wont) as a man's name and as a woman's name :—

Signior Baptista, will you be so strange ?—*Tam. of S.*, i. 1.

Gonzago is the duke's name ; *his wife, Baptista.*—*Hamlet*, iii. 2.

He has used four names apparently in remembrance of old familiar Stratford-on-Avon names :—

Here comes fair Mistress *Anne* [the name of one of the poet's sisters as well as of his wife].—*Merry W.*, i. 1.

Come apace, good *Audrey :** I will fetch up your goats, *Audrey*. And how, *Audrey ?* Am I the man yet?—*As You L.*, iii. 3.

*Bardolph.**—*Merry W.*, 1 and 2 *H. IV.*, *H. V.*

Captain *Fluellen,** you must come presently.—*Hen. V.*, iii. 2.

---

* All these three names have been ascertained to have belonged to neighbours in Shakespeare's native town.

He uses some familiar forms of Christian names [*See* VARIATIONS]:—

For *Dickon* [Richard] thy master is bought and sold—*R. III.*, v. 3 (*Scroll*).
Jockey [John] of Norfolk, be not too bold.—*Ibid.*, v. 3 (*Scroll*).
Wilt thou not, *Jule* [Juliet]?—*R. & Jul.*, i. 3.
It is such another *Nan* [Anne].—*Merry W.*, i. 4.

He uses some common names to express generalisation ; "the usual run of men or women," or 'just such kind of people':—

> Some mumble-news, some trencher-knight, some *Dick*,
> That smiles his cheek in years.—*Love's L. L.*, v. 2.
> To beg of *Hob* and *Dick*, that do appear,
> Their needless vouches ?—*Coriol.*, ii. 3.
> Since every *Jack* became a gentleman,
> There 's many a gentle person made a *Jack*.—*R. III.*, i. 3.
> Our wooing doth not end like an old play ;
> *Jack* hath not *Jill*.—*Love's L. L.*, v. 2.

Be the *Jacks* fair within, the *Jills* fair without.—*Tam. of S.*, iv. 1.
Some men must love my lady, and some *Joan*.—*Love's L. L.*, iii. 1.
Well, now can I make any *Joan* a lady.—*John*, i. 1.
As *Tib's* rush for *Tom's* forefinger.—*All's W.*, ii. 2.

In several passages Shakespeare denotes the then custom of using "Jack" as an expression of contempt :—

Little better than played the *Jack* with us.—*Temp.*, iv. 1.
By gar, I will kill de *Jack* priest.—*Merry W.*, i. 4.
He is de coward *Jack* priest of de vorld.—*Ibid.*, ii. 3.
Or do you play the flouting *Jack*, to tell us.—*M. Ado*, i. 1.
She did call me rascal fiddler, and twangling *Jack*.—*Tam. of S.*, ii. 1.
A mad-cap ruffian, and a swearing *Jack*.—*Ibid.*, ii. 1.
Tell me flatly I am no proud *Jack*, like Falstaff.—1 *H. IV.*, ii. 4.
The prince is a *Jack*, a sneak-cup.—*Ibid.*, iii. 3.
If I be not Jack Falstaff, then am I a *Jack*.—*Ibid.*, v. 4.
Abus'd by silken, sly, insinuating *Jacks*.—*R. III.*, i. 3.
Lustier than he is, and twenty such *Jacks*.—*R. & Jul.*, ii. 4.

In the following passages Shakespeare has recorded the custom that prevailed in his time of giving particular names to particular houses, especially houses of entertainment and houses of commerce :—

Go bear it to *the Centaur*, where we host.—*Com. of E.*, i. 2.
Home to your house, *the Phœnix*, sir, to dinner.—*Ibid.*, i. 2.
Bring it, I pray you, to *the Porcupine ;* for there 's the house.—*Ibid.*, iii. 1.
And let us to *the Tiger* all to dinner.—*Ibid.*, iii. 1.
In Genoa, where we were lodgers at *the Pegasus*.—*Tam. of S.*, iv. 4.
> Where do the palmers lodge, I do beseech you ?—
> At *the Saint Francis* here, beside the port.—*All's W.*, iii. 5.
At *the Elephant*, is best to lodge. . . . To *the Elephant*.—*Tw. N.*, iii. 3.
The duke being at *the Rose*, within the parish St. Laurence, Poultry.—*H. VIII.*, i. 2.
Lead to the Sagittary* the raised search.—*Oth.*, i. 1.

---

* It has been supposed by some commentators that an inn is here meant; and by another (Mr. Charles Knight) that an official residence at the Venetian arsenal is meant. But, inasmuch as Cassio's question, "What makes he here?" shows that it is neither Othello's own "lodging" nor his usual military quarters, and moreover that the senate send "several quests" in search of him, we believe "the Sagittary" to be

He has also noted the custom which formerly prevailed of giving particular names to particular rooms, especially in taverns or houses of public entertainment ; and which custom lasted even to as late a period as Goldsmith's time, who, in his pleasant comedy of " She Stoops to Conquer," makes his heroine, when impersonating a barmaid, exclaim, " attend *the Lion* there ; pipes and tobacco for *the Angel ; the Lamb* has been outrageous this half-hour " :—

'Twas in *the Bunch of Grapes*, where, indeed, you have a delight to sit, have you not ?—I have so, because it is an open room, and good for winter.—*M. for M.*, ii. 1.

Score a pint of bastard in *the Half Moon*. . . . Look down into *the Pomegranate*, Ralph.—1 *H. IV.*, ii. 4.

Sitting in my *Dolphin*-chamber.—2 *H. IV.*, ii. 1.

He has given particular names of pirates ; the first being that of a Ragusan vessel (called a " Ragozine," from the island of Ragusa, or Ragosa) ; the second having possibly been suggested by the fact that Don Pedro de Valdes was an admiral in the fleet of the Spanish Armada ; the dramatist thinking that to assign this hostile admiral's name to a " pirate," was likely to prove a popular point with an Elizabethan audience :—

One *Ragozine*, a most notorious pirate.—*M. for M.*, iv. 3.

These roguing thieves serve the great pirate *Valdes*.—*Per.*, iv. 2.

He has given particular names of ships ; the first in the following list, being an Italian vessel, it is well named in honour of the great Genoese admiral, *Andrea* Doria :—

And see my wealthy *Andrew* dock'd in sand.—*Mer. of V.*, i. 1.

The *Antoniad*, the Egyptian admiral, with all their sixty, fly.—*Ant. & C.*, iii. 8.

That *the bark Expedition* put forth to-night; and then were you hindered by the sergeant, to tarry for *the hoy Delay*.—*Com. of E.*, iv. 3.

That took the *Phœnix* and her fraught from Candy ;
And this is he that did the *Tiger* board.—*Tw. N.*, v. 1.

Her husband 's to Aleppo gone, master o' the *Tiger*.*— *Macb.*, i. 3.

'Faith, he to-night hath boarded a land *carrack*.—*Oth.*, i. 2.

Who sent whole armadas of *carracks* to be ballast at.—*Com. of E.*, iii. 2.

The ooze, to show what coast thy sluggish *crare*
Might easiliest harbour in ?—*Cym.*, iv. 2.

Than three great *argosies ;* besides two *galliasses*,
And twelve tight *galleys*.—*Tam. of S.*, ii. 1.

He hath an *argosy* bound to Tripolis, another to the Indies.—*Mer. of V.*, i. 3.

The ship is here put in, a *Veronessa*.—*Oth.*, ii. 1.

Particular names of horses :—

When Bolingbroke rode on *roan Barbary*.—*R. II.*, v. 5.

---

some newly taken house, bearing the classical name and sign of a certain fabulous beast, described in Caxton's " History of the Destruction of Troy," as being half horse, half man, with " eyen red as a cole, and shotte well with a bowe." That Othello subsequently says to Iago :—" Ancient, conduct them ; *you best know the place*," confirms our idea that the dramatist intended it as some secluded residence to which the Moorish general had conveyed his lately made bride, and that its whereabouts was known only to himself and to his trusted officer, the supposed " honest Iago."

* Sir W. C. Trevelyan has pointed out that in " Hakluyt's Voyages " there are several letters and journals of a voyage made to *Aleppo* in the ship *Tiger*, of London, in the year 1583.

Let him let the matter slip, and I 'll give him my horse, *grey Capilet.**—*Tw. N.*, iii. 4.
I 'd give *bay Curtal* and his furniture.—*All's W.*, ii. 2.
I pr'ythee, Tom, beat *Cut's* saddle, put a few.—1 *H. IV.*, ii. 1.
Than *Dobbin* my phill-horse has on his tail.—*Mer. of V.*, ii. 2.
Now here he fights on *Galathe* his horse.—*Tr. & Cr.*, v. 5.
Saddle *White Surrey* for the field to-morrow.—*R. III.*, v. 3.

Particular names of dogs :—

He will spend his mouth, and promise, like *Brabbler* the hound.—*Tr. & Cr.*, v. 1.
I had rather hear *Lady*, my *brach*, howl.—1 *H. IV.*, iii. 1.
When *Lady*, the *brach*, may stand by the fire and stink.—*Lear*, i. 4.

> Huntsman, I charge thee, tender well my hounds :
> Trash *Merriman*—the poor cur is emboss'd ;
> And couple *Clowder* with the deep-mouth'd *brach*.
> Saw'st thou not how *Silver* made it good
> At the hedge-corner, in the coldest fault?
> I would not lose the dog for twenty pound.—
> Why, *Belman* is as good as he, my lord . . .
> . . . if *Echo* were as fleet.—*Tam. of S.*, *Induc.* 1.

Sowter will cry upon 't, for all this.—*Tw. N.*, ii. 5.

> The little dogs and all,
> *Tray*, *Blanch*, and *Sweet-heart*, see, they bark at me.—*Lear*, iii. 6.

Where 's my spaniel *Troilus* ?—*Tam. of S.*, iv. 1.
Hope is a *curtail-dog* in some affairs.—*Merry W.*, ii. 1.
She had transformed me to a *curtail-dog*, and made me turn i' the wheel.—*Com. of E.*, iii. 2.

> *Mastiff*, *greyhound*, *mongrel* grim,
> *Hound* or *spaniel*, *brach* or *lym*,
> Or *bobtail tike*, or *trundle-tail*.—*Lear*, iii. 6.

> As *hounds*, *greyhounds*, *mongrels*, *spaniels*, *curs*,
> *Shoughs*, *water-rugs*, and demi-wolves are cleped
> All by the name of dogs.—*Macb.*, iii. 1.

Particular names for cats :—

I am as melancholy as a *gib* cat, or a lugged bear.—1 *H. IV.*, i. 2.
From a bat, a *gib*, such dear concernings hide ?—*Hamlet*, iii. 4.
I come, *Graymalkin !*—*Macb.*, i. 1.

> Why, what is *Tybalt ?*—More than prince of cats,
> I can tell you.—*R. & Jul.*, ii. 4.

Particular names for birds :—

I hear the strain of strutting *chanticleer*.—*Temp.*, i. 2 (*Song*).
My lungs began to crow like *chanticleer*.—*As You L.*, ii. 7.

> Another way I have to man my *haggard*,
> To make her come, and know her keeper's call;
> That is, to watch her, as we watch these *kites*
> That bate, and beat, and will not be obedient.—*Tam. of S.*, iv. 1.

Not, like the *haggard*, check at every feather.—*Tw. N.*, iii. 1.
As coy and wild as *haggards* of the rock.—*M. Ado*, iii. 1.

> And, ten to one, *old Joan* had not gone out.—
> But what a point, my lord, your falcon made,
> And what a pitch she flew above the rest !—2 *H. VI.*, ii. 1.

---

* That " capel " was a name for a horse, we learn from two lines in Chaucer :—
> To kepe him on his *capel* out of the slough,
> And if he falle from of his *capel* eftsone.

> *Maniple's Prol.*, CANT. TALES.

Thou art woman-tir'd, unroosted by thy *Dame Partlet* here.—*W. T.*, ii. 3.

How now, *Dame Partlet* the hen! have you.—1 *H. IV.*, iii. 3.

Philip? sparrow! James, there's toys abroad.—*John*, i. 1.

Philomel, with melody, sing in our sweet lullaby.—*Mid. N. D.*, ii. 3 *(Song)*.

> By this, lamenting *Philomel* had ended
> The well-tun'd warble of her nightly sorrow.—*Lucrece*, Stanza 155.

> Who finds the *partridge* in the *puttock's* nest,
> But may imagine how the bird was dead,
> Although the *kite* soar with unbloodied beak?—2 *H. VI.*, iii. 2.

An *owl*, a *puttock*, or a herring without a roe.—*Tr. & Cr.*, v. 1.

I chose an *eagle*, and did avoid a *puttock*.—*Cym.*, i. 2.

The *ruddock* would, with charitable bill.—*Cym.*, iv. 2.

A name for a hare :—

> By this, poor *Wat*, far off upon a hill,
> Stands on his hinder legs with listening ear,
> To hearken if his foes pursue him still.—*V. & Adon.*, Stanza 117.

The name of a bear (it having been a custom to give to the most known of these animals in bear-baiting exhibitions, the names of their leaders or keepers) :—

I have seen *Sackerson* loose twenty times, and have taken him by the chain.—*Merry W.*, i. 1.

A name for a toad :—

Paddock calls: anon!—*Macb.*, i. 1.

Sober, wise, would from a *paddock*, from a.—*Hamlet*, iii. 4.

Names for fiends :—

Amaimon sounds well; *Lucifer*, well; *Barbason*, well; yet they are all devils' additions, the names of fiends.—*Merry W.*, ii. 2.

He of Wales, that gave *Amaimon* the bastinado.—1 *H. IV.*, ii. 4.

I am not *Barbason;* you cannot conjure me.—*H. V.*, ii. 1.

This is the foul fiend, *Flibbertigibbet :* he begins.—*Lear*, iii. 4.

Frateretto calls me; and tells me Nero is.—*Ibid.*, iii. 6.

Hopdance cries in Tom's belly for two white herring.—*Ibid.*, iii. 6.

How now, *Mephistophilus!*—*Merry W.*, i. 1.

Modo he's called, and *Mahu*.– *Lear*, iii. 4.

It would control my dam's god, *Setebos*.—*Temp.*, i. 2.

Peace, *Smulkin;* peace, thou fiend!—*Lear*, iii. 4.

Names of certain fruits :—

I am withered like an old *apple-john*.—1 *H. IV.*, iii. 3.

What the plague hast thou brought there? *apple-johns?* thou knowest Sir John cannot endure an *apple-john* . . . the prince once set a dish of *apple-johns* before him.—2 *H. IV.*, ii. 4.

> Feed him with *apricocks*, and *dewberries*,
> With purple *grapes*, green *figs*, and *mulberries*.—*Mid. N. D.*, iii. 1.

Or a *codling* when 'tis almost an apple.—*Tw. N.*, i. 5.

There is a dish of *leather-coats* for you.—2 *H. IV.*, v. 3.

We will eat a last year's *pippin* of my own graffing.—*Ibid.*, v. 3.

I will make an end of my dinner; there's *pippins* and cheese to come.—*Merry W.*, i. 2.

Ripe as a *pomewater*, who now hangeth.—*Love's L. L.*, iv. 2.

Thou a *poprin pear!*—*R. & Jul.*, ii. 1.

Thy wit is a very bitter *sweeting*; it is a.—*R. & Jul.*, ii. 4.

Saffron, to colour the *warden* pies.—*W. T.*, iv. 2.

Names of certain fish :—

Pray you, sir, use the *carp* as you may.—*All's W.*, v. 2.

To change the *cod's* head for the *salmon's* tail.—*Oth.*, ii. 1.

And there is *salmons* in both.—*H. V.*, iv. 7.

If the young *dace* be a bait for the old *pike*.—2 *H. IV.*, iii. 2.

I will praise an *eel* with the same praise.—*Love's L. L.*, i. 2.

> Or is the adder better than the *eel*
> Because his painted skin contents the eye ?—*Tam. of S.*, iv. 3.

As the cockney did to the *eels*, when she put them.—*Lear*, ii. 4.

> But fish not, with this melancholy bait,
> For this fool-*gudgeon*, this opinion.—*Mer. of V.*, i. 1.

Ashamed of my soldiers, I am a soused *gurnet*.—1 *H. IV.*, iv. 2.

Then am I a shotten *herring*.—*Ibid.*, ii. 4.

Or a *herring* without a roe, I would not care.—*Tr. & Cr.*, v. 1.

Without a roe, like a dried *herring*.—*R. & Jul.*, ii. 4.

As *pilchards* are to *herrings*, the husband 's the bigger.—*Tw. N.*, iii. 1.

Our old *ling* and our Isbels o' the country are nothing like your old *ling* and your Isbels o' the court.—*All's W.*, iii. 2.

Breeds fleas like a *loach*.—1 *H. IV.*, ii. 1.

You may buy land now as cheap as stinking *mackerel*.—*Ibid.*, ii. 4.

A kind of, not of the newest, *poor-john*. A strange fish !—*Temp.*, ii. 2.

'Tis well thou art not fish ; if thou hadst, thou hadst been *poor-john*.—*R. & Jul.*, i. 1.

I am stung like a *tench*.—Like a *tench* !—1 *H. IV.*, ii. 1.

Here comes the *trout* that must be caught with tickling.—*Tw. N.*, ii. 5.

Groping for *trouts* in a peculiar river.—*M. for M.*, i. 2.

Fantastical pet names for a sword :—

Have we not *Hiren* here? . . . Then feed, and be fat, my fair *Calipolis*.—2 *H. IV.*, ii. 4.

The names of special places :—

Smell like *Bucklersbury* in simple-time.—*Merry W.*, iii. 3.

To old *Free-town*, our common judgment-place.—*R. & Jul.*, i. 1.

> Goose, if I had you upon *Sarum plain*,
> I 'd drive you home to *Camelot*.—*Lear*, ii. 2.

A *Cotswold* man . . . behind *Gray's Inn* . . . at *Stamford* fair . . . the windmill in *Saint George's Fields* . . . before I came to *Clement's Inn* . . . I remember at *Mile End Green* . . . the feats he hath done about *Turnbull Street*.—2 *H. IV.*, iii. 2.

And he has some invented names of places :—

They say, he is already in the forest of *Arden*.—*As You L.*, i. 1.

My father was that Sebastian of *Messaline*, whom I know you have heard of.—*Tw. N.*. ii. 1.

With the spirit and vivacity of a true wit, Shakespeare is prolific in nicknames :—

Let him be clapped on the shoulder and called *Adam*.—*M. Ado*, i. 1.

Young *Adam* Cupid, he that shot so trim.—*R. & Jul.*, ii. 1.

Well said, *Adversity* ! and what need these tricks.—*Tr. & Cr.*, v. 1.

A la stoccata carries it away.—*R. & Jul.*, iii. 1.

Draw, you whoreson cullionly *barbermonger*, draw.—*Lear*, ii. 2.

Thou whoreson little *Bartholomew boar-pig*, when wilt.—2 *H. IV.*, ii. 4.

This bed-presser, this *horseback-breaker*, this *huge hill of flesh.*—1 *H. IV.*, ii. 4.

Thou *bitch-wolf's son*, canst thou not hear ?—*Tr. & Cr.*, ii. 1.

Here's a *Bohemian Tartar* tarries the.—*Merry W.*, iv. 5.

He dreamt the *boar* had rased off his helm . . . to fly the *boar* before the *boar* pursues . . . the *boar* will use us kindly.—*R. III.*, iii. 2.

Away, you *bottle-ale-rascal!* you *basket-hilt stale juggler*, you!—2 *H. IV.*, ii. 4.

Why strew'st thou sugar on that *bottled spider.*—*R. III.*, i. 3.

The very conveyances of his land will hardly lie in this *box.*—*Hamlet*, v. 1.

Come, come, thou *boy-queller*, show thy face.—*Tr. & Cr.*, v. 5.

I will hold my peace when Achilles' *brach* bids me.—*Ibid.*, ii. 1.

And that damned *brawn* shall play Dame Mortimer.—1 *H. IV.*, ii. 4.

Marry, hang thee, *brock !*—*Tw. N.*, ii. 5.

Thou *cacodemon!* there thy kingdom is.—*R. III.*, i. 3.

You whoreson *candle-mine*, you, how vilely.—2 *H. IV.*, ii. 4.

Alas, poor wretch! ah, poor *capocchia !*—*Tr. & Cr.*, iv. 2.

And a whole bookful of these *quondam carpet-mongers.*—*M. Ado*, v. 2.

Some *carry-tale*, some *please-man*, some *slight zany*, some *mumble-news*, some *trencher-knight.*—*Love's L. L.*, v. 2.

Those soft parts of conversation that *chamberers* have.—*Oth.*, iii. 3.

How now, how now, *chop-logic !* what is this?—*R. & Jul.*, iii. 5.

Why, thou *clay-brained guts*, thou *knotty-pated fool*, thou *whoreson, obscene, greasy tallow-keech.*—1 *H. IV.*, ii. 4.

Reprieves for you and your *coach-fellow*, Nym.—*Merry W.*, ii. 2.

Cobloaf !—He would pun thee into shivers.—*Tr. & Cr.*, ii. 1.

Cry to it, nuncle, as the *cockney* did to the eels.—*Lear*, ii. 4.

With Satan : hang him, foul *collier !*—*Tw. N.*, iii. 4.

Go, go, you *cot-quean*, go ; get you to bed.—*R. & Jul.*, iv. 4.

A goodly count, *Count Confect ;* a sweet gallant.—*M. Ado*, iv. 1.

> Most smiling, smooth, detested parasites,
> *Courteous destroyers, affable wolves, meek bears,*
> You *fools of fortune, trencher friends, time's flies,*
> *Cap and knee slaves, vapours,* and *minute-jacks !*—*Timon*, iii. 6.

There is three *cousin-germans* that has cozened.—*Merry W.*, iv. 5.

If thou hast her not i' the end, call me *cut.*—*Tw. N.*, ii. 3.

Away, you *cut-purse rascal!* you *filthy bung* [*See* CANT TERMS], away!—2 *H. IV.*, ii. 4.

For thou dost know, O *Damon dear*, this.—*Hamlet*, iii. 2.

Be-lee'd and calm'd by *debitor and creditor*, this *counter-caster.*—*Oth.*, i. 1.

Like three German devils, three *Doctor Faustuses.*—*Merry W.*, iv. 5.

That same *dog-fox*, Ulysses.—*Tr. & Cr.*, v. 4.

Dromio, thou *Dronio,** thou *snail*, thou *slug*, thou *sot !*—*Com. of E.*, ii. 2.

Then fly, false thanes, and mingle with the English *epicures.*—*Macb.*, v. 3.

'Faith, here's an *equivocator*, that could swear in both the scales against either scale ; who committed treason enough for God's sake, yet could not equivocate to heaven: O, come in, *equivocator.*—*Ibid.*, ii. 3.

How now, my *eyas-musket !*—*Merry W.*, iii. 3.

To be abus'd by one that looks on *feeders.*—*Ant. & C.*, iii. 11.

And, look, whether the *fiery Trigon*, his man.—2 *H. IV.*, ii. 4.

---

* The Folio prints this word ' Dromio,' and most editors alter it to ' drone '; but we believe it to be a jocose alteration of Dromio's name, to indicate the lazy insect to which he is likened, in addition to " snail " and " slug."

That *fire-drake* did I hit three times. . . . I missed the *meteor* once.—*H. VIII.*, v. 3.

'Tis such another *fitchew!* marry, a perfumed one.—*Oth.*, iv. 1.

I am none of his *flirt-gills;* I am none of his *skains-mates.*—*R. & Jul.*, ii. 4.

Is he dead, my *Francisco?* ha, bully? What says my *Esculapius?* my *Galen?* my *heart of elder?* ha! is he dead, *bully stale?* is he dead?—*Merry W.*, ii. 3.

Word of denial: *froth and scum*, thou liest.—*Ibid.*, i. 1.

Thrust him down-stairs! know we not *Galloway nags?*—*2 H. IV.*, ii. 4.

To be the pillage of a *giglot* wench.—*1 H. VI.*, iv. 7.

At point (O *giglot* fortune!) to master Cæsar's sword.—*Cym.*, iii. 1.

Why, thou *globe of sinful continents*, what a life.—*2 H. IV.*, ii. 4.

Is not this a lamentable thing, *grandsire*, that.—*R. & Jul.*, ii. 4.

Ere I would drown myself for the love of a *guinea-hen* [*See* CANT TERMS], I would change my humanity.—*Oth.*, i. 3.

Stolen from me by the *hangmen* boys in the.—*Two G. of V.*, iv. 4.

And the little *hangman* dare not shoot at him.—*M. Ado*, iii. 2.

How now, my *headstrong!* where have you been gadding?—*R. & Jul.*, iv. 2.

Are these your *herd?* Must these have voices.—*Coriol.*, iii. 1.

Before he should thus stoop to the *herd.*—*Ibid.*, iii. 2.

When he perceived the common *herd* was glad he refused.—*Jul. C.*, i. 2.

Thou *hilding* of a devilish spirit.—*Tam. of S.*, ii. 1.

Out on her, *hilding!*—*R. & Jul.*, iii. 5.

Thou elvish-mark'd, abortive, rooting *hog!*—*R. III.*, i. 3.

If I tell thee a lie, spit in my face, call me *horse.*—*1 H. IV.*, ii. 4.

O *hound of Crete*, think'st thou my spouse to get?—*H. V.*, ii. 1.

Romeo! humours! madman! passion! lover!—*R. & Jul.*, ii. 1.

Given *Hydra* here to choose an officer.—*Coriol.*, iii. 1.

Pish for thee, *Iceland dog!* thou prick-eared *cur of Iceland!*—*H. V.*, ii. 1.

To be disgraced by an *inkhorn mate.*—*1 H. VI.*, iii. 1.

Come, my young soldier, put up your *iron.*—*Tw. N.*, iv. 1.

I will wink, and hold out mine *iron.*—*H. V.*, ii. 1.

> Put up thy sword betime;
> Or I'll so maul you and your *toasting-iron* —*John*, iv. 3.

Without drawing their massy *irons* and.—*Tr. & Cr.*, ii. 3.

> Yon *island-carrions*, desperate of their bones,
> Ill-favouredly become the morning field:
> Their *ragged curtains* poorly are let loose.—*H. V.*, iv. 2.

You little *Jack-a-Lent*, have you been true to us?—*Merry W.*, iii. 3.

Is as arrant a villain and a *Jack-sauce.*—*H. V.*, iv. 7.

Some *jay* of Italy, whose mother was her painting.—*Cym.*, iii. 4.

We'll teach him to know turtles from *jays.*—*Merry W.*, iii. 3.

Like *John-a-dreams*, unpregnant of my cause.—*Hamlet*, ii. 2.

I wonder that such a *keech* can with his very.—*H. VIII.*, i. 1.

Unto this *king of smiles*, this Bolingbroke.—*1 H. IV.*, i. 3.

What, my dear *Lady Disdain!* are you yet living?—*M. Ado*, i. 1.

E'en so, and now my *Lady Worm's.*—*Hamlet*, v. 1.

What, *lamb*, what *lady-bird!*—*R. & Jul.*, i. 3.

Why *lamb!* why, lady! fie, you *slug-a-bed!*—*Ibid.*, iv. 5.

How now, *lambs!*—*Tr. & Cr.*, iv. 4.

Thy tender *lambkin* now is king.— *2 H. IV.*, v. 3.

For, *lambkins*, we will live.—*H. V.*, ii. 1.

This *lapwing* runs away with the shell on his head.—*Hamlet*, v. 2.

Farewell, thou *latter-spring!* Farewell, *All-hallown summer!*—*1 H. IV.*, i. 2.

Fetch forth the *lazar kite of Cressid's kind.—H. V.,* ii. 1.

Behold where *Madam Mitigation comes !—M. for M.,* i. 2.

Thou whoreson *mad compound of majesty.—2 H. IV.,* ii. 4.

The kitchen *malkin* pins her richest lockram.—*Coriol.,* ii. 1.

Whilst ours was blurted at, and held a *malkin.—Per.,* iv. 4.

And that arrant *malmsey-nose-knave,* Bardolph.—*2 H. IV.,* ii. 1.

A whining *mammet,* in her fortune's tender.—*R. & Jul.,* iii. 5.

This is no world to play with *mammets.—1 H. IV.,* ii. 3.

Mars his idiot ! do, *rudeness ;* do, *camel ;* do, do.—*Tr. & Cr.,* ii. 1.

And how doth the *martlemas,* your master ?—*2 H. IV.,* ii. 2.

This is a riddling *merchant* for the nonce.—*1 H. VI.,* ii. 3.

What saucy *merchant* was this that was.—*R. & Jul.,* ii. 4.

That base *minnow of thy mirth.—Love's L L.,* i. 1 (*Letter*).

Minion, thou liest : is 't not Hortensio ?—*Tam. of S.,* ii. 1.

Mistress minion, you, . . . out, you *green-sickness carrion !* out, you *baggage !* you *tallow face !—R. & Jul.,* iii. 5.

Mistress Thersites !—Tr. & Cr., ii. 1.

Mome, malt-horse, capon, coxcomb, idiot, patch !—Com. of E., iii. 1.

Thou *mongrel beef-witted lord !—Tr. & Cr.,* ii. 1.

Ha ! the prince and *Monsieur Love !—M. Ado,* ii. 3.

A word, *Monsieur Mock-water.—Merry W.,* ii. 3.

What says *Monsieur Remorse ?—1 H. IV.,* i. 2.

Now I would pray our *Monsieurs* to think.—*H. VIII.,* i. 3.

That stale old *mouse-eaten dry cheese,* Nestor.—*Tr. & Cr.,* v. 4.

You have been a *mouse-hunt* in your time.—*R. & Jul.,* iv. 4.

You *muddy rascal.* . . . Hang yourself, you *muddy conger,* hang yourself !—*2 H. IV.,* ii. 4.

Yet I, a dull and *muddy-mettled rascal,* peak.—*Hamlet,* ii. 2.

Ay, marry, was it, *muscle-shell.—Merry W.,* iv. 5.

My fool usurps my body.—*Lear,* iv. 2.

Thus do I ever make *my fool* my purse.— *Oth.,* i. 3.

Now, *my sick fool* Roderigo, whom love has turn'd.—*Ibid.,* ii. 3.

Would not this *nave of a wheel* have his ears cut off ?—*2 H. IV.,* ii. 4.

Stand, rogue, stand ; you *neat slave,* strike.—*Lear,* ii. 2.

Good night, my good *owl. —Love's L. L.,* iv. 1.

I bade the vile *owl* go learn me the tenor.—*Tr. & Cr.,* ii. 1.

Out on ye, *owls !* nothing but songs of death ?—*R. III.,* iv. 4.

Come, come, you *paraquito,* answer me.—*1 H. IV.,* ii. 3.

He 's a rogue, and a *passy-measures pavin.—Tw. N.,* v. 1.

And now reigns here a very, very—*peacock.—Hamlet,* iii. 2.

But the *peaking cornuto* her husband.—*Merry W.,* iii. 5.

So I do still, by these *pickers and stealers.—Hamlet,* iii. 2.

What, ho, *Pilch !* . . . What, *Patch-breech,* I say !—*Per.,* ii. 1.

Will you pluck your sword out of his *pilcher* by the ears ?—*R. & Jul.,* iii. 1.

Peace, good *pint-pot !* peace, good *tickle-brain !—1 H. IV.,* ii. 4.

To be so pester'd with a *popinjay.—Ibid.,* i. 3.

Do not, *porcupine,* do not : my fingers itch.—*Tr. & Cr.,* ii. 1.

More than *prince of cats,* I can tell you.—*R. & Jul.,* ii. 4.

The *black prince,* sir ; alias, *the prince of darkness* . . . but, sure, he is *the prince of the world.—All's W.,* iv. 5.

The *prince of darkness* is a gentleman.—*Lear,* iii. 4.

You are a *princox ;* go : be quiet, or.—*R. & Jul.,* i. 5.

Very wisely, *puppies !—W. T.*, iv. 3.

As many inches as you have oceans. *Puppies !—Cym.*, i. 3.

I shall be with you presently, good master *puppy.—H. VIII.*, v. 3.

How now, blown Jack! how now, *quilt!—*1 *H. IV.*, iv. 2.

You *rag*, you *baggage*, you *pole-cat*, you *ronyon !—Merry W.*, iv. 2.

Thy father, that poor *rag*, must be thy subject.—*Timon*, iv. 3.

Thou *rag of honour !* thou detested.—*R. III.*, i. 3.

Lash hence these overweening *rags* of France.—*Ibid.*, v. 3.

Tybalt, you *rat-catcher*, will you walk?—*R. & Jul.*, iii. 1.

" Aroint thee, witch!" the *rump-fed ronyon* cries.—*Macb.*, i. 3.

Hang him, mechanical *salt-butter rogue !—Merry W.*, ii. 2.

Ah, thou *say*, thou *serge*, nay, thou *buckram lord !—*2 *H. VI.*, iv. 7.

Out, *scab !*—Nay, patience, or we break.—*Tw. N.*, ii. 5.

Well said, i' faith, Wart; thou art a good *scab.—*2 *H. IV.*, iii. 2.

What say you, *Scarlet and John ?—Merry W.*, i. 1.

Thy ambition, thou *scarlet sin*, robb'd this.—*H. VIII.*, iii. 2.

Or I shall break that merry *sconce* of yours.—*Com. of E.*, i. 2.

Or I will beat this method in your *sconce.—Sconce* call you it? So you would leave battering, I had rather have it a head: an you use these blows long, I must get a sconce* for my head, and ensconce it too.—*Ibid.*, ii. 2.

To knock him about the *sconce* with a dirty shovel.—*Hamlet*, v. 1.

Away, you *scullion !* you *rampallian !* you *fustilarian !—*2 *H. IV.*, ii. 1.

Thou *scurvy valiant ass !* thou art here.—*Tr. & Cr.*, ii. 1.

You *shames of Rome !* you herd of— . . . You *souls of geese*, that bear the shapes of men.—*Coriol.*, i. 4.

Is *Signior Montanto* returned from the wars.—*M. Ado*, i. 1.

I would not be *Sir Nob* in any case.—*John*, i. 1.

As who should say—I am *Sir Oracle.—Mer. of V.*, i. 1.

This ancient morsel, this *Sir Prudence*, who.—*Temp.*, ii. 1.

By *Sir Smile*, his neighbour.—*W. T.*, i. 2.

Ay, *Sir Tike*, who more bold ?—*Merry W.*, iv. 5.

And at this sport, *Sir Valour* dies.—*Tr. & Cr.*, i. 3.

The prince is a Jack, a *sneak-cup.—*1 *H. IV.*, iii. 3.

If I would time expend with such a *snipe.—Oth.*, i. 3.

Ay, do, do; thou *sodden-witted lord !—Tr. & Cr.*, ii. 1.

O *Spartan dog*, more fell than anguish.—*Oth.*, v. 2.

Away, you *starveling*, you *elf-skin*, you *dried neat's tongue, bull's pizzle*, you *stockfish* . . . you *tailor's yard*, you *sheath*, you *bow-case*, you *vile standing-tuck.—*1 *H. IV.*, ii. 4.

Thou *stool for a witch !—Tr. & Cr.*, ii. 1.

O, my *sweet beef*, I must still be good.—1 *H. IV.*, iii. 3.

And that same *sword-and-buckler Prince of Wales.—Ibid.*, i. 3.

I warrant you, no *tell-tale*, nor no *breed-bate.—Merry W.*, i. 4.

What a full fortune doth the *thick-lips* owe, if.—*Oth.*, i. 1.

What wouldst thou have, boor ? what, *thick-skin ?—Merry W.*, iv. 5.

By inches, thou *thing of no bowels*, thou !—*Tr. & Cr.*, ii. 1.

Thou *thin man in a censer* . . . you *blue-bottle rogue !* you *filthy famished correctioner* . . . you *starved bloodhound !—Goodman death ! goodman bones !—*Thou *atomy*, thou !—come, you *thin thing !—*2 *H. IV.*, v. 4.

---

* " Sconce " is here used in its original sense of a ' protective fortification.'

> Thou liest, thou *thread*, thou *thimble*,
> Thou *yard, three-quarters, half-yard, quarter, nail!*
> Thou *flea*, thou *nit*, thou *winter-cricket* thou!
> Brav'd in mine own house with a *skein of thread?*
> Away, thou *rag*, thou *quantity*, thou *remnant.—Tam. of S.*, iv. 3.

A base, proud, shallow, beggarly, *three-suited, hundred-pound*, filthy, *worsted-stocking knave;* a *lily-livered, action-taking knave;* a whoreson *glass-gazing, super-serviceable, finical rogue; one-trunk-inheriting slave.—Lear*, ii. 2.

Toadstool, learn me the proclamation.—*Tr. & Cr.*, ii. 1.

> To the descent and dust below thy foot,
> A most *toad-spotted traitor.—Lear*, v. 3.

I pressed me none but such *toasts and butter.*—1 *H. IV.*, iv. 2.

I 'll tell thee what, thou damned *tripe-visaged rascal* . . . thou *paper-faced villain.*— 2 *H. IV.*, v. 4.

Hear you this *Triton of the minnows ?—Coriol.*, iii. 1.

Or an old *trot* with ne'er a tooth in her head.—*Tam. of S.*, i. 2.

Ah, ha, boy! say'st thou so? art thou there, *true-penny ?—Hamlet*, i. 5.

A *tun of man* is thy companion. Why dost thou converse with that *trunk of humours*, that *bolting-hutch of beastliness*, that *swoln parcel of dropsies*, that *huge bombard of sack*, that *stuffed cloak-bag of guts*, that *roasted Manningtree ox with the pudding in his belly*, that *reverend vice*, that *grey iniquity*, that *father ruffian*, that *vanity in years?* . . . that *villainous abominable misleader of youth*, Falstaff, that *old white-bearded Satan.*—1 *H. IV.*, ii. 4.

Turk Gregory never did such deeds in arms.—*Ibid.*, v. 3.

We 'll use this *unwholesome humidity*, this *gross watery pumpion.—Merry W.*, iii. 3.

Where be my horses? speak well of them, *varletto.—Ibid.*, iv. 5.

To *velvet-guards*, and Sunday citizens.—1 *H. IV.*, iii. 1.

> I see them lording it in London streets,
> Crying—" *Villiago!*" unto all they meet.—2 *H. VI.*, iv. 8.

Speak, then, thou *vinewd'st leaven*, speak.—*Tr. & Cr.*, ii. 1.

Dost know this *water-fly ?—Hamlet*, v. 2.

I do allow this *wen* to be as familiar with me.—2 *H. IV.*, ii. 2.

O this *woodcock!* what an ass it is!—*Tam. of S.*, i. 2.

Who was wont to call them *woollen vassals, things created to buy and sell with groats.—Coriol.*, iii. 2.

How now, *wool-sack!* what mutter you ?—1 *H. IV.*, ii. 4.

A rascally *yea-forsooth knave* . . . the whoreson *smooth-pates* do now wear nothing but high shoes.—2 *H. IV.*, ii. 1.

Thou whoreson *zed*, thou *unnecessary letter!* . . . Spare my grey beard, you *wagtail!—Lear*, ii. 2.

PARTS OF SPEECH DIVERSELY USED.

Much expressiveness and inclusiveness of effect is produced by the mode in which Shakespeare occasionally uses various parts of speech with different power from that which is strictly their own. He sometimes uses nouns as verbs :—

And make him with our pikes and partisans
A grave: come *arm* him [where the effect is succinctly expressed of ' take him up in your arms '].—*Cym.*, iv. 3.

Scald rhymers *ballad* us out o' tune: the quick comedians extemporally will *stage* us. —*Ant. & C.*, v. 2.

And thou, his yoke-fellow of equity, *bench* by his side.—*Lear*, iii. 6.

Blanket my loins; *elf* all my hair in knots.—*Ibid.*, ii. 3.

To *book* our dead, and then to bury them.—*H. V.*, iv. 7.

And I will *boot* thee with what gift beside.—*Ant. & C.*, ii. 5.

I shall see some squeaking Cleopatra *boy* my greatness.—*Ibid.*, v. 2.

There thou may'st *brain* him . . . or *paunch* him.—*Temp.*, iii. 2.

I 'll *buckler* thee against a million.—*Tam. of S.*, iii. 2.

No farther personal power to *business* with the king.—*Hamlet*, i. 2.

Will the cold brook, candied with ice, *caudle* thy morning taste.—*Timon*, iv. 3.

That such as we *cave* here, hunt here, are outlaws.— *Cym.*, iv. 2.

The blessed gods purge all infection from our air, whilst you do *climate* here —
W. T., v. 1.

In my rights, by me invested, he *compeers* the best.—*Lear*, v. 3.

Dost *dialogue* with thy shadow ?—*Timon*, ii. 2.

All my right of her I do *estate* unto Demetrius.—*Mid. N. D.*, i. 1.

My becomings kill me, when they do not *eye* well to you.—*Ant. & C.*, i 3.

And rather *father* thee than *master* thee.—*Cym.*, iv. 2.

Foot it featly here and there.—*Temp.*, i. 2 (*Song*).

And *foot* me, as you spurn a stranger cur.—*Mer. of V.*, i. 3.

I 'll knock her back, *foot* her home again.—*Cym.*, iii. 5.

The holy eagle stoop'd, as to *foot* us.—*Ibid.*, v. 4.

He *furnaces* the thick sighs from him.—*Ibid.*, i. 7.

Adoptious christendoms, that blinking Cupid *gossips.*—*All's W.*, i. 1.

And ditches *grave* you all !—*Timon*, iv. 3.

Or *hoop* his body more with thy embraces.—*W. T.*, iv. 3.

Go bear it to the Centaur, where we *host.*—*Com of E.*, i. 2.

I will bring you where you shall *host.*—*All's W.*, iii. 5.

To *hovel* thee with swine and rogues forlorn.—*Lear*, iv. 7.

That were the most, if he should *husband* you.—*Ibid.*, v. 3.

Yet neither pleasure's art can *joy* my spirits.—*Per.*, i. 2.

And *knee* the way into his mercy.—*Coriol.*, v. 1.

I could as well be brought to *knee* his throne.—*Lear*, ii. 4.

And rather woo those that would *mischief* me.—*Timon*, iv. 3.

You shall *nose* him as you go up the stairs into.—*Hamlet*, iv. 3.

Will these moss'd trees . . . *page* thy heels.—*Timon*, iv. 3.

With ridiculous and awkward action. . . . he *pageants* us.—*Tr. & Cr.*, i. 3.

And *pall** thee in the dunnest smoke of hell.—*Macb.*, i. 5.

And his own letter . . . must fetch him in he *papers.*—*H. VIII.*, i. 1.

That mine own servant should *parcel* the sum of my disgraces.—*Ant. & C.*, v. 2.

That relish all as sharply, *passion* as they.—*Temp.*, v. 1.

But with this I *passion* to say wherewith.—*Love's L. L.*, i. 1 (*Letter*).

For if thou *path*, thy native semblance on.—*Jul. C.*, ii. 1.

When the thunder would not *peace* at my bidding.—*Lear*, iv. 6.

Which, failing, *periods* his comfort.—*Timon*, i. 1.

And nature prompts them . . . to *prince* it.—*Cym.*, iii. 3.

Quoit him down, Bardolph, like a.—*2 H. IV.*, ii. 4.

Which calls me pupil, or hath *read*† to me ?—*1 H. IV.*, iii. 1.

---

* "Pall" has been variously explained by several previous commentators; but we believe it to be one of Shakespeare's expressively framed verbs from nouns, and signifying 'cover as with a funereal pall.'

† "Read" is here used for 'given counsel or information'; "read" being an antique noun, signifying 'counsel,' 'advice,' 'imparted wisdom.'

The things of fame, that do *renown* this city.—*Tw. N.*, iii. 3.
Life-rendering pelican, *repast* them with my blood.—*Hamlet*, iv. 5.
Come, seeling night, *scarf* up the tender eye of pitiful day.—*Macb.*, iii. 2.
I 'll *silence** me e'en here.—*Hamlet*, iii. 4.

> That even her art *sisters* the natural roses;
> Her inkle, silk, *twin* with the rubied cherry.—*Per.*, v. (*Gower*).

Sin-dieted man, that *slaves* your ordinance.—*Lear*, iv. 1.
Thou dost *stone* my heart, and mak'st me.—*Oth.*, v. 2.
Rather than *story* him in his own hearing.—*Cym.*, i. 5.
The smiles of knaves *tent* in my cheeks.—*Coriol.*, iii. 2.
A birth, indeed, which *throes* thee much to yield.—*Temp.*, ii. 1.
The time's with labour; and *throes* forth, each minute, some.—*Ant & C.*, iii. 7.
I should . . . *uproar* the universal peace.—*Macb.*, iv. 3.

> That the first face of neither, on the start,
> Can *woman* me unto 't.—*All's W.*, iii. 2.

For all the sun sees, or the close earth *wombs*.—*W. T.*, iv. 3.
He *words* me, girls, he *words* me, that I.—*Ant. & C.*, v. 2.

He sometimes uses nouns adjectively:—

Blow, villain, till thy sphered *bias* cheek outswell.—*Tr. & Cr.*, iv. 5.
Hence, *broker*-lackey! ignomy and shame.—*Ibid.*, v. 11.
On the pendent boughs her *coronet* weeds clambering.—*Hamlet*, iv. 7.
Virtue is of so little regard in these *costermonger* times.—*2 H. IV.*, i. 2.
Looks with such *ferret* and such fiery eyes.—*Jul. C.*, i. 2.
Is of so *flood-gate* and o'erbearing nature.—*Oth.*, i. 3.
Yet *god*† Achilles still cries, "Excellent!"—*Tr. & Cr.*, i. 3.
That the weaker sort may wish *god*† Marcius home again.—*Coriol.*, iv. 6.

> Yet gives he not till judgment guide his bounty,
> Nor dignifies an *impair* ‡ thought with breath.—*Tr. & Cr.*, iv. 5.

That I some *lady* trifles have reserv'd.—*Ant. & C.*, v. 2.
Such *neighbour* nearness to our sacred blood.—*R. II.*, i. 1.
Rumour'd through the *peasant* towns between.—*2 H. IV.* (*Induc.*)
Oh, what a rogue and *peasant* slave am I!—*Hamlet*, ii. 2.
'Twas this flesh begot those *pelican* daughters.—*Lear*, iii. 4.
Think this *pilot* thought; so with his steerage.—*Per.*, iv. 4 (*Gower*).
I should have fatted all the *region* kites.—*Hamlet*, ii. 2.
Look on me with your *welkin* eye.—*W. T.*, i. 2.
'Tis *wonder*, that thy life and wits at once.—*Lear*, iv. 7.
'Tis *wonder*, that an invisible instinct should.—*Cym.*, iv. 2.

---

* "Silence" has been altered by Hanmer and others to 'sconce'; but "silence me" appears to us to be here used by Shakespeare to express 'silently station myself.'

† In both these passages, it appears to us, that "god" is put into the mouth of a speaker who uses it as a scoffing epithet, implying that the person thus alluded to is deified by his admirers. In the passage from "Troilus and Cressida," both Folio and Quartos have the word "god," though some editors have changed it to 'good'; in the passage from "Coriolanus" the Folio prints 'good,' though it seems evident that the author intended "god," from this epithet having been similarly used in "Troilus and Cressida," from the circumstance of Cominius saying soon after, "He is their god," and from the expression subsequently employed by Coriolanus himself, "Nay, *godded* me, indeed."

‡ For our explanation of "impair," *See* Varied Meanings combined in One Word, &c.

In this latter expression, " wonder " may either be used adjectively, to signify ' wonderful ' ; or it may be used elliptically, to imply ' a wonder,' or ' matter for wonder.'

In the following passage, Shakespeare uses a noun adverbially :—

But he 's *vengeance* proud, and loves not the.—*Coriol.*, ii. 2.

In the two following passages, Shakespeare uses a noun as a term of address :—

Well said, *Adversity !* and what need these tricks ?—*Tr. & Cr.*, v. 1.

And you, *enchantment*—worthy enough a herdsman.—*W. T.*, iv. 3.

In the following passage, Shakespeare uses a noun framed from a compound salutation :—

Greater than both, by the *all-hail* hereafter !—*Macb.*, i. 5.

And, in the following, a noun framed from a compound verb :—

The *let-alone* lies not in your good will.—*Lear*, v. 3.

And, in the following, a noun framed from a defective verb :—

Mark you his absolute " *shall* " ? . . . with his peremptory " *shall*," being but the horn and noise . . . who puts his " *shall*," his popular " *shall* " against.—*Coriol.*, iii. 1.

And, in the following, a noun framed from other verbs :—

O, that " *had !* " how sad a passage 'tis !—*All's W.*, i. 1.

For this " *would* " changes, and hath abatements and delays . . . and then this " *should* " is like a spendthrift sigh, that hurts by easing.—*Hamlet*, iv. 7.

He sometimes uses participles framed from nouns :—

Therefore my son i' the ooze is *bedded*.—*Temp.*, iii. 3.

Your *bedded* hair, like life in excrements.—*Hamlet*, iii. 4.

Supple and courteous to the people, *bonneted*, without.—*Coriol*, ii. 2.

That hath so *cowarded* and chas'd your blood out.—*H. V.*, ii. 2.

Or worth, in thee make thy words *faith'd*.—*Lear*, ii. 1.

Being so *father'd* and so *husbanded* ?—*Jul. C.*, ii. 1.

For he is *footed* in this land already.—*H. V.*, ii. 4.

There is part of a power already *footed*.—*Lear*, iii. 3.

Swithold *footed* thrice the old.—*Ibid.* iii. 4 (*Song*).

The traitors late *footed* in the kingdom ?—*Ibid.*, iii. 7.

Were they not *forc'd* with those that should be ours.—*Macb.*, v. 5.

Julius Cæsar, who at Philippi the good Brutus *ghosted*.—*Ant. & C.*, ii. 6.

Above the measure of a father ; nay, *godded* me, indeed.—*Coriol.*, v. 3.

Are you so *gospell'd*, to pray for this good man.—*Macb.*, iii. 1.

Kingdom'd * Achilles in commotion rages.—*Tr. & Cr.*, ii. 1.

A hand that kings have *lipp'd*, and trembled kissing.—*Ant. & C.*, ii. 5.

One *minded* like the weather, most unquietly.—*Lear*, iii. 1.

And with him there lie *mudded*.—*Temp.*, iii. 3.

I wish myself were *mudded* in that oozy bed.—*Ibid.*, v. 1.

---

* We take " kingdom'd " to signify ' dominated by his turbulent inward condition or " state of man " ' ; since we think the following lines serve to illustrate Shakespeare's use of " kingdom'd " here :—

> " And the *state of man*,
> Like to a little *kingdom*, suffers then
> The nature of an insurrection."—*Jul. C.*, ii. 1.

'Tis a sufferance *panging* as soul and body's severing.—*H. VIII.*, ii. 3.

'Twas Ariadne, *passioning* for Theseus' perjury.—*Tw. G. of V.*, iv. 4.

So am I *purposed.*—*Lear*, ii. 4.

My throat of war be turn'd, which *quired* with my drum.—*Coriol.*, iii. 2.

Still *quiring* to the young-ey'd cherubins.—*Mer. of V.*, v. 1.

These *roguing* thieves serve the great pirate.—*Per.*, iv. 2.

And made a cistern for *scal'd* snakes !—*Ant. & C.*, ii. 5.

But you have found, *scaling* his present bearing with his past, that he 's your fixed enemy. —*Coriol.*, ii. 3.

The *scarfed* bark puts from her native bay.—*Mer. of V.*, ii. 6.

My sea-gown *scarf'd* about me.—*Hamlet*, v. 2.

He smote the *sledded* Polack on the ice.—*Ibid.*, i. 1.

The hearts that *spaniel'd* me at heels.—*Ant. & C.*, iv. 10.

I am *sprighted* with a fool; frighted and angered.—*Cym.*, ii. 3.

My third comfort, *starr'd* most unluckily.—*W. T.*, iii. 2.

O ill-*starr'd* wench ! pale as thy smock.—*Oth.*, v. 2.

By the forge that *stithied* Mars his helm.—*Tr. & Cr.*, iv. 5.

Who *stock'd* my servant ?—*Lear*, ii. 4.

And *stock'd*, punished, and imprisoned.—*Ibid.*, iii. 4.

And person of my master, *stocking* his messenger.—*Ibid.*, ii. 2.

Of love or bounty, you were *straited* for a reply.—*W. T.*, iv. 3.

Though the catalogue of his endowments had been *tabled* by his side.—*Cym.*, i. 5.

And bring thee cords made like a *tackled* stair.—*R. & Jul.*, ii. 4.

I thank you, you have *testerned* me.—*Tw. G. of V.*, i. 1.

Still *virginalling* upon his palm ?—*W. T.*, i. 2.

Horns *whelk'd* and *wav'd* like the *enridged* sea.—*Lear*, iv. 6.

Your *loop'd* and *window'd* raggedness.—*Ibid.*, iii. 4.

Wouldst thou be *window'd* in great Rome.—*Ant. & C.*, iv. 12.

Nor my wish, to have him see me *woman'd.*—*Oth.*, iii. 4.

So rare a *wonder'd* father and a wife.—*Temp.*, iv. 1.

In the following passages, he uses a participle substantively :—

Since my *becomings* kill me, when they do not.—*Ant. & C.*, i. 3.

And all my powers do their *bestowing* lose.—*Tr. & Cr.*, iii. 2.

Would, to the *bleeding* and the grim alarm, excite.—*Macb.*, v. 2.

The chronicles of my *doing.*—*H. VIII.*, i. 2.

These *couchings* and these lowly courtesies.—*Jul. C.*, iii. 1.

Joy's soul lies in the *doing.*—*Tr. & Cr.*, i. 2.

Your *having* in beard is a younger brother's revenue.—*As You L.*, iii. 2.

Our content is our best *having.*—*H. VIII.*, ii. 3.

But par'd my present *havings*, to bestow.—*Ibid.*, iii. 2.

Whose rarest *havings* made the blossoms dote.—*Lover's Comp.*, Stanza 34.

She had all the royal *makings* of a queen.—*H. VIII.*, iv. 1.

And he employs thus several participle's that are more frequently used in this manner; such as "baking," "beginning," "painting," "reading," "understanding," "wedding," "wooing," "writing," &c.

In the following he uses a conjunction substantively :—

And many such like *as's* of great charge.—*Hamlet*, v. 2.

You may avoid that too, with an "*if*" . . . your "*if*" is the only peace-maker; much virtue in "*if*."—*As You L.*, v. 4.

Talk'st thou to me of "*ifs*" ?—*R. III.*, iii. 4.

In the following, he uses interjections substantively :—

She did, with an "*alas*," I would fain say, bleed tears.—*W. T.*, v. 2.

Their loud applause and *aves* vehement.—*M. for M.*, i. 1.

Crier Hobgoblin, make the fairy *o-yes*.—*Merry W.*, v. 5.

Fame with her loudest *o-yes* cries.—*Tr. & Cr.*, iv. 5.

His daughter's woe and heavy *well-a-day*.—*Per.*, iv. 4 (*Gower*).

In the following he uses substantively a word which is both an adjective and an adverb :—

From th' extremest *upward* of thy head, to the.—*Lear*, v. 3.

In the following passages he uses an adverb as a noun :—

In russet *yeas*, and honest kersey *noes*.—*Love's L. L.*, v. 2.

That "*only*" came well in.—*Tam. of S.*, ii. 1.

Dies in his own *too-much*.—*Hamlet*, iv. 7.

A lady's *verily* is as potent as a lord's . . . by your dread *verily*, one of them you shall be.—*W. T.*, i. 2.

They say every *why* hath a *wherefore*.—*Com. of E.*, ii. 2.

How if your husband start some other *where*.—*Ibid.*, ii. 1.

I know his eye doth homage some other *where*.—*Ibid.*, ii. 1.

This is not Romeo, he's some other *where*.—*R. & Jul.*, i. 1.

Thou losest here, a better *where* to find.—*Lear*, i. 1.

In the following he uses an adverb adjectively :—

Are as interpreters of my *behind-hand* slackness.—*W. T.*, v. 1.

So, my state, *seldom*, but sumptuous, showed like a feast.—*1 H. IV.*, iii. 2.

Blunting the fine point of *seldom* pleasure.—*Sonnet* 52.

> Ere twice the sun hath made his journal greeting
> To th' *under* generation, you shall find.—*M. for M.*, iv. 3.

With the spleen of all the *under* fiends.*—*Coriol.*, iv. 5.

Approach, thou beacon to this *under* globe.—*Lear*, ii. 2.

> Lo, in the orient when the gracious light
> Lifts up his burning head, each *under* eye
> Doth homage to his new-appearing sight.—*Sonnet* 7.

In the following he makes a petulant speaker use an adjective as a verb and as a noun [*See* COINED WORDS]:—

Thank me no thankings, nor *proud* me no *prouds*.—*R. & Jul.*, iii. 5.

He occasionally uses even short phrases substantively:—

The hardest voice of her behaviour, to be Englished rightly, is, "*I am Sir John Falstaff's.*"—*Merry W.*, i. 3.

Here's too much "*out upon thee !*"—*Com. of E.*, iii. 1.

Indeed, your "*O Lord, sir !*" is very sequent to your whipping.—*All's W.*, ii. 2.

This "*once again*," but that your highness pleas'd, was once superfluous.—*John*, iv. 2.

Better at home, if "*would I might*" were "*may*."—*Tr. & Cr.*, i. 1.

Letting "*I dare not*" wait upon "*I would*."—*Macb.*, i. 7.

And with an absolute, "*Sir, not I*," the cloudy messenger.—*Ibid.*, iii. 6.

> "*But yet*" is as a gaoler to bring forth
> Some monstrous malefactor.—*Ant. & C.*, ii. 5.

He sometimes uses verbs substantively :—

Without the sensible and true *avouch* of mine.—*Hamlet*, i. 1.

Sextus Pompeius hath given the *dare* to Cæsar.—*Ant. & C.*, i. 3.

---

* "The under fiends" is equivalent to 'the fiends below,' 'the fiends of the lower regions.'

I true! how now! what wicked *deem* is this ?—*Tr. & Cr.*, iv. 4.

For the *fail* of any point in 't shall not only be.—*W. T.*, ii. 3.

By his highness' *fail* of issue.—*Ibid.*, v. 1.

How grounded he his title to the crown upon our *fail ?*—*H. VIII.*, i. 2.

The danger which my realms stood in by this my issue's *fail.*—*Ibid.*, ii. 4.

Shall be false and perjur'd, from thy great *fail.*—*Cym.*, iii. 4.

Troy; within whose strong *immures* the.—*Tr. & Cr.* (*Prologue*).

According to your ladyship's *impose*, I am.—*Two G. of V.*, iv. 3.

Our fortune lies upon this *jump.*—*Ant. & C.*, iii. 8.

Bear the guilt of our great *quell.*—*Macb.*, i. 7.

And send forth us, to make our sorrow'd *render.*—*Timon*, v. 2.

May drive us to a *render* where we have liv'd.—*Cym.*, iv. 4.

Take no stricter *render* of me than my all.—*Ibid.*, v. 4.

The *solve* is this—that thou dost common grow.—*Sonnet* 69.

That we come short of our *suppose* thus far.—*Tr. & Cr.*, i. 3.

While counterfeit *supposes* blear'd thine eyne.—*Tam. of S.*, v. 1.

There has been much *to do* on both sides.—*Hamlet*, ii. 2.

What 's sweet to do, *to do* will aptly find.—*Lover's Comp.*, *Stanza* 13.

With every gale and *vary* of their masters.—*Lear*, ii. 2.

That, on the *view* and *know* of these contents.—*Hamlet*, v. 2.

Will I not, Pompey; it is not the *wear.*—*M. for M.*, iii. 2.

Motley's the only *wear.*—*As You L.*, ii. 7.

Of the new'st and fin'st, fin'st *wear*-a?—*W. T.*, iv. 3 (*Song*).

In the following passage he uses a verb as a noun-adjective :—

And be a *thwart* disnatur'd torment to her!—*Lear*, i. 4.

Sometimes he uses verbs framed from adjectives :—

None does offend, none—I say, none; I'll *able* 'em.—*Ibid.*, iv. 6.

And it shall go hard but I will *better* the instruction.—*Mer. of V.*, iii. 1.

Each day still *better* other's happiness; until.—*R. II.*, i. 1.

Not unlike, each way, to *better* yours.—*Coriol.*, iii. 1.

If that ever my low fortunes *better*, I'll pay.—*Per.*, ii. 1.

Since they do *better* thee in their command.—*Ibid.*, iv. 6.

What you do still *betters* what is done.—*W. T.*, iv. 3.

> It toucheth us, as France invades our land,
> Not *bolds* the king, with others, whom, I fear.—*Lear*, v. 1.

Deep clerks she *dumbs;* and with her neeld.—*Per.*, v. (*Gower*).

Madam, the care I have had to *even* your content.—*All's W.*, i. 3.

To make him *even* o'er the time he has lost.—*Lear*, iv. 7.

> There 's more to be consider'd; but we'll *even*
> All that good time will give us.*—*Cym.*, iii. 4.

It *faints* me, to think what follows.—*H. VIII.*, ii. 3.

---

* It is to be noted that in each of these three passages Shakespeare uses the word "even" with largely inclusive effect. In the first, "to even your content" includes the combined significations of 'to keep pace with your wishes,' 'to act conformably with your wishes,' 'to make the accomplishment of your desires easy'; in the second, the phrase implies 'to make him pass in review the interval that has elapsed, and endeavour to render its events smooth and easy of comprehension to himself'; and in the third, the phrase comprises the multiplied effect of 'we will make our attempts keep pace with the time allowed us for endeavour,' 'we will accomplish all that time will give us leave to try for,' 'we will meet smoothly and with even temper all that time brings,' and 'we will accept thankfully all that good time grants.' *See* VARIED MEANINGS COMBINED IN ONE WORD OR SENTENCE, in justification of our ascribing these largely inclusive significations to Shakespeare's words.

And makes Diana's rangers *false* themselves.—*Cym.*, ii. 3.
And I, poor monster, *fond* as much on him.—*Tw. N.*, ii. 2.
And god-like reason to *fust* in us unus'd.—*Hamlet*, iv. 4.
This day shall *gentle* his condition.—*H. V.*, iv. 3.
That which most with you should *safe* my going.—*Ant. & C.*, i. 3.
How poor Andromache *shrills* her dolours forth !—*Tr. & Cr.*, v. 3.
And *violenteth* in a sense as strong.—*Ibid.*, iv. 4.

In the following passage he frames a verb from a word used both as a noun and as an adjective :—

Which we will *niggard* with a little rest.—*Jul. C.*, iv. 3.

In the following he uses a verb humorously framed from a pronoun :—

If thou *thou'st* him some thrice, it shall.—*Tw. N.*, iii. 2.

And, in the following, verbs humorously framed from nouns :—

A French song and a fiddle has no fellow.—
The devil *fiddle* 'em !—*H. VIII.*, i. 3.
You are grand-jurors, are ye? we 'll *jure* ye, i' faith.—1 *H. IV.*, ii. 2.

He sometimes uses participles framed from adjectives :—

He hath, indeed, better *bettered* expectation.—*M. Ado*, i. 1.
Which, *bettered* with his own learning.—*Mer. of V.*, iv. 1 (*Letter*).
Which I have *better'd* rather than decreas'd.—*Tam. of S.*, ii. 1.
But since he is *better'd*, we have therefore odds.—*Hamlet*, v. 2.
And the *bettering* of my mind with that.—*Temp.*, i. 2.
Bettering thy loss makes the bad-causer worse.—*R. III.*, iv. 4.
Nay, if he *coy'd* to hear Cominius speak.—*Coriol.*, v. 1.
Shall acquire no honour *demuring* upon me.—*Ant. & C.*, iv. 12.
Till I am *even'd* with him, wife for wife.—*Oth.*, ii. 1.
Spoke was beastly *dumb'd* by him.—*Ibid.*, i. 5.
Fairing the foul with art's false borrow'd face.—*Sonnet* 127.
Nay, not sure, in a thing *falsing*.—*Com. of E.*, ii. 2.
Best you *saf'd* the bringer out of the host.—*Ant. & C.*, iv. 6.
I would I knew not why it should be *slow'd*.—*R. & Jul.*, iv. 1.
All his visage *wann'd :* tears in his eyes.—*Hamlet*, ii. 2.

In the following passages he uses participles humorously framed from nouns [*See* COINED WORDS]:—

Aufidius got off . . . I would not have been so *fidiused* for all the chests in Corioli.
—*Coriol.*, ii. 1.
To see how the sea *flap-dragoned* it.—*W. T.*, iii. 3.
He hath *out-villained* villainy so far, that the rarity.—*All's W.*, iv. 3.

And in the following he uses a proper name humorously as a verb:—

Come, Mother Pratt ; come, give me your hand.—
I 'll "*prat*" her.—*Merry W.*, iv. 2.

PASSAGES OF INCOMPLETE EXPLANATION.

Shakespeare has some passages, where much is dramatically inferred in very few words ; thus sparing needless diffuseness and prolixity in detailing circumstances already known to the perusers or spectators of the play. These passages generally occur in the closing scenes, where the plot is wound up, and the characters come to a mutual understanding; therefore much is taken for granted, or left for supposed subsequent explanation among themselves, in order to avoid recapitulation before the audience. Some of his commentators, not perceiving this intentional succinctness on the part of the dramatist, have accused him of oversight, omission, forgetfulness, inexplicitness, &c., &c.; but we think that the following collected instances will serve to show that, far from denoting any of these alleged defects, they evince systematic art with care and skill in dramatic provision. He will often throw in an apparently trivial phrase, which really serves to indicate a point that it is requisite should be conveyed and known; yet doing this so slightly, that it demands attention on the part of those who read or see the play : and thus it comes, that so frequently when fault is found with Shakespeare's composition, it is the carelessness of the observer, and not the carelessness of the writer, which deserves blame. The two first passages we shall cite afford instances of the slight by-touches he occasionally introduces, to convey a circumstance needful to be noted, yet not demanding lengthy explanation:—

There is no better way than *that they spoke of.—Merry W.*, iv. 4.

Here allusion is made to the proposal already made by Mistress Ford and Mistress Page, supposed to have been " spoken of " before entering on the scene, and which their husbands proceed to discuss.

But, *they say*, the duke will be here to-morrow,—*M. for M.*, iv. 3.

By the words " they say," put into Lucio's mouth here, the fact is indicated that the duke's return is now generally reported.

My wife, more careful for *the latter-born*,
Had fasten'd him unto a small spare mast. . . .
My *youngest boy*, and yet my eldest care,
At eighteen years became inquisitive
After his brother.—*Com of E.*, i. 1.

Here, in order perhaps to convey the effect of the confusion of the wreck, the description is given somewhat confusedly ; so that the particulars of the mother's having fastened the " latter-born " to the mast, while she herself became fastened to the other end where her elder twin son was secured, thus leaving the " youngest boy " under the charge of her husband, must be well borne in mind, so that the present details may tally with the fact of Æmilia's having reached Ephesus with the *elder* Antipholus, and Ægeon's having had the *younger* Antipholus with him at Syracuse.

Are you a suitor to *the maid you talk of ?—Tam. of S.*, i. 2.

Here reference is made to a subject as if it had been named ; while, in fact, it has only been implied. But though there has been no actual mention of Bianca among the speakers, it is well understood that she is meant by them.

Petruchio is my name ; Antonio's son,
A man well known throughout all Italy.—
I know him well ; you are welcome for his sake.—
Saving your tale, Petruchio, I pray,
Let us, that are poor petitioners, *speak too.—Ibid.*, ii. 1.

By this expedient of Gremio's interruption, the needless repetition of Petruchio's stating his father's death to Baptista is saved.

Lucentio is your name—of whence, I pray ?—*Tam. of S.*, ii. 1.

Here the dramatist allows the disguised Tranio's assumed name of Lucentio to be supposed to have become known to the speaker; possibly by its having been marked upon the lute, or inscribed in the volumes presented to Baptista.

Had you not lately an intent . . . to go to Paris ?—*All's W.*, i. 3.

Although there has been no express mention of Helena's "intent" having become known to the Countess, the dramatist here allows the point to be inferred.

Methought you said you saw one here in court could witness it.—*I did*, my lord, but loath am to produce so bad an instrument: his name's Parolles.—*Ibid.*, v. 3.

Notwithstanding that there has been no actual speech made by Diana to this effect, yet, knowing that the audience are already aware of the point, and that it is needful to introduce Parolles, the dramatist permits her having adverted to some one who could "witness" for her to be taken for granted :—

> That I am Viola : which to confirm,
> I'll bring you to a captain in this town,
> Where lie my maiden weeds ; by whose gentle help
> I was preserv'd, to serve this noble count. . . .
> The captain that did bring me first on shore
> Hath my maid's garments ; he, upon some action,
> Is now in durance ; at Malvolio's suit. . . .
> Pursue him, and entreat him to a peace :
> He hath not told us of the captain yet.—*Tw. N.*, v. 1.

By the above slight indications, the dramatist sketches events already known to the audience ; not only avoiding their recapitulation, but also leaving undetailed the needless particulars of "Malvolio's suit" against the sea-captain.

> Thou wouldst have poison'd good Camillo's honour,
> To have him kill a king.—*W. T.*, iii. 3.

Although Leontes' confession of his misdeed took place during Paulina's absence from the scene, our dramatist permits her to make the above speech as if aware of the self-accusation, since it has become known to the audience.

> Teeth hadst thou in thy head when thou wast born,
> To signify, thou cam'st to bite the world :
> And, if the rest be true which I have heard,
> *Thou cam'st—*
> I'll hear no more : die, prophet in thy speech ;
> For this, among the rest, was I ordain'd . . .
> Indeed, '*tis true, that Henry told me of ;*
> For I have often heard my mother say, &c.—3 *H. VI.*, v. 6.

Shakespeare purposely allows King Henry's speech to be broken off in the midst of his scoffing at the preposterous circumstances attending Richard's birth, while allowing Richard to allude to them as having been "told" ; because they are not only recounted immediately after by Richard himself, but were well known and popularly believed.

The noble *Brutus hath told you* Cæsar was ambitious.—*Jul. C.*, iii. 2.

The dramatist here causes it to be inferred that Antony has heard of Brutus's having told the people this.

I must to England; you know that?—Hamlet, iii. 4.

Although there has been no express mention that Hamlet obtains this information previously to his here announcing it to his mother, yet King Claudius having twice mentioned his determination of despatching the prince to England, first to Polonius, and then to Rosencrantz and Guildenstern, it may be gathered that such a court decree has reached Hamlet's ears; besides that his own words immediately after, "there's letters sealed," imply that the decree has been officially announced to him. His subsequently choosing to express surprise when the king tells him he is to set out for England immediately, is but in consonance with his assumed flightiness of manner when speaking to his " uncle-father."

> What! *fifty of my followers, at a clap !*
> Within a fortnight !—*Lear*, i. 4.

This disjointed exclamation of the frantic old king suffices to indicate the fact that Goneril has suddenly dismissed half his train of knights within two short weeks of the time when he gave to her and Regan his kingdom.

> To seek him on the mountains near to Milford;
> Where, in a frenzy, in my master's garments,
> Which he enforc'd from me, away he posts
> With unchaste purpose, and with oath to violate
> My lady's honour.—*Cym.*, v. 5.

It is true that Cloten mentioned nothing to Pisanio of his " unchaste purpose" in the dialogue held between them (act iii., sc. 5); but the dramatist leaves to be inferred that Pisanio is aware of it, inasmuch as he causes Cloten to say to Pisanio, when the latter returns with Posthumus's clothes, " The third is, that thou wilt be a voluntary mute to my design," which conveys the effect that Pisanio is informed, or is to be informed, of what this " design " is.

> Sit, sir, *I will recount it to you :*
> But see, *I am prevented.—Per.*, v. 1.

The audience, knowing already the circumstances, are spared by this dramatic expedient, the needless repetition of " the cause " of Pericles' " sorrow."

> You shall prevail,
> Were it to woo my daughter; for *it seems*
> *You have been noble towards her.—Ibid.*, v. 2.

Although there has been nothing stated concerning Lysimachus having behaved nobly towards Marina, yet, since the readers or spectators of the play know this to be the case, the dramatist allows it to be thus referred to as a circumstance known to her father.

PASSAGES OF POETICAL LICENCE IN ANTICIPATION.

With the true imaginative force of a great poet, Shakespeare has some passages which deal with that which is to be as if it were already past, and treat as something done that which is still unperformed. [*See*

PARADOXICAL PHRASEOLOGY.] Of this kind is John Keats's startlingly bold expression, in the twenty-seventh stanza of his " Isabella ":—

> " So the two brothers and *their murder'd man*
> Rode past fair Florence."

It is such audacities of imaginative writing as these which fill poetical appreciators with transport, and which utterly dismay wretched conventionalists like Mr. Steevens, who stigmatises the passage we shall here below cite from " Romeo and Juliet" as being among " those miserable conceits with which our author too frequently counteracts his own pathos." The fact of writing such a comment as that upon such a passage as the one in question, strikes us as proving " miserable conceit" in the commentator himself, who conceives himself capable of passing judgment on a poetical idea of which he is incapable of perceiving the profound beauty and pathos. The intensity of emotional feeling—which regards as elapsed and irretrievable that which is dreaded and impending, or, as triumphantly effected that which is eagerly desired—was thoroughly comprehended and expressed by Shakespeare ; and the following passages bear witness to this :—

> Pr'ythee, bring me
> To the dead bodies of my queen and son :
> One grave shall be for both . . . once a day I'll visit
> The chapel *where they lie.*—*W. T.*, iii. 2.

> Great king, within this coffin I present
> Thy *buried fear.*—*R. II.*, v. 6.

> Here shall they make their ransom on the sand,
> Or with their blood stain this *discolour'd* shore.—2 *H. VI.*, iv. 1.

Upon them ! *Victory sits on our helms.*—*R. III.*, v. 3.

Death, lie thou there, *by a dead man interr'd.*—*R. & Jul.*, v. 3.

And fortune, on *his damned quarry* smiling.—*Macb.*, ?. 2.

The above expression—judging by the sense in which Shakespeare uses the word " quarry " elsewhere [*See* PECULIAR USE OF WORDS]— appears to us to signify ' Macdonwald's herd of fellows doomed to become a heap of slaughtered creatures '—already considered as a ' heap of carrion.'

I am dead, Horatio . . . Horatio, *I am dead.*—*Hamlet*, v. 2.

> And more, much more; the time will bring it out ;
> 'Tis past, and *so am I.*—*Lear*, v. 3.

My friend *is dead ;* 'tis done at your request.—*Oth.*, iii. 3.

Minion, your dear *lies dead.*—*Ibid.*, v. 1.

PASSAGES OF SINGLE WORDS.

Among the numerous varieties in Shakespeare's style, is that of occasional passages where a series of single words succeed each other :—

> So minutes, hours, days, months, and years,
> Pass'd over to the end they were created.—3 *H. VI.*, ii. 5.

> Observe degree, priority, and place,
> Insisture, course, proportion, season, form,
> Office, and custom, in all line of order.—*Tr. & Cr.*, i. 3.

> The trumpets, sackbuts, psalteries, and fifes,
> Tabors, and cymbals, and the shouting Romans.—*Coriol.*, v. 4.
> Day, night, hour, tide, time, work, play,
> Alone, in company, still my care hath been
> To have her matched.—*R. & Jul.*, iii. 5.
>
> Accurs'd, unhappy, wretched, hateful day!—*Ibid.*, iv. 5.
> 　　　　　　　　　　　　The ear,
> Taste, touch, smell, pleas'd from thy table rise.—*Timon*, i. 2.
> Are all thy conquests, glories, triumphs, spoils,
> Shrunk to this little measure?—*Jul. C.*, iii. 1.
> Who can be wise, amaz'd, temperate, and furious,
> Loyal and neutral, in a moment?—*Macb.*, ii. 3.
> Hoo! hearts, tongues, figures, scribes, bards, poets, cannot
> Think, speak, cast, write, sing, number, hoo!—*Ant. & C.*, iii. 2.

And, in the following passage, he gives us a succession of proper names, poetically collected, such as Milton delighted in and gave so felicitously :—

> 　　　　　　　　He hath assembled
> Bocchus, the king of Lybia; Archelaus,
> Of Cappadocia; Philadelphos, king
> Of Paphlagonia; the Thracian king, Adallas;
> King Malchus of Arabia; king of Pont;
> Herod of Jewry; Mithridates, king
> Of Comagene; Polemon and Amintas,
> The kings of Mede and Lycaonia,
> With a more larger list of sceptres.—*Ibid.*, iii. 6.

PASSAGES WHERE AN ORIGINAL WORD IS INTRODUCED INTO A USUAL FORM OF PHRASE.

Shakespeare occasionally so employs a word of his own introduction into a usual form of phrase as to give peculiar or duplicate effect to the sentence; and this mode of his, not having been duly observed by commentators and editors, has led them into the belief of error and misprint existing where there is, on the contrary, originality and power of diction :—

> Whose shadow the dismissed bachelor loves,
> Being *lass*-lorn.—*Temp.*, iv. 1.

By using "lass" in combination with "lorn," instead of the ordinary expression ' *love*-lorn,' our poet is able to have the word " loves " in the preceding line.

> He went but forth to wash him in the Hellespont, and, being taken with the cramp, was drowned: and the foolish *chroniclers* of that age found it was—Hero of Sestos.—*As You L.*, iv. 1.

Hanmer and others altered " chroniclers " to ' coroners ': but by using the word " found " in the sentence, Shakespeare imparts the effect of ' coroners ' to " chroniclers," while allowing it to stand for ' historians.'

> Pacing through the forest,
> Chewing the *food* of sweet and bitter fancy.—*Ibid.*, iv. 3.

It has been supposed that " food " is a misprint for ' cud '; but by the employment of " chewing " in the phrase, our dramatist imparts

the effect of ' cud ' to the word " food," which he frequently uses elsewhere in connection with " fancy," or "love."

> Then go thou forth ;
> And Fortune *play* upon thy prosperous helm,
> As thy auspicious mistress !—*All's W.*, iii. 3.

By the felicitous introduction of the word " play " into this sentence,
the poet gives the duplicate effect of ' shine ' (as the sunbeams play
upon an object) and ' smile' (as a lady looks favouringly on her chosen
lover) to the expression here used.

By my troth, sir, if I were to *live* this present hour, I will tell true.—*Ibid.*, iv. 3.

The word " live" has been suspected of error in the above passage ;
but by introducing it instead of the more generally used word ' die '
in this phrase, Shakespeare has given the inclusive effect to Parolles'
speech of ' if I were to die this present hour or allowed to live through it.'

> Our fancies are more giddy and unfirm,
> More longing, wavering, sooner lost and *worn*,
> Than women's are.—*Tw. N.*, ii. 4,

Johnson, and some editors since, would change " worn " to ' won '
in this passage; but Shakespeare, by introducing the word " worn,"
in connection with " lost," not only conveys the impression of the
ordinarily employed ' won,' but also allows it to imply ' worn out,'
' worn away.'

Indeed, brother-in-law was the farthest off you could have been to him ; and then
your blood had been the dearer, by I know how much an ounce.—
Very wisely, puppies.—*W. T.*, iv. 3.

Hanmer and others opine that ' not' ought to be placed between
" know " and " how," in the above passage ; but by omitting the ' not '
in a phrase where it is ordinarily used, our dramatist, besides giving
the effect of characteristically blundering phraseology to the rustic
speaker, also affords an opportunity for Autolycus's sly rejoinder to
come with appropriateness.

Ye shall have a hempen caudle, then, and the help of hatchet.—2 *H. VI.*, iv. 7.

Because there is an old slang term, ' pap with a hatchet,' Farmer
proposed to change Shakespeare's expression here to the better known
one.   But by using a slight variation from it, the dramatist not only
recalls the popular phrase, but adds the effect of similar ones which he
uses elsewhere : as, " Wisdom's warrant and *the help of school* "
(" Love's Labour 's Lost," v. 2) ; " Witches and *the help of hell* " (" First
Part of King Henry VI.," ii. 1) ; and " A man that were to sleep your
sleep, and a *hangman to help* him to bed " (" Cymbeline," v. 4).

> I have, thou gallant Trojan, seen thee oft,
> Labouring for destiny, make cruel way
> Through ranks of Greekish youth ; and I have seen thee,
> As hot as Perseus, spur thy Phrygian steed,
> Despising many forfeits and subduements,
> When thou hast hung thy advanced sword i' the air,
> Not letting it decline on the declin'd,
> That I have said to some my standers-by,
> " Lo, Jupiter is yonder, dealing *life !* "—*Tr. & Cr.*, iv. 5.

By using the word "life" here in an expression where 'death' is more generally employed, the dramatist conveys the idea of Hector's hewing his way through his enemies, yet sparing those among them who are already struck to earth; thus confirming his brother Troilus's remonstrance to him in act v., sc. 3, where he says, "Brother, you have a vice of mercy in you, which better fits a lion than a man. . . . When many times the captive Grecians fall, even in the fan and wind of your fair sword, you bid them rise, and live." Thus consistently does Shakespeare work.

For the nobles *receive* so to heart the banishment of that worthy Coriolanus, that they are in a ripe aptness to take all power from the people.—*Coriol.*, iv. 3.

By employing the word "receive" instead of the more usual one, 'take,' the impression is strengthened in the first clause of the sentence, and better allows the subsequent occurrence of "take" in the second clause.

> If, Tullus,
> Not yet thou know'st me, and seeing me, dost not
> *Think* me for the man I am, necessity
> Commands me name myself.—*Ibid.*, iv. 5.

Pope altered "think" to 'take' here; but by retaining Shakespeare's own word, we have the forcible and double effect of 'take me for the man I am,' and of 'recognise me in thy thought for the man I am.' This skilful method of introducing unhackneyed words into conventional and well-known phrases, forms one of the peculiar merits of Shakespeare's masterly style.

You shall perceive that a Jack guardant cannot *office* me from my son Coriolanus.—*Ibid.*, v. 2.

By using the word "office" instead of the more common expression 'keep,' the dramatist gives the effect of 'Jack in office' as an additional taunt to the contemptuous term "Jack guardant."

Doth not rosemary and Romeo begin both with a letter?—Ay, nurse; what of that? both with an R.—Ah, mocker! that's the dog's *name;* R is for the dog. No; I know it begins with some other letter.—*R. & Jul.*, ii. 4.

There is an old saying that "R is the dog's letter"; but Shakespeare varies the phrase by substituting "name" for 'letter,' partly because it imparts an effect of blundering confusion to the nurse's diction, and partly because "name" thus forms the antecedent to "it" in the next clause of the sentence.

I will carry no *crotchets:* I'll re you, I'll fa you; do you note me?—*Ibid.*, iv. 5.

Shakespeare makes Peter vary the formerly well-known phrase, 'I'll not carry coals' (meaning 'I'll not put up with insults') by introducing the word "crotchets," for the sake of having a jocose fling at the musician who is bantering him.

Is not my lord seen yet?—Not yet.—I wonder on't; he was wont to shine at seven.—*Timon*, iii. 4.

By using the word "shine" instead of 'appear' in this phrase, the idea of Timon's being like the sun is suggested, and well introduces the imagery of the speech that is made in rejoinder.

> I cannot think but your age has forgot me ;
> It could not else be, I should prove so base,
> To sue, and be denied such common grace :
> My wounds *ache at* you.—*Timon*, iii. 5.

By the phraseology here, Shakespeare gives the double effect of ' my wounds blush for your shameless ingratitude ' and ' my wounds ache afresh at your cruel hardness.'

Why, man, they *did make love to* this employment.—*Hamlet*, v. 2.

This variation from the more usual phrase, ' courted this employment,' gives increased force to the accusation of base suing for a base office.

And we shall talk before we fight.—Most meet that first we come to *words.*—*Ant. & C.*, ii. 6.

By the introduction of " words " into this form of phrase, Shakespeare neatly infers ' before coming to blows ' as its understood completion.

And not resting here, accuses him of letters he had formerly wrote to Pompey ; *upon his own appeal* seizes him.—*Ibid.*, iii. 5.

The phrase, thus constructed, gives the duplicate effect of ' on his own responsibility,' and ' on his own accusation solely '; since " appeal " is here used in the sense which it bears in common law—that of ' accusation.'

> Follow the noise so far as we have quarter ;
> Let 's see how it will *give off.*—*Ibid.*, iv. 3.

By employing this expression instead of either of the commoner ones, ' give over,' or ' leave off,' the poet imparts an effect of the speakers being unusually impressed by the supernatural sounds they hear.

PECULIAR CONSTRUCTION.

Some of Shakespeare's constructional peculiarities in phraseology deserve special notification. He occasionally has phrases of transposed or even of involved construction :—

One of them is *a plain* [plainly a] fish.—*Temp.*, v. 1.

Yet in this life lie hid *more thousand deaths* [a thousand more deaths than I have enumerated, or than the one that is life's ending].—*M. for M.*, iii. 1.

Here is the head ; I 'll carry it myself.—
Convenient is it [it is convenient that you should do so].—*Ibid.*, iv. 3.

And I, with *your two helps* [the help of you two], will so practise on Benedick.—*M. Ado*, ii. 1.

I will fetch my gold, and have *our two wagers* [the wagers of us two] recorded.—*Cym.*, i. 5.

These, and *your three motives* [the motives of you three] to the battle, with I know not how much more, should be demanded.—*Ibid.*, v. 5.

I shall desire *you of more acquaintance* [more acquaintance of you], good Master Cobweb.—*Mid. N. D.*, iii. 1.

I humbly do desire *your grace of pardon* [pardon of your grace] ; I must away this night.—*Mer. of V.*, iv. 1.

Till that the *weary very means* [very means, becoming weary] do ebb ?—*As You L.*, ii. 7.

> *If yourself,*
> Whose aged honour cites a virtuous youth,
> *Did ever, in so true a flame of liking,*
> *Wish chastely, and love dearly, that your Dian*
> *Was both herself and love* * [if ever you wished chastely and loved dearly in so pure

and true a flame as that your Diana was both herself and love itself].—*All's W.*, i. 3.

I am commanded here, and *kept a coil with* [a coil is kept up with me],—" Too young " and " the next year."—*Ibid.*, ii. 1.

The last that e'er I took her leave at court [the last time that ever I took leave of her at court].—*Ibid.*, v. 3.

> I could not find him at the Elephant :
> Yet *there he was* [he had been there].—*Tw. N.*, iv. 3.

So long I *daily vow to use it* [vow to use it daily].—*W. T.*, iii. 2.

This *avouches the shepherd's son* [the shepherd's son avouches].—*Ibid.*, v. 2.

'A pops me out *at least from* [from at least] fair five hundred pound a year.— *John*, i. 1.

Why, then, your fears (which, as they say, attend the steps of wrong) *should move you* [why, then, should your fears move you] to mew up your tender kinsman.— *Ibid.*, iv. 2.

But my fair name (*despite of death, that lives* [that, despite of death, lives] upon my grave).—*R. II.*, i. 1.

With rival-hating envy, *set on you* [set you on] to wake our peace.—*Ibid.*, i. 3.

Violent fires soon *burn out themselves* [burn themselves out].—*Ibid.*, ii. 1.

> He hath not money for these Irish wars,
> *His burdenous taxes notwithstanding* [notwithstanding his burdenous taxations].— *Ibid.*, ii. 1.

Nor friends, nor foes, to me welcome you are [neither as friends nor as foes are you welcome to me].—*Ibid.*, ii. 3.

The worst is worldly loss thou canst unfold [the worst that thou canst unfold is worldly loss].—*Ibid.*, iii. 2.

Revolt our subjects ? [Do our subjects revolt ?]—*Ibid.*, iii. 2.

Me rather had [I had rather] my heart might feel your love.—*Ibid.*, iii. 3.

> Mounted upon a hot and fiery steed,
> *Which his aspiring rider seem'd to know* [which seem'd to know his aspiring rider].— *Ibid.*, v. 2.

> Nor I, nor any man, that *but man is* [is but man],
> With nothing shall be pleas'd.—*Ibid.*, v. 5.

Was he not proclaim'd by Richard, that *dead is* [is dead], the next of blood ?— 1 *H. IV.*, i. 3.

Whose wrongs *in us God pardon !* [God pardon in us !].—*Ibid.*, i. 3.

What a *candy deal of* [deal of candy] courtesy.—*Ibid.*, i. 3.

Homo is a *common name* [name common] to all men.—*Ibid.*, ii. 1.

I know his death will be a march of twelve-score [I know that a march of twelve-score will be the death of him].—*Ibid.*, ii. 4.

Make *blind itself* [itself blind] with foolish tenderness.—*Ibid.*, iii. 2.

The dauphin, *whom of succour we entreated* [of whom we entreated succour].— *H. V.*, iii. 3.

So that here men are punished, for before-breach of the king's laws, in *now the king's quarrel* [the king's quarrel now].—*Ibid.*, iv. 1.

But all's not done ; yet *keep the French the field* [the French keep the field].— *Ibid.*, iv. 6.

---

* Besides " love " here meaning ' love itself,' it means " Love," as used for the goddess of love, Venus ; since Shakespeare has more than once employed " Love " thus [*See* TITLES].

Lives he [does he live], good uncle?—*H. V.*, iv. 6.

Peace to this meeting, wherefore we are met [peace, for which we are here met, be to this meeting]!—*Ibid.*, v. 2.

This Gloster should be quickly rid the world [the world should be quickly rid of this Gloster].—2 *H. VI.*, iii. 1.

Men's flesh preserv'd so whole do seldom win [men, whose flesh is preserved so whole, do seldom win].—*Ibid.*, iii. 1.

Until my mis-shap'd trunk that bears this head [until my head, that this mis-shaped trunk bears] be round impaled with a glorious crown.—3 *H. VI.*, iii. 2

I can add colours to the cameleon ;
Change shapes with Proteus for advantages [advantageously compete with Proteus in changing shapes].—*Ibid.*, iii. 2.

And to that end *I shortly mind to leave you* [I intend soon to leave you].—*Ibid.*, iv. 1.

So *your dislikes* [the dislikes of you], to whom I would be pleasing,
Do cloud my joys with danger and with sorrow.—*Ibid.*, iv. 1.

Thus yields *the cedar to the axe's edge* [to the axe's edge the cedar],
Whose arms gave shelter to the princely eagle.—*Ibid.*, v. 2.

Thus doth he force the swords of wicked men
To turn *their own points on their masters' bosoms* [their points on their masters' own bosoms].—*R. III.*, v. 1.

I am sorry *my integrity should breed*
(And service to his majesty and you)
So deep suspicion, where all faith was meant [my integrity and service to his majesty and you should breed].—*H. VIII.*, iii. 1.

Have been more *than could my studied purposes requite* [than my studied purposes could requite].—*Ibid.*, iii. 2.

You have as little honesty as honour ;
That, in the way of loyalty and truth
Toward the king, my ever royal master,
Dare mate* a sounder man than Surrey can be,
And all that love his follies [you have as little honesty as honour, who dare impugn a sounder man (on the score of loyalty and truth towards my royal master, the king) than Surrey and all who love his follies can be].—*Ibid.*, iii. 2.

An ordinary groom is for such payment [such payment is fit only for an ordinary groom].—*Ibid.*, v. 1.

They would shame to make me wait else at door [else they would shame to make me wait at the door].—*Ibid.*, v. 2.

That loves his mistress *more than in confession*
With truant vows to her own lips he loves [more than he protests he loves her when he vows constancy and kisses her].—*Tr. & Cr.*, i. 3.

Hector shall have a great catch, if he knock out *either of your brains* [the brains of either of you].—*Ibid.*, ii. 1.

Diomed has got that same scurvy doting foolish *young knave's sleeve of Troy* [young knave of Troy's sleeve] there in his helm.—*Ibid.*, v. 4.

The policy of those crafty swearing rascals . . . *is not proved* [is proved to be not] worth a blackberry.—*Ibid.*, v. 4.

My work hath *yet not* [not yet] warm'd me.—*Coriol.*, i. 5.

Of all the treasure *in this field achiev'd and city* [achiev'd in this field and city].—*Ibid.*, i. 9.

What good condition can a treaty find
I' the part that is at mercy? [What good condition can the side that is at the mercy of the other find in a treaty?]—*Ibid.*, i. 10.

Thereto witness may my surname, Coriolanus [my surname of Coriolanus may bear witness thereto].—*Ibid.*, iv. 5.

I also am longer to live most weary [I also am most weary to live longer].—*Ibid.*, iv. 5.

---

* For Shakespeare's varied use of the word "mate," *see* PECULIAR USE OF WORDS.

This so never-needed help [this never so much needed help].—*Coriol.*, v. 1.

Nay, an you *begin to rail on society once* [once begin to rail on society], I am sworn not to regard you.—*Timon*, i. 2.

Not nature, to whom all sores lay siege, can bear great fortune, but by contempt of nature [human nature, liable to the assaults of every misfortune, can never bear great fortune without showing contempt for its fellow-creatures].—*Ibid.*, iv. 1.

So soon we shall drive back *of Alcibiades th' approaches wild* [the wild approaches of Alcibiades].—*Ibid.*, v. 2.

Crimes, like lands, are not inherited [crimes are not inherited, as lands are].—*Ibid.*, v. 5.

And roars, as doth the lion, in the Capitol [and roars in the Capitol, as the lion roars].—*Jul. C.*, i. 3.

O Rome, *I make thee promise* [I make promise to thee].—*Ibid.*, ii. 1.

That every like is not the same, O Cæsar,
The heart of Brutus yearns to think upon! [O Cæsar, the heart of Brutus grieves to think that everything which seems like another is not always the same as that other!]
—*Ibid.*, ii. 2.

Speak, then, to me, *who neither beg nor fear*
Your favours nor your hate [who neither beg your favours nor fear your hate].—*Macb.*, i. 3.

Which is now *our point of second meeting* [the point (or object) of our second meeting].—*Ibid.*, iii. 1.

Free from our feasts and banquets bloody knives [free our feasts and banquets from bloody knives].—*Ibid.*, iii. 6.

Our suffering country under a hand accurs'd! [our country suffering under an accursed hand!]—*Ibid.*, iii. 6.

Pour in *sow's blood, that hath eaten* her nine farrow [the blood of a sow that hath eaten].—*Ibid.*, iv. 1.

Having ever seen *in the prenominate crimes*
The youth you breathe of guilty [the youth you breathe of guilty in the prenominate crimes].—*Hamlet*, ii. 1.

But, good Laertes, *will you do this* [if you will do this], keep close within your chamber.—*Ibid.*, iv. 7.

Grop'd I to find *out them* [them out].—*Ibid.*, v. 2.

And *your large speeches may your deeds approve* [may your deeds prove equal to your large speeches].—*Lear*, i. 1.

So *distribution should* [should distribution] undo excess.—*Ibid.*, iv. 1.

I marvel, our mild husband *not met us* [met us not, or, did not meet us] on the way.—*Ibid.*, iv. 2.

What cannot be preserv'd when fortune takes,
Patience her injury a mockery makes [when fortune takes what cannot be preserved, patience makes a mockery of her injury].—*Oth.*, i. 3.

His barque is stoutly timber'd, and his pilot
Of very expert and approv'd allowance [of very allowed and proved expertness].—*Ibid.*, ii. 1.

I humbly do beseech *you of* [of you] your pardon.—*Ibid.*, iii. 3.

This fellow's of exceeding honesty,
And knows all qualities, with a learned spirit,
Of human dealings [and knows with an experienced spirit all qualities of human dealings].—*Ibid.*, iii. 3.

How this Herculean Roman *does become*
The carriage of his chafe [makes his chafed bearing become him].—*Ant. & C.*, i. 3.

That he which is was wish'd until he were [that the man who is in power was wished for until he came to be in power].—*Ibid.*, i. 4.

Lepidus flatters both,
Of both is flattered; but he *neither loves* [loves neither of them]
Nor *either cares* [does either of them care] for him.—*Ibid.*, ii. 1.

Your wife and brother made wars upon me; and their contestation *was theme for you* [had you for its theme], you were the word of war.—*Ant. & C.*, ii. 2.

If Cleopatra heard you, *your reproof were well deserv'd of rashness* [the reproof you would receive from her would be well deserved for your rashness].—*Ibid.*, ii. 2.

Leap thou, attire and all, through *proof of harness* [armour of proof] to my heart.—*Ibid.*, iv. 8.

Her life in Rome would be eternal in our triumph [her living presence in Rome would render our triumph eternal].—*Ibid.*, v. 1.

And golden Phœbus *never be beheld of eyes again so royal!* [never again be beheld by eyes so royal!].—*Ibid.*, v. 2.

And *you shall hear the legions, now in Gallia, sooner landed in our not-fearing Britain* [you shall sooner hear that the legions, now in Gallia, are landed in our not-fearing Britain] than have tidings of any penny tribute paid.—*Cym.*, ii. 4.

From whose so many weights of baseness *cannot
A dram of worth be drawn* [a dram of worth cannot be drawn].—*Ibid.*, iii. 5.

Many years, though Cloten then but young, you see, not wore him from my remembrance [though Cloten then was but young, you see many years have not worn him from my remembrance].—*Ibid.*, iv. 4.

Than be so, better to cease to be [better to cease to be than to be so].—*Ibid.*, iv. 4.

Fairer than *those for preservation cas'd, or shame* [those cased for preservation or shame].—*Ibid.*, v. 3.

Why, do ye take it [why, then, take it].—*Per.*, ii. 1.

Opinion's but a fool, that makes us scan
The outward habit by the inward man [the inward man by the outward habit].—*Ibid.*, ii. 2.

For a more blust'rous birth had never babe [for never had babe a more blusterous birth].—*Ibid.*, iii. 1.

We are near Tharsus.—*Thither, gentle mariner, alter thy course for Tyrė* [alter thy course, which is now for Tyre, to go thither (to Tharsus)].—*Ibid.*, iii. 1.

In your supposing once more put your sight of heavy Pericles [once more put what you behold of the melancholy Pericles under the influence of your imagination].—*Ibid.*, v. (*Gower*).

He has a few phrases where objects are mentioned and references made in order of succession contrary to usual arrangement:—

What would you have, you curs,
That like nor *peace* nor *war?* the one *affrights* you,
The other *makes you proud.*—*Coriol.*, i. 1.

In all shapes that man goes up and down in from *fourscore* to *thirteen*, this spirit walks in.—*Timon*, ii. 2.

Till he unseam'd him from the *nave* to the *chops.*—*Macb.*, i. 2.

Thou hast it now—*king*, *Cawdor*, *Glamis*, all.—*Ibid.*, iii. 1.

They are apt enough to *dislocate* and *tear*
Thy *flesh* and *bones.*—*Lear*, iv. 2.

If *knife*, *drugs*, *serpents*, have *edge*, *sting*, or *operation*, I am safe.—*Ant. & C.*, iv. 13.

And will to *ears* and *tongues* be *theme* and *hearing* ever.—*Cym.*, iii. 1.

He sometimes has phrases where verbs and pronouns are transposed:—

But is my husband coming?—Ay, in good sadness, *is he.*—*Merry W.*, iv. 2.

And there *will she* sit in her smock.—*M. Ado*, ii. 3.

Like a demi-god here *sit I* in the sky.—*Love's L. L.*, iv. 3.

There *lay he*, stretch'd along like a wounded knight.—*As You L.*, iii. 2.

Then again *worries he* his daughter with clipping her.—*W. T.*, v. 2.

You are so fretful, you cannot live long.—Why, there *is it.*—1 *H. IV.*, iii. 3.

The very same day *did I* fight with one Sampson.—2 *H. IV.*, iii. 2.

My soul shall *thine keep* company to heaven.—*H. V.*, iv. 6.

But *gather we* [let us gather] our forces out of hand.—1 *H. VI.*, iii. 2.

Why, then from Ireland *come I* with my strength.—2 *H. VI.*, iii. 1.

Sprawl'st thou ? [dost thou sprawl ?] take that.—3 *H. VI.*, v. 5.

Now *march we* [let us march] hence.—*Ibid.*, v. 5.

> The son of Clarence *have I* pent up close ;
> His daughter meanly *have I* match'd in marriage.—*R. III.*, iv. 3.

That shall not serve your turn ; that *shall it* not.—*Tr. & Cr.*, iii. 1.

Dar'st thou [dost thou dare], Cassius, now.—*Jul. C.*, i. 2.

Now *sit we* [let us sit] close about this taper.—*Ibid.*, iv. 3.

Come, *go we* [let us go] to the king.—*Macb.*, iv. 3.

Near Birnam wood *shall we* well meet them ; that way *are they* coming.—*Ibid.*, v. 2.

> Well, *march we* [let us march] on,
> To give obedience where 'tis truly ow'd :
> *Meet we* [let us meet] the medicine of the sickly weal ;
> And with him *pour we* [let us pour], in our country's purge,
> Each drop of us . . .
> *Make we* [let us make] our march towards Birnam.—*Ibid.*, v. 2.

The day almost *itself professes* yours.—*Ibid.*, v. 7.

This to me in dreadful secrecy *impart they did.*—*Hamlet*, i. 2.

Com'st thou [dost thou come] to beard me in Denmark ?—*Ibid.*, ii. 2.

Pray can I not, though inclination be as strong.—*Ibid.*, iii. 3.

Why so earnestly *seek you* [do you seek] to put up that letter ?—*Lear*, i. 2.

Thy half o' the kingdom *hast thou* not forgot.—*Ibid.*, ii. 4.

Shut your mouth, dame ; or with this paper *shall I* stop it.—*Ibid.*, v. 3.

It is too true an evil : *gone she is.*—*Oth.*, i. 1.

Even out of that *will I* cause these of Cyprus to mutiny.—*Ibid.*, ii. 1.

Thus *do they*, sir : they take the flow o' the Nile.—*Ant. & C.*, ii. 7.

Fight I will no more, but yield me to the.—*Cym.*, v. 3.

Also, phrases where epithets and nouns are transposed :—

If *love ambitious* sought a match of birth.—*John*, ii. 2.

Why the *law Salique*, that they have in France.—*H. V.*, i. 2.

That the *land Salique* is in Germany.—*Ibid.*, i. 2.

The sword, the mace, the *crown imperial* . . .
Not all these laid in *bed majestical.*—*Ibid.*, iv. 1.

Tears virginal shall be to me even as the dew.—*2 H. VI.*, v. 2.

In peril of precipitation from off the *rock Tarpeian.*—*Coriol.*, iii. 3.

That seems to speak *things strange.*—*Macb.*, i. 2.

But *treasons capital*, confess'd and proved.—*Ibid.*, i. 3.

My dull brain was wrought with *things forgotten.*—*Ibid.*, i. 3.

The *borders maritime* lack blood to think on 't.—*Ant. & C.*, i. 4.

Whilst I wore his *sword Philippan.*—*Ibid.*, ii. 5.

Are you good *men and true ?*—*M. Ado*, iii. 3.

Thou hast a cruel *nature and a bloody.*—*H. VIII.*, v. 2.

He cannot flatter, he—an honest *mind and plain.*—*Lear*, ii. 2.

> For he hath laid strange *courtesies and great*
> Of late upon me.—*Ant. & C.*, ii. 2.

There are some passages where our great dramatist gives inconsecutive construction, in order to mark agitation in the speaker [*See* SOLILOQUIES and VARIATIONS] :—

> I am more proud to be Sir Roland's son,
> His youngest son ;—and would not change that calling,
> To be adopted heir to Frederick.—*As You L.*, i. 2.

Orlando begins with the words, "I am more proud to be," which seems to require 'than' before "to be adopted"; but Duke Frederick's previous speech having roused the noble young man into indignation, he replies with a natural half-incoherence of expression.

> This ring was mine; and when I gave it Helen,
> I bade her, if her fortunes ever stood
> Necessitied to help, that by this token
> I would relieve her.—*All's W.*, v. 3.

The king, by the expression "necessitied to help" implies 'necessitied *to ask* for help'; and thus the effect of appeal by presentation of the ring is given to the sentence, which allows the words, "that by this token I would relieve her," to follow naturally. The king's deep displeasure at Bertram's conduct causes him to speak with this succinctness and condensed utterance.

> Let me speak a little. This youth that you see here
> I snatch'd one half out of the jaws of death;
> Reliev'd him with such sanctity of love,—
> And to his image, which methought did promise
> Most honourable worth, did I devotion.—*Tw. N.*, iii. 4.

In this outburst of passionate feeling, the inconsecutive construction serves admirably to denote the emotion with which Antonio speaks; and "such," which seems to require 'that' or 'as' to follow up the sentence, being succeeded by a break in the speech, artistically conveys the impression of the broken voice and bitter feeling of the utterer.

> 'A made a finer end, and went away, an it had been any christom child.—*H. V.*, ii. 3.

The word "finer" is used by the hostess as if she were going to say 'finer than any christom child'; but, in her slipshod style and her grief at the recollection of Falstaff's death, she changes the construction of her sentence half way by the introduction of the words, "and went away," which requires the 'as if it had been any christom child,' to complete the sense of what she thus secondly says.

> The king, on his own royal disposition,
> And not provok'd by any suitor else;
> Aiming, belike, at your interior hatred,
> That in your outward action shows itself
> Against my children, brothers, and myself,
> Makes him to send; that thereby he may gather
> The ground of your ill-will, and so remove it.—*R. III.*, i. 3.

The inconsequence observable in the construction of this speech serves well to mark the perturbed condition of the queen, as she thus replies to Gloster's insidious attack:—

> A man, young lady! lady, such a man,
> As all the world—why he's a man of wax.—*R. & Jul.*, i. 3.

Here the nurse's interrupted diction is somewhat similar to that of the hostess, just before cited; but nursey's flustered incompetence to finish her phrase arises from her wishing to show how impossible it is adequately to express her sense of County Paris's matchless excellence.

> But myself,
> Who had the world as my confectionary;
> The mouths, the tongues, the eyes, and hearts of men
> At duty more than I could frame employment

> That numberless upon me stuck, as leaves
> Do on the oak, have with one winter's brush
> Fell from their boughs, and left me open, bare
> For every storm that blows;—I, to bear this,
> That never knew but better, is some burden:
> Thy nature did commence in sufferance, time
> Hath made thee hard in 't.—*Timon*, iv. 3.

To our thinking, the disconnected construction in this fine passage aids well the dramatist's purpose of indicating the passionate indignation of Timon against his professedly cynical tormentor and against his faithless friends.

> No, not an oath: if not the face of men,
> The sufferance of our souls, the time's abuse,—
> If these be motives weak, break off betimes,
> And every man hence to his idle bed.—*Jul. C.*, ii. 1.

The break in the consecution of constructional progress perceptible here, helps to mark the eager earnestness of the speaker.

> Impatient of my absence,
> And grief that young Octavius with Mark Antony
> Have made themselves so strong;—for with her death
> That tidings came;—with this she fell distract,
> And, her attendants absent, swallow'd fire.—*Ibid.*, iv. 3.

The disjointed framing of this speech has excellent effect in denoting the profound sorrow of Brutus at the loss of his wife beneath his assumed stoicism of courage upon hearing the news.

> What are you, then, determined to do?—
> Even by the rule of that philosophy
> By which I did blame Cato for the death
> Which he did give himself:—I know not how,
> But I do find it cowardly and vile,
> For fear of what might fall, so to prevent
> The time of life: arming myself with patience
> To stay the providence of some high powers
> That govern us below.—*Ibid.*, v. 1.

The inconsecutive construction here well represents the speaker as a man rather deliberating with himself, and pursuing an inward train of thought, than giving a direct answer to a question.

> Here, as before, never, so help you mercy,
> How strange or odd soe'er I bear myself—
> As I perchance, hereafter shall think meet
> To put an antick disposition on—
> That you, at such times seeing me, never shall,
> With arms encumber'd thus, or this head-shake,
> Or by pronouncing of some doubtful phrase,
> As, " Well, well, we know ; "—or, " We could, an if we would ; "—
> Or, " If we list to speak ; "—or, " There be, an if they might; "—
> Or such ambiguous giving out, to note
> That you know aught of me : this not to do,
> So grace and mercy at your most need help you,
> Swear.—*Hamlet*, i. 5.

Excellently does the immethodical phraseology in this speech help to depict the tumult of the speaker's mind at the present juncture ; partly occupied with the awe inspired by the recent appearance of his father's spirit, partly with the conception of his plan for the future in assuming madness.

> When by no means he could . . .
> Persuade me to the murder of your lordship;
> But that I told him, the revenging gods
> 'Gainst parricides did all their thunders bend;
> Spoke, with how manifold and strong a bond
> The child was bound to the father;—sir, in fine,
> Seeing how loathly opposite I stood
> To his unnatural purpose, in fell motion,
> With his prepared sword, he charges home
> My unprovided body, lanc'd mine arm.—*Lear*, ii. 1.

The ill-following sentences here serve to represent Edmund's hurriedly concocted narration of the pretended fray between himself and his brother, whom he is seeking to ruin in their father's opinion.

> Why, the hot-blooded France, that dowerless took
> Our youngest born, I could as well be brought
> To knee his throne, and, squire-like, pension beg
> To keep base life afoot.—*Ibid.*, ii. 4.

The disturbed mode of construction in this speech consists perfectly with the agitation of the hapless old king's mind.

> What hath been seen,
> Either in snuffs and packings of the dukes;
> Or the hard rein which both of them have borne
> Against the old kind king; or something deeper,
> Whereof perchance these are but furnishings;—
> But, true it is, from France there comes a power
> Into this scatter'd kingdom.—*Ibid.*, iii. 1.

The irregularity of the construction here has characteristic effect, as suiting with the wild circumstances of the scene, with the mysteriously hinted nature of the communication, and with the concealed rank of the speaker.

> She is abus'd, stol'n from me, and corrupted
> By spells and medicines bought of mountebanks;
> For nature so preposterously to err—
> Being not deficient, blind, or lame of sense—
> Sans witchcraft could not.—*Oth.*, i. 3.

The inconsecutive construction in the phrase, " For nature so preposterously to err, sans witchcraft could not," accords well with the father's perturbation of mind.

> I do beseech you—
> Though I perchance am vicious in my guess,
> As, I confess, it is my nature's plague
> To spy into abuses, and oft my jealousy
> Shapes faults that are not—that your wisdom yet,
> From one that so imperfectly conceits,
> Would take no notice; nor build yourself a trouble
> Out of his scattering and unsure observance.—*Ibid.*, iii. 3.

The halting construction of this speech well gives the effect of Iago's putting on a hesitating, unwilling manner; half expressing, half suppressing his suggestions, and whetting his victim's anxiety to hear more by bidding him desire to hear no more.

Occasionally, Shakespeare has phrases of confused construction, for the sake of giving some special effect :—

> Who cannot want the thought, how monstrous
> It was for Malcolm and for Donalbain
> To kill their gracious father? damned fact!

> How it did grieve Macbeth ! did he not straight,
> In pious rage, the two delinquents tear,
> That were the slaves of drink and thralls of sleep ?
> Was not that nobly done ?   Ay, and wisely too ;
> For 'twould have angered any heart alive
> To hear the men deny 't.—*Macb.*, iii. 6.

The construction of the first sentence here is so contrived as to give superficially the effect of, ' Who can fail to have the thought how monstrously wicked it was, &c.,' while in reality meaning, ' Who cannot be without the thought that Malcolm and Donalbain could be so monstrously wicked as to kill, &c.' The ambiguity of the mode of expression harmonises completely with the strain of irony and mocking question throughout the whole speech.

> Those wicked creatures yet do look well-favour'd,
> When others are more wicked ; not being the worst
> Stands in some rank of praise.   I 'll go with thee :
> Thy fifty yet doth double five-and-twenty,
> And thou art twice her love.—*Lear*, ii. 4.

Pope proposed to alter " art " to 'hast' here ; but the phraseology is peculiarly Shakespearian—that is, better than conventionally correct. The introduction of the word " art " into this sentence gives the characteristic touch of confused idea to Lear's diction, besides according with the passionate vehemence and imaginative force that distinguish his mode of expression.   He embodies the " love " here ; making it the representation of his daughters, valued according to their relative amount of affection towards him.

> Thou hadst been better have been born a dog,
> Than answer my wak'd wrath.—*Oth.*, iii. 3.

The redundancy of the first " been " in that sentence, far from being a blemish, seems to us to aid in conveying the effect of agitated utterance.

Shakespeare has very many phrases of condensed and elliptical construction.   [*See* Elliptical Style and Elliptically used Words]:—

> Who were below him
> He us'd as creatures of another place ;
> And bow'd his eminent top to their low ranks,
> Making them proud of his humility,
> *In their poor praise he humbled* [in praising whom he humbled himself].—*All's W.*, i. 2.

> Can't no other,
> *But, I your daughter, he must be my brother ?* [Can it be no otherwise than were I your daughter, he must be my brother ?]—*Ibid.*, i. 3.

> I have spoke
> With one that, in her sex, her years, profession,
> Wisdom, and constancy, *hath amaz'd me more*
> *Than I dare blame my weakness* [hath filled me with more well-grounded astonishment than with weak credulity deserving blame].—*Ibid.*, ii. 1.

> Beware of them, Diana ; their promises, enticements, oaths, tokens, and all these engines of lust, *are not the things they go under* [are not the things under the names of which they go].—*Ibid.*, iii. 5.

> And the misery is, example, that so terribly shows in the wreck of maidenhood, cannot for all that *dissuade succession* [warn against following in the same path].—*Ibid.*, iii. 5.

> Yet, good deed, Leontes,
> I love thee *not a jar o' the clock behind*
> *What lady she her lord* [not so much as a tick of the clock less than any lady loves her lord, however dearly she may love him].—*W. T.*, i. 2.

I never heard of such another encounter, which lames report to follow it, and *undoes description to do it* [ruins description in attempting to describe it].—*W. T.*, v. 2.

My lord of Hereford, my message is to you.—

My lord, *my answer is—to Lancaster* [I will make my answer when you address me as Duke of Lancaster, which is my title now, and not lord of Hereford].—*R. II.*, ii. 3.

Little are we beholden to your love,
And little look'd for at your helping hands [And little was this small amount of love looked for at your hands which should have helped us].—*Ibid.*, iv. 1.

Arrest them *to the answer of the law* [to make their answer to the law].—*H. V.*, ii. 2.

Scorn and defiance ; *slight regard, contempt,*
And anything that may not misbecome
The mighty sender, *doth he prize you at* [he esteems you worthy of no other than slight regard and contempt].—*Ibid.*, ii. 4.

It may be, his enemy is a gentleman *of great sort, quite from the answer of his degree* [of great rank, quite removed from a corresponding level of low degree with that of the soldier, and therefore exempt from being called upon to render him an answer].—*Ibid.*, iv. 7.

Me seemeth [it seems to me], then, it is no policy.—2 *H. VI.*, iii. 1.

A sceptre shall it have—*have I a soul* [as surely as I have a soul]—on which I 'll toss the flower-de-luce of France.—*Ibid.*, v. 1.

Suppose, my lords, he did it unconstrain'd,
Think you 'twere prejudicial *to his crown?* [to the due hereditary succession of his crown].—3 *H. VI.*, i. 1.

The broken rancour of your high-swoln hearts,
But lately splinter'd, knit and join'd together,
Must gently be preserv'd, cherish'd, and kept [The unsound rancour of your proud hearts, like a newly set limb but lately splinted, must be carefully tended until it become perfectly sound and whole].—*R. III.*, ii. 2.

This, this All-Souls' day to my fearful soul
Is the determin'd respite of my wrongs [This All-Souls' day is the period to which my trembling soul sees that the punishment of its misdeeds has been respited].—*Ibid.*, v. 1.

That blind priest, like the eldest son of fortune,
Turns what he list [turns as he pleases whatever event he chooses to turn, as if it were the wheel of fortune].—*H. VIII.*, ii. 2.

How tastes it? is it bitter? *forty pence, no* [I 'll wager forty pence that it is not].—*Ibid.*, ii. 3.

Of which there is not one . . . but will deserve,
For virtue and true beauty of the soul,
For honesty and decent carriage,
A right good husband, *let him be a noble* [even though he should be a nobleman].—*Ibid.*, iv. 2.

You are potently oppos'd ; and with a malice
Of as great a size [as great as is the power that opposes you].—*Ibid.*, v. 1.

What was purpos'd
Concerning his imprisonment, was rather
(If there be faith in men) meant for his trial,
And fair purgation to the world, than malice,—
I 'm sure, *in me* [it was so meant by me].—*Ibid.*, v. 2.

All princes *living with her* [living at the same epoch with herself].—*Ibid.*, v. 4.

His youth in flood [though his youthful blood be in full flow],
I 'll prove this truth with my three drops of blood.—*Tr. & Cr.*, i. 3.

And sometimes we are devils to ourselves,
When we will tempt the frailty of our powers,
Presuming on their changeful potency [presuming too far on the strength of that which is variable, unstable, and fallible].—*Ibid.*, iv. 4.

To pray Achilles see us at our tent [To pray that Achilles will come and see us at our tent].—*Ibid.*, v. 10.

He cannot temperately transport his honours
From where he should begin, and end [from where he should begin to where he should end].—*Coriol.*, ii. 1.

I would they would forget me, *like the virtues*
Which our divines lose by them [as they forget the virtues which our divines vainly endeavour to implant in them].—*Ibid.*, ii. 3.

Put not your worthy rage into your tongue ;
One time will owe another [some other time will give you the opportunity which the present time denies you].—*Ibid.*, iii. 1.

And you will rather show our general louts
How you can frown, than spend a fawn upon them,
For the inheritance of their loves, and safeguard
Of what *that want* [the want of that love] might ruin.—*Ibid.*, iii. 2.

To beg of thee, it is my more dishonour
Than thou of them [it is more dishonour for me to beg of thee than it is dishonour for thee to beg of them].—*Ibid.*, iii. 2.

Fortune's blows,
When most struck home, being gentle wounded, craves
A noble cunning [when Fortune's blows are most struck home, to be gentle, although wounded, demands a noble philosophy].—*Ibid.*, iv. 1.

Thy sight, which should make our eyes flow with joy, hearts dance with comforts,
constrains them weep, and shake with fear and sorrow [the sight of thee, which should make our eyes flow with joy and our hearts dance with comfort, constrains our eyes to weep, and our hearts to shake with fear and sorrow].—*Ibid.*, v. 3.

Oh, she is rich in beauty ; only poor,
That, when she dies, *with beauty dies her store* [with her individual beauty dies so large a store of beauty].—*R. & Jul.*, i. 1.

Going to find a barefoot brother out,
One of our order, *to associate me*
Here in this city visiting the sick [to bear me company, he being here in this city visiting the sick].—*Ibid.*, v. 2.

He does deny him, in respect of his,
What charitable men afford to beggars [he refuses to give him that which, in comparison with his own means, is but the usual alms afforded by charitable men to beggars].—*Timon*, iii. 2.

Had his necessity made use of me,
I would have put my wealth into donation,
And the best half should have return'd to him [I would have treated my wealth as if it had been Timon's gift, and would have sent him back the larger half].—*Ibid.*, iii. 2.

If there be such valour in the bearing, *what make we abroad ?* [What do we do out fighting? or what makes us go forth into the field ?]—*Ibid.*, iii. 5.

Dry up *thy marrows, vines, and plough-torn leas* [the marrows of thy vines and plough-torn leas].—*Ibid.*, iv. 3.

Willing misery
Outlives incertain pomp, is crown'd before :
The one is filling still, never complete ;
The other, at high wish : best state, contentless,
Hath a distracted and most wretched being,
Worst than the worst, content.
Thou shouldst desire to die, being miserable [Willing misery outlives uncertain grandeur, its desires are sooner and more surely fulfilled : the one is ever craving, never satisfied ; the other is always at the height of its wishes : the best of states, without content, has a distracted and most wretched existence, worse than the very worst of states, with content.   Thou shouldst desire to die, being unwillingly miserable].
—*Ibid.*, iv. 3.

Not a man
Shall pass his quarter, or offend the stream
Of regular justice in your city's bounds,

But shall be render'd to your public laws
At heaviest answer [that he may make answer to its heaviest decrees and penalties].
—*Timon*, v. 5.

He hath left them you,
And to your heirs for ever,—*common pleasures*,
To walk abroad, and recreate yourselves [pleasures to be enjoyed by you all in common, where you may walk abroad and recreate yourselves].—*Jul. C.*, iii. 2.

Did not great Julius bleed for justice' sake?
What villain touched his body, that did stab,
And not for justice? [Who among those that assailed Cæsar was a villain that stabbed him otherwise than for justice?]—*Ibid.*, iv. 3.

Yet, countrymen, oh, yet hold up your heads!—
What bastard doth not? [Who is it that would prove himself degenerate by not holding up his head and still maintaining the fight?].—*Ibid.*, v. 4.

Think upon what hath chanc'd; and, at more time,
The interim having weigh'd it [the interim having allowed of its being duly balanc'd in our minds], let us speak our free hearts each to other.—*Macb.*, i. 3.

Thy letters have transported me beyond
This ignorant present [this present moment unacquainted with the existence of that which hereafter will exist].—*Ibid.*, i. 5.

I will advise you where to plant yourselves;
Acquaint you with *the perfect spy o' the time* [the precise time when you may espy him coming].—*Ibid.*, iii. 1.

The head is not more native to the heart,
The hand more instrumental to the mouth,
Than is the throne of Denmark to thy father [The head is not more naturally co-operative with the heart, or the hand more actively useful to the mouth, than the throne of Denmark is willing to be serviceable to thy father].—*Hamlet*, i. 2.

That, on the supervise, *no leisure bated* [no abatement of time allowed].—*Ibid.*, v. 2.

Answer my life my judgment [Let my life be answerable for my judgment].—*Lear*, i. 1.

World, world, oh, world!
But that thy strange mutations make us hate thee,
Life would not yield to age [we should never be willing to surrender life even in old age].—*Ibid.*, iv. 1.

Mean you to espouse him?—
The let-alone lies not in your good will [The relinquishment of the match depends not upon your will, however much your will might desire that relinquishment].—*Ibid.*, v. 3.

In night, and *on the court and guard of safety* [on the very spot and guarding-place of safety].—*Oth.*, ii. 3.

This broken joint between you and her husband entreat her to splinter; and, my fortunes against any lay worth naming, *this crack of your love shall grow stronger than it was before* [the bond injured by this crack in your love shall become stronger than it was before (see the similarly constructed passage above quoted from "King Richard III.," ii. 2)].—*Ibid.*, ii. 3.

I have made my way through *more impediments*
Than twenty times your stop [more impediments than twenty times as much as that by which you would stop me].—*Ibid.*, v. 2.

I would have broke mine eye-strings; crack'd them, but
To look upon him; till the *diminution*
Of space [diminution caused by space] had pointed him sharp as my needle.—*Cym.*, i. 4.

Slaver with lips as common as the stairs
That mount the Capitol [by which the Capitol is mounted].—*Ibid.*, i. 7.

How we may steal hence; and for the gap
That we shall make in time, *from our hence-going*
And our return [from the period of our hence-going until that of our return (See the similarly constructed passage above quoted from "Coriolanus," ii. 1)], to excuse.
—*Ibid.*, iii. 2.

Why hast thou gone so far,
To be unbent [to have thy bow unbent] when thou hast ta'en thy stand,
The elected deer before thee?—*Cym.*, iii. 4.

Must I repent?
I cannot do it better than in gyves,
Desir'd more than constrain'd [I cannot repent better than in gyves, desiring to do so more than constrained to do so].—*Ibid.*, v. 4.

This man is better than the man he slew,
As well descended as thyself; and *hath*
More of thee merited than a band of Clotens
Had ever scar for [hath merited more of thee than a whole band of Clotens ever received a single scar to entitle them to claim].—*Ibid.*, v. 5.

Shakespeare has some passages of very peculiar and condensed construction, where a comparison is made [*See* ELLIPSES OF COMPARISON] :—

And for womanhood, Maid Marian *may be the deputy's wife of the ward to thee* [might be wife to the deputy of the ward if compared in fitness with thee].—*1 H. IV.*, iii. 3.

Upon their ancient malice, will forget,
With the least cause, these his new honours; *which,*
That he will give them, make I as little question
As he is proud to do't [which cause, that he will give them, I as little question as that he is proud enough to do it, and proud of doing it].—*Coriol.*, ii. 1.

Like madness is the glory of this life,
As this pomp shows to a little oil and root [Just such madness is the glory of this life, as the pomp of this feast appears when compared with the philosopher's frugal repast of a little oil and a few roots].—*Timon*, i. 2.

What if this cursed hand *were thicker than itself with brother's blood* [were steep'd in brother's blood to the thickness of itself].—*Hamlet*, iii. 3.

Sometimes Shakespeare uses the present or future tense in the kind of sentence where the participle is generally used :—

Though bride and bridegroom *wants* [are wanting] for to supply the places at the table.—*Tam. of S.*, iii. 2.

Your betters have endured *me say* [my saying] my mind.—*Ibid.*, iv. 3.

I know not how I shall assure you farther,
But *I shall lose* [by losing] the grounds I work upon.—*All's W.*, iii. 7.

Sometimes he uses the present tense in the kind of sentence where other forms of phraseology are generally used :—

You are the first that *rears* [are to rear] your hand.—*Jul. C.*, iii. 1.

I cannot say whore—*it does abhor me* [it is abhorrent to me], now I speak the word.—*Oth.*, iv. 2.

Sometimes he uses the infinitive mood in the kind of sentence where other forms of phraseology are employed :—

I fly not death, *to fly* [by flying] his deadly doom.—*Two G. of V.*, iii. 1.

Heaven would that she these gifts should have,
And *I to live* [that I should live] and die her slave.—*As You L.*, iii. 2 (*Verses*).

His private arbours, and new-planted orchards, . . .
To walk [where you may walk] abroad, and recreate yourselves.—*Jul. C.*, iii. 2.

Myself the while *to draw* [might draw] the Moor apart.—*Oth.*, ii. 3.

What a plague mean ye *to colt* [by colting] me thus?—*1 H. IV.*, ii. 2.

Who, then, shall blame his pester'd senses *to recoil and start* [for recoiling and starting], when all that is within him does condemn itself for being there?—*Macb.*, v. 2.

And, for I am richer than *to hang* [to be hung] by the walls, I must be ripp'd.—*Cym.*, iii. 4.

And how achiev'd you these endowments, which you make more rich *to owe* [by possessing them].—*Per.*, v. 1.

Sometimes he uses the participle in the kind of sentence where other forms of phraseology are ordinarily employed :—

And, now *I am remember'd* [I remember], scorn'd at me.—*As You L.*, iii. 5.

But if you *be remember'd* [remember], I did not bid.—*Tam. of S.*, iv. 3.

My person ; which I weigh not, *being* [if it be] of those virtues vacant.—*H. VIII.*, v. 1.

How *have I been behaved* [can I have behaved] that he might stick the small'st opinion on my least misuse ?—*Oth.*, iv. 2.

What's her price, Boult ?—I cannot *be bated* [get them to bate me] one doit of a thousand pieces.—*Per.*, iv. 3.

Sometimes he has sentences with verbs somewhat pleonastically employed :—

Admit him *entrance*, Griffith.—*H. VIII.*, iv. 2.

> We shall not *spend* a large *expense* of time,*
> Before we reckon with your several loves.—*Macb.*, v. 7.

> That we the pain of *death* would hourly *die*,
> Rather than die at once !—*Lear*, v. 3.

Shakespeare has some passages where one sentence is followed up by a second illustrating the first ; and sometimes with a repeated word :—

> Dost think I am *so* muddy, *so* unsettled,
> To appoint myself in this vexation.—*W. T.*, i. 2.

> Take pity of your town and of your people,
> *Whiles yet* my soldiers are in my command ;
> *Whiles yet* the cool and temperate wind of grace
> O'erblows the filthy and contagious clouds.—*H. V.*, iii. 3.

> In him there is a hope of government ;
> That, in his nonage, council under him,
> And, in his full and ripen'd years, himself,
> No doubt, shall then, and till then, govern well.—*R. III.*, ii. 3.

> There 's his period to sheathe his knife in us. —*H. VIII.*, i. 2.

> After my death I wish *no other* herald,
> *No other* speaker of my living actions,
> To keep mine honour from corruption,
> But such an honest chronicler as Griffith.—*Ibid.*, iv. 2.

> Know you not
> How your state stands i' the *world*, with the whole *world* ?—*Ibid.*, v. 1.

> Now shall we see to-morrow,
> An act that very chance doth throw upon him,
> Ajax renown'd.—*Tr. & Cr.*, iii. 3.

> No, Cassius ; for the eye sees not itself,
> But by reflection, by some other things.—*Jul. C.*, i. 2.

> Tell me—*but* truly—*but* then speak the truth,
> Do you not love my sister ?—*Lear*, v. i.

> To take the widow,
> Exasperates, makes mad, her sister.—*Ibid.*, v. 1.

> Let 's teach ourselves that honourable stop,
> Not to out-sport discretion.—*Oth.*, ii. 3.

> Her tongue will not obey her heart, nor can
> Her heart inform her tongue—the swan's down feather,
> That stands upon the swell at the full of tide,
> And neither way inclines.—*Ant. & C.*, ii. 2.

---

* *See* our remarks upon this passage under REPEATED WORDS.

Most monster-like, be shown
For poor'st diminutives, *for** doits.—*Ant. & C.*, iv. 10.

I, that with my sword
Quarter'd the world, and o'er green Neptune's back
With ships made cities, condemn myself to lack
The courage of a woman ; less† noble mind
Than she which by her death our Cæsar tells,
" I am conqueror of myself."—*Ibid.*, iv. 12.

Thou art sworn, Eros,
That, *when* the exigent should come (which now
Is come indeed), *when* I should see behind me
The inevitable prosecution of
Disgrace and horror, that, on my command,
Thou then wouldst kill me.—*Ibid.*, iv. 12.

I never do him wrong
But he does buy my injuries to be friends ;
Pays dear for my offences.—*Cym.*, i. 2.

A wooer more hateful *than* the foul expulsion is
Of thy dear husband, *than* that horrid act
Of the divorce he 'd make !—*Ibid.*, ii. 1.

Woe is my heart that the poor soldier, that so richly fought,
Whose rags sham'd gilded arms, *whose* naked breast
Stepp'd before targes of proof, cannot be found.—*Ibid.*, v. 5.

I never saw *such* noble fury in so poor a thing ;
Such precious deeds in one that promis'd naught
But beggary and poor looks.—*Ibid.*, v. 5.

Our heir apparent is a king !
Who dream d, *who* thought of such a thing ?—*Per.*, iii. (*Gower*).

Occasionally Shakespeare gives emphatic effect to a speech by introducing a precisely repeated word and phrase :—

Now does he feel
His secret murders sticking on his hands ;
Now minutely revolts upbraid his faith-breach ;
Those he commands move only in command,
Nothing in love : *now does he feel* his title
Hang loose about him, like a giant's robe
Upon a dwarfish thief.—*Macb.*, v. 2.

PECULIAR REPLIES.

Shakespeare occasionally introduces peculiarly phrased replies,
where the form of answer does not seem precisely to cohere with the
form of question just put :—

---

* It has been proposed to change the first " for " in the present passage into ' to,'
assuming " poor'st diminutives " to signify ' meanest and most insignificant persons ' ;
whereas " poor'st diminutives " is here used for ' smallest and lowest coins,' as
" poorest piece " is used in " Coriolanus," iii. 3.

† ' To be of ' is elliptically understood before " less noble mind " ; and under
ELLIPTICAL STYLE we have shown several instances of passages similarly constructed,
though the present one has been suspected of error, and altered by emendators.   If
Shakespeare's mode of occasionally employing the infinitive mood be borne in mind,
it will be seen that " condemn myself to lack " means ' condemn myself for lacking ' ;
and then, according to his elliptical style, allows " less noble mind " to imply ' condemn
myself for being of less noble mind.'

When *are you married*, madam ?—

Why, *every day to-morrow* [*See* Note at p. 357, IDIOMS, for our explanation of this reply].—*M. Ado*, iii. 1.

Hate him not, for my sake.—

Why should I not ? doth he not deserve well ?—*As You L.*, i. 3.

After " why should I not," we must understand ' not hate him ? ' Celia implying, ' Why should I not love him ? ' as is shown by what Rosalind says immediately after.

Can it be possible that no man saw *them ?* . . .

I cannot hear of any that did see *her.*—*Ibid.*, ii. 2.

Duke Frederick asks after both ladies ; while the courtier, in his reply, mentions the duke's daughter only.

Thou knowest, winter tames man, woman, and beast ; for it hath tamed my old master, and my new mistress, and *myself*, fellow Curtis.—

Away, you three-inch fool ! *I am no beast.*—*Tam. of S.*, iv. 1.

Grumio having made himself out to be " a beast," and then called the other servant " fellow Curtis," includes him in the imputation, thereby eliciting Curtis's indignant disclaimer.

It shall do you no harm to learn.—

To be young again, if we could.—*All's W.*, ii. 2.

The old Countess follows up the Clown's remark as if it were an incomplete sentence.

How goes all in France ?—

From France to England.—*John*, iv. 2.

The messenger makes part of the king's inquiry form the implied commencement of his own ; as if he said :—

' All goes now from France to England.'

I had a mighty cause

To wish him dead, but thou *hadst none* to kill him.—

No had, my lord ! why, did you not provoke me ?—*Ibid.*, iv. 2.

" No had," as well as ' no did,' ' no does,' and ' no will,' were idiomatic retorts formerly in use.

How now, good Blunt ! thy looks *are* full of speed.—

So *hath* the business that I come to speak of.—*1 H. IV.*, iii. 2.

The reply here omits the " full of " included in the question, and accepts it as if it had been ' thy looks *have* speed in them ' ; thus consisting well with the hurry of the speaker.

Have you laid fair the bed ? *are* all things well,

According as I gave directions ?—

'Tis, my good lord.—*2 H. VI.*, iii. 2.

Here, although the question is put in the plural, the reply is given in the singular ; implying, ' 'tis done,' ' all that you have ordered is performed.'

In any case, *be not too rough* in terms ;

For he is fierce, and cannot brook hard language.—

I *will*, my lord.—*Ibid.*, iv. 9.

In this case, ' not be too rough ' is elliptically understood after " I will."

> Tell me, my friend, *art thou the man* that slew him ?—
> *I was,* an 't like your majesty.—*2 H. VI.,* v. 1.

Instead of the usual ' I am,' Iden answers, " I was," to signify ' it was I that slew him.'

> *You forget*
> That we are those which chas'd you from the field,
> And slew your fathers, and with colours spread
> March'd through the city to the palace-gates.—
> *Yes,* Warwick, I remember it to my grief.—*3 H. VI.,* i. 1.

Here " yes " implies ' yes, I do ' ; and forms the reply to " you forget," as if that were equivalent to ' you do not remember.'

> No, Warwick, no ; while life upholds this arm,
> *This arm* upholds the house of Lancaster.—
> *And I* the house of York.—*Ibid.,* iii. 3.

To have preserved literal consistency of phraseology, " And I," might here have been ' And mine.'

> The *packet,* Cromwell, gave it you the king ?—
> To his own hand, in his bedchamber.—
> Look'd he o' th' inside of the *paper* ?—
> *Presently*
> He did unseal *them :* and the first he view'd,
> He did it with a serious mind.—*H. VIII.,* iii. 2.

Here " them " is used as if the questions implied ' the contents of the " packet " or " paper." '

> *Would we were all discharg'd.*—
>   *I fear it.*—*Timon,* ii. 2.

Here " discharged " means ' paid ' (' that all our debts were discharged ') ; and " I fear it " implies, ' I fear that we shall not be paid ' (' have our debts discharged ').

> Cæsar, *thou canst not die by traitors' hands,*
> Unless thou bring'st them with thee.—
>   *So I hope.*—*Jul. C.,* v. 1.

This reply signifies, ' I hope not to die by traitors' hands.'

> Of Albany's and Cornwall's powers *you heard not ?*—
> *'Tis so,* they are a-foot.—*Lear,* iv. 3.

Here " 'tis so " implies, ' yes, I did hear of them, and it is as was rumoured,' ' it is just as we expected.'

> *Save you,* worthy general !—
>   *With all my heart,* sir.—*Oth.,* iv. 1.

' I thank you ' is elliptically understood before ' with all my heart.' [*See* Mode of Address or Salutation.]

> What shall be said *to* thee ?
>   *Why, anything :*
> *An honourable murderer, if you will.*—*Ibid.,* v. 2.

In accordance with usual phraseology, the word " to," in the question, might be ' of. '

> *Whence are you ?*—
> *A poor Egyptian yet.*—*Ant. & C.,* v. 1.

The answer implies, ' I come from Egypt ; and as yet I have been no more than a poor Egyptian, though now no less than a messenger from Egypt's queen to Octavius Cæsar.'

I came unto your court for honour's cause,
And not to be a rebel to her state ;
And he that otherwise accounts of me,
This sword shall prove he 's honour's enemy.—
No! here comes my daughter, *she can witness it.—Per.,* ii. 5.

The reply signifies, 'she can witness that you are a traitor, as I have said you are.'

Shakespeare occasionally introduces retorts where a somewhat similar word is used :—

Where is *my lady ?*—
Here; what would *my lord ?—Mer. of V.,* ii. 9.
Save you, *fair queen.*—
And you, *monarch.*—
No.—And *no.—All's W.,* i. 1.
Hail, *royal prince !*—
Thanks, *noble peer.—R. II.,* v. 5.
But, hear you, *my lord.*—
What say'st thou, *my lady ?*—1 *H. IV.,* ii. 3.
My lord the prince,—
How now, *my lady the hostess !—Ibid.,* ii. 4.

Who am I, sir ?—*My lady's father.*—My lady's father! *my lord's knave.—Lear,* i. 4.
Sir, sir,—Yes, *my lord,* yes.—*Ant. & C.,* iii. 9.
What 's *your lordship's pleasure ?—Your lady's person.—Cym.,* ii. 3.
O, my *all-worthy lord !—All-worthy villain !—Ibid.,* iii. 5.

Sometimes he introduces a half-scornful rejoinder in the form of inquiry :—

Thanks, i' faith ; for silence is only commendable
In a neat's tongue dried, and a maid not vendible.—
*Is that anything now ? *—Mer. of V.,* i. 1.
To tell you where he lodges, is to tell you where I lie.—
Can anything be made of this ?—Oth., iii. 4.

He sometimes uses a form of rejoinder that draws attention to a purposed obscurity of style in the question [*See* DRAMATIC LAWS AND ART] :—

I understand you not : my griefs are dull.—*Love's L. L.,* v. 2.
How blow ? how blow? *speak to be understood.—Ibid.,* v. 2.

He not unfrequently has a word used in one sense, and replied to as if it were used in another sense :—

How cam'st thou in this *pickle* ['mess'] ?—
I have been in such a *pickle* ['brine'] . . . I shall not fear fly-blowing.—*Temp.,* v. 1.
So, by your *circumstance* ['argumentative statement'], you call me fool.—So, by your *circumstance* ['actual state or condition'], I fear you'll prove.—*Two G. of V.,* i. 1.
The music *likes* ['pleases'] you not.—
You mistake ; the musician *likes* ['loves'] me not.—*Ibid.,* iv. 2.
I have a brother is *condemn'd* ['doomed' or 'sentenced'] to die. . . .
Why, every fault's *condemn'd* ['censured'] ere it be done.—*M. for M.,* ii. 2.
What a plague mean ye to *colt* ['cheat,' 'trick,' 'deceive'] me thus ?—Thou liest;
thou art not *colted* ['provided with a horse or colt'], thou art *uncolted* ['deprived of thy horse'].—1 *H. IV.,* ii. 2.

---

* The Folio prints this, ' It is that any thing now': but the very similar phrase in
" Othello " (above quoted) makes it probable that Shakespeare intended to write,
" Is that anything now ? "

And therein you are *senseless* ['unconscious,' 'purposely without perception'].—
Senseless ['devoid of sense,' 'stupid']! not so.—*Cym.*, ii. 3.

In the following passage he uses a form of question in a peculiar manner :—

Will you be gone ['Are you going'] ?—*Coriol.*, iv. 2.

PECULIAR USE OF WORDS.*

Shakespeare often uses words with peculiar force of meaning, and sometimes in a sense not ordinarily assigned. It is requisite to bear this in mind when judging certain passages that present some difficulty of interpretation, if his practice in this respect be not remembered; and frequently, by observing how he employs a word in one instance, it will aid in denoting how he similarly employs it in another, where perhaps the whole signification of the phrase is less obvious. In some cases, he uses words in a sense that they bore when he wrote, but which they have since lost; in others, he uses words in the sense they strictly bear as derived from classical original sources ; and, in others, with a degree of latitude in signification, as indirectly pertaining to them. But, in every case, as it appears to us, he uses words with expressive and effective power.

Being all this time *abandoned* ['banished,' 'interdicted'] from your bed.—*Tam. of S., Induc.* 2.

If she be so *abandon'd* ['given up,' 'given over'] to her sorrow.—*Tw. N.*, i. 4.

O long and tedious night! *abate* ['curtail,' 'diminish'] thy hours.—*Mid. N. D.*, iii. 2.

Abate ['suppressing,' 'leaving out,' 'excepting'] throw at novum.—*Love's L. L.*, v. 2.

Which once in him *abated* ['reduced to lower temper,' 'let down'].—*2 H. IV.*, i. 1.

Abate ['blunt,' 'put down,' 'repress,' 'subdue,' 'lower,' 'depress'; and 'diminish,' 'make fewer,' 'lessen the number of.' *See* VARIED MEANINGS, &c., for instances of Shakespeare's thus including many senses in one expressive word] the edge of traitors, gracious Lord.—*R. III.*, v. 4.

Deliver you as most *abated* ['depressed,' 'subdued,' 'cast down,' 'dispirited'] captives.—*Coriol.*, iii. 3.

Let no man *abide* ['endure the consequence of,' 'incur the penalty of'] this deed.—*Jul. C.*, iii. 1.

We are the queen's *abjects* ['lowest of subjects'].—*R. III.*, i. 1.

I say, none ; I'll *able* ['empower'] 'em.—*Lear*, iv. 6.

The night-crow cried, *aboding* ['foreboding,' 'presaging'] luckless time.—*3 H. VI.*, v. 6.

Be *absolute* ['firm,' 'decided'] for death.—*M. for M.*, iii. 1.

I am *absolute* ['certain,' 'positive,' 'decided'] 'twas very Cloten.—*Cym.*, iv. 2.

As just, as *absolute* ['complete in excellence,' 'accomplished in merit'] as Angelo.—*M. for M.*, v. 1.

Contends in skill with *absolute* ['fully accomplished,' 'completely excellent'] Marina.—*Per.*, iv. (*Gower*).

I am mightily *abus'd* ['confused,' 'bewildered,' 'perplexed with false illusions'].—*Lear*, iv. 7.

Then Edgar was *abus'd* ['maligned,' 'calumniated'].—*Ibid.*, iii. 7.

---

* It is to be observed that we here give to several of Shakespeare's words—in many cases—more varied and quite different significations from those given by other glossarists and commentators.

Do not *abuse* ['deceive,' 'mislead,' 'delude'] me.—*Lear*, iv. 7.

The Moor 's *abus'd* ['deceived,' 'misled'] by some.—*Oth.*, iv. 2.

You are a great deal *abus'd* ['deceived'] in too bold.—*Cym.*, i. 5.

My master is *abus'd* ['deluded,' 'beguiled'].—*Ibid.*, iii. 4.

Enforcement shall *acquittance* ['acquit'] me from all.—*R. III.*, iii. 7.

And think it no *addition* ['advantageous circumstance'].—*Oth.*, iii. 4.

With swinish phrase soil our *addition* ['title'].—*Hamlet*, i. 4.

All the *additions* ['titles belonging'] to a king.—*Lear*, i. 1.

Where great *additions* ['titles'] swell.—*All's W.*, ii. 3.

Beasts of their particular *additions* ['titles to distinction'].—*Tr. & Cr.*, i. 2.

Address ['prepare,' 'apply'] yourself to entertain them.—*W. T.*, iv. 3.

Were all *addressed* ['prepared'] to meet you.—*Love's L. L.*, ii. 1.

Nor time nor place did then *adhere* ['cohere,' 'suit'].—*Macb.*, i. 7.

Why, everything *adheres* ['coheres,' 'consists,' 'suits'] together.—*Tw. N.*, iii. 4.

To whom he more *adheres* ['is attached'].—*Hamlet*, ii. 2.

That *admiration* ['wonder,' 'amazement'] did whoop at them.—*H. V.*, ii. 2.

At this encounter do so much *admire* ['wonder'].—*Temp.*, v. 1.

Nor *admire* ['wonder,' 'marvel'] not in thy mind.—*Tw. N.*, iii. 4.

With most *admir'd* ['wondered at,' 'wonderful,' 'marvellous'] disorder.—*Macb.*, iii. 4.

That is an *advertisement* ['warning'] to a proper maid in Florence.—*All's W.*, iv. 3.

This *advertisement* ['notice,' 'warning,' 'intelligence'] is five days old.—1 *H. IV.*, iii. 2.

Never did lack *advice* ['reflection,' 'consideration'], so much.—*All's W.*, iii. 4.

So hot a speed with such *advice* ['consideration,' 'deliberation'] dispos'd.—*John*, iii. 4.

Advise ['bethink,' 'reflect,' 'take heed,' 'be careful'] you what you say.—*Tw. N.*, iv. 2.

Were you well *advised* ['bethought,' 'considered']?—*Love's L. L.*, v. 2.

I will *advise* ['inform'] you where to plant.—*Macb.*, iii. 1.

The French, *advised* ['informed'] by good intelligence.—*H. V.*, ii. (*Chorus*).

You were *advised* ['aware'] his flesh was.—2 *H. IV.*, i. 1.

He does neither *affect* ['like,' 'have inclination for'] company.—*Timon*, i. 2.

I am in all *affected* ['inclined,' 'disposed'] as yourself.—*Tam of S.*, i. 1.

For *affection* ['constitutional tendency or impulse,' 'innate disposition or inclination'], master of passion.—*Mer. of V.*, iv 1.

The appetite and *affection* ['constitutional tendency'] common of the whole body.—*Coriol.*, i. 1.

Seem all *affin'd* ['united by affinity'] and kin.—*Tr. & Cr.*, i. 3.

In any just term am *affin'd* ['bound by any due claim of affinity'] to love the Moor.—*Oth.*, i. 1.

If partially *affin'd* ['swayed by any link of affinity'], or leagu'd in office.—*Ibid.*, ii. 3.

Her picture, *affront* ['confront,' 'meet'] his eye.—*W. T.*, v. 1.

May here *affront* ['confront,' 'encounter,' 'meet'] Ophelia.—*Hamlet*, iii. 1.

Your preparation can *affront* ['confront'] no less.—*Cym.*, iv. 3.

Gave the *affront* ['encounter,' 'confronting,' 'meeting in attack'] with them.—*Ibid.*, v. 3.

Might be *affronted* ['confronted,' 'met,' 'matched'] with the match and weight of such.—*Tr. & Cr.*, iii. 2.

Fearing lest my jealous *aim* ['suspicion'] might err.—*Two G. of V.*, iii. 1.

I have some *aim* ['guess,' 'surmise,' 'conjecture'].—*Jul. C.*, i. 2.

I *aimed* ['guessed'] so near, when I suppos'd.—*R. & Jul.*, i. 1.

That will *allow* ['approve,' 'prove'] me very worth.—*Tw. N.*, i. 2.

Allow ['approve'] us as we prove.—*Tr. & Cr.*, iii. 2.

In your *allowance* ['estimation,' 'admission'], o'erweigh.—*Hamlet*, ii. 2.

Put it on by your *allowance* ['approval,' 'sanction'].—*Lear*, i. 4.

Generally *allowed* ['approved'] for your many.—*Merry W.*, ii. 2.

To her *allowing* ['approving,' 'sanctioning'] husband.—*W. T.*, i. 2.

His roguish madness *allows* ['lends,' 'adapts'] itself to anything.—*Lear*, iii. 7.

You do *amaze* ['bewilder,' 'confuse'] her.—*Merry W.*, v. 5.

Lest your retirement do *amaze* ['throw into confusion'] your friends —1 *H. IV.*, v. 4.

For I was *amaz'd* ['bewildered,' 'confounded'] under the tide.—*John*, iv. 2.

I am *amaz'd* ['confused,' 'perplexed,' 'bewildered'], methinks.—*Ibid.*, iv. 3.

More *amaz'd* ['confounded,' 'overpowered'] than had I seen.—*Ibid.*, v. 2.

I am *amaz'd* ['bewildered,' 'perplexed'] with matter.—*Cym.*, iv. 3.

That fell *anatomy* ['skeleton'] which cannot hear.—*John*, iii. 4.

A mere *anatomy* ['skeleton'], a mountebank.—*Com. of E.*, v. 1.

I'll eat the rest of the *anatomy* ['body,' 'corporeal frame'].—*Tw. N.*, iii. 2.

In what vile part of this *anatomy* ['body'] doth.—*R. & Jul.*, iii. 3.

Let's, then, determine with the *ancient* ['experienced.' *See* ELDER for examples of the mode in which Shakespeare uses that word, as we think he here uses the word "ancient"] of war on our proceedings.—*Lear*, v. 1.

Arrest them to the *answer* ['retributive justice'] of the law.—*H. V.*, ii. 2.

Great the *answer* ['reprisal,' 'retaliation'] be the Britons must take.—*Cym.*, v. 3.

Than to *answer* ['sustain,' 'endure,' 'bear the penalty'] with thy uncovered body this extremity.—*Lear*, iii. 4.

How can her contempt be *answer'd* ['excused,' 'extenuated,' 'explained'].—*Cym.*, iii. 5.

Nature, drawing of an *antic* ['a grotesque figure,' 'a distorted form'], made a foul blot.—*M. Ado*, iii. 1,

Pageant, or *antic* ['grotesque exhibition'], or firework. . . . We will have, if this fadge not, an *antic*.—*Love's L. L.*, v. 1.

Three such *antics* ['grotesque figures'] do not amount.—*H. V.*, iii. 2.

Wherein of *antres* ['caverns': Latin, *antrum*] vast and deserts idle, rough.—*Oth.*, i. 3.

It is *apparent* ['evident,' 'obvious'] foul play.—*John*, iv. 2.

These *apparent* ['manifest,' 'visible,' 'evident'] prodigies.—*Jul. C.*, ii. 1.

Scorn me so *apparently* ['openly,' 'evidently']. - *Com. of E.*, iv. 1.

The boisterous late *appeal* ['accusation'].—*R. II.*, i. 1.

To *appeal* ['accuse'] each other of high treason.—*Ibid.*, i. 1.

Upon his own *appeal* ['accusation'], seizes him.—*Ant. & C.*, iii. 5.

As for the rest *appeal'd* ['accused,' 'alleged,' 'charged,' 'made the subject of appeal'].—*R. II.*, i. 1.

Your favour is well *appeared* ['made to appear,' 'manifested,' 'shown'] by your tongue.—*Coriol.*, iv. 3.

This youth, howe'er distress'd, *appears* ['shows,' 'makes manifest'] he hath had good ancestors.—*Cym.*, iv. 2.

Philosophy will I *apply* ['ply,' 'practise diligently,' 'apply the mind to'].—*Tam. of S.*, i. 1.

Nestor shall *apply* ['apply to additional instances,' 'demonstrate by farther illustration'] thy latest words.—*Tr. & Cr.*, i. 3.

So unsettled, to *appoint* ['point out for blame,' 'mark out for censure,' 'stigmatise,' 'asperse'] myself in this vexation.—*W. T.*, i. 2.

My care to have you royally *appointed* ['accoutred,' 'equipped'].—*Ibid.*, iv. 3.

A pirate of very warlike *appointment* ['accoutrement,' 'equipment.'] gave us chase.—*Hamlet*, iv. 6 (*Letter*).

Your best *appointment* ['equipment for a voyage,' also implying 'spiritual preparation and supplyment'] make with speed.—*M. for M.*, iii. 1.

How long have you professed *apprehension* ['quick-wittedness,' 'intellectual smart-ness']?— *M. Ado*, iii. 4.

How such an *apprehension* ['conception,' 'construed belief'] may turn the tide of fearful faction.—1 *H. IV*., iv. 1.

Took from you the *apprehension* ['appreciation,' 'perception'] of his present portance.—*Coriol*., ii. 3.

Whose *apprehensive* ['fastidiously perceiving,' 'squeamishly observant'] senses all but new things disdain.—*All's W*., i. 2.

Makes it *apprehensive*.['intellectually ready,' 'prompt to perceive and understand'] quick.—2 *H. IV*., iv. 3.

And men are flesh and blood, and *apprehensive* ['capable of comprehending,' pos-sessed of intelligence'].—*Jul. C*., iii. 1.

Task me to my word ; *approve* ['prove'] me, lord.—1 *H. IV*., iv. 1.

> I shall not fail to *approve* ['confirm'] the fair conceit
> The king hath of you.—*H. VIII*., ii. 3.

Does *approve* ['testify,' 'prove,'] by his lov'd mansionry.—*Macb*., i. 6.

He may *approve* ['confirm the witness of,' 'add proof to the testimony of'] our eyes, and speak to it.—*Hamlet*, i. 1.

Thou dost *approve* ['attest,' 'prove'] thyself the.—*Cym*., iv. 2.

Which must *approve* ['prove,' 'attest'] thee honest.—*Ibid*., v. 5.

That which well *approves* ['proves,' 'testifies'] you're great.—*All's W*., iii. 7.

Which *approves* ['proves'] him an intelligent party.—*Lear*, iii. 5.

He *approves* ['proves true,' 'confirms'] the common.—*Ant. & C*., i. 1.

He that is *approv'd* ['proved to be'] in this offence.—*Oth*., ii. 3.

I have well *approv'd* ['proved'] it, sir.—*Ibid*., ii. 3.

Make known to their *approvers* ['provers,' 'testers'; 'those who put them to the proof'] they are people such.—*Cym*., ii. 4.

I, most jocund, *apt* ['ready' 'prompt'], and willingly.—*Tw. N*., v. 1.

I am most *apt* ['ready,' 'willing'] to embrace your offer.—*Ibid*., v. 1.

Not find myself so *apt* ['ready,' 'thoroughly disposed,' 'willing'] to die.—*Jul. C*., iii. 1.

A heart as little *apt* * ['pliant,' 'inclinable,' 'accommodating,' 'conformable'] as yours.—*Coriol*., iii. 2.

She is young and *apt* ['easily led,' 'pliant,' 'facile'].—*Timon*, i. 1.

So kind, so *apt* ['compliant,' 'ready to confer a benefit'], so blessed a disposition — *Oth*., ii. 3.

My worthy *arch* ['chief'] and patron.—*Lear*, ii. 1.

---

* The word "apt" has been suspected of error in this passage ; but if the mode in which Shakespeare employs the word "apt" in the other passages we have here cited be observed, we think it will be perceived that "apt" is right, and bears the meaning we assign—a meaning included among those borne by the Latin word *aptus*. It may be expedient here to mention (in reference to "antres," "apt," "contrive," &c., cited under the present heading) that we had originally written a heading entitled "CLASSICALLY DERIVED WORDS," which minutely discussed Shakespeare's employ-ment of such words. It showed that his use of them with their strickly primitive sense in reference to their classical derivation clearly demonstrates the injustice (not unfrequently committed by former commentators) of attributing to him a deficiency of knowledge in the classical languages ; and showed, on the contrary, that he possessed a very accurate acquaintance with the sources whence many English terms are derived. We cancelled that heading, from a desire to condense the present book ; but we now draw attention to such words as "accite," "agnise," "artificial," "aspersion," "cadent," "concent," "conduce," "consist," "crescive," "crisp," "dissemble," "erring," "expostulate," "extracting," "extravagant," "fact," "gests," "impose," "imposition," "indign," injury," "lin'd," "lineaments," "plants," "prevent," "remotion," "speculation," "stomach," "verbal," "virtue," &c., as proofs of our assertion.

For bearing, *argument* ['powers of conversation'], and valour.—*M. Ado*, iii. 1.

Much like an *argument* ['animated conversation,' 'controversy'] that fell out last night.—*Cym.*, i. 5.

Imports the *argument* ['subject'] of the play.—*Hamlet*, iii. 2.

The *argument* ['subject,' 'theme'] of your praise.—*Lear*, i. 1.

Prove a notable *argument* ['subject for raillery']—*M. Ado*, i. 1.

You would not make me such an *argument* ['subject for mockery'].—*Mid. N.D.*, iii. 2.

Sheath'd their swords for lack of *argument* ['subject for contest'].—*H. V.*, iii. 1.

Look you *arm* ['prepare'] yourself to fit your fancies.—*Mid. N. D.*, i. 1.

Arm ['prepare'] you, I pray you, to this speedy voyage.—*Hamlet*, iii. 3.

Those pleasures live that *art* ['acquired knowledge,' 'learning'] would comprehend.—*Love's L.L.*, iv. 2 (*Letter*).

I have as much of this in *art* ['studied philosophy,' 'acquired reasoning'] as you, but yet my nature.—*Jul. C.*, iv. 3.

More matter, with less *art* ['ingenuity in word-twisting,' 'dexterity of language']. . . . I use no *art* at all. . . . I will use no *art*.—*Hamlet*, ii. 2.

On objects, *arts* ['artful practices,' 'dexterities in scheming'], and imitations.—*Jul. C.*, iv. 1.

With whom we may *articulate* ['enter into articles'].—*Coriol.*, i. 9.

These things, indeed, you have *articulated* ['set forth in articles'].—*1 H. IV.*, v. 1.

Did you *assay* ['endeavour to win'] him to any pastime ?—*Hamlet*, iii. 1.

By no *assay* ['test,' 'trial'] of reason.—*Oth.*, i. 3.

He it is that hath *assum'd* ['acquired,' 'attained,' 'reached,' 'summed up'] unto this age.—*Cym.*, v. 5.

May *astonish* ['confound,' 'stun'] these fell lurking curs.—*2 H. VI.*, v. 1.

You have *astonished* ['stunned,' 'confounded'] him.—*H. V.*, v. 1.

Every man *attach* ['take hold of'] the hand of his fair mistress.—*Love's L. L.*, iv. 3.

Or I'll *attach* ['seize,' 'arrest'] you by this officer.—*Com. of E.*, iv. 1.

Hath *attach'd* ['seized,' 'taken possession of'] our merchants' goods at Bordeaux.—*H. VIII.*, i. 1.

Who am myself *attach'd* ['seized,' 'overcome'] with weariness.—*Temp.*, iii. 3.

I had thought weariness durst not have *attached* ['seized upon,' 'taken possession of,' 'laid hold of'] one of so high blood.—*2 H. IV.*, ii. 2.

May worthy Troilus be half *attach'd* ['possessed,' 'overcome or overpowered'] with that which here.—*Tr. & Cr.*, v. 2.

Give as soft *attachment* ['seizure,' 'holding in repose'] to thy senses.—*Ibid.*, iv. 2.

When earthly things made even *atone* ['accord,' 'agree,' 'combine,' 'unite,' 'are at one'] together.—*As You L.*, v. 4.

He and Aufidius can no more *atone* ['be of one mind,' 'accord,' 'agree'] than violentest contrariety.—*Coriol.*, iv. 6.

Since we cannot *atone* ['reconcile,' 'make agree or accord'] you, we shall see.—*R. II.*, i. 1.

To *atone* ['reconcile'] your fears with my.—*Timon*, v. 5.

The present need speaks to *atone* ['reconcile'] you.—*Ant. & C.*, ii. 2.

Glad I did *atone* ['reconcile'] my countryman and you.—*Cym.*, i. 5.

He desires to make *atonement* ['reconciliation'] between.—*R. III.*, i. 3.

But freshly looks, and overbears *attaint* ['weariness,' 'depression'] with cheerful semblance.—*H. V.*, iv. (*Chorus*).

I am *attended* ['awaited,' 'expected'] at the cypress grove.— *Coriol.*, i. 10.

Attends ['awaits,' 'expects'] thee at the orchard end.—*Tw. N.*, iii. 4.

Much *attribute* ['attributed merit'] he hath.—*Tr. & Cr.*, ii. 3.

That is *attributive* ['attributive of merit,' 'ascriptive of merit': in both the present and the previous passage '*merit*' is involved in the word "attribute" and "attributive"].—*Ibid.*, ii. 2.

To give her the *avaunt* ['dismissal,' 'discarding']!—*H. VIII.*, ii. 3.

Averring ['confirmatory,' 'evidential'] notes of.—*Cym.*, v. 5.

Thrust from the company of *awful* ['respectable,' 'law-respecting,' 'order-reverencing'] men.—*Two G. of V.*, iv. 1.

An *awful* ['lawful,' 'legitimately authorised'] rule, and right supremacy.—*Tam. of S.*, v. 2.

We come within our *awful* ['lawfully appointed,' 'just,' 'rightful'] banks again.—2 *H. IV.*, iv. 1.

That will prove *awful* ['worthy of respect,' and 'lawful in conduct'] both in deed and word —*Per.*, ii. (*Gower*).

No sinister nor no *awkward* ['distorted,' 'perverted,' 'indirect'] claim.—*H. V.*, i. 2.

Twice by *awkward* ['contrary,' 'unpropitious,' 'adverse'] wind from England's bank.—2 *H. VI.*, iii. 2.

To the world and *awkward* ['adverse,' 'unpropitious,' 'untoward,' 'calamitous'] casualties.—*Per.*, v. 1.

Protest me the *baby* ['doll'] of a girl.—*Macb.*, iii. 4.

Here ye lie *baiting of* ['swilling refreshment from,' 'taking a draught from.' In support of our interpretation of the word "baiting," we cite from Beaumont and Fletcher's "Scornful Lady," act ii., sc. 2: "If you grow dry before you end your business, pray take a *bait* here; I have a fresh hogshead for you."] bombards.—*H. VIII.*, v. 3.

Balk ['wrangle,' 'altercate,' 'bandy,' 'interchange': "balk logic" was formerly used as we now use 'chop logic'] logic with.—*Tam. of S.*, i. 1.

Knights *balk'd* ['heaped up,' 'piled in heaps': 'a balk' was a ridge of land or bank of earth, laid up between two furrows; and 'to balk' was to throw up the earth so as to form these ridges, banks, or heaps] in their own blood.—1 *H. IV.*, i. 1.

As my farthest *band* ['bond'] shall pass.—*Ant. & C.*, iii. 2.

Release me from my *bands* ['bonds'] with.—*Temp. (Epilogue)*.

To be so *bared* ['shaved'] before his death.—*M. for M.*, iv. 2.

Or the *baring* ['shaving'] of my beard.—*All's W.*, iv. 1.

Each *battle* ['main body of an army,' 'collective embattled force'] sees the other's umber'd face.—*H. V.*, iv. (*Chorus*).

The king himself is rode to view their *battle* ['embattled force'].—*Ibid.*, iv. 3.

Their *battles* ['battalions,' 'embattled forces'] are at hand.—*Jul. C.*, v. 1.

I'll rent the fairest house in it after three-pence a *bay* ['architectural portion of a building:' it is as if the Clown said, 'at the rate of three-pence per floor or story,' 'at the rate of three-pence per window-range'].—*M. for M.*, ii. 1.

A dog, and *bay* ['pertinaciously or harassingly bark at'] the moon . . . *bay* not me.—*Jul. C.*, iv. 3.

Here wast thou *bay'd* ['chased barkingly and brought to bay.' *See* VARIED MEANINGS, &c.], brave hart; here didst thou fall.—*Ibid.*, iii. 1.

They *bay'd* ['chased and brought to bay,' 'hunted with pertinacious barking'] the bear with hounds.—*Mid. N. D.*, iv. 1.

Waving his *beam* ['lance'] upon the.—*Tr. & Cr.*, v. 5.

It must not *bear* ['achieve,' 'obtain,' 'bear off.' *See* "Carry" thus used, under the present heading] my daughter.—*Timon*, i. 1.

With more facile question *bear* ['win,' 'achieve,' 'carry,' 'prevail'] it.—*Oth.*, i. 3.

I will *beard* ['defy,' 'confront'] him.—1 *H. IV.*, iv. 1.

Am I dar'd, and *bearded* ['defied'] to my face.—1 *H. VI.*, i. 3.

Was *beastly* ['in a beast-like manner'] dumb'd.—*Ant. & C.*, i. 5.

We are *beastly* ['beast-like,' 'like animals'].—*Cym.*, iii. 3.

Which you shun *beastly* ['like beasts'].—*Ibid.*, v. 3.

Thine eyes and thoughts *beat* ['are longingly bent,' 'are anxiously fixed'] on a crown, the treasure of thy heart.—2 *H. VI.*, ii. 1.

A turn or two I 'll walk, to still my *beating* ['anxiously throbbing,' 'intently occupied '] mind.—*Temp.*, iv. I.

Do not infest your mind with *beating* ['anxiously dwelling,' 'intently occupying '], on the strangeness.—*Ibid.*, v. I.

Speak fair, *become* ['render becoming,' 'give some grace to'] disloyalty.—*Com. of E.*, iii. 2.

As those two eyes *become* ['adorn,' 'set off,' 'grace,' 'give loveliness to'] that heavenly face ?—*Tam. of S.*, iv. 5.

When he intendeth to *become* [' grace,' 'adorn,' 'embellish with his presence'] the field.—*John*, v. i.

That integrity which should *become* [' becomingly adorn,' 'befittingly invest'] it.—*Coriol.*, iii. I.

How this Herculean Roman does *become* ['render becoming'] the carriage of his chafe.—*Ant. & C.*, i 3.

For vilest things *become* ['appear becoming,' 'become becoming'] themselves in her.—*Ibid.*, ii. 2.

It well *becomes* ['adorns,' 'graces,' 'sets off,' 'ornaments,' 'embellishes'] the ground.—*As You L.*, iii. 2.

As I am a soldier, a name that, in my thoughts, *becomes* ['adorns,' 'graces'] me best.—*H. V.*, iii. 3.

Observe how Antony *becomes* ['makes becoming,' 'suffers to befit him,' 'sustains appropriately'] his flaw.—*Ant. & C.*, iii. 10.

Pisa . . . gave me my *being* [' existence,' 'birth'].—*Tam. of S.*, i. I.

To shift his *being* [' abode,' 'place and mode of existence'], is to exchange one misery with another.—*Cym.*, i. 6.

That men of few words are the *best* ['bravest'] men.—*H. V.*, iii. 2.

Do your *best* ['highest,' 'divinest'] wills, and make me.—*Cym.*, v. I.

How should I *bestow* ['place,' ' put,' ' stow away'] him ?—*Merry W.*, iv. 2.

Bestow ['place in order,' 'range'] yourself with speed.—*H. V.*, iv. 3.

And so *bestow* ['place,' ' put,' ' dispose'] these papers.—*Jul. C.*, i. 3.

In heedfull'st reservation to *bestow* ['lay by,' 'put away,' 'place in security,' 'treasure up,' 'carefully keep'] them.—*All's W.*, i. 3.

How might we see Falstaff *bestow* [' behave,' 'comport'] himself to-night in his true colours.—*2 H. IV.*, ii. 2,

Of female favour, and *bestows* [' comports,' 'behaves,' 'demeans'] himself like a ripe sister.—*As You L.*, iv. 3.

In what safe place you have *bestow'd* ['stowed away,' 'deposited in safety'] my money ?—*Com. of E.*, i. 2.

Our bloody cousins are *bestow'd* [' placed,' 'refuged'] in England, and in Ireland.—*Macb.*, iii. I.

All my powers do their *bestowing* ['governance,' 'due conduct,' 'proper management,' 'fit control'] lose.—*Tr. & Cr.*, iii. 2.

When I first my wedded mistress saw *bestride** ['pass over,' 'cross over.' *See* "Stride" thus used under the present heading] my threshold.—*Coriol.*, iv. 5.

I am *bid* ['invited'] forth to supper . . . I am not *bid* for love.—*Mer. of V.* ii. 5.

I will *bid* [' invite'] the duke to the nuptial . . . *bid* your friends.—*As You L.*, v. 2

Provide the feast, father, and *bid* [' invite'] the guests.—*Tam. of S.*, ii. I.

I 'll lead you to some *biding* [' dwelling,' 'place for rest and shelter,' 'place where you may bide'].—*Lear*, iv. 6.

My mind hath been as *big* ['swelling,' 'haughty,' 'unbending,' 'unsubmissive'] as one of yours.—*Tam. of S.*, v. 2.

---

* The word is here used without its usual sense of '*step* across'; since a Roman bride was *borne over* her husband's threshold, that she might not so much as touch it in passing.

It will wear the surplice of humility over the black gown of a *big* ['proud,' 'arrogant,' 'haughty'] heart.—*All's W.*, i. 3.

I mock at death with as *big* ['haughty,' 'unbending,' 'unflinching,' 'unyielding'] heart as thou.—*Coriol.*, iii. 2.

To repay that money will be a *biting* ['keen,' 'sore'] affliction.—*Merry W.*, v. 5.

Lie not guiltless here under some *biting* ['keenly piercing,' 'acutely painful,' 'sorely distressing'] error.—*M. Ado*, iv. 1.

We're nail'd for our advantage on the *bitter* ['cruel,' 'barbarous,' 'agonising'] cross.—1 *H. IV.*, i. 1.

The *bitter* ['cruel,' 'unrelenting,' 'inexorable'] disposition of the time will have it so.—*Tr. & Cr.*, iv. 1.

And do such *bitter** ['cruel,' 'deadly,' 'fatal,' 'inexorable'] business as the day would quake to look on.—*Hamlet*, iii. 2.

Bitter ['cruel,' 'agonising,' 'deadly'] torture shall winnow the truth from falsehood.—*Cym.*, v. 5.

Out of the *blank* ['mark,' 'point whereat to aim'] and level of my brain.—*W. T.*, ii. 3.

As level as the cannon to his *blank* ['mark'].—*Hamlet*, iv. 1.

Stood within the *blank* ['mark,' 'aim-point'] of his displeasure.—*Oth.*, iii. 4.

Muffle your false love with some show of *blindness* ['concealment'].—*Com. of E.*, iii. 2.

The fashion of his hat; it ever changes with the next *block* ['mould,' 'form,' 'shape'].—*M. Ado*, i. 1.

More than the common *blocks* [in allusion to the moulds used for shaping hats upon: 'hat-heads,' 'block-heads'].—*W. T.*, i. 2.

This' a good *block* ['hat,' 'well-shaped hat'].—*Lear*, iv. 6.

It better fits my *blood* ['disposition'] to be disdained.—*M. Ado*, i. 3.

Against whose charms faith melteth into *blood* ['impulsive affection,' 'passionate love'].—*Ibid.*, ii. 1.

Let thy *blood* ['passions,' 'ungoverned impulses'] be thy direction till thy death.—*Tr. & Cr.*, ii. 3.

Strange unusual *blood* ['disposition,' 'propensity,' inclination'], when man's worst sin is, he does too much good!—*Timon*, iv. 2.

Excitements of my reason and my *blood* ['passions'], and let all sleep?—*Hamlet*, iv. 4.

Though the conflict be sore between that and my *blood* ['natural affection'].—*Lear*, iii. 5.

Were't my fitness to let these hands obey my *blood* ['natural impulse,' 'prompting of passion'].—*Ibid.*, iv. 2.

Or did the letters work upon his *blood* ['passions'], and new-create this fault?—*Oth.*, iv. 1.

I know young *bloods* ['temperaments'] look for a time of rest.—*Jul. C.*, iv. 3.

Our *bloods* ['constitutional impressions,' 'natural dispositions,' 'native impulses or temperaments'] no more obey the heavens than our courtiers.—*Cym.*, i. 1.

Led on by *bloody* ['full of blood,' 'sanguine'] youth . . . base and *bloody* [in the combined senses of 'full of blood,' 'sanguine,' and of 'bloodthirsty,' 'sanguinary'] insurrection.—2 *H. IV.*, iv. 1.

How now, *blown* [in the combined senses of 'out of breath,' and 'swollen'] Jack! how now, quilt!—1 *H. IV.*, iv. 2.

No *blown* ['swollen,' 'tumid,' 'inflated'] ambition doth our arms incite.—*Lear*, iv. 3.

A vent of blood, and something *blown* ['swollen,' 'puffed, 'tumid'].—*Ant. & C.*, v. 2.

Look how imagination *blows* ['swells,' 'puffs up'] him.—*Tw. N.*, ii. 5.

---

* The word "bitter" has been suspected of error in this passage by some commentators; but see how Shakespeare uses it in the other passages here collectively cited.

This *blows* [in the sense of ' swells, and with the effect of ' strikes '] my heart.—*Ant. & C.,* iv. 6.

Not to seem senseless of the *bob* [' sharp hit,' ' fling,' ' scoff, ' sarcasm '].—*As You L.,* ii. 7.

You shall not *bob* [' cheat,' ' trick '] us out of our melody.—*Tr. & Cr.,* iii. 1.

I have *bobbed* [' fleered,' ' flouted,' ' scoffed at '] his brain more than he has beat my bones.—*Ibid.,* ii. 1.

Gold and jewels that I *bobb'd* [' fooled,' ' tricked,' ' cheated '] from him, as gifts to Desdemona.—*Oth.,* v. 1.

You *boggle* [' shuffle,' ' shift,' ' evade '] shrewdly.—*All's W.,* v. 3.

You have been a *boggler* [' shuffler,' ' evader '] ever.—*Ant. & C.,* iii. 11.

With a base and *boisterous* [' rough,' ' fierce,' ' lawless '] sword enforce a thievish living on the common road ?—*As You L.,* ii. 3.

Feeling what small things are *boisterous* [' rough,' ' fierce,' ' pain-giving '] there.—*John,* iv. 1.

May I be *bold* [' justified,' ' confident '] to think these spirits ?—*Temp.,* iv. 1.

As I am *bold* [' confident,' ' sure,' ' secure '] her honour will remain hers.—*Cym.,* ii. 4.

My love hath in 't a *bond* [' warrant,' ' justification,' ' authorised right '], whereof the world takes note.—*All's W.,* i. 3.

To seal love's *bonds* [' plighted vows '] new-made.—*Mer. of V.,* ii. 6.

The *bonds* [' pledged vows,' ' plighted assurances of faith and troth '] of heaven are slipp'd.—*Tr. & Cr.,* v. 2.

Like sanctified and pious *bonds* * [' pledged assurances of faith and troth '], the better to beguile.—*Hamlet,* i. 3.

By that time will our *book* [' contract of articles or indentures '], I think, be drawn.—1 *H. IV.,* iii. 1.

A beggar's *book* [' book-learning,' ' bookish attainments '] outworths a noble's blood.—*H. VIII.,* i. 1.

To *book*† [' enregister,' ' enter in the note, list, or scroll '] our dead, and then to bury them.—*H. V.,* iv. 7.

You, to your rights; with *boot* [' extra advantage,' ' increase '].—*Lear,* v. 3.

I will *boot* [' profit,' ' advantage,' ' give extra '] thee with what gift beside thy modesty can beg.—*Ant. & C.,* ii. 5.

Make *boot* [' profit,' ' advantage,'] of his distraction.—*Ibid.,* iv. 1.

Like the south, *borne* [' laden,' ' charged,' ' freighted '] with black vapour, doth begin to melt, and drop.—2 *H. IV.,* ii. 4.

You shall have your *bosom* [' cherished wish,' ' fullest and heartiest desire '] on this wretch.—*M. for M.,* iv. 3.

Into the *bosom* [' private confidence ' and ' favourable opinion '] of that same noble prelate.—1 *H. IV.,* i. 3.

To speak your *bosom* [' secret thoughts and wish '] freely.—*Oth.,* iii. 1.

Disgorge thy glutton *bosom* [including the senses of ' stomach' and ' popular affection or favourable opinion '] of the royal Richard.—2 *H. IV.,* i. 3.

How shall this *bosom multiplied* [' multifarious stomach,' ' general stomach '] digest the senate's courtesy ?—*Coriol.,* iii. 1.

To pluck the *common bosom* [' popular affection,' ' favour of the commonalty,' ' common people's inclination '] on his side.—*Lear,* v. 3.

---

* The word " bonds " in this passage has been suspected of error by several commentators; but see how it is used by Shakespeare in the other passages we have here cited.

† It has been proposed by some emendators to change " book " to ' look' here; but inasmuch as the passage above cited from the " First Part of King Henry IV." shows that " book " was used for a note or paper, as in the course of the next scene a paper or " note " of the number slain is given to the king, and as Shakespeare frequently forms a noun into an expressive verb [*See* PARTS OF SPEECH DIVERSELY USED], we believe " book " to be the word written by him in the present passage.

In your embowell'd *bosoms* ['stomachs'].—*R. III.*, v. 2.

Is *bound* ['held fast,' 'hemmed in'] in shallows.—*Jul. C.*, iv. 3.

Made him *brave* ['defy,' 'attack'] me upon the watch.—*Oth.*, v. 2.

Brav'd ['defied,'] in mine own house . . . thou hast *braved* [in the combined sense of 'defied' and 'made fine'] many men.—*Tam. of S.*, iv. 3.

Youth, and cost, and witless *bravery* ['finery,' 'showy dress'] keeps.—*M. for M.*, i. 4.

That says his *bravery* ['finery,' 'expensive clothing'] is not on my cost.—*As You L.*, ii. 7.

The *bravery* ['defiant and ostentatious character'] of his grief.—*Hamlet*, v. 2.

In my vantbrace put this wither'd *brawn* ['arm'].—*Tr. & Cr.*, i. 3.

Hew thy target from thy *brawn* ['arm'].—*Coriol.*, iv. 5.

He cannot choose but *break* ['become bankrupt'].—*Mer. of V.*, iii. 1.

He'll but *break* ['give vent to,' 'utter'] a comparison or two.—*M. Ado*, ii. 1.

That made you *break* ['disclose,' 'communicate'] this enterprise to me?—*Macb.*, i. 7.

The fool has an excellent *breast* ['singing-voice'].—*Tw. N.*, ii. 3.

Your digestion sake, an after-dinner's *breath* ['exercise,' 'relaxation'].—*Tr. & Cr.*, ii. 3.

To the uttermost, or else a *breath* ['exercise,' 'relaxation,' 'recreation'].—*Ibid.*, iv. 5.

A night is but small *breath* ['breathing time'] and little pause to answer matters of this consequence.—*H. V.*, ii. 4.

Created for men to *breathe* ['exercise'] themselves upon thee.—*All's W.*, ii. 3.

I am not yet well *breathed* ['exercised,' 'entered into action'; including the sense of 'made to breathe hard,' 'put out of breath'].—*As You L.*, i. 2.

A most incomparable man; *breath'd* ['exercised,' 'inured by practice'], as it were, to an untirable.—*Timon*, i. 1.

Sick for *breathing* ['exercise,' 'exertion,' 'action'] and exploit.—*All's W.*, i. 2.

Here is a lady that wants *breathing* ['exercise'] too.—*Per.*, ii. 3.

There is a *brief* ['short note,' 'memorandum'] how many sports are ripe.—*Mid. N. D.*, v. 1.

Expedient on the now-born *brief* ['command'].—*All's W.*, ii. 3.

She told me, in a sweet verbal *brief* ['short speech'].—*Ibid.*, v. 3.

Shall draw this *brief* ['small written note'] into as huge a volume.—*John*, ii. 1.

This is the *brief* ['short list,' 'note,' 'memorandum'] of money, plate, and jewels, I am possess'd of.—*Ant. & C.*, v. 2.

Postures beyond *brief** ['transient'] nature.—*Cym.*, v. 5.

Go, put on thy defences.—*Briefly* ['immediately,' 'soon,' 'in a short time'], sir.—*Ant. & C.*, iv. 4.

I'll *bring* ['accompany,' 'escort'] thee on thy way.—*R. II.*, i. 3.

Let me *bring* ['accompany'] thee to Staines.—*H. V.*, ii. 3.

I'll *bring* ['accompany'] you to the gates.—*Tr. & Cr.*, v. 2.

Bring ['escort,' 'accompany'] me on the way a little.—*Oth.*, iii. 4.

From *broad* ['bold,' 'unreserved'] words, and 'cause he.—*Macb.*, iii. 6.

His pranks have been too *broad* ['unreserved,' 'audacious'] to bear with.—*Hamlet*, iii. 4.

Who can speak *broader* ['more openly,' 'more unreservedly'] than he that has no house to put his head in?—*Timon*, iii. 4.

And therefore may be *broke* ['broken with,' 'broken off from'] without offence.—1 *H. VI.*, v. 5.

Love to Richard is a strange *brooch* ['ornament,' 'jewel,' 'precious article'] in this all-hating world.—*R. II.*, v. 5.

He is the *brooch* ['distinguishing ornament'], indeed, and gem of all the nation.—*Hamlet*, iv. 7.

---

* The whole passage, as it appears to us, signifies 'postures (or attitudes) surpassing the transient postures (or attitudes) of nature.'

Ever shall be *brooch'd* ['ornamented,' 'adorned,' 'decorated'] with me.—*Ant. & C.*, iv. 13.

I have no *brother* ['parallel,' 'counterpart'].—3 *H. VI.*, v. 6.

Like strengthless hinges, *buckle* ['bend'] under life.—2 *H. IV.*, i. 1.

In single combat thou shalt *buckle* ['engage,' 'contend'] with me.—1 *H. VI.*, i. 2.

Too strong for me to *buckle* ['contend,' 'strive'] with.—*Ibid.*, v. 3.

But *buckle* ['interchange contendingly'] with thee blows twice two for one.—3 *H. VI.*, i. 4.

Be *buckled* ['engaged,' 'contended'] with.—1 *H. VI.*, iv. 4.

This jewel holds his *building* ['firm placing,' 'strong and solid position,' 'fixture'] on my arm.—*Per.*, ii. 1.

Not pay for the glasses you have *burst* ['broken']?—*Tam. of S., Induc.* 1.

Hath been often *burst* ['broken'], and now repaired with knots.—*Ibid.*, iii. 2.

How her bridle *burst* ['broke']; how I lost.—*Ibid.*, iv. 1.

And of *buxom* ['stout,' 'lusty,' 'vigorous'] valour.—*H. V.*, iii. 6.

So *buxom* ['fresh,' 'lively'], blithe, and full of face.—*Per.*, i. (*Gower*).

Shall *buy* ['pay for'] this treason, even with the dearest blood your bodies bear.—3 *H. VI.*, v. 1.

Then *by-peeping* ['leering,' 'ogling,' 'casting side-way glances'] in an eye base and unlustrous.—*Cym.*, i. 7.

And would not change that *calling* ['appellation,' 'the right to be called thus'], to be adopted heir.—*As You L.*, i. 2.

Shall flout me out of my *calling* ['avocation'].—*Ibid.*, iii. 3.

Candied ['hardened': including a play on the word, as if it were spelt 'candid'] be they, and melt, ere they molest!—*Temp.*, ii. 1.

Let the *candied* ['sugary,' 'fawningly sweet': including an ironical play on the word, as if it were spelt 'candid'] tongue lick absurd pomp.—*Hamlet*, iii. 2.

Thou art the *cap* ['chief'] of all the fools.—*Timon*, iv. 3.

To poor we thine enmity's most *capital* ['chiefly affecting life,' 'mainly injurious']—*Coriol.*, v. 3.

Douglas, Mortimer, *capitulate* ['treat by agreement, drawn up into heads or chapters.' See "Articulate" under the present heading, as thus used] against us.—1 *H. IV.*, iii. 2.

In this *captious* [See VARIED MEANINGS, &c., for our full interpretation of the word as used in the present passage by Shakespeare] and intenible sieve.—*All's W.*, i. 3.

Sent our sons and husbands *captivate* ['as captives,' 'taken into captivity'].—1 *H. VI.*, ii. 3.

Women have been *captivate* ['made captive,' 'taken into captivity'] ere now.—*Ibid.*, v. 3.

Whom fortune *captivates* ['takes captive'].—3 *H. VI.*, i. 4.

Carded ['debased by mixing'] his state.—1 *H. IV.*, iii. 2.

And *careful* ['full of care or trouble'] hours.—*Com. of E.*, v. 1.

Mingled his royalty with *carping* ['jesting,' bantering,' 'rallying,' 'word-catching'] fools.—1 *H. IV.*, iii. 2.

Our reverend cardinal *carried* ['carried through,' 'conducted.' See IDIOMS for various uses of this verb].—*H. VIII.*, i. 1.

The greater part *carries* it ['prevails,' 'carries the day'].—*Coriol.*, ii. 3.

He shall not *carry* ['prevail over,' 'conquer'] him.—*Tr. & Cr.*, v. 6.

He can *carve* ['divide and dispense food at table;' also 'make a peculiar sign with the little finger,' that was considered an accomplishment in persons of gallantry] too.—*Love's L. L.*, v. 2.

She discourses, she *carves* ['makes the sign with the little finger to engage the favoured person's attention'], she gives the leer of invitation.—*Merry W.*, i. 3.

Let it be *cast* ['cast up,' 'computed,' 'reckoned'], and paid —2 *H. IV.*, v. 1.

He hath bought a pair of *cast* ['left off,' 'discarded'] lips of Diana.—*As You L.*, iii. 4.

Our general *cast* [' dismissed '] us thus early.—*Oth.*, ii. 3.

You are but now *cast* [' dismissed,' ' discharged,' ' cashiered '] in his mood.—*Ibid.*, ii. 3.

Whereon it came that I was *cast* [' dismissed from office,' ' cashiered ']—*Ibid.*, v. 2.

And *catch* [' secure ' ' ensure,' ' surely obtain '], with his surcease, success.—*Macb.*, i. 7.

Such temperate order in so fierce a *cause** [' course,' ' proceeding '], doth want example.—*John*, iii. 4.

Upon the spot of this enforced *cause* [' procedure,' ' motived course of action,' as well as ' side taken in a contest '].—*Ibid.*, v. 2.

Working so grossly in a natural *cause* [' procedure,' ' motived course of action,' as well as ' adopted side'].—*H. V.*, ii. 2.

And power i' the truth o' the *cause* [' procedure,' ' course of action '].—*Coriol.*, iii. 3.

Stand to me in this *cause* [' procedure,' ' course of action,' as well as ' matter for consideration,' ' ground of future possible debate '].—*Ibid.*, v. 3.

He cannot buckle his distemper'd *cause* [' course of conduct,' ' motived action,' ' impelled procedure,' ' career '] within the belt of rule.—*Macb.*, v. 2.

By the image of his *cause* [' course of proceeding,' ' conduct,' as well as ' motive,' ' urging occasion of hostility '], I see the portraiture of his.—*Hamlet*, v. 2.

Sith I am enter'd in this *cause* [' course of action,' ' purposed proceeding,' as well as ' side ' or ' party '] so far.—*Oth.*, iii. 3.

Should *censure* [' pass judgment,' ' give an opinion,' ' criticise '] thus on lovely gentlemen.—*Two G. of V.*, i. 2.

Censure [' judge,' ' form your own opinion of'] me in your wisdom.—*Jul. C.*, iii. 2.

Take each man's *censure* [' opinion '], but reserve.—*Hamlet*, i. 3.

In mouths of wisest *censure* [' opinion,' ' judgment '].—*Oth.*, ii. 3.

Remains the *censure* [' sentence,' ' judgment,' ' condemnation '] of this hellish villain.—*Ibid.*, v. 2.

Despatch those *centuries* [' companies of a hundred men '] to our aid.—*Coriol.*, i. 7.

A *century* [' company of a hundred men'] send forth.—*Lear*, iv. 4.

Said a *century* [' hundred '] of prayers.—*Cym.*, iv. 2.

Flies each bound it *chafes* [' chafingly makes,' ' takes with much chafing '].— *Timon*, i. 1.

Resign thy *chair* [' assumed royal seat or position,' ' usurped throne '], and where I stand.—3 *H. VI.*, v. 5.

Is the *chair* [' throne,' ' regal seat'] empty?—*R. III.*, iv. 4.

The foil of England's *chair* [' throne'] where he.—*Ibid.*, v. 3.

Not a tomb so evident as a *chair* [' public rostrum,' ' cathedra,' ' pulpit for public orations'] to extol what it hath done.—*Coriol.*, iv. 7.

Let him go up into the public *chair* [' rostrum '].—*Jul. C.*, iii. 2.

Who may I rather *challenge* [' accuse '] for unkindness.—*Macb.*, iii. 4.

Where nature doth with merit *challenge* [' claim as due'].—*Lear*, i. 1.

So much I *challenge* [' claim as due'] that I may.—*Oth.*, i. 3.

And not of any *challenge* [' claim,' ' pretext'] of desert.—1 *H. VI.*, v. 4.

These white flakes had *challeng'd* [' claimed,' ' demanded '] pity of them.— *Lear*, iv. 7.

Which *challenges* [' proclaims ': including the effect of ' provokes confutation '] itself as honour's born.—*All's W.*, ii. 3.

Through the ashes of my *chance* [' fortune,' ' lot '].—*Ant. & C.*, v. 2.

Think what a *chance* [' prospect of fortune '] thou.—*Cym.*, i. 6.

As we *change* [' exchange,' ' interchange '] our courtesies.—*All's W.*, iii. 2.

---

* In the present passage, as in the one from " King Henry V." and the one from " Macbeth," commentators have wished to alter the word " cause ;" but we think that all the passages we here cite, serve to show that Shakespeare employed the word " cause " peculiarly, and with so much of the same kind of meaning, as to testify that it should be retained in the text of all these passages.

He that I gave it to in *change* ['exchange'] promised.—*H. V.*, iv. 8.

But with them *change* * ['exchange'] of honours.—*Coriol.*, ii. 1.

I'll *change* ['exchange,' 'interchange'] that name with you.—*Hamlet*, i. 2.

To *change* ['exchange'] the cod's head for the salmon's tail.—*Oth.*, ii. 1.

Do not seek to take your *change*† ['change of fortune,' 'reverse,' 'vicissitude'] upon you.—*As You L.*, i. 3.

It is but *change* ['change of fortune,' 'vicissitude,' 'alternation'], Titinius; for Octavius is overthrown.—*Jul. C.*, v. 3.

Did deserve his *change* ['reverse,' 'altered fortune'].—*Ant. & C.*, iii. 6.

In his own *change* ['changed conduct,' 'change of conduct,' 'altered behaviour'] or by ill officers.—*Jul. C.*, iv. 2.

Why should this *change* ['conflicting interchange,' 'disturbing mutation'] of thoughts, the sad companion.—*Per.*, i. 2.

In *changing* ['exchanging,' 'interchanging'] hardiment with great Glendower.— 1 *H. IV.*, i. 3.

My thoughts I'll *character* ['write,' 'inscribe,' 'express in graven characters'].— *As You L.*, iii. 2.

Produce my very *character* ['handwriting'].—*Lear*, ii. 1.

And *charm* ['bind as by a spell,' 'subdue by magic influence'] her chattering tongue.—*Tam. of S.*, iv. 2.

Or I will *charm* ['spell-bind'] your tongue.—3 *H. VI.*, v. 5.

Go to, *charm* ['silence as by a magic spell'] your tongue.—*Oth.*, v. 2.

When I am reveng'd upon my *charm* ['spell,' 'bewitchment,' 'sorceress,' 'enchantress'], I have done all . . . this grave *charm*, whose eye beck'd forth my wars — *Ant. & C.*, iv. 10.

She was a *charmer* ['enchantress,' 'sorceress,' 'one who deals in charms and spells'], and could almost read the thoughts.—*Oth.*, iii. 4.

This is the *chase* ['the beast that is being hunted or chased'].—*W. T.*, iii. 3.

Single out some other *chase* ['object chased,' 'prey pursued'].—3 *H. VI.*, ii. 4.

The goodness that is *cheap* ['held of small value,' 'parted with on easy terms'] in beauty, makes beauty brief in goodness.—*M. for M.*, iii. 1.

Man's life is *cheap* ['of little value,' 'worth as little'] as beast's.—*Lear*, ii. 4.

The *childing* ['teeming,' 'fruitful,' 'productive'] autumn.—*Mid. N. D.*, ii. 2.

If thou shouldst strive to *choose* ['resist,' 'refrain,' 'do other than this.' *See* IDIOMS for "choose" thus used].—*All's W.*, ii. 3.

The princess, sweet *chuck* [a term of endearment or familiarity, varied from 'chick' or 'chicken'].—*Love's L. L.*, v. 1.

Sweet *chucks* ['term of familiarity'] beat not.—*Ibid.*, v. 2.

Wind about my love with *circumstance* ['circumlocution,' 'superfluous words,' 'needless instances'].—*Mer. of V.*, i. 1.

Who, in his *circumstance* ['circumstantial argument,' 'detailed discussion'], expressly proves that no man is.—*Tr. & Cr.*, iii. 3.

Without more *circumstance* ['circumlocution'] at all.—*Hamlet*, i. 5.

With a bombast *circumstance* ['circumlocution'] horribly stuffed.—*Oth.*, i. 1.

I must be *circumstanc'd* ['content to yield to circumstances'].—*Ibid.*, iii. 4.

Whose aged honour *cites* ['denotes,' 'betokens'] a virtuous youth.—*All's W.*, i. 3.

---

* In the present passage, some commentators would alter "change" to 'charge'; but the passages we here cite, show that Shakespeare occasionally uses "change" in the sense of 'exchange,' and we believe that in this instance "change of honours" means 'exchange of titles,' with reference to the new surname of Coriolanus in lieu of the former name, Caius Marcius.

† Some commentators propose to substitute 'charge' for "change" in this passage; but we have shown that elsewhere also Shakespeare uses "change" in the sense of 'altered fortune,' 'reverse,' 'vicissitude.'

I think it *cites* ['summons,' 'urges,' 'incites'] us, brother, to the field.—3 *H. VI.*, ii. 1.

The rude sea grew *civil* ['gentle,' 'less rough'] at her song.—*Mid. N. D.*, ii. 2.

And many a *civil* ['unbarbarous,' 'civilised'] monster.—*Oth.*, iv. 1.

If any thing that 's *civil* ['civilised'], speak; if savage.—*Cym.*, iii. 6.

The *civil'st* ['most civilised'] place of all this isle.—2 *H. VI.*, iv. 7.

Roaming *clean* ['completely'] through the bounds of Asia.—*Com. of E.*, i. 1.

And disfigur'd *clean* ['completely,' 'quite,' 'utterly,' 'thoroughly'].—*R. II.*, iii. 1.

This is *clean* ['quite'] *kam* ['irrelevant,' 'beside the purpose'].—*Coriol.*, iii. 1.

Clean ['quite'] from the purpose of the things.—*Jul. C.*, i. 3.

It is *clean* ['quite'] out of the way.—*Oth.*, i. 3.

Ere *clean* ['completely,' 'quite'] it o'erthrow nature.—*Cym.*, iii. 6.

And a *clear* ['pure,' 'sinless'] life ensuing.—*Temp.*, iii. 3.

Roots, you *clear* ['pure,' 'immaculate'] heavens!—*Timon*, iv. 3.

So *clear* ['pure,' 'free from blemish,' 'spotless'] in his great office.—*Macb.*, i. 7.

Persever in that *clear* ['pure,' 'innocent,' 'immaculate'] way thou goest.—*Per.*, iv. 6.

Lest my life be cropp'd to keep you *clear* ['unsuspected,' 'free from chance of detection'].—*Ibid.*, i. 1.

I require a *clearness* ['freedom from suspicion for myself,' and also 'neatness and completeness in the task you undertake'].—*Macb.*, iii. 1.

The earth this *climate* ['portion of the firmament'] overlooks.—*John*, ii. 2.

That, in a Christian *climate* ['country,' 'region'].—*R. II.*, iv. 1.

Unto the *climate* ['country,' 'region'] that they point upon.—*Jul. C.*, i. 3.

Whilst you do *climate* ['dwell,' 'reside,' 'remain,' 'breathe the atmosphere'] here!—*W. T.*, v. 1.

Till famine *cling* ['shrivel,' 'shrink,' 'wither'] thee.—*Macb.*, v. 5.

Let me *clip* ['embrace'] you in arms as sound.—*Coriol.*, i. 6.

Here I *clip* ['embrace'] the anvil of my sword.—*Ibid.*, iv. 5.

Clip ['embrace'] your wives, your friends.—*Ant. & C.*, iv. 8.

No grave upon the earth shall *clip* ['inclose,' 'infold'] in it a pair so famous.—*Ibid.*, v. 2.

Hark, how the villain would *close* ['conciliate by,' 'agreeing with,' 'by coming round to the same opinion with'] now, after his.—*M. for M.*, v. 1.

To *close* ['conciliate by finally assenting,' 'by agreeing'] with us ?—2 *H. IV.*, ii. 4.

He *closes* ['ends by agreeing,' 'finally comes to the concluding point of assent'] with you in this consequence.—*Hamlet*, ii. 1.

That *close* ['secret-looking,' 'reserved'] aspect of his.—*John*, iv. 2.

Go *closely* ['secretly,' 'privately'] in with me.—*Ibid.*, iv. 1.

Meaning to keep her *closely* ['secretly,' 'privately,' 'in concealment'] at my cell.—*R. & Jul.*, v. 3.

We have *closely* ['secretly,' 'privately,' 'hiddenly': also implying 'indirectly,' 'in so covert a manner that he shall not know it is I who have done so'] sent for Hamlet hither.—*Hamlet*, iii. 1.

All dedicated to *closeness* ['privacy,' 'seclusion'].—*Temp.*, i. 2.

All in haste she *coasteth* ['advances,' 'runs'] to the cry.—*V. & Adon.*, Stanza 145.

That give a *coasting* ['sidling,' 'conciliatory,' 'alluring,' 'enticing,' 'advancing to meet half way'] welcome ere it* comes.—*Tr. & Cr.*, iv. 5.

How he *coasts* ['insidiously proceeds,' 'encroachingly advances'], and hedges his own way.—*H. VIII.*, iii. 2.

As *cognisance* ['badge,' 'visible token'] of my blood-drinking hate.—1 *H. VI.*, ii. 4.

The *cognisance* ['token,' 'visible proof,' 'evidence'] of her incontinency is this.—*Cym.*, ii. 4.

---

* *See* RELATIVELY USED PRONOUNS for our explanation of "it," as employed in this passage.

Move the hearers to *collection* ['make collective deduction,' 'draw conclusions'] ; they aim at it.—*Hamlet*, iv. 5.

I can make no *collection* [' collective deduction,' 'conclusion drawn from aggregate premises'] of it.—*Cym.*, v. 5.

A fellow of the self-same *colour* [' kind,' 'complexional character.' *See* IDIOMS for " colour " thus used].—*Lear*, ii. 2.

Against all *colour* ['show of right,' ' ostensible right'], here did put the yoke upon us.—*Cym.*, iii. 1.

Her *combinate* [' betrothed,' ' bound by contract '] husband.—*M. for M.*, iii. 1.

A solemn *combination* [' marriage contract'] shall be made of our dear souls.— *Tw. N.*, v. 1.

Thy faith my fancy to thee doth *combine* ['contract,' 'affiance,' 'bind'].— *As You L.*, v. 4.

I am *combined* [' bound'] by a sacred vow.—*M. for M.*, iv. 3.

Comes [' becomes,' ' comes to be'] dear'd by being lack'd.—*Ant. & C.*, i. 4.

Infects one *comma* [' jot,' ' iota,' 'the smallest imaginable point': in reference to the smallest mark in punctuation, 'the least stop'] in the course I hold.—*Timon*, i. 1.

And stand a *comma* [' link of amicably harmonious connection:' in reference to the least of all the sensible intervals in music. *See* MUSICAL TERMS] 'tween their amities. —*Hamlet*, v. 2.

Commend [' deliver,' ' convey,' 'commit'] the paper to his gracious hand.— *All's W.*, v. 1.

His glittering arms he will *commend* [' commit'] to rust.—*R. II.*, iii. 3.

Justice *commends* [' commits'] the ingredients of our.—*Macb.*, i. 7.

There is our *commission* [' warrant of authority'], from which we would not have you warp.—*M. for M.*, i. 1.

Seals a *commission* ['authorising warrant'] to a blank of danger.—*Tr. & Cr.*, iii. 3.

Bore the *commission* [' authorised power,' 'representativeship'] of my place and person.—*Lear*, v. 3.

Blunted with *community* ['commonness,' 'usualness,' ' frequency'].—1 *H. IV.*, iii. 2.

New friends and stranger *companies* ['associates,' ' society '].—*Mid. N. D.*, i. 1.

His *companies* [' associates,' ' companions'] unletter'd.—*H. V.*, i. 1.

What an equivocal *companion* ['fellow': used as a term of contempt] is this!— *All's W.*, v. 3.

These jigging fools ? *Companion* [' fellow '], hence !—*Jul. C.*, iv. 3.

Entrance to such *companions* [' fellows '].—*Coriol.*, iv. 5.

That such *companions* [' fellows '] thou'dst unfold.—*Oth.*, iv. 2.

The most *comparative* [' given to humorous similes,' ' full of droll comparisons'], rascalliest, sweet young prince.—1 *H. IV.*, i. 2.

Every beardless vain *comparative* [' one given to make sallies of comparison,' ' dealer in jesting similes '].—*Ibid.*, iii. 2.

A *comparison* [' jocose simile,' ' witticism of analogy'] or two on me.—*M. Ado*, ii. 1.

Full of *comparisons* [' jesting similes '] and wounding flouts.—*Love's L. L.*, v. 2.

To lay his gay *comparisons* [' comparative advantages '] apart.—*Ant. & C.*, iii. 11.

To *compass* [' gain,' ' achieve '] her I 'll use my skill.—*Two G. of V.*, ii. 4.

Bragged of that he could not *compass* ['achieve,' ' perform,' ' fulfil '].—*Merry W.*, iii. 3.

That were hard to *compass* [' achieve '].—*Tw. N.*, i. 2.

To *compass* [' gain,' ' attain,' ' obtain '] such a boundless happiness !—*Per.*, i. 1.

He and his *competitors* [' consociates,' ' confederates'] in oath.—*Love's L. L.*, ii. 1.

The *competitors* [' confederates,' ' allies,' ' colleagues '] enter.—*Tw. N.*, iv. 2.

No, my *complete* [' accomplished '] master.—*Love's L. L.*, iii. 1.

This man so *complete* [' fully accomplished'].—*H. VIII.*, i. 2.

Complete [' accomplished'] in mind and feature.—*Ibid.*, iii. 2.

Thou great and *complete* [' accomplished '] man.—*Tr. & Cr.*, iii. 3.

That honourable, *complete* ['accomplished'], free-hearted gentleman.—*Timon*, iii. 1.

Then it is the *complexion* ['nature,' 'constitutional tendency'] of them all to leave the dam.—*Mer. of V.*, iii. 1.

Good my *complexion* ['bloom of countenance,' and 'natural propensity,' 'constitutional tendency'].—*As You L.*, iii. 2.

The o'ergrowth of some *complexion* ['natural propensity, 'constitutional tendency'], oft breaking down the.—*Hamlet*, i. 4.

On my *complexion* ['constitutional temperament'].—*Ibid.*, v. 2.

Of her own clime, *complexion* ['fair skin,' and 'temperament'], and degree.—*Oth.*, iii. 3.

If we *compose* ['come to an agreement'] well here.—*Ant. & C.*, ii. 2.

I crave our *composition* ['compact,' 'agreement'] may be written.—*Ibid.*, ii: 6.

There is no *composition* ['consistency,' 'coincidence,' 'congruity'] in these news.—*Oth.*, i. 3.

But it was a strong *composure* ['composition,' 'consociation,' 'combination'] a fool could disunite.—*Tr. & Cr.*, ii. 3.

Thou art of sweet *composure* ['composition,' 'compounded qualities'].—*Ibid.*, ii. 3.

As his *composure* ['native component qualities'] must be rare indeed.—*Ant. & C.*, i. 4

And have the dates in *compt* ['duly taken account,' 'regularly summed-up order'].—*Timon*, ii. 1.

And what is theirs, in *compt* ['trust'].—*Macb.*, i. 6.

When we shall meet at *compt* ['the last great account'].—-*Oth.*, v. 2.

Using *conceit* ['conception,' 'comprehension,' 'power of understanding'] alone.—*John*, iii. 3.

If it had *conceit* ['power of conceiving thought'], would die, as I am like to do.—*Per.*, iii. 1.

Force his soul so to his own *conceit* ['conception,' 'idea'], that, from her working . . . his whole function suiting with forms to his *conceit?*—*Hamlet*, ii. 2.

Some horrible *conceit* ['conception,' 'idea'].—*Oth.*, iii. 3.

One that so imperfectly *conceits* ['conceives,' 'imagines'].—*Ibid.*, iii. 3.

Well *conceited* ['conceived,' 'imagined'], Davy.—*2 H. IV.*, v. 1.

With her modest eyes and still *conclusion* ['final manner,' 'sedate demeanour, 'reticence'] shall acquire no.—*Ant. & C.*, iv. 13.

So that, *conclusions* ['logical experiments,' 'deductions,' 'arguments'] to be as kisses, if your four negatives make your.—*Tw. N.*, v. 1.

To try *conclusions* ['experiments'], in the basket creep.—*Hamlet*, iii. 4.

She hath pursu'd *conclusions* ['experiments'] infinite—*Ant. & C.*, v. 2.

If he have the *condition* ['inherent qualities,' 'native disposition'] of a saint.—*Mer. of V.*, i. 2.

Than my *condition* ['innate disposition,' 'natural tendency or quality']; which hath been smooth.—*1 H. IV.*, i. 3. .

A good English *condition* ['disposition,' 'moral quality'].—*H. V.*, v. 1.

My *condition* ['natural disposition'] is not smooth.—*Ibid.*, v. 2.

I have a touch of your *condition* ['temper,' 'disposition'].—*R. III.*, iv. 4.

Much prevail'd on your *condition* ['mood,' 'state of mind,' 'temper,' 'disposition'].—*Jul. C.*, ii. 1.

She's full of most blessed *condition* ['qualities of nature,' 'moral disposition'].—*Oth.*, ii. 1.

And then, of so gentle a *condition* ['disposition,' 'native character'].—*Ibid.*, iv. 1.

I, in my *condition* ['official capacity'], shall better speak of you.—*2 H. IV.*, iv. 3.

Well express'd in our *condition* ['pictorial capacity'].—*Timon*, i. 1.

Soft *conditions* ['qualities,' 'dispositions'] and our hearts.—*Tam. of S.*, v. 2.

Govern our *conditions* ['dispositions,' 'tempers,' 'individual qualities'].—*Lear*, iv. 3.

Our *conditions* ['dispositions,' 'characters'] so differing.—*Ant. & C.*, ii. 2.

And gentle thy *conditions* ['qualities,' 'disposition']!—*Per.*, iii. 1.

Give him courteous *conduct* ['escort'] to this place.—*Mer. of V.*, iv. 1.

And desire some *conduct* ['escort,' 'convoy'] of the lady.—*Tw. N.*, iii. 4.

More than nature was ever *conduct* ['conductor'] of.—*Temp.*, v. 1.

I will be his *conduct* ['conductor'].—*R. II.*, iv. 1.

Thou hast been *conduct* ['conductor'] of my shame.—2 *H. VI.*, ii. 4.

He did *confound* ['spend,' 'dissipate,' 'cause to pass away'] the best part of an hour in.—1 *H. IV.*, i. 3.

How couldst thou in a mile *confound* ['spend,' 'lose,' 'consume'] an hour.— *Coriol.*, i. 6.

Let's not *confound* ['lose,' 'spend,' 'consume'] the time.—*Ant. & C.*, i. 1.

The interim, pray you, all *confound* ['consume'].—*Per.*, v. 2 (*Gower*).

So keen and greedy to *confound* ('destroy,' 'ruin,' 'cause to perish'] a man.— *Mer. of V.*, iii. 2.

Jutty his *confounded* ['being consumed by the action of the waves,' and 'confused,' 'bewildered,' 'overwhelmed' from their perpetual dash and drenching] base.— *H. V.*, iii. 1.

Have *confounded* ['destroyed,' 'caused to perish'] one the other, or have fallen both.—*Cym.*, i. 5.

Decline to your *confounding* ['destructive'] contraries.—*Timon*, iv. 1.

With some sweet *consort* ['company of musicians'].—*Tw. G. of V.*, iii. 2.

Wilt thou be of our *consort* ['band,' 'gang,' 'fellowship'].—*Ibid.*, iv. 1.

Grows to something of great *constancy* ['consistency'; in its combined senses of 'congruity and substantiality'].—*Mid. N. D.*, v. 1.

Oh, *constancy* ['firmness,' 'steadfastness'], be strong.—*Jul. C.*, ii. 4.

Cassius, be *constant* ['firm,' 'self-possessed'].—*Ibid.*, iii. 1.

I was *constant* ['decided,' 'firmly resolved'] Cimber should be banish'd, and *constant* do remain to keep him so.—*Ibid.*, iii. 1.

This hour a *constant* ['steadfast,' 'determined,' 'resolute'] will to publish our daughters' several dowers.—*Lear*, i. 1.

Bring his *constant* ['firm,' 'decided,' 'settled'] pleasure.—*Ibid.*, v. 1.

To find the mind's *construction* ['interpretation,' 'exponent'] in the face.— *Macb.*, i. 4.

Your own honour to *contain* ['retain,' 'keep'] the ring.—*Mer. of V.*, v. 1.

We can *contain* ['restrain,' 'keep control over'] ourselves.—*Tam. of S.*, *Induc.* 1.

Oh, *contain* ['restrain,' 'control'] yourself.—*Tr. & Cr.*, v. 2.

Contain ['control,' 'restrain'] thyself, good friend.—*Timon*, ii. 2.

Ay, my *continent* ['container,' 'includer'] of beauty.—*Love's L. L.*, iv. 1.

The *continent* ['container'] and summary of my fortune.—*Mer. of V.*, iii. 2.

That orbed *continent* ['container of heat and light'] the fire that.—*Tw. N.*, v. 1.

Not tomb enough and *continent* ['container,' 'recipient'] to hide the slain.— *Hamlet*, iv. 4.

You shall find in him the *continent* ['container and campriser'] of what part a gentleman would see.—*Ibid.*, v. 2.

Have a *continent* ['containing,' 'restraining'] forbearance.—*Lear*, i. 2.

Be stronger than thy *continent* ['container,' 'the body containing the heart'].— *Ant. & C.*, iv. 12.

Have overborne their *continents* ['containers,' 'the banks that contain the stream of water'].—*Mid. N. D.*, ii. 2.

Thou globe of sinful *continents* ['contents,' 'propensities therein contained'].— 2 *H. IV.*, ii. 4.

Rive your concealing *continents* ['exterior inclosures'].—*Lear*, iii. 2.

An untirable and *continuate* ['continuous,' 'continual,' 'continued,' 'incessant'] goodness.—*Timon*, i. 1.

In a more *continuate* [' uninterrupted '] time.—*Oth.*, iii. 4.

From the body of *contraction* [' wedded union,' ' wedlock '] plucks the very soul.—*Hamlet*, iii. 4.

These false and most *contrarious* [' contrary to fact ' and ' contradictory to each other '] quests.—*M. for M.*, iv. 1.

Please ye we may *contrive* [' spend,' ' pass away,' ' wear out ': from the preterite *contrivi* of the Latin verb *contero*] this afternoon.—*Tam. of S.*, i. 2.

Was 't you that did so oft *contrive* [' plot '] to kill him ?—*As You L.*, iv. 3.

The Fates with traitors do *contrive* [' plot,' ' conspire '].—*Jul. C.*, ii. 3.

Thou hast *contrived* [' plotted,' ' schemed '] against the very life.—*Mer. of V.*, iv. 1.

And his more braver daughter, could *control* [' confute,' ' bring a contrary account '] thee.—*Temp.*, i. 2.

Notice of your *conventicles* [' secret meetings for conspiracy '].—2 *H. VI.*, iii. 1.

Holy, cold, and still *conversation* [' conduct,' ' behaviour,' ' moral procedure '].—*Ant. & C.*, ii. 6.

The good in *conversation* [' moral conduct,' ' behaviour '].—*Per.*, ii. (*Gower*).

From the *conversation* [' secret anxious discussion '] of my thoughts.—*All's W.*, i. 3.

I will *converse* [' hold communion,' ' confer '] with iron-witted fools and unrespective boys.—*R. III.*, iv. 2.

To *converse* [' hold communion,' ' have intercourse,' ' have commerce '] with him that is wise.—*Lear*, i. 4.

One that *converses* [' holds communion,' ' has commerce '] more with the buttock of the night, than with the forehead.—*Coriol.*, ii. 1.

" *Convey* " [' steal '] the wise it call.—*Merry W.*, i. 3.

You may *convey* [' conduct stealthily,' ' carry on clandestinely or furtively '] your pleasures.—*Macb.*, iv. 3.

Convey [' artfully manage,' ' dexterously carry through '] the business as I shall find means.—*Lear*, i. 2.

I fear, there is *conveyance* [' unfair management,' ' fraudulent dealing '].—1 *H. VI.*, i. 3.

Thy sly *conveyance* [' artifice,' ' crafty dealing '].—3 *H. VI.*, iii. 3.

Conveyers [' tricksters,' ' defrauders '] are you all.—*R. II.*, iv. 1.

A whole armado of *convicted* [' condemned,' ' doomed to perdition,' ' marked out for destruction '] sail.—*John*, iii. 4.

The holy suit which fain it would *convince* [' conquer,' ' obtain by conquest '].—*Love's L. L.*, v. 2.

With wine and wassail so *convince* [' overpower,' ' overcome,' ' subdue '].—*Macb.*, i. 7.

To *convince* [' overcome,' ' conquer,' ' defeat '] the honour of my mistress.—*Cym.*, i. 5.

This truth shall ne'er *convince* [' overcome,' ' confute,' ' refute '].—*Per.*, i. 2.

Their malady *convinces* [' defeats,' ' baffles,' ' conquers '] the great assay of art.—*Macb.*, iv. 3.

We freely *cope* [' pay,' ' remunerate,' ' reward,' ' recompense '] your courteous pains withal.—*Mer. of V.*, iv. 1.

I love to *cope* [' encounter,' ' engage in conversation with '] him in these sullen fits.—*As You L.*, ii. 1.

In the fear to *cope* [' encounter,' ' meet opposingly '] malicious censurers.—*H. VIII.*, i. 2.

Noble as the adversary I come to *cope* [' encounter,' ' engage in fight with '].—*Lear*, v. 3.

And is again to *cope* [' encounter,' ' meet in amorous assignation '] your wife.—*Oth.*, iv. 1.

He yesterday *coped* [' encountered,' ' engaged in fight with '] Hector in the battle.—*Tr. & Cr.*, i. 2.

As e'er my conversation *cop'd* [' encountered '] withal.—*Hamlet*, iii. 2.

It was the *copy* [' copious subject '] of our conference.—*Com. of E.*, v. 1.

The whole matter and *copy* [' copious transcript '] of the father.—*W. T.*, ii. 3.

Be *copy* ['model,' 'pattern,' 'example'] now to men of.—*H. V.*, iii. 1.

But in them nature's *copy's* ['example,' 'specimen,' and 'copyhold tenure'] not eterne.—*Macb.*, iii. 2.

Adorn his temples with a *coronet* ['crown'].—1 *H. VI.*, v. 4.

This *coronet* ['crown'] part between you.—*Lear*, i. 1.

Bears the *cost* ['wealth,' 'riches,' 'costly goods'] of princes.—*As You L.*, ii. 7.

Worth all our mundane *cost* ['possessions'].—*Per.*, iii. 2.

Her amber hairs for foul have amber *coted* ['gone side by side with,' 'surpassed,' 'outvied,' and 'caused to be quoted,' 'observed,' 'noted.' *See* PRONUNCIATION].—*Love's L. L.*, iv. 3.

We *coted* ['passed beside,' 'passed by,' 'overtook'] them on the way.—*Hamlet*, ii. 2.

That England shall *couch* ['crouch,' 'humbly bend'] down.—*H. V.*, iv. 2.

These *couchings* ['humble bendings,' 'crouchings'] and these.—*Jul. C.*, iii. 1.

Emptying our bosoms of their *counsel* ['interchanged confidence,' 'mutually exchanged secrets'] sweet.—*Mid. N. D.*, i. 1.

Is all the *counsel* ['interchanged confidence'] that we two.—*Ibid.*, iii. 2.

What to your sworn *counsel* ['secrecy'] I have spoken.—*All's W.*, iii. 7.

Did ever keep your *counsels* ['secrets,' 'confidences'].—*Mid. N. D.*, iii. 2.

Are enter'd in our *counsels* ['proceedings proposed in council'].—*Coriol.*, i. 2.

To *countenance* ['entertain,' 'receive,' 'welcome'] my mistress.—*Tam. of S.*, iv. 1.

Have *countenance* ['sanction,' 'support'] in this world to drown or hang themselves.—*Hamlet*, v. 1.

Fair Portia's *counterfeit* ['likeness,' 'portrait']!—*Mer. of V.*, iii. 2.

Thou draw'st a *counterfeit* ['likeness,' 'portrait'] best in all.—*Timon*, v. 1.

What *counts* ['marks,' 'lines'] harsh fortune casts upon my face.—*Ant. & C.*, ii. 6.

This soft *courage* ['heart,' 'spirit,'] makes your followers faint.—3 *H. VI.*, ii. 2.

I'd such a *courage* ['spirit,' 'will,' 'strength of desire,' 'ardour'] to do him good.—*Timon.*, iii. 3.

I will gyve thee in thine own *courtship* ['courtesy,' 'courteous behaviour'].—*Oth.*, ii. 1.

Sirs, *cover* ['prepare the table,' 'spread the meal'] the while.—*As You L.*, ii. 5.

Why, then, *cover* ['lay the cloth,' 'prepare the table for the meal'], and set them down.—2 *H. IV.*, ii. 4.

While I thy amiable cheeks do *coy* ['fondle,' 'caress,' 'smooth,' 'pat,' 'stroke'].—*Mid. N. D.*, iv. 1.

When he was a *crack* ['boy,' 'young lad'], not thus high.—2 *H. IV.*, iii. 2.

A *crack* ['lively boy'], madam.—*Coriol.*, i. 3.

Ethiops of their sweet complexion *crack* ['boast'].—*Love's L. L.*, iv. 3.

Were *crack'd* ['boasted,' 'vaunted'] of kitchen trulls.—*Cym.*, v. 5.

What *cracker* ['boaster'] is this same, that deafs.—*John*, ii. 1.

Being compact of *credit* ['credulity'] that you love us.—*Com. of E.*, iii. 2.

There I found this *credit* ['oral intelligence,' 'verbal message'], that he did range the town to seek me out.—*Tw. N.*, iv. 3.

And the rich *crop* ['produce'] of sea and land.—*Cym.*, i. 7.

Who can *cross* ['contradict,' 'controvert,' 'dispute,' 'refute'] it?—*Per.*, iv. 4.

You common *cry* ['pack'] of curs!—*Coriol.*, iii. 3.

You and your *cry* ['pack']!—*Ibid.*, iv. 6.

Wherein your *cunning* ['skill,' 'artistic knowledge or proficiency'] can assist me much.—*Tam. of S., Induc.* 1.

Craves a noble *cunning* ['wisdom,' 'philosophy'].—*Coriol.*, iv. 1.

Shame, that they wanted *cunning* ['wisdom,' 'judgment'].—*Timon*, v. 5.

In ignorance, and not in *cunning* ['knowledge,' 'intentional deed'].—*Oth.*, iii. 3.

My better *cunning* ['skill'] faints under his chance.—*Ant. & C.*, ii. 3.

Virtue and *cunning* ['knowledge,' 'wisdom'] were endowments.—*Per.*, iii. 2.

Yea, *curb* ['bend,' 'bow': French, *courber*] and woo.—*Hamlet*, iii. 4.

Mocked thee for too much *curiosity* ['careful regard to luxurious appointments,' 'fastidious refinement'].—*Timon*, iv. 3.

For *curious* ['scrupulous,' 'carefully precise'] I cannot be with you —*Tam. of S.*, iv. 4.

Nature, rather *curious* ['excessively careful,' 'scrupulously painstaking': as derived from the Latin *cura*, 'care,' 'concern.' *See* Note at page 529 for Shakespeare's practice in this respect] than in haste, hath well composed thee.—*All's W.*, i. 2.

So fraught with *curious* ['particular,' 'requiring special care'] business.—*W. T.*, iv. 3.

His body couched in a *curious* ['carefully arranged and elaborately ornamented' as well as 'care-fraught.' *See* VARIED MEANINGS, &c., for Shakespeare's inclusive mode of employing words] bed.—3 *H. VI.*, ii. 5.

Mar a *curious* ['elaborate,' 'complicated,' 'involved'] tale in telling it.—*Lear*, i. 4.

Though you be therein *curious* ['scrupulous in inquiry,' 'particular in examination,' 'careful in investigating'] the least cause.—*Ant. & C.*, iii. 2.

I am something *curious* ['careful,' 'particular,' 'anxious,' 'solicitous'].—*Cym.*, i. 7.

Wherein so *curiously* ['carefully,' 'regardfully'] he had set this counterfeit.—*All's W.*, iv. 3.

She's too *curst* ['shrewish,' 'pert,' 'perverse'].—Too *curst*.—*M. Ado.*, ii. 1.

I was never *curst* ['shrewish,' 'spiteful,' 'scolding'].—*Mid. N. D.*, iii. 2.

With *curst* ['harsh,' 'scolding,' 'severe'] speech I threatened.—*Lear*, ii. 1.

Nor *curstness* ['wrangling,' 'ill-temper'] grow to the matter.—*Ant. & C.*, ii. 2.

Look, with a spot I *damn* ['doom,' 'condemn'] him.—*Jul. C.*, iv. 1.

Perform 't, or else we *damn* ['doom,' 'condemn'] thee.—*Ant. & C.*, i. 1.

Mark'd with a blot, *damn'd* ['doomed'] in the book of Heaven.—*R. II.*, iv. 1.

Fortune, on his *damned* ['doomed'] quarry smiling.—*Macb.*, i. 2.

Oh, wilt thou *darkling** ['in the dark,' 'in darkness'] leave me?—*Mid. N. D.*, ii. 3.

And we were left *darkling* ['in the dark'].—*Lear*, i. 4.

Darkling ['in darkness'] stand the varying shore.—*Ant. & C.*, iv. 13.

I cannot *daub* ['keep up this miserable show of imitation,' 'this wretched mimicry'] it farther.—*Lear*, iv. 1.

So smooth he *daub'd* ['overlaid,' 'spread over disguisingly'] his vice with show of virtue.—*R. III.*, iii. 5.

By charms, by spells, by the figure, and such *daubery* ['delusion,' 'imposition,' 'trickery,' 'fraud,' 'jugglery'] as this is.—*Merry W.*, iv. 2.

The king was slily finger'd from the *deck* ['pack of cards'].—3 *H. VI.*, v. 1.

When I have *deck'd* ['sprinkled'] the sea with drops.—*Temp.*, i. 2

Not letting it *decline* ['fall'] on the *declin'd* ['fallen'].—*Tr. & Cr.*, iv. 5.

Being advanc'd, *declines* ['falls'], and then men die.—*Coriol.*, ii. 1.

Far more to you do I *decline* ['incline,' 'bend towards'].—*Com. of E.*, iii. 2.

Decline ['bend,' 'incline'] your head.—*Lear*, iv. 2.

And rats, and such small *deer* ['animals in general'].—*Ibid.*, iii. 4.

Defeat ['disfigure'] thy favour with a usurped beard.—*Oth.*, i. 3.

The ground of my *defeatures* ['impaired looks,' 'disfigurements'].—*Com. of E.*, ii. 2.

Strange *defeatures* ['disfigurements'] in my face.—*Ibid.*, v. 1.

For God *defend* ['forbid'] the lute should be like.—*M. Ado*, ii. 1.

Take my *defiance* ['denial,' 'rejection']; die, perish.—*M. for M.*, iii. 1.

Breaths that I *defied* ['abjured,' 'rejected'] not.—*As You L.* (*Epilogue*).

But I *defy* ['refuse,' 'reject'] all angels.—*Merry W.*, ii. 2.

I *defy* ['reject,' 'refuse,' 'renounce'] all counsel.—*John*, iii. 4.

---

* Besides its direct meaning of 'in the dark,' "darkling," as Shakespeare employs it, includes the meaning of 'baffled,' 'deserted,' 'bereft of light and help.'

I *defy* ['denounce'] the tongues of soothers.—1 *H. IV.*, iv. 1.

That's a *degree* ['step,' 'advance'] to love.—*Tw. N.*, iii. 1.

In these *degrees* ['steps'] have they made a pair of stairs to marriage.—*As You L.*, v. 2.

Shall of his *demerits* ['high merits': from the Latin *demereo. See* Note at page 529] rob Cominius.—*Coriol.*, i. 1.

My *demerits* ['merits'] may speak, unbonneted.—*Oth.*, i. 2.

If not *denounc'd* ['interdicted,' 'proclaimed to be prohibited'], against us, why should not we be there in person?—*Ant. & C.*, iii. 7.

The *denunciation* ['proclamation'] lack of outward order.—*M. for M.*, i. 3.

You *denied* ['refused'] to fight with me.—*W. T.*, v. 2.

You kill me to *deny* ['refuse'] it.—*M. Ado*, iv. 1.

If they *deny* ['refuse'] to come.—*Tam. of S.*, v. 2.

Deny ['refuse'] to speak with me?—*Lear*, ii. 4.

Ere we *depart* ['part,' 'separate'], we'll share a bounteous time.—*Timon*, i. 1.

Willingly *departed* ['parted'] with a part.—*John*, ii. 2.

Like life and death's *departing* ['parting,' 'separation'].—3 *H. VI.*, ii. 6.

That shall still *depend* ['remain dependents'].—*Lear*, i. 4.

Our jealousy does yet *depend* ['hang in suspense'].—*Cym.*, iv. 3.

Depose him ['take his deposition,' 'examine him upon oath'] in the justice of his cause.—*R. II.*, i. 3.

The term of a *despised* ['worthless,' 'unvalued'] life.—*R. & Jul.*, i. 4.

What's to come of my *despised* ['worthless,' 'unvalued'] time.—*Oth.*, i. 1.

Sickness hath *determin'd* ['ended,' 'terminated'] me.—2 *H. IV.*, iv. 4.

To my *determin'd* * ['brought to a prospect of termination'] time thou gav'st new date.—1 *H. VI.*, iv. 6.

The *determin'd* * ['terminating period of'] respite.—*R. III.*, v. 1.

As it *determines* ['dissolves,' 'melts away,' 'comes to an end'], so dissolve my life!—*Ant. & C.*, iii. 11.

Trembles under his *devouring* † ['destroying'] paws.—3 *H. VI.*, i. 3.

That can my speech *diffuse* ['disorder,' 'render wild, irregular, uncouth, and rough'].—*Lear*, i. 4.

With some *diffused* ['wild,' 'irregular,' 'discordant'] song.—*Merry W.*, iv. 4.

Stern looks, *diffus'd* ['disorderly,' 'negligent,' 'wild,' 'irregular'] attire.—*H. V.*, v. 2.

Vouchsafe, *diffus'd* ['strange,' 'irregular,' 'uncouth,' including the sense of 'widely spread,' 'copiously dispers'd'] infection of a man.—*R. III.*, i. 2.

Blot in thy *digressing* ['transgressing,' 'erring,' 'deviating from the right course'] son.—*R. II.*, v. 3.

I may example my *digression* ['transgression,' 'deviating from the right way,' 'passing out of bounds'] by some.—*Love's L. L.*, i. 2.

You feel the *dint* ['deep impression,' 'strong effect'] of pity.—*Jul. C.*, iii. 2.

Your rule *direct* ['convey,' 'delegate'] to any.—*Per.*, i. 2.

Disable ['disparage,' 'depreciate,' 'undervalue'] all the benefits of your own country.—*As You L.*, iv. 1.

He *disabled* ['disparaged,' 'depreciated,' 'impugned'] my judgment.—*Ibid.*, v. 4.

Unhousel'd, *disappointed* ['unappointed,' 'unprepared,' 'spiritually unprovided.' *See* "Appointment" as used in the passage cited from "Measure for Measure" under the present heading], unanel'd.—*Hamlet*, i. 5.

---

* In both these passages where "determined" is used, the construction is peculiar. *See* PECULIAR CONSTRUCTION.

† This use of "devouring" for 'destroying,' and not for 'eating ravenously,' has been adopted by Milton in his "Lycidas":—

"Besides what the grim wolf, with privy *paw*
Daily *devours* apace."

Do *discandy* ['liquefy,' 'dissolve.' *See* "Candied" under the present heading as used in "The Tempest," ii. 1], melt their sweets.—*Ant. & C.*, iv. 10.

By the *discandying* ['melting,' 'liquefying'] of this pelleted storm.—*Ibid.*, iii. 11.

I will *discase* ['take off my outer garments.' *See* "Uncase" under the present heading] me, and myself present, as I was sometime Milan.—*Temp.*, v. 1.

Therefore *discase* ['take off thy outer garments'] thee instantly.—*W. T.*, iv. 3.

No *discourse of reason* ['ratiocination,' 'power of arguing rationally'], nor fear of bad success.—*Tr. & Cr.*, ii. 2.

A beast, that wants *discourse of reason* ['ratiocination,' 'reasoning faculty'], would have mourn'd longer.—*Hamlet*, i. 2.

All instance, all *discourse* ['ratiocination,' 'reasonable argument'] that I am ready to distrust mine eyes.—*Tw. N.*, iv. 3.

He that made us with such large *discourse* ['capacity for ratiocination,' 'faculty of reasoning,' 'power of argument'].—*Hamlet*, iv. 4.

At large *discoursed* ['treated of,' 'set forth from point to point'] in this paper here.—*R. II.*, v. 6.

Send *discoverers* ['investigators,' 'scouts'] forth to know.—*2 H. IV.*, iv. 1.

By diligent *discovery* ['investigation,' 'exploring,' 'scouting'].—*Lear*, v. 1.

To fob off our *disgrace* ['misfortune,' 'unhappiness': as the Italians use their word *disgrazia*. *See* also "Fault" under the present heading] with a tail.—*Coriol.*, i. 1.

Do what you will, *dishonour* ['indignity'] shall be humour.—*Jul. C.*, iv. 3.

I never heard any soldier *dislike* ['express aversion'] to it.—*M. for M.*, i. 2.

I did *dislike* ['express aversion to'] the cut of a certain courtier's beard.—*As You L.*, v. 4.

The stream of his *dispose* ['mood,' 'inclination,' 'that to which he is disposed'], without observance or respect of any.—*Tr. & Cr.*, ii. 3.

Please you to *dispose* ['place,' 'range'] yourselves.—*Timon*, i. 2.

She had *disposed* ['arranged,' 'adjusted matters'] with Cæsar.—*Ant. & C.*, iv. 12.

Boyet is *disposed* ['inclined to be too free in talk,' 'inclined to unseemly merriment'].—*Love's L. L.*, ii. 1.

He does well enough if he be *disposed* ['in the humour for freedom in mirth,' 'ready to ndulge in licence of fun or in broad talk'].—*Tw. N.*, ii. 3.

With my *disposer* ['indulger in frolicsome mirth,' 'incliner to free talk,' 'inciter to gaiety'], Cressida.—*Tr. & Cr.*, iii. 1.

That's a feeling *disputation* ['argument,' 'discussion'].—*1 H. IV.*, iii. 1.

In *disputation* ['debating terms,' 'parleying,' 'argumentative treaty'] I kiss his conquering hand.—*Ant. & C.*, iii. 11.

A few *disputations* ['arguments,' 'discussions'] with you.—*H. V.*, iii. 2.

Dispute ['discuss,' 'argue upon'] his own estate?—*W. T.*, iv. 3.

Let me *dispute* ['reason,' 'argue,' 'debate'] with thee of thy estate.—*R. & Jul.*, iii. 3.

Though my soul *disputes* ['debates,' 'argues,' 'logically discusses'] well with my sense.—*Tw. N.*, iv. 3.

I will *dissemble* ['disguise,' 'conceal.' *See* Note at page 529] myself in't.—*Tw. N.*, iv. 2.

Dissemble ['disguise,' 'hide,' 'conceal'] not your hatred.—*R. III.*, ii. 1.

By *dissembling* ['making unlike to others,' 'creating with a want of resemblance to the rest of mankind'] nature.—*Ibid.*, i. 1.

Proceeding on *distemper* ['intemperance,' 'intoxication'], shall not.—*H. V.*, ii. 2.

Thorough this *distemperature* ['mutual displeasure,' 'disagreement,' 'disturbance'] we see the seasons alter.—*Mid. N. D.*, ii. 2.

The day looks pale at his *distemperature* ['disturbance,' 'disorder'].—*1 H. IV.*, v. 1.

Marvellous *distemper'd* ['disordered,' 'disturbed'].—*Hamlet*, iii. 2.

Full of supper and *distempering* ['intoxicating'] draughts.—*Oth.*, i. 1.

Which *distinction* ['distinctly detailed relation'] should be rich in.—*Cym.*, v. 5.

Would I flame *distinctly* ['separately'], then meet, and join.—*Temp.*, i. 2.

His power went out in such *distractions* ['detachments,' 'separate bodies'].—*Ant. & C.*, iii. 7.

Go to the feast, revel and *domineer* ['roister,' 'have an orgy' 'be uproariously festive'].—*Tam. of S.*, iii. 2.

There's a *double* ['deceitful,' 'deluding'] tongue.—*M. Ado*, v. 1.

Swear by your *double* ['deceitful,' 'full of duplicity'] self.—*Mer. of V.*, v. 1.

I am not a *double* ['deceitful,' 'delusive'] man.—1 *H. IV.*, v. 4.

A voice potential as *double* ['forcible,' 'strong,' and 'armed with duplicate power to divorce or to imprison'] as the duke's.—*Oth.*, i. 1.

I *doubt* ['dread,' 'fear'] he will be dead or ere I come.—*John*, v. 6.

More than you *doubt* ['dread'] the change on 't.—*Coriol.*, iii. 1.

I *doubt* ['fear'], it is no other but the main.—*Hamlet*, ii. 2.

> *Doubt* ['have a misgiving, a dread or half-belief'] thou the stars are fire;
> *Doubt* that the sun doth move;
> *Doubt* truth to be a liar;
> But never *doubt* ['disbelieve'] I love.—*Ibid.*, ii. 2 (*Letter*).

Do not *doubt* ['dread,' 'fear,' 'have a misgiving of'] that.—*Oth.*, iii. 3.

Since *doubting* ['dreading,' 'having a misgiving that'] things go ill often hurts more than to be sure.—*Cym.*, i. 7.

Sweet *draught* ['receptacle for ordure']: sweet, quoth 'a !—*Tr. & Cr.*, v. 1.

Drown them in a *draught* ['receptacle for ordure'].—*Timon*, v. 1.

And *draw* ['withdraw'] thy action.—2 *H. IV.*, ii. 1.

Supposed dead and *drown'd* ['submerged in water ;' without including the sense of 'destroyed by water'].—*Per.*, v. 3.

> To such as may the passive *drugs* ['drudges'] of it
> Freely command.—*Timon*, iv. 3.

Duck ['bow'] with French nods and apish.—*R. III.*, i. 3.

The learned pate *ducks* ['bows'] to the golden fool.—*Timon*, iv. 3.

Silly *ducking* ['fawningly bowing'] observants.—*Lear*, ii. 2.

She was in her *dull* ['drowsy'] and sleeping hour.—*Mid. N. D.*, iii. 2.

Unless some *dull* ['drowsy,' 'slumberous,' 'lulling,' 'sleep-inducing'] and favourable hand will whisper music.—2 *H. IV.*, iv. 4.

'Tis a good *dulness* ['drowsiness'] and give it way.—*Temp.*, i. 2.

Never palates more the *dung* ['grossly material products of the earth'], the beggar's nurse and Cæsar's.—*Ant. & C.*, v. 2.

Our *dungy* ['material'] earth alike feeds beast as man.—*Ibid.*, i. 1.

The face to sweeten of the whole *dungy* ['material'] earth.—*W. T.*, ii. 1.

He gave you all the *duties* ['qualities duly belonging to'] of a man.—1 *H. IV.*, v. 2.

Vex him with *eager* ['sharp,' 'sour,' 'acrimonious': French, *aigre*,] words.—3 *H. VI.*, ii. 6.

A nipping and an *eager* ['sharp,' 'keen'] air.—*Hamlet*, i. 4.

Like *eager* ['sour,' 'acid,' 'sharp'] droppings into milk. —*Ibid.*, i. 5.

Let them go to *ear* ['plough,' 'till'] the land.—*R. II.*, iii. 2.

Our ills told us is as our *earing* ['ploughing,' 'tilling'].—*Ant. & C.*, i. 2.

I have had *earnest* ['money given in token that a bargain is ratified']; but I cannot in conscience take it.—*W. T.*, iv. 3.

If not, I have lost my *earnest* ['sum paid down as a pledge of intention to purchase'].—*Per.*, iv. 3.

She is the hopeful lady of my *earth* ['landed estates;' also 'corporeal or material self'].—*R. & Jul.*, i. 2.

Turn back, dull *earth* ['corporeal or material part of me,' 'my earthlier portion'], and find thy centre out.—*Ibid.*, ii. 1.

But to the *earth* ['inhabitants of earth'] some special good doth give.—*Ibid.*, ii. 3.

Vile *earth* [' corporeal portion of me '] to earth resign.—*R. & Jul.*, iii. 2.

O that that *earth* [' corporeal form,' ' material body '], which kept the world in awe.
—*Hamlet*, v. 1.

Poor soul, the centre of my sinful *earth* [' body,' ' corporeal or material portion '].—
Sonnet 146.

Was this *easy* [' easy to be borne,' ' a light offence '] ?—*2 H. IV.*, v. 2.

Never win a soul so *easy* [' light,' ' fickle,' ' facile '; also including the effect of
' easily '] as that Englishman's.—*H. V.*, ii. 2.

These faults are *easy* [' slight,' ' venial,' ' unimportant '; also including the effect of
' easily '], quickly answered.—*2 H. VI.*, iii. 1.

The *easy* [' unimportant,' ' inconsiderable,' ' insignificant,' ' of small consequence ']
groans of old women.—*Coriol.*, v. 2.

Hinder them from what this *ecstasy* [' excitement of mind '] may now provoke them
to.—*Temp.*, iii. 3.

Mark how he trembles in his *ecstasy* [' aberration of mind '] !—*Com. of E.*, iv. 4.

Blasted with *ecstasy* [' alienation of mind '].—*Hamlet*, iii. 1.

The *ecstasy* [' violent emotion,' ' mental disturbance'] hath so much overborne her.
—*M. Ado*, ii. 3.

Laid good 'scuse upon your *ecstasy* ['violent disturbance of mind,' ' fit of strong
emotion '].—*Oth.*, iv. 1.

Thou wast the cause, and* most accurs'd *effect* [' deed,' ' that which was effected '].
—*R. III.*, i. 2.

The *effect* [' purport,' ' tenor '] of what I wrote ?—*Hamlet*, v. 2.

Lest with this piteous action you convert my stern *effects* [' deeds,' ' those which
are to be effected ']—*Ibid.*, iii. 4.

How much more *elder* [' more experienced,' ' more advanced in judgment as well as
years '] art thou than thy looks [*See* ELDER, &c.].—*Mer. of V.*, iv. 1.

And I the *elder* [' more potent,' ' more mighty'] and more terrible.—*Jul. C.*, ii. 2.

Thou whoreson, impudent, *embossed* ['swollen,' ' protuberant'] rascal.—*1 H.IV.*, iii. 3.

An *embossed* [' swollen,' ' protuberant '] carbuncle.—*Lear*, ii. 4.

The poor cur is *emboss'd* ['foaming at the mouth,' 'panting for breath,' and 'wearied
out'].—*Tam. of S.*, *Induc.* 1.

We have almost *emboss'd* [' run down,' ' hunted down'] him.—*All's W.*, iii. 6.

The boar of Thessaly was never so *emboss'd* ['foaming at the mouth'].—
Ant. & C., iv. 11.

Our lock'd *embrasures* [' embraces,' ' embracements '].—*Tr. & Cr.*, iv. 4.

In the instant of our *encounter* [' amorous meeting'].—*Merry W.*, iii. 5.

If the *encounter* [' amorous meeting'] acknowledge itself.—*M. for M.*, iii. 1.

This amiable *encounter* [' amorous meeting'].—*M. Ado*, iii. 3.

With your strange *encounter* [' address,' ' mode of accosting '] much amaz'd me.—
Tam. of S., iv. 5.

Appoints him an *encounter* [' amorous meeting'].—*All's W.*, iii. 7.

The loose *encounters* ['amorous advances'] of lascivious men.—*Two G. of V.*, ii. 7.

The vile *encounters* [' amorous meetings'] they have had.—*M. Ado*, iv. 1.

Arm, wenches, arm! *encounters* [' encounterers,' ' amorous enterprisers or advancers']
mounted are against your peace.—*Love's L. L.*, v. 2.

Oh, these *encounterers*† ['amorous enterprisers'], so glib of tongue, that give a
coasting welcome ere it comes.—*Tr. & Cr.*, iv. 5.

---

* ' Thine was the ' is elliptically understood between " and " and " most " in this passage.

† The instances here collected of the mode in which Shakespeare often uses
" encounter " and " encounters," serve to show the sense in which he employs
" encounterers " in the present passage; while we think that " it " implies ' amorous
advance ' as implied in the mention of " encounterers." *See* RELATIVELY USED
PRONOUNS.

The cardinal is the *end* ['origin,' 'ultimate cause'] of this.—*H. VIII.*, ii. 1.

When you were more *endear'd* ['dearly pledged,' 'engaged by more dear motives'] to it than now.—*2 H. IV.*, ii. 3.

Enforce ['urge,' 'forcibly instance'] his pride.—*Coriol.*, ii. 3.

Enforce ['urge against'] him with his envy.—*Ibid.*, iii. 3.

Enforce ['urge'] the present execution of.—*Ibid.*, iii. 3.

To *enforce* ['urge'] no farther the griefs between ye.—*Ant. & C.*, ii. 2.

To be *engag'd* ['pledged as a hostage,' 'detained as prisoner of war'] in Wales — 1 *H. IV.*, iv. 3.

Westmoreland, that was *engag'd* ['detained as hostage'].—*Ibid.*, v. 2.

So much *engraffed* ['attached'; as a graft is bound to the parent stock of a plant] to Falstaff.—*2 H. IV.*, ii. 2.

For this they have *engrossed* ['accumulated'] and pil'd up.—*Ibid.*, iv. 4.

Shall *enter* ['give me entrance into his service,' 'cause him to entertain me in his service'] me with him.—*Ant. & C.*, iv. 12.

All that serv'd Brutus, I will *entertain* ['receive them into my service'] them.— *Jul. C.*, v. 5.

So please you *entertain* ['receive me in your service'] me.—*Cym.*, iv. 2.

Already in the *entertainment* ['in military pay'].—*Coriol.*, iv. 3.

If your lady strain his *entertainment* ['restoration to military pay and office'] with any strong.—*Oth.*, iii. 3.

The keenness of thy sharp *envy* ['hatred,' 'malice,' 'ill-will'].—*Mer. of V.*, iv. 1.

By addition of his *envy* ['malice']!—*Ant. & C.*, v. 2.

If this foul deed were by to *equal* ['be compared with'] it.—*3 H. VI.*, v. 5.

And *erring* ['straying,' 'roving'] spirit hies.—*Hamlet*, i. 1.

Betwixt an *erring* ['wandering,' 'erratic,' 'roving'] barbarian and a.—*Oth.*, i. 3.

It is the very *error* ['errant' or 'wandering' as well as 'mistaken path'] of the moon.—*Ibid.*, v. 2.

For thy *escape* ['elopement,' 'flight'; including the effect of 'prank,' 'irregular act.' *See* "Scape," subsequently quoted under the present heading] would teach me tyranny.— *Oth.*, i. 3.

Thousand *escapes* ['sallies,' 'words uttered wantonly and with levity'] of wit make thee the father.—*M. for M.*, iv. 1.

I do *estate* ['confer,' 'bestow'] unto Demetrius.—*Mid. N. D.*, i. 1.

Will I *estate* ['settle,' 'confer,' 'bestow'] upon you.—*As You L.*, v. 2.

Though my *estate* ['condition,' 'position in life'] be fallen.—*All's W.*, iii. 7.

Will show you his *estate* ['general condition,' 'state of means or resources, health, and spirits'] . . . my *estate* is very low.—*Mer. of V.*, iii. 2.

'Twas of some *estate* ['high rank,' 'distinguished condition'].—*Hamlet*, v. 1.

Such difference betwixt their two *estates* ['conditions,' 'ranks in life'].—*All's W.*, i. 3.

I speak not this in *estimation* ['reckoning upon conjecturally,' 'counting upon from sanguine surmise'] as what.—*1 H. IV.*, i. 3.

Had he himself *eternity* ['immortality'], and could.—*W. T.*, v. 2.

He wants nothing of a god but *eternity* ['immortality'].—*Coriol.*, v. 4.

Do not stain the *even* ['serene,' 'equable,' &c. *See* Note on the word "Even" at page 498] virtue of our enterprise.—*Jul. C.*, ii. 1.

Not a tomb so *evident* ['obviously sure,' 'manifestly certain'] as a chair to extol what.—*Coriol.*, iv. 7.

We must find an *evident* ['sure,' 'certain,' 'inevitable'] calamity.—*Ibid.*, v. 3.

That *excellent* ['excelling in wickedness,' 'surpassing,' 'egregious'] grand tyrant of the earth.—*R. III.*, iv. 4.

Much asham'd of my *exchange* ['disguise,' 'exchange of women's for men's clothes']. —*Mer. of V.*, ii. 6.

Dally with my *excrement* ['hair,' 'beard'], with my mustachio.—*Love's L. L.*, v. 1.

Pocket up my pedler's *excrement* ['beard'].—*W. T.*, iv. 3.

The *execution* ['employment,' 'performance,' 'exercise'] of his wit, hands, heart to wrong'd Othello's service !—*Oth.*, iii. 3.

You are from me *exempt* ['cut off,' 'taken away'].—*Com. of E.*, ii. 2.

This our life, *exempt* ['cut off,' 'apart,' 'secluded'] from public haunt.—*As You L.*, ii. 1.

And *exempt* ['cut off,' 'excluded'] from ancient gentry.—1 *H. VI.*, ii. 4.

Who would not wish to be from wealth *exempt* ['free,' 'released'].—*Timon*, iv. 2.

In debt for your last *exercise* ['homily,' 'religious discourse'].—*R. III.*, iii. 2.

That show of such an *exercise* ['devotional reading,' 'religious perusal'] may colour your lonelinesss.—*Hamlet*, iii. 1.

Like *exhibition* ['allowance of money,' 'stipend'] thou shalt have from me.—*Two G. of V.*, i. 3.

Confin'd to an *exhibition* ['stipendiary allowance'] !—*Lear*, i. 2.

Due reference of place and *exhibition* ['provision,' 'allowance'].—*Oth.*, i, 3.

Nor any petty *exhibition* ['stipend,' 'displayed offer'].—*Ibid.*, iv. 3.

No *exorciser* ['raiser of spirits:' not, as is more usual, 'layer of spirits'] harm thee.—*Cym.*, iv. 2 (*Song*).

Behold and hear our *exorcisms* ['conjurations for raising spirits'].—2 *H. VI.*, i. 4.

Is there no *exorcist* ['raiser of spirits'] beguiles the.—*All's W.*, v. 3.

Like an *exorcist* ['raiser of spirits'] has conjur'd up my mortified spirit.—*Jul. C.*, ii. 1.

In forwarding this dear *expedience* ['expedition,' 'enterprise'].—1 *H. IV.*, i. 1.

The cause of our *expedience* ['expedition,' 'haste,' 'despatch'] to the queen.—*Ant. & C.*, i. 2.

With much *expedient* ['expeditious'] march.—*John*, ii. 1.

Do this *expediently* ['expeditiously'], and turn him going.—*As You L.*, iii. 1.

Extended ['seized'] Asia from Euphrates.—*Ant & C.*, i. 2.

Make an *extent* ['seizure'] upon his house and lands.—*As You L.*, iii. 1.

Unjust *extent* ['seizure,' 'assault'] against thy peace.—*Tw. N.*, iv. 1.

Which by no means we may extenuate ['mitigate in severity,' 'diminish in force'].—*Mid. N. D.*, i. 1.

Thinking by this *face* ['show of courage'] to fasten.—*Jul C.*, v. 1.

To *face* ['garnish' as with a facing or trimming] the garment of rebellion with some fine colour.—1 *H. IV.*, v. 1.

Doth not flatter, *face* ['wear a deceitful appearance'] or feign.—1 *H. VI.*, v. 3.

To *face* ['impudently assert'] me out of my wits.—*Tw. N.*, iv. 2.

For fear I should be *faced* ['impudently taunted'] out of my way.—*H. V.*, iii. 7.

He's of a most *facinorous* ['rebellious,' 'refractory,' 'contumacious': from the Italian *facinoroso*] spirit that will not acknowledge.—*All's W.*, ii. 3.

Not sin, and yet a sinful *fact* ['deed'].—*Ibid.*, iii. 7.

Those of your *fact* ['deed,' 'sin,' 'crime,' 'guilt'] are so.—*W. T.*, iii. 2.

Becoming well thy *fact* ['deed,' 'crime'].—*Per.*, iv. 4.

With their *faint* ['feeble,' 'weak,' 'spiritless,' 'faint-hearted'] reply this answer join.—*Timon*, iii. 3.

Perceived a most *faint* ['languid,' 'spiritless'] neglect.—*Lear*, i. 4.

That *fair* ['beauty.' *See* PARTS OF SPEECH DIVERSELY USED], for which love groan'd.—*R. & Jul.*, i. 5 (*Chorus*).

Having no *fair* ['beauty'] to lose.—*V. & Adon.*, Stanza 181.

Inward worth, nor outward *fair* ['beauty'].—*Sonnet* 16.

Every *fair* ['beauty'] from *fair* sometime declines.—*Ibid.* 18.

To your *fair* ['beauty'] no painting set.—*Ibid.* 83.

To this great *fairy* ['enchantress'] I'll commend.—*Ant. & C.*, iv. 8.

Hath sense withal of its own *fall** ['downfall'].—*Timon*, v. 2.

Ours is the *fall* ['downfall,' 'defeat'], I fear.—*Ibid.*, v. 3.

Whose *fall* ['downfall,' 'ruin,' 'destruction'] the mark of his ambition is.—*Ibid.*, v. 4.

I know not what may *fall* ['befall,' 'happen,' 'occur'].—*Jul. C.*, iii. 1.

No disgrace shall *fall* ['befall'] you for refusing.—*Ant. & C.*, iii. 7.

Her mantle she did *fall* ['let fall,' 'drop'].—*Mid. N. D.*, v. 1.

Here she did *fall* ['let fall,' 'drop'] a tear.—*R. II.*, iii. 4.

Fall ['drop'] not a tear, I say.—*Ant. & C.*, iii. 9.

Well thank'd, whate'er *falls* ['befalls'] more.—*All's W.*, v. 1.

Each drop she *falls* ['lets fall,' 'drops'] would prove.—*Oth.*, iv. 1.

Forty *fancies* ['favourite songs, gay and fanciful'] prick'd in 't.—*Tam. of S.*, iii. 2.

They were his *fancies* ['favourite fanciful songs'].—*2 H. IV.*, iii. 2.

So full of shapes is *fancy* ['love,' 'enamoured imagination'].—*Tw. N.*, i. 1.

I am, and by my *fancy* ['love,' 'affection'].—*W. T.*, iv. 3.

In May's new-*fangled* ['decked out'] shows.—*Love's L. L.*, i. 1.

Be not, as is our *fangled* ['frivolously decked out,' 'fantastically fashioned'] world, a garment nobler.—*Cym.*, v. 4.

The *farced* ['stuffed,' 'compounded of highly seasoned epithets': French, *farci*. *See* "Forced" under the present heading] title running 'fore the king.—*H. V.*, iv. 1.

I prattle out of *fashion* ['conventional form'].—*Oth.*, ii. 1.

'Tis our *fast* ['firm,' 'steadfast'] intent to shake.—*Lear*, i. 1.

Strong and *fastened* ['confirmed,' 'inveterate,' 'steadfast in guilt'] villain!—*Ibid.*, ii. 1.

The native mightiness and *fate* ['power decreed to him by fate,' 'performance appointed him by destiny'] of him.—*H. V.*, ii. 4.

'Tis your *fault* ['ill-luck,' 'mishap,' 'misfortune'], 'tis your *fault*: 'tis a good dog.—*Merry W.*, i. 1.

'Tis my *fault* ['misfortune'], Master Page.—*Ibid.*, iii. 3.

The more my *fault* ['misfortune'], to 'scape.—*Per.*, iv. 3.

I know your *favour* ['aspect,' 'look,' 'countenance'] well.—*Tw. N.*, iii. 4.

As I do know your outward *favour* ['aspect,' 'appearance'].—*Jul. C.*, i. 2.

To alter *favour* ['aspect'] ever is to fear.—*Macb.*, i. 5.

To this *favour* ['appearance'] she must come.—*Hamlet*, v. 1.

And stain my *favours* ['features,' 'looks'] in a bloody mask.—*1 H. IV.*, iii. 2.

But let my *favours* ['silken scarf worn over armour'] hide thy mangled face.—*Ibid.*, v. 4.

And hold'st it *fear* ['danger,' 'that which is to be feared,' 'cause of fear,' *See* WORDS LIKE "BLAME," &c.], or sin, to speak a truth.—*2 H. IV.*, i. 1.

And indent with *fears* ['causers of fear,' 'those likely to inspire fear'], when they have lost.—*1 H. IV.*, i. 3.

All these bold *fears* ['causers of fear'] thou see'st.—*2 H. IV.*, iv. 4.

Come down with *fearful* ['secretly timid'] bravery.—*Jul. C.*, v. 1.

He's gentle, and not *fearful*† ['timid'].—*Temp.*, i. 2.

Pursue these *fearful* ['timid'] creatures.—*V. & Adon.*, Stanza 113.

Doth my simple *feature* ['general personal appearance'] content you?—*As You L.*, iii. 3.

---

* "Fall," in this passage, has been variously altered by various commentators; but we think that the mode in which Shakespeare uses it in the two other passages here cited from the same play serves to show that he intended to use it in the sense we assign, in the present instance.

† Some interpreters explain "gentle, and not fearful" here to mean, 'mild, not formidable'; but we believe it to mean 'of noble nature, and not timid.' *See* "Gentle" as used in the present heading; and "Fearful" as used in the above-cited passages.

Be-monster not thy *feature* ['personal appearance'].—*Lear*, iv. 2.

Report the *feature* ['personal appearance,' 'general aspect'] of Octavia.—*Ant. & C.*, ii. 5.

For *feature* ['personal appearance,' 'general shapeliness'], laming the shrine of Venus.—*Cym.*, v. 5.

I will your very faithful *feeder* ['menial,' 'hired servant,' and 'pasturer or feeder of sheep'] be.—*As You L.*, ii. 4.

One that looks on *feeders* ['menials,' 'hired servants'].—*Ant. & C.*, iii. 11.

Have secret *feet* ['footing'] in some of our best ports.—*Lear*, iii. 1.

That *fell* ['cruel,' 'barbarous,' 'tyrannous,' 'grim'] anatomy.—*John*, iii. 4.

Of that *fell* ['cruel,' 'tyrannous'] poison which assaileth him.—*Ibid.*, v. 7.

To be your *fellow* ['companion,' 'equal'] you may deny me.—*Temp.*, iii. 1.

Nor after my degree, but *fellow* ['companion,' 'equal'].—*Tw. N.*, iii. 4.

Cannot parallel a *fellow* ['equal'] to it.—*Macb.*, ii. 3.

My brother's servants were then my *fellows* ['equals'].—*Temp.*, ii. 1.

Put into contempt the suits of princely *fellows* ['equals'].—*Cym.*, iii. 4.

A *fetch* ['contrivance,' 'trick,' 'stratagem'] of warrant.—*Hamlet*, ii. 1.

Mere *fetches* ['pretences,' 'excuses,' 'feints']; the images.—*Lear*, ii. 4.

Temperate order in so *fierce* ['rash,' 'hasty,' 'sudden,' 'precipitate'] a cause.—*John*, iii. 4.

This *fierce* ['hasty,' 'rapid,' 'brief'] abridgment hath.—*Cym.*, v. 5.

The valu'd *file* ['list'] distinguishes . . . a station in the *file*.—*Macb.*, iii. 1.

Three performers are the *file* ['line of soldiers,' 'range of combatants'], when all the rest do nothing.—*Cym.*, v. 3.

Are his *files* ['lines of soldiers'] as full as thy report?—*Timon*, v. 3.

Yet *fil'd* ['kept pace with'] my abilities.—*H. VIII.*, iii. 2.

Have I *fil'd* ['defiled'] my mind.—*Macb.*, iii. 1.

His tongue *filed* ['polished'], his eye.—*Love's L. L.*, v. 1.

Thou art too *fine* ['evasive,' 'prevaricating,' 'wily'] in thy evidence.—*All's W.*, v. 3.

Say, the *firm* ['constant.' See "Constant," under the present heading, sometimes used for 'firm'] Roman to great Egypt sends.—*Ant. & C.*, i. 5.

Too *flattering* ['illusively'] sweet to be substantial.—*R. & Jul.*, ii. 2.

If I may trust the *flattering* ['illusive'] truth of sleep.—*Ibid.*, v. 1.

Observe how Antony becomes his *flaw* ['breach of fortune' and 'storm of fortune']. —*Ant. & C.*, iii. 10.

I do not fear the *flaw* ['stormy blast'].—*Per.*, iii. 1.

Sudden as *flaws* * ['sudden gusts of wind'] congealed.—*2 H. IV.*, iv. 4.

Oh, these *flaws* ['sudden gusts'] and starts.—*Macb.*, iii. 4.

Shall break into a hundred thousand flaws ['fragments,' 'shivers'].—*Lear*, ii. 4.

As seasons *fleet* ['pass away in succession'].—*2 H. VI.*, ii. 4.

Our sever'd navy too have knit again, and *fleet* ['float.' This is an antique form of the word], threatening most.—*Ant. & C.*, iii. 11.

To darkness *fleet* ['float rapidly,' 'pass quickly away'], souls that fly backwards!—*Cym.*, v. 3.

False, *fleeting* ['fluctuating,' 'vacillating,' 'inconstant,' 'changeable'], perjur'd Clarence.—*R. III.*, i. 4.

Now the *fleeting* ['inconstant,' 'variable,' 'changeable'] moon no planet is of mine.—*Ant. & C.*, v. 2.

You are well *fleshed* ['commenced and practised in the use of your weapon']; come on.—*Tw. N.*, iv. 1.

---

* It has been asserted that here "flaws" signifies 'small blades of ice'; but from the tenor of the passage, and from Shakespeare's use of the word "flaws" elsewhere, we incline to think he employed it with the meaning we assign.

Princes, *flesh'd* ['satiated'] with conquest.—*2 H. IV.*, i. 1.

And the *flesh'd* ['practised,' 'experienced' 'accustomed to butchery'] soldier, rough and hard of heart.—*H. V.*, iii. 3.

Albeit they were *flesh'd* ['practised'] villains.—*R. III.*, iv. 3.

Challenged Cupid at the *flight* ['sharp slender arrow used for flying long distances'].—*M. Ado*, i. 1.

The *flighty* ['swift,' 'rapidly conceived'] purpose.—*Macb.*, iv. 1.

Does your business *follow* ['concern,' 'pursue as its object'] us?—*All's W.*, ii. 1.

I have *follow'd* ['inimically and emulatively pursued'] thee to this.—*Ant. & C.*, v. 1.

What *folly* ['indiscretion,' 'lightness,' 'levity'] I commit.—*Tr. & Cr.*, iii. 2.

Tempt me no more to *folly* ['light conduct'].—*Ibid.*, v. 2.

She turn'd to *folly* ['light conduct,' 'wantonness'].—*Oth.*, v. 2.

Feeds his vulture *folly* ['wantonness,' 'depravity'].—*Lucrece, Stanza* 80.

Or tyrant *folly* ['wantonness,' 'depravity'] lurk.—*Ibid.*, 122.

This is a *fond* ['foolish,' 'witless,' 'crazed'] and desperate creature.—*All's W.*, v. 3.

Be not *fond* ['foolish,' 'weak'], to think that Cæsar.—*Jul. C.*, iii. 1.

An idle and *fond* ['foolish,' 'weak'] bondage.—*Lear*, i. 2 (*Letter*).

Stoop'd, as to *foot* ['clutch in talons'] us.—*Cym.*, v. 4.

Forage ['range forth in search of prey'], and run to.—*John*, v. 1.

Lion's whelp *forage* ['ravagingly prey,' 'destructively ramp or range'] in blood of French nobility.—*H. V.*, i. 2.

Canst thou not *forbear* ['bear with'] me half an hour?—*2 H. IV.*, iv. 4.

To *forbear* ['bear with,' 'tolerate,' 'endure'] the absence of.—*Per.*, ii. 4.

He shall live a man *forbid* ['bewitched,' 'under a spell or charm'].—*Macb.*, i. 3.

Law by the nose, when he would *force* ['enforce'] it?—*M. for M.*, iii. 1.

And *force* ['enforce,' 'urge'] them with a constancy.—*H. VIII.*, iii. 2.

Why *force* ['enforce,' 'urge'] you this?—*Coriol.*, iii. 2.

Much is the *force* ['power' 'influence,' 'efficacy,' 'favourable agency'] of heaven-bred poesy.—*Two G. of V.*, iii. 2.

Thy fair virtue's *force* ['essential excellence,' 'virtuous property or quality'] perforce doth move me.—*Mid. N. D.*, iii. 1.

Had *force* ['influence' and 'virtuous exellence'] and knowledge more than was ever man's.—*W. T.*, iv. 3.

Force ['stuff,' 'cram.' *See* "Farced" under the present heading] him with praises: pour in, pour in.—*Tr. & Cr.*, ii. 3.

By that *forced* ['perverted from truth,' 'wryed from fact,' 'false'] baseness which he has put upon't!—*W. T.*, ii. 3.

With these *forc'd* ['perverted from truth,' 'false'] thoughts.—*Ibid.*, iv. 3.

So *forcing* ['falsely imputing,' 'wrongfully charging'] faults upon Hermione, I little like.—*Ibid.*, iii. 1.

To make of him a *formal* ['sane,' 'rational'] man again.—*Com. of E.*, v. 1.

This is evident to any *formal* ['sane,' 'rational'] capacity.—*Tw. N.*, ii. 5.

Flow henceforth in *formal* ['well-regulated,' 'sedate'] majesty.—*2 H. IV.*, v. 2.

With untir'd spirits and *formal* ['orderly,' 'well-regulated,' 'discreet,' 'judicious'] constancy.—*Jul. C.*, ii. 1.

On our *former* ['foremost'] ensign two mighty.—*Ibid.*, v. 1.

The *fortitude* ['fortified strength'] of the place is best known.—*Oth.*, i. 3.

I have now *found* ['detected,' 'found out'] thee.—*All's W.*, ii. 3.

I have *found* ['detected'] thee.—*Ibid.*, ii. 4.

The first that *found* ['detected'] me.—*Ibid.*, v. 2.

Heaven save the *foundation* ['religious house or establishment where alms were given']!—*M. Ado*, v. 1.

I think *foundations* ['religious establishments where relief is given'] fly the wretched.—*Cym.*, iii. 6.

And these hard *fractions* ['broken sentences,' 'fragmentary phrases'].—*Timon*, ii. 2.

Chid I for that at frugal nature's *frame* ['order,' 'ordination,' 'disposal of events']?—*M. Ado*, iv. 1.

Ever out of *frame* ['order'].—*Love's L. L.*, iii. 1.

That yarely *frame* ['perform,' 'fulfil'] the office.—*Ant. & C.*, ii. 2.

Frank ['freely bounteous,' 'open-handed,' 'generous in gifts'] nature, rather curious than in haste.—*All's W.*, i. 2.

Doth the old boar feed in the old *frank* ['sty,' 'place to fatten hogs in']?—2 *H. IV.*, ii. 2.

He is *frank'd* ['styed'] up to fatting for his pains.—*R. III.*, i. 3.

And the *free* ['pure,' 'chaste,' 'free from vicious taint'] maids.—*Tw. N.*, ii. 4.

More *free* ['chaste,' 'pure'] than he is jealous.—*W. T.*, ii. 3.

He did solicit you in *free* ['open,' 'unreserved'] contempt.—*Coriol.*, ii. 3.

Being *free* ['liberal'] itself, it thinks all others so.—*Timon*, ii. 2.

We that have *free* ['unguilty,' 'free from crime'] souls.—*Hamlet*, iii. 2.

With his *free* ['freely rendered,' 'spontaneously offered'] duty recommends.—*Oth.*, i. 3.

When this advice is *free* ['liberal,' 'spontaneous'] I give.—*Ibid.*, ii. 3.

I think it *freely* ['sincerely,' 'genuinely']; and, betimes.—*Ibid.*, ii. 3.

We'll learn our *freeness* ['generosity,' 'liberality,' 'magnanimity'] of a son-in-law. —*Cym.*, v. 5.

He hath got his *friend* ['sweetheart,' 'mistress,' 'loveress'] with child.—*M. for M.*, i. 5.

Lady, will you walk about with your *friend* ['admirer,' 'lover']?—*M. Ado*, ii. 1.

Which *fronted* ['affronted,' 'opposed'] mine own peace.—*Ant. & C.*, ii. 2.

She's fram'd as *fruitful* ['bountiful,' 'generous'] as the free elements.—*Oth.*, ii. 3.

What a *full* ['plenarily good'] fortune does the.—*Ibid.*, i. 1.

Commands like a *full* ['fully accomplished'] soldier.—*Ibid.*, ii. 1.

Blithe, and *full* ['fully beautiful,' 'plenarily attractive'] of face.—*Per.*, i. (*Gower*).

My *full* ['whole,' 'entire,' 'complete'] life doth sway.—*As You L.*, iii. 2.

He was *furnish'd* ['equipped,' 'accoutred'] like a hunter.—*Ibid.*, iii. 2.

I am not *furnished* ['appareled,' 'attired'] like a beggar.—*Ibid.* (*Epilogue*).

Semblably *furnish'd* ['accoutred'] like the king.—1 *H. IV.*, v. 3.

Whereof perchance these are but *furnishings* ['outward appendages']—*Lear*, iii. 1.

Now will I stir this *gamester* ['mettlesome young spark,' 'forward young fellow'].—*As You L.*, i. 1.

A common *gamester* ['prostitute'] to the camp.—*All's W.*, v. 3.

Love not a *gaping* ['loud-voiced,' 'noisy,' 'discordant,' 'yelling'] pig . . . cannot abide a *gaping* pig —*Mer. of V.*, iv. 1.

With fatal mouths *gaping* ['open-jawed,' 'wide-stretched,' and 'roaring'] on girded Harfleur.—*H. V.*, iii. (*Chorus*).

Leave your *gaping* ['roaring,' 'shouting,' 'bawling'].—*H. VIII.*, v. 3.

Who never leave *gaping* ['stretching their jaws and roaring or bawling'] till they've swallowed the whole parish.—*Per.*, ii. 1.

Break the heart of *generosity* ['nobility,' 'those of high rank'], and make bold power look pale.—*Coriol.*, i. 1.

The *generous* ['high-born,' 'nobly ranked'] and gravest citizens.—*M. for M.*, iv. 6.

The *generous* ['distinguished,' 'high-born'] islanders.—*Oth.*, iii. 3.

He's *gentle* ['well born,' 'noble'], and not fearful.—*Temp.*, i. 2.

He said he was *gentle* ['well born,' 'of superior race and rank'], but unfortunate.—*Cym.*, iv. 2.

To show us so much *gentry* ['gentility,' 'gentleness,' 'courtesy'] and good will.—*Hamlet*, ii. 2.

All *gilt* ['ruddy.' *See* "Golden" thus used as applied to blood, under the present heading] with Frenchmen's blood.—*John*, ii. 2.

For the *gilt* ['gold,' 'gold coin'] of France.—*H. V.*, ii. (*Chorus*).

More laud than *gilt* ['gold'] o'er-dusted.—*Tr. & Cr.*, iii. 3.

Take a pride to *gird* ['gibe,' 'jeer'] at me.—*2 H. IV.*, i. 2.

He will not spare to *gird* ['gibe,' 'jeer'] the gods.—*Coriol.*, i. 1.

Men's reports *give* ['adjudge,' 'consider'] him much wrong'd.—*Ant. & C.*, i. 4.

Thus *given* ['granted,' 'permitted'] Hydra here to choose.—*Coriol.*, iii. 1.

Than may be *given* ['granted,' 'allowed'] you.—*Hamlet*, i. 3.

Is the desire that's *glorious* ['high-raised,' 'exalted'].—*Cym.*, i. 7.

They whom youth and ease have taught to *gloze* ['talk speciously,' 'insinuate,' 'flatter'].—*R. II.*, ii. 1.

Unjustly *gloze* ['speciously set forth,' 'misconstrue,' 'misinterpret,' 'misrepresent'] to be the realm of France.—*H. V.*, i. 2.

I will *gloze* ['talk speciously,' 'beguilingly,' 'insinuatingly,' 'conciliatingly'] with him.—*Per.*, i. 1.

Have *glozed* ['talked speciously,' 'argued plausibly'], but superficially.—*Tr. & Cr.*, ii. 2.

Lay these *glozes* ['special pleadings,' 'sophistical representations'] by.—*Love's L. L.*, iv. 3.

His silver skin lac'd with his *golden* ['ruddy'] blood.—*Macb.*, ii. 3.

With as few *good* ['brave,' 'spirited'] deeds.— *H. V.*, iii. 2.

Antonio is a *good man* ['man of credit,' 'man of reputed wealth and substance'] . . . in saying he is a *good man.*—*Mer. of V.*, i. 3.

The patricians, *good* ['of good credit,' 'of substantial possession'].—*Coriol.*, i. 1.

As our *good* ['advantage,' 'interest,' 'profit,' 'benefit'] wills.—*Ibid.*, ii. 1.

Some *good* ['valid,' 'substantial,' 'real,' 'unfeigned'] necessity touches his friend.—*Timon*, ii. 2.

If they have any *goodness* ['justice,' 'righteousness,' 'candour'], the trial just and noble.—*H. VIII.*, ii. 2.

That *goodness* ['justice,' 'righteousness,' 'virtue'] of gleaning.—*Ibid.*, iii. 2.

I have commended to his *goodness* ['favour,' 'propitiousness'] the model of our chaste loves, his young daughter.—*Ibid.*, iv. 2.

And the chance of *goodness* ['success,' 'favourable issue,' 'justice.' *See* VARIED MEANINGS, &c.] be like.—*Macb.*, iv. 3.

What the *good-year* ['pestilence,' 'plague': an ironical form of the Italian imprecation, *mal anno*], my lord!—*M. Ado*, i. 3.

The *good years* ['pestilence'] shall devour them.—*Lear*, v. 3.

My fame is shrewdly *gor'd* ['bloodily torn,' 'wounded' as by the horn of an animal; and 'smirch'd,' 'polluted,' 'soiled,' as derived from the Saxon word *gor*, 'dirt,' 'mud,' 'filth'].—*Tr. & Cr.*, iii. 3.

Gor'd ['torn,' 'wounded,' and 'smirched,' 'soiled,' 'polluted'] mine own thoughts.—*Sonnet* 110.

'Tis *government* ['self-control,' 'modest submission and discretion,' 'moral discipline'] that makes them seem divine.—*3 H. VI.*, i. 4.

Wife-like *government* ['discretion,' 'modest deportment,' 'self-control,' 'moral discipline'], obeying in commanding.—*H. VIII.*, ii. 4.

Put your *grace* ['virtue'] in your pocket, sir.—*Tw. N.*, v. 1.

Mickle is the powerful *grace* ['virtuous property'] that lies in herbs.—*R. & Jul.*, ii. 3.

One shamed that was never *gracious* ['graced by fortune,' 'favoured by destiny'].—*As You L.*, i. 2.

Not such a *gracious* ['well-graced by nature'] creature born.—*John*, iii. 4.

Antonio, *gratify* ['recompense,' 'reward'] this gentleman.—*Mer. of V.*, iv. 1.

As we do *gratify* ['recompense,' 'reward by handsome treatment'] this gentleman.—*Tam. of S.*, i. 2.

This *grave* ['fatal,' 'deadly,' 'destructive'] charm.—*Ant. & C.*, iv. 10.

When you were *gravelled* ['stuck fast,' 'brought to a standstill,' 'run aground'] for lack of matter.—*As You L.*, iv. 1.

Come, come, you talk *greasily* ['grossly,' 'coarsely'].—*Love's L. L.*, iv. 1.

And *greasy* ['foul,' 'gross,' 'coarse'] reliques of her o'er-eaten faith.—*Tr. & Cr.*, v. 2.

My heart as *great* ['haughty,' 'swelling,' 'unsubmissive.' See "Big" under the present heading].—*Tam. of S.*, v. 2.

That folly and *green* ['immature,' 'inexperienced'] minds look after.—*Oth.*, ii. 1.

Be jogging whiles your boots are *green* ['freshly greased'].—*Tam. of S.*, iii. 2.

Since griefs are *green* ['fresh,' 'vividly in remembrance'].—*2 H. IV.*, iv. 4.

The memory be *green* ['fresh,' 'vivid'].—*Hamlet*, i. 2.

Tybalt, yet but *green* ['recently'] in earth.—*R. & Jul.*, iv. 3.

The promise of his *greener* ['less mature'] days.—*H. V.*, ii. 4.

We have done but *greenly* ['unwisely,' 'with unripe judgment'].—*Hamlet*, iv. 5.

It *greets* ['it presents itself to,' 'it appears to'] me as an enterprise.—*Per.*, iv. 4.

Where lies your *grief* ['pain']?—*John*, iv. 1.

To build a *grief* ['grievance'] on.—*2 H. IV.*, iv. 1.

And find our *griefs* ['grievances'] heavier.—*Ibid.*, iv. 1.

No farther the *griefs* ['grievances'] between ye.—*Ant. & C.*, ii. 2.

I'll speak more *gross* ['openly,' 'plainly,' 'palpably'].—*M. for M.*, ii. 4.

Now to all sense 'tis *gross* ['obvious,' 'evident'] you love.—*All's W.*, i. 3.

The truth of it stands off as *gross* ['obviously'] as black from white.—*H. V.*, ii. 2.

If 'tis not *gross* ['obvious,' 'evident'] in sense.—*Oth.*, i. 2.

Who is so *gross* ['obtuse,' 'dull,' 'stupid'], that cannot see.—*R. III.*, iii. 6.

This palpable *gross* ['clumsy,' 'lumbering'] play hath well.—*Mid. N. D.*, v. 1.

Is *growing* ['accruing,' 'coming as a right'] to me by Antipholus.—*Com. of E.*, iv. 1.

Knowing how the debt *grows* ['accrues,' 'is owing'] I will pay it.—*Ibid.*, iv. 4.

No profit *grows* ['accrues'] where is no pleasure ta'en.—*Tam. of S.*, i. 1.

To *guard* ['ornament,' 'trim'] a title that was rich before.—*John*, iv. 2.

Sometime *guarded* ['trimmed'] with fragments, and the *guards* ['ornamental lace or borderings trimming the edge'] are but slightly basted on neither.—*M. Ado*, i. 1.

Give him a livery more *guarded* ['trimmed,' 'ornamented'] than his fellows.—*Mer. of V.*, ii. 2.

To invest and cover in priestly *guards* ['trimmings'].—*M. for M.*, iii. 1.

As that ungentle *gull* ['callow bird,' 'unfledged nestling'], the cuckoo's bird.—*1 H. IV.*, v. 1.

Timon will be left a naked *gull* ['unfledged bird' and 'dupe'].—*Timon*, ii. 1.

Oh, *gull* ['dupe']! oh, dolt!—*Oth.*, v. 2.

I should think this a *gull* ['trick,' 'imposture'] but.—*M. Ado*, ii. 1.

I will *gyve* ['fetter,' 'shackle'] thee in thine own courtship.—*Oth.*, ii. 1.

Convert his *gyves* ['fetters,' 'restraints'] to graces.—*Hamlet*, iv. 7.

I cannot do it better than in *gyves* ['fetters'].—*Cym.*, v. 4.

Against the *hair* ['nature,' 'quality'] of your professions.—*Merry W.*, ii. 3.

The quality and *hair* ['nature,' 'character'] of our attempt.—*1 H. IV.*, iv. 1.

Or the blank verse shall *halt* ['be imperfect'] for't.—*Hamlet*, ii. 2.

So bang'd the Turks, that their designment *halts* ['suffers check,' 'is rendered imperfect'].—*Oth.*, ii. 1.

And by the *happy* ['opportune,' 'fortunately found'] hollow of a tree escap'd.—*Lear*, ii. 3.

Tell him wherein you 're *happy* [' accomplished,' ' gifted '].—*Cym.*, iii. 4.

He doth fill fields with *harness* [' armour'] in the realm.—1 *H. IV.*, iii. 2.

At least we 'll die with *harness* [' armour'] on our backs.—*Macb.*, v. 5.

This *harness'd* [' armed,' ' clad in armour'] mask.—*John*, v. 2.

Restrain'd, and out of *haunt* [' company,' ' general concourse '].—*Hamlet*, iv. 1.

In a riotous *head* [' force,' ' throng'] o'erbears.—*Ibid.*, iv. 5,

By raising of a *head* [' collective force,' ' insurrectionary body of men'].—1 *H. IV.*, i. 3.

Let our best *heads* [' chiefs,' ' principal officers '] know.—*Ant. & C.*, iv. 1.

Hearken [' inquire,' ' endeavour to obtain the knowledge of'] after their offence (*See* Bacon's " Essay on Plantations ").—*M. Ado*, v. 1.

Well, *hearken* [' wait for,' ' bide the coming of'] the end.—2 *H. IV.*, ii. 4.

Daughter, whom you *hearken* [' hanker,' ' desire eagerly'] for.—*Tam. of S.*, i. 2.

Said I *hearken'd* [' longed,' ' desired,' ' hankered'] for your death.—1 *H. IV.*, v. 4.

Old Gremio is *hearkening* [' eaves-dropping,' and ' hankering after,' ' anxiously seeking to obtain '] still.—*Tam. of S.*, iv. 4.

Boldness comes to me now, and brings me *heart* [' courage '].—*Tr. & Cr.*, iii. 2.

Restores his *heart* [' spirit,' ' courage,' ' valour '].—*Ant. & C.*, iii. 11.

Beguil'd me to the very *heart* [' core,' ' depth '] of loss.—*Ibid.*, iv. 10.

The *heart* [' central point '] and place of general wonder.—*Per.*, iv. (*Gower*).

The *heat* [' course,' ' race,' ' chase,' ' pursuit.' *See* IDIOMS for " Heat" thus used] is past; follow no farther.—2 *H. IV.*, iv. 3.

In *heavy* [' griev'd '] *satisfaction* [' conviction '].—*All's W.*, v. 3.

On the *heavy* [' dark '] middle of the night.—*M. for M.*, iv. 1.

It is a *heavy* [' grievous' and ' dark '] night.—*Oth.*, v. 1.

To *help* [' cure,' ' heal'] him of his blindness,
And being *help'd* [' cured '] inhabits there.—*Two G. of V.*, iv. 2 (*Song*).

Not *helping* [' healing,' ' curing'], death's my fee ;
But if I *help* [' cure '], what do you promise me ?—*All's W.*, ii. 1.

Ye shall have a hempen caudle then, and the *help* [' cure,' ' healing'] of hatchet.—2 *H. VI.*, iv. 7.

Though what they do impart
Help [' heal'] nothing else, yet do they ease the heart.—*R. III.*, iv. 4.

I, sick withal, the *help* [' cure,' ' healing '] of bath desir'd.—*Sonnet* 153.

We rest your *hermits* [' beadsmen,' ' persons dedicated to constant prayer on your behalf'].—*Macb.*, i. 6.

Flouting ; we cannot *hold* [' hold back,' ' refrain '].—*As You L.*, v. 1.

Doth the news *hold* [' hold good,' ' remain uncontradicted '] of good.—*R. III.*, ii, 3.

Dost thou *hold* [' keep to,' ' abide by '] there still ?—*Ant. & C.*, ii. 5.

Holy [' righteous,' ' virtuous,' ' of good character and blameless life '] Gonzalo, honourable man.—*Temp.*, v. 1.

Holy [' virtuous,' ' good '], fair, and wise is she.—*Two G. of V.*, iv. 2 (*Song*).

You have a *holy* [' good,' ' virtuous'] father, a graceful gentleman.—*W. T.*, v. 1.

I will pay thy graces *home* [' fully'], both in word and deed.—*Temp.*, v. 1.

To know her estimation *home* [' fully,' ' thoroughly'].—*All's W.*, v. 3.

That, trusted *home* [' fully,' ' to the utmost extent.' *See* IDIOMS for " Home" thus used] might yet enkindle you unto the crown.—*Macb.*, i. 3.

But you say she 's *honest* [' pure,' ' chaste '].—*All's W.*, iii. 6.

An *honest* [' creditable,' ' honourable'] man and a good housekeeper.—*Tw. N.*, iv. 2.

Honest [' auspicious,' ' lucky': with reference to the *dies honestissimus* of Cicero, as employed in the old English almanacks, which put down lucky and unlucky days, &c.] ! good fellow, what's that ? If it be a day fits you, search.—*Per.*, ii. 1.

All her deserving is a reserved *honesty* [' purity,' ' chastity '].—*All's W.*, iii. 5.

'Tis now your *honour* [' honourable duty or task'], daughter, to explain.—*Per.*, ii. 2.

The rabblement *hooted* [' hurrahed,' ' howled approval'].—*Jul. C.*, i. 2.

The people fall a-*hooting* [' shouting approval'].—*Love's L. L.*, iv. 2 (*Verses*).

In *hooting* [' shouting approval'] at Coriolanus' exile.—*Coriol.*, iv. 6.

I cannot *hope* [' expect'] Cæsar and Antony shall.—*Ant. & C.*, ii. 1.

Centaur, where we *host* [' take up our quarters.' *See* PARTS OF SPEECH DIVERSELY USED].—*Com. of E.*, i. 2.

Take the shadow of this tree for your good *host* [' shelter,' ' protection'].—*Lear*, v. 2.

A most *humorous* [' full of strange whimsical fancies and cynical notions'] sadness.—*As You L.*, iv. 1.

No marvel he's so *humorous* [' wayward,' ' eccentric,' 'whimsical'].—1 *H. IV.*, iii. 1.

As *humorous* [' wayward,' ' petulant'] as winter.—2 *H. IV.*, iv. 4.

A *humorous* [' petulant,' ' testy'] patrician.—*Coriol.*, ii. 1.

Consorted with the *humorous* [' humid,' ' teeming with damp vapours,' and ' full of strange humours and whimsical fancies'] night.—*R. & Jul.*, ii. 1.

Naught but *humour* [' caprice,' ' waywardness'] sways him.—*Timon*, iii. 6.

Dishonour shall be *humour* [' hasty temperament,' ' petulance'].—*Jul. C.*, iv. 3.

How to *humour* [' bend the inclination of,' ' bring round the liking of,' ' induce,' ' manage'] your cousin, that she shall fall in love.—*M. Ado*, ii. 1.

I would *humour* [' propitiate'] his men with the.—2 *H. IV.*, v. 1.

He should not *humour* [' influence disposition,' ' sway inclination'] me.—*Jul. C.*, i. 2.

So neighbour'd to his youth and *humour* [' inclination,' ' disposition'].—*Hamlet*, ii. 2.

Were he in favour, as in *humour* [' disposition,' ' character'], alter'd.—*Oth.*, iii. 4.

We'll go dress our *hunt* [' game,' ' that which has been hunted'].—*Cym.*, iii. 6.

Your serving-man and your *husband* [' husbandman'].—2 *H. IV.*, v. 3.

While I play the good *husband* [' economist'] at home.—*Tam. of S.*, v. 1.

Borrowing dulls the edge of *husbandry* [' economy'].—*Hamlet*, i. 3.

'Tis not our *husbandry* [' diligence,' ' assiduity,' ' economical prudence'].—*Per.*, iii. 2.

Brier, or *idle* [' profitless,' ' good for nothing'] moss.—*Com. of E.*, ii. 2.

You said that *idle* [' profitless,' ' worthless'] weeds.—*R. III.*, iii. 1.

Vast and deserts *idle* [' unprofitable,' ' unfertile,' ' unproductive,' ' unfruitful,' ' barren,' ' sterile'].—*Oth.*, i. 3.

Heaven cease this *idle* [' senseless'] humour in . . . but very *idle* [' senseless,' ' meaningless'] words.—*Tam. of S.*, *Induc.* 2.

An *idle* [' futile,' ' senseless,' ' given to meaningless babble,' ' crack-brained'] lord, I swear.—*All's W.*, ii. 5.

In his *idle* [' wild,' ' rash,' ' impetuous,' and ' inconsiderate,' ' light-minded'] fire.— *Ibid.*, iii. 7.

I am no *idle* [' meaningless,' ' inconsiderate,' ' insensate'] votarist.—*Timon*, iv. 3.

I must be *idle* [' meaningless in manner,' ' crazy, insensate, and purposeless in behaviour'].—*Hamlet*, iii. 2.

I begin to find an *idle* [' senseless'] and fond.—*Lear*, i. 2 (*Letter*).

If *idle* [' futile,' ' vain,' ' superfluous'] talk will once be necessary.—*Ant. & C.*, v. 2.

In *ignorant* [' uncommunicative,' ' uninforming'] concealment.—*W. T.*, i. 2.

This *ignorant* [' unknowing,' ' uninformed,' ' unconscious'] present.—*Macb.*, i. 5.

Myself, the *ignorant* [' unconscious,' ' unknowing'] motive.—*Ant. & C.*, ii. 2.

I am *ignorant* [' resolved to appear unconscious or unknowing'] in what I am commanded.—*Cym.*, iii. 2.

Where *ill* [' bad,' ' evil,' ' wicked'] men were.—*Ibid.*, v. 5.

My shipwreck's now no *ill* [' evil'], since I.—*Per.*, ii. 1.

Without the *illness* [' evilness,' ' badness,' wickedness'] should attend it.—*Macb.*, i. 5.

With any branch or *image* [' representative,' ' relative,' ' one who bears any resemblance or affinity'] of thy state.—*All's W.*, ii. 1.

From any *image* [' shadow'] of offence done to any man.—*Tw. N.*, iii. 4.

The *image* ['created earthly semblance'] of his Maker.—*H. VIII.*, iii. 2.

Looking on his *images* ['offspring,' 'children who resemble him'].—*R. III.*, ii. 2.

On objects, arts, and *imitations* ['simulations of fairness and truth'].—*Jul. C.*, iv. 1.

Did I *impale* ['encircle'] him with the regal crown.—3 *H. VI.*, iii 3.

Round *impaled* ['encircled'] with a glorious crown.—*Ibid.*, iii. 2.

Do I *impart* ['confer,' 'bestow,' 'dispense'] towards you.—*Hamlet*, i. 2.

In this I'll be *impartial* ['not taking part,' 'remaining neutral'] : be you judge of your own cause.—*M. for M.*, v. 1.

Which would be great *impeachment* ['imputation,' 'ground of reproach,' and 'hindrance,' 'drawback,' 'detriment': French, *empêchement*] to his age.—*Two G. of V.*, i. 3.

March on to Calais without *impeachment* ['hindrance,' 'obstruction,' 'impediment'].—*H. V.*, iii. 6.

Devis'd *impeachments* ['accusations'] to imprison.—*R. III.*, ii. 2.

What occasion of *import* ['importance,' 'moment,' 'consequence'] hath.—*Tam. of S.*, iii. 2.

For some purpose of *import* ['importance'].—*Oth.*, iii. 3.

At Sir Toby's great *importance* ['importunacy,' 'entreaty'].—*Tw. N.*, v. 1.

Could not say if the *importance* ['import,' 'occasioning cause'] were joy or sorrow.—*W. T.*, v. 2.

Upon *importance* ['import,' 'matter,' 'subject,' 'cause'] of so slight.—*Cym.*, i. 5.

His *important* ['importunate'] blood will.—*All's W.*, iii. 7.

My mourning and *important* ['importunate'] tears hath pitied.—*Lear*, iv. 4.

I will search *impossible* ['the most unlikely,' 'the most absurdly improbable'] places.—*Merry W.*, iii. 5.

In devising *impossible* ['ludicrously improbable,' 'difficult of belief'] slanders —*M. Ado*, ii. 1.

Jest upon jest, with such *impossible* ['almost incredible'] conveyance.—*Ibid.*, ii. 1.

Ever believe such *impossible* ['wildly incredible,' 'ridiculously improbable'] passages of grossness.—*Tw. N.*, iii. 2.

Our *imputation* ['imputed excellence,' 'attributed merit.' *See* "Attribute" and "Attributive" under the present heading] shall be oddly pois'd. —*Tr. & Cr.*, i. 3.

In the *imputation* ['attributed merit,' ·imputed excellence'] laid on him.—*Hamlet*, v. 2.

And would *incense* ['instigate,' 'incite'] me to murder.—*W. T.*, v. 1.

Your brother *incensed* ['incited'] me to slander.—*M. Ado*, v. 1.

Make him by *inch-meal* ['an inch at a time'] a disease !—*Temp.*, ii. 2.

Though *inclination* ['desire'] be as sharp as will.—*Hamlet*, iii. 3.

The *inclining* ['compliant,' 'kindly disposed'] Desdemona.—*Oth.*, ii. 3.

We will *include* ['close in,' 'put to conclusion'] all jars.—*Two. G. of V.*, v. 4.

Everything *includes* ['closes,' 'shuts,' 'narrows,' 'compresses,' 'reduces'] itself in power.—*Tr. & Cr.*, i. 3.

That the *inclusive* ['closing in,' 'encircling'] verge.—*R. III.*, iv. 1.

Which they will climb *incontinent* ['incontinently,' 'immediately'].—*As You L.*, v. 2.

He will return *incontinent* ['immediately'].—*Oth.*, iv. 3.

With an *indifferent* ['impartial'] eye.—*R. II.*, ii. 3.

No judge *indifferent* ['impartial'].—*H. VIII.*, ii. 4.

As the *indifferent* ['averagely well treated,' 'impartially used'] children of the earth.—*Hamlet*, ii. 2.

Though *indirect* ['wrongful,' 'unrighteous'], yet *indirection* ['unrighteousness'] thereby grows *direct* ['righteous'].—*John*, iii. 1.

Haste so *indirectly* ['wrongfully,' 'unrighteously'] shed.—*Ibid.*, ii. 1.

Man, and best *indu'd* ['endowed,' 'gifted'].—*H. V.*, ii. 2.

And *indu'd* ['endowed with qualities that fitted her,' 'gifted with powers that qualified her'] unto that element.—*Hamlet*, iv. 7.

And it *indues* ['endows,' 'gifts'] our other.—*Oth.*, iii. 4.

A nature but *infected* ['diseased,' 'morbid,' 'poisoned by reverse and disappoint-ment']; a poor.—*Timon*, iv. 3. .

These poor *informal* ['deranged,' 'of disordered intellect.' *See* "Formal" under the present heading] women are no more but.—*M. for M.*, v. 1.

And thought I stood *ingag'd* ['pledged'].—*All's W.*, v. 3.

Learning and *ingenious* ['intellectual,' 'scientific'] studies.—*Tam. of S.*, i. 1.

And have *ingenious* ['intelligent,' 'acutely perceptive,' 'keenly appreciative'] feeling of my huge sorrows!—*Lear*, iv. 6.

Ingeniously ['ingenuously,' 'sincerely'] I speak.—*Timon*, ii. 2.

If trembling I *inhabit* ['remain within doors,' 'stay in any habitation or inhabited place'] then, protest me.—*Macb.*, iii. 4.

All which it *inherit* ['possess'] shall dissolve.—*Temp.*, iv. 1.

Or else nothing, will *inherit* ['obtain possession of'] her.—*Two G. of V.*, iii. 2.

That can *inherit* ['possess'] us so much as of a thought.—*R. II.*, i. 1.

But to the girdle do the gods *inherit* ['possess'].—*Lear*, iv. 6.

Yet am I *inland* ['urbanely,' 'polishedly,' 'refinedly'] bred.—*As You L.*, ii. 7.

In his youth an *inland* ['dwelling in civilised and refined places'] man.—*Ibid.*, iii. 2.

Thou most beauteous *inn* ['dwelling-place,' 'habitation'], Why should hard-favour'd grief be lodg'd in thee.—*R. II.*, v. 1.

My desires had *instance* ['plea'] and argument to.—*Merry W.*, ii. 2.

Gives me this *instance* ['intimation'].—*M. for M.*, iv. 3.

I have receiv'd a certain *instance* ['intimation,' 'information,' 'assurance'] that Glendower is dead.—*2 H. IV.*, iii. 1.

An old, an old *instance* ['maxim,' 'axiom'], Beatrice.—*M. Ado*, v. 2.

What *instance* ['axiom'] for it?—*Tr. & Cr.*, v. 11.

Any tragic *instance* ['indication'] of our harm.—*Com. of E.*, i. 1.

A better *instance* ['token,' 'evidence'], come.—*As You L.*, iii. 2.

Wherefore, what's the *instance* ['proof,' 'evidence,' 'that which is to be brought forward or instanced']?—*All's W.*, iv. 1.

Examples of every minute's *instance* ['occurring proof,' 'evidence,' 'manifestation'].—*2 H. IV.*, iv. 1.

What *instance* ['ground of evidence,' 'testifying circumstance'] gives Lord Warwick for his vow?—*2 H. VI.*, iii. 2.

His fears are shallow, without *instance* ['cause,' 'ground,' 'basis'].—*R. III.*, iii. 2.

Instance ['evidence'], oh, *instance!* strong as.—*Tr. & Cr.*, v. 2.

It sends some precious *instance* ['token,' 'manifestation'] of itself after the thing it loves.—*Hamlet*, iv. 5.

So far exceed all *instance* ['example'].—*Tw. N.*, iv. 3.

Gave thee no *instance* ['motive,' 'reason'] why.—*H. V.*, ii. 2.

And *instances* ['evidences'] as infinite of love.—*Two G. of V.*, ii. 7.

Offer them *instances* ['proofs,' 'evidences'].—*M. Ado*, ii. 2.

But not with such familiar *instances* ['tokens,' 'manifestations,' 'earnest enforce-ments'], nor with.—*Jul. C.*, iv. 2.

Wise saws and modern *instances* ['axioms,' 'adages'].—*As You L.*, ii. 7.

Had lack'd a master, but for these *instances* ['causes,' 'reasons'].—*Tr. & Cr.*, i. 3.

The *instances* ['motives,' 'grounds of inducement'] that second marriage move.—*Hamlet*, iii. 2.

A most *intelligencing* ['carrying intelligence,' 'conveying information'] bawd!—*W. T.*, ii. 3.

And dare not be *intelligent* ['explicit,' 'communicative,' 'conveyant of intelligence'] to me?—*Ibid.*, i. 2.

Spies and speculations *intelligent* ['knowing,' 'cognisant,' and 'conveying intel-ligence'] of our state.—*Lear*, iii. 1.

An *intelligent* ['knowing' and 'communicating'] party to the advantages of France.—*Lear*, iii. 5.

Our posts shall be swift and *intelligent* [' conveyant of intelligence,' ' communicative of intelligence'] betwixt us.—*Ibid.*, iii. 7.

How *intend* [' mean,' ' interpret,' understand'] you, practis'd ?—*Ant. & C.*, ii. 2.

Intend [' pretend,' ' affect'] a kind of zeal.—*M. Ado*, ii. 2.

I *intend* [' pretend'] that all is done in reverend care.—*Tam. of S.*, iv. 1.

That is *intended* [' understood,' ' implied'] in the general's name.—*2 H. IV.*, iv. 1.

Intending [' pretending'] deep suspicion.—*R. III.*, iii. 5.

And so *intending* [' pretending'] other serious matters.—*Timon*, ii. 2

But what I protest *intendment* [' intention'] of doing.—*Oth.*, iv. 2.

For *intermission* [' pause,' ' interposition of time,' ' hesitation'] no more pertains to me, my lord, than you.—*Mer. of V.*, iii. 2.

Cut short all *intermission* [' pause,' ' interposition of time,' ' interval of suspense'].—*Macb.*, iv. 3.

Which are too *intrinse* [' intricate'] t' unloose.—*Lear*, ii. 2.

This knot *intrinsicate* [' intricate'] of life at once untie.—*Ant. & C.*, v. 2.

Take the cruel *issue* [' deed,' ' act,' ' procedures'] of these bloody men.—*Jul. C.*, iii. 1.

Therefore your *issues* [' acts,' ' deeds,' ' procedure'], being foolish.—*Cym.*, ii. 2.

A princess, no worse *issu'd* [' descended by birth'].—*Temp.*, i. 2.

But *issu'd* [' descended by birth'] from the progeny of kings.—*1 H. VI.*, v. 4.

Take hence this *Jack* [' fellow': used contemptuously. *See* PARTICULAR NAMES], and whip him.—*Ant. & C.*, iii. 11.

Braggarts, *Jacks* [' fellows,' ' jackanapes'], milksops !—*M. Ado*, v. 1.

And be not *jealous* [' suspicious,' ' doubtful,' ' mistrustful'] on me.—*Jul. C.*, i. 2.

But our *jealousy* [' suspicion,' ' mistrust'] does yet depend.—*Cym.*, iv. 3.

That giants may *jet* [' strut,' ' stalk'] through.—*Ibid.*, iii. 3.

How he *jets* [' struts,' ' walks pompously'] under his advanced plumes !—*Tw. N.*, ii. 5.

I see the *jewel* [' ornament'] best enamelled.—*Com. of E.*, ii. 1.

Wear this *jewel* [' ornament'] for me,—'tis my picture.—*Tw. N.*, iii. 4.

He's for a *jig* [' ballad'], or a tale of bawdry.—*Hamlet*, ii. 2.

Do with these *jigging* [' rhyming,' ' ballad-making'] fools ?—*Jul. C.*, iv. 3.

Make friends of them, *jointing* ['joining in confederacy,' ' combining conjointly'] their force 'gainst Cæsar.—*Ant. & C.*, i. 2.

They may *joll* [' strike,' ' clash,' ' knock'] horns together.—*All's W.*, i. 3.

Hath made his *journal* [' daily'] greeting.—*M. for M.*, iv. 3.

Stick to your *journal* [' daily'] course.—*Cym.*, iv. 1.

But his *Jovial* [' Jove-like'] face.—*Ibid.*, iv. 2.

Our *Jovial* [' Jove-named,' ' Jupiter-styled'] star reign'd at his birth.—*Ibid.*, v. 4.

How the knave *jowls* [' hurls the cheek-bone of'] it to the ground.—*Hamlet*, v. 1.

Joy'd [' glad,' ' joyful,' ' happy'] are we, that you are.—*Cym.*, v. 5.

Shall have *judicious* [' judicial'] hearing.—*Coriol.*, v. 5.

To *jump* [' risk,' ' hazard,' ' jeopardise'] a body with a dangerous physic.—*Ibid.*, iii. 1.

We'd *jump* [' risk'] the life to come.—*Macb.*, i. 7.

Or *jump* [' risk,' ' hazard'] the after-enquiry.—*Cym.*, v. 4.

Our fortune lies upon this *jump* [' chance,' ' venture,' ' risk'].—*Ant. & C.*, iii. 8.

Do cohere and *jump* [' coincide,' ' concur'], that I am.—*Tw. N.*, v. 1.

But though they *jump* [' coincide,' ' agree,' ' consist'] not.—*Oth.*, i. 3.

So *jump* [' just immediately,' ' exactly,' ' precisely'] upon this bloody question.—*Hamlet*, v. 2.

And bring him *jump* [' precisely,' ' exactly'] when he.—*Oth.*, ii. 3.

Seldom or never *jumpeth* [' accords,' ' consists,' ' corresponds'] with the heart.—*R. III.*, iii. 1.

And in some sort it *jumps* ['agrees,' 'suits'] with my humour as well as waiting in the court. —1 *H. IV.*, i. 2.

And here *justified* ['testified,' 'borne witness to,' 'avouched'] by us, a pair of kings. —*W. T.*, v. 3.

While greasy Joan doth *keel* ['cool by clearing off the scum'] the pot.— *Love's L. L.*, v. 2 (*Song*).

This place is famous for the creatures of prey that *keep* ['dwell.' *See* IDIOMS for various use of "keep"] upon 't — *W. T.*, iii. 3.

Doth Calchas *keep* ['dwell,' 'reside']?—*Tr. & Cr.*, iv. 5.

And where they *keep* ['dwell,' 'reside'], what company.—*Hamlet*, ii. 1.

Shall I *keep* ['guard,' 'take care of'] your hogs, and eat husks.—*As You L.*, i. 1.

The house doth *keep* ['guard,' 'take care of'] itself.—*Ibid.*, iv. 3.

Cannot *keep* ['retain,' 'keep in'] the battery.—*Ant. & C.*, iv. 12.

Keep ['observe,' 'preserve,' 'maintain,' 'keep up'] leets and law-days.—*Oth.*, iii. 3.

Call you that *keeping* ['taking care of,' 'training,' 'educating'] for a gentleman of my birth.—*As You L.*, i. 1.

That *keeps* ['stays,' 'remains,' 'dwells,' 'resides'] here in court.—*Love's L. L.*, iv. 3.

While he himself *keeps* ['remains,' 'stays'] in the cold field?—3 *H. VI.*, iv. 3.

The Earl of Pembroke *keeps* ['remains with'] his regiment.—*R. III.*, v. 3.

That thy spirit which *keeps* ['guards,' 'protects,' 'guides'] thee.—*Ant. & C.*, ii. 3.

This habitation, where thou *keep'st* ['dwellest,' 'keepest station'], hourly afflict.— *M. for M.*, iii. 1.

Poor house, that *keep'st* ['guardest,' 'takest care of'] thyself.—*Cym.*, iii. 6.

Men, that I have *kept* ['kept company,' 'dwelt'] withal.—*Two G. of V.*, v. 4.

Cur that ever *kept* ['dwelt,' 'associated'] with men.—*Mer. of V.*, iii. 3.

Where the madcap duke his uncle *kept* ['dwelt,' 'resided'].—1 *H. IV.*, i. 3.

Long *kept* ['maintained'] in Bretagne at our mother's cost.—*R. III.*, v. 3.

If the cat will after *kind* ['nature'].—*As You L.*, iii. 2 (*Verses*).

Your cuckoo sings by *kind* ['nature'].—*All's W.*, i. 3 (*Verses*).

That in their *kind* ['way,' 'mode,' 'natural fashion'] they speak it.—*Ibid.*, i. 3.

More than kin and less than *kind* ['naturally and affectionately attached'].— *Hamlet*, i. 2.

Treacherous, *kindless* ['unnatural'] villain.—*Ibid.*, ii. 2.

The bishop hath a *kindly* ['lenient' and 'kinsmanly'] gird.—1 *H. VI.*, iii. 1.

Thou hast most *kindly* ['amiably' and 'aptly'] hit it.—*R. & Jul.*, ii. 4.

Or else my *kingdom* ['kingship,' 'kinghood'] stands on brittle glass.—*R. III.*, iv. 2.

My good *knave* ['lad,' 'attendant': German, *knabe*, 'a boy'], Eros . . . my *knave.*— *Ant. & C.*, iv. 12.

A couple of Ford's *knaves* ['lads,' 'servants'].—*Merry W.*, iii. 5.

With this *knife* ['dagger'] I'll help it presently.—*R. & Jul.*, iv. 1.

Nor by a hired *knife* ['dagger'].—*Ant. & C.*, v. 1.

That you *know* ['recognise'] me not, till time.—*Lear*, iv. 7.

Yet to be *known* ['recognised'] shortens my.—*Ibid.*, iv. 7.

You and I have *known* ['been acquainted'], sir.—*Ant. & C.*, ii. 6.

We have *known* ['been acquainted'] together in Orleans.—*Cym.*, i. 5.

Shall *lack* ['feel the loss of'] you first.—*All's W.*, i. 2.

And *lack* ['fail,' 'cease'] not to lose still.—*Ibid.*, i. 3.

Have sure more *lack* ['failure,' 'want'] of reason.—*M. for M.*, v. 1.

Your *lack* ['failure,' 'want'] of love or bounty.—*W. T.*, iv. 3.

But the feet were *lame* ['imperfect'].—*As You L.*, iii. 2.

Not deficient, blind, or *lame* ['imperfect'] of sense.—*Oth.*, i. 3.

Most *lame* ['imperfect,' 'inefficient'] and impotent conclusion!—*Ibid.*, ii. 1.

On the *lame* ['imperfect'] feet of my rhyme.—*Per.*, iv. (*Gower*).

Made *lame* * ['imperfect,' 'defective'] by fortune's dearest spite. . . .
So then I am not *lame*, poor, nor despis'd.—*Sonnet* 37.

Are they not *lamely* ['imperfectly,' 'inefficiently'] writ ?—*Two G. of V.*, ii. 1.

Speak of my *lameness* ['imperfection,' 'inefficiency'], and I straight will *halt* ['be imperfect,' 'inefficient'].—*Sonnet* 89.

The careless *lapse* ['falling into fault,' 'slip,' 'gliding into error'] of youth and ignorance.—*All's W.*, ii. 3.

To *lapse* ['fall into error,' 'commit a fault'] in fulness
Is sorer than to lie for need.—*Cym.*, iii. 6.

If I be *lapsed* ['found carelessly straying,' 'negligently wandering'] in this place, I shall pay dear.—*Tw. N.*, iii. 3.

That, *lapsed* ['blameably negligent'] in time and passion, let's go by the important acting.—*Hamlet*, iii. 4.

That verity would without *lapsing* ['deviating into error or untruth'] suffer.—*Coriol.*, v. 2.

Larded ['garnished'] with sweet flowers.—*Hamlet*, iv. 5 (*Song*).

Where hearing should not *latch* ['catch the sound of,' 'effectually hold in'] them.—*Macb.*, iv. 3.

For it no form delivers to the heart of bird, of flower, or shape, which it doth *latch* ['catch the sight of,' 'effectually hold in'].—*Sonnet* 113.

Hast thou yet *latch'd* ['smeared,' 'anointed': French, *lécher*, 'to lick'] the Athenian's eyes with the love-juice.—*Mid. N. D.*, iii. 2.

The world may *laugh* ['smile auspiciously,' 'wear a favourable aspect'] again.—*2 H. VI.*, ii. 4.

Had he been *lay* ['secular,' 'not clerical,' 'of the laity'], my lord.—*M. for M.*, v. 1.

A dreadful *lay* ['wager,' 'bet,' 'stake'] !—*2 H. VI.*, v. 2.

My fortunes against any *lay* ['wagered stake'] worth.—*Oth.*, ii. 3.

When I *lay* ['lodged,' 'dwelt'] at Clement's Inn.—*2 H. IV.*, iii. 2.

With a fearful soul *leads* ['leads a life of.' *See* ELLIPTICALLY USED WORDS for other verbs employed with similarly inclusive force of effect] discontented steps in.—*R. III.*, iv. 4.

You must not *learn* ['teach': the original Saxon *lœran* meant both to 'teach' and to 'learn'; from *lœre*, 'knowledge,' 'skill,' 'learning,' which might either be instilled or acquired] me how to remember.—*As You L.*, i. 2.

And *learn* ['teach'] me how to lose a winning match.—*R. & Jul.*, iii. 2.

Both do *learn* ['teach'] me how to respect you.—*Oth.*, i. 3.

Hast thou not *learn'd* ['taught'] me how to make.—*Cym.*, i. 6.

Mercury endue thee with *leasing* ['lying'], for thou.—*Tw. N.*, i. 5.

Almost stamp'd the *leasing* ['lying'].—*Coriol.*, v. 2.

To *leave* ['part with,' 'give away,' 'relinquish'] her token.—*Two G. of V.*, iv. 4.

Love me and *leave* ['relinquish,' 'give away'] me not . . . he would not *leave* it.—*Mer. of V.*, v. 1.

I may not *leave* ['yield,' 'relinquish,' 'resign'] it so.—*R. III.*, iv. 1.

Leave ['cease,' 'desist'] to afflict my heart.—*2 H. VI.*, ii. 1.

Bid the music *leave* ['cease,' 'leave off'].—*H. VIII.*, iv. 2.

Their functions *leave* ['cease'] to do.—*Hamlet*, iii. 2.

Let us *leave* ['cease,' 'leave off,' 'discontinue this discourse'] here, gentlemen.—*Cym.*, i. 5.

Here, there, and everywhere he *leaves* ['leaves them dead'].—*Tr. & Cr.*, v. 5.

---

* It has strangely been questioned whether this passage does not prove that Shakespeare was a cripple and had a limping leg or a club-foot; but, surely, the other passages here collected serve to show the sense in which he often uses the words "lame," "lamely," and "lameness." *See* also "Halt" and "Halts" under the present eading.

She gives the *leer* [' side-glance '] of invitation.—*Merry W.*, i. 3.

A Rosalind of a better *leer* [' complexion,' ' look,' ' countenance,' ' appearance ': Saxon, *hleare*, ' face,' ' visage '] than you.—*As You L.*, iv. 1.

Where you shall be an everlasting *leiger* [' permanently resident embassador '].—*M. for M.*, iii. 1.

Unpeople her of *leigers* [' resident embassadors '] for her sweet.—*Cym.*, i. 6.

They that least *lend* [' manifestly give '] it you.—*All's W.*, i. 2.

Take or *lend* [' bestow,' ' confer,' ' give voluntarily '].—*Cym.*, iii. 6.

To draw it out in *length* [' prolongation,' ' deferred conclusions '].—*Mer of V.*, iii. 2.

There is such *length* [' prolonged suffering '] in grief.—*R. II.*, v. 1.

All *length** [' lingering,' ' deferred conclusion,' ' length of endurance and existence '] is torture.—*Ant. & C.*, iv. 12.

That God had *lent*† [' conferred or bestowed upon '] us but this only child.—*R. & Jul.*, iii. 5.

As heaven had *lent* [' conferred upon '] her all his grace.—*Per.*, i. (*Gower*).

That I may know the *let* [' impediment,' ' hindrance,' ' obstacle '] why gentle Peace should not expel.—*H. V.*, v. 2.

Thy kinsmen are no let [' hindrance '] to me.—*R. & Jul.*, ii. 2.

What *lets* [' hinders,' ' prevents '] but one may enter.—*Tw. G. of V.*, iii. 1.

If nothing *lets* [' hinders,' ' prevents,' ' impedes '] to make us happy both but this.—*Tw. N.*, v. 1.

I 'll make a ghost of him that *lets* [' hinders '] me.—*Hamlet*, i. 4.

Out of the blank and *level* [' range,' ' space within aim '] of my brain.—*W. T.*, ii. 3.

My life stands in the *level* [' range,' ' space wherein aim can hit '] of your dreams.—*Ibid.*, iii. 2.

I stood i' the *level* [' range,' ' space for aim '] of a full-charg'd confederacy—*H. VIII.*, i. 2.

Her acquaintance grew with this *lewd* [' idle,' ' ignorant,' ' wicked '] fellow.—*M. Ado*, v. 1.

Detain'd for *lewd* [' wicked,' ' vile,' ' base '] employments.—*R. II.*, i. 1.

Such *lewd* [' idle,' ' foolish,' ' witless,' ' unwise '], such mean attempts.—1 *H. IV.*, iii. 2.

Is *liable* [' apt,' ' adaptable '], congruent, and measurable for the afternoon.—*Love's L. L.*, v. 1.

And reason to my love is *liable* [' subordinate '].—*Jul. C.*, ii. 2.

That *liberal* [' free-spoken '] shepherds give.—*Hamlet*, iv. 7.

Profane and *liberal* [' licentious '] counsellor.—*Oth.*, ii. 1.

I 'll be in speaking *liberal* [' free,' ' unrestrained '] as the air.—*Ibid.*, v. 2.

Does he *lie* [' lodge,' ' sojourn '] at the Garter ?—*Merry W.*, ii. 1.

She must *lie* [' lodge,' ' dwell,' ' reside,' ' take up abode '] here on mere necessity.—*Love's L. L.*, i. 1.

There doth my father *lie* [' lodge,' ' sojourn '].—*Tam. of S.*, iv. 4.

Where Lieutenant Cassio *lies* [' lodges,' ' resides '].—*Oth.*, iii. 4.

Short summers *lightly* [' commonly,' ' ordinarily,' ' usually '] have a forward spring.—*R. III.*, iii. 1.

I weigh it *lightly* [' as a trifle,' ' slightly '].—*Ibid.*, iii. 1.

---

* It has been proposed to change " length " in this passage to 'life ; but the other passages we cite, where Shakespeare employs "length " in a similar sense, show that he probably so used the word here likewise.

† If " lent " be the correct word in this passage (and it is so given in the Folio and all the Quarto copies excepting the First Quarto, which gives ' sent,' it bears the sense we here assign : but—considering that Capulet, in act i., sc. 2., says, " earth hath swallow'd all my hopes but she," which conveys the idea that he had had other children who died young—we have an impression that possibly " left " was the word written by Shakespeare in the present passage.

And will not *lightly* ['easily,' 'facilely'] trust the messenger.—*Com. of E.*, iv. 4.

And believe 't not *lightly* ['easily,' 'readily'].—*Coriol.*, iv. 1.

But by loving *likelihood* ['similitude '].—*H. V.*, v. (*Chorus*).

To tear her *limb-meal* ['a limb at a time,' 'limb from limb.' *See* "Inch-meal" under the present heading].—*Cym.*, ii. 4.

Who gave his blood to *lime* ['cement'] the stones together.—3 *H. VI.*, v. 1.

The bird that hath been *limed* ['caught' as by bird-lime] . . . where my poor bird was *lim'd.*—*Ibid.*, v. 6.

I have *limed* ['caught,' 'captivated'] her.—*Tw. N.*, iii. 4.

Limit ['appoint'] each leader to his several charge.— *R. III.*, v. 3.

There is boundless theft in *limited* ['appointed,' 'stated,' 'set'] professions.— *Timon*, iv. 3.

'Tis my *limited* ['appointed'] service.—*Macb.*, ii. 3.

We will not *line* ['strengthen'] his thin bestained cloak with our pure honours.— *John*, iv. 3.

Sent for you to *line* ['strengthen,' 'give sustainment or support to'] his enterprise.— 1 *H. IV.*, ii. 3.

Or did *line* ['strengthen,' 'reinforce,' 'support,' 'sustain'] the rebel with hidden help and vantage.—*Macb.*, i. 3.

Within the *list* ['boundary,' 'limit'] of too cold an adieu.—*All's W.*, ii. 1.

Within the weak *list* ['limit'] of a country's fashion.—*H. V.*, v. 2.

The ocean, overpeering of his *list* ['boundary,' 'limit'].—*Hamlet*, iv. 5.

Confine yourself but in a patient *list* ['boundary'].—*Oth.*, iv. 1.

Or star, or what I *list* ['choose,' 'please,' 'desire,' 'like'], or ere I.—*Tam. of S.*, iv. 5.

When I have *list* ['inclination,' 'desire'] to sleep.—*Oth.*, ii. 1.

List ['listen to'] a brief tale.—*Lear*, v. 3.

List ['listen to'] me. The lieutenant to-night.—*Oth.*, ii. 1.

Ah, you sweet *little* [with an effect of fondness, and without an effect of smallness] rogue, you.—2 *H. IV.*, ii. 4.

For *little* [with similar effect] England you 'd venture.—*H. VIII.*, ii. 3.

Be sure you be not *loose* ['unreticent,' 'unguarded in speech'].—*Ibid.*, ii. 1.

A kind of men so *loose* ['unreticent,' 'unrestrained,' 'undisciplined'] of soul.— *Oth.*, iii. 3.

Ere I will yield my virgin patent up unto his *lordship* ['marital dominion'].— *Mid. N. D.*, i. 1.

As you swear them *lordship* ['marital guardianship'].—*All's W.*, v. 3.

Let *Love* ['the Queen of love,' 'Venus'], being light.—*Com. of E.*, iii. 2.

Forerun fair *Love* ['Venus'], strewing her way.—*Love's L. L.*, iv. 3.

For the love of *Love* ['Venus'] and her soft hours.—*Ant. & C.*, i. 1.

Tell me, *Love's* ['Venus's'] master, shall we meet to-morrow?—*V. & Adon.*, Stanza 98.

She 's *Love* ['Venus'], she loves, and yet she.—*Ibid.*, 102.

Love ['Venus'] lack'd a dwelling, and made him her place.—*Lover's Comp.*, Stanza 12.

Lustick ['vigorous,' 'robust,' 'active,' 'alert'], as the Dutchman says.—*All's W.*, ii. 3.

Your dolphin is not *lustier* ['more vigorous'].—*Ibid.*, ii. 3.

Yet I am strong and *lusty* ['vigorous'] . . . a *lusty* winter.—*As You L.*, ii. 3.

He would unhorse the *lustiest* ['most vigorous'] challenger.—*R. II.*, v. 3.

Be *mad* ['wild with high spirits,' 'extravagantly gay'] and merry.—*Tam. of S.*, iii. 2.

A *mad* ['mad-cap,' 'wild-spirited'] fellow met me.—1 *H. IV.*, iv. 2.

How now, *mad* ['frolicsome,' 'mad-cap'] wag!—*Ibid.*, iv. 2.

They will talk of *mad* ['frolicsome,' 'mad-cap'] Shallow yet.—2 *H. IV.*, iii. 2.

The doors are *made* ['fastened,' 'barred.' *See* IDIOMS for "Made" variously used] against you.—*Com. of E.*, iii. 1.

Our best friends *made* [' secured '], and our best means.—*Jul. C.*, iv. 1.

Goes it against the *main* [' mainland '] of Poland.—*Hamlet*, iv. 4.

Swell the curled waters 'bove the *main* [' mainland '].—*Lear*, iii. 1.

'Twixt the heaven and the *main* [' ocean,' ' sea '].—*Oth.*, ii. 1.

Make [' fasten,' ' bar '] the doors upon a woman's wit.—*As You L.*, iv. 1.

Which thou must *make* [' secure '] thy friends.—*2 H. IV.*, iv. 4.

He would shine on those that *make* [' adjust,' ' form,' ' mould '] their looks by his.—*Ant. & C.*, i. 5.

Such a wife as my thoughts *make* [' consider,' ' esteem,' ' believe '] thee.—*Ibid.*, iii. 2.

Our fears do *make* [' cause us to seem.' *See* ELLIPTICAL STYLE for several instances of " Make " thus used] us traitors.—*Macb.*, iv. 2.

Preparation *makes* [' speeds.' *See* IDIOMS] for Cyprus.—*Oth.*, i. 3.

That which *makes* [' accomplishes,' ' completes '] him.—*Cym.*, i. 5.

Fortune did *malign* [' injure,' ' damage,' ' harm '] my state.—*Per.*, v. 1.

A *mankind* [' masculine,' ' male-sexed '] witch!—*W. T.*, ii. 3.

Are you *mankind** [' masculine,' ' manlike,' ' mannish,' ' of male kind ']?—*Coriol.*, iv. 2.

If thou never sawest good *manners* [' conduct,' ' behaviour '], then thy *manners* [' morals,' ' ways '] must be wicked.—*As You L.*, iii. 2.

He, a *marble* [' impenetrable statue '] to her tears.—*M. for M.*, iii. 1.

Who was most *marble* [' hard-natured,' ' unimpressionable '] there changed colour.—*W. T.*, v. 2.

Will pierce into a *marble* [' hard '] heart.—*3 H. VI.*, iii. 1.

Now, by yond' *marble* [' cruel,' ' inexorable '] heaven.—*Oth.*, iii. 3.

Live you, the *marble* [' inexorable,' ' impenetrable '] breasted tyrant, still.—*Tw. N.*, v. 1.

If his chief good and *market* [' purchase made,' ' bargain gained,' ' profit made '] of his time be but to sleep and feed?—*Hamlet*, iv. 4.

Shall I come to you at evening *mass* [' service,' ' office,' ' prayer,' " evening mass " being here used for ' vespers ']?—*R. & Jul.*, iv. 1.

'Tis our *match* [' compact,' ' agreement '].—*Cym.*, iii. 6.

With tender Juliet *match'd* [' compared '], is now not fair.—*R. & Jul.*, i. 5 (*Chorus*).

Dare *mate* [' oppose,' ' attack,' ' challenge,' ' impugn '] a sounder man than Surrey can be.—*H. VIII.*, iii. 2.

I think you are all *mated* [' confused,' ' bewildered,' ' confounded '] or stark mad.—*Com. of E.*, v. 1.

My mind she has *mated* [' bewildered,' ' dismayed].—*Macb.*, v. 1.

I am amaz'd with *matter* [' affairs that demand attention '].—*Cym.*, iv. 3.

More *matter* [' substantial speaking,' ' sedately made statement '], with less art.—*Hamlet*, ii. 2.

Oh, *matter* [' rationally sedate statement '] and *impertinency* [' that which is not pertinent,' ' irrelevancy '] mix'd!—*Lear*, iv. 6.

Were he *meal'd* [' mingled,' ' mixed '] with that which he corrects.—*M. for M.*, iv. 2.

Nay, he can sing a *mean* [' tenor part.' *See* MUSICAL TERMS].—*Love's L. L.*, v. 2.

A *measure* [' a dignified dance, with slow and measured steps '], full of state and ancientry.—*M. Ado*, ii. 1.

To tread a *measure* [' dance '] with you on this grass.—*Love's L. L.*, v. 2.

Am starv'd for *meat* [' food '], giddy for lack of sleep.—*Tam. of S.*, iv. 3.

What you want in *meat* [' food '], we 'll have in drink.—*2 H. IV.*, v. 3.

You want much of *meat* † [' food,' ' victuals '].—*Timon*, iv. 3.

---

* In the present passage, the word " mankind " is used by the asker in this sense, tauntingly; but is replied to by the answerer in the sense of ' human,' ' of humankind.'

† The word " meat " in this passage has been variously altered by various emendators; but it is used in its general sense of ' food ' here, as well as in the other passages above cited.

For *meddle* [' deal with,' ' engage with him '] you must.—*Tw. N.*, iii. 4.

Money's a *meddler* [' dealer '], that doth utter.—*W. T.*, iv. 3 (*Song*).

I have seen a *medicine* [' one who brings remedial aid,' ' healer.' *See* THINGS IMPERSONATED] that 's able to breathe life into.—*All's W.*, ii. 1.

Meet we the *medicine* [' healer,' ' physician,' ' one bringing remedial aid '] of the sickly weal.—*Macb.*, v. 2.

To one so *meek* [' lowly,' ' subdued,' ' bowed by misfortune '].—*Ant. & C.*, v. 2.

Desire, all recreant, poor, and *meek* [' brought low,' ' humbled ']. — *Lucrece*, *Stanza* 102.

You *memory* [' memorial '] of old Sir Roland !—*As You L.*, ii. 3.

A good *memory* [' memorial '] and witness of the.—*Coriol.*, iv. 5.

Brought thee to their *mercies* [' discretionary powers to spare or to destroy '].—*Tw. N.*, v. 1.

Life lies in the *mercy* [' discretionary power '] of the duke only.—*Mer. of V.*, iv. 1.

The sovereign *mercy* [' power to spare or condemn '] of the king.—*R. II.*, ii. 3.

Engag'd my friend to his *mere* [' thorough,' ' utter,' ' extreme '] enemy.—*Mer. of V.*, iii. 2.

To the *mere* [' utter,' ' complete '] undoing of all.—*H. VIII.*, iii. 2.

Of your *mere* [' entirely,' ' absolutely '] own.—*Macb.*, iv. 3.

The *mere* [' absolute,' ' complete,' ' utter '] perdition of the.—*Oth.*, ii. 2.

To thy *mere* [' utter,' ' complete '] confusion.—*Cym.*, iv. 2.

He being the *mered* [' absolutely limited,' ' entirely confined,' ' solely included '] question.—*Ant. & C.*, iii. 11.

Merely [' absolutely,' ' thoroughly '] our own traitors.—*All's W.*, iv. 3.

Heaven knows, is *merely* [' exclusively,' ' absolutely,' ' genuinely '] love.—*Timon*, iv. 3.

See where she comes from shrift with *merry* [' cheerful '] look.—*R. & Jul.*, iv. 2.

Say I am *merry* [' cheerful '].—*Jul. C.*, iii. 4.

Tell me of a *mess* [' portion,' ' quantity,' ' measure '] of porridge.—*Merry W.*, iii. 1.

To borrow a *mess* [' measure,' ' quantity '] of vinegar.—*2 H. IV.*, ii. 1.

Which fate and *metaphysical* [' supernatural,' ' preternatural,'] aid doth seem.—*Macb.*, i. 5.

And forth my *mimic* [' actor '] comes.—*Mid. N. D.*, iii. 2.

Hold up your head, and *mince* [' walk demurely '].—*Merry W.*, v. 1.

I know no ways to *mince* [' talk affectedly, smoothly, or ceremoniously '] in love.—*H. V.*, v. 2.

Love doth *mince* [' palliate,' ' smooth '] this matter.—*Oth.*, ii. 3.

Mince [' palliate,' ' mitigate '] not the general tongue.—*Ant. & C.*, i. 2.

That *minces* [' is affectedly demure in '] virtue.—*Lear*, iv. 6.

Turn two *mincing* [' demure,' ' affectedly small '] steps.—*Mer. of V.*, iii. 4.

Nothing so much as *mincing* [' affected '] poetry.—*1 H. IV.*, iii. 1.

Saving your *mincing* [' affected self-denial,' ' demureness '].—*H. VIII.*, ii. 3.

That man might ne'er be wretched for his *mind* [' generosity of disposition,' ' high-mindedness,' ' liberality of spirit '].—*Timon*, i. 2.

Sent to me first, but for my *mind's* [' understanding's '] sake.—*Ibid.*, iii. 3.

Do thee wrong to *mind* [' remind '] thee of it.—*H. V.*, iv. 3.

I *mind* [' am in the mind,' ' am disposed or inclined '] to tell him plainly — *3 H. VI.*, iv. 1.

I *minded* [' reminded '] him how royal 'twas.—*Coriol.*, v. 1.

How you stand *minded* [' disposed '] in the.—*H. VIII.*, iii. 1.

Belike she *minds* [' is disposed '] to play the Amazon.—*3 H. VI.*, iv. 1.

We do not come as *minding* [' wishing,' ' being in the mind '] to content you.—*Mid. N. D.*, v. 1 (*Prologue*).

Minding [' remembering,' ' being reminded of'] true things by what their mockeries be.—*H. V.*, iv. (*Chorus*).

Not *minding* ['choosing,' 'being in the mind'] longer to withhold vengeance.—*Per.*, ii. 4.

Among a *mineral* ['metallic vein,' 'lode'] of metals base.—*Hamlet*, iv. 1.

Minion ['pet,' 'darling': used contemptuously], thou liest.—*Tam. of S.*, ii. 1.

But this your *minion* ['favourite,' 'darling'] whom.—*Tw. N.*, v. 1.

He covets less than *misery* ['miserliness'] itself would give.—*Coriol.*, ii. 2.

O noble *misery* ['miserable conduct,' 'mean behaviour'], to be i' the field, and ask, what news, of me!—*Cym.*, v. 3.

*Mislike** ['dislike mistakenly,' 'disapprove erroneously'] me not for my complexion.—*Mer. of V.*, ii. 1.

'Tis not my speeches that you do *mislike* ['affect to dislike'], but 'tis my presence.—2 *H. VI.*, i. 1.

Setting your scorns and your *mislike* ['unjust dislike'] aside.—3 *H. VI.*, iv. 1.

If he *mislike* ['dislike and take amiss'] my speech, and what is done, tell him.—*Ant. & C.*, iii. 11.

You spend your passion on a *mispris'd* ['mistaken'] mood.—*Mid. N. D.*, iii. 2.

Misprising ['taking amiss,' 'depreciating,' 'disparaging,' 'despising'] what they look on.—*M. Ado*, iii. 1.

There is some strange *misprision* ['mistake,' 'misconception'] in the princes.—*Ibid.*, iv. 1.

Of thy *misprision* ['mistake'] must perforce.—*Mid. N. D.*, iii. 2.

Misprision ['mistake'] in the highest degree!—*Tw. N.*, i. 5.

In vile *misprision* ['scorn,' 'disdain,' 'depreciation'] shackle up my love and her desert.—*All's W.*, ii. 3.

We cannot *miss* ['do without'] him.—*Temp.*, i. 2.

I should have a heavy *miss* ['loss,' 'want'] of thee.—1 *H. IV.*, v. 4.

He saith she is immodest, blames her *'miss*† ['misbehaviour,' 'misconduct'].—*V. & Adon.*, Stanza 9.

Did gibe my *missive* ['messenger'] out of audience.—*Ant. & C.*, ii. 2.

Came *missives* ['messengers'] from the king.—*Macb.*, i. 5 (*Letter*).

Opinion on my least *misuse* ['misconduct,' 'misdeed'].—*Oth.*, iv. 2.

Wise girls to *mock* ['use despitefully and disdainfully:' 'treat hardly' as well as 'scoff at,' 'make game of'] our lovers so.—*Love's L. L.*, v. 2.

Misery makes sport to *mock* ['use tormentingly,' 'treat cruelly,' as well as 'treat disdainfully and scoffingly'] itself.—*R. II.*, ii. 1.

Which doth *mock* ‡ ['disdain,' 'spurn,' 'tear wrathfully'] the meat it feeds on.—*Oth.*, iii. 3.

In time the rod becomes more *mock'd* ['treated disdainfully and derisively'] than fear'd.—*M. for M.*, i. 4.

For gnarling sorrow hath less power to bite the man that *mocks* ['treats it harshly and contemptuously'] at it, and sets it light.—*R. II.*, i. 3.

But a clod and *model* ['image,' 'copy,' 'representation'] of confounded royalty.—*John*, v. 7.

Who was the *model* ['copy,' 'representation'] of thy father's life.—*R. II.*, i. 2.

That small *model* ['portion heaped into the form of the human body'] of the barren earth which serves as paste.—*Ibid.*, iii. 2.

---

* In all the four instances where Shakespeare uses this word, he employs it with a shade of meaning different from 'dislike'; and therefore it were well to preserve so expressive a word as mislike in our accustomed language.

† "Amiss" was used in Shakespeare's time for 'misdeed'; and he himself uses "amiss" for 'mishap' in the following passage:—

Each toy seems prologue to some great *amiss*.—*Hamlet*, iv. 5.

‡ "Mock" has been changed in the present passage by Hanmer and others, to 'make'; but the other instances we have here collected of Shakespeare's use of this word, suffice to show that he probably employed it likewise in the present passage.

Which was the *model* [' copy :' ' modelled upon the pattern '] of that Danish seal.— *Hamlet*, v. 2.

Full of wise saws and *modern* [' common,' ' trite,' ' hackneyed,' ' conventional '] instances.—*As You L.*, ii. 7.

Betray themselves to every *modern* [' common,' ' ordinary '] censure.—*Ibid.*, iv. 1.

Scorns a *modern* [' common,' ' ordinary,' ' usual '] invocation.—*Ibid.*, iii. 4.

Which *modern* [' common,' ' ordinary'] lamentation might have mov'd.—*R. & Jul.*, iii. 2.

Likelihoods of *modern* [' ordinary '] seeming do.—*Oth.*, i. 3.

As we greet *modern* [' ordinary '] friends withal.—*Ant. & C.*, v. 2.

How far a *modern* [' ordinary '] quill doth.—*Sonnet* 83.

Joy could not show itself *modest* ['decorous,' 'moderate'] enough without.— *M. Ado*, i. 1.

Within the *modest* ['decorous '] limits of order.—*Tw. N.*, i. 3.

Reverence to your calling makes me *modest* ['reticent,' ' forbearing,' 'moderate'].— *H. VIII.*, v. 2.

I am doubtful of your *modesties* [' powers of discretion '].—*Tam. of S.*, *Induc.* 1.

If it be husbanded with *modesty* ['moderation,' ' discretion '].—*Ibid.*, *Induc.* 1.

Thy religious truth and *modesty* [' forbearance,' ' mildness '].—*H. VIII.*, iv. 2.

Win straying souls with *modesty* ['moderation,' ' mildness'] again.—*Ibid.*, v. 2.

In a friend, it is cold *modesty* ['moderation,' ' reticence,' 'forbearance'].—*Jul. C.*, iii. 1.

Follow him thither with *modesty* [' moderation '] enough.—*Hamlet*, v. 1.

Methinks my *moiety* [' portion,' ' share,'] north from Burton.—1 *H. IV.*, iii. 1.

A *moiety* [' portion '] competent was gaged.—*Hamlet*, i. 1.

Can make choice of either's *moiety* [' portion,' ' share '].—*Lear*, i. 1.

The clear eye's *moiety* [' portion,' ' share '] and the dear.—*Sonnet* 46.

Idly sit to hear my nothings *monster'd* ['made wonders of,' ' lauded as something extraordinary '].—*Coriol.*, ii. 2.

To *monstrous* [' unnatural,' ' unwonted,' ' exceptional,' ' extraordinary '] quality . . . unto some *monstrous* state.—*Jul. C.*, i. 3.

Goodness and he fill up one *monument* [' tomb,' ' sepulchre']!—*H. VIII.*, ii. 1.

Our *monuments* [' tombs,' ' sepulchres '] shall be the maws of kites.—*Macb.*, iii. 4.

Who, in my *mood* [' wrath,' 'resentment'], I stabb'd.—*Two G. of V.*, iv. 1.

As hot a Jack in thy *mood* ['wrath '] . . . as soon moved to be *moody* ['wrathful'], and as soon *moody* to be moved.—*R. & Jul.*, iii. 1.

But *moody* [' gloomily pensive '] and dull melancholy.—*Com of E.*, v. 1.

Music, *moody* ['melancholy,' ' pensive'] food of us that trade in love.—*Ant. & C.*, ii. 5.

Will be here with *mop* [' grimace,'] and *mow* [' wryed mouth,'].—*Temp.*, iv. 1.

To *mope* ['wander blindly and blunderingly'] with his fat-brained followers so far out of his knowledge.—*H. V.*, iii. 7.

Could not so *mope* [' dully go astray,' ' blindly wander '].—*Hamlet*, iii. 4.

And were brought *moping* [' dully and bewilderedly straying'] hither.—*Temp.*, v. 1.

Flibbertigibbet, of *mopping* ['grimacing'] and *mowing* ['making mouths'].— *Lear*, iv. 1.

You have some *moral* [' occult signification,' ' pointed meaning'] in this Benedictus. —*M. Ado*, iii. 4.

The meaning or *moral* ['signification '] of his signs.—*Tam. of S.*, iv. 4.

I pray thee, *moralize* [' expound '] them.—*Ibid.*, iv. 4.

I *moralize* [' make out,' ' ingeniously frame'] two meanings in one word.— *R. III.*, iii. 1.

Did he not *moralize* [' deduce a moral from ' ' draw and utter a moral lesson from '] this spectacle?—*As You L.*, ii. 1.

Thou hear'st me *moralize* ['utter moral deductions '], applying this to that, and so to so.—*V. & Adon.*, Stanza 119.

Nor could she *moralize* ['interpret,' 'discover the meaning of'] his wanton sight.— *Lucrece, Stanza* 15.

As all is *mortal* ['subject to death'] in nature, so is all nature *mortal* ['excessive,' 'abundant'] in folly.—*As You L.*, ii. 4.

Even to a *mortal* ['deadly'] arbitrement.—*Tw. N.*, iii. 4.

That tend on *mortal* ['deadly'] thoughts.—*Macb.*, i. 5.

Which to read would be even *mortal* ['deadly,' 'fatal'] to me.—*Cym.*, iii. 4.

One *mortal* ['fatal,' 'deadly'] night drove him to this.—*Per.*, v. 1.

Dumain is *mortified* ['dead to worldly allurements,' 'ascetic'].—*Love's L. L.*, i. 1.

Excite the *mortified* ['ascetic,' 'dead to passion'] man.—*Macb.*, v. 2.

Oh, excellent *motion* ['puppet-show']! Oh, exceeding puppet!—*Two G. of V.*, ii. 1.

He compassed a *motion* ['puppet-show'] of the Prodigal Son.—*W. T.*, iv. 2.

And he is a *motion* ['puppet'] ungenerative.—*M. for M.*, iii. 2.

And are no fairy? *motion* ['puppet']?—*Per.*, v. 1.

But from the inward *motion* ['intelligential faculty,' 'insight,' 'inspiration'] to deliver.—*John*, i. 1.

I see it in my *motion* ['secret impulse of conviction,' 'mental prompting,' 'divinatory insight or inspiration'], have it not in my tongue.—*Ant. & C.*, ii. 3.

For there's no *motion* ['impulse,' 'inclination'] that tends to vice in man.— *Cym.*, ii. 5.

I have a *motion* ['proposal,' 'appeal,' 'solicitation'] much imports your good.— *M. for M.*, v. 1.

I'll make the *motion* ['proposal']: stand here.—*Tw. N.*, iii. 4.

Unshak'd of *motion** ['proposal,' 'appeal,' 'solicitation'].—*Jul. C.*, iii. 1.

Give ear to his *motions* ['proposals,' 'appeals'], Master Slender.—*Merry W.*, i. 1.

But from sincere *motions* ['impulses of indignation'].—*H. VIII.*, i. 1.

To be my *motive* ['moving power,' 'active means,' 'agent,' 'promoter'] and helper to a husband.—*All's W.*, iv. 4.

Every joint and *motive* ['portion instrumental in producing motion,' 'motive organ'] of her body.—*Tr. & Cr.*, iv. 5.

What's your dark meaning, *mouse* [formerly used as a term of endearment or familiarity], of this light word?—*Love's L. L.*, v. 2.

Good my *mouse* [similarly used] of virtue.—*Tw. N.*, i. 5.

Call you his *mouse* [similarly used].—*Hamlet*, iii. 4.

Move ['penetrate,' 'pierce,' 'wound'] the still-piercing air, that sings with piercing.— *All's W.*, iii. 2.

And rather *muse* ['wonder,' 'be at a loss for the reason'] than ask why I entreat you.—*Ibid.*, ii. 5.

Do not *muse* ['wonder,' 'marvel'] at me.—*Macb.*, iii. 4.

He will discredit our *mystery* ['trade'].—*M. for M.*, iv. 2.

Not to have us thrive in our *mystery* ['trade'].—*Timon*, iv. 3.

I am glad I have found this *napkin* ['handkerchief'].—*Oth.*, iii. 3.

Dip their *napkins* ['handkerchiefs'] in his sacred blood.—*Jul. C.*, iii. 2.

Which *native* ['by nature,' 'naturally'] she doth owe.—*Love's L. L.*, i. 2.

Could never be the *native* ['origin,' 'source,' 'cause of birth,' 'natural engenderer'] of our so frank donation.—*Coriol.*, iii. 1.

That a monster should be such a *natural* ['idiot']!—*Temp.*, iii. 2.

This drivelling love is like a great *natural* ['idiot'].—*R. & Jul.*, ii. 4.

Nature ['natural strength,' 'native constitution'] and sickness debate it at their leisure.—*All's W.*, i. 2.

---

* It has been questioned whether "motion" bears the signification assigned by us in this passage; but we think the other instances here cited of similar use by Shakespeare of "motion" in this sense, show it to be the correct one.

That death and *nature* ['natural strength,' 'native constitution'] do contend about them.—*Macb.*, ii. 2.

This *naughty* ['good for nothing,' 'worthless,' 'bad,' 'wicked'] man shall face to face be brought to Margaret.—*M. Ado*, v. 1.

But a *naughty* ['good for naught,' 'worthless,' 'bad'] orator.—*All's W.*, v. 3.

And this *neglection* ['neglect'] of degree it is.—*Tr. & Cr.*, i. 3.

If *neglection* ['neglect,' 'negligence'] should therein make me vile.—*Per.*, iii. 3.

I speak the truth the *next* ['nearest,' 'directest'] way.—*All's W.*, i. 3.

Home, home, the *next* ['nearest'] way.—*W. T.*, iii. 3.

Is the *next* ['nearest,' 'readiest'] way to draw new.—*Oth.*, i. 3.

The respects thereof are *nice* ['insignificant,' 'unimportant,' 'over-scrupulously weighed'] and trivial.—*R. III.*, iii. 7.

That every *nice* ['slight,' 'unimportant'] offence.—*Jul. C.*, iv. 3.

Nor the lady's, which is *nice* ['mincing,' 'affected,' 'modish'].—*As You L.*, iv. 1.

I am not so *nice* ['foolishly particular,' 'sillily fastidious'], to change true rules for odd inventions.—*Tam. of S.*, iii. 1.

Hence, therefore, thou *nice* ['over-luxurious,' 'effeminate'] crutch !—*2 H. IV.*, i. 1.

Nice ['punctilious,' 'precise,' 'prudish,' 'fastidious'] customs court'sy to great kings. —*H. V.*, v. 2.

Or *nicely* ['subtly,' 'sophistically'] charge your understanding soul with opening titles miscreate.—*Ibid.*, i. 2.

Stretch their duties *nicely* ['punctiliously,' 'precisely,' 'with scrupulous exactness']. —*Lear*, ii. 2.

Inflame too *nicely* ['scrupulously'].—*Per.*, iv. 1.

See if thou canst find out Sneak's *noise* ['street-band,' 'company of itinerant musicians'].—*2 H. IV.*, ii. 4.

And what *noise* ['musical sound'] is this ?—*Macb.*, iv. 1.

Fame doth *noise* ['report,' 'rumour'] abroad, Navarre hath.—*Love's L. L.*, ii. 1.

The *noise* ['report,' 'rumour'] goes, this.—*Tr. & Cr.*, i. 2.

A trull, that *noises* ['loudly menaces,' 'turbulently threatens'] it against us.— *Ant. & C.*, iii. 6.

Some base *notorious* ['that should be noted,' 'that ought to be exposed to notoriety'] knave.—*Oth.*, iv. 2.

'Tis a *notorious* ['that should be noted and exposed'] villain.—*Ibid.*, v. 2.

Such fiery *numbers* ['verses,' 'rhythmical lines'] as the prompting eyes.—*Love's L. L.*, iv. 3.

The *numbers* ['verses,' 'versification'] altered !—*Tw. N.*, ii. 5.

Inland bred, and know some *nurture* ['education,' 'cultivation'].—*As You L.*, ii. 7.

The *object* ['spectacle'] of our misery is.—*Coriol.*, i. 1.

Your best *object* ['object of affection'], the argument of.—*Lear*, i. 1.

One that feeds on *objects* ['objects of pursuit,' 'objects to be attained'], arts, and imitations.—*Jul. C.*, iv. 1.

My *oblivion* ['obliviousness,' 'defective memory'] is a very Antony.—*Ant. & C.*, i. 3.

And so *obsequious* ['lavish of obsequies'] will thy father be.—*3 H. VI.*, ii. 5.

To do *obsequious* ['deferential,' and 'lavish of obsequies'] sorrow.—*Hamlet*, i. 2.

Make her fault her husband's *occasion* ['occasioning,' 'occasioned by'].—*As You L.*, iv. 1.

Stronger than his just *occasion* ['that which might have occasioned resentment'], made him give.—*Ibid.*, iv. 3.

We do *o'er-count* ['outnumber'] thee.—At land, indeed, thou dost *o'er-count* ['out number'; including the effect of 'overreach'] me of my father's house.— *Ant. & C.*, ii. 6.

May *offer* ['attack,' 'assail,' 'make hostile attempt'], but not hold.—*2 H. IV.*, iv. 1.

Offer ['attack,' 'assail,' 'make hostile advance'] nothing here.—*H. V.*, ii. 1.

We of the *offering* ['assailing,' 'challenging,' 'commencing hostilities'] side must keep aloof.—1 *H. IV.*, iv. 1.

With all the *office* [' duty,' 'dedicated service '] of my heart.—*Oth.*, iii. 4.

Now turn the *office* ['dedicated service,' 'duteous observance'] of their view upon a tawny front.—*Ant. & C.*, i. 1.

I 'll rack thee with *old* [' excessive,' 'abundant'] cramps.—*Temp.*, i. 2.

Here will be an *old* ['excessive,' 'abundant'] abusing.—*Merry W.*, i. 4.

Here will be *old* [' excessive,' 'extreme '] utis.—2 *H. IV.*, ii. 4.

He should have *old* [' abundant'] turning of the key.—*Macb.*, ii. 3.

Meet the *old* ['usual,' 'ordinary'] course of death.— *Lear*, iii. 7.

This is the *old* [' former '] man still.—*Timon*, iii. 6.

Passion stands for true *old* ['of primitive simplicity,' 'genuine,' and ' excessive '] woe.—*Per.*, iv. 4 (*Gower*).

If the *old* [used to imply familiarity, without implying age] fantastical duke of dark corners.—*M. for M.*, iv. 3.

One that *old* [similarly used] Frederick.—*As You L.*, i. 2.

For all the *old* [partly with the effect of familiarity and petulant mention, partly with that of 'hackneyed in worldly ways,' partly as being older than the speaker] gentleman's saying.—*Ibid.*, v. 1.

How now, *old* [implying familiarity] lad ?—*Tam. of S.*, iv. 1.

Go thy ways, *old* [similarly used] lad ; for thou.—*Ibid.*, v. 2.

*Old** [in Shakespeare's time sometimes applied to men of what would now be considered middle age] John of Gaunt.—*R. II.*, i. 1.

To crush our *old*† [similarly applied] limbs in ungentle steel.—1 *H. IV.*, v. 1.

My glass shall not persuade me I am *old*‡ . . .—*Sonnet* 22.

> But when my glass shows me myself indeed,
> Beated and chopp'd with tann'd *antiquity.—Ibid.* 62.

I would not believe her lips in *opening* [' disclosing,' 'revealing'] it.—*Cym.*, v. 5.

To steel a strong *opinion* [' reputation,' 'estimation'] to themselves ?—*Tr. & Cr.*, i. 3.

Then we did our main *opinion* ['reputation,' ' estimation '] crush.—*Ibid.*, i. 3.

The smallest *opinion* ['ill opinion,' 'misconstruction'] on my least misuse.—*Oth.*, iv. 2.

Rear the higher our *opinion* [' opinion of ourselves,' 'self-estimation '] that our stirring can.—*Ant. & C.*, ii. 1.

Be *opposite* ['antagonistic,' 'contradictious,' 'hostile'] with a kinsman.—*Tw. N.*, ii. 5 (*Letter*).

And his *opposite* [' antagonist,' ' opponent,' ' adversary '], the youth.—*Ibid.*, iii. 2.

The most skilful, bloody, and fatal *opposite* [' adversary '] that you could possibly have found.—*Ibid.*, iii. 4.

In single *opposition* [' contest,' 'combat '].—1 *H. IV.*, i. 3.

More remarkable in single *oppositions* [' encounters,' 'combats'].—*Cym.*, iv. 1.

In our *orbs* [' orbits,' ' spheres '] we 'll live.—*Per.*, i. 2.

Having our fair *order* [' arrangement,' 'compact '] written down.—*John*, v. 2.

To *order* [' arrange,' 'settle, 'establish'] peace between them.—*H. V.*, v. (*Chorus*).

Speak in the *order* [' pre-arranged ceremonial,' ' appointed course '] of his funeral.—*Jul. C.*, iii. 1.

Send fair-play *orders*§ [' arrangements,' 'proposed measures '].—*John*, v. 1.

---

* John of Gaunt was then fifty-eight years of age.

† Henry IV. was then about thirty-six years of age.

‡ Shakespeare, when his Sonnets were first published, was forty-five years of age.

§ Some emendators have proposed to change " orders " to ' offers ' here ; but the other passages we have collectively cited, where " order" and " orders " are used in the sense given, serve to show that probably " orders " was thus used by Shakespeare in this passage also.

Plots, *orders* ['arrangements,' 'proposed measures '], preventions, excitements to the field.—*Tr. & Cr.*, i. 3.

Like some *ore* ['gold,' 'precious metal'] among a mineral of metals base.—*Hamlet*, iv. 1.

This *orient* ['eastern,' and 'bright'] pearl.—*Ant. & C.*, i. 5.

It is marvel he *out-dwells* ['outstays,' 'overpasses'] his hour.—*Mer. of V.*, ii. 6.

Seal up the mouth of *outrage* ['raging out,' 'storming aloud,' 'uproar,' 'clamour,' 'outcry'] for a while.—*R. & Jul.*, v. 3.

Her pretty action did *outsell* ['exceed in value'] her gift.—*Cym.*, ii. 4.

Of all compounded, *outsells* ['outvalues'] them all.—*Ibid.*, iii. 5.

Outwent ['outdid,' 'excelled'] her, motion and breath left out.—*Ibid.*, ii. 4.

Made the *overture* ['opening,' 'disclosure,' 'discovery'] of thy treasons to us.—*Lear*, iii. 7.

The great danger which this man's life did *owe* ['threaten to cause,' 'menace,' 'occasioning,' 'possess for'] you.—*Coriol.*, v. 5.

Targets like the men that *owe* ['own,' 'possess'] them.—*Ant. & C.*, iv. 8.

The jeweller that *owes* ['owns'] the ring is sent for.—*All's W.*, v. 3.

With those infirmities she *owes* ['owns,' 'possesses'].—*Lear*, i. 1.

Hath it been *ow'd* ['owned,' 'possessed'] and worn.—*All's W.*, v. 3.

Never may that state or fortune fall into my keeping, which is not *ow'd* ['held by me as owing or due'] to you!—*Timon*, i. 1.

Who I believe was *pack'd* ['joined as a conspirator,' 'combined as an accomplice'] in all this wrong.—*M. Ado*, v. 1.

Here's *packing* ['conspiring,' 'joining in a plot or scheme'], with a witness, to deceive us all!—*Tam. of S.*, v. 1.

In snuffs and *packings* ['factious conspiracies,' 'private confederacies'] of the dukes. —*Lear*, iii. 1.

But was *paid* ['punished,' 'paid out'] for my learning.—*Merry W.*, iv. 5.

I am *paid* ['punished'] for 't now.—*Ant. & C.*, ii. 5.

Remember he was *paid* ['punished'] for that.—*Cym.*, iv. 2.

Take *pain* ['trouble,' 'care'] to allay with some cold.—*Mer. of V.*, ii. 2.

Hath ta'en much *pain* ['trouble'] in the king's business.—*H. VIII.*, iii. 2.

Your knowledge, your personal *pain* ['trouble'].—*Per.*, iii. 2.

When our deep plots do *pall* ['become spiritless,' 'lifeless,' 'without vigour and vitality'].—*Hamlet*, v. 2.

Where do the *palmers* ['pilgrims'] lodge.—*All's W.*, iii. 5.

Is holy *palmers'* ['pilgrims''] kiss.—*R. & Jul.*, i. 5.

Oh, sir, *pardon* ['excuse'] me!—*Ant. & C.*, iv. 12.

What shall be next, *pardon* ['excuse'] old Gower.—*Per.*, ii. (*Gower*).

A *parish* ['parish full,' 'great number,' 'large amount'] of such Clotens.—*Cym.*, iv. 2.

Since presently your souls must *part* ['part from,' 'depart from'] your bodies.—*R. II.*, iii. 1.

To *part* ['share,' 'divide into just parts'] the glories of this happy day.—*Jul. C.*, v. 5.

Your exultation *partake* ['mutually share,' 'participate,' 'impart'] to every one.—*W. T.*, v. 3.

And our mind *partakes* ['imparts,' 'gives participation of'] her private actions to your secrecy.—*Per.*, i. 1.

For his *particular* ['individual self'], I'll receive him.—*Lear*, ii. 4.

The wittiest *partition* [in the double sense of 'partition wall' and 'sect,' 'propounder of doctrine'] that ever I heard discourse.—*Mid. N. D.*, v. 1.

The *party* ['person,' 'individual'] is gone, fellow Hector.—*Love's L. L.*, v. 2.

Your *party* ['certain person,' 'individual'] in converse.—*Hamlet*, ii. 1.

And being at that *pass* ['point,' 'extremity'] you would.—*Com. of E.*, iii. 1.

And *pass* ['assure,' 'convey'] my daughter a sufficient dower.—*Tam. of S.*, iv. 4.

We 'll *pass* [' transact,' ' accomplish '] the business.—*Tam. of S.*, iv. 4.

Nay, an thou *pass* [' pass your jokes,' ' play jesting tricks '] upon me, I 'll no more with thee.—*Tw. N.*, iii. 1.

As for these silken-coated slaves, I *pass* [' care,' ' heed,' ' regard '] not.—*2 H. VI.*, iv. 2.

Were I alone to *pass* [' pass through,' ' encounter,' ' experience '] the difficulties.—*Tr. & Cr.*, ii. 2.

That I may *pass* [' pass by,' ' omit '] this doing.—*Coriol.*, ii. 3.

We may not *pass* [' pass sentence '] upon his life.—*Lear*, iii. 7.

Thus might he *pass* [' pass away,' ' expire,' ' die '] indeed.—*Ibid.*, iv. 6.

Oh, let him *pass* [' pass away,' ' die ']! he hates him that.—*Ibid.*, v. 3.

As my farthest band shall *pass* [' be staked '] on thy approof.—*Ant. & C.*, iii. 2.

The stirring *passage* [' throng of passers-by '] of the day.—*Com. of E.*, iii. 1.

No watch? no *passage* [' passers-by ']? murder!—*Oth.*, v. 1.

That " had," how sad a *passage* [' indication of what passes '] 'tis!—*All's W.*, i. 1.

In thy *passages* [' evil courses '] of life, make me.—*1 H. IV.*, iii. 2.

So cried and shrieked at it, that it *passed* [' surpassed belief '].—*Merry W.*, i. 1.

This *passes* [' surpasses belief,' ' exceeds credence '].—*Ibid.*, iv. 2.

Hath look'd upon my *passes* [' evil courses,' ' passages of misconduct '].—*M. for M.*, v. 1.

'Tis a *passing* [' exceeding,' ' surpassing '] shame.—*Two G. of V.*, i. 2.

Is she not *passing* [' exceedingly,' ' surpassingly '] fair?—*Ibid.*, iv. 4.

Relish all as sharply, *passion* [' feel emotionally and intensely '] as they.—*Temp.*, v. 1.

This *passion* [' emotional grief,' ' passionate sorrow '], and the death of a dear friend.—*Mid. N. D.*, v. 1.

I feel my master's *passion* [' emotion,' ' passionate indignation '].—*Timon*, iii. 1.

Oh, well-painted *passion* [' distressful emotion ']!—*Oth.*, iv. 1.

This borrow'd *passion* [' distress,' ' grief '] stands for true.—*Per.*, iv. 4 (*Gower*).

Make *passionate* [' full of emotional sadness '] my sense of hearing.—*Love's L. L.*, iii. 1.

She is sad and *passionate* [' overwhelmed by emotional distress '] at your highness' tent.—*John*, ii. 2.

'Twas Ariadne, *passioning* [' lamenting passionately,' ' mourning distressfully '] for Theseus' perjury.—*Two G. of V.*, iv. 4.

Dumbly she *passions* [' mourns,' ' grieves '].—*V. & Adon.*, *Stanza* 177.

Till that his *passions* [' angry emotions '], like a.—*2 H. IV.*, iv. 4.

Had the *passions* [' angry emotions,' ' throes of passion '] of thy heart burst out.—*1 H. VI.*, iv. 1.

Do breed love's settled *passions* [' emotions,' ' passionate feelings '] in my heart.—*Ibid.*, v. 5.

But his *passions* [' emotions,' ' throes of passion '] move me so.—*3 H. VI.*, i. 4.

'Tis *past* [' passed away,' ' transpired,' ' expired,' ' gone '], and so am I.—*Lear*, v. 3.

For if thou *path* [' walk forth,' ' walk abroad '], thy native semblance on.—*Jul. C.*, ii. 1.

They stay upon your *patience* [' sufferance,' ' permission '].—*Hamlet*, iii. 2.

By your gracious *patience* [' permission '] I will.—*Oth.*, i. 3.

Rascal, *peak* [' act sneakingly, pitifully, hesitatingly '], like John-a-dreams.—*Hamlet*, ii. 2.

The *peaking* [' sneaking,' ' pitiful '] cornuto.—*Merry W.*, iii. 5.

A domineering *pedant* [' schoolmaster '] o'er the boy.—*Love's L. L.*, iii. 1.

Mercatante, or a *pedant* [' schoolmaster,' ' preceptor,' ' tutor '].—*Tam. of S.*, iv. 2.

This it is to be a *peevish* [' perverse,' ' wilful,' ' wayward '] girl.—*Two G. of V.*, v. 2.

'Tis but a *peevish* [' wayward,' ' perverse,' and ' silly,' ' insignificant '] boy.—*As You L.*, iii. 5.

That same *peevish* [' wayward,' ' wilful,' ' perverse '] messenger.—*Tw. N.*, i. 5.

When Richmond was a little *peevish* [' silly,' ' foolish,' ' insignificant '] boy.—*R. III.*, iv. 2.

A *peevish* ['foolishly wilful'] schoolboy.—*Jul. C.*, v. 1.

I'll *perfect* ['fully acquaint or inform'] him withal.—*M. for M.*, iv. 3.

Thou art *perfect* ['certain,' 'fully informed,'] then.—*W. T.*, iii. 3.

I am *perfect* ['sure,' 'certain,' 'well informed'] that the Pannonians and Dalmatians.—*Cym.*, iii. 1.

Being once *perfected* ['fully informed or instructed'] how to grant suits.—*Temp.*, i. 2.

Her sweet *perfection** ['perfectioning'; in allusion to the then prevailing and beautiful doctrine that marriage was the perfectioning of a human being].—*Tw. N.*, i. 1.

To die, even when they to *perfection* [used not only in reference to the perfected beauty of the full-blown rose, but also in allusion to the perfected loveliness and excellence of a woman matched with her chosen manly counterpart in married union] grow!—*Ibid.*, ii. 4.

And she a fair divided excellence, whose fulness of *perfection* [used with similar allusion] lies in him.—*John*, ii. 2.

And now newly *performed* ['finished,' 'completed,' 'achieved'] by that rare Italian master.—*W. T.*, v. 2.

Contempt his scornful *perspective* [a glass presenting a distortedly reflected image] did lend me, which warp'd the line of.—*All's W.*, v. 3.

A natural *perspective* [a glass presenting a different object from the one held before it to be reflected therein], that is and is not!—*Tw. N.*, v. 1.

Like *perspectives* [glasses made to present distortedly or undistortedly reflected images according to the position in which these glasses were held], which rightly gaz'd upon, show nothing but confusion.—*R. II.*, ii. 2.

Awake the *pert* ['brisk,' 'alert,' 'lively'] and nimble spirit of mirth.—*Mid. N. D.*, i. 1.

Appear, and *pertly* ['briskly,' 'alertly'].—*Temp.*, iv. 1.

Yond' walls, that *pertly* ['saucily,' 'defiantly'] front your town.—*Tr. & Cr.*, iv. 5.

Peruse ['observe,' 'examine,' 'scan'] the traders.—*Com. of E.*, i. 2.

Peruse ['examine,' 'scan'] them well.—*All's W.*, ii. 3.

I have *perused* ['examined,' 'scanned'] her well—*H. VIII.*, ii. 3.

I have with exact view *perus'd* ['examined'] thee.—*Tr. & Cr.*, iv. 5.

And *pervert* ['divert,' 'turn from its course'] the present wrath he hath against himself.—*Cym.*, ii. 4.

I'll pour this *pestilence* ['poison'] into his ear.—*Oth.*, ii. 3.

The blood I drop is rather *physical* ['wholesome,' 'salutary'].—*Coriol.*, i. 5.

Is it *physical* ['wholesome,' 'salutary'] to walk unbraced.—*Jul. C.*, ii. 1.

I'll *pick* ['pitch,' 'hurl,' 'toss'] you o'er the pales.—*H. VIII.*, v. 3.

High as I could *pick* ['pitch,' 'cast,' 'throw,' 'hurl'] my lance.—*Coriol.*, i. 1.

He is too *picked* ['finical,' 'foppish,' 'over-particular and precise'], too spruce, too affected.—*Love's L. L.*, v. 1.

My *picked* ['foppish,' 'coxcombical,' 'finical'] man of countries.—*John*, i. 1.

The age is grown so *picked* ['over-precise,' 'excessively particular'], that the toe of the peasant comes.—*Hamlet*, v. 1.

Such *picking* ['petty,' 'insignificant'] grievances.—*2 H. IV.*, iv. 1.

By smiling *pick-thanks* ['pickers of occasion to be thanked or rewarded,' 'pickers of opportunity to curry favour'] and base newsmongers.—*1 H. IV.*, iii. 2.

My eyes on thy *picture* ['image'], and my heart.—*Love's L. L.*, iv. 1 (*Letter*).

Going to see the queen's *picture* ['painted statue'].—*W. T.*, v. 2.

With mine own *picture* ['portrait'] on the top of it.—*2 H. IV.*, iv. 3.

His *picture* ['portrait,' 'description'] I will send far and near.—*Lear*, ii. 1.

Hath alter'd that good *picture* ['image']?—*Cym.*, iv. 2.

---

* The Folio adds an "s" to "perfection" in this passage; but the other passages we cite, where Shakespeare uses the word "perfection," appear to us to prove that he also used it in the present passage and in the sense we assign. [*See* 'S' ADDED OR OMITTED IN THE FIRST FOLIO].

Plain words best *pierce* ['penetrate'] the ear.—*Love's L. L.*, v. 2.

The bruised heart was *pierced* ['penetrated,' 'reached,' 'arrived at'] through the ear.—*Oth.*, i. 3.

Tents, thus proudly *pight* ['pitched,' 'fixed,' 'placed'] upon our Phrygian plains.—*Tr. & Cr.*, v. 11.

Found him *pight* ['pitched,' 'fixed,' 'settled,' 'resolved'] to do it.—*Lear*, ii. 1.

Straight-*pight* ['pitched,' 'fixed,' 'poised,' 'placed'] Minerva.—*Cym.*, v. 5.

Two and thirty, a *pip* [a spot or mark on a card, determining its suit and value] out.—*Tam. of S.*, i. 2.

The heart and *place* ['resting-spot,' 'dwelling-place,' 'residence'] of general wonder.—*Per.*, iv. (*Gower*).

Love lack'd a dwelling, and made him her *place* ['resting-place,' 'residence'].—*Lover's Comp.*, Stanza 12.

I 'll *plain* ['make plain or clear,' 'elucidate'] with speech.—*Per.*, iii. (*Gower*).

The king hath cause to *plain* ['complain'].—*Lear*, iii. 1.

Plaining ['complaining'] comes too late.—*R. II.*, 1. 3.

Piteous *plainings* ['complainings,' 'wailings'] of the pretty babes.—*Com. of E.*, i. 1.

Some o' their *plants* ['soles of the feet'] are ill-rooted already.—*Ant. & C.*, ii. 7.

As *plates* ['silver coin or pieces of money'] dropp'd from his pocket.—*Ibid.*, v. 2.

The Romans *plausibly* ['applausively,' 'applaudingly,' 'with acclamation'] did give consent.—*Lucrece*, Stanza 265.

His *plausive* ['worthy of applause, praise, or admiration'] words.—*All's W.*, i. 2.

It must be a very *plausive* ['plausible'] invention.—*Ibid.*, iv. 1.

The form of *plausive* ['worthy of applause,' 'meritorious,' 'attractive'] manners.—*Hamlet*, i. 4.

I am glad your grace is grown so *pleasant* ['facetious,' 'indulging in pleasantry'].—*H. VIII.*, i. 4.

Come, you are *pleasant* ['indulging in pleasantry'].—*Ibid.*, ii. 3.

I will *please* ['give as a gratuity,' 'recompense,' 'pay.' *See* "Gratify" under the present heading] you what you will demand.—*Com. of E.*, iv. 4.

Guarded, to know your *pleasure* ['decision,' 'determination'].—*Hamlet*, iv. 3.

Bring his constant *pleasure* ['decision,' 'determination'].—*Lear*, v. 1.

But this single *plot* [literally 'a piece of ground'; here, figuratively applied to the human body, 'piece of earth.' *See* "Earth" under the present heading] to lose, this mould of Marcius.—*Coriol.*, iii. 2.

Fight for a *plot* ['small piece of ground'] whereon the numbers cannot try the cause.—*Hamlet*, iv. 4.

An argument that he is *pluck'd* ['stripped,' 'deprived of all'], when hither he sends so poor a pinion of his wing.—*Ant. & C.*, iii. 10.

Growing to a *plurisy* ['superabundance,' 'superfluence,' 'plethora'], dies in his own too-much.—*Hamlet*, iv. 7.

Makes his approaches to the *port* ['gate'] of Rome.—*Ant. & C.*, i. 3.

All *ports* ['gates'] I 'll bar.—*Lear*, ii. 1.

The apprehension of his present *portance* ['bearing,' 'carriage'].—*Coriol.*, ii. 3.

And *portance* ['conduct,' 'bearing'] in my travels.—*Oth.*, i. 3.

More than can thy *portage* ['safe conveyance into life'] quit.—*Per.*, iii. 1.

And this the regal seat: *possess* ['take possession of,' 'occupy'] it, York.—*3 H. VI.*, i. 1.

Things rank and gross in nature *possess* ['hold possession of,' 'occupy'] it merely.—*Hamlet*, i. 2.

Be a child o' the time.—*Possess** ['take possession of,' 'occupy'] it, I 'll make answer.—*Ant. & C.*, ii. 7.

---

* Some commentators have supposed "possess" not to be the right word in the present passage; but the mode in which Shakespeare has used it in the two other previously cited passages we think serves to show that "possess" is the word he employed in the present passage also.

Possess ['inform,' 'tell'] the people in Messina.—*M. Ado*, v, 1.

Possess ['inform'] us, *possess* us.—*Tw. N.*, ii. 3.

I have *possess'd* ['informed'] him my most.—*M. for M.*, iv. 1.

He is, sure, *possess'd* ['taken possession of by an evil spirit,' 'insane'], madam.—*Tw. N.*, iii. 4.

How long hath this *possession* ['insanity'] held the man ?—*Com. of E.*, v. 1.

Thou art to *post* ['hasten'] after with oars.—*Two G. of V.*, ii. 3.

Is *posted* ['hastened'], as the agent of our cardinal, to second all his plot.—*H. VIII.*, iii. 2.

His guilt should be but idly *posted* over ['put aside,' 'put by,' 'let pass unpunished'] because his purpose.—*2 H. VI.*, iii. 1.

Nor *posted* off ['put off,' 'postponed,' 'deferred'] their suits with slow delays.—*3 H. VI.*, iv. 8.

And *posts* ['hastens'] like the commandment of a king.—*Tr. & Cr.*, i. 3.

The *posts* ['messengers who travel post-haste and bring news, letters, or dispatches'] come tiring on.—*2 H. IV. (Induc.)*

I have foundered nine-score and odd *posts* ['post-horses'].—*Ibid.*, iv. 3.

The *posture* of ['mode of placing or giving'] your blows are yet unknown.—*Jul. C.*, v. 1.

Of the duke and her is *practice* ['artifice,' 'designing scheme'] only.—*Lear*, ii. 4.

This is *practice* ['machination,' 'artful device'], Gloster.—*Ibid.*, v. 3.

Fall'n in the *practice* ['snare,' 'machination'] of a cursed slave.—*Oth.*, v. 2.

Sworn unto the *practices* ['treacherous schemes,' 'plots,' 'devices'] of France.—*H. V.*, ii. 2.

My *practices* ['devices,' 'stratagems'] ride easy !—*Lear*, i. 2.

Will so *practise* ['plot,' 'act contrivingly and schemingly'] on Benedick, that.—*M. Ado*, ii. 1.

He will *practise* ['plot,' 'scheme,' 'treacherously contrive'] against thee by poison.—*As You L.*, i. 1.

Have *practis'd* ['conspired,' 'plotted'] dangerously against your state.—*2 H. VI.*, ii. 1.

How intend you, *practis'd* ['acted on behalf of' or 'treacherously plotted'] ?—*Ant. & C.*, ii. 2.

Return the *precedent* ['original copy,' 'rough draught'] to these lords again.—*John*, v. 2.

The *precedent* ['original draught'] was full as long a-doing.—*R. III.*, iii. 6.

His sweating palm, the *precedent* ['indication,' 'prognostic,' 'augury'] of pith and livelihood.—*V. & Adon., Stanza 5.*

Those *precepts* ['warrants'] cannot be served.—*2 H. IV.*, v. 1.

As send *precepts* ['warrants'] to the Leviathan.—*H. V.*, iii. 3.

If Messala will *prefer* ['recommend,' 'present for acceptance'] me to you.—*Jul. C.*, v. 5.

Should not sooner than thine own worth *prefer* ['recommend'] thee.—*Cym.*, iv. 2.

I shall then have to *prefer* ['promote,' 'advance'] them.—*Oth.*, ii. 1.

Ere I arise, I will *prefer* ['advance,' 'promote'] my sons.—*Cym.*, v. 5.

Our play is *preferred* ['proffered,' 'proposed,' 'presented for acceptance'].—*Mid. N. D.*, iv. 2.

He is *preferr'd* ['recommended'] by thee to us.—*Cym.*, iv. 2.

Pregnancy ['intellectual capacity,' 'fertility of thought'] is made a tapster, and hath his quick wit.—*2 H. IV.*, i. 2.

You're as *pregnant* ['skilled,' 'proficient,' 'fully instructed'] in as art.—*M. for M.*, i. 1.

'Tis very *pregnant* ['full of self-evident fact'] the jewel.—*Ibid.*, ii. 1.

To your own most *pregnant* ['ready,' 'prompt to listen and apprehend'] and vouchsafed ear.—*Tw. N.*, iii. 1.

If ever truth were *pregnant* ['full of self-evident fact'] by circumstance.—*W. T.*, v. 2.

The Grecians are most prompt and *pregnant* ['ready,' 'aptly disposed'].—*Tr. & Cr.*, iv. 4.

How *pregnant* ['full of apt meaning'] sometimes his replies are!—*Hamlet*, ii. 2.

Crook the *pregnant* ['quick,' 'ready,' 'prompt'] hinges of the knee.—*Ibid.*, iii. 1.

As it is a most *pregnant* ['full of plausibility'] and unforced position.—*Oth.*, ii. 1.

'Twere *pregnant* ['full of probability'] they should square between themselves.—*Ant. & C.*, ii. 1.

Hath the *pregnant* ['apt,' 'prompt'] instrument of wrath.—*Per.*, iv. (*Gower*).

Preposterous ['out of due order,' 'misplacing and misplaced'] ass, that never read so far.—*Tam of S.*, iii. 1.

In so *preposterous* ['out of the usual course': though the Clown probably intends it for 'prosperous'] estate as we are.—*W. T.*, v. 2.

That befall *preposterously* ['contrary to due course,' 'perversely'].—*Mid. N. D.*, iii. 2.

The *presence* ['presence-chamber'] strew'd.—*R. II.*, i. 3.

Cardinals wait in the *presence* ['presence-chamber'].—*H. VIII.*, iii. 1.

A feasting *presence* ['presence-chamber'] full of light.—*R. & Jul.*, v. 3.

Work the peace of the *present* ['present time'].—*Temp.*, i. 1.

Even at this *present* ['present time'].—*W. T.*, i. 2.

To sit here at this *present* ['present time'].—*H. VIII.*, v. 2.

No farther than this *present* ['present time']?—*Coriol.*, iii. 3.

Beyond this ignorant *present** ['present time'].—*Macb.*, i. 5.

I'll make division of my *present* ['present store,' 'sum of money that I have at present'] with you.—*Tw. N.*, iii. 4.

This is from the *present* ['present consideration or point of discussion'].—*Ant. & C.*, ii. 6.

But his *present* ['that which he presents'] is a wither'd branch.—*Per.*, ii. 2.

What *present* ['presented letter'] hast thou there?—*Love's L. L.*, iv. 3.

By these *presents* ['presented bills'].—*As You L.*, i. 2.

When I *presented* ['represented,' 'enacted'] Ceres.—*Temp.*, iv. 1.

Great Hercules is *presented* ['represented'] by this imp.—*Love's L. L.*, v. 2.

Presently ['at present,' 'immediately']? Ay, with a twink.—*Temp.*, iv. 1.

I will seek him, sir, *presently* ['immediately'].—*Lear*, i. 2.

Would shake the *press* ['crowd,' 'throng'].—*H. VIII.*, iv. 1.

Break among the *press* ['crowd'], and find.—*Ibid.*, v. 3.

Who is it in the *press* ['crowd'] that calls.—*Jul. C.*, i. 2.

I have misused the king's *press* ['impress,' 'commission to forcibly enlist'] damnably.—*1 H. IV.*, iv. 2.

I *press* ['impress,' 'enlist'] me none but.—*Ibid.*, iv. 2.

The gibbets, and *pressed* ['impressed,' 'enlisted'] the dead bodies.—*Ibid.*, iv. 2.

And I am *prest* ['ready,' 'prompt,' 'disposed'] unto it.—*Mer. of V.*, i. 1.

Prest ['ready'] for this blow.—*Per.*, iv. (*Gower*).

Publisher of this *pretence* ['intention,' 'purpose,' 'design'].—*Two G. of V.*, iii. 1.

The *pretence* ['intention,' 'purpose,' 'design'] whereof being by circumstances.—*W. T.*, iii. 2 (*Indictment*).

Against the undivulg'd *pretence* ['intention'] I fight.—*Macb.*, ii. 3.

And to no other *pretence* ['design'] of danger.—*Lear*, i. 2.

To keep your great *pretences* ['intentions,' 'designs'] veil'd.—*Coriol.*, i. 2.

Their disguising, and *pretended* ['intended'] flight.—*Two G. of V.*, ii. 6.

Such black payment as thou hast *pretended* ['intended'].—*Lucrece, Stanza* 83.

---

* In this passage Pope proposed to add the word 'time' after "present"; but the four passages we have precedingly cited show that Shakespeare several times uses "present" for 'present time.'

It is a *pretty* ['apt,' 'appropriate,' 'felicitous'] mocking of the life.—*Timon*, i. 1.

But had most *pretty* ['apt,' 'appropriate'] things to say.—*Cym.*, i. 4.

Tread a course *pretty* ['felicitous,' 'fair,' 'prosperous,' 'propitious'], and full of view.—*Ibid.*, iii. 4.

A *pretty* ['apt,' 'felicitous'] moral.—*Per.*, ii. 1.

Both the degrees *prevent* ['anticipate'] my curses.—*2 H. IV.*, i. 2.

So to *prevent* ['anticipate'] the time of life.—*Jul. C.*, v. 1.

But we are *prevented* ['anticipated'].—*Tw. N.*, iii. 1.

That happiness and *prime* ['the spring of youth'] can happy call.—*All's W.*, ii. 1.

Were they as *prime* ['forward,' 'eager,' 'wantonly disposed'] as goats.—*Oth.*, iii. 3.

Prospero the *prime* ['first,' 'principal,' 'chief'] duke, being so reputed in dignity.—*Temp.*, i. 2.

My *prime* ['first,' 'principal,' 'chief'] request which I do last pronounce.—*Ibid.*, i. 2.

For there is no *primer* ['more first in importance,' 'more early urgent,' 'chiefer'] business.—*H. VIII.*, i. 2.

A violet in the youth of *primy* ['early,' 'spring-like'] nature.—*Hamlet*, i. 3.

The very *principals* ['strongest rafters of a building'] did seem to rend.—*Per.*, iii. 2.

It is war's *prize* ['privilege'] to take all vantages—*3 H. VI.*, i. 4.

'Tis *prize* ['privilege'] enough to be his son.—*Ibid.*, ii. 1.

Then had my *prize* ['value'] been less.—*Cym.*, iii. 6.

What *profane* ['gross-spoken,' 'coarse-languaged,' 'impure,' 'unhallowed'] wretch art thou?—*Oth.*, i. 1.

Is he not a most *profane* ['infamous,' 'unhallowed'] and liberal counsellor?—*Ibid.*, ii. 1.

The mourning brow of *progeny* ['offspring'] forbid.—*Love's L. L.*, v. 2.

And this same *progeny* ['offspring,' 'race'] of evils.—*Mid. N. D.*, ii. 2.

Doubting thy birth and lawful *progeny* ['race,' 'descent'].—*1 H. VI.*, iii. 3.

Issu'd from the *progeny* ['race,' 'descent'] of kings.—*Ibid.*, v. 4.

The whip of your bragg'd *progeny* ['progenitors'].—*Coriol.*, i. 8.

I cannot *project* ['put forth,' 'set forth,' 'make out a statement of'] mine own cause so well.—*Ant. & C.*, v. 2.

There is a *prone* ['deferential,' 'submissive,' 'supplicatory'] and speechless dialect. —*M. for M.*, i. 3.

I am not *prone* ['given,' 'addicted,' 'readily disposed'] to weeping.—*W. T.*, ii. 1.

As *prone* ['inclined,' 'disposed,' 'readily given'] to mischief.—*H. VIII.*, i. 1.

I never saw one so *prone* ['prompt,' 'ready,' 'willing,' 'alertly disposed'].—*Cym.*, v. 4.

To *propagate* ['promote the advantage of'] their states.—*Timon*, i. 1.

Only for *propagation* ['promoting the bestowal or payment of'] a dower remaining in the coffer of.—*M. for M.*, i. 3.

Imagination, *proper* ['pertaining,' 'appropriate'] to madmen.—*2 H. IV.*, i. 3.

Do justice on my *proper* ['own'] son.—*Ibid.*, v. 2.

Though our *proper* ['own'] son stood in your action.—*Oth.*, i. 3.

For he is a *proper* ['comely,' 'finely proportioned,' 'well-made'] man.—*Two G. of V.*, iv. 1.

This Lodovico is a *proper* ['comely,' 'good-looking'] man.—*Oth.*, iv. 3.

Though I owe my revenge *properly* ['personally,' 'as regards myself'], my remission lies.—*Coriol.*, v. 2.

They have here *propertied* ['made a property of,' 'taken possession of'] me.—*Tw. N.*, iv. 2.

I am too high-born to be *propertied* ['made a property of,' 'controlled,' 'held in subjection'].—*John*, v. 2.

Subdues and *properties* ['makes his property,' 'appropriates,' 'subjects'] to his love. —*Timon*, i. 1.

The *property* ['intrinsic quality,' 'that which is inherent in,' 'properly belonging to'] by what it is should go, not by the title.—*All's W.*, ii. 3.

Custom hath made it in him a *property* ['quality,' 'habit,' 'adopted calling or avocation'] of easiness.—*Hamlet*, v. 1.

That great *property* ['propriety,' 'beseeming quality'] which still should go with Antony.—*Ant. & C.*, i. 1.

But thou, 'gainst all *proportion* ['relative fitness,' 'proportionate likelihood'], didst bring in wonder to wait on.—*H. V.*, ii. 2.

And *propose* ['imagine to yourself'] a son.—2 *H. IV.*, v. 2.

The toged consuls can *propose* ['discourse,' 'hold forth'] as learnedly as he.—*Oth.*, i. 1.

To listen our *propose* ['conversation': French, *propos*].—*M. Ado*, iii. 1.

Beatrice *proposing* ['conversing,' 'discoursing'] with the prince.—*Ibid.*, iii. 1.

That sleep and feeding may *prorogue* ['linger on,' 'weary out,' 'gradually lull and subdue'] his honour.—*Ant. & C.*, ii. 1.

But to *prorogue* ['linger out the period of,' 'protract the wearisome duration of'] his grief.—*Per.*, v. 1.

And nothing may *prorogue* ['defer'] it.—*R. & Jul.*, iv. 1.

Than death *prorogued* ['deferred,' postponed,' 'delayed'].—*Ibid.*, ii. 2.

Lend your *prosperous* ['propitious,' 'favourable'] ear.—*Oth.*, i. 3.

Provokes ['urges,' 'impels'] the mightiest hulk.—1 *H. VI.*, v. 5.

Our gentle flame *provokes* ['evokes,' 'calls forth,' 'elicits'] itself, and, like the current, flies each bound it chafes.—*Timon*, i. 1.

Sleep, and that thou oft *provok'st* ['invokest,' 'callest forth,' 'encouragest'].—*M. for M.*, iii. 1.

Thou shalt have a share in our *purchase* ['booty,' 'stolen goods'].—1 *H. IV.*, ii. 1.

The *purchase* ['advantage,' 'gain,' profit'] is to make men glorious.—*Per.* i. (*Gower*).

I sought the *purchase* ['achievement,' 'acquisition'] of a glorious beauty.—*Ibid.*, i. 2.

For what in me was *purchas'd* ['purloined,' 'obtained by indirect means'], falls upon thee in a.—2 *H. IV.*, iv. 4.

Hereditary, rather than *purchas'd* ['acquired,' 'voluntarily procured'].—*Ant. & C.*, i. 4.

The *purple* ['encrimsoned'] testament of bleeding war.—*R. II.*, iii. 3.

With *purple* ['encrimsoned'] faulchion, painted.—3 *H. VI.*, i. 4.

With *purple* ['dark red,' 'crimson'] fountains issuing from your veins.—*R. & Jul.*, i. 1.

All with *purpled* ['encrimsoned'] hands dy'd in.—*John*, ii. 2.

Whilst your *purpled* ['encrimsoned'] hands do reek.—*Jul. C.*, iii. 1.

To be his *purveyor* ['precursor']: but he rides well.—*Macb.*, i. 6.

Lest they desire, upon this *push* ['emergency,' 'special occasion'], to trouble your joys.—*W. T.*, v. 3.

This *push* ['emergency,' 'exigence,'] will cheer me ever.—*Macb.*, v. 3.

We 'll put the matter to the present *push* ['test,' 'trial'].—*Hamlet*, v. 1.

And made a *push* ['pish,' 'pshaw'] at chance and sufferance—*M. Ado*, v. 1.

Push ['pish']! did you see my cap?—*Timon*, iii. 6.

My *quaint* ['ingenious,' 'dexterous,' and 'gracefully fantastic'] Ariel, hark in thine ear.—*Temp.*, i. 2.

For a fine, *quaint* ['tasteful,' 'well-fancied'], graceful, and excellent fashion.—*M. Ado*, iii. 4.

And wonders at our *quaint* ['delicately graceful,' 'prettily fantastic'] spirits.—*Mid. N. D.*, ii. 3.

Tell *quaint* ['ingenious,' 'cleverly fantastic'] lies, how honourable ladies sought my love.—*Mer. of V.*, iii. 4.

The lines are very *quaintly* ['ingeniously,' 'cleverly,' 'dexterously'] writ.—*Two G. of V.*, ii. 1.

A ladder, *quaintly* ['cleverly,' 'deftly,' 'dexterously.'] made of cords.—*Two G. of V.*, iii. 1.

Unless it may be *quaintly* ['tastefully,' 'gracefully,' 'with elegant appropriateness,' 'ingeniously'] ordered.—*Mer. of V.*, ii. 4.

Breathe his faults so *quaintly* ['dexterously,' 'adroitly'], that they may seem.—*Hamlet*, ii. 1.

With your fine fancies *quaintly* ['ingeniously,' 'skilfully'] eche.—*Per.*, iii. (*Gower*).

Whose *qualification* ['allayed anger,' 'appeasement'] shall come into no true taste again but by.—*Oth.*, ii. 1.

Rests by you only to be *qualified* ['allayed,' 'appeased'].—*John*, v. 1.

Till some little time hath *qualified* ['allayed,' 'appeased'] the heat of his displeasure.—*Lear*, i. 2.

Craftily *qualified* ['allayed,' 'weakened' with water] too.—*Oth.*, ii. 3.

Strive to *qualify* ['pacify'], and bring him.—*W. T.*, iv. 3.

Because you are not of our *quality* ['sort,' 'kind,' 'way of thinking,' 'mode of opinion'].—1 *H. IV.*, iv. 3.

Even to the very *quality* ['individual nature,' 'moral and mental identity'] of my lord.—*Oth.*, i. 3.

Task Ariel, and all his *quality* ['qualification,' 'gift'].—*Temp.*, i. 2.

What *quality* ['calling,' 'avocation,' 'profession'] are they of?—*M. for M.*, ii. 1.

Will they pursue the *quality* ['profession of actor'] no longer than they can sing?—*Hamlet*, ii. 2.

Give us a taste of your *quality* ['theatrical powers,' 'professional ability'].—*Ibid.*, ii. 2.

Yet, if that *quarrel* ['square-headed arrow'], fortune, do divorce it from the bearer.—*H. VIII.*, ii. 3.

I'd make a *quarry* ['heap of slaughtered game' and 'the portion of it given to the hounds,' 'offal,' 'carrion'] with thousands of these quarter'd slaves.—*Coriol.*, i. 1.

On his damned *quarry* ['heap of slaughtered creatures,' 'heap of carrion'] smiling.—*Macb.*, i. 2.

On the *quarry* ['slaughtered heap'] of these murder'd deer.—*Ibid.*, iv. 3.

This *quarry* ['heap of dead creatures'] cries on havoc.—*Hamlet*, v. 2.

Not a man shall pass his *quarter* ['military station,' 'post'], or offend.—*Timon*, v. 5.

In *quarter* ['military station,' 'post'], and in terms.—*Oth.*, ii. 3.

Quail, crush, conclude and *quell* ['destroy,' 'kill']!—*Mid. N. D.*, v. 1.

The guilt of our great *quell* ['murder,' 'assassination']?—*Macb.*, i. 7.

She will not *quench* ['abate her warmth,' 'grow cool']—and let instructions enter where.—*Cym.*, i. 6.

Or cease your *quest* ['seeking,' 'pursuit,' 'suit'] of love?—*Lear*, i. 1.

Expense can stead the *quest* ['search'].—*Per.*, iii. (*Gower*).

These false and most contrarious quests ['spyings,' 'inquisitions'] upon thy doings!—*M. for M.*, iv. 1.

Three several *quests* ['seekers'] to search you out.—*Oth.*, i. 2.

When the bravest *questant* ['seeker,' 'aspirant'] shrinks.—*All's W.*, ii. 1.

Hot *questrists* ['seekers'] after him.—*Lear*, iii. 7.

Hermia, *question* ['inquire into,' 'examine'] your desires.—*Mid. N. D.*, i. 1.

And *question* ['inquire into,' 'examine into'] this most bloody piece of work—*Macb.*, ii. 3.

With more facile *question* ['dispute,' 'contest'] bear it.—*Oth.*, i. 3.

The *question* ['statement of the reasons,' 'debated argument'] of his death is enrolled in the Capitol.—*Jul. C.*, iii. 2.

Might be my *question* ['subject of discourse,' 'theme of animadversion'].—*Ant. & C.*, ii. 2.

And had much *question* ['conversation,' 'discourse,' 'debate'] with him.—*As You L.*, iii. 4.

Thou com'st in such a *questionable* ['conversable,' 'inviting question'] shape, that I will speak to thee.—*Hamlet*, i. 4.

How *quick* ['lively,' 'vital'] and fresh art thou!—*Tw. N.*, i. 1.

The mercy that was *quick* ['alive,' 'living'] in us but late.—*H. V.*, ii. 2.

The *quick* ['lively,' 'quick-witted'] comedians.—*Ant. & C.*, v. 2.

Quicken ['revive,' 'live again'] with kissing.—*Ibid.*, iv. 13.

Is fated to us when we do *quicken* ['begin to live'].—*Oth.*, iii. 3.

Some *quillets* ['sophistical quibbles'] how to cheat the devil.—*Love's L. L.*, iv. 3.

His *quillets* ['legal sophistries'], his cases.—*Hamlet*, v. 1.

Like doth *quit* ['requite'] like.—*M. for M.*, v. 1.

I *quit* ['acquit'] them all.—*Ibid.*, v. 1.

To *quit* ['procure requital or redress'] me of them throughly.—*M. Ado*, iv. 1.

To *quit* ['acquit,' 'remit'] the fine for one half.—*Mer of V.*, iv. 1.

Till thou canst *quit* ['acquit'] thee by thy brother's mouth.—*As You L.*, iii. 1.

Here I *quit* ['acquit'] him.—*All's W.*, v. 3.

To *quit* ['requite,' 'render an equivalent for'] their grief.—*R. II.*, v. 1.

I would I could *quit* ['acquit myself of,' 'disculpate myself from'] all offences with as clear excuse.—1 *H. IV.*, iii. 2.

And I sall *quit* ['retaliate,' 'make reprisals,' 'reply.' 'answer you with arguments in return'] you with gud leve, as I may pick occasion.—*H. V.*, iii. 2.

So we were *quit* ['free from,' 'away from'] here.—*Ibid.*, iv. 1.

God safely *quit* ['free,' 'rid,' 'deliver'] her of her burden.—*H. VIII.*, v. 1.

To *quit* ['give retaliation or reprisal'] him with this arm.—*Hamlet*, v. 2.

Draw: seem to defend yourself: now *quit* ['acquit'] you well.—*Lear*, ii. 1.

To *quit* ['requite,' 'redress'] this horrid act.—*Ibid.*, iii. 7.

And say, "God *quit* ['requite,' 'reward'] you!"—*Ant. & C.*, iii. 11.

As he shall like, to *quit* ['requite,' 'retaliate upon'] me.—*Ibid.*, iii. 11.

More than can thy portage *quit* ['requite,' 'compensate for'].—*Per.*, iii. 1.

There was a little *quiver* ['nimble,' 'active,' 'quick'] fellow.—2 *H. IV.*, iii. 2.

 And how *quote* ['note,' 'remark,' 'observe'] you my folly?—
 I *quote* it in your jerkin.—*Two G. of V.*, ii. 4.

He's *quoted* ['noted,' 'observed,' 'remarked'] for a most perfidious slave.—*All's W.*, v. 3.

Mark'd, *quoted* ['noted,' 'observed'], and sign'd.—*John*, iv. 2.

And *quoted* ['noted,' 'observed,' 'examined'] joint by joint.—*Tr. & Cr.*, iv. 5.

A *race* ['root,' or 'spray-formed piece': Spanish, *raiz* or *rayz*, 'root'] or two of ginger.—*W. T.*, iv. 2.

Leave not a *rack* ['light scudding cloud of the upper region'] behind.—*Temp.*, iv. 1.

The *rack* ['train of thin vaporous cloud in upper air'] stand still.—*Hamlet*, ii. 2.

The *rack* ['vaporous scud of upper air'] dislimns.—*Ant. & C.*, iv. 12.

And *rack* ['torture into semblance of evil,' 'stretch into enormity'] thee in their fancies!—*M. for M.*, iv. 1.

Then we *rack* ['exaggerate,' 'overstrain,' 'stretch to the utmost'] the value.—*M. Ado*, iv. 1.

That shall be *rack'd* ['stretched,' 'strained,'] even to the uttermost.—*Mer. of V.*, i. 1.

That have *rack'd* ['strained every nerve,' 'stretched authority to the utmost'] for Rome.—*Coriol.*, v. 1.

Not separated with the *racking* ['train of scudding vapoury'] clouds.—3 *H. VI.*, ii. 1.

The wide arch of the *rang'd* ['well-ordered,' 'well-arranged'] empire fall!—*Ant. & C.*, i. 1.

Which yet distinctly *ranges* ['stands in goodly order'], in heaps and piles of ruin.—*Coriol*, iii. 1.

If I keep not my *rank* [' rate of talking,' ' way of following up one joke with another ']. —*As You L.*, i. 2.

The right butter-woman's *rank* ['rate of going in single file on horseback'] to market.—*Ibid.*, iii. 2.

Though it be as *rank* [' foul-scented '] as a fox.—*Tw. N.*, ii. 5.

Deserves a name as *rank* [' gross,' ' coarse '] as any flax-wench.— *W. T.*, i. 2.

How *rank* [' high-grownly,' ' exuberantly,' 'excessively'] soever rounded in with danger.—*Tr. & Cr.*, i. 3.

In *rank* [' high-grown,' ' rampant '] Achilles must.—*Ibid.*, i. 3.

Is *rank'd* [' occupied by ranks of men '] with all deserts.—*Timon*, i. 1.

I will physic your *rankness* ['high-grown insolence '].—*As You L.*, i. 1.

Leaving our *rankness* [' excess,' ' over-fulness,' ' exuberance '] and irregular course.— *John*, v. 4.

What, dear sir, thus *raps* you ['transports you,' ' carries you away,' ' seizes your imagination '] ? Are you well?—*Cym.*, i. 7.

That he seems *rapt* ['transported,' ' in a state of mental abstraction'] withal.— *Macb.*, i. 3.

Look how our partner's *rapt* ['involved in abstraction,' ' carried away into a fit of thought '].—*Ibid.*, i. 3.

Into a *rapture* [' fit;' ' ecstasy or transport of weeping'] lets her baby cry.— *Coriol.*, ii. 1.

Spite of all the *rapture* [' seizure,' ' violent snatching away '] of the sea.—*Per.*, ii. 1.

And a most *rare* ['choice,' ' admirable'] speaker.—*H. VIII.*, i. 2.

How *rarely* [' choicely,' ' admirably'] does it meet with this time's guise.—*Timon*, iv. 3.

Did dream the boar did *rase* ['tear or strike off as by tusks'] his helm.—*R. III.*, iii. 4.

The boar had *rased* [' torn or struck as by tusks '] off.—*Ibid.*, iii. 2.

Sorrow were ever *ras'd* [' erased,' ' effaced '].—*Per.*, i. 1.

That with no rash [' hasty,' ' speedy '] potion.—*W. T.*, i. 2.

Jesters and *rash* [' speedily burnt out or exhausted '] bavin wits.—1 *H. IV.*, iii. 2.

One of them *rates* [' equals in value'] all.—*Ant. & C.*, iii. 9.

God make incision in thee! Thou art *raw* [used in the double sense of ' sore ' and ' ignorant,' ' inexperienced,' ' immature,' ' green '].—*As You L.*, iii. 2.

And yet but *raw* [' ignorant,' ' inexpert,' ' inefficient,' 'inadequate'] neither, in respect of his quick sail.—*Hamlet*, v. 2.

In our more *rawer* [' inexperienced,' ' inexpert,' ' inefficient'] breath ?—*Ibid.*, v. 2.

Upon their children *rawly* [' rashly ' and ' unprovidedly,' ' in immature age '] left.— *H. V.*, iv. 1.

Why in that *rawness* [' rashness,' ' want of mature consideration ' and ' unprovided-ness '] left you wife and child.—*Macb.*, iv. 3.

Roses on my *razed* [' cut,' ' slashed ': French, *rasé*] shoes.—*Hamlet*, iii. 2.

And two *razes* [' pieces,' ' packets.' *See* " Race " under the present heading: probably the terms, originally derived from the same source, came to be applied to ginger in the piece, or in the packet] of ginger.—1 *H. IV.*, ii. 1.

Therein should we *read* [' peruse exhaustively,' ' possess ourselves entirely of'] the very bottom and the soul of hope.—*Ibid.*, iv. 1.

And recks not his own *read* [' monition,' ' precept,' ' lesson '].—*Hamlet*, i. 3.

Is she *ready* [' dressed.' *See* " Unready" under the present heading] ?—*Cym.*, ii. 3.

Hear him but *reason* [' discourse '] in divinity.—*H. V.*, i. 1.

No, we'll *reason* [' talk,' ' parley'] with him.—*R. III.*, i. 4.

But *reason* [' talk,' ' parley '] with the fellow.—*Coriol.*, iv. 6.

And *reason* [' discretion,' ' propriety of language'] to my love is liable.—*Jul. C.*, ii. 2.

I *reason'd* [' conversed,' ' discoursed '] with a Frenchman.—*Mer. of V.*, ii. 8.

Why is this *reason'd* [' discussed '] ?—*Lear*, v. 1.

What are you *reasoning* [' talking,' ' discussing'] with yourself ?—*Two G. of V.*, ii. 1.

But doth *rebate* ['beat back,' 'repress,' 'subdue,' 'dull,' 'render obtuse'] and blunt his natural edge.—*M. for M.*, i. 5.

His present *reconciliation* ['atonement,' 'submission,' 'act of conciliation'] take.—*Oth.*, iii. 3.

Ere I could *recover* ['attain,' 'reach to'] the shore.—*Temp.*, iii. 2.

If I cannot *recover* ['attain,' 'obtain'] your niece.—*Tw. N.*, ii. 3.

Gives his potent *regiment* ['rule,' 'power,' 'command,' 'authority,' 'government'] to a trull.—*Ant. & C.*, iii. 6.

I'll have grounds more *relative* ['pertinent,' 'nearly concerning,' 'closely connected'] than this.—*Hamlet*, ii. 2.

But we shall *relish* ['have some remaining taint'] of it.—*Ibid.*, iii. 1.

That never *relish'd* ['had any taint'] of a base descent.—*Per.*, ii. 5.

Although this lord of weak *remembrance* ['memory'].—*Temp.*, ii. 1.

With this *remembrance* ['reminder,' 'admonition'].—*2 H. IV.*, v. 2.

Make rash *remonstrance* ['re-showing,' 're-demonstration'] of my hidden power.—*M. for M.*, v. 1.

Touch'd with that *remorse* ['pity,' 'compassion'].—*Ibid.*, ii. 2.

Show thy mercy and *remorse* ['pity,' 'compassion'], more strange.—*Mer. of V.*, iv. 1.

Wise, *remorseful* ['compassionate,' 'tender-hearted'].—*Two G. of V.*, iv. 3.

All thy safety were *remotion* ['removing to a distance'].—*Timon*, iv. 3.

This *remotion* ['removal,' 'moving away'] of the duke.—*Lear*, ii. 4.

Lov'd the life *remov'd* ['secluded,' 'retired'].—*M. for M.*, i. 4.

So *removed* ['sequestered,' 'retired,' 'remote from other habitations'] a dwelling.—*As You L.*, iii. 2.

And he did *render* ['describe,' 'declare'] him the most unnatural.—*Ibid.*, iv. 3.

Make their sorrow'd *render* ['declaration,' 'avowal'].—*Timon*, v. 2.

Repair ['revive,' 'renovate'] me with thy presence.—*Two G. of V.*, v. 4.

It much *repairs* ['revives,' 'renovates'] me to talk of.—*All's W.*, i. 2.

A cause for thy *repeal* ['recall from exile'], we.—*Coriol.*, iv. 1.

Repeal ['recall'] thee home again.—*Two G. of V.*, v. 4.

That she *repeals* ['causes to be recalled'] him for.—*Oth.*, ii. 3.

The first view shall kill all *repetition* ['recrimination'].—*All's W.*, v. 3.

To these ill-tuned *repetitions* ['recriminations'].—*John*, ii. 1.

The most *replenish'd* ['consummate,' 'plenarily qualified'] villain.—*W. T.*, ii. 1.

The most *replenished* ['consummate'] sweet work.—*R. III.*, iv. 3.

In the *reproof* ['disproof,' 'confutation,' 'refutation'] of this.—*1 H. IV.*, i. 2.

In *reproof* ['disproof,' 'refutation'] of many tales.—*Ibid.*, iii. 2.

'Tis so, I cannot *reprove* ['disprove,' 'refute,' 'disallow'] it.—*M. Ado*, ii. 3.

Reprove ['disprove,' 'refute'] my allegation, if you can.—*2 H. VI.*, iii. 1.

How will the world *repute* ['consider,' 'deem,' 'account'] me.—*Two G. of V.*, ii. 7.

All in England did *repute* ['consider'] him dead.—*1 H. IV.*, v. 1.

Do *repute* ['consider'] his grace the rightful heir.—*2 H. VI.*, v. 1.

Yet, by *reputing* ['spreading the reputation,' 'boasting'] of his high descent.—*Ibid.*, iii. 1.

Reserve ['preserve,' 'keep carefully,' 'guard from injury'] that excellent complexion.—*Per.*, iv. 1.

Reserve ['preserve'] them for my love.—*Sonnet 32*.

Reserve ['preserve'] their character with golden quill.—*Ibid.*, 85.

To be in a due *resolution* ['conviction,' 'assurance'].—*Lear*, i. 2.

To *resolve* me ['satisfy my mind,' 'decide my case'] now.—*3 H. VI.*, iii. 2.

Resolve ['satisfy,' 'inform'] your angry father.—*Per.*, ii. 5.

We would be *resolv'd* ['satisfied,' 'assured'], before we hear.—*H. V.*, i. 2.

To be *resolv'd* ['assured'] if Brutus so unkindly.—*Jul. C.*, iii. 2.

As a form of wax *resolveth* ['dissolveth'] from.—*John*, v. 4.

You in my *respect* ['regard,' 'consideration'] are all the world.—*Mid. N. D.*, ii. 2.

Humour than advis'd *respect* ['consideration,' 'motive'].—*John*, iv. 2.

And this *respect* ['consideration,' 'motive'] beside.—*Ibid.*, v. 4.

You are very *respectively* ['regardfully,' 'with much consideration'] welcome.—*Timon*, iii. 1.

For my *respects* ['motives,' 'originating causes of action'] are better than they seem.—*All's W.*, ii. 5.

The *respects* ['motives,' 'grounds of action,' 'considerations that prompt procedure'] thereof are nice.—*R. III.*, iii. 7.

When it is mingled with *respects* ['scrupulous considerations,' 'over-prudential regardfulnesses'].—*Lear*, i. 1.

From the *restful* ['peaceful,' 'quiet'] English court.—*R. II.*, iv. 1.

When *resty* ['inert,' 'sluggish,' 'idle,' 'too full of rest'] sloth finds the down pillow hard.—*Cym.*, iii. 6.

Rise, *resty* ['inert,' 'too long resting'] muse.—*Sonnet* 100.

Nor *resumes* no care ['takes no recapitulatory care,' 'takes no summing-up care'] of what is to continue.—*Timon*, ii. 2.

To whom I will *retail* ['recount,' 'relate'] my conquest won.—*R. III.*, iv. 4.

As 'twere *retail'd* ['related,' 'retold,' 'recounted'] to all posterity.—*Ibid.*, iii. 1.

The king is merciful, if you *revolt* ['turn back,' 'return': Italian, *revoltare*].—2 *H. VI.*, iv. 2.

The red plague *rid* ['destroy'] you, for.—*Temp.*, i. 2.

And will *rid* ['destroy'] his foe.—*R. II.*, v. 4.

You have *rid* ['destroyed'] this sweet young prince!—3 *H. VI.*, v. 5.

Willingness *rids* ['gets rid of,' 'consumes'] way.—*Ibid.*, v. 3.

It is the *right* ['true,' 'exact,' 'precise'] butter-women's rank.—*As You L.*, iii. 2.

I answer you *right* ['exactly like'] painted cloth.—*Ibid.*, iii. 2.

Denied him *rivality* ['equal rank in consociation'].—*Ant. & C.*, iii. 5.

The *rivals* ['sharers,' 'partners,' 'associates'] of my watch.—*Hamlet*, i. 1.

I must be *round* ['frank,' 'bluntly candid'] with you.—*Tw. N.*, ii. 3.

I must be *round* ['plain,' 'frank,' 'outspoken'] with him.—*Timon*, ii. 2.

I went *round* ['bluntly,' 'straightforwardly'] to work.—*Hamlet*, ii. 2.

Our little life is *rounded* * ['encompassed' and 'completed'] with a sleep.—*Temp.*, iv. 1.

How rank soever *rounded* ['encompassed'] in with danger.—*Tr. & Cr.*, i. 3.

Rounded ['whispered sinisterly'] in the ear with that.—*John*, ii. 2.

He answered me in the *roundest* ['bluntest,' 'bluffest'] manner, he would not.—*Lear*, i. 4.

Whispering, *rounding* ['murmuring sinisterly'], Sicilia is.—*W. T.*, i. 2.

Come *roundly* ['directly,' 'straightforwardly'] to thee.—*Tam. of S.*, i. 2.

Take it on you at the first so *roundly* ['bluntly,' 'roughly'].—*Ibid.*, iii. 2.

The king's *rouse* ['deep draught'] the heavens shall bruit.—*Hamlet*, i. 2.

There o'ertook in 's *rouse* ['carouse'].—*Ibid.*, ii. 1.

They have given me a *rouse* ['deep draught'] already.—*Oth.*, ii. 3.

The *rout* ['company,' 'crowd'] is coming.—*Tam. of S.*, iii. 2.

Sleep yslaked hath the *rout* ['company,' 'assemblage'].—*Per.*, iii. (*Gower*).

How this foul *rout* ['tumult,' 'brawl'] began.—*Oth.*, ii. 3.

Were our *royal* ['loyal,' 'allegiant'] faiths martyrs.—2 *H. IV.*, iv. 1.

---

* It has been debated in what sense Shakespeare uses the word "rounded" in the present passage. We believe it to be used (according to his inclusive mode of employing words) in the duplicate sense of 'encompassed' and 'completed'; human life being 'encompassed,' while it lasts, with a "sleep" of dreams and images, and being 'completed' at its close by a "sleep" of eternal peace and rest.

Shown at full their *royal* ['loyal,' 'allegiant'] minds.— *H. VIII.,* iv. 1.

Royal ['sumptuous,' 'magnificent'] cheer, I warrant you.—*Timon,* iii. 6.

Which promises *royal* ['supreme,' 'a high degree of'] peril.—*Ant. & C.,* iv. 8.

And in his *royalty* ['exaltedness,' 'elevated quality'] of nature.—*Macb.,* iii. 1.

You think we are *ruffians* ['rufflers,' 'bullies,' 'swaggerers,' 'roisterers'].—*Oth.,* i. 1.

The bleak winds do sorely *ruffle* ['roughly blow'].—*Lear,* ii. 4.

Favours you should not *ruffle* ['roughly treat,' 'tear,' or 'rend'] thus.—*Ibid.,* iii. 7.

Deck thy body with his *ruffling* ['flaunting,' 'showy'] treasure.—*Tam. of S.,* iv. 3.

What night-*rule* ['revel'] now about this?—*Mid. N. D.,* iii. 2.

Means for this uncivil *rule* ['revel'].—*Tw. N.,* ii. 3.

I heard a bustling *rumour* ['noise,' 'uproar,' 'tumultuous sound': Italian, *rumore*], like a fray.—*Jul. C.,* ii. 4.

Hath *rush'd* ['pushed,' 'thrust'] aside the law.—*R. & Jul.,* iii. 3.

Spur them to *ruthful* ['rueful,' 'woeful,' 'that which produces ruth or pity'] work —
—*Tr. & Cr.,* v. 3.

In *sad* ['serious,' 'sedate'] confidence.—*M. Ado,* i. 3.

He is *sad* ['serious,' 'grave'] and civil.—*Tw. N.,* iii. 4.

My father and the gentlemen are in *sad* ['serious'] talk.—*W. T.,* iv. 3.

The conference was *sadly* ['seriously'] borne.—*M. Ado,* ii. 3.

Accords not with the *sadness* ['seriousness'] of my suit.—3 *H. VI.,* iii. 2.

By doing everything *safe* ['productive of security'] toward your love and honour.—
Macb., i. 4.

But Banquo's *safe* ['secure from doing harm,' 'securely despatched']?—Ay, my good lord: *safe* ['securely stowed away'] in a ditch he bides.—*Ibid.,* iii. 4.

Are his wits *safe* ['steady,' 'stable,' 'in sound condition']?—*Oth.,* iv. 1.

In all *safe* ['sound,' 'sure'] reason he must have.—*Cym.,* iv. 2.

That which most with you should *safe* ['render safe'] my going.—*Ant. & C.,* i. 3.

Best you *saf'd* ['safely conveyed,' 'rendered safe the going of'] the bringer out of the host.—*Ibid.,* iv. 6.

And on a *safer* ['staider,' 'sounder'] judgment.—*Coriol.,* ii. 3.

The *safer* ['sounder,' 'steadier,' 'staider'] sense will ne'er.—*Lear,* iv. 6.

My blood begins my *safer* ['staider,' 'steadier'] guides.—*Oth.,* ii. 3.

Deliver him to *safety* ['safe custody'].—*John,* iv. 2.

Or pick a *sallet* ['salad,' 'mixture of herbs'] . . . . but for a *sallet* ['helmet' 'head-piece'] my brain-pan had.—2 *H. VI.,* iv. 10.

There were no *sallets* ['pungent sentences,' 'piquant phrases,' 'phrases seasoned with salt or ribald meanings'] in the lines.—*Hamlet,* ii. 2.

Whose *salt* ['salacious,' 'lustful,' 'gross'] imagination yet hath wrong'd.—
M. for M., v. 1.

Salt ['wanton,' 'impure,' 'licentious'] Cleopatra.—*Ant. & C.,* ii. 1.

For certain drops of *salt* ['tears'].—*Coriol.,* v. 5.

Would make a man a man of *salt* ['tears'].—*Lear,* iv. 6.

All things had been *savage* ['wild,' 'uncultivated'] here.—*As You L.,* ii. 7.

If *savage* ['wild'] take or lend.—*Cym.,* iii. 6.

Coughing drowns the parson's *saw* ['axiom,' 'promulgated doctrine'].—*Love's L. L.,* v. 2 (*Song*).

Approve the common *saw* ['axiom,' 'proverb,' 'adage'].—*Lear,* ii. 2.

Full of wise *saws* ['axioms,' 'proverbial sayings'] and.—*As You L.,* ii. 7.

The rascally, *scald* ['sorry,' 'scurvy'] beggarly . . . *scald* knave.—*H. V.,* v. 1.

And *scald* ['sorry,' 'scurvy'] rhymers ballad us.— *Ant. & C.,* v. 2.

The corrupt deputy *scaled* ['deprived of his false surface'].—*M. for M.,* iii. 1.

Like *scaled* ['covered with scales' and 'dispersed,' 'scattered'] *sculls* ['shoals'] before the belching whale.—*Tr. & Cr.,* v. 5.

Scaling ['weighing,' 'balancing' as in scales] his present bearing with his past.—*Coriol.*, ii. 3.

Sure, some *scape* ['prank, 'irregularity,' 'wild freak, 'dissolute act'] . . . I can read waiting-gentlewoman in the *scape.*—*W. T.*, iii. 3.

Day, quoth she, night's *scapes* ['wanton deeds,' 'dissolute acts'] doth open lay.—*Lucrece, Stanza* 107.

Scarf ['bandage,' 'veil'] up the tender eye of.—*Macb.*, iii. 2.

The *scarfed* ['adorned with streamers and pennons'] bark.—*Mer of V.*, iii. 6.

My sea-gown *scarf'd* ['wrapped,' 'folded'] about me.—*Hamlet*, v. 2.

So every *scope* ['extent of licence'] by the immoderate use.—*M. for M.*, i. 3.

No *scope**['free course of operation,' 'ordained or appointed agency'] of Nature, no distemper'd day, no common wind.—*John*, iii. 4.

Be angry when you will, it shall have *scope* ['free course,' 'extended limit'].—*Jul. C.*, iv. 3.

An anchor's cheer in prison be my *scope* ['appointed limit of fare'].—*Hamlet*, iii. 2.

I will not *seal* ['confirm,' 'ratify'] your knowledge.—*Coriol.*, ii. 3.

Now must your conscience my acquittance *seal* ['confirm,' 'ratify'].—*Hamlet*, ii. 7.

The power to *seal* ['effectually close'] th' accuser's lips.—*Lear*, iv. 6.

Our peace we'll ratify; *seal* ['confirm'] it with feasts.—*Cym.*, v. 5.

The best brine a maiden can *season* ['preserve sweet, fresh, and lasting'] her praise in.—*All's W.*, i. 1.

All this to *season* ['preserve sweet, fresh, and lasting'] a brother's dead love.—*Tw. N.*, i. 1.

Season ['temper,' 'modify,'] your admiration for awhile with an attent ear.—*Hamlet*, i. 2.

My blessing *season* ['temper wisely,' 'make pleasant and profitable'] this in thee!—*Ibid.*, i. 3.

As you may *season* ['temper,' 'modify,' 'qualify'] it in the charge.—*Ibid.*, ii. 1.

When mercy *seasons* ['tempers,' 'qualifies'] justice.—*Mer. of V.*, iv. 1.

Directly *seasons* ['tempers,' 'moulds,' and 'confirms,' 'establishes'] him his enemy.—*Hamlet*, iii. 2.

Which *seasons* ['gives zest or relish to,' 'renders more pleasant and acceptable'] comfort.—*Cym.*, i. 7.

Being *season'd* ['made more pleasant'] with a gracious voice.—*Mer. of V.*, iii. 2.

So *season'd* ['rendered acceptable'] with your faithful love to me.—*R. III.*, iii. 7.

All *season'd* ['long-established,' 'time-matured'] office.—*Coriol.*, iii. 3.

This castle hath a pleasant *seat* ['site,' 'situation'].—*Macb.*, i. 6.

Mock your workings in a *second* ['deputed,' 'representative'] body.—*2 H. IV.*, v. 2.

Divulge Page himself for a *secure* ['over-trusting'] and wilful Actæon.—*Merry W.*, iii. 2.

Open the door, *secure* ['rashly confident'], fool-hardy king.—*R. II.*, v. 3.

Secure ['reassure'] thy heart.—*Timon*, ii. 2.

Upon my *secure* ['supposed safe,' 'fancied secure'] hour.—*Hamlet*, i. 5.

Heaven *secure* ['keep safe,' 'guard,' 'protect'] him!—*Ibid.*, i. 5.

Our means *secure* ['render over-confident or rashly trusting'] us, and our mere defects prove.—*Lear*, iv. 1.

I do not so *secure* ['feel over-confident'] me in the error, but the main article.—*Oth.*, i. 3.

But *securely* ['over-confidently'] done.—*Tr. & Cr.*, iv. 5.

Through our *security* ['over-confidence,' 'blind reliance'], grows strong.—*R. II.*, iii. 2.

---

* "Scope" in this passage has been suspected of error by some commentators; but we think that the other passages here collectively cited where Shakespeare uses "scope," suffice to show that he probably employed it in this case also with similar meaning.

Too much *security* ['over-trust,' 'rash reliance'].—*H. V.*, ii. 2.

Security ['over-confidence'] is mortals' chiefest enemy.—*Macb.*, iii. 5.

Toys of feather'd Cupid *seel* ['blind,' 'close up,' 'incapacitate'] with wanton dulness my.—*Oth.*, i. 3.

Come, *seeling* ['blinding'] night.—*Macb.*, iii. 2.

These, indeed, *seem* ['wear an appearance of being,' 'give a semblance of existence'], for they are actions that.—*Hamlet*, i. 2.

Still *seem* ['wear the same appearance or looks'] as does the king.—*Cym.*, i. 1.

Nothing she does, or *seems* ['appears to be,' 'looks'] but smacks of something greater than herself.—*W. T.*, iv. 3.

Seeming, seeming ['hypocrisy,' 'simulated virtue,' 'appearance of goodness'], I will proclaim thee.—*M. for M.*, ii. 4.

Out on thee! *Seeming* ['simulated virtue,' 'appearance of innocence']! I will write against it.—*M. Ado*, iv. 1.

This hath some *seeming* ['appearance of likelihood'].—*Cym.*, v. 5.

Out of *self-bounty* ['inherent generosity'], he abus'd.—*Oth.*, iii. 3.

Tomboys, hir'd with that *self-exhibition* ['self-same stipend'] which your own coffers yield!—*Cym.*, i. 7.

To knit their souls . . . in *self-figured knot* ['a knot tied or formed by themselves']. —*Ibid.*, ii. 3.

I'll tell thee what befell me on a day
In this *self-place* ['self-same spot'] where now we mean to stand.—3 *H. VI.*, iii. 1.

Do not curst wives hold that *self-sovereignty* ['sovereignty vested in self'] only for praise sake, when they strive to be lords o'er their lords?—*Love's L. L.*, iv. 1.

His *semblable* ['resemblance,' 'likeness,' 'brother-man,' 'fellow-creature'], yea, himself, Timon disdains.—*Timon*, iv. 3.

His *semblable* ['resemblance,' 'likeness'] is his mirror.—*Hamlet*, v. 2.

The *semblable* ['similar,' 'resembling'] coherence of his men's spirits and his.— 2 *H. IV.*, v. 1.

Thousands more of *semblable* ['similar,' 'like'] import.—*Ant. & C.*, iii. 4.

Semblably ['similarly,' 'in semblance'] furnish'd like the king himself.— 1 *H. IV.*, v. 3.

And all is *semblative* ['resembling,' 'seemingly,' 'apparently'] a woman's part.— *Tw. N.*, i. 4.

Spirit of *sense* ['sense of touch'] hard as the.—*Tr. & Cr.*, i. 1.

That most pure spirit of *sense* ['sense of sight'].—*Ibid.*, iii. 3.

Pierce his ready *sense* ['sense of hearing'].--*Coriol.*, ii. 2.

Sense ['perception,' 'appreciation,' 'power of discrimination'] sure, you have . . . that *sense* is apoplex'd . . . nor *sense* to ecstasy was ne'er so thralled.—*Hamlet*, iii. 4.

Their wives have *sense* ['sensuous perception'] like them.—*Oth.*, iv 3.

I would your cambric were *sensible* ['sensitive,' 'capable of feeling'] as your finger. —*Coriol.*, i. 3.

Without the *sensible* ['faculty of the senses'] and true avouch of mine own eyes.— *Hamlet*, i. 1.

An answerable *sequestration* ['mutual retirement from each other's company, 'reciprocal separation'].—*Oth.*, i. 3.

Sir Valentine and *servant* ['suitor'] to you.—*Two G. of V.*, ii. 1.

Servant ['suitor'],—Mistress?—*Ibid.*, ii. 4.

Till necessity be *serv'd* ['ministered to,' 'attended to'].—*As You L.*, ii. 7.

What touches us ourself shall be last *serv'd* * ['attended to'].—*Jul. C.*, iii. 1.

---

* This passage has been altered by those who affirm that the verb "to serve" is used in relation to *persons*, not to *things;* but the passage we here cite from "As You Like It" shows that Shakespeare employs "serv'd" in both passages with similar effect.

Like heralds 'twixt two dreadful battles *set* * ['appointed'].—*John*, iv. 2.

Old Adam's likeness, *set* ['appointed'] to dress this garden.—*R. II.*, iii. 4.

I have *set* ['staked'] my life upon a cast.—*R. III.*, v. 4.

To *set* ['stake'] upon one battle all our liberties.—*Jul. C.*, v. 1.

I would *set* ['stake'] my life on any chance.—*Macb.*, iii. 1.

Set ['stake'] less than thou throwest.—*Lear*, i. 4.

Thou may'st not coldly *set* ['rate,' 'estimate,' 'reckon,' 'value'] our sovereign process.—*Hamlet*, iv. 3.

I'll *set* ['send admonishingly and controllingly'] those to you that can speak.—*Ibid.*, iii. 4.

On the score for *sheer* ['pure,' 'unmixed,' and 'purely,' 'merely,' 'solely'] ale.—*Tam. of S., Induc.* 2.

Thou *sheer* ['pure,' 'clear,' 'transparent,' 'unmixed'], immaculate, and silver fountain.—*R. II.*, v. 3.

I must coney-catch, I must *shift* ['act fraudulently'].—*Merry W.*, i. 3.

But *shift* ['act furtively,' 'remove clandestinely'] away.—*Macb.*, ii. 3.

To *shift* ['change,' 'remove'] his being.—*Cym.*, i. 6.

Be bitter with him and passing *short* ['curt,' 'sharp,' 'snappish'].—*As You L.*, iii. 5.

Till some certain *shot* ['reckoning,' 'amount'] be paid.—*Two G. of V.*, ii. 5.

A little, lean, old, chapped, bald, *shot* ['shooter'].—*2 H. IV.*, iii. 2.

Ah, foul *shrewd* ['untoward,' 'disastrous'] news!—*John*, v. 5.

Do my lord of Canterbury a *shrewd* ['evil,' 'mischievous,' 'malicious'] turn, and he is your friend.—*H. VIII.*, v. 2.

We shall find of him a *shrewd* ['mischievous,' and 'slily clever,' 'artful,' 'cunning'] contriver.—*Jul. C.*, ii. 1.

This last day was a *shrewd* ['mischievous,' 'harmful,' 'disastrous'] one to us.—*Ant. & C.*, iv. 9.

I will give him a present *shrift* ['hearing confession and giving absolution'].—*M. for M.*, iv. 3.

Now hath done his *shrift* ['hearing confession and giving absolution'].—*3 H. VI.*, iii. 2.

His board a *shrift* ['confessional'].—*Oth.*, iii. 3.

I will here *shroud* ['take shelter'], till the dregs.—*Temp.*, ii. 2.

Put yourself under his *shroud* ['shelter,' 'protection'].—*Ant. & C.*, iii. 11.

Hardly shall I carry out my *side* ['game,' 'cause,' 'object of attainment'], her husband being alive.—*Lear*, v. 1.

To be the *siege* ['seat': French, *siége*] of this moon-calf?—*Temp.*, ii. 2.

Upon the very *siege* ['official seat'] of justice.—*M. for M.*, iv. 2.

From men of royal *siege* ['seat,' 'throne'].—*Oth.*, i. 2.

We'll *sift* ['examine'] this matter farther.—*All's W.*, v. 3.

Well, we shall *sift* ['examine,' 'test,' 'try'] him.—*Hamlet*, ii. 2.

On *silly* ['innocent,' 'harmless,' 'helpless'] women or poor.—*Two G. of V.*, iv. 1.

It is *silly* ['simple,' 'plain'] *sooth* ['truth'].—*Tw. N.*, ii. 4.

Man, in a *silly* ['simple,' 'plain,' 'homely,' 'rustic'] habit.—*Cym.*, v. 3.

A *single* ['simple,' 'plain,' 'insignificant,' 'individual'] thing, as I am now.—*Temp.*, i. 2.

Single ['singly,' 'simply,' 'plainly'] I'll resolve you.—*Ibid.*, v. 1.

But the plain *single* ['simple,' and 'one only'] vow that is.—*All's W.*, iv. 2.

Your wit *single* ['simple,' 'feeble,' 'weakly,' 'slender,' 'slight']?—*2 H. IV.*, i. 2.

Pomp was *single* ['simple,' 'plain,' and 'unmarried' to grandeur], but now married to one above itself.—*H. VIII.*, i. 1.

I speak it with a *single* ['simple,' 'guileless'] heart.—*Ibid.*, v. 2.

---

* The word "set" has been altered by some emendators in the present passage; but we have shown it to be the word probably used by Shakespeare, inasmuch as he employs it in the same sense in the passage here cited from "King Richard II."

Shakes so my *single* [' simple,' ' individual,' ' imperfect,' ' fallible,' 'weak,' 'feeble '] state of man.—*Macb.*, i. 3.

Were poor and *single* [' simple,' 'weak,' ' feeble,' ' ineffectual,' and ' individual,' ' one only'] business.—*Ibid.*, i. 6.

Due to some *single* [' individual,' ' sole '] breast ?—*Ibid.*, iv. 3.

To scant my *sizes* [' allotted portions of food,' ' allowances of provision '].—*Lear*, ii. 4.

Skipper [' nimble, forward and frivolous youth '], stand back.—*Tam. of S.*, ii. 1.

Of modesty thy *skipping* [' frivolous,' ' light,' 'forward '] spirit.—*Mer. of V.*, ii. 2.

In so *skipping* [' light,' ' frivolous,' ' trivial,' ' vain,' ' irrational'] a dialogue.—*Tw. N.*, i. 5.

The *skipping* [' frivolous,' ' unbefittingly nimble and frequent in motion '] king, he ambled up and down.—*2 H. IV.*, iii. 2.

Make the gruel thick and *slab* [' sticky,' ' glutinous '].—*Macb.*, iv. 1.

What a beast am I to *slack* [' neglect,' ' delay attending to '] it.—*Merry W.*, iii. 4.

If then they chanc'd to *slack* [' neglect,' ' be remiss to'] you.—*Lear*, ii. 4.

So *slander* [' injure,' ' disgrace,' ' abuse '] any moment's leisure.—*Hamlet*, i. 3.

As *slanderous* [' disgraceful'] death's-man.—*Lucrece, Stanza* 143.

We have been too *slight* [' negligent'] in sufferance.—*Cym.*, iii. 5.

The rogues *slighted* [' negligently tossed,' ' flung,' ' threw '] me into the river with as little remorse.—*Merry W.*, iii. 5.

Your most dreadful laws so loosely *slighted* [' treated with contempt'].—*2 H. IV.*, v. 2.

My letters . . . were *slighted* [' treated contemptuously and negligently'] off.— *Jul. C.*, iv. 3.

To part so *slightly* [' negligently,' ' carelessly'] with your wife's first gift.— *Mer. of V.*, v. 1.

Gone *slightly* [' easily'] o'er low steps.—*H. VIII.*, ii. 4.

Should *slip* [' fall into transgression,' ' err '] so grossly.—*M. for M.*, v. 1.

We 'll *slip* you [' let your fault pass by,' ' omit to reprove or punish you'] for a season.—*Cym.*, iv. 3.

The *slip* [' piece of false money ' and ' sly escape '], sir, the *slip*.—*R. & Jul.*, ii. 4.

That you *slipp'd* [' err'd '] not with any but with us.—*W. T.*, i. 2.

Lucentio *slipp'd* [' let loose from the straps of leather in which hounds are held'] me like his greyhound.—*Tam. of S.*, v. 1.

Wild, and usual *slips* [' errors '] as are companions.—*Hamlet*, ii. 1.

Stand like greyhounds in the *slips* [' straps of leather in which hounds are held '], straining upon the start.—*H. V.*, iii. 1.

To pull at a *smack* [' tincture,' ' twang,' ' flavouring quality'] o' the contrary.— *All's W.*, ii. 3.

A *smack* [' smattering'] of all neighbouring languages —*Ibid.*, iv. 1.

They *smack* [' savour,' ' have a tincture, a flavour '] of honour both.—*Macb.*, i. 2.

Some *smatch* [' smack,' ' savour,' ' taste,' ' flavour'] of honour in it.—*Jul. C.*, v. 5.

And *smile* [' smile derisively,' ' smile in derision'] at Troy !—*Tr. & Cr.*, v. 11.

All the regions do *smilingly* [' derisively,' ' contemptuously'] revolt.—*Coriol.*, iv. 6.

I 'll *smoke* [' smoke-dry,' and ' make game of,' ' detect the pretensions of'] your skin-coat.—*John*, ii. 1.

He was first *smoked* [' found out,' ' detected,' and ' smoke-dried'] by the old lord Lafeu.—*All's W.*, iii. 6.

Smooth [' flatter '], deceive, and cog.—*R. III.*, i. 3.

Seem'd not to strike, but *smooth* [' flatter,' ' cajole '].—*Per.*, i. 2.

You 'll mar the light by taking it in *snuff* [' anger,' and ' burnt candle-wick '].— *Love's L. L.*, v. 2.

Either in *snuffs* [' offences taken,' ' angers conceived'] and packings of the dukes.— *Lear*, iii. 1.

The fitchew, nor the *soiled* [' pampered,' ' high-fed,' ' full of blood'] horse.—*Ibid.*, iv. 6.

Not making any scruple of her *soilure* [' defilement,' ' pollution,' ' stain '].— *Tr. & Cr.*, iv. 1.

To rejoice and *solace* ['take comfort,' 'take delight'] in.—*R. & Jul.*, iv. 5.

And *solace* ['take delight,' 'take joy'] i' the dungeon by a snuff?—*Cym.*, i. 7.

Which have *solicited* ['urged thereto,' 'prompted this decision'].—*Hamlet*, v. 2.

This supernatural *soliciting* ['prompting,' 'urging upon the attention'] cannot be ill.—*Macb.*, i. 3.

We 'll have a posset for 't *soon* ['by-and-by'] at night.—*Merry W.*, i. 4.

He looks like *sooth* ['truth'].—*W. T.*, iv. 3.

If I say *sooth* ['truth'], I must report.—*Macb.*, i. 2.

To *sooth* ['give an air of truth to'] your forgery.—3 *H. VI.*, iii. 3.

Ay, *sooth* ['in truth,' 'truly'] ; so humbled.—*Oth.*, iii. 3.

You *sooth'd* ['flattered'] not, therefore hurt not.—*Coriol.*, ii. 2.

I defy the tongues of *soothers* ['flatterers'].—1 *H. IV.*, iv. 1.

Is *sorer* ['worse,' 'more criminal,' 'more injurious'] than to lie for need.—*Cym.*, iii. 6.

Of *sorriest* ['grimmest,' 'dismallest'] fancies.—*Macb.*, iii. 2.

This is a *sorry* ['grim,' 'ghastly'] sight.—*Ibid.*, ii. 2.

The place of death and *sorry* ['sorrowful,' 'dreadful,' 'dismal'] execution.—*Com. of E.*, v. 1.

If it *sort* ['fall out,' 'happen'] not well.—*M. Ado*, iv. 1.

Glad that all things *sort* ['happen,' 'concur'] so well.—*Ibid.*, v. 4.

Well may it *sort* ['fit,' 'suit,' 'agree,' 'cohere'], that.—*Hamlet*, i. 1.

All my pains is *sorted* ['tended'] to no proof.—*Tam. of S.*, iv. 3.

Could *speak* ['proclaim,' 'declare,' 'describe'] thee out.—*H. VIII.*, ii. 4.

Let me *speak* ['declare,' 'proclaim,' 'describe'] myself.—*Ibid.*, iii. 1.

Speak ['declare,' 'describe'] to me what thou art.—*Jul. C.*, iv. 3.

Whose general graces *speak* ['declare,' 'express'] that which none else can utter.—*Ant. & C.*, ii. 2.

Where that and other *specialties* ['papers containing special statements or specified particulars'] are bound.—*Love's L. L.*, ii. 1.

Let *specialties* ['legal papers containing specified particulars'] be therefore drawn between us.—*Tam. of S.*, ii. 1.

For *speculation* ['sight,' 'power of sight'] turns not to itself.—*Tr. & Cr.*, iii. 3.

No *speculation* ['power of sight,' 'faculty of sight'] in those eyes.—*Macb.*, iii. 4.

My *speculative* ['seeing,' 'visual'] and offic'd instruments.—*Oth.*, i. 3.

And *sped* ['succeeded,' 'prospered'] you, sir ?—*Merry W.*, iii. 5.

So be gone ; you are *sped* ['settled,' 'despatched'].—*Mer. of V.*, ii. 9 (*Scroll*).

Married, but you two are *sped* ['settled,' 'ruined,' 'done for'].—*Tam. of S.*, v. 2.

I am *sped* ['settled,' 'despatched,' 'done for'].—*R. & Jul.*, iii. 1.

I long to hear how they *sped* ['succeeded,' 'got on'] to-day.—*Tr. & Cr.*, iii. 1.

You shall know how I *speed* ['proceed,' 'get on,' 'succeed'].—*Merry W.*, ii. 2.

And fear of the queen's *speed* ['hap,' 'fortune,' 'course of success or failure'] is gone. —*W. T.*, iii. 2.

Blossom, *speed* ['proceed,' 'run future course,' 'succeed,' 'prosper'] thee well!—*Ibid.*, iii. 3.

To go *speed* ['succeed,' 'prosper'] elsewhere.—3 *H. VI.*, iv. 1.

Is this your *speeding* ['success,' 'prospering'] ?—*Tam. of S.*, ii. 1.

To-morrow all for *speeding* ['obtaining success,' 'achieving success'] do their best.—*Per.*, ii. 3.

Treachers, by *spherical* ['pertaining to the spheres,' 'spheres-belonging'] predominance.—*Lear*, i. 2.

The over-merry *spleen* ['fit of laughter'].—*Tam. of S., Induc.* 1.

If you desire the *spleen* ['immoderate mirth'], and will laugh yourselves into stitches. —*Tw. N.*, iii. 2.

That, in a *spleen* ['paroxysm of haste'], unfolds.—*Mid. N. D.*, i. 1.

Swifter *spleen* [' outburst of speed '] than powder can enforce.—*John*, ii. 2.

Hotspur, govern'd by a *spleen* [' fit of hasty temper '].—1 *H. IV.*, v. 2.

You are all in all in *spleen* [' choler,' ' wrath '], and nothing.—*Oth.*, iv. 1.

Broken joint . . . entreat her to *splinter* [' splint '].—*Ibid.*, ii. 3.

Broken rancour . . . but lately *splinter'd* [' splinted '].—*R. III.*, ii. 2.

Which *spungy* [' moist,' 'showery '] April at thy hest.—*Temp.*, iv. 1.

From the *spungy* [' moist,' ' damp '] south to this part of the west.—*Cym.*, iv. 2.

Other ventures he hath, *squandered* [' scattered,' ' dispersed '] abroad.—*Mer. of V.*, i. 3.

The *squandering* [' variously directed,' ' widely dispensed '] glances of the fool.—*As You L.*, ii. 7.

But they do *square* [' quarrel ']; that all their elves.—*Mid. N. D.*, ii. 1.

They should *square* [' quarrel,' ' differ '] between themselves.—*Ant. & C.*, ii. 1.

Mine honesty and I begin to *square* [' differ '].—*Ibid.*, iii. 11.

If report be *square* ['just,' ' equitable '] to her.—*Ibid.*, ii. 2.

I have not kept my *square* [' due regularity of conduct '].—*Ibid.*, ii. 3.

I will be *squar'd* [' regulated '] by this.—*W. T.*, iii. 3.

Is there no young *squarer* [' quarreller,' ' brawler,' ' rioter '] now that will.—*M. Ado*, i. 1.

Into the *staggers* [' unsteady courses,' ' misguided deviations from the right path '] and the careless lapse.—*All's W.*, ii. 3.

That *staggers* [' gives this bewildering shock to '] my person.—*R. II.*, v. 5.

How come these *staggers* [' reelings of the brain and totterings of the frame '] on me ?—*Cym.*, v. 5.

For *stale* [' decoy,' ' lure,' ' bait '] to catch these thieves.—*Temp.*, iv. 1.

Poor I am but his *stale* [' a shelter from whence to attack game,' and ' that which has become flavourless and unpalatable '].—*Com. of E.*, ii. 2.

A contaminated *stale* [' woman hackneyed in evil courses '] such as Hero.—*M. Ado*, ii. 2.

To make a *stale* [' commonised ware,' and ' checked figure,' like a king at chess when checkmated] of me amongst these mates ?—*Tam. of S.*, i. 1.

To cast thy wand'ring eyes on every *stale* [' lure,' ' bait,' ' decoy,' and ' common worthless fellow '].—*Ibid.*, iii. 1.

Had he none else to make a *stale* [' butt,' ' dupe,' ' pretence,' ' stalking-horse '] but me ?—3 *H. VI.*, iii. 3.

So *stale* [' commonise,' ' degrade,' ' lower '] his palm.—*Tr. & Cr.*, ii. 3.

I will venture to *stale* 't* [' make flat, insipid, poor, or too common,' ' deteriorate by repetition '] a little more.—*Coriol.*, i. 1.

Or did use to *stale* [' degrade,' ' debase,' ' render poor and common '] with ordinary oaths my love.—*Jul. C.*, i. 2.

Nor custom *stale* [' make flat, vapid, or insipid,' ' wear out,' ' exhaust '] her infinite variety.—*Ant. & C.*, ii. 2.

An she *stand* [' withstand,' ' make show of resistance '] him but a little.—*Tam. of S.*, i. 2.

Being nature's livery, or fortune's *star* [' influence on a human being's destiny '].—*Hamlet*, i. 4.

A prince, out of thy *star* [' sphere,' ' rank of life,' ' appointed destiny or course of fortune '].—*Ibid.*, ii. 2.

In my *stars* [' sphere,' ' rank of life,' ' appointed course of fortune '] I am above thee.—*Tw. N.*, ii. 5 (*Letter*).

Shall I so much dishonour my fair *stars* [' rank of life,' ' birth,' ' station '], on equal terms to give.—*R. II.*, iv. 1.

---

* The Folio prints ' scale 't ' instead of " stale 't " in this passage ; but we think the mode in which Shakespeare uses the verb " to stale " in the other passages above cited, serve to show that he probably employed the same word in the same sense here likewise.

Mak'st my blood cold, and my hair to *stare* ['stand on end,' 'stick upright'].— *Jul. C.*, iv. 3.

With hair up-*staring* ['standing,' 'sticking'].—*Temp.*, i. 2.

Aches contract and *starve* ['destroy,' 'perish,' 'disable'] your supple joints!— *Timon*, i. 1.

Lest the bargain should catch cold and *starve* ['perish,' 'die'].—*Cym.*, i. 5.

Need and oppression *starveth* ['dwell perishingly,' 'sit starvingly'] in thine eyes. —*R. & Jul.*, v. i.

Beggars, *starving* ['longing,' 'hungrily pining'] for a time of pell-mell havoc and confusion.—1 *H. IV.*, v. 1.

Instruments of fear and warning unto some monstrous *state* ['state of things, affairs, or events'].—*Jul. C.*, i. 3.

Thorough the hazards of this untrod *state* ['state of things'] with all true faith.— *Ibid.*, iii. 1.

Sitting in my *state* ['raised seat, with a canopy over it,' 'chair of dignity'].— *Tw. N.*, ii. 5.

This chair shall be my *state* ['throne,' 'royal seat'].—1 *H. IV.*, ii. 4.

A *station* ['attitude,' 'position assumed when standing'] like the herald Mercury.— *Hamlet*, iii. 4.

Her motion and her *station* ['attitude when standing,' 'state of repose,' 'remaining still'] are as one.—*Ant. & C.*, iii. 3.

My substance should be *statue* ['representative image,' 'embodied shape.' *See* "Picture," under the present heading] in thy stead.—*Two G. of V.*, iv. 4.

The *statue* ['figure painted in imitation of nature'] is but newly fix'd, the colour's not dry.—*W. T.*, v. 3.

To *stay* ['await'] the providence of some.—*Jul. C.*, v. 1.

Vouchsafe awhile to *stay* ['restrain yourselves'],
And I will show you.—*John*, ii. 2.

Here's a *stay* ['restraint,' 'prudent restrainer'; with the included sense of 'prop,' 'support.' *See* VARIED MEANINGS, &c., for fuller explanation of this passage], that shakes.—*Ibid.*, ii. 2.

What hope, what *stay* ['point of reliance,' 'available support'], when this was.— *Ibid.*, v. 7.

Can *stead* ['aid,' 'assist' 'promote'] the quest.—*Per.*, iii. (*Gower*).

Which since have *steaded* ['benefited,' 'aided'] much.—*Temp.*, i. 2.

My intercession likewise *steads* ['benefits'] my foe.—*R. & Jul.*, ii. 3.

How *stiff* ['stubborn,' 'hard,' 'unyielding'] is my vile sense.—*Lear*, iv. 6.

This is *stiff* ['stubborn,' 'hard,' 'harsh,' 'disagreeable'] news.—*Ant. & C.*, i. 2.

And swears she'll never *stint* ['cease,' 'stop'].—*Per.*, iv. 4 (*Gower*).

It *stinted* ['stopped,' 'ceased,' 'desisted'] and said, "Ay."—*R. & Jul.*, i. 3.

Now will I *stir* ['incite,' 'instigate'] this gamester.—*As You L.*, i. 1.

Should *stir* ['incite,' 'urge'] me most to my revenge.—*Hamlet*, v. 2.

An undergoing *stomach* ['courage,' 'fortitude'] to bear.—*Temp.*, i. 2.

A man of an unbounded *stomach* ['pride,' 'haughtiness'].—*H. VIII.*, iv. 2.

If you must believe, *stomach* ['take resentfully or wrathfully'] not all.—*Ant. & C.*, iii. 4.

And sharpens the *stomach* ['appetite'].—*Per.*, iv. 1.

Not a time for private *stomaching* ['quarrelling,' 'indulging in resentments'].— *Ant. & C.*, ii. 2.

He is of a noble *strain* ['stock,' 'descent,' 'race,' 'lineage'].—*M. Ado*, ii. 1.

The *strain* ['race'] of man's bred out into baboon and monkey.—*Timon*, i. 1.

Unless he know some *strain* ['propensity,' 'tendency to evil'] in me.—*Merry W.*, ii. 1.

I would all of the same *strain* ['vicious tendency, propensity, or inclination'] were in the same distress.—*Ibid.*, iii. 3.

Make no *strain* ['difficulty of doubt,' 'demur'] but that Achilles.—*Tr. & Cr.*, i. 3.

I do not *strain* ['demur'] at the position.—*Tr. & Cr.*, iii. 3.

Note, if your lady *strain* ['urge,' 'press'] his entertainment.—*Oth.*, iii. 3.

You are so *strait* ['narrow-minded,' 'parsimonious,' 'niggardly'] and so ingrateful, you deny me that.—*John*, v. 7.

Some *strait* ['strict,' 'rigorous,' 'pinching'] decrees that lie too heavy on the commonwealth.—*1 H. IV.*, iv. 3.

You were *straited* ['put to straits or difficulties'] for a reply.—*W. T.*, iv. 3.

Howsoever, *strange* ['marvellous,' 'out of nature'], and admirable.—*Mid. N. D.*, v. 1.

Hot ice and wondrous *strange** ['marvellous,' 'unnatural,' 'anomalous,' 'prodigious'] snow.—*Ibid.*, v. 1.

Strong reasons make *strange* ['unusual,' 'anomalous'] actions.—*John*, iii. 4.

You owe this *strange* ['marvellous,' 'portentous,' 'supernatural'] intelligence.—*Macb.*, i. 3.

Heard i' the air; *strange* ['marvellous,' 'extraordinary,' 'portentous'] screams of death.—*Ibid.*, ii. 3.

Hours dreadful and things *strange* ['marvellous,' 'portentous,' 'unnatural'].—*Ibid.*, ii. 4.

You make me *strange* ['feel strangely,' 'feel doubtful and unacquainted'] even to the disposition that I owe.—*Ibid.*, iii. 4.

I will be *strange* ['distant,' 'reserved'], *stout* ['proud,' 'lofty,' 'dignified,' 'haughty,' 'arrogant'], in yellow stockings.—*Tw. N.*, ii. 5.

He is *strange* ['foreign,' 'a foreigner'] and peevish.—*Cym.*, i. 7.

I am something curious, being *strange* ['foreign,' 'a foreigner'].—*Ibid.*, i. 7.

Fame answering the most *strange* ['unusual,' 'uncommon,' 'extraordinary'] enquire.—*Per.*, iii. (*Gower*).

Ungird thy *strangeness* ['reserve,' 'distance,' 'stiffness'].—*Tw. N.*, iv. 1.

The father of some *stratagem* ['dire event,' 'disastrous occurrence,' 'calamity']: the times are wild.—*2 H. IV.*, i. 1.

What *stratagems* ['direful events,' 'calamitous incidents'], how fell, how butcherly. —*3 H. VI.*, ii. 5.

A prison for a debtor, that not dares to *stride* ['overpass,' 'cross over,' 'go beyond'] a limit.—*Cym.*, iii. 3.

Strong ['confirmed'] and *fasten'd* ['inveterate'] villain !—*Lear*, ii. 1.

Whose death 's, indeed, the *strongest* ['most likely,' 'most strongly probable'] in our censure.—*Per.*, ii. 4.

Fetch our *stuff* ['luggage,' 'baggage'] from thence.—*Com. of E.*, iv. 4.

Shall I fetch your *stuff* ['luggage'] from ship-board?—*Ibid.*, v. 1.

All parts of his *subjection* ['duty as a subject'] loyally.—*Cym.*, iv. 3.

When I had *subscrib'd* ['submitted'] to mine own fortune.—*All's W.*, v. 3.

Subscrib'd ['yielded,' 'surrendered'] his power!—*Lear*, i. 2.

Subscribes ['yields,' 'gives way,' 'defers'] to tender objects.—*Tr. & Cr.*, iv. 5.

And Death to me *subscribes* ['yields,' 'gives way'].—*Sonnet* 107.

You owe me no *subscription* ['submission,' 'deference,' 'obedience'].—*Lear*, iii. 2.

Like to a bowl upon a *subtle* ['smooth'] ground.—*Coriol.*, v. 2.

Give me leave to try *success* ['issue,' 'consequence,' 'that which follows'].— *All's W.*, i. 3.

In whose *success* ['succession,' 'descent'] we are gentle.—*W. T.*, i. 2.

And so *success* ['succession,' 'sequence,' 'following on'] of mischief shall be borne.—*2 H. IV.*, iv. 2.

Ere long have knowledge of my *success* ['progress,' 'that which follows or happens, —whether good or bad'].—*Coriol.*, v. 1.

---

* Some emendators have proposed to alter the word "strange" in the present passage, in the one from "King John," and in the one from "Pericles"; but we think the mode in which Shakespeare uses "strange," in the six first instances here collectively cited, shows it to be most probably employed also by him in these three passages.

Bring me their opinions of success ['what will follow or happen,' 'what will be the issue'].—*Jul. C.*, ii. 2.

My speech should fall into such vile *success* ['consequence'] as my thoughts aim not at.—*Oth.*, iii. 3.

What is the *success* ['issue,' 'following thereon'] ?—*Ant. & C.*, iii. 5.

Jealous in honour, *sudden* ['hasty,' 'rash,' 'passionate,' 'violent'] and quick in quarrel.—*As You L.*, ii. 7.

As *sudden* ['hasty'] as flaws congealed in the.—*2 H. IV.*, iv. 4.

Deceitful, *sudden* ['hasty,' 'rash,' 'violent-tempered,' 'passionate'], malicious.—*Macb.*, iv. 3.

No man's virtue nor *sufficiency* ['ability,' 'capacity,' 'efficiency,' 'competent power'] to be so moral.—*M. Ado*, v. 1.

And some *sufficient* ['capable,' 'efficient,' 'competent'] witnesses.—*Tam. of S.*, iv. 4.

That *suggest* ['incite,' 'tempt'] by treasons.—*H. V.*, ii. 2.

They do *suggest* ['tempt,' 'entice'] at first with heavenly shows.—*Oth.*, ii. 3.

Tender youth is soon *suggested* ['tempted,' 'enticed,' 'allured'].—*Two G. of V.*, iii. 1.

To thy *suggestion* ['instigation,' 'incitement'], plot.—*Lear*, ii. 1.

Our solemn hymns to *sullen* ['melancholy'] dirges.—*R. & Jul.*, iv. 5.

I have a salt and *sullen* ['churlish,' 'vexatious'] rheum offends me.—*Oth.*, iii. 4.

Come short of our *suppose* ['supposition,' 'that which we supposed possible'] so far.—*Tr. & Cr.*, i. 3.

While counterfeit *supposes* ['appearances,' 'assumed characters,' 'incidents calculated to inspire supposition'] bleared thine eyne.—*Tam. of S.*, v. 1.

Lest I *surcease* ['cease'] to honour mine own truth.—*Coriol.*, iii. 2.

No pulse shall keep his native progress, but *surcease* ['cease,' 'stop'].—*R. & Jul.*, iv. 1.

And catch, with his *surcease* ['cessation,' 'stop'], success.—*Macb.*, i. 7.

If we recover that, we are *sure* ['safe'] enough.—*Two G. of V.*, v. 1.

You are both *sure* ['reliable,' 'trustworthy'], and will assist me ?—*M. Ado*, i. 3.

Though thou stand'st more *sure* ['securely,' 'stably'] than I could do.—*2 H. IV.*, iv. 4.

Still close as *sure* ['steady,' 'steadfast,' 'to be relied on'].—*Cym.*, i. 7.

Surprise ['take by storm,' 'overpower,' 'make conquest of'] her with discourse of my dear faith.—*Tw. N.*, i. 4.

I intend but only to *surprise* ['capture,' 'make conquest of'] him.—*3 H. VI.*, iv. 2.

So *surpris'd* ['overcame,' 'overpowered'] my sense.—*W. T.*, iii. 1.

He liv'd from all attainder of *suspect* ['suspicion'].—*R. III.*, iii. 5.

Clear yourself from all *suspects* ['suspicions'].—*2 H. VI.*, iii. 1.

Let us *sway* ['sweep heavily yet impetuously'] on, and face them in the field.—*2 H. IV.*, iv. 1.

When all the *sway* ['ponderous swing'] of earth.—*Jul. C.*, i. 3.

Now *sways* ['sweeps heavily yet impetuously'] it this way, like a mighty sea.—*3 H. VI.*, ii. 5.

Or, rather, *swaying* ['preponderating,' 'leaning,' 'giving weight of influence'] more upon our part.—*H. V.*, i. 1.

So *swift* ['quick,' 'brisk,' 'alert'] and excellent a wit.—*M. Ado*, iii. 1.

He is very *swift* ['quick-witted,' 'ready with his jests'] and sententious.—*As You L.*, v. 4.

She *swore* ['averred,' 'affirmed'], in faith, 'twas strange.—*Oth.*, i. 3.

If that thy valour stand on *sympathy* ['equality,' 'parity of rank'].—*R. II.*, iv. 1.

Sympathy ['parity,' 'similarity,' 'equality'] in years, manners, and beauties.—*Oth.*, ii. 1.

Affection fall into *taint* ['attaint,' 'imputation of blame,' 'accusation of injustice'].—*Lear*, i. 1.

Abjure the *taints* ['attaints,' 'imputations,' 'accusations'] I laid upon myself.—*Macb.*, iv. 3.

Nero will be *tainted* ['touched'] with remorse.—3 *H. VI.*, iii. 1.

Or *tainting* ['attainting,' 'impugning,' 'throwing a slur upon'] his discipline.—*Oth.*, ii. 1.

To *take* ['engage,' 'take possession of'] your imagination.—*Per.*, iv. 4 (*Gower*).

And *take* ['destroy,' 'blast,' 'annihilate'] the one by the other.—*Coriol.*, iii. 1.

And *takes* ['strikes,' 'blasts,' 'bewitches,' 'affects with disease'] the cattle.—*Merry W.*, iv. 4.

No fairy *takes* ['blasts,' 'bewitches'], nor witch hath power.—*Hamlet*, i. 1.

You *taking* ['blighting,' 'blasting,' 'infecting'] airs.—*Lear*, ii. 4.

Bless thee from whirlwinds, star-blasting, and *taking* ['blighting,' 'infection']!—*Ibid.*, iii. 4.

Every tongue brings in a several *tale* ['heavy reckoning,' 'account of misdeeds'], and every *tale* condemns me.—*R. III.*, v. 3.

As thick as *tale* ['successive reckoning,' 'counting one after the other'], came post with post.—*Macb.*, i. 3.

And both as light as *tales* ['reckoned numbers' and 'trivial stories'].—*Mid. N. D.*, iii. 2.

Five *talents* ['sums of about £243 15*s.*, English, each'] is his debt.—*Timon*, i. 1.

Beyond all *talents* ['sums of wealth'].—*Cym.*, i. 7.

Behold these *talents* ['rich tresses'] of their hair.—*Lover's Comp.*, Stanza 30.

He is as *tall* ['able,' 'bold'; including the effect of 'high in stature'] a man of his hands as any.—*Merry W.*, i. 4.

Thou 'rt a *tall* ['brave,' 'reliable'] fellow.—*Tam. of S.*, iv. 4.

He's as *tall* ['stout,' 'able,' 'bold,' 'valorous'] a man as any 's in.—*Tw. N.*, i. 3.

I am not *tall* ['stout,' 'vigorous,' 'robust'] enough to.—*Ibid.*, iv. 2.

A *tall* ['valorous,' 'able-bodied,' 'stout,' 'bold'] gentleman.—2 *H. IV.*, iii. 2.

I *task* ['summon as testimony,' 'cite in proof'] the earth to the like.—*R. II.*, iv. 1.

Task'd ['taxed'] the whole state.—1 *H. IV.*, iv. 3.

How show'd his *tasking* ['challenging,' 'citing,' 'summoning']? seem'd it in contempt?—*Ibid.*, v. 2.

Purposely on others, to *taste* ['test,' 'try,' 'prove'] their valour.—*Tw. N.*, iii. 4.

Let me *taste* ['try,' 'prove,' 'put to the test'] my horse.—1 *H. IV.*, iv. 1.

But, *tasting* ['experiencing'] it, their counsel.—*M. Ado*, v. 1.

By *tasting* ['trying,' 'testing,' and 'experiencing'] of our wrath?—*Cym.*, v. 5.

That *tell* ['assert,' 'say'] you have good faces.—*Coriol.*, ii. 1.

With moderate haste might *tell* ['count,' 'reckon'] a hundred.—*Hamlet*, i. 2.

As thou canst *tell* ['count,' 'reckon'] in a year.—*Lear*, ii. 4.

What damned minutes *tells* ['counts'] he o'er.—*Oth.*, iii. 3.

Where you may *temper* ['mould'] her, by your persuasion.—*Two G. of V.*, iii. 2.

To *temper* ['mould,' 'work to proper consistency'] clay.—*Lear*, i. 4.

Rightly *temper* ['mould themselves consistently'] with the stars.—3 *H. VI.*, iv. 6.

A poison, I would *temper* [ostensibly used in the sense of 'mix,' 'prepare,' really used in the sense of 'mingle,' 'allay,' 'weaken by introduction of innocuous matter'] it.—*R. & Jul.*, iii. 5.

A man of such a feeble *temper* ['temperament,' 'constitutional quality'] should so get the start of.—*Jul. C.*, i. 2.

Of subtle, tender, and delicate *temperance* ['temperature'].—*Temp.*, ii. 1.

It is a poison *temper'd* ['mixed,' 'prepared'] by himself.—*Hamlet*, v. 2.

I have him already *tempering* ['manipulating,' 'preparing for use, like soft wax'] between my finger and my thumb, and shortly will I seal with him.—2 *H. IV.*, iv. 3.

Which I *tender* ['hold,' 'prize,' 'value,' 'esteem'] dearly.—*As You L.*, v. 2.

Thou mak'st some *tender* ['loving regard,' 'affectionate care'] of my life.—1 *H. IV.*, v. 4.

The *tent* ['roll of lint used by surgeons in searching a wound'] that searches to the bottom of the worst.—*Tr. & Cr.*, ii. 2.

Nor *tent* ['curatively search'] to bottom that.—*Cym.*, iii. 4.

The *thewes* ['muscular strength,' 'bodily vigour,' 'sinewy power'], the stature, bulk.—2 *H. IV.*, iii. 2.

Have *thewes* ['muscles,' 'sinews,' 'physical strength'] and limbs like to their ancestors.—*Jul. C.*, i. 3.

Does not grow alone in *thewes* ['muscular power,' 'physical strength,' 'sinewy vigour'] and bulk.—*Hamlet*, i. 3.

Think ['take to heart,' 'grieve,' 'reflect mournfully,' 'give way to sorrowful pensiveness'], and die.—*Ant. & C.*, iii. 9.

Begot of *thought* ['melancholy reverie'], conceived of spleen.—*As You L.*, iv. 1.

She pin'd in *thought* ['mournful reflection']; and.—*Tw. N.*, ii. 4.

Take *thought* ['anxious reflection'], and die for Cæsar.—*Jul. C.*, ii. 1.

Sicklied o'er with the pale cast of *thought* ['melancholy reverie'].—*Hamlet*, iii. 1.

Thought ['melancholy,' 'mournfulness,' 'sadness'] and affliction, passion.—*Ibid.*, iv. 5.

If swift *thought* ['grieving reflection,' 'taking to heart'] break it not, a swifter mean shall outstrike *thought*, but *thought* will do 't, I feel.—*Ant. & C.*, iv. 6.

Thou shalt be pinch'd as *thick* ['numerously spotted and indented'] as honey-comb.—*Temp.*, i. 2.

Thick ['ply me quickly and plentifully with questions'], *thick*, spare not me.—*All's W.*, ii. 2.

Speaking *thick* ['rapidly,' 'quickly,' 'fast,' 'in close succession,' 'in swift accumulation'] which nature made his blemish.—2 *H. IV.*, ii. 3.

As *thick* ['rapidly in succession'] as tale.—*Macb.*, i. 3.

My heart beats *thicker* ['more rapidly,' 'faster'] than a fev'rous pulse.—*Tr. & Cr.*, iii. 2.

All *thin* ['thinly clad,' 'bare'] and naked.—*R. III.*, ii. 1.

Than these *thin* ['slender,' 'bare'] *habits* ['assumptions,' 'cloaks of speech'] and poor likelihoods.—*Oth.*, i. 3.

I have a mind presages me such *thrift* ['gain,' 'profit,' 'advantage,' 'prosperity,' 'thriving'] that I should.—*Mer. of V.*, i. 1.

To the doer's *thrift* ['advantage,' 'benefit'].—*Cym.*, v. 1.

A man *throng'd* ['pierced,' 'beset,' and 'hard pressed'] with cold.—*Per.*, ii. 1.

Here one, being *throng'd* ['pressed,' 'crowded'] bears back.—*Lucrece, Stanza* 203.

Abate *throw* ['cast of the dice'] at Novum.—*Love's L. L.*, v. 2.

You can fool no more money out of me at this *throw* ['time,' 'while;' and 'cast of the dice,' and 'cast of a fishing-net'].—*Tw. N.*, v. 1.

Thou whoreson little *tidy* ['plump,' 'well-conditioned'] Bartholomew boar-pig.—2 *H. IV.*, ii. 4.

My queen's a squire more *tight* ['adroit,' 'dexterous,' 'handy'] at this than thou.—*Ant. & C.*, iv. 4.

Bear you these letters *tightly* ['adroitly,' 'briskly'].—*Merry W.*, i. 3.

'Tis true that you have lately *told* ['foretold'] us.—*Coriol.*, i. 1.

I will buy me a son-in-law in a fair, and *toll* ['pay toll for the liberty of selling'] this one.—*All's W.*, v. 3.

To be partner'd with *tomboys* ['hoydens,' 'bold roistering wenches'].—*Cym.*, i. 7.

I did dream of money-bags *to-night* ['last night'].—*Mer. of V.*, ii. 5.

He took good rest *to-night* ['last night'].—*W. T.*, ii. 3.

We shall have reveilling *to-night* ['this coming night'].—*M. Ado*, i. 1.

Of feasting forth *to-night* ['this coming night'].—*Mer. of V.*, ii. 5.

This night ['this coming night'] he meaneth with.—*Two G. of V.*, ii. 6.

If for *this night* ['this coming night'] he entreat you.—*M. for M.*, iii. 1.

Meant to acknowledge it *this night* ['this coming night'] in a dance.—*M. Ado*, i. 2.

Tell me how it came *this night* ['last night'], that I.—*Mid. N. D.*, iv. 1.

Half my power *this night* ['last night'], passing.—*John*, v. 6.

Where it did mark, it *took* ['blasted,' 'struck annihilatingly '].—*Coriol.*, ii. 2.

Must bide the *touch* ['test,' 'proof,' 'trial'].--1 *H. IV.*, iv. 4.

Now do I play the *touch* ['touchstone'], to try if.—*R. III.*, iv. 2.

Oh, thou *touch* ['touchstone,' 'test'] of heart!—*Timon*, iv. 3.

A *touch* ['perceptive sense,' 'susceptibility of being touched by'], a feeling of their afflictions.—*Temp.*, v. 1.

So excellent a *touch* ['denotement,' 'indication,' 'trait'] of modesty.—*Tw. N.*, ii. 1.

Give your friend some *touch* ['hint,' 'inkling,' 'indication '] of your late business. —*H. VIII.*, v. 1.

One *touch* ['sympathetic feeling,' 'perceptive trait,' 'keen sense'] of nature makes the whole world kin.—*Tr. & Cr.*, iii. 3.

He wants the natural *touch* ['spark of feeling,' 'sympathetic perception or sense ']. —*Macb.*, iv. 2.

A *touch* ['keen sense,' 'acute perception,' 'pang,' 'throe'] more rare subdues all pangs, all fears.—*Cym.*, i. 2.

Spirits are not finely *touch'd* ['gifted with acute perception,' 'endowed with keen sense'] but to fine issues.—*M. for M.*, i. 1.

How seems he to be *touched* ['affected'] ?—*Ibid.*, iv. 2.

You *touch'd* ['hit upon,' 'penetrated'] my vein at first.—*As You L.*, ii. 7.

What villain *touch'd* ['pierced'] his body, that did stab, and not for justice ?— *Jul. C.*, iv. 3.

Some lively *touches* ['traits,' 'hints,'] of my daughter's favour.—*As You L.*, v. 4.

With more urgent *touches* ['points of interest,' 'motives '].—*Ant. & C.*, i. 2.

Upon the rack of this *tough* ['inexorable,' 'pitiless,' 'unrelenting,' 'unyielding'] world stretch him out longer.—*Lear*, v. 3.

All my joy *trace* ['attend,' 'follow closely,' 'keep up with '] the *conjunction* ['union,' 'match,' 'marriage']!—*H. VIII.*, iii. 2.

And all unfortunate souls that *trace* ['follow,' 'succeed'] him in his line.—*Macb.*, iv. 1.

Who else would *trace* ['follow,' 'emulate,' 'imitate '] him.—*Hamlet*, v. 2.

Thus *translate* ['reveal,' 'describe'] him to me.—*Tr. & Cr.*, iv. 5.

You must *translate* ['explain,' 'reveal']: 'tis fit we understand.—*Hamlet*, iv. 1.

Or some enchanted *trifle* ['phantasm,' 'illusion '].—*Temp.*, v. 1.

Win us with honest *trifles* ['illusions,' 'unsubstantial predictions '] to betray us in deepest consequence.—*Macb.*, i. 3.

With pomp, with *triumph* ['stately pageant,' 'processional show '], and with revelling. —*Mid. N. D.*, i. 1.

Hold those justs and *triumphs* ['pageants,' 'celebrations '].—*R. II.*, v. 2.

Marry, how ? *Tropically* ['metaphorically,' 'figuratively,' 'by means of a trope.' *See* "Spherical," under the present heading].—*Hamlet*, iii. 2.

To be no *true* ['honest'] man.—*M. Ado*, iii. 3.

Shall have all *true* ['rightful,' 'just'] rites.—*Jul. C.*, iii. 1.

That lies enclosed in this *trunk* ['body'].—*W. T.*, i. 2.

Are empty *trunks* ['bodies'; with an allusion to richly carved 'chests'], o'erflourish'd by the devil.—*Tw. N.*, iii. 4.

Having sworn *truth* ['fidelity,' 'constancy '], ever will be true.—*Ibid.*, iv. 3.

Thy father bears the *type* ['crown,' 'symbol of sovereignty'] of King of Naples.— 3 *H. VI.*, i. 4.

The high imperial *type* ['crown,' 'symbol of royalty'] of this earth's glory.— *R. III.*, iv. 4.

His *umbrage* ['shadow'], nothing more.—*Hamlet*, v. 2.

And his *unbookish* ['ignorant,' 'inexperienced'] jealousy must construe.—*Oth.*, iv. 1.

Uncase ['take off outer garments'] thee; take my colour'd hat and cloak.—*Tam. of S.*, i. 1.

Pompey is *uncasing* ['taking off his outer garments'] for the combat?—*Love's L. L.*, v. 2.

How able such a work to *undergo* ['undertake' and 'sustain'].—2 *H. IV.*, i. 3.

You *undergo* ['undertake to support'] too strict a paradox.—*Timon*, iii. 5.

To *undergo* ['undertake'] with me an enterprise.—*Jul. C.*, i. 3.

Virtues . . . as infinite as man may *undergo* ['sustain,' 'possess'].—*Hamlet*, i. 4.

Undergo ['undertake'] those employments.—*Cym.*, iii. 5.

His name and credit shall you *undertake* ['assume'].—*Tam. of S.*, iv. 2.

Lordship should *undertake* ['engage with,' 'fight with'] every companion.—*Cym.*, ii. 1.

I pr'ythee, now, *ungird* ['unbend,' 'relax'] thy strangeness.—*Tw. N.*, iv. 1.

I should judge now *unhappily* ['mischievously'].—*H. VIII.*, i. 4.

Oh, most *unhappy* ['ill-conditioned'] woman!—*Com. of E.*, iv. 4.

Arm'd for some *unhappy* ['offensive,' 'abusive,' 'uncivil'] words.—*Tam. of S.*, ii. 1.

A shrewd knave and an *unhappy* ['ill-conditioned'].—*All's W.*, iv. 5.

Dubbed with *unhatched* ['unhacked'] rapier.—*Tw. N.*, iii. 4.

Or some *unhatch'd* ['undeveloped'] treason.—*Oth.*, iii. 4.

Bid them farewell, Cordelia, though *unkind* ['unnatural' and 'unaffectionate.' *See* "Kindless," under the present heading].—*Lear*, i. 1.

She had not brought forth thee, but died *unkind* ['without offspring,' 'childless'].—*V. & Adon.*, Stanza 34.

And not *unluckily* ['perversely'], against the bias.—*Tam. of S.*, iv. 5.

This *unprevailing* ['unavailing'] woe.—*Hamlet*, i. 2.

An *unquestioned* ['avoiding question.' *See* "Questionable," under the present heading] spirit, which you have not.—*As You L.*, iii. 2.

What, all *unready* ['undressed,' 'half-dressed'] so?—1 *H. VI.*, ii. 1.

Like a green girl, *unsifted* ['untried, 'untested,' 'inexperienced.' *See* "Sifted," under the present heading] in such perilous circumstance.—*Hamlet*, i. 3.

So my *untruth* ['disloyalty'] had not provok'd.—*R. II.*, ii. 2.

Let all *untruths* ['unfaithfulness,' 'inconstancy'] stand by thy stained name.—*Tr. & Cr.*, v. 2.

Ay, tell me that, and *unyoke* ['have done,' 'give over,' 'cease,' 'desist': from the unyoking of oxen at the end of their labour].—*Hamlet*, v. 1.

He lent it me awhile, and I gave him *use* ['interest,' 'usurious advantage'] for it.—*M. Ado*, ii. 1.

Make *use* ['interest,' 'profit'] now, and provide.—*H. VIII.*, iii. 2.

These things are beyond all *use* ['usual event,' 'customary occurrence'], and I do fear them.—*Jul. C.*, ii. 2.

The other half in *use* ['trust,' 'present power over,' 'for future transferred possession'] to render it.—*Mer. of V.*, iv. 1.

My full heart remains in *use* ['trust,' 'pledge,' 'guarantee for future possession'] with you.—*Ant. & C.*, i. 3.

If I have *us'd* ['behaved,' 'conducted'] myself unmannerly.—*H. VIII.*, iii. 1.

Of two *usuries* ['iniquitous pursuits,' 'improper practices'], the merriest was put down.—*M. for M.*, iii. 2.

Did you but know the city's *usuries* ['unfair ways,' 'imposing practices,' 'extortionate dealings'].—*Cym.*, iii. 3.

Champion me to the *utterance* ['uttermost,' 'extremity': French, *outrance*].—*Macb.*, iii. 1.

Behoves me keep at *utterance* ['uttermost,' 'extreme of defiance'].—*Cym.*, iii. 1.

That doth *utter* ['sell,' 'vend'] all men's ware-a.—*W. T.*, iv. 3 (*Song*).

Not *utter'd* ['sold'] by base sale of.—*Love's L. L.*, ii. 1.

And *utters* ['sells' and 'speaks'] it again.—*Ibid*, v. 2.

Death to any he that *utters* ['sells,' 'vends'] them.—*R. & Jul.*, v. 1.

Then *vail* ['lower'] your ignorance.—*Coriol.*, iii. 1.

Did *vail* ['lower,' 'stoop'] their crowns, to his supremacy.—*Per.*, ii. 3.

Vail ['pay homage,' 'give deferential honour'] to her mistress Dian.—*Per.*, iv. (*Gower*).

With thy *vailed* ['lowered,' 'drooped'] lids.—*Hamlet*, i. 2.

Vailing ['lowering'] her high-top lower than her ribs.—*Mer. of V.*, i. 1.

To be a little *vain* ['untrue,' 'hyperbolical,' 'adulatory'].—*Com. of E.*, iii. 2.

There's no man is so *vain* ['wanting in good sense,' 'unwise,' 'foolish'], that would refuse so fair.—*Ibid.*, iii. 2.

Whose high respect and rich *validity* ['value,' 'worth'] did lack a parallel.— *All's W.*, v. 3.

Of what *validity* ['value'] and pitch soever.—*Tw. N.*, i. 1.

Some *vanity* ['illusion,' 'magic show,' 'vision'] of mine art.—*Temp.*, iv. 1.

If I were much in love with *vanity* ['frivolity,' 'light pursuit']!—1 *H. IV.*, v. 4.

So light is *vanity* ['vain delight,' 'trivial pursuit'].—*R. & Jul.*, ii. 6.

When the doctor spies his *vantage* ['opportunity'] ripe.— *Merry W.*, iv. 6.

With his next *vantage* ['favourable opportunity'].—*Cym.*, 1. 4.

For that *vast* ['dark and desolate space'] of night.—*Temp.*, i. 2.

Shook hands, as over a *vast* ['wide extent of distance,' 'large space'].—*W. T.*, i. 1.

In the dead *vast* ['dark and desolate space'] and middle of the night.—*Hamlet*, i. 2.

Who, like a late-sack'd island, *vastly* ['in a waste and desolate manner'] stood.— *Lucrece, Stanza* 249.

Our play leaps o'er the *vaunt* ['van,' 'avant,' 'previous portion,' 'beginning'].— *Tr. & Cr. (Prologue)*.

Did promise most *venerable* ['admirable,' 'worshipable,' 'that which is to be revered or venerated'] worth.—*Tw. N.*, iii. 4.

Could do no *vengeance* ['mischief,' 'harm'] to me.—*As You L.*, iv. 3 (*Letter*).

A trusty *villain* ['bondman,' 'vassal'], sir.—*Com. of E.*, i. 2.

My *villain* ['serf,' 'feudal retainer,' 'vassal'].—*Lear*, iii. 7.

May *vie* ['compete,' 'parallel,' 'be equal in'] honour with you.—*Per.*, iii. 1.

With the dove of Paphos might the crow *vie* ['compete in'] feathers white.— *Ibid.*, iv. (*Gower*).

Kiss on kiss she *vied* ['proffered in competition'] so fast.—*Tam. of S.*, ii. 1.

Trust to thy single *virtue* ['valour,' 'courage'].—*Lear*, v. 3.

Oh, infinite *virtue* ['valour,' 'courage'] com'st thou.—*Ant. & C.*, iv. 8.

This *visitation* ['consolatory advent'] shows it.—*Temp.*, iii. 1.

That you have lent him *visitation* ['consoling advent or repair'].—*M. for M.*, iii. 2

Hath got the *voice* ['suffrage,' 'vote'] in hell for excellence.—*H. V.*, ii. 2.

The people must have their *voices* ['suffrages,' 'votes'].—*Coriol.*, ii. 2.

Doth spit and *void* ['eject'] his rheum upon.—*H. V.*, iii. 5.

Or *void* ['quit,' 'leave,' 'depart from'] the field.—*Ibid.*, iv. 7.

If you'll *vouchsafe* ['please to accept.' *See* ELLIPTICALLY USED WORDS for other instances of "vouchsafe" thus used] me.—*M. Ado*, iii. 2.

Vouchsafe ['be pleased to approve and accept'] my labour.—*Timon*, i. 1.

'Tis a *vulgar* ['commonly or publicly known'] proof.—*Tw. N.*, iii. 2.

That buildeth on the *vulgar* ['common,' 'plebeian,' 'general,' 'popular'] heart — 2 *H. IV.*, i. 3.

The most *vulgar* ['commonly or generally known'] to sense.—*Hamlet*, i. 2.

Most sure and *vulgar* ['commonly or generally known,' 'publicly reported'].— *Lear*, iv. 6.

That *vulgars* ['common people'] give bold'st titles.—*W. T.*, ii. 1.

So *vulgarly* ['publicly and coarsely'] and personally accus'd.—*M. for M.*, v. 1.

The English bottoms have *waft* ['wafted'] o'er.—*John*, ii. 1.

When he, *wafting* ['turning'] his eyes to the contrary.—*W. T.*, i. 2.

Who *wafts* ['waves to,' 'beckons to'] us yonder.—*Com. of E.*, ii. 2.

Whom Fortune with her ivory hand *wafts* ['waves,' 'beckons'] to her.—*Timon*, i. 1.

Too weak to *wage* ['maintain'] an instant trial.—*1 H. IV.*, iv. 4.

And choose to *wage* ['contend,' 'wage war'] against.—*Lear*, ii. 4.

To wake and *wage* ['maintain,' 'carry on,' 'encounter,' 'undertake'] a danger profitless.—*Oth.*, i. 3.

His taints and honours *waged* ['maintained contending strength'] equal with him.—*Ant. & C.*, v. 1.

Nor the commodity *wages* ['equals,' 'maintains equal pace'] not with the danger.—*Per.*, iv. 3.

Which here we *waken* ['rouse into energy.' *See* IDIOMS for other passages where "awake" and "wake" are similarly used] to our country's good.—*R. III.*, iii. 7.

Doth *want* ['stand in need of'] her proper limbs.—*Ibid.*, iii. 7.

Makes the *wappen'd* ['worn out,' 'stale.' Shakespeare uses the epithet "o'er-worn," applied to a widow, in the first scene of "King Richard III."] widow wed again.—*Timon*, iv. 3.

Sent to *warn* ['summon'] them to his royal presence.—*R. III.*, i. 3.

Who is it that hath *warn'd* ['summoned'] us to the walls?—*John*, ii. 1.

With wine and *wassail* ['feasting'] so convince.—*Macb.*, i. 7.

At wakes and *wassails* ['feastings'], meetings.—*Love's L. L.*, v. 2.

She shall *watch* ['keep awake'] all night.—*Tam. of S.*, iv. 1.

The longest night that e'er I *watched* ['kept awake'].—*Two G of V.*, iv. 2.

Sick to-morrow for this night's *watching* ['keeping awake'].—*R. & Jul.*, iv. 4.

Was well worth *watching* ['keeping awake'].—*Cym.*, ii. 4.

Ween ['imagine,' 'think,' 'suppose'] you of better luck.—*H. VIII.*, v. 1.

Weening ['thinking,' 'imagining'] to redeem.—*1 H. VI.*, ii. 5.

The world to *weet* ['know,' 'be aware'] we stand up peerless.—*Ant. & C.*, i. 1.

The *weird* ['witch,' 'fatal,' 'prophetic'] sisters.—*Macb.*, i. 3.

These *weird* ['witch,' 'fatal,' 'prophetic'] sisters saluted me.—*Ibid.*, i. 5 (*Letter*).

He that *went* [was 'dressed,' 'attired,' or 'apparelled'] like a base-viol, in a case of leather.—*Com. of E.*, iv. 3.

How looked he? Wherein *went* ['was dressed'] he?—*As You L.*, iii. 2.

And he *went* ['was dressed'] still in this fashion.—*Tw. N.*, iii. 4.

Never lack'd gold, and yet *went* ['dressed'] never gay.—*Oth.*, ii. 1.

Oh, how the *wheel* ['burden' of a ballad; also suggesting the idea of the instrument of torture called "the wheel"] becomes it!—*Hamlet*, iv. 5.

Had first been *whole* ['sound in health,' 'well,' 'not ill,' 'unsick'], ere he by sickness had.—*1 H. IV.*, iv. 1.

And not *wholesome* ['favourable,' 'beneficial,' 'propitious'] to our cause.—*H.VIII*, iii. 2.

Speak to them, I pray you, in *wholesome* ['propitiatory,' 'gracious,' 'conciliatory'] manner.—*Coriol.*, ii. 3.

If it shall please you to make me a *wholesome* ['gracious,' 'favourable'] answer . . . make you a *wholesome* ['rational,' 'sane,' 'healthy'] answer.—*Hamlet*, iii. 2.

Good morrow, good *wife* ['woman.' Falstaff says it in this sense, while Dame Quickly takes it in the sense of 'married woman'].—*Merry W.*, ii. 2.

A cause between an orange-*wife* ['woman'] and a fosset-seller.—*Coriol.*, ii. 1.

A fellow almost damn'd in a fair *wife** ['woman'].—*Oth.*, i. 1.

Though inclination be as sharp as *will* ['determination'].—*Hamlet*, iii. 3.

To the perpetual *wink* ['closed eyes'] for aye might put this ancient morsel.—*Temp.*, ii. 1.

Although you judge I *wink* ['have my eyes closed'].—*Two G. of V.*, i. 2.

I'll *wink* ['shut my eyes'] and couch.—*Merry W.*, v. 5.

---

* "Wife" has been suspected of error in this passage: but if the mode be observed in which the word is used in the other passages here cited, and "wives" as cited a little farther on, we think it will be seen to be the correct reading.

To *wish* ['recommend'] him wrestle with affection.—*M. Ado*, iii. 1.

I will *wish* ['recommend'] him to her father.—*Tam. of S.*, i. 1.

And *wish* ['recommend'] thee to a shrewd.—*Ibid.*, i. 2.

When man was *wish'd* ['recommended,' 'desired,' 'enjoined'] to love his enemies. —*Timon*, iv. 3.

Only shape thou thy silence to my *wit* ['intelligence,' 'sagacity'].—*Tw. N.*, i. 2.

Shall suffer what *wit* ['ingenuity,' 'skill in cruelty,' 'barbarous invention'] can make heavy.—*W. T.*, iv. 3.

Away with scrupulous *wit* ['policy,' 'ingenuity']! now arms must rule.— 3 *H. VI.*, iv. 7.

Since brevity is the soul of *wit* ['wisdom,' 'intelligential acuteness'].—*Hamlet*, ii. 2.

Now please you *wit* ['know,' 'understand'] the epitaph is.—*Per.*, iv. 4 (*Gower*).

As *witting* ['knowing'] I no other comfort have.—1 *H. VI.*, ii. 5.

If I drown myself *wittingly* ['knowingly'].—*Hamlet*, v. 1.

The deep-revolving *witty* ['sagacious,' 'perspicacious,' and 'ingenious,' 'full of clever devices'] Buckingham.—*R. III.*, iv. 2.

You must be *witty* ['alert-minded,' 'quick-witted'] now.—*Tr. & Cr.*, iii. 2.

With men, with *wives* ['women'] and boys.—*H. V.*, v. (*Chorus*).

Lest that thy *wives* ['women'] with spits, and boys with stones.—*Coriol.*, iv. 4.

Men, *wives* ['women'] and children, stare.—*Jul. C.*, iii. 1.

Like a *wood* ['mad,' 'distracted,' 'crazy'] woman!—*Two G. of V.*, ii. 3.

Raging *wood* ['mad'] did flesh his.—1 *H. VI.*, iv. 7.

Am I a *woodman* ['huntsman,' 'sportsman,' 'one who chases female game'], ha?— *Merry W.*, v. 5.

He's a better *woodman* ['huntsman,' 'sportsman,' 'a chaser of female game'] than thou takest him for.—*M. for M.*, iv. 3.

Have proved best *woodman* ['huntsman,' 'sportsman'].—*Cym.*, iii. 6.

What, the sword and *the word* ['the Scriptures,' 'Holy Writ']! Do you study them both, master parson?—*Merry W.*, iii. 1.

Do set *the word* ['Holy Writ'] itself against *the word*—*R. II.*, v. 5.

The hopeless *word* ['short phrase,' 'sentence'] of "never to return."—*Ibid.*, i. 3.

A time for such a *word* ['sentence'].—*Macb.*, v. 5.

Now to my *word* ['watchword']; it is, "Adieu, adieu! remember me."—*Hamlet*, i. 5.

Give the *word* ['watchword,' 'password'].—*Lear*, iv. 6.

The *word* ['motto'], "Lux tua vita mihi."—*Per.*, ii. 2.

Some *words* ['dispute,' 'contention'] there grew 'twixt.—1 *H. VI.*, ii. 5.

To fill the world with *words* ['disputing,' 'wrangling']?—3 *H. VI.*, v. 5.

Not so rich in *worth* ['rank,' 'wealth,' 'worldly position or estimation'] as beauty.—*W. T.*, v. 1.

Not for the *worth* ['amount of value'] that hangs upon our quarrel.—*Tr. & Cr.*, ii. 3.

And to have his *worth* ['pennyworth,' 'full amount,' 'fill,' 'full swing'] of contradiction.—*Coriol.*, iii. 3.

Found this trespass *worth* ['deserving of'] the shame which here it suffers.— *Lear*, ii. 4.

Me, wretch, more *worth* ['deserving,' 'meriting'] your vengeance.—*Cym.*, v. 1.

A peevish schoolboy, *worthless* * ['unworthy'] of such honour.—*Jul. C.*, v. 1.

He has much *worthy* ['deserved,' 'merited'] blame laid upon him for.—*All's W.*, iv. 3.

---

* Shakespeare often uses words ending in "less" with some latitude of signification; and he is followed in this practice by a poet of our own day, who, in his poem of "Vivien," uses the word "selfless" to express 'unselfish.' So Shakespeare uses "artless," "aweless," "kindless," "mindless," "needless," "opposeless," "sightless," "timeless," "topless," "trustless," "viewless," "woundless," &c., with quite peculiar meaning.

To *worthy* ['merited'] danger and deserved death.—*R. II.*, v. 1.

For a score of kingdoms you should *wrangle* ['dispute,' 'contend overbearingly'], and I would call it fair play.—*Temp.*, v. 1.

And *wrangle* ['dispute,' 'altercate'] with my reason.—*Tw. N.*, iv. 3.

To those that *wring* ['writhe,' 'feel acutely'] under the load of sorrow.—*M. Ado*, v. 1.

He *wrings* ['writhes in anguish,' 'feels acutely'] at some distress.—*Cym.*, iii. 6.

Patiently to bear my *wroth* ['that which causes writhing'; 'misfortune,' 'calamity,' 'disaster'].—*Mer. of V.*, ii. 9.

Yare ['alertly,' 'promptly'], *yare!* Take in the top-sail.—*Temp.*, i. 1.

You shall find me *yare* ['ready,' 'prompt,' 'apt'].—*M. for M.*, iv. 2.

That *yarely* ['alertly,' 'dexterously'] frame the office.—*Ant. & C.*, ii. 2.

Whom *zeal* ['religious virtue,' 'piety'] and charity brought to the field as God's own soldier.—*John*, i. 2.

With tears of innocency and terms of *zeal* ['piety,' 'religious fervour,' 'holiness'].— 1 *H. IV.*, iv. 3.

Shakespeare occasionally uses the word " there " in reference to some place *inferred*, rather than directly mentioned :—

> He came too late, the ship was under sail :
> But *there* the duke was given to understand,
> That in a gondola were seen together
> Lorenzo and his amorous Jessica.—*Mer. of V.*, ii. 8.

And sometimes in reference to a time or circumstance, not to a place :—

> Why, as I told thee, tis a custom with him
> I' the afternoon to sleep: *there* thou may'st brain him.—*Temp.*, iii. 2.

Bearing in mind the above-named peculiarities of our author when occasionally using the word " there," we are inclined to believe it to have been employed by him in the following passage, although it has been suspected of misprint in the First Folio. If " our most quiet *there* " be what Shakespeare wrote, we take it to signify ' the supreme quiet which we enjoyed in the stream of time ' :—

> We see which way the stream of time doth run,
> And are enforc'd from our most quiet *there*
> By the rough torrent of occasion.—2 *H. IV.*, iv. 1.

The word " though " is also used by Shakespeare in a peculiar manner ; allowing it to bear almost the sense of ' since,' ' if,' ' being that,' ' inasmuch as ' :—

Sowter will cry upon 't, for all this, *though* it be as rank as a fox.—*Tw. N.*, ii. 5.

There 's a medlar for thee, eat it.—On what I hate I feed not.—Dost hate a medlar ? —Ay, *though* it look like thee.—*Timon*, iv. 3.

I would abate her nothing ; *though* I profess myself her adorer, not her friend.— *Cym.*, i. 5.

And, in the following passage, with the sense of ' granting that,' ' allowing that,' ' admitting that ' :—

For *though* the camomile, the more it is trodden on, the faster it grows, yet youth the more it is wasted, the sooner it wears.—1 *H. IV.*, ii. 4.

There are certain words that were affectedly and hackedly used by some of the fops, would-be fine gentlemen, or martial-mannered fellows, of Shakespeare's time, that are recorded by him in a few passages of his plays as thus used :—

A soldier is better *accommodated* than with a wife [*See* AFFECTED PHRASEOLOGY].— 2 *H. IV.*, iii. 2.

Captain! * thou abominable damned cheater, art thou not ashamed to be called *captain?* An *captains* were of my mind, they would truncheon you out, for taking their names upon you before you have earned them. You a *captain!* you slave, for what? . . . He a *captain!* Hang him, rogue! . . . A *captain!* these villains will make the word *captain* as odious . . . therefore *captains* had need look to it.—2 *H. IV.*, ii. 4.

I might say *element*, but the word is over-worn.—*Tw. N.*, iii. 1.

You are idle, shallow things: I am not of your *element.*—*Ibid.*, iii. 4.

Slice! that's my *humour* . . . good *humours* . . . nuthook's *humour* [*See* the diction of NYM throughout this play].—*Merry W.*, i. 1.

I have a *humour* to knock you . . . that's the *humour* of it [*See* the diction of NYM throughout this play also].—*H. V.*, ii. 1.

As odious as the word *occupy;* which was an excellent good word before it was ill sorted.—2 *H. IV.*, ii. 4.

To *occupy* the argument no longer.—*R. & Jul.*, ii. 4.

O Lord, sir! . . . *O Lord, sir!* [*See* the rest of the dialogue in this scene.]—*All's W.*, ii. 2.

I will tell her, sir, that you do *protest ;* which, as I take it, is a gentlemanlike offer. —*R. & Jul.*, ii. 4.

The lady *protests* too much, methinks.—*Hamlet*, iii. 2.

My love to thee is sound, *sans* crack or flaw.—*Sans*, "*sans*," I pray you.—*Love's L. L.*, v. 2.

Sans teeth, *sans* eyes, *sans* taste, *sans* everything.—*As You L.*, ii. 7.

Come, come ; *sans* compliment, what news abroad ?—*John*, v. 6.

Taste your legs, sir: put them to motion.—My legs do better understand me, sir, than I understand what you mean by bidding me *taste* my legs.—*Tw. N.*, iii. 1.

I pr'ythee *vent* thy folly somewhere else: thou know'st not me.—*Vent* my folly! he has heard that word of some great man, and now applies it to a fool: *vent* my folly! . . . tell me what I shall *vent* to my lady: shall I *vent* to her that thou art coming ?—*Tw. N.*, iv. 1.

By *welkin* and her stars!—*Merry W.*, i. 3.

By thy favour, sweet *welkin*, I must sigh in thy face.—*Love's L. L.*, iii. 1.

Who you are, and what you would, are out of my *welkin.*—*Tw. N.*, iii. 1.

PERSONAGES IN THE OLD MORALITIES, &c.

In the course of Shakespeare's dramas there are to be found allusions to certain allegorical personages who figured in the old moralities, mysteries, or miracle-plays that were formerly enacted for popular entertainment :—

Which is the wiser here? *Justice* or *Iniquity ?*—*M. for M.*, ii. 1.

Merely, thou art *Death's Fool.*—*Ibid.*, iii. 1.

> Like to the old *Vice* . . . with dagger of lath,
> In his rage and his wrath,
> Cries, ah, ha! to the *Devil :*
> Like a mad lad,
> Pare thy nails, dad ;
> Adieu, goodman drivel.—*Tw. N.*. iv. 2 (*Song*).

---

* The mode in which the title of " captain " was adopted by fellows having no claim to bear it is satirised by a dramatist who wrote at a later date than Shakespeare ; for Farquhar, in his comedy of the " Beaux' Stratagem," makes Gibbet the highwayman observe : " Captain is a good travelling name, and so I take it ; it stops a great many foolish inquiries that are generally made about gentlemen that travel ; it gives a man an air of something, and makes the drawers obedient—and thus far I am a captain, and no farther."—Act iii., sc. 2.

That reverend *Vice*, that grey *Iniquity*, that father ruffian, that *Vanity* in years.—
1 *H. IV.*, ii. 4.

The slave of life, and life *Time's Fool.—Ibid.*, v. 4.

And now is this *Vice's* dagger become a squire.—2 *H. IV.*, iii. 2.

Thus, like the formal *Vice*, *Iniquity*, I moralise two meanings in one word.—
R. III., iii. 1.

Let my lady apprehend no *Fear :* in all Cupid's pageant there is presented no
monster.—*Tr. & Cr.*, iii. 2.

Oh, I am *Fortune's Fool !—R. & Jul.*, iii. 1.

It out-herods *Herod :* pray you, avoid it.—*Hamlet*, iii. 2.

A *Vice* of kings; a cut-purse of the empire.—*Ibid.*, iii. 4.

And take *Vanity*, the puppet's part, against.—*Lear*, ii. 2.

I am even the natural *Fool of Fortune.—Ibid.*, iv. 6.

Thy angel becomes a *Fear*, as being o'erpower'd.—*Ant. & C.*, ii. 3.

> Or tie my treasure up in silken bags,
> To please the *Fool* and *Death.—Per.*, iii. 2.

He also alludes to certain personages in the pageants and puppet-
shows of his time :—

When loud *Rumour* speaks? . . . upon my tongues continual slanders ride. . . .
Who but *Rumour*, who but only I, make fearful musters? . . . *Rumour* is a pipe blown
by surmises. . . . Why is *Rumour* here ? . . . from *Rumour's* tongues they bring.—
2 *H. IV. (Induc.)*

I was then *Sir Dagonet* in Arthur's show.—*Ibid.*, iii. 2.

And also to certain figurers in the morris-dances of the period :—

And for womanhood, *Maid Marian* may be the deputy's wife of the ward to thee.—
Ibid., iii. 3.

The *hobby-horse* is forgot.—*Love's L. L.*, iii. 1.

With the *hobby-horse*, whose epitaph is, " For, oh, for, oh, the *hobby-horse* is forgot."
—*Hamlet*, iii. 2.

PHYSICAL INDICATIONS.

Our great dramatic poet gives occasional touches of physical indication, that forcibly heighten the effect of personal truth in actual
condition of the characters he draws. Some of these indications serve
to enhance prosaic and even humorous effect; while others aid in
strengthening the impression of excitement or anguish. Ludicrously
well, for instance, are denoted the remnants of sea-sickness still hanging
about Stephano, together with the effects of his constant application to
the bottle containing the wine he has saved, by his mode of adjuring
Trinculo not to embrace him with too demonstrative a hug of con-
gratulation :—

Pr'ythee, *do not turn me about; my stomach is not constant.—Temp.*, ii. 2.

Afterwards, in the same play, how pointedly is Prospero's disturbance
of mind marked, by the desire to calm his restlessness by motion :—

> Sir, I am vex'd :
> Bear with my weakness; my old brain is troubled :
> Be not disturb'd with my infirmity.
> If you be pleas'd, retire into my cell,
> And there repose : *a turn or two I 'll walk*,
> *To still my beating mind.—Ibid.*, iv. 1.

With what skill is augmented the impression of Constance's agony of grief and incipient frenzy, when she is made to tear off her head-dress, unable to bear the sense of heat upon her brain, with the words :—

> *I will not keep this form upon my head,*
> When there is such disorder in my wit.—*John*, iii. 1.

The approach of death is vividly painted to the imagination by such a touch as the following :—

> *His eye is hollow, and he changes much.*—2 *H. IV.*, iv. 4.

And the physical peculiarities attendant upon dying moments are with marvellous truth enumerated in the following passage :—

> 'A made a finer end, and went away, an it had been any christom child ; 'a parted even just between twelve and one, even at the turning o' the tide : for after I saw him *fumble with the sheets*, and *play with flowers*, and *smile upon his fingers' ends*, I knew there was but one way ; for *his nose was as sharp as a pen*, and *'a babbled of green fields*. . . . So *'a bade me lay more clothes on his feet :* I put my hand into the bed and felt them, and *they were cold as any stone ;* then I felt to his knees, and so upward and upward, and *all was as cold as any stone.*—*H. V.*, ii. 3.

The contrast between the visible appearance presented by the corse of one who has died a natural death and of one who has met with a violent death is thus graphically depicted :—

> See, *how the blood is settled in his face.*
> Oft have I seen a timely-parted ghost,
> *Of ashy semblance, meagre, pale, and bloodless,*
> Being all descended to the heart ;
> Who, in the conflict that it holds with death,
> Attracts the same for aidance 'gainst the enemy ;
> Which with the heart there cools, and ne'er returneth
> To blush and beautify the cheek again.
> But see, *his face is black and full of blood ;*
> *His eye-balls farther out than when he liv'd,*
> *Staring full ghastly like a strangled man ;*
> *His hair uprear'd, his nostrils stretch'd with struggling ;*
> *His hands abroad display'd, as one that grasp'd*
> *And tugg'd for life, and was by strength subdued :*
> *Look on the sheets, his hair, you see, is sticking ;*
> *His well-proportion'd beard made rough and rugged,*
> Like to the summer's corn by tempest lodg'd.
> It cannot be but he was murder'd here ;
> The least of all these signs were probable.—2 *H. VI.*, iii. 2.

Again he portrays the near approach of death in striking corporeal denotements :—

> Do you note
> *How much her grace is alter'd on the sudden ?*
> *How long her face is drawn ?   How pale she looks,*
> *And of an earthy cold ?   Mark her eyes !* . . .
> *Mine eyes grow dim.*   Farewell, my lord.—*H. VIII.*, iv. 2.

Even so slight a sentence as the following serves strongly to indicate the travelled and hungry condition of the banished exile, when he enters the dwelling of the man who has so long been his foe :—

> A goodly house : *the feast smells well.*—*Coriol.*, iv. 5.

Lear's exclamation, affecting to pass off the choking sensations of his grief and indignation as a fit of the disease called "the mother" or *hysterica passio*, aids powerfully in showing the emotions that surge within him :—

> O, how this mother *swells up toward my heart!*
> Hysterica passio—*down, thou climbing sorrow,*
> Thy element's below !—*Lear*, ii. 4.

The following passing phrase, uttered by the worn-out old king, as he yields to Kent's persuasions that he will lie down and take some rest, helps to indicate the state of exhaustion into which he has fallen, and to show how fatigue and want of food make themselves felt amid the other miseries of that maddening night:—

> Make no noise, make no noise; draw the curtains:
> So, so, so, *we'll go to supper* i' the morning: so, so, so.—*Ibid.*, iii. 4.

That his poor old frame has been severely shaken by exposure throughout that tempestuous night, and that he shivers with more than distressful emotion as he pours forth his wandering words, is conveyed by the brief phrase :—

> They told me I was everything; 'tis a lie,—*I am not ague-proof.*—*Ibid.*, iv. 6.

Again, the sensation of pressure and impeded circulation in the extremities, indicated in the following few words, gives augmented effect of suffering by the addition of physical distress to mental distress :—

> Now, now, now, now :
> *Pull off my boots : harder, harder :*—so.—*Ibid.*, iv. 6.

Then, again, one of the most intensely yet condensedly expressed denotements of mingled bodily pain and consciousness of mental infirmity ever penned, is where the old king gives utterance to that pathetic appeal, which actually makes us *feel* the sensation of wounded writhing within the head that it implies :—

> Use me well ;
> You shall have ransom.   Let me have a surgeon ;
> *I am cut to the brains.*—*Ibid.*, iv. 6.

In the following sentences, the poet not only shows us the poor old eyesight worn by age and grief, but subtly indicates the dimness of vision that precedes death :—

> Who are you?
> *Mine eyes are not o' the best:* I'll tell you straight . . .
> *This is a dull sight.*   Are you not Kent?—*Ibid.*, v. 3.

And, lastly, the dramatist has doubly denoted the oppression of grief and the difficult drawing of dying breath, in these few pathetically simple words:—

> *Pray you, undo this button:* thank you, sir.—*Ibid.*, v. 3.

In the following brief phrase, Shakespeare presents to us a physical condition arising from emotional disturbance—the perturbed ill-at-ease body, the fret of limb, the longing for motion, that accompanies fever of the mind :—

> Oh, pardon me; *'twill do me good to walk.*—*Oth.*, iv. 3.

And soon after, a remark is made that serves to trace a period when exterior calm succeeds to uncontrollable agitation.   Having resolved to put his supposed injurer to death, Othello is able to suppress those starts of speech and that fierceness of glance which were irrepressible while his soul was tossed with doubt and racked with suspense; and therefore it is, that Emilia says :—

> How goes it now? *he looks gentler than he did.—Oth.*, iv. 3.

But subsequently, in the dread moment of fulfilling his intended vengeance, the Moor's tortures of contending wrath and anguish are brought forcibly forth by the outward tokens here introduced :—

> And yet I fear you; for you are fatal then,
> *When your eyes roll so.* . . . .
> Alas! *why gnaw you so your nether lip?*
> Some bloody passion *shakes your very frame.—Ibid.*, v. 2.

With what verity of naturalness is the pathos of the situation heightened, where we behold heart-weary Imogen arriving at the cave among the Welsh mountains, by the touches of bodily fatigue and privation that the poet of Nature has thrown in :—

> I see a man's life is a tedious one:
> *I have tir'd myself;* and for two nights together
> Have made the ground my bed. *I should be sick*
> *But that my resolution helps me.* Milford,
> When from the mountain-top Pisanio show'd thee,
> Thou wast within a ken : O Jove ! I think
> Foundations fly the wretched : such, I mean,
> Where they should be reliev'd. . . . My dear lord !
> Thou art one of the false ones : *now I think on thee,*
> *My hunger's gone ; but even before, I was*
> *At point to sink for food.—Cym.*, iii. 6.

And the suddenly awakened desire for food upon the revival of joy in one previously given up to affliction has been denoted by Shakespeare in the following passage, where Pericles asks Lysimachus :—

> *Shall we refresh us,* sir, upon your shore,
> And give you gold for such provision
> As our intents will need ?—*Per.*, v. 2.

PLEONASMS.

Shakespeare has a few passages affording instances of the superflously repeated or redundant words that were sometimes used in a sentence by writers of his period ; and were then not considered objectionable :—

> *Of* what kind should this cock come *of ?—As You L.*, ii. 7.
> This wide and universal theatre
> Presents more woeful pageants than the scene
> Where*in* we play *in.—Ibid.*, ii. 7.
> Amity, too, of your brave father, *whom,*
> Though bearing misery, I desire my life
> Once more to look on *him.—W. T.*, v. 1.
> Oh, how it yearn'd my heart, *when* I beheld,
> In London streets, that coronation-day,
> *When* Bolingbroke rode on roan Barbary !—*R. II.*, v. 5.

Of Salisbury, who can report *of* him.—2 *H. VI.*, v. 3.

I come no more to make you laugh : things *now*,
That bear a weighty and a serious brow,
Sad, high, and working, full of state and woe,
Such noble scenes as draw the eye to flow,
We *now* present.—*H. VIII.* (*Prologue*).

   All the whole time
I was my chamber's prisoner.—*Ibid.*, i. 1.

To whom as great a charge as little honour
He meant to lay *upon*.—*Ibid.*, i. 1.

And sleep in dull cold marble, where no mention
Of me more must be heard *of*.—*Ibid.*, iii. 2.

In what enormity is Marcius poor *in*, that you two have not in abundance ?—*Coriol.*, ii. 1.

That fair, *for* which love groan'd *for* and would die.—*R. & Jul.*, i. 5 (*Chorus*).

   Now his friends are dead,
Doors, that were ne'er acquainted with their wards
Many a bounteous year, must be employ'd
Now to guard sure their master.—*Timon*, iii. 3.

And which, without desert, because thine eye
Presumes to reach, *all thy whole* heap must die.—*Per.*, i. 1.

The men of Tyrus *on* the head
Of Helicanus would set *on*
The crown of Tyre.—*Ibid.*, iii. (*Gower*).

There are two passages in Shakespeare that wear the superficial appearance of being pleonastic ; but in both passages the charge of pleonasm arises from insufficient knowledge of the mode in which Shakespeare uses some words :—

These *dangerous unsafe* lunes i' the king, beshrew them !—*W. T.*, ii. 2.

Here, " dangerous " is used in the sense of 'severe,' 'sharp,' 'keen,' 'menacing,' more than in its directer sense of ' perilous.'

Why such unplausive eyes are *bent*, why *turn'd* on him.—*Tr. & Cr.*, iii. 3.

To this Steevens objects, proposing to alter the passage, saying : " If the eyes were *bent* on him, they were *turn'd* on him. This tautology, therefore, together with the redundancy of the line, plainly show that we ought to read, with Sir Thomas Hanmer, ' Why such unplausive eyes are bent on him.' " In the first place, Shakespeare uses the word " bent " (in reference to eyes) to express a frown, a stern look, an angry glance; therefore, in the above line, " bent " appears to us to express ' cast frowningly,' rather than in the sense of 'inclined'; which does away with the alleged " tautology " : and, in the second place, " the redundancy of the line " is merely consistent with many lines in Shakespeare, containing more than the usual strict ten feet.

We find several instances of Shakespeare's using a second epithet, or sometimes a second verb, bearing almost similar meaning with the first ; which, at the time he wrote, was not considered a fault of pleonasm, but as giving emphasis and additional force to the phrase :—

The *inaudible* and *noiseless* foot of Time.—*All's W.*, v. 3.

That *old* and *antique* song we heard last night.—*Tw. N.*, ii. 4.

Not all the water in the *rough rude* sea.—*R. II.*, iii. 2.

Did he suspire, that *light* and *weightless* down perforce must move.—2 *H. IV.*, iv. 4.

To buy a *slobbery* and a *dirty* farm.—*H. V.*, iii. 5.

Or given my heart a winking, *mute* and *dumb.*—*Hamlet*, ii. 2.
And in my hearing be you *mute* and *dumb.*—*Lucrece, Stanza* 161.
But doth *rebate* and *blunt* his natural edge.—*M. for M.*, i. 5.
To *prate* and *talk* for life and honour.—*W. T.*, iii. 2.
To *plot, contrive*, or *complot* any ill 'gainst us.—*R. II.*, i. 3.

He has also expressions that may be accused of being pleonastic ; but which, to our minds, bear a certain energy and spirit with fitness of characteristic context in them that give them poetic propriety :—

> It was the *swift celerity* of his death,
> Which I did think with slower foot came on,
> That brain'd my purpose.—*M. for M.*, v. 1.
> Forwearied in this action of *swift speed.*—*John*, ii. 1.
> Doth Arthur live ? oh, haste thee to the peers,
> Throw this report on their *incensed rage*,
> And make them tame to their obedience ! . . .
> Oh, answer not ; but to my closet bring
> The angry lords with all *expedient* haste !*—*John*, iv. 2.

Whereas, in the " First Part of King Henry VI." there are pleonasms so needless and so wanting in vigour, that they have been among the many points of style in that play which have always formed proofs to us of its being for the most part not his composition. Compare the following vapid tautologies of diction with those we have above cited:—

In private will I talk with thee *apart.*—1 *H. VI.*, i. 2.
Or will you *blame* and *lay the fault* on me ?—*Ibid.*, ii. 1.
To gather our soldiers, *scatter'd* and *dispers'd.*—*Ibid.*, ii. 1.
I see report is *fabulous* and *false.*—*Ibid.*, ii. 3.
Where is the *best* and *safest* passage in ?—*Ibid.*, iii. 2.
Are *glad* and *fain* by flight to save themselves.—*Ibid.*, iii. 2.
In France, amongst a *fickle wavering* nation.—*Ibid.*, iv. 1.
Than I am able to *instruct* or *teach.*—*Ibid.*, iv. 1.
Your *angry choler* on your enemies.—*Ibid.*, iv. 1.
Than yet can be *imagin'd* or *suppos'd.*—*Ibid.*, iv. 1.
Of an *invincible unconquer'd* spirit.—*Ibid.*, iv. 2.
This *speedy* and *quick* appearance argues proof.—*Ibid.*, v. 3.

And there is a tame as well as pleonastic expression in another play which seems to us to contain internal proof that it is not wholly written by Shakespeare :—

My mercy dried their *water-flowing tears.*—3 *H. IV.*, iv. 8.

There are a few idiomatic phrases, that are pleonastic in their form, which Shakespeare uses :—

How and which way I may bestow myself.—*Two G. of V.*, iii. 1.
I 'll take the sacrament on 't, *how and which way* you will.—*All's W.*, iv. 3.
If I know *how or which way* to order these affairs.—*R. II.*, ii. 2.

> Then *how or which way* should they first break in ?—
> Question, my lords, no farther of the case,
> *How or which way.*—1 *H. VI.*, ii. 1.
> Signor Antonio, *many a time and oft*,
> In the Rialto, you have rated me.—*Mer. of V.*, i. 3.

---

* " Expedient " is generally, as here, used by Shakespeare as an equivalent for ' expeditious.'

And *many a time and oft* myself have heard.—2 *H. VI.*, ii. 1.
Many a time and often I have dined with him.—*Timon*, iii. 1.
Many a time and oft have you climb'd up to walls.—*Jul. C.*, i. 1.
Time and the hour runs through the roughest day.—*Macb.*, i. 3.

And there is a pleonastic legal phrase which Shakespeare has used :—

There might you have beheld one joy crown another, *so, and in such manner*, that it seemed sorrow wept to take leave of them.—*W. T.*, v. 2.

POETIC BEAUTIES.

Such a heading as the present, when treating of a writer like Shakespeare, would seem to involve countless citations ; but we merely propose to enumerate a few of his passages containing poetic beauties of a peculiar kind—where effects of actual colour or sound are presented to the senses by his artistic pen.   Some of his picturesquely graphic presentments, marking locality, we have enumerated under our heading entitled DRAMATIC LAWS AND ART ; but here we bring together those more particularly conveying hues and tones.   In the following address to Iris, for instance, how the poet fills our eyes with resplendent colouring of sky and earth :—

> Hail, many-colour'd messenger, that ne'er
> Dost disobey the wife of Jupiter :
> Who, with thy saffron wings, upon my flowers
> Diffusest honey-drops, refreshing showers ;
> And with each end of thy blue bow dost crown
> My bosky acres and my unshrubb'd down,
> Rich scarf to my proud earth ; why hath thy queen
> Summon'd me hither, to this short grass'd green ?—*Temp.*, iv. 1.

While, in the few following words, he puts before our sight the very impression of that rainbow-tinted moisture which swells into an eye ready to brim over with tears, and makes it look rounder and larger through its medium :—

> What 's the matter,
> That this distemper'd messenger of wet,
> The many-coloured Iris, rounds thine eye ?—*All's W.*, i. 3.

And how gorgeously he floods the following lines with blended rosy, golden, and sea-green hues, where Oberon, the fairy-king, says :—

> I with the morning's love have oft made sport ;
> And, like a forester, the groves may tread,
> Even till the eastern gate, all fiery-red,
> Opening on Neptune with fair blessed beams,
> Turns into yellow gold his salt-green streams.—*Mid. N. D.*, iii. 2.

And with what power of condensed expression has he depicted vast spread of imagined colouring in this brief phrase :—

> Will all great Neptune's ocean wash this blood
> Clean from my hand ?   No ; this my hand will rather
> The multitudinous seas incarnardine,
> Making the green—one red.—*Macb.*, ii, 2.

In the following passage, the tumultuous raging of the sea, the frantic cries of the drowning wretches, the noise and uproar of the scene are brought to our very ears by Miranda's words :—

> If by your art, my dearest father, you have
> Put the wild waters in this roar, allay them.
> The sky, it seems, would pour down stinking pitch,
> But that the sea, mounting to the welkin's cheek,
> Dashes the fire out.   Oh, I have suffer'd
> With those that I saw suffer ! a brave vessel,
> Who had, no doubt, some noble creatures in her,
> Dash'd all to pieces.   Oh, the cry did knock
> Against my very heart !—*Temp.*, i. 2.

The beauty and the fitful play of the magic harmony sent to lure Ferdinand onward to the spot where he will meet with Miranda, is made to vibrate upon our senses as well as upon those of the speaker, in this passage :—

> Where should this music be ?   I' th' air or th' earth ?
> It sounds no more : and sure, it waits upon
> Some god o' th' island.   Sitting on a bank,
> Weeping again the king my father's wreck,
> This music crept by me upon the waters,
> Allaying both their fury, and my passion,
> With its sweet air : thence I have follow'd it,
> Or it hath drawn me rather : but 'tis gone.
> No, it begins again.—*Ibid.*, i. 2.

The strangeness and loveliness of the sounds that float about the enchanted island are brought full upon our fancied hearing, where even the savage Caliban is made to express the soothing effect they have upon his senses :—

> The isle is full of noises,
> Sounds, and sweet airs, that give delight, and hurt not.
> Sometimes a thousand twangling instruments
> Will hum about mine ears ; and sometime voices,
> That, if I then had wak'd after long sleep,
> Will make me sleep again.—*Ibid.*, iii. 2.

And with what grand sonorous tone is the murmur of universal nature in the ear of a conscience-stricken soul described, where King Alonso exclaims :—

> Methought, the billows spoke, and told me of it,
> The winds did sing it to me ; and the thunder,
> That deep and dreadful organ-pipe, pronounc'd
> The name of Prosper ; it did base my trespass.—*Ibid.*, iii. 3.

The following passage not only occasions us to hear the spirit-stirring sounds of the chase, together with that peculiar effect of "bells" produced by hounds baying in chorus, but it brings to our appreciation that special and almost indescribable charm that certain thrilling "discord" amid a monotony of melodious sound possesses for the educated musical ear :—

> My love shall hear the music of my hounds. . . .
> We will, fair queen, up to the mountain's top,
> And mark the musical confusion
> Of hounds and echo in conjunction.—
> I was with Hercules and Cadmus once,
> When in a wood of Crete they bay'd the bear

With hounds of Sparta : never did I hear
Such gallant chiding ; for, besides the groves,
The skies, the fountains, every region near
Seem'd all one mutual cry : I never heard
So musical a discord, such sweet thunder.—
My hounds are bred out of the Spartan kind,
So flew'd, so sanded ; and their heads are hung
With ears that sweep away the morning dew ;
Crook-kneed, and dew-lapp'd, like Thessalian bulls ;
Slow in pursuit, but match'd in mouth like bells,
Each under each.   A cry more tuneable
Was never holla'd to, nor cheer'd with horn,
In Crete, in Sparta, nor in Thessaly.—*Mid. N. D.*, iv. 1.

To those who have felt the full voluptuous effect of a melodious cadence in music, the following brief but most characteristic expression —a " dying fall "—will recall the exact kind of subsiding notes that drop off into silence :—

That strain again ! it had a dying fall :
Oh, it came o'er my ear like the sweet south,
That breathes upon a bank of violets,
Stealing and giving odour !—*Tw. N.*, i. 1.

And, in the next passage, how the words " move still, still so," give the alternate rise and fall, the to-and-fro undulation of the water, the easy swing of each wave, in most harmonious flow of combined movement and sound :—

When you do dance, I wish you
A wave o' the sea, that you might ever do
Nothing but that ; move still, still so,
And own no other function.—*W. T.*, iv. 3.

The following passages afford instances—among numberless that might be cited—of Shakespeare's exquisite ear for poetic cadence at the close of a line or sentence :—

For where thou art, there is the world itself,
With every several pleasure in the world ;
And where thou art not, desolation.—2 *H. VI.*, iii. 2.
                    Nay, forsooth, my friends,
They that must weigh out my afflictions,
They that my trust must grow to, live not here ;
They are, as all my other comforts, *far hence,*
In mine own country, lords.—*H. VIII.*, iii. 1.
Shipwreck'd upon a kingdom, where no pity,
No friends, no hope ; no kindred weep for me ;
Almost no grave allow'd me : like the lily,
That once was mistress of the field and flourish'd,
I'll hang my head and perish.—*Ibid.*, iii. 1.
I have touch'd the highest point of all my greatness ;
And, from that full meridian of my glory,
I haste now to my setting : I shall fall
Like a bright exhalation in the evening,
And no man see me more.—*Ibid.*, iii. 2.
And when he falls, he falls like Lucifer,
Never to hope again.—*Ibid.*, iii. 2.
And oh ! you mortal engines, whose rude throats
The immortal Jove's dread clamours counterfeit,
Farewell ! Othello's occupation's gone !—*Oth.*, iii. 3.

POINTS LEFT FOR IMPROVISATION.

It was not unfrequently a practice with the dramatists of Shakespeare's time, to leave certain points in their plays for filling up as occasion served, or as the ingenuity of the actor entrusted with the part in which this point occurred might suggest. This was often the case, where a song had to be introduced; the choice of which was left to the singer or to the theatrical manager: and it was sometimes the case, in the course of the clown's part; some of the scraps of quoted ballad, or impromptu levity, which he had to utter, being left to the memory or extempore wit of the performer to supply. Occasionally, the popular favourites who enacted the clowns, chose to indulge in what, in stage technicality, is called "gag," by introducing a quantity of extraneous jest or ribaldry of their own invention, irrespective of any such introduction being signified by the author of the play. It is to this practice that Hamlet alludes, where he says:

And let those that play your clowns speak *no more than is set down for them :* for there be of them that will themselves laugh, to set on some quantity of barren spectators to laugh too; *though in the meantime,* some necessary question of *the play be then to be considered :* that's villanous, and shows a most pitiful ambition in the fool that uses it.—*Hamlet,* iii. 2.

Into Hamlet's mouth, also, Shakespeare has put allusion to the legitimately written drama, and to those plays where the actor is at liberty to substitute his own words. There were formerly extemporal dramas, in imitation of the Italian *commedie all' improviso,* where the performers had to invent the dialogue for themselves :—

The best actors in the world, either for tragedy, comedy, history, pastoral, pastoral-comical, historical-pastoral, tragical-historical, tragical-comical-historical-pastoral, scene individable, or poem unlimited : Seneca cannot be too heavy, nor Plautus too light. For *the law of writ* and *the liberty,* these are the only men.—*Ibid.,* ii. 2.

The following passages of *stage direction* (which we here give as printed in the Folio of 1623) afford a specimen of Shakespeare's occasionally permitting a point of dialogue to be supplied by the performer :—

> *Mortimer.* Good father, tell her that she and my aunt Percy
> Shall follow in your conduct speedily.
>   [*Glendower speaks to her in Welsh, and she answers him in the same.*]
> *Glendower.* She's desperate here; a peevish, self-will'd harlotry,
> One that no persuasion can do good upon.   [*The Lady speakes in Welsh.*
> *Mortimer.* I understand thy looks: that pretty Welsh
> Which thou pour'st down from these swelling heavens
> I am too perfect in; and, but for shame,
> In such a parley should I answer thee.   [*The Lady againe in Welsh.*
> I understand thy kisses, and thou mine,
> And that's a feeling disputation:
> But I will never be a truant, love,
> Till I have learn'd thy language; for thy tongue
> Makes Welsh as sweet as ditties highly penn'd,
> Sung by a fair queen in a summer's bower,
> With ravishing division to her lute.
> *Glendower.* Nay, if you melt, then will she run mad.
>   [*The Lady speakes againe in Welsh*].—1 *H. IV.,* iii. 1.

And the following passages of *stage direction* (which we also give as printed in the Folio of 1623) show that Shakespeare occasionally adopted the then practice of sometimes leaving an introduced song or piece of music to the selection of the performer or management : —

> *Hotspur.* Peace! she sings.—[*Heere the Lady sings a Welsh Song.*]—
> 1 *H. IV.*, iii. 1.
>
> *Sir Andrew.* Good, i' faith. Come, begin.—[*Catch sung.*]—*Tw. N.*, ii. 3.
>
> *Brutus.* It was well done ; and thou shalt sleep again ;
> I will not hold thee long : if I do live,
> I will be good to thee.—[*Musicke, and a Song.*]—*Jul. C.*, iv. 3.

In the following passage there is a *stage direction* of a similar kind, which we here give as printed in the 1664 Folio edition of " Pericles " ; since that play was not included in the 1623 Folio edition of Shakespeare's plays :—

> *Lysimachus.* Come, let us leave her ;
> And the gods make her prosperous.—[*The Song.*]—*Per.*, v. 1.

In the following passage there is a word which has been supposed to have been the indication of a song, or the commencement of a song, usually sung by the boy who performed Moth ; but we are inclined to think that " Concolinel " forms a few syllables strung together to express warbling, or humming a tune, as we now use 'la li ra, la li ra,' &c. Armado's comment—" Sweet air ! "—seems to us to confirm our idea :—

> *Armado.* Warble, child ; make passionate my sense of hearing.
> *Moth (Singing).* Concolinel.
> *Armado.* Sweet air !—*Love's L. L.*, iii. 1.

POWER IN WRITING SILENCE; AND PERFECT IMPRESSION THROUGH IMPERFECT EXPRESSION.

Shakespeare, among his other vast gifts and resources in dramatic art, has shown an admirable power of indicating silence in certain of his characters, by the comment upon their abstinence from speech which he has put into the mouths of other characters. When Hermione descends from the pedestal where she has impersonated a statue of herself, she utters no word. Not only is her heart suffocating with unutterable emotions in this moment of restoration to life and love after a sixteen years' self-imposed seclusion and silence, but she is exactly the woman to give no other than mute token of reconciliation when she throws herself into her husband's arms, and forgives him the injustice he once did her. Her reticence is thus marked, by the comment of others :—

> *Leontes (Embracing her).* Oh, she's warm !
> If this be magic, let it be an art
> Lawful as eating.
> *Polixenes.* She embraces him.
> *Camillo.* She hangs about his neck.—*W. T.*, v. 3.

Perdita's reticent dignity of soul (inherited from her mother) as well as her innate love of truth and candid nature are well indicated by her maintaining silence while Polixenes rebukes his son and reproaches her, and again while Leontes receives her and Florizel, who relates a feigned history of themselves :—

> Mark your divorce, young sir, &c.—*W. T.*, iv. 3.
> She came from Libya, &c.—*Ibid.*, v. 1.

The habitual quietude and soft stillness of Virgilia, her silent weeping and suppressed excitement, when she meets her husband on his return from the Volscian war, are excellently denoted by her husband's words of greeting :—

> *Coriolanus.*   My gracious silence, hail!
> Wouldst thou have laugh'd had I come coffin'd home,
> That weep'st to see me triumph? Ah, my dear,
> Such eyes the widows in Corioli wear,
> And mothers that lack sons.—*Coriol.*, ii. 1.

Later on, the same characteristic silent distress is indicated on her part ; where, after the first irrepressible burst of anguish in the exclamation, "Oh, heavens, oh, heavens!" she remains speechless until the close of the scene where her husband is escorted by his friends to the gates of Rome, whence he is banished ; and she gives only silent response to his repeated adieus :—

> Farewell, my wife,—my mother: . . .
> Come, my sweet wife, my dearest mother, and
> My friends of noble touch ; when I am forth,
> Bid me farewell, and smile.—*Ibid.*, iv. 1.

Again, her quiet grieving is indicated by the contrast of Volumnia's fierce reproaches to the tribunes ; and by the characteristic rebuke given by the Roman matron to her meek daughter-in-law :—

> Come, let's go :
> Leave this faint puling, and lament as I do,
> In anger, Juno-like. Come, come, come.—*Ibid.*, iv. 2.

Yet again, Virgilia's habitual silence, and Volumnia's as habitual torrent of words, are most artistically conveyed by the following injunction, given without waiting for the speech it enjoins:—

> Daughter, speak you:
> He cares not for your weeping.—*Ibid.*, v. 3.

In the following passage Macduff's silent anguish is forcibly depicted by making Malcolm first exclaim at the horror of Rosse's tidings, and then turn to the bereaved husband and father, who is unable to utter a syllable on the first shock of hearing them :—

> *Malcolm.*   Merciful Heaven!
> What, man! ne'er pull your hat upon your brow ;
> Give sorrow words : the grief that does not speak
> Whispers the o'er-fraught heart, and bids it break.—*Macb.*, iv. 3.

For the mode in which our dramatist ingeniously draws speechlessness, we refer our readers to the examination of four of his characters of few words:—

Dull.—*Love's L. L.*, i. 2; iv. 2; and v. 1.
James Gurney.*—*John*, i. 1.
Francis.—1 *H. IV.*, ii. 4.
Silence.—2 *H. IV.*, iii. 2, and v. 3.

Shakespeare has a most potent art in conveying perfect impression of a speaker's meaning, through imperfectly expressed speech. Occasionally this imperfect expression conveys the effect of emotional agitation in the speaker; sometimes a threat, an inuendo, or a half-uttered insinuation, that the speaker wishes his interlocutor to understand without explicit utterance; and sometimes, incapacity on the part of the speaker to put into words all that is meant [*See* UNFINISHED SENTENCES]:—

If you prove a mutineer, the next tree! The poor monster's my subject, and he shall not suffer indignity.—*Temp.*, iii. 2.

> Would I were dead, but that, methinks, already—
> What was he, that did make it?—*W. T.*, v. 3.

> I had a thing to say,—but let it go . . .
> I would into thy bosom pour my thoughts:
> But, ah! I will not: yet I love thee well. . . .
> Good Hubert, Hubert, Hubert, throw thine eye
> On yond' young boy: I'll tell thee what, my friend,
> He is a very serpent in my way;
> And wheresoe'er this foot of mine doth tread,
> He lies before me: dost thou understand me?
> Thou art his keeper.—*John*, iii. 3.

I have known thee these twenty-nine years, come peascod-time; but an honester and truer-hearted man,—well, fare thee well.—2 *H. IV.*, ii. 4.

Wished, my lord! the gods grant,—Oh, my lord!—What should they grant? What makes this pretty abruption?—*Tr. & Cr.*, iii. 2.

An 'twere to give again,—but 'tis no matter.—*Coriol.*, ii. 3.

He had, sir, a kind of face, methought,—I cannot tell how to term it.—He had so; looking as it were,—Would I were hanged, but I thought there was more in him than I could think.—*Ibid.*, iv. 5.

I have it, and soundly too:—your houses!—*R. & Jul.*, iii. 1.

> Will't hold? will't hold?—
> It does: but time will—and so—
> I do conceive.—*Timon*, iii. 6.

> If you shall cleave to my consent,—when 'tis,
> It shall make honour for you.—*Macb.*, ii. 1.

> Or by pronouncing of some doubtful phrase,
> As, "Well, well, we know"; or, "We could, an if we would";
> Or, "If we list to speak"; or, "There be, an if they might";
> Or such ambiguous giving out, to note
> That you know aught of me.—*Hamlet*, i. 5.

> Approach, thou beacon to this under globe,
> That by thy comfortable beams I may
> Peruse this letter! Nothing, almost, sees miracles
> But misery: I know 'tis from Cordelia,
> Who hath most fortunately been inform'd
> Of my obscured course; and shall find time
> From this enormous state,—seeking to give

---

* Of whom Coleridge, in one of his "Table-Talks," says: "For an instance of Shakespeare's powers *in minimis*, I generally quote James Gurney's character in "King John." How individual and comical he is with the four words allowed to his dramatic life!"

> Losses their remedies,—All weary and o'er-watched,
> Take vantage, heavy eyes, not to behold
> This shameful lodging.—*Lear*, ii. 2.

The imperfect expression, the confused and inconsecutive phraseology, the disjointed sentences, in the above speech, appear to us to give perfectly the impression of the speaker's reflections upon the probable contents of the letter which he defers reading until the sun shall have risen, and his yielding to the sleep that meanwhile creeps over him:—

> Why should she write to Edmund?   Might not you
> Transport her purposes by word?   Belike,
> Something—I know not what—I 'll love thee much ;
> Let me unseal the letter.—
> 　　　　　　　　　　　Madam, I had rather—
> I know your lady does not love her husband.—*Ibid.*, iv. 5.
>
> And so I am, I am . . . No cause, no cause.—*Ibid.*, iv. 7.
>
> Nothing, my lord : or if—I know not what.—*Oth.*, iii. 3.

Handkerchief,—confessions,—handkerchief ! to confess, and be hanged for his labour ;—first, to be hanged, and then to confess : I tremble at it.   Nature would not invest herself in such shadowing passion, without some instruction.   It is not words that shake me thus :—Pish !—Noses, ears, and lips.   Is it possible ?   Confess !—Handkerchief !—O devil !—*Ibid.*, iv. 1.

> And she 's obedient, as you say,—obedient,
> Very obedient.   Proceed you in your tears.—
> Concerning this, sir,—O well-painted passion !—
> I am commanded home.—Get you away ;
> I 'll send for you anon.—Sir, I obey the mandate,
> And will return to Venice.—Hence ! avaunt !—*Ibid.*, iv. 1.
>
> O Desdemona !—away ! away ! away !—*Ibid.*, iv. 2.
>
> Sir, you and I must part,—but that 's not it ;
> Sir, you and I have lov'd,—but there's not it ;
> That you know well : something it is I would,—
> O, my oblivion is a very Antony,
> And I am all forgotten.—*Ant. & C.*, i. 3.

My noble brother ! . . . Sir, look well to my husband's house ; and— . . . I 'll tell you in your ear.—*Ibid.*, iii. 2.

Then, Antony,—but now,—well, on.—*Ibid.*, iv. 4.

> 　　　　　　　　　　　　　The augurers
> Say, they know not,—they cannot tell ;—look grimly,
> And dare not speak their knowledge.—*Ibid.*, iv. 10.
>
> There are no more such masters : I may wander
> From east to occident, cry out for service,
> Try many, all good, serve truly, never
> Find such another master.—*Cym.*, iv. 2.
>
> Why did you throw your wedded lady from you ?
> Think that you are upon a rock ; and now
> Throw me again.—
> 　　　　　　　Hang there like fruit, my soul,
> Till the tree die !—*Ibid.*, v. 5.
>
> 　　　　　　　Voice and favour !—
> You are, you are—oh, royal Pericles !—*Per.*, v. 3.

PRONUNCIATION.

There are some peculiarities in the mode of occasionally pronouncing some words used by Shakespeare that require bearing in mind when judging certain passages of his plays ; either to properly comprehend the metre of the lines where such words occur, or to appreciate the quibble involved in a similar sound :—

Fill all thy bones with *aches* [pronounced as a dissyllable], make thee roar.—*Temp.*, i. 2.

" *Aches* " [pronounced as dissyllable] contract and starve your supple joints !—*Timon*, i. 1.

If you love an *addle egg* [similar sound] as well as you love an *idle head*, you would eat chickens i' the shell.—*Tr. & Cr.*, i. 2.

Al'ce [' Alice'] madâm, or Joan madam ?—*Tam. of S.*, *Induc.* 2.

And in such *alligant* [' elegant' or, perhaps, ' eloquent.' *See* CORRUPTIONS] terms.—*Merry W.*, ii. 2.

Their bands i' the vaward are the *Antiates* [as trisyllable].—*Coriol.*, i. 6.

Be called thieves of the day's *beauty* [pronounced as ' booty'].—1 *H. IV.*, i. 2.

La force de ton *bras* [pronouncing final *s*: similar sound].—Brass, cur !—*H. V.*, iv. 4.

And all the *ceremony* [as trisyllable] of this compàct.—*Tw. N.*, v. 1.

She never had so sweet a *changeling* [as trisyllable].—*Mid. N. D.*, ii. 1.

These are the parents to these *children* [as trisyllable].—*Com. of E.*, v. 1.

But *civil* [pronounced as ' Seville'], count,—*civil* as an orange.—*M. Ado*, ii. 1.

Be valu'd 'gainst your wife's *commandment* [as quadrisyllable].—*Mer. of V.*, iv. 1.

And what says my *conceal'd* [similar sound] lady to our *cancell'd* love ?—*R. & Jul.*, iii. 3.

Sir, the *contempts* [' contents '] thereof are as touching me.—*Love's L. L.*, i. 1.

Whereas the *contràry* [as quadrisyllable] bringeth bliss.—1. *H. VI.*, v. 5.

Her amber hairs for foul have amber *coted* [' quoted' was sometimes thus pronounced. *See* PECULIAR USE OF WORDS].—*Love's L. L.*, iv. 3.

And that hath *dazzled* [as trisyllable] my reason 's light.—*Two G. of V.*, ii. 4.

I could too well feel his blows, and withal so *doubtfully* [used punningly in reference to two words of somewhat similar sound—' doughtily ' and ' redoubtably '], that I could scarce understand them.—*Com. of E.*, ii. 1.

Ducdame [as trisyllable], *ducdame*, *ducdame*.—*As You L.*, ii. 5 (*Song*).

Fire [as dissyllable] that 's closest kept burns most of all.—*Two G. of V.*, i. 2.

Why, what a peevish *fool* [similar sound] was that of Crete, that taught his son the office of a *fowl !*—3 *H. VI.*, v. 6.

I am here with thee and thy *goats* [similar sound] as the most capricious poet, honest Ovid, was among the *Goths.*—*As You L.*, iii. 3.

She was the sweet-marjoram of the salad, or rather, the herb of *grace* [similar sound].—They are not salad-herbs, you knave ; they are nose-herbs.—I am no great Nebuchadnezzar, sir, I have not much skill in *grass.*—*All's W.*, iv. 5.

Edward and Richard, like a brace of *greyhounds* [as monosyllable ; having sometimes formerly been written ' grewnds'].—3 *H. VI.*, ii. 5.

By my troth, I am exceeding ill : heigh-ho !—

For a hawk, a horse, or a husband ?—

For the letter that begins them all, H [the word ' ache' was formerly pronounced *aitch*].—*M. Ado*, iii. 4.

These oracles are *hardly* [as trisyllable] attain'd.—2 *H. VI.*, i. 4.

These ears of mine, thou know'st, did *hear* [as dissyllable] thee.—*Com. of E.*, v. 1.

Brought hither Henry *Hereford* [as dissyllable], thy bold son.—*R. II.*, i. 1.

A ship you sent me to, to *hire* [as dissyllable] waftage.—*Com. of E.*, iv. 1.

Sign'd in thy spoil, and crimson'd in thy *lethe* [as monosyllable].—*Jul. C.*, iii. 1.

That my master is become a notable *lover* [similar sound] ?—I never knew him otherwise.—Than how?—A notable *lubber.*—*Two G. of V.*, ii. 5.

That now is lying in *Marseilles'* [as trisyllable] road.—*Tam. of S.*, ii. 1.

His grace is at *Marseilles* [as trisyllable] ; to which place.—*All's W.*, iv. 4.

I deny your *major* [used punningly in reference to its similarity of sound with ' mayor ']: if you will deny the sheriff, so.—1 *H. IV.*, ii. 4.

I am now, sir, muddied in Fortune's *mood* ['mud' was formerly pronounced somewhat like "mood"], and smell somewhat strong of her strong displeasure.—*All's W.*, v. 2.

It is much that the *Moor* [similar sound] should be *more* than reason.—*Mer. of V.*, iii. 5.

Speak it in French, king; say, pardonnez *moy* [pronounced in Shakespeare's time so as to allow of its rhyming with "destroy"].— Dost thou teach pardon pardon to destroy?—*R. II.*, v. 3.

Ayez pitié de *moy* [pronounced as above explained].—*Moy* [supposed to be a contraction of 'moidore'; a Portuguese coin, worth about twenty-seven shillings] shall not serve; I will have forty *moys*.—*H. V.*, iv. 4.

I ay me stark *nak'd* [as monosyllable], and let the water-flies.—*Ant. & C.*, v. 2.

There's not a note of mine that's worth the *noting* [similar sound].—Why, these are very crotchets that he speaks; note, notes, forsooth, and *nōthing* !—*M. Ado*, ii. 3.

No hearing, no feeling, but my sir's song, and admiring the *nōthing* [pronounced as above with a long ō; affording a pun with 'noting'] of it.—*W. T.*, iv. 3.

By the compulsion of their *ordnance* [as trisyllable].—*John*, ii. 1.

In second accent of his *ordnance* [as trisyllable].—*H. V.*, ii. 4.

But to *parfect* ['perfect'] one man in one poor man.—*Love's L. L.*, v. 2.

Good-morrow master *person* ['parson'].—Master *person*—quasi *pers-on* ['pierce was sometimes formerly pronounced 'perse,' and 'one' like 'on']. And if one should be pierced, which is the one?—*Ibid.*, iv. 2.

Well, if *Percy* [sometimes corruptly pronounced 'Piercy'] be alive, I'll pierce him.—1 *H. IV.*, v. 3.

Dumain was at my service, and his sword: No *point* [used as the French negative for 'none,' and in reference to the "point" of a sword], quoth I.—*Love's L. L.*, v. 2.

Hath turned my feignèd *prayer* [as dissyllable] on my head.—*R. III.*, v. 1

Cousin, go draw our *puissance* [as trisyllable] together.—*John*, iii. 1.

For every one *pursents* ['presents'] three.—*Love's L. L.*, v. 2.

I *quote* [sometimes formerly pronounced like 'coat'] it in your jerkin.—*Two G. of V.*, ii. 4.

Renege [pronounced with a hard *g*, as if written 'reneag,' which is the spelling in the quarto copy of this play], affirm, and turn their halcyon beaks.—*Lear*, ii. 2.

The buckles on his breast, *reneges* [pronounced with a hard *g*, and as a dissyllable] all temper.—*Ant. & C.*, i. 1.

I myself *reprehend* ['represent'] his own person.—*Love's L. L.*, i. 1.

Oh, how this spring of love *resembleth* [as quadrisyllable].—*Two G. of V.*, i. 3.

That shall *reverberate* [as trisyllable] all as loud as thine.—*John*, v. 2.

That I have room with *Rome* [sometimes pronounced like "room"] to curse awhile.—*Ibid.*, iii. 1.

Rome [sometimes pronounced like "roam"] shall remedy this.—Roam thither, then.—1 *H. VI.*, iii. 1.

An he begin once, he'll rail in his *rope-tricks* [the speaker confounds this with the somewhat similarly sounding word 'rhetoric' or 'rhetorics'; and accordingly quibbles upon it in this sense, by introducing the term "figure" immediately afterwards]. I'll tell you what, sir, an she stand him but a little, he will throw a figure in her face.—*Tam. of S.*, i. 2.

Is not l'envoy a *salve* [although not pronounced like the Latin form of salutation, *salve*, Moth chooses to pun upon the English epithet for unguent, as though it were so, merely because they are spelt alike]?—*Love's L. L.*, iii. 1.

Good, good, my lord; the *secrets* [as trisyllable] of nature.—*Tr. & Cr.*, iv. 2.

And these two Dromios, one in *semblance* [as trisyllable].—*Com. of E.*, v. 1.

Why, thou peevish *sheep* [similar sound], what *ship* of Epidamnum stays for me?—*Ibid.*, iv. 1.

He is shipp'd already, and I have play'd the *sheep* [pronounced 'ship' in Warwick-shire and some other counties of England] in losing him.—*Two G. of V.*, i. 1.

Two hot *sheeps* [similar sound], marry.—And wherefore not *ships?*—*Love's L. L.*, ii. 1.

He that knows better how to tame a *shrew* [sometimes pronounced 'shrow'; which gives the requisite rhyme here and in the following passages where the word is used], now let him speak: 'tis charity to show. —*Tam. of S.*, iv. 1.

> Your husband, being troubled with a *shrew*,
> Measures my husband's sorrow by his woe.—*Ibid.*, v. 2.

> Now, go thy ways; thou hast tam'd a curst *shrew*,
> 'Tis a wonder, by your leave, she will be tam'd so.—*Ibid.*, v. 2.

> Oh, that your face were not so full of O's!—
> A pest of that jest! and I beshrew all *shrews*.—*Love's L. L.*, v. 2.

Erect his *statua* [the Folio prints this word throughout all the passages where it is used by Shakespeare, 'statue'; but it was often pronounced as a trisyllable in his time, and he uses it trisyllabically in the four passages here cited. Not only was it frequently pronounced as a trisyllable when Shakespeare lived, but it was often spelt " statua "; and on the assumption that he wrote it thus when he used it as a trisyllable, we have preserved that form in our editions of his works where these passages occur] and worship it.—*2 H. VI.*, iii. 2.

She dreamt to-night she saw my *statua*.—*Jul. C.*, ii. 2.

Even at the base of Pompey's *statua*.—*Ibid.*, iii. 2.

But, like dumb *statuas*, or breathing stones.—*R. III.*, iii. 7.

Who is the *suitor* [pronounced like 'shooter']? who is the *suitor?* . . . Why, she that bears the bow.—*Love's L. L.*, iv. 1.

Our *targes* [pronounced with a hard *g*, as a monosyllable] undinted.—*Ant. & C.*, ii. 6.

Stepped before *targes* [as monosyllable] of proof.—*Cym.*, v. 5.

No, sir; but it is *vara* ['very'] fine.—*Ibid.*, v. 2.

Veal ['well'] quoth the Dutchman.—*Ibid.*, v. 2.

A quick *venew* [an English form of the French word, *venue*; used as a term of the fencing-school for a 'hit'] of wit.—*Ibid.*, v. 1.

Three *veneys* [a slip-shod form of 'venews'] for a dish of stewed prunes.—*Merry W.*, i. 1.

Shakespeare has two passages of sarcastically and mimickingly made blunders :—

Simple. I may not *conceal* ['reveal'] them, sir.—
Falstaff. Conceal them, or thou diest.—*Ibid.*, iv. 5.

Nurse. If you be he, sir, I desire some *confidence* ['conference'] with you.—
Benvolio. She will *indite* ['invite'] him to some supper.—*R. & Jul.*, ii. 4.

And he has three droll specimens of drunken mispronunciation :—

I have heard the Ptolemies' *pyramises* ['pyramis' was a form of "pyramid" used in Shakespeare's time; but its plural is excellently put into the mouth of the soaked Lepidus] are very goodly things.—*Ant. & C.*, ii. 7.

Do me right, and dub me knight: *samingo* [muddled contraction of 'San Domingo'].—*2 H. IV.*, v. 3.

They are scoundrels and *substractors* [bousy blunder for 'detractors'] that say so of him.—*Tw. N.*, i. 3.

The following passages mark affected pronunciation :—

Such rackers of orthography, as to speak dout, fine, when he should say doubt; det when he should pronounce debt,—d, e, b, t, not, d, e, t: he clepeth a calf, cauf: half hauf; neighbour *vocatur* nebour; neigh abbreviated ne. This is abhominable,—which he would call abominable.—*Love's L. L.*, v. 1.

Chirrah!—*Quare* chirrah, not sirrah?—*Ibid.*, v. 1.

Fair princess, you have lost much good *sport* [finically pronounced *spawt* or 'spot'].—*Sport* ['spot']! of what colour?—*As You L.*, i. 2.

Against the which he has *imponed* ['impawned'], as I take it, six French rapiers. . . Why is this *imponed* ['impawned'], as you call it ?—*Hamlet*, v. 2.

Shakespeare has appended a final " a " to certain words used by Doctor Caius, by way of marking his French pronunciation of them :—

A box, a *green-a* box : do intend vat I speak ? a *green-a* box . . . come, *take-a* your rapier, and come after my heel to de court. . . . Verefore shall I be *content-a ?* . . . *Peace-a* your tongue ! *Speak-a* your tale . . . Sir Hugh *send-a* you? . . . You jack'nape, *give-a* dis letter to Sir Hugh. . . . It is no *matter-a* for dat : do not you *tell-a* me.— *Merry W.*, i. 4.

I shall *procure-a* you de good guest, de earl.—*Ibid.*, ii. 3.

I pray you, *let-a* me speak a word vit your ear : verefore vill you not *meet-a* me ? . . . Have you *make-a* de sot of us, ha, ha ?—*Ibid.*, iii. 1.

De maid is *love-a* me : my *nursh-a* Quickly tell me so much.—*Ibid.*, iii. 2.

[*See* SPELLING OF FOREIGN WORDS.]

There are two passages where a word occurs that may have been intended to be pronounced differently from the usual mode, to mark the sense in which Shakespeare wished to have it understood :—

I take him to be a soul of great article ; and his infusion of such *dearth* and rareness, as, &c.—*Hamlet*, v. 2.

Here—as including the sense of 'dearness,' 'value,' as well as that of ' scarcity '—" dearth," instead of being pronounced ' dirth,' may have been intended to be pronounced ' deerth.' [*See* VARIED MEANINGS, &c.]

Yet this *imperseverant* thing loves him in my despite.—*Cym.*, iv. 1.

Here, " imperseverant," including the sense of 'obstinately persevering' and that of 'unperceiving,' 'undiscerning,' may not have been pronounced 'imperseveerant,' but 'imperceiverant.' [*See* VARIED MEANINGS COMBINED IN ONE WORD OR SENTENCE.]

PROVINCIAL TERMS.

Shakespeare, the Warwickshire born and London sojourning man, used several provincial expressions in his plays ; and these sturdy sterling country words, coming amid the general refinement of his style, are among the many points that give us cause to perceive the advantage of his having had rural as well as urban experiences in his life—all tending to make him the grand *universal* poet and dramatist that he was :—

For the blood-*bolter'd* ['clotted,' 'smeared'] Banquo smiles upon me.—*Macb.*, iv. 1.

Throw the quean in the *channel* ['kennel,' 'gutter'].—*2 H. IV.*, ii. 1.

Till famine *cling* ['shrivel,' 'shrink,' 'wither'] thee.—*Macb.*, v. 5.

Whether your *costard* ['head'] or my *ballow* ['pole,' 'staff,' or 'cudgel'] be the harder.—*Lear*, iv. 6.

When I have *deck'd* ['sprinkled'] the sea with drops full salt.—*Temp.*, i. 2.

But *fettle* ['prepare,' 'make ready,' 'adjust,' 'put in order'] your fine joints 'gainst Thursday next.—*R. & Jul.*, iii. 5.

Where hearing should not *latch* ['catch,' 'catch the sound of'] them.—*Macb.*, iv. 3.

For selling the dukedom of Maine.—

And good reason ; for thereby is England *mained* ['maimed' : by using the provincial form of the word here, opportunity is given for the pun between it and " Maine "], and fain to go with a staff.—*2 H. VI.*, iv. 2.

Shall the blessed sun of heaven prove a *micher* ['truant,' 'skulker,' 'lurker'], and eat blackberries?—1 *H. IV.*, ii. 4.

We cannot *miss* ['do without'] him.—*Temp.*, i. 2.

Swithold footed thrice the *old* ['wold'].—*Lear*, iii. 4.

Thou want'st a rough *pash* ['head:' usually applied to a young bull-calf, whose horns are sprouting], and the shoots that I have.—*W. T.*, i. 2.

I'll give you leave to *powder* ['salt': 'powdered beef' is still used in some English provinces for 'corned beef' or 'salted beef'] me, and eat me too, to-morrow.— 1 *H. IV.*, v. 4.

He would *pun* ['pound'] thee into shivers with his fist, as a sailor breaks a biscuit.— *Tr. & Cr.*, ii. 1.

I have rubb'd this young *quat* ['pimple,' 'pustule': here used as a nick-name] almost to the sense.—*Oth.*, v. 1.

It is the pasture lards the *rother's* ['horned beast's'] sides, the want that makes him lean.—*Timon*, iv. 3.

The above passage appears thus misprinted in the Folio: 'It is the Pastour Lards, the Brothers sides, The want that makes him leaue.' Rowe corrected the word "pasture"; the second Folio, the word "lean;" and Mr. Singer, in 1842, suggested the word "rother," which has since been generally adopted as the right word. In Holloway's "General Provincial Dictionary" it is stated that there is a market in Stratford-upon-Avon, called "the *rother* market"; a point that brings the word home to Shakespeare's own knowledge and familiar use, giving every probability to its being the one he here employed.

And take thou my oblation, poor but free,
Which is not mix'd with *seconds* ['inferior kind of flour:' here used figuratively for 'less pure matter'].—*Sonnet* 125.

PUNCTUATION.

The punctuation in the First Folio edition of Shakespeare's plays is often so inaccurate as to leave much doubt with regard to the mode in which he himself intended certain passages should be punctuated and interpreted. A few of the most notable of these we here collectively cite; giving first each passage as printed in the Folio, and secondly as printed in our own and most modern editors' text:—

> There is more in it; Cosen Ganimed.
> There is more in it.—Cousin!—Ganymede!—*As You L.*, iv. 3.

In the above passage the old printer seems to have taken "Cosen" to be merely a term of address; whereas if this had been intended by the dramatist he would have made Celia address Rosalind as *Brother* Ganymede. But by the word "Cousin" Shakespeare evidently meant to indicate that Celia, in her alarm at seeing Rosalind faint, for an instant forgets their assumed characters of relationship, and calls upon her by the old accustomed title; then, recollecting herself, says, "Ganymede!"

> Here art thou in appointment fresh and faire,
> Anticipating time. With starting courage,
> Giue with thy Trumpet a loud note to Troy
> Thou dreadfull *Aiax*, that the appauled aire
> May pierce the head of the great Combatant,
> And hale him hither.

> Here art thou in appointment fresh and fair,
> Anticipating time with starting courage.
> Give with thy trumpet a loud note to Troy,
> Thou dreadful Ajax ; that the appallèd air
> May pierce the head of the great combatant,
> And hale him hither.—*Tr. & Cr.*, iv. 5.

By placing the full stop after "time" instead of after "courage," the Folio printer disjoins the first phrase, and brings the word "with" twice into the second phrase of the above speech.

> All the contagion of the South, light on you,
> You Shames of Rome : You Heard of Byles and Plagues
> Plaister you o're, that you may be abhorr'd
> Farther then seene, and one infect another
> Against the Winde a mile :

> All the contagion of the south light on you,
> You shames of Rome ! you herd of—Boils and plagues
> Plaster you o'er ; that you may be abhorred
> Farther than seen, and one infect another
> Against the wind a mile !—*Coriol.*, i. 4.

By omitting the dash between "herd of" and "Boils" the impetuous break in Marcius's speech is lost, and the sentence is rendered meaningless.

> May these same instruments, which you prophane,
> Neuer sound more : when Drums and Trumpets shall
> I' th' field proue flatterers, let Courts and Cities be
> Made all of false-fac'd soothing :
> When Steele growes soft, as the Parasites Silke,
> Let him be made an Ouerture for th' Warres :

> May these same instruments, which you profane,
> Never sound more, when drums and trumpets shall
> I' the field prove flatterers ! Let courts and cities be
> Made all of false-fac'd soothing,
> When steel grows soft as the parasite's silk !
> Let them be made an overture for the wars !—*Ibid.*, i. 9.

The Folio's colon after "more" and its misprinting 'him' for "them" in the closing line, destroys the author's meaning ; which appears to us to be a desire that the "instruments" shall not be profaned into flourishers of laudation, but shall be reserved for preluders to war.

> Will all great *Neptunes* Ocean wash this blood
> Cleane from my Hand ? no : this my Hand will rather
> The multitudinous Seas incarnardine,
> Making the Greene one, Red.

> Will all great Neptune's ocean wash this blood
> Clean from my hand ? No ; this my hand will rather
> The multitudinous seas incarnardine,
> Making the green—one red.—*Macb.*, ii. 2.

The Folio printer, by putting a comma after "one," destroys the force of the image and sense of the line, which we believe to be, 'making the green of the seas one entire red colour.'

> *Kent.* No, my good Lord, I am the very man.
> *Lear.* Ile see that straight.
> *Kent.* That from your first of difference and decay,
> Haue follow'd your sad steps.
> *Lear.* Your are welcome hither.
> *Kent.* Nor no man else :

> *Kent.* No, my good lord; I am the very man—
> *Lear.* I 'll see that straight.
> *Kent.* That, from your first of difference and decay,
> Have follow'd your sad steps,—
>   *Lear.*   You are welcome hither.
>   *Kent.* Nor no man else.—*Lear*, v. 3.

From the Folio having placed no indication of interruption at the close of Kent's brief speeches here, it has generally been unperceived that they are consecutive phrases with which he attempts to explain his identity, and make his old master comprehend that he has followed him throughout his distressed wanderings. So much has this want of perception been produced by the Folio's defective punctuation in the present dialogue, that various explanations have been given of Kent's words, " Nor no man else," by those who have failed to perceive that they are the conclusion of his attempted explanation to Lear.

> Put out the Light, and then put out the Light :
> Put out the light, and then—Put out the light !—*Oth.*, v. 2.

By placing no stop between " then " and " put," the Folio printer gives no indication of the dramatist's intention to make the speaker interrupt himself with a repetition of his own words, that begin the line, and afterwards proceed to the reflections which they awaken.

> Yea, and furred mosse besides. When flowres are none
> To winter-ground thy Coarse—
> Yea, and furr'd moss besides, when flowers are none,
> To winter-ground thy corse.—*Cym.*, iv. 2.

The full stop put by the Folio printer after " besides," and the dash after " corse," makes incomplete and incomprehensible this close to one of our poet's most exquisitely written speeches.

>   Let vs bury him,
> And not protract with admiration, what
> Is now due debt. To th' graue.

>   Let us bury him,
> And not protract with admiration what
> Is now due debt. To the grave !—*Ibid.*, iv. 2.

In all our editions of Shakespeare's works, we have retained the punctuation of the Folio, by placing a full stop after the word " debt " in this last-quoted passage; but we have long entertained a strong impression that he wrote the line thus,—' Is now due debt to the grave.'

Shakespeare has given a specimen of one of the favourite jokes with authors of his time ; which was, to produce a perfectly contrary sense to the clauses of a speech by wrong punctuation. It is in the Prologue to the Interlude enacted by the clowns before Duke Theseus :—

> If we offend, it is with our good will.
>   That you should think, we come not to offend,
> But with good will. To show our simple skill,
>   That is the true beginning of our end.

Consider, then, we come but in despite.
We do not come as minding to content you,
Our true intent is. All for your delight,
We are not here. That you should here repent you,
The actors are at hand ; and, by their show,
You shall know all, that you are like to know.—*Mid. N. D.*, v. 1.

And, in order that the purposed mispunctuation should not escape notice, the dramatist has put into the mouth of two of the assembled audience an amused comment :—

Theseus. This fellow doth not stand upon points.
Lysander. He hath rid his prologue like a rough colt ; he knows not the stop.

RECURRENCE OF PARTICULAR POINTS.

We have discovered recurrent traces of special features of style marking certain plays by Shakespeare, which lead us to fancy that he thought in that particular mode while he was writing that particular drama.   Sometimes it is a peculiar word, sometimes a peculiar manner of construction, sometimes a peculiar fashion of employing epithets or terms in an unusual sense.   Throughout the play of " A Midsummer Night's Dream " the word " respect " is used somewhat peculiarly ; so as to convey the idea of ' regard ' or ' consideration,' rather than the more usually assigned one of ' reverence ' or ' deference ' :—

Or else misgraffèd in *respect* of years.—*Mid. N. D.*, i. 1.
And she *respects* me as her only son.—*Ibid.*, i. 1.
What worser place can I beg in your love
(And yet a place of high *respect* with me),
Than to be used as you use your dog ?—*Ibid.*, ii. 2.
Nor doth this wood lack worlds of company,
For you in my *respect* are all the world.—*Ibid.*, ii. 2.
And what poor duty cannot do,
Noble *respect* takes it in might, not merit.—*Ibid.*, v. 1.

It is only in this play that the word " aby " and its abbreviated form " 'by " are to be found :—

Lest, to thy peril, thou *aby* it dear.—*Ibid.*, iii. 2.
Take not her part ; for, if thou dost intend
Never so little show of love to her,
Thou shalt *aby* it.—*Ibid.*, iii. 2.
Nay, then, thou mock'st me. Thou shalt *'by* this dear,
If ever I thy face by daylight see.—*Ibid.*, iii. 2.

In " The Merchant of Venice " the word " imposition " is twice used in the sense of an injunction laid upon a person :—

Unless you may be won by some other sort than your father's *imposition*, depending on the caskets.—*Mer. of V.*, i. 2.

I do desire you
Not to deny this *imposition ;*
The which my love, and some necessity,
Now lays upon you.—*Ibid.*, iii. 4.

A somewhat similar and somewhat peculiar form of phrase also occurs twice in this play :—

> *I never did repent for doing good,*
> Nor shall not now.—*Mer. of V.*, iii. 4.
> My mind was *never yet more mercenary.*—*Ibid.*, iv. 1.

In the play of " As You Like It " the word " occasion " is twice used with exceptionally elliptical force. The first time, the sentence implies ' make out her fault to be her husband's occasioning' or ' to be occasioned by her husband '; the second time, the sentence implies ' stronger than his sense of that which might justly have occasioned his resentful abandonment of his brother':—

> O, that woman that cannot make her fault her husband's *occasion*, let her never nurse her child herself, for she will breed it like a fool.—*As You L.*, iv. 1.
> But kindness, nobler ever than revenge,
> And nature, stronger than his just *occasion*,
> Made him give battle to the lioness.—*Ibid.*, iv. 3.

A peculiar idiomatic expression occurs twice in " All's Well that Ends Well." In the first passage it implies ' subscribed to,' ' confessed to having,' ' owned to,' ' gave tokens of possessing'; in the second passage, it implies ' give evidence of the right to be called,' ' show that I am worthy to be styled,' ' may proclaim myself to be':—

> I'd give bay Curtal and his furniture,
> My mouth no more were broken than these boys',
> And *writ* as little beard.—*All's W.*, ii. 3.
> I must tell thee, sirrah, I *write* man ; to which title age cannot bring thee.—*Ibid.*, ii. 3.

In the play of " Twelfth Night " we trace more than one allusion to the astrological belief that prevailed in Shakespeare's time respecting the influence of certain stars and constellations upon the human disposition and upon individual temperament :—

> I did think by the excellent constitution of thy leg, it was *formed under the star* of a galliard. . . . Shall we set about some revels ?—What shall we do else ? *were we not born under Taurus ?—Taurus ! That's sides and heart.*—No, sir, *it is legs and thighs.*—*Tw. N.*, i. 3.
> I know *thy constellation is right apt*
> *For this affair.*—*Ibid.*, i. 4.

A marked feature in " The Winter's Tale " is the numerous elisional contractions [*See* ELISIONAL ABBREVIATIONS] contained in its diction ; and Shakespeare has several times introduced into this play the impressive iteration of a word with felicitous effect :—

> There is no tongue that moves, *none, none* i' the world,
> So soon as yours, could win me.—*W. T.*, i. 2.
> My lord *the king, the king !*—*Ibid.*, iii. 2.
> When I have said, cry, Woe ! *the queen, the queen,*
> The sweet'st, dear'st creature's dead.—*Ibid.*, iii. 2.
> When you do dance, I wish you
> A wave o' the sea, that you might ever do
> Nothing but that ; move *still, still* so,
> And own no other function.—*Ibid.*, iv. 3.
> Stars, stars,
> And all eyes else dead coals.—*Ibid.*, v. 1.

In this play we find rather unusually numerous indications of gesture and look [*See* INDICATIONS OF CONDUCT, &c.].

In this play Shakespeare has twice used the word "best" as an epithet of affectionate esteem :—

> What cheer ?   How is 't with you, *best* brother ?—*W. T.*, i. 2.
>
> My *best* Camillo !   We must disguise ourselves.—*Ibid.*, iv. 1.

And in this play he has not only twice used the word "forced" in the peculiar sense of 'perverted from truth,' 'wryed from fact,' 'false'; he has also used "forcing" to express 'falsely imputing,' 'wrongfully charging':—

> For ever
> Unvenerable be thy hands, if thou
> Tak'st up the princess by that *forcèd* baseness
> Which he has put upon 't !—*Ibid.*, ii. 3.
>
> With these *forc'd* thoughts, I pr'ythee, darken not
> The mirth o' the feast.—*Ibid.*, iv. 3.
>
> These proclamations,
> So *forcing* faults upon Hermione,
> I little like.—*Ibid.*, iii. 1.

In the play of "King John" there is a very remarkable abundance of passages with repeated similar words [*See* REPEATED WORDS], and of passages with not only double iteration, but triple iteration of the same word :—

> You are *forsworn, forsworn.*—*John*, iii. 1.
>
> *Arm, arm,* you heavens, against these perjur'd kings !—*Ibid.*, iii. 1.
>
> *Hear me !* O, *hear me !*—*Ibid.*, iii. 1.
>
> Lo, *now ! now* see the issue of your peace !—*Ibid.*, iii. 4.
>
> I am not mad ; *too well, too well* I feel
> The different plague of each calamity.—*Ibid.*, iii. 4.
>
> But from the inward motion to deliver
> *Sweet, sweet, sweet* poison for the age's tooth.—*Ibid.*, i. 1.
>
> *War ! war !* no peace! peace is to me a *war,*—*Ibid.*, iii. 1.
>
> Good *Hubert, Hubert, Hubert,* throw thine eye
> On yond' young boy.—*Ibid.*, iii. 3.
>
> No, I defy all counsel, all redress,
> But that which ends all counsel, true redress,
> *Death, death :* O, amiable lovely *death !*—*Ibid.*, iii. 4.

In this play, also, twice occurs an expression which is to be found nowhere else used by Shakespeare.   It is "lord of thy presence" and "lord of our presence," employed to signify 'master of thine own individuality,' and 'master of our own individuality.'   In the first of the two passages, we think it is meant to include the sense of 'master of that fine manly person inherited from Cœur-de-Lion,' as well as 'master of thine own self or individuality':—

> Whether hadst thou rather be a Faulconbridge,
> And like thy brother, to enjoy thy land,
> Or the reputed son of Cœur-de-Lion,
> *Lord of thy presence*, and no land beside?—*Ibid.*, i. 1.
>
> In us, that are our own great deputy,
> And bear possession of our person here ;
> *Lord of our presence*, Angiers, and of you.—*Ibid.*, ii. 2.

In the historical tragedy of Richard II. there are several instances of defective lines; of transposed construction [*See* PECULIAR CONSTRUCTION]; of nouns used elliptically [*See* ELLIPTICALLY USED WORDS]; of antique contracted forms of words and a marked prevalence of compound epithets. There are also three peculiar expressions which Shakespeare has used in this play only :—

> Where, then, alas! may I *complain myself?*—*R. II.*, i. 2.
> And toil'd with works of war, *retir'd himself*
> To Italy.—*Ibid.*, iv. 1.
> He is our cousin, cousin ; but *'tis doubt,*
> When time shall call him home from banishment,
> Whether our kinsman come to see his friends.—*Ibid.*, i. 4.
> Depress'd he is already ; and depos'd,
> *'Tis doubt,* he will be.—*Ibid.*, iii. 4.

In the " First Part of King Henry IV." there is an immense number of nick-names [*See* PARTICULAR NAMES] ; but this is naturally accounted for by the presence of fertile-brained Sir John Falstaff and his associates, since the same peculiarity is observable in each of the plays where he figures.

We observe that in the " Second Part of King Henry IV." " accite " and " accites " are both used ; but nowhere else by Shakespeare* :—

> And what *accites* your most worshipful thought to think so ?—*2 H. IV.*, ii. 2.
> Our coronation done, we will *accite,*
> As I before remember'd, all our state.—*Ibid.*, v. 2.

In the play of " King Henry V." the amplified form of " vasty," instead of the simpler and more usual one of " vast," occurs no fewer than three times :—

> Can this cockpit hold
> The *vasty* fields of France ?—*H. V.*, i. (*Chorus*).
> He might return to *vasty* Tartar back.—*Ibid.*, ii. 2.
> To take mercy
> On the poor souls, for whom this hungry war
> Opens his *vasty* jaws.—*Ibid.*, ii. 4.

The " First Part of King Henry VI." contains so many recurrent points of variously bad style, that they combine to establish our conviction that this play was not Shakespeare's composition. We think it was merely retouched by him for the purpose of stage representation ; as the points in it are few where we see manifest tokens of his master-hand. One of these is the passage of five lines, in act i., sc. 2, commencing, " Glory is like a circle in the water " ; and which passage, be it observed, has a remarkable air of irrelevancy in the speech, as if it had been introduced by some other hand than the one that wrote the main dialogue of the scene. Another portion that we think gives token of Shakespeare's manner is the fourth scene of the second act, describing the incident in the Temple Garden which gave rise to the adoption of

---

* There is an instance of "accited," occurring in "Titus Andronicus;" but we do not believe that revolting play to have been one of our author's productions.

the red rose and the white rose as badges of the factions of Lancaster and York; for it is written with a spirit and vigour in the diction, a general air of strength with simplicity, and of energy without bombast, that we vainly look for throughout the rest of the play—with the exception of dying Mortimer's speech at the commencement of sc. 5, act ii., which we also find much in Shakespeare's style. But the numerous points of un-Shakespearian diction strike us at every page. See, for example, how often the little word " so " is clumsily used :—

> The battles of the Lord of hosts he fought ;
> The church's prayers made him *so* prosperous.—1 *H. VI.*, i. 1.
>
> Else ne'er could they hold out *so* as they do.—*Ibid.*, i. 2.
>
> Here, said they, is the terror of the French,
> The scare-crow that affrights our children *so.*—*Ibid.*, i. 4.
>
> How now, my lords ! what all unready *so ?*—*Ibid.*, ii. 1.
>
> Didst thou at first, to flatter us withal,
> Make us partakers of a little gain,
> That now our loss might be ten times *so* much ?—*Ibid.*, ii. 1.
>
> Madam, according as your ladyship desir'd,
> By message crav'd, *so* is Lord Talbot come.—*Ibid.*, ii. 3.
>
> Fly to revenge my death, if I be slain.—
> He that flies *so* will ne'er return again.—*Ibid.*, iv. 5.

And how awkwardly " quite " is used :—

> Paris, Guysors, Poictiers, are all *quite* lost.—*Ibid.*, i. 1.
>
> France is revolted from the English *quite,*
> Except some petty towns of no import.—*Ibid.*, i. 1.
>
> The king, thy sovereign, is not *quite* exempt
> From envious malice of thy swelling heart.—*Ibid.*, iii. 1.
>
> And should (if I were worthy to be judge)
> Be *quite* degraded, like a hedge-born swain
> That doth presume to boast of gentle blood.—*Ibid.*, iv. 1.
>
> Henceforth I charge you, as you love our favour,
> *Quite* to forget this quarrel and the cause.—*Ibid.*, iv. 1.

And " about " :—

> I do remember it ; and here take my leave,
> To go *about* my preparation.—*Ibid.*, i. 1.
>
> I was employ'd in passing to and fro,
> *About* relieving of the sentinels.—*Ibid.*, ii. 1.

And " likewise" :—

> Most of the rest slaughter'd or took, *likewise.*—*Ibid.*, i. 1.
>
> I would his troubles *likewise* were expired,
> That so he might recover what was lost.—*Ibid.*, ii. 5.

And " now " :—

> *Now* will it best avail your majesty
> To cross the seas, and to be crown'd in France.—*Ibid.*, iii. 1.
>
> And *now* no more ado, brave Burgundy,
> But gather we our forces out of hand,
> And set upon our boasting enemy.—*Ibid.*, iii. 2.

And " then," and " enough," uncouthly brought in at the end of a line :—

Was Mahomet inspired with a dove ?
Thou with an eagle art inspir'd, *then.*—1 *H. VI.*, i. 2.
Bright star of Venus, fall'n down on the earth,
How may I reverently worship thee *enough !*—*Ibid.*, i. 2.

And the untragic mode in which " O, no " is twice made to commence the Third Messenger's replies :—

What ! wherein Talbot overcame?   Is 't so?
O, no ; wherein Lord Talbot was o'erthrown.—*Ibid.*, i. 1.

Is Talbot slain ? then I will slay myself,
For living idly here in pomp and ease,
Whilst such a worthy leader, wanting aid,
Unto his dastard foemen is betray'd.—
O, no, he lives ; but is took prisoner.—*Ibid.*, i. 1.

Then the peculiar sense in which certain words are used :—

In single combat thou shalt *buckle* [' contend '] with me.—*Ibid.*, i. 2.
            All our general force
Might with a sally of the very town
Be *buckled* [' engaged '] with.—*Ibid.*, iv. 4.
My ancient incantations are too weak,
And hell too strong for me to *buckle* [' contend '] with.—*Ibid.*, v. 3.
And sent our sons and husbands *captivate* [' taken captive '].—*Ibid.*, ii. 3.
Tush, women have been *captivate* [' taken captive '] ere now.—*Ibid.*, v. 3.
But mark : as, in this *haughty* [' lofty,' ' exalted '] great attempt,
They laboured to plant the rightful heir.—*Ibid.*, ii. 5.
I am vanquish'd ; these *haughty* ['exalted'] words of hers
Have batter'd me like roaring cannon-shot,
And made me almost yield upon my knees.—*Ibid.*, iii. 3.
Knights of the garter were of noble birth,
Valiant and virtuous, full of *haughty* [' high,' ' lofty '] courage,
Such as were grown to credit by the wars.—*Ibid.*, iv. 1.

And then the ludicrously stiff phrases of announcement, so thoroughly un-Shakespearian, that recur again and again in this play :—

I must inform you of a dismal fight
Betwixt the stout Lord Talbot and the French.—*Ibid.*, i. 1.
The circumstance I 'll tell you more at large.—*Ibid.*, i. 1.
I 'll to the Tower, with all the haste I can,
To view th' artillery and munition ;
And then I will proclaim young Henry king.—
To Eltham will I, where the young king is,
Being ordain'd his special governor ;
And for his safety there I 'll best devise.—
Each hath his place and function to attend :
I am left out ; for me nothing remains.
But long I will not be Jack-out-of-office :
The king from Eltham I intend to steal,
And sit at chiefest stern of public weal.—*Ibid.*, i, 1.
I am come to survey the Tower this day.—*Ibid.*, i. 3.
I must go victual Orleans forthwith.—*Ibid.*, i. 5.
Agreed : *I 'll to yon corner.*—
                    And I to this.—
And here will Talbot mount, or make his grave.—*Ibid.*, ii. 1.

And also the number of lame and tame lines; which not even Shakespeare's own assertion to that effect could make us believe to be his writing :—

> Among the soldiers this is muttered,—
> *That here you maintain several factions.—1 H. VI.*, i. 1.
>
> A third man thinks, without expense at all,
> *By guileful fair words peace may be obtain'd.—Ibid.*, i. 1.
>
> Ten thousand soldiers with me I will take,
> *Whose bloody deeds shall make all Europe quake.—Ibid.*, i. 1.
>
> Chief master-gunner am I of this town ;
> *Something I must do to procure me grace.—Ibid.*, i. 4.
>
> How wert thou handled, being prisoner?
> *Or by what means got'st thou to be releas'd ?—Ibid.*, i. 4.
>
> *I grieve to hear what torments you endur'd ;*
> *But we will be reveng'd sufficiently.—Ibid.*, i. 4.
>
> *Let me have your express opinions,*
> *Where is best place to make our battery next.—Ibid.*, i. 4.
>
> Stay, stay, I say !
> And, if you love me, as you say you do,
> *Let me persuade you to forbear awhile.—Ibid.*, iii. 1.
>
> But kings and mightiest potentates must die,
> *For that 's the end of human misery.—Ibid.*, iii. 2.
>
> Now let us on, my lords, and join our powers ;
> *And seek how we may prejudice the foe.—Ibid.*, iii. 3.
>
> *To say the truth, this fact was infamous,*
> And ill beseeming any common man,
> Much more a knight, a captain, and a leader.—*Ibid.*, iv. 1.
>
> Fain would I woo her, yet I dare not speak :
> *I 'll call for pen and ink, and write my mind.—Ibid.*, v. 3.

The fustian style of the threats, too, mere rant and balderdash, are utterly unlike Shakespeare, except when he is writing Pistol's diction :—

> Priest, beware your beard ;
> *I mean to tug it, and to cuff you soundly :*
> Under my feet I stamp thy cardinal's hat ;
> In spite of Pope or dignities of church,
> *Here by the cheeks I 'll drag thee up and down.—Ibid.*, i. 3.
>
> But, O, the treacherous Fastolfe wounds my heart !
> *Whom with my bare fists I would execute,*
> *If I now had him brought into my power.—Ibid.*, i. 4.
>
> *Your hearts I 'll stamp out with my horse's heels,*
> *And make a quagmire of your mingled brains.—Ibid.*, i. 4.
>
> *O, were mine eye-balls into bullets turn'd,*
> *That I, in rage, might shoot them at your faces !—Ibid.*, iv. 7.
>
> May never glorious sun reflex his beams
> Upon the country where you make abode ;
> But darkness and the gloomy shade of death
> Environ you, till mischief and despair
> *Drive you to break your necks, or hang yourselves !—Ibid.*, v. 4.

Then the wretchedly poor similes :—

> Let frantic Talbot triumph for awhile,
> And *like a peacock sweep along his tail ;*

We 'll pull his plumes, and take away his train,
If Dauphin and the rest will be but rul'd.—1 *H. VI.*, iii. 3.

As plays the sun upon the glassy streams,
Twinkling another counterfeited beam,
So seems this gorgeous beauty to mine eyes.—*Ibid.*, v. 3.

A number of flatly tautological expressions disfigure the diction in this play [*See* PLEONASMS, page 611] :—

Warlike and *martial* Talbot, Burgundy.—*Ibid.*, iii. 2.

Presumptuous vassals, are you not asham'd,
With this immodest clamorous outrage
To *trouble* and *disturb* the king and us ?—*Ibid.*, iv. 1.

More *rancorous spite*, more *furious raging broils*,
Than yet can be *imagin'd* or *suppos'd*.—*Ibid.*, iv. 1.

I may *revolve* and *ruminate* my grief.—*Ibid.*, v. 5.

Also an ineffective repetition :—

Thy *humble* servant vows obedience
And *humble* service till the point of death.—*Ibid.*, iii. 1.

Also an ambiguously and awkwardly worded sentence ; where " that grudge one thought " may be meant to express 'that think one grudging thought,' or (if " grudge " be used in an old sense it bore of ' murmur,' ' complain ') it may be meant to express ' that mutter to themselves one thought' :—

So perish they
That grudge one thought against your majesty.—*Ibid.*, iii. 1.

Also two glaring dramatic discrepancies, utterly at variance with our great dramatist's artistic method in such particulars. In an early scene of the play Joan of Arc is made to say she is of lowly birth, and subsequently to say she is of royal birth.   In another early scene Winchester appears *already as a cardinal;* yet in the fifth act he is spoken of *as a newly made cardinal.*   These are inconsistencies not in accordance with Shakespeare's style :—

Dauphin, *I am by birth a shepherd's daughter,*
My wit untrain'd in any kind of art.—*Ibid.*, i. 2.

First, let me tell you whom you have condemn'd :
Not me begotten of a shepherd swain,
But issu'd from the progeny of kings.—*Ibid.*, v. 4.

The Cardinal of Winchester forbids . . .
I 'll canvass thee in thy broad *cardinal's hat.* . . .
Under my feet I stamp thy *cardinal's hat.* . . .
Cardinal, I 'll be no breaker of the law. . . .
This *cardinal 's* more haughty than the devil.—*Ibid.*, i. 3.

What ! *is my lord of Winchester install'd,*
And call'd unto a cardinal's degree?—*Ibid.*, v. 1.

Also several instances of lumberingly transposed construction, utterly un-Shakespearian in manner :—

Sad tidings bring I to you out of France.—*Ibid.*, i. 1.
Farewell, my masters ; *to my task will I.*—*Ibid.*, i. 1.
A holy maid hither with me I bring.—*Ibid.*, i. 2.

In open market-place *produc'd they me.*—1 *H. VI.*, i. 4.

Here is Sir William Lucy, *who with me*
Set from our o'er-match'd forces forth for aid.—*Ibid.*, iv. 4.

For fly he could not, if he would have fled;
And fly would Talbot never, though he might.—*Ibid.*, iv. 4.

Finally, we meet frequently in this play with a questioning phraseology; an introduction of bald, irrelevant queries, that give an inexpressibly undramatic and platitudinising effect to the dialogue, and which are essentially unlike Shakespeare's style:—

His sparkling eyes, replete with wrathful fire,
More dazzled and drove back his enemies
Than mid-day sun fierce bent against their faces.
What should I say? his deeds exceed all speech:
He ne'er lift up his hand, but conquerèd.—
We mourn in black: *why mourn we not in blood?* . . .
What, *shall we curse the planets of mishap,*
That plotted thus our glory's overthrow?
Or shall we think the subtle-witted French
Conjurors and sorcerers, that, afraid of him,
By magic verses have contriv'd his end?—*Ibid.*, i. 1.

The battles of the Lord of hosts he fought:
The church's prayers made him so prosperous.—
The church! where is it? Had not churchmen pray'd,
His thread of life had not so soon decay'd.—*Ibid.*, i. 1.

The Dauphin crownèd king! all fly to him!
O, whither shall we fly from this reproach?—*Ibid.*, i. 1.

Now we are victors, upon us he smiles.
What towns of any moment but we have?
At pleasure here we lie, near Orleans.—*Ibid.*, i. 2.

Let's raise the siege: *why live we idly here?*
Talbot is taken, whom we wont to fear.—*Ibid.*, i. 2.

Who ever saw the like? What men have I!—*Ibid.*, i. 2.

One to ten!
Lean raw-bon'd rascals! *who would e'er suppose*
They had such courage and audacity?—*Ibid.*, i. 2.

What! *am I dar'd, and bearded to my face?*—*Ibid.*, 1. 3.

Where is my strength, my valour, and my force?
Our English troops retire, I cannot stay them.—*Ibid.*, i. 5.

Heavens, can you suffer hell so to prevail?
My breast I'll burst with straining of my courage.—*Ibid.*, i. 5.

Divinest creature, bright Astræa's daughter,
How shall I honour thee for this success?
Thy promises are like Adonis' gardens,
That one day bloom'd, and fruitful were the next.—*Ibid.*, i. 6.

Why ring not out the bells throughout the town?
Dauphin, command the citizens make bonfires.—*Ibid.*, i. 6.

Now, quiet soul, depart when Heaven please,
For I have seen our enemies' overthrow.
What is the trust or strength of foolish men?
They, that of late were daring with their scoffs,
Are glad and fain by flight to save themselves.—*Ibid.*, iii. 2.

Thanks, gentle duke. *But where is Pucelle now?*
I think her old familiar is asleep:
Now where's the Bastard's braves, and Charles his gleeks?
What, all a-mort? Rouen hangs her head for grief
That such a valiant company are fled.—*Ibid.*, iii. 2.

O monstrous treachery!　*Can this be so,—*
That in alliance, amity, and oaths,
*There should be found such false dissembling guile ?—*1 *H. VI.*, iv. 1.

Alas, *what joy shall noble Talbot have,*
To bid his young son welcome to his grave ?
Away ! vexation almost stops my breath,
That sunder'd friends greet in the hour of death.—*Ibid.*, iv. 3.

Fie, De la Poole ! disable not thyself;
Hast not a tongue ? is she not here thy prisoner ?
Wilt thou be daunted at a woman's sight ?
Ay, beauty's princely majesty is such,
Confounds the tongue, and makes the senses rough.—*Ibid.*, v. 3.

And therefore, lords, since he affects her most,
It most of all these reasons bindeth us,
In our opinions she should be preferr'd.
For what is wedlock forced but a hell,
An age of discord and continual strife ?
Whereas the contrary bringeth bliss,
And is a pattern of celestial peace.
Whom should we match with Henry, being a king ?
But Margaret, that is daughter to a king ?—Ibid., v. 5.

We have taken some pains to collect the above instances of recurrently vicious style in the play of the " First Part of King Henry VI."; glad of this opportunity to testify by intrinsic evidence how dissimilar the majority of its diction is to Shakespeare's mode of composition, and how well-founded is our belief that but a very minute portion of it is his writing.

The " Second Part of King Henry VI." contains several examples of words in their contracted form ; and in it there occur an epithet and a word each twice repeated, which our author has not used elsewhere :—

With you, mine alder-*liefest* sovereign.—2 *H. VI.*, i. 1.

My *liefest* liege to be mine enemy.—*Ibid.*, iii. 1.

Before the wound do grow *uncurable.*—*Ibid.*, iii. 1.

But fly you must: *uncurable* discomfit
Reigns in the hearts of all our present parts.—*Ibid.*, v. 2.

In the " Third Part of King Henry VI." the word " prize " is twice used in the unusual sense of ' privilege ':—

It is war's *prize* to take all vantages.—3 *H. VI.*, i. 4.

Methinks 'tis *prize* enough to be his son.—*Ibid.*, ii. 1.

An idiomatic expression—" in place," signifying ' in company,' ' present,' ' among those assembled '—occurs twice in this play:—

But what said Henry's queen?
For I have heard that she was there *in place.*—*Ibid.*, iv. 1.

Yet in this one thing let me blame your grace,
For choosing me when Clarence is *in place.*—*Ibid.*, iv. 6.

A similar phrase is twice introduced :—

Environed he was with many foes;
And stood against them, as *the hope of Troy*
Against the Greeks.—*Ibid.*, ii. 1.

Farewell, my Hector, and *my Troy's true hope.*—*Ibid.*, iv. 8.

And another similar phrase occurs twice; which has caused some misapprehension in commentators, who suppose the phrase to be both times applied to Warwick. This supposition probably arose from the confused effect given to the first passage where the phrase occurs by the employment of "thine" in the first two lines of the speech, when Edward is addressing Warwick; and by the employment of "thee," "thou," and "thy," immediately afterwards, when Edward appeals to the divine power. Another cause for the supposition is, that in the second passage where the phrase occurs, Margaret unmistakably addresses it to Warwick, who was popularly known by the name of 'Warwick, the king-maker':—

> O, Warwick, I do bend my knee with thine;
> And in this vow do chain my soul to thine!
> And, ere my knee rise from the earth's cold face,
> I throw my hands, mine eyes, my heart to thee,
> Thou *setter up and plucker down of kings*,—
> Beseeching thee, if with thy will it stands,
> That to my foes this body must be prey,
> Yet that thy brazen gates of Heaven may ope,
> And give sweet passage to my sinful soul!—*3 H. VI*, ii. 3.
>
> Peace, impudent and shameless Warwick,—
> Proud *setter up and puller down of kings!—Ibid.*, iii. 3.

In "King Richard III." we see an iterated word used more than once to express eagerness [*See* ITERATED WORDS]; "that" several times used redundantly:—

> Till *that* the duke give order for.—*R. III.*, i. 4.
> How *that* the guilty kindred of the queen.—*Ibid.*, ii. 1.
> If *that* our noble father be alive?—*Ibid.*, ii. 2.
> When *that* he bids good-morrow with such.—*Ibid.*, iii. 4.
> Be branded, if *that* right were right.—*Ibid.*, iv. 4.
> You speak as if *that* I had slain my.—*Ibid.*, iv. 4.

And the word "reason" employed in the sense of 'talk inquiringly or arguingly,' 'parley,' no fewer than four times:—

> I am, in this, commanded to deliver
> The noble Duke of Clarence to your hands:
> I will not *reason* what is meant hereby,
> Because I will be guiltless of the meaning.—*Ibid.*, i. 4.
>
> Strike!—
> No, we'll *reason* with him.—*Ibid.*, i. 4.
>
> You cannot *reason* almost with a man
> That looks not heavily and full of dread.—*Ibid.*, ii. 3.
>
> Away towards Salisbury! while we *reason* here,
> A royal battle might be won and lost.—*Ibid.*, iv. 4.

The play of "King Henry VIII." abounds with tokens of Shakespeare's thinking and writing in a particular manner at the period when he composed this magnificent historical drama. In the first place there is a marked prevalence of contractions by elision [*See* ELISIONAL ABBREVIATIONS]; so much so that one of them, assuming it to be a mere habit of his pen at the time when he wrote this play, we have never retained in the text of any of our editions of his works. It is the elisional form of " 'em " for 'them '; and inasmuch as we believe it to have been merely a temporary trick of handwriting, not intended by him to be either spoken or printed thus, we think it should be omitted from such passages as the following (a few only of those where " 'em " is given for " them " in the Folio throughout this play), where it mars the effect, and where it is certainly not in accordance with Shakespeare's usual style in passages of kindred staidness.   Be it observed, also, that it cannot be intended as a mark of *characteristic* diction, since it occurs in speeches made by various speakers, and speakers of lofty character and diction.   For instance, in one of the Duke of Norfolk's speeches, giving a stately description of the royal meeting at the Field of the Cloth of Gold :—

> When these suns
> (For so they phrase *'em*) by their heralds challeng'd
> The noble spirits to arms, they did perform
> Beyond thought's compass.—*H. VIII.*, i. 1.

In Queen Katharine's speech of noble remonstance to her husband :—

> I am solicited, not by a few,
> And those of true condition, that your subjects
> Are in great grievance : there have been commissions
> Sent down among *'em*, which hath flaw'd the heart
> Of all their loyalties.—*Ibid.*, i. 2.

In the king's speech at the festal dance in York Place :—

> I have half a dozen healths
> To drink to these fair ladies, and a measure
> To lead *'em* once again.—*Ibid.*, i. 4.

In Buckingham's speech as he is led to death :—

> But those that sought it I could wish more Christians :
> Be what they will, I heartily forgive *'em* :
> Yet let *'em* look they glory not in mischief,
> Nor build their evils on the graves of great men ;
> For then my guiltless blood must cry against *'em*.—*Ibid.*, ii. 1.

And in Wolsey's speech of denouncement to the hostile lords :—

> Follow your envious courses, men of malice ;
> You have Christian warrant for *'em*, and, no doubt,
> In time will find their fit rewards.—*Ibid.*, iii. 2.

There are likewise to be traced, throughout the present play, several instances of a redundant form of phrase [*See* PLEONASMS] ; very numerous examples of ellipsis [*See* ELLIPTICAL STYLE] ; many passages of irony [*See* IRONICAL PHRASES] ; unusually frequent and detailed stage directions, [*See* STAGE DIRECTIONS AND ENTRANCES] ; frequent sentences of constructional conciseness [*See* PECULIAR CONSTRUCTION] ; and an abundance of parentheses, of which we will quote no more than those occurring in the first act only :—

When these suns
(For so they phrase them) by their heralds challeng'd
The noble spirits to arms.—*H. VIII.*, i. 1.

I advise you
(And take it from a heart that wishes towards you
Honour and plenteous safety), that you read
The cardinal's malice and his potency
Together.—*Ibid.*, i. 1.

But this top-proud fellow,
(Whom from the flow of gall I name not, but
From sincere motions) by intelligence,
And proofs as clear as founts in July, when
We see each grain of gravel, I do know
To be corrupt and treasonous.—*Ibid.*, i. 1.

This holy fox,
Or wolf, or both (for he is equal ravenous
As he is subtle, and as prone to mischief
As able to perform 't; his mind and place
Infecting one another, yea, reciprocally),
Only to show his pomp as well in France
As here at home.—*Ibid.*, i. 1.

Now this follows
(Which, as I take it, is a kind of puppy
To the old dam, treason),—Charles the emperor,
Under pretence to see the queen his aunt
(For 'twas indeed his colour, but he came
To whisper Wolsey), here makes visitation:
. . . Let the king know
(As soon he shall by me), that thus the cardinal
Does buy and sell his honour as he pleases.—*Ibid.*, i. 1.

Yet the king our master
(Whose honour Heaven shield from soil!), even he escapes not
Language unmannerly.—*Ibid.*, i. 2.

You shall hear
(This was his gentleman in trust) of him
Things to strike honour sad.—*Ibid.*, i. 2.

Neither the king nor 's heirs
(Tell you the duke) shall prosper.—*Ibid.*, i. 2.

They must either
(For so run the conditions) leave those remnants
Of fool and feather, that they got in France,
With all their honourable points of ignorance
Pertaining thereunto (as fights and fireworks;
Abusing better men than they can be,
Out of a foreign wisdom); renouncing clean.—*Ibid.*, i. 3.

I am glad they are going
(For, sure, there's no converting of them): now,
An honest country lord, as I am, beaten
A long time out of play.—*Ibid.*, i. 3.

There are also in this play three instances of a peculiar form of question occasionally used by Shakespeare; in which the usually employed word "not" is omitted, and allowed to be elliptically understood:—

What friend of mine
That had to him deriv'd your anger, did I
Continue in my liking? nay, gave [I *not*] notice
He was from thence discharg'd?—*Ibid.*, ii. 4.

> Which of the peers
> Have uncontemn'd gone by him, or at least
> [Have *not* been] Strangely neglected ?—*H. VIII.*, iii. 2.

>   At what ease
> Might [*not*] corrupt minds procure knaves as corrupt
> To swear against you ?—*Ibid.*, v. 1.

And, finally, in this play " out " is twice peculiarly used :—

> The honourable board of council *out* ['left out,' ' omitted '].—*Ibid.*, i. 1.
> Could speak thee *out* ['completely '].—*Ibid.*, ii. 4.

In the play of " Troilus and Cressida " we meet with a remarkable recurrence of words framed by Shakespeare from classical derivatives, or words used by him in their more strictly classical sense [*See* COINED WORDS]; several instances of words terminating in "ive," such as " directive," " persistive," " protractive," " tortive," " unplausive," and " unrespective"; several instances of the antique form of possessive case, "his" instead of ''s'; and several examples of certain words used in peculiar senses :—

> This man, lady, hath robbed many beasts of their particular *additions* ['titles to distinction']; he is as valiant as the lion, churlish as the bear, slow as the elephant.— *Tr. & Cr.*, i. 2.

> Bull-bearing Milo his *addition* [' title of distinction '] yield
> To sinewy Ajax.—*Ibid.*, ii. 3.

> We will not name desert before his birth; and, being born, his *addition* ['title'] shall be humble.—*Ibid.*, iii. 2.

> I came to kill thee, cousin, and bear hence
> A great *addition* [' title to distinction '] earned in thy death.—*Ibid.*, iv. 5.

> Whilst *emulation* [' envious rivalry '] in the army crept.—*Ibid.*, ii. 2.

> The obligation of our blòod forbids
> A gory *emulation* ['contest '] 'twixt us twain.—*Ibid.*, iv. 5.

> A good quarrel to draw *emulous* ['hostile'] factions and bleed to death upon.— *Ibid.*, ii. 3.

> He is not *emulous* [' full of arrogant rivalry '] as Achilles is.—*Ibid.*, ii. 3.

> Whose glorious deeds but in these fields of late,
> Made *emulous* [' enviously rivalling'] missions 'mongst the gods themselves,
> And drave great Mars to faction.—*Ibid.*, iii. 3.

> When *rank* [' coarse,' ' gross '] Thersites opes his mastiff jaws.—*Ibid.*, i. 3.

> How *rank* [' overgrownly '] so ever rounded in with danger.—*Ibid.*, i. 3.

> The seeded pride
> That hath to this maturity blown up
> In *rank* [' rampantly arrogant'] Achilles must or now be cropp'd,
> Or, shedding, breed a nursery of like evil,
> To overbulk us all.—*Ibid.*, i. 3.

> Thou shouldst not bear from me a Greekish member
> Wherein my sword had not impressure made
> Of our *rank* [' rampant'] feud.—*Ibid.*, iv. 5.

The play of " Coriolanus " exhibits a prevalence of words elisionally contracted [*See* ELISIONAL ABBREVIATIONS]; which tends to mark the period of its composition as coeval with the one whereat Shakespeare wrote his " Winter's Tale " and " King Henry VIII." There are also in " Coriolanus " several passages containing instances of indefinitely expressed conditional time ; and it presents recurrent token of words used peculiarly and in peculiar senses.   For instance, he uses " have " more than once in this play with especial force :—

He hath deserved worthily of his country : and his ascent is not by such easy degrees as those who, having been supple and courteous to the people, bonneted, without any farther deed to *have* them at all into their estimation and report.— *Coriol.*, ii. 2.

And since the wisdom of their choice is rather to *have* my hat than my heart, I will practise the insinuating nod, and be off to them most counterfeitly.—*Ibid.*, ii. 3.

And, in confirmation of our idea that the particular force of " have " was just then in his mind, we observe that he employs in this play an unusual noun framed therefrom :—

> It is held,
> That valour is the chiefest virtue, and
> Most dignifies the *haver.—Ibid.*, ii. 2.

He also uses the word " end," in various passages of this play, with much force of ellipsis :—

> He cannot temperately transport his honours
> From where he should begin, and [to where he should] *end ;* but will
> Lose those he hath won.—*Ibid.*, ii. 1.

> It shall be to him, then, as our good wills,
> A sure destruction.—
> So it must fall out
> To him, or our authorities.   For an *end* [of this sort],
> We must suggest the people in what hatred
> He still hath held them.—*Ibid.*, ii. 1.

> He covets less
> Than misery itself would give ; rewards
> His deeds with doing them ; and is content
> To spend the time [thus, as the due mode] to *end* it.—*Ibid.*, ii. 2.

> Serv'd his designments
> In mine own person ; holp to reap the fame
> Which he did *end* [by making] all his.—*Ibid.*, v. 5.

In this play, likewise, " enforce " (and, in one instance, " force," as an abbreviation of " enforce ") is used to express ' urge ' and ' urge against ' :—

> *Enforce* his pride,
> And his old hate unto you.—*Ibid.*, ii. 3.

> In this point charge him home,—that he affects
> Tyrannical power : if he evade us there,
> *Enforce* him with his envy to the people.—*Ibid.*, iii. 3.

> And when such time they have begun to cry,
> Let them not cease, but with a din confus'd
> *Enforce* the present execution
> Of what we chance to sentence.—*Ibid.*, iii. 3.

> Why *force* you this ?—*Ibid.*, iii. 2.

In " Romeo and Juliet " we are struck with the rarity of elliptical sentences ; one of the points in its diction which lead us to believe it to be an early written play of our dramatist.   We also find in it a multitude of conceits, quibbles, and plays on words ; another point of style which marks it as one of Shakespeare's more youthful productions [*See* BITTER PUNS, &c.] The word " earth " is peculiarly used in three passages of this tragedy :—

> Earth hath swallow'd all my hopes but she,
> She is the hopeful lady of my *earth.—R. & Jul.*, i. 2.

The latter expression giving the doubly included meaning of ' she is the hopeful inheritrix of my landed estates,' and ' she is the sole surviving issue of my body, in whom I have centred all my hopes ' ; because Shakespeare sometimes uses " earth" for 'land' or 'landed possessions, and because he employs " earth " in the two next quoted examples from this play to express ' corporeal part,' ' material part,' ' the earthly portion of a human being ' :—

> Can I go forward when my heart is here ?
> Turn back dull *earth*, and find thy centre out.
> > [*He climbs the wall, and leaps down within it.*]—*Ibid.*, ii. 1.
> O, break, my heart ! poor bankrupt, break at once !
> To prison, eyes, ne'er look on liberty !
> Vile *earth*, to earth resign ; end motion here ;
> And thou and Romeo press one heavy bier !—*Ibid.*, iii. 2.

The rather uncommon verb " prorogue " (which Shakespeare in only two other plays uses, introducing it but once in each of them, and then in a different sense from the one in which he here employs it) is twice employed in the present play to express ' delay,' ' defer,' ' put off,' ' postpone ' :—

> My life were better ended by their hate,
> Than death *prorogued*, wanting of thy love.—*Ibid.*, ii. 2.
> I hear thou must, and nothing may *prorogue* it,
> On Thursday next be married to this county.—*Ibid.*, iv. 1.

In " Timon of Athens " we have remarked a recurrent use of " to " and " to be " in passages where the construction is peculiar and rendered somewhat obscure by the mode in which these words are introduced ; as, for instance :—

> But [it is requisite] *to* support him after,—*Timon*, i. 1.
> Nor has he with him [wherewith] *to* supply his life.—*Ibid.*, iv. 2.
> Who would be so mock'd with glory ? or *to* ['who would '] live
> But in a dream of friendship ?
> *To* [' who would '] have his pomp, and all what state compounds,
> But only painted, like his varnish'd friends ?—*Ibid.*, iv. 2.
> That I had no angry wit *to be* [' by being '] a lord.*—*Ibid.*, i. 1.
> Was [created] *to be* so unwise, [and yet] *to be* so kind.—*Ibid.*, ii. 1.

And also three instances in one scene, of " when " being elliptically understood [*See* ELLIPTICAL STYLE].

In " Julius Cæsar " we find an idiomatic phrase (signifying ' bear a

---

* This sentence has been suspected of error, and has been variously altered ; but, we think, other similarly constructed sentences used by Shakespeare show this one to be correct as it stands, and that it bears the double signification of ' that being a lord, I should have no angry wit,' and ' that I had given up (Apemantus's) angry wit in order to be a lord.'

hard opinion of,' 'bear ill-will,' 'bear a grudge') thrice repeated, which is used nowhere else by Shakespeare :—

> Cæsar doth *bear me hard ;* but he loves Brutus.—*Jul. C.*, i. 2.
> Caius Ligarius doth *bear Cæsar hard.*—*Ibid.*, ii. 1.
> I do beseech ye, if you *bear me hard.*—*Ibid.*, iii. 1.

We also meet herein with three instances of " but " used peculiarly and transposedly: the first phrase signifying, 'Where none but Brutus may find it'; the second 'Do but send him hither'; and the third, 'Do but pluck his name out of his heart ' :—

> Take this paper,
> And look you lay it in the prætor's chair,
> *Where Brutus may but find it.*—*Ibid.*, i. 3.
> *Send him but hither*, and I 'll fashion him.—*Ibid.*, ii. 1.

It is no matter, his name 's Cinna; *pluck but his name out of his heart*, and turn him going.—*Ibid.*, iii. 3.

In this play likewise the words " constancy " and " constant " are repeatedly used to express ' self-possession,' ' firmness,' ' steadiness,' and ' self-possessed,' ' firm,' ' steady' :—

> But bear it as our Roman actors do,
> With untir'd spirits and formal *constancy.*—*Ibid.*, ii. 1.
> I have made strong proof of my *constancy*,
> Giving myself a voluntary wound
> Here, in the thigh: can I bear that with patience,
> And not my husband's secrets ?—*Ibid.*, ii. 1.
> O, *constancy*, be strong upon my side,
> Set a huge mountain 'tween my heart and tongue !—*Ibid.*, ii. 4.
> Cassius, be *constant :*
> Popilius Lena speaks not of our purposes.—*Ibid.*, iii. 1.
> But I am *constant* as the northern star,
> Of whose true-fix'd and resting quality
> There is no fellow in the firmament . . .
> Let me a little show it, even in this,—
> That I was *constant* Cimber should be banish'd,
> And *constant* do remain to keep him so.—*Ibid.*, iii. 1.

" Slight" is twice used in this drama as an epithet of contempt:—

> This is a *slight* unmeritable man.—*Ibid.*, iv. 1.
> Away, *slight* man !—*Ibid.*, iv. 3.

There are three allusions in this play to time by the clock, which of course has subjected Shakespeare to the charge of anachronism [*See* Alleged Discrepancies, &c.]. But not only was the impression of current time evidently strong in the author's mind while he wrote this piece, it was also imperatively requisite that he should maintain the impression of present dramatic time well before the imagination of his audience, in order to counterbalance the effect of prolonged dramatic time, which it was incumbent upon him to give for the due lapse of events between the opening and the close of the play [*See* Dramatic Time]:—

> Peace ! *count the clock.*—
> *The clock hath stricken* three.—*Ibid.*, ii. 1.

What is 't *o'clock ?*—
> Cæsar, *'tis strucken* eight.—*Jul. C.*, ii. 2.
> Set our battles on :
> 'Tis three *o'clock ;* and, Romans, yet ere night
> We shall try fortune in a second fight.—*Ibid.*, v. 3.

In " Macbeth " there is a notable prevalence of compound words and of simply plain common words in even some of the most strikingly grand passages [*See* FAMILIAR AND HOMELY EXPRESSIONS]. There are also several instances of the word " even " elliptically understood [*See* ELLIPTICAL STYLE].

There are to be observed in the tragedy of " Hamlet " a recurrence of words punningly used, and of scraps of doggerel verse : both of which, however, are attributable to the peculiar mental condition of the hero, whose assumed madness and veritable melancholy take these means of venting their many wayward moods. The first words uttered by Hamlet contain a pun :—

A little more than kin, and less than *kind.*—*Hamlet*, i. 2.

And the next speech, of a single line :—

Not so, my lord ; I am too much i' the *sun.*—*Ibid.*, i. 2.

And so on, throughout the play :—

Excellent well, you are a *fish-monger.*—*Ibid.*, ii. 2.

All which, sir, though I most powerfully and potently believe, yet I hold it not *honesty* to have it thus set down.—*Ibid.*, ii. 2.

> What should we say, my lord ?—
> Why, anything—*but to the purpose.*—*Ibid.*, ii. 2.

Nay, then, *I have an eye of you.*—*Ibid.*, ii. 2.

O, my old friend ! thy face is valanced since I saw thee last ; comest thou to *beard* me in Denmark ?—*Ibid.*, ii. 2.

Pray Heaven, your voice, like a piece of uncurrent gold, be not *cracked within the ring.*—*Ibid.*, ii. 2.

> Why should the poor be flatter'd ?
> No, let the *candied* tongue lick absurd pomp.—*Ibid.*, iii. 2.

I did enact Julius Cæsar : I was killed i' the Capitol ; Brutus killed me.—It was a *brute* part of him to kill so *capital* a calf there.—*Ibid.*, iii. 2.

Nay, then, let the devil wear black, for I 'll have a suit of *sables.*—*Ibid.*, iii. 2.

To *withdraw with you :* Why do you go about to recover the wind of me, as if you would drive me into a toil?—*Ibid.*, iii. 2.

Call me what instrument you will, though you can *fret* me, you cannot *play upon* me.—*Ibid.*, iii. 2.

> Indeed, this counsellor
> Is now most *still*, most *secret*, and most *grave*,
> Who was in life a foolish prating knave.—*Ibid.*, iii. 4.

The body is with the king, but *the king is not with the body.*—*Ibid.*, iv. 2.

A certain convocation of politic *worms* are e'en at him.—*Ibid.*, iv. 3.

This might be the pate of a politician, which this ass now *o'er-reaches.*—*Ibid.*, v. 1.

Why may not that be the skull of a lawyer ? . . . Why does he suffer this rude knave now to knock him about the sconce with a dirty shovel, and will not tell him of his *action of battery?* . . . The very length of his lands will hardly lie in this *box ;* and must the inheritor himself have no more, ha ?—*Ibid.*, v. 1.

They are *sheep* and *calves* which seek out *assurance* in that.—*Ibid.*, v. 1.

Thou dost *lie in 't*, to be in 't and say it is thine : 'tis for the dead, not for the quick ; therefore thou liest.—*Hamlet*, v. 1.

> Give us the foils. Come on.—
>   Come, one for me.—
> I 'll be your *foil*, Laertes : in mine ignorance
> Your skill shall, like a star i' the darkest night,
> Stick fiery off indeed.—*Ibid.*, v. 2.

> Here, thou incestuous, murderous, damned Dane,
> Drink off this potion :—is thy *union* here ?
> Follow my mother.—*Ibid.*, v. 2.

Not only does Hamlet occasionally doggerelise, as if he were quoting scraps from some remembered popular rhyme or verse ; but he sometimes lapses into a rhyming couplet amid his own blank-verse speeches :—

> But I have that within which passeth *show ;*
> These but the trappings and the suits of *woe.*—*Ibid.*, i. 2.

> The time is out of joint :—O, cursèd *spite,*
> That ever I was born to set it *right !*—*Ibid.*, i. 5.

> As hell whereto it goes. My mother *stays :*
> This physic but prolongs thy sickly *days.*—*Ibid.*, iii. 3.

> A bloody deed ! Almost as bad, good *mother,*
> As kill a king, and marry with his *brother.*—*Ibid.*, iii. 4.

> I must be cruel, only to *be kind :*
> Thus bad begins, and worse remains *behind.*—*Ibid.*, iii. 4.

> Is now most still, most secret, and most *grave,*
> Who was in life a foolish prating *knave.*—*Ibid.*, iii. 4.

The passages where the prince seems to be repeating quoted scraps are these :—

> Then came each actor on his ass.—*Ibid.*, ii. 2.

> One fair daughter, and no more,
> The which he loved passing well.—*Ibid.*, ii. 2.

> As by lot, God wot.—*Ibid.*, ii. 2.

> It came to pass, as most like it was.—*Ibid.*, ii. 2.

> Why, let the strucken deer go weep,
>   The hart ungalled play ;
> For some must watch, while some must sleep ;
>   So runs the world away.—*Ibid.*, iii. 2.

> For thou dost know, O Damon dear,
>   This realm dismantled was
> Of Jove himself ; and now reigns here
>   A very, very—peacock.—*Ibid.*, iii. 2.

> For if the king like not the comedy,
> Why, then, belike,—he likes it not, perdy.—*Ibid.*, iii. 2.

> Imperial Cæsar, dead and turn'd to clay,
> Might stop a hole to keep the wind away :
> O that that earth, which kept the world in awe,
> Should patch a wall t' expel the winter's flaw !—*Ibid.*, v. 1.

> Let Hercules himself do what he may,
> The cat will mew, the dog will have his day.—*Ibid.*, v. 1.

Even in his letter to Ophelia, Hamlet (in accordance with an antique fashion for lovers) addresses his mistress partly in doggerel verse :—

> Doubt thou the stars are fire ;
> Doubt that the sun doth move ;
> Doubt truth to be a liar ;
> But never doubt I love.—*Hamlet*, ii. 2.

There is also a recurrence of iterated words in the present play [*See* ITERATED WORDS]; which is likewise referable to a characteristic point of diction in the prince, who makes this one token of the mental derangement which he assumes.

Certain words are, more than once during the five acts, used in peculiar and various senses :—

It is a nipping and an *eager* [' sharp,' ' keen '] air.—*Ibid*., i. 4.

And, with a sudden vigour, it doth posset
And curd, like *eager* [' sharp,' ' acid,' ' sour '] droppings into milk, the thin and wholesome blood : so did it mine.—*Ibid*., i. 5.

> *Season* [' temper,' ' modify '] your admiration for a while
> With an attent ear.—*Ibid*., i. 2.

Farewell: my blessing *season* [' temper,' ' turn to profit '] this in thee !—*Ibid*., i. 3.

My lord, that would dishonour him.—
Faith, no ; as you may *season* [' temper,' ' qualify '] it in the charge.—*Ibid*., ii. 1.

And who in want a hollow friend doth try,
Directly *seasons him* [' tempers him into,' ' moulds him into '; also including the sense of ' inures, habituates, or accustoms him to become '] his enemy.—*Ibid*., iii. 2.

In " King Lear " are observable a recurrence of double comparatives ; an unusual number of interrupted speeches [*See* UNFINISHED SENTENCES]; a marked frequency of compound epithets ; and several instances of verbs formed from nouns [*See* PARTS OF SPEECH DIVERSELY USED]. Also, there are in this tragedy a few words peculiarly employed :—

> Am I in France ?—
> In your own kingdom, sir.—
> Do not *abuse* [' delude '] me.—*Lear*, iv. 3.

He is attended with a desperate train ;
And what they may incense him to, being apt
To have his ear *abus'd* [' beguiled '], wisdom bids fear.—*Ibid*., ii. 4.

Then Edgar was *abus'd* [' slandered,' ' falsely accused '].—*Ibid*., iii. 7.

> Ah ! dear son Edgar,
> The food of thy *abusèd* [' deceived '] father's wrath !—*Ibid*., iv. 1.

O, you kind gods,
Cure this great breach in his *abusèd* [' ill-used,' ' injured '] nature !—*Ibid*., iv. 7.

I am mightily *abus'd* [' bewildered,' ' perplexed '].—*Ibid*., iv. 7.

That thought *abuses* [' deceives,' ' wrongs '] you.—*Ibid*., v. 1.

For equalities are so weighed, that *curiosity* [' carefullest scrutiny '] in neither can make choice of either's moiety.—*Ibid*., i. 1.

> Wherefore should I
> Stand in the plague of custom, and permit
> The *curiosity* [' scrupulousness,' ' punctiliousness '] of nations to deprive me,
> For that I am some twelve or fourteen moonshines
> Lag of a brother ? Why bastard? wherefore base ?—*Ibid*., i. 2.

I have perceived a most faint neglect of late ; which I have rather blamed as mine own jealous *curiosity* [' susceptible punctilio,' ' over-scrupulous care for deference '] than as a very pretence and purpose of unkindness.—*Ibid*., i. 4.

Servants, who seem no less,
Which are to France the spies and speculations
*Intelligent** ['aware' and 'communicative'] of our state.—*Lear*, iii. 1.

This is the letter he spoke of, which approves him an *intelligent* ['informed' and 'communicative'] party to the advantages of France.—*Ibid.*, iii. 5.

Our posts shall be swift and *intelligent* ['communicative of intelligence,' 'conveyant of intelligence'] betwixt us.—*Ibid.*, iii. 7.

In "Othello," there are recurrent instances of words ending in 'ce' and 'te':—

Not with vain thanks, but with *acceptance* bounteous.—*Oth.*, iii. 3.

If this be known to you, and your *allowance*.—*Ibid.*, i. 1.

Of very expert and approv'd *allowance*.—*Ibid.*, ii. 1.

For every minute is expectancy
Of more *arrivance*.—*Ibid.*, ii. 1.

What needs this *iterance*, woman?—*Ibid.*, v. 2.

Out of his scattering and unsure *observance*.—*Ibid.*, iii. 3.

That we should, with joy, *pleasance*, revel, and applause, transform ourselves into beasts!—*Ibid.*, ii. 3.

This sight would make him do a desperate turn,
Yea, curse his better angel from his side,
And fall to *reprobance*.—*Ibid.*, v. 2.

But I shall, in a more *continuate* time,
Strike off this score of absence.—*Ibid.*, iii. 4.

Wherein none can be so *determinate* as the removing of Cassio.—*Ibid.*, iv. 2.

To such *exsufflicate* and blown surmises.—*Ibid.*, iii. 3.

In this play we find "to do" twice used for 'ado':—

To have so much *to do*,
To bring him in!—*Ibid.*, iii. 3.

I have much *to do*,
But to go hang my head all at one side.—*Ibid.*, iv. 3.

And we meet with two instances of "trash" used as a contemptuous epithet:—

If this poor *trash* of Venice.—*Ibid.*, ii. 1.

Gentlemen all, I do suspect this *trash*
To be a party in this injury.—*Ibid.*, v. 1.

Then, too, we have several examples of words used in peculiar senses:—

After some time to *abuse* ['misinform'] Othello's ear
That he is too familiar with his wife.—*Ibid.*, i. 3.

I'll have our Michael Cassio on the hip;
Abuse ['misrepresent'] him to the Moor in the rank garb.—*Ibid.*, ii. 1.

If you think other,
Remove your thought; it doth *abuse* ['deceive' 'wrong'] your bosom.—*Ibid.*, iv. 2.

That there be women do *abuse* ['betray,' 'wrong'] their husbands
In such gross kind?—*Ibid.*, iv. 3.

Are there not charms,
By which the property of youth and maidhood
May be abused ['deluded,' 'injured']?—*Ibid.*, i. 1.

---

* *See* ELLIPTICALLY USED WORDS for farther explanation of this word.

That thou hast practis'd on her with foul charms;
Abus'd ['injured,' 'deluded'] her delicate youth with drugs or minerals
That weaken motion.—*Oth.*, i. 2.

She is *abus'd* ['deluded,' 'injured'], stol'n from me, and corrupted
By spells and medicines bought of mountebanks.—*Ibid.*, i. 3.

Her delicate tenderness will find itself *abused* ['beguiled'].—*Ibid.*, ii. 1.

I would not have your free and noble nature,
Out of self-bounty, be *abus'd* ['cheated,' 'beguiled'].—*Ibid.*, iii. 3.

She's gone; I am *abus'd* ['betrayed,' 'beguiled']; and my relief
Must be to loathe her.—*Ibid.*, iii. 3.

I swear, 'tis better to be much *abus'd* ['deceived,' 'injured'],
Than but to know 't a little.—*Ibid.*, iii. 3.

The Moor's *abus'd* ['deceived,' 'deluded'] by some most villainous knave.—*Ibid.*, iv. 2.

I therefore apprehend and do attach thee
For an *abuser* ['injurer,' 'impostor'] of the world, a practiser
Of arts inhibited and out of warrant.—*Ibid.*, i. 2.

For, I do know, the state,—
However this may gall him with some check,—
Cannot with safety *cast* ['cashier'] him.—*Ibid.*, i. 1.

Our general *cast* ['dismissed'] us thus early for the love of his Desdemona.—*Ibid.*, ii. 3.

You are but now *cast* ['cashiered'] in his mood.—*Ibid.*, ii. 3.

How he upbraids Iago, that he made him
Brave me upon the watch; whereon it came
That I was *cast* ['cashiered'].—*Ibid.*, v. 2.

What a *full* ['plenarily good,' 'complete'] fortune does the thick-lips owe,
If he can carry 't thus!—*Ibid.*, i. 1.

For I have serv'd him, and the man commands
Like a *full* ['fully accomplished,' 'complete'] soldier.—*Ibid.*, ii. 1.

Is this the noble Moor whom our *full* ['complete,' 'entire,' and 'fully competent to judge'] senate
Call all-in-all sufficient?—*Ibid.*, iv. 1.

The verb "affin'd" is used in this play twice, and in no other, excepting once in "Troilus and Cressida"; while the noun "affinity" occurs nowhere else than in the present tragedy:—

Now, sir, be judge yourself,
Whether I in any just term am *affin'd*
To love the Moor.—*Ibid.*, i. 1.

If partially *affin'd*, or leagu'd in office,
Thou dost deliver more or less than truth,
Thou art no soldier.—*Ibid.*, ii. 3.

The Moor replies,
That he you hurt is of great fame in Cyprus
And great *affinity*.—*Ibid.*, iii. 1.

We find in "Antony and Cleopatra" various recurrent features of style: marked condensation in the diction with elliptical force of construction [*See* ELLIPTICAL STYLE]; more than one instance of "he," "him," and "his" used in abstract; frequent employment of a turn of phrase which resembles one used in Italy [*See* ITALIAN IDIOM]; and several sentences where "but" is used exceptively. The peculiar expressions "discandy" and "discandying" are introduced by Shakespeare into no play besides the present one:—

> The hearts
> That spaniel'd me at heels, to whom I gave
> Their wishes, do *discandy*, melt their sweets
> On blossoming Cæsar.—*Ant. & C.*, iv. 10.
> Together with my brave Egyptians all,
> By the *discandying* of this pelleted storm,
> Lie graveless.—*Ibid.*, iii. 11.

The play of " Cymbeline " abounds with contracted forms of words [*See* ELISIONAL ABBREVIATIONS] and with extremely condensed phraseology [*See* ELLIPTICAL STYLE]. There are several passages where the pronoun is varied in the same sentence when referring to the. same antecedent; there are three passages where " sir " is used as a noun ; and there are some sentences where " for " is peculiarly used in this play.

In " Pericles " there is a marked introduction of antiquated words and of words with the final syllable " en," such as " killen," " lien," " perishen," and " thoughten."

There are some vestiges of coincident thought and style in certain plays by Shakespeare that seem to denote his having written the productions bearing these tokens of similarity at the same period of his career. For instance, we find the word " defeature " in " Venus and Adonis " (stated by himself, in his preface to this poem, to be " the first heir of my invention "), and the word " defeatures " twice in the " Comedy of Errors " (evidently an early composition), but in no other of his plays :—

> To mingle beauty with infirmities,
> And pure perfection with impure *defeature*.—*V. & Adon.*, Stanza 123.
> Then is he the ground of my *defeatures*.—*Com. of E.*, ii. 1.
> And careful hours, with Time's deformed hand,
> Have written strange *defeatures* in my face.—*Ibid.*, v. 1.

The contracted plural form of " corse' " for ' corses,' and the unusual form of " strond " for ' strand' occur in both the opening scenes of the two Parts of " King Henry IV.," and in no other of his dramas :—

> A thousand of his people butchered ;
> Upon whose dead *corse'* there was such misuse.—1. *H. IV.*, i. 1.
> My lord, your son had only but the *corse'*,
> But shadows, and the shows of men, to fight.—2 *H. IV.*, i. 1.
> To be commenc'd in *stronds* afar remote.—1 *H. IV.*, i. 1.
> So looks the *strond*, whereon th' imperious flood
> Hath left a witness'd usurpation.—2 *H. IV.*, i. 1.

There are evidences of special coincident points in the " Second Part of King Henry IV.," and in the comedy of " Much Ado About Nothing " ; and singularly enough as regards our theory, the entry in the Registers of the Stationers' Company makes mention of both these plays together: " 23 Aug: 1600. And. Wise. Wm. Apsley] Two books, the one called ' Muche Adoe about Nothing,' and the other, ' The Seconde Parte of the History of King Henry IIII., with the Humours of Sir John Falstaff: wrytten by Mr. Shakespeare." Farthermore, two of these special coincident points coexist in an evidently early written play by our dramatist, " Love's Labour's Lost," and one of the two in still another early written play, " Romeo and Juliet " ; but in no other of his dramas. One of these points is an allusion to the custom of engraving or carving figures on an " agate " ; the other is in reference to a particular fashion of wearing-apparel, called a " slop " or " slops," which were large loose trousers :—

If low, *an agate very vilely cut.—M. Ado*, iii. 1.

His heart, like *an agate, with your print impress'd.—Love's L. L.*, ii. 1.

I was never manned with *an agate* till now.—*2 H. IV.*, i. 2.

A German from the waist downward, all *slops.—M. Ado*, iii. 2.

O, rhymes are guards on wanton Cupid's hose:
Disfigure not his *slop.—Love's L. L.*, iv. 3.

What said Master Dumbleton about the satin for my short cloak and my *slops* ?—
2 H. IV., i. 2.

Signior Romeo, bon jour! there's a French salutation to your French *slop.*—
R. & Jul., ii. 4.

In " Romeo and Juliet " there are some signal tokens of Shakespeare's correspondent mode of thinking at the time he wrote this tragedy and at the time he wrote the play of " Love's Labour's Lost." One is a recurrent allusion to books as a figurative illustration of human looks :—

Study his bias leaves, and makes his *book* thine eyes.—*Love's L. L.*, iv. 2 (*Verses*).

From women's eyes this doctrine I derive,—
They are the ground, the *books*, the academes,
From whence doth spring the true Promethean fire. . . .
They are the *books*, the arts, the academes,
That show, contain, and nourish all the world.—*Ibid.*, iv. 3.

Read o'er the *volume* of young Paris' face,
And find delight writ there with beauty's pen ;
Examine every married lineament,
And see how one another lends content ;
And what obscur'd in this fair *volume* lies,
Find written in the margin of his eyes.
This precious *book* of love, this unbound lover,
To beautify him, only lacks a cover :
The fish lives in the sea ; and 'tis much pride,
For fair without the fair within to hide.
That *book* in many's eyes doth share the glory,
That in gold clasps locks in the golden story.—*R. & Jul.*, i. 3.

Was ever *book* containing such vile matter,
So fairly bound ?—*Ibid.*, iii. 2.

Another similar point in these two plays is the heaping up of hyperbolical and antithetical expressions :—

This wimpled, whining, purblind, wayward boy ;
This senior-junior, giant-dwarf, Dan Cupid ;
Regent of love-rhymes, lord of folded arms,
Th' anointed sovereign of sighs and groans,
Liege of all loiterers and malcontents,
Dread prince of plackets, king of cod-pieces,
Sole imperator and great general
Of trotting paritors.—*Love's L. L.*, iii. 1.

Here's much to do with hate, but more with love :—
Why, then, O brawling love ! O loving hate !
O anything, of nothing first create !
O heavy lightness ! serious vanity !

Mis-shapen chaos of well-seeming forms !
Feather of lead, bright smoke, cold fire, sick health !
Still-waking sleep, that is not what it is !
This love feel I, that feel no love in this.—*R. & Jul.*, i. 1.

O, serpent heart, hid with a flowering face !
Did ever dragon keep so fair a cave ?
Beautiful tyrant ! fiend angelical !
Dove-feather'd raven ! wolvish-ravening lamb !
Despised substance of divinest show !
Just opposite to what thou justly seem'st,
A damned saint, an honourable villain !
O, nature ! what hadst thou to do in hell,
When thou didst bower the spirit of a fiend
In mortal paradise of such sweet flesh ?—*Ibid.*, iii. 2.

There is also a seemingly trivial point of coincidence in these two plays : but, joined with other concurrent particulars, it seems to us to be significant. It is that in these two plays alone has Shakespeare used the woman's name of " Rosaline ; " but in both plays he has assigned it to characters bearing points of personal and even dispositional resemblance. Rosaline in " Love's Labour 's Lost " appears to us to be the finished picture of which Rosaline in " Romeo and Juliet " is but the outlined sketch ; Rosaline in " Love's Labour 's Lost " is the most highly wrought female figure on that dramatic canvas, while Rosaline in " Romeo and Juliet " is merely mentioned, not seen, though limned with distinct touches, and brought vividly before our mental vision. Rosaline in " Love's Labour 's Lost " is emphatically stated to be a dark beauty, with exquisitely beautiful and expressive eyes. [*See* passage quoted at page 478.]

Even when Biron, vexed at being unable to resist his passion for her, attempts to disparage her charms, he uses an expression that precisely describes a dark beauty whose skin looks dazzlingly fair by contrast with her pencilled brows and brilliantly black eyes :—

And, among three, to love the worst of all ;
A *whitely* wanton with a velvet brow,
With two pitch balls stuck in her face for eyes.—*Love's L. L.*, iii. 1.

And the expressions employed by Mercutio when speaking of Rosaline in " Romeo and Juliet " tally remarkably with the above :—

Ah ! that same *pale* hard-hearted wench, that Rosaline,
Torments him so, that he will sure run mad. . . .
Alas, poor Romeo, he is already dead ! stabbed with a *white wench's black eye.*—*R. & Jul.*, ii. 4.

Rosaline in " Love's Labour 's Lost " is proof against the solicitations of her admirer, and dooms him to a twelvemonth's severe probation in absence and hard service ; while Rosaline in " Romeo and Juliet " is deaf to her lover's suit, repels all his advances with rigour, and is called by his friend " hard-hearted." We have always had the strong impression that both the highly painted portrait of Rosaline in " Love's Labour 's Lost " and the sketched delineation of Rosaline in " Romeo and Juliet " were taken from one and the same life-original—some lady known to him ; and, to our thinking, probably likewise identical with the dark beauty so graphically described in Sonnets 127, 130, 131, 132. In this last-named Sonnet we have again presented to our beholding the individual bright-eyed, dark-complexioned, pitiless-hearted charmer that he depicted in the two dramatic portraitures. [*See* passage quoted at page 479.]

RELATIVELY USED PRONOUNS.

Shakespeare often uses a pronoun in reference to some person or thing not precisely stated, but in reference to an implied particular:—

If the French be lords of this loud day, *he* [the Dauphin : implied in " the French "] means to recompense the pains you take.—*John*, v. 4.

His second marriage shall be publish'd, and *her* [the lady he is going to marry : implied in " his second marriage "] coronation.—*H. VIII.*, iii. 2.

And bid me, when my fate would have me wive, to give it *her* [my wife : implied in " wive "].—*Oth.*, iii. 4.

The ears are senseless that should give us hearing, to tell *him* [the king : implied in " the ears "] *his* commandment is fulfill'd.—*Hamlet*, v. 2.

What ! all so soon asleep ? I wish mine eyes would. . . . Do not omit the heavy offer of *it* [sleep : implied in " asleep "].—*Temp.*, ii. 1.

If you are arm'd to do, as sworn to do, subscribe to your deep oaths, and keep *it* [that which you have " sworn to do "] too.—*Love's L. L.*, i. 1.

I know not why I am so sad : *it* [sadness : implied in " sad "] wearies me : you say *it* wearies you.—*Mer. of V.*, i. 1.

All my plots and purposes, how to get clear of . . . let me know *it* [your plan : implied in " plots and purposes, how to "].—*Ibid.*, i. 1.

You are lov'd, sir : they that least lend *it* [love : implied in " lov'd "] you, shall lack you first.—*All's W.*, i. 2.

Most *it* [the impression collectively produced by " the celestial habits," &c.] caught me, the celestial habits . . . and the reverence of the grave wearers.—*W. T.*, iii. 1.

If your father had been victor there, he ne'er had borne *it* [the honour of being " victor "] out of Coventry.—*2 H. IV.*, iv. 1.

Who are the late commissioners ?—I one, my lord : your highness bade me ask for *it* [commission : implied in " commissioners "] to-day.—*H. V.*, ii. 2.

Her father . . . hath pawn'd the Sicils and Jerusalem, and hither have they sent *it* [the sum raised by having " pawn'd " &c.] for her ransom.—*3 H. VI.*, v. 7.

Be not easily won to our requests ; play the maid's part,—still answer nay, and take *it* [that of which " requests " beg acceptance].—*R. III.*, iii. 7.

No doubt we bring *it* [the concerted scheme implied in the previous dialogue].—*Ibid.*, iii. 7.

I wish the bastards dead ; and I would have *it* [the deed implied in the previous wish] suddenly perform'd.—*Ibid.*, iv. 2.

If I chance to talk a little wild, forgive me ; I had *it* [the trick of talking " a little wild "] from my father.—*H. VIII.*, i. 4.

The king loves you ; beware you lose *it* [the king's love : implied in " the king loves you "] not.—*Ibid.*, iii. 1.

Till I find more than will or words to do *it* [the fulfilment of your malicious command that I should " render up the great seal "] . . . I dare and must deny *it*.—*Ibid.*, iii. 2.

How eagerly ye follow my disgraces, as if *it* [the sight of " my disgraces "] fed ye ! —*Ibid.*, iii. 2.

Oh, these encounterers, so glib of tongue, that give a coasting welcome ere *it* [amorous encounter: implied in "encounterers"] comes.—*Tr. & Cr.*, iv. 5.

Time will one day end *it* [this uncertainty as to the issue of the war].—So to him we leave *it.*—*Ibid.*, iv. 5.

It [the concession made to "the rabble" in having "granted them five tribunes"] will in time win upon power, and throw.—*Coriol.*, i. 1.

He has *it* [the consulship: implied in the previous dialogue] now; and, by his looks, methinks 'tis warm at his heart.—*Ibid.*, ii. 3.

He's gone, and we'll no farther . . . let us seem humbler after *it* [his banishment: implied in "he's gone"] is done, than when *it* was a-doing.—*Ibid.*, iv. 2.

He that hath a will to die by himself fears *it* [death: implied in "to die"] not from another.—*Ibid.*, v. 2.

If not most mortal to him. But let *it* [death: implied in "mortal"] come.— *Ibid.*, v. 3.

Love you the maid? Ay, my good lord; and she accepts of *it* [my love: implied in "love you"].—*Timon*, i. 1.

It [the prevention of Cæsar's becoming king: implied in the remainder of the soliloquy] must be by his death.—*Jul. C.*, ii. 1.

When I ask'd you what the matter was, you stared upon me with . . . hoping *it* [that which ails you: implied in "ask'd you what the matter was"] was but an effect of humour . . . *It* will not let you eat, nor talk, nor sleep: and, could *it* work so much upon your shape, as *it* hath.—*Jul. C.*, ii. 1.

Than your particular demands will touch *it* [the "enquiry" respecting "his behaviour"].—*Hamlet*, ii. 1.

If she should break *it* [her vow: implied in the previous speech] now!—'Tis deeply sworn.—*Ibid.*, iii. 2.

The present death of Hamlet. Do *it* [this deed: implied in "death of Hamlet"], England . . . till I know 'tis done.—*Ibid.*, iv. 3.

Goes *it* [military expedition: implied in "powers" sent "against some part of Poland"] against the main.—*Ibid.*, iv. 4.

He hath borne me on his back a thousand times; and now how abhorred in my imagination *it* [the idea of having been "borne on" the "back," and having "kissed" the "lips" of one whose fleshless skull is now in the speaker's hand] is! my gorge rises at *it.*—*Ibid.*, v. 1.

It must be shortly known to him from England. . . . *It* [the period ere "it must be known"] will be short.—*Ibid.*, v. 2.

I'll not endure *it* [this suspicion: implied in the context].—I do repent me that I put *it* to you.—*Oth.*, iii. 3.

But entertain *it* [my proposal: implied in the context], and, though thou think me poor.—*Ant. & C.*, ii. 7.

To him again: tell him he wears the rose of youth. . . . I'll write *it* [this that I had told you to "tell him"]; follow me.—*Ibid.*, iii. 11.

For thee, fellow, who needs must know of her departure . . . we'll enforce *it* [confession of the knowledge of her departure: implied in "know of her departure"] from thee by a sharp torture.—*Cym.*, iv. 3.

You snatch some hence for little faults; that's love, to have them fall no more: you some permit to second ills with ills, each elder worse, and make them dread *it* [sudden punishment for crime (implied in "snatch some hence") and a long course of sin: implied in "to second ills with ills"], to the doer's thrift.—*Ibid.*, v. 1.

On either side I come to spend my breath, which neither . . . but end *it* [my life: implied in "my breath"] by some means.—*Ibid.*, v. 3.

That box I gave you . . . *It* [the drug within the "box": the contents implied by that which contained them] poison'd me.—*Ibid.*, v. 5.

It [our sense of being treated by Helicanus with less confidence than Escanes: implied in the previous speech] shall no longer grieve without reproof.—And curs'd be he that will not second *it* [our intended "reproof"].—*Per.*, ii. 4.

Well, I commend her choice; and will no longer have *it* [the marriage: implied in "her choice"] be delayed.—*Per.*, ii. 5.

Here comes my daughter, she can witness *it* [the truth of what I have asserted].—*Ibid.*, ii. 5.

That she is dead. Nurses are not the fates, to foster *it* [life: implied in "she is dead"], nor ever to preserve.—*Ibid.*, iv. 4.

Yet long'st,—but in a fainter kind: O, not like me; for *mine* [my longing: implied in "long'st"] 's beyond beyond.—*Cym.*, iii. 2.

The moment on 't [the deed implied in the context]; for 't must be done to-night.—*Macb.*, iii. 1.

They can well on horseback: but this gallant had witchcraft in 't [horsemanship: implied in "horseback"].—*Hamlet*, iv. 7.

Ha! false to me? . . . her stolen hours of lust? I saw 't [her falsehood: implied in "false" and "hours of lust"] not, thought *it* not, *it* harm'd not me.—*Oth.*, iii. 3.

I slew him there . . . Deny 't [that you "slew him"] again. I have spoke *it*, and I did *it*.—*Cym.*, v. 5.

He hath a witchcraft over the king in's tongue . . . his spell in *that* [ascendency: implied in "witchcraft over the king"] is out.—*H. VIII.*, iii. 2.

For your highness' good I ever labour'd more than mine own; *that* [devoted to your service: implied in "for your highness' good I ever labour'd"] I am, have, and will be.—*Ibid.*, iii. 2.

For the inheritance of their loves, and safeguard of what *that want* [the want of that love: implied in "loves"] might ruin.—*Coriol.*, iii. 2.

I have not kept my square; but *that* [conduct: implied in the context] to come shall all be done by rule.—*Ant. & C.*, ii. 3.

Nay, nay, Octavia, not only *that* [the speaker's ground of complaint against Octavius Cæsar: implied in the context],—*that* were excusable, *that*, and thousands more of semblable import.—*Ibid.*, iii. 4.

If in your country wars you chance to die, *that* [the battle-field: implied in "wars"] is my bed too, lads.—*Cym.*, iv. 4.

There shalt thou know thy charge; and there receive money and order for *their* [the foot soldiers implied in "thy charge," which has been previously mentioned as "a charge of foot"] furniture.—*1 H. IV.*, iii. 3.

They lost France, and made his England bleed; which oft our stage hath shown; and, for *their* [the plays of "King Henry VI.": implied in "oft our stage hath shown"] sake, in your fair minds let *this* ['present play' understood] acceptance take.—*H. V.*, v. 2 (*Chorus*).

While I to this hard house . . . return, and force *their* [the hard-hearted inmates: implied in "this hard house"] scanted courtesy.—*Lear*, iii. 2.

I'll take my leave, and leave you to the hearing of the cause; hoping you'll find good cause to whip *them* [the persons whose "cause" is to be heard] all.—*M. for M.*, ii. 1.

Have stolen his bird's nest.—I will but teach *them* [the birds: implied in "bird's nest"] to sing, and restore *them* to the owner.—If *their* singing answer your saying.—*M. Ado*, ii. 1.

The complaints I have heard of you I do not all believe . . . you lack not folly to commit *them* [the knaveries implied in "complaints," and subsequently expressed], and have ability enough to make such knaveries yours.—*All's W.*, i. 3.

The soul of this man is his clothes . . . I have kept of *them* [such creatures as "this man"] tame, and know *their* natures.—*Ibid.*, ii. 5.

As true as I believe you think *them* [those who occasion your grief: implied in the context] false, that give you cause to prove my saying true.—*John*, iii. 1.

Be not easily won to our requests . . . if you plead as well for *them* [the objects urged by your "requests"] as I can say nay to thee for myself.—*R. III.*, iii. 7.

I think he'll be to Rome as is the osprey to the fish. . . . First, he was a noble servant to *them* [the Romans: implied in "Rome"].—*Coriol.*, iv. 7.

A leg of Rome shall not return to tell what crows have peck'd *them* [the Romans: implied in "Rome"] here.—*Cym.*, v. 3.

Bring me no more reports; let *them* [my nobles: implied in subsequent mention of "thanes"] fly all.—*Macb.*, v. 3.

'Tis meet that some more audience than a mother, since nature makes *them* [mothers: implied in "mother"] partial, should o'erhear the speech.—*Hamlet*, iii. 3.

I am glad at soul I have no other child; for thy escape would teach me tyranny, to hang clogs on *them* [children: implied in "child"].—*Oth.*, i. 3.

Flew on him, and amongst *them* [those present: implied in the description of the scene] fell'd him dead.—*Lear*, iv. 2.

Yond's that same knave that leads him to *these places* [haunts of dissipation: implied in the description of Bertram's corrupt morals].—*All's W.*, iii. 5.

Oh, could this kiss be printed in thy hand, that thou might'st think upon *these* [lips: implied in "kiss" and in "through whom a thousand sighs are breath'd"] by the seal, through whom a thousand sighs are breathed for thee!—*2 H. VI.*, iii. 2.

Who call'd here of late?—None, since the curfew rung.—Not Isabel?—No.—*They* [the persons of whom the speaker is thinking, and whose advent he expects; viz., "Isabel" and the messenger with the "countermand for Claudio": implied in the previous inquiry and subsequent dialogue] will, then, ere 't be long. . . . Now are *they* come.—*M. for M.*, iv. 2.

The land is burning; Percy stands on high; and either *they* [the insurgents who are the cause that "the land is burning," and of whom "Percy" is a leader] or we must lower lie.—*1 H. IV.*, iii. 3.

All the temporal lands, which men devout by testament have given to the church, would *they* [the Commons who "urg'd" the Parliament "bill" against the clergy] strip from us.—*H. V.*, i. 1.

He, more incens'd against your majesty than all the rest, discharg'd me. . . . *They* [those persons implied in "he" and "all the rest"] shall have wars, and pay for *their* presumption.—*3 H. VI.*, iv. 1.

Go levy men, and make prepare for war; *they* [the expected foes: implied in "war"] are already, or quickly will be landed.—*Ibid.*, iv. 1.

Anon he's there afoot, and there *they* [the objects of Hector's assault: implied in the descriptive context] fly or die.—*Tr. & Cr.*, v. 5.

Nor get a messenger to bring it thee, so fearful were *they* [those who would not bear a message from dread of the pestilence: implied in "messenger"] of infection.—*R. & Jul.*, v. 2.

Down from the waist *they* [prudes: implied in the previous description, which takes "yon simpering dame" as a type of such pretenders to virtue] are centaurs, though women all above.—*Lear*, iv. 6.

Look where *they* [Antony and Cleopatra: implied in the description of his subjugation to her charms] come.—*Ant. & C.*, i. 1.

To rage the city turn, that him and his *they* [the citizens: implied in "the city"] in his palace burn.—*Per.*, v. 3 (*Gower*).

That you will take your instant leave o' the king, and make this haste as your own good proceeding. . . . That, having *this* [the king's permission to depart (implied in "leave"), with the understanding that it is her own wish to go: implied in "make this haste as your own," &c.] obtained, you presently attend his farther pleasure.—*All's W.*, ii. 4.

Let *this* [the paper containing the "notes" of the compact between the Dauphin and the revolted English nobles] be copied out, and keep *it* safe for our remembrance.—*John*, v. 2.

What, in Heaven's name, doth become of *this* [the money thus raised: implied in the previous account of the king's extortionate proceedings]?—Wars have not wasted *it*.—*R. II.*, ii. 1.

By the necessary form of *this* [the circumstance of Northumberland's previous conduct in being "great friends" and then "in two years after" being "at wars" with the speaker of the "prophecy"], King Richard might create a perfect guess that great Northumberland.—*2 H. IV.*, iii. 1.

In little room confining mighty men . . . most greatly liv'd *this star of England* [Henry V.: implied in "mighty men"].—*H. V.*, v. 2 (*Chorus*).

We 'll be there before the stream o' the people; and *this* [change to resentment: implied by the previous discussion] shall seem, as '*t*is, their own, which we have goaded onward.—*Coriol.*, ii. 3.

I would not take *this* [the extreme pathos of the meeting between the speaker's blind father and the distracted king: implied by the passing scene] from report; *it* is, and my heart breaks at *it*.—*Lear*, iv. 6.

O Imogen! thou hast lost by *this* [the discovery of thy brothers: implied in the context] a kingdom.—*Cym.*, v. 5.

We have not spoke us yet of torch-bearers.—'*T*is [the mask in question: implied in "torch-bearers" and subsequently mentioned] vile, unless *it* may be quaintly order'd, —*Mer. of V.*, ii. 4.

New-made honour doth forget men's names; '*t*is [the remembrance of men's names: implied as the reverse of "doth forget men's names"] too respective and too sociable for your conversion.—*John*, i. 1.

I will, sir, flatter my sworn brother, the people, to earn a dearer estimation of them; '*t*is [the practice of flattering: implied in "flatter"] a condition they account gentle. —*Coriol.*, ii. 3.

Some news is come, that turns their countenances.—'*T*is [the panic thus occasioned: implied in previous dialogue] this slave.—*Ibid.*, iv. 6.

I have already fit ('*t*is [a suit: implied in "doublet, hat, hose," &c.] in my cloak-bag) doublet, hat, hose, all that answer to them.—*Cym.*, iii. 4.

The disorder 's such as war were hood-wink'd.—'*T*is [this discomfiture: implied in "the disorder"] their fresh supplies.—*Ibid.*, v. 2.

To satisfy, if of my freedom '*t*is [my life: implied in "my all" and stated farther on in the speech] the main part, take no stricter render of me, than my all.—*Ibid.*, v. 4.

She has a leathern hand, a freestone-colour'd hand; I verily did think that her old gloves were on, but '*t*was [the sun-tanned surface that I saw: implied in "leathern" and "freestone-colour'd"] her hands.—*As You L.*, iv. 3.

I play a merchant's part, and venture madly on a desperate mart.—'*T*was [a marriageable and saleable daughter: implied in "mart"] a commodity lay fretting by you; *t*will bring you gain.—*Tam. of S.*, ii. 1.

By relating tales of others' griefs, see if '*t*will [this relation, implied in "relating"] teach us to forget our own.—*Per.*, i. 4.

My honour 's at the stake; *which* [risk of losing "my honour"] to defeat, I must produce my power.—*All's W.*, ii. 3.

Time was, I did him a desired office, dear almost as his life; *which gratitude* [gratitude for which "desired office"] through flinty Tartar's bosom would peep forth. —*Ibid.*, iv. 4.

Commend the paper to his gracious hand; *which* [the act of commending the paper: implied in "commend the paper"], I presume, shall render you no blame.— *Ibid.*, v. 1.

As true, as I am now unhappy: *which* [unhappiness: implied in "unhappy"] is more than history can pattern.—*W. T.*, iii. 2.

To deliver sweet, sweet, sweet poison for the age's tooth, *which* [delivery of poison: implied in "to deliver poison"], . . . I mean to learn.—*John*, i. 1.

And beat our watch, and rob our passengers; *which* [beating and robbing: implied in "beat" and "rob"] he, young wanton and effeminate boy, takes on the point of honour.—*R. II.*, v. 3.

Men shall deal unadvisedly sometimes, *which* [unadvised dealing: implied in "deal unadvisedly"] after-hours give leisure to repent.—*R. III.*, iv. 4.

And, not reform'd, may prove pernicious. — *Which reformation* [implied in "reformed"] must be sudden too.—*H. VIII.*, v. 2.

That plats the manes of horses in the night; and bakes the elf-locks in foul sluttish hairs, *which* [entangled mass: implied in "plats" and "bakes"] once untangled, much misfortune bodes.—*R. & Jul.*, i. 4.

Here, as I point my sword, the sun arises: *which* [the quarter where "the sun arises"] is a great way growing on the south.—*Jul. C.*, ii. 1.

Let your highness command upon me; to the *which* [commands: implied in "command"] my duties are with a most indissoluble tie for ever knit.—*Macb.*, iii. 1.

You made it known to us.—I did so; and went farther, *which* [farther revealment: implied in "made it known" and "went farther"] is now our point of second meeting.—*Ibid.*, iii. 1.

The impediment most profitably removed, without the *which* [removal: implied in "removed"] there were no expectation of our prosperity.—*Oth.*, ii. 1.

Therefore have we our written purposes before us sent; *which* [proposal: implied in "written purposes"], if thou hast consider'd, let us know if 'twill tie up thy discontented sword.—*Ant. & C.*, ii. 6.

It is great to do that thing that ends all other deeds; *which* [the act by which death is self-inflicted: implied in "that thing" and "deeds"] shackles accidents, and bolts up change; *which* [the condition of death thus caused] sleeps, and never palates more the dung.—*Ibid.*, v. 2.

Promising to pay our wonted tribute, from the *which* [payment: implied in "pay"] we were dissuaded.—*Cym.*, v. 5.

The king hath not deserv'd my service, nor your loves; *who* [you: implied in "your"] find in my exile the want.—*Ibid.*, iv. 4.

He hath given his empire up to a whore; *who* [Antony and Cleopatra: implied in "he" and "whore"] now are levying the kings o' the earth for war.—*Ant. & C.*, iii. 6.

Then lead me hence; with *whom* [those who occupy the spot implied in "hence"] I leave my curse.—*1 H. VI.*, v. 4.

We are no tyrant, but a Christian king; unto *whose* [Christ's: implied in "Christian"] grace our passion is as subject as are our wretches fetter'd in our prisons.—*H. V.*, i. 2.

Who are the late commissioners? . . . There is *yours* [your commission: implied in "commissioners"]; there *yours* . . . *this* same is *yours*; read *them*.—*Ibid.*, ii. 2.

In some instances he employs a pronoun in reference to a not immediately preceding antecedent:—

He must observe their mood on whom he jests. . . . This is a practice as full of labour as a wise man's art: for folly, that *he* ["he" (meaning a man who wishes to play the fool well); not "a wise man"] wisely shows, is fit.—*Tw. N.*, iii. 1.

This was her first remembrance from the Moor; my wayward husband hath a hundred times woo'd me to steal it; but she so loves the token, for *he* ["the Moor"; not "my husband"] conjur'd her she should evermore keep it.—*Oth.*, iii. 3.

By this, your king hath heard of great Augustus; Caius Lucius will do 's commission throughly; and I think *he*'ll ["your king"; not "Caius Lucius"] grant the tribute.—*Cym.*, ii. 4.

The regent made in Mitylin, to greet the king. So *he* ["the regent"; not "the king"] thriv'd that *he* is promis'd to be wiv'd to fair Marina; but in no wise till *he* ["the king"; not "the regent"] had done *his* sacrifice.—*Per.*, v. 2 (*Gower*).

By helping Baptista's eldest daughter to a husband, we set his youngest free. . . . Sweet Bianca! . . . his wooing that would thoroughly woo *her* [Katharina, the "eldest daughter"; not "Bianca," the "youngest"] wed *her*, and rid the house of *her*!—*Tam of S.*, i. 1.

Love forswore me in my mother's womb: and, for I should not deal in *her* ["Love" (meaning Venus); not "mother"] soft laws, *she* did corrupt frail nature with some bribe.—*3 H. VI.*, iii. 2.

The harlot king is quite beyond mine arm. . . . How does the boy? . . . Go, see how he fares. Fie, fie! no thought of *him* ["the king"; not "the boy"]; the very thought.—*W. T.*, ii. 3.

Oh, well did he become that lion's robe, that did disrobe the lion of that robe!—It lies as sightly on the back of *him* [the Archduke of Austria (of whom Faulconbridge speaks thus contemptuously in the third person); not "he" (in allusion to Richard Cœur-de-lion)] as great Alcides' shoes.—*John*, ii. 1.

The duke cannot deny the course of law, for the commodity that strangers have with us in Venice: if *it* ["the course of law"; not "the commodity"] be denied.— *Mer. of V.*, iii. 3.

It is very meet the lord Bassanio live an upright life; for having such a blessing in his lady, he finds the joys of heaven here on earth; and if on earth he do not mean *it* [to "live an upright life"; not to "find the joys of heaven here on earth"] then in reason.—*Ibid.*, iii. 5.

Thy gown? why, ay: come, tailor, let us see 't. . . . You shall hop without my custom, sir: I 'll none of *it* [the "gown"; not the "custom"]; hence!—*Tam. of S.*, iv. 3.

Thou art all unjust; and, that thou art so, there I throw my gage, to prove *it* ["that thou art so"; not "my gage"] on thee to th' extremest point of mortal breathing: seize *it* ["my gage"; not "th' extremest point"] if thou dar'st.— *R. II.*, iv. 1.

We will consider of your suit; and come some other time. . . . 'Twere pity they should lose their father's lands.—Be pitiful, dread lord, and grant *it* [my "suit"; not "their father's lands"], then.—3 *H. VI.*, iii. 2.

But mine honesty shall not make poor my greatness, nor my power work without *it* ["mine honesty"; not "my greatness"].—*Ant. & C.*, ii. 2.

The law hath not been dead, though it hath slept: those many had not dar'd to do that evil, if the first, that did th edict infringe, had answer'd for his deed: now '*t*is ["the law"; not the "deed"] awake.—*M. for M.*, ii. 2.

I have a pain upon my forehead here.—Faith, that 's with watching; '*t*will [the pain"; not the "forehead"] away again: let me but bind *it* [your "forehead"] hard, within this hour *it* will be well.—*Oth.*, iii. 3.

He brought a Grecian queen. . . . Why keep we her? the Grecians keep our aunt: is *she* [the "Grecian queen"; not "our aunt"] worth keeping? why, *she* is a pearl.— *Tr. & Cr.*, ii. 2.

I found her trimming up the diadem on her dead mistress; tremblingly *she* ["her," Charmian; not the "dead mistress"] stood . . . but *she* [the "dead mistress," Cleopatra; not "her," Charmian] looks like sleep.—*Ant. & C.*, v. 2.

The temple of virtue was she; yea and *she* ["virtue"; not "she"] herself.— *Cym.*, v. 5.

That youth is surely in their company.—Send to his brother: fetch *that* gallant ["that youth"; not "his brother"] hither.—*As You L.*, ii. 2.

I cannot believe this crack to be in my dread mistress. . . . I have lov'd thee,— make *that* [the "crack" in thy "dread mistress's" fidelity; not the fact of thy having "lov'd" me] thy question, and go rot!—*W. T.*, i. 2.

A space whose every cubit seems to cry out. . . . Say, this were death that now hath seized *them* [the sleeping king and his lords, seen to fall into sudden slumber during the scene; and not to "every cubit"]; why, they were no worse than now *they* are.—*Temp.*, ii. 1.

I fear no uncles dead.—Nor none that live, I hope.—An if they live, I hope I need not fear . . . with a heavy heart, thinking on *them* ["uncles dead"; not those "that live"], go I unto the Tower.—*R. III.*, iii. 1.

There is at hand Paris your brother, and Deiphobus, the Grecian Diomed, and our Antenor. . . . How my achievements mock me! I will go meet *them* ["Paris," "Deiphobus," "Diomed," and "Antenor"; not "my achievements"].—*Tr. & Cr.*, iv. 2.

And gave me up to tears.—I blame you not; for, hearing this, I must perforce compound with mistful eyes, or *they* ["tears"; not "eyes"] will issue too.— *H. V.*, iv. 6.

You were ever good at sudden commendations, bishop. . . . I come not to hear such flattery now, and in my presence; *they* ["commendations"; not flatteries, implied in "flattery"] are too thin and base to hide offences.—*H. VIII.*, v. 2.

I hope to see Romans as cheap as Volscians. *They* [those who have been previously described as "within," at "their feast"; not either "Romans" or "Volscians"] are rising, *they* are rising.—*Coriol.*, iv. 5.

There are certain ladies most desirous of admittance. . . . The five best senses acknowledge thee their patron; and come freely . . . *they* [the "ladies"; not the "five best senses"] only now come but to feast thine eyes.—*Timon*, i. 2.

Every reason excites to this, that my lady loves me. . . . Jove, I thank thee.—I will smile: I will do everything that *thou* ["my lady"; not "Jove"] wilt have me.—*Tw. N.*, ii. 5.

Thou didst smile, infused with a fortitude from heaven, when I have deck'd the sea with drops full salt, under my burden groan'd; *which* [when "thou didst smile"; not when I "groaned"] rais'd in me.—*Temp.*, i. 2.

I have your own letter that induc'd me to the semblance I put on; with the *which* ["letter"; not "semblance"] I doubt not but do myself much right.—*Tw. N.*, v. 1 (*Letter*).

My life stands in the level of your dreams, *which* ["life"; not "dreams"] I'll lay down.—*W. T.*, iii. 2.

And so the prince obscur'd his contemplation under the veil of wildness; *which* ["contemplation"; not "wildness"], no doubt, grew like the summer grass.—*H. V.*, i. 1.

The commoners . . . will forget, with the least cause, these his new honours; *which* ["cause"; not "honours"] that he will give them make I as little question.—*Coriol.*, ii. 1.

There shall I try, in my oration, how the people take the cruel issue of these bloody men; according to the *which* ["how the people take"; not the "issue"], thou.—*Jul. C.*, iii. 1.

Brave Macbeth . . . like valour's minion, carv'd out his passage till he fac'd the slave; *which* ["Macbeth"; not "the slave"] ne'er shook hands.—*Macb.*, i. 2.

Our will became the servant to defect; *which* ["will"; not "defect"] else should free have wrought.—*Ibid.*, ii. 1.

Hath nature given them eyes to see this vaulted arch and the rich crop of sea and land, *which* ["eyes"; not "sea and land"] can distinguish 'twixt the fiery orbs above. —*Cym.*, i. 7.

I find that she, which late was in my nobler thoughts most base, is now the praised of the king; *who* ["she"; not "the king"] so ennobled, is, as 'twere, born so.—*All's W.*, ii. 3.

One of my fellows had the speed of him; *who* ["one of my fellows"; not "him"], almost dead for breath.—*Macb.*, i. 5.

Though you in swearing shake the throned gods, *who* ["you"; not "the gods"] have been false to Fulvia.—*Ant. & C.*, i. 3.

No more kin to me, than I to your highness; *who* ["I" not "your highness"], being born your vassal.—*Cym.*, v. 5.

My mother was the daughter of a king; *who* ["my mother"; not "a king"] died the minute I was born.—*Per.*, v. 1.

The smaller is his daughter: the other is daughter to the banish'd duke, and here detained by her usurping uncle to keep his daughter company; *whose* [not "her uncle" and "his daughter"; but "the smaller" and "the other"] loves are dearer than the natural bond of sisters.—*As You L.*, i. 2.

The great prerogative and rite of love . . . puts it off to a compell'd restraint; *whose* ["the rite of love"; not "a compell'd restraint"] want and whose delay is.—*All's W.*, ii. 4.

Come, Camillo, and take her by the hand, *whose* ["Camillo"; not "her"] worth and honesty.—*W. T.*, v. 3.

As for the brat of this accursed duke, *whose* ["brat"; not "duke"] father slew my father.—*3 H. VI.*, i. 3.

Thus yields the cedar to the axe's edge, *whose* ["cedar"; not "axe"] arms gave shelter to the princely eagle.—*Ibid.*, v. 2.

Bring in our daughter, clothed like a bride, for the embracements even of Jove himself; at *whose* ["our daughter"; not "Jove"] conception, till Lucina reigned, Nature.—*Per.*, i. 1.

He occasionally uses not only pronouns, but other words in relation to a not immediately preceding antecedent :—

Upon the right hand I; keep thou the left.—Why do you cross me in this exigent?—I do not cross you; but I will *do so* [take " the right hand"; not " cross you"].—*Jul. C.*, v. i.

Will you to Scone?—No, cousin, I 'll to Fife.—Well, I will *thither* ["to Scone"; not " to Fife"].—*Macb.*, ii. 4.

REPEATED WORDS.

A marked peculiarity in Shakespeare's style is the fearless mode in which he frequently repeats the same word or words in a line, phrase or speech; thereby giving an emphatic effect to the passage :—

> This he wish'd :
> I *after him*, do *after him* wish too.—*All's W.*, i. 2.
> A man, who is the abstract of *all* faults
> That *all* men follow.—
> I must not think there are
> Evils enow to darken *all* his goodness.—*Ant. & C.*, i. 4.
> *All* is lost !
> . . . Bid them *all* fly ;
> For when I am reveng'd upon my charm,
> I have done *all :*—bid them *all* fly ; be gone.
> . . . *All* come to this? . . .
> . . . this pine is bark'd,
> That overtopp'd them *all*.—*Ibid.*, iv. 10.
> She is *all* happy as the fair'st of all.—*Per.*, v. i.
> Would that *alone, alone* he would detain.—*Com. of E.*, ii. i.
> Yet I, *alone, alone* do me oppose
> Against the Pope.—*John*, iii. i.
> But I *alone, alone* must sit and pine.—*Lucrece, Stanza* 114.
> Yes, yes, Sir Thomas,
> There are that dare ; *and* I myself have ventur'd
> To speak my mind of him : *and*, indeed, this day.—*H. VIII.*, v. i.
> Sweet, rouse yourself; *and* the weak wanton Cupid
> Shall from your neck unloose his amorous fold,
> *And*, like a dew-drop from the lion's mane,
> Be shook to air.—*Tr. & Cr.*, iii. 3.
> The boatswain whistles, *and*
> The master calls, *and* trebles their confusion.—*Per.*, iv. i.
> Your uncle York is join'd with Bolingbroke ;
> *And all your* northern castles yielded up,
> *And all your* southern gentlemen in arms
> Upon his party.—*R. II.*, iii. 2.
> Edmund, I *arrest* thee
> On capital treason ; and, in thy *arrest*,
> This gilded serpent.—*Lear*, v. 3.
> It likes us well. Young princes close your hands.—
> And your lips, too ; for I am well *assur'd*
> That I did so when I was first *assur'd*.—*John*, ii. 2.
> *Beware*
> Of entrance to a quarrel ; but, being in,
> Bear 't, that th' opposed may *beware* of thee.—*Hamlet*, i. 3.

Why ask I that ? my mangled *body shows*,
My blood, my want of strength, my sick heart *shows*,
That I must yield my *body* to the earth.—*3 H. VI.*, v. 2.

My lord, you must tell us where the *body* is, and go with us to the *king*.—The *body*
is with the *king*, but the *king* is not with the *body*. The *king* is a thing.—*Hamlet*, iv. 2.

First he was
A noble servant to them ; *but* he could not
Carry his honours even : whether 'twas pride,
Which out of daily fortune ever taints
The happy man ; whether defect of judgment,
To fail in the disposing of those chances
Which he was lord of ; or whether nature,
Not to be other than one thing, not moving
From the casque to the cushion, *but* commanding peace
Even with the same austerity and garb
As he controll'd the war ; *but* one of these
(As he hath spices of them all, not all,
For I dare so far free him,) made him fear'd,
So hated, and so banish'd ; *but* he has a merit,
To choke it in the utterance.—*Coriol.*, iv. 7.

The skies are painted with unnumber'd sparks,
They are all fire, and every one doth shine ;
But there's *but* one in all doth hold his place.—*Jul. C.*, iii. 1.

He might not *but* refuse you ; *but* he protests he loves you,
And needs no other suitor *but* his likings,
To take the saf'st occasion by the front
To bring you in again.—*Oth.*, iii. 1.

No, Cassius ; for the eye sees not itself,
But *by* reflection, *by* some other things.—*Jul. C.*, i. 2.

No place will please me so, no mean of death,
As here *by** Cæsar, and *by* you cut off,
The choice and master spirits of this age.—*Ibid.*, iii. 1.

I *charge* thee use her well, even for my *charge*.—*Tr. & Cr.*, iv. 4.

For me, the ransom of my bold attempt
Shall be this *cold* corse on the earth's *cold* face.—*R. III.*, v. 3.

O happy Leonatus ! I may say :
The *credit* that thy lady hath of thee
Deserves thy trust ; and thy most perfect goodness
Her assur'd *credit*.—*Cym.*, i. 7.

This night methinks is but the daylight sick ;
It looks a little paler : 'tis a *day*,
Such as the *day* is when the sun is hid.—*Mer. of V.*, v. 1.

You breathe these *dead* news in as *dead* an ear.—*John*, v. 7.

For that is good *deceit*
Which mates him *first* that *first* intends *deceit*.—*2 H. VI.*, iii. 1.

We have no reason to *desire* it,
Commended to our master, not to us :
Yet, ere you shall depart, this we *desire*,—
As friends to Antioch, we may feast in Tyre.—*Per.*, i. 3.

Clifford, *devise* excuses *for thy faults*.—
While we *devise* fell tortures *for thy faults*.—*3 H. VI.*, ii. 6.

Doubt thou the stars are fire ;
Doubt that the sun doth move ;
Doubt truth to be a liar ;
But never *doubt* I love.—*Hamlet*, ii. 2 (*Letter*).

---

* This first " by " in the line is used in the sense of ' by the side of.'

From whence though willingly I came to Denmark,
To show my *duty* in your coronation ;
Yet now, I must confess, that *duty* done,
My thoughts and wishes bend again toward France.—*Hamlet*, i. 2.

Entreat her *fair ;* and by my soul, *fair* Greek,
If e'er thou stand at mercy of my sword,
Name Cressid, and thy life shall be as safe
As Priam is in Ilion.—
                    Fair lady Cressid,
So please you, save the thanks this prince expects :
The lustre in your eye, heaven in your cheek,
Pleads your *fair* usage.—*Tr. & Cr.*, iv. 4.

Expose thyself to *feel* what wretches *feel.*—*Lear*, iii. 4.

                    Know thou *first*,
I lov'd the maid I married ; never man
Sighed truer breath ; but that I see thee here,
Thou noble thing ! more dances my rapt heart,
Than when I *first* my wedded mistress saw
Bestride my threshold.—*Coriol.*, iv. 5.

Wherein we are not destitute *for* want,
But weary *for* the staleness.—*Per.*, v. 1.

                    We may again
Give to our tables meat, sleep to our nights ;
Free from our feasts and banquets bloody knives ;
Do faithful homage, and receive *free* honours.—*Macb.*, iii. 6.

And give to dust, that is a little *gilt*,
More laud than *gilt* o'er-dusted.—*Tr. & Cr.*, iii. 3.

For where there is advantage to be *given*,
Both more and less have *given* him the revolt.—*Macb.*, v. 4.

My queen and son are *gone* to France for aid ;
And, as I hear, the great commanding Warwick
Is thither *gone*, to crave the French king's sister
To wife for Edward.—3 *H. VI.*, iii. 1.

I hope, sir, I have your *good* will to have mine own *good* fortunes.—*All's W.*, ii. 4.

                    The greatest *grace* lending *grace*,
Ere twice the horses of the sun shall bring
Their fiery torcher his diurnal ring.—*Ibid.*, ii. 1.

                    Sir, we have all
Great cause to give *great* thanks.—*Coriol.*, v. 4.

                    The Moor replies,
That he you hurt is of *great* fame in Cyprus,
And *great* affinity.—*Oth.*, iii. 1.

                    And *having* woo'd
A villain to attempt it, who *having* drawn to do 't.—*Per.*, v. 1.

                    I have
Incens'd the lords o' the council, that *he is*
(For so I know *he is*, they know *he is*)
A most arch heretic.—*H. VIII.*, v. 1.

My sole earth's *heaven*, and my *heaven*'s claim.—*Com. of E.*, iii. 2.

Therefore, merchant, I 'll limit thee this day,
To seek thy *help* by beneficial *help.*—*Ibid.*, i. 1.

Such harmony is in immortal souls ;
But whilst this muddy vesture of decay
Doth grossly close *it** in, we cannot hear *it.*—*Mer. of V.*, v. 1.

---

* The first " it " in this line refers to 'the human soul,' as implied in " immortal souls," previously mentioned ; and the second " it " refers to " harmony." *See* the first passage quoted under ANTITHETICAL STYLE (page 24), where " it " refers to ' work ' as implied in " labours."

> Must I repent?
> I cannot do *it* better than in gyves,
> Desir'd more than constrained: to satisfy,
> If of my freedom '*t*is the main part, take
> No stricter render of me than my all.—*Cym.*, v. 4.

In both the above passages, Shakespeare has used "it" (or "'t") consecutively, but in reference to two different objects. In the latter passage, from "Cymbeline," "it" refers to "repent," and "'t" refers to "life," as implied in "my all" and as actually stated farther on in the speech [*See* RELATIVELY USED PRONOUNS]. In judging such condensedly expressed passages, it is needful to bear well in mind Shakespeare's peculiar and various modes of constructional diction; for which purpose our enumeration of his several similarly constructed passages will materially serve.

> I am not an impostor, that proclaim
> Myself against the level of mine aim;
> But *know I think*, and *think I know* most sure,
> My art is not past power, nor you past cure.—*All's W.*, ii. 1.

> To *know* my deed, 'twere best not *know* myself.—*Macb.*, ii. 2.

> But I believe, although I seem so loath,
> I am the *last* that will *last* keep his oath.—*Love's L. L.*, i. 1.

> Was it so *late*, friend, ere you went to bed,
> That you do lie so *late?*—*Macb.*, ii. 3.

> Landlord of England art thou now, not king:
> Thy state of *law* is bond slave to the *law*.—*R. II.*, ii. 1.

> Their weapons like to lightning came and went;
> Our soldiers',—like the night-owl's *lazy* flight,
> Or like a *lazy* thresher with a flail,—
> Fell gently down, as if they struck their friends.—*3 H. VI.*, ii. 1.

> I'll take my *leave*, and *leave* to you the hearing.—*M. for M.*, ii. 1.

> Ay, good *leave* have you; for you will have *leave*,
> Till youth take *leave*, and *leave* you to the crutch.—*3 H. VI.*, iii. 2.

> I *like* the work well; ere it be demanded,
> (As *like* enough it will] I'd have it copied.—*Oth.*, iii. 4.

> We are beastly; subtle as the fox for prey;
> *Like* war-*like* as the wolf for what we eat.—*Cym.*, iii. 3.

> Do you see this? *Look* on her,—*look*,—her lips,—
> *Look* there, look there!—*Lear*, v. 3.

> But, you must know, your father *lost* a father;
> That father *lost*, *lost* his.—*Hamlet*, i. 2.

> Now, for *love* of *Love* and her soft hours.—*Ant. & C.*, i. 1.

> I met a courier, one mine ancient friend;
> Whom, though in general part we were oppos'd,
> Yet our old love *made* a particular force,
> And *made* us speak like friends.—*Timon*, v. 3.

> O, I am known
> Of *many* in the army: *many* years,
> Though Cloten then but young, you see, not wore him
> From my remembrance.—*Cym.*, iv. 4.

> But Heaven hath pleas'd it so,
> To punish *me with this*, and *this with me*.—*Hamlet*, iii. 4.

> I will come after you, with what good speed
> Our *means* will make us *means*.—*All's W.*, v. 1.

> Why all these things change, from their ordinance,
> Their natures, and pre-formed faculties,
> To *monstrous* quality;—why, you shall find
> That Heaven hath infus'd them with these spirits,
> To make them instruments of fear and warning
> Unto some *monstrous* state.—*Jul. C.*, i. 3.

> This night I hold an old accustom'd feast,
> Whereto I have invited many a guest
> Such as I love; and you, among the store,
> One *more*, most welcome, makes my number *more*.—*R. & Jul.*, i. 2.

> And my *more*-having would be as a sauce
> To make me hunger *more*.—*Macb.*, iv 3.

> Witness our too much memorable shame
> When Cressy battle fatally was struck,
> And all our princes captiv'd by the hand
> Of that *black* name, Edward, *Black* Prince of Wales;
> Whiles that his *mountain* sire,—on *mountain* standing,
> Up in the air, crown'd with the golden sun,—
> Saw his heroical seed, and smil'd to see him,
> Mangle the work of nature.—*H. V.*, ii. 4.

The epithet "mountain," which by some commentators has been thought not Shakespeare's word here, on account of its being repeated in the same line, we think likely to be his for that very reason; since our collected passages under the present heading, serve to show how perfectly in his style is a repeated word. Moreover "mountain," as applied to the father of the Black Prince, not only gives the effect of 'lofty,' 'exalted,' but it has reference to the Welsh descent of Edward III., he being son to Edward II. (surnamed 'of Caernarvon'), born among the mountains of Wales.

> And, could it work so *much* upon your shape,
> As it hath *much* prevail'd on your condition,
> I should not know you, Brutus.—*Jul. C.*, ii. 1.

> Then I (as one that am the tongue of these,
> To sound the purposes of all their hearts),
> Both for *myself and them* (but, chief of all,
> Your safety, for the which *myself and them*
> Bend their best studies), heartily request
> Th' enfranchisement of Arthur.—*John*, iv. 2.

The second "them" in this sentence was altered by Pope to 'they'; but the grammatical licence of "them" used instead of 'they,' and the repetition of the same words, are both in accordance with Shakespeare's style.

> And the ebb'd man, *ne'er* lov'd till *ne'er* worth love,
> Comes dear'd by being lack'd.—*Ant. & C.*, i. 4.

>   What wouldst thou beg, Laertes,
> That shall *not* be my offer, *not* thy asking?
> The head is *not* more native to the heart,
> The hand more instrumental to the mouth,
> Than is the throne of Denmark to thy father.—*Hamlet*, i. 2.

> And that would set my teeth *nothing* on edge,
> *Nothing* so much as mincing poetry.—*1 H. IV.*, iii. 1.

Nay, an he do *nothing* but speak *nothing*, he shall be *nothing* here.—*2 H. IV.*, ii. 4.

> Alas, poor country,—
> Almost afraid to know itself! It cannot
> Be call'd our mother, but our grave: where *nothing*,
> But who knows *nothing*, is once seen to smile.—*Macb.*, iv. 3.
>
> Now the good gods forbid
> That our renowned Rome, whose gratitude
> Towards her deserved children is enroll'd
> In Jove's own book, like an unnatural dam
> Should *now* eat up her own !—*Coriol.*, iii. 1.
>
> *Now* might I do it, pat, *now* he is praying ;
> And *now* I 'll do 't.—*Hamlet*, iii. 3.

O, of this contradiction you shall now be quit.   *O*, the charity of a penny cord !—*Cym.*, v. 4.

Some modern editors have omitted this first " O " ; but observe how Shakespeare has a similar repetition of the exclamation " O " in the next example we give from this very play, and also observe that the jailer again prefaces a remark with an " O " in his last speech of the present scene.   It is as if the dramatist meant it as a characteristic of this speaker's diction.

> *O*, my gentle brothers,
> Have we thus met ?   *O*, never say hereafter
> But I am truest speaker.—*Ibid.*, v. 5.
>
> This is not strong enough to be believ'd
> *Of* one persuaded well *of*.—
>   Never talk on 't.—*Ibid.*, ii. 4.

I 'll none *of it ;* hence ! make your best *of it.*—*Tam. of S.*, iv. 3.

> O, the blest gods ! so will you wish *on* me,
> When the rash mood is *on.*—*Lear*, ii. 4.
>
> And *once again* bestride our foaming steeds,
> And *once again* cry—Charge upon our foes !
> But never *once again* turn back and fly.—*3 H. VI.*, ii. 1.
>
> If then *one* is, or hath, or means to be,
> That *one* meets Hector; if none else, I am he.—
> Tell him of Nestor, *one* that was a man
> When Hector's grandsire suck'd : he is old now ;
> But if there be not in our Grecian host
> *One* noble man that hath *one* spark of fire,
> To answer for his love, tell him from me.—*Tr. & Cr.*, i. 3.
>
> Nay, weep not, gentle Eros ; there is left us
> *Ourselves* to end *ourselves.*—*Ant. & C.*, iv. 12.
>
> Better be with the dead,
> Whom we, to gain our *peace*, have sent to *peace*,
> Than on the torture of the mind to lie
> In restless ecstacy.—*Macb.*, iii. 2.

Several editors have adopted the alteration made by the Second Folio of the first " peace " in the above line to ' place '; whereby we think that much of the force and antithetical point of the passage is lost.   As it stands, the repeated word is completely in Shakespeare's manner, and it precisely describes that which Macbeth has endeavoured to " gain," in order to appease his restless ambition and to give expected fulness of content to all his after days.

> The foe is merciless, and will not *pity ;*
> For at their hands I have deserv'd no *pity.*—*3 H. VI.*, ii. 6.

Do you know this house to be a *place* of such resort, and will come to it ?   I hear say, you are of honourable parts, and are governor of this *place.*—*Per.*, iv. 6.

Deposing thee before thou wert *possess'd,*
Which art *possess'd* now to depose thyself.—*R. II.*, ii. 1.

The *present* eye praises the *present* object.—*Tr. & Cr.*, iii. 3.

Amongst them
Whose eyes are on this sovereign lady fix'd,
One do I personate of lord Timon's frame,
Whom Fortune with her ivory hand wafts to her;
Whose *present* grace to *present* slaves and servants
Translates his rivals.—*Timon*, i. 1.

It has been proposed to alter the second "present" in the above line to 'peasant'; but the emphatic repetition is in Shakespeare's manner, and draws special attention to the point he wishes to enforce—namely, that it is Timon's "present" prosperity which makes "present" slaves and servants of those around him, as his 'future' downfall will make 'future' ingrates of those who now worship him.

But now mischance hath trod my title down,
And with dishonour laid me on the ground;
Where I must take like *seat* unto my fortune,
And to my humble *seat* conform myself.—3 *H. VI.*, iii. 3.

This *service* is not *service*, so being done,
But being so allow'd.—*Cym.*, iii. 3.

From forth thy reach he would have laid thy *shame,*
. . . Wert thou regent of the world,
It were a *shame* to let this land by lease;
But for thy world enjoying but this land,
Is it not more than *shame* to *shame* it so?—*R. II.*, ii. 1.

Live in thy *shame*, but die not *shame* with thee.—*Ibid.*, ii. 1.

Why ask I that? my mangled body *shows,*
My blood, my want of strength, my sick heart *shows,*
That I must yield my body to the earth.—3 *H. VI.*, v. 2.

So come my soul to bliss, as I speak true;
So speaking as I think, I die,—I die.—*Oth.*, v. 2.

I *sometimes* do believe, and *sometimes* do not;
As those that *fear* they hope, and know they *fear.*—*As You L.*, v. 4.

O, but impatience waiteth on true *sorrow :*
And see where comes the breeder of my *sorrow.*—3 *H. VI.*, iii. 3.

I have *spirit* to do anything that appears not foul in the truth of my *spirit.*—*M. for M.*, iii. 2.

Here the first "spirit" is used in the sense of courage or courageous enterprise; the second "spirit" in the sense of conscience, spiritual perception of right and wrong. It is a rule in ordinary constructional style that the same word should not be used in a different sense in the same sentence; but we have shown several examples of Shakespeare's breaking through this rule with excellent effect. He made his own rules; making them so ably, and working by them so advantageously, as to render them worthy of adoption by others. For dramatic diction, where the object is to produce prompt and striking impression, Shakespeare's bold originality in laws of construction is worth far more than the tame decrees of merely strict phraseologists.

To England will I *steal*, and there I'll *steal.*—*H. V.*, v. 1.

If you will *take* this audit, *take* this life,
And cancel these cold bonds.—*Cym.*, v. 4.

What is the matter,
That being pass'd for consul with full voice,
I am so dishonour'd, *that* the very hour
You take it off again ?—*Coriol.*, iii. 3.

                          Woe is my heart,
That the poor soldier, *that* so richly fought,
Whose rags sham'd gilded arms, *whose* naked breast
Stepp'd before targes of proof, cannot be found.—*Cym.*, v. 5.

They shall have none, I swear, but these my joints,—
Which, if they have as I will leave *'em them*,
Shall yield *them* little, tell the Constable.—*H. V.*, iv. 3.

You may *think* perchance that I *think* you are *in love :* nay, by 'r lady, I am *not* such a fool to *think* what I *list ; nor* I *list not* to *think* what I can; *nor*, indeed, I can*not think*, if I would *think* my heart out of *thinking*, that you are *in love, or* that you will be *in love, or* that you can be *in love*.—*M. Ado*, iii. 4.

In this passage Shakespeare is evidently showing how repetition of words may be carried to excess ; since he has made the speaker, Margaret, a would-be imitatress of her mistress, Beatrice, in playful word-catching. It is not only, like most imitations, inferior to the original, but it is a caricature. He has elsewhere taken care to mark how the fashion of playing upon a repeated word may run into exaggeration, by making Polonius check himself when he is overstraining his reiteration of the words " tender " and " tenders :"—

He hath, my lord, of late made many *tenders*
Of his affection to me.—
Affection ! pooh ! you speak like a green girl,
Unsifted in such perilous circumstance.
Do you believe his *tenders*, as you call them ?—
I do not know, my lord, what I should *think*.—
Marry, I 'll teach you : *think* yourself a baby;
That you have ta'en these *tenders* for true pay,
Which are not sterling. *Tender* yourself more dearly ;
Or,—not to crack the wind of the poor phrase,
Wronging it thus,—you 'll *tender* me a fool.—*Hamlet*, i. 3.

Those that I reverence, *those* I *fear*,—the wise :
At fools I laugh, not *fear* them.—*Cym.*, iv. 2.

               If thou please
To take me *to* thee, as I was *to* him
I 'll be *to* Cæsar.—*Ant. & C.*, v. 1.

Our *tongues* and sorrows do sound deep
Our woes into the air ; our eyes do weep,
Till *tongues* fetch breath that may proclaim them louder.—*Per.*, i. 4.

The second " tongues " in this passage has been altered by Malone and others to ' lungs '; but, besides that the repetition is consistent with Shakespeare's style, we find in " King Richard II.," i. 3, the expressions, " Which robs my *tongue* from *breathing* native breath," and " The *tongue's* office should be prodigal to *breathe* th' abundant dolour of the heart."

If this poor *trash* of Venice, whom I *trash*
For his quick hunting, stand the putting on.—*Oth.*, ii. 1.

In the First Folio and in the Second and Third Quartos, the second " trash " in the above line is printed ' trace ' (probably an old form of ' trass ' or " trash "), while the First Quarto misprints it ' crush.' The very repetition of the word makes, in our opinion, for the correctness of the reading in the text; while the phrase "for his quick hunting" shows that a sporting term is intended, " trash " being an expression of the chase for ' check,' ' stop,' ' keep back.'

> And appetite, a *universal* wolf,
> So doubly seconded with will and power,
> Must make perforce a *universal* prey,
> And last eat up himself.—*Tr. & Cr.*, i. 3.

I serve here *voluntary*.—Your last service was sufferance, 'twas not *voluntary*,—no man is beaten *voluntary*: Ajax was here the *voluntary*, and you as under an impress.—*Ibid.*, ii. 1.

My mother greets me kindly: is she *well ?*—
She is not *well;* but yet she has her health: she's very merry; but yet she is not *well:* but thanks be given, she's very *well*, and wants nothing i' the world; but yet she is not *well*.—If she be very *well*, what does she ail, that she's not very *well ?*—Truly, she's very *well* indeed, but for two things.—*All's W.*, ii. 4.

The above is a specimen of the skirmishing with repeated words, which was one of the means by which professional fool-jesters entertained their employers.

> *Well*, I am glad that all things sort so *well*.—*M. Ado*, v. 4.
>> Will you to Scone ?—
> No, cousin, I'll to Fife.—
>> *Well*, I will thither.—
> *Well*, may you see things *well* done there,—adieu,—
> Lest our old robes sit easier than our new !—*Macb.*, ii. 4.
> Wilt thou, O God, fly from such gentle lambs,
> And throw them in the entrails of the wolf?
> *When* didst thou sleep, *when* such a deed was done ?—*R. III.*, iv. 4.

In the Second Folio the first " when " in this line was changed to ' why ;' but the word is firstly used in the sense of ' at what time before this' or ' when ere now '; and, secondly, in the sense of ' at the time that' or ' while.' Moreover, this near repetition of the word " when " appropriately gives it the effect of an impatient exclamation, such as it sometimes formerly bore.

> But, what's your *will ?*—
> Your answer, sir, is enigmatical :
> But for my *will*, my *will* is, your good *will*
> May stand with ours, this day to be conjoin'd
> In the state of honourable marriage.—*M. Ado*, v. 4.

You may as well go about to turn the sun to ice *with* fanning in his face *with* a peacock's feather.—*H. V.*, iv. 1.

> Thou told'st me they were stol'n into this *wood;*
> *And* here am I, *and wood* within this *wood*
> Because I cannot meet my Hermia.—*Mid. N. D.*, ii. 2.

The second time " wood " occurs in the above passage, it bears one of the senses it formerly had—' wild,' ' distracted,' ' mad.'

I must take out the *work !* A likely piece of *work*, that you should find it in your chamber, and not know who left it there! This is some minx's token, and I must take out the *work !* There, give it your hobby-horse: wheresoever you had it, I'll take out no *work* on 't.—*Oth.*, iv. 1.

> I will to-morrow
> (And betimes I will) to the weird sisters :
> More shall they speak; for now I am bent to know,
> By the *worst* means, the *worst*.—*Macb.*, iii. 4.

Sometimes Shakespeare gives a nearly similar word in the same sentence :—

> Peace, ho ! for shame ! *confusion's* cure lives not
> In these *confusions.—R. & Jul.*, iv. 5.
> When thou hast hung thy advancèd sword i' the air,
> Not letting it *decline* on the *declin'd.—Tr. & Cr.*, iv. 5.
> *Deposing* thee before thou wert *possess'd*,
> Which art *possess'd* now to *depose* thyself.—*R. II.*, ii. 1.
> And give to *dust*, that is a little *gilt*,
> More laud than *gilt* o'er-*dusted.—Tr. & Cr.*, iii. 3.
> Were he as *famous*, and as bold in war,
> As he is *fam'd* for mildness, peace, and prayer.—3 *H. VI.*, ii. 1.
> Deny to speak with me ?   They are sick ? they are weary ?
> They have travell'd hard to-night ?   Mere *fetches;*
> The images of revolt and flying off.
> *Fetch* me a better answer.—*Lear*, ii. 4.
>
> O, world, thy slippery turns !   Friends now fast sworn,
> Whose double bosoms seem to wear one heart,
> Whose *hours*, whose bed, whose meal, and exercise,
> Are still together, who twin, as 'twere, in love
> Unseparable, shall within this *hour*,
> On a dissension of a doit, break out
> To bitterest enmity.—*Coriol.*, iv. 4.

It has been proposed to change " hours " to ' house ' here : but not only would the alteration deprive the passage of the nearness of " hours " and " hour," which is in Shakespeare's style ; it would also destroy the antithetical force of the entire sentence, which signifies, ' Strange that friends whose *hours* have been perpetually spent together, should within *a single hour* break out to bitterest enmity.' As a corroboration, too, the passage describing mutual friendship in " Two Gentlemen of Verona," ii. 4, contains the same word here employed : " From our infancy we have convers'd and spent our *hours* together."

> Though *indirect*,
> Yet *indirection* thereby grows *direct.—John*, iii. 1.

The whole speech, from which this example is cited, abounds with instances of repeated similar words ; affording a most characteristic specimen of sophistical argument dressed in specious terms confusedly intervolved and reiterated :—

> I may disjoin my hand, but not my *faith.*—
> So mak'st thou *faith* an enemy to *faith ;*
> And, like a civil war, sett'st *oath* to *oath*,
> Thy *tongue* against thy *tongue*.   O, let thy vow
> *First* made to *Heaven, first* be to *Heaven perform'd*,—
> That is, to be the champion of our church !
> What since thou *swor'st* is *sworn* against *thyself:*
> And may not be *performèd* by *thyself:*
> For that which thou hast *sworn* to do *amiss*
> Is not *amiss* when it is *truly done ;*
> And being not *done*, where *doing* tends to ill,
> The *truth* is then most *done* not *doing* it :
> The better act of purposes *mistook*
> Is to *mistake* again ; though *indirect*,
> Yet *indirection* thereby grows *direct*,

And *falsehood falsehood* cures ; as *fire* cools *fire*
Within the scorched veins of one new burn'd.
It is *religion* that doth make vows kept ;
But thou hast *sworn against religion,*
By what thou *swear'st against* the thing thou *swear'st ;*
And mak'st an *oath* the *surety* for thy *truth*
Against an *oath :* the truth thou art *unsure*
To *swear, swears only* not to be *forsworn ;*
Else, what a mockery should it be to *swear !*
But thou dost *swear only* to be *forsworn ;*
And most *forsworn,* to keep what thou dost swear.—*John,* iii. 1.

In the same play there are two other speeches that contain an abundance of repeated similar words ; which makes for our theory (stated under the heading of RECURRENCE OF PARTICULAR POINTS) respecting Shakespeare's special modes of thinking and writing in certain plays :—

If lusty *love should go* in quest of beauty,
Where should he find it fairer *than in Blanch ?*
If zealous *love should go* in search of virtue,
Where should he find it purer *than in Blanch ?*
If *love* ambitious sought a match of birth,
Whose veins bound richer blood than Lady *Blanch ?*
Such as she is, in beauty, virtue, birth,
Is the young Dauphin every way *complete,*—
If not *complete* of, say, *he is not she ;*
And she again *wants* nothing, to name *want,*
If *want* it be not, that *she is not he :*
He is the half part of a blessèd man,
Left to be finished by such a *she ;*
And *she* a fair divided excellence,
Whose fulness of perfection lies in him.
O, *two* such silver currents, when they join,
Do glorify the banks that bound them in ;
And *two* such shores to *two* such streams made one,
Two such controlling bounds shall you be, kings,
To these *two* princes, if you marry them.—*Ibid.,* ii. 2.
I am not *mad :* this hair I tear is mine ;
My name is Constance ; I was Geffrey's wife ;
Young Arthur is my son, and he is lost :
I am not *mad ;* I would to heaven I were !
For then 'tis like I should forget myself :
O, if I could, what grief should I forget !
Preach some philosophy to make me *mad,*
And thou shalt be canóniz'd, cardinal ;
For, being not *mad,* but sensible of grief,
My *reasonable* part produces *reason*
How I may be deliver'd of these woes,
And teaches me to kill or hang myself :
If I were *mad,* I should forget my son,
Or *madly* think a babe of clouts were he.
I am not *mad : too well, too well* I feel
The different plague of each calamity.—*Ibid.,* iii. 4.
                              Nay, certainly to-night,
For *look,* how fresh she *looks !* They were too rough,
That threw her in the sea.—*Per.,* iii. 2.
And the ebb'd man, ne'er *lov'd* till ne'er worth *love,*
Comes dear'd by being lack'd.—*Ant. & C.,* i. 4.
Oft have you (*often* have you thanks therefore)
Desir'd my Cressid in right great exchange.—*Tr. & Cr.,* iii. 3.

> While we were interchanging thrusts and blows,
> Came more and more, and fought on *part* and *part*,
> Till the prince came, who *parted* either *part.—R. & Jul.*, i. 1.

> That he is not only *plaguèd* for *her sin*,
> But God hath made *her sin* and *her* the *plague*
> On this removèd issue, *plagu'd* for *her*,
> And with *her plague, her sin;* his *injury*
> *Her injury*,—the beadle to *her sin;*
> *All* punish'd in the person of this child,
> *And all* for *her;* a *plague* upon *her!*—
> Thou unadvisèd scold, I can produce
> A *will* that bars the title of thy son.—
> Ay, who doubts that? *A will!* a wicked *will;*
> A woman's *will;* a canker'd grandam's *will!*—
> Peace, lady! pause, or be more temperate;
> It *ill* beseems this presence to cry aim
> To these *ill*-tunèd repetitions.—*John*, ii. 1.

> The Moor already changes with my *poison:*—
> Dangerous conceits are, in their natures, *poisons*,
> Which at the first are scarce found to distaste,
> But, with a little act upon the blood,
> Burn like the mines of sulphur. I did say so:—
> Look, where he comes!—*Oth.*, iii. 3.

The word "poison" has been objected to as probably erroneous; whereas we not only think its proximity to "poisons" shows it to be in accordance with Shakespeare's style, but we think the one word is used in direct reference to the other, as illustrative comment, thus: 'The Moor already changes with the *poison* I have administered to him— for dangerous fancies such as I have suggested to his mind are, in their inflaming quality, *poisons*, which, &c.' The very words that follow— "I did say so: look where he comes!"—serve to support our view of the passage; since they imply, 'I have just said that the poisonous ideas I have suggested burn fiercely; and see where he comes to confirm my words by his pangs of restless misery!'

> For young hot colts, being *rag'd*, do *rage* the more.—*R. II.*, ii. 1.

To avoid the effect of repetition, various substitutions have been proposed for "rag'd"; but, in our opinion, "rag'd" was here used by Shakespeare as an abbreviated form of 'enraged' (to express 'fretted,' 'irritated,' 'provoked'), for the sake of producing that very repetitional effect which offends some of his would-be emendators, but in which he delighted, and which delights those who admire his spirited style.

> There, take the paper: see it be *return'd;*
> Or else *return* no more into my sight.—*Two G. of V.*, i. 2.

> And when we have our armours buckled on,
> The venom'd vengeance ride upon our swords,
> Spur them to *ruthful* work, rein them from *ruth.—Tr. & Cr.*, v. 3.

> O miracle of men!—him did you leave,
> (*Second* to none, *unseconded* by you)
> To look upon the hideous god of war
> In disadvantage.—*2 H. IV.*, ii. 3.

> But I *love* thee
> By *love's* own sweet constraint, and will for ever
> Do thee all rights of *service.*—

> Ay, so you *serve* us,
> Till we *serve* you ; but when you have our roses,
> You *barely* leave our thorns to prick ourselves,
> And mock us with our *bareness.—All's W.,* iv. 2.

By changing the word " barely " to ' basely,' Rowe showed that he did not perceive the Shakespearian emphasis of repetition which marks the whole of this passage, or the Shakespearian condensation whereby the last sentence is made succinctly and poetically to express, ' You leave us deprived of all save our stings of conscience, and then reproach us with our deprivation.'

> *Shame* come to Romeo !—
> > Blister'd be thy tongue
> For such a wish ! he was not born to *shame :*
> Upon his brow *shame* is *ashamed* to sit.—*R. & Jul.,* iii. 2.
> So come my soul to bliss, as I *speak* true ;
> So *speaking* as I think, I die,—I die.—*Oth.,* v. 2.
> We shall not *spend* a large *expense* of time
> Before we reckon with your several loves,
> And make us even with you.—*Macb.,* v. 7.

Although in this passage we have left the word " expense " in the text of all our editions of the poet, and although we here cite it among our examples of nearly similar words repeated, yet we feel by no means confident that it is not a misprint ; perhaps for either ' extent ' or ' expanse,' which have been suggested as probably supplying the original word.

> And with some sweet oblivious antidote
> Cleanse the *stuff'd* bosom of that perilous *stuff*
> Which weighs upon the heart ?—*Ibid.,* v. 3.

See FAMILIAR AND HOMELY EXPRESSIONS for an explanation of our views upon the above passage.

> And I, like one lost in a *thorny* wood,
> That *rents* the *thorns,* and is *rent* with the *thorns,*
> Seeking a *way,* and straying from the *way ;*
> Not knowing how to find the open air,
> But toiling desperately to find it out,—
> *Torment* myself to catch the English crown :
> And from that *torment* I will free myself,
> Or hew my *way* out with a bloody axe.
> Why, I can *smile,* and murder while I *smile.*—3 *H. VI.,* iii. 2.
> If, like a Christian, thou hadst *truly* borne
> Betwixt our armies *true* intelligence.—1 *H. IV.,* v. 5.
> For I have ever *verified* my friends
> (Of whom he 's chief) with all the size that *verity*
> Would without lapsing suffer.—*Coriol.,* v. 2.

There have not been wanting objectors to the word " verified " in this sentence : but not only does its similarity to " verity " offer likelihood of its being what Shakespeare wrote, taking it to be used in the sense of ' affirmed the excellence of,' ' asserted the merit of,' ' borne witness to the worth of,' it may also be taken to bear the sense of ' spoken the truth of,' in which case the sentence would be quite in his style, as implying, ' I have always spoken the truth of my friends as largely as truth would allow without ceasing to be truth.'

> This he *wish'd*
> I, after him, do after him *wish* too.—*All's W.,* i. 2.

RHYMES.

Several of Shakespeare's plays contain passages and even whole speeches written in rhyme; but among these rhymed portions, there are a few that present instances of a non-rhyming couplet occurring :—

> Cricket, to Windsor chimneys shalt thou *leap ;*
> Where fires thou find'st unrak'd, and hearths un*swept.—Merry W.*, v. 5.

> These lily *lips*,
> This cherry *nose.—Mid. N. D.*, v. 1.

> May I, sweet lady, beg a kiss of *you ?—*
> You may.—
>   I do desire it.—
>   Why, beg, *then.—Tr. & Cr.*, iv. 5.

> Here's that, which is too weak to be a *sinner*,
> Honest water, which ne'er left man i' the *mire.—Timon*, i. 2.

> And winking Mary-buds *begin*
>   To ope their golden eyes ;
> With every thing that pretty *is :*
>   My lady sweet, arise.—*Cym.*, ii. 3 (*Song*).

He also occasionally gives an imperfectly rhyming couplet; and, when he wrote, considerable licence was taken in forming rhymes from words that merely sounded somewhat alike :—

> In very likeness of a roasted *crab ;*
> And, when she drinks, against her lips I *bob.—Mid. N. D.*, ii. 1.

> May be the lady.   Thou shalt know the *man*
> By the Athenian garments he hath *on.—Ibid.*, ii. 2.

> Ay, that left *pap*,
> Where heart doth *hop.—Ibid.*, v. 4.

> Nay, by Saint *Jamy*,
> I hold you a *penny*,
> A horse and a *man*
> Is more than *one*,
> And yet not *many.—Tam. of S.*, iii. 2.

> Great Hector's sister did Achilles *win ;*
> But our great Ajax bravely beat down *him.—Tr. & Cr.*, iii. 3.

> If my cap would buy a *halter :*
> So the fool follows *after.—Lear*, i. 4.

> To sing a song that old was *sung*,
> From ashes ancient Gower is *come ;* . . .
> The fairest in all *Syria*,—
> I tell you what mine authors *say :* . . .
> With whom the father liking *took*,
> And her to incest did *provoke.—Per.*, i. (*Gower*).

> And, to remember what he *does*,
> Build his statue to make him *glorious :* . . .
> Good Helicane hath stay'd at *home*,
> Not to eat honey like a *drone*. . . .
> How Thaliard came full bent with *sin*,
> And hid intent to murder *him ;* . . ,
> Make such unquiet that the *ship*
> Should house him safe, is wreck'd and *split.—Ibid.*, ii. (*Gower*).

> The mutiny he there hastes t' *oppress ;*
> Says to them, if King *Pericles*
> Come not home in twice six *moons,*
> He, obedient to their *dooms.* . . .
> This stage the ship, upon whose *deck*
> The sea-tost Pericles appears to *speak.—Per.,* iii. (*Gower*).
> Dionyza doth *appear,*
> With Leonine, a *murderer.—Ibid.,* iv. (*Gower*).
> Now our sands are almost *run ;*
> More a little, and then *dumb.—Ibid.,* v. 2. (*Gower*).

We find a few instances of Shakespeare's giving a single unrhymed line among several that rhyme :—

> This grisly beast, which Lion hight by *name.—Mid. N. D.,* v. 1.
> I 'll do, I 'll do, and I 'll *do.* . . .
> I' the shipman's *card* . . .
> Look what I have.—
> > Show me, show *me.—* . . .
> Thus do go about, *about :* . . .
> Peace ! the charm 's wound *up.—Macb.,* i. 3.

In the above-cited instances, we believe that the defective rhyming was intentional on the part of our author ; in the first-cited instance, to denote the slipshod style of the doggerel that forms the dialogue in the Interlude of " Pyramus and Thisbe " (and which we have always cherished a conviction Shakespeare intended to be taken as written by Peter Quince himself ; because in the Folio we find, " *Enter the Prologue Quince,*" and because, in act iv., sc. 1, Bottom says :—

> I will get Peter Quince *to write a ballad* of this dream,

showing that Quince is an author as well as stage-manager and deliverer of the prologue) ; and in the second-cited instance, to give the effect of ruggedness and irregularity to the diction of those wild, weird creatures, the witches.

Sometimes Shakespeare passes from couplet rhyming to alternate rhyming : as in the speeches of the Chorus, Gower ; which are for the most part in couplet, but which at the opening of act v. are given in alternate rhymes :—

> Marina thus the brothel 'scapes, and *chances*
> > Into an honest house, our story *says.*
> She sings like one immortal, and she *dances*
> > As goddess-like to her admired *lays.—Per.* v. (*Gower*).

In a few cases, Shakespeare allows himself to rhyme with the same word :—

> Our prayers do out-pray his ; then let them *have*
> That mercy which true prayers ought to *have.—R. II.,* v. 3.
> To seek her as a bed-*fellow,*
> In marriage pleasures play-*fellow.—Per.* i. (*Gower*).
> Where our scenes seem to live.   I do beseech *you*
> To learn of me, who stand i' the gaps to teach *you.—Ibid.,* iv. 4 (*Gower*).
> Potent at court : he, none but he, shall have *her,*
> Though twenty thousand worthier come to crave *her.—Merry W.,* iv. 4.

In the two last-quoted examples there is merely a licence that would always be and is now permissible in playful rhyming ; inasmuch as the rhyme lies in the penultimate word, and the final word counts for no more than a mute half-foot at the end of the line.

Shakespeare, in accordance with a practice of other dramatists, frequently terminates a scene with a rhyming couplet :—

Prospero, my lord, shall know what I have *done :*
So, king, go safely on to seek thy *son.*—*Temp.*, ii. 1.

If I can check my erring love, I *will ;*
If not, to compass her I 'll use my *skill.*—*Two G. of V.*, ii. 4.

To Master Brook you yet shall hold your *word ;*
For he to-night shall lie with Mistress *Ford.*—*Merry W.*, v. 5.

Is more to bread than stone : hence shall we *see,*
If power change purpose, what our seemers *be.*—*M. for M.*, i. 4.

Hopeless, and helpless, doth Ægeon *wend,*
But to procrastinate his lifeless *end.*—*Com. of E.*, i. 1.

For others say thou dost deserve, and *I*
Believe it better than reporting*ly.*—*M. Ado*, iii. 1.

Well, I will love, write, sigh, pray, sue, *groan :*
Some men must love my lady, and some *Joan.*—*Love's L. L.*, iii. 1.

A fortnight hold we this solem*nity,*
In nightly revels and new jol*lity.*—*Mid. N. D.*, v. 1.

Where money is ; and I no question *make,*
To have it of my trust, or for my *sake.*—*Mer. of V.*, i. 1.

After my flight. Now go we in con*tent*
To liberty, and not to banish*ment.*—*As You L.*, i. 3.

Seize thee that list : if once I find thee *ranging,*
Hortensio will be quit with thee by *changing.*—*Tam. of S.*, iii. 1.

Begone to-morrow ; and be sure of *this,*
What I can help thee to, thou shalt not *miss.*—*All's W.*, i. 3.

Away before me to sweet beds of *flowers :*
Love-thoughts lie rich, when canopied with *bowers.*—*Tw. N.*, i. 1.

Strong reasons make strange actions : let us *go :*
If you say ay, the king will not say *no.*—*John*, iii. 4.

Come home with me to supper ; I will *lay*
A plot shall show us all a merry *day.*—*R. II.*, iv. 1.

I 'll so offend, to make offence a *skill ;*
Redeeming time, when men think least I *will.* –1 *H. IV.*, i. 2.

Get posts and letters, and make friends with *speed,*—
Never so few, and never yet more *need.*—2 *H. IV.*, i. 1.

Cheerly to sea ; the signs of war *advance :*
No king of England, if not king of *France.*—*H. V.*, ii. 2.

Come, let us four to dinner : I dare *say*
This quarrel will drink blood another *day.*—1 *H. VI.*, ii. 4.

And force, perforce, I 'll make him yield the *crown,*
Whose bookish rule hath pull'd fair England *down.*—2 *H. VI.*, i. 1.

Now therefore let us hence ; and lose no *hour,*
Till we meet Warwick with his foreign *power.*—3 *H. VI.*, iv. 1.

Clarence still breathes ; Edward still lives and *reigns ;*
When they are gone, then must I count my *gains.*—*R. III.*, i. 1.

That little thought, when she set footing *here,*
She should have bought her dignities so *dear.*—*H. VIII.*, iii. 1.

Two curs shall tame each other : pride *alone*
Must tarre the mastiffs on, as 'twere their *bone.*—*Tr. & Cr.*, i. 3.

Come, let 's away. When, Caius, Rome is *thine,*
Thou art poor'st of all ; then shortly art thou *mine.*—*Coriol.*, iv. 7.

Farewell : thou canst not teach me to *forget.*—
I 'll pay that doctrine, or else die in *debt.*—*R. & Jul.*, i. 1.

I 'll ever serve his mind with my best *will* :
Whilst I have gold, I 'll be his steward *still.*—*Timon,* iv. 2.
And, after this, let Cæsar seat him *sure* ;
For we will shake him, or worse days *endure.*—*Jul. C.,* i. 2.
Away, and mock the time with fairest *show* :
False face must hide what the false heart doth *know.*—*Macb.,* i. 7.
Till then sit still, my soul : foul deeds will *rise,*
Though all the earth o'ewhelm them, to men's *eyes.*—*Hamlet,* i. 2.
Let me, if not by birth, have lands by *wit* :
All with me 's meet that I can fashion *fit.*—*Lear,* i. 2.
For if such actions may have passage *free,*
Bond-slaves and pagans shall our statesmen *be.*—*Oth.,* i. 2.
Ah, women, women ! come ; we have no *friend*
But resolution, and the briefest *end.*—*Ant. & C.,* iv. 13.
Do as I bid thee : there 's no more to *say* ;
Accessible is none but Milford *way.*—*Cym.,* iii. 2.
Thaliard, adieu ! Till Pericles be *dead,*
My heart can lend no succour to my *head.*—*Per.,* i. 1.

" The Winter's Tale " is the only one of Shakespeare's plays which does not afford an instance of the dialogue in a scene ending with a rhyming couplet.

' S ' ADDED OR OMITTED IN THE FIRST FOLIO.

Among the many typographical inaccuracies of the 1623 Folio, is that of adding a final ' s ' to a word which should obviously not have it appended, and of omitting a final ' s ' or ' 's ' in a word which obviously requires either of these conclusions. It is needful therefore to bear in mind this peculiar error of the First Folio printer, when judging certain passages written by Shakespeare ; and we here collectively cite several passages that have given rise to debate upon the point in question. The italicised words in the following passages are printed in the 1623 Folio with an erroneously added ' s ':—

A man who is the *abstract* of all faults
That all men follow.—*Ant. & C.,* i. 4.
Farther than he is *Cæsar.*—*Ibid.,* iii. 11.
She, Eros, has pack'd cards with *Cæsar.*—*Ibid.,* iv. 12.
                                    Their discipline
(Now mingled with their *courage*) will make known.—*Cym.,* ii. 4.
Most miserable is the *desire* that 's glorious.—*Ibid.,* i. 7.
Whose subdu'd eyes . . . *drop* tears as fast.—*Oth.,* v. 2.
By the *hangman** boys in the market-place.—*Tw. G. of V.,* iv. 4.
There hath been in Rome strange *insurrection.*—*Coriol.,* iv. 3.
                                    Our bloods
No more obey the heavens than our courtiers
Still seem as does the *king.*—*Cym.,* i. 1.
My *lord*†, farewell.—*H. VIII.,* i. 2.

---

* Shakespeare elsewhere (" Much Ado About Nothing," iii. 2) uses " hangman " as a nick-name. *See* PARTICULAR NAMES.

† As Abergavenny accompanies Buckingham to the Tower, the latter takes leave merely of Norfolk.

For affection,
Master of passion, sways it to the mood
Of what it likes or loathes.—*Mer. of V.*, iv. 1.

I have assailed her with *music*, but she.—*Cym.*, ii. 3.

And see, a book of prayer in his hand,—
True *ornament* to know a holy man.—*R. III.*, iii. 7.

When liver, brain, and heart,
These sovereign thrones, are all supplied and fill'd
(Her sweet *perfection**) with one self king!—*Tw. N.*, i. 1.

Will nothing stick our *person* to arraign.—*Hamlet*, iv. 5.

The *son* of Duncan,
From whom this tyrant holds the due of birth,
Lives in the English court.—*Macb.*, iii. 6.

So foolish *sorrow* bids your stones farewell.—*R. III.*, iv. 1.

I am not made of *stone*, but penetrable to.—*Ibid.*, iii. 7.

What a full fortune does the *thick*-lips owe, if he.—*Oth.*, i. 1.

Have broke their sleeps with *thought*, their brains with care.—*2 H. IV.*, iv. 4.

With witchcraft of his *wit*, with traitorous gifts,
(O wicked wit, and gifts, that have the power
So to seduce!) won to his shameful lust.—*Hamlet*, i. 5.

For this the foolish over-careful fathers
Have broke their sleeps. . . .
For this they have engrossed and pil'd up
The canker'd heaps of strange-achievèd gold;
For this they have been thoughtful to invest
Their sons with arts and martial exercises:
When, like the bee, tolling from every flower
The virtuous sweets,
Our thighs pack'd with wax, our mouths with honey,
We bring it to the hive; and, like the bees,
Are murder'd for our pains. This bitter taste
Yield† his engrossments to the ending father.—*2 H. IV.*, iv. 4.

The italicised words in the following passages are printed in the 1623 Folio with the final ' s ' or ' 's ' omitted :—

How parted with your *brothers?* How first met them?—*Cym.*, v. 5.

Ye see, I drink the water of mine *eyes*.—*3 H. VI.*, v. 4.

Left and abandon'd of his velvet *friends*.—*As You L.*, ii. 1.

Be that you seem, truly your country's *friends*.—*Coriol.*, iii. 1.

His sons he there proclaim'd the *kings* of kings.—*Ant. & C.*, iii. 6.

The *legions*, now in Gallia, sooner landed.—*Cym.*, ii. 4.

I have fair *meanings*, sir.—
And fair words to them.—*Ant. & C.*, ii. 6.

Half all *men's* hearts are his.—*Cym.*, i. 7.

Hath he not passed the *nobles* and the *commons?*—*Coriol.*, iii. 1.

Takes no account
How things go from him; nor *resumes* no care
Of what is to continue.—*Timon*, ii. 2.

---

* *See* PECULIAR USE OF WORDS (page 576) for explanation of the mode in which the word " perfection " is used, in the present passage and in two others, by Shakespeare, with reference to the beautiful doctrine that prevailed in his time of marriage being the perfectioning of a human being.

† The previous context of this sentence shows that the word " engrossments " refers to the " heaps " which the over-careful fathers have " engrossed and pil'd up "; therefore the construction is—' His engrossments *yield* this bitter taste to the ending father.'

How many ages hence
Shall this our lofty scene be acted over
In *states* unborn and accents yet unknown !—*Jul. C.*, iii. 1.
She 's a lady
So tender of rebukes, that words are *strokes*,
And strokes death to her.—*Cym.*, iii. 5.
But even the very middle of my heart
Is warm'd by the rest, and *takes* it thankfully.—*Ibid.*, i. 7.
The *things* I have forsworn to grant may never
Be held by you denials.—*Coriol.*, v. 3.
So our *virtues*
Lie in the interpretation of the time.—*Ibid.*, iv. 7.

The first line in the following passage is printed thus in the First
Folio : 'When many times the captiue Grecian fals '; but the word
" them," in the third line, shows the ' s ' to be misplaced :—

When many times the captive *Grecians fall*,
Even in the fan and wind of your fair sword,
You bid them rise, and live.—*Tr. & Cr.*, v. 3.

In the earliest printed editions of " Pericles " (which is not included
among the plays in the 1623 Folio) there occur some of these additions
and omissions of the final ' s ' or ' 's ' in a word.   The italicised words
in the following passages have an erroneously added ' s ' :—

By Cleon train'd in *music*, letters.—*Per.*, iv. (*Gower*).
His woful queen we leave at Ephesus,
Unto Diana *there* a votaress.—*Ibid.*, iv. (*Gower*).

And the italicised words in the following passages have the final ' s '
or ' 's ' omitted :—

Sure, *all* 's effectless; yet nothing we 'll omit.—*Ibid.*, v. 1.
This cannot be : my *daughter* 's buried.—*Ibid.*, v. 1.
Whose *death* 's, indeed, the strongest in our censure.—*Ibid.*, ii. 4.
And *leaves* us to our free election.—*Ibid.*, ii. 4.
Where now his *son* 's like a glow-worm in the night.—*Ibid.*, ii. 3.

SARCASMS.

Into the mouths of two of his gentlest women, Shakespeare has put
bitter sarcasms ; worded quietly, but none the less forcible and intense
for their very temperance of expression.   Cordelia, led in captive with
her cruelly aggrieved father, inquires :—

Shall we not see *these daughters and these sisters ?*—*Lear*, v. 3.

And Imogen, in reply to Cymbeline's storm of reproaches at the very
moment he banishes her husband from her side, says :—

I beseech you, sir,
Harm not yourself with your vexation :
I am senseless of your wrath ; a touch more rare
Subdues all pangs, all fears.—*Cym.*, i. 2.

Again, when Pisanio, telling Imogen that he has received her husband's command to kill her, adding, " Oh, gracious lady, since I

receiv'd command to do this business I have not slept one wink," she, with sarcastic quietude, replies :—

> *Do 't and to bed then.—Cym.*, iii. 4.

With equal yet quite another force of effect, Shakespeare has put into the mouths of vehement and vicious-natured women sarcastic speeches remarkable for quiet wording, yet strength of sneer. Lady Macbeth, when her husband is aghast at the apparition of the murdered man sitting at the very festal board in the seemingly empty seat, exclaims :—

> Shame itself!
> *Why do you make such faces ?* When all 's done,
> *You look but on a stool.—Macb.*, iii. 4.

Goneril greets Edmund with the words :—

> Welcome, my lord : I marvel *our mild husband*
> Not met us on the way.—*Lear*, iv. 2.

Cleopatra asks after Marc Antony's wife Fulvia by an epithet which, in the mouth of the imperial courtesan, is a superb scoff :—

> What says *the married woman ?—Ant. & C.*, i. 3.

And she afterwards alludes to his wife Octavia with terms that, used by the " Serpent of old Nile," signify profoundest scorn :—

> Your wife Octavia, with her *modest eyes*
> And *still conclusion*, shall acquire no honour
> *Demuring* upon me.—*Ibid.*, iv. 13.

Dionyza heaps contempt upon her husband Cleon's less unscrupulous character and his remorse for their joint deed in words of cutting taunt that are akin to Lady Macbeth's diction. They are well worthy the same dramatist's hand who, later on in his career, depicted that grandly drawn impersonation of criminal ambition :—

> *Cleon* . . . What canst thou say
> When noble Pericles shall demand his child ?
> *Dionyza.* That she is dead. *Nurses are not the fates,*
> *To foster, nor ever to preserve.*
> She died at night ; I 'll say so. Who can cross it ?
> *Unless you play the pious innocent,*
> And *for an honest attribute* cry out,
> " She died by foul play " . . .
> . . . *Be one of those that think*
> *The petty wrens of Tharsus will fly hence,*
> *And open this to Pericles. I do shame*
> *To think of what a noble strain you are,*
> *And of how coward a spirit.* . . .
> *You are like one that superstitiously*
> *Doth swear to the gods that winter kills the flies.—Per.*, iv. 4.

SATIRE.

Amid the numberless indirect satires upon the crimes, the vices, the errors, the follies, and the mistakes of mankind, that may be traced through all his plays and characters, there are to be found some passages of more direct satire in Shakespeare's works. He satirises a fashion that prevailed in his time of painting the cheeks; together with other feminine affectations of manner:—

I have heard of your paintings too, well enough; God hath given you one face, and you make yourselves another: you jig, you amble, and you lisp, and nickname God's creatures, and make your wantonness your ignorance.—*Hamlet*, iii. 1.

And another fashion, of wearing false hair:—

> Oh, if in black my lady's brows be deckt,
> It mourns that painting and usurping hair
> Should ravish doters with a false aspect!—*Love's L. L*, iv. 3.
>
> So are those crisped snaky golden locks,
> Which make such wanton gambols with the wind,
> Upon supposed fairness, often known
> To be the dowry of a second head,
> The skull that bred them in the sepulchre.—*Mer. of V.*, iii. 2.

And others, of foppishly curling the hair, and trimming or dyeing the beard:—

A serving-man, proud in heart and mind; that curled my hair; wore gloves in my cap.—*Lear*, iii. 4.

The wealthy curled darlings of our nation.—*Oth.*, i. 3.

The barber's man hath been seen with him; and the old ornament of his cheek has already stuffed tennis-balls.—Indeed, he looks younger than he did, by the loss of a beard.—*M. Ado*, iii. 2.

What beard were I best to play it in? . . . I will discharge it in either your straw-colour beard, your orange-tawny beard, your purple-in-grain beard, or your French-crown-colour beard, your perfect yellow.—*Mid. N. D.*, i. 2.

Others, of fantastical styles in dress, and fanatical adoption of foreign modes:—

There is no appearance of fancy in him, unless it be a fancy that he hath to strange disguises; as, to be a Dutchman to-day, a Frenchman to-morrow; or in the shape of two countries at once; as, a German from the waist downward, all slops, and a Spaniard from the hip upward, no doublet. Unless he have a fancy to this foolery, as it appears he hath, he is no fool for fancy, as you would have it appear he is.—*M. Ado*, iii. 2.

And one Deformed is one of them; I know him; 'a wears a lock [meaning a long lock of hair, sometimes called a love-lock; a fashion originally introduced from the Continent by young gallants, and afterwards adopted by ruffianly fellows and thieves].—*Ibid.*, iii. 3.

How oddly he is suited! I think he bought his doublet in Italy, his round hose in France, his bonnet in Germany, and his behaviour everywhere —*Mer. of V.*, i. 2.

Farewell, Monsieur Traveller; look, you lisp, and wear strange suits; disable all the benefits of your own country; be out of love with your nativity, and almost chide God for making you that countenance you are; or I will scarce think you have swam in a gondola.—*As You L.*, iv. 1.

Your son was misled with a snipt-taffeta fellow there, whose villanous saffron would have made all the unbaked and doughy youth of a nation of his colour . . . that red-tailed humble-bee I speak of.—*All's W.*, iv. 5.

> Report of fashions in proud Italy,
> Whose manners still our tardy apish nation
> Limps after, in base imitation.—*R. II.*, ii. 1.
>
> Duck with French nods and apish courtesy.—*R. III.*, i. 3.
>
> Is 't possible the spells of France should juggle
> Men into such strange mysteries?—
> New customs,
> Though they be never so ridiculous,
> Nay, let 'em be unmanly, yet are follow'd.—

> As far as I see, all the good our English
> Have got by the late voyage is but merely
> A fit or two o' the face; but they are shrewd ones;
> For when they hold 'em, you would swear directly
> Their very noses had been counsellors
> To Pepin or Clotharius, they keep state so.—
> They have all new legs, and lame ones: one would take it,
> That never saw them pace before, the spavin
> Or springhalt reign'd among them.—
>   Death! my lord,
> Their clothes are after such a pagan cut too,
> That, sure, they 've worn out Christendom.—*H. VIII.*, i. 3.

A great man, I 'll warrant; I know by the picking on 's teeth.—*W. T.*, iv. 3.

>   Now your traveller,—
> He and his toothpick at my worship's mess;
> And when my knightly stomach is suffic'd,
> Why then I suck my teeth, and catechise
> My picked man of countries:—" My dear sir,"
> Thus, leaning on mine elbow, I begin,
> " I shall beseech you "—that is question now;
> And then comes answer like an Absey-book:
> " Oh, sir," says answer, " at your best command;
> At your employment; at your service, sir;"
> " No, sir," says question, " I, sweet sir, at yours:"
> And so, ere answer knows what question would,—
> Saving in dialogue of compliment,
> And talking of the Alps and Appenines,
> The Pyrannean, and the river Po,—
> It draws towards supper in conclusion so.
> But this is worshipful society.—*John*, i. 1.

In the following passages he satirises a fashion affected by amorous young gentlemen of wearing slovenly attire:—

Oh, that you had mine eyes; or your own eyes had the lights they were wont to have when you chid at Sir Proteus for going ungartered!—

What should I see then?—

Your own present folly, and her passing deformity; for he, being in love, could not see to garter his hose; and you, being in love, cannot see to put on your hose.—*Two G. of V.*, ii. 1.

A beard neglected,—which you have not . . . your hose should be ungartered, your bonnet unbanded, your sleeve unbuttoned, your shoe untied, and everything about you demonstrating a careless desolation; but you are no such man,—you are rather point-device in your accoutrements, as loving yourself, than seeming the lover of any other.—*As You L.*, iii. 2.

> Lord Hamlet,—with his doublet all unbrac'd;
> No hat upon his head; his stockings foul'd,
> Ungarter'd and down-gyved to his ancle;
> Pale as his shirt; his knees knocking each other;
> And with a look so piteous in purport
> As if he had been loosed out of hell
> To speak of horrors,—he comes before me.—
> Mad for thy love?—*Hamlet*, ii. 1.

In the following he satirises several accomplishments in which those who wished to acquire the reputation of being dashing fellows strove for proficiency :—

I am sworn brother to a leash of drawers; and can call them all by their Christian names, as,—Tom, Dick, and Francis. They take it already upon their salvation, that though I be but Prince of Wales, yet I am the king of courtesy; and tell me flatly I am no proud Jack, like Falstaff; but a Corinthian, a lad of mettle, a good boy, (by the Lord, so they call me,) and when I am king of England, I shall command all the good lads in Eastcheap.   They call drinking deep, dyeing scarlet; and when you breathe in your watering, they cry "Hem!" and bid you play it off.   To conclude, I am so good a proficient in one quarter of an hour, that I can drink with any tinker in his own language during my life.—1 *H. IV.*, ii. 4.

He plays at quoits well; and eats conger and fennel; and drinks off candles'-ends for flap-dragons; and rides the wild mare with the boys; and jumps upon joint-stools;. and swears with a good grace; and wears his boot very smooth, like unto the sign of the leg; and breeds no bate with telling of discreet stories; and such other gambol faculties he has, that show a weak mind and an able body, for the which the prince admits him: for the prince himself is such another; the weight of a hair will turn the scales between their avoirdupois.—2 *H. IV.*, ii. 4.

In the next he satirises the vice of immoderate drinking :—

I learned it in England, where, indeed, they are most potent in potting: your Dane, your German, and your swag-bellied Hollander . . . are nothing to your English . . . he drinks you, with facility, your Dane dead drunk; he sweats not to overthrow your Almain; he gives your Hollander a vomit, ere the next pottle can be filled.—*Oth.*, ii. 3.

In the next he satirises a set of boasters who gain false reputation for courage and military experience :—

Why, 'tis a gull, a fool, a rogue, that now and then goes to the wars, to grace himself, at his return into London, under the form of a soldier.   And such fellows are perfect in the great commanders' names: and they will learn you by rote where services were done;—at such and such a sconce, at such a breach, at such a convoy; who came off bravely, who was shot, who disgraced, what terms the enemy stood on; and this they con perfectly in the phrase of war, which they trick up with new-tuned oaths: and what a beard of the general's cut, and a horrid suit of the camp, will do among foaming bottles, and ale-washed wits, is wonderful to be thought on.— *H. V.*, iii. 6.

And, in the next, another set of vapouring braggarts :—

> Scambling, out-facing, fashion-mong'ring boys,
> That lie, and cog, and flout, deprave, and slander,
> Go anticly, and show outward hideousness,
> And speak off half a dozen dangerous words,
> How they might hurt their enemies, if they durst.—*M. Ado*, v. 1.

In the following passages he satirises the absurd "laws of the duello," and the coxcombries of professed duellists :—

Cupid's butt-shaft is too hard for Hercules' club; and therefore too much odds for a Spaniard's rapier.   The first and second cause will not serve my turn; the passado he respects not, the duello he regards not: his disgrace is to be called boy; but his glory is, to subdue men.—*Love's L. L.*, i. 2.

I have had four quarrels, and like to have fought one.—And how was that ta'en up?— Faith, we met, and found the quarrel was upon the seventh cause.—How seventh cause? . . . how did you find the quarrel on the seventh cause?—Upon a lie seven times removed . . . I did dislike the cut of a certain courtier's beard: he sent me word, if I said his beard was not cut well, he was in the mind it was: this is called the Retort courteous.   If I sent him word again, it was not well cut, he would send me word, he cut it to please himself: this is called the Quip modest.   If again, it was not well cut, he disabled my judgment: this is called the Reply churlish.   If again, it was not well cut, he would answer, I spake not true: this is called the Reproof valiant.   If again, it was not well cut, he would say, I lie: this is called the Countercheck quarrelsome: and so to the Lie circumstantial and the Lie direct.—And how oft did you say, his beard was not well cut?—I durst go no farther than the Lie circumstantial, nor he durst not give me the Lie direct; and so we measured swords and parted.—Can you nominate in order now the degrees of the lie?—Oh, sir, we quarrel in print, by the book; as you have books for good manners: I will name you the degrees.   The first, the Retort courteous; the second, the Quip modest; the third, the Reply churlish; the fourth, the Reproof valiant; the fifth, the Countercheck quarrelsome; the sixth, the

Lie with circumstance; the seventh, the Lie direct. All these you may avoid, but the Lie direct; and you may avoid that too, with an "if." I knew when seven justices could not take up a quarrel; but when the parties were met themselves, one of them thought but of an "if," as, "If you said so, then I said so": and they shook hands, and swore brothers. Your "if" is the only peace-maker; much virtue in "if."—*As You L.,* v. 4.

But thou liest in thy throat * . . . Thou killest me like a rogue and a villain.—Still you keep on the windy side of the law.†—*Tw. N.,* iii. 4.

There's no remedy, sir; he will fight with you for's oath sake: marry, he hath better bethought him of his quarrel, and he finds that now scarce to be worth talking of: therefore draw, for the supportance of his vow; he protests he will not hurt you . . . Come, Sir Andrew, there's no remedy; the gentleman will, for his honour's sake, have one bout with you; he cannot by the duello avoid it: but he has promised me, as he is a gentleman and a soldier, he will not hurt you.—*Ibid.,* iii. 4.

He is the courageous captain of compliments. He fights as you sing prick-song, keeps time, distance, and proportion; rests me his minim rest, one, two, and the third in your bosom: the very butcher of a silk button, a duellist, a duellist; a gentleman of the very first house,—of the first and second cause: ah, the immortal passado! the punto reverso! the hay!—*R. & Jul.,* ii. 4.

In the following he holds up to ridicule quarrellers for quarrelling's sake; and renders the satire the more pungent by putting it into the mouth of one who picks a quarrel on the very first occasion, and loses his life thereby:—

Thou art like one of those fellows that, when he enters the confines of a tavern, claps me his sword upon the table, and says, "God send me no need of thee!" and, by the operation of the second cup, draws it on the drawer, when, indeed, there is no need . . . thou wilt quarrel with a man that hath a hair more, or a hair less, in his beard, than thou hast: thou wilt quarrel with a man for cracking nuts, having no other reason, but because thou hast hazel eyes; what eye, but such an eye, would spy out such a quarrel? Thy head is as full of quarrels, as an egg is full of meat; and yet thy head hath been beaten as addle as an egg, for quarrelling. Thou hast quarrelled with a man for coughing in the street, because he hath wakened thy dog that hath lain asleep in the sun: didst thou not fall out with a tailor for wearing his new doublet before Easter? with another, for tying his new shoes with old riband?—*Ibid.,* iii. 1.

In the following there is keen satire and fine irony of commendation implying profoundest censure, upon the reckless squandering of life and wealth in a quarrel for supposed national aggrandisement :—

Truly to speak, and with no addition,
We go to gain a little patch of ground,
That hath in it no profit but the name.
To pay five ducats, five, I would not farm it;
Nor will it yield to Norway, or the Pole,
A ranker rate, should it be sold in fee.—
Why, then the Polack never will defend it.—

---

* The phrase "in thy throat" was reckoned by the laws of duelling an inexpiable affront, when appended to the form of giving the lie. "Thou liest" might be explained away; but "thou liest in thy throat" was an affront that could only be washed out by blood.

† This refers to another appended phrase, pronounced by the laws of duelling to be an inexpiable offence, save by fighting. It was just permissible to tell a gentleman he behaved "like a rogue and a villain"; but not to say "like a rogue and a villain, *as thou art.*" Fabian hoaxingly comforts Sir Andrew by assuring him that the wording of his challenge keeps him on the safe side, and screened from the consequences of infringing the laws of honour as laid down by the duellists' code; but he omits to point out the sentence ("thou liest in thy throat") whereby he violates them.

Yes, 'tis already garrison'd.—
Two thousand souls, and twenty thousand ducats,
Will not debate the question of this straw ;
This is the imposthume of much wealth and peace,
That inward breaks, and shows no cause without
Why the man dies. . . . Examples, gross as earth, exhort me :
Witness this army, of such mass and charge,
Led by a delicate and tender prince ;
Whose spirit, with divine ambition puff'd,
Makes mouths at the invisible event ;
Exposing what is mortal, and unsure,
To all that fortune, death, and danger, dare,
Even for an egg-shell.   Rightly to be great,
Is not to stir without great argument,
But greatly to find quarrel in a straw,
When honour's at the stake. . . . I see
The imminent death of twenty-thousand men,
That, for a fantasy and trick of fame,
Go to their graves like beds ; fight for a plot
Whereon the numbers cannot try the cause,
Which is not tomb enough and continent
To hide the slain.—*Hamlet*, iv. 4.

And, in the following few lines, he gives a pungent satire upon soldiering as a profitable profession :—

What would you have me do ? go to the wars, would you ; where a man may serve seven years for the loss of a leg, and have not money enough in the end to buy him a wooden one ?—*Per.*, iv. 6.

In the following passages he satirises the affectation of larding discourse with French scraps and phrases :—

Pourquoi, my dear knight ?—What is *pourquoi?* do or not do ?—*Tw. N.*, i. 3.

Dieu vous garde, monsieur.—*Et vous aussi ; votre serviteur.*—I hope, sir, you are and I am yours.—*Ibid.*, iii. 1.

Speak it in French, king ; say, *pardonnez moy.* . . . The chopping French we do not understand.—*R. II.*, v. 3.

That is the *rendezvous* of it. . . . *Coupe le gorge !* that is the word.—*H. V.*, ii. 1.

These strange flies, these fashion-mongers, these *pardonnez-mois*, who stand so much on the new form, that they cannot sit at ease on the old bench ?   Oh, their *bons*, their *bons !* . . . Signior Romeo, *bon jour !* there's a French salutation to your French slop.—*R. & Jul.*, ii. 4.

In the following he satirises affectedly dashing and fantastical talk [*See* Affected Phraseology] :—

Noble heroes, my sword and yours are kin.   Good sparks and lustrous, a word, good metals :—you shall find in the regiment of the Spinii one Captain Spurio, with his cicatrice, an emblem of war ; here on his sinister cheek ; it was this very sword entrenched it : say to him, I live ; and observe his reports for me. . . . Mars dote on you for his novices ! . . . Use a more spacious ceremony to the noble lords ; you have restrained yourself within the list of too cold an adieu : be more expressive to them : for they wear themselves in the cap of the time, there do muster true gait, eat, speak, and move under the influence of the most received star ; and though the devil lead the measure, such are to be followed : after them, and take a more dilated farewell. —*All's W.*, ii. 1.

In the following he satirises would-be philosophers :—

They say miracles are past ; and we have our philosophical persons, to make modern and familiar, things supernatural and causeless.   Hence is it that we make trifles of terrors ; ensconcing ourselves into seeming knowledge, when we should submit ourselves to an unknown fear.—*Ibid.*, ii. 3.

In the following passages he has a gird at the pedantry of logic and rhetoric :—

Then learn this of me : to have, is to have ; for it is a figure in rhetoric, that drink, being poured out of a cup into a glass, by filling the one doth empty the other ; for all your writers do consent that *ipse* is he : now, you are not *ipse*, for I am he.—*As You L.*, v. 1.

For, as the old hermit of Prague, that never saw pen and ink, very wittily said to a niece of King Gorboduc, " That, that is, is ; " so I, being master parson, am master parson ; for what is that, but that ? and is, but is ?—*Tw. N.*, iv. 2.

In the following passages he mocks at the fashion of affecting melancholy—an affectation which was evidently a special object of detestation to his cheerful and appreciative nature :

They say you are a melancholy fellow.—
I am so ; I do love it better than laughing.—
Those that are in extremity of either are abominable fellows, and betray themselves to every modern censure worse than drunkards.—
Why, 'tis good to be sad and say nothing.—
Why, then, 'tis good to be a post.—
I have neither the scholar's melancholy, which is emulation : nor the musician's, which is fantastical ; nor the courtier's, which is proud ; nor the soldier's, which is ambitious ; nor the lawyer's, which is politic ; nor the lady's, which is nice ; nor the lover's, which is all these ; but it is a melancholy of mine own, compounded of many simples, extracted from many objects ; and, indeed, the sundry contemplation of my travels ; which, by often rumination, wraps me in a most humorous sadness.—
A traveller ! By my faith, you have great reason to be sad : I fear you have sold your own lands, to see other men's : then, to have seen much, and to have nothing, is to have rich eyes and poor hands.—
Yes, I have gained my experience.—
And your experience makes you sad : I had rather have a fool to make me merry, than experience to make me sad ; and to travel for it too !—*As You L.*, iv. 1.

By my troth, I take my young lord to be a very melancholy man . . . he will look upon his boot and sing ; mend the ruff, and sing ; ask questions, and sing ; pick his teeth, and sing. I know a man that had this trick of melancholy sold a goodly manor for a song.—*All's W.*, iii. 2.

> Yet, I remember, when I was in France,
> Young gentlemen would be as sad as night,
> Only for wantonness.—*John*, iv. 1.

In the following passages he satirises the assumption of its being an aristocratic privilege to swear :—

Not swear it, now I am a gentleman ? Let boors and franklins say it, I 'll swear it.—*W. T.*, v. 2.

> Swear me, Kate, like a lady as thou art,
> A good mouth-filling oath : and leave " in sooth,"
> And such protest of pepper gingerbread,
> To velvet-guards, and Sunday citizens.—*1 H. IV.*, iii. 1.

A rascally yea-forsooth knave ! to bear a gentleman in hand, and then stand upon security !—*2 H. IV.*, i. 2.

In the following he satirises persons who are fidgettily anxious to claim high relationship :—

Like those that are kin to the king ; for they never prick their finger but they say, " There is some of the king's blood spilt." " How comes that ? " says he, that takes upon him not to conceive. The answer is as ready as a borrower's cap, " I am the king's poor cousin, sir."—
Nay, they will be kin to us, or they will fetch it from Japhet.—*Ibid.*, ii. 2.

In the following he amusingly depicts the cutting coolness with which upstarts treat those who have suddenly become their inferiors in rank :—

> " Good den, Sir Richard " :—" God-a-mercy, fellow " ;—
> And if his name be George, I 'll call him Peter ;
> For new-made honour doth forget men's names,—
> 'Tis too respective and too sociable
> For your conversion.—*John*, i. 1.

In the following he notes the vulgar anxiety for precedence and priority :—

> Make not a city feast of it, to let the meat cool ere we can agree upon the first place : sit, sit.—*Timon*, iii. 6.

In the following brief dialogue he pithily sets forth the style in which ' back-stairs interest ' is used and succeeds in swaying the course of public justice :—

> *Davy*. I beseech you, sir, to countenance William Visor of Wincot against Clement Perkes of the hill.
> *Shallow*. There are many complaints, Davy, against that Visor : that Visor is an arrant knave, on my knowledge.
> *Davy*. I grant your worship that he is a knave, sir ; but yet, God forbid, sir, but a knave should have some countenance at his friend's request. An honest man, sir, is able to speak for himself, when a knave is not. I have served your worship truly, sir, this eight years ; and if I cannot once or twice in a quarter bear out a knave against an honest man, I have but a very little credit with your worship. The knave is mine honest friend, sir ; therefore, I beseech your worship, let him be countenanced.
> *Shallow*. Go to ; I say, he shall have no wrong.—2 *H. IV.*, v. 1.

In the following passage, and in several others [*See* ALLITERATION], Shakespeare ridicules the fashion of versifying with a profusion of words having the same commencing letter:—

> Whereas, with blade, with bloody blameful blade,
> He bravely broach'd his boiling bloody breast.—*Mid. N. D.*, v. 1.

In the concluding portion of the following he, in his own subtle vein of quiet humour, satirises the foppery of give-and-take criticism ; implying praise, implying censure, yet giving definitely neither:—

> The play, I remember, pleased not the million ; 'twas caviare to the general : but it was (as I received it, and others, whose judgments in such matters cried in the top of mine) an excellent play, well digested in the scenes, set down with as much modesty as cunning. I remember, *one said there were no sallets in the lines to make the matter savoury, nor no matter in the phrase that might indict the author of affectation ; but called it an honest method, as wholesome as sweet, and by very much more handsome than fine.*—*Hamlet*, ii. 2.

And, in the following, he satirises a wretched affectation (which prevailed in his time, and which has subsisted since among other persons besides " statists ") of writing an illegible hand as a mark of supposed superiority, and holding a clear handwriting to be a mere vulgar and mechanical accomplishment :—

> I sat me down ;
> Devis'd a new commission ; wrote it fair :—
> I once did hold it, as our statists do,
> A baseness to write fair, and labour'd much
> How to forget that learning ; but, sir, now
> It did me yeoman's service.—*Ibid.*, v. 2,

SCENIC ARRANGEMENTS.

In Shakespeare's time, stage scenery and machinery were of so meagre a kind that the dramatic author had need to rely greatly upon the vividness of his own descriptions and the imagination of his audiences, to aid in conveying impression of locality and situation.

When we remember how inadequate were theatrical representative appointments at the period he wrote, we can the more keenly appreciate our author's being equal to the need there was for power of description in such passages as those that place before our eyes the loveliness of the enchanted island in "The Tempest"; the sylvan beauties of the forest of Arden in "As You Like It"; the moonlit wood-glades in "A Midsummer Night's Dream"; the battle-fields of Agincourt, Shrewsbury, and Tewkesbury in his historical plays; his castle platforms, blasted heaths, and midnight tempests in his tragedies of "Hamlet," "Macbeth," and "Lear." When we think of the inefficient representation of shipboard that existed in his time, we the better recognise the marvellous force and poetry of his diction in such passages as those that open the play of "The Tempest," and the one that opens the third act of "Pericles"; passages that set the actors in these scenes face to face with the roar of the elements, and let us positively behold them exposed to the full sweep of the storm, on a sea-washed deck. So poor were the scenic resources in the Elizabethian era, that they consisted of little more than mere walls, hung round with well-worn tapestry. A curtain, technically called "a traverse," formed an occasional substitute for a scene, and was used as an indication of adjoining apartments, an inner room, &c.; a few boards put together served to represent towers, battlements, caves, tombs, or other such needed accessories.

The upper portion of the stage decoration, technically called "the heavens," represented the sky; but when the performance was of a tragic character, the upper and side portions of the stage were hung with black. To this particular, there is probably figurative reference in the following passage :—

Hung be the heavens with black, yield day to night.—1 *H. VI.*, i. 1.

The back of the stage was fitted up with a raised platform or balcony to which curtains were appended; and this was used when it was requisite that some of the characters in the drama should be supposed to appear at a window, or to be occupying any other elevated position overlooking the front portion of the stage, where the rest of the performers were. In the following passages, we find trace of this antique stage arrangement; and we give them as printed in the First Folio, in order the more clearly to make these particulars apparent :—

Enter aloft the drunkard with attendants, some with apparel, Bason and Ewer, and other appurtenances, and Lord.—Tam. of S., Induc. 2.

[*Exeunt.*] *The Presenters aboue speakes.*

1 *Man.* My lord, you nod, you do not minde the play.

Beg. Yes by Saint Anne do I, a good matter surely: Comes there any more of it?

Lady. My lord, 'tis but begun.

Beg. 'Tis a verie excellent peece of worke, Madame Ladie: would 'twere done. *They sit and marke.—Ibid.*, i. 1.

Enter Elianor aloft. [*See* STAGE DIRECTIONS, &c.]—2 *H. VI.*, i. 4.
Enter Richard aloft, between two Bishops.—*R. III.*, iii. 7.
Enter the King, and Buts, at a Windowe aboue.
   Buts. Ile shew your Grace the strangest sight.
   King. What's that Buts?
   Butts. I thinke your Highnesse saw this many a day.
   Kin. Body a me: where is it?
   Butts. There, my Lord:
The high promotion of his Grace of Canterbury,
Who holds his State at dore 'mongst Purseuants,
Pages, and Foot-boyes.—*H. VIII.*, v. 2.
               Enter Romeo and Juliet aloft.
  Jul. Wilt thou be gone? It is not yet neere day.—*R. & Jul.*, iii. 3.
Enter Cleopatra, and her Maides aloft, with Charmian and Iras.
   Cleo. Oh, Charmian, I will neuer go from hence. . . .
       . . . Oh, come, come, come.
               They heaue Anthony aloft to Cleopatra.
And welcome, welcome.—*Ant. & C.*, iv. 13.

The scantiness of stage appointments may be estimated by the fact that frequently a change of scene from an exterior to an interior was signified by the mere introduction of a few tables and chairs; or even by two or three words, indicative of altered place, put into the mouth of one of the speakers. In the first of the following passages, the commencement of the scene takes place in the lobby before the Council Chamber; but proceeds to display the inside of the Council Chamber itself: though the change is only indicated in the First Folio by this stage direction:—

A Councell Table brought in with Chayres and Stooles, and placed under the State. Enter Lord Chancellour, places himselfe at the vpper end of the Table, on the lefte hand: A Seate being left void aboue him, as for Canterburies Seate. Duke of Suffolke, Duke of Norfolke, Surrey, Lord Chamberlaine, Gardiner, seat themselves in Order on each side. Cromwell at lower end, as Secretary.—*H. VIII.*, v. 2.

In the second passage, there is no indication whatever in the First Folio of the locality in which the scene takes place: but the dialogue denotes that we are first supposed to see the " street " where the Soothsayer encounters Cæsar, where Artemidorus presents his petition, and where Decius presents that of Trebonius, while the imperial procession is on its way to the Capitol; and that we are subsequently supposed to behold Cæsar and his train enter the Capitol itself, where he takes his seat amid the assembled " senate." The exigencies of the successive scene require that both the outside and the inside of the Capitol should be visible to the audience during the progress of representation; but there is no other denotement in the Folio of the shifting scene than what may be gathered from the dialogue itself:—

   What! urge you your petitions in the street?
   Come to the Capitol. . . .
       . . . What is now amiss
   That Cæsar and his senate must redress?—*Jul. C.*, iii. 1.

In the third passage, the requirements of the scene demand that both the outside and the inside of Cleopatra's monument should be seen by the audience as the action progresses; and the modern editions of this play give stage directions, &c. (made up for the most part from

Plutarch's narrations of the incidents here dramatised by Shakespeare), that shall explain the situation ; but in the First Folio edition no indication is given of the scenic arrangements, which can only be inferred [*See* STAGE DIRECTIONS, &c.] :—

> You see how easily she may be surpris'd :
> Guard her till Cæsar come.
> Royal queen !
> O Cleopatra, thou art taken, queen !—*Ant. & C.*, v. 2.

In the fourth passage, the situation requires that we should see the deck of the ship, and then the cabin where Thaisa is lying apparently dead ; but the original editions give no stage direction. It is probable that at the nurse's words, " Here she lies, sir," the speaker put by a curtain—most likely the one called " a traverse "—and disclosed the recumbent figure of Pericles' wife, whom he proceeds to address in those affecting farewell terms :—

> *Lychorida.* Here she lies, sir.
> *Pericles.* A terrible child-bed hast thou had, my dear ;
> No light, no fire : the unfriendly elements
> Forgot thee utterly ; nor have I time
> To give thee hallow'd to thy grave, but straight
> Must cast thee, scarcely coffin'd, in the ooze ;
> Where, for a monument upon thy bones,
> And aye-remaining lamps, the belching whale
> And humming waters must o'erwhelm thy corpse,
> Lying with simple shells.—*Per.*, iii. 1.

In the fifth passage, the original copies of the play give no stage direction ; but the words, " Behold him," imply that a curtain was withdrawn, discovering Pericles absorbed in grief :—

> *Lysimachus.* May we not see him ?
> *Helicanus.* You may ;
> But bootless is your sight ; he will not speak
> To any.
> *Lysimachus.* Yet let me obtain my wish.
> *Helicanus.* Behold him.
> This was a goodly person,
> Till the disaster that, one mortal night,
> Drove him to this.—*Ibid.*, v. 1.

One of the stage usages of former times was the adoption of a particular garment ; which gave token that its wearer was supposed to be invisible to the audience and to the other personages engaged in the scene. It is probable that the following passage denotes the assuming such a garment by Oberon, when he says :—

> But who comes here ? *I am invisible ;*
> And I will overhear their conference.—*Mid. N. D.*, ii. 2.

Among the expedients for supplying the deficiencies of former stage representation, it was not unfrequently the custom to introduce an explanatory " apology " or " prologue," by way of justification, vindication, or elucidation :—

You shall present before her the Nine Worthies. . . . Where will you find men worthy enough to present them ?—Joshua, yourself ; myself, or this gallant gentleman, Judas Maccabæus ; this swain, because of his great limb or joint, shall pass Pompey the great ; the page Hercules,—Pardon, sir ; error : he is not quantity enough for

that Worthy's thumb : he is not so big as the end of his club.—Shall I have audience ?
he shall present Hercules in minority : his enter and exit shall be strangling a snake ;
and I will have *an apology* for that purpose.—An excellent device ! so, if any of the
audience hiss, you may cry, " Well done, Hercules ! now thou crushest the snake ! "
that is the way to make an offence gracious, though few have the grace to do it.—
Love 's L. L., v. 1.

I believe we must leave the killing out, when all is done.—Not a whit : I have a
device to make all well. Write me *a prologue ;* and let *the prologue* seem to say,
we will do no harm with our swords, and that Pyramus is not killed indeed. . . .
Therefore *another prologue* must tell he is not a lion.—*Mid. N. D.*, iii. 1.

It is among Shakespeare s merits, and forms one of the many proofs
of his being a dramatist far in advance of his own time, that he introduced such clumsy expedients as those just cited merely in burlesque
performances like the Show of the " Nine Worthies " and the Interlude
of " Pyramus and Thisbe."

SHAKESPEARE'S SELF-ILLUSTRATION AND COMMENT.

Shakespeare, of all other writers the least egoistical, gives little or no
token of himself in his writings. Shakespeare, the most perfect of
dramatists, lets little of his own individuality appear in his dramatic
characters. The only two instances we can recall where there is direct
introduction of his actual identity, in the whole course of his plays, are
the following :—

If you be not too much cloyed with fat meat, *our humble author* will continue the
story with Sir John in it.—2 *H. IV. (Epilogue).*

Thus far, with rough and all-unable pen,
Our bending author hath pursued the story.—*H. V.*, v. 2 *(Chorus).*

In the brief prefaces to his two Poems, " Venus and Adonis " and
" Lucrece " there is of course absolute personal mention ; but, to our
thinking, it is instinct with modest, manly feeling, earnest fervour, and
noble self-dedication to exalted attachment and exalted purpose : just
the expression—at once reticent yet ardent—to be expected from the
devoted friend and author, William Shakespeare. In the " Sonnets,"
there is the same spirit of modesty, fervour, and self-dedication ; but in
more intense degree, and with the utmost veiledness of diction. So
remarkable a self-revelation, couched in terms that tell nothing whatever of the person writing or the person addressed—so wonderful an
outpouring of inner heart thoughts and emotions, with no word of
betrayal concerning individual identity—we believe never existed, as
in those Sonnets. So warm with very heart-blood are they, so glowing
and impassioned are their every sentence, that we can never read them
without being moved to our own heart's core; yet there is in them
not a syllable that declares the personality of either their object or their
author.

But though, throughout his plays, there is little token of himself, yet
there are here and there certain touches from which we may gather
traces of his own tastes, predilections, opinions, and tendencies.
Markedly is deducible his passionate sense of friendship, attachment,

and preference, from several passages in his dramas [*See* APPRECIATION OF FRIENDSHIP and PARTICULAR NAMES]; while as forcibly are denoted his firm faith and pure morality by such passages as the following :—

> Who by repentance is not satisfied,
> Is nor of Heaven, nor earth ; for these are pleas'd.
> By penitence th' Eternal's wrath 's appeas'd.—*Two G. of V.*, v. 4.

> Heaven doth with us, as we with torches do,—
> Not light them for themselves; for if our virtues
> Did not go forth of us, 'twere all alike
> As if we had them not. Spirits are not finely touch'd
> But to fine issues.—*M. for M.*, i. 1.

> Our remedies oft in ourselves do lie,
> Which we ascribe to Heaven: the fated sky
> Gives us free scope ; only, doth backward pull
> Our slow designs when we ourselves are dull.—*All's W.*, i. 1.

> If powers divine
> Behold our human actions (as they do),
> I doubt not, then, but innocence shall make
> False accusation blush, and tyranny
> Tremble at patience.—*W. T.*, iii. 2.

> Heaven has an end in all.—*H. VIII.*, ii. 1.

> He, that hath the steerage of my course,
> Direct my sail!—*R. & Jul.*, i. 4.

> Love, give me strength! and strength shall help afford.—*Ibid.*, iv. 1.

> My long sickness
> Of health and living now begins to mend,
> And nothing brings me all things.—*Timon*, v. 2.

> Therein, ye gods, you make the weak most strong;
> Therein, ye gods, you tyrants do defeat:
> Nor stony tower, nor walls of beaten brass,
> Nor airless dungeon, nor strong links of iron,
> Can be retentive to the strength of spirit.—*Jul. C.*, i. 3.

> I do find it cowardly and vile,
> For fear of what might fall, so to prevent
> The time of life :—arming myself with patience,
> To stay the providence of some high powers
> That govern us below.—*Ibid.*, v. 1.

> Nature, crescent, does not grow alone
> In thewes and bulk; but, as this temple waxes,
> The inward service of the mind and soul
> Grows wide withal.—*Hamlet*, i. 3.

> Words without thoughts never to Heaven go.—*Ibid.*, iii. 3.

> Sure, He, that made us with such large discourse,
> Looking before and after, gave us not
> That capability and godlike reason,
> To fust in us unus'd.—*Ibid.*, iv. 4.

> There's a divinity that shapes our ends,
> Rough-hew them how we will.—*Ibid.*, v. 2.

There is a special providence in the fall of a sparrow. If it be now, 'tis not to come; if it be not to come, it will be now ; if it be not now, yet it will come: the readiness is all.—*Ibid.*, v. 2.

> Men must endure
> Their going hence, even as their coming hither :
> Ripeness is all.—*Lear*, v. 2.

> The gods are just, and of our pleasant vices
> Make instruments to plague us.—*Ibid.*, v. 3.

> Stoop, boys : this gate
> Instructs you how to adore the heavens, and bows you
> To morning's holy office . . . . Hail, thou fair heaven !
> We house i' the rock, yet use thee not so hardly
> As proud livers do.—Hail, heaven !—Hail, heaven !—*Cym.*, iii. 3.

> Though those that are betray'd
> Do feel the treason sharply, yet the traitor
> Stands in worse case of woe.—*Ibid.*, iii. 4.

There are none want eyes to direct them the way I am going, but such as wink, and will not use them.—*Ibid.*, v. 4.

> Love all, trust a few,
> Do wrong to none: be able for thine enemy
> Rather in power than use ; and keep thy friend
> Under thy own life's key : be check'd for silence,
> But never tax'd for speech.—*All's W.*, i. 1.

> Give thy thoughts no tongue,
> Nor any unproportion'd thought his act.
> Be thou familiar, but by no means vulgar.
> The friends thou hast, and their adoption tried,
> Grapple them to thy soul with hooks of steel ;
> But do not dull thy palm with entertainment
> Of each new-hatch'd, unfledg'd comrade.   Beware
> Of entrance to a quarrel ; but, being in,
> Bear 't, that th' opposed may beware of thee.
> Give every man thine ear, but few thy voice :
> Take each man's censure, but reserve thy judgment. . . .
> Neither a borrower, nor a lender be :
> For loan oft loses both itself and friend ;
> And borrowing dulls the edge of husbandry.
> This above all,—to thine own self be true ;
> And it must follow, as the night the day,
> Thou canst not then be false to any man.—*Hamlet*, i. 3.

The following two passages show his delicate sense of propriety in the matter of self-praise, and in the perception of what is due in questions of courtesy and frankness between man and man :—

> If it be so,
> How little is the cost I have bestow'd
> In purchasing the semblance of my soul
> From out the state of hellish cruelty !
> This comes too near the praising of myself;
> Therefore, no more of it.—*Mer. of V.*, iii. 4.

I perceive in you so excellent a touch of modesty, that you will not extort from me what I am willing to keep in ; therefore it charges me in manners the rather to express myself. . . . A lady, sir, though it was said she much resembled me, was yet of many accounted beautiful : but, though I could not, with such estimable wonder, overfar believe that, yet thus far I will boldly publish her,—she bore a mind that envy could not but call fair.—*Tw. N.*, ii. 1.

The following passages serve to evidence his trust in time as the solver of many a perplexity and present difficulty :—

> Time is the nurse and breeder of all good.—*Two G. of V.*, iii. 1.

> We must away ;
> Our waggon is prepar'd, and time revives us :
> All's well that ends well : still the fine 's the crown.—*All's W.*, iv. 4.

> What else may hap, to time I will commit.—*Tw. N.*, i. 2.

> O Time, thou must untangle this, not I ;
> It is too hard a knot for me t' untie !—*Ibid.*, ii. 2.

I must be patient till the heavens look
With an aspect more favourable.—*W. T.*, ii. 1.

Let time shape, and there an end.—*2 H. IV.*, iii. 2.

What means do you make to him ?—
Not any; but abide the change of time;
Quake in the present winter's state, and wish
That warmer days would come.—*Cym.*, ii. 4.

We 'll even all that good time will give us.—*Ibid.*, iii. 4.

All other doubts, by time let them be clear'd;
Fortune brings in some boats that are not steer'd.—*Ibid.*, iv. 3.

From the following we may gather his love of cheerfulness and brightness of temper [*See* Satire for his denouncements of cultivated melancholy] :—

With mirth and laughter let old wrinkles come ;
And let my liver rather heat with wine
Than my heart cool with mortifying groans.
Why should a man, whose blood is warm within,
Sit like his grandsire cut in alabaster ?
Sleep when he wakes ? and creep into the jaundice
By being peevish ?—*Mer. of V.*, i. 1.

He hears merry tales, and smiles not: I fear he will prove the weeping philosopher when he grows old, being so full of unmannerly sadness in his youth.—*Ibid.*, i. 2.

Frame your mind to mirth and merriment,
Which bars a thousand harms and lengthens life.—*Tam. of S., Induc.* 2.

Falstaff. . . . This same young sober-blooded boy doth not love me ; nor a man cannot make him laugh.—*2 H. IV.*, iv. 3.

Seldom he smiles ; and smiles in such a sort
As if he mock'd himself, and scorn'd his spirit
That could be mov'd to smile at anything.
Such men as he be never at heart's ease
Whiles they behold a greater than themselves ;
And therefore are they very dangerous.—*Jul. C.*, i. 2.

From the following may clearly be inferred his love of music, with belief in its potent and benign influence :—

My mirth it much displeas'd, but pleas'd my woe.—
'Tis good; though music oft hath such a charm
To make bad good, and good provoke to harm.—*M. for M.*, iv. 1.

And bring your music forth into the air.
How sweet the moonlight sleeps upon this bank !
Here will we sit, and let the sounds of music
Creep in our ears: soft stillness and the night
Become the touches of sweet harmony.
Sit, Jessica: look, how the floor of heaven
Is thick inlaid with patines of bright gold:
There 's not the smallest orb which thou behold'st
But in his motion like an angel sings,
Still quiring to the young-ey'd cherubins:
Such harmony is in immortal souls;
But whilst this muddy vesture of decay
Doth grossly close it in, we cannot hear it.

Enter Musicians.

Come, ho ! and wake Diana with a hymn :
With sweetest touches pierce your mistress' ear,
And draw her home with music.   [*Music.*

Jessica. I am never merry when I hear sweet music.
Lorenzo. The reason is your spirits are attentive :
For do but note a wild and wanton herd,

Or race of youthful and unhandled colts,
Fetching mad bounds, bellowing and neighing loud,
Which is the hot condition of their blood;
If they but hear perchance a trumpet sound,
Or any air of music touch their ears,
You shall perceive them make a mutual stand,
Their savage eyes turn'd to a modest gaze,
By the sweet power of music: therefore the poet
Did feign that Orpheus drew trees, stones, and floods;
Since naught so stockish, hard, and full of rage,
But music for the time doth change his nature.
The man that hath no music in himself,
Nor is not mov'd with concord of sweet sounds,
Is fit for treasons, stratagems, and spoils;
The motions of his spirit are dull as night,
And his affections dark as Erebus:
Let no such man be trusted.   Mark the music.—*Mer. of V.*, v. 1.

The cause why music was ordain'd!
Was it not to refresh the mind of man,
After his studies, or his usual pain?—*Tam. of S.*, iii. 1.

Music, awake her; strike!   [*Music*].—*W. T.*, v. 3.

                    [*Music.*]   Music do I hear?
Ha, ha! keep time;—how sour sweet music is,
When time is broke and no proportion kept!
So is it in the music of men's lives.
And here have I the daintiness of ear
To check time broke in a disorder'd string;
But, for the concord of my state and time,
Had not an ear to hear my true time broke.
I wasted time, and now doth time waste me; . . .
This music mads me; let it sound no more;
For though it have holp madmen to their wits,
In me it seems it will make wise men mad.
Yet, blessing on his heart that gives it me!
For 'tis a sign of love; and love to Richard
Is a strange brooch in this all-hating world.—*R. II.*, v. 5.

Let there be no noise made, my gentle friends;
Unless some dull and favorable hand
Will whisper music to my weary spirit.—
Call for the music in the other room.—*2 H. IV.*, iv. 4.

                    So please your majesty
That we may wake the king; he hath slept long.
Be govern'd by your knowledge, and proceed
I' the sway of your own will . . .
Please you draw near.   Louder the music there!—*Lear*, iv. 7.

The rough and woful music that we have,
Cause it to sound, beseech you. . . .
The music there! I pray you, give her air.
Gentlemen, this queen will live.—*Per.*, iii. 2.

That Shakespeare had a love for actors and a reverence for their vocation, which was likewise his own adopted profession, may be gathered from such passages as the following:—

I do not know the man I should avoid
So soon as that spare Cassius; . . . he loves no plays,
As thou dost, Antony; he hears no music.—*Jul. C.*, i. 2.

What players are they?—

Even those you were wont to take delight in, the tragedians of the city. . . . Good my lord, will you see the players well bestowed? Do you hear, let them be well used; for they are the abstracts and brief chronicles of the time.—*Hamlet*, ii. 2.

In the following words there is probably allusion to his own Globe theatre ; the sign of which was *Hercules carrying the Globe :*—

> Do the boys carry it away ?
> Ay, that they do, my lord; Hercules and his load too.—*Hamlet*, ii. 2.

And in the four first lines of the following, how vividly is brought to our mind the possibility that Shakespeare himself, with that extreme modesty which characterised him, and which led him to play only short parts in his own plays, often felt the eyes of the audience turned carelessly in his own direction while some better actor and the player of a more prominent part had just quitted scene :—

> As in a theatre, the eyes of men,
> After a well-graced actor leaves the stage,
> Are idly bent on him that enters next,
> Thinking his prattle to be tedious;
> Even so, or with much more contempt, men's eyes
> Did scowl on Richard.—*R. II.*, v. 2.

We find pleasant token of his liking for brother authors ; not only in traces of his calling to memory such writers as Virgil, Ovid, Plutarch, Boccaccio, Rabelais, Montaigne, Chaucer, Petrarch, Raleigh, and Spenser, but in actual quotations from his own contemporaries : as in the two first of the following passages, from Christopher Marlowe ; and in the third, from Sir Philip Sidney :—

> " To shallow rivers, to whose falls
> Melodious birds sing madrigals;
> There will we make our beds of roses,
> And a thousand fragrant posies."—*Merry W.*, iii. 1.
> Dead shepherd, now I find thy saw of might—
> " Who ever lov'd that lov'd not at first sight ? "—*As You L.*, iii. 5.
> " Have I caught my heavenly jewel ? "—*Merry W.*, iii. 3.

In the following passage he puts upon record his admiration of Italy ; which he has made the scene of several of his most romantic plays :—

> And toil'd with works of war, retir'd himself
> To Italy ; and there, at Venice, gave
> His body to that pleasant country's earth.—*R. II.*, iv. 1.

In the following touches we fancy we can perceive indications of two special points in feminine beauty which engaged Shakespeare's peculiar interest and attention as sources of attractiveness to himself; for though in the first passage " hair " seems to be lightly and playfully treated, yet, be it observed, it forms *the climax* to the enumerated requisites for winning favour :—

Till all graces be in one woman, one woman shall not come in my grace. Rich she shall be, that 's certain ; wise, or I 'll none; virtuous, or I 'll never cheapen her : fair, or I 'll never look on her; mild, or come not near me ; noble, or not I for an angel; of good discourse, an excellent musician, and her *hair* shall be of what colour it please God.—*M. Ado*, ii. 3.

> Bid him
> Report the feature of Octavia, her years,
> Her inclination, *let him not leave out*
> *The colour of her hair.*—*Ant. & C.*, ii. 5.
> Her *hair*, what colour ?—*Ibid.*, iii. 3.

> Her *voice* was ever soft,
> Gentle, and low,—an excellent thing in woman.—*Lear*, v. 3.

The following words seem to us to picture Shakespeare's own mode of sitting down to write—eager, full of his subject, the words coming at will; his teeming brains beginning a play, and seeing all its scope and bearings, ere he had well penned down the opening lines :—

> Ere I could make a prologue to my brains,
> They had begun the play,—I sat me down;
> Devis'd a new commission; wrote it fair.—*Hamlet*, v. 2.

In such points as the following, we feel as if we witnessed the author's relish of his own fun, where he makes Falstaff twice remain by himself to chuckle and witticise over the peculiarities of Justice Shallow; and where he makes Enobarbus fairly run himself out of breath in his jesting dialogue with Agrippa on the absurdities of Lepidus :—

> As I return, I will fetch off these justices: I do see the bottom of Justice Shallow. Lord, lord! how, &c.—*2 H. IV.*, iii. 2.

> If I were sawed into quantities, I should make four dozen of such bearded hermits' staves as Master Shallow. It is a wonderful thing to see, &c.—*Ibid.*, v. 1.

> 'Tis a noble Lepidus.—A very fine one: oh, how he loves Cæsar!—Nay, but how dearly, &c.—*Ant. & C.*, iii 2.

And in a repeated particular like the following, how pleasantly we detect his own enjoyment of a happy image and epithet :—

> And then the lover,
> *Sighing like furnace*, with a woful ballad
> Made to his mistress' eyebrow.—*As You L.*, ii. 7.

> There is a Frenchman his companion, one
> An eminent monsieur, that, it seems, much loves
> A Gallian girl at home : *he furnaces*
> *The thick sighs from him.*—*Cym.*, i. 7.

In scores of such vestiges as the following, we are able to discern his taste, knowledge, and observation, in rural natural philosophy :—

> The strawberry grows underneath the nettle,
> And wholesome berries thrive and ripen best,
> Neighbour'd by fruit of baser quality:
> And so the prince obscur'd his contemplation
> Under the veil of wildness; which, no doubt,
> Grew like the summer grass fastest by night;
> Unseen, yet crescive in his faculty.—*H. V.*, i. 1.

> Now, ere the sun advance his burning eye,
> The day to cheer, and night's dank dew to dry,
> I must up-fill this osier cage of ours
> With baleful weeds and precious-juiced flowers.—*R. & Jul.*, ii. 3.

> Whiles yet the dew's on ground, gather those flowers.—*Cym.*, i. 6.

The following passages have often made us speculate upon the question as to whether Will Shakespeare, notwithstanding his evident knowledge of the popular creed that beef is injurious to clearness of intellect, found this good old English* meat toothsome and wholesome for his masculine appetite :—

> What say you to a piece of beef and mustard?—
> A dish that I do love to feed upon.—*Tam. of S.*, iv. 3.

---

* For this national predilection, witness the old song :—
> Oh, the roast beef of old England!
> And, oh, the old English roast beef!

I am a great eater of beef, and I believe that does harm to my wit.—*Tw. N.*, i. 3.
Thou mongrel beef-witted lord!—*Tr. & Cr.*, ii. 1.

It is interesting to notice how this most modest and least self-obtrusive of writers has occasionally and unconsciously commented upon his own writing; and we have frequently smiled, when coming upon such passages as the following, to remark how the exigencies of the dramatic dialogue and situation, as well as the eloquent power in the words themselves, have forced upon the author the necessity of not only commenting upon his own phrases, but of commending them:—

> O! it is excellent,
> To have a giant's strength; but it is tyrannous
> To use it like a giant.—
> > *That's well said.*—*M. for M.*, ii. 2.

> Go to your bosom:
> Knock there, and ask your heart what it doth know
> That's like my brother's fault; if it confess
> A natural guiltiness such as his,
> Let it not sound a thought upon your tongue
> Against my brother's life.—
> > *She speaks, and 'tis*
> *Such sense,* that my sense breeds with it.—*Ibid.*, ii. 2.

For aught I see, they are as sick that surfeit with too much, as they that starve with nothing: it is no mean happiness, therefore, to be seated in the mean: superfluity comes sooner by white hairs: but competency lives longer.—
Good sentences, and well pronounced.—*Mer. of V.*, i. 2.

> How dost thou like this tune?—
> It gives a very echo to the seat
> Where love is thron'd.—
> > *Thou dost speak masterly.*—*Tw. N.*, ii. 4.

> And what's her history?—
> A blank, my lord. She never told her love,
> But let concealment, like a worm i' the bud,
> Feed on her damask cheek: she pin'd in thought;
> And, with a green and yellow melancholy,
> She sat like patience on a monument,
> Smiling at grief. *Was not this love indeed?*—*Ibid.*, ii. 2.

> What you do
> Still betters what is done. *When you speak,* sweet,
> *I'd have you do it ever.*—*W. T.*, iv. 3.

> I cannot say it is pity
> She lacks instructions, for *she seems a mistress*
> *To most that teach.*—*Ibid.*, iv. 3.

> *Arthur.* Are you sick, Hubert? you look pale to-day:
> In sooth, I would you were a little sick,
> That I might sit all night, and watch with you:
> I warrant, I love you more than you do me.
> > *Hubert (Aside). His words do take possession of my bosom.*—*John,* iv. 1.

Falstaff. Men of all sorts take a pride to gird at me: the brain of this foolish-compounded clay, man, is not able to invent anything that tends to laughter, *more than I invent*, or is invented on me: *I am not only witty in myself*, but the cause that wit is in other men.—*2 H. IV.*, i. 2.

> O my son,
> God put it in thy mind to take it hence,
> That thou might'st win the more thy father's love,
> *Pleading so wisely* in excuse of it!—*Ibid.*, iv. 4.

So did he turn, and over Suffolk's neck
He threw his wounded arm, and kiss'd his lips;
And so, espous'd to death, with blood he seal'd
A testament of noble-ending love.
The pretty and sweet manner of it forc'd
Those waters from me which I would have stopp'd;
But I had not so much of man in me,
And all my mother came into mine eyes,
And gave me up to tears.—
                               I blame you not;
For, *hearing this, I must perforce compound
With mistful eyes*, or they will issue too.—*H. V.*, iv. 6.

Tell me, wherein have I offended most?
Have I affected wealth, or honour? Speak.
Are my chests filled up with extorted gold?
Is my apparel sumptuous to behold?
Whom have I injur'd, that ye seek my death?
These hands are free from guiltless blood shedding,
This breast from harbouring foul deceitful thoughts.
O, let me live!—

I feel remorse in myself with his words; but I'll bridle it: he shall die, an it be but
or *pleading so well* for his life.—*2 H. VI.*, iv. 7.

These tears are my sweet Rutland's obsequies;
And every drop cries vengeance for his death,
'Gainst thee, fell Clifford, and thee, false Frenchwoman.—
Beshrew me, but *his passions move me so*,
That hardly can I check my eyes from tears.—*3 H. VI.*, i. 4.

Live each of you the subjects to his hate,
And he to yours, and all of you to God s!—
*My hair doth stand on end to hear her curses.—
And so doth mine.—R. III.*, i. 3.

                               The honour'd gods,
Keep Rome in safety, and the chairs of justice
Supplied with worthy men! plant love among us!
Throng our large temples with the shows of peace,
And not our streets with war!—
                               Amen, amen.
A noble wish.—Coriol., iii. 3.

                               Dismay'd not this
Our captains, Macbeth and Banquo?—
                               Yes;
As sparrows eagles, or the hare the lion.
If I say sooth, I must report they were
As cannons overcharg'd with double cracks;
So they redoubled strokes upon the foe:
Except they meant to bathe in reeking wounds,
Or memorize another Golgotha,
I cannot tell;—
But I am faint, my gashes cry for help.—
*So well thy words become thee as thy wounds;
They smack of honour* both.—*Macb.*, i. 2.

I would not take this* from report; *it is,
And my heart breaks at it.—Lear*, iv. 6.

First, *a very excellent good-conceited thing;* after, a wonderful sweet air, with
admirable rich words to it,—and then let her consider.

---

* "This" means the pathetic meeting between the speaker's blind father and the distracted king. We explain this, because the passage has been strangely misunderstood; one commentator complaining that there is 'some obscurity here.'

Song.

Hark, hark! the lark at heaven's gate sings,
   And Phœbus 'gins arise,
His steeds to water at those springs
   On chalic'd flowers that lies;
And winking Mary-buds begin
   To ope their golden eyes;
With every thing that pretty is,
   My lady sweet, arise;
      Arise, arise!—*Cym.*, ii. 3.

                Kneel not to me:
The power that I have on you is to spare you;
The malice towards you to forgive you: live,
And deal with others better.—

Nobly doom'd!—Ibid., v. 5.

SIMILES.

Shakespeare is always apt and forcible in his similes. He uses one, which that fine old genuine poet Chaucer also used, more apparent in its truth at the time these authors wrote than now; inasmuch as glass formerly was sufficiently blue in colour to imply the azure tint in the grey, while the crystal clearness is presented to the imagination :—

Her eyes are *grey as glass.—Two G. of V.*, iv. 4.

The following, among innumerable others that might be cited, serve to evince the strength and pertinence of Shakespeare's similes :—

But were they *false as o'er-dy'd blacks.—W. T.*, i. 2.

I have removed Falstaff's horse, and he *frets like a gummed velvet.—1 H. IV.*, ii. 2.

There 's *no more valour* in that Poins *than in a wild-duck.—Ibid.*, ii. 2.

There 's *no more faith* in thee *than in a stewed prune;* nor *no more truth* in thee *than in a drawn fox.—Ibid.*, iii. 3.

And how poetically and condensedly expressed is the following :—

His faults, in him, seem as the spots of heaven, more fiery by night's blackness.—*Ant. & C.*, i. 4.

Some of his similes are very elliptically expressed :—

This third, dull lead, with warning *all as blunt* [as the lead is dull].—*Mer. of V.*, ii. 7.

We are no tyrant, but a Christian king;
Unto whose [Christ's] grace our passion is as subject
As are our wretches fetter'd in our prisons [subject to our grace].—*H. V.*, i. 2.

To seel her father's eyes up close as [the grain of] oak.—*Oth.*, iii. 3.

There is characteristic confusion of expression in Fluellen's simile :—

If he be perjured, see you now, his reputation is as arrant a villain and a Jack-sauce, as ever his plack shoe trod upon Got's ground and his earth.—*H. V.*, iv. 7.

But in a few other of Shakespeare's similes also, we find somewhat peculiarly constructed and condensed phraseology [See Ellipses of Comparison] :—

Sleep kill those pretty eyes,
And give as soft attachment to thy senses
As infants' empty of all thought!—*Tr. & Cr.*, iv. 2.

> They call him Troilus; and on him erect
> A second hope, as fairly built as Hector.—*Tr. & Cr.*, iv. 5.
> 　　　　　　And call thee back
> With twenty hundred thousand times more joy
> Than thou went'st forth in lamentation.—*R. & Jul.*, iii. 3.
> 　　　　　　Oh, sweetest, fairest lily!
> My brother wears thee not the one half so well
> As when thou grew'st thyself.—*Cym.*, iv. 2.
> 　　　　　　One sand another
> Not more resembles that sweet rosy lad
> Who died, and was Fidele.—*Ibid.*, v. 5.

Shakespeare has some humorous similes or comparisons. In the first of the following passages, the humour is delightful of making Falstaff draw a possible likeness between his huge self in the first place to so small an object as a peppercorn, and in the second place to an animal that drags liquor about outside of him, while the speaker drags it about inside of him :—

An I have not forgotten what the inside of a church is made of, I am a peppercorn, a brewer's horse.—*1 H. IV.*, iii. 3.

You two never meet, but you fall to some discord; you are both, in good troth, as rheumatic as two dry toasts.—*2 H. IV.*, ii. 4.

His wit is as thick as Tewksbury mustard; there is no more conceit in him than is in a mallet.—*Ibid.*, ii. 4.

In the two following passages, Shakespeare uses an old proverbially employed comparison. A "door-nail" was the nail or lump of iron on which ancient door-knockers struck ; and, being subject to innumerable blows, it became a type of ultra deadness :—

> What, is the old king dead?—
> As nail in door.—*Ibid.*, v. 3.

If I do not leave you all as dead as a door-nail.—*2 H. VI.*, iv. 10.

In the following passage, he uses ironical similes :—

Why, it hath bay-windows transparent as barricadoes, and the clear stories toward the south-north are as lustrous as ebony.—*Tw. N.*, iv. 2.

In the following passages he uses the kind of meaningless comparisons, that have often been popularly favourite in familiar colloquial English :—

> What, are they broken?—
> No, they are both as whole as a fish.—*Two G. of V.*, ii. 5.

Peas and beans are as dank here as a dog.—*1 H. IV.*, ii. 1.

I am stung like a tench.—*Ibid.*, ii. 1.

The following passage contains a simile and poetical image perfectly worthy of Shakespeare himself; and though it occurs in a play of which we believe only certain portions were written by him, yet its diction is so completely his, that it appears to us to be unmistakably from his pen. It is noteworthy, however, that the five italicised lines (the three first of which form this simile) have a remarkable air of irrelevancy, as if introduced into the speech by some other hand than the one that wrote the speech itself and the main part of the scene :—

> Assign'd am I to be the English scourge.
> This night the siege assuredly I'll raise :
> *Expect Saint Martin's summer, halcyon days,*

Since I have entered into these wars.
Glory is like a circle in the water,
Which never ceaseth to enlarge itself,
Till, by broad spreading, it disperse to naught.
With Henry's death the English circle ends;
Dispersed are the glories it included.
Now am I like that proud insulting ship
Which Cæsar and his fortune bare at once.—1 *H. VI.*, i. 2.

SOLILOQUIES.

In several of his soliloquies, Shakespeare gives precisely that perplexity of expression, that half-obscure diction, which tallies with the
incomplete form that thought takes when a man communes with himself. A crowd of ideas cross the mind, a confusion of images present
themselves to the fancy, and become compounded into a train of
musing; and this is what soliloquy represents. It is thinking aloud.
And as the process of thinking takes but partially defined shape, so the
great dramatist delineates it, in many cases, with this natural indefiniteness. For instance, where the duke in " Measure for Measure "
is left alone by the calumnious ribald, Lucio, he falls into reflection upon
the impossibility there is for rulers to escape from slander; and when
left alone by Escalus, he resumes his reverie, branching into consideration of the need there is that rulers should set good example; this
branch of thought expressing itself in elliptically succinct sentences,
like the mere traces of ideas. Even the brief eight-foot line here adopted
by the poet, aids in giving this effect :—

He, who the sword of heaven will bear,
Should be as holy as severe;
Pattern in himself to know,
Grace to stand, and virtue go;
More nor less to others paying,
Than by self-offences weighing.
Shame to him whose cruel striking
Kills for faults of his own liking!
Twice treble shame on Angelo,
To weed my vice, and let his grow!
O, what may man within him hide,
Though angel on the outward side!
How may likeness, made in crimes,
Making practice on the times,
To draw with idle spiders' strings
Most pond'rous and substantial things !—*M. for M.*, iii. 2.

Observe how elliptically the third and fourth lines are allowed to
imply, ' should be himself a pattern whereby to know how grace ought
to bear itself, and how virtue ought to proceed ; ' and how in the
thirteenth line, ' be ' has to be elliptically understood before " made " in
order to furnish the consecution between the latter word and "to
draw." Again, the duke resumes this same reverie (even in the next
act and scene), when Mariana and Isabella leave him; and while
they confer together, he falls into reflection upon the theme that chiefly
engages his thoughts :—

> O, place and greatness, millions of false eyes
> Are stuck upon thee! volumes of report
> Run with these false and most contrarious quests
> Upon thy doings! thousand escapes of wit
> Make thee the father of their idle dream,
> And rack thee in their fancies.—*M. for M.*, iv. 1.

See how condensedly " contrarious " is made to express the double meaning of ' contrary to fact ' and ' contradictory to each other ; ' while " rack thee in their fancies " is allowed to imply ' stretch thy doings into enormity in their surmise,' ' torture thy conduct into the semblance of evil in their idea,' and 'mangle thy reputation by their false representations.'

> Even so it was with me when I was young ;
> If ever we are nature's, these are ours; this thorn
> Doth to our rose of youth rightly belong;
> Our blood to us, this to our blood is born ;
> It is the show and seal of nature's truth,
> Where love's strong passion is impress'd in youth :
> By our remembrances of days foregone,
> Such were our faults ;—or then we thought them none.—*All's W.*, i. 3.

Very marked is the close assemblage of ideas and elliptical construction in this soliloquy. It exactly represents the effect of broken or interrupted thought, checked by other crossing or interposing thoughts ; and of the passing of these through the mind, presented to the speaker's imagination rather than uttered aloud. The old countess first reflects, ' Even thus it was with me when I was young like Helena ; ' then she proceeds to the more general consideration, ' If ever we have been thoroughly natural, or true to nature, such as these are our impulses ; this thorn and spur to love is an innate part of the rose and loveliness of youth ; as our blood is native to us, so is this impulse of affection native to our blood (" blood " signifying ' inherent quality or disposition ') ; it is the evidence and token of nature's truth where love's strong passion is felt in youth ; and by our own remembrances of our past days, we know that such were our own impulsive faults—or, rather, we then thought them no faults, but natural feelings.'

> I will, my lord: God give your grace good rest ! [CLARENCE *sleeps.*
> Sorrow breaks seasons and reposing hours,
> Makes the night morning, and the noon-tide night.
> Princes have but their titles for their glories,
> An outward honour for an inward toil ;
> And, for unfelt imaginations,
> They often feel a world of restless cares :
> So that, between their titles and low name,
> There 's nothing differs but the outward fame.—*R. III.*, i. 4.

The two lines previous to the concluding couplet we interpret thus :— ' And, instead of pleasures of imagination which they never experience, they often experience a multitude of restless cares.' This is a reflection naturally growing out of Clarence's description of his late dreams ; which, instead of being filled with images of beauty and peace, are crowded with troublous and terrible visions. The passage is rendered somewhat obscure in effect from the employment of the word " for " ; which is twice used in its ordinary sense, and the third time is used in the sense of ' instead of.' But there is also intentional obscurity of effect; as representing the dimly expressed thoughts that pass through the brain of a soliloquiser.

> Farewell, a long farewell, to all my greatness!
> This is the state of man: to-day he puts forth
> The tender leaves of hope; to-morrow blossoms,
> And bears his blushing honours thick upon him;
> The third day comes a frost, a killing frost,
> And,—when he thinks, good easy man, full surely
> His greatness is a-ripening,—nips his root,
> And then he falls as I do. I have ventur'd,
> Like little wanton boys that swim on bladders,
> This many summers in a sea of glory;
> But far beyond my depth: my high-blown pride
> At length broke under me; and now has left me,
> Weary and old with service, to the mercy
> Of a rude stream, that must for ever hide me.
> Vain pomp and glory of this world, I hate ye:
> I feel my heart new open'd. O, how wretched
> Is that poor man that hangs on princes' favours!
> There is betwixt that smile we would aspire to,
> That sweet aspect of princes, and their ruin,
> More pangs and fears than wars or women have:
> And when he falls, he falls like Lucifer,
> Never to hope again.—*H. VIII.*, iii. 2.

Throughout this soliloquy the pronouns are made to vary most remarkably, changing in accordance with the fluctuations of thought that pour through the speaker's mind. First, there is, " *my* greatness;" then come, " *he* puts forth," " *his* blushing honours thick upon *him*," " when *he* thinks," " *his* greatness," " *his* root," and " *he* falls," closing with " as *I* do." This is succeeded by the more directly personal " *I* have ventur'd," " *my* depth," " *my* high-blown pride," " broke under *me*," " left *me*," " hide *me*," " *I* hate ye," and " *I* feel *my*." Then, again, comes the more general reflection, " that poor man, &c.," followed by a kind of parenthetical observation respecting " that smile *we* would aspire to," and " that sweet aspect of princes, and *their* ruin; " and when the speaker has ended it, he returns suddenly to the close of the reflection upon him who " when *he* falls, *he* falls, &c." The expression " their ruin " elliptically implies ' the ruin caused by their wrath.'

> This she? no, this is Diomed's Cressida:
> If beauty have a soul, this is not she;
> If souls guide vows, if vows be sanctimonies,
> If sanctimony be the gods' delight,
> If there be rule in unity itself,
> This is not she. O, madness of discourse,
> That cause sets up with and against itself!
> Bi-fold authority! where reason can revolt
> Without perdition, and loss assume all reason
> Without revolt: this is, and is not, Cressid!
> Within my soul there doth conduce a fight
> Of this strange nature, that a thing inseparate
> Divides more wider than the sky and earth,
> And yet the spacious breadth of this division
> Admits no orifice for a point, as subtle
> As Arachne's broken woof, to enter.

This passionate speech is not addressed to Ulysses, although he is with its speaker, Troilus. It is an outburst of distracted thought, an attempt to persuade himself that the false woman he has just seen is not his Cressida, even while conscious that she is no other than her own heartless self. It is a series of abrupt agitated sentences, yet with a link of consecution running through them all; it disputes identity, and tries to disprove the individuality his own eyes have witnessed. The expression, "if there be rule in unity itself," means, 'if there be truth in identity;' that one person cannot be more or other than one. "Discourse" is here used for 'ratiocination;' "conduce" has its classical sense of 'lead together,' 'assemble;' and "a fight" signifies the elements of a fight, the contending forces, the conflicting feelings, the battling emotions that surge and meet tumultuously within the speaker's soul, brought together by the strength of passion. Lastly, we take "a thing inseparate," &c., to mean, 'a thing so inseparable as personal individuality'—Cressida's identity with herself—'becomes in my mind more widely divided than are the sky and the earth, and yet I am perfectly aware that in all this space which my imagination would fain establish, there exists no opening for admission of proof even so minute as a spider's web.'

> How if, when I am laid into the tomb,
> I wake before the time that Romeo
> Come to redeem me? There's a fearful point!
> Shall I not, then, be stifled in the vault,
> To whose foul mouth no healthsome air breathes in,
> And there die strangled ere my Romeo comes?
> Or, if I live is it not very like,
> The horrible conceit of death and night,
> Together with the terror of the place,—
> As in a vault, an ancient receptacle,
> Where, for these many hundred years, the bones
> Of all my buried ancestors are pack'd;
> Where bloody Tybalt, yet but green in earth,
> Lies festering in his shroud; where, as they say,
> At some hours in the night spirits resort;—
> Alack, alack, is it not like that I,
> So early waking,—what with loathsome smells,
> And shrieks like mandrakes' torn out of the earth,
> That living mortals, hearing them, run mad;—
> O, if I wake, shall I not be distraught,
> Environed with all these hideous fears?
> And madly play with my forefathers' joints?
> And pluck the mangled Tybalt from his shroud?
> And, in this rage, with some great kinsman's bone,
> As with a club, dash out my desperate brains.—*R. & Jul.*, iv. 3.

The construction is inconsecutive in this soliloquy; admirably serving to mark the wild agitation of the speaker. Juliet commences with, "If I live is it not very like," &c.; then goes on to appal herself with images of horror till she resumes with, "Alack, alack, is it not like that I, so early waking," &c., and again loses herself in terrors until she breaks off unfinishedly and a third time resumes disjointedly with, "O, if I wake, shall I not," &c.

> Good king, that must approve the common saw,—
> Thou out of heaven's benediction com'st

> To the warm sun!
> Approach, thou beacon to this under globe,
> That by thy comfortable beams I may
> Peruse this letter! Nothing, almost, sees miracles
> But misery: I know 'tis from Cordelia,
> Who hath most fortunately been inform'd
> Of my obscurèd course; and shall find time
> From this enormous state,—seeking to give
> Losses their remedies,—All weary and o'er-watch'd,
> Take vantage, heavy eyes, not to behold
> This shameful lodging.
> Fortune, good night: smile once more; turn thy wheel!   [*Sleeps.*
> *Lear*, ii. 2.

Besides the usual natural inexplicitness of wording which Shakespeare gives to some of his soliloquies, he here still farther marks disconnection of ideas and disjunction of sentences. Kent, put into the stocks by Lear's granite-natured daughter Regan, resolves to sleep out the time of his ignoble punishment; and, left by himself, while dropping off into slumber, he muses upon passing events. He first illustrates his fear that the old king will be likely to receive even worse treatment from Regan than that which he has experienced from Goneril by allusion to the old adage, " He goes out of God's blessing to the warm sun," viz., from good to worse; then he bids the sun arise, that by its beams he may see to read a letter that he has received from Cordelia; then comes a passing reflection upon there being no condition like a lowly one for seeing miracles—suggested by his own disguise as a serving-man, which may perchance enable him to behold the miracle of redress for the present unnatural state of affairs; then he returns to consideration of the letter from Cordelia, who has had intelligence of his disguised procedure, and who,* he trusts, shall find time and opportunity from this irregular state of things (to convert it into duer order)—endeavouring to give lost positions their due remedies (by reinstating her father in his kingdom, and restoring the speaker to his earldom); lastly, finding himself unable to pursue his train of ideas or to express them coherently, he interrupts himself with, " All weary and o'erwatch'd," &c., and resolves to rest.

> O Posthumus! alas,
> Where is thy head? where's that?   Ah me, where's that?
> Pisanio might have kill'd thee at the heart,
> And left this head on.—*Cym.*, v. 2.

The finely dramatic soliloquy, of which this is a portion, admirably serves to depict the condition of mind in which its speaker, Imogen, awakes from the trance produced by the drug she has swallowed; and, in the passage here cited, the expression " this head "—which has been objected to and even altered by some of the commentators—appears to us to be advisedly used by Shakespeare for the purpose of marking the perturbation of the soliloquiser.

> I heard no letter from my master since
> I wrote him Imogen was slain: 'tis strange:

---

* The " who " before " hath most fortunately," is elliptically understood as repeated before " shall find time."

> Nor hear I from my mistress, who did promise
> To yield me often tidings; neither know I
> What is betid to Cloten; but remain
> Perplex'd in all: the heavens still must work.
> Wherein I am false I am honest; not true, to be true;
> These present wars shall find I love my country,
> Even to the note o' the king, or I'll fall in them.—*Cym.*, iv. 3.

The phrase, "I heard no letter from my master," has been pronounced inaccurate, and proposals have been made to change "I heard" to 'I've had,' or 'I had.' But "I heard" not only accords with, "Nor hear I from my mistress," it seems like a familiarism of soliloquy or thinking aloud; since there is a familiar idiom, 'I heard no word from him,' when it is meant that no letter has been received. The whole phraseology of this soliloquy is in the same tone of concise expression: "not true, to be true," signifying, 'I am apparently not true to my employers, in order that I may be true to my own master and mistress'; and "even to the note o' the king," meaning, 'even until the proof I give of it shall attract the king's notice.'

> Why should this change of thoughts,
> The sad companion, dull-ey'd melancholy,
> Be my so us'd a guest as not an hour,
> In the day's glorious walk, or peaceful night
> (The tomb where grief should sleep), can breed me quiet?
> Here pleasures court mine eyes, and mine eyes shun them,
> And danger, which I fear'd, is at Antioch,
> Whose arm seems far too short to hit me here:
> Yet neither pleasure's art can joy my spirits,
> Nor yet the other's distance comfort me.
> Then it is thus: the passions of the mind,
> That have their first conception by mis-dread,
> Have after-nourishment and life by care;
> And what was first but fear what might be done,
> Grows elder now, and cares it be not done.—*Per.*, i. 2.

The musing fit is here denoted by the style of diction, which is dreamily reflective. To follow the train of idea, it is requisite to bear in mind that "this change of thoughts" implies both 'this conflicting interchange of thoughts, the one with the other in my mind,' and 'this alteration of my thoughts from their previous cheerfuller course'; and also to bear in mind that "elder" is here used in the peculiar manner in which Shakespeare sometimes employs this word. In the present passage it includes the senses of 'larger,' 'stronger,' 'more confirmed,' 'more established,' and 'more advanced in time,' 'having attained to a later period.'

As instances of Shakespeare's power in writing brief but most effective soliloquies, we cite the two following; each intensely significant in its peculiar kind. The one is where Troilus is awaiting the coming of Cressida, when she is to give herself to his arms in fulness of possession:—

> I am giddy; expectation whirls me round.
> The imaginary relish is so sweet
> That it enchants my sense: what will it be,
> When that the watery palate tastes indeed

> Love's thrice-repurèd* nectar ? death, I fear me ;
> Swooning destruction ; or some joy too fine,
> Too subtle-potent, turn'd too sharp in sweetness,
> For the capacity of my ruder powers :
> I fear it much ; and I do fear besides,
> That I shall lose distinction in my joys ;
> As doth a battle, when they charge on heaps
> The enemy flying.—*Tr. & Cr.*, iii. 2.

The other is where we first see Lady Macbeth *alone*, after her achievement of royalty—that object of ambition for which she has bartered all self-respect, all peace of mind. It is a wonderful condensation of moral homily into three lines and a half of soliloquy :—

> Naught's had, all's spent,
> Where our desire is got without content :
> 'Tis safer to be that which we destroy,
> Than, by destruction, dwell in doubtful joy.—*Macb.*, iii. 2.

There are three notable instances given by our supreme dramatist of a person permitting the thoughts to wander off into soliloquy spoken aside, in the presence of others ; when an engrossing subject wholly occupies the mind and will not be contented to lie silently undiscussed, but must needs have the vent of self-communing at once. In each case, the language is singularly veiled—even obscure—as befits the theme reflected upon ; and serves to show Shakespeare's refinement in expression combined with vigour in dealing with the most hallowed as well as the most unhallowed subjects of meditation :—

> But, O, strange men !
> That can such sweet use make of what they hate,
> When saucy trusting of the cozen'd thoughts
> Defiles the pitchy night ! so lust doth play
> With what it loathes, for that which is away :
> But more of this hereafter.—*All's W.*, iv. 4.

> Affection ! thy intention stabs the centre ;
> Thou dost make possible things not so held,
> Communicat'st with dreams !—(how can this be ?)—
> With what's unreal thou coactive art,
> And fellow'st nothing : then 'tis very credent,
> Thou may'st co-join with something ; and thou dost,—
> And that beyond commission ; and I find it,—
> And that to the infection of my brains,
> And hardening of my brows.—*W. T.*, i. 2.

> This supernatural soliciting
> Cannot be ill ; cannot be good :—if ill,
> Why hath it given me earnest of success,
> Commencing in a truth ? I am thane of Cawdor :
> If good, why do I yield to that suggestion
> Whose horrid image doth unfix my hair,
> And make my seated heart knock at my ribs,

---

* The Quarto reading of " repured " seems to us to be greatly preferable to the Folio reading, ' reputed.' " Thrice-repured," signifying ' thrice-purified,' ' trebly pure, ' quintessentially refined,' seems to us far more likely to be Shakespeare's word ; as he constantly maintains the principle that love is the purest of essences, as well as the most purifying and ennobling. By way of illustrating this principle of his, no less than for the sake of determining the right word in the present passage, we have observed how very frequently in his works the word " pure " and the word " love " are to be found in combination.

> Against the use of nature? Present fears
> Are less than horrible imaginings :
> My thought, whose murder yet is but fantastical,
> Shakes so my single state of man, that function
> Is smother'd in surmise ; and nothing is
> But what is not.—*Macb.,* i. 3.

There are some peculiar forms used in soliloquy, of which instances are to be found in Shakespeare's plays. One form is as if the speaker were addressing an imaginary auditor :—

My grandam, having no eyes, *look you,* wept herself blind at my parting. Nay, I'll show *you* the manner of it. . . . *Now, sir,* this staff is my sister; for, *look you,* she is as white as a lily, and as small as a wand. . . . *Mark* the moan she makes. Now, the dog all this while sheds not a tear, nor speaks a word; but *see* how I lay the dust with my tears.—*Two G. of V.,* ii. 3.

I am but a fool, *look you ;* and yet I have the wit to think, my master is a kind of a knave. . . . "Item, she can milk;" *look you,* a sweet virtue in a maid with clean hands.—*Ibid.,* iii. 1.

> *Now, sir,* the sounds that tell what hour it is,
> Are clamorous groans, that strike upon my heart,
> Which is the bell.—*R. II.,* v. 5.

O, *you shall see* him laugh, till his face be like a wet cloak ill laid up !—2 *H. IV.,* v. 1.

It is this same form of appeal to an imaginary auditor that is used in the following passage, not an address to any one of the bystanders ; and it serves to give a heightened effect of impassioned derision to the words which Queen Margaret utters, as she sets a paper crown on the defeated York's head :—

Ay, marry, *sir,* now looks he like a king !—2 *H. VI.,* i. 4.

What a pagan rascal is this! an infidel! Ha! *you shall see now,* in very sincerity of fear and cold heart, will he to the king, and lay open all our proceedings.—1 *H. IV.,* ii. 3.

Soft! who art thou? Sir Walter Blunt! *there's honour for you !*—*Ibid.,* v. 3.

> *Soft you now !*
> The fair Ophelia.—*Hamlet,* iii. 1.

There is another form employed in soliloquy which Shakespeare has used in the magnificent speech of self-communing that he has put into the mouth of Henry V. after having the night interview in disguise with the three soldiers of his camp, Bates, Court, and Williams. At the opening of the soliloquy " our " is used in reference to those in whose person the king is musingly speaking ; though he immediately follows it by " we " in reference to himself, as speaking in his own person. This is admirably true to nature : it is precisely that inexact mode of expression which thoughts take in the mind, and which soliloquy represents :—

> Upon the king! let us *our* lives, *our* souls,
> *Our* debts, *our* careful wives,
> *Our* children, and *our* sins, lay on the king!
> We must bear all. O, hard condition,
> Twin-born with greatness, subject to the breath
> Of every fool, whose sense no more can feel
> But his own wringing !—*H. V.,* iv. 1.

Still another form is used in the soliloquy spoken by York, at the close of the opening scene in the " Second Part of King Henry VI.,"

where he employs the word " thine " to express that which belongs to
the community generally, and to himself in particular; since he goes on
to say that the realms of England, France, and Ireland seem to be a
portion of his own flesh and blood, and that he had hope of possessing
France as he hoped to possess England :—

> Anjou and Maine are given to the French;
> Paris is lost; the state of Normandy
> Stands on a tickle point, now they are gone:
> Suffolk concluded on the articles:
> The peers agreed; and Henry was well pleas'd
> To change two dukedoms for a duke's fair daughter.
> I cannot blame them all: what is 't to them?
> 'Tis *thine* they give away, and not their own.—*2 H. VI.*, i. 1.

And yet another form is used in the same play :—

> This devil here shall be my substitute;
> For that John Mortimer, which now is dead,
> In face, in gait, in speech, he doth resemble:
> By this I shall perceive the commons' mind,
> How they affect the house and claim of York.
> *Say*, he be taken, rack'd, and tortur'd,
> I know no pain they can inflict upon him,
> Will make him say I mov'd him to those arms.
> *Say*, that he thrive (as 'tis great like he will),
> Why, then from Ireland come I with my strength,
> And reap the harvest which that rascal sow'd.—*Ibid.*, iii. 1.

Occasionally Shakespeare with excellent dramatic effect makes a
soliloquy commence abruptly, with a reference to something or some
one unspecified, except by a pronoun :—

> I have sent after *him : he* says *he* 'll come;
> How shall I feast *him ?* what bestow of *him ?*
> For youth is bought more oft than begg'd or borrow'd.—*Tw. N.*, iii. 4.

Here, not only is the person alluded to spoken of vaguely and left
unnamed, but the diction is likewise so hurried and sketchy, that it
leaves to be elliptically understood ' if,' ' supposing,' or ' granted that,'
before " he says he 'll come."

> Leave me solely: go,
> See how he fares. [*Exit* ATTENDANT.] Fie, fie! no thought of *him ;*
> The very thought of my revenges that way
> Recoil upon me: in *himself* too mighty,
> And in *his* parties, *his* alliance,—let *him* be,
> Until a time may serve: for present vengeance,
> Take it on *her*.—*W. T.*, ii. 3.

Here, the pronoun " he " refers to Mamillius, who has just been
spoken of; but " him," in the same line, refers to Polixenes, who has
not been mentioned. The speaker first gives the order respecting his
little son Mamillius; and then, the moment the Attendant departs,
resumes his bitter musing upon his supposed injurer, Polixenes.

> My birth-place hate I, and my love 's upon
> This enemy town. I 'll enter: if *he* slay me,
> *He* does fair justice: if *he* give me way,
> I 'll do *his* country service.—*Coriol.*, iv. 4.

> It must be by *his* death: and for my part,
> I know no personal cause to spurn at *him*,
> But for the general. *He* would be crown'd:
> How that might change *his* nature, there 's the question.—*Jul. C.*, ii. 1.

SPELLING OF FOREIGN WORDS.

Shakespeare gave an anglicised spelling of certain foreign words, as a means of indicating to the actors the mode in which these words should be pronounced. Thus, he spells *Petruccio*, " Petruchio ; " showing that the Italian " cc " before " i " is sounded as " ch " is sounded in English :—

My good friend *Petruchio !* How do you all at Verona ?—*Tam. of S.*, i. 2.

In the following passage the word " Strachy " has much puzzled several of the commentators ; who have proposed various substitutions. But we believe it to be Shakespeare's way of anglicising the spelling of the Italian word *Stracci.* In Florio's Dictionary, a book proved to be well known to Shakespeare, we find the word printed " *Straccij*," and there explained to mean 'rags, clouts, tatters, torne or rent rags.' Our dramatist has put " Strachy " into the mouth of Malvolio with a " the " before it, as if it were the name of a noble family of Italy, like the Strozzi, the Orsini, &c. ; thus, while " the lady of the Strachy " seems to be the title of a lady of rank, it really bears the significance of ' the lady of rags-and-tatters,' forming a humorous analogy with " the yeoman of the wardrobe." In corroboration of our belief, we find, under the word *Vestiario* in Florio's Dictionary, ' one that sels clothes ready made. Also a wardrobe keeper, or *a yeoman of a wardrobe*.' The Italian form of ' j ' for a final ' i,' as printed in Florio, gives very much the effect of the final ' y,' as printed in the First Folio, and as probably written by Shakespeare in the word " Strachy " :—

The lady of the *Strachy* married the yeoman of the wardrobe.—*Tw. N.*, ii. 5.

In the following passage, although modern editions agree to print the word " capriccio " rightly in its Italian form, yet the First Folio, and probably Shakespeare himself in his original manuscript, in order to suggest to the actors the mode of pronunciation, spelt the word thus, —' caprichio ' :—

Will this *capriccio* hold in thee, art sure ?—*All's W.*, ii. 3.

Similarly, in the Folio (and probably by Shakespeare himself) " Capucius " is spelt ' Capuchius':—

You should be lord ambassador from the emperor,
My royal nephew, and your name *Capucius.*—*H. VIII.*, iv. 2.

In the following passage, the name of the Clown is spelt "Lavatch," to convey to the actors an idea of the pronunciation of what is evidently intended for a French word. It has been believed by some commentators that this was intended for *La Vache*, in punning allusion to the name of the actor who played the part, either Richard *Cowley* or John Lowine (lowing). But we incline to think that it was probably intended for *Lavage ;* which, in familiar French language, is used to express ' slop,' ' puddle,' ' washiness.' The context seems to warrant our supposition :—

Good Monsieur *Lavatch*, give my lord Lafeu this letter : I have ere now, sir, been better known to you, when I have held familiarity with fresher clothes; but I am now, sir, muddied in fortune's mood, and smell somewhat strong of her strong displeasure. —*All's W.*, v. 2.

In the following instance, modern editions give the French name, "Biron," with its proper orthography; but the First Folio prints it sometimes 'Beroune' and sometimes 'Berowne,' to show that the accent is laid on the last syllable, and to indicate something of its mode of pronunciation. This latter seems to have been 'Biroon;' since, in the passage we cite, the name is made to rhyme with "moon":—

> My love, her mistress, is a gracious moon;
> She an attending star, scarce seen a light.—
> My eyes are, then, no eyes, nor I *Biròn:*
> Oh, but for my love, day would turn to night!—*Love's L. L.,* iv. 3.

In the following instance, Shakespeare spells the French name he uses with its due orthography; although in French, it would be pronounced without sounding the final 't.' However, in the passage we cite, he gives us reason to suppose that in his time this letter may have been sounded; since he makes the name rhyme with "debt":—

> And consciences, that will not die in debt,
> Pay him the due of honey-tongued *Boyet.*—*Ibid.,* v. 2.

STAGE DIRECTIONS AND ENTRANCES.

It is interesting to observe the meagreness of the stage directions in the earliest printed copies of Shakespeare's plays, probably those which he himself gave in his original manuscript copies, and which formed the only indications of some of those fine dramatic situations known to us as occurring in his dramas. Modern editions of his plays have given fuller and more precisely detailed versions of these old stage directions; mostly gathered from the text of the dialogue and the requisites of the stage situation implied by the incidents of the story or plot, or from historical sources recording the particulars dramatised. In some cases the old stage directions have been merely amplified or slightly varied in the wording :—

(Folio.)—*Enter Claudio, Prince, and three or foure with Tapers.*—*M. Ado,* v. 3.

(Modern.)—Scene III.—*The inside of a church. Enter* Don Pedro, Claudio, *and* Attendants, *with music and tapers.*—*Ibid.,* v. 3.

(Folio.)—*Clow.* I haue a reasonable good eare in musicke. Let us haue the tongs and the bones. *Musicke Tongs, Rurall Musicke.*—*Mid. N. D.,* iv. 1.

(Modern.)—*Bottom.* I have a reasonable good ear in music: let us have the tongs and the bones. [The stage direction omitted; since Titania goes on to ask, "Or, say sweet love, what thou desir'st to eat": which gives it to be inferred that it was not the poet-author, but the theatrical manager, who inserted this stage direction, that a treat might be afforded to those among the audience who had asses' ears as well as Bully Bottom.—*Ibid.,* iv. 1.

(Folio.)—*Enter the Witch, the two Priests, and Bullingbroke. . . . Enter Elianor aloft* [*See* Scenic Arrangements for a description of the platform or balcony at the back of the stage, in use formerly for those scenes where some of the actors were to occupy a window, a terrace, or other elevated position].—2 *H. VI.,* i. 4.

(Modern.)—Scene IV.—*London. The* Duke of Gloster's *garden. Enter* Margery Jourdain, Hume, Southwell, *and* Bolingbroke. . . . *Enter* Duchess *above; and presently* Hume.—*Ibid.,* i. 4.

(Folio.)—*Enter two or three running ouer the Stage,* from the *Murther of Duke Humfrey. . . . King sounds. . . . Noyse within. Enter Warwicke, and many Commons. . . . Bed put forth.*—2 *H. VI.*, iii. 2.

(Modern.)—SCENE II.—*Bury. A room in the palace. Enter certain* MURDERERS, *hastily. . . . The* KING *swoons . . . Noise within. Enter* WARWICK *and* SALISBURY. *The* COMMONS *press to the door. . . .* WARWICK *goes into an inner chamber.* SALISBURY *retires to the* COMMONS *at the door. . . . The doors of the inner chamber are thrown open, and* GLOSTER *is discovered dead in his bed;* WARWICK *and others standing by it.*—*Ibid.*, iii. 2.

(Folio.)—*Enter the King, Salisbury, and Warwicke to the Cardinal in bed.*—*Ibid.*, iii. 3.

(Modern.)—SCENE III.—*London.* CARDINAL BEAUFORT'S *bedchamber. Enter* KING HENRY, SALISBURY, WARWICK, *and others. The* CARDINAL *in bed;* ATTENDANTS *with him.*—*Ibid.*, iii. 3.

(Folio.)—*Alarum. Fight at Sea. Ordnance goes off. Enter Lieutenant, Suffolke, and others.*—*Ibid.*, iv. 1.

(*Modern.*)—SCENE I.—*Kent. The sea-shore near Dover. Firing heard at sea. Then enter, from a boat, a* CAPTAIN, *a* MASTER, *a* MASTER'S MATE, WALTER WHITMORE *and others; with them* SUFFOLK *disguised, and other* GENTLEMEN *prisoners.*—*Ibid.*, iv. 1.

(Folio.)—*Enter Gabriel* [supposed to have been meant for the name of the actor (possibly, Gabriel Spencer) who played the part].—3 *H. VI.*, i. 2.

(Modern.)—*Enter a* MESSENGER.—*Ibid.*, i. 2.

(Folio.)—*Enter one blowing* [this quaint description of the panting Messenger's arrival is illustrated by Shakespeare's own words in "The Merry Wives of Windsor," iii. 3: "Here's Mistress Page at the door, sweating and *blowing*, and looking wildly, and would need speak with you presently"].—*Ibid.*, ii. 1.

(Modern.)—*Enter a* MESSENGER.—*Ibid.*, ii. 1.

(Folio.)—*Enter Sinklo, and Humfrey, with Crosse-bowes in their hands* [supposed to have been meant for the two actors who played the parts.—These vestiges of Shakespeare's fellow-actors are interesting, and worth tracing].—*Ibid.*, iii. 1.

(Modern.)—SCENE I.—*A Chase in the North of England. Enter two* KEEPERS, *with cross-bows in their hands.*—*Ibid.*, iii. 1.

(Folio.)—*Enter Henry the Sixt, and Richard, with the Lieutenant on the Walles.* [This shows that the Lieutenant, though within sight and hearing of the royal prisoner, was intended to be aloof mounting guard; and that the outside as well as inside of the apartment were supposed to be apparent to the audience. *See* SCENIC ARRANGEMENTS.]—*Ibid.*, v. 6.

(Modern.)—SCENE VI.—*London. A room in the Tower.* King HENRY *is discovered sitting with a book in his hand, the* LIEUTENANT *attending. Enter* GLOSTER.—*Ibid.*, v. 6.

(Folio.)—*Exit Lord Chamberlaine, and the King drawes the Curtaine and sits reading pensiuely.* [This "curtaine" was "the traverse"; for an account of which *see* SCENIC ARRANGEMENTS.]—*H. VIII.*, ii. 2.

(Modern.)—*Exit* LORD CHAMBERLAIN. NORFOLK *opens a folding-door. The* KING *is discovered sitting, and reading pensively.*—*Ibid.*, ii. 2.

(Folio.)—*Thunder. Enter the three Witches. . . . Enter Hecat, and the other three Witches.*—*Macb.*, iv. 1.

(Modern.)—SCENE I.—*A dark cave. In the middle, a cauldron boiling. Thunder. Enter the three* WITCHES. *. . . Enter* HECATE. [The sentence, "the other three witches," is omitted; because it appears improbable that Shakespeare intended more than the three weird sisters already known to Macbeth to be upon the stage during his present interview with them, and because it was sometimes in old plays the custom to make a stage direction that announced the entrance of a fresh person on the scene likewise recapitulate those already present.]—*Ibid.*, iv. 1.

In other cases, stage directions have been given in modern editions of Shakespeare's plays, although in the early printed copies no stage directions at all were given with these passages ; the needful particulars being either deduced from the dialogue text, from the situation, or from known historical details :—

Thurio. Farewell.   [*Exeunt* THURIO *and Musicians.*
           Enter SILVIA *above, at her window.*
Proteus. Madam, good even to your ladyship.—*Two G. of V.*, iv. 2.
Eglamour. . . . Madam, madam !
           Enter SILVIA *above, at her window.*
Silvia. Who calls?—*Ibid.*, iv. 3.
Grumio. . . . and thereby hangs a tale.
Curtis. Let 's ha' 't, good Grumio.
Grumio. Lend thine ear.
Curtis. Here.
Grumio (Striking him). There.
Curtis. This is to feel a tale, not to hear a tale.—*Tam. of S.*, iv. 1.

    SCENE IV.—*Grounds adjoining* OLIVIA'S *house.*—*Tw. N.*, iii. 4.

There is no stage direction in the Folio to indicate the place where this scene passes ; and in most modern editions it is stated to be " Olivia's garden " ; but the incidents that take place towards the end of the scene—the duel, the entrance of Antonio, the coming of the officers—all show it to be more public ground than the garden inclosure round the Countess's house ; and accordingly, in our editions of the poet, this stage direction stands as here given.

Shepherd. . . . (*Seeing the child*) Good luck, an 't be thy will ! what have we here ? Mercy on 's, a barne ; a very pretty barne ! . . . I 'll take it up for pity: yet I 'll tarry till my son come.—*W. T.*, iii. 3.

Some modern editions give " taking up the child " in the above passage ; but the text shows that the Shepherd merely sees the babe lying on the ground at first, and does not " take it up " till afterwards.

    SCENE I.—*Northampton. A room in the castle.*—*John*, iv. 1.

" Northampton " has generally been made the locality of this scene ; because there is mention of " Northamptonshire " in the first scene of the play, and because Northampton is known to have been occasionally the royal residence in the time of King John. However, history records Valaise to have been the place of Prince Arthur's imprisonment, and Rouen to have been that of his death.

        [*Trumpet sounds.*]
    What lusty trumpet thus doth summon us ?—*Ibid.*, v. 2.

This stage direction—given in all modern editions, because of the words in the text that follow it—we think is also implied in a previous passage of the same scene, where Lewis the Dauphin says : " And even there, methinks an angel spake ; look, where the holy legate comes apace " ; because the sounding of a trumpet often precedes a stage entrance of importance, especially on the battle-field, and because it is poetically and dramatically appropriate that the trumpet-call which heralds the approach of " the holy legate " should suggest the idea of an angel's proclamation.

    SCENE II.—*London. A room in* PRINCE HENRY'S *house.*—1 *H. IV.*, i. 2.

Most modern editions give the stage direction here, " Another room in the Palace." But, from several passages in the plays where Prince

Hal figures, we learn that he does not frequent the court ; while, from tradition, we learn that he had a residence granted to him as Prince of Wales, not far from Eastcheap, one of his favourite haunts.

> *Warkworth. Before* NORTHUMBERLAND'S *castle. Enter* RUMOUR, *painted*
> *full of tongues.*
> Upon my tongues continual slanders ride. . . .
> . . . from Rumour's tongues
> They bring smooth comforts false, worse than true wrongs.—2 *H. IV.* (*Induc.*)

The stage direction, "painted full of tongues," is printed in the Quarto copy, though not in the Folio copy of this play ; and the text shows it to be needed.

> *King Henry.* I pray you, take me up, and bear me hence
> Into some other chamber : softly, pray. [*They convey the* KING *into an inner part*
> *of the room, and place him on a bed.—Ibid.,* iv. 4.
>
> EPILOGUE (*Spoken by a Dancer*). . . . If my tongue cannot entreat you to acquit me, will you command me to use my legs ? and yet that were but light payment to dance out of your debt. . . . My tongue is weary ; when my legs are too, I will bid you good night.—*Ibid.* (*Epilogue*).
>
> This monument of the victory will I bear. [*Puts on part of* SIR HUMPHREY STAFFORD'S *armour*]—2 *H. VI.,* iv. 3.

The above stage direction is derived from a passage in Holinshed, that records the circumstance.

> *Enter* IDEN, *with* SERVANTS *behind.*
> *Cade.* . . . Yet, come thou and thy five men, and if I do not leave you all as dead as a door-nail, I pray God I may never eat grass more.
> *Iden.* Nay, it shall ne'er be said, while England stands,
> That Alexander Iden, an esquire of Kent,
> Took odds to combat a poor famish'd man.—*Ibid.,* iv. 10.

The Folio makes no mention of the "Servants" in the stage direction which states Iden's entrance ; but—not only does the stage direction in the older drama to which Shakespeare's "Second Part of King Henry VI." succeeded, speak of "Master Alexander Iden and his men,"—the words in the text of the above passage ("and thy five men," "you all," and "took odds") warrant the inclusion of the Servants.

> [GLOSTER *and* CLARENCE *whisper.*
> Come, Clarence, come ; thou wilt, if Warwick call.
> *Clarence.* Father of Warwick, know you what this means ?
> [*Taking the red rose out of his hat.*
> Look here, I throw my infamy at thee.—3 *H. VI.,* v. 1.

The two stage directions in the above passage are supplied from the older drama on the same subject which preceded Shakespeare's "Third Part of King Henry VI. ; " Clarence's words requiring the accompanying explained action.

> SCENE V.—*Antium. A public place.—Coriol.,* v. 5.

The Folio giving no stage direction announcing the locality of this scene, some modern editors have placed it in "Antium," others in "Corioli ; " but many reasons (expressed at length in our Annotated Edition of Shakespeare's plays) cause us to believe that our dramatist intended it should be "Antium."

> No, no ; this shall forbid it : lie thou there. [*Laying down her dagger.*]—*R. & Jul.,* iv. 3.

This stage direction is authorised by the reading of the 1597 Quarto of this play which gives Juliet's line in the text thus:—"This shall forbid it. *Knife*, lye thou there"; and, in a previous scene, Juliet has said to the friar, "With *this knife* I'll help it presently."

> SCENE I.—*Rome. A room in* ANTONY'S *house.* . . .
> But, Lepidus, go you to Cæsar's house;
> Fetch the will hither, and we shall determine
> How to cut off some charge in legacies.
> *Lepidus.* What! shall I find you here?
> *Octavius.* Or here, or at the Capitol.—*Jul. C.*, iv. 1.

Although Shakespeare probably remembered that in North's Plutarch it is stated "all three met together (to wit, Cæsar, Antonius, and Lepidus) in an iland enuironed round about with a little river," the text shows that the dramatist intended to place this scene in "Rome."

> SCENE II.—*A room in the castle.*—*Oth.*, iv. 2.

It has been asserted that there is some difficulty in ascertaining where this scene takes place; as, at its commencement, the words "shut the door" imply an apartment in the castle, while, at its close, Roderigo's careless entry seems to bespeak some place outside adjoining the castle. But other passages of the play indicate that a portion of the castle is used as a guard-room; and Roderigo may well be supposed to seek Iago there, not find him, and pursue his search in other adjacent apartments. If it be borne in mind that Roderigo is partially disguised, according to Iago's advice in act i., sc. 3. ("defeat thy favour with a usurped beard"), he is not likely to dread being recognised as the man who gave Brabantio intelligence of Othello's having married Desdemona, and therefore need have no hesitation in entering Othello's house at Cyprus.

> SCENE II. ALEXANDRIA. *The monument.* Enter CLEOPATRA, CHARMIAN, *and* IRAS.
> . . . *Enter, below, to the gates of the monument,* PROCULEIUS, GALLUS, *and*
> SOLDIERS. . . . PROCULEIUS *and two of the Guard ascend the monument by a*
> *ladder, and come behind* CLEOPATRA. *Some of the Guard unbar and open the gates,*
> *discovering the lower room of the monument.* . . . *Brings* CLEOPATRA *down into*
> *the lower room of the monument, and delivers her to* DOLABELLA.—*Ant. & C.*, v. 2.

Most modern editions give the former portion of the above stage directions thus, in accordance with the description of the scene and incident of Cleopatra's capture, as given in North's Plutarch; whence, in all probability, Shakespeare drew his details: but, in our editions of his plays, we have appended the latter portion of the above stage directions relative to "the lower room of the monument," because North's Plutarch adds "*came down* into the monument," after describing Proculeius's having gained access to the "high window," and because the circumstances of the whole scene, as depicted by Shakespeare, require that Cleopatra should be withinside her monument until the very end. We believe that, consistently with the scanty scenic arrangements which were all that existed in our dramatist's time, the stage representation of this scene may have been somewhat thus: Cleopatra and her women at first appeared on the platform or balcony (supposed to be the "high window" of an upper room in "the monument;" as in act iv., sc. 13, where the stage directions in the

Folio describe " Cleopatra and her maides aloft," and "they heaue Anthony *aloft* to Cleopatra ") ; that Proculeius, Gallus, and the guard enter from the side-scene towards the front of the stage: that they parley with Cleopatra, she above, they below : that Proculeius and two of the guard ascend to the platform by means of a ladder; that he makes her his prisoner, while the guards below removed some rude token of gates, that left to view the back portion of the stage immediately beneath the platform, which portion was supposed to be the lower room of the monument, containing the bed upon which Cleopatra ultimately falls and " dies : " that Dolabella enters from the side scene near the front of the stage, and that to his care Proculeius delivers Cleopatra, after having brought her down from the platform to the portion of the stage beneath : that she remains thus at the back of the stage, supposed to be in the lower room of her monument; while at the front of the stage successively Cæsar and his train come and go, the Clown brings in the basket of figs containing the concealed asp, the guards rush in in alarm, and finally Cæsar and his train return to find her and her women dead. In such small space, and with such large demands on the imagination, did actors and audience formerly contrive to give and receive theatrical representation : frequently the inside and the outside of a building being supposed visible at one and the same time, within the most restricted compass of stage and stage appointments.

Imogen. . . . I am sick still ; heart-sick : Pisanio, I'll now taste of thy drug. [*Swallows some*].—*Cym.*, iv. 2.

The Folio giving no stage direction here, it might be imagined that the words in the text, " I 'll now taste of thy drug," were possibly no more than an indication that Imogen intends to take some of the drug when she returns to the cave and will be alone ; but the probability is that the author meant this to be the juncture at which she swallows some in sight of the audience.

Pericles. Let none disturb us. [HELICANUS *and* LORDS *stand aloof.*] Why should this change.—*Per.*, i. 2.

As it is evident that Pericles, after the first four words, utters his speech in soliloquy, we inserted the above stage direction in our editions of Shakespeare's works.

In old stage directions it was sometimes the habit to give announcement of the entrance of a character at too early a point of the scene ; and we find instances of this habit in the First Folio copy of Shakespeare's plays :—

(Folio.)—*Scena Quinta. Enter Falstaffe, Mistris Page, Mistris Ford, Euans, Anne Page, Fairies, Page, Ford, Quickly, Slender, Fenton, Caius, Pistoll.—Merry W.*, v. 5.

(Modern.)—SCENE V. *Another part of the park. Enter* FALSTAFF *disguised as Herne, with a buck's head on.*

Falstaff. The Windsor bell hath struck twelve. . . . Who comes here ? my doe ?

Enter MISTRESS FORD *and* MISTRESS PAGE.

Mrs. Ford. Sir John ! art thou there, my deer ? . . .

Falstaff. . . . Would never cross me thus.

Enter SIR HUGH EVANS, *as a Satyr;* PISTOL, *as Hobgoblin;* ANNE PAGE, *as the Fairy Queen, attended by her brother and others as Fairies, with waxen tapers on their heads.*

Queen. Fairies, black, grey, green, and white, &c., &c.—*Ibid.*, v. 5.

(Folio.) —And perturbation followes her.
Enter Claudio and Beatrice, Leonato, Hero.

Pedro.—Looke heere she comes.—*M. Ado*, ii. 1.

(Modern.)—I cannot endure my Lady Tongue.   [*Exit.*
Enter CLAUDIO, BEATRICE, HERO, and LEONATO.

D. Pedro. Come, lady, come; you have lost the heart of Signior Benedick.—*Ibid.*, ii. 1.

(Folio.)—*Enter Florizell, Perdita, Shepherd, Clowne, Polixenes, Camillo, Mopsa, Dorcas, Servants, Autolicus.*

Flo. These your vnvsuall weeds, to each part of you
Do 's giue a life.—*W. T.*, iv. 3.

(Modern.)—SCENE III.—BOHEMIA. *A lawn before a shepherd's cottage. Enter* FLORIZEL *and* PERDITA.

Flo. These your unusual weeds to each part of you
Do give a life . . .
. . . See, your guests approach:
Address yourself to entertain them sprightly,
And let 's be red with mirth.
Enter SHEPHERD, *with* POLIXENES *and* CAMILLO, *disguised;* CLOWN, MOPSA, DORCAS, *and other* SHEPHERDS *and* SHEPHERDESSES. . . .
Enter AUTOLYCUS, singing.—Ibid., iv. 3.

(Folio.)—*Actus Quintus. Scena Prima. Enter Leontes, Cleomenes, Dion, Paulina, Servants: Florizel, Perdita.*—*Ibid.*, v. 1.

(Modern.)—ACT V. SCENE I.—*Sicilia. A room in the palace of* LEONTES. *Enter* LEONTES, CLEOMENES, DION, PAULINA, *and others.*

Cleo. Sir, you have done enough, and have perform'd
A saint-like sorrow. . . .
Leontes. They are come.
Re-enter CLEOMENES, with FLORIZEL, PERDITA, and others.—Ibid., v. 1.

(Folio.)—*Enter Henry Prince of Wales, Sir John Falstaffe, and Pointz.*—1 *H. IV.*, i. 2.
(Modern.)—Enter PRINCE HENRY and FALSTAFF.

Falstaff. Now, Hal, what time of day is it, lad? . . .
Prince Henry. I see a good amendment of life in thee,—from praying to purse-taking.
Enter POINS, at a distance.—Ibid., i. 2.

(Folio.)—Who knocks so hard?
Whence come you? What 's your will?
Enter Nurse.

Nurse. Let me come in,
And you shall know my errand;
I come from Lady Iuliet.
Fri. L. Welcome, then.—*R. & Jul.*, iii. 3.

(Modern.)—Who knocks so hard? whence come you? what 's your will?
Nurse (Within). Let me come in, and you shall know my errand; I come from Lady Juliet.
Fri. L. Welcome, then.
Enter NURSE.—Ibid., iii. 3.

(Folio.)—*Aper.* Much.
Sound Tucket. Enter the Maskers of Amazons, with Lutes in their hands, dauncing and playing.

Timon. What meanes that trumpe? How now?
Enter Seruant.

Ser. Please youe my Lord, there are certaine Ladies most desirous of admittance.
Tim. Ladies? What are their wils?

Ser. There comes with them a fore-runner my Lord, which beares that office, to signifie their pleasures.

Tim. I pray let them be admitted.

Enter Cupid with the Maske of Ladies.

Cup. Haile to thee, worthy Timon. . . .

Timo. They'r wecome all, let 'em haue kind admittance. Musicke, make their welcome.

Luc. You see, my Lord, how ample y' are belou'd.

Aper. Hoyday,

What a sweepe of vanitie comes this way.—*Timon*, i. 2.

(Modern.)—*Apem.* Much !   [*Tucket sounded.*

Timon. What means that trump ?

Enter a SERVANT.

How now !

Servant. Please you, my lord, there are certain ladies most desirous of admittance.

Timon. Ladies! what are their wills ?

Servant. There comes with them a fore-runner, my lord, which bears that office to signify their pleasures.

Timon. I pray, let them be admitted.

Enter CUPID.

Cupid. Hail to thee, worthy Timon. . . .

Timon. They're welcome all; let them have kind admittance. Music, make their welcome!   [*Exit* CUPID.

First Lord. You see, my lord, how ample you 're belov'd.

[*Music.*] *Re-enter* CUPID, *with a Mask of Ladies as Amazons, with lutes in their hands, dancing and playing.*

Apem. Hey day! what a sweep of vanity comes this way!—*Ibid.*, i. 2.

(Folio.)—*Lear* . . . Off, off, you Lendings : Come, vnbutton heere.

Enter Gloucester, with a Torch.

Foole. . . . Looke, heere comes a walking fire. . . .

Kent. How fares your Grace ?

Lear. What 's he ?—*Lear*, iii. 4.

(Modern.)—*Lear.* . . . Off, off, you lendings ! come, unbutton here.

[*Tearing off his clothes.*

Fool. Look, here comes a walking fire. . . .

Kent. How fares your grace ?

Enter GLOSTER, with a torch.

Lear. What 's he ?—*Ibid.*, iii. 4.

In several of his plays, Shakespeare inserts stage directions indicating pageants, processions, visions, apparitions, &c. ; and the Folio gives these stage directions, for the most part, with sufficient detail :—

Solemne and strange musicke : and Prosper on the top * *(inuisible) : Enter seuerall strange shapes, bringing in a Banket ; and dance about it with gentle actions of salutations, and inuiting the King, &c., to eate, they depart. . . . Thunder and Lightning. Enter Ariell (like a Harpey) claps his wings vpon the Table, and with a quient deuice the Banquet vanishes. . . . He vanishes in Thunder : then (to soft musicke) Enter the shapes againe, and daunce (with mockes and mowes) and carrying out the Table.—Temp.*, iii. 3.

Soft musick. Enter IRIS. . . . *Iuno descends. . . . Enter* CERES. . . . *Iuno and Ceres whisper and send* Iris *on employment. . . . Enter certaine Nimphes. . . . Enter certaine Reapers (properly habited), they ioyne with the Nimphes, in a gracefull dance, towards the end whereof, Prospero starts sodainly and speakes, after which to a strange hollow and confused noyse, they heauily vanish. . . . A noyse of Hunters heard. Enter diuers Spirits in shape of Dogs and Hounds, hunting them about : Prospero and Ariel setting them on.—Ibid.*, iv. 1.

* " *Prosper on the top* " signifies that PROSPERO enters above ; on the platform or balcony at the back of the stage, explained under SCENIC ARRANGEMENTS.

Flor. Trum.   Enter the Prologue.   Quince. . . . Tawyer,* with a Trumpet before them. Enter Pyramus and Thisby, Wall, Moone-shine, and Lyon.—Mid. N. D., v. 1.

Enter Morochus, a tawnie Moore all in white, and three or foure followers accordingly with Portia, Nerrissa and their traine.   Flo. Cornets.—Mer. of V., ii. 1.

Enter Hymen,† Rosalind, and Celia.   Still Musicke.—As You L., v. 4.

Heere a Daunce of Shepheards and Shepheardesses. . . . Heare a Dance of twelue Satyres.—W. T., iv. 3.

The Trumpets sound.   Enter King Henrie the Fift, Brothers, Lord Chiefe Iustice.— 2 *H. IV.,* v. 5.

Alarum, and Chambers ‡ goe off. . . . Enter the King, Exeter, Bedford, and Gloucester. Alarum: Scaling Ladders at Harflew. . . . Alarum, and Chambers goe off.—H. V., iii. 1.

*Enter Fiends. . . . They walke, and speake not. . . . They hang their heads. . . . They shake their heads. . . . They depart.—*1 *H. VI.,* v. 3.

Heere doe the ceremonies belonging, and make the circle, Bullingbrooke or Southwell reades, Coniuro te, &c. *It Thunders and Lightens terribly: then the Spirit riseth. . . . Thunder and Lightning.   Exit Spirit.—*2 *H. VI.,* i. 4.

Enter the Ghost of Prince Edward, Sonne to Henry the Sixt. . . . Enter the Ghost of Henry the Sixt. . . . Enter the Ghost of Clarence. . . . Enter the Ghosts of Riuers, Gray, and Vaughan. . . . Enter the Ghost of Lord Hastings. . . . Enter the Ghosts of the two young Princes. . . . Enter the Ghost of Anne, his wife. . . . Enter the Ghost of Buckingham.—R. III., v. 3.

Enter Cardinall Wolsey, the Purse borne before him, certaine of the Guard, and two Secretaries with papers ; The Cardinall in his passage, fixeth his eye on Buckingham, and Buckingham on him, both full of disdaine. . . . Exeunt Cardinall, and his Traine. . . . Enter Brandon, a Sergeant at Armes before him, and two or three of the Guard.—H. VIII., i. 1.

Cornets.   Enter King Henry, leaning on the Cardinal's Shoulder, the Nobles, and Sir Thomas Louell : the Cardinall places himself vnder the Kings feete on his right side. . . . A noyse within crying roome for the Queen, vsher'd by the Duke of Norfolke.   Enter the Queene, Norfolke and Suffolke : She kneels.   King riseth from his State, takes her vp, kisses and placeth her by him.—Ibid., i. 2.

Hoboies.   A small Table vnder a State for the Cardinall, a longer Table for the Guests. Then enter Anne Bullen, and diuers other Ladies, and Gentlemen, as guests at one Doore ; at another Doore enter Sir Henry Guilford. . . . Enter L. Chamberlaine, L. Sands, and Louell. . . . Hoboyes.   Enter Cardinall Wolsey, and takes his State. . . . Drum and Trumpet, Chambers§ discharged. . . . All rise, and Tables remou'd. . . . Hoboyes.   Enter King and others as Maskers, habited like Shepheards, vsher'd by the Lord Chamberlaine.   They passe directly before the Cardinall, and gracefully salute him. . . . Choose Ladies, King, and An Bullen. . . . Musicke, Dance. . . . Whisper. . . . Exeunt with Trumpets.—Ibid., i. 4.

Enter Buckingham from his Arraignment, Tipstaues before him, the Axe with the edge towards him, Halberds on each side, accompanied with Sir Thomas Louell, Sir Nicholas Vaux, Sir Walter Sands, and common people, &c.—Ibid., ii. 1.

Trumpets, sennet,‖ and cornets.   Enter two Vergers, with short siluer wands ; next them two Scribes, in the habite of Doctors : after them, the Bishop of Canterbury alone ; after him, the Bishops of Lincoln, Ely, Rochester, and S. Asaph : Next them, with some small distance, followes a Gentleman bearing the Purse, with the great Seale,

---

* " Tawyer " was probably the name of the trumpeter.

† Although this stage direction does not include them, there must have been intended a train of chorister spirits accompanying Hymen, who says, " Whiles a wedlock hymn *we* sing."

‡ " Chambers " were small pieces of ordnance, used on festive occasions and for stage purposes.

§ It was the discharge of chambers in the present scene of this play that was supposed to have occasioned the fire which burned down the Globe Theatre in 1613.

‖ " Sennet " meant a particular blast on the trumpet, differing somewhat from a flourish [*See* MUSICAL TERMS].

and a Cardinals Hat : then two Priests, bearing each a Siluer Crosse : then a Gentleman Vsher bare-headed, accompanyed with a Sergeant at Armes, bearing a Siluer Mace : then two Gentlemen bearing two great Siluer Pillers. After them, side by side, the two Cardinals, two Noblemen, with the sword and mace. The King takes place vnder the Cloth of State. The two Cardinalls sit vnder him as Iudges. The Queene takes place some distance from the King. The Bishops place themselues on each side the Court in manner of a Consistory : Below them the Scribes. The Lords sit next the Bishops. The rest of the Attendants stand in conuenient order about the Stage. . . . The Queene makes no answer, rises out of her Chaire, goes about the Court, comes to the King, and kneeles at his Feete. Then speakes. . . . She Curtsies to the King, and offers to depart. . . . Exit Queene, and her Attendants. . . . Exeunt in manner as they enter'd.—H. VIII., ii. 4.

Enter King, reading of a Scedule. . . . King takes his Seat, whispers Louell, who goes to the Cardinall. . . . Exit King, frowning upon the Cardinall, the Nobles throng after him smiling, and whispering. . . Enter to Woolsey, the Dukes of Norfolke and Suffolke, the Earle of Surrey, and the Lord Chamberlaine. . . . Exeunt all but Wolsey. . . . Enter Cromwell, standing amazed.—Ibid., iii. 2.

Enter two Gentlemen, meeting one another. . . . Hoboyes. The Order of the Coronation.—*1. A liuely Flourish of Trumpets. 2. Then, two Iudges. 3. Lord Chancellor, with Purse and Mace before him. 4. Quirristers singing. Musicke. 5.* Maior of London, *bearing the Mace. Then* Garter, *in his Coate of Armes, and on his head he wore a gilt Copper Crowne. 6.* Marquesse Dorset, *bearing a Scepter of Gold, on his head, a Demy Coronall of Gold. With him, the Earle of* Surrey, *bearing the Rod of Siluer with the Doue, Crowned with an Earles Coronet. Collars of Esses. 7.* Duke of Suffolke, *in his Robe of Estate, his Coronet on his head, bearing a long white Wand, as High Steward. With him, the Duke of* Norfolke, *with the Rod of Marshalship, a Coronet on his head. Collars of Esses. 8. A* Canopy, *borne by foure of the* Cinque-Ports, *vnder it the Queene in her Robe, in her haire, richly adorned with Pearle, Crowned. On each side her, the Bishops of* London *and* Winchester. *9. The* Olde Dutchesse of Norfolke, *in a Coronall of Gold, wrought with Flowers, bearing the Queenes Traine. 10. Certaine* Ladies *or* Countesses, *with plaine Circlets of Gold, without Flowers. Exeunt first passing ouer the Stage in Order and State, and then, A great Flourish of Trumpets.—Ibid., iv. 1.*

Enter Katherine Dowager, sicke, lead betweene Griffith, her gentleman Vsher, and Patience her Woman. . . . Sad and solemne Musicke. . . . The Vision. Enter solemnely tripping, &c. [*See* Dumb Shows *for this stage direction, given at length.*]

Enter Trumpets sounding : Then two Aldermen, L. Maior, Garter, Cranmer, Duke of Norfolke with his Marshals Staffe, Duke of Suffolke, two Noblemen bearing great standing bowles for the Christening Guifts : Then foure Noblemen bearing a Canopy, vnder which the Dutchesse of Norfolke, Godmother, bearing the Childe richly habited in a Mantle, &c. Traine borne by a Lady : Then followes the Marchionesse Dorset, the other Godmother, and Ladies. The Troupe passe once about the Stage, and Garter speakes.—Ibid., v. 4.

Enter the Ghost of Cæsar.—Jul. C., iv. 3.

Enter the Ghost of Banquo, and sits in Macbeths place. . . . Enter Ghost.—Macb., iii. 4.

Thunder. 1. Apparition, an Armed Head. . . . He descends. . . . Thunder. 2. Apparition, a Bloody Childe. . . . Descends. . . . Thunder. 3. Apparition, a Childe Crowned, with a tree in his hand. . . . Descend. . . . Hoboyes. . . . A Shew of eight Kings, and Banquo last, with a glasse in his hand.—Ibid., iv. 1.

Enter the Ghost. . . . Exit the Ghost. . . . Enter Ghost againe. . . . Exit Ghost.—Hamlet, i. 1.

Enter Ghost. . . . Ghost beckons Hamlet. . . . Exeunt Ghost and Hamlet.—Ibid., i. 4.

Enter Ghost and Hamlet. . . . Exit. . . . Ghost cries vnder the Stage.—Ibid., i. 5.

Enter Ghost. . . . Exit.—Ibid., iii. 4.

Enter King, Queene, Laertes, and a Coffin, with Lords attendant.—Ibid., v. 1.

Enter Lucius, Iachimo, and the Romaine Army at one doore : and the Britaine Army at another : Leonatus Posthumus following like a poore Souldier. They march ouer, and goe out. Then enter againe in skirmish Iachimo and Posthumus ; he vanquisheth and disarmeth Iachimo, and then leaues him. . . . The Battaile continues, the Britaines fly, Cymbeline is taken : Then enter to his rescue, Bellarius, Guiderius, and Aruiragus. . . . Enter Posthumus, and seconds the Britaines. They rescue Cymbeline, and Exeunt.—Cym., v. 2.

Enter Cymbeline, &c., [See DUMB SHOWS; where this stage direction is given at length.]—*Ibid.*, v. 3.

Solemne musicke. Enter (as in an Apparition) Sicillius Leonatus, Father to Posthumus, an old man, attyred like a warriour, leading in his hand an ancient Matron (his wife, and Mother to Posthumus) with Musicke before them. Then, after other Musicke, followes the two young Leonati (Brothers to Posthumus) with Wounds as they died in the Warrs. They circle Posthumus round as he lies sleeping. . . . Iupiter descends in Thunder and Lightning, sitting vppon an Eagle : hee throws a Thunder-bolt. The Ghostes fall on their Knees. . . . Ascends. . . . Vanish.— Ibid., v. 4.

In the First Folio there are a few stage directions which contain mention of certain characters that appear nowhere else in the play ; and it is probable that they were characters afterwards omitted by the author, although suffered by inadvertence to remain in the original version used for theatrical representation :—

Enter Leonato, Gouernor of Messina, Imogen his wife, Hero his daughter, and Beatrice his neece, with a Messenger.—M. Ado, i. 1.

Enter Leonato, his brother, his wife, Hero his daughter, and Beatrice his neece, and a kinsman.—Ibid., ii. 1.

Leonato's " wife " is omitted in all modern editions, as she takes no part in the play ; while they substitute the particular mention of a " kinsman " by " others." This " kinsman " probably meant the " cousin " to whom Leonato refers in act i., sc. 2, where he says to Antonio, " How now, brother ! where is *my cousin, your son ?* hath he provided this music ? "

Flourish. Enter Lewis the French King, his sister Bona, his Admirall, call'd Bourbon ; Prince Edward, Queene Margaret, and the Earle of Oxford. Lewis sits, and riseth vp againe.—3 H. VI., iii. 3.

As the French Admiral does not figure in the dialogue, his name is substituted in modern versions of this stage direction by the word " attended."

Enter Enobarbus, Lamprius, a Soothsayer, Rannius, Lucillius, Charmian, Iras, Mardian the Eunuch, and Alexas.—Ant. & C., i. 2.

Modern editions omit the names of Lamprius, Rannius, and Lucillius, as they are personages not introduced by Shakespeare into the speech or action of the play. But the first of these three names possesses an interest for us, inasmuch as it may indicate an original intention on the part of the dramatist to introduce into this play a character and historical authority thus mentioned in North's Plutarch:—" I have heard my grandfather *Lampryas* report, that one Philotas, a Physitian, borne in the city of Amphion, told him that he was at that present time in Alexandria, and studied Physicke : and that having acquaintance with one of Antonius cookes, he tooke him with him to Antonius house (being a young man desirous to see things) to shew him the wonderful sumptuous charge and preparation of one only supper."

There are a few stage situations, in the course of Shakespeare's dramas, which have no accompanying stage direction either in the ancient or modern editions of his works; yet which require bearing in mind, duly to comprehend the passages where they occur:—

> *Gonzalo.* Beseech you, sir, be merry; you have cause
> (So have we all) of joy; for our escape
> Is much beyond our loss. . . .
> *Alonso.* Prithee, peace.
> *Sebastian.* He receives comfort like cold porridge.
> *Antonio.* The visitor will not give him o'er so. . . .
> *Adrian.* Though this island seem to be desert,— . . .
> *Francisco.* Sir, he may live:
> I saw him beat the surges under him,
> And ride upon their backs. . . . I not doubt
> He came alive to land.
> *Alonso.*   No, no; he's gone.
> *Sebastian.* Sir, you may thank yourself for this great loss,
> That would not bless our Europe with your daughter.—*Temp.*, ii. 1.

During the above dialogue, we must imagine the speakers to be arranged in two separate groups: King Alonso surrounded by his faithful adherents, Gonzalo, Adrian, Francisco, and the rest, engaged in endeavouring to comfort him; while Sebastian and Antonio remain apart together, commenting sneeringly upon the others.

> *Countess.* . . . No more of this, Helena,—go to, no more; lest it be rather thought you affect a sorrow than to have.
> *Helena.* I do affect a sorrow, indeed; but I have it too.
> *Lafeu.* Moderate lamentation is the right of the dead; excessive grief the enemy to the living.
> *Helena.* If the living be enemy to the grief, the excess makes it soon mortal.
> *Bertram.* Madam, I desire your holy wishes.
> *Lafeu.* How understand we that?
> *Countess.* Be thou blest, Bertram!—*All's W.*, i. 1.

The Countess, at the commencement of the above passage, leaves Helena, and goes over to Bertram; so that the following speeches, crossing each other [*See* CROSSING SPEECHES], show that the mother and son are engaged together, while Lafeu remains near Helena, addressing her.

> *Lafeu.* Do all they deny her?—*Ibid.*, ii. 3.

This denotes that Lafeu is within sight, but not within hearing of what is taking place; since he supposes that the young lords, each in turn, refuse Helena, and does not discover that it is she who successively declines to take them.

> *Leontes.* Is he won yet?—*W. T.*, i. 2.

These words indicate that Leontes has remained somewhat apart, playing with his little son Mamillius, while Hermione fulfils his wish of pleading with Polixenes for a longer sojourn.

> And hither am I come,
> A prologue arm'd,—but not in confidence
> Of author's pen or actor's voice; but suited
> In like conditions as our argument.—*Tr. & Cr.* (*Prologue*).

This gives us to understand that the person appointed to speak the present prologue was clad in armour, consistently with the "argument" of the play; instead of being dressed in the customary suit of black worn by the speaker of a prologue in Shakespeare's time.

> *Hamlet.* . . . Nymph, in thy orisons
> Be all my sins remember'd.
>   *Ophelia.*   Good, my lord,
> How does your honour for this many a day ?
>   *Hamlet.* I humbly thank you; well, well, well.
>   *Ophelia.* My lord, I have remembrances of yours
> That I have longed long to re-deliver;
> I pray you, now receive them.
>   *Hamlet.*   No, not I ;
> I never gave you aught. . . .
> Where 's your father ? . . . It hath made me mad.—*Hamlet*, iii. 1.

In the above dialogue there is token that—after the first involuntary greeting, in which he addresses her in his old tone of gentleness and affection—Hamlet instinctively perceives Ophelia's meeting him to be the suggestion of others, by whom they are both watched; and he immediately falls into his resolved course of wildness, levity, and mad harshness.

> *Kent.* Good my lord, take his offer; go into the house. . . .
> . . . Importune him once more to go, my lord. . . .
>   *Gloster.* . . . I do beseech your grace,—
>   *Lear.*   Oh, cry you mercy, sir.
> Noble philosopher, your company.
>   *Edgar.* Tom 's a-cold.
>   *Gloster.* In, fellow, there, into the hovel: keep thee warm.
>   *Lear.* Come, let 's in all.
>   *Kent.*   This way, my lord.
>   *Lear.*   With him ;
> I will keep still with my philosopher.
>   *Kent.* Good my lord, soothe him ; let him take the fellow.
>   *Gloster.* Take him you on.
>   *Kent.* Sirrah, come on ; go along with us.
>   *Lear.* Come, good Athenian.—*Lear*, iii. 4.

It must be imagined that " the house "—probably some cottage or farmhouse belonging to one of Gloster's tenants—lies on the opposite side of the stage from that on which lies " the hovel." When Gloster says, " I do beseech your grace," he attempts to lead the king in the direction of the shelter he has provided in the farmhouse ; but Lear will not leave his " philosopher," and Gloster bids the Bedlam " fellow " go into the " hovel," that he may be out of the king's sight, who then proposes to follow him thither, by saying, " Let 's in all." Kent endeavours to draw Lear away ; but, finding him resolved to " keep still with " his " philosopher," begs Gloster to humour the king and " let him take the fellow " with him. Gloster accedes, and bids Kent himself take the fellow with them in the direction they desire to go : this is done, and they all quit the stage together.

SUPERNATURAL MUSIC.

Several times in the course of his dramas Shakespeare introduces supernatural music ; and always with charming effect, aiding the dramatic impression he intends to convey :—

>   [*Solemn and strange music*
>   *Alonso.* What harmony is this ? My good friends, hark !
>   *Gonzalo.* Marvellous sweet music ! . . .
> [*Then, to soft music, enter the Shapes again.*]—*Temp.*, iii. 3

Soft music. A masque. Enter IRIS.—*Temp.,* iv. I.

Prospero. . . . When I have required
Some heavenly music (which even now I do)
To work mine end upon their senses, that
This airy charm is for, I 'll break my staff,
Bury it certain fathoms in the earth,
And, deeper than did ever plummet sound,
I 'll drown my book.   [*Solemn music.*]—*Ibid.,* v. I.

Oberon. . . . Titania, music call; and strike more dead
Than common sleep, of all these five the sense.
Titania. Music, ho ! music such as charmeth sleep !
                                    [*Still music.* . . .
Oberon. Sound, music !   [*Still music.*]—*Mid. N. D.,* iv. I.

[*Still music.*]   *Enter* HYMEN, *leading* ROSALIND *in woman's clothes, and* CELIA.—
As You L., v. 4.

Rosalind, being supposed by the persons on the stage to be brought to their forest assemblage through magic means, is imagined to be escorted by some spirit impersonating Hymen, and attended by enchanted music.

Glendower. Do so;
And those musicians that shall play to you,
Hang in the air a thousand leagues from hence ;
And straight they shall be here : sit and attend. . . .
          [GLENDOWER *speaks some words in Welsh, and music is heard.*
Hotspur. Now I perceive the devil understands Welsh;
And 'tis no marvel he 's so humorous.
By 'r lady, he 's a good musician.—1 *H. IV.,* iii. I.

The sly comment put into Hotspur's mouth lets us into the secret that probably the Welsh chieftain has some such instrument as an Æolian harp placed under the control of one of his people, commissioned, at a signal, to set it playing; although Glendower would fain have it believed to be produced by such agency as that to which he alludes when he says he can " call spirits from the vasty deep."

                              [*Music as of hautboys underground.*
Fourth Soldier. Peace ! what noise ?
First Soldier.   List, list !
Second Soldier. Hark !
First Soldier.   Music i' the air.
Third Soldier.   Under the earth.
Fourth Soldier. It signs well, does it not ?
Third Soldier.   No.
First Soldier.   Peace, I say !
What should this mean ?
Second Soldier. 'Tis the god Hercules, whom Antony lov'd,
Now leaves him.—*Ant. & C.,* iv. 3.

The dramatist derived this incident, of supernatural music heard at night when Antony's fortunes were waning, from North's Plutarch; and excellently is it turned to account.

                                        [*Solemn music.*
Belarius.   My ingenious instrument !
Hark, Polydore, it sounds ! But what occasion
Hath Cadwal now to give it motion ?   Hark!
Guiderius. Is he at home?
Belarius.   He went hence even now.
Guiderius. What does he mean ? since death of my dear'st mother
It did not speak before. All solemn things
Should answer solemn accidents.—*Cym.,* iv. 2.

Although this "solemn music" is naturally accounted for, and the "ingenious instrument" was probably intended to be of similar kind to the one that Glendower has at his command, yet the awe-stricken words with which its sound is noted by those whose ear it thus unexpectedly comes upon, give it all the effect of supernatural music.

> *Pericles.*   I embrace you.
> Give me my robes.   I am wild in my beholding.
> Oh, heavens bless my girl!   But, hark, what music?
> Tell Helicanus, my Marina, tell him
> O'er, point by point, for yet he seems to doubt,
> How sure you are my daughter.   But, what music?
>   *Helicanus.* My lord, I hear none.
>   *Pericles.* None?
> The music of the spheres!   List, my Marina.
>   *Lysimachus.* It is not good to cross him; give him way.
>   *Pericles.* Rarest sounds!   Do ye not hear?
>   *Lysimachus. Music?*   My lord, I hear—
>   *Pericles.* Most heavenly music!
> It nips me into listening, and thick slumber
> Hangs upon mine eyes: let me rest [*Sleeps*].—*Per.*, v. 1.

It has been suggested by some commentators that the word "music," which we have italicised in Lysimachus's speech, should be transposed from the dialogue and placed as a stage direction; but we cannot think this was intended by Shakespeare. We think he meant Lysimachus to repeat the word used by Pericles, as a mode of humouring his fancy that he hears "rarest sounds;" these "rarest sounds" being purely a visionary music, the spiritual echo of the king's harmonious condition of soul, which is tuned to rapture by the recent recovery of his supposed dead child Marina. To us this seems to be an extremely beautiful idea of the poet—making the divine strains of vouchsafed "heavenly music" merely audible to the entranced senses of Pericles himself.

TAKING ONE BIRD FOR ANOTHER.

To take one bird for another was anciently in English proverbial use to signify want of discernment, as to know one bird from another was similarly employed to signify discrimination. In "The Three Lords of London," 1590, we find, "No more skill than take a falcon for a buzzard"; the "buzzard" being the 'bald-kite,' a degenerate hawk. Nares quotes, from *Comenii Janua. Lond. ed*, 1662, a sentence that serves in illustration,—"'Between hawk and buzzard,' means, 'between a good thing and a bad of the same kind': the hawk being the true sporting bird, the buzzard a heavy lazy fowl of the same species"; and Singer affirms that "there is an old Italian proverb—'*Saper discerner i Tordi da Stornelli*,' for 'to know one thing from another.'"

Shakespeare has several allusions to this figurative form of proverbial expression:—

> We'll teach him to know turtles from jays.—*Merry W.*, iii. 3.

The turtle has long been held as a type of true love; while 'a jay' was a term for a wanton woman.

> Ay, for a turtle, as he takes a buzzard.—*Tam. of S.*, ii. 1.
> I took this lark for a bunting.—*All's W.*, ii. 5.

The bunting is a bird that has some resemblance to a skylark, but without its fine song, and with so little caution as to be easily snared.

> I know a hawk from a handsaw.—*Hamlet*, ii. 2.

This is in direct reference to an old English proverb, given verbatim in Ray's "Proverbs," page 196, ed. 1768, thus:—"He knows not a hawk from a hand-saw." Both Ray and the Folio edition of Shakespeare give "hand-saw," which is a corruption of 'hernshaw'; 'hernshaw' being provincially used for a 'heron,' though strictly meaning a 'heronry.' We believe that the dramatist purposely put the corrupt form of "hernshaw" into Hamlet's mouth for the very reason that there is additional strongly apparent diversity between "a hawk" and "a hand-saw." Had the prince said 'a hawk from a hernshaw' there would have been merely the effect of the proverbial knowledge between one bird and another; but saying, "a hawk from a handsaw," there is not only the proverbial and well-understood phrase of discrimination, there is *also* the effect of discerning a bird from a carpenter's tool—just the sort of asserted power of distinguishing which a madman would claim; and therefore well suiting Hamlet's assumption of madness. Shakespeare, as we have frequently shown in the course of the present work, has this largely inclusive force of effect in many of his phrases; and we believe this to be one of these phrases.

There is indirect reference to the proverbial expression of judgment shown by being able to distinguish between bird and bird, in the following passage :—

> I chose an eagle, and did avoid a puttock.—*Cym.*, i. 2.

A puttock is a 'kite,' an inferior species of hawk.

TECHNICALITIES.

The poetry and truth lying at the core of even the most prosaic subjects—the mode in which a great poet and dramatist will illustrate a poetical or passionate sentence by an allusion to a practical object—the special knowledge as well as varied information possessed by Shakespeare—are all evidenced by the numerous technicalities used by him. His interest in the particulars of knowledge, as well as in knowledge itself, led him not only to become acquainted with multiform pursuits, but made him also take pains to become conversant with the proper terms employed in those pursuits. Thus, he uses many technicalities belonging to falconry and hawking :—

> How now, my *eyas-musket*! what news with you ?—*Merry W.*, iii. 3.

This was a term for a 'young sparrow-hawk': "eyas" meaning a nestling or unfledged bird, from the French *nias* or *niais* ('a nias' becoming corrupted by malpronunciation into 'an eyas'); and "musket" being derived from the old French *mouschet* or *mousquet*, a male sparrow-hawk.

> Nay, do not fly: I think we have *watch'd* you now.—*Merry W.*, v. 5.

To "watch" a hawk meant to tame it by preventing it from sleeping; therefore the above phrase is equivalent to 'I think we have broken you of your wild habits.'

> This outward-sainted deputy—
> Whose settled visage and deliberate word
> Nips youth i' the head, and follies doth *enmew*,
> As falcon doth the fowl.—*M. for M.*, iii. 1.

The term "enmew," strictly signifying to encage or retain in the mew where hawks are kept, is here employed to express inclosing with intent to destroy, as the falcon soars and circles round the fowl it makes its prey.

> My falcon now is *sharp*, and passing empty;
> And, till she *stoop*, she must not be *full-gorg'd*,
> For then she never looks upon her *lure*.
> Another way I have to *man* my *haggard*,
> To make her come, and know her keeper's call;
> That is, to *watch* her, as we *watch* these kites
> That *bate* and beat, and will not be obedient.—*Tam. of S.*, iv. 1.

"Sharp" means 'sharp-set,' 'hungry;' "stoop," besides its sense of 'yield,' 'bend,' 'submit,' is used in its technical sense of coming down as a trained falcon upon its prey; "full gorg'd" is 'fully fed'; "lure" is the stuffed bird made to represent that kind of living one which it is intended that the falcon shall pursue; to "man" a hawk is to tame it; and a "haggard" is a wild unreclaimed hawk.

> And with what wing the *stannyel checks* at it.—*Tw. N.*, ii. 5.

A "stannyel" is a stonehawk; and "checks" is the technical expression in falconry when a hawk forsakes its appointed prey, and flies at inferior birds that chance to come in view.

> And, like an eagle o'er his *aiery*, towers,
> To *souse* annoyance that comes near his nest.—*John*, v. 2.

"Aiery," sometimes spelt 'eyry' (from the Teutonic *eyren*, eggs), means a bird's brood; to "tower" is used in falconry to express the spiral flight or soaring higher and higher of an eagle or hawk; and to "souse" is a technicality in hawking for the sudden plunge or stoop which the bird makes when darting down upon its prey.

> *Imp* out our drooping country's *broken wing*.—*R. II.*, ii. 1.

To 'imp a hawk' was the term for an operation whereby any feathers that the bird might have lost or injured were artificially supplied.

> Which makes him *prune* himself, and bristle up
> The crest of youth against your dignity.—1 *H. IV.*, i. 1.

A hawk is said to "prune" itself, when it picks and ruffles its feathers in order to dress them and set them in good condition.

> All plum'd like estridges (that with the wind
> *Bated*, like eagles having lately bath'd).—*Ibid.*, iv. 2.

To "bate" means to flutter and beat the wings, and also to sedulously spread and ruffle the feathers, as birds do after bathing, in order that the air may speedily dry them. We think that Rowe's alteration of " with " to ' wing,' adopted by many other editors, spoils this passage ; while the original Folio word appears to us to give the author's meaning—the sentence, describing the impression produced by the plumed warriors, being parenthetical.

> Never anybody saw it but his lackey : 'tis a *hooded* valour ; and when it appears, it will *bate.—H. V.*, iii. 7.

Besides the allusion to the fact that when a hawk is unhooded it beats, flaps, or flutters its wings, there is included a play upon the word " bate " in its sense of ' abate,' ' diminish,' ' dwindle.'

> Though his affections are higher mounted than ours, yet, when they *stoop*, they *stoop with the like wing.* [*See* previous explanation of " stoop."]—*Ibid.*, iv. 1.

> For our approach shall so much *dare the field*,
> That England shall couch down in fear, and yield.—*Ibid.*, iv. 2.

Birds are said to be " dared " when by the falcon in the air they are terrified from rising, so that they may sometimes be taken by the hand.

> Between two hawks, which *flies the higher pitch.*—1 *H. VI.*, ii. 4.
> Believe me, lords, for *flying at the brook,*
> I saw not better sport these seven years' day :
> Yet, by your leave, *the wind was very high ;*
> And, ten to one, old Joan *had not gone out.—*
> But what a point, my lord, your falcon made,
> And *what a pitch she flew* above the rest ! . . .
> No marvel, an it like your majesty,
> My lord protector's hawks do *tower* so well ;
> They know their master loves to be aloft,
> And bears his thoughts above his falcon's *pitch.*—2 *H. VI.*, ii. 1.

" Flying at the brook," or ' flying at birds of the brook,' meant hawking at water-fowl ; and authorities in falconry assert that hawks are very sensitive to wind.

> Methinks I should not thus be led along,
> *Mail'd up* in shame.—*Ibid.*, ii. 4.

A hawk was said to be " mailed up " when she was wrapped up in a cloth or handkerchief, that she might not stir her wings or struggle.

> Neither the king, nor he that loves him best,
> The proudest he that holds up Lancaster,
> Dares stir a wing, if Warwick *shake his bells.*—3 *H. VI.*, i. 1.

Hawks had small bells hung upon them ; the sound of which was supposed to daunt birds that were hawked at.

> Whose haughty spirit, wingèd with desire,
> Will cost my crown, and like an empty eagle,
> *Tire* on the flesh of me and of my son !—*Ibid.*, i. 1.

To " tire" was to tear with the beak, to peck like a bird of prey, to feed voraciously. The word " cost," in this passage, may elliptically signify ' cost me ; ' but we think it very likely to have been a Folio misprint for ' foot ' (in the sense of ' clutch ') as Shakespeare uses that expression in the passage we below quote from " Cymbeline," v. 4, where reference is also made to an " eagle."

> This day should Clarence closely be *mew'd up.*—*R. III.*, i. 1.
> More pity that the eagles should be *mew'd*,
> While kites and buzzards prey at liberty.—*Ibid.*, i. 1.

The "mew" was the place where hawks were kept, and in which they were confined while moulting.

> Our *aiery* buildeth in the cedar's top,
> And dallies with the wind, and scorns the sun. . . .
> Your *aiery* buildeth in our *aiery's* nest.—*R. III.*, i. 3.
>   [*See* "aiery" previously explained.]

You must be *watched ere you be made tame*, must you?—*Tr. & Cr.*, iii. 2.
The *falcon* as the *tercel*, for all the ducks i' the river.—*Ibid.*, iii. 2.

"The falcon" is the female hawk, "the tercel" is the male hawk.

> Hist! Romeo, hist! Oh, for a falconer's voice,
> To *lure* this *tassel-gentle* back again!—*R. & Jul.*, ii. 2.

"Tassel-gentle" is a corruption of 'tiercel-gentle' or 'tercel-gentle.' The term "tiercel" was applied to the male of the goshawk, because it is a 'tierce' or 'third,' less than the female; and the epithet "gentle" was appended, because this kind of hawk is easily tamed, and because it was a favourite with persons of gentle birth.

> *Hood* my *unmann'd* blood, *bating* in my cheeks,
> With thy black mantle.—*Ibid.*, iii. 2.

See "hooded," "man," and "bated," as previously explained under the present heading.

> To-night she is *mew'd* up to her heaviness.—*Ibid.*, iii. 4.
>   Come, *seeling* night,
> Scarf up the tender eye of pitiful day.—*Macb.*, iii. 2.

"Seeling" means 'blinding'; it being the custom to *seel* the eyes of a hawk by sewing its upper and under lids together, in order to accustom it to its hood.

> Did you say all? Oh, hell-kite! All?
> What! all my pretty chickens and their dam
> At one fell *swoop*?—*Macb.*, iv. 3.

This is the expression used for the sweeping flight with which a bird of prey descends upon the object of its pursuit.

There is, sir, an *aiery* of children, little *eyases*, that cry out on the top of question.—*Hamlet*, ii. 2.

See "aiery" and "eyas-musket," previously explained.

> If he be now return'd,
> As *checking at* his voyage.—*Ibid.*, iv. 7.

"Checking at" means 'flying startingly from'; see "checks," previously explained.

> Oh, *well-flown, bird!*—*Lear*, iv. 6.

This was the falconer's exclamation when the hawk was successful in her flight.

> I'll *watch him tame*, and talk him out of patience.—*Oth.*, iii. 3.
> To *seel* her father's eyes up close as oak.—*Ibid.*, iii. 3.

See "seeling," previously explained.

>   If I do prove her *haggard*,
> Though that her *jesses* were my dear heart-strings,
> I'd *whistle her off*, and *let her down the wind*,
> To prey at fortune.—*Ibid.*, iii. 3.

" Haggard " was the term for a degenerate, wild, irreclaimable, or unreclaimed hawk ; " jesses " were short thongs or straps of leather attached to the foot of the hawk, which the falconer twisted round his hand, to hold the bird firmly on the fist ; " whistle her off " meant ' dismiss her ; ' and as the falconer always let fly the hawk against the wind, because if she flew with the wind behind her she seldom returned, so, if a hawk for any reason were dismissed, she was " let down the wind," to shift for herself.

> But when we in our viciousness grow hard
> (Oh, misery on 't !), the wise gods *seel* our eyes.—*Ant. & C.*, iii. 11.
> When thou shalt be *disedg'd* by her
> That now thou *tir'st on.*—*Cym.*, iii. 4.

" Disedg'd " means the edge of appetite taken off ; for " tir'st," see " tire," previously explained.

> The holy eagle
> *Stoop'd*, as to *foot* us : . . . his royal bird
> *Prunes* the immortal wing, and *cloys his beak.*—*Ibid.*, v. 4.

To " foot " is to ' clutch in the talons.' "Cloys," ' cleys,' or ' clees,' are old forms of ' claws ; ' and to claw their beaks is an accustomed action with eagles and hawks.

Shakespeare uses several technicalities of hunting and sporting :—

> How to deny them, whom t' advance, and whom
> To *trash* for *over-topping.*—*Temp.*, i. 2.

These are terms of the chase. To " trash " meant to check, stop, or correct a hound ; " over-topping " meant outrunning the rest of the pack.

> For *stale* to catch these thieves.—*Ibid.*, iv. 1.

A " stale " was a fowling term ; and meant a decoy, lure, or bait.

> I 'll warrant we 'll unkennel the fox. Let me stop this way first. So, now *uncape.*
> —*Merry W.*, iii. 3.

To " uncape " is to ' unearth.'

> If I *cry out* thus upon *no trail*, never trust me when I *open* again.—*Ibid.*, iv. 2.

To " cry out " and to " open " mean to bark at sight of the game ; and " trail " is the track of scent left by its passage over the ground.

> Divide me like *a bribed buck*, each a haunch : I will keep my sides to myself, my shoulders for *the fellow of this walk*, and my horns I bequeath your husbands. Am I a *woodman*, ha ?—*Ibid.*, v. 5.

A " bribed buck " was a buck cut up into portions for distribution : from French, *bribe*, a piece or portion ; " the fellow of this walk " means the forester. " Woodman " was a title given to the forester's attendant ; and meant one generally skilled in the sport of hunting game.

> I am glad, though you have ta'en a special *stand* to strike at me, that your arrow hath glanced.—*Ibid.*, v. 5.

A " stand " was a refuge-place formed with boughs, wherein ladies might station themselves to witness the sport of deer-shooting, and from whence they might even take part in it, by aiming at the game driven by the keepers near to them

He's a better *woodman* than thou takest him for.—*M. for M.*, iv. 3.

Here, as in the passage from "The Merry Wives of Windsor," "woodman" is used in an equivocal sense, for a hunter of game, or sportsman.

A hound that *runs counter*, and yet *draws dry-foot* well.—*Com. of E.*, iv. 2.

To "run counter" meant to run in a contrary direction from the game, by following on a wrong scent ; and to "draw dry-foot" meant to track by the print left by the foot of the game. The terms are here used with a play on the words.

That I will have a *recheat* winded in my forehead, or hang my bugle in an invisible *baldrick*, all women shall pardon me.—*M. Ado*, i. 1.

A "recheat" was a note sounded on a hunting-horn to call back the hounds when they pursued a wrong scent, from the old French *recet*, used for *retraite ;* and a "baldrick" was the belt in which the hunting-horn or "bugle" was slung.

Stalk on, stalk on ; the fowl sits.—*Ibid.*, ii. 3.

This was a phrase used in reference to the 'stalking-horse' ; a real or painted and stuffed animal, from behind which sportsmen used to shoot at their game.

The deer was, as you know, *sanguis,—in blood.* . . . it was *a buck of the first head.* . . . 'twas *a pricket* . . . ; some say *a sore ;* . . . then *sorel* jumps from thicket.—*Love's L. L.*, iv. 2.

"In blood" signified in season, in good condition, fit for killing ; "a buck of the first head" was the term given to a buck in its fifth year ; "a pricket," in its second year ; "a sore" in its fourth year ; "a sorel," in its third year.

The noblest deer hath them as huge as the *rascal.*—*As You L.*, iii. 3.

"Rascal" was the term for lean deer.

He uses his folly like *a stalking-horse*, and under the presentation of that, he shoots his wit.—*Ibid.*, v. 4.

See above for the explanation of "stalking-horse."

> *Trash* Merriman,—the poor cur is *emboss'd ;*
> And couple Clowder with the deep-mouth'd *brach.*
> Saw'st thou not, boy, how Silver made it good
> At the hedge corner, *in the coldest fault ?*
> I would not lose the dog for twenty pound.—
> Why, Belman is as good as he, my lord ;
> He *cried upon it* at the merest loss,
> And twice to-day pick'd out the dullest scent.—*Tam. of S.*, Induc. 1.

"Trash" has been previously explained ; "emboss'd" signifies foaming at the mouth, panting for breath, and wearied out ; "brach" means a bitch-hound ; and "in the coldest fault" means 'when the scent was at the coldest and the dogs were most at fault.'

We have almost *embossed him.*—*All's W.*, iii. 6.

The expression here signifies 'run him down,' 'hunted him down,' 'wearied him out.'

We'll make you some sport with the fox, ere we *case him.*—*Ibid.*, iii. 6.

Meaning, strictly, ' skin him '; figuratively, ' strip him of his deceitful coverings,' ' unmask him.'

> This same coxcomb *that we have i' the wind.*—*All's W.*, iii. 6.

Besides signifying ' that we have scent of,' the phrase meant ' that we have got the upper hand of.'

> Come, my young soldier, put up your iron : you are *well fleshed ;* come on.—*Tw. N.*, iv. 1.

The phrase signified ' well initiated and well trained '; it being the custom to initiate and train dogs by giving them flesh to eat, and to establish them in practice by satiating them with it.

> And then to sigh, as 'twere *the mort o' the deer.*—*W. T.*, i. 2.

This was the name given to a prolonged note blown on the hunting-horn at the death of the deer.

> Before the game 's a-foot, thou still *lett'st slip.*—1 *H. IV.*, i. 3.

To " let slip" was to free the dogs from the leash in which they were held till the game was in view.

> No more truth in thee than *a drawn fox.*—*Ibid.*, iii. 3.

A fox drawn from his cover to be hunted.

> Come, you thin thing ! come, you *rascal !*—2 *H. IV.*, v. 4.
> Turn head, and stop pursuit; for coward dogs
> Most *spend their mouths*, when what they seem to threaten
> Runs far before them.—*H. V.*, ii. 4.

To " spend their mouths " is to bark superfluously.

> I see you stand like greyhounds in *the slips*,
> Straining upon the start. The game 's a-foot.—*Ibid.*, iii. 1.

" Slips " are straps of leather by which hounds are held in couples, so as to let two start together.

> If we be English deer, be, then, *in blood ;*
> Not *rascal-like*, to fall down with a pinch,
> But rather, moody-mad and desperate stags,
> Turn on the bloody hounds with heads of steel,
> And make the cowards *stand* aloof *at bay.*—1 *H. VI.*, iv. 2.
> Thou *rascal*, that art worst *in blood* to run.—*Coriol.*, i. 1.
>   I 'd make a *quarry*
> With thousands of these quarter'd slaves.—*Ibid.*, i. 1.

A " quarry" meant not only a heap of slaughtered game, but also the offal portion given to hounds as a reward for having hunted well.

> When they shall see, sir, his crest up again, and the man *in blood*, they will out of their burrows, like conies after rain, and revel all with him.—*Ibid.*, iv. 5.
>   Here wast thou *bay'd*, brave hart ;
> Here didst thou fall ; and here thy hunters stand,
> Sign'd in thy spoil, and crimson'd in thy lethe.—*Jul. C.*, iii. 1.

" Bay'd " here means ' brought to bay.'

> Fortune on his damned *quarry* smiling.—*Macb.*, i. 2.
> Were, on the *quarry* of these murder'd deer,
> To add the death of you.—*Ibid.*, iv. 3.

Why do you go about *to recover the wind* of me, as if you would drive me into a toil ?—*Hamlet*, iii. 2.

This means 'to take advantage by getting to the windward.' See " have i' the wind," previously explained.

> How cheerfully *on the false trail they cry* !
> Oh, this is *counter*, you false Danish dogs !—*Hamlet*, iv. 5.

See " trail " and " counter," previously explained.

> This *quarry* cries on havoc.—*Ibid.*, v. 2.
> You, Polydore, have prov'd best *woodman*, and
> Are master of the feast.—*Cym.*, iii. 6.

Shakespeare uses a technicality of angling :—

> I am angling now,
> Though you perceive not how I *give line.*—*W. T.*, i. 2.

And many technicalities of archery :—

> Behold her that *gave aim* to all thy oaths,
> And entertain'd them deeply in her heart :
> How oft hast thou with perjury *cleft* the root.—*Two G. of V.*, v. 4.

" Gave aim " means 'formed the mark ; ' and " cleft " means 'pierced' or 'hit.'

> To these violent proceedings all my neighbours shall *cry aim.*—*Merry W.*, iii. 2.

An expression of encouragement used first among archers, and afterwards colloquially, to signify incitement or approval.

> I 'll make a *shaft* or a *bolt* on 't.—*Ibid.*, iii. 4.

A " shaft " was a sharp arrow used by skilful archers; a " bolt " was a blunt one, employed to shoot birds; so that the phrase in the text became a proverbial phrase, signifying, 'I'll do it either cleverly or clumsily,' 'hit or miss.'

> Believe not that the *dribbling* dart of love
> Can pierce a complete bosom.—*M. for M.*, i. 4.

A poor marksman was called ' a dribbler.'

> Challenged Cupid at the *flight ;* and my uncle's fool, reading the challenge, subscribed for Cupid, and challenged him at the *bird-bolt.*—*M. Ado*, i. 1.

A " flight " was a long sharp arrow; the " bird-bolt " was a short, thick, blunt one, the use of which was permitted to fools and jesters.

> Cupid's *butt-shaft* is too hard for Hercules' club.—*Love's L. L.*, i. 2.

A " butt-shaft " was an arrow used for shooting at butts with ; the " butt " being the place on which the mark to be aimed at was set.

> Hereby, upon the edge of yonder coppice ;
> A *stand* where you may make the fairest shoot.—*Ibid.*, iv. 1.
> *Wide o' the bow-hand !* i' faith, your hand is out.—
> Indeed, 'a must shoot nearer, or he 'll ne'er *hit the clout.*—
> An if my hand be out, then belike your hand is in.—
> Then will she get the upshot by *cleaving the pin.*—*Ibid.*, iv. 1.

" Wide o' the bow-hand " meant a shot too much to the left of the mark ; " the clout " was the white mark at which archers took aim ; and " cleaving the pin " meant hitting the centre of the butts.

> 'Twas I won the wager, though you *hit the white.*—*Tam. of S.*, v. 2.

This term meant to win by hitting the centre of the target, which was generally painted white.

His death will be a march of *twelve-score.*—1 *H. IV.*, ii. 4.

This, in archery language meant 'twelve-score yards.'

He drew a good bow;—and dead! he shot a fine shoot: . . . he would have *clapped in the clout* at *twelve-score;* and carried you *a fore-hand shaft a fourteen and fourteen and a half.*—2 *H. IV.*, iii. 2.

" A fore-hand shaft " was an arrow peculiarly constructed for shooting straightforward.

Shot thorough the ear with a love-song; the very *pin* of his heart *cleft* with the blind bow-boy's *butt-shaft.*—*R. & Jul.*, ii. 4.

The " pin " was the black nail in the centre of the " clout " or white mark at which archers took aim.

So that my arrows,
Too slightly timber'd for so loud a wind,
Would have reverted to my bow again,
And not where I had aim'd them.—*Hamlet*, iv. 6.

This shows knowledge of an axiom in archery, that '*light shafts* cannot stand in a *rough wind.*'

Let me still remain the true *blank* of thine eye.—*Lear*, i. 1.

This was another term for the white mark at which shooters aimed.

That fellow handles his bow like a *crow-keeper:* draw me a *clothier's yard.* . . . i' *the clout, i' the clout.*—*Ibid.*, iv. 6.

For the purpose of keeping crows from the corn, a fellow with a bow and arrow, or a stuffed figure similarly armed, were employed; and " a clothier's yard " meant an arrow the length of a clothier's yard.

Shakespeare uses some technicalities of gunnery :—

What's this? a sleeve? 'tis like *a demi-cannon.*—*Tam. of S.*, iv. 3.

This was a great gun, six and a half inches diameter in the bore, twelve feet long; carrying a shot six inches one-sixth diameter, and thirty-two pounds weight.

The harlot king
Is quite beyond mine arm, out of the *blank*
And *level* of my brain, plot-proof,—*W. T.*, ii. 3.

The " blank " means the ' mark '; the " level " means the ' range,' the ' space within aim.'

My life stands in the *level* of your dreams.—*Ibid.*, iii. 2.

Such as fear the report of a *caliver* worse than a struck fowl, or a hurt wild-duck.— 1 *H. IV.*, iv. 2.

A " caliver " (which is a corruption of ' caliber ') was a hand-gun, smaller and lighter than a musket, with a bore, or caliber, of a particular size.

Put me a *caliver* into Wart's hand. . . . Come, manage me your *caliver.*— 2 *H. IV.*, iii. 2.

As level as the cannon to his *blank.*—*Hamlet*, iv. 1.

This,
Like to a *murdering-piece*, in many places
Gives me superfluous death.—*Ibid.*, iv. 5.

The name given to a small piece of ordnance, that had several barrels. It was charged with bullets, nails, old iron, &c.; and with it could be kept up a murderously raking fire.

I have words to speak in thine ear will make thee dumb ; yet are they much too light for the *bore* of the matter.—*Hamlet*, iv. 6 (*Letter*).

The " bore " means the caliber or circumferential size of a gun barrel.

And stood within the *blank* of his displeasure.—*Oth.*, iii. 4.

And several military technicalities :—

He that *sets up his rest* to do more exploits with his *mace* than a *morris-pike.—Com. of E.*, iv. 3.

The expression " sets up his rest " is here used in the double sense it bore as a gaming technicality and as a military technicality ; as the latter, meaning planted the " rest " in which pikes were occasionally fixed to receive a charge during an engagement. " Mace " is here used in the double sense it bore as a sergeant's staff of office, and as the weapon employed both in battles and tournaments ; and a " morris-pike " meant a Moorish pike ; that being a military weapon much used in the sixteenth century.

He had the honour to be the officer at a place there called Mile End, to instruct for *the doubling of files.—All's W.*, iv. 3.

In reference to the military evolution of ' marching in double file,' or two by two.

He that is well hanged in this world needs to *fear no colours.* . . . I can tell thee where that saying was born, of, I *fear no colours* . . . In the wars.—*Tw. N.*, i. 5.

The phrase was of military origin, signifying ' fear no foe, under whatever colours he may fight ' ; but it came to be familiarly used, meaning ' fear no threats or danger, under whatever aspect they may approach.'

Cry, *havock*, kings ! back to the stained field.—*John*, ii. 2.

" Havock " was the word used in war as a declaration that no quarter should be given.

Tut, tut ; good enough to *toss.*—1 *H. IV.*, iv. 2.

" To toss " here means to be tossed upon a pike ; the expression for handling the weapon called a pike being to " toss."

Hold, Wart, *traverse ;* thus, thus, thus.—
Come, *manage* me your caliver . . . he would *manage*
You his piece thus.—2 *H. IV.*, iii. 2.

" Traverse " was an ancient military term for " march " ; and " manage " was the technical military expression, applied to arms or weapons, signifying ' handle,' ' manipulate,' ' use.'

To a loud trumpet or *a point of war.—Ibid.*, iv. 1.

This was the term for a warlike flourish, a martial call to arms played on some instrument.

Fear no colours : go with me to dinner.—*Ibid.*, v. 5.
The soldiers should have *toss'd* me on their pikes
Before I would have granted to that act.—3 *H. VI.*, i. 1.
Do not cry *havock*, where you should but hunt
With modest warrant.—*Coriol.*, iii. 1.

The centurions and their charges, distinctly billeted, already *in the entertainment*, and to be on foot at an hour's warning.—*Ibid.*, iv. 3.

This expression meant ‘ in pay.’

> All places yield to him ere he *sits down.—Coriol.*, iv. 7.

To ‘ sit down before a place ’ meant ‘ prepare to capture it,’ ‘ commence besieging it.’

> *Kill, kill, kill, kill, kill* him !—
> *Hold, hold, hold, hold !—Ibid.*, v. 5.

The first of these exclamations was the word formerly given, when an onset was made upon the enemy ; the second was the phrase used when parting combatants.

> Cry, “ *Havock*,” and let slip the dogs of war.—*Jul. C.*, iii. 1.
> Nor heaven peep through the blanket of the dark,
> To cry, *Hold, hold !—Macb.*, i. 5.
> And damn’d be him that first cries, “ *Hold*, enough ! ”—*Ibid.*, v. 7.
> This quarry cries on *havock.—Hamlet*, v. 2.
> Then, *kill, kill, kill, kill, kill, kill !—Lear*, iv. 6.
> Dispose of them, of me ; *the walls are thine.—Ibid.*, v. 2.

This is equivalent to ‘ the besieged city surrenders.’

> *Traverse ;* go ; provide thy money.—*Oth.*, i. 3.
> If the general camp, *pioneers*, and all.—*Ibid.*, iii. 3.

These were generally degraded soldiers ; appointed to be “ pioneers,” as a punishment for misbehaviour.

He uses some technicalities of tilting and tourneying :—

> Sir, I shall *meet* your wit *in the career*, an you *charge* it *against* me.   I pray you choose another subject.
> Nay, then give him another staff: this last was *broke cross.—M. Ado*, v. 1.

To “ meet in the career ” meant to encounter at full gallop ; and it was reckoned a great disgrace to have the lance broken across the body of an opponent, instead of by a thrust with the point.

> Full merrily
> Hath this brave *manage*, this *career* been run.—*Love's L. L.*, v. 2.

“ Manage ” meant the controlment or government of a horse.

> I would I had ; so I had *broke* thy pate,
> And ask’d thee mercy for ’t.—
> Good faith, *across.—All's W.*, ii. 1.

See “ broke cross,” previously explained.

> I am courtier *cap-à-pé.—W. T.*, iv. 3.

This expression, meaning ‘ from head to foot,’ was originally employed to express clad in a complete suit of armour ; but came to be more generally applied.

> Which now the *manage* of two kingdoms must
> With fearful bloody issue arbitrate.—*John*, i. 1.
> Or, if misfortune miss the first *career*,
> Be Mowbray’s sins so heavy in his bosom,
> That they may break his foaming courser’s back,
> And throw the rider headlong in the lists.—*R. II.*, i. 2.
> Stay, the king hath thrown his *warder* down.—*Ibid.*, i. 3.

This was a kind of truncheon or staff, held by the umpire who presided at trials by combat ; when thrown up, it was a signal to charge ; when " thrown down," a signal to desist.

> And *stickler*-like the armies separates.—*Tr. & Cr.*, v. 9.

A " stickler" was the name given to the person appointed as umpire in combats or trials of skill, and to decide when the contest should cease ; which he signified by interposing the *stick*, staff, or wand that he bore for the purpose.

> Rather than so, come, fate, into the list,
> And champion me *to the utterance !*—*Macb.*, iii. 1.

Derived from the French phrase *à l'outrance ;* signifying ' to the uttermost,' ' to extremity,' or ' unto death.'

> Arm'd at all points exactly, *cap-à-pé.*—*Hamlet*, i. 2.
> Behoves me keep *at utterance.*—*Cym.*, iii. 1.

Several technicalities of fencing and duelling :—

> Come from thy *ward*,
> For I can here disarm thee with this stick,
> And make thy weapon drop.—*Temp.*, i. 2.

" Ward " means ' posture of defence.'

In these times you stand on *distance*, your *passes*, *stoccadoes*, and I know not what : 'tis the heart, Master Page ; 'tis here, 'tis here. I have seen the time, with my *long sword*, I would have made you four tall fellows skip like rats.—*Merry W.*, ii. 1.

" Distance," " passes," and " stoccadoes " were terms used in rapier-fencing ; while the " long sword " was often a weapon of such length as to require both hands used in raising it.

To see thee fight, to see thee *foin*, to see thee *traverse ;* to see thee here, to see thee there ; to see thee pass thy *punto*, thy *stock*, thy *reverse*, thy *distance*, thy *montànt*.—*Ibid.*, ii. 3.

" Foin " was to make a fencing-thrust ; " traverse " was to baffle by shifting place ; " punto," " stock," " reverse," and " montànt " were terms derived from the Italian fencing-school.

> Sir boy, I 'll whip you from your *foining* fence.—*M. Ado*, v. 1.
> If he be, he knows how to *turn his girdle.*—*Ibid.*, v. 1.

A phrase familiarly used as a challenge to fight. It arose from the practice of wearing the sword at the back ; so that, to bring it round ready for use, the belt or girdle had to be turned or shifted. The belt was fastened in front by a buckle, which, in wrestling, used to be turned behind, to give the adversary a fairer grasp at the girdle ; and thus the phrase, as a challenge, had a double origin.

Thy wit is as quick as the greyhound's mouth—it catches.—And yours as blunt as the fencer's foils, which hit, but hurt not.—A most manly wit, Margaret ; it will not hurt a woman : and so, I pray thee, call Beatrice : *I give thee the bucklers.*—*Ibid.*, v. 2.

This phrase originated at sword and buckler practice, and passed into current use, signifying, ' I yield,' ' I own myself defeated.'

The first and second cause will not serve my turn ; the *passado* he respects not, the *duello* he regards not.—*Love's L. L.*, i. 2.

Technical terms derived from the treatises of Italian writers on the art of defence.

Dismount thy *tuck*, be yare in thy preparation.—*Tw. N.*, iii. 4.

The "tuck" was a rapier (in later times called 'a small sword'); from the Italian *stocco.*

Hob, nob, is his word; give't or take't.—*Tw. N.,* iii. 4.

This phrase, used in drinking as well as fighting, is probably a corruption of ' hab or nab,' and derived from the Saxon, *habban,* to have, and *nabban,* not to have.

I had *a pass* with him, rapier, scabbard, and all, and he gives me the *stuck in,* with such a mortal motion, that it is inevitable; and on the answer, he pays you as surely as your feet hit the ground they step on: they say he has been fencer to the Sophy.— *Ibid.,* iii. 4.

" Stuck in " is derived from the Italian *stoccata,* ' thrust.'

He cannot *by the duello* avoid it.—*Ibid.,* iii. 4.

Thou knowest my old *ward ;*—here I lay, and thus I bore my point.—1 *H. IV.,* ii. 4.

He fights as you sing prick-song, keeps *time, distance,* and *proportion ;* rests me his minim rest, one, two, and the third in your bosom: the very butcher of a silk button, a duellist, a duellist ; a gentleman *of the very first house,—of the first and second cause :* ah! the immortal *passado !* the *punto reverso !* the *hay !—R. & Jul.,* ii. 4.

The expression " of the very first house " and " of the first and second cause " are styles of excellence in the art of quarrelling, as belonging to one who would be master of all its degrees, according to the books and treatises upon this subject. " Hay" is derived from the Italian word *hai,* ' thou hast it ' ; and was used when a thrust told upon an opponent, as in modern fencing phraseology " ha ! " is employed.

A la stoccata carries it away. . . . Come, sir, your *passado.*—*Ibid.,* iii. 1.

If he by chance escape your venom'd *stuck.*—*Hamlet,* iv. 7.

Come ; no matter vor your *foins.*—*Lear,* iv. 6.

Several marine and nautical technicalities :—

Bring her *to try with main-course.* . . . *Lay her a-hold, a-hold! set her two courses :* off to sea again ; lay her off.—*Temp.,* i. 1.

" To try with main-course " is explained in Smith's Sea Grammar, 1627, thus :—' To hale the tacke aboord, the sheat close aft, the boling set up, and the helm tied close aboord ; ' to " lay her a-hold " is to bring the ship to lie as near the wind as she can ; and " set her two courses " means to set two of the three largest and lowest sails.

Clap on more sails; pursue; up with your *fights ;*
Give fire; she is my prize, or ocean whelm them all!—*Merry W.,* iv. 2.

" Fights " was the name for waist-cloths hung round a ship to prevent the men from being seen during an engagement.

The ship is *under sail,* and here she comes amain.—*Love's L. L.,* v. 2.

My ventures are not in one *bottom* trusted.—*Mer. of V.,* i. 1.

Will you *hoist sail,* sir ? here lies your way.—No, good *swabber ;* I am to *hull* here a little longer.—*Tw. N.,* i. 5.

" Swabber" is the sweeper of a deck ; and to " hull " is to drive to and fro upon the water without sails or rudder.

A bawbling vessel was he captain of,
For shallow *draught* and bulk unprizable;
With which such scathful grapple did he make
With the most noble *bottom* of our fleet.—*Ibid.,* v. 1.

You had much ado to make his anchor hold:
When you cast out, *it still came home.*—*W. T.,* i. 2.

Meaning, ' it could not be made to take hold.'

> Than now the English *bottoms* have waft o'er.—*John*, ii. 1.
> Provokes the mightiest *hulk* against the tide.—1 *H. VI.*, v. 5.
> And there they *hull*, expecting but the aid.—*R. III.*, iv. 4.
>   Thus *hulling* in
> The wild sea of my conscience, I did steer
> Toward this remedy.—*H. VIII.*, ii. 4.
> And *sounded all the depths and shoals* of honour.—*Ibid.*, iii. 2.
> Light boats sail swift, though greater *hulks draw deep.*—*Tr. & Cr.*, ii. 3.
> Mine honour *keeps the weather* of my fate.—*Ibid.*, v. 3.

This phrase means, ' has the advantage of the wind,' ' keeps to windward'; figuratively used to express, ' maintains superiority over.'

> Omitted, all the voyage of their life
> Is *bound* in shallows and in miseries.—*Jul. C.*, iv. 3.

" Bound " is here used as it is in such sea-terms as ' weatherbound,' or ' windbound '; and therefore well expresses ' held fast,' ' hemmed in,' ' kept still.'

> She once being *loof'd*,
> The noble ruin of her magic, Antony,
> Claps on his sea-wing.—*Ant. & C.*, iii. 8.

" Loof'd " is an old form of ' luffed '; which means, ' brought close to the wind,' ' sailed before the wind,' ' went to windward.'

> *Slack the bolins* there! . . . But *sea-room*, an the brine and cloudy billow kiss the moon, I care not. . . . Your queen must *overboard* . . . she must *overboard* straight. —*Per.*, iii. 1.

"Bolins" is a sailorly pronunciation of ' bow-lines ': meaning the ropes by which the sails of a ship are governed when the wind is unfavourable, and which are slackened when it is high.

Several technicalities of horsemanship and farriery :—

> And so conclusions passed the *careires.*—*Merry W.*, i. 1.

This was a term of the *manège*, for running at full speed.

> Ay, that I will, *come cut and long-tail*, under the degree of a squire.—*Ibid.*, iii. 4.

A " cut " meant a horse with a docked tail; and " long-tail," a horse with an undocked tail. The phrase " come cut and long-tail " was used proverbially to express, ' whatever kind may come.'

> Sir, *give him head :* I know he 'll prove a jade.—*Tam. of S.*, i. 2.

This term means letting the rein or bridle lie loose, so as to give the horse his own course.

> His horse hipped with an old mothy saddle, and stirrups of no kindred ; besides, possessed with *the glanders*, and like to *mose in the chine;* troubled with *the lampass*, infected with *the fashions*, full of *windgalls*, sped with *spavins*, *raied with the yellows*, past cure of *the fives*, stark spoiled with *the staggers*, begnawn with *the bots*, *swayed in the back*, and *shoulder-shotten; ne'er legged before.*—*Ibid.*, iii. 2.

These are all diseases and defects to which horses are subject.

> The poor jade is *wrung in the withers.* . . . That is the next way to give poor jades *the bots.*—1 *H. IV.*, ii. 1.

" Wrung " means ' strained ' or ' wryed,' and also ' galled ' or ' hurt'; " the withers " is the joining of the shoulder-blades at the bottom of the neck and mane of a horse.

> I will not change my horse with any that treads but on four *pasterns.*—*H. V.*, iii. 7.

The " pastern " is that part of the leg of a horse between the joint next the foot and the coronet of the hoof.

> Their wounded steeds fret *fetlock* deep in gore.—*H. V.*, iv. 7.

The " fetlock " is a tuft of hair that grows behind the pastern-joint of a horse.

> And *given* unto the house of York such *head*,
> As thou shalt reign but by their sufferance.—3 *H. VI.*, i. 1.
>
> Let the galled jade wince, our *withers are unwrung*.—*Hamlet*, iii. 2.

Some technicalities of bear-baiting :—

> Are these thy bears ? we 'll *bait* thy bears to death,
> And manacle the *bear-ward* in their chains,
> If thou dar'st bring them to the *baiting-place*.—2 *H. VI.*, v. 1.
>
> Or as a bear, encompass'd round with dogs,—
> Who having *pinch'd* a few, and made them cry,
> The rest stand all aloof, and bark at him.—3 *H. VI.*, ii. 1.
>
> Let us do so, for we are *at the stake*,
> And *bay'd* about with many enemies.—*Jul. C.*, iv. 1.
>
> They have *tied me to a stake ;* I cannot fly,
> But, bear-like, I must fight *the course*.—*Macb.*, v. 7.
>
> I am *tied to the stake*, and I must stand *the course*.—*Lear*, iii. 7.

Several, of gaming :—

> Let vultures gripe thy guts ! for *gourd and fullam* holds,
> And *high and low* beguile the rich and poor.—*Merry W.*, i. 3.

These were gamblers' names for false dice.

> He that *sets up his rest* to do more exploits.—*Com. of E.*, iv. 3.

This expression is here partly used in its sense as a military technicality [*See* the passage, as previously explained, under the present heading], and partly in its sense as a gaming technicality ; as the latter, it was used at the game of primero, signifying to remain satisfied with the hand then held. Thence, it came to mean being resolved or determined ; also, to have made up one's mind, or to be convinced.

> She hung about my neck; and kiss on kiss
> She *vied* so fast, protesting oath on oath.—*Tam. of S.*, ii. 1.

" Vied " signifies ' proffered in competition ; ' to " vie " and " re-vie " were terms used in the game of primero, signifying to stake or wager the goodness of one hand of cards against another.

> Gremio is *out-vied*.—*Ibid.*, ii. 1.
>
> Yet I have *fac'd it with a card of ten*.—*Ibid.*, ii. 1.

Meaning, ' made a bold stand by playing one of the highest cards in the pack.'

> Since you *set up your rest* 'gainst remedy.—*All's W.*, ii. 1.
>
> The odds for *high and low*'s alike.—*W. T.*, v. 1.
>
> If what *in rest* you have in right you hold.—*John*, iv. 2.
>
> Who *sets* me else ? By Heaven, I 'll *throw* at all.—*R. II.*, iv. 1.

" Sets " meant ' offers a wager,' ' defies competition '; and " throw," to cast the dice.

> There lies *a cooling card*.—1 *H. VI.*, v. 3.

This was the term for a card so decisive as to cool the courage of an adversary.

> But whiles he thought to steal the single *ten*,
> The *king* was slily finger'd from the *deck !*—3 *H. VI.*, v. 1.

" Deck " was an old term for a pack of cards.

> Yes, if I *make my play.—H. VIII.*, i. 4.

Meaning, ' win the game.'

> And hardly shall I *carry out my side.—Lear*, v. 1.

' Succeed in winning the game.'

> Or Cassio him, or each do kill the other,
> Every way *makes my game.—Oth.*, v. 1.
>
>> She, Eros, has
> *Pack'd cards* with Cæsar, and false play'd my glory
> Unto an enemy's *triumph.—Ant. & C.*, iv. 12.

To " pack cards " meant to shuffle them unfairly ; and " triumph " is, 'trump-card.'

> Nature wants stuff to *vie* strange forms with fancy.—*Ibid.*, v. 2.

Some technicalities of bowling :—

> Commodity, the *bias* of the world ;
> The world, who of itself is peized well,
> Made to *run even* upon even ground,
> Till this advantage, this vile drawing *bias*,
> This sway of motion, this commodity,
> Makes it take head from all indifferency,
> From all direction, purpose, course, intent :
> And this same *bias*, this commodity,
> This cheat, this broker, this all-changing word,
> Clapp'd on the outward *eye* of fickle France,
> Hath drawn him from his own determined aid.—*John*, ii. 2.

" Bias " is the weight lodged on one side of a bowl, which turns it from the straight line ; and " eye " was the term for the aperture in which the weight or " bias " that sways it is lodged.

> Madam, we'll play at bowls.—
> 'Twill make me think the world is full of *rubs*,
> And that my fortune runs against the *bias.—R. II.*, iii. 4.

" Rubs " are the inequalities of ground that hinder the motion of a bowl.

> So, so ; *rub* on, and *kiss the mistress.—Tr. & Cr.*, iii. 2.

The " mistress " or " jack " is the name for the smaller bowl, used as a mark for the other bowls ; and when any of them " kiss " and remain close to it, an advantage is gained.

> To sleep ! perchance to dream : ay, there's the *rub.—Hamlet*, iii. 1.
>
> Whose disposition, all the world knows,
> Will not be *rubb'd* nor *stopp'd.—Lear*, ii. 2.

Was there ever man had such luck ! when I *kissed the jack*, upon an *upcast* to be hit away !—*Cym.*, ii. 1.

A few instances of tennis and racket :—

> Well *bandied* both ; a *set* of wit well play'd.—*Love's L. L.*, v. 2.

To " bandy " is to send the ball from one to another ; and a " set " means a game.

But that the *tennis-court keeper* knows better than I ; for it is a low ebb of linen with thee when thou *keepest not racket* there.—*2 H. IV.*, ii. 2.

This passage shows that racket-players usually played, as the phrase goes, ' in their shirt-sleeves ' ; so that when Master Poins' stock of linen was worn out, he could not frequent the tennis-court, because he could not take off his coat while keeping up the game.

> When we have match'd our *rackets* to these *balls*,
> We will, in France, by God's grace, *play a set*
> Shall *strike* his father's crown *into the hazard*.
> Tell him he hath *made a match* with such a *wrangler*
> That all the *courts* of France will be disturb'd
> With *chases*.—*H. V.*, i. 2.

The " hazard " was a portion of the tennis-court into which the ball was occasionally struck; " wrangler " meant a player who runs back, yet does not cease to contend; and " chases " meant contests between tennis-players, during which the object is on each side to keep up the ball.

> She would be as swift in motion as a ball;
> My words would *bandy* her to my sweet love,
> And his to me.—*R. & Jul.*, ii. 5.

Some of wrestling :—

> We all were sea-swallow'd, though some *cast* again.—*Temp.*, ii. 1.

The word " cast " is here used in various senses [*See* Varied Meanings Combined, &c.]; but as employed in wrestling it means ' thrown.'

A disposition to come in disguised against me to *try a fall*.—*As You L.*, i. 1.

The eldest of the three wrestled with Charles, the duke's wrestler; which Charles in a moment *threw* him, and broke three of his ribs.—*Ibid.*, i. 2.

You shall *try but one fall*.—*Ibid.*, i. 2.

It is young Orlando that *tripped up* the wrestler's heels and your heart, both, in an instant.—*Ibid.*, iii. 2.

Being too strong for him, though he took up my legs sometime, yet I made a shift to *cast* him.—*Macb.*, ii. 3.

Nor *tripped* neither, you base foot-ball player.—*Lear*, i. 4.

Flattering his displeasure, *tripp'd me behind*.—*Ibid.*, ii. 2.

Some convivial technicalities :—

> Why, now you have *done me right*.—
> *Do me right*, and dub me knight.—*2 H. IV.*, v. 3.

These phrases signified ' pledged me,' or ' pledge me,' and ' drunk as deep as I do,' or ' drink as deep as I do.'

> Should find a *running banquet* ere they rested.—*H. VIII.*, i. 4.
> Besides the *running banquet* of two beadles.—*Ibid.*, v. 3.

This was the term given to a light repast taken hastily; and generally consisted of fruit, cakes, sweetmeats, wines, &c.

> By the mass, you'll *crack a quart* together.—*2 H. IV.*, v. 3.
> I pray, come and *crush a cup of wine*.—*R. & Jul.*, i. 2.

These were phrases in use formerly, equivalent to the modern one of ' crack a bottle.'

> We'll teach you to *drink deep* ere you depart.—*Hamlet*, i. 2.
> To the health of our general!
> I am for it, lieutenant; and I'll *do you justice*.—*Oth.*, ii. 3.

Meaning, ' drink as much as you do '; ' honour your toast.'

The technical call to tapsters, and the technical reply of tapsters :—

> Spent with crying " *Bring in!* "—*1 H. IV.*, i. 2.
> Francis!—*Anon, anon, sir.*—*Ibid.*, ii. 4.

Some theatrical technicalities :—

> Though some *cast* again ;
> And by that destiny, to *perform* an act,
> Whereof what's past is *prologue ;* what to come,
> In yours and my *discharge.—Temp.*, ii. 1.

See " cast," previously explained as a term in wrestling ; which is one of the senses the word bears in this passage. It also includes the sense of ' cast ' (or selected) for a part in a play. " Discharge " was formerly sometimes used for ' enact ' or ' act ' a part in a play.

> When I *presented* Ceres, I thought to have told thee.—*Ibid.*, iv. 1.

" Presented " was sometimes used for ' represented,' ' enacted,' or ' performed.'

> Go get us *properties*, and tricking for our fairies.—*Merry W.*, iv. 4.

" Properties " are stage necessaries.

> Speak, count, 'tis your *cue.—M. Ado*, ii. 1.

The " cue " means the concluding words of a speech, which give warning to the next speaker that his turn is come to speak.

> Great Hercules is *presented* by this imp.—*Love's L. L.*, v. 2.

I will *discharge* it in either your straw-colour beard . . . here are your *parts* . . . there will we *rehearse* . . . I will draw a bill of *properties* . . . take pains; be *perfect.—Mid. N. D.*, i. 2.

Here 's a marvellous convenient place for our *rehearsal*. This green plot shall be our stage, this hawthorn-brake our *'tiring-house.—Ibid.*, iii. 1.

This was the place wherein the actors attired themselves—their dressing-room.

So every one according to his *cue* . . . you speak all your *part* at once, *cues* and all. Pyramus, enter: your *cue* is past; it is, " never tire."—*Ibid.*, iii. 1.

You have not a man in all Athens is able to *discharge* Pyramus but he.—*Ibid.*, iv. 2.

Say, what *abridgment* have you for this evening ?—*Ibid.*, v. 1.

An " abridgment " was a brief performance, or short entertainment.

> Had you not come upon your *cue*, my lord,
> William Lord Hastings had pronounc'd your *part*,
> I mean, your voice, for crowning of the king.—*R. III.*, iii. 4.
> How chances it they *travel ?—Hamlet*, ii. 2.

This was the term for those actors who went about the country giving performances at various places ; something equivalent to ' strolling players.'

> And are most tyrannically *clapped* for 't.—*Ibid.*, ii. 2.

Familiarly used for ' applauded.'

So berattle the common stages (so they call them) . . . if they should grow themselves to *common* players.—*Ibid.*, ii. 2.

This word " common " was technically used to express what is more modernly called ' strolling.'

> Look, where my *abridgment* comes.—*Ibid.*, ii. 2.

Shakespeare uses several musical technicalities [*See* MUSICAL TERMS] ; and a few of painting :—

> To sit and draw
> His arched brows, his hawking eye, his curls,
> In our heart's *table.—All's W.*, i. 1.

This was the term for the panel, canvas, or other substance upon which a picture is painted.

> Drawn in the flattering *table* of her eye.—*John*, ii. 2.
> That, though the truth of it *stands off* as gross
> As black from white, my eye will scarcely see it.—*H. V.*, ii 2.
> So 'tis; this *comes off* well and excellent.—*Timon*, i. 1.

" Stands off " and " comes off " are used as ' stands out ' or ' stands forth ' are used by artists to express ' is brought into relief,' ' is made boldly and distinctly prominent.'

> To this well-painted piece is Lucrece come,
> To find a face where all distress is *stel'd*.—*Lucrece*, Stanza 207.
> Mine eye hath play'd the painter, and hath *stel'd*
> Thy beauty's form in *table* of my heart.—*Sonnet* 24.

" Stel'd " is ' delineated.'

He uses a technicality of inlaying:—

> As venerable Nestor, *hatched in silver*.—*Tr. & Cr.*, i. 3.

To " hatch in silver " was the term for inlaying the fine silver hair-like lines which formed an ornamental design upon the hilts of swords, handles of daggers, and stocks of pistols; and the lines of the graver upon a plate of metal are still called ' hatchings:' French, *haché*, engraved.

And technicalities of cutlery :—

> In few, his death (whose spirit lent a fire
> Even to the dullest peasant in his camp)
> Being bruited once, took fire and heat away
> From the best *temper'd* courage in his troops;
> For from his metal was his party steel'd;
> Which once in him *abated*, all the rest
> Turn'd on themselves, like dull and heavy lead.—*2 H. IV.*, i. 1.

" Temper'd " is brought to a proper degree of hardness; and " abated " means reduced to lower temper, or, as the workmen call it, ' let down.'

Some of weaving and winding :—

> Therefore, as you unwind her love from him,
> Lest it should *ravel* and be good to none.
> You must provide to *bottom* it on me.—*Tw. G. of V.*, iii. 2.

" Ravel " here means ' become entangled '; and " bottom " is a term used by seamstresses for that on which silk or thread is wound.

> I fear not Goliath with a weaver's *beam;* because I know also life is a shuttle.—*Merry W.*, v. 1.

The " beam " is a cylindrical piece of wood belonging to the loom on which the web is gradually rolled as it is woven; and a " shuttle " is the implement with which the weaver shoots the cross threads.

> O Fates, come, come, cut *thread* and *thrum*.—*Mid. N. D.*, v. 1.

The " thrum " is the end of a weaver's warp.

> Beat me to death with a *bottom* of brown thread.—*Tam. of S.*, iv. 3.
> And must I *ravel out* my weav'd-up follies ?—*R. II.*, iv. 1.

To " ravel out " is to ' unweave ' or ' unknit.'

> Thou idle immaterial skein of *sleave-silk.*— *Tr. & Cr.*, v. 1.

" Sleave-silk " is ' raw silk,' ' unwrought silk.'

> If I should pay you for 't as 'tis extoll'd,
> It would *unclew* me quite.—*Timon*, i. 1.

To " unclew " is to ' unwind,' ' undo.'

> Sleep that knits up the *ravell'd sleave* of care.—*Macb.*, ii. 2.
> Make you to *ravel* all this matter *out.*—*Hamlet*, iii. 4.
> Be 't when she weav'd the *sleided silk.*—*Per.*, iv. (*Gower*).

This means ' unwrought silk,' prepared for weaving by passing it through the weaver's *sley* or reed-comb.

Some of heraldry :—

> They may give the dozen white luces in their *coat.*—
> It is an old *coat.* . . . I may *quarter*, coz ?—
> You may, by marrying.—*Merry W.*, i. 1.

" Coat" means ' coat of arms '; and " quarter" means bear as an appendage to the hereditary arms.

> Ford 's a knave, and I will aggravate his *style ;* thou, Master Brook, shalt know him for knave and cuckold.—*Ibid.*, ii. 2.

" Style" is a term of the herald's office for special appellation and titles.

> Each fair instalment, *coat*, and several *crest*,
> With loyal *blazon*, evermore be blest !—*Ibid.*, v. 5.

" Blazon " is here used for heraldic denotement.

> If he have wit enough to keep himself warm, let him *bear it for a difference* between himself and his horse.—*M. Ado*, i. 1.

" A difference " is a heraldic term for ' a distinction.'

> I think your *blazon* to be true.—*Ibid.*, ii. 1.

" Blazon " is here used in its sense of the art of explaining coats of arms and heraldic colours.

> So we grew together,
> Like to a double cherry, seeming parted ;
> But yet a union in partition,
> Two lovely berries moulded on one stem ;
> So, with two seeming bodies, but one heart ;
> Two of the first, like *coats* in heraldry,
> Due but to one, and crowned with one *crest.*—*Mid. N. D.*, iii. 2.

This passage refers to a heraldic technicality ; the speaker meaning that their two bodies having but one heart between them, are like the coats of arms of a married couple, which are emblazoned as two, yet are surmounted but by one crest.

> I swear I 'll cuff you, if you strike again.—
> So may you lose your *arms :*
> If you strike me, you are no gentleman ;
> And if no gentleman, why then no *arms.*—
> A herald, Kate ? Oh, put me in thy books !—
> What is your *crest ?* a coxcomb ?—*Tam. of S.*, ii. 1.
> From mine own windows torn my household *coat*,
> Raz'd out my *impress*, leaving me no sign,
> Save men's opinions and my living blood,
> To show the world I am a gentleman.—*R. II.*, iii. 1.

The family coat of arms was frequently blazoned on the stained glass forming the window-panes of old mansions. The " impress " is the heraldic motto or device, belonging to the coat of arms ; formerly spelt ' imprese,' as derived from the Italian *impresa*, ' motto.'

> With man's blood paint the ground, *gules*, *gules.*—*Timon*, iv. 3.

This is the term, in heraldic nomenclature, for ' red.'

> The rugged Pyrrhus,—he whose *sable* arms,
> Black as his purpose . . .
> Hath now this dread and black complexion smear'd
> With heraldry more dismal ; head to foot
> Now is he total *gules :* horridly trick'd
> With blood of fathers, mothers, daughters, sons.—*Hamlet*, ii. 2.

He uses some collegiate and scholastic technicalities :—

> Yes, for a score of kingdoms you should *wrangle*,
> And I would call it fair play.—*Temp.*, v. 1.

" Wrangle " is here used partly in its sense as a technical expression at the game of tennis [*See* the word " wrangler," previously explained, under the present heading], and partly in its sense as a term in logic, for ' dispute,' ' altercate.'

> What maintenance he from his friends receives,
> Like *exhibition* thou shalt have from me.—*Two G. of V.*, i. 3.

The term " exhibition " is still used in the universities for a stipend.

> Rightly reasoned, and in his own *division.*—*M. Ado*, v. 1.

This was a term for the parts or sections into which an oration is divided.

> It is the wittiest *partition* that ever I heard discourse, my lord.—*Mid. N. D.*, v. 1.

" Partition " and " partition wall " are terms employed by Hooker and other controversialists somewhat in the same sense that ' sect ' is now used.

> Of all the learned and *authentic* fellows.—*All's W.*, ii. 3.

This was an epithet applied to a physician regularly educated and licensed to practise ; the Latin phrase in the diploma of a licentiate being still *authentice licentiatus.*

> So far exceed all instance, all *discourse*,
> That I am ready to distrust mine eyes,
> And *wrangle* with my reason, that persuades me
> To any other trust but that I am mad.—*Tw. N.*, iv. 3.

" Discourse " was a scholarly term for ' ratiocination.'

> I deny your *major.*—*1 H. IV.*, ii. 4.

A " major premiss " is a term in logic signifying the first proposition of a syllogism.

> And learning, a mere hoard of gold kept by a devil, till sack *commences it*, and sets it in *act* and use.—*2 H. IV.*, iv. 3.

To " commence" is a collegiate term for 'take an academic degree'; and " act " is the term used at both universities for the exercise or ceremony observed when taking a degree.

> Subscrib'd his power ! confin'd to *exhibition !*—*Lear*, i. 2.
> To bandy hasty words, to scant my *sizes.*—*Ibid.*, ii. 4.

This expression means ' allotted portions of food,' ' allowances of provision'; and the term ' sizar ' is still used at Cambridge for that class of students who live there on a stated allowance.

> Let's have one other *gaudy* night.—*Ant. & C.*, iii. 11.

In the colleges of both universities, ' gaudy days ' is the term used for feast days : Latin, *gaudium*, joy, mirth, rejoicing.

> Hir'd with that self-*exhibition*
> Which your own coffers yield !—*Cym.*, i. 7.

He uses several legal technicalities [*See* LEGAL PHRASES] ; and one of land-buying :—

These wise men, that give fools money, get themselves a good report after *fourteen years' purchase.*—*Tw. N.*, iv. 1.

" After " is here used in the sense of ' according to the rate of ' ; and as it seems that when Shakespeare wrote, *twelve* years' purchase was about the current price of land, the phrase in the text implies an exorbitant price.

He uses one mining technicality :—

Art thou there, *true-penny ?*—*Hamlet*, i. 5.

This is a term used by miners for a particular indication in the soil of the direction in which ore may be found.

A few millers' and bakers' technicalities :—

I bought you a dozen of shirts to your back.—
Dowlas, filthy dowlas: I have given them away to bakers' wives, and they have made *bolters* of them.—1 *H. IV.*, iii. 3.

" Bolters " are sieves ; used for sifting or bolting meal.

He that will have a cake out of the wheat must tarry the grinding.—Have I not tarried ?—Ay, the grinding; but you must tarry the *bolting.*—Have I not tarried ?—Ay, the *bolting ;* but you must tarry the *leavening.*—Still have I tarried.—Ay, to the *leavening :* but here 's yet in the word " hereafter," the *kneading*, the making of the cake, the heating of the oven, and the baking.—*Tr. & Cr.*, i. 1.

> And take thou my oblation, poor but free,
> Which is not mix'd with *seconds.*—*Sonnet* 125.

This is the term for the second kind of flour, which is collected after the smaller bran is sifted.

He uses an agricultural technicality, employed when he wrote, as the word ' lay ' is now :—

> We 'll make foul weather with despised tears ;
> Our sighs and they shall *lodge* the summer corn.—*R. II.*, iii. 3.
> Like to the summer's corn by tempest *lodg'd.*—2 *H. VI.*, iii. 2.
> Though bladed corn be *lodg'd*, and trees blown down.—*Macb.*, iv. 1.

And a few technicalities of natural history :—

My doe with the black *scut.*—*Merry W.*, v. 5.

This term was given to the tail of those animals whose tails are very short, such as of a hare, a deer, &c.

As the coney, that you see dwell where she is *kindled.*—*As You L.*, iii. 2.

This means ' brought forth,' ' born.'

As that ungentle *gull*, the cuckoo's bird.—1 *H. IV.*, v. 1.

This was a term for an unfledged nestling, a callow bird.

So many days my ewes have been with young:
So many weeks ere the poor fools will *yean.*—3 *H. VI.*, ii. 5.

This means ' bring forth young.'

Lord Timon will be left *a naked gull.*—*Timon*, ii. 1.

This, as well as " gull," was a technical term for a callow or unfledged bird.

> There 's something in his soul,
> O'er which his melancholy sits on brood ;
> And, I do doubt, the hatch and the *disclose*
> Will be some danger.—*Hamlet*, iii. 1.

This was the term applied to the first coming of birds from the shell.

> Anon, as patient as the female dove,
> When that her golden couplets are *disclos'd,*
> His silence will sit drooping.—*Hamlet,* v. 1.

A few technicalities of astrology :—

> Were we not *born under Taurus?*—
> *Taurus!* That 's *sides and heart.*—
> No, sir; it is *legs and thighs.*—*Tw. N.,* i. 3.

To be " born under Taurus," the Bull, which is the second constellation in the Zodiac, is supposed by the speaker to imply a tendency to joviality and revelry. The expressions " sides and hearts," " legs and thighs," refer to the system that associated particular portions of the human body with the predominance of particular constellations; evidences of which system used to appear in almanacs of former date.

> *Saturn and Venus this year in conjunction!* What says the almanack to that?—And, look, whether *the fiery Trigon,* his man, be not lisping to his master's old tables.—2 *H. IV.,* ii. 4.

The " conjunction" alluded to is stated by astrological works to have been never known to occur ; and " the fiery Trigon " is a term applied by astrologers to the meeting of Aries, Leo, and Sagittarius.

And technicalities of palmistry and chiromancy :—

> Well, if any man in Italy have a fairer *table* which doth offer to swear upon a book,— I shall have good fortune! go to, here 's a *simple line of life!* here 's a small trifle of wives!—*Mer. of V.,* ii. 2.

" Table" was the term for the palm of the hand ; and " the line of life " meant the curved line proceeding downwards, inside the hand, from the thumb towards the wrist.

He uses some technical terms of state formulas :—

> I 'll give him my commission
> To let him there a month behind the *gest*
> Prefix'd for 's parting.—*W. T.,* i. 2.

This was the name given to the scroll containing the several stages, or resting-places, in a king's progress ; from the old French, *giste,* a place to lie or lodge at.

> Nothing but to show you how a king may go a *progress* through the guts of a beggar. —*Hamlet,* iv. 3.

> If that his majesty would aught with us,
> We shall express our duty *in his eye.*—*Ibid.,* iv. 4.

This was a term used in state formulas for ' in his presence.'

And he uses some technicalities of ecclesiastical service:—

> Look, how the floor of heaven
> Is thick inlaid with *patines* of bright gold.—*Mer. of V.,* v. 1.

A " patine " (from the Latin, *patina*) is the small plate of gold used with the chalice in the administration of the Eucharist.

> For he hath stolen a *pax,* and hanged must 'a be.—*H. V.,* iii. 6.

This was a small plate, sometimes made of precious metal, bearing a sacred image upon it, and presented to the congregation during the

celebration of mass, for them to bestow upon it 'the kiss of peace':
Latin, *pax*, peace.

> Cut off even in the blossoms of my sin,
> *Unhousel'd*, disappointed, *unanel'd.*—*Hamlet*, i. 5.

The former of these terms signifies 'without having received the
sacrament'; the latter, 'without extreme unction.'

[See ELLIPTICALLY USED WORDS for names formed from technical
implements.]

TERMS OF DEFIANCE OR CHALLENGE.

There are several passages in Shakespeare's plays that refer to the
practice among combatants of daring each other to some wild and
lonely place, out of the reach of help or interference, and these passages
aid in confirming the propriety of retaining a word in one passage
which has been suspected of error :—

> This is true that I say: an I had thee in place where [thou and I could fight
> uninterruptedly] thou shouldst know it.—*Tam. of S.*, iv. 3.

> I do defy him, and I spit at him ;
> Call him a sland'rous coward and a villain :
> Which to maintain, I would allow him odds ;
> And meet him, were I tied to run a-foot
> Even to the frozen ridges of the Alps,
> Or any other ground inhabitable,*
> Wherever Englishman durst set his foot.—*R. II.*, i. 1.

> If I dare eat, or drink, or breathe, or live,
> I dare meet Surrey in a wilderness.—*Ibid.*, iv. 1.

> Or be alive again,
> And dare me to the desert with thy sword,
> If trembling I inhabit then, protest me
> The baby of a girl.—*Macb.*, iii. 4.

This is the passage which has been supposed incorrect by some
commentators ; who have proposed to alter the words " inhabit then."
But we think they are precisely in Shakespeare's style, as forming
direct antithesis with " dare me to the desert." He elsewhere
employs " inhabit " as an intransitive verb, to express 'remain,'
'dwell'; and here the sense is, 'remain within doors,' 'stay in any
habitation or inhabited place when thou challengest me forth.'

> If I had thee in Lipsbury pinfold, I would make thee care for me.—*Lear*, ii. 2.

> Goose, if I had you upon Sarum plain,
> I'd drive ye cackling home to Camelot.—*Ibid.*, ii. 2.

> I would they were in Afric both together ;
> Myself by with a needle, that I might prick
> The goer-back.—*Cym.*, i. 2.

---

* Here used for 'not habitable,' 'unhabitable,' or 'uninhabitable': Latin, *inhabitabilis.*

THINGS IMPERSONATED.

With very spirited effect, Shakespeare occasionally impersonates objects, treating them as if they were living and acting creatures :—

> Arm, wenches, arm ! *encounters* mounted are
> Against your peace.—*Love's L. L.*, v. 2.

> I have seen
> A *medicine* that 's able to breathe life into a stone,
> Quicken a rock, and make you dance canary.—*All's W.*, ii. 1.

> Bring in *the admiration*.—*Ibid.*, ii. 1.

> A thousand *knees*
> Ten thousand years together, naked, fasting,
> Upon a barren mountain.—*W. T.*, iii. 2.

I have *eyes* under my service which look upon his removedness ; from whom I have this intelligence.—*Ibid.*, iv. 1.

> Whom he loves ·
> (He bade me say so) more than all the *sceptres*
> And those that bear them, living.—*Ibid.*, v. 1.

> But for my *hand*, as unattempted yet,
> Like a poor beggar, raileth on the rich.—*John*, ii. 2.

> He should have his uncle Gaunt a father,
> To rouse his *wrongs*, and chase them to the bay.—*R. II.*, ii. 3.

> Then *murders*, *treasons*, and detested *sins*,
> The cloak of night being pluck'd from off their backs,
> Stand bare and naked, trembling at themselves.—*Ibid.*, iii. 2.

> No more the thirsty *entrance of this soil*
> Shall daub her lips with her own children's blood ;
> No more shall trenching war channel her fields,
> Nor bruise her flowerets with the armed hoofs
> Of hostile *paces :* those opposed *eyes* . . .
> Shall now, in mutual well-beseeming ranks,
> March all one way, and be no more oppos'd
> Against acquaintance, kindred, and allies.—*1 H. IV.*, i. 1.

> Shall we buy treason ? and indent with *fears*,
> When they have lost and forfeited themselves ?—*Ibid.*, i. 3.

> Why doth the crown lie there upon his pillow,
> Being so troublesome a bedfellow ?
> O polish'd *perturbation !* golden *care !*
> That keep'st the ports of slumber open wide
> To many a watchful night ! . . .

> . . . O *majesty !*
> When thou dost pinch thy bearer, thou dost sit
> Like a rich armour worn in heat of day,
> That scalds with safety.—*2 H. IV.*, iv. 4.

> All these bold *fears*,
> Thou seest, with peril I have answer'd.—*Ibid.*, iv. 4.

> *Murder*, indeed, that bloody sin, I tortur'd
> Above the felon, or what trespass else.—*2 H. VI.*, iii. 1.

> No bending *knee* will call thee Cæsar now.—*3 H. VI.*, iii. 1.

The *drum* [*See* ELLIPTICALLY USED WORDS for other similar instances] your honour hears marcheth from Warwick.—*Ibid.*, v. 1.

I had rather be a tick in a sheep, than such a valiant *ignorance*.—*Tr. & Cr.*, iii. 3.

> I have some *wounds* upon me, and they smart
> To hear themselves remember'd.—*Coriol.*, i. 9.

> Stalls, bulks, windows,
> Are smother'd up, leads fill'd, and ridges hors'd

With variable *complexions ;* all agreeing
In earnestness to see him.—*Coriol.,* ii. 1.

     So shall my lungs
Coin words till their decay against those *meazels,*
Which we disdain should tetter us, yet sought
The very way to catch them.—*Ibid.,* iii. 1.

Lest you should chance to whip your *information.*—*Ibid.,* iv. 6.

    You that stood so much
Upon the voice of *occupation.*—*Ibid.,* iv. 6.

    You have made fair hands,
You and your *crafts !* you have crafted fair !—*Ibid.,* iv. 6.

My wife comes foremost; then the honour'd *mould*
Wherein this trunk was fram'd, and in her hand
The grand-child to her blood ! – *Ibid.,* v. 3.

Now old *desire* doth in his death-bed lie,
And young *affection* gapes to be his heir.—*R. & Jul.,* i. 5 *(Chorus).*

Romeo ! *humours !* madman ! *passion !* lover !—*Ibid.,* ii. 1.

Two of the fairest *stars* in all the heaven,
Having some business, do entreat her eyes
To twinkle in their spheres till they return.—*Ibid.,* ii. 2.

For naught so vile that on the earth doth live,
But to the *earth** some special good doth give.—*Ibid.,* ii. 3.

     As if that *name*
Shot from the deadly level of a gun,
Did murder her ; as that *name's* cursed hand
Murder'd her kinsman. Oh, tell me, friar, tell me,
In what vile part of this anatomy
Doth my *name* lodge ?—*Ibid.,* iii. 3.

    The base o' the mount
Is rank'd with all *deserts,* all kind of *natures,*
That labour on the bosom of this sphere
To propagate their states.—*Timon,* i. 1.

So noble a master fall'n ! All gone ! and not
One friend to take his *fortune* by the arm,
And go along with him !—*Ibid.,* iv. 2.

His coward *lips* did from their colour fly.—*Jul. C.,* i. 2.

   Danger knows full well
That Cæsar is more dangerous than he.—*Ibid.,* ii. 2.

Came *missives* from the king, who all-hailed me, " Thane of Cawdor."—*Macb.,* i. 5 *(Letter).*

   What are these *faces ?*—*Ibid.,* iv. 2.

Great *tyranny,* lay thou thy basis sure,
For *goodness* dare not check thee ! wear thou thy wrongs,
The title is affeer'd !—*Ibid.,* iv. 3.

Unspeak mine own detraction: here abjure
The *taints* and *blames* I laid upon myself,
For strangers to my nature.—*Ibid.,* iv. 3.

Meet we the *medicine* of the sickly weal ;
And with him pour we, in our country's purge,
Each drop of us.—*Ibid.,* v. 2.

   Whiles I see *lives,* the gashes
Do better upon them.—*Ibid.,* v. 7.

To *reason* most absurd ; whose common theme
Is death of fathers, and who still hath cried,
From the first corse till he that died to-day,
" This must be so."—*Hamlet,* i. 2.

---

 * Here used for the ' inhabitants of earth,' ' human beings.'

The very place puts toys of desperation,
Without more motive, into every *brain*
That looks so many fathoms to the sea,
And hears it roar beneath.—*Hamlet*, i. 4.

For we will fetters put upon this *fear*,
Which now goes too free-footed.—*Ibid.*, iii. 3.

For in the fatness of these pursy times,
Virtue itself of *vice* must pardon beg,
Yea, curb and woo for leave to do him good.—*Ibid.*, iii. 4.

Which are to France the spies and *speculations*
Intelligent of our state.—*Lear*, iii. 1.

Hide thee, thou bloody *hand*.—*Ibid.*, iii. 2.

While I to this hard *house*
(More hard than is the stone whereof 'tis rais'd ;
Which even but now, demanding after you,
Denied me to come in) return, and force
Their scanted courtesy.—*Ibid.*, iii. 2.

To be tender-minded
Does not become a *sword*.—*Ibid.*, v. 3.

What comfort to *this great decay* may come
Shall be applied : for us, we will resign,
During the life of *this old majesty*,
To him our absolute power.—*Ibid.*, v. 3.

This *grief* is crowned with consolation ; your old *smock* brings forth a new petticoat :
and, indeed, the *tears* live in an onion that should water this sorrow.—*Ant. & C.*, i. 2.

His speech sticks in my heart.—
Mine *ear* must pluck it thence.—*Ibid.*, i. 5.

And have my learning from some true *reports*
That drew their swords with you.—*Ibid.*, ii. 2.

Did gibe my *missive* out of audience.—*Ibid.*, ii. 2.

From the barge
A strange invisible perfume hits the sense
Of the adjacent *wharfs*.   The *city* cast
Her people out upon her ; and Antony,
Enthron'd i' the market-place, did sit alone,
Whistling to the *air ;* which, but for vacancy,
Had gone to gaze on Cleopatra too,
And made a gap in nature.—*Ibid.*, ii. 2.

If our *eyes* had authority, here they might take two thieves kissing.—*Ibid.*, ii. 6.

A lower *place*, note well,
May make too great an act.—*Ibid.*, iii. 1.

The Kings of Mede, and Lycaonia,
With a more larger list of *sceptres*.—*Ibid.*, iii. 6.

In his livery
Walk'd *crowns* and *crownets*.—*Ibid.*, v. 2.

What shall I need to draw my sword ; the *paper*
Hath cut her throat already.   No, 'tis *slander ;*
Whose edge is sharper than the sword : whose tongue
Outvenoms all the worms of Nile ; whose breath
Rides on the posting winds, and doth belie
All corners of the world : kings, queens, and states,
Maids, matrons, nay, the secrets of the grave
This viperous *slander* enters.—*Cym.*, iii. 4.

Whose naked *breast*
Stepp'd before targes of proof.—*Ibid.*, v. 5.

These *mouths*, whom but of late, earth, sea, and air,
Were all too little to content and please,

> Although they gave their creatures in abundance;
> As houses are defil'd for want of use,
> They are now starv'd for want of exercise:
> Those *palates*, who, not yet two summers younger,.
> Must have inventions to delight the taste,
> Would now be glad of bread, and beg for it.—*Per.*, i..4..

> O let those *cities*, that of plenty's cup
> And her prosperities so largely taste,
> With their superfluous riots, hear these *tears* !—*Ibid.*, i. 4.

Shakespeare uses several bold and peculiar sentences of figurative and metaphorical phraseology ; a few of which he has repeated with slight variations in the wording :—

> Oh, thou that dost inhabit in my breast,
> Leave not the mansion so long tenantless,
> Lest, *growing ruinous, the building fall,*
> And leave no memory of what it was!—*Tw. G. of V.*, v. 4.

> Shall love, *in building, grow so ruinous ?*—*Com. of E.*, iii. 2

> But *the strong base and building of my love*
> Is as the very centre of the earth,
> Drawing all things to it.—*Tr. & Cr.*, iv. 2.

> *Who might be your mother,*
> That you insult, exult, and all at once,
> Over the wretched ?—*As You L.*, iii. 5.

>   Some jay of Italy,
> *Whose mother was her painting*, hath betray'd him.—*Cym.*, iii. 4.

These two passages seem to us to contain some scoff understood when Shakespeare wrote, implied in reference to a would-be beauty's "mother"; and the latter of the two passages has the same kind of figurative mode of saying, 'the producer of whose beauty was her rouged face,' or 'whose sole origin of comeliness was her painted complexion,' as the following three passages have of asserting a man to be 'made by his attire :' according to the old proverbial axiom, 'Fine feathers make fine birds':—

> Know'st me not by my clothes ?—
>   .   No, nor *thy tailor*, rascal,
> *Who is thy grandfather : he made those clothes,*
> *Which*, as it seems, *make thee.*—*Ibid.*, iv. 2.

> You cowardly rascal, nature disclaims in thee : *a tailor made thee.*—*Lear*, ii. 2.

> *The soul of this man is his clothes.*—*All's W.*, ii. 5.

In another passage of the same play Shakespeare has reversed this figurative expression with much humour, to express men of no more understanding than will serve them to invent new styles of dress :—

> *Whose judgments are mere fathers of their garments.*—*Ibid.*, i. 2.

>   His honour,
> *Clock to itself, knew the true minute* when
> Exception bid him speak, and *at this time*
> *His tongue obey'd his hand.*—*Ibid.*, i. 2.

> But *what linsey-woolsey hast thou to speak to us* again !—*Ibid.*, iv. 1.

> I am in love; but *a team of horse shall not pluck that from me ;* nor who 'tis I love.
> —*Two G. of V.*, iii. 1.

> Though *our silence be drawn from us with cars*, yet peace.—*Tw. N.*, ii. 5.

> I think *oxen and wain-ropes cannot hale them* together.—*Ibid.*, iii. 2.

> I am yet *so near the manners of my mother*, that, upon the least occasion more, *mine eyes will tell tales of me.*—*Ibid.*, ii. 1.

And *all my mother came into mine eyes,*
And gave me up to tears.—H. V., iv. 6.
Unthread the rude eye of rebellion,
And welcome home again discarded faith.—*John,* v. 4.
Thus out of season, *threading dark-ey'd night.—Lear,* ii. 1.
　　　　　　Will you again *unknit*
This churlish knot of all-abhorred war?—1 *H. IV.,* v. 1.
And these same thoughts people *this little world.—R. II.,* v. 5.
Strives in *his little world of man* to out-scorn.—*Lear,* iii. 1.
To *face the garment of rebellion*
With some fine colour, that may please the eye
Of fickle changelings and poor discontents.—1 *H. IV.,* v. 1.
To rank our chosen truth with such a show
As *fool and fight* is.—*H. VIII. (Prologue).*
　　　　　　They must either
(For so run the conditions) leave those remnants
Of *fool and feather,* that they got in France.—*Ibid.,* i. 3.

It appears to us that, in the one instance, Shakespeare used " fool and
fight " to express ' buffoons and mock battles ' or ' buffoonery and
battling '; and, in the other, " fool and feather " to express ' folly and
levity ' or ' foppery and frippery.'

A beggar's book outworths a noble's blood.—Ibid., i. 1.
Honour's train is longer than his foreskirt.—Ibid., ii. 3.
　　　　　　That his bones,
When he has run his course and sleeps in blessings,
May have *a tomb of orphans' tears* wept on them.—*Ibid.,* iii. 2.
Still *in thy right hand carry gentle peace,*
To silence envious tongues.—*Ibid.,* iii. 2.
Here is the steed, we the caparison.—Coriol., i. 9.
Is 't possible that so short a time can alter the condition of a man ?—
There is differency between a grub and a butterfly ; yet your butterfly was a grub.
This Marcius *is grown from man to dragon : he has wings ; he's more than a creeping
thing.—Ibid.,* v. 4.
　　　　　　Therefore this project
Should have a back or second, that might hold,
If this *should blast in proof.—Hamlet,* iv. 7.
How shall your houseless heads and unfed sides,
Your *loop'd and window'd* raggedness, defend you
From seasons such as these ?—*Lear,* iii. 4.
Might I but live *to see thee in my touch,*
I 'd say I had eyes again !—*Ibid.,* iv. 1.
I see it feelingly.—Ibid., iv. 6.
They flattered me like a dog; and *told me I had white hairs in my beard ere the
black ones were there.—Ibid.,* iv. 6.
　　　　　　When we shall hear
The rain and wind beat dark December.—Cym., iii. 3.
Thus smiling, *as some fly had tickled slumber,*
Not as death's dart, being laugh'd at.—*Ibid.,* iv. 2.

He also uses some poetical licences of expression that trouble and
perplex the literal and conventional critics ; but which delight the
appreciators of such audacities in imaginative and unprosaic composition :—

When service should in my old limbs lie lame,
And unregarded age in corners thrown.—As You L., ii. 3.

Join with the present sickness that I have;
And *thy unkindness be like crooked age,*
To crop at once a too-long wither'd flower.—*R. II.*, ii. 1.

　　　　Famine is in thy cheeks,
Need and oppression starveth in thine eyes,
Contempt and beggary hang upon thy back.—*R. & Jul.*, v. 1.

When all *our offices have been oppress'd*
With riotous feeders ; when *our vaults have wept*
With drunken spilth of wine ; when *every room*
Hath blaz'd with lights, and bray'd with minstrelsy.—*Timon*, ii. 2.

　　　　Leak'd is our barque ;
And we, poor mates, stand on *the dying deck,*
Hearing the surges threat : we must all part
Into *this sea of air.*—*Ibid.*, iv. 2.

A mote it is to trouble the mind's eye.—*Hamlet*, i. 1.

　　　　Methinks I see my father.—
O where, my lord?—
　　　　　　　In my mind's eye, Horatio.—*Ibid.*, i. 2.

And am fall'n out with my more headier will,
To take the indispos'd and sickly fit
For the sound man.—*Lear*, ii. 4.

　　　　I 'll look no more ;
Lest my brain turn, and *the deficient*
Sight topple down headlong.—*Ibid.*, iv. 6.

TITLES.

Shakespeare occasionally uses the names of their countries as titles for sovereigns :—

The King of Sicilia means to pay *Bohemia* the visitation which he justly owes him.
—*W. T.*, i. 1.

No jocund health that *Denmark* drinks to-day.—*Hamlet*, i. 2.

　　　　Then bid adieu to me, and say the tears
　　　　Belong to *Egypt.*—*Ant. & C.*, i. 3.

O, whither hast thou led me, *Egypt ?* . . . *Egypt*, thou knew'st too well, my heart was to thy rudder tied.—*Ibid.*, iii. 9.

What *England* says, say briefly, gentle lord.—*John*, ii. 1.

　　　　And here, from gracious *England*, have I offer
　　　　Of goodly thousands . . . gracious *England* hath
　　　　Lent us good Siward and ten thousand men.—*Macb.*, iv. 3.

Now say, Chatillon, what would *France* with us ?—*John*, i. 1.

Call *France ;* who stirs ?　Call *Burgundy.*—*Lear*, i. 1.

Myself present as I was sometime *Milan.*—*Temp.*, v. 1.

　　　　Was *Milan* thrust from Milan, that his issue
　　　　Should become kings of Naples ?—*Ibid.*, v. 1.

Pause there, *Morocco*, and weigh thy value.—*Mer. of V.*, ii. 7.

Myself am *Naples ;* who, with mine eyes.—*Temp.*, i. 2.

When he th' ambitious *Norway* combated.—*Hamlet*, i. 1.

What from our brother *Norway ?*—*Ibid.*, ii. 2.

Sicilia cannot show himself over-kind to *Bohemia.*—*W. T.*, i. 1.

What means *Sicilia ?*—He something seems unsettled.—*Ibid.*, i. 2.

Bold Iachimo, *Sienna's* brother.—*Cym.*, iv. 2.

He has used several foreign titles :—

Fetch you a hair off the great *Cham's* beard.—*M. Ado*, ii. 1.
But our *count-cardinal* has done this.—*H. VIII.*, i. 1.
Look upon the years of Lewis *the Dauphin.*—*John*, ii. 2.
Thou 'rt an emperor, Cæsar, *Keisar*, and Pheezar.—*Merry W.*, i. 3.
Two faults, *madonna*, that drink and good counsel.—*Tw. N.*, i. 5.
The *magnifico* is much belov'd.—*Oth.*, i. 2.
The duke himself, and the *magnificoes* of greatest.—*Mer. of V.*, iii. 2.
But what is the sport, *monsieur*, that the.—*As You L.*, i. 2.
Bring you the length of *Prester John's* foot.—*M. Ado*, ii. 1.
Now, *signior*, where 's the count ?—*Ibid.*, ii. 1.
> That slew *the Sophy*, and a Persian prince
> That won three fields of *Sultan* Solyman.—*Mer. of V.*, ii. 1.
A pension of thousands to be paid from *the Sophy.*—*Tw. N.*, ii. 5.
They say he has been fencer to *the Sophy.*—*Ibid.*, iii. 4.

He sometimes uses " grace " to a royal personage as well as to a duke or duchess :—

Your *grace* [to a queen] shall stay behind.—*John*, iii. 3.
How brooks your *grace* [to a king] the air.—*R. II.*, iii. 2.
That called your *grace* [to a duchess] to breakfast.—*R. III.*, iv. 4.
Begg'd your *grace's* [to a duke] pardon.—*R. II.*, i. 1.

He sometimes applies ' duke,' ' peer,' or ' prince,' to a king :—

That are vow-fellows with this virtuous *duke.*—*Love's L. L.*, ii. 1.
Gonzago is the *duke's* name.—*Hamlet*, iii. 2.
King Stephen was a worthy *peer.*—*Oth.*, ii. 3 (*Song*).
Young *prince* of Tyre, you have at large receiv'd.—*Per.*, i. 1.

In the following passage, " duke " is used for ' commander ': Latin, *dux*, a leader :—

Be merciful, great *duke* . . . abate thy rage, great *duke !*—*H. V.*, iii. 2.

In the following the princess is addressed as " your majesty," to mark that she has become *queen* by her father's death :—

How fares *your majesty ?*—*Love's L. L.*, v. 2.

In the following, Cleopatra is alluded to by a peculiar title that was appropriate, her father and her brother having both been called Ptolemy, which was the name borne by a long line of Egyptian kings :—

> Is not more manlike
> Than Cleopatra ; nor *the queen of Ptolemy*
> More womanly than he.—*Ant. & C.*, i. 4.

Shakespeare occasionally uses " princes " for ' noblemen,' or ' magnates ' :—

> With other *princes* that may best be spar'd . . .
> Now these, her *princes*, are come home again.—*John*, v. 7.
Commend me to the *princes* in our camp.—*H. V.*, iv. 1.

In the following passage he uses a Welsh title, signifying ' son of ' :—

And Rice *Ap* Thomas, with a valiant crew.—*R. III.*, iv. 5.

In the following he employs a title anciently given to a noble youth trained up to arms :—

Child Rowland to the dark tower came.—*Lear*, iii. 4 (*Song*).

And in the following he employs a title anciently given to men equivalent to ' Master ' :—

This senior-junior, giant-dwarf, *Dan* Cupid.—*Love's L. L.*, iii. 1.

In the following passage Shakespeare uses " the " as it was formerly sometimes used in England (and as *la* and *il* are still sometimes used in Italy) as a distinctive prefatory appellation for a distinguished person or one of high birth :—

Such attribution should *the* Douglas have.—1 *H. IV.*, iv. 1.

And in the following we believe him to have used " the " (as its equivalent is still used in Italy) as a term of distinction for a noble family [*See* SPELLING OF FOREIGN WORDS for our farther remarks on this passage] :—

The lady of *the* strachy married the yeoman of the wardrobe.—*Tw. N.*, ii. 5.

Shakespeare occasionally uses certain titles—as they were formerly sometimes used—rather indiscriminately applied :—

A noble *duke*,* in nature as in name.—*Tw. N.*, i. 2.
The *count** himself here hard by woos her.—*Ibid.*, i. 3.
The Earl [for ' duke '] of Hereford was reputed then.—2 *H. IV.*, iv. 4.

Shakespeare occasionally uses " county," an old form of ' count '; and " counties " for noblemen generally :—

Princes and *counties !* surely a princely testimony.—*M. Ado*, iv. 1.
Then is there the *County* Palatine.—*Mer. of V.*, i. 2.
A ring the *county* wears.—*All's W.*, iii. 7.
Peevish messenger, the *county's* man.—*Tw. N.*, i. 5.
Juliet, the *county* stays.—*R. & Jul.*, i. 3.
Noble gentleman, the *County* Paris.—*Ibid.*, iii. 4.

He occasionally uses " thane" for ' thaneship,' or ' title of thane':—

Those that gave the *thane* of Cawdor to me . . . the crown, besides the *thane* of Cawdor.—*Macb.*, i. 3.

He not unfrequently (according to a former custom) uses " your honour " for ' your lordship ' :—

I crave *your honour's* pardon . . . Save *your honour !* . . . Heaven keep *your honour !* . . . Save *your honour !*—*M. for M.*, ii. 2.
I hope I shall know *your honour* better. . . . Grace! not so, friend ; *honour* and *lordship* are my titles.—*Tr. & Cr.*, iii. 1.
All happiness to *your honour !*—*Timon*, i. 1.
> *Your honour* has through Ephesus pour'd forth
> Your charity.—*Per.*, iii. 2.

He employs " worship," according to a former custom, for an appropriate title to a knight or a squire :—

Give your *worship* [to a knight] good-morrow.—*Merry W.*, ii. 2.
He and his tooth-pick at my *worship's* [the speaker uses this expression as showing that he has recently been created a knight] mess ; and when my knightly stomach is suffic'd.—*John*, i. 1.
I may not go in without *your worship* [to a squire].—*Merry W.*, i. 1.
Have not *your worship* [to a squire] a wart above your eye ?—*Ibid.*, i. 4.

---

* " Duke " and " count " are both applied to Orsino ; not only in these two passages, but again in the course of this play.

He uses duplicate titles that denote official dignity :—

Got my *lord chamberlain* his liberty.—*R. III.*, i. 1.
Chosen *lord chancellor* in your place.—*H. VIII.*, iii. 2.
They are worn, *lord consul*, so, that we shall.—*Coriol.*, iii. 1.
My *lord embassador*, these letters are for you.—3 *H. VI.*, iii. 3.
Am bound to beg of my *lord general*.—*Coriol.*, i. 9.

> And we create, in absence of ourself,
> Our uncle York *lord governor* of England.—*R. II.*, ii. 1.

Stay, my *lord legate :* you shall first.—1 *H. VI.*, v. 1.
Answer you so the *lord protector ?*—*Ibid.*, i. 3.

He uses titles derived from the articles borne by those to whom the titles are applied [*See* ELLIPTICALLY USED WORDS] :—

Thou shalt be my lieutenant, monster, or my *standard.*—*Temp.*, iii. 2.

He uses the title of " Doctor" in reference to learned men *not* of the medical profession :—

Good *Doctor* Pinch, you are a conjuror.—*Com. of E.*, iv. 4.
Go, Lovel, with all speed to *Doctor* Shaw.*—*R. III.*, iii. 5.

He uses both forms of the following title :—

No less flowing than *Marchioness†* of Pembroke.—*H. VIII.*, ii. 3.
Duchess of Norfolk, and lady *Marquess†* Dorset.—*Ibid.*, v. 2.

He uses " Dame " as a female title :—

Dame Eleanor gives gold. . . . *Dame* Eleanor's aspiring humour.—2 *H. VI.*, i. 2.
She shall not strike *Dame* Eleanor unreveng'd.—*Ibid.*, i. 3.
Stand forth, *Dame* Eleanor Cobham, Gloster's wife.—*Ibid.*, ii. 3.
Where Henry and *Dame* Margaret kneel'd to me.—*Ibid.*, i. 2.
Why, then, *Dame* Margaret was ne'er thy joy.—*Ibid.*, iii. 2.
By thy *Dame* Partlet here.—*W. T.*, ii. 3.
How now, *Dame* Partlet the hen !—1 *H. IV.*, iii. 3.
Why, how now, *dame !* whence grows this.—*Tam of S.*, ii. 1.
My old *dame* will be undone now.—2 *H. IV.*, iii. 2.
Bless you, fair *dame !* I am not to you known.—*Macb.*, iv. 2.
Our veil'd *dames* commit the war of white and damask, in their nicely-gawded cheeks.—*Coriol.*, ii. 1.

In conformity with the custom of his time, Shakespeare uses " Mistress " for an unmarried as well as for a married woman :—

Mistress Ann Page ?   She has brown hair.—*Merry W.*, i. 1.
Mistress Bianca, bless you with such grace.—*Tam. of S.*, iv. 2.
Where, good *Mistress* Mary ?—*Tw. N.*, i. 5.
Ah, ha ! *Mistress* Ford and *Mistress* Page.—*Merry W.*, ii. 2.

Also, in conformity with the custom of his time, he occasionally uses " Master " as a title for a grown man :—

How, now, *Master* Ford !—*Merry W.*, ii. 1.
Let us see honest *Master* Page.—*Ibid.*, i. 1.
Good *Master* Fang, hold him sure ; good *Master* Snare, let him not 'scape.— 2 *H. IV.*, ii. 1.

---

* A popular preacher, and brother to the Lord Mayor, Edmund Shaw.
† " Marchioness " is formed by adding the English feminine termination to the Latin title *marchio*, a marquis, one who looks to the marches or bounds of the country ; while " marquess " is derived from the French *marquise*.

In the following passage, "Master" is facetiously used *with* "esquire":—

There will I visit *Master* Robert Shallow, *esquire.—2 H. IV.*, iv. 2.

In accordance with a usage that prevailed when he wrote, he frequently gives the title of "Sir" to a clergyman:—

Sir Hugh, persuade me not.—*M. W.*, i. 1.

Shakespeare uses terms of relationship with much latitude:—

Your kind *aunt* [for 'third cousin'], Duchess of Burgundy.—*3 H. VI.*, ii. 1.

Provost, my *brother* [in official authority] Angelo will not be alter'd.—*M. for M.*, iii. 2.

Brother [king] of England, how may we.—*John*, ii. 2.

And, *brother* [-in-law], here's the Earl of Wiltshire's.—*3 H. VI.*, i. 1.

Thy *brother's* [for 'half-brother's'] blood the thirsty.—*Ibid.*, ii. 3.

      Dream on thy *cousins* * [nephews] smother'd in the Tower . . .
      Thy nephews' souls bid thee despair and die!—*R. III.*, v. 3.

You are a *brother* [member of our council] of us.—*H. VIII.*, v. 1.

The sunset of my *brother's* [for 'brother-in-law's'] son.—*R. & Jul.*, iii. 5.

Sir, 'tis your *brother* [-in-law] Cassius at the door.—*Jul. C.*, ii. 1.

Back, Edmund, to my *brother* [-in-law].—*Lear*, iv. 2.

How is't, *brother* [officer]?—*Oth.*, v. 1.

To make you *brothers* [-in-law], and to knit.—*Ant. & C.*, ii. 2.

Good *brother* [-in-law], let me request you off.—*Ibid.*, ii. 7.

Are the *brothers* [-in-law] parted?—*Ibid.*, iii. 2.

Brother [soldier], good night: to-morrow is.—*Ibid.*, iv. 3.

Cousins [kinsmen, relations], you know what.—*M. Ado*, i. 2.

How now, daughter, and *cousin* [niece]!—*As You L.*, i. 2.

Cousin [kinsman], look not sad.—*John*, iii. 3.

Our *cousin* [kinsman] Hereford and fell.—*R. II.*, i. 2.

Cousin [nephew], farewell: no farther go.—*1 H. IV.*, i. 3.

My dear *cousin* [kinsman], I, as a child.—*R. III.*, ii. 2.

Welcome, dear *cousin* [nephew], my thoughts' sovereign.—*Ibid.*, iii. 1.

Good-morrow, *cousin* [niece] Cressid. . . . How do you, *cousin* [niece]?—*Tr. & Cr.*, i. 2.

Sit, good *cousin* [kinsman] Capulet.—*R. & Jul.*, i. 5.

Forgive me, *cousin* [kinsman]!—*Ibid.*, v. 3.

Cousins [kinsmen], a word, I pray you.—*Macb.*, i. 3.

Our bloody *cousins* [kinsmen] are bestow'd.—*Ibid.*, iii. 1.

Cousin [kinsman] Hamlet, you know the wager?—*Hamlet*, v. 2.

And, dear *coz* [brother-in-law], to you the.—*1 H. IV.*, iii. 1.

My dearest *coz* [kinswoman], I pray you, school yourself.—*Macb.*, iv. 2.

'Tis true, fair *daughter* [-in-law]; and this.—*John*, iii. 1.

No, be assur'd you shall not find me, *daughter* [step-daughter], after the slander of most stepmothers, evil-ey'd unto you.—*Cym.*, i. 2.

Whoo! ho! ho! *father* [anticipatedly, for 'father-in-law'] Page!—Son [anticipatedly, for 'son-in-law'], how now, *son!*—*Merry W.*, v. 5.

My *father* [anticipatedly, for 'father-in-law'] Capulet will have it so.—*R. & Jul.*, iv. 1.

Cæsarion, whom they call my *father's* [by adoption] son.—*Ant. & C.*, iii. 6.

Your Cæsar's *father* [by adoption] oft, when he.—*Ibid.*, iii. 9.

---

* This passage affords an instance of "cousins" and "nephews" used in the same speech, applied to the same persons, while addressing the same individual.

Depos'd his *nephew* [cousin] Richard.—*1 H. VI.*, ii. 5.

You 'll have your *nephews* [grandchildren] neigh to you.—*Oth.*, i. 1.

My niece [grand-daughter] Plantagenet led in.—*R. III.*, iv. 1.

Get thee to Plashy, to my *sister* [-in-law] Gloster.—*R. II.*, ii. 2.

As much to you, good *sister* [-in-law].—*R. III.*, iv. 1.

Keep you our *sister* [-in-law] company. . . . farewell, dear *sister* [-in-law].—*Lear*, iii. 7.

Not till Monday, my dear *son* [anticipatedly for 'son-in-law'].—*M. Ado*, ii. 1.

Acquaint her here of my *son* [anticipatedly for 'son-in-law'] Paris' love.—*R. & Jul.*, iii. 4.

I scarce did know you, *uncle* [-in-law].—*Oth.*, v. 2.

Cassibelan, thine *uncle* [for 'great uncle'].—*Cym.*, iii. 1.

He sometimes introduces terms of relationship as used ecclesiastically :—

I will, as 'twere a *brother* of your order.—*M. for M.*, 1. 4.

Going to find a bare-foot *brother* out.—*R. & Jul.*, v. 2.

'Tis meet so, *daughter*, but lest you do repent.—*M. for M.*, ii. 3.

My leisure serves me, pensive *daughter*, now.—*R. & Jul.*, iv. 1.

To make confession to this *father* ? . . . at leisure, holy *father*, now.—*Ibid.*, iv. 1.

Bless you, good *father* friar.—*M. for M.*, iii. 2.

> No longer staying but to give *the mother*
> Notice of my affair.—*Ibid.*, i. 5.

One Isabel, a *sister*, desires access to you.—*Ibid.*, ii. 4.

Vouchsafe a word, young *sister*, but one word.—*Ibid.*, iii. 1.

Son, I have overheard what hath passed.—*Ibid.*, iii. 1.

Young *son*, it argues a distemper'd head. . . . That's my good *son*. . . . Be plain good *son*.—*R. & Jul.*, ii. 3.

He occasionally introduces terms of relationship as used by young persons in reverence to age :—

Pardon, old *father*, my mistaking eyes. . . .
Now I perceive thou art a reverend *father*. . . .
Do, good old *grandsire*, . . . I do assure thee, *father*, so it is.—*Tam. of S.*, iv. 5.

Lord Timon, hear me speak.—Freely, good *father*.—*Timon*, i. 1.

Therefore, thou happy *father*, think that the clearest gods. . . . Well pray you, *father*. . . . Sit you down, *father;* rest you. . . . Come, *father*,* I 'll bestow you with a friend.—*Lear*, iv. 6.

Shakespeare has made allusion to some of the adoptive titles of relationship which were occasionally used among intimate friends at the time he wrote :—

> My cousin Juliet.—
> Is she your *cousin* ? —
> Adoptedly ; as school-maids change their names
> By vain, though apt, affection.—*M. for M.*, i. 5.

Shall I call you *father* ?—Ay, my good *son*.—*Tr. & Cr.*, ii. 3.

He call'd me *father* : but what o' that ?—*Coriol.*, v. 1.

Love thee no worse than thy old *father* Menenius does.—*Ibid.*, v. 2.

Timon has been this lord's *father*.—*Timon*, iii. 2.

I am a *mother* to you.—Mine honourable mistress.—Nay, a *mother*. . . . I say, I am your *mother*. . . . You are my *mother*, madam.—*All's W.*, i. 3.

---

* Beautifully has the dramatist made Edgar avail himself in this scene of the customary mode of addressing a venerable old man, in order to indulge himself with giving Gloster the paternal appellation, truly his.

Cannot office me from my *son* Coriolanus. . . . Oh, my *son*, my *son!* thou art preparing fire.—*Coriol.*, v. 2.

He uses some familiarly abbreviated forms in titles of relationship :—

I may quarter, *coz ?*—*Merry W.*, i. 1.
Good-morrow, *coz.* . . . Help to dress me, good *coz.*—*M. Ado*, iii. 4.
I pray thee, Rosalind, sweet my *coz*, be merry.—*As You L.*, i. 2.
No, *coz*, I rather weep.—*R. & Jul.*, i. 1.
Pare thy nails, *dad.*—*Tw. N.*, iv. 2 (*Song*).
Since I first call'd my brother's father *dad.*—*John*, ii. 2.
Was wont to cheer his *dad* in mutinies ?—3 *H. VI.*, i. 4.

He introduces some familiarly applied titles of relationship :—

The wisest *aunt*, telling the saddest tale.—*Mid. N. D.*, ii. 1.
Are summer songs for me and my *aunts* [*See* CANT TERMS].—*W. T.*, iv. 2 (*Song*).
How now, *nuncle !* . . . Mark it, *nuncle.*—*Lear*, i. 4.

This familiar contraction of ' mine uncle ' was the usual appellation of the professional fool for his employer and his superiors.

Shakespeare uses some facetious titles :—

Bull Jove, sir, had an amiable low.—*M. Ado*, v. 4.
Coragio ! *bully*-monster, coragio!—*Temp.*, v. 1.
Bless thee, *bully* doctor.—*Merry W.*, ii. 3.
Bully knight ! *bully* Sir John ! . . . Let her descend, *bully.*—*Ibid.*, iv. 5.
What say'st thou, *bully* Bottom ?—*Mid. N. D.*, iii. 1.
I love the lovely *bully.*—*H. V.*, iv. 1.
Come, *captain*, we must be neat ; not neat, but cleanly, *captain.*—*W. T.*, i. 2.
Hear ye, *captain*, are you not at leisure ?—1 *H. VI.*, v. 3.
Cavalero justice, I say ! . . . Tell him, *cavalero* justice.—*Merry W.*, ii. 1.
Master Page, and eke *Cavalero* Slender.—*Ibid.*, ii. 3.
But to help *Cavalery* Cobweb to scratch.—*Mid. N. D.*, iv. 1.
Monsieur Cobweb, good *monsieur*, get your weapons. . . . Where 's *Monsieur* Mustard-seed ?—*Ibid.*, iv. 1.
Ha ! the prince and *Monsieur* Love !—*M. Ado*, ii. 3.

And in the following passage he uses a playfully coined title :—

What her is this ?—Why, *Doctor She.*—*All's W.*, ii. 1.

In the following passages he uses a corrupted form of a title, and jocosely corrupted names :—

Why, your *dolphin* [Dauphin] is not lustier.—*Ibid.*, ii. 3.
Pucelle or puzzel, *dolphin* [Dauphin] or dog-fish.—1 *H. VI.*, i. 4.
Dolphin [Dauphin] my boy, my boy, sessa !—*Lear*, iii. 4.
Twopence a-piece of *Yead* [Ned] Miller.—*Merry W.*, i. 1.
Hear ye, *Yedward* [Edward] ; if I tarry at home.—1 *H. IV.*, i. 2.

He occasionally uses the titles derived from avocations, which were customary in his time :—

Sot, didst see *Dick Surgeon*, sot ?—*Tw. N.*, v. 1.
Turned upside down since *Robin Ostler* died.—1 *H. IV.*, ii. 1.
What 's to do here, *Thomas Tapster ?*—*M. for M.*, i. 2.
Yea, marry, *William cook*, bid him come hither. . . . But for *William cook :* are there no young pigeons ?—2 *H. IV.*, v. 1.
Twopence a-piece of *Yead Miller*, by these gloves.—*Merry W.*, i. 1.

He has more than one allusion to the custom that prevailed formerly of servants assuming their employers' names :—

Hear me call Margaret, *Hero.*—*M. Ado*, ii. 2.
I have to-night wooed Margaret, the Lady Hero's gentlewoman, *by the name of Hero.*—*Ibid.*, iii. 3.
Good even, *Varro :* what ! . . . and yours too, *Isidore ?*—*Timon*, ii. 2.

He has used several familiar titles :—

Goodman Verges, sir, speaks a little off the matter.—*M. Ado*, iii. 5.
Via, *goodman* Dull ! thou hast spoken no.—*Love's L. L.*, v. 1.
Since the old days of *goodman* Adam to the.—1 *H. IV.*, ii. 4.
I think he be, but *goodman* Puff of Barson.—2 *H. IV.*, v. 3.
Did not *goodwife* Keech, the butcher's wife.—*Ibid.*, ii. 1.
What, ho, *gossip* Ford ! what, ho !—*Merry W.*, iv. 2.
Come, in then, and call me *gossip* Quickly.—2 *H. IV.*, ii. 1.
Give them their charge, *neighbour* Dogberry. . . . Come hither, *neighbour* Seacoal.—*M. Ado*, iii. 3.
Come, *neighbour* Mugs, we 'll call up the gentlemen.— 1 *H. IV.*, ii. 1.

He has introduced some titles of imaginary and typical personages :—

By *Sir Smile*, his neighbour.—*W. T.*, i. 2.
This might be *my lord such-a-one*, that praised *my lord such-a-one's* horse . . . e'en so, and now *my Lady Worm's.*—*Hamlet*, v. 1.
When *Signior Sooth* here does proclaim.—*Per.*, i. 2.

He sometimes appends " sir " to a title in stern address :—

Come, *sir boy*, come, follow me; *sir boy*, I 'll.—*M. Ado*, v. 1.
Stay, *sir king :* this man is better than.—*Cym.*, v. 5.

He sometimes uses " Love " for ' the queen of love,' ' Venus ' [*See* PECULIAR USE OF WORDS for other instances]:—

That your Dian was both herself and *love.**—*All's W.*, i. 3.
For the love of *Love* and her soft hours.—*Ant. & C.*, i. 1.

Sometimes, in accordance with a usage of his time, he employs " lover " as a term for ' friend,' said by men to each other [*See* APPRECIATION OF FRIENDSHIP, &c.] :—

Farewell, my lord: I as your *lover* speak.—*Tr. & Cr.*, iii. 3.
The mighty gods defend thee ! Thy *lover*, Artemidorus.—*Jul. C.*, ii. 3 (*Letter*).
Romans, countrymen, and *lovers !* hear me for.—*Ibid.*, iii. 2.
That we may, *lovers* in peace, lead on.—*Ibid.*, v. 1.

He sometimes, also in accordance with a usage of his time, applies the term " lover " to a woman as well as to a man :—

Your brother and his *lover* have embraced.—*M. for M.*, i. 5.
        Most like a noble lord in love, and one
        That had a royal *lover.*—*Cym.*, v. 5.

---

* In this passage the word " love " means ' love itself ' as well as ' the queen of love. Venus.'

UNFINISHED SENTENCES.

Shakespeare, in his skill as a dramatist, knew the full value of introducing upon occasion an unfinished sentence : sometimes broken off by the speaker's self-interruption to imply something left unsaid, to imply an inuendo or a threat, to imply some interposed gesture or action, or to imply agitation and incapacity of expression ; sometimes broken off by interruption from an interlocutor, or by other speakers ; sometimes interrupted by a sudden entrance ; sometimes even interrupted by death itself, when utterance is checked by departing breath, and the speaker expires leaving his sentence unended. In the Folio, these unfinished sentences are generally indicated by a dash (that is, a long line or a line composed of short hyphen-marks, thus - - -) ; but, in several cases, are so imperfectly indicated (by a full stop, by a comma, by no stop at all, or even by a blank space) that it is difficult to decide whether an interrupted sentence is really intended by the dramatist, or whether the printer may not have made a blunder, and even (in the last-mentioned case) have left the passage incompletely given. However, in the majority of instances, the context of the passage resolves the difficulty ; and the dramatist's intention is manifest. First, then, for the passages of self-interruption :—

Trinculo, keep a good tongue in your head : if you prove a mutineer, the next tree—*Temp.*, iii. 2.

It is so, indeed ; he is no less than a stuffed man : but for the stuffing,—well, we are all mortal—*M. Ado*, i. 1.

What ! I am not bestraught : here 's—*Tam. of S., Induc.* 2.

The Folio concludes the above speech with a line or dash ; and we believe it to denote that Sly breaks off his speech with a nod of the head, and a half-uttered ' here 's to your health,' as he drinks the proffered wine.

I 'll have no more pity of his age, than I would have of—I 'll beat him an if I could but meet him again !—*All's W.*, ii. 3.

> Would I were dead, but that, methinks already—
> What was he, that did make it ?   See, my lord,
> Would you not deem it breath'd ? and that those veins
> Did verily bear blood ?—*W. T.*, v. 3.

Because the Folio prints the above passage with a full stop after " already " instead of a dash, there have not been wanting critics who have supposed the line to be one which was originally followed by another, omitted by the printer ; whereas we feel it to be precisely one of those abrupt breaks in a passionate speech, which our Shakespeare knew to be full of eloquent implication. The whole of the context shows the speaker to be impressed with the conviction that what he looks upon moves, breathes, exists ; and we take the imperfectly expressed sentence : ' Would I were dead with her, but that methinks already she moves and breathes, and lives again to me ! '

> He writes me here that inward sickness,—
> And that his friends by deputation could not
> So soon be drawn.—1 *H. IV.*, iv. 1.

In the above passage, the Folio merely puts a comma after " sickness "; but who does not feel that it is Hotspur's characteristic way of breaking off a phrase, and leaving its completion to be understood by the listener ?

> I cannot speak ; if my heart be not ready to burst,—well, sweet Jack, have a care of thyself.—2 *H. IV.*, ii. 4.

> Well, fare thee well: I have known thee these twenty-nine years, come peascod-time; but an honester and truer-hearted man,—well, fare thee well.—*Ibid.*, ii. 4.

> > Thou shalt not die, whiles—
> > He beckons with his hand, and smiles on me.—1 *H. VI.*, i. 4.

> > I dare presume, sweet prince, he thought no harm.—
> > An if I wist he did,—but let it rest.—*Ibid.*, iv. 1.

> > Hard to seem won : but I was won, my lord,
> > With the first glance that ever—pardon me,
> > If I confess much, you will play the tyrant.—*Tr. & Cr.*, iii. 2.

The Folio misprints 'glance; that ever pardon me!' But thoroughly characteristic of the coquettish Cressida is that affected sudden pause in her speech ; half pretendedly modest, half calculating, in its self-check. True Shakespeare ! even in his delineation of an untrue woman !

> > Five tribunes to defend their vulgar wisdoms,
> > Of their own choice : one 's Junius Brutus,
> > Sicinius Velutus, and I know not—'Sdeath !
> > The rabble should have first unroof'd the city,
> > Ere so prevail'd with me.—*Coriol.*, i. 1.

Though the Folio puts a full stop after " and I know not," it is obviously a sentence broken off by the speaker's haughty petulance.

> > You shames of Rome ! you herd of—Boils and plagues
> > Plaster you o'er ; that you may be abhorr'd
> > Farther than seen, and one infect another
> > Against the wind a mile !—*Ibid.*, i. 4.

The Folio misprints thus, ' you Heard of Byles and Plagues ; ' depriving the passage of meaning, and of the characteristically impetuous break in Marcius's speech.

> An 'twere to give again,—but 'tis no matter.—*Ibid.*, ii. 3.

> He had, sir, a kind of face, methought,—I cannot tell how to term it.—*Ibid.*, iv. 5.

> He had so; looking as it were,—Would I were hanged, but I thought there was more in him than I could think.—*Ibid.*, iv. 5.

> > Well said, my hearts ! you are a princox ; go :
> > Be quiet, or—More light, more light !—*R. & Jul.*, i. 5.

> > I am sick at heart,
> > When I behold—Seyton, I say !—*Macb.*, v. 3.

> > I am sorry,—
> > What, have you given him any hard words of late?—*Hamlet*, ii. 1.

> Ay, sir, but " while the grass grows,"—the proverb is something musty.—*Ibid.*, iii. 2.

> So please you,—[*Exit.*]—*Lear*, i. 4.

In the above passage, the steward Oswald leaves his sentence unfinished, and abruptly goes from the old king's presence, purposely to manifest negligence and disrespect, in accordance with Goneril's orders.

> > Fiery ? the fiery duke ? Tell the hot duke, that—
> > No, but not yet: may be, he is not well.—*Ibid.*, ii. 4.

> Thy sister 's naught : O Regan, she hath tied
> Sharp-tooth'd unkindness, like a vulture here— [*Points to his heart.*
> I can scarce speak to thee ; thou 'lt not believe
> With how deprav'd a quality—O Regan !—*Lear*, ii. 4.
>
> Give ear, sir, to my sister ;
> For those that mingle reason with your passion,
> Must be content to think you old, and so—
> But she knows what she does.—*Ibid.*, ii. 4.
>
> Your old kind father, whose frank heart gave all,—
> O, that way madness lies ; let me shun that.—*Ibid.*, iii. 4.
>
> In, boy ; go first. You houseless poverty,—
> Nay, get thee in. I 'll pray, and then I 'll sleep.—*Ibid.*, iii. 4.
>
> Why should she write to Edmund ? might not you
> Transport her purposes by word ? Belike,
> Something—I know not what : I 'll love thee much ;
> Let me unseal the letter.—*Ibid.*, iv. 5.
>
> She that, so young, could give out such a seeming,
> To seel her father's eyes up close as oak,—
> He thought 'twas witchcraft :—but I am much to blame. —*Oth.*, iii. 3.
>
> Put out the light, and then—Put out the light !
> If I quench thee, thou flaming minister,
> I can again thy former light restore,
> Should I repent me.—*Ibid.*, v. 2.

Although the Folio prints " then " without any stop or dash after it, we think there is every reason to believe that the dramatist intended an unfinished sentence here ; Othello interrupting himself in saying he will put out the light, and then proceed to the fulfilment of his purposed vengeance, by the reflections suggested by his own words, " Put out the light " ; which he repeats and descants upon as applying to his own intended deed.

> Where is thy lady ? or, by Jupiter—
> I will not ask again. Close villain,
> I 'll have this secret from thy heart, or rip
> Thy heart to find it.—*Cym.*, iii. 5.

Next, for the passages where the speaker is interrupted by some other speaker or speakers :—

> *Dogberry.* Come, let them be opinioned.
> *Verges.* Let them be in the hands—
> *Conrade.* Off, coxcomb !—*M. Ado*, iv. 2.

The Folio misprints this as all one speech ('Let them be in the hands of Coxcombe'), and assigns it to the Sexton : whereas, " Let them be in the hands" is evidently a portion of an order given by Verges in confirmation of Dogberry's previous one, " Let them be opinioned," because both Verges and Dogberry are spoken of elsewhere in the play as " *officers* " of the watch ; and " Off, coxcomb!" is obviously spoken by one of the delinquents, because Dogberry immediately afterwards says, " Let him write down—the prince's *officer, coxcomb.*"

> *Gremio.* Hark you, sir : you mean not her to—
> *Tranio.* Perhaps, him and her, sir ; what have you to do?—*Tam. of S.*, i. 2.
>
> *Parolles.* Hadst thou not the privilege of antiquity upon thee,—
> *Lafeu.* Do not plunge thyself too far in anger.—*All's W.*, ii. 3.

Sir Toby. There is sixpence for you ; let's have a song.
Sir Andrew. There's a testril of me too : if one knight give a—
Clown. Would you have a love-song, or a song of good life?—*Tw. N.,* ii. 3.

The Folio places neither stop nor blank after "give a" in the above passage ; so that it may be a printer's omission of some flabby reason given by Sir Andrew for his giving a similar piece of money to the one given by his brother "knight." Nevertheless, taken as a broken speech, it serves well to denote Aguecheek's limp attempt to imitate his knightly model, trying to give a reason, and failing from sheer incompetence to express himself.

Camillo. I have lov'd thee,—
Leontes. Make that thy question, and go rot !—*W. T.,* i. 2.
Winchester. But he shall know, I am as good—
Gloster. As good !
Thou bastard of my grandfather !—*1 H. VI.,* iii. 1.
Suffolk. If thou wilt condescend to be my—
Q. Margaret. What ?
Suffolk. His love.—*Ibid.,* v. 3.
Gloster. She should have stay'd in France, and starved in France
Before—
Cardinal. My lord of Gloster, now you grow too hot.—*2 H. VI.,* i. 1.
Suffolk. All the foul terrors in dark-seated hell—
Q. Margaret. Enough, sweet Suffolk ; thou torment'st thyself.—*Ibid.,* iii. 2.
Say. You men of Kent,—
Dick. What say you of Kent ?—*Ibid.,* iv. 7.
Say. This tongue hath parley'd unto foreign kings
For your behoof,—
Cade. Tut ! when struck'st thou one blow in the field ?—*Ibid.,* iv. 7.
Clifford. And till I root out their accursed line,
And leave not one alive, I live in hell.
Therefore—
Rutland. O, let me pray before I take my death !—*3 H. VI.,* i. 3.
K. Henry. And, if the rest be true which I have heard,
Thou cam'st—
Gloster. I'll hear no more : die, prophet, in thy speech.—*Ibid.,* v. 6.
Q. Margaret. Thou rag of honour ! Thou detested—
Gloster. Margaret.—*R. III.,* i. 3.
Clarence. Who sent you hither ? Wherefore do you come ?
Both Murderers. To, to, to—
Clarence. To murder me ?—*Ibid.,* i. 4.
Pandarus. I will not dispraise your sister Cassandra's wit, but—
Troilus. O Pandarus ! I tell thee, Pandarus,—*Tr. & Cr.,* i. 1.
Hector. But I'll endeavour deeds to match these words,
Or may I never—
Ajax. Do not chafe thee, cousin.—*Ibid.,* iv. 5.
Lartius. Hadst thou beheld—
Martius. Pray, now, no more : my mother,
Who has a charter to extol her blood,
When she does praise me, grieves me.—*Coriol.,* i. 9.
Brutus. But since he hath
Serv'd well for Rome,—
Coriolanus. What do you prate of service !—*Ibid.,* iii. 3.
Cominius. Know,
I pray you,—
Coriolanus. I'll know no farther.—*Ibid.,* iii. 3.

Cominius. Hear me, my masters, and my common friends,--
Sicinius. He's sentenc'd ; no more hearing.—*Coriol.*, iii. 3.
    Cominius.   Then if I would
Speak that—
    Sicinius. We know your drift : speak what ?—*Ibid.*, iii. 3.
    Third Conspirator. Sir, his stoutness
When he did stand for consul, which he lost
By lack of stooping,—
    Aufidius.   That I would have spoke of.—*Ibid.*, v. 5.
    First Conspirator. When he had carried Rome, and that we look'd
For no less spoil than glory,—
    Aufidius.   There was it ;
For which my sinews shall be stretch'd upon him.—*Ibid.*, v. 5.
    Romeo. Lady, by yonder blessed moon I swear,
That tips with silver all these fruit-tree tops,—
    Juliet. O, swear not by the moon, th' inconstant moon.—*R. & Jul.*, ii. 2.
    Romeo.   If my heart's dear love—
    Juliet. Well, do not swear : although I joy in thee,
I have no joy of this contract to-night.—*Ibid.*, ii. 2.
    Romeo.   So thrive my soul,—
    Juliet. A thousand times good night !—*Ibid.*, ii. 2.

Richly deserving of notice is the mode in which, during the above love-dialogue (certainly the most poetically beautiful and dramatically true to youthful nature ever penned!), the author has made Juliet repeatedly interrupt her lover in his protestations with the breathless eagerness of a rapture that cannot doubt its bliss, and needs no assurances to convince her of that truth which her own truth of love has already told her. The Folio, it is true, gives no typographical token of these being interrupted speeches; but the poet and dramatist's intention is made clearly evident by his own exquisite power of composition, which will not permit us to misunderstand his meaning.

    First Lord. I am so far already in your gifts,—
    All. So are we all.—*Timon*, i. 2.
    Second Lord. It does : but time will—and so—
    Third Lord. I do conceive.—*Ibid.*, iii. 6.
    Metellus. Stand fast together, lest some friend of Cæsar's
Should chance—
    Brutus. Talk not of standing. Publius, good cheer.—*Jul. C.*, iii. 1.
    Cassius. Brutus, this sober form of yours hides wrongs ;
And when you do them—
    Brutus.   Cassius, be content ;
Speak your griefs softly.—*Ibid.*, iv. 2.
    Second Murderer.   We shall, my lord,
Perform what you command us.
    First Murderer.   Though our lives—
    Macbeth. Your spirits shine through you.—*Macb.*, iii. 1.
    Servant. There is ten thousand—
    Macbeth.   Geese, villain ?
    Servant.   Soldiers, sir.—*Ibid.*, v. 3.
    Bernardo. The bell then beating one,—
    Marcellus. Peace ! break thee off ; look, where it comes again.—*Hamlet*, i. 1.
    Hamlet. When Roscius was an actor in Rome,—
    Polonius. The actors are come hither, my lord.—*Ibid.*, ii. 2.
    Player King.   And, haply, one as kind
For husband shalt thou—

Player Queen.   O, confound the rest!
Such love must needs be treason in my breast.—*Hamlet*, iii. 2.

First Clown. I'll put another question to thee: if thou answerest me not to the purpose, confess thyself—
Second Clown. Go to.—*Ibid.*, v. 1.

Albany. How far your eyes may pierce, I cannot tell:
Striving to better, oft we mar what's well.
Goneril. Nay, then—
Albany. Well, well; the event.—*Lear*, i. 4.

Cornwall. To this chair bind him.   Villain, thou shalt find—
            ' [REGAN *plucks his beard.*
Gloster. By the kind gods, 'tis most ignobly done
To pluck me by the beard.—*Ibid.*, iii. 7.

Regan.   Wherefore
To Dover?   Wast thou not charg'd at peril—
Cornwall. Wherefore to Dover?   Let him answer that.—*Ibid.*, iii. 7.

Cornwall. If you see vengeance,—
Servant.   Hold your hand, my lord.—*Ibid.*, iii. 7.

Regan. Let me unseal the letter.
Oswald.   Madam, I had rather—
Regan. I know your lady does not love her husband.—*Ibid.*, iv. 5.

Gentleman. O, here he is: lay hand upon him.   Sir,
Your most dear daughter—
Lear. No rescue?   What, a prisoner?—*Ibid.*, iv. 6.

Gentleman.   Good sir,—
Lear. I will die bravely.—*Ibid.*, iv. 6.

Desdemona.   Trust me, I could do much,—
Othello. Pr'ythee, no more: let him come when he will;
I will deny thee nothing.—*Oth.*, iii. 3.

Dolabella.   Though he be honourable,—
Cleopatra. He'll lead me, then, in triumph?
Dolabella. Madam, he will; I know it.—*Ant. & C.*, v. 2.

First Guard. Cæsar hath sent—
Charmian.   Too slow a messenger.—*Ibid.*, v. 2.

Iachimo.   A piece of work
So bravely done, so rich, that it did strive
In workmanship and value; which I wonder'd
Could be so rarely and exactly wrought,
Since the true life on't was—
Posthumus.   This is true;
And this you might have heard of here, by me,
Or by some other.—*Cym.*, ii. 4.

Philario. This is not strong enough to be believ'd
Of one persuaded well of—
Posthumus.   Never talk on 't.—*Ibid.*, ii. 4.

Iachimo. Methinks I see him now,—
Posthumus.   Ay, so thou dost,
Italian fiend!—*Ibid.*, v. 5.

Imogen.   Peace, my lord; hear, hear—
Posthumus. Shall's have a play of this?—*Ibid.*, v. 5.

Pericles.   But, what music?
Helicanus. My lord, I hear none.
Pericles. None?
The music of the spheres!   List, my Marina.
Lysimachus. It is not good to cross him; give him way.
Pericles. Rarest sounds!   Do ye not hear?
Lysimachus.   Music? my lord, I hear—
Pericles. Most heavenly music!—*Per.*, v. 1.

Notwithstanding that the ancient copies (both Folios and Quartos) of this play put a full stop after " hear " in the above passage, we believe that Shakespeare intended it should be a half-uttered assent of Lysimachus to Pericles, whom, he has just said, " it is not good to cross," and whom he humours by repeating the word "music ?" questioningly, and then adding words that shall let the prince suppose others besides himself hear the divine strains which lullingly fill his senses. Some modern editors, instead of leaving the word " music " in Lysimachus's speech, place it in the margin as a stage direction; which, in our opinion, literalises a poetical passage. It seems to us that the dramatist meant that the " music " to which Pericles so repeatedly refers should be understood as a purely imaginary music, the spiritual echo of his own harmonious condition of soul, which is tuned to rapture by the recent recovery of his supposed dead child.

And next, for the passages where the speaker is interrupted by the entrance of some person :—

> A far more glorious star thy soul will make,
> Than Julius Cæsar or bright—
> > *Enter a* MESSENGER.
> *Messenger.* My honourable lords, health to you all!—1 *H. VI.*, i. 1.

> *King.* And that, I hope, will teach you to imagine,—
> > *Enter a* MESSENGER.
> How now! what news ?
> *Messenger.*   Letters, my lord, from Hamlet :
> This to your majesty ; this to the queen.—*Hamlet*, iv. 7.

> > Epicurean cooks
> Sharpen with cloyless sauce his appetite ;
> That sleep and feeding may prorogue his honour
> Even till a Lethe'd dulness !—
> > *Enter* VARRIUS.
> > How now, Varrius !
> *Varrius.* This is most certain that I shall deliver.—*Ant. & C.*, ii. 1.

> > Your crown's awry ;
> I'll mend it, and then play—
> > *Enter the* GUARD, *rushing in.*
> *First Guard.* Where is the queen ?—*Ibid.*, v. 2.

> *Cloten.* I will conclude to hate her, nay, indeed,
> To be reveng'd upon her. For, when fools shall—
> > *Enter* PISANIO.
> Who is here ? What, are you packing, sirrah ?—*Cym.*, iii. 5.

> And not your knowledge, your personal pain, but even
> Your purse, still open, hath built Lord Cerimon
> Such strong renown as time shall never—
> > *Enter two* SERVANTS, *with a chest.*
> *First Servant.* So, lift there.—*Per.*, iii. 2.

Then come the instances where the speaker is interrupted by death :—

> > O, I could prophesy,
> But that the earthy and cold hand of death
> Lies on my tongue : no, Percy, thou art dust,
> And food for—[*Dies.*]—1 *H. IV.*, v. 4.

> Nay, I will take thee too: [*Applying another asp to her arm.*
> What should I stay—[*Falls on a bed, and dies.*]—*Ant. & C.,* v. 2.

And then come instances where Shakespeare causes a speaker to be interrupted in his sentence, and to continue it afterwards :—

> *Juliet.*   *But if thou mean'st not well,*
> *I do beseech thee,*—
> *Nurse (Within).* Madam !
> *Juliet.*   By-and-by, I come :—
> *To cease thy suit, and leave me to my grief.*—*R. & Jul.,* ii. 2.

> *Polonius. Upon my honour,*—
> *Hamlet.* Then came each actor on his ass,—
> *Polonius. The best actors in the world.*—*Hamlet,* ii. 2.

> *Hamlet. The king is a thing*—
> *Guildenstern.* A thing, my lord !
> *Hamlet. Of nothing :* bring me to him.—*Ibid.,* iv. 2.

> *Lear. Who is it that can tell me who I am ?*—
> *Fool. Lear's shadow,*—
> *Lear. I would learn that ;* for, by the marks of sovereignty, knowledge, and reason,
> I should be false persuaded I had daughters.
> *Fool. Which they will make an obedient father.*—*Lear,* i. 4.

In the above passage, both speakers continue their interrupted sentence ; the old king pursuing his own train of thought and speech, while the Fool half replies to, half comments upon, his master's wild questioning. The old copies give this passage with deplorable inaccuracy ; the Folio giving it incompletely, the Quartos making the words " Lear's shadow " a part of Lear's own speech.

> *Lear. I gave you all*—
> *Regan.*   And in good time you gave it.
> *Lear. Made you my guardians, my depositaries ;*
> *But kept a reservation to be follow'd*
> *With such a number.*—*Ibid.,* ii. 4.

> *Lear.* This is a dull sight. Are you not Kent ?
> *Kent.*   The same,
> Your servant Kent. Where is your servant Caius ?
> *Lear.* He 's a good fellow, I can tell you that ;
> He 'll strike, and quickly too : he 's dead and rotten.
> *Kent.* No, my good lord ; *I am the very man*—
> *Lear.* I'll see that straight.
> *Kent. That, from your first of difference and decay,*
> *Have follow'd your sad steps,*—
> *Lear.*   You are welcome hither.
> *Kent. Nor no man else.*—*Ibid.,* v. 3.

Malone strangely interpreted the words, " Nor no man else," to be a reply to Lear's previous sentence, and to signify, 'I welcome! No, nor no man else!' Whereas we think they are evidently intended as the conclusion of Kent's attempt to make his old master comprehend the identity between Kent and Caius, and that it is he himself, and " no man else," who has followed the injured king from first to last.

> *Iago.* A thing for me ! *It is a common thing*—
> *Emilia.* Ha?
> *Iago. To have a foolish wife.*—*Oth.,* iii. 3.

> *Dolabella. If it might please you,*—
> *Cleopatra.* His face was as the heavens ; and therein stuck
> A sun and moon, which kept their course, and lighted
> The little O, the earth.

> *Dolabella.*   *Most sovereign creature,—*
> *Cleopatra.* His legs bestrid the ocean: his rear'd arm
> Crested the world: his voice . . .
>   . . . realms and islands were
> As plates dropp'd from his pocket.
> *Dolabella.*   *Cleopatra,—Ant. & C.,* v. 2.

Shakespeare has given two specimens of an entire dialogue where this kind of interruption is characteristically carried on. One is where the vulgar-minded and vulgar-mannered Parolles perpetually breaks in upon lord Lafeu's observations; while the old nobleman steadily cuts him and his intrusive nothings, by pursuing his own train of thought without noticing the fellow's ill-breeding. The dialogue commences thus :—

> *Lafeu. To be relinquished of the artists,—*
> *Parolles.* So I say; both Galen and Paracelsus.
> *Lafeu. Of all the learned and authentic fellows,—*
> *Parolles.* Right; so I say.
> *Lafeu. That gave him out incurable,—*
> *Parolles.* Why, there 'tis; so say I too, &c.—*All's W.,* ii. 3.

The other dialogue is where Pandarus endeavours to deliver Troilus's message to Paris; but is perpetually interrupted by Helen's banter, teasing the old go-between to sing. It runs thus :—

> *Pandarus.* I have business to my lord, dear queen. *My lord, will you vouchsafe m a word?*
> *Helen.* Nay, this shall not hedge us out: we'll hear you sing, certainly.
> *Pandarus.* Well, sweet queen, you are pleasant with me. *But, marry, thus, my lord,—my dear lord, and most esteemed friend, your brother Troilus,—*
> *Helen.* My lord Pandarus; honey-sweet lord,—
> *Pandarus.* Go to, sweet queen, go to:—*commends himself most affectionately to you,—*
> *Helen.* You shall not bob us out of our melody; &c.—*Tr. & Cr.,* iii. 1.

VARIATIONS.

It has been complained, by sticklers for what they call consistency, that Shakespeare has given repetitions of certain sentences from previous scenes in some of his plays, with verbal variations that show inattention and negligence on the part of the author. To our thinking, they, on the contrary, show his attention to nature and his care to make his characters speak consistently with dramatic verisimilitude. In all the passages where these variations in wording occur, we shall find that there was some excellent reason for the dramatist's making the speaker deviate from strict accuracy of repetition; either to denote hurry, or agitation, or heedlessness, or purposed incorrectness in the person speaking. With regard to the first of the following passages, we must premise that the Folio copy and the Quarto copies vary in their version of the text; and that our version adopts one phrase from the Quartos. The phrase is, " *what* goes here?" which was originally misprinted '*who* goes heare?' Just as, a little farther on in the scene, the Folio misprints 'who' for "what," where Mrs. Page exclaims, " What a taking was he in, when your husband asked *what* was in the basket!" 'Who' for 'what' was formerly by no means an unfrequent misprint.

Ford. How now! *what goes here? whither bear you this?*
Servant. To the laundress, forsooth.—*Merry W.*, iii. 3.

Mrs. Page. What a taking was he in, *when your husband asked what was in the basket!*—*Ibid.*, iii. 3.

Falstaff. Being thus crammed in the basket, a couple of Ford's knaves, his hinds, were called forth by their mistress, to carry me in the name of foul clothes to Datchet Lane: they took me on their shoulders; met the jealous knave their master in the door, *who asked them once or twice what they had in their basket.*—*Ibid.*, iii. 5.

That Ford challenges the contents of the basket is sufficiently indicated; and to object that Mrs. Page does not repeat the exact words of his inquiry, appears to us to show no better appreciation of the dramatist's intention than if objection were made at her observing "*what a taking was he in, when,*" &c., on the ground that she could not see or know how dismayed Falstaff was, since he was hidden beneath the heap of linen. This mode of giving *the spirit* of a hurried incident, when related by the parties concerned, instead of *its letter*, is in accordance with Shakespeare's truth to nature and actual fact.

"Who chooseth me shall get as much as he deserves."—*Mer. of V.*, ii. 7.
"Who chooseth me shall get as much as he deserves."—*Ibid.*, ii. 7.
"Who chooseth me shall get as much as he deserves."—*Ibid.*, ii. 9.
"Who chooseth me shall have as much as he deserves."—*Ibid.*, ii. 9.

Because the inscription on the silver casket is three times worded with the word "get," it has been contended by critics that "have" should be 'get' the fourth time the inscription is cited; but we think that inasmuch as the speaker is here agitatedly quoting from memory the inscription previous to reading the "schedule," he does so most naturally with a slight verbal difference.

Look on his letter, madam, here's my passport.
[*Reads*] "When thou canst get the ring upon my finger, which never shall come off, and show me a child begotten of thy body, that I am father to, then call me husband."—*All's W.*, iii. 2.

                              There is your ring;
And, look you, here's your letter; this it says:
"When from my finger you can get this ring
And are by me with child," &c. This is done:
Will you be mine, now you are doubly won?—*Ibid.*, v. 3.

In the former instance Helena is *reading* the letter; in the latter she is *quoting* it; which points the dramatist has marked by putting the letter itself in prose, while he puts its quoted substance into blank verse, as forming part of her speech. But though one feels sure she knows its every cruel sentence by heart, yet the very inaccuracy of the cited words serves to indicate the quivering of the lip that repeats them, and the shaking of the hand that holds out the paper containing them.

I marvel your ladyship takes delight in such a barren rascal: . . . unless you laugh and minister occasion to him, he is gagged.—*Tw. N.*, i. 5.

[*Reads*] "If this fall into thy hand, revolve. In my stars I am above thee; but be not afraid of greatness: some are born great, some achieve greatness, and some have greatness thrust upon them."—*Ibid.*, ii. 5 (*Letter*).

Fool, there was never man so notoriously abused: I am as well in my wits, fool, as thou art.—*Ibid.*, iv. 2.

Why, " some are born great, some achieve greatness, and some have greatness thrown upon them." I was one, sir, in this interlude,—one Sir Topas, sir; but that's all one. " By the Lord, fool, I am not mad "; but do you remember? " Madam, why laugh you at such a barren rascal? an you smile not he's gagged": and thus the whirligig of time brings in his revenges.—*Tw. N.*, v. i.

It has been suggested that "thrown" should be 'thrust'; in order to consist (!) with the wording of the letter. Certainly not; the dramatist, making the whole speech a jocular taunt of the Clown to Malvolio, causes the wag to lightly quote a prominent sentence from the letter, with the same inaccurate wording that he uses when reminding the puritanical steward of certain other recent matters of grudge and reprisal between them. The salient expressions " barren rascal," " he's gagged," and the denial of imputed insanity are recalled; but with precisely that variation from exactness which we find in real life, and therefore in Shakespeare's page.

Master, there is three carters, three shepherds, three neat-herds, three swine-herds, that have made themselves all men of hair,—they call themselves saltiers; and they have a dance. . . . Pray, let us see these four threes of herdsmen.—*W. T.*, iv. 3.

Because of these last words it has been proposed to change " carters " to ' goat-herds; ' but it is thoroughly in characteristic accordance with nature that the farm-servant should know precisely what are the several callings of the rustics who personate these " men of hair," and should designate them specially; while the king, hearing chiefly the repetition words " shepherds," " neat-herds " and " swine-herds," speaks of the whole twelve as " these four threes of *herdsmen*."

> Lord Marshal, command our officers at arms
> Be ready to direct these home alarms.—*R. II.*, i. i.
>
> Marshal, demand of yonder champion
> The cause of his arrival here in arms.—*Ibid.*, i. 3.
>
> Marshal, ask yonder knight in arms,
> Both who he is, and why he cometh hither
> Thus plated in habiliments of war.—*Ibid.*, i. 3.

Because the word " lord " is omitted before " marshal " in the second and third of the above passages, and because the omission would improve the metre, Steevens and others leave out " lord " in the first passage. But Shakespeare sometimes disregards the exact quantity of feet in a line; especially where a title or a proper name occurs. Besides, it is not improbable that he made Richard say " Lord Marshal " in the first scene, by way of marking this officer's rank and form of title to the audience.

" Item, that the duchy of Anjou and the county of Maine shall be released and delivered to the king her father"—
> Uncle, how now!—
> > Pardon me, gracious lord;
> Some sudden qualm hath struck me at the heart,
> And dimm'd mine eyes, that I can read no farther.—
> Uncle of Winchester, I pray, read on.—
[*Reads*] " Item, it is farther agreed between them, that the duchies of Anjou and Maine shall be released and delivered over to the king her father."—2 *H. VI.*, i. i.

The variation in the wording of this item of the treaty has been objected to by Malone and others, who accuse Shakespeare of " in- accuracy " and " inconsistency." We believe it to be one of those inaccuracies and inconsistencies which the dramatist purposely commits for the sake of giving natural effect to certain passages, where varied wording is true to nature in the situation he is representing. In the present case, Gloster, while reading, gathers the main purport of the distasteful item, and blurts it out in abstract ; while Winchester, bid to "read on," does so with more verbal precision.

> [*Reads*] " What fates await the Duke of Suffolk ?"
> By water shall he die, and take his end.
> [*Reads*] " What shall befall the Duke of Somerset?" . . .
> [*Reads*] " Tell me what fate awaits the Duke of Suffolk ?
> By water shall he die, and take his end,
> What shall betide the Duke of Somerset ?"—2 *H. VI.*, i. 4.

The questions in the above passage are first propounded to the spirit by Bolingbroke the conjuror ; who, having made himself acquainted with their purport, words them rather according to their known substance than with verbal implicitness to the form in which the duchess has written them down. Although holding the paper in his hand, and formally appearing to read from it, yet he delivers the questions with just that want of literal exactness which is natural under such circumstances. The second time it is York who reads them from the paper where they are written, together with the answers that have been added from the spirit's rejoinder ; and he, of course, reads verbatim what he finds penned down. This, we think, accounts for the variation between the forms of the same questions ; and even shows a certain amount of dramatic propriety in the variation.

> If ever he have wife, let her be made
> More miserable by the death of him,
> Than I am made by my young lord and thee !—*R. III.*, i. 2.
> When he, that is my husband now,
> Came to me, as I follow'd Henry's corse ;
> When scarce the blood was well wash'd from his hands,
> Which issu'd from my other angel husband,
> And that dead saint which then I weeping follow'd ;
> O, when, I say, I look'd on Richard's face,
> This was my wish, —" Be thou," quoth I, " accurs'd,
> For making me, so young, so old a widow !
> And, when thou wedd'st, let sorrow haunt thy bed ;
> And be thy wife (if any be so mad)
> More miserable by the life of thee
> Than thou hast made me by my dear lord's death ! "—*Ibid.*, iv. 1.

In the penultimate line of the last-cited passage, the Quarto copies give ' death ' instead of " life," and give other minor differences in this sentence, which cause it to correspond more closely with the words previously used by Anne in act i., sc. 2, that she is now quoting. But the Folio reading, which we adopt, is in accordance with other variations which Anne here makes ; for she not only repeats her own words with natural inexactness, she also describes herself as having addressed Richard, when, in fact, she addressed the corse of King Henry VI.

> How far off lie these armies ?—
> Within this mile and half.—*Coriol.*, i. 4.
> The citizens of Corioli have issu'd,
> And given to Lartius and to Marcius battle ;
> I saw our party to their trenches driven,
> And then I came away.—

> Though thou speak'st truth,
> Methinks thou speak'st not well.   How long is't since ?—
> Above an hour, my lord.—
> 'Tis not a mile ; briefly we heard their drums :
> How could'st thou in a mile confound an hour,
> And bring thy news so late ?—*Coriol.*, i. 6.

In the first of the two above-cited passages Steevens proposed to omit the words " and half " from the conclusion of the line, because he complains that they disturb the measure, and because, he says, it is mentioned in the second passage that " 'tis not a mile " between the two armies.   But, not only does Shakespeare occasionally give lines of more or fewer than ten feet, he sometimes purposely gives these variations in reports of distance or numbers on a battle-field, as being peculiarly natural to the scene.

> Draw Benvolio; beat down their weapons.
> Gentlemen, for shame, forbear this outrage !
> Tybalt,—Mercutio,—the prince expressly hath
> Forbidden bandying in Verona streets :
> Hold, Tybalt !—Good Mercutio. —*R. & Jul.*, iii. 1.
>   Romeo he cries aloud,
> " Hold, friends ! friends, part ! " and, swifter than his tongue,
> His agile arm beats down their fatal points,
> And 'twixt them rushes.—*Ibid.*, iii. 1.

Here, in the account which Benvolio gives of the fray, he repeats Romeo's words with just that variation in literal precision which is in accordance with repetitions of the kind in real life.

> All hail, Macbeth ! that shalt be king hereafter.—*Macb.*, i. 3.
> These weird sisters saluted me, and referred me to the coming on of time, with,
> " Hail, king that shalt be ! "—*Ibid.*, i. 5 (*Letter*).

In his letter to his wife, Macbeth quotes the witches' prognostic with natural deviation from its exact wording.

> Be bloody, bold, and resolute ; laugh to scorn
> The power of man, for none of woman born
> Shall harm Macbeth.—*Ibid.*, iv. 1.
>   The spirits that know
> All mortal consequences have pronounced me thus,—
> " Fear not, Macbeth; no man that's born of woman
> Shall e'er have power upon thee."—*Ibid.*, v. 3.
> Macbeth shall never vanquish'd be, until
> Great Birnam wood to high Dunsinane hill
> Shall come against him.—*Ibid.*, iv. 1.
> I pull in resolution ; and begin
> To doubt th' equivocation of the fiend,
> That lies like truth : " Fear not, till Birnam wood
> Do come to Dunsinane."—*Ibid.*, v. 5.

In both the last-quoted instances, Macbeth repeats the oracular sentences of the apparitions summoned by the witches, with the slight verbal alteration that Shakespeare introduces on these occasions with so natural an effect.

> How look I,
> That I should seem to lack humanity
> So much as this fact comes to ?   [*Reading*] " Do't: the letter
> That I have sent her, by her own command
> Shall give thee opportunity."—*Cym.*, iii. 2

Let thine own hands take away her life: I shall give thee opportunity at Milford Haven: she hath my letter for the purpose —*Cym.*, iii. 4.

In the first of the above two citations, Pisanio is glancing at the cruel contents of his master's letter, and giving the substance of a sentence from it, so as to form part of his own blank-verse speech ; in the latter, Imogen is reading the letter itself, which is in prose : these combined circumstances account for Shakespeare's having, according to his wont in such cases, given the due amount of variation proper to dramatically artistic effect. Another point in connection with this letter is that no portion of it which is read aloud contains any command respecting a token to be sent ; though Pisanio says to Imogen :—

> I 'll give but notice you are dead, and send him
> Some bloody sign of it ; for 'tis commanded
> I should do so.—*Ibid.*, iii. 4.

But it may be supposed that this command has been added in a postscript, or in a portion of the letter left unread by Imogen, when she has perused its first bitter sentences.

> Upon a time,—unhappy was the clock
> That struck the hour !—it was in Rome,—accurs'd
> The mansion where !—'twas at a feast,—O, would
> Our viands had been poison'd, or at least
> Those which I heav'd to head !—the good Posthumus,—
> What should I say ! he was too good to be
> Where ill men were ; and was the best of all
> Amongst the rest of good ones,—sitting sadly,
> Hearing us praise our loves of Italy
> For beauty, &c.—*Ibid.*, v. 5.

The above description does not precisely tally with the circumstances of the incident as it actually occurred in the fifth scene of the first act ; but we have shown that Shakespeare occasionally gives these variations in particular detail ; and, in the present case, he may either have given it for the sake of producing the effect of that inaccuracy of memory which often marks the narration of a past occurrence even in persons habitually truthful, or in order to denote Iachimo's innate untruthfulness and unscrupulousness, which lead him to falsify in minor matters as in those of greater moment.

> Speak, Pyramus. Thisby, stand forth.—
> *Thisby, the flowers of odious savours sweet,—*
> " Odours, odours."—
> ——*odours savours sweet :*
> *So hath thy breath, my dearest Thisby, dear.*
> *But hark ! a voice ; stay thou but here awhile,*
> *And by-and-by I will to thee appear.* [*Exit.*
> Must I speak now ?

Ay, marry, must you ; for you must understand, he goes but to see a noise that he heard, and is to come again.

> *Most radiant Pyramus, most lily-white of hue,*
> *Of colour like the red rose on triumphant brier,*
> *Most brisky juvenal, and eke most lovely Jew,*
> *As true as truest horse, that yet would never tire,*
> *I 'll meet thee, Pyramus, at Ninny's tomb.*

" Ninus' tomb," man ! Why, you must not speak that yet ; that you answer to Pyramus : you speak all your part at once, cues and all. Pyramus, enter : your cue is past, it is, " never tire."

> O,—*As true as truest horse, that yet would never tire.*—
> > *Re-enter* PUCK, *and* BOTTOM *with an ass's head.*
>
> *If I were, fair Thisby, I were only thine.*—*Mid. N. D.*, iii. 1.
> *I see a voice : now will I to the chink,*
> *To spy an I can hear my Thisby's face.*
> *Thisby !—*
> *My love ! thou art my love, I think.—*
> *Think what thou wilt, I am thy lover's grace;*
> *And, like Limander, am I trusty still.—*
> *And I like Helen, till the Fates me kill.—*
> *Not Shafalus to Procrus was so true.—*
> *As Shafalus to Procrus, I to you.—*
> *O, kiss me through the hole of this vile wall !—*
> *I kiss the wall's hole, not your lips at all.—*
> *Wilt thou at Ninny's tomb meet me straightway ?—*
> *'Tide life, 'tide death, I come without delay.—Ibid.*, v. 1.

By the above extracts, it will be seen that the dialogue of the interlude is made to vary *at performance* from what it is *at rehearsal* ; and we believe that Shakespeare purposely did this to avoid the flat effect upon his audience which an exact repetition would have produced. He preferred giving an inexactitude to giving a platitude.

He occasionally has some variations in stated times :—

> But this new governor
> Awakes me all the enrolled penalties,
> Which have, like unscour'd armour, hung by the wall
> So long, that *nineteen zodiacs have gone round*,
> And none of them been worn.—*M. for M.*, i. 3,
>
> We have strict statutes, and most biting laws,—
> The needful bits and curbs to headstrong steeds,—
> Which for these *fourteen years* we have let sleep.—*Ibid.*, i. 4.

See ALLEGED ANACHRONISMS, &c., for an explanation of the above variation in stated time ; and for two other similar instances.

> Impute it not a crime
> To me or my swift passage, that I slide
> O'er *sixteen years*, and leave the growth untried
> Of that wide gap.—*W. T.*, iv. (*Chorus*).
>
> It is *fifteen years* since I saw my country.—*Ibid.*, iv. 1.

In making Camillo speak of a fifteen years' interval, while Time, as Chorus, mentions sixteen years as having elapsed since the events that happened in the play during the first three acts, Shakespeare gives one of those variations in statement which come naturally from a person supposed to talk without strict precision of a past period.

In some cases, the dramatist gives a variation of construction in one speech [*See* PECULIAR CONSTRUCTION]; and he does this with a view to characteristic effect—generally, to mark agitation in the speaker. He has occasional variations of an auxiliary verb in the same sentence :—

> " The time *shall* come," thus did he follow it,
> " The time *will* come, that foul sin, gathering head,
> Shall break into corruption ":—so went on.—*2 H. IV.*, iii. 1.
>
> I *will* hold my peace when Achilles' brach bids me, *shall* I ?—*Tr. & Cr.*, ii. 1.

He now and then varies the form in names of places ; sometimes for the sake of metre, sometimes for the sake of rhyme :—

> Let what is dear in *Sicily* be cheap.—*W. T.*, i. 2

Purchase the sight again of dear *Sicilia.—W. T.*, iv. 3.
Young prince of *Tyre*, you have at large receiv'd.*—Per.*, i. 1.
Our son and daughter shall in *Tyrus* reign.*—Ibid.*, v. 3.
        In her unholy service. Patience, then,
        And think you now are all in *Mitylen.—Ibid.*, iv. 4 (*Gower*).
Sir, there's a barge put off from *Mitylene.—Ibid.*, v. 1.
        What minstrelsy, and pretty din,
        The regent made in *Mitylin.—Ibid.*, v. 2. (*Gower*).

He occasionally gives variation in names of persons ; sometimes to suit the metre, sometimes as a token of familiarity, sometimes even to denote a humorous alteration made by the speaker—as in the first case we cite:—

Who, Sir Andrew *Aguecheek ?*——*Tw. N.*, i. 3.
For here comes Sir Andrew *Ague-face.—Ibid.*, i. 3.
There is *Anne* Page, which is daughter to Master George Page.—*Merry W.*, i. 1.
Therefore no more turn me to him, sweet *Nan.—Ibid.*, iii. 4.
Thou blushest, *Antony*, and that blood of thine.—*Ant. & C.*, i. 1.
Is Cæsar with *Antonius* priz'd so slight?—*Ibid.*, i. 1.
By thee, old *Capulet*, and Montague.—*R. & Jul.*, i. 1.
Her body sleeps in *Capels'* monument.—*Ibid.*, v. 1.
O *Cressida !* but that the busy day.—*Tr. & Cr.*, iv. 2.
Make *Cressid's* name the very crown of falsehood.—*Ibid.*, iv. 2.
The Grecian *Diomed*, and our Antenor.—*Tr. & Cr.*, iv. 2.
We must give up to *Diomedes'* hand the lady Cressida.—*Ibid.*, iv. 2.
Gentle son *Edward*, thou wilt stay with me ?—3 *H. VI.*, i. 1.
O *Ned*, sweet *Ned !* speak to thy mother, boy!—*Ibid.*, v. 5.
Good morrow, *Ned.*—1 *H. IV.*, i. 2.
Hear ye, *Yedward ;* if I tarry at home.—*Ibid.*, i. 2.
        Here's to thee, Menas !
                  Enobarbus, welcome !—*Ant. & C.*, ii. 7.
        You see, we have burnt our cheeks, strong *Enobarbe*
        Is weaker than the wine.—*Ibid.*, ii. 7.
Now, *Hal*, what time of day is it, lad ?—1 *H. IV.*, i. 2.
Harry, I do not only marvel where thou spendest thy time.—*Ibid.*, ii. 4.
Three times hath *Henry* Bòlingbroke made head.—*Ibid.*, iii. 1.
Made love to Nedar's daughter, *Helena.—Mid. N. D.*, i. 1.
Helen, to you our minds we will unfold.—*Ibid.*, i. 1.
No more of this, *Helena*,—go to, no more.—*All's W.*, i. 1.
Little *Helen*, farewell : if I can remember thee.—*Ibid.*, i. 1.
Because she's kin to me, therefore she's not so fair as *Helen.—Tr. & Cr.*, i. 1.
Nell, he is full of harmony.—*Ibid.*, iii. 1.
Thou speak'st like a physician, *Helicanus.—Per.*, i. 2.
Follow me, then. Lord *Helicane*, a word.—*Ibid.*, ii. 4.
I got possession of *Julietta's* bed.—*M. for M.*, i. 3.
With character too gross is writ on *Juliet.—Ibid.*, i. 3.
God forbid ! Where's this girl ? What, *Juliet.—R. & Jul.*, i. 3.
Wilt thou not, *Jule ?* and, by my holy-dame.—*Ibid.*, i. 3.
Her name is *Katharina* Minola.—*Tam. of S.*, i. 2.
Till *Katharine* the curst have got a husband.—*Ibid.*, i. 2.
I pr'ythee, sister *Kate*, untie my hands.—*Ibid.*, ii. 1.
To our most fair and princely cousin *Katharine.—H. V.*, v. 2.

Do you like me, *Kate ?*—*H. V.*, v. 2.
Katharine our queen, before the primest creature.—*H. VIII.*, ii. 4.
Go thy ways, *Kate.*—*Ibid.*, ii. 4.
Good *Margaret*, run thee to the parlour.—*M. Ado*, iii. 1.
No, pray thee, good *Meg*, I 'll wear this.—*Ibid.*, iii. 4.
A stoop of wine, *Maria!*—*Tw. N.*, ii. 3.
Marian, I say! a stoop of wine !—*Ibid.*, ii. 3.
Mistress *Mary*, if you prized my lady's favour.—*Ibid.*, ii. 3.
O *Pandarus !* I tell thee, *Pandarus.*—*Tr. & Cr.*, i. 1.
I cannot come to Cressid but by *Pandar.*—*Ibid.*, i. 1.
You did supplant your brother *Prospero.*—*Temp.*, ii. 1.
From bogs, fens, flats, on *Prosper* fall, and make him.—*Ibid.*, ii. 2.
Hard-favour'd *Richard ? Richard*, where art thou ?—3 *H. VI.*, v. 5.
And thou mis-shapen *Dick*,—I tell ye all.—*Ibid.*, v. 5.
For *Dickon* thy master is bought and sold.—*R. III.*, v. 3 (*Scroll*).
And I had his, Sir *Robert* his, like him.—*John*, i. 1.
I would not be Sir *Nob* in any case.—*Ibid.*, i. 1.
How his companion, youthful *Valentine.*—*Two G. of V.*, i. 3.
With *Valentinus* in the emperor's court.—*Ibid.*, i. 3.

Shakespeare sometimes gives variation in a form of address or of mention ; and, generally, with some definite dramatic purpose:—

Mrs. Overdone. What's to do here, *Thomas* Tapster? Let's withdraw.—*M. for M.*, i. 2.

Escalus. What's your name, master tapster ?—
Clown. Pompey.—*Ibid.*, ii. 1.

Lucio. Art going to prison, *Pompey ?*—*Ibid.*, iii. 2.

The fact that his mistress calls the tapster-clown " Thomas," would lead us to suspect that he impudently gives Escalus an '*alias*' in the second of the above instances ; but as Lucio addresses him by the same name that he gives to Escalus, we take " Pompey " to be a familiar appellation bestowed upon him by waggish customers and adopted by himself.

Antipholus S. What's her name ?
Dromio S. Nell, sir.—*Com. of E.*, iii. 2.

Dromio S. Where *Dowsabel* did claim me for her husband.—*Ibid.*, iv. 1.

We presume that Dromio invents a name in both instances for the kitchen-wench : first, " Nell " to afford a pun with " an ell," in allusion to her breadth of proportions ; secondly, " Dowsabel," by way of a fleer at her assault upon him—to ' dowse,' in old English parlance, signifying to give a blow on the face, to strike.

Parolles. O, *my knave*,—how does my old lady ?—*All's W.*, ii. 4.

Parolles. Good *Monsieur Lavatch*, give my lord Lafeu this letter : I have ere now, sir, been better known to you, when I have held familiarity with fresher clothes.—*Ibid.*, v. 2.

The contrast between the braggart's lordly style of addressing the Clown in the first instance, and his cringing style of address in the latter instance, is admirably characteristic.

King John. Kneel thou down, *Philip*, but arise more great,—
Arise Sir *Richard* and *Plantagenet.*—*John*, i. 1.

King John. Hubert, keep this boy. *Philip*, make up.—*Ibid.*, iii. 2.

Salisbury. Sir Richard, what think you ?—*Ibid.*, iv. 3.

Salisbury. Stand by, or I shall gall you, *Faulconbridge.*—*Ibid.*, iv. 3.

In the second of the above cases, it has been objected that the king, who has knighted Philip Faulconbridge by the title of Sir Richard Plantagenet, should call him "Philip"; but the old familiar name is used here, as in the fourth of the above cases. In other passages of the play the dramatist has maintained the same variations, as if to denote that the renownedly brave man was popularly known by both his former and his subsequent denominations.

> Duchess. Here comes my son *Aumerle*.
> York.   *Aumerle* that was;
> But that is lost for being Richard's friend,
> And, madam, you must call him *Rutland* now.—*R. II.*, v. 2.
>
> Duchess. Strike him, *Aumerle*. Poor boy, thou art amaz'd.—*Ibid.*, v. 2.
> Duchess. By pardoning *Rutland*, my transgressing boy.—*Ibid.*, v. 3.

Most naturally, the mother calls her son by the old familiar name in the moment of urging him to prevent the servant from aiding York in his journey to court for the purpose of revealing the discovered treason; but, as naturally, she calls her son by the new name assigned to him by Bolingbroke when imploring the latter to grant her boy's pardon.

> Prince Henry. Call in Falstaff: I'll play Percy, and that damned brawn shall play *Dame Mortimer* his wife.—*1 H. IV.*, ii. 4.
>
> Mortimer. Good father, tell her that she and *my aunt Percy* shall follow in your conduct speedily.—*Ibid.*, iii. 1.
>
> Hotspur. Come, *Kate*, I'll have your song too.—*Ibid.*, iii. 1.

Prince Henry calls Lady Percy by her maiden name, "Dame *Mortimer*." Mortimer speaks of her as his kinswoman, and by her married name, "my aunt Percy"; and Hotspur addresses his wife by her Christian name, "Kate."

> Glendower. Sit, cousin *Percy*; sit, good cousin *Hotspur*;
> For by that name as oft as *Lancaster*
> Doth speak of you, his cheek looks pale.—*Ibid.*, iii. 1.
>
> Glendower. Three times hath *Henry Bolingbroke* made head
> Against my power.—*Ibid.*, iii. 1.

Very natural is Glendower's calling Percy by his surname of "Hotspur," in order to recall its effect upon King Henry; whom he, again most naturally, adverts to by his simple patronymic of "Lancaster," and by his family name of "Henry Bolingbroke," which has the effect of implying that he is a usurper and no true monarch.

> Sir, *ancient* Pistol's below, and would speak with you.—*2 H. IV.*, ii. 4.
>
> No, good *Captain* Pistol; not here, sweet *captain.*—*Ibid.*, ii. 4.
>
> Come, *Lieutenant* Pistol.—*Ibid.*, v. 5.
>
> I tell thee what, *Corporal* Bardolph.—*Ibid.*, ii. 4.
>
> Good-morrow, *Lieutenant* Bardolph.—*H. V.*, ii. 1.

By the above variation in the titles given by these swashbucklers to one another, it should seem that the dramatist intended to convey the indefiniteness of their respective grades, as being altogether a pretence; and that occasionally they themselves were at a loss to remember what was the special title that each had assumed.

> First, you know, *Caius Marcius* is chief enemy to the people.—*Coriol.*, i. 1.
>   And from this time,
> For what he did before Corioli, call him,

> With all th' applause and clamour of the host,
> *Caius Marcius Coriolanus.—Coriol.*, i. 9.

> My gentle *Marcius*, worthy *Caius*, and
> By deed-achieving honour newly nam'd,—
> What is it ? *Coriolanus* must I call thee ?—*Ibid.*, ii. 1.

> A little of that worthy work perform'd
> By *Caius Marcius Coriolanus ;* whom
> We meet here, both to thank, and to remember
> With honours like himself —*Ibid.*, ii. 2.

> Sit, *Coriolanus ;* never shame to hear
> What you have nobly done.—*Ibid.*, ii. 2.

> A fearful army, led by *Caius Marcius*,
> Associated with Aufidius, rages
> Upon our territories.—*Ibid.*, iv. 6.

> To his surname, *Coriolanus*, 'longs more pride
> Than pity to our prayers.—*Ibid.*, v. 3.

How naturally sometimes the old familiar name, sometimes the honourably gained added name, is used in the above passages !

> Do you know this noble gentleman, *Edmund ?—Lear*, i. 1.

> True or false, it hath made thee *Earl of Gloster.—Ibid.*, iii. 5.

> Back, *Edmund*, to my brother.—*Ibid.*, iv. 2.

> My most dear *Gloster !—Ibid.*, iv. 2.

> Lord *Edmund* spake not with your lord at home ?—*Ibid.*, iv. 5.

> And give the letters, which thou find'st about me,
> To *Edmund, Earl of Gloster.—Ibid.*, iv. 6.

In each of the above-quoted instances the variation of form in name and title is made with dramatically appropriate effect.

> One *Michael Cassio*, a Florentine.—*Oth.*, i. 1.

> Good *Michael*, look you to the guard to-night.—*Ibid.*, ii. 3.

> Come, *lieutenant*, I have a stoop of wine.—*Ibid.*, ii. 3.

> Now, 'mongst this flock of drunkards,
> Am I to put our *Cassio* in some action
> That may offend the isle.—*Ibid.*, ii. 3.

> How comes it, *Michael*, you are thus forgot ?—*Ibid.*, ii. 3.

> *Cassio*, I love thee ;
> But never more be officer of mine.—*Oth.*, ii. 3.

Admirably are the above differences of appellation made to conduce to dramatic purpose. Iago speaks of his brother officer first by his full name to Roderigo ; later on he speaks of him sneeringly as " our Cassio," but he addresses him by the title of " lieutenant," which so excites his own secret envy. And even still more marked is the mode in which Othello familiarly and affectionately calls his favourite subaltern by his Christian name " Michael," *before* the young man's transgression, but *never afterwards*.

> Good *Enobarbus*, 'tis a worthy deed.—*Ant. & C.*, ii. 2.

> Why, *Enobarbus*, when Antony found Julius Cæsar dead.—*Ibid.*, iii. 2.

> More, *Domitius ;* my lord desires you presently.—*Ibid.*, iii. 5.

> He will not fight with me, *Domitius.—Ibid.*, iv. 2.

Shakespeare makes this character generally addressed by his chief name of " Enobarbus "; but, in two cases, by his pre-name of " Domitius." In one case by Antony's personal attendant Eros, and in the other case by Antony himself.

Shakespeare occasionally gives varieties in corrupt pronunciations, which have a humorous as well as a natural effect; blunderers often hitting upon wrong utterances, though sometimes stumbling upon right ones :—

Sir Hugh Evans. There is also another device in my prain, which, peradventure, prings *goot* discretions with it.—*Merry W.*, i. 1.

Sir Hugh Evans. Can you carry your *good* will to the maid?—*Ibid.*, i. 1.

Dr. Caius. Vere is *dat* knave Rugby?—*Ibid.*, i. 4.

Dr. Caius. I pray you, bear vitness *that* me have stay six or seven, two, tree hours for him.—*Ibid.*, ii. 3.

Hostess Quickly. I pray ye, since my *exion* is entered.—2 *H. IV.*, ii. 1.

Hostess Quickly. Master Fang, have you entered the *action?*—*Ibid.*, ii. 1.

Hostess Quickly. Good Captain *Peesel*, be quiet.—*Ibid.*, ii. 4.

Hostess Quickly. No, good Captain *Pistol;* not here.—*Ibid.*, ii. 4.

VARIED MEANINGS COMBINED IN ONE WORD OR SENTENCE.

A peculiar feature in Shakespeare's style is his masterly manner of comprising in a single felicitously chosen epithet a variety of significations, thus expressed at one and the same moment—a grand essential for a dramatist, whose aim is to produce at the first hearing of his lines, a prompt comprehension of the idea or ideas he intends to convey. Coleridge says: "The play of assimilation, the meaning one sense chiefly, and yet keeping both senses in view, is perfectly Shakespearian." And this remark is strongly exemplified in certain words and phrases used by him :—

> Mark, then, *abounding* valour in our English;
> That, being dead, like to the bullet's grazing,
> Break out into a second course of mischief,
> Killing in relapse of mortality.—*H. V.*, iv. 3.

Here, the word "abounding" is used with such force of witty as well as energetic force, that it conveys the effect of 'a bounding' as well as 'abundant;' and gives wonderful impetus and spirit to the passage.

> So in *approof* lives not his epitaph
> As in your royal speech.—*All's W.*, i. 2.

"Approof" here conveys the double effect of 'proof' and 'approval.'

> I am disgrac'd, impeach'd, and *baffled* here.—*R. II.*, i. 1.

Thus put into the mouth of the king-checked Norfolk, the word "baffled" includes the triple signification of 'foiled' or 'defeated,' of 'reviled' or 'abused,' and of 'degraded,' in allusion to the technical term for punishing a recreant knight by hanging him up by the heels, —old French, *baffoler.*

> Have I not heard these islanders shout out,
> "*Vive le roi!*" as I have *bank'd* their towns?—*John*, v. 2.

In conjunction with its context in the speech, "bank'd" here comprises the three meanings of 'thrown up embankments in front of assailed towns,' ' skirted those towns that stood on the river's banks,' and ' gained towns, placing them in bank as tricks at games of cards.'

> Never anybody saw it but his lackey: 'tis a hooded valour; and when it appears it will *bate.—H. V.*, iii. 7.

The last word combines the expression technically used by falconers of a hawk, which, when it is unhooded, is said to " bate "—that is, to ' beat,' ' flap,' or ' flutter' its wings, with the abbreviated form of ' abate,' in the sense of ' diminish,' ' dwindle.'

> Let us do so: for we are at the stake,
> And *bay'd* about with many enemies.—*Jul. C.*, iv. 1.

The word " bay'd " here has the comprehensive force of ' encompassed,' of ' brought to a stand,' as when a stag is at bay, and of ' baited ' or ' barked at,' as a hunted animal, or one bound to a stake, is bayed at by dogs.

> O Antony,
> Thou mine of bounty, how wouldst thou have paid
> My better service, when my turpitude
> Thou dost so crown with gold! This *blows* my heart.—*Ant. & C.*, iv. 6.

The forcible expression " blows " gives the *sense* of ' swells ' and the *effect* of ' strikes.'

> And so, great powers,
> If you will take this audit, take this life,
> And cancel these cold *bonds.—Cym.*, v. 4.

Here " bonds " is used with triple play on the word; in reference to the legal instrument so called, to the iron shackles on the speaker's limbs, and to the sense in which the poet sometimes elsewhere employs " bond " as that whereon the term of " life " is held.

> For that will physic the great myrmidon
> Who *broils* in loud applause.—*Tr. & Cr.*, i. 3.

What a capital expression, that " broils ! " How it suggests the image of a man who swells and sweats in the fire of applause, as broiling meat swells, spits, fumes, and exudes, above the red coals; and how well it includes the sense of ' is quarrelsome,' ' is resentful,' ' is hostilely arrogant ! '

> Lean but upon a rush,
> The cicature and *capable* impressure
> Thy palm some moment keeps.—*As You L.*, iii. 3.

Here he makes " capable " equivalent to the compound expression ' able-to-be-received,' with the included meaning of ' visible ' or ' able-to-be-seen.'

> Even so my bloody thoughts, with violent pace,
> Shall ne'er look back, ne'er ebb to humble love,
> Till that a *capable* and wide revenge
> Swallow them up.—*Oth.*, iii. 3.

Here he makes " capable " convey the combined senses of ' capacious,' ' comprehensive,' ' capable of receiving,' and ' capable of satisfying.'

> To sit and draw
> His arched brow, his hawking eye, his curls,
> In our heart's table,—heart too *capable*
> Of every line and trick of his sweet favour.—*All's W.*, i. 1.

Here he uses "capable" to express 'susceptible' and 'able to receive.'

> His form and cause conjoin'd, preaching to stones,
> Would make them *capable.—Hamlet*, iii. 4.

Here "capable," besides the sense of 'able to understand,' includes the sense of 'susceptible,' 'able to feel.'

> I know I love in vain, strive against hope ;
> Yet, in this *captious* and intenible sieve,
> I still pour in the waters of my love,
> And lack not to lose still.—*All's W.*, i. 3.

Bearing well in mind the various senses in which Shakespeare uses the word "capable," also the possibility that "captious" may bear an included sense as derived from the Latin *captiosus*, 'deceitful' or 'fallacious,' and likewise that "captious" may here be partly intended as a contraction of 'capacious,' we feel that Helena implies in this single sentence the following varied meanings. She figuratively calls the object upon which she profitlessly lavishes her hopeless love a "sieve," that is, capable of receiving but not of holding or retaining : she believes this object to be 'capable of receiving' love, because he is in her eyes worthy of all love ; she allows that the object of her love is 'fallacious' to hope and 'deceives' expectation ; and she asserts it to be 'capacious' in extent of merit.

> She from whom
> We all were sea-swallow'd, though some *cast* again ;
> And, by that destiny, to perform an act,
> Whereof what 's past is prologue.—*Temp.*, ii. 1.

Here the word "cast" includes the sense of 'brought up after swallowing,' 'flung ashore,' 'thrown in wrestling,' and 'appointed for a part in a play.' The commentators, who differ as to the sense in which some of Shakespeare's expressions are to be taken—one affirming that he meant this, a second contending that he meant the other, and a third pronouncing that he intended *merely* to say so and so—seldom seem to perceive his large-minded mode of assembling several significances in a single concentrated word.

> Romeo is banish'd ; and all the world to nothing,
> That he dares ne'er come back to *challenge* you.—*R. & Jul.*, iii. 5.

As the verb "challenge" is here employed, it combines in itself the varied meaning of 'to claim you,' 'to declare you his,' and 'to call you to answer for what you do,' 'to accuse you.' The word is used in both these senses by writers of Shakespeare's time ; and it was his method to include several meanings in one comprehensive expression.

> That is honour's scorn,
> Which *challenges* itself as honour's born,
> And is not like the sire.—*All's W.*, ii. 3.

Here "challenges," while signifying 'proclaims,' is so judiciously introduced into the sentence as to convey the effect of honour's challenging or provoking confutation, at the same time that it proclaims itself.

> More *charming*
> With their own nobleness (which could have turn'd
> A distaff to a lance), gilded pale looks,
> Part shame, part spirit renew'd.—*Cym.*, v. 3.

" Charming," in the present passage—as in several others written by Shakespeare—combines the sense of ' influencing as by a spell,' ' actuating as by enchantment,' with the sense of ' enchanting,' ' prepossessing,' ' attractive.'

> He 'll call you to so hot an answer for it,
> That caves and womby vaultages of France
> Shall *chide* your trespass, and return your mock
> In second accent of his ordnance.—*H. V.*, ii. 4.

Inasmuch as Shakespeare elsewhere uses " chides " and " chiding " to express a peculiarly characterised sound, he here uses " chide " to express ' resound,' ' re-echo,' as well as ' rebuke,' ' reprove.'

> The count is neither sad, nor sick, nor merry, nor well; but *civil*, count,—*civil* as an orange, and something of that jealous complexion.—*M. Ado*, ii. 1.

Into the witty Beatrice's mouth has Shakespeare put an epithet here, which, besides a quibble on " civil " and ' Seville,' includes a gibe at Claudio's being sour and bitter, and sweet, like the fruit in question; at his being ' courteous and polite' though with a touch of crabbedness; at his being ' meek and mild ' though grumpy withal ; and at his being ' sober and grave ' while the others are merry : because in all of these senses has the poet used this word " civil " elsewhere.

> For 't must be done to-night,
> And something from the palace; always thought
> That I require a *clearness :* and with him
> (To leave no rubs nor botches in the work)
> Fleance his son, that keeps him company,
> Whose absence is no less material to me
> Than is his father's, must embrace the fate
> Of that dark hour.—*Macb.*, iii. 1.

" Clearness," as here used, implies both that the speaker requires he should be kept clear from suspicion, and that he requires neatness and completeness in the deed undertaken.

> Love's feeling is more soft and sensible
> Than are the tender horns of *cockled* snails.—*Love's L. L.*, iv. 3.

The term here italicised comprises the double meaning of ' shelled,' like a cockle-fish, and of ' spiral-formed,' from the Latin *cochlea*, a screw.

> Cry to it, nuncle, as the *cockney* did to the eels when she put 'em i' the paste alive.—*Lear*, ii. 4.

" Cockney " was formerly used both for a ' ninny ' and for a ' cook '; while Shakespeare, in the present passage, includes reference to both these meanings.

He employs it in one other passage only (" Twelfth Night," act iv., sc. 1) ; but there he employs the epithet more according to the sense it bears at present—as a term of contempt for a simpleton born and bred in the metropolis, bigoted to its ways, and knowing nothing beyond them.

> For in that sleep of death what dreams may come,
> When we have shuffled off this mortal *coil*,
> Must give us pause.—*Hamlet*, iii. 1.

By introducing the word " coil " in this sentence, the poet not only allows it to bear the sense it then bore of ' tumult,' ' bustle,' ' worry,' 'turmoil,' 'fuss,' but he permits it to poetically convey the effect of that which oppressively encircles, like a coil of heavy rope or the coil of a serpent around its prey.

> What is your will?—
> That I may *compass* yours.—*Two G. of V.*, iv. 2.

Shakespeare elsewhere uses " compass " as ' achieve ' is used; to express either ' gain,' ' obtain,' ' acquire,' or ' perform,' ' fulfil,' ' complete ': therefore here the speaker is made to infer that he wishes both to gain a knowledge of Silvia's will, and to perform its behests.

> Gentlemen, you are welcome to Elsinore. Your hands, come: the appurtenance of welcome is fashion and ceremony: let me *comply* with you in this garb.—*Hamlet*, ii. 2.
> He did *comply* with his dug, before he sucked it.—*Ibid.*, v. 2.

In both the above passages, Shakespeare uses the word " comply " inclusively; he gives it its more usual sense, ' to be complaisant, obsequious, or deferential to '; and also a sense which it formerly bore of ' enfold,' ' embrace,' ' caress,' ' fondle.'

> Three thousand ducats, due unto the Jew,
> We freely *cope* your courteous pains withal.—*Mer. of V.*, iv. 1.

Since Shakespeare elsewhere uses the word " cope " to express ' encounter,' or ' meet in interchange of word or deed '; since one of the original meanings of the word is ' a covering for the head '; and since there is an old verb, ' to cope, cowp, chap, or buy '—his employment of " cope " in the present passage allows the line to combinedly express, ' We freely encounter in exchange your courteous pains withal,' ' we freely crown your courteous pains withal,' and ' we freely reward (or purchase) your courteous pains withal.'

> Thou know'st that Banquo, and his Fleance, lives.—
> But in them nature's *copy* 's not eterne.—*Macb.*, iii. 2.

Here " copy " not only means ' example ' or ' specimen ' of humanity, but includes reference to the technical legal term for a ' lease ' held by *copyhold* tenure; in which the tenant holds an estate *for life* merely, and not in perpetuity.

> I take him to be a soul of great article; and his infusion of such *dearth* and rareness, as.—*Hamlet*, v. 2.

Here *dearth* includes the sense of ' dearness,' ' value,' as well as that of ' scarcity '; and may have been pronounced *deerth*.

> Therefore these stops of thine fright me the more;
> For such things in a false disloyal knave
> Are tricks of custom; but in a man that's just
> They 're close *delations*, working from the heart,
> That passion cannot rule.—*Oth.*, iii. 3.

" Delations," as here used by Shakespeare, combines in itself the two several meanings which it bore in his time, of something accused, and something carried or conveyed; so that by employing the expression " close delations" he signifies ' secret accusations,' ' inwardly conceived impugnings,' ' quietly conveyed intimations.'

> Let me yet know of you whither you are bound.—No, sooth, sir; my *determinate* voyage is mere *extravagancy*.—*Tw. N.*, ii. 1.

In the word " determinate," Shakespeare here blends the two meanings of ' determined upon,' and ' wherein terminating '; and in the word

" extravagancy " he blends the two meanings of ' wandering ' and ' vacillation.'

> I purpose not to wait on fortune till
> These wars *determine.—Coriol.*, v. 3.

The last word, as here employed, gives the inclusively large meaning of ' end,' ' conclude,' ' terminate,' and also ' decide,' ' resolve the point at issue.'

> I, after him, do after him wish too,
> Since I nor wax nor honey can bring home,
> I quickly were *dissolved* from my hive,
> To give some abourers room.—*All's W.*, i. 2.

The word " dissolved " is here most elegantly and Shakespearianly used ; conveying, as it does, the idea of the speaker's being *melted* away from his waxen cell of life, and subjected to *dissolution* or death.

> Then in my tent, Cassius, *enlarge* your griefs.—*Jul. C.*, iv. 2.

By the mode in which our author has here introduced the word " enlarge," it combines the senses it bears in both the familiar expressions, ' to enlarge upon a theme,' and ' to enlarge a prisoner.'

> This *ensign* here of mine was turning back ;
> I slew *the coward*, and did take *it* from *him*.—*Ibid.*, v. 3.

Shakespeare has here availed himself of the then mode of employing " ensign " both for a ' standard ' and a ' standard-bearer,' by making it succinctly serve a double purpose in this sentence.

> Thy life is dear ; for all, that life can rate
> Worth name of life, in thee hath *estimate.—All's W.*, ii. 1.

By his employment of the word " estimate " here, Shakespeare has given the duplicate effect to the sentence of ' in thee may be reckoned,' and ' in thee hath estimable existence.'

[*See* Note upon the word " even " (page 498) under PARTS OF SPEECH DIVERSELY USED.]

> And his honour
> Clock to itself, knew the true minute when
> *Exception* bid him speak.—*Ibid.*, i. 2.

The word " exception " is employed here with comprehensive force ; including both its meanings of ' offence ' and of ' a case specially excluded from a general rule.' It represents that against which the person alluded to took exception, rousing him to speak sharply, and the exceptional case which urged him to do so. Now, when we use ' exception ' in the sense of ' offence,' ' cavil,' or ' objection,' we use with it the words ' take ' and ' against ' (to take exception against a thing or person) ; but in Shakespeare's mode of introducing an expressive word in an elliptically constructed sentence, he often employs it so as to give its effect without accompanying it by its usual concomitants.

> The grave doth gape, and doting death is near ;
> Therefore *exhale.—H. V.*, ii. 1.

Pistol is here made, in one significant word, to bid Nym ' hale,' ' haul,' ' lug,' or ' draw out your weapon,' and also, ' breathe out your last breath.'

Captain Jamy is a marvellous falorous gentleman, that is certain ; and of great *expedition* and knowledge in the auncient wars, upon my particular knowledge of his directions : he will maintain his argument as well as any military man in the 'orld, in the disciplines of the pristine wars of the Romans.—*H. V.*, iii. 2.

Into Fluellen's mouth, the dramatist has characteristically put a word that (as derived from the Latin *expedire ;* one of the senses of which is, ' to show,' ' declare,' ' set forth in speech ') signifies ' power of expounding,' and also signifies ' readiness,' ' expertness.'

> Exchange me for a goat,
> When I shall turn the business of my soul
> To such *exsufflicate* and blown surmises,
> Matching thy inference,—*Oth.*, iii. 3.

The Shakespearian word, " exsufflicate," as traced to the low Latin *exsufflare*, 'to spit down upon,' which was an ancient form of exorcising, implies ' despicable,' ' contemptible,' ' abhorrent,' ' repudiated '; as having affinity with the Italian *suffolare*, to 'whisper,' it implies ' whispered,' ' breathed '; and as possessing some resemblance to ' sufflation ' (which means ' a puffing up,' ' a making to swell with blowing '), it implies ' puffed up,' ' blown out,' ' exaggerated,' ' extravagant ' : so that we take the expression, as here used, to include something of all these significations.

> And what art thou, thou idol ceremony ? . . .
> . . . No, thou proud dream,
> That play'st so subtly with a king's repose :
> I am a king that *find* thee.—*H. V.*, iv. 1.

Here, besides its sense of ' meet with,' ' possess,' the word " find " comprises that of ' find out,' ' see through,' ' discover the veritable quality of,' ' penetrate the true essence of.'

> They *flattered* me like a dog ; and told me I had white hairs in my beard ere the black ones were there.—*Lear*, iv. 6.

The word " flattered " here includes two of the senses which the French verb *flatter* bears, 'to fawn upon' as a dog does, and 'to stroke' as one strokes a dog ; besides conveying its usual meaning of ' to praise or compliment falsely.'

> Observe how Antony becomes his *flaw*,
> And what thou think'st his very action speaks
> In every power that moves.—*Ant. & C.*, iii. 10.

" Flaw " is here employed with double force, to express ' breach of fortune,' ' cracked fortune,' as well as ' tempest of fortune,' ' storm of fortune.'

> Do faithful homage, and receive *free* honours ;
> All which we pine for now.—*Macb.*, iii. 6.

By the mode in which he has used the word " free " here, Shakespeare gives the phrase inclusively to imply, ' free from pollution in the hand that confers these honours,' ' free from the taint of servility in us that accept them,' and ' free from fear and constraint in their possession.'

> Nay, but I bar to-night : you shall not *gage* me
> By what we do to-night.—*Mer. of V.*, ii. 2.

He uses " gage " here not only in the sense of ' engage,' ' limit,' ' confine,' ' restrain,' ' restrict,' but also (as if it were spelt ' gauge ') in the sense of ' judge,' ' measure,' ' estimate.'

> Behold the ordnance on their carriages,
> With fatal mouths *gaping* on girded Harfleur.—*H. V.*, iii. (*Chorus*).

The poet, by his introduction of this word in the present passage, gives both picture and sound to the imagination. In his time, "gaping," besides meaning 'wide open,' meant 'bawling,' 'roaring,' 'noisy,' 'loud'; therefore he causes us not only to see the wide-stretched jaws of the monster cannon, but to hear their roar.

> Between the acting of a dreadful thing
> And the first motion, all the interim is
> Like a phantasma, or a hideous dream:
> The *Genius* and the *mortal instruments*
> Are then in council; and the state of man,
> Like to a little kingdom, suffers then
> The nature of an insurrection.—*Jul. C.*, ii. 1.

According to our poet's grandly inclusive style, the word " Genius " here signifies both the Christianly understood ' soul' and the paganly understood attendant ' spirit'; while " mortal instruments " comprise the signification of both ' natural passions ' and ' bodily powers.'

> Now we'll together; and the chance of *goodness*
> Be like our warranted quarrel!—*Macb.*, iv. 3.

Inasmuch as Shakespeare occasionally employs " goodness" to express ' propitiousness,' ' favour' [*See* PECULIAR USE OF WORDS], and in some other cases to express ' justice,' the above sentence gives the bifold effect of ' May the chance of favourable issue be as great as the warrant for our contest!' and ' May our chance of justice be great as the justice of our cause!'

> Dry up thy marrows, vines, and plough-torn leas;
> Whereof ingrateful man, with liquorish draughts
> And morsels unctuous, *greases* his pure mind,
> That from it all consideration slips!—*Timon*, iv. 3.

By the single word " greases " here, Shakespeare condensedly expresses ' pollutes,' ' renders gross,' no less than ' clogs as with fat,' and ' imparts a smeary surface to'; so that by one felicitously employed verb, he presents the idea that over-eating-and-drinking sullies the mind, impedes its action, and deprives it of power to retain its thinking faculty.

> *Green*, indeed, is the colour of lovers.—*Love's L. L.*, i. 2.

It has been maintained that by " green " here is intended *either* an allusion to jealousy, *or* to green-hued eyes, *or* to the willow, as the badge of unsuccessful love. But we believe that here the poet, according to his frequent wont, included very many other allusions in the epithet he employs in this passage. " Green " has sometimes been used as an emblem of ' hope'; and thus is suitable for favoured lovers. " Green " has occasionally been made significant of ' desertion'; and is therefore applicable to forsaken or rejected lovers. " Green " is used by Shakespeare, as well as by other writers of his time, as a synonym for ' pale' and ' sickly'; therefore is appropriate for forlorn lovers and love-sick persons. " Green " is emblematic of youth and spring, the season of lovers; and " green " is often used, even to this day, as a term for ' inexperienced,' ' unripe in judgment,' ' immature,' ' raw,' which applies to novices in love.

The satirical rogue says here, that old men have grey beards; that their faces are wrinkled; their eyes purging thick amber and plum-tree gum; and that they have a plentiful lack of wit, together with most weak hams: all of which, sir, though I most powerfully and potently believe, yet I hold it not *honesty* to have it thus set down.— *Hamlet*, ii. 2.

" Honesty," as here used, besides including one of the senses in which the French use their word *honnêteté*, 'politeness,' 'civility,' ' courtesy,' ' decorum,' also comprises the English meaning of ' truth,' ' candour.'

> The youngest son of Priam, a true knight;
> Not yet mature, yet matchless: firm of word;
> Speaking in deeds, and deedless in his tongue;
> Not soon provok'd, nor, being provok'd, soon calm'd:
> His heart and hand both open, and both free;
> For what he has he gives, what thinks he shows;
> Yet gives he not till judgment guide his bounty,
> Nor dignifies an *impair* thought with breath.—*Tr. & Cr.*, iv. 5.

The fact that there have been proposals to alter the word " impair " here, and substitute the word " impure," appears to us to have arisen from failure in perceiving Shakespeare's mode of using expressions that combine several meanings in one word. As derived from the Latin *impar*, our poet's expression " impair " signifies ' unequal,' ' unsuitable,' ' unbefitting,' ' unworthy '; as derived from the Latin *imparatus*, " impair " signifies ' unprepared,' ' unready,' or ' perplexed,' 'entangled '; and as used (substantively) by Ben Jonson, by Chapman, and by Brown, " impair " (adjectively used) signifies ' injurious,' ' impairing,' ' deteriorating,' ' detractive.' Now we conceive that our author intended to blend somewhat of all the above meanings into the single epithet " impair " as above employed by him; and, to change it for another, would be not only to deprive the passage of its full intended force, but it would be to banish from our language a comprehensive adjective framed for us by a most original-minded writer.

The lines of my body are as well-drawn as his; no less young, more strong, not beneath him in fortunes, beyond him in the advantage of the time, above him in birth, alike conversant in general services, and more remarkable in single oppositions: yet this *imperseverant* thing loves him in my despite.—*Cym.*, iv. 1.

The word here used comprises the sense of ' undiscerning,' ' unperceiving ' (as though it were spelt ' imperceiverant '), and also the sense of ' obstinately persevering,' or ' excessively persevering.' [*See* Pronunciation.]

> Youth no less becomes
> The light and careless livery that it wears,
> Than settled age his sables and his weeds,
> *Importing* health and graveness.—*Hamlet*, iv. 7.

Here importing is used with double significance: it means ' of importance to,' in its reference to " health "; and it means 'implying,' in its reference to " graveness."

> Peace, children, peace! The king doth love you well:
> *Incapable* and shallow innocents,
> You cannot guess who caus'd your father's death.—*R. III.*, iii. 3.

Here he employs " incapable " to express ' unable to understand,' ' unconscious,' as well as ' helpless.'

> Thou,
> Conspir'd with that *irregulous* devil, Cloten,
> Hast here cut off my lord.—*Cym.*, iv. 2.

The word " irregulous " has not been met with in any other author ; and we take it to have been invented by Shakespeare to combine the senses of ' irregular,' ' disorderly,' ' lawless,' ' licentious,' as well as of ' anomalous,' ' mongrel,' ' monstrous,' ' out of ordinary rule in every way.'

> I was not made a horse ;
> And yet I bear a burden like an ass,
> Spur-gall'd and tir'd by *jauncing* Bolingbroke.—*R. II.*, v. 5.

Besides its meaning of ' hard-riding,' ' rough-riding,' which " jauncing " bears as derived from the old French verb *jancer* (which Cotgrave explains, " To stir a horse in the stable till he sweat withal "), the epithet here applied to Bolingbroke admits the additional sense of ' ostentatiously airy,' ' showily at ease,' as conveyed by the familiar word ' jaunty.'

> And hope *to joy* is little less in joy,
> Than hope enjoy'd.—*Ibid.*, ii. 3.

Here " to joy " is made to include both its senses of ' to be glad,' and ' to enjoy.'

> His last offences to us
> Shall have *judicious* hearing.—*Coriol.*, v. 5.

As Shakespeare here employs the word " judicious," it comprises the meanings of ' just,' ' skilful in judgment,' and ' judicial ' ; " judicious " and ' judicial ' having frequently been used formerly the one for the other.

> I have a *kind* soul that would give you thanks,
> And knows not how to do it but with tears.—*John*, v. 7.

" Kind," as here used, includes the several meanings of ' kindly ' or ' tenderly disposed,' of ' kindred in feeling with that which you express towards me,' and of ' touched with natural emotion.'

> Sweet king ! the bishop hath a *kindly* gird.—1 *H. VI.*, iii. 1.

Here, " kindly " includes the meaning of ' mild,' or ' gentle,' of ' befitting from one kinsman to another,' and of ' akin to the question in hand.'

> Yet, in this captious and intenible sieve,
> I still pour in the waters of my love,
> And *lack* not to lose still.—*All's W.*, i. 3.

By the mode in which " lack " is used in this sentence, it not only gives the sense of ' And am not without more love in reserve to go on losing,' but also, ' And fail not to lose still.'

> Pardon me, Julius ! Here wast thou bay'd, brave hart;
> Here didst thou fall ; and here thy hunters stand,
> Sign'd in thy spoil, and crimson'd in thy *lethe.*—*Jul. C.*, iii. 1.

Here " lethe " has, by Shakespeare's inclusive mode of using a word, the triple poetical meaning of the term as derived from the Latin *lethum*, ' death ' (pronounced monosyllabically), of the term as used by hunters to signify the blood shed by a deer at its fall, and as a classical term applied to the waters of oblivion ; thus causing it condensedly to express ' death-blood,' ' death-stream,' or ' death-flood.'

> Yet I have not seen
> So *likely* an embassador of love.—*Mer. of V.*, ii. 9.

The word "likely," as here employed, comprises the double sense of 'probable' and 'pleasing.'

> You know my father left me some prescriptions
> Of rare and prov'd effects, such as his reading
> And *manifest* experience had collected
> For general sovereignty.—*All's W.*, i. 3.

"Manifest," as an epithet applied to "experience" in this passage, gives the comprehensive effect of 'experience that made manifest certain facts to his own mind,' 'experience that manifested itself in its results,' and 'experience that he was manifestly known to possess.' Moreover, so ingeniously is the epithet here introduced, that it almost conveys the additional effect of '*practical* experience'; especially, when we regard the word "manifest" in its original acceptation, as derived from the Latin—that which is palpable to the hand.

> Well, niece, I hope to see you one day fitted with a husband.—Not till God make men of some other metal than earth. Would it not grieve a woman to be over-mastered with a piece of valiant dust? to make an account of her life to a clod of way-ward *marl*?—*M. Ado*, ii. 1.

By the selection of this name for a peculiar kind of clayey earth, and causing the insolently witty Beatrice to use it as a type of husbandhood, the dramatist has caused her not only to hint at the 'obstinacy' and 'unyieldingness,' which she assumes to be properties of manly nature, but also contemptuously by implication to call it *manure;* since Bacon, in his Natural History, says, "*Marl* is the best *compost.*"

> And do not stand on quillets how to slay him :
> Be it by gins, by snares, by subtlety,
> Sleeping or waking, 'tis no matter how,
> So he be dead ; for that is good deceit
> Which *mates* him first that first intends deceit.—2 *H. VI.*, iii. 1.

Here "mates" signifies not only 'to confound,' 'to destroy,' but also 'to circumvent,' 'to defeat by stratagem,' as the word is used in the terms 'check-mate' and 'stale-mate,' technically belonging to the game of chess.

> As for my country I have shed my blood,
> Not fearing outward force, so shall my lungs
> Coin words till their decay against those *meazels*,
> Which we disdain should tetter us, yet sought
> The very way to catch them.—*Coriol.*, iii. 1.

Coriolanus is here made to use the expression "meazels" both in its sense of 'lepers' and of 'leprosies'; thus by one significant word, hurling contemptuous defiance at the men he is abusing, and scorning the diseases which he affects to think he may catch from them.

> What a wretched and peevish fellow is this king of England, to *mope* with his fat-brained followers so far out of his knowledge.—*H. V.*, iii. 7.

Here the word "mope" conveys not only the sense of 'move dejectedly,' but also the sense of 'wander blindly'; because the old compound term, *mope*-eyed (as derived from the Greek original of *myopy*, 'shortsightedness') signified 'half-blind,' 'purblind.'

> Strike, you slave; stand, rogue, stand; you *neat* slave, strike.—*Lear*, ii. 2.

The epithet "neat," here applied by Kent to the object of his wrath and scorn, possesses comprehensive force of allusive signification. It signifies 'spruce,' 'dapper,' 'cleanly,' in allusion to the steward's being a "*glass-gazing, finical* rogue"; it signifies 'unclean,' like black or 'neat cattle' (from the Saxon *neten*); and it signifies 'villanous,' as referring to the 'neat land,' or *terra villanorum*, which was land let out to feudal tenants. Thus the word "neat" is largely appropriate for the foppish yet dirtily servile creature, the arrogant yet serf-devoted steward, Oswald.

> So, if the time thrust forth
> A cause for thy repeal, we shall not send
> O'er the vast world to seek a single man;
> And lose advantage, which doth ever cool
> I' the absence of the *needer.*—*Coriol.*, iv. 1.

The closing word of this passage is completely in Shakespeare's comprehensive style; including as it does the effect of the man needing the advantage of which there is a prospect, and of the man needed home by his friends who want him to profit by it.

> Therefore, you men of Harfleur,
> Take pity of your town and of your people,
> Whiles yet my soldiers are in my command;
> Whiles yet the cool and temperate wind of grace
> *O'erblows* the filthy and contagious clouds
> Of heady murder, spoil, and villany.—*H. V.*, iii. 3.

Here "o'erblows" is not only used to express 'prevails over,' 'acts controllingly upon,' it also includes the sense of 'disperses'; as we say 'the storm is *blown over*,' for 'the storm is dispersed.'

> Oh, you mighty gods!
> This world I do renounce, and, in your sights,
> Shake patiently my great affliction off:
> If I could bear it longer, and not fall
> To quarrel with your *opposeless* wills,
> My snuff and loathed part of nature should
> Burn itself out.—*Lear*, iv. 6.

The epithet "opposeless" here conveys the combined effect of 'useless to oppose,' and 'ought not to be opposed.'

> This *orient* pearl.—*Ant. & C.*, i. 5.

As an epithet applied to a "pearl" the word "orient" is doubly appropriate; since it signifies both 'eastern' and 'bright.'

> Can such things be,
> And *overcome* us like a summer's cloud,
> Without our special wonder?—*Macb.*, iii. 4.

"Overcome us" here, besides the effect of 'pass over us,' also implies 'subdue our spirits,' 'impress our senses,' as a sudden dark cloud overspreading the summer sky would do.

> Come, thou monarch of the vine,
> Plumpy Bacchus with *pink* eyne!—*Ant. & C.*, ii. 7 (*Song*).

In the expressions 'pink-eyed' and 'pink-sterned' as applied to eyes and to ships, the word "pink" signified 'small,' 'little,' 'narrow'; but by using the term "pink eyne" in reference to Bacchus, the poet combines the effect of eyes not only half closed, but also reddened by inebriation.

> Be pilot to me, and thy *places* shall
> Still neighbour mine.—*W. T.*, i. 2.

The word " places," as here used by King Polixenes, combines the meaning of position as to fortune, and spot wherein to dwell ; since we subsequently find that the speaker confers manifold dignities and honours upon Camillo, and keeps him ever near to himself in Bohemia.

> Were you sent hither to *praise* me ?—*Tw. N.*, i. 5.

Here the word " praise " is made playfully to combine the meanings of ' extol ' and of ' appraise '; as if written, *'praise*.

> And fortune, on his damnèd quarry smiling.—*Macb.*, i. 2.

" Quarry " having been a technical term of the chase, applied both to a heap of slaughtered game and to the offal portion of the venison just killed, which was thrown to the hounds, the poet here employed the word inclusively to express those who were·already doomed to become ' a heap of slain ' and ' a heap of carrion.'

> Plantagenet doth *quit* Plantagenet,
> Edward for Edward pays a dying debt.—*R. III.*, iv. 4.

The verb " quit " here comprehensively expresses both ' *requite* the death of' and ' *acquit* the crime of.'

> Their eyes o'ergalled with *recourse* of tears.—*Tr. & Cr.*, v. 3.

" Recourse," as here used,. includes the sense of ' repeated flowing,' ' recurrence,' ' recoursing,' and the sense of ' access,' ' repair thither,' ' frequent resort.'

> What should it be that he respects in her,
> But I can make *respective* in myself.—*Two G. of V.*, iv. 4.

Julia uses the expression " respective " to imply ' worthy of being regarded,' and ' of relative worth to what is beautiful in Silvia.'

> Now, by this hand, I gave it to a youth,—
> A kind of boy ; a little *scrubbèd* boy,
> No higher than thyself, the judge's clerk.—*Mer. of V.*, v. 1.

The italicised epithet combines the sense of ' stunted,' ' stubbed,' or ' stubby,' like a dwarf tree or shrub (' shrub ' and ' scrub ' being at one time used synonymously ; witness the name of ' Wormwood Scrubs,' which was originally a place covered with low shrubs or brushwood), and the sense of ' scrubby,' ' contemptible,' ' pitiful,' ' shabby.'

> You gentle gods, give me but this I have,
> And *sear* up my embracements from a next
> With bonds of death !—*Cym.*, i. 2.

" Sear " in this passage expresses inclusively the dry withering of death, as well as the closing with wax by those " bonds of death," cerecloths, sometimes written searecloths.

> And who in want a hollow friend doth try,
> Directly *seasons* him his enemy.—*Hamlet*, iii. 2.

Shakespeare here uses the word " seasons " not only to express a sense in which he sometimes uses it, ' tempers,' ' moulds,' but also to express ' inures,' ' habituates,' ' accustoms to become.'

> But is there any else longs to *see* this broken music in his sides ?—*As You L.*, i. 2.

Rosalind here employs the verb " see " in allusion to witnessing the so-called " sport " as well as to looking at the skill with which the wrestler plies his " broken music " of " rib-breaking "; to that she may fairly (in wit-play) apply " see " to hearing a sound.

> Not with fond *shekels* of the tested gold.—*M. for M.*, ii. 2.

Inasmuch as " shekels " meant both a Jewish coin and a Jewish weight, Shakespeare, by using the term here, conveys the idea of minted gold and heavy amount of gold.

> Let 's hence, and hear
> How the despatch is made ; and in what fashion,
> More than his *singularity*, he goes
> Upon this present action.—*Coriol.*, i. 1.

The word " singularity " comprises the meaning of ' individual capacity,' ' special appointment,' and ' peculiarity ' or ' own particular pride of disposition.'

> We 'll make you some sport with the fox, ere we case him. He was first *smoked* by the old lord Lafeu : when his disguise and he is parted, tell me what a sprat you shall find him.—*All's W.*, iii. 6.

By employing the word " smoked " in this passage, Shakespeare has contrived to combine suggestion of analogy with the " case " or skin, implication of the ' smoke-dried ' fish that turns out to be a " sprat," besides inference of the tracking out by scent which agrees with " fox," and which furnishes the jocose verb for ' finding out a pretender,' that is still in familiar use.

> For life, I prize it as I weigh grief, which I would *spare*.—*W. T.*, iii. 2.

" Spare " is here used partly in its sense of ' part with,' ' do without,' ' let go '; partly in its sense of ' forbear from destroying,' or ' shield from destruction '; partly in its sense of ' avoid encountering '; so that the whole sentence conveys to our mind the inclusive meaning: ' I estimate life as I estimate grief—things that I could willingly part with ; while the one I would avoid destroying, and the other I would avoid encountering.'

> Here 's a *stay*,
> That shakes the rotten carcase of old Death
> Out of his rags !—*John*, ii. 2.

By the term " stay," banteringly applied by Faulconbridge here to the Citizen of Angiers, the speaker not only calls him a ' restraint ' or ' prudent restrainer ' (in reference to the Citizen's having previously said : " Hear us, great kings, vouchsafe awhile to *stay*," that is, ' to restrain yourselves,' ' to hold your hands,' ' to forbear '); but he also, by this term, calls him ' a prop,' ' a support,' since Shakespeare elsewhere (and in this very play) uses " stay " in the latter sense.

> Rather proclaim it, Westmoreland, through my host,
> That he which hath no *stomach* to this fight,
> Let him depart.—*H. V.*, iv. 3.

" Stomach " is here used in its combined sense of ' appetite ' or ' inclination,' and of ' courage ' or ' valour.'

> To satisfy,
> If of my freedom 'tis the main part, take
> *No stricter* render of me than my all.—*Cym.*, v. 4.

Here, " no stricter," besides meaning ' no more restricted,' ' no more limited,' ' no straiter,' ' no narrower,' ' no less,' is also made to include the sense of ' no more strictly equivalent.'

> It tutors Nature: artificial *strife*
> Lives in these touches, livelier than life.—*Timon*, i. 1.

By here using the comprehensive word " strife," Shakespeare includes the sense of Art's contention with Nature to outdo her, the sense of contrast in colours and forms, and the sense of artistic ' striving,' ' endeavour to excel.'

> But he that *temper'd* thee bade thee stand up,
> Gave thee no instance why thou shouldst do treason.—*H. V.*, ii. 2.

Johnson, in proposing to alter " temper'd " to ' tempted' here, would have substituted a tame and restrictedly significant word for the poet's largely significant expression. By " temper'd " is not only expressed, ' moulded thee to his will,' ' rendered thee fit for his purpose,' ' made thee pliant,' but also is implied ' governed' (as derived from the Latin *temperare*, one of the senses of which is ' to rule,' ' govern'), and moreover ' brought thee to the requisite degree of callousness,' as metals are brought to a due degree of hardness by *tempering*.

> And worthier than himself
> Here *tend* the savage strangeness he puts on.—*Tr. & Cr.*, ii. 3.

" Tend," in the present passage, combines the two senses of ' attend to ' and ' attend upon.'

> Fire answers fire ; and through their paly flames
> Each battle sees the other's *umber'd* face.—*H. V.*, iv. (*Chorus*).

By the finely poetical word " umber'd," as here introduced, the combined effect is produced of ' brownly enshadowed,' being partly framed from the brown colour ' umber,' and partly from ' umbrated,' shadowed.

> And while thou livest, dear Kate, take a fellow of plain and *uncoined* constancy.—*Ibid.*, v. 2.

Into this single epithet, which refers to the purity of gold before it is converted into current coin, the poet condenses the various significations of ' genuine,' ' unalloyed,' ' unmade,' ' unput-forth,' ' unprofessed,' ' unprotested.'

> Disguise the holy strength of their command,
> And *underwrite* in an *observing* kind
> His humorous predominance.—*Tr. & Cr.*, ii. 3.

" Underwrite " is here made to include the double meaning of ' take note of' and ' subscribe to'; the latter bearing the sense of ' submit to,' ' defer to '; while " observing " is likewise so employed as to convey the combined signification of ' remarking,' and of ' paying observance to.'

> Oh, *undistinguish'd* space of woman's will !
> A plot upon her virtuous husband's life;
> And the exchange, my brother !—*Lear*, iv. 6.

By the word " undistinguish'd " here employed, the double sense is given to the sentence of an excess in licentious will too unlimited to be discerned or distinguished, and a will so undistinguishing as to prefer the vicious Edmund to the virtuous Albany.

> The glow-worm shows the matin to be near,
> And 'gins to pale his *uneffectual* fire.—*Hamlet*, i. 5.

By this epithet the double effect is given of the glow-worm's light shining without giving heat, and no longer showing when morning appears.

Though there was no great matter in the ditty, yet the note was very *untuneable* —
You are deceived, sir : we kept time, we lost not our time.—*As You L.*, v. 3.

As in Shakespeare's day " untuneable " was sometimes used for ' out
of time ' as well as ' out of tune,' Master Touchstone's accusation
includes both charges by the word the poet has put into his mouth.

Arm, arm, my lord ; the foe *vaunts* in the field.—*R. III.*, v. 3.

By the verb " vaunts," the double effect is here produced of ' boasts
itself' and ' precedes us ' ; as derived from the French *vanter*, to boast,
and *avant*, before.

> He thinks, nay, with all confidence he swears,
> As he had seen 't, or been an instrument
> To *vice* you to 't, that you have touch'd his queen
> Forbiddenly.—*W. T.*, i. 2.

By his formation of the verb to " vice " here, Shakespeare condensedly expresses the act of ' viciously urges or incites ' ; since he infers
the impelling action of a vice by its screw power, and the operation of
vice or unvirtuousness.

> Down, down I come ; like glistering Phaeton,
> *Wanting* the manage of unruly jades.—*R. II.*, iii. 3.

" Wanting," as here employed, combines the effect of ' lacking ' and
' desiring.'

> No, I will rob Tellus of her *weed*,
> To strew thy green with flowers.—*Per.*, iv. 1.

" Tellus," being a mythological name for the earth as a goddess, the
word " weed " here includes the double meaning of ' garment ' and
' wild-flower.'

> Well, Angelo, *your evil quits you well.*—*M. for M.*, v. 1.

This phrase bears comprehensive interpretation ; being equivalent to
' your course of evil leaves you befittingly,' ' the fear you have suffered
acquits you of your misdeeds,' and ' you receive in requital good for
evil.'

> *To offend, and judge, are distinct offices,*
> *And of opposed natures.*—*Mer. of V.*, ii. 9.

This little speech, that Portia utters to herself, contains several
meanings. It serves to express that the province of the casket-con-
tents is not to give offence, but to pronounce sentence ; it also serves
as a rejoinder to the hurt prince's inquiry, by remarking that to be
wanting in desert and wanting in judgment are two different things ;
and it promulgates a maxim in English law which prohibits a man from
being a judge in his own cause, or in a cause wherein he is interested
—thus again, in still another sense, serving as a comment upon what
the Prince of Arragon has just said.

> Wear this for me, *one out of suits with Fortune*,
> That could give more, but that her hand lacks means.—*As You L.*, i. 2.

By this phrase, Shakespeare combines many metaphorical allusions ;
for it may be taken as implying, ' deprived of Fortune's livery or badge,'
' not in accord or unsuited with Fortune,' ' unpossessed of the trump-
suits in Fortune's cards,' and ' out of favour with Fortune.'

> The common executioner,
> Whose heart the accustom'd sight of death makes hard,
> Falls not the axe upon the humbled neck

> But first begs pardon: will you sterner be
> Than he that *dies and lives by* bloody drops ?—*As You L.*, iii. 5.

The phrase "dies and lives by," taken connectedly, implies 'continues to the end of his life familiar with'; but, taken separately, signifies 'stains his hands in, and gains his living by.' Those commentators who will not, or cannot, perceive Shakespeare's extremely *inclusive* style, are always contending that he means this *or* he means that, by a phrase; whereas, in most cases, he includes *both* meanings.

> Impossible be strange attempts to *those*
> *That weigh their pains in sense.*—*All's W.*, i. 1.

By this sentence Shakespeare condensedly expresses two significations: 'those persons who estimate the pains they take by the amount of trouble and suffering involved,' and 'those persons who calculate the difficulties of their "strange attempts" ('unusual undertakings') by 'reason and common-sense probability of success.'

> My life upon 't, young though thou art, thine eye
> Hath stay'd upon some favour that it loves;—
> Hath it not, boy ?—
>   *A little, by your favour.*—*Tw. N.*, ii. 4.

This reply is made by Viola, ostensibly, in the sense of 'A little, by your leave'; but she says it, secretly, in the sense of 'I have somewhat allowed mine eye to rest upon your own countenance'; including, moreover, 'I have now and then permitted mine eye to dwell upon your face, when favoured by your not observing that I looked at you.'

> Learn this, Thomas,
> And thou shalt prove a shelter to thy friends;
> A hoop of gold to bind thy brothers in,
> That the united vessel of their blood,
> Mingled with *venom of suggestion*
> (As, force perforce, the age will pour it in),
> Shall never leak.—*2 H. IV.*, iv. 4.

By "the venom of suggestion" is doubly meant the evil temptations that youth meets with, and the poisonous insinuations that may be poured in the future king's ear by those who wish to produce disunion between him and his brothers.

> Piece out our imperfections with your thoughts;
> Into a thousand parts divide one man,
> And *make imaginary puissance.*—*H. V.*, i. (*Chorus*).

This expression may be taken to include the twofold meaning of 'exert your powers of imagination,' and 'create in your imagination a numerous armed force.'

> I do retort the "solus" in thy bowels;
> For *I can take*, and Pistol's cock is up,
> And flashing fire will follow.—*Ibid.*, ii. 1.

Mine ancient's menace elliptically comprises the triple sense of 'I can take fire,' 'I can take offence,' and 'I can take a meaning.'

> Yon island carrions, *desperate of their bones*,
> Ill-favour'dly become the morning field.—*Ibid.*, iv. 2.

This phrase succinctly and forcibly conveys the joint signification of 'in desperate condition from their bones starting through their skins,' and 'ready desperately to risk their remaining bones, their mere skeleton.'

> And *given* unto the house of York *such head*,
> As thou shalt reign but by their sufferance.—3 *H. VI.*, i. 1.

"Given such head," is here idiomatically used for 'given such power,' 'given such dominion'; and metaphorically, for 'given such licence,' 'such freedom from restraint': 'to give a horse his head,' signifying 'to let him have his own way.'

> I am the shadow of poor Buckingham,
> Whose figure even this instant cloud puts on,
> *By darkening my clear sun.* —*H. VIII.*, i. 1.

The whole passage has been found difficult of explanation; and proposals have been made for altering it. But we think that the inclusive force of the closing clause of the sentence permits our interpretation of the whole thus: 'I am but the shadow of poor Buckingham, and even my shadowy figure this cloud of misfortune assumes and absorbs into itself, *by coming between me and my sun of prosperity*, and *by extinguishing my light of life for ever*.

> Nay, forsooth, my friends,
> They that must *weigh out* my afflictions,
> They that my trust must grow to, live not here.—*Ibid.*, iii. 1.

Here, "weigh out" gives the twofold impression of 'outweigh,' 'counterbalance,' or 'compensate for,' and of 'estimate,' 'judge the weight of.'

> The citizens,
> I am sure, have shown at full their royal minds;
> As, *let 'em have their rights*, they 're ever forward
> In celebration of this day with shows,
> Pageants, and sights of honour.—*Ibid.*, iv. 1.

Thus used, "let 'em have their rights" bears the double meaning of 'to give them their due,' and 'if they have their rights accorded to them.'

> The purpose is conspicuous even as substance,
> *Whose grossness little characters sum up.*—*Tr. & Cr.*, i. 3.

The last line includes the several meanings of 'the bulk of which is formed by small amounts,' 'which may be calculated by small marks of the pen,' and 'which may be estimated by persons of small intelligence.'

> *Like to a lonely dragon, that his fen*
> *Makes fear'd and talk'd of more than seen.*—*Coriol.*, iv. 1.

The construction of the above sentence allows it to convey two meanings: 'Like a lonely dragon, that his pestilential fen makes feared and talked of more than seen,' and, 'like a lonely dragon that makes his fenny retreat feared and talked of more than seen.' Both meanings apply well to Coriolanus, whose withdrawal to some unknown place causes him to be dreaded and talked of during absence, and whose known fierce nature causes this intended place of retreat to become a subject of fear and wondering conjecture.

> Only make trial *what your love can do*
> *For Rome, towards Marcius.*—*Ibid.*, v. 1.

By the skill with which this phrase is constructed, it may be taken to imply both 'what your love towards Marcius can do for Rome,' and 'what your love can do for Rome, in your advances made to Marcius.'

She is the hopeful lady of my earth.—R. & Jul., i. 2.

As referring to the old French legal term for heiress, *fille de terre*, and because Shakespeare sometimes uses " earth " for ' land' or ' landed possessions,' this line signifies, ' she is the hopeful inheritrix of my landed estates'; but as he employs the word " earth " in the present play to express ' corporeal part,' ' material part,' ' the earthly portion of man,' this line also signifies, ' she is my sole surviving offspring, in whom I have centred all my hopes.'

> Oh, how my heart abhors
> To hear him nam'd,—and cannot come to him,
> *To wreak the love I bore* my cousin Tybalt
> Upon his body that hath slaughter'd him !—*Ibid.,* iii. 5.

This phrase is said with a double sense ; Juliet meaning her mother to understand it as meaning ' to revenge the loss I suffer in the love I bore'; and herself really meaning by it, ' to bestow entirely the love I bore.'

> *'Tis conceiv'd to scope.—Timon,* i. 1.

From the various senses in which Shakespeare elsewhere uses the word " scope," we may conclude that he intended the present phrase to comprise the double meaning of ' it is conceived with large scope or compass of imagination,' and ' it is conceived with apt fulfilment of its purposed scope or drift.'

> *There is no time so miserable but a man may be true.—Timon,* iv. 3.

This is one of Shakespeare's crystallised pieces of wit, sparkling with many-sided meanings. The speaker is probably intended to express by it, ' There is no time so miserable but a man may be true to his adopted profession ' (his " trade," his " mystery "—that of thieving !) ; but it also admits of the interpretations, ' there is no time so miserably late but a man may turn honest ' (the word " true " often being used in Shakespeare's time for ' honest '), and ' there is no time so miserable but a man may find consolation in being true to himself and to virtue.'

> Well, *to our work alive.—Jul. C.,* iv. 3.

This phrase, as here introduced, possesses triple signification : ' let us now devote ourselves to the work which we survivors have to do,' ' let us attend to our work that concerns the living,' and ' let us proceed to our work with animation.'

> But now, my cousin Hamlet, and my son—
> A little more than kin, and less than kind.—
> How is it that the clouds still hang on you ?—
> Not so, my lord; *I am too much i' the sun.—Hamlet,* i. 2.

The prince, by this expression, means three things : that he is too much in the glare of his uncle's nuptial festivities so soon after his father's death ; that he has exchanged a righteous condition for a corrupt one (in reference to the old proverb, " out of God's blessing into the warm sun ") ; and that he deplores (by a play on the word) that he has become *son* as well as nephew to the usurping king, by the hateful marriage of the latter.

> Thou mixture rank, *of midnight weeds collected.—Hamlet*, iii. 2.

This phrase gives the double effect of 'collected from midnight weeds,' and 'made of weeds collected or gathered at midnight.'

> *To withdraw with you.* Why do you go about to recover the wind of me, as if you would drive me into a toil ?—*Ibid.*, iii. 2.

By the above muttered four words, Hamlet, observing the two spies drawing a little apart to watch and track him, implies not only, ' Now, then, to draw away a little as you do,' but also ' to track you in your own manner '; because elsewhere Shakespeare uses the word " draw " in the sense it bears as a term of the chase for track by the scent, trail, or foot-print of the animal pursued. That this latter meaning is included we think is evidenced by the hunting technicality (" recover the wind ") occurring so immediately after.

> 'Tis meet that some more audience than a mother,
> Since nature makes them partial, should o'erhear
> The speech, *of vantage.—Ibid.*, iii. 3.

This expression, besides meaning ' with the advantage of conceal-ment,' ' having the advantage of being hidden,' also includes the sense of ' for the sake of advantage,' ' for future benefit.'

> Your son and daughter *found this trespass worth*
> *The shame which here it suffers.—Lear*, ii. 4.

Here the double meaning is implied of, ' found this trespass deserv-ing of the shame which here it suffers,' and ' found it worth while to put me to the shame which I here undergo for this trespass.'

> Dear daughter, I confess that I am old;
> *Age is unnecessary :* on my knees I beg
> That you 'll vouchsafe me raiment, bed, and food.—*Ibid.*, ii. 4.

This phrase comprises the two significations of ' living to be old is needless,' and ' age needs but the merest necessaries of life.'

> She that herself will sliver and disbranch
> From *her material sap*, perforce must wither,
> And come to deadly use.—*Ibid.*, iv. 2.

This expression means, literally, ' the sap of the parent tree or trunk ; ' it means, figuratively, ' her own parental blood,' ' the blood of her old father '; and it means, elliptically, ' the parent stock which supplies her vital sap.' " Material " has here especial force of apt signification ; *materia*, in Latin, besides signifying ' material,' ' matter,' ' substance,' also signifying ' timber,' ' wood,' ' the trunk of a tree.'

> Oh, then it mov'd her.—
> Not to a rage : patience and sorrow strove
> Who should express her goodliest. You have seen
> Sunshine and rain at once : her smiles and tears
> Were like *a better way.—Ibid.*, iv. 3.

This phrase (which has been variously altered by various emendators) is, as it stands, thoroughly Shakespearian in its inclusive mode of referring to two clauses of the speech ; it implies ' her mingled "smiles and tears " expressed her feelings *in a better way* than either " patience " or " sorrow " could do separately,' and it also implies, ' her " smiles and tears " showed that she was " mov'd," " not to a rage," but to *a better way* of expressing her deep feeling.'

> Cassio's a proper man: let me see now;
> To get his place, and *to plume up my will*
> In double knavery.—*Oth.*, i. 3.

In the mouth of Iago, this expression has varied significance of effect; as if any project that involved reduplication of knavery were a feather in the cap of his depraved will—a thing to plume himself upon as a feat of intellectual volition—and as if, moreover, he meant to give wings of speed to his purpose by investing it with twin wickednesses, and to dress it up finely in the plumage of trickery. So suggestive and inclusive are the words Shakespeare chooses, that a crowd of images are presented to the mind by their expressive conciseness.

> Eternity was in our lips and eyes,
> Bliss in *our brows' bent.*—*Ant. & C.*, i. 3.

This phrase comprises the sense of 'the arched curve of our eyebrows,' 'the bending of our brows in expressive mobility,' and 'the half frown of our brows when knit in sudden anger.' Cleopatra, in these five little words, reminds Antony of the rapture he has felt at every varying turn of those flexile and bewitching brows of hers.

> Oh, my oblivion is a very Antony,
> And *I am all forgotten.*—*Ibid.*, i. 3.

This combines the double sense of 'I am entirely forgotten' and 'I am thoroughly forgetful.'

> *Why should excuse be born or e'er begot ?*—*Cym.*, iii. 2.

This phrase means not only 'Why should excuse be framed before the act is done for which excuse will be necessary?' it also means 'Why should excuse be born or ever be begotten?' 'Why should excuse be made or ever be conceived?' It is characteristic of the noble-souled Imogen that she should deplore the necessity for excuse, —the next thing to deception.

> Now, if you could wear a mind
> Dark as your fortune is, and but disguise
> That which, to appear itself, must not yet be
> But by self-danger, you should tread a course
> Pretty and *full of view ;* yea, haply, near
> The residence of Posthumus,—so nigh, at least,
> That though his actions were not visible, yet
> Report should render him hourly to your ear
> As truly as he moves.—*Ibid.*, iii. 4.

Here, "full of view" includes the combined meanings of 'full of promising or auspicious aspect in itself,' 'full of means of observation for yourself,' and 'full in view of others.'

> I'll make my will, then ; and, as sick men do,
> Who know the world, *see heaven*, but, feeling woe,
> Gripe not at earthly joys, as erst they did.—*Per.*, i. 1.

This phrase elliptically conveys the twofold effect of 'see a heaven of delight in their mundane pleasure,' and 'see heaven itself only as a distant goal to be attained.' The whole passage is condensedly expressed; but we interpret it to mean, 'As sick men do, who know the world, seeing a heaven of delight in its pleasures while they lasted, and seeing heaven itself only as a distant object of attainment; but feeling illness and sorrow, care no longer for earthly joys as once they did.'

VERBS PECULIARLY USED.

Shakespeare occasionally makes a verb do double or multiplied duty in a sentence [*See* ELLIPTICAL STYLE] :—

> And Ferdinand, her brother, *found* a wife
> Where he himself was lost ; Prospero [found] his dukedom
> In a poor isle ; and all of us [found] ourselves
> When no man was his own.—*Temp.*, v. 1.

> To be in love, where scorn is *bought* with groans ;
> Coy looks [bought] with heart-sore sighs ; one fading moment's mirth
> [Bought] With twenty watchful, weary, tedious nights.—*Tw. G. of V.*, i. 1.

> Now *are* our brows bound with victorious wreaths ;
> Our bruised arms [are] hung up for monuments ;
> Our stern alarums [are] *chang'd* to merry meetings,
> Our dreadful marches [are changed] to delightful measures.—*R. III.*, i. 1.

> Wrong *hath but* wrong, and blame [hath but] the due of blame.—*Ibid.*, v. 1.

> An honest country lord, as I am, beaten
> A long time out of play, may bring his plain-song,
> And *have* an hour of hearing ; and by 'r lady,
> [Have it] Held current music too.—*H. VIII.*, i. 3.

> One fire *drives out* one fire ; one nail [drives out] one nail ;
> Rights by rights fouler [do fail], strengths by strengths *do fail.*—*Coriol.*, iv. 7.

In this last-cited passage various alterations have been made by various commentators, who believe the line to be incorrect ; but we think that if it be compared with the several other instances here collectively quoted of Shakespeare's mode of allowing a verb to perform double and even multiplied duty in a phrase, it will be found to be quite correct.

> But passion *lends them* power [to meet], time [lends them] means, *to meet.*—*R. & Jul.*, i. 5 (*Chorus*).

> Thus much of this will *make* black, white ; [make] foul, fair ; [make] wrong, right ; [make] base, noble ; [make] old, young ; [make] coward, valiant.—*Timon*, iv. 3.

> Thou *wouldst have* plung'd thyself
> In general riot ; [wouldst have] melted down thy youth
> In different beds of lust ; and never [wouldst have] learn'd
> The icy precepts of respect, but [wouldst have] follow'd
> The sugar'd game before thee. But myself,
> *Who had* the world as my confectionary ;
> [Who had] The mouths, the tongues, the eyes, and hearts of men
> At duty, more than I could frame employment.—*Ibid.*, iv. 3.

> As fire *drives out* fire, so pity [drives out] pity.—*Jul. C.*, iii. 1.

> *Dismay'd* not this
> Our captains, Macbeth and Banquo ?—
> Yes ;
> As sparrows [dismay] eagles, or the hare [dismays] the lion.—*Macb.*, i. 2.

> This tyrant, whose sole name blisters our tongues,
> Was once thought honest : you have lov'd him well ;
> He hath not touch'd you yet. I am young ; but something
> You may *discern* of him through me ; and [discern] wisdom
> To offer up a weak, poor, innocent lamb
> To appease an angry god.—*Ibid.*, iv. 3.

" Discern " is the word given by the Folio in this passage, and we believe it to have been Shakespeare's word, though altered to 'deserve' by Theobald and every editor since his time excepting ourselves. The alterers of the word complain that there is no verb to which "wisdom" can refer; but if the original word " discern " be retained, we have a verb doing double duty in a sentence, according to Shakespeare's frequent practice in this respect; and the sense of the whole passage is then consistent, thus : ' I am young, but something you may perceive of Macbeth in me [Malcolm has stated that Macbeth " was once thought honest," and afterwards taxes himself with vices], and also you may perceive the wisdom of offering up, &c.'

> Why day *is* day, night [is] night, and time is time.—*Hamlet*, ii. 2.
> > Do not look upon me;
> Lest with this piteous action you convert
> My stern effects : then what I have to do
> *Will want* true colour; [will want] tears, perchance for blood.—*Ibid.*, iii. 4.
> Fairest Cordelia, that *art* most rich, *being* poor;
> [Art] Most choice, [being] forsaken; and [art] most loved, [being] despis'd!—*Lear*, i. 1.
> > *Let there be no* honour,
> Where *there is* beauty; [let there be no] truth, where [there is] semblance; [let there be no] love,
> Where there 's another man.—*Cym.*, ii. 4.
> > 'Tis wonder,
> That an invisible instinct *should frame them*
> To royalty unlearn'd; [should frame them to] honour untaught;
> [Should frame them to] Civility not seen from other; [should frame them to] valour,
> That wildly grows in them, but yields a crop
> As if it had been sow'd!—*Ibid.*, iv. 2.
> Thy name *well fits* thy faith; thy faith [well fits] thy name.—*Ibid.*, iv. 2.
> > *Take* that life, beseech you,
> Which I so often owe: but [take] your ring first;
> And here [take] the bracelet of the truest princess.—*Ibid.*, v. 5.
> *Here have you seen* a mighty king
> His child, I wis, to incest bring;
> [Here have you seen] A better prince, and benign lord,
> That will prove awful both in deed and word.—*Per.*, ii. (*Gower*).
> *He will* repent the breadth of his great voyage;
> [He will] Blame both my lord and me.—*Ibid.*, iv. 1.

Shakespeare occasionally uses a verb peculiarly and arbitrarily in reference to its accompanying pronouns :—

> No? hath not? Rosalind lacks, then, the love
> Which teacheth *thee* that *thou* and I am one.—*As You L.*, i. 3.

The use of " am " here gives succinctly the effect of the speaker's saying, ' which should teach thee, as it teaches me, that thou and I are (or " am ") one.' It should always be remembered, in judging Shakespeare's phraseology, that the great art of a dramatist is to give *promptly conveyed impression* to his sentences; and in this art Shakespeare is eminently an adept.

> And, I beseech you, hear *me*, who *professes*
> *Myself* your loyal servant, your physician,
> Your most obedient counsellor; yet that *dares*
> Less appear so, in comforting your evils,
> Than such as most seem yours.—*W. T.*, ii. 3.

By putting the verbs " professes " and "dares" in the third person, the effect is conveyed of Paulina's speaking of another, while she thus confidently asserts her own fidelity to the king.

> Even so *myself bewails* good Gloster's case
> With sad unhelpful tears ; and with dimm'd eyes
> *Look* after him, and cannot do him good,—
> So mighty are his vowed enemies.—2 *H. VI.*, iii. 1.

" Bewails " gives the effect of Henry's speaking of himself in the third person as a helpless being ; while " look " allows ' I ' to be elliptically understood before the latter verb, and produces the more directly forcible effect of personal feeling.

> Casca, *you* are the first that *rears your* hand.—*Jul. C.*, iii. 1.

Either ' you are the first that rear your hand ' or ' you are the first that rears his hand ' would be more accordant to usual construction ; but the sentence, as written by the dramatist, gives the effect of hurried speaking, and is expressively consistent with the stage situation.

In the following passage Shakespeare uses a verb (as he frequently uses a pronoun : *See* RELATIVELY USED PRONOUNS) with reference to an implied particular; this implied particular being the *circumstance* of " two boys, an old man, &c." :—

> Two boys, an old man twice a boy, a lane,
> Preserv'd the Britons, *was* the Romans' bane.—*Cym.*, v. 3.

In the following passage he uses a verb in the plural, referring to an antecedent in the singular :—

> Priam's six-gated *city*,
> Dardan, and Tymbria, Ilias, Chetas, Trojan,
> And Antenorides, with massy staples,
> And corresponsive and fulfilling bolts,
> *Sperr* up the sons of Troy.—*Tr. & Cr. (Prologue).*

He sometimes uses neuter and passive verbs actively :—

> But ere we could *arrive* the point propos'd.—*Jul. C.*, i. 2.
>> Those powers that the queen
> Hath rais'd in Gallia have *arriv'd* our coast.—3 *H. VI.*, v. 3.
> And now, *arriving* a place of potency.—*Coriol.*, ii. 3.
> That gallant spirit hath *aspir'd* the clouds.—*R. & Jul.*, iii. 1.
> Now let the general trumpet blow his blast,
> Particularities and petty sounds
> To *cease !*—2 *H. VI.*, v. 2.
> Take an oath to *cease* this civil war.—3 *H. VI.*, i. 1.
> A certain stuff, which, being ta'en, would *cease*
> The present power of life.—*Cym.*, v. 5.
> Be not *ceas'd* with slight denial.—*Timon*, ii. 1.
> And afterward *consort* you till bed-time.—*Com. of E.*, i. 2.
> Sweet health and fair desires *consort* your grace !—*Love's L. L.*, ii. 1.
> Thou, wretched boy, that didst *consort* him here.—*R. & Jul.*, iii. 1.
> Who to Philippi here *consorted* us.—*Jul. C.*, v. 1.
> What mutter you, or what *conspire* you, lords ?—3 *H. VI.*, i. 1.
> That do *conspire* my death with devilish plots.—*R. III.*, iii. 4.
> And *expire* the term of a despised life.—*R. & Jul.*, i. 4.
> Let us be keen, and rather cut a little,
> Than *fall** and bruise to death.—*M. for M.*, ii. 1.
> Here did she *fall* a tear.—*R. II.*, iii. 4.

---

* " Fall " is here used for ' strike down,' ' fell to the earth,' as a tree is felled.

To-morrow in the battle think on me,
And *fall* thy edgeless sword.—*R. III.*, v. 3.

And make him *fall* his crest.—*Tr. & Cr.*, i. 3.

They *fall* their *crests*, and, like deceitful jades.—*Jul. C.*, iv. 2.

Wafting his eyes to the contrary, and *falling*
A lip of much contempt, speeds from me.—*W. T.*, i. 2.

The common executioner. . . .
Falls not the axe upon the humbled neck.—*As You L.*, iii. 5.

Each drop she *falls* would prove a crocodile.—*Oth.*, iv. 1.

We must not make a scarecrow of the law,
Setting it up to *fear* the birds of prey.—*M. for M.*, ii. 1.

The people *fear* me ; for they do observe.—*2 H. IV.*, iv. 4.

Thou seest what's past,—go *fear* thy king withal.—*3 H. VI.*, iii. 3.

Something *fears* me to think of.—*Lear*, iii. 5.

There will she hide her to *listen* our propose.—*M. Ado*, iii. 1.

And now, Octavius, *listen* great things.—*Jul. C.*, iv. 1.

I pray thee, *moralise* them.—*Tam. of S.*, iv. 4.

I *moralise* two meanings in one word.—*R. III.*, iii. 1.

Your exultation *partake* to every one.—*W. T.*, v. 3.

Our mind *partakes* her private actions to your secrecy.—*Per.*, i. 1.

Who o'er the white sheet *peers* her whiter chin.—*Lucrece, Stanza* 68.

Because thy flinty heart, more hard than they,
Might in thy palace *perish* Margaret.—*2 H. VI.*, iii. 2.

Hadst thou, like us, from our first swath, *proceeded*
The sweet degrees that this brief world affords.—*Timon*, iv. 3.

Relish your nimble notes to pleasing* ears.—*Lucrece, Stanza* 161.

Retir'd himself to Italy.—*R. II.*, iv. 1.

Aches contract and *starve* your supple joints.—*Timon*, i. 1.

Oh, how it *yearn'd* my heart when I beheld.—*R. II.*, v. 5.

He occasionally uses an active verb as a neuter verb :—

This sickly land might *solace* as before.—*R. III.*, ii. 3.

But one thing to rejoice and *solace* in.—*R. & Jul.*, iv. 5.

To hide me from the radiant sun, and *solace*
I' the dungeon by a snuff ?—*Cym.*, i. 7.

That, in this case of justice, my accusers,
Be what they will, may stand forth face to face,
And freely *urge* against me.—*H. VIII.*, v. 2.

In the following passages, the verb " inform " is used variously and with some peculiarity :—

Haply thou mayst *inform* something to save thy life.—*All's W.*, iv. 1.

He will betray us all unto ourselves :
Inform on that.—*Ibid.*, iv. 1.

Let him alone ; he did *inform* the truth.—*Coriol.*, i. 4.

It is the bloody business which *informs*
Thus to mine eyes.—*Macb.*, ii. 1.

Shakespeare so frequentiy uses " inhabit " as an intransitive verb, that it confirms our belief in its being the correct word in the last of the following passages [*See* TERMS OF DEFIANCE OR CHALLENGE for our remarks on the passage in question] :—

On this island, where man doth not *inhabit*.—*Temp.*, iii. 3.

Oh, thou that dost *inhabit* in my breast.—*Two G. of V.*, v. 4.

---

* " Pleasing " is here used for ' pleased.'

There's none but witches do *inhabit* here.—*Com. of E.,* iii. 2.
And Lapland sorcerers *inhabit* here.—*Ibid.,* iv. 3.
A fearful eye thou hast: where is that blood
That I have seen *inhabit* in those cheeks ?—*John,* iv. 2.
Disorder, horror, fear, and mutiny,
Shall here *inhabit.*—*R. II.,* iv. 1.
     And, in those holes
Where eyes did once *inhabit,* there were crept.—*R. III.,* i. 4.
And dare me to the desert with thy sword;
If trembling I *inhabit* then, protest me.—*Macb.,* iii. 4.

WEIGHTS AND MEASURES.

There are a few of these mentioned by Shakespeare, which thus
obtain a certain interest in recordation :—

How much your chain weighs to the utmost *carrat.*—*Com. of E.,* iv. 1.
Therefore, thou, best of gold, art worst of gold:
Other, less fine in *carat,* is more precious.—*2 H. IV.,* iv. 4.

This word, which was spelt variously, carat, carrat, caract, charact,
and charect, signifies a weight of four grains, by which gold and gems
are weighed ; and has been derived either from *carat,* a bean, used by
Orientals for weighing gold, or from the Arabian, *kirat,* a weight.

Every tithe soul, 'mongst many thousand *dismes* [tenths]
Hath been as dear as Helen.—*Tr. & Cr.,* ii. 2.

For, like an ass, whose back with *ingots* [lumps of gold, masses of precious metal]
bows.—*M. for M.,* iii. 1.

    Realms and islands were
As *plates* [silver coin or pieces of money: Spanish, *plata*] dropp'd from his pocket.—
Ant. & C., v. 2.

Not with fond *shekels* of the tested gold.—*M. for M.,* ii. 2.

" Shekels " is printed in the Folio and in ancient versions of the
Bible ' sickles.' It signified both a Jewish coin and a Jewish weight ;
and our word ' scale,' to weigh, is indirectly derived from the Hebrew
word "shekel." As employed here by Shakespeare, "shekels" conveys
the idea of minted gold and heavy amount of gold.

Ay, my good lord, five *talents* is his debt. . . . Three *talents* on the present; in
future, all.—*Timon,* i. 1.

I do return those *talents,* doubled with thanks.—*Ibid.,* i. 2.

Let the request be fifty *talents* . . . bid them send o' the instant a thousand *talents*
to me. . . . I clear'd him with five *talents* . . . to be remember'd with those five
talents.—*Ibid.,* ii. 2.

Having great and instant occasion to use fifty *talents.*—*Ibid.,* iii. 1.

To borrow so many *talents* . . . to supply his instant use with so many *talents* . . .
he cannot want fifty-five hundred *talents.*—*Ibid.,* iii. 2.

Mine, fifty *talents.*—*Ibid.,* iii. 4.

In all the above passages, Shakespeare by " talents " refers to the
Attic talent, which has been calculated to amount in worth to rather
more than fifty-six pounds of silver, or to be equivalent to about
£243 15s. of modern English money. A " talent "—being a term
originally applied to a large weight of gold or silver, then to a large

sum in gold or silver coin—became subsequently used to express a thing of indefinite but great value ; and Shakespeare thus uses the word in the following two passages :—

> Not he : but yet Heaven's bounty towards him might
> Be us'd more thankfully.   In himself 'tis much ;
> In you,—which I 'count his,—beyond all *talents.—Cym.,* i. 7.

> And, lo, behold these *talents* of their hair,
> With twisted metal amorously impleach'd,
> I have receiv'd from many a several fair.—*Lover's Comp.,* Stanza 30.

I have a great desire to a *bottle* [bundle: French, *botte*] of hay.—*Mid. N. D.,* iv. 1.

Give me thy *mete-yard* [yard-measure, yard-wand], and spare not me.—*Tam. of S.,* iv. 3.

> By many a dearn and painful *perch* [a measure of five yards and a half]
> Of Pericles the careful search . . .
> Is made.—*Per.,* iii. *(Gower).*

> Go brew me a *pottle* of sack finely.—*Merry W.,* iii. 5.

> Ere the next *pottle* can be filled.—*Oth.,* ii. 3.

> By the mass, you 'll crack a quart together,—ha !
> Will you not, Master Bardolph ?—
> Yea, sir, in a *pottle-pot.*—2 *H. IV.,* v. 3.

" Pottle," from the old French, *potel,* was originally a measure containing two quarts ; but was familiarly used for a tankard or pot, from which wine or beer was drunk.   Master Bardolph's reply shows that it was certainly of capacious dimensions.

> Marian, I say, a *stoop* of wine !—*Tw. N.,* ii. 3.

> Fetch me a *stoop* of liquor.—*Hamlet,* v. 1.

> Set me the *stoops* of wine upon that table.—*Ibid.,* v. 2.

> Come, lieutenant, I have a *stoop* of wine.—*Oth.,* ii. 3.

The " stoop " was a measure containing about half a gallon (Dutch, *stoope*), and came to be used for a flagon, bowl, or vessel for holding drinking liquor.

Shakespeare uses two idiomatic terms of quantity, familiarly employed :—

> Three veneys for a *dish* of stewed prunes.—*Merry W.,* i. 1.

> I have here a *dish* of doves that I would bestow upon your worship.—*Mer. of V.,* ii. 2.

> For a quart of ale is a *dish* for a king.—*W. T.,* iv. 2 *(Song).*

> Moving such a *dish* of skimmed milk.—1 *H. IV.,* ii. 3.

It is observable that in the two latter passages " dish " is used for a vessel that contains liquid ; as in our grandmothers' days it was the custom to say ' a dish of tea ' for ' a cup of tea.'

> I had as lief you would tell me of a *mess* of porridge.—*Merry W.,* iii. 1.

> Coming in to borrow a *mess* of vinegar.—2 *H. IV.,* ii. 1.

WOMEN'S PARTS PLAYED BY BOYS.

There are several passages in Shakespeare's dramas that refer to the custom which existed in his time of boys or very young men (sometimes masked) enacting the women's parts in stage plays ; a custom that it is requisite to bear in mind for the due comprehension of these passages :—

Francis Flute the bellows-mender. . . . You must take Thisby on you. . . . Nay, 'faith; let not me play a woman; I have a beard coming.—That's all one: you shall play it in a mask, and you may speak as small as you will.—*Mid. N. D.*, i. 2.

> About my stature: for, at Pentecost,
> When all our pageants of delight were play'd,
> Our youth got me to play the woman's part,
> And I was trimm'd in Madam Julia's gown.—*Two G. of V.*, iv. 4.

This is said by Julia herself, disguised as the page, Sebastian.

It is not the fashion to see the lady the epilogue; but it is no more unhandsome than to see the lord the prologue. . . . If I were a woman, I would kiss as many of you as had beards that pleased me.—*As You L.* (*Epilogue*).

This epilogue is spoken by Rosalind.

What! my young lady and mistress! By'r lady, your ladyship is nearer heaven, than when I saw you last, by the altitude of a chopine. Pray God, your voice, like a piece of uncurrent gold, be not cracked within the ring.—*Hamlet*, ii. 2.

Hamlet is here addressing the *growing* youth who enacts the stage heroines, and who has reached the age when the boyish treble voice is changing to the manly tenor or bass, which will soon unfit him for any longer playing the lady characters.

> *Cleopatra.* . . . The quick comedians
> Extemporally will stage us, and present
> Our Alexandrian revels; Antony
> Shall be brought drunken forth, and I shall see
> Some *squeaking* Cleopatra *boy* my greatness
> I' the posture of a wench.—*Ant. & C.*, v. 2.

WORDS LIKE " BLAME," &c.

Shakespeare occasionally uses some words for the *causes* of that which they directly signify; and he does this consistently with a familiar usage in English diction. By way of illustration—we remember that droll effect was obtained from this in one of the elder Mathews's Entertainments, where an old lady aboard a vessel while the sea is running high, asks in great trepidation, " There's no fear, is there, captain?" To which he replies, " Oh, dear, yes, ma'am! plenty of fear, but no danger " :—

And shall my youth be guilty of such *blame*? [fault, error].—1 *H. VI.*, iv. 5.

Wrong hath but wrong, and *blame* the due of *blame*.—*R. III.*, v. 1.

'Tis his own *blame* : h'ath put himself from rest.—*Lear*, ii. 4.

My high-repented *blames* [errors], dear sovereign, pardon to me.—*All's W.*, v. 3.

Danger [dread of danger] deviseth shifts ; wit waits on fear.—*V. & Adon.*, Stanza 115.

And send *discoverers* [scouts, investigators] forth to know the numbers of our enemies.—2 *H. IV.*, iv. 1.

> Here is the guess of their true strength and forces
> By diligent *discovery* [search, exploring, investigation].—*Lear*, v. 1.

> Or in the night, imagining some *fear* [danger],
> How easy is a bush suppos'd a bear!—*Mid. N. D.*, v. 1.

> That shows the ignorant a kind of *fear*
> Before not dreamt of.—1 *H. IV.*, iv. 1.

> Thou shak'st thy head, and hold'st it *fear*, or sin,
> To speak a truth.—2 *H. IV.*, i. 1.

> There is no *fear* in him; let him not die.—*Jul. C.*, ii. 1.

Present *fears* [dangers, objects of fear] are less than horrible imaginings.—*Macb.*, i. 3.

No *meed* [desert, merit], but he repays sevenfold above itself.—*Timon*, i. 1.

In his *meed*, he 's unfellowed.—*Hamlet*, v. 2.

Each one already blazing by our *meeds* [meritorious deeds, acts deserving meed or reward].—3 *H. VI.*, ii. 1.

> And, by the *merit* [guerdon, reward, recompense] of vile gold, dross, dust,
> Purchase corrupted pardon of a man.—*John*, iii. 1.

> A dearer *merit*, not so deep a maim
> As to be cast forth in the common air.—*R. II.*, i. 3.

We answer others' *merits* [deeds which merit or deserve punishment] in our name — *Ant. & C.*, v. 2.

The greatest *obloquy* [disgrace] i' the world in me to lose . . . the greatest *obloquy* i' the world in me.—*All's W.*, iv. 2.

May one be pardon'd and retain the *offence* [gain for which the offence was committed]?—*Hamlet*, iii. 3.

My noble master will appear such as he is, full of *regard* [that which is worthy of regard] and honour.—*Jul. C.*, iv. 2.

My young master doth expect your *reproach* [this is said as a blunder for 'approach'; but it is replied to in the sense of 'discredit,' 'defeat,' 'disgrace,' that which incurs reproach].—So do I his.—*Mer. of V.*, ii. 5.

> In whose comparison all whites are ink,
> Writing their own *reproach*.—*Tr. & Cr.*, i. 1.

To do upon *respect* [that which should cause or command respect, that which is entitled to respect] such violent outrage.—*Lear*, ii. 4.

There is no *terror* [peril, that which inspires terror], Cassius, in your threats.—*Jul. C.*, iv. 3.

You have brought a *trembling* [that which may well cause trembling, a calamity to tremble at] upon Rome, such as was never so incapable of help.—*Coriol.*, iv. 6.

See PECULIAR USE OF WORDS for " chase " and " hunt " used in a similar manner.